Street by Street

STAFFORDSHIRE

PLUS ALDRIDGE, ALSAGER, ASHBOURNE, BROWNHILLS, MARKET DRAYTON, PELSALL, WOLVERHAMPTON

Enlarged Areas Burton upon Trent, Lichfield, Stafford, Stoke-on-Trent, Tamworth

Ist edition May 2001

© Automobile Association Developments Limited 2001

This product includes map data licensed from Ordnance Survey® with the permission of the Controller of Her Majesty's Stationery Office. © Crown copyright 2000. All rights reserved. Licence No: 399221.

Published by AA Publishing (a trading name of Automobile Association Developments Limited, whose registered office is Norfolk House, Priestley Road, Basingstoke, Hampshire, RG24 9NY. Registered number 1878835).

Mapping produced by the Cartographic Department of The Automobile Association.

A CIP Catalogue record for this book is available from the British Library.

Printed by in Italy by Printer Trento srl

The contents of this atlas are believed to be correct at the time of the latest revision. However, the publishers cannot be held responsible for loss occasioned to any person acting or refraining from action as a result of any material in this atlas, nor for any errors, omissions or changes in such material. The publishers would welcome information to correct any errors or omissions and to keep this atlas up to date. Please write to Publishing, The Automobile Association, Fanum House, Basing View, Basingstoke, Hampshire, RG21 4EA.

Ref: MX096

Key to map pages	ii-iii
Key to map symbols	iv-1
Enlarged scale pages	2-13
Street by Street	14-311
Index – towns & villages	312-313
Index – streets	314-349
Index – featured places	349-355

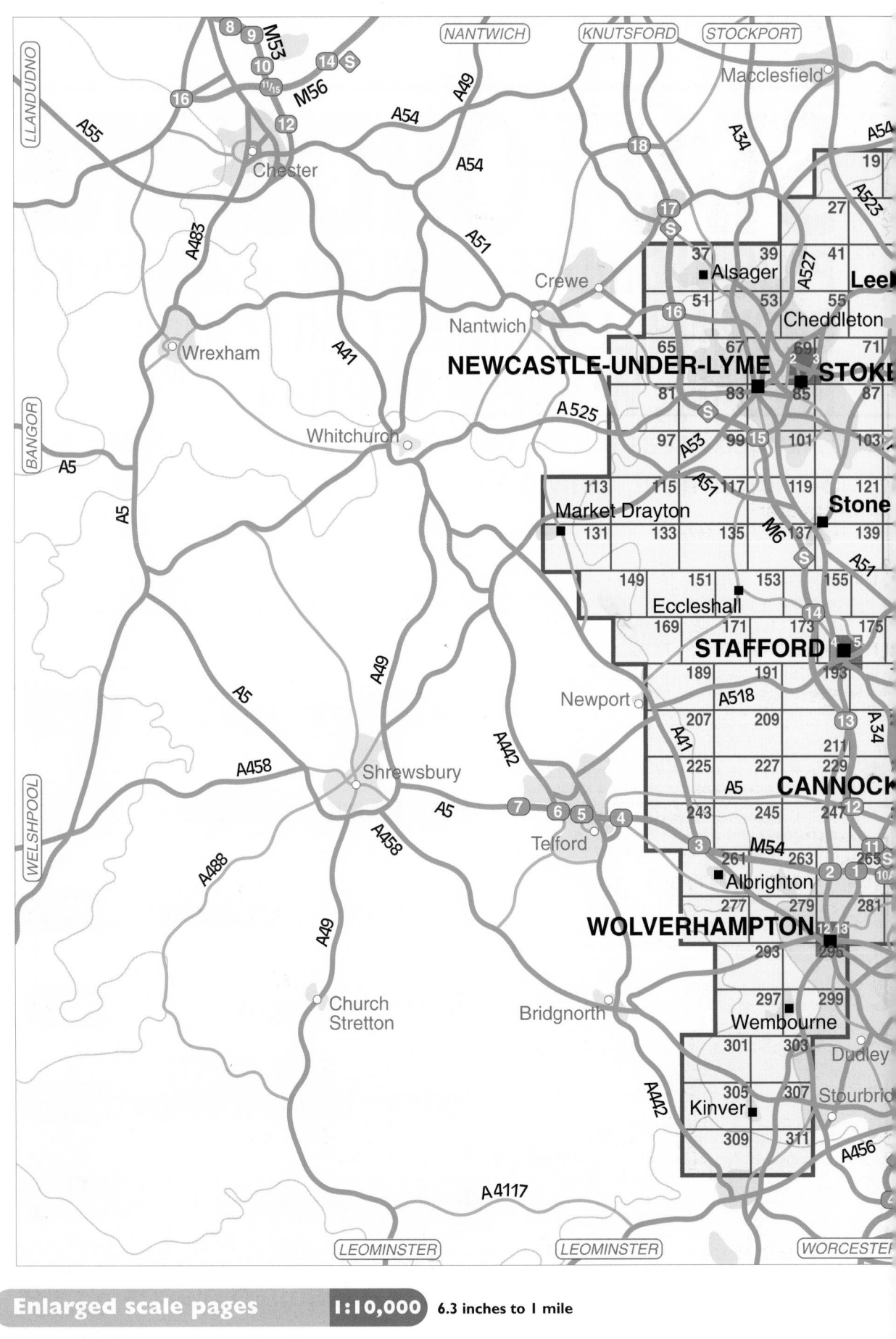

ii

0   1/4   miles   1/2   3/4

0   1/4   1/2   kilometres   3/4   1   1 1/4

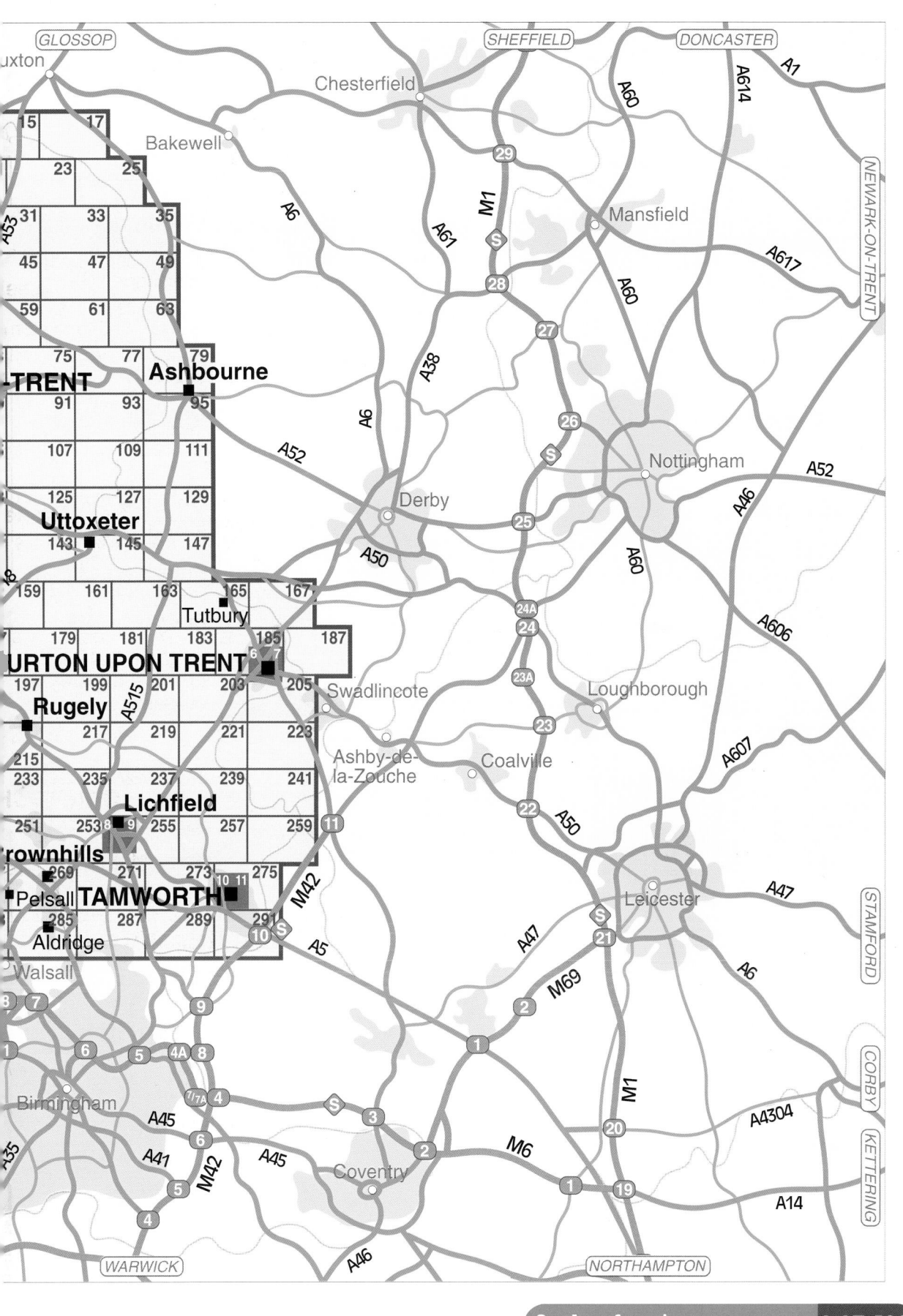

GLOSSOP
SHEFFIELD
DONCASTER
uxton
Chesterfield
Bakewell
A1
A614
A60
A6
A61
M1
Mansfield
A617
NEWARK-ON-TRENT
15 17
23 25
31 33 35
A53
45 47 49
59 61 63
75 77 79 Ashbourne
-TRENT
91 93 95
A60
A38
28
27
26
A52
Nottingham
A52
107 109 111
A6
125 127 129
Uttoxeter
143 145 147
25
Derby
A46
159 161 163 165 167
Tutbury
179 181 183 185 187
URTON UPON TRENT 6 7
197 199 201 203 205
Rugely
A515
217 219 221 223
215
233 235 237 239 241
Lichfield 8 9
251 253 255 257 259
rownhills
269 271 273 275
Pelsall TAMWORTH 10 11
285 287 289 291
Aldridge 10
Walsall
A50
A50
A606
A607
Swadlincote
24A
24
23A
Loughborough
23
Ashby-de-
la-Zouche
Coalville
22
A47
A5
11
M42
A60

8 7
1
9
6 5 4A 8
7 7A 4
Birmingham
A45
A41
A42
A45
6
A35
5
4
WARWICK
A46
Leicester
A47
21
M69
2
1
Coventry
3
2
M6
1
19
NORTHAMPTON
STAMFORD
CORBY
KETTERING
M1
A4304
A6
A14

3.6 inches to I mile   **Scale of main map pages 1:17,500**

0   1/2   miles   1
0   1/2   1   kilometres   1 1/2   2

iv

Junction 9	Motorway & junction
Services	Motorway service area
	Primary road single/dual carriageway
Services	Primary road service area
	A road single/dual carriageway
	B road single/dual carriageway
	Other road single/dual carriageway
	Restricted road
	Private road
← ←	One way street
	Pedestrian street
	Track/ footpath
	Road under construction
	Road tunnel
P	Parking

P+	Park & Ride
	Bus/coach station
	Railway & main railway station
	Railway & minor railway station
	Underground station
	Light railway & station
+++++	Preserved private railway
LC	Level crossing
●—●—●—	Tramway
-------	Ferry route
....	Airport runway
-·-·-	Boundaries- borough/ district
vvvvv	Mounds
93	Page continuation 1:17,500
7	Page continuation to enlarged scale 1:10,000

River/canal lake, pier		Toilet with disabled facilities
Aqueduct lock, weir		Petrol station
465 ▲ Winter Hill	Peak (with height in metres)	PH	Public house
	Beach	PO	Post Office
	Coniferous woodland		Public library
	Broadleaved woodland	_i_	Tourist Information Centre
	Mixed woodland		Castle
	Park		Historic house/ building
	Cemetery	Wakehurst Place NT	National Trust property
	Built-up area	M	Museum/ art gallery
	Featured building	†	Church/chapel
	City wall		Country park
A&E	Accident & Emergency hospital		Theatre/ performing arts
	Toilet		Cinema

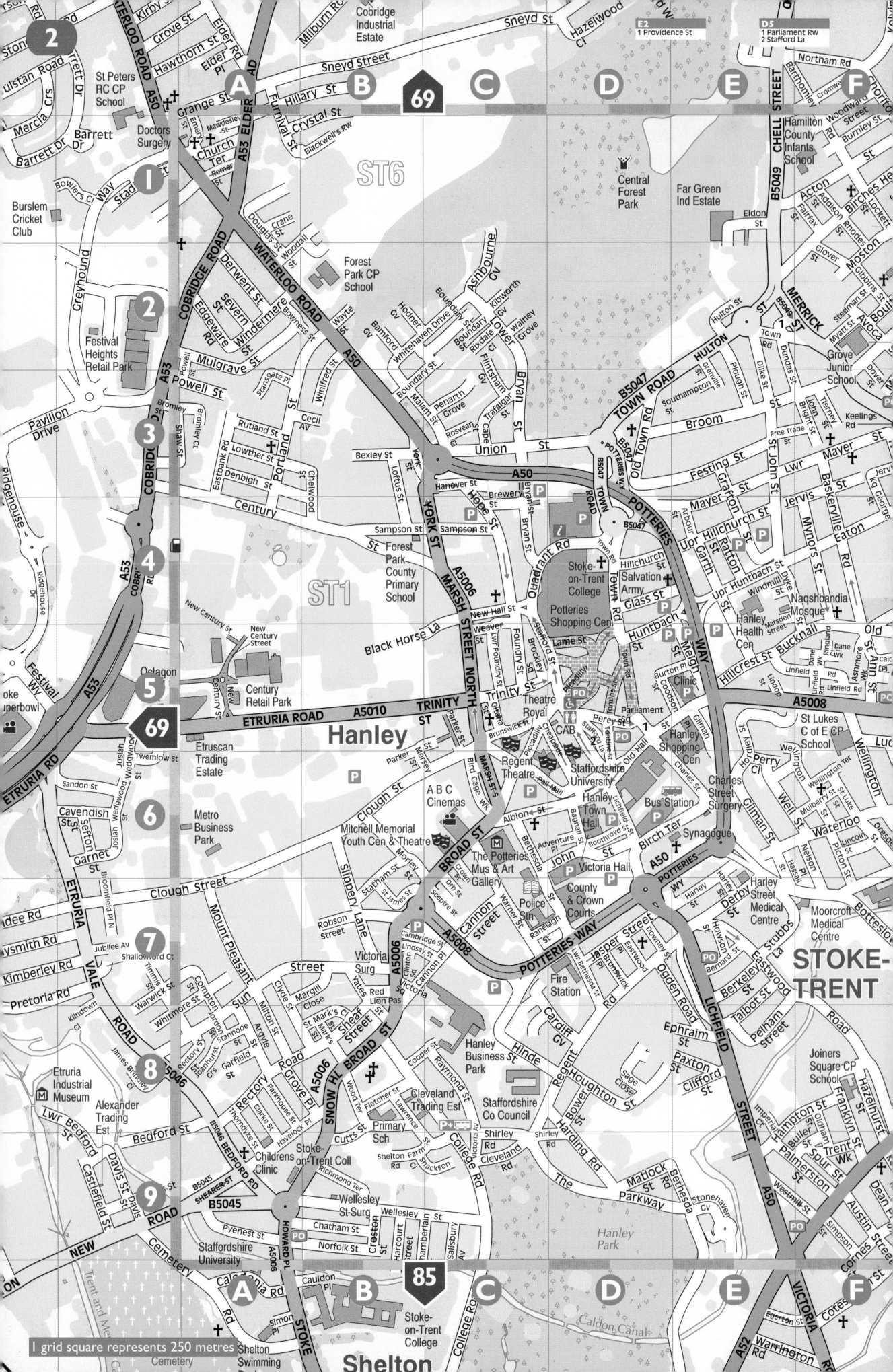

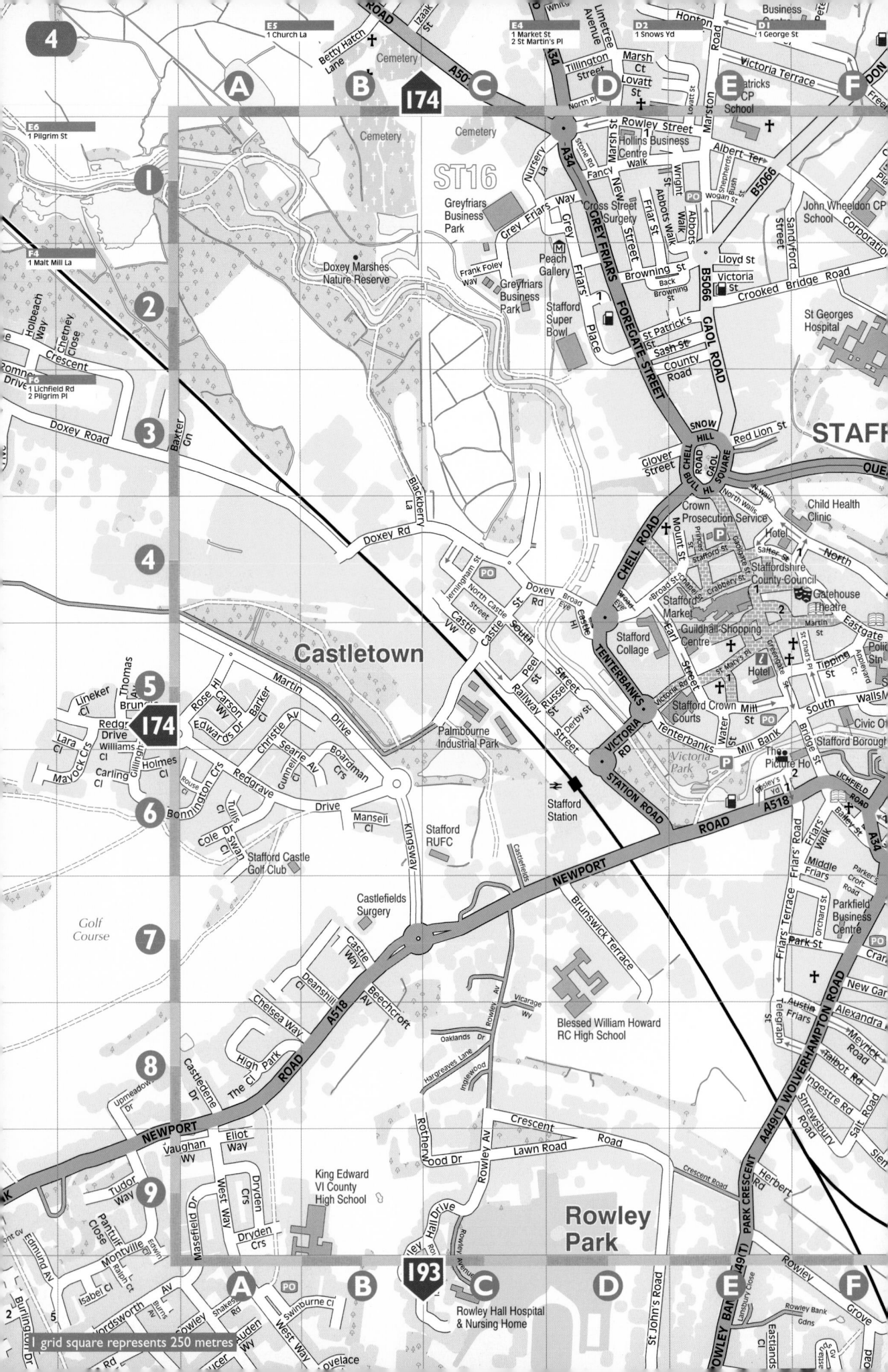

1 grid square represents 250 metres

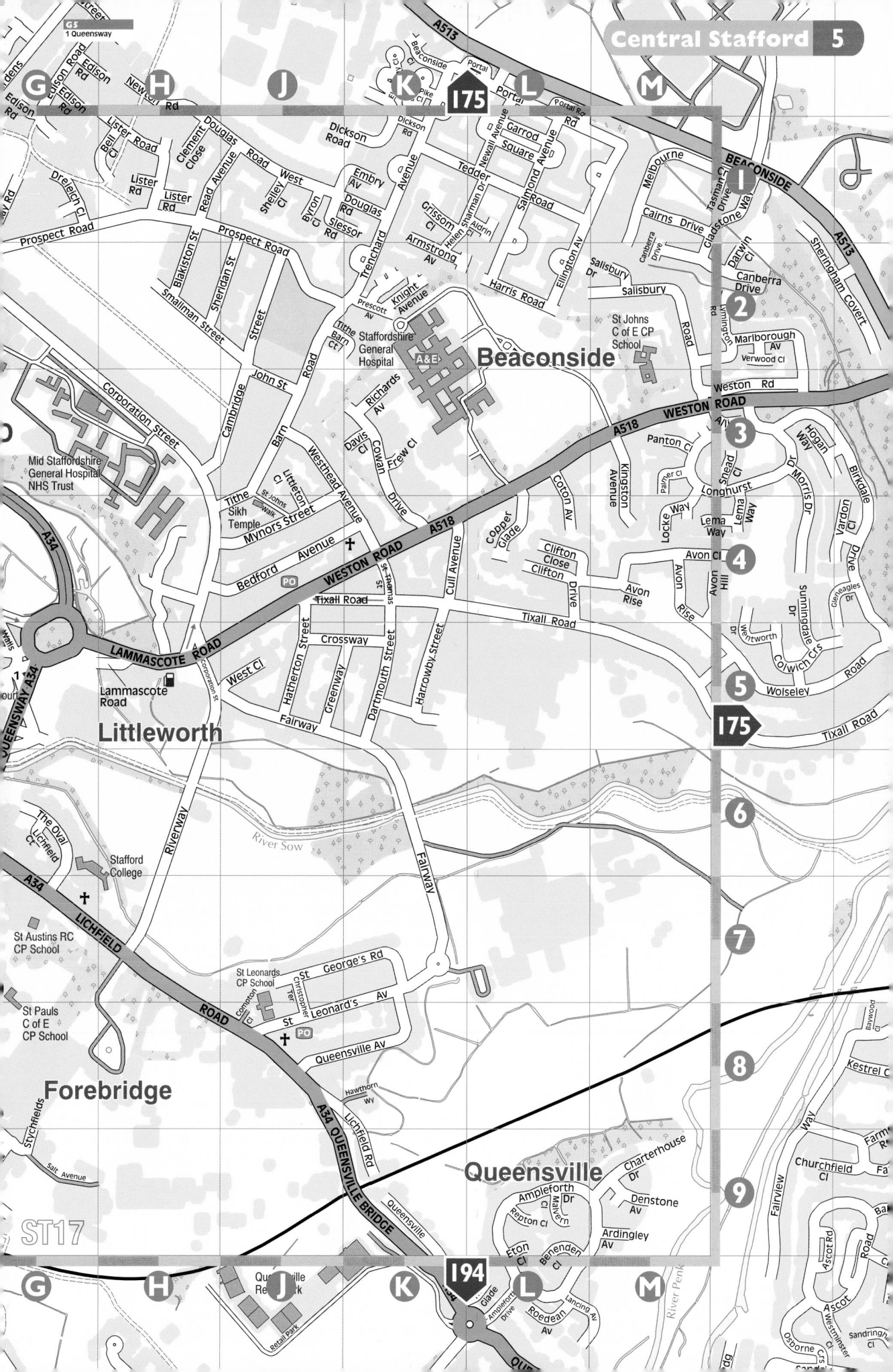

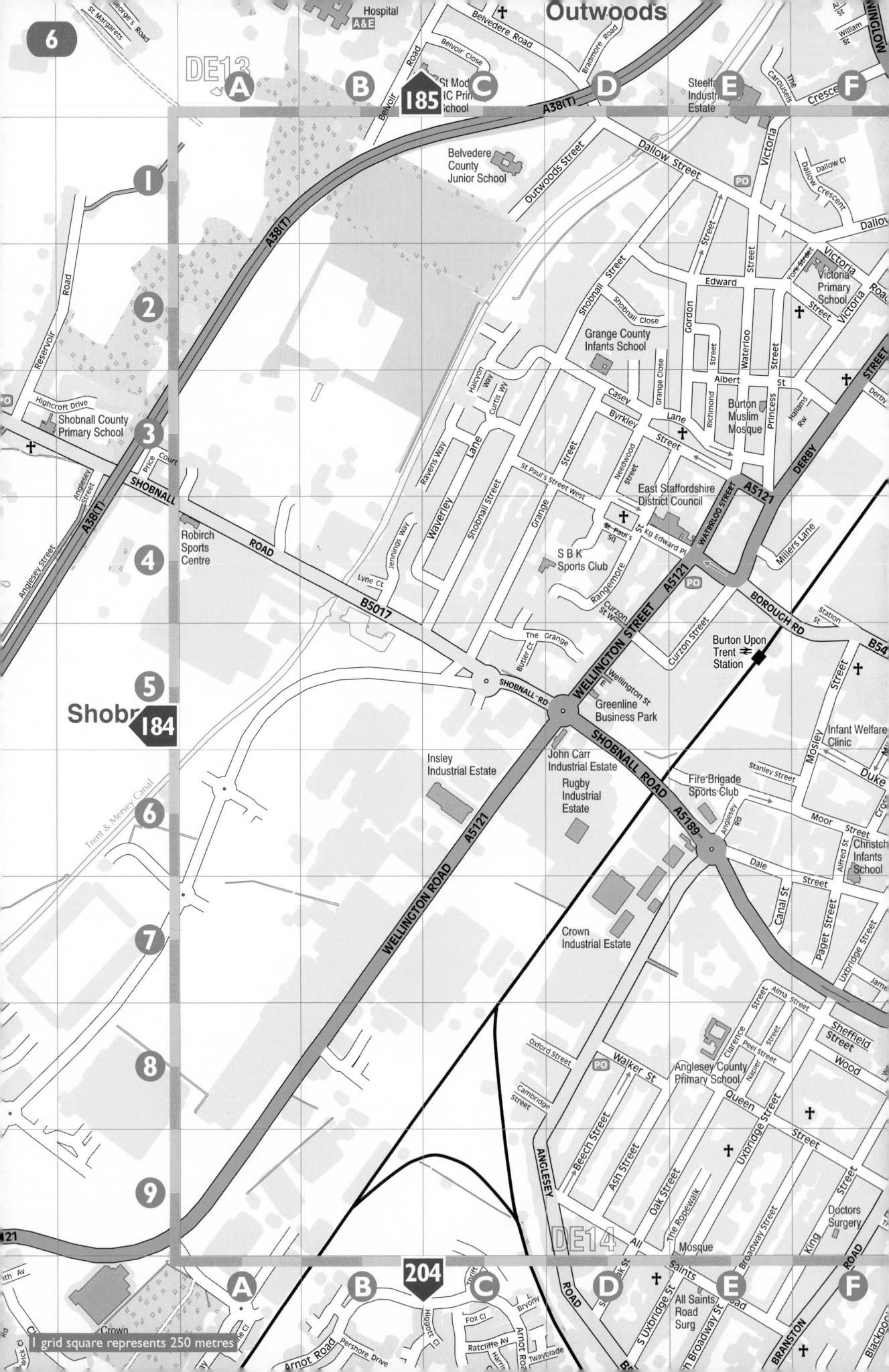

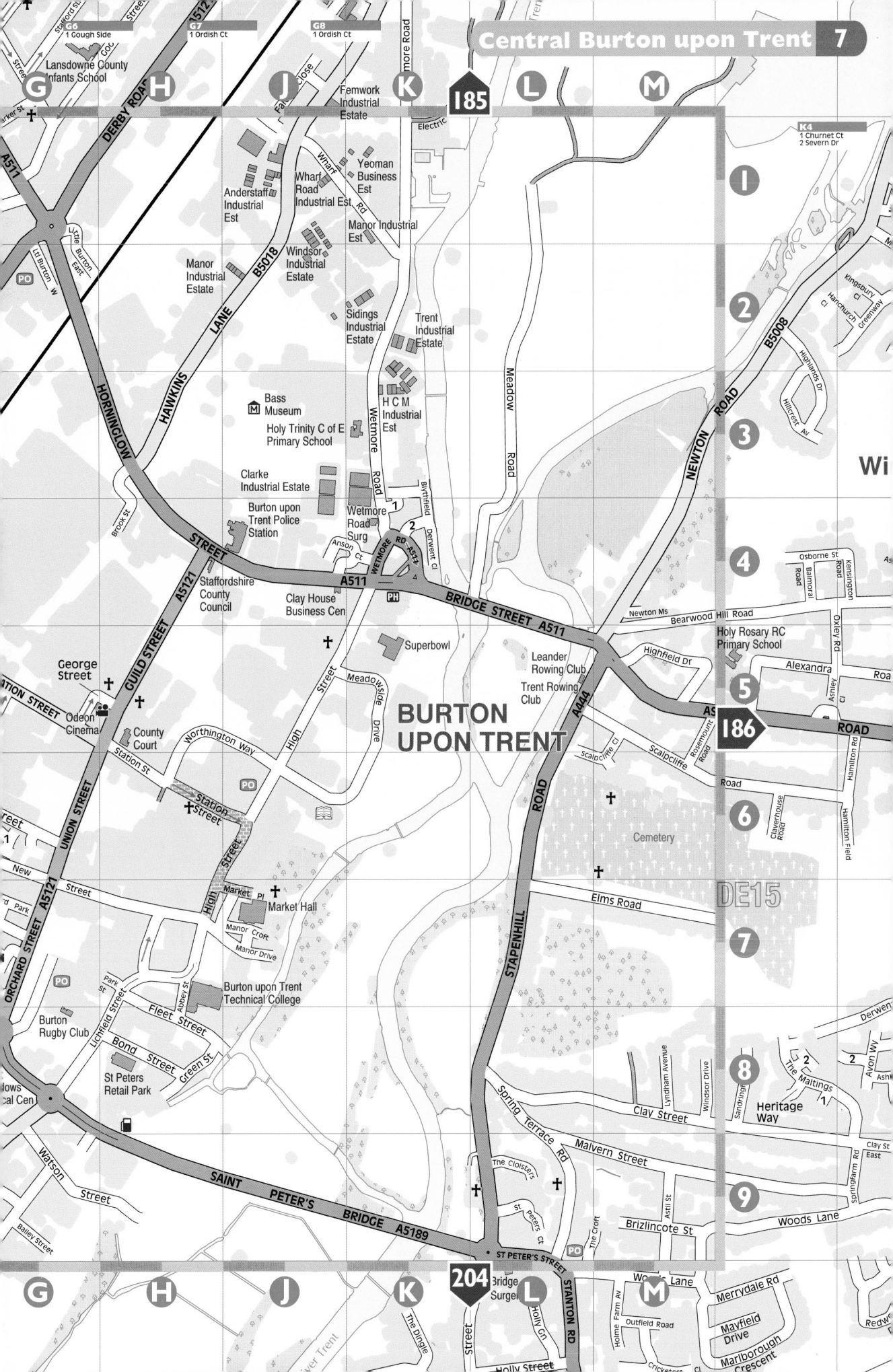

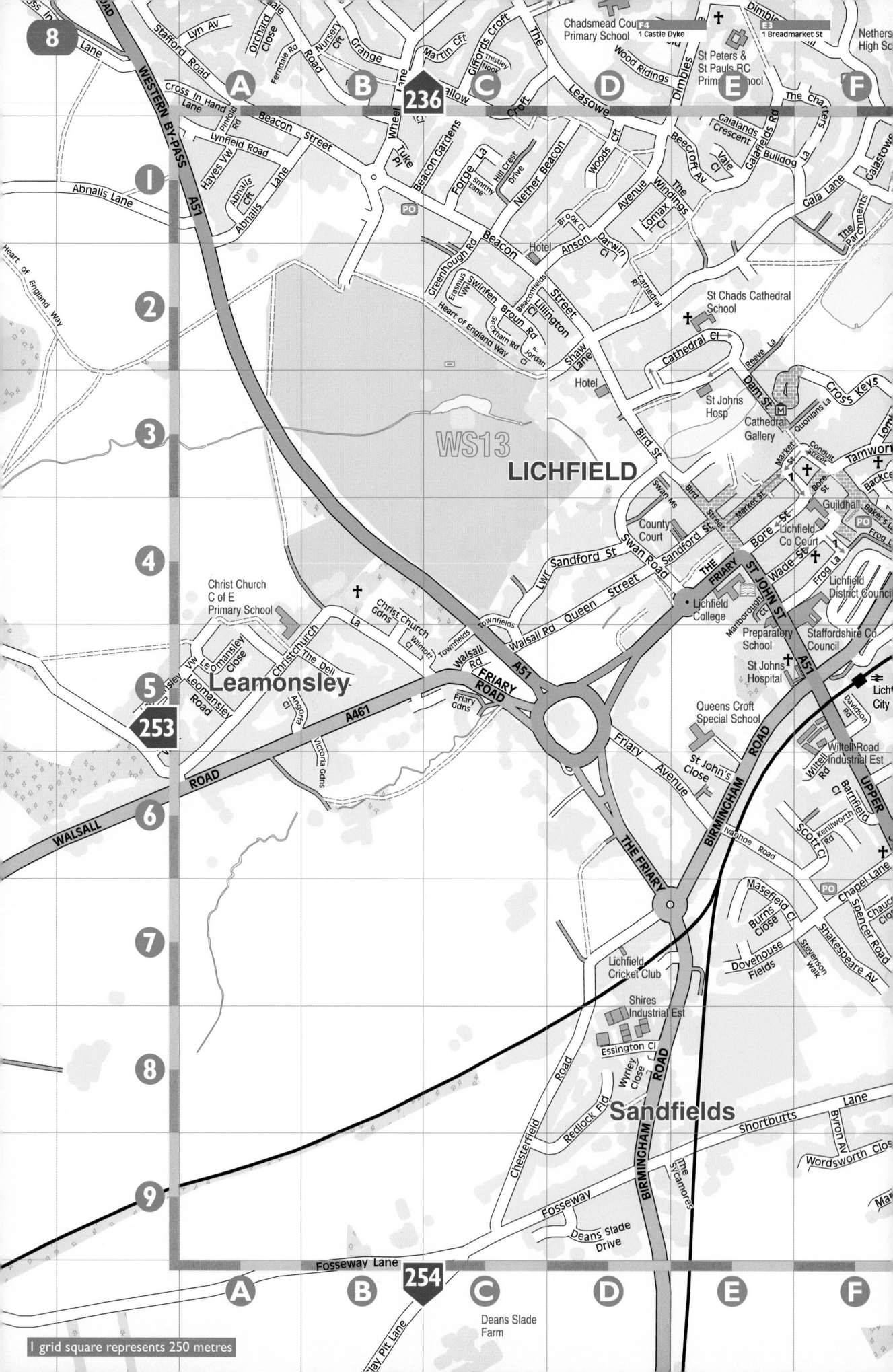

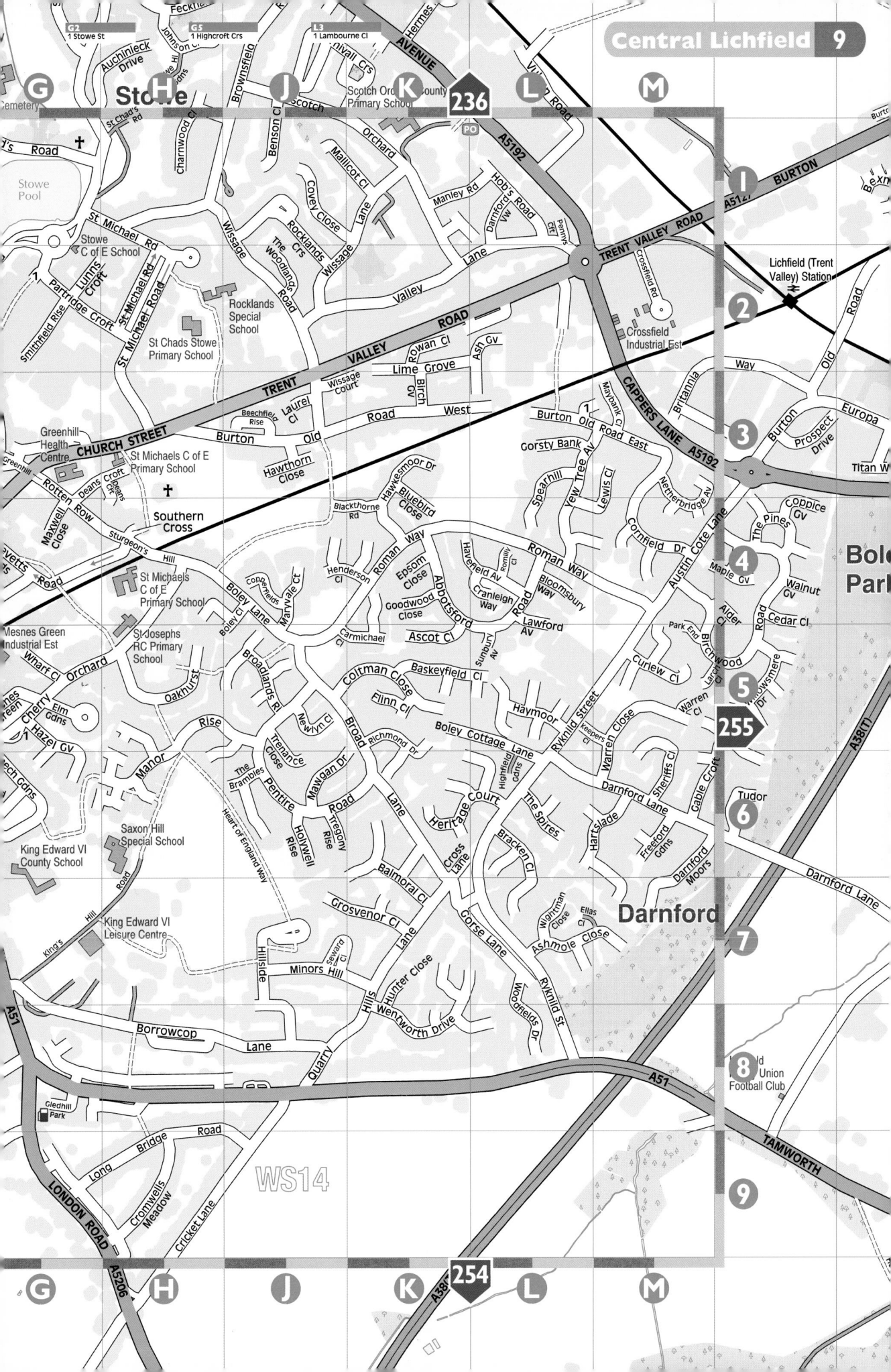

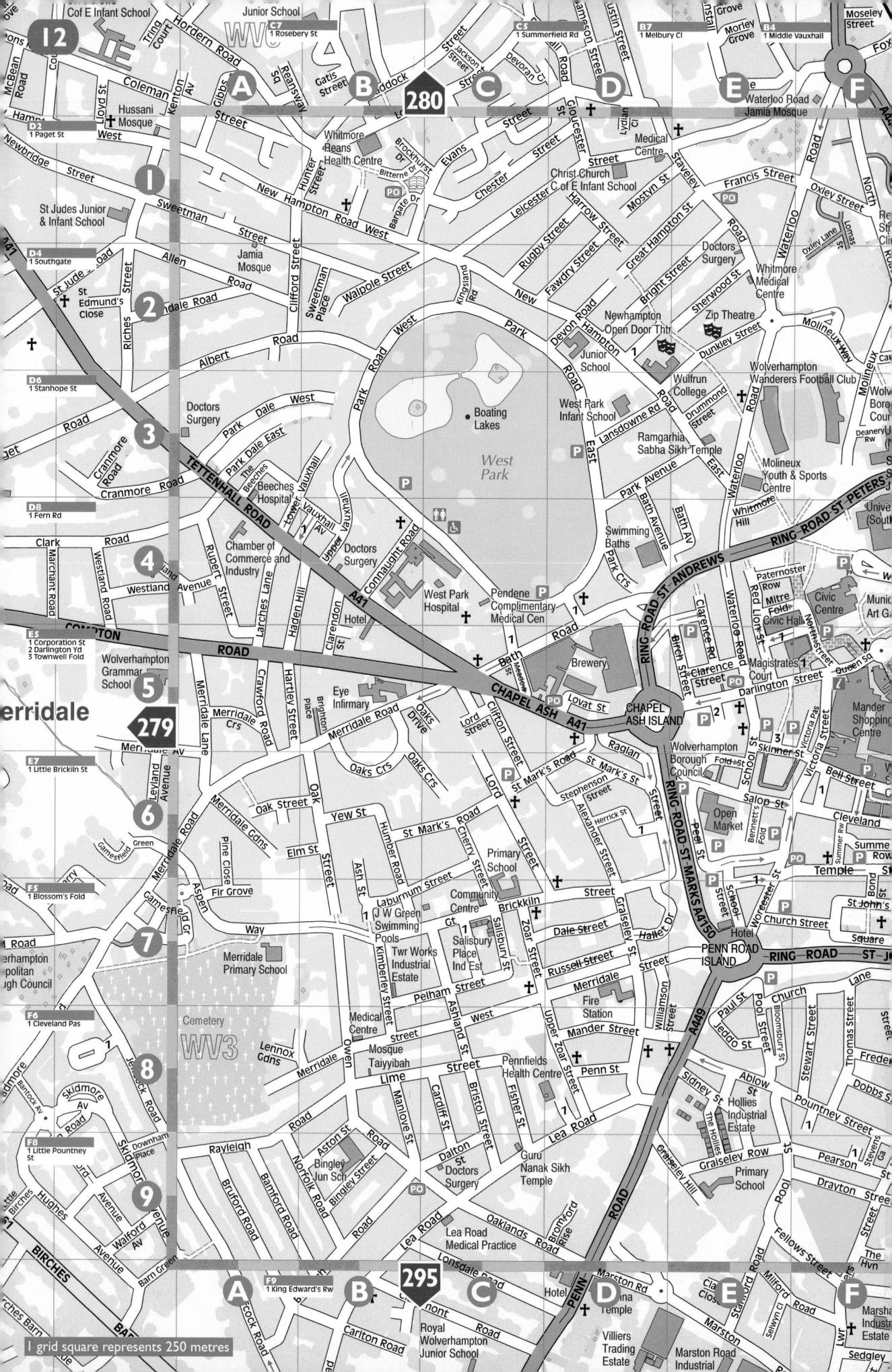

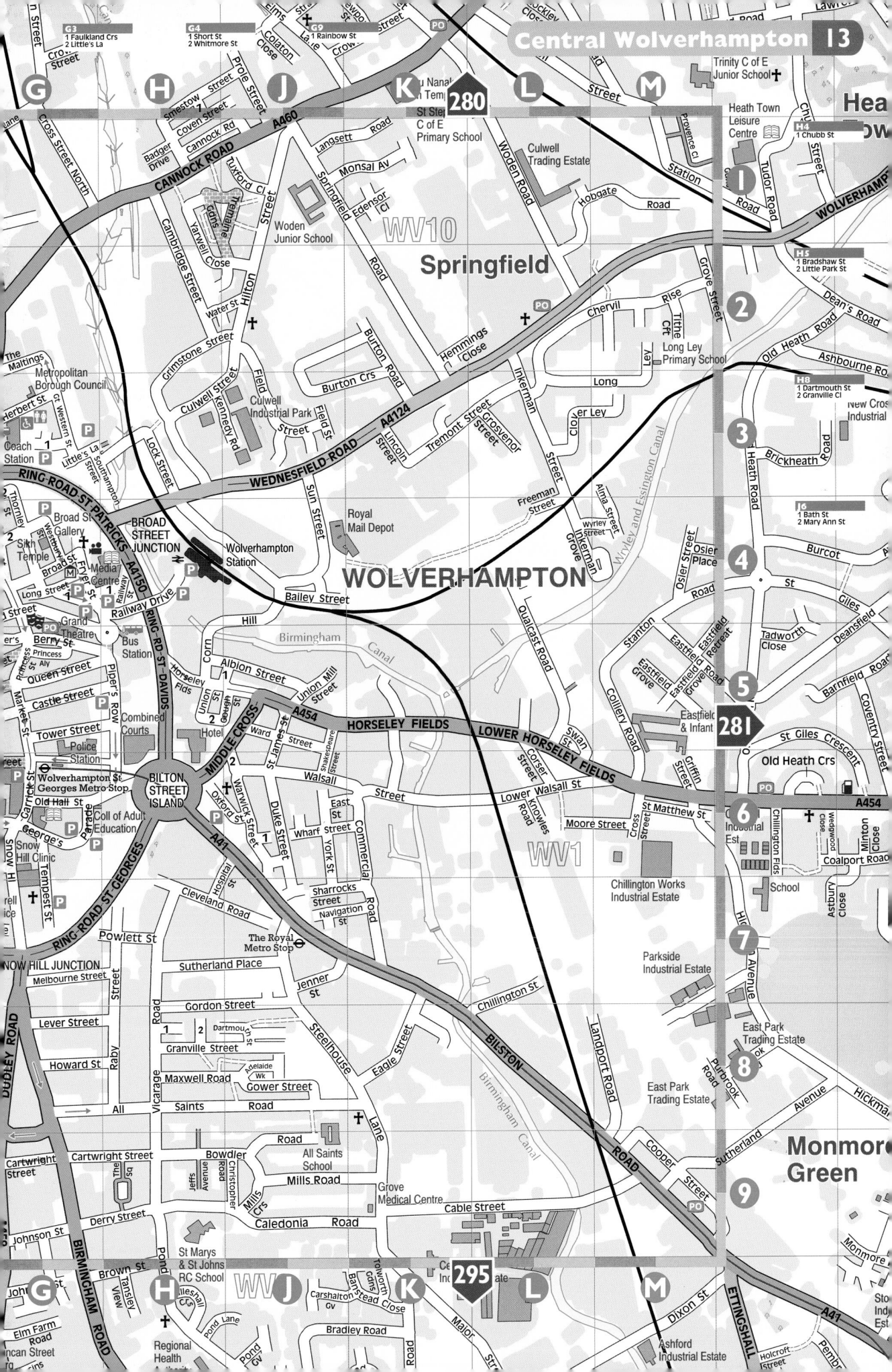

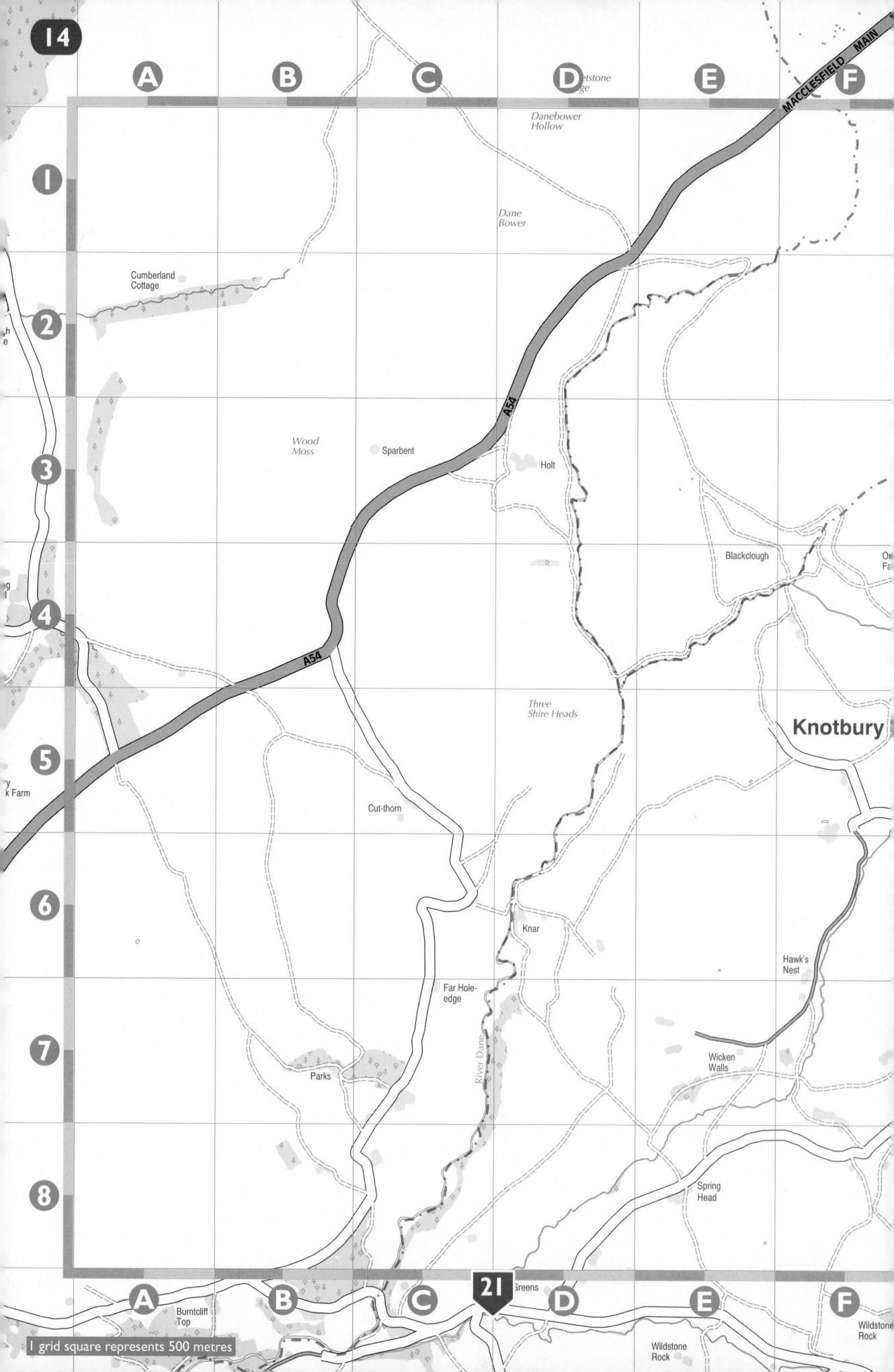

14

A B C D E F

Danebower
Hollow

I

Dane
Bower

Cumberland
Cottage

2

Wood
Moss   Sparbent   Holt

3

Blackclough   Or
Fa

A54

4

A54   Three
Shire Heads   Knotbury

5

Cut-thorn

k Farm

Knar

6

Hawk's
Nest

Far Hole-
edge

7

River Dane   Wicken
Walls

Parks

Spring
Head

8

21

Greens

A B C D E F

Burntcliff
Top   Wildstone
Rock

Wildstone
Rock

Macclesfield Main

G H J K L M

1

2

3

Turncliff

Leap Edge

Fairthorn

Thirkelow

Axe Edge

Drystone Edge

Axe Edge End

Wallnook

Brand Side

Brand Top

4

16

Howe Green

Dove Head

River Dove

Bra End

5

Hilltop

6

Wolf Edge

New Lodge Farm

Gamballs Green

Colshaw

Summerhill

Tenter

7

Hollinsclough Rake

Brown Lane

Flash Head

Flash C of E Primary School

Flash

PO

Nield Bank

Dun Cow's Grove

Moseley

8

Blackbank

Under Hill Farm

Wilson Knowl

G H J K L M

22

Thick Withins

Edgetop

551 ▲ Axe Edge

Derbyshire County

Staffordshire County

A53

A B C D E F

University
of Sheffield

Haslin Rd
Dolby Road
Heathfield
Nook Road
Barso...

Hillhead Lane

1

2

The
Frith

Hillhead
Farm

3

Thirkelow

4

15

Greensides

Upper
Edge

5

Brand
End

Booth
Farm

Stoop
Farm

Tor
Rock

6

Leycote

Fough

Dowall
Hall

Tenterhill

7

insclough Rake

Moor Side

Hollins
Farm

River Dove

Moseley

8

Hollinsclough Rake

Stannery

Hollinsclough

Hollinsclough
School

A B C 23 D E F

1 grid square represents 500 metres

Edgetop

Hollinsclough

Nabend

G H J K L M

I

2 Ch

3

4

5

6

7

8

Back Dale

Horseshoe Dale

SK17

Shallow Grange

Brierlow Bar Farm

A5270

A5270

Farditch Farm

The Ditch

Netherlow Farm

Brierlow Bar

A515

Townend Farm

Nether Low

Brierlow Grange

Hindlow

B5053

Hind Low

Brier Low

BUXTON ROAD

Sterndale Moor

A515

Great Low

Greatlow

Harley Grange

Jericho Farm

Hatch-a-Way

Earl Sterndale

Fernydale

Dale View

Earl Sterndale School

Glutton Grange

PO

Glutton Bridge

Abbotside Farm

B5053

Fox Hole Cave

OLD COALPIT LANE

Common

Street

Well Road

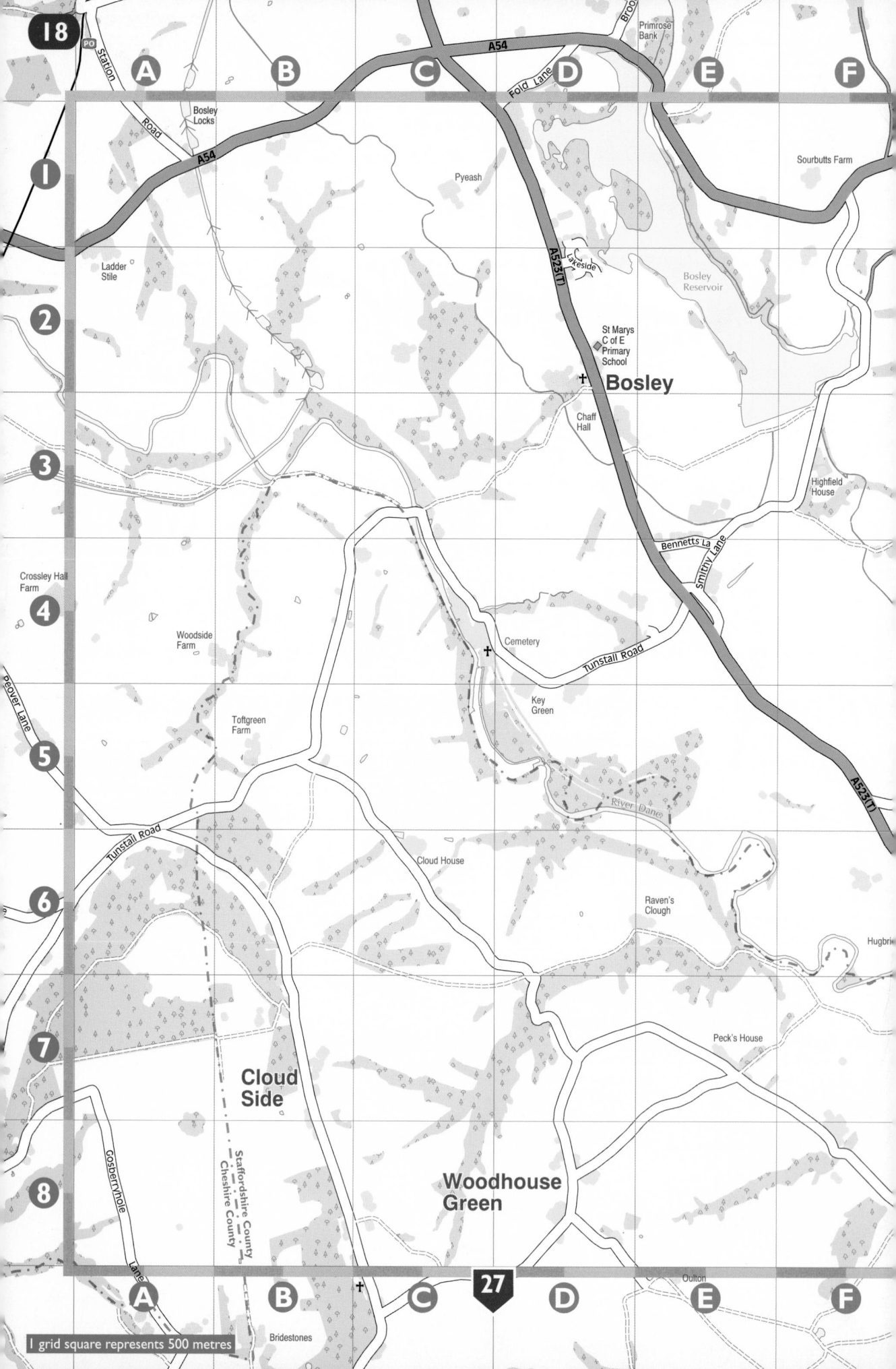

18

PO

Station Road

A

Bosley Locks

B

C

A54

A54

Fold Lane

D

Brook

Primrose Bank

E

F

Sourbutts Farm

1

Ladder Stile

Pyeash

A523(T)

Lakeside

Bosley Reservoir

2

St Marys C of E Primary School

† Bosley

Chaff Hall

3

Highfield House

Bennetts Lane

Smithy Lane

Crossley Hall Farm

4

Woodside Farm

Cemetery

†

Tunstall Road

Peover Lane

5

Toftgreen Farm

Key Green

River Dane

A523(T)

6

Tunstall Road

Cloud House

Raven's Clough

Hugbri

7

Cloud Side

Peck's House

Gosberryhole Lane

Staffordshire County
Cheshire County

8

Woodhouse Green

Oulton

A

B

Bridestones

†

C

27

D

E

F

Hammertor

G DUMBERS H J K L M

Turnhurst

Bosley Minn

Swallowdale

Wincle Minn

Greasley

Bennettshill

Lanehead

Wincle C of E Primary School

1

Wincle

2

Broomhill

Barlow Hill

Hawkslee

Wincle Grange

3

PI

eadow

Shell Brook

Gritstone Trail

4

Lower Minnend

Minn-End-Lane

Higher Minnend

Whitelee

20

Bearda

5

Barleighford Farm

Gig Hall

bridge Farm

Gritstone Trail

Gritstone Trail

Cheshire County

Hollinhall

6

River Dane

Staffordshire County

Gritstone Trail

Gritstone Trail

7

Wallhill

Wormhill

Thompson

Heatonlow

Mow Cop Trail

Brandy-Lee

8

Heaton

Street

Rushton C of E Primary School

28

G H J K L M

Rushton Bank

Rushton Spencer

A523(T)

Sugar

Lane

Minn-End-Lane

20

Hammerton
Moss

Allmeadows

Midgley Farm

Pearls

A **B** **C** **D** **E** **F**

Burnt
House Farm

River Dane

Helmesley

I
Wincle C of E
Primary School

Back
Forest Farm

Back Dane

Cheshire Cou
Staffordshire Co

Wincle

2

River Dane

Lud's Church
(Cave)

Back
Forest

3

PH

Hangingstone
Farm

Paddock

High
Forest

Danebridge

4

Swythamley
Hall

19

Hillylees

Old Springs

Clough
Head

5

Bearda

Highridge

Buxton
Brow

Old
Smithy

Hollinhall

6

Bent
End Farm

Pool Farm

Turner's
Pool

Meadows

7

Neild's
Farm

PO

Old Hag

Greenhouse

Gun
End House

Cliff

Thornyleigh

8

Gun End
Farm

Isle

A **B** **C** **29** **D** **E** **F**

Horse
Haylands

Oldhay
Top

1 grid square represents 500 metres

22

15

31

21

A — Hill
B
C
D
E
F

Blackbank

Wilson Knowl

Wildstone Rocks

1

Flash Bottom

Daffodil Farm

Sunnydale Farm

Thick Withins

Edgetop

2

Smallshaw Farm

Roundhill

3

Adder's Green

Morridge Top

High Ash

Gib Torr

A53

4

Pyeclough Farm

Merril Grove Farm

5

Royal Cottage

Newstone Farm

6

Badger's Croft

A53

7

Stake Gutter

bersend

8

Ramshaw

Ramshaw Rocks

A
B
Dry Stones
C
Morridge
D
E
F

Folly

1 grid square represents 500 metres

G H J 16 K L M

Hollinsclough Rake

Hollinsclough
Hollinsclough
School

Nabend

1

Hollinsclough
Moor

Coatestown

Moss
Carr

2

Tunstead

Ball Bank
House Farm

3

Hole
Carr

Fawside
Edge

Fawside

4

Lo

Marnshaw
Head

**Hardings
Booth**

24

Heath
House

Barrow
Moor

5

Oakenclough
Hall

Shining
Ford

Hillend

The Lane

Fawfieldhead

6

School
Clough

7

e
rns

Hallhill

Bank
House

The
Bent

sgrove

Newtown

8

Boosley
Grange

G H J 32 K L M

Lady Edge

Glutton
Bridge

A B C **17** D E F

I

B5053

Fox Hole
Cave

Underhill

High
Wheeldon

2

Tunstead

Under
the Hill

Derbyshire County

Staffordshire County

River Dove

3

BUXTON ROAD

Lane Head

Crowdecote

St Bartholomews
C of E Primary
School

Church Street

Gauledge
Lane

1 | 3

2 | 4
PO

High Street

Fawside

Windyridge

Longnor

Leek Road

4

Edgetop

23

Heath
House

Upper
Whitle

5

Knowsley
Cross

Under
Whitle

The
Cottage

6

Waterhouse
Farm

River Manifold

Over
Boothlow

Top
Farm

School
Clough

Brownspit

7

The Ferns

Lower
Boothlow

Race
Hous

The
Bent

Fernyknowle

Ridge
Farm

The
Low

Ridge End
Farm

8

Bridge
End

Ludburn

A B C **33** D Pool E Hill
End F

Flat
Head

The
Holmes

1 grid square represents 500 metres

G H J K L M

Hurdlow Town

The Whim

High Peak Trail

B5055

Endmoor

LANE

I

Sparklow

2

Cronkston Grange

3

Cronkston Lodge

Waggon Low

High Peak Trail

Cotesfield

4

A515

Mosey Low

5

Custard Field Farm

Pilsbury Lodge

6

River Dove

Pilsbury

7

Vincent House

Derbyshire County

Staffordshire County

8

High Farm

G H J 34 K L M

Harris Close

Hide Lane

G   H   J   18   K   L   M

High Lee

Rushton
Bank

I

Bridestones

Dial Lane

Biddulph
Common

dulph Park

Earlsway House

Beat Lane

Lane-end

Askerbank

Bandridge Lane

2

Beat Lane

Rushtonhall

3

Lee House

Green Meadows
Farm

Pyat's
Barn

Hays

Endon
Hays

4

Common   Road

Park   Road

Newtown

Ashmore
House

Dingle Lane

Oxhay

28

iddulph

Tallash

5

Butterlands
Farm

Top Road

6

Staffordshire Moorlands Walks

Troughstone
Farm

**The
Hollands**

Porter's
Farm

7

Heath
Hay

The

Hollands

Shirkley
Hall

Hurst   Road

Ellases Lane

Stanways   Lane

Hot Lane

Broad
Meadows

8

Under the Hill

Over the Hill

Dam Lane

School Lane

Moor
2 First School

Park Lane

Rudyard

Rails Farm

Top Road

G   H   J   41   K   L   M

Church   La

Ridgefie

Fairfields
Rd

PO

Cedar Tree

Cottside

roomfields

Lane

A B C 19 D Heaton E F

High Lee

I

Rushton
Bank

Rushton
Spencer

Askerbank Lane

Bandridge Lane

Rushton C of E
Primary School

Sugar Street

A523(T)

Mow Cop Trail

Heaton
House Farm

Axstones
Spring

Overh
Farm

2

Beat Lane

Ryecroft
Gate

Rushtonhall

3

Lee House

Reacliffe Road

Wolf-Dale

Intakes

Fairborough

Endon
L

4

Leeside

Staffordshire

Moorlands

Barnswood

27

Barns
Lee

Walks

A523(T)

5

Cliffe Park

Rudyard
Reservoir

Hunt
House

6

Birch Trees
Farm

7

Reacliffe Road

Rea Cliffe
Farm

Greentree
Farm

Green Lane

Rudyard
Manor

8

St Michaels
First School

Heath House Lane

42

Horton Lodge
Special School

The Crescent

Lake

Hotel

Willgate Farm

A B C D E F

G H J 20 K L M

Gun End
Farm

Isle

Oldhay
Top

Horse
Haylands

Stockmeadows

Gree

373
▲
Gun Hill

Lodge
Farm

Wetwood

Redshaw

Burntoak
Hollins

Meerbrook ✝

Haddon

Oxhay

Alder
Lee

30

Titteswort
Reservoir

wners

Gunside

Rudyard
Hall

Park
House

North
Hillswood

Red Earth
Farm

Staffordshire Moorlands Walks

Fould

Upper Foker

Lower Foker
Farm

G H 43 K L M

Poolend

South Hillswood
Farm

MACCLESF

I
2
3
4
5
6
7
8

A   B   Five
Clouds   C   21   D   E   Summi   F

Roach Side
Farm

I

ckmeadows

Greenlane

Lodge
Farm

2

3

4

29

5

6

7

North
Hillswood

8

Pheasant
Clough

Well
Farm

Windygates

Far House

The
Roaches
House

Naychurch

Frith
Bottom

Staffordshire Moorlands Walks

Benthead

Upper
Hulme

A53

River

Whitty   Lane

Nether
Hay

Knd

Whitty   Lane

Middle
Hulme

Tittesworth
Reservoir

Walks

Blackshaw Moor
C of E First
School

Hotel

Blackshaw Moor

Staffordshire

Moorlands

A53

Troutsdale
Farm

Ley Fields

Thorncliff

A   B   C   Upper
Tittesw   44   D   E   F

G   H   J   **22**   K   L   M

Boarsgrove

1 Round Knowl

2

3

4

32

5

6

7 Hob Hay

8

Dry Stones

Morridge

Folly

Oxbatch

Swainsmoor

Strines

Merryton Low

Hurdlow

Mermaid

Feltysitch

Brindley Croft

Whitehouse

Triangle

Highfields Farm

Royledge

New York

Sheepwalk

Upper Green

Lower Green Farm

G   H   J   **45**   K   L   M

Upper Acre

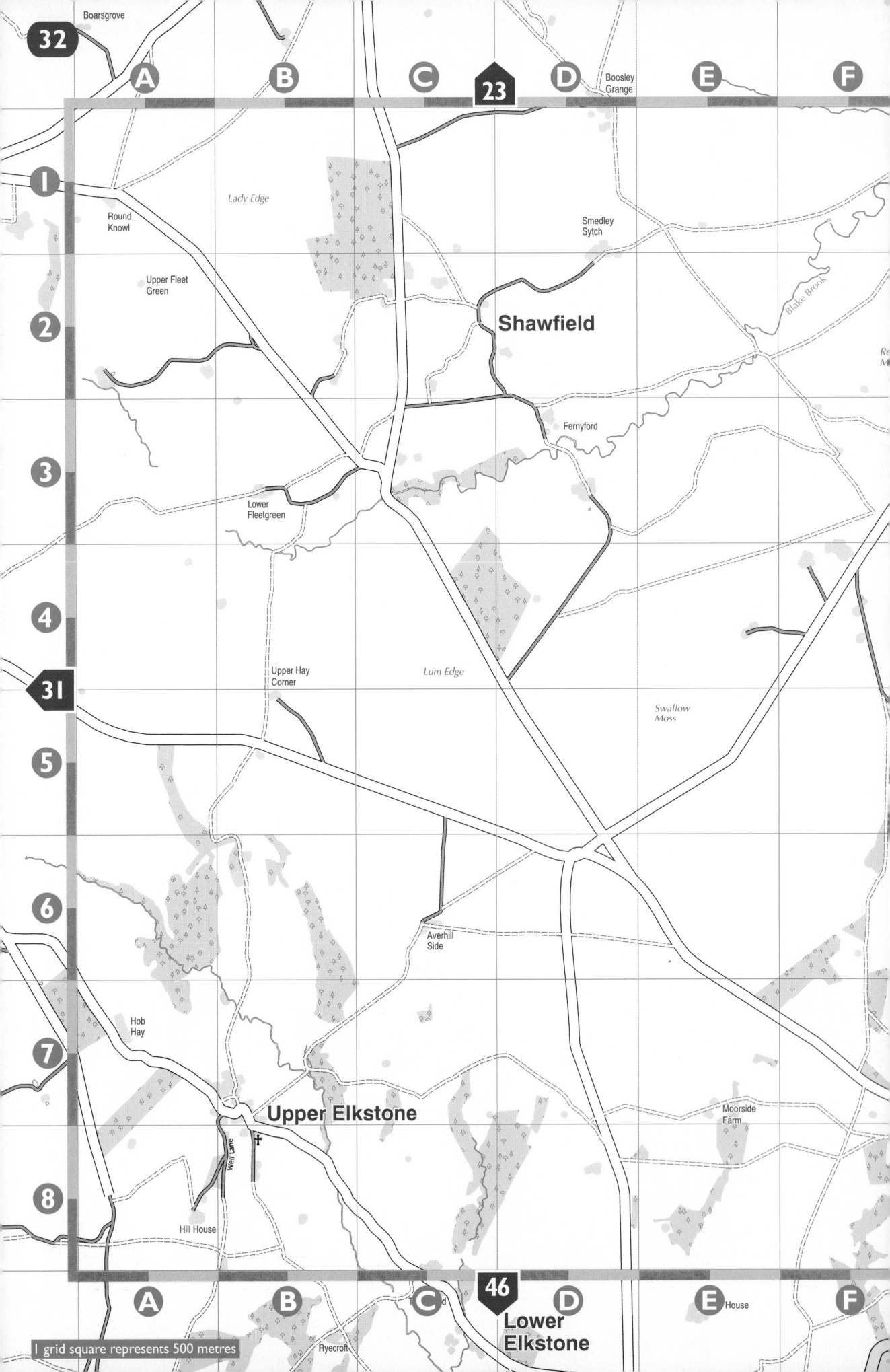

Boarsgrove

A   B   C   23   D   E   F

Boosley
Grange

1
Round
Knowl

Lady Edge

Smedley
Sytch

Blake Brook

Upper Fleet
Green

2
Shawfield

Re
M

Fernyford

3
Lower
Fleetgreen

4

Upper Hay
Corner

Lum Edge

31

*Swallow
Moss*

5

6

Averhill
Side

Hob
Hay

7

Moorside
Farm

Upper Elkstone

8
Well Lane

Hill House

A   B   C   46   D   E   House   F

Ryecroft

Lower
Elkstone

Ⓐ Ⓑ Ⓒ ◆25 Ⓓ Ⓔ Ⓕ

① High Sheen Farm
Harris Close
Hide Lane

Slate House Farm

Sprink

② Bank Top Farm
Long Dale

Sheen PO
Pown Street

③ Fold Farm
Moat Hall
Hide Lane
Bank Side

④ Bridge-end
Dig Street
Hartington
Harrots Lane

◆33 Stonewell Lane
Church St
Hartington C of E School
B5054

⑤ River Dove
Parsons Cl
MILL LANE
Hall Bank
Reynards Lane
Highfield Lane

⑥ Banktop
The Raikes
MILL LANE
Crossland Sides

B5054

⑦ Lower Hurst Farm
Derbyshire County
Staffordshire County
Brighton

⑧ Upper Hurst
Beresford Dale

Harecops
Beresford Lane

Ⓐ Ⓑ Ⓒ ◆48 Ⓓ Ⓔ Ⓕ

I grid square represents 500 metres

G   H   J   K   L   M

Newhaven
Lodge

I

Leanlow
Farm

Tissington Trail

Hartington-moor
Farm

High Peak Trail

2

Brundcliffe

B5054

3

Hand
Dale

Newhaven
Cottage

Tissington Trail

A515

Friden

4

Old
House

Heathcote

Newhaven

5

Harding's Lane

Stanedge
Grange

A515

6

Lane

Dale
End

Tissington Trail

Ivy
House

7

Cliffs Road

Cotterill
Farm

Percival
Close

Biggin

† Biggin
C of E
School

Biggin
Grange

Drury Lane

Greenhead
Crescent

Woollaton Lane

Woollaton Lane

Cardlemere

Dalehead

Greenhead

Tissington Trail

Bank
House

8

Lane

Cliffs Road

Back Lane

Hassall GrGn

G6
1 Dunnockswood

H6
1 Smith Cl

J4
1 Rowan Cl

J5
1 Brookfield Dr

H7
1 Bude Cl
2 Sandside Rd

J7
1 Gawsworth Cl
2 Tatton Cl

K6
1 The Butts
2 Woodland Ct

South Cheshire Way

Townsend

Thurlwood

Rode Heath

Lawton Heath End

Lawton Heath

Lawton-gate

ALSAGER

38

51

G7, K5
Street names for
these grid squares
are listed at the
back of the index

M2
1 Fernleaf Cl

M3
1 Birchfield Av
2 Maple Pl
3 Willow Tree Gv

L3
1 Byron Cl

L8
1 Chestnut Dr
2 Sycamore Av

K7
1 Woolaston Dr

L2
1 Burns Cl
2 Scott Cl

G7
1 Dorchester Cl

G8
1 Back Heathcote St
2 Swallow Cl

H4
1 Chapel Cl
Farm

Cheshire's Close

G H J K L M

Roe Park

Cheshire Ring Canal Walk

Old House Green

Ramsdell Hall

Roepark Farm

Roe Park

Hayhill

LC

Drumber Lane

Close Farm

Staffordshire County

Staffordshire Way

Congleton Road

Old-Man of Mow

Castle Road

Station Road

Birch Tree Lane

Wood Street

High Street

Close

Mow Cop Castle (NT)

Tower Hill

Akesmoor Lane

Spring Bank

The Bank

Grays Cl

The Bank

Meadowside Lane

Mount Pleasant Road

Station Road

Top Station Rd

Manor Rd

Lower High

Well St

Pr Bourne

St Thomas

Church Lane

Moorland

Road

Hill Road

The Bank

Mill Lane

The Brake Village

Westfield Rd

Chapel St

Hillside

Chapel Museum

Mow Cop Road

Sands Road

Tower Road

Hill Road

Mow Cop

PO

M

No

40

Mount Pleasant

Chapel St

Central Street

North Street

Church Street

Woodcock Lane

Halls

Rockside

Fords Lane

Castle CP School

Biddulph Road

Brown

West St

Wilmer Crs

Clare St

PO

South Street

Mow Cop Road

Mellors Bank

Dale View

Holly Lane

Lees Road

The Hollow

High View

Dale Green Road

Dales Green

Harriseahead

High Street

Wain Lee

Mow

Lee

Brieryhurst

Aldenay Lane

Harriseahead

Chapel Lane

Clare Street

Brown Lane

Long Lane

Stadmorslow Lane

Stadmo

Cob

Moor Road

Lawton St

PO

Church St

High St

Bank

Willowcroft Way

Thursfield CP School

Laurel Drive

Aspen Close

Cottonwood Grove

Staffordshire County
City of Stoke-on-Trent

The Rookery

Maryhill Cl

Gloucester Road

Maryhill CP School

Calleys

Newchapel Road

Brieryhurst

Rigby Road

Hillary Rd

Hazel Place

St Andrews Drive

Acacia Gardens

Woodhall Road

Bullocks House Road

Thursfield Lodge

Comprehensive School

Moss Pl

Park View

Saisbd

Castleview

Everest Road

Rookery Road

Birkdale Drive

Lark Av

Starling

Kite

Merlin Way

Wild Goose Av

Newchapel

Dorset Place

Bank

PO

Whitehill

Highfield Avenue

Spey Drive

Lapwing Road

Pennyfields Road

High Street

Warwick

William

Rutland

Surtey Rd

Tawney Cl

Derwent Crs

Tern Avenue

Marsh Av

Newtown

Lamb Street

Dove Bank CP School

Whitehill Road

Nabbswood

Medina Rd

Diamond

Brights

Wingnay Road

Dairy Gdns

Kidsgrove Medical Centre

Lordshire Pl

Jasmin Wy

Woodruff

Attwood St

Powy Dr

Weir Gv

Whitefield Rd

Whitehill

Station Rd

Handley

LIVERPOOL

Town Hall

Kiline Bank Rd

Wellington

Mount

Kingswood

Larkfield

Parklands

53

K7
1 Osprey Vw

J8
1 Phoenix Cl
2 Sparrowbutts Gv

J7
1 Astbury Cl
2 Thursfield Av

M
Lorraine

H8
1 Burnwood Gv
2 Magpie Crs
3 Mossfield Crs
4 Nabbs Cl
5 Silvermine Cl
6 Tilewright Cl
7 Wheelock Wy
CP School

PO

G H J K L M

ckm

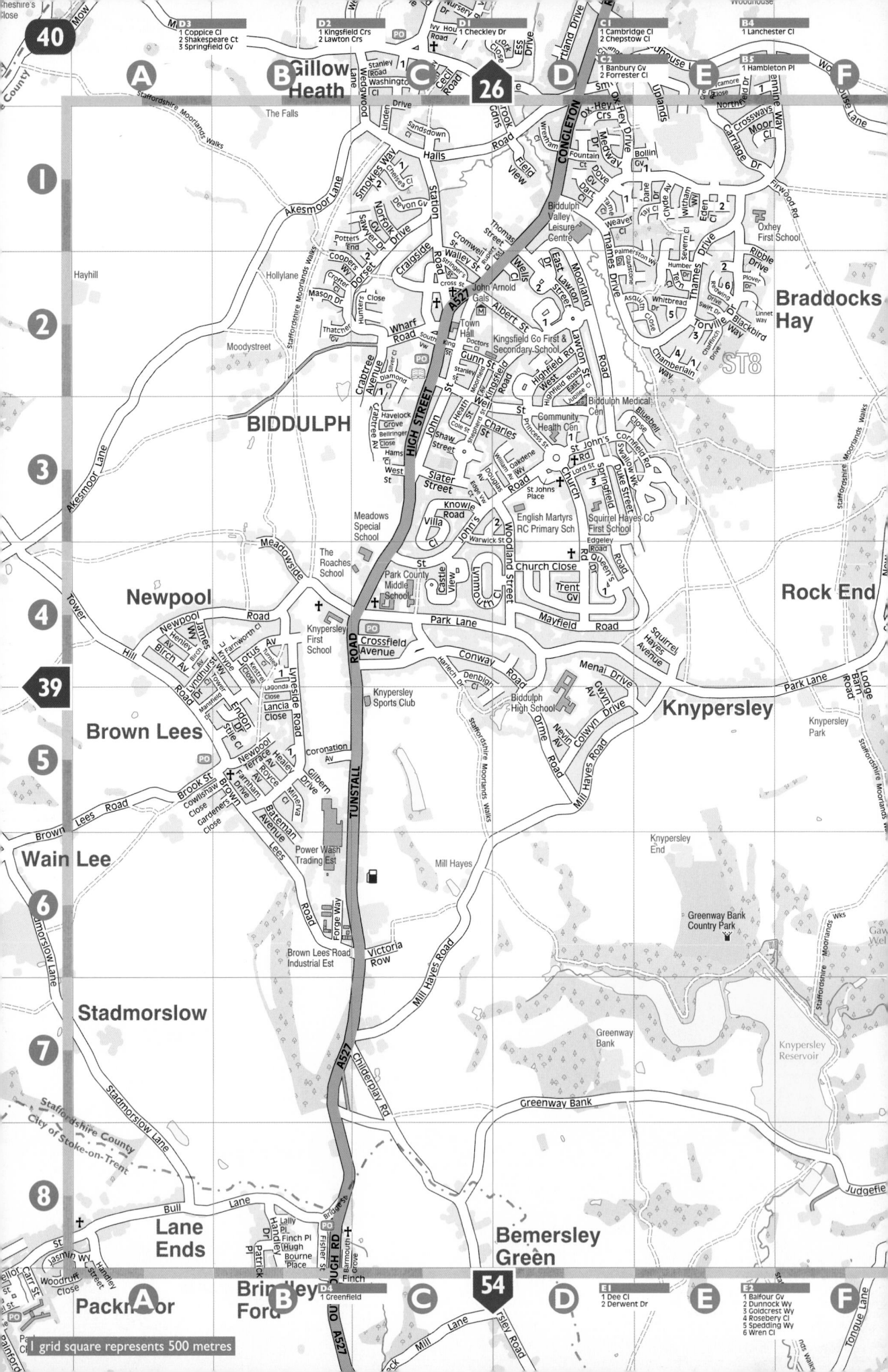

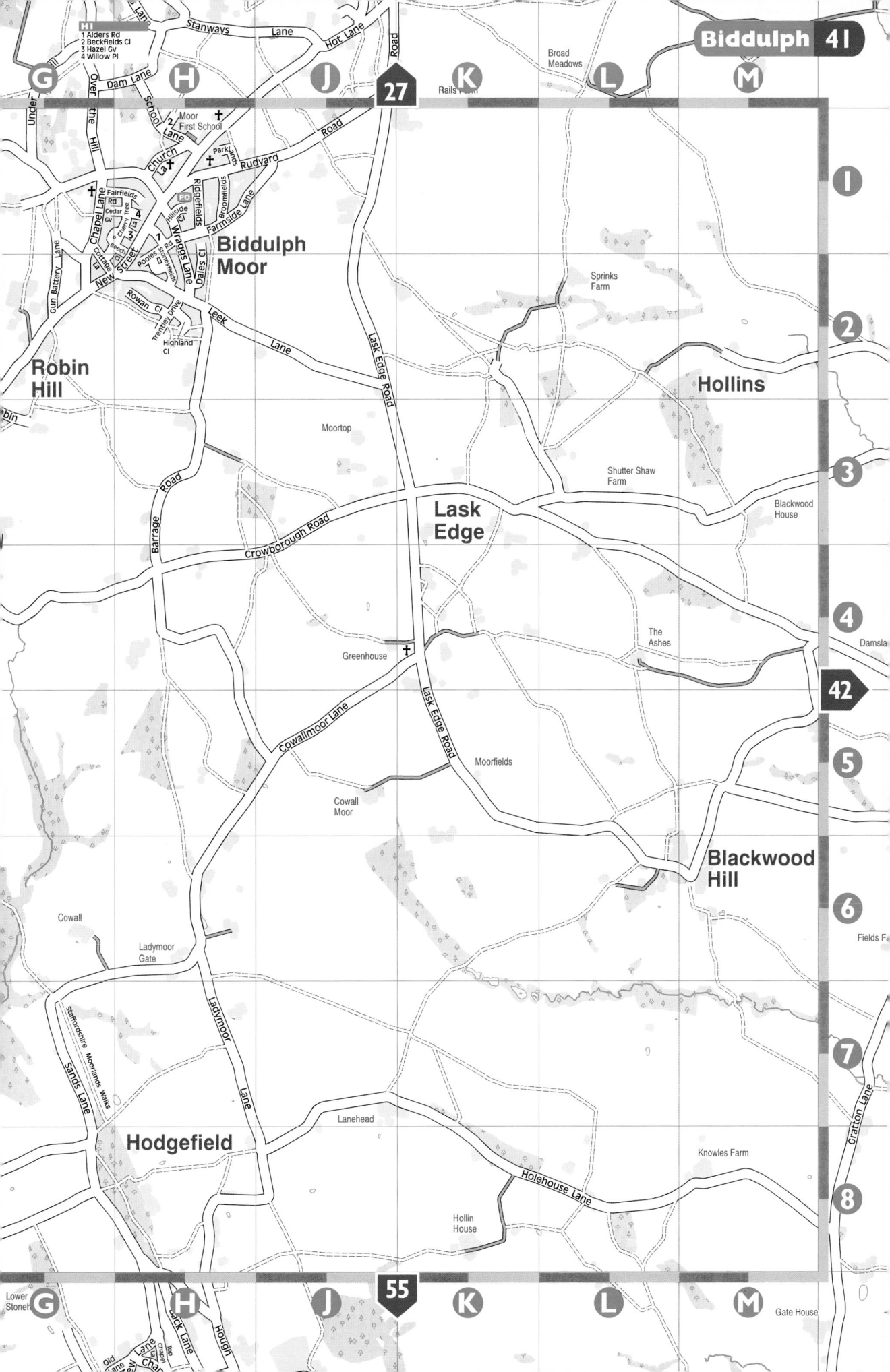

H1
1 Alders Rd
2 Beckfields Cl
3 Hazel Gv
4 Willow Pl

Stanways Lane
Hot Lane
Road

G   H   J   27   K   Broad Meadows   L   M   I

Moor First School
School Lane
Dam Lane
Over the Hill
Under the Hill
Park Jms
Rudyard
Church La
Rudyard Road

Rails Farm

Fairfields Rd
Cedar Gv
Cherry Tree
Ridgefields
Broomfields
Broomfields
Farmside Lane
Hillside
PO

Biddulph Moor

Chapel Lane
Cottage La
Beech Cl
Pooles
New Street
Wraggs Lane
Dales Cl

Rowan Cl
Trentlea Drive
Highland Cl

Leek Lane

Sprinks Farm

2

Robin Hill

Hollins

obin

Moortop

Lask Edge Road

Shutter Shaw Farm

3

Blackwood House

Barrage Road

Crowborough Road

Lask Edge

4

Damsla

Greenhouse

The Ashes

42

Cowallmoor Lane

Lask Edge Road

Moorfields

5

Cowall Moor

Blackwood Hill

6

Cowall

Fields Fa

Ladymoor Gate

Ladymoor Lane

7

Staffordshire Moorlands Walks
Sands Lane

Lanehead

Gratton Lane

8

Hodgefield

Holehouse Lane

Knowles Farm

Hollin House

Lower Stoneh

dCK Lane
Hough
Chapel
Lane
Old

G   H   J   **31**   K   L   M

I

2

3

4

46

5

6

7

8

G   H   J   **59**   K   L   M

Lower
Green
Farm

Upper
Acre

Manor Farm

Meadows

Old
Mixon Hay

New
Mixon Hay

Mixon

Golden
Hill

ST13

Dunlea
Farm

Harvey Gate

Newhouse
Farm

Morridge

White Lea
Farm

Wellington
Farm

Waterhouse

Butterton
Moor End

Douse Lane

High
Cross

Onecote
Lane Head

Onecote
Grange

Intake Farm

Douse Lane

Onecote

PH

Onecote
CP School

Moor Top

Moorside

Wetley Lane

Moor Top

Slate Ho

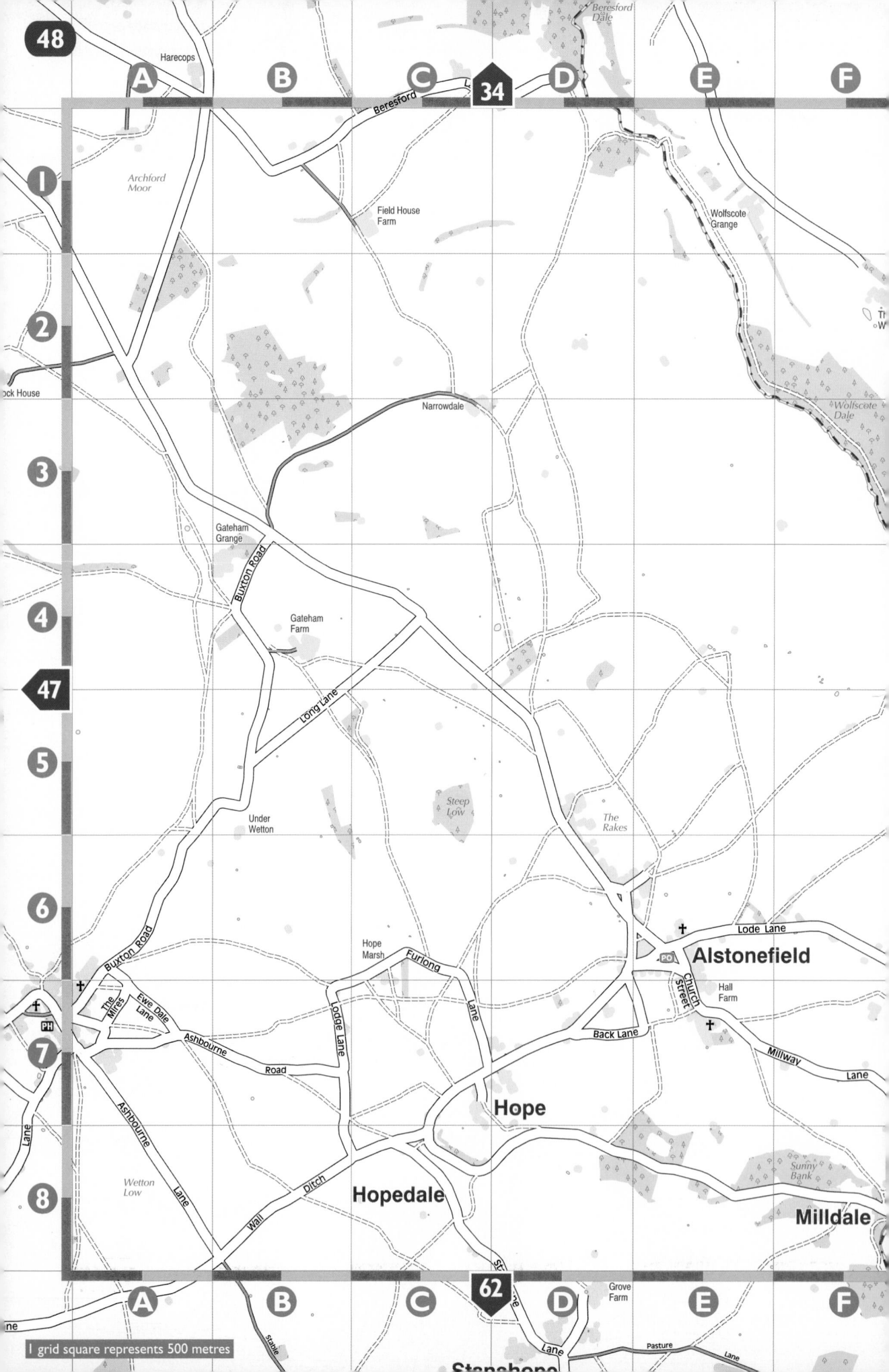

G H J K L M

Woollaton Lane

Dalehead

Greenhead

Woollaton Lane

35

I

Liffs Road

Back Lane

Back Lane

Bigginmoor
Farm

2

Biggin
Dale

Tissington Trail

A515

3

4

Liffs Road

Tissington Trail

Coldeaton

Hawkslow
Farm

Crosslow

Alsop Moor
Cottages

5

River Dove

Lane

Oxdales
Farm

A515

Iron Tors

Tissington Trail

6

Crosslow Lane

Staffordshire County

Derbyshire County

Crosslowbank

Lode
House

Dam Lane

7

A515

Alsop en le Dale

Lode Lane

Tissington Trail

The

Shining Tor

Pinch

Dam Lane

Oxclose Lane

8

Green

Lane

63

Dar

Parwich

Gag L

A515

Tissington Trail

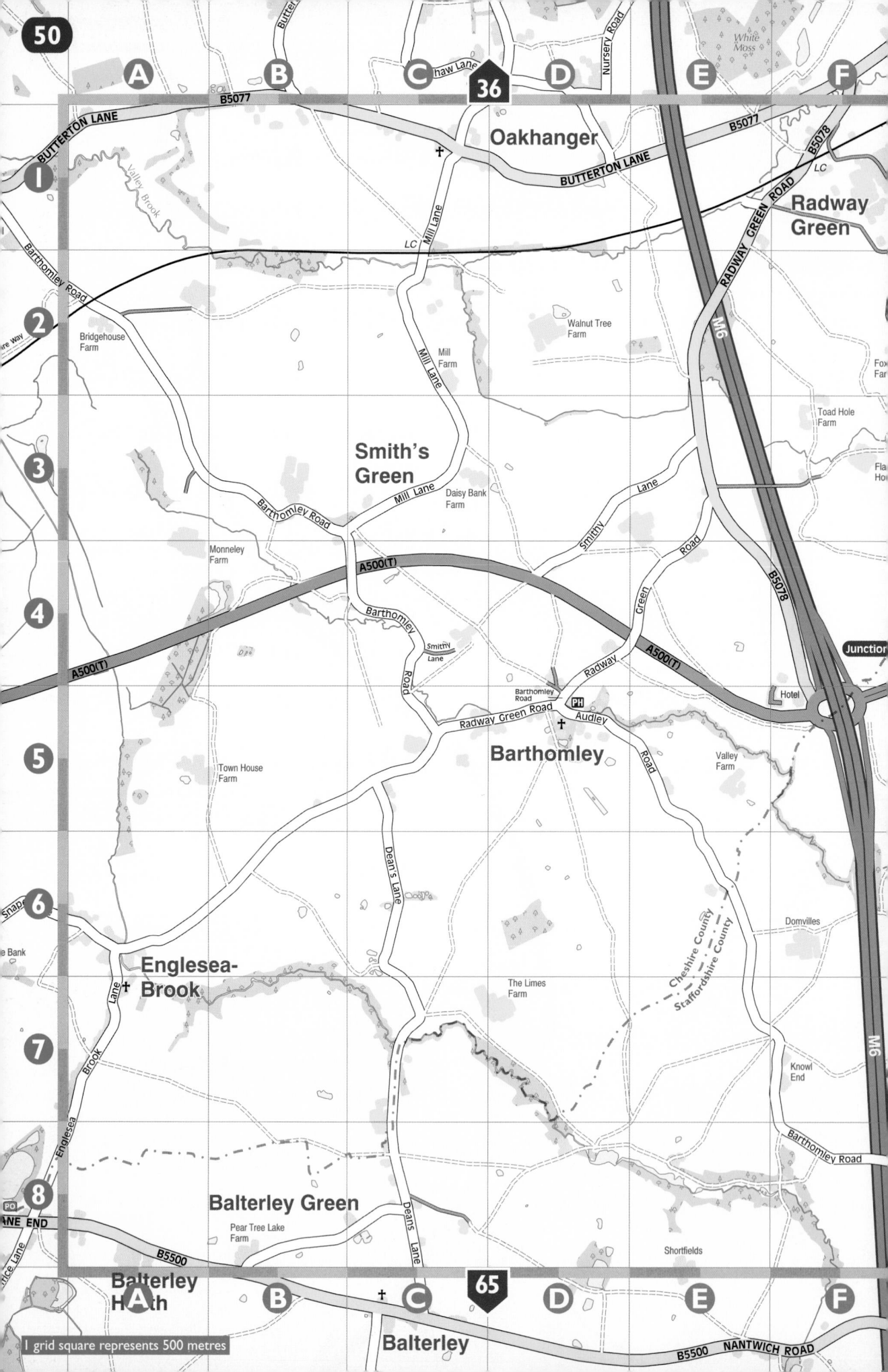

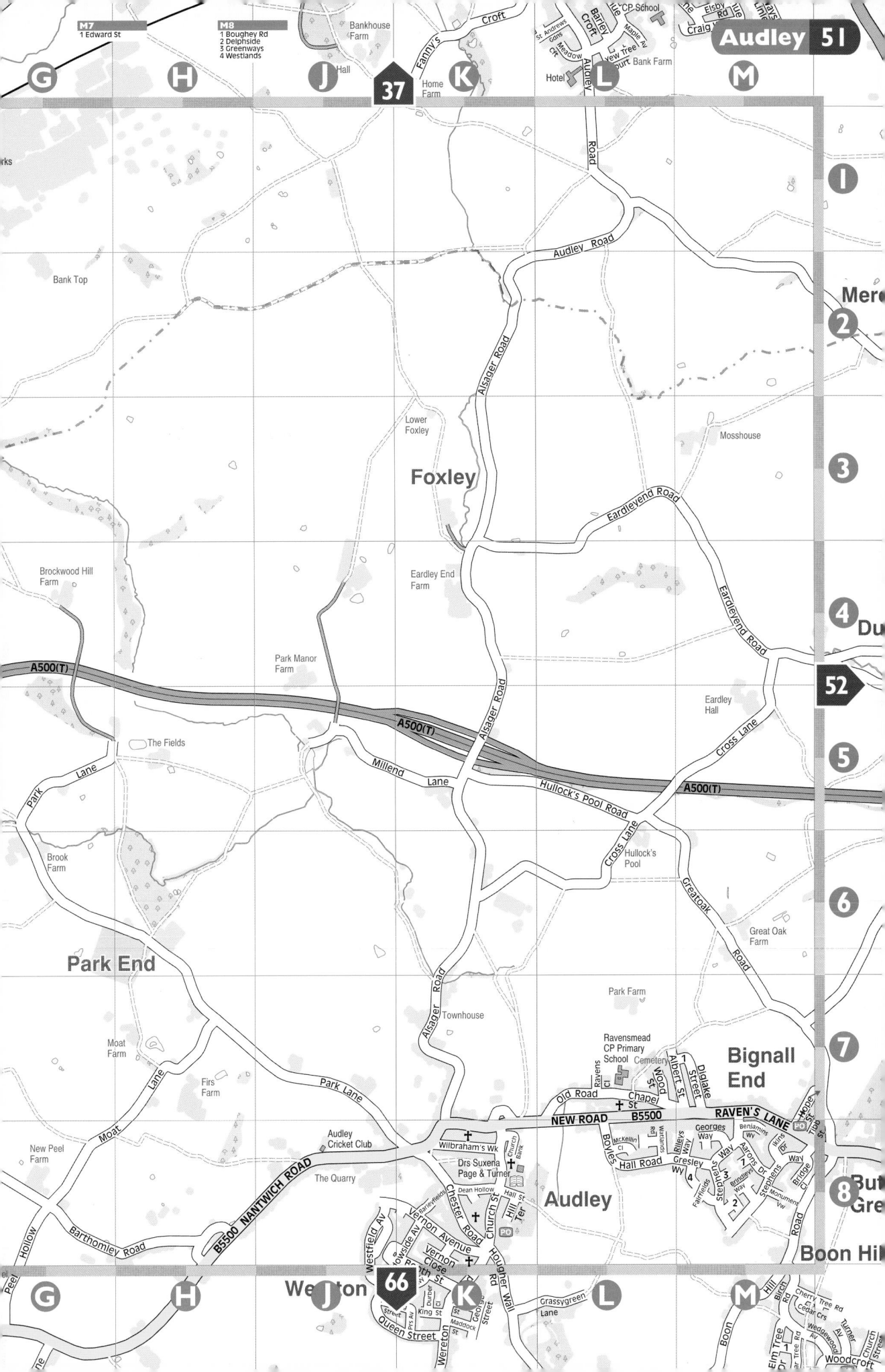

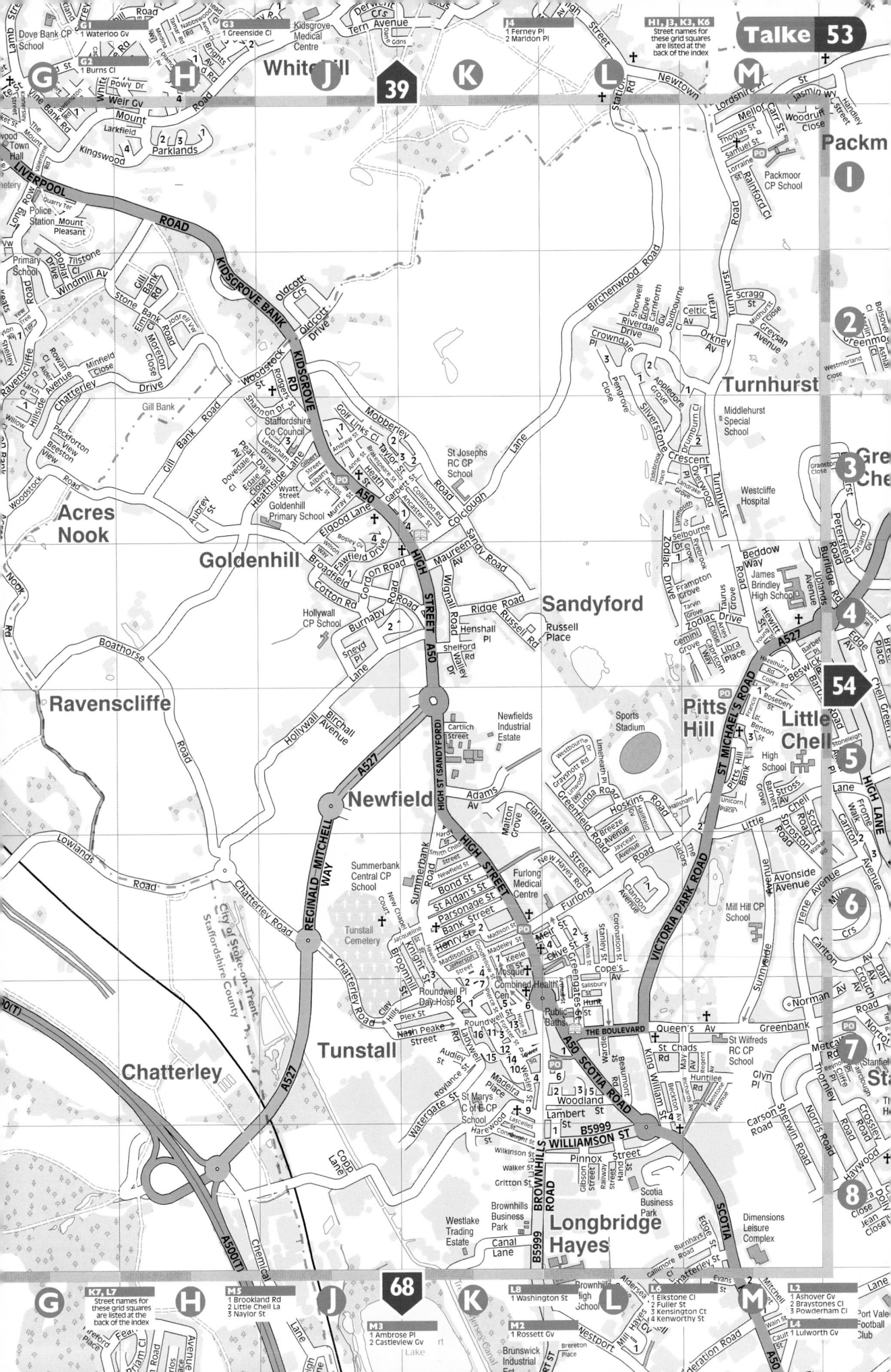

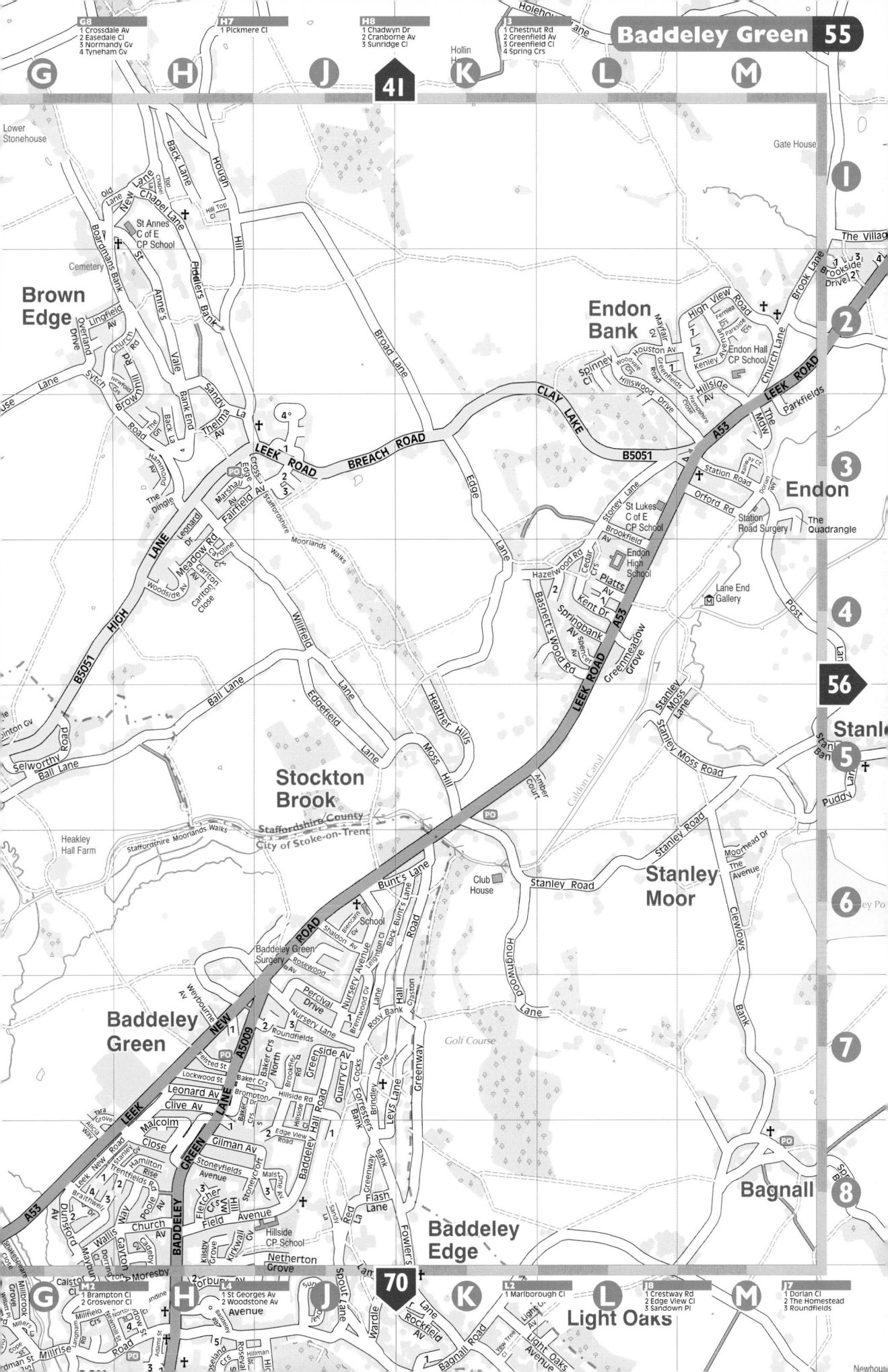

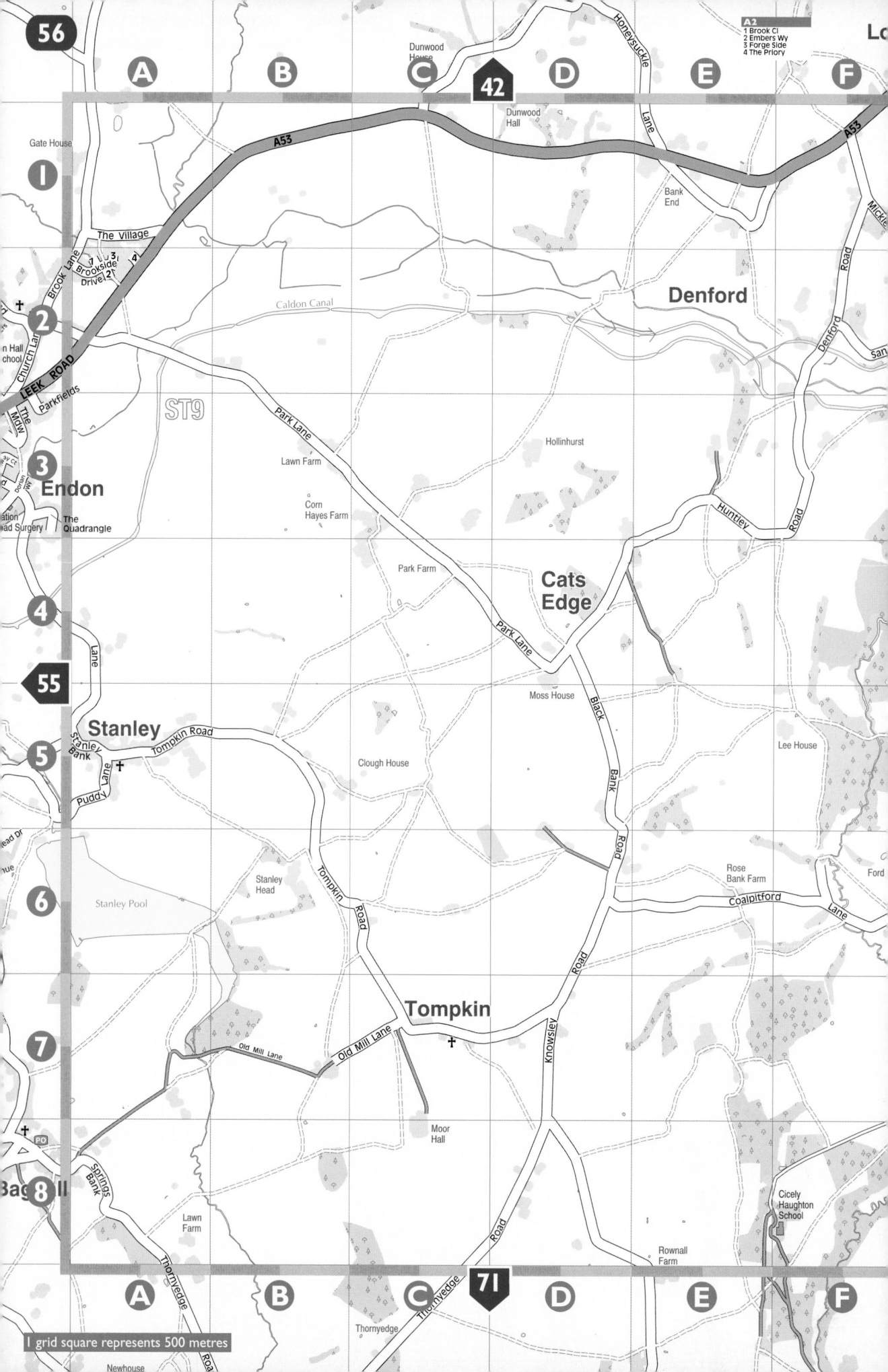

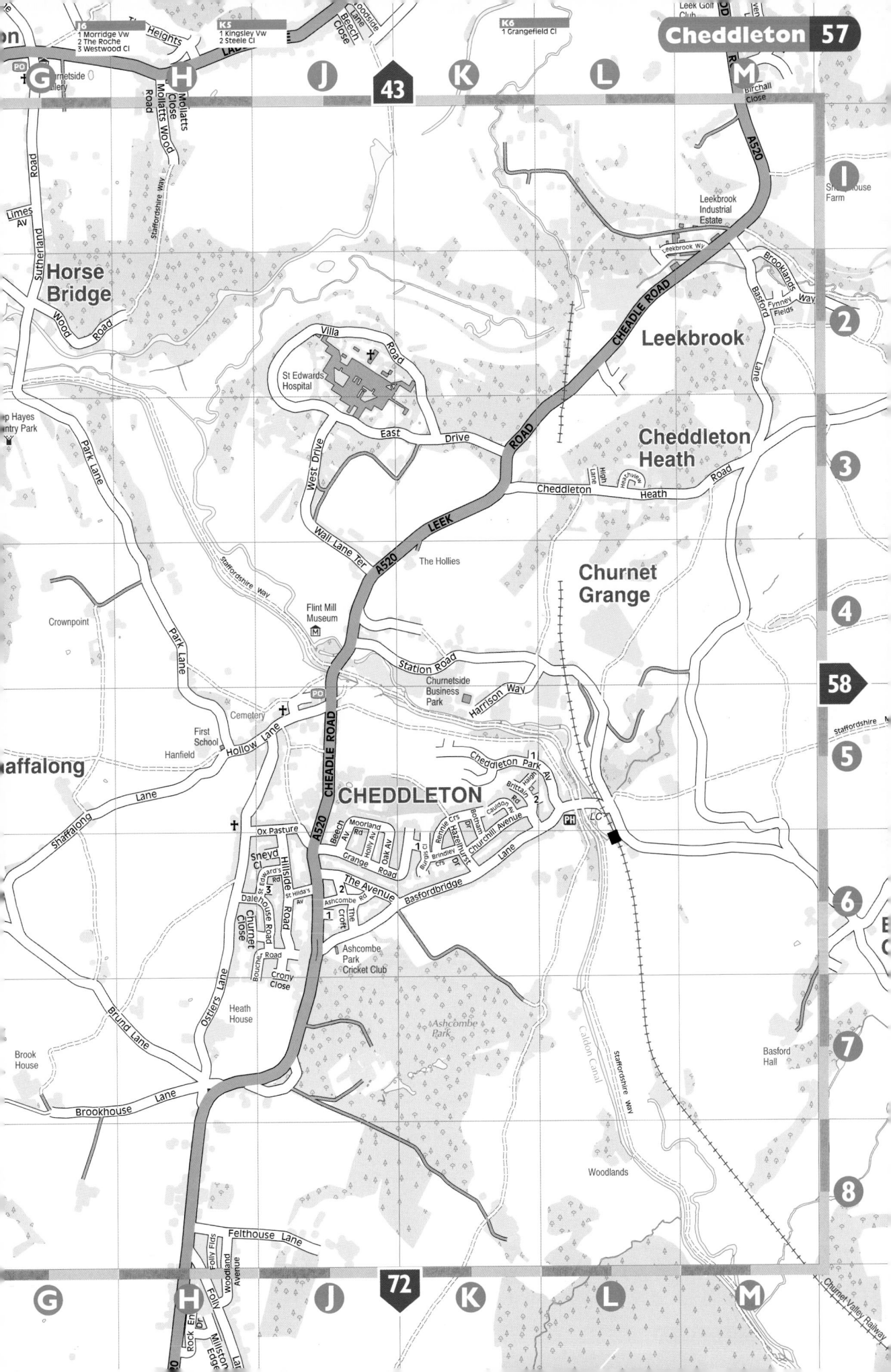

Middle Cliff

58

A B C 44 D E F

Fairfield

Birchall Close

A520

1 Sheephouse Farm

Longshaw

Brooklands Way

Basford Fynney Lane

2 Fynneylane

Roost Hill

Revedge

Ballfields

Apes

3 Ringehay

Combes Brook

4

Staffordshire Moorlands Walks

57

Staffordshire Moorlands Walks

Sharpcliffe Hall

5 Basford Grange

6 **Basford Green**

Low Wood

Staffordshire Moorlands Walks

Crab Tree Farm

7 Bas Hall

Whitehough

8 Hills Farm

Coltstone

Mosslee Hall

Church Lane

Chesnet Valley Railway

A B C 73 D E F

1 grid square represents 500 metres

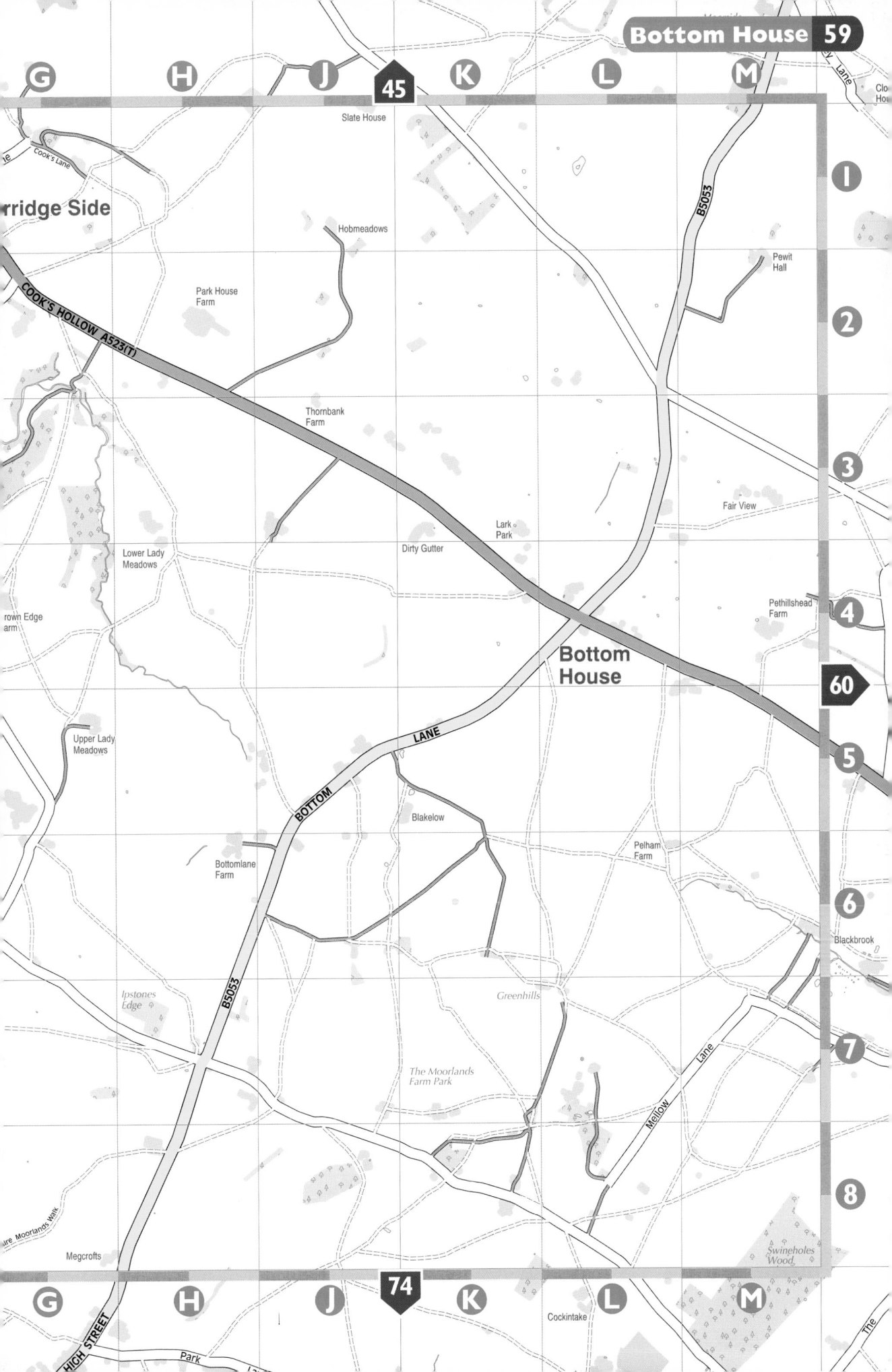

G H J **45** K L M

I
2
3
4
60
5
6
7
8

Slate House

Hobmeadows

Park House
Farm

COOK'S HOLLOW A523(T)

Thornbank
Farm

Lark
Park

Dirty Gutter

Lower Lady
Meadows

**Bottom
House**

Upper Lady
Meadows

LANE

Blakelow

Pelham
Farm

Bottomlane
Farm

B5053

Ipstones
Edge

Greenhills

The Moorlands
Farm Park

Mellow Lane

Megcrofts

Swineholes
Wood

G H J **74** K L M

HIGH STREET

Cockintake

ridge Side

Cook's Lane

B5053

Pewit
Hall

Fair View

Pethillshead
Farm

Blackbrook

rown Edge
arm

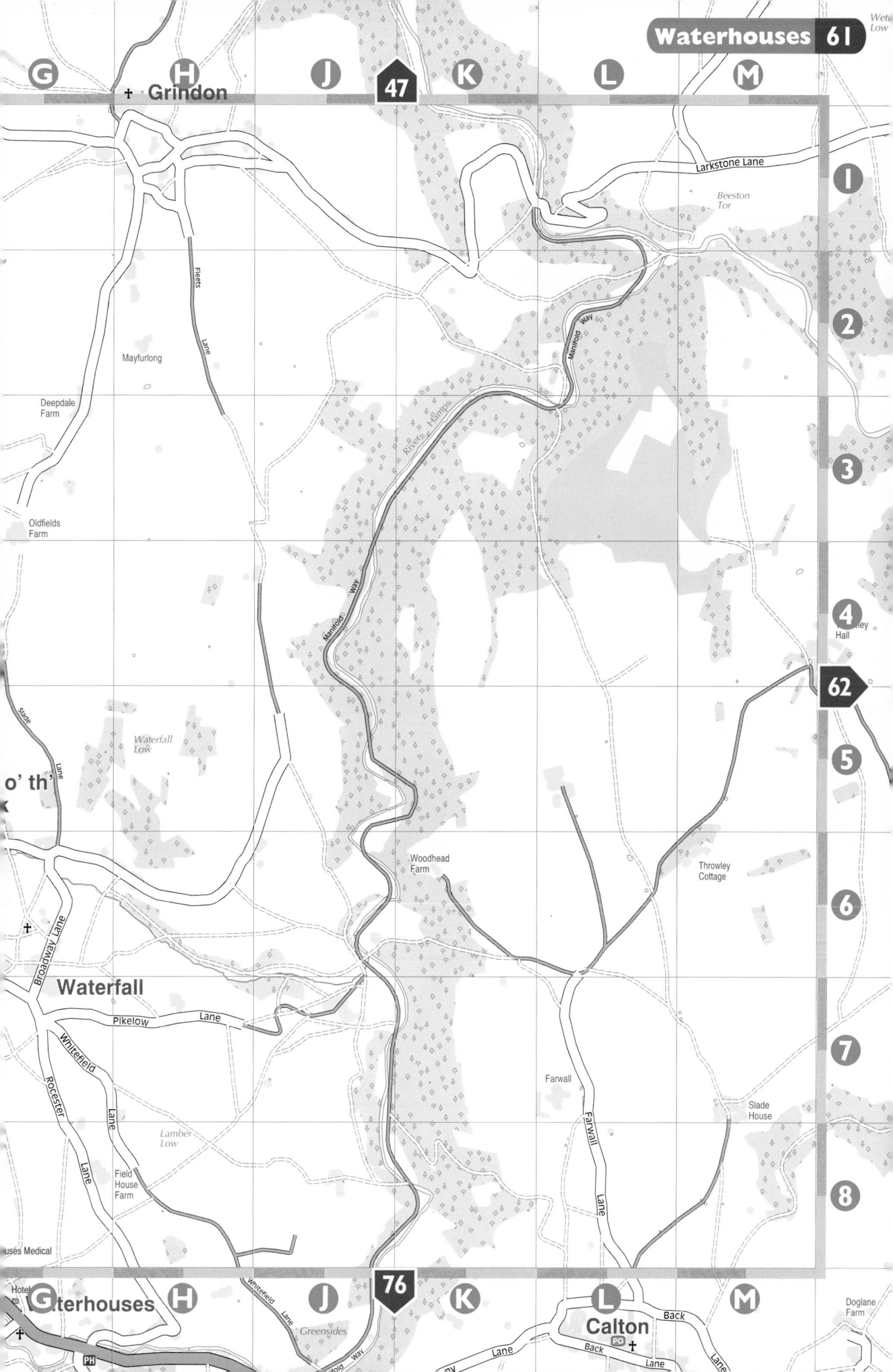

G ✝ **Grindon** H J ◆47 K L M

Larkstone Lane

Beeston Tor

I

2

3

4

Hall

62

5

Fleets Lane

Mayfurlong

Deepdale Farm

River Hamps

Manifold Way

Oldfields Farm

Manifold Way

Waterfall Low

Woodhead Farm

Throwley Cottage

6

o' th'

★

7

✝ Broadlaw Lane

Waterfall

Pikelow Lane

Lane

Whitefield Lane

Rocester Lane

Lamber Low

Field House Farm

Farwall

Farwall Lane

Slade House

8

...uses Medical

Hotel

G **...terhouses** H J ◆76 K L M

Whitefield Lane

Greensides

✝

PH

Calton PO ✝

Back Lane

Back Lane

Doglane Farm

Lane

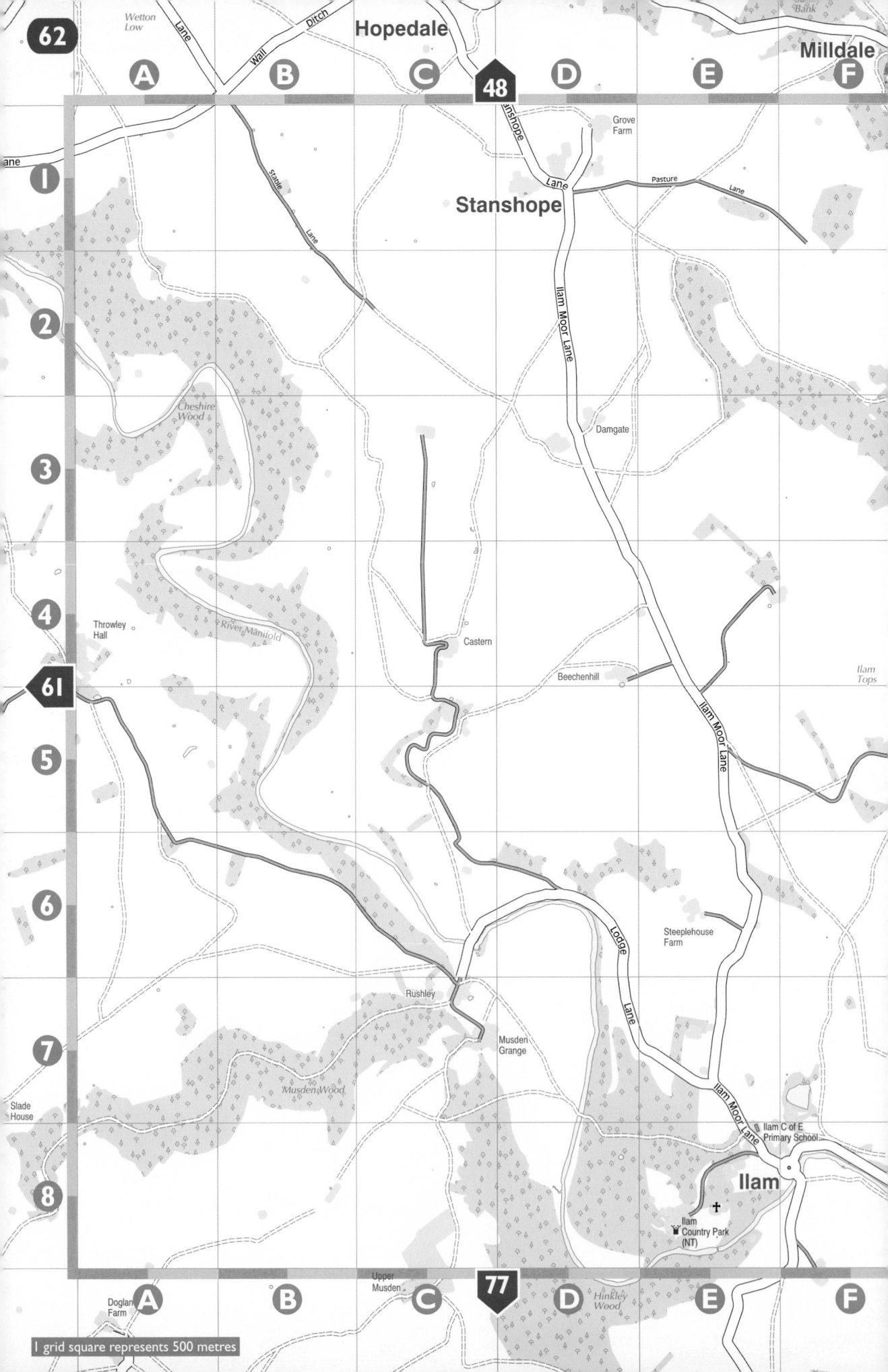

A7
1 Foundry La
2 Northfleet St

A4
1 Abbey St
2 Avonwick Gv
3 Perivale Cl

A5
1 Cluny Pl

A **B** **C** **D** **E** **F**

55

Ba Deley Edge

Light Oaks

Jack Hay

Milton

Staffordshire County
City of Stoke-on-Trent

Woodhead

Woodhead Road

Greenfield

Kerry Hill

Holehouse Farm

Abbey Surgery

Carmountside CP School

Abbey Farm

Birches Head Road

Leek Road Surgery

The New Abbey Friar

ST2

Abbey Hulton

Abbey Hulton CP School

Our Lady & St.Benedict RC Primary School

Abbey Hill Special School

Newhouse Special Sch

North Staffordshire Combined Healthcare N H S Trust

Eaves Lane

Brookhouse Lane

Hanley Hayes

Hanley Town Football Club

Heath House La

Bucknall

Townsend Primary School

Stewart's Farm

Ash Hall

Werrington Road

Finney Gardens Sports Ground

Primary Sch

Police Station

Mitchell County High School

Ash Bank Road

Ash Bank

Townsend

Eaton Park CP School

Dividy Road Surg

St Maria Goretti RC Primary School

Simfields

Berry Hill County High School

B8
1 Arclid Wy
2 Cranfield Pl
3 Hammoon Gv

C5
1 Kennermont Rd

C6
1 Dickens St

C8
1 Brecon Wy
2 Oakham Wy

D1
1 Ingleborough Pl

D7
1 Cairn Cl
2 Mulliner Cl
3 Redland Dr

A8, B1, D8
Street names for these grid squares are listed at the back of the index

Berry Hill

1 grid square represents 500 metres

G6
1 Heather Cl
2 Newton Ct

G7
1 Holly Dr
2 Laurel Crs

H6
1 Brentwood Ct
2 Brentwood Gv
3 Haven Crs
4 Kennedy Wk

J6
1 Highbury Rd
2 Irvine Rd

Rownall

Armshead

Withystakes

asherwall

Cellarhead

Werrington

Rownall
Farm

Lawn
Farm

Newhouse
Farm

Lark
Hall

The
Grove

Brookhouse

Thornyedge

Rownall
Hall

Ladyfields

Newfields

Round
Meadows

Heath Avenue

Moorside
High School

Moorside

Southlowe
Av

The
Oval

Toll
Bar
Rd

Withystakes Rd

CELLARHEAD ROAD

Wilton Av

Wetley Av

Armshead Road

Mount C

Kaydor
Cl

Kaydor
Cl

Philip La

Howard
Cl

Caroline
Cl

Park

Moss

Alan Dr

Milford
Av

Moonland
Cl

Moonard

Sandy

Hill

Park

Park
Crs

Park

Park
Dr

Park
Rd

Russell

James

Whitmore
Av

Johnstone Av

Hillside Road

Cotehill Road

Lansdowne Crs

Brentwood Dr

Windmill
Vw

Oak Mount Rd

Ash Bank Rd

Draw-Well

Draw-Well

Avenue

Quarry
Close

Uplands Croft

Marsh Crs

Washerwall

Langford

Meigh

Ferndale

Beaufort

Somerton Rd

Westacre Dr

Kenton

Fernlee

Alford

Hewitt

Uplands

Uplands Av

Stonehouse
Road

Werrington
County Infants
School

PO

A52

ASH BANK ROAD

LEEK ROAD

Grove
Farm

Foxearth

Junior Sch

Werrington
Village Surgery

Salters
Cl

Salters
Cl

HM Young Offenders
Institution Werrington House

Chartwell

Chatsworth

Blithfield

Shugboro

Drive

Capesthorne

Moreton

Haddon

Beaulieu

Close

Clough
Lane

Hulme
Lane

Salters Lane

Saltway
School

Salthouse
Farm

Rouch

Windycote

St
Co
CP

School

Mill Lane

Thornyedge
Road

Washerwall Lane

Rownall Road

Thornyedge

Hulme

56

87

72

LEE

A52

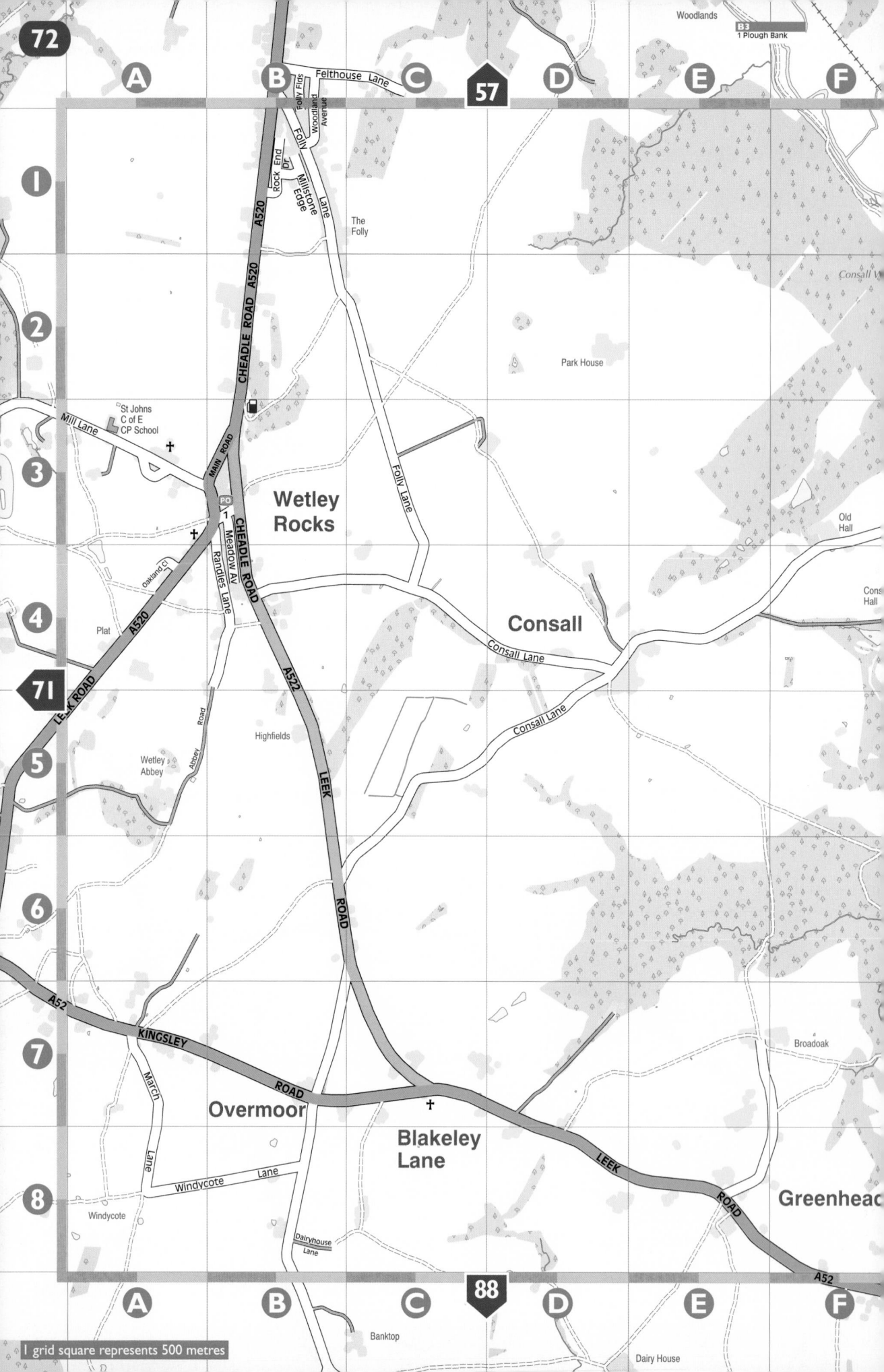

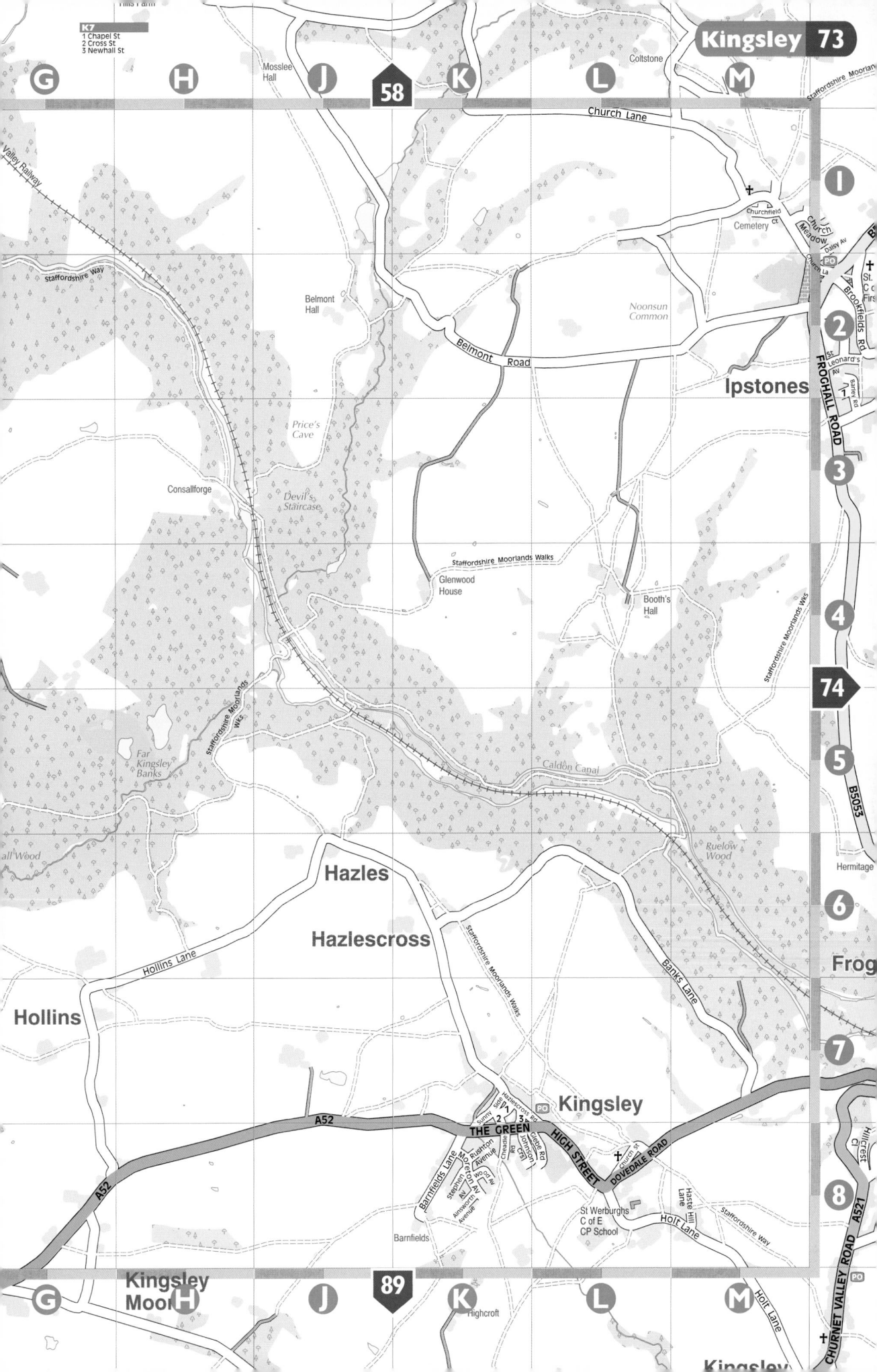

A Megcrofts   B   C   59   D   E   F

A2
1 Regent Ct

Swine
Wood

I
Churchfield
Cemetery Ct
Church Meadow
Dalby Av
Church La
PO

Park Lane
Crowgutter
Cockintake

B5053 HIGH STREET

Staffordshire Moorlands Walks
Higher Parkhead

2
stones
St. Leonards
C of E
First School
Mayfair Av
St Leonard's Av
Brookfields Rd
Barley Rd
FROGHALL ROAD

Ipstones
Park
Ipstones
Park
Farm
Parknook
Black

3
Town Head
Blackbank
Wood

Park Lane

Cloughhead
Shav
Lane

4
Staffordshire Moorlands Wks
Staffordshire Moorlands Walks
PO
Foxt

73

Shirley
Farm

5
B5053
Oldridge
Whiston
Common

6
Hermitage
Staffordshire Moorlands Walks
Staffordshire Moorlands Wks
Blakeley
Lane

Froghall

7
A52
A52
Leys
Brookside
PO
Black
Jubilee
Drive
Whiston Hall
Golf Club
Blake
Farm

St Mildreds
C.of E
CP School
Brookfield Ct
Whiston Eaves La
Whiston

8
Hillcrest Ct
Hillcrest
Avenue
Sidney Drive
A521
Banktop
Eavesford
Ross Road
Eaves Lane
shire Way
Holt Lane

NET VALLEY ROAD
PO

A   B   C   90   D   E   Whiston   F
Eaves

G H J 60 K L M

Waterhouses

Crowtrees Ind
Industrial Est

Waterhouses Med
Practice

Hotel
W

1

Crowtrees

Birch Head

Broomyshaw

Butt's Lane

Cow Lane

Cemetery

2

Church Lane

Church Bank

PH

Cau

3

Walls

Moorend

Cauldon Low

Duke's Lane

4

Stoney Lane

Windy
Harbour

76

W-Wall Lane

Lanehead

5

Cotton Lane

PO

A52

Ellastone Road

**Hoften's
Cross**

6

**Upper
Cotton**

Westfields

Moorhouse

Main

B5417

Road

Moorside

7

Cotton Lane

Staffordshire Moorlands Wks

Tenement
Farm

8

Blakeley Lane

Cemetery

G H J 91 K L M

Moneystone

Threelows

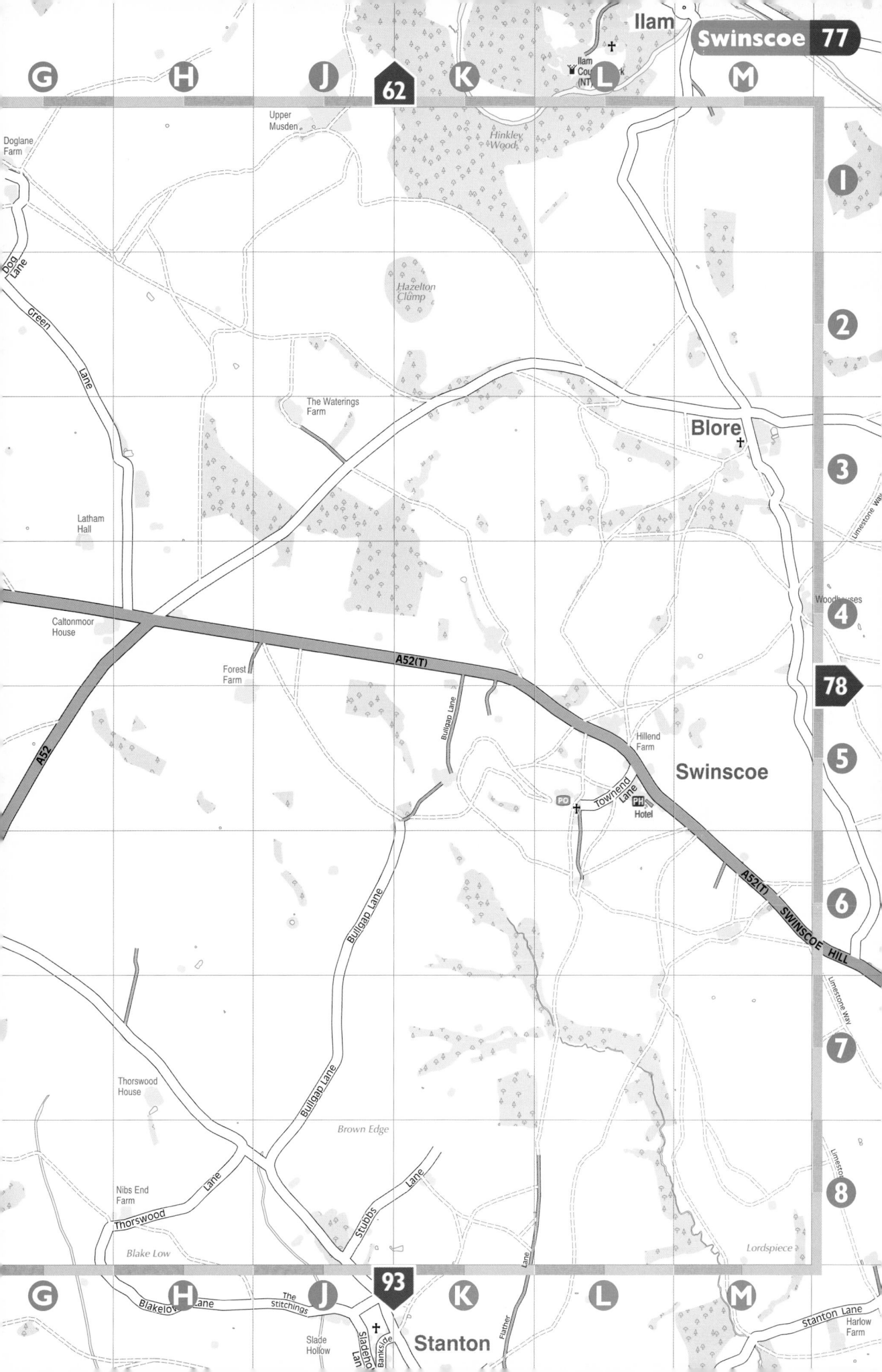

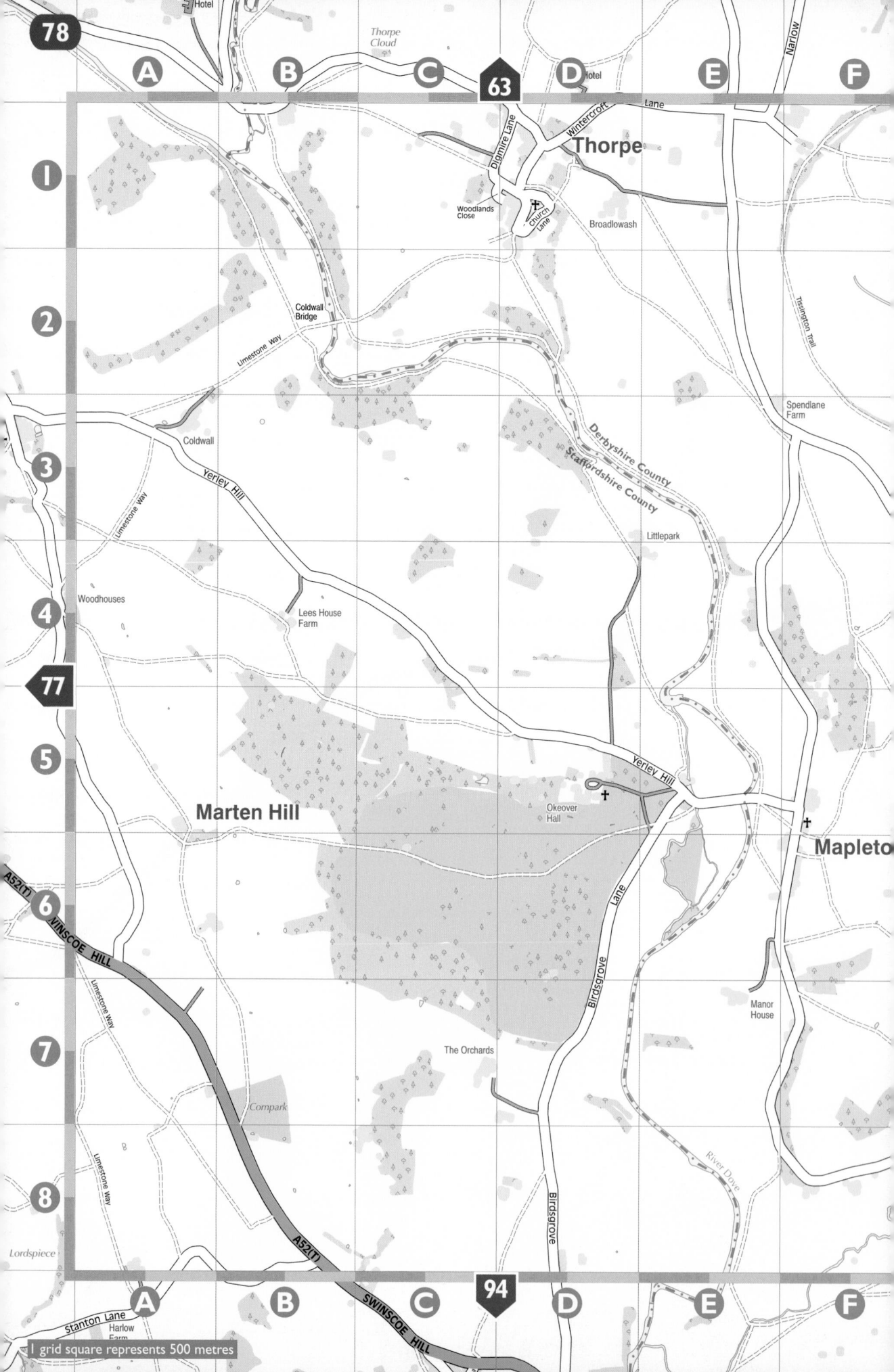

A B C D E F

63

1

Thorpe Cloud

Hotel

Thorpe

Wintercroft Lane

Digmire Lane

Hotel

Church Lane

Woodlands Close

Broadlowash

2

Coldwall Bridge

Limestone Way

Derbyshire County

Staffordshire County

Spendlane Farm

Tissington Trail

3

Coldwall

Yerley Hill

Limestone Way

Littlepark

4

Woodhouses

Lees House Farm

5

Marten Hill

Okeover Hall

Yerley Hill

Mapleto

6

A52(T)

SWINSCOE HILL

Limestone Way

Birdsgrove Lane

Manor House

7

The Orchards

Limestone Way

Compark

8

Lordspiece

A52(T)

River Dove

A B C D E F

SWINSCOE HILL

94

Stanton Lane

Harlow Farm

I grid square represents 500 metres

64

A B C D E F

Randilow
Farm

The Grange

Ley
Ground

1

A51

Checkley Lane

Checkley

LONDON ROAD

2

Bridgemere
Hall

Checkley
Green

Checkley
Brook

3

Checkley
Wood

4

Bridgemere
Farm

Checkley Wood
Farm

5

Blake Hall
Farm

Bridgemere
Garden World

Phynsons Hayes
Farm

Hollyhurst
Farm

mirals
rse

6

Holdings Lane

County
County

Flash Farm

Field Farm

7

The Greaves
Farm

Onnel

8

Syllenhurst
Farm

Gravenhunger
Moss

Candle Lane

Cherry Tree Lane

NANTWICH ROAD

Blaizefield
Close

A B C D E F

AUDLEM ROAD

St Leonard's Way

Farmfields
Rise

Kenrick
Close

PH

PO

Wo

96

A5 WCASTLE ROAD

Bulkeley Hall

Woore County
Primary School

Woore
Hall

1 grid square represents 500 metres

G H J K L M

65

A531

MAIN ROAD

M6

1

2

I

KEELE ROAD

Meadows County P School

Bowseywood Farm

Lower Thornhill

Higher Thornhill

Bowsey Wood Road

Heighley Castle Way

Woodland Hills

Hidden Hills

Madeley Manor

College Close

Windy Arbour

New Road

Holm Oak Drive

Beck Road

Salisbury

Furnace Lane

Woodside Road

Arbour Close

Greenmeadows Road

Police Station

Staffordshire County Council

A525 NEWCASTLE ROAD

Little Madeley

3

PO

Mill Lane

Middle Madeley

Bevan Place

Apple Court

Pear Tree Drive

The Bridle Path

Primrose Dell

Beresford Dale

Plover Field

Bower End

Moss Lane Surgery

Moss Lane

Morningside

Cherry Hill

Merlin Green

Bramble Lea

Madeley High School

Waterside Close

4

Bower End Lane

John Offley Road

Birch Dale

Moor Hall

Izaac Walton Way

POOLSIDE A525

The Holborn

Pastoral Close

Knightley

82

Lane

Hungerford House Farm

5

Madeley

Sir John Offley C of E Primary School

Vicarage Lane

Castle Lane

Nethersel

Hey Lane

Field House

Red Lane

BAR HILL

Bar Hill House Farm

Station Road

Manor Road

6

Onneley Golf Club

Hotel

PH

Hey House

7

Station Road

Manor Farm

8

New Terrace

G H J K L M

97

Aston

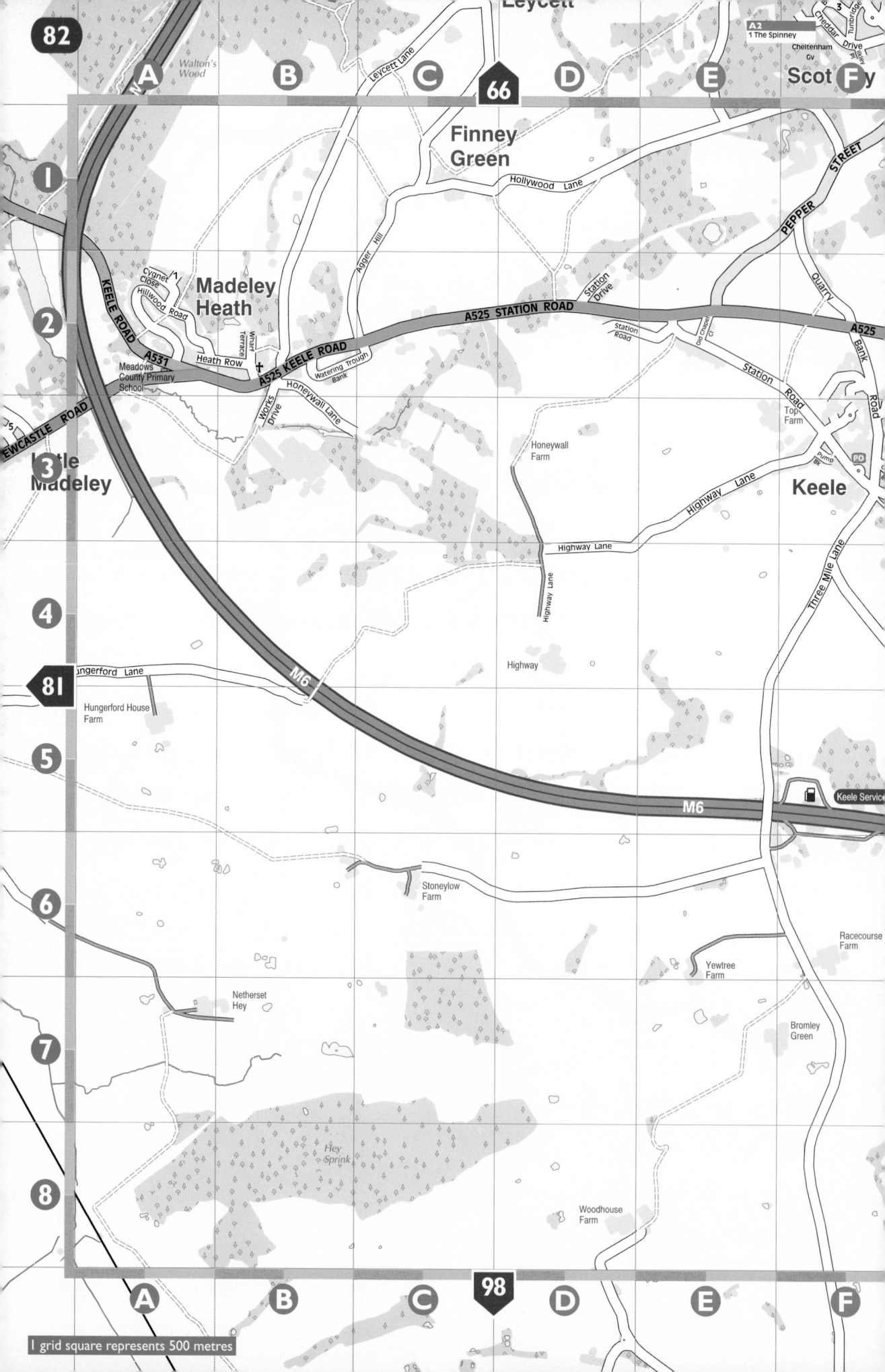

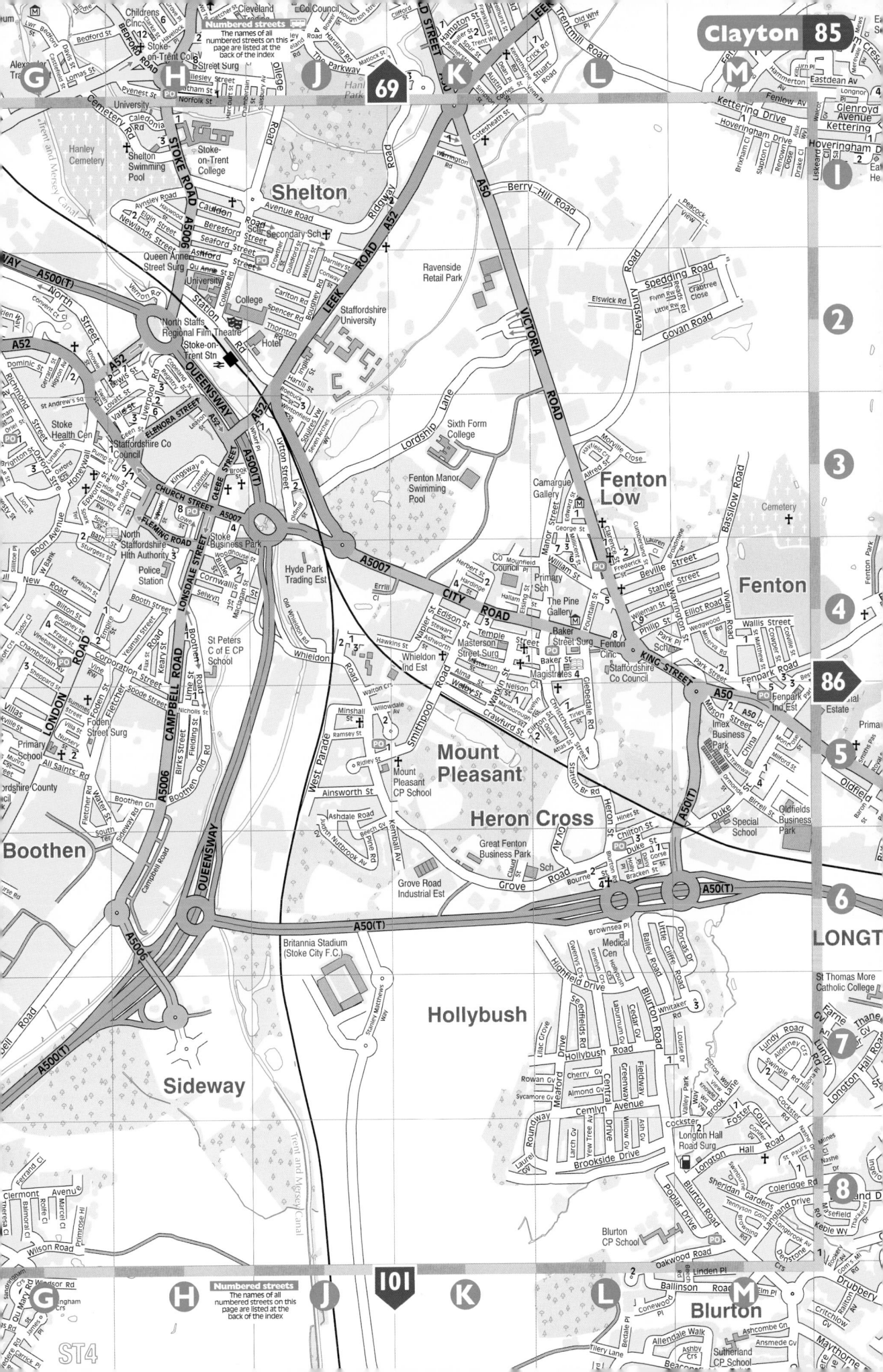

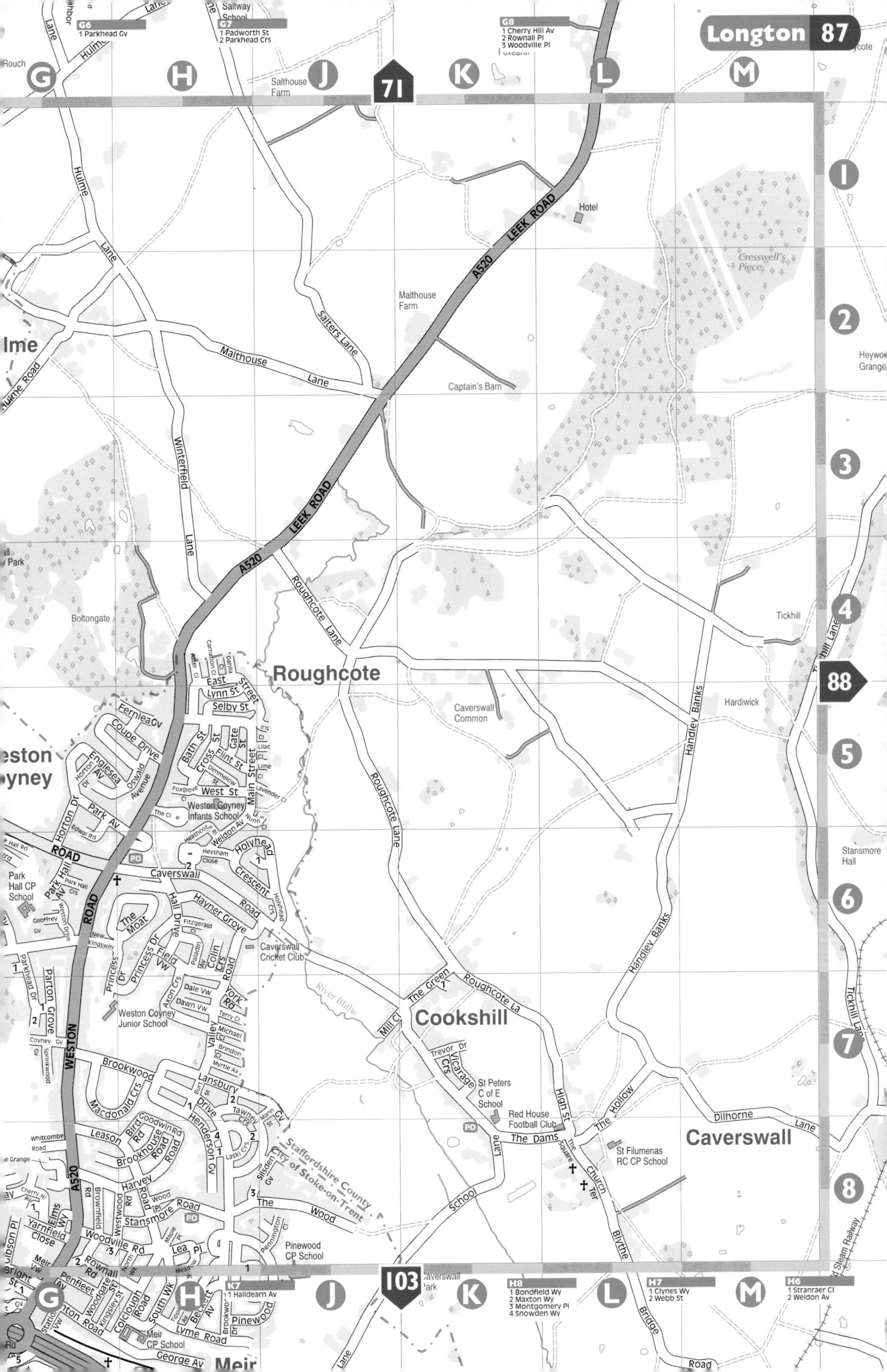

G6
1 Parkhead Gv

G7
1 Padworth St
2 Parkhead Crs

G8
1 Cherry Hill Av
2 Rownall Pl
3 Woodville Pl

G **H** **J** **71** **K** **L** **M**

I

Salthouse Farm

2

Heywood Grange

Malthouse Farm

Cresswell's Piece

LEEK ROAD A520

Hotel

3

Captain's Barn

Ime

Malthouse Lane

Salters Lane

Winterfield Lane

LEEK ROAD A520

Tickhill

4

Boltongate

Roughcote Lane

Roughcote

Caverswall Common

Hardiwick

Handley Banks

Tickhill Lane

88

Fernlea Gv

Coupe Drive

Englesea Av

Carnation Cl
Dahlia
East Lynn St
Selby St
Iris Cl
Lilac Cl

West St
Bath St
Cross St
Flint St
Gate St
Dimmelow St
Main Street
FoxGlove Cl
Lavender Cl
Lime Cl

5

Weston Coyney

Park Av
Coupe Drive
Horton Dr
Oswald Av
Edwal Rd

Weston Coyney Infants School
The Cl
Nunn Cl

Stansmore Hall

Roughcote Lane

6

Park Hall Rd

ROAD
PO
Caverswall Road

Heathcote Cl
Weldon Av
Holyhead
Crescent
Heysham Close

Holyhead Crs

Handley Banks

Park Hall
Park Hall Crs
Geoffrey Gv

The Moat
Hall Drive
New Kingsway
Fitzgerald Cl
Palatin

Hayner Grove
Colin Cl
York Rd

Axon Crs
Dale Vw
Dawn Vw
Terry Cl

Caverswall Cricket Club

River Blithe

The Green

Roughcote La

7

Parkhead Dr
Parton Grove

Princess Dr
Princess Field
Coyney Gv
Springwood

Weston Coyney Junior School

Michael Cl
Brindon Cl
Myrtle Av

Mill Cl

Cookshill

Trevor Dr
Vicarage Crs

The Hollow

Ticknill Lane

WESTON

Brookwood
Macdonald Crs

Lansbury Drive
Burt Cl
Tawney Cl
Mann St

Laski Crs

Goodwin Rd
Bird Rd
Brookhouse Road

St Peters C of E School

Red House Football Club

High St

St Filumenas RC CP School

Dilhorne Lane

Caverswall

8

Whitcombe Road
The Grange
Cherry Hl
Yarnfield Close

Leason

Harvey Road
Westwood
Brownfield Rd

Stansmore Road
PO

Wood Cl

Staffordshire County
City of Stoke-on-Trent

The Wood
Pennington Cl

School Lane

The Dams
PO
The Square

The Church Ter

Blythe

Mid Steam Railway

A520

Melr
Bright

Penfleet
Rownall Rd
Woodgate
Colclough
Kingsley Rd
Road
Bevcott Av

Halldearn Av

Lyme Road
Pinewood

Pinewood CP School

Caverswall Park

Blythe Bridge Road

G **H** **J** **103** **K** **L** **M**

H8
1 Bondfield Wy
2 Maxton Wy
3 Montgomery Pl
4 Snowden Wy

H7
1 Clynes Wy
2 Webb St

H6
1 Stranraer Cl
2 Weldon Av

Meir CP School

George Av **Meir**

Windycote Lane

Windycote

A **B** Dairyhouse Lane **C** 72 **D** **E** **F**

Greenhead

A52

1

resswell's iece

Banktop

Dairy House

Dairyhouse Lane

2

Heywood Grange

Summerhill

Tickhill Lane

Hatchley

3

Whitehurst

◆

Foxfield Light Railway

Whitehurst Lane

4

Tickhill Lane

87

Godleybrook

†

Godleybarn Lane

Birchenfields Lane

5

Cartwright's Drumble

Godley Lane

6

Stansmore Hall

Dilhorne Endowed Primary School

Godley School Lane

Newclosefield

High St

Sarver Lane

Dilhorne

The Dale

New Road

Dilhorne Recreation Centre

†

Callow Hill Lane

7

Tickhill Lane

Caverswall Road

Dilhorne Road

The Common

Lane

LC

A521

8

Foxfield Steam Railway

Field House

Callow Hill Farm

Boundary

† Little

A **B** **C** 104 **D** CHEADLE ROAD **E** **F**

74

106

89

Whiston
Eaves

Crowtrees

Dustystile

North Staffordshire Railway

Staffordshire Way

Lockwood
Close

Lockwood
Hall

Lockwood Road

Chapel La

Burton
Crescent

Holt Lan

CHURNET VALLEY ROAD A521

Banktop

PO

Eavesford

Eaves Lane

Ros

River Churnet

Chu

East Wall
Farm

Wood
House
Farm

Hawksmoor
Nature
Reserve

Hayes
Wood

Lightoaks

Parkfields

Cherry
Lane

ST10

Lockwood Road

Hawksmoor
Wood

Highshutt

OAKAMOOR   ROAD   B5417

Greendale

Lane

Staffordshire   Way

Stoney Dale

Greendale

Oldfurnace

Lower Grange
Farm

Hill Top

Lambskin
Dale

Chapel   Lane

Threa
Woo

Staffordshire Wa

ASHBOURNE

Beech

Moss

ROAD   B5032

Lane

Lane

Lady Lane

Threapwood

Bradley
Elms

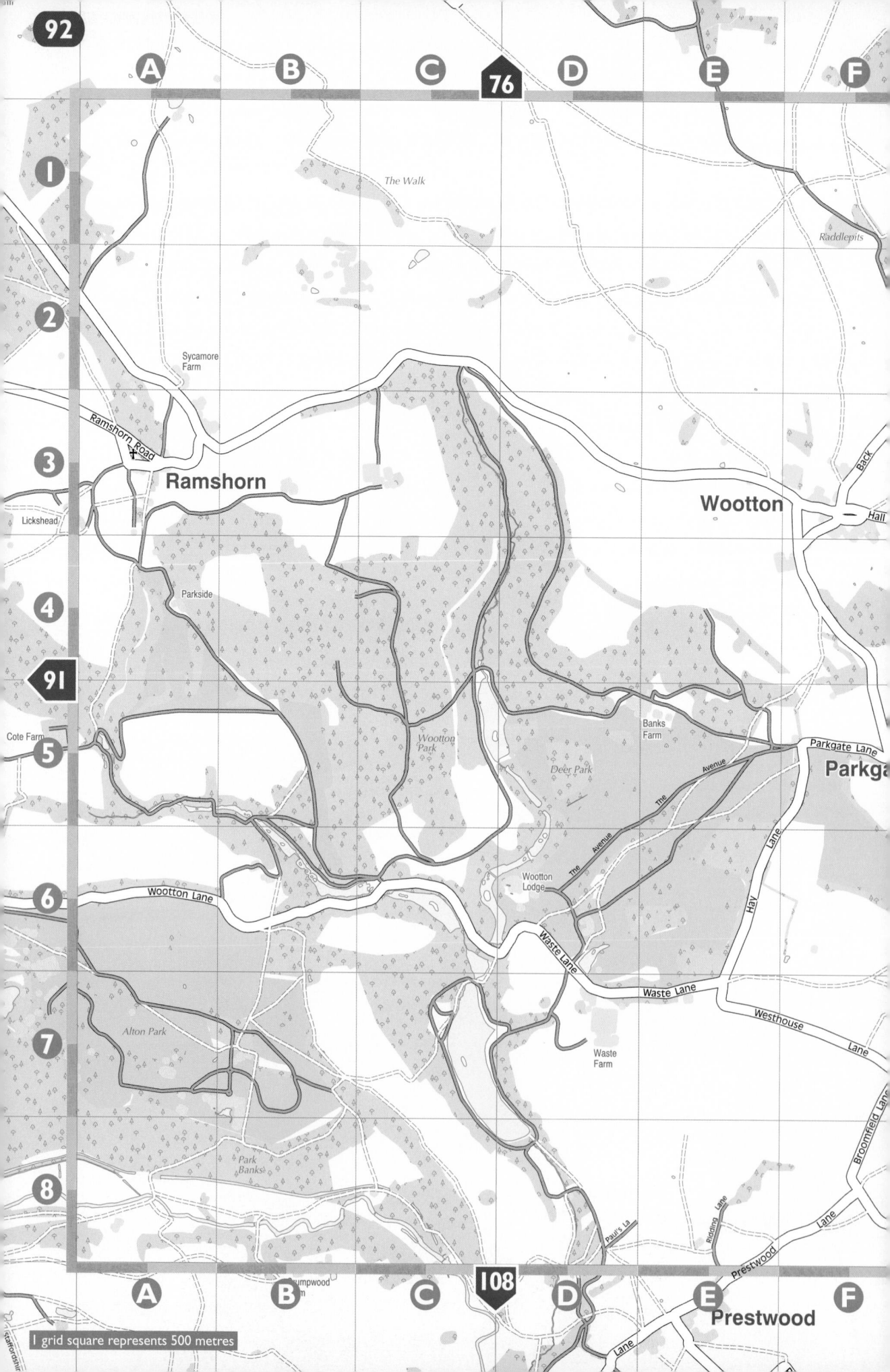

A B C **76** D E F

I

The Walk

Raddlepits

2

Sycamore
Farm

Ramshorn Road

3

Lickshead

Ramshorn

Wootton

Hall Back

Parkside

4

91

Banks
Farm

Cote Farm

5

Deer Park

Parkgate Lane

Parkga

The Avenue

Wootton
Park

Hay Lane

6

Wootton Lane

Wootton
Lodge

The Avenue

Waste Lane

Waste Lane

Westhouse
Lane

7

Alton Park

Waste
Farm

Broomfield Lane

8

Park
Banks

Paul's La

Ridding Lane

Prestwood Lane

Lane

A B C **108** D E **Prestwood** F

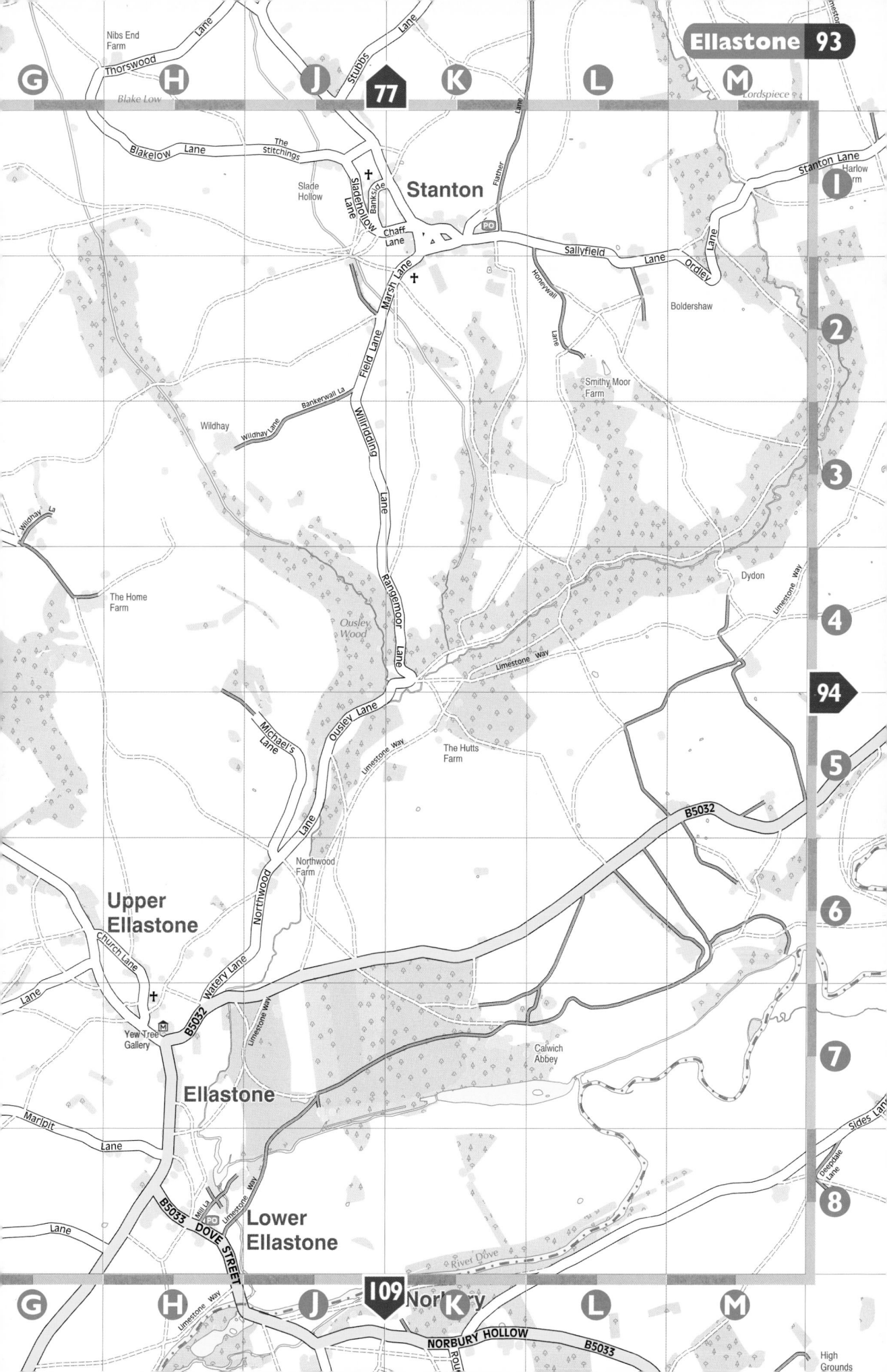

G H J **77** K L M

I

Nibs End Farm

Thorswood Lane

Blake Low

Blakelow Lane

The Stitchings

Slade Hollow

Sladehollow Lane

Bankside

Chaff Lane

Stanton

Stubbs Lane

Flather Lane

PO

Sallyfield Lane

Ordley Lane

Stanton Lane

Harlow Farm

Lordspiece

2

Marsh Lane

Field Lane

Honeywall Lane

Boldershaw

Smithy Moor Farm

3

Wildhay Lane

Bankerwall La

Wildhay

Willridding Lane

Dydon

Limestone Way

4

Wildhay La

The Home Farm

Ousley Wood

Rangemoor Lane

Limestone Way

94

5

Michael's Lane

Ousley Lane

Limestone Way

The Hutts Farm

B5032

6

Upper Ellastone

Northwood Lane

Northwood Farm

7

Church Lane

Watery Lane

B5032

Yew Tree Gallery

Limestone Way

Calwich Abbey

Ellastone

Lane

Marlpit Lane

8

Sides Lane

Drepale Lane

B5033

DOVE STREET

Mill La

PO

Limestone Way

Lower Ellastone

River Dove

Lane

G H J **109** K L M

NorbY ry

NORBURY HOLLOW

B5033

High Grounds

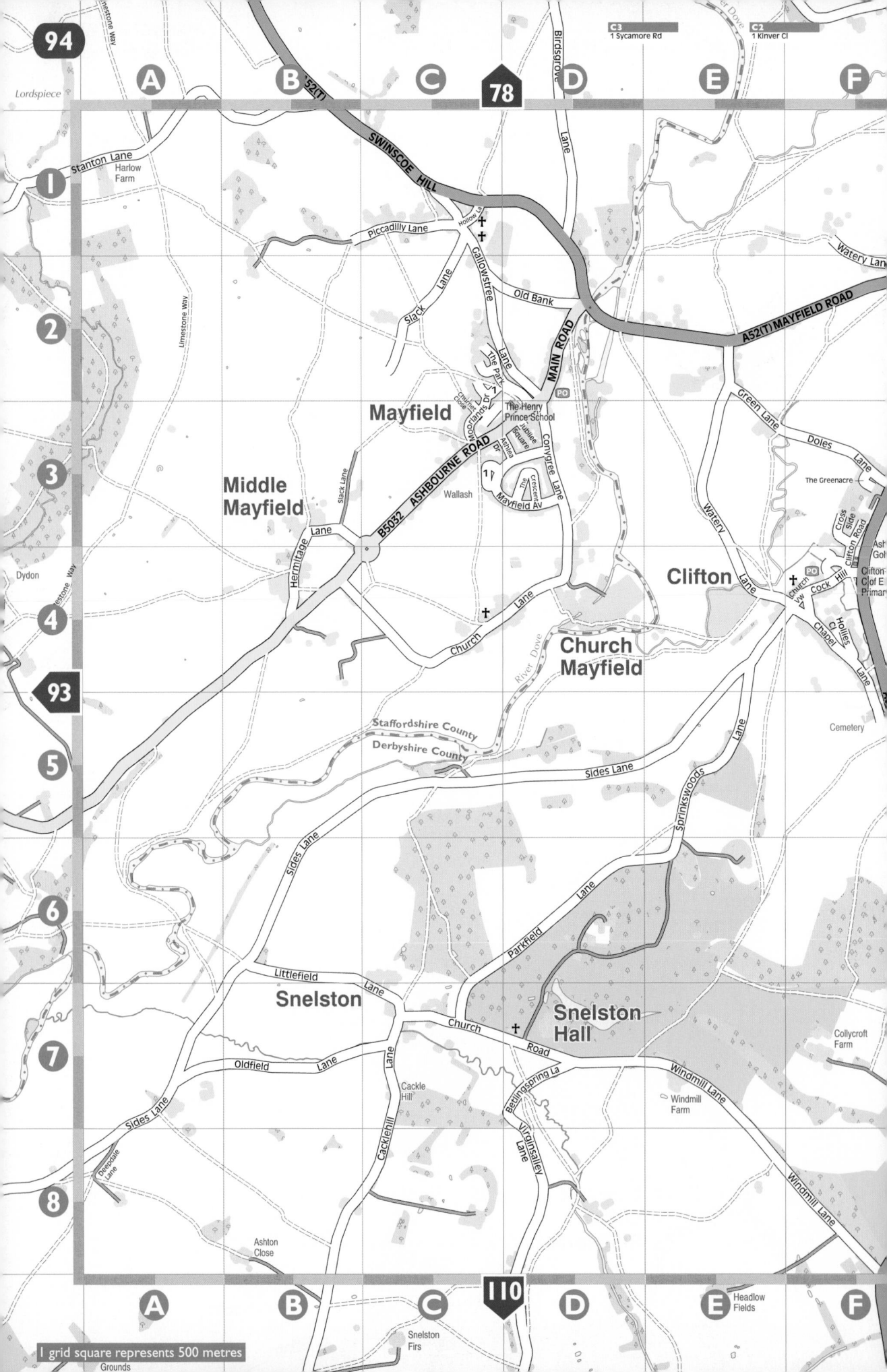

G   H   J   **81**   K   L   M

I
2
3
4
98
5
6
7
8

Aston Cliff

Farm

School Lane

Aston

Lunts Farm

Holloway Lane

Holloway Farm

Radwood

Camp

Maerway Lane

Slymans

Willoughbridge

Dorothy Clive

A51

Sidway

Badger Lane

Wood Lane

Sidway Mill Farm

Wayside Farm Equine Hospital

Blackbrook

A51

Park House

The Bogs

Wharmadine Lane

Moss Lane

NEWCASTLE ROAD

G   H   J   83   K   L   M

1

2

3

4

100

5

6

7

8

WHITMORE ROAD

Shutlanehead

A53

Butterton

Park Road

New Hayes Farm

A5182

TRENTHAM ROAD

Whisper Lane

Acton Farm

Acton

Actonhill Farm

Model Farm

Hanchurch

The Pleck

WHITMORE ROAD

A53

Whitmore

Newhouse Farm

Drayton Rd

Harley Thorn La

Harley

Swynnerton Old Park

Shelton under Harley

Harley Thorns

Bent Lane

Springfields

Dog Lane

Stableford

A51

The Rowe

G   H   A51   117   J   K   L   M

G1
1 Cornelious St
2 Crossland Pl WestWood
3 Ednam Pl
4 Redwood Pl
5 Saracen Wy

G3
1 Bewcastle Gv
2 Bridestowe Cl
3 Danemead Cl
4 Fairlight Gv
5 Goosemoor Gv
6 Ingleton Gv
7 Partridge Cl
8 Polperro Wy

H1
1 Briarwood Pl
2 Denewood Pl
3 Farmwood Cl

H5
1 Golborn Av

G H J 87 K L M

Meir

Moor Green 2

BLYTHE BRIDGE 3

Blythe Bridge Station 104

Gorstybirch 5

6

Stallington 7

8

G H J 121 K L M

G **H4, J3, L4, M4**
Street names for
these grid squares
are listed at the
back of the index

H **G2, G4, G6, H3**
Street names for
these grid squares
are listed at the
back of the index

J **121**

K **K6**
1 Stallington Cl

L **J4**
1 Bonnard Cl

M **J2**
1 Willowood Gv

K3
1 Portland Cl

Fulford

A B C D E F

88

A521

B2
1 Bankhouse Rd

A4
1 Cypress Gv

Callow Hill
Farm

A3
1 Blythe Mount Pk
2 Blythe Rd

A2
1 Dolespring Cl
2 Greenwood Rd
3 Rushton Wy
4 Stratford Cl
5 Willow Wy

Boundar

Little Rd

1

Foxfield Steam Railway

Caversw

CHEADLE ROAD

2

Moor
Green

Spring
Gdns

Parkend

New Cl Av

Cemetery

Mount
Pleasant

Draycott
Cross

Chapel Street

East Bank Ride

Field
House

Dilhorne Road

BrookGate

Portland
Drive

York

Portland Dr

Beverley Crs

Springfield Dr

Hillside Av

Old Road

Meadow Cl

Well St

Park

Forsbrook

Manifold Rd

Trent Rd

Church

Dove Rd

Penk Rd

CHEADLE ROAD   A521

Scarratt Dr

Scarratt

William

Birch Gv

3

Forsbrook C of E
Infants School

Beeches County
Junior School

Mount Pl

Draycott Old Road

Blythe Bridge
High School

Police
Station

Bridgwood Rd

Brook Cl

Blythe
Marsh

ROAD

PO

Wesley St

The Av

Mount Rd

Glebe

Stonehouses

LC

Marsh CP
School

Green Lane

Elmwood Drive

Ashwood

Oakdene

Draycott Old Road

Stuart Av

Draycott Manor
CP School

Grange Farm

Cheadle Road

4

Blythe View

ton Rd

arlstone Av

Beechwood Cl

Limewood Cl

Dr

Maple

Ashwood Cl

Uttoxeter Road

New Rd

Clemans

Poplar

Elmwood

Chestnut

Laburnum

Pinewood Crs

Cedar Av

A521

Woodlands Lane

Marsh
House

Draycott in
the Moors

Church La

103

ST11

Draycott
Sports
Centre

Uttoxeter Road

Cresswell Lane

PO

5

A50(T)

6

A50(T)

7

Leacroft
Hall

Saverley
Green

Cresswell

PH

LC

Cresswell Old Road

A50(T)

Sandon Road

Rookery Crs

Newton

8

Meadowside

Leese House
Farm

A B C D E F

C4
1 Manor Cl

122

C8
1 Sandon Cl

Westgate

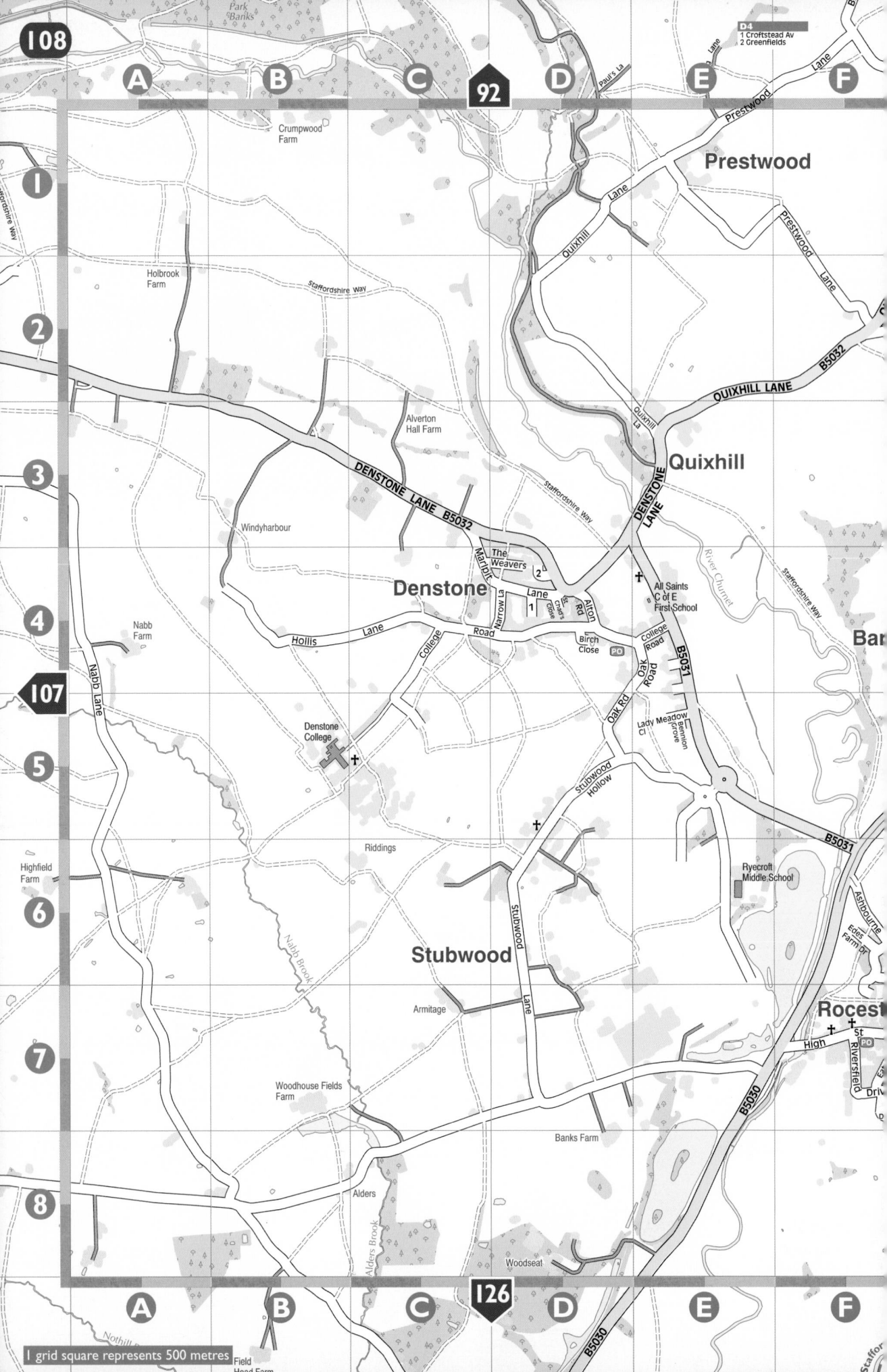

G6
1 Coronation Crs

**Lower
Ellast**

G Lane

H DOVE STREET
B5033
PO
Mill La
Limestone Way

J e

93

K
River Dove

L

M

+Norbury

NORBURY HOLLOW
B5033

I
Grounds

Greenlane
Farm

GREEN

2

Riverside
Doveleys

Limestone Way

River Dove

Mill Lane

Roughlow Lane

Bowlingalley Lane

Lid Lane

Norbury C of E
Primary School

Lid Lane

3

Swinholm
Farm

Meadow Lane

Mill Lane

Bag Lane

Roston

The Hollow

PO

4

Derbyshire County
Staffordshire County

Undertown Lane

110

gap

Dovecliff
Farm

5

I

5030

Doveflats

6

Dove Lane

Dove First
School

La

Long
Chimneys

7

West Vw

Marston
Park

Mill Street

Mill Bank Drive

Daisybank
Farm

8

Staffordshire Way

Abbotsholme
School

G Lane

H

J

127

K

L **Thurvaston** **M**

Cubley Lane

aston

A

Ashton Close B

C

94

D

E

F

Headlow Fields

High Grounds

1

Snelston Firs

2 LANE B5033

Snapes Lane

Virginsalley Lane

Darley Moor

A515

Snelston Common

COCKSHEAD LANE B5033

3

4 Roston Common

Birchwood Park

Manor House

109

Birchwoodmoor

5

Cubley Wood Farm

Hollies Lane

Hollies Lane

Woodhay Farm

6

A515

Long Chimneys

Sandhills Farm

7

Cubley Common

8

A515

Cubley Lane A

B

C

128

D

E

F

Great Cubley

1 grid square represents 500 metres

G   H   J   **95**   K   L   M

Edlaston

Edlaston Lane

Orchard   Lane

Wyaston Grove

Darley Moor Motor Cycle Race Track

Wyaston

Rodsley Lane

1

2

Shirley Oldpark Farm

Hales Green

3

Rodsleywood

4

Park Farm

Priory

Rodsley Lane

Gravelly Bank Mews

5

Leapley Lane

R

Rodsley

Yeaveley

6

Riddings

Boothay Farm

7

8

Bentley Brook

Bentley Fields Open Farm

Leapley Lane

G   H   J   **129** Alkmonton   K   L   M

Top House

E8
1 Caernarvon Cl
2 Kenilworth Cl

D8
1 Annefield Cl
2 Grosvenor Ct
3 Smithfield Cl

D7
1 Llewellyn
Roberts Wy

C8
1 Cheshire Gdns

A **B** **C** **D** **E** **F**

1
2
3
4
5
6
7
8

Shropshire Union Canal

Ridgwardine

A529

New House
Farm

A529

ADDERLEY ROAD

Betton Wood

Betton
Moss

Moss Lane

Brownhills

Spoonley

Shropshire Union Canal

Victoria
Wharf

ADDERLEY ROAD

Mitton Drive

Bert Smith Way

Talbot Way

Maer Lane
Industrial Estate

Campbell Road

Greenfields Lane

Rush Lane

Maer Lane

CHESHIRE STREET

Greenfields Road

Ashbourne Drive

Laburnum Close

Rowan Road

Warwick Close

Windsor Dr

Sandringham Close

Balmoral Drive

Abbey Way

Fairfields Road

Smithfield Road

Grosvenor Road

Longlands Primary School

Longlands Lane

Grove Gardens

Watersdale Drive

Sambrook Crescent

Betton Road

Newcastle Road

Hinsley Crescent

Kingsley Dr

Mill

A53

Broomhall
Grange

A **B** **C** **D** **E** **F**

Meadow Close

Cort Way

The Par

Pezenas
Drive

Tower
Close

Longslow Road

Cemetery Road

F8
1 Millfield Gra

Draytonmoor Groove

Ashmore Road

FROGMORE

SMITHFIELD

130
PO

Cheshire Street

Cross St

STAFFORD ST

Queens St

Stafford Street

Grove Upper
Comprehensive
School

Newcastle Road

The Health
Centre

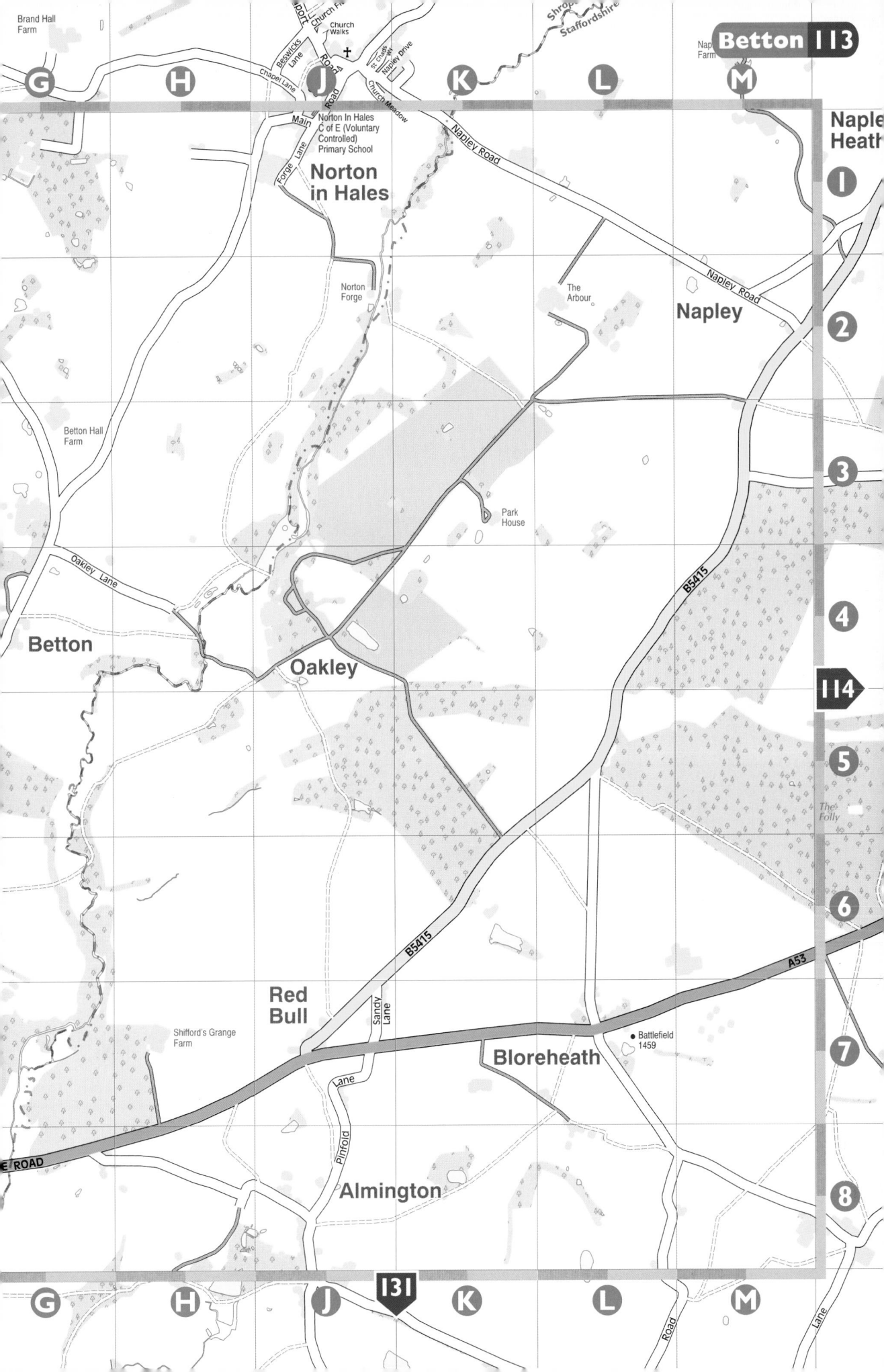

Brand Hall
Farm

G   H   J   K   L   M

Church Fi
Church
Walks
Napley Drive

Chapel Lane

Beswicks Lane

Church Meadow

Shrop
Staffordshire

Napley
Farm

Napley
Heath

1

Norton in Hales
C of E (Voluntary
Controlled)
Primary School

Main

Forge Lane

**Norton
in Hales**

Napley Road

The
Arbour

Napley

2

Norton
Forge

Betton Hall
Farm

3

Park
House

B5415

4

Oakley Lane

Betton

Oakley

114

5

The
Folly

6

B5415

A53

**Red
Bull**

Shifford's Grange
Farm

Sandy
Lane

Battlefield
1459

Bloreheath

7

E ROAD

Lane

Pinfold

Almington

8

G   H   J   K   L   M

Road

Lane

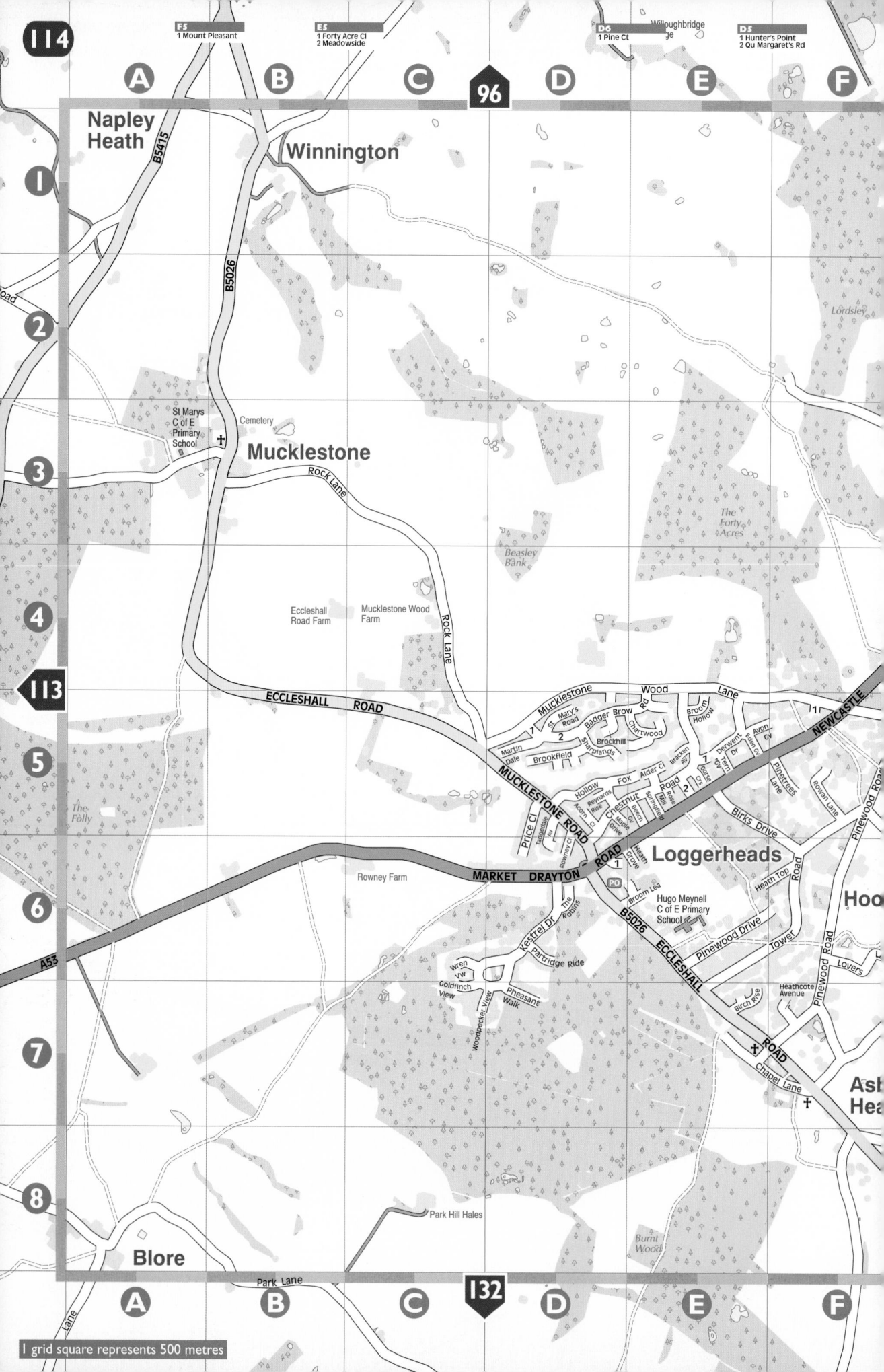

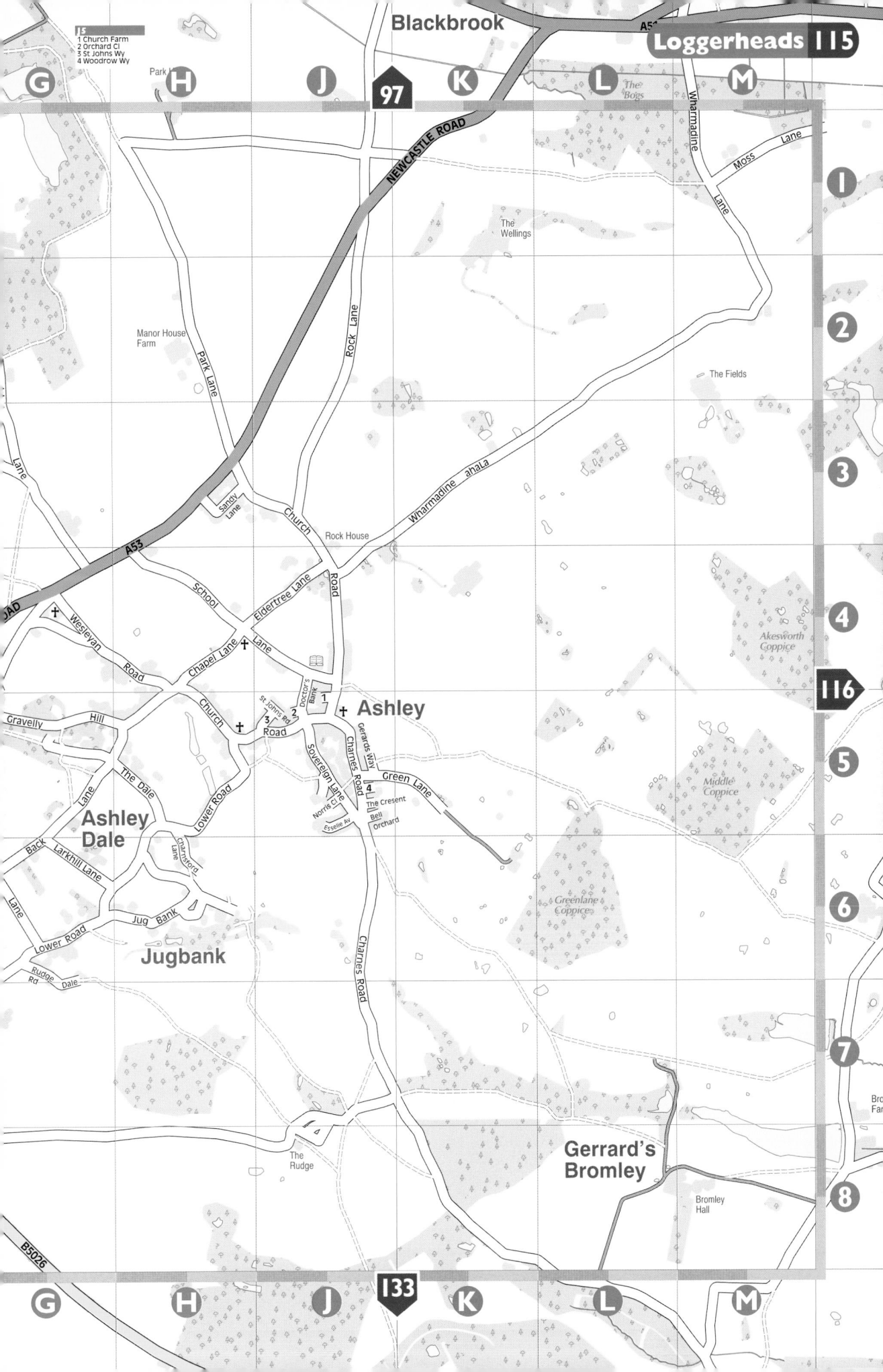

Blackbrook

5
1 Church Farm
2 Orchard Cl
3 St Johns Wy
4 Woodrow Wy

G   H   J   97   K   L   M

1

2

3

4

116

5

6

7

8

Park Lane

Manor House Farm

Sandy Lane

A53

School Lane

Chapel Lane

Church Road

Wesleyan Road

Gravelly   Hill

The Dale

Ashley Dale

Back Larkhill Lane

Lane

Lower Road

Charnsford Lane

Jug Bank

Lower Road

Rudge Rd   Dale

B5026

Jugbank

Eldertree Lane

Rock Lane

Church Road

St Johns Rd

Doctor's Bank

Sovereign Lane

Norris Cl

Esselle Av

Charnes Road

Gerards Way

The Cresent

Bell Orchard

Green Lane

✝ **Ashley**

Rock House

NEWCASTLE ROAD

Wharmadine   Lane

Wharmadine   Lane

Moss Lane

The 'Bogs

The Wellings

The Fields

Akesworth Coppice

Middle Coppice

Greenlane Coppice

Charnes Road

The Rudge

Gerrard's Bromley

Bromley Hall

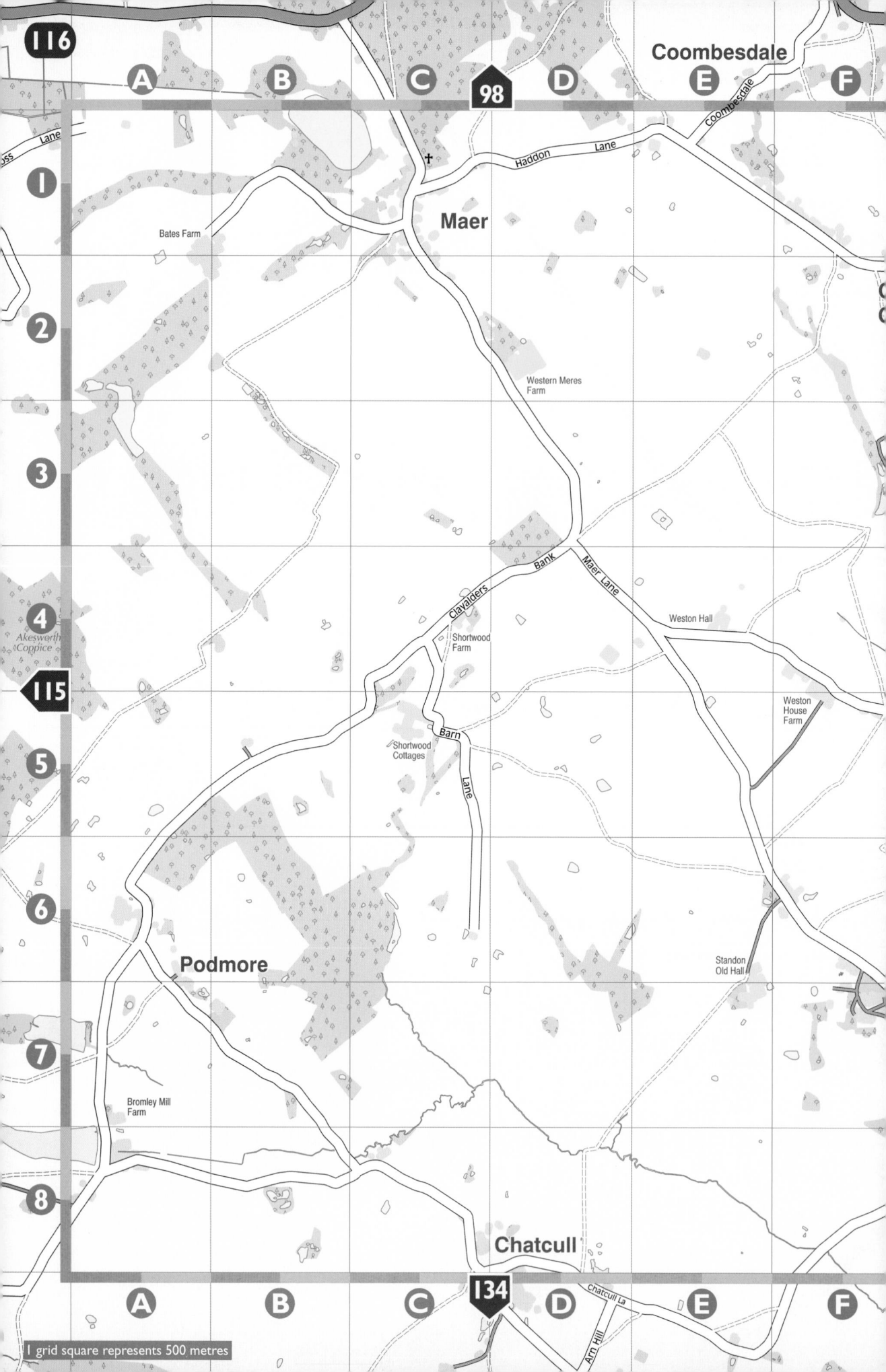

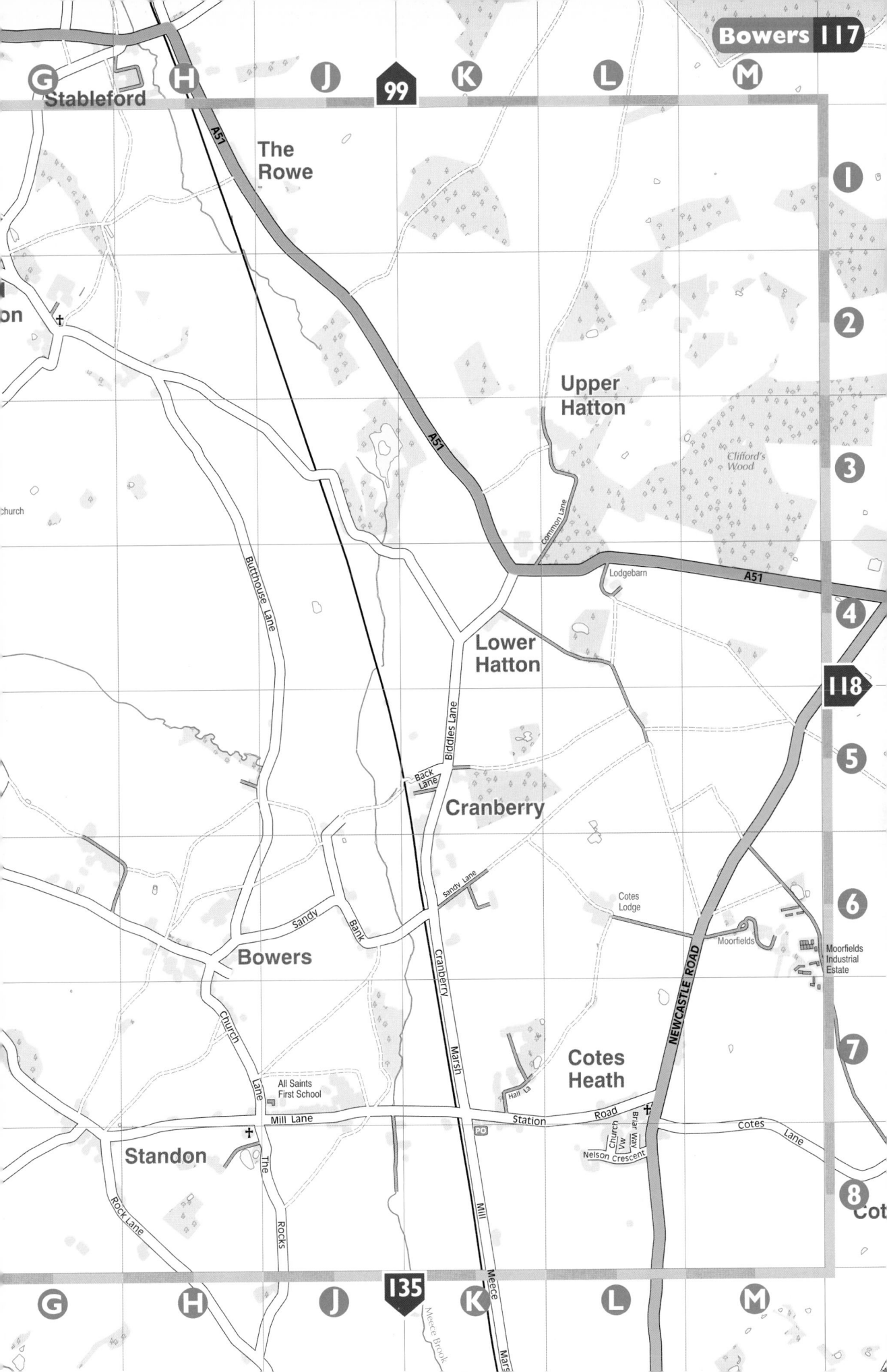

G **Stableford** H J **99** K L M

The Rowe

A51

I 1

2

Upper Hatton

Clifford's Wood

3

Common Lane

Lodgebarn A51

4

Lower Hatton

118

Biddles Lane

Back Lane

5

Cranberry

Sandy Lane

Butthouse Lane

Cranberry Marsh

Cotes Lodge

6

NEWCASTLE ROAD

Moorfields

Moorfields Industrial Estate

church

Sandy Bank

Bowers

7

Church Lane

Cotes Lane

Mill Lane

All Saints First School

Cotes Heath

Station Road

Hall La

PO

Church Vw

Briar Way

Nelson Crescent

Cotes Lane

Rock Lane

The Rocks

Standon

8

Cot

G H J **135** K L M

Meece Brook

Meece

Mars

A B C 100 D E F

B6
1 Fitzherbert Cl
2 Lawrence Dr
3 The Mill Wy
4 Monks Wy

Beechcliff La.

1

Harley Lane
A519
Old Lane
Top Lane

Beechdale Lane
Beech Dl Rd
Groundslow F

2
Beech House
Farm
✝
Winghouse Lane

3
A519
Bottom Lane
M6
Wing
House
Chase Lane

4
A51
Long Compton
Farm

5
Sandyford
Farm
A51

6
Moorfields
Industrial
Estate
Swynnerton
Fairbanks Wk
The Hay
Barns 7 Old La 3
2 4
Weavers Wk
Early Lane
PO
✝
Blakelow

7
Swynnerton
RC Primary
School
Park View
Frobisher
Drive Wk
✝
Swynnerton
Park
Hall Lane
M6

8
Cotes
Swynnerton
Grange

Lane
Blackflats Road
A B 136 C D E F
Pilstones Road

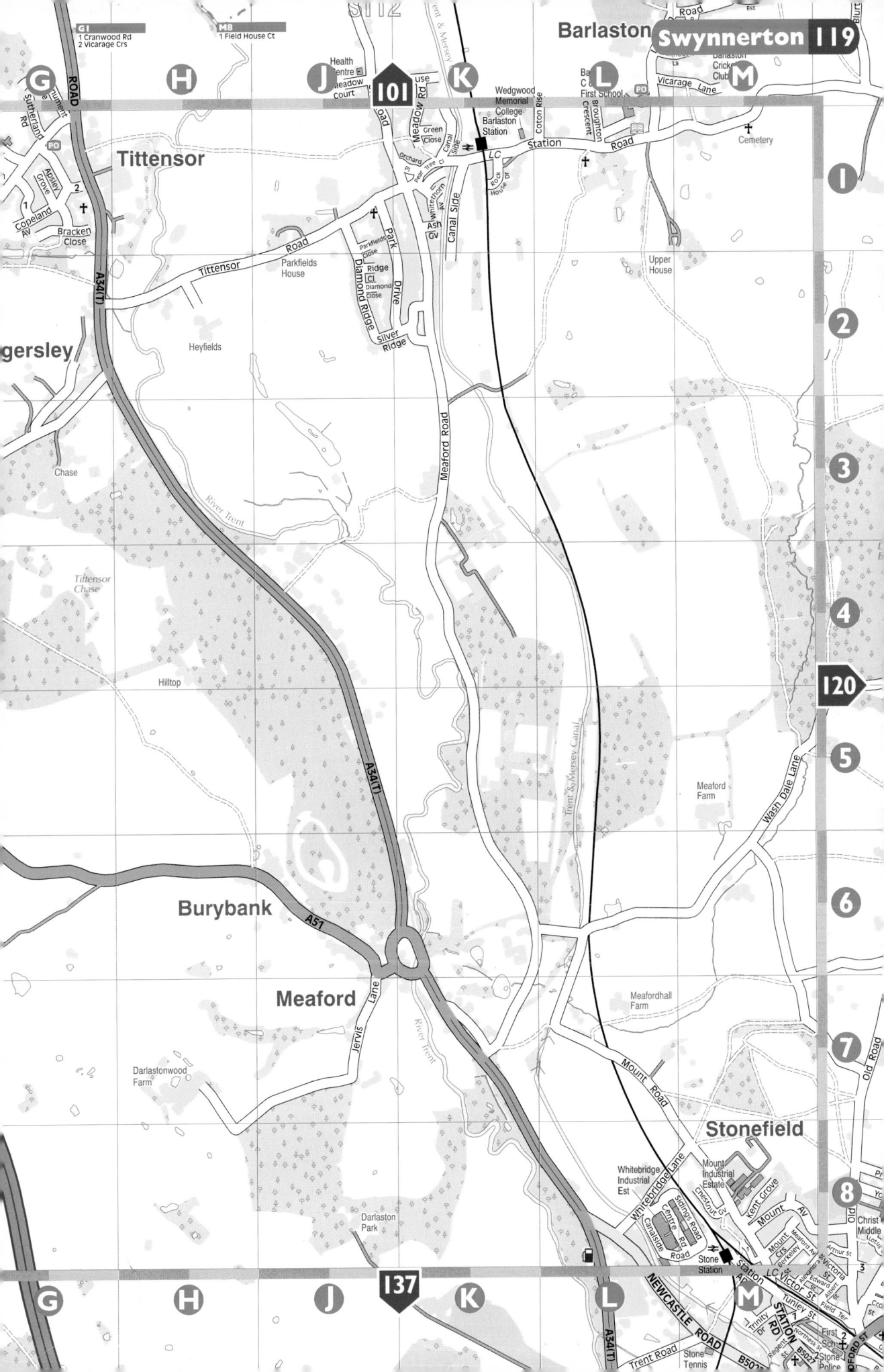

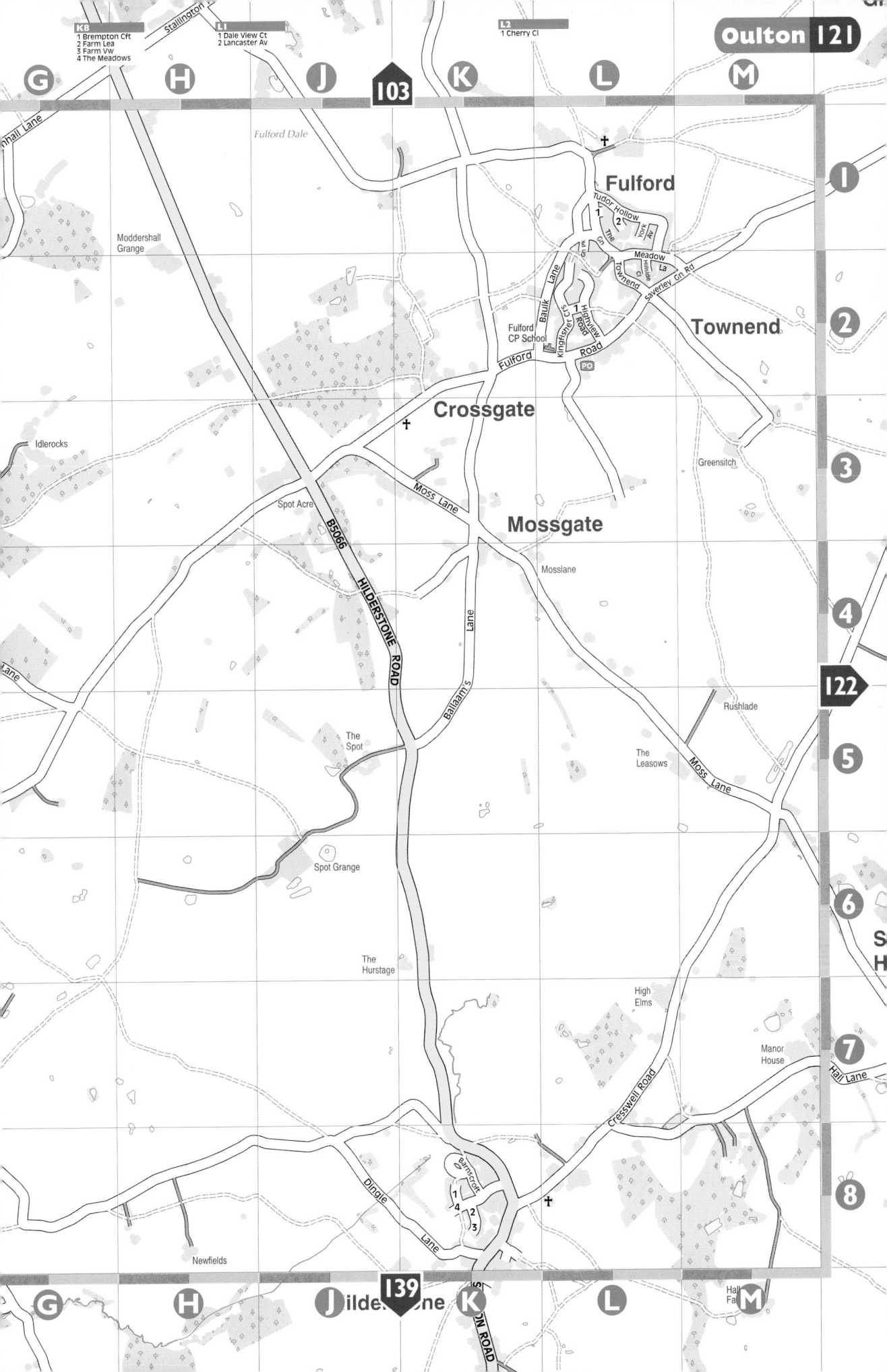

K8
1 Brempton Cft
2 Farm Lea
3 Farm Vw
4 The Meadows

L1
1 Dale View Ct
2 Lancaster Av

L2
1 Cherry Cl

G   H   J   K   L   M

I

Fulford Dale

Moddershall
Grange

Fulford

Tudor Hollow
The Gro
York Av
Meadow
Townend
Hillside
Saverley Gn Rd

2

Townend

Baulk Lane
Highview Road
Kingfisher Ct's
Fulford
CP School
Fulford Road
PO

Idlerocks

† **Crossgate**

Greensitch

3

Spot Acre

Moss Lane

Mossgate

Mosslane

B5066
HILDERSTONE ROAD

4

Lane

122

Rushlade

Ballaam's Lane

The
Leasows

Moss Lane

5

The
Spot

6

Spot Grange

The Hurstage

High
Elms

Manor
House

7

Hall Lane

Cresswell Road

Dingle Lane

Farmscroft
1
4
2
3

†

Newfields

Hall
Fa

ilderstone
N ROAD

8

S
H

S
H

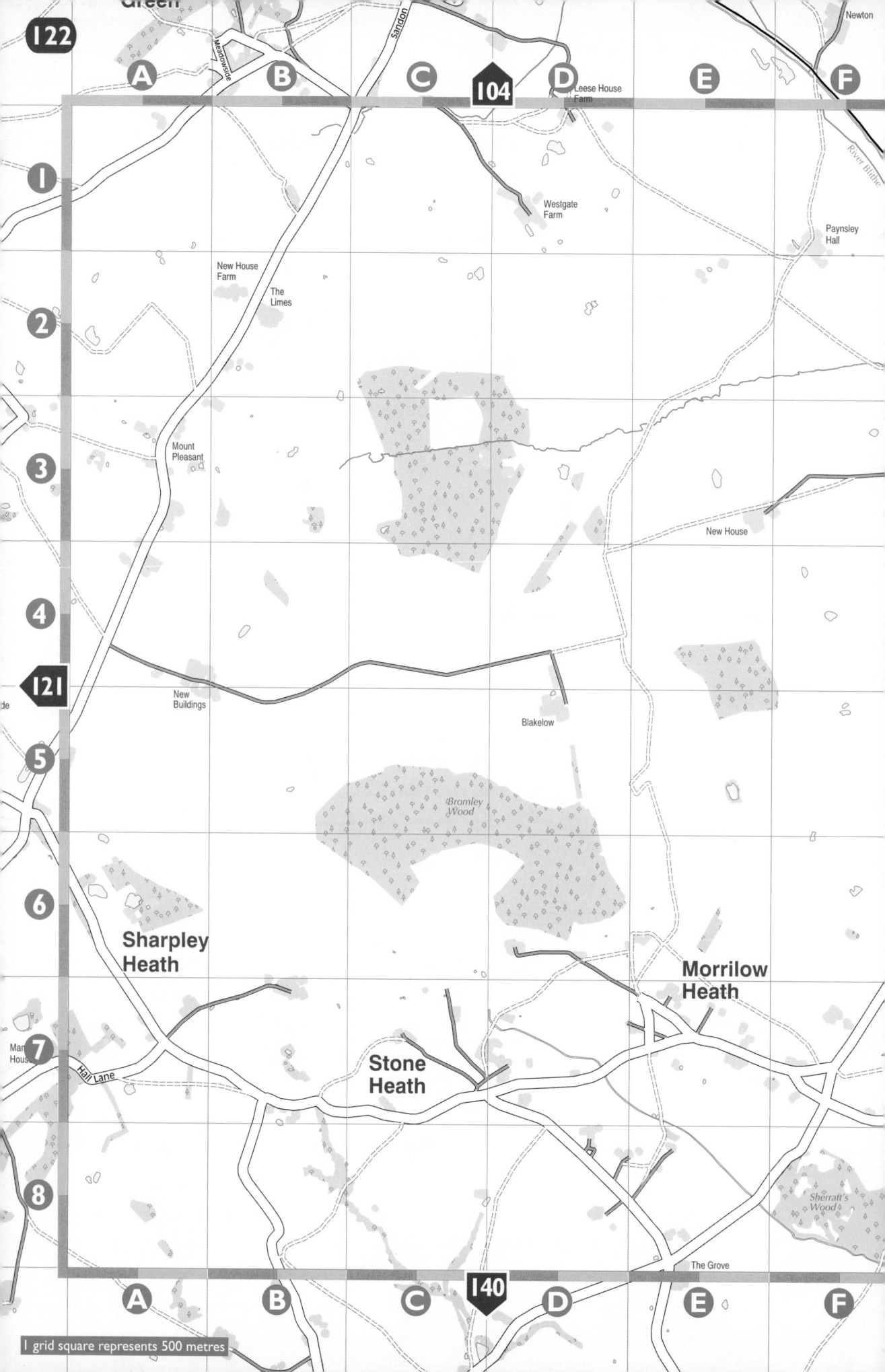

Green

Newton

A B C 104 D E F

Sandon

River Blithe

1

Westgate Farm

Paynsley Hall

New House Farm

The Limes

2

Mount Pleasant

3

New House

4

121

New Buildings

Blakelow

5

Bromley Wood

6

Sharpley Heath

Morrilow Heath

Man House

7

Hall Lane

Stone Heath

8

Sherratt's Wood

The Grove

A B C 140 D E F

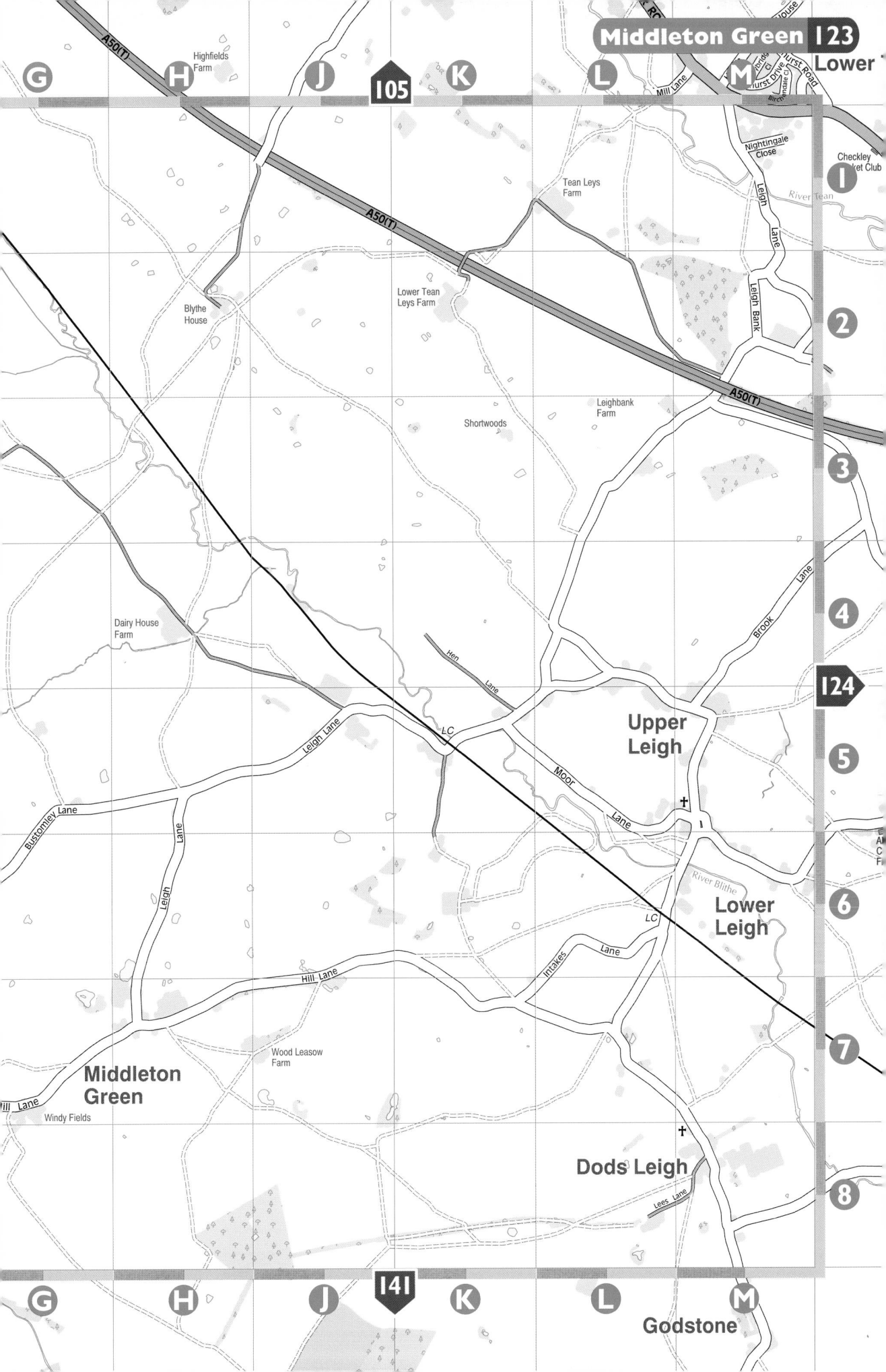

G H J **105** K L M

I

2

3

4

124

5

6

7

8

A50(T)

A50(T)

Highfields
Farm

Tean Leys
Farm

Lower Tean
Leys Farm

Blythe
House

Shortwoods

Leighbank
Farm

Checkley
ket Club

River Tean

Nightingale
Close

Leigh Lane

Leigh Bank

Dairy House
Farm

Hen Lane

LC

Leigh Lane

Bustomley Lane

Leigh Lane

Brook Lane

**Upper
Leigh**

Moor Lane

River Blithe

LC

**Lower
Leigh**

Hill Lane

ill Lane

**Middleton
Green**

Windy Fields

Wood Leasow
Farm

Intakes Lane

Lane

Dods Leigh

Lees Lane

G H J **141** K L M

Godstone

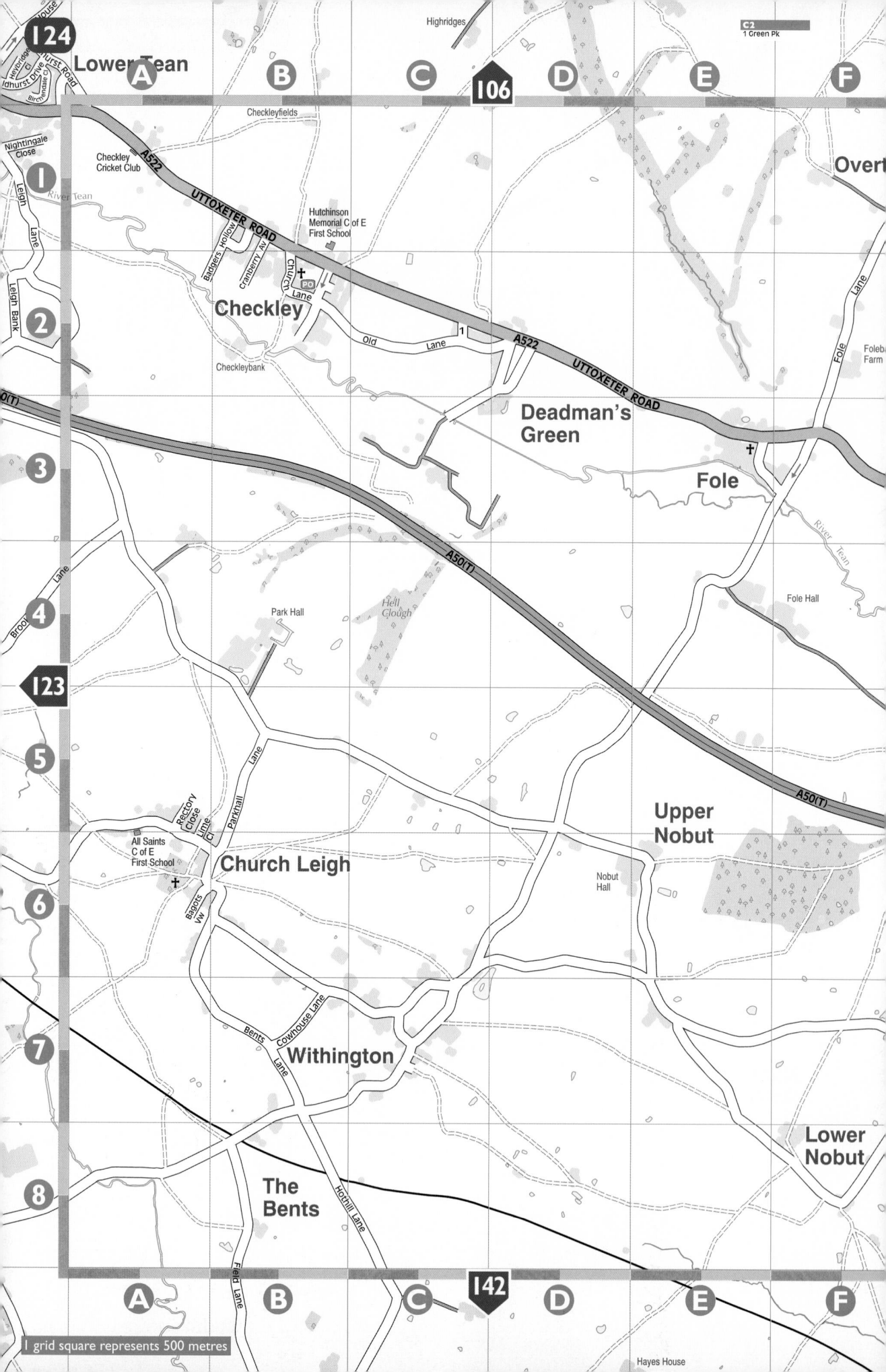

124

Lower Tean

Highridges

106

Over

A522 UTTOXETER ROAD

Checkleyfields

Nightingale Close

Leigh Lane

River Tean

Checkley Cricket Club

Badgers Hollow

Cranberry Av

Church Lane

Hutchinson Memorial C of E First School

PO

Checkley

Old Lane

1

A522

UTTOXETER ROAD

Fole Lane

Foleb Farm

Leigh Bank

Checkleybank

Deadman's Green

Fole

River Tean

0(T)

A50(T)

Fole Hall

Brook Lane

Park Hall

Hell Clough

123

Parkhall Lane

Rectory Close

Lime Cl

All Saints C of E First School

Church Leigh

Bagots Vw

Upper Nobut

Nobut Hall

A50(T)

Bents Lane

Cowhouse Lane

Withington

Lower Nobut

The Bents

Hothill Lane

Field Lane

142

Hayes House

C2
1 Green Pk

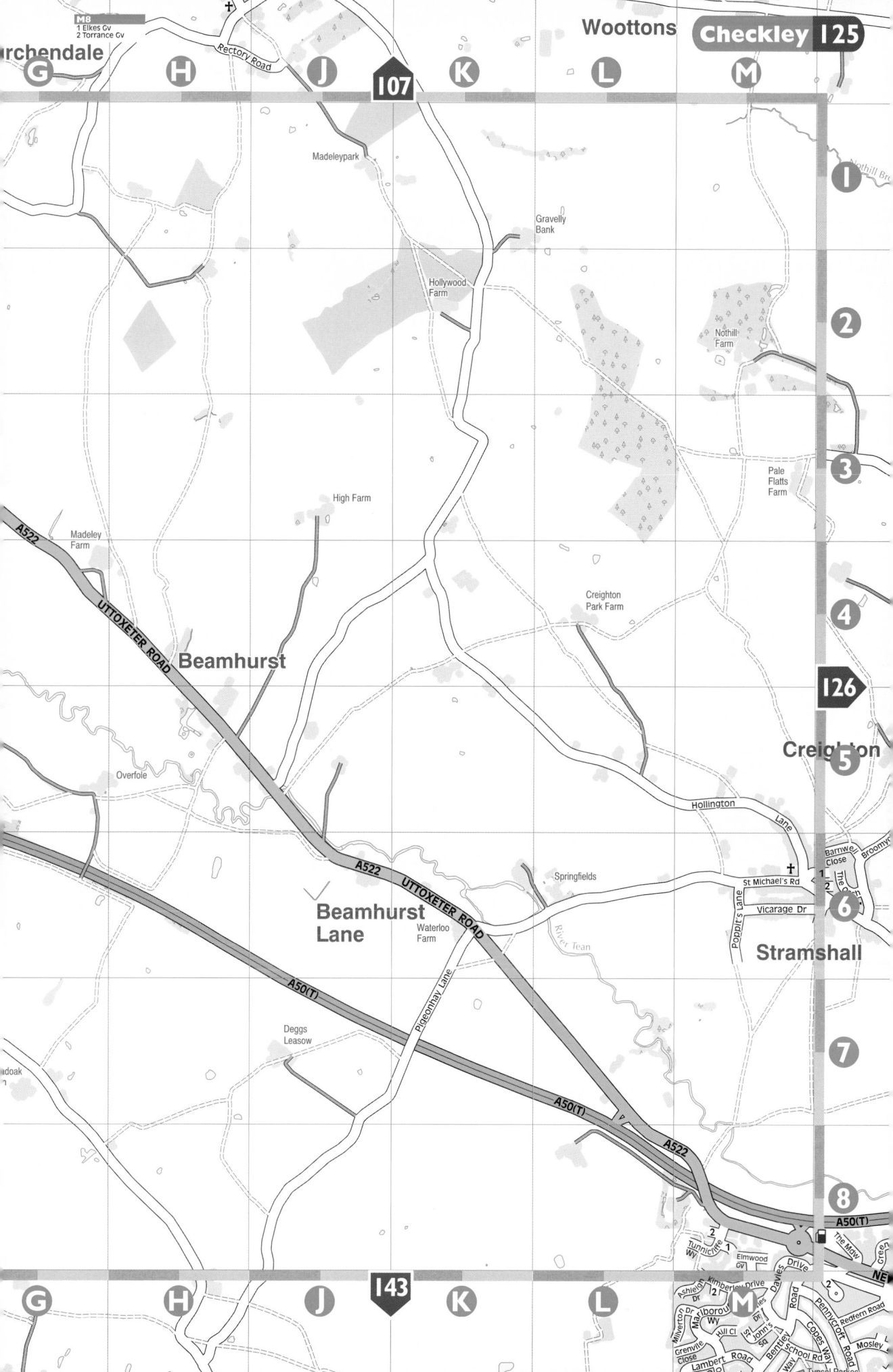

A B C 110 D E A515 F

Cubley Lane

Rough
Grounds

Great
Cubley

PO

I

Shaw Lane

Shaw
Lane Farm

Little
Cubley

2

Riggs Lane

3

Malcomsley

A515

Hollyhurst Lane

Hollyhurst
Farm

Cubley
Carr

4

Brook
Farm

Foston Brook

Cubley
Lodge

5

Vernon's
Oak Farm

Potter
Somersal

Bowling Alley Lane

Oak Lane

A515

Coton Wood
Farm

6

Somersal
House

Sudbury
Coppice

Somersal
Herbert

7

Hill Somersal

A515

8

A B C 146 D E F

1 grid square represents 500 metres

G H J K L M

Bentley Brook

Bentley Fields
Open Farm

Leapley L

Alkmonton

1

Top
House
Farm

2

Middleton
Park

Alkmonton
Old Hall

3

High Grounds
Farm

Ashbourne Road

Dairy
House
Farm

4

Awdishaw Lane

Boylestonfield

5

Boylestone

Chapel Lane

6

Sappertonfield Lane

Bartonpark

New Road

Harehill

Foston Brook

7

Twisses Bank

Marjory Lane

Lees Hall
Farm

Gorsty
Fields

8

Sapperton

I grid square represents 500 metres

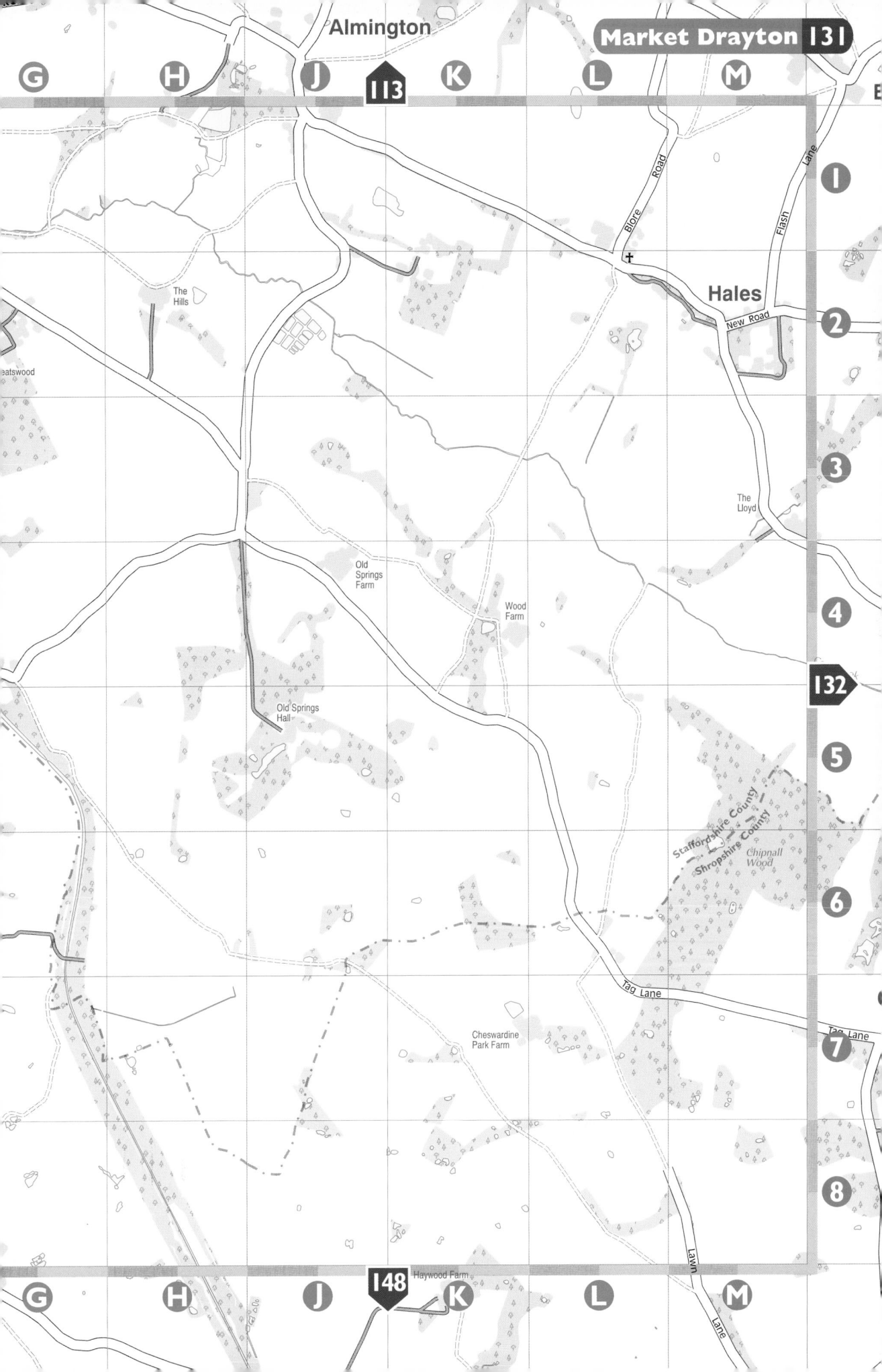

G H J K L M

113

Blore Road

Flash Lane

I

The Hills

✝

Hales

New Road

2

eatswood

3

The Lloyd

Old
Springs
Farm

Wood
Farm

4

132

Old Springs
Hall

5

Staffordshire County
Shropshire County

Chipnall
Wood

6

Tag Lane

Tag Lane

Cheswardine
Park Farm

7

8

Lawn Lane

148 Haywood Farm

132

114

I

A Blore B Park Hill Hales C D E F

Burnt Wood

Flash Lane

Park Lane

Park Lane

2

New Road

Park Springs

Bishop

3

The Lloyd

The Nook Farm

Golden Farm

Glass Houses

4

Coal Brook

131

Chipnall Lees

5

County

Chipnall Wood

6

Lipley Farm

Chipnall

Moss Lane

Tag Lane

7

Moss Lane

Lipley

8

Cheswardine Hall

Lipley Hall Farm

A B C **149** D E F

I grid square represents 500 metres

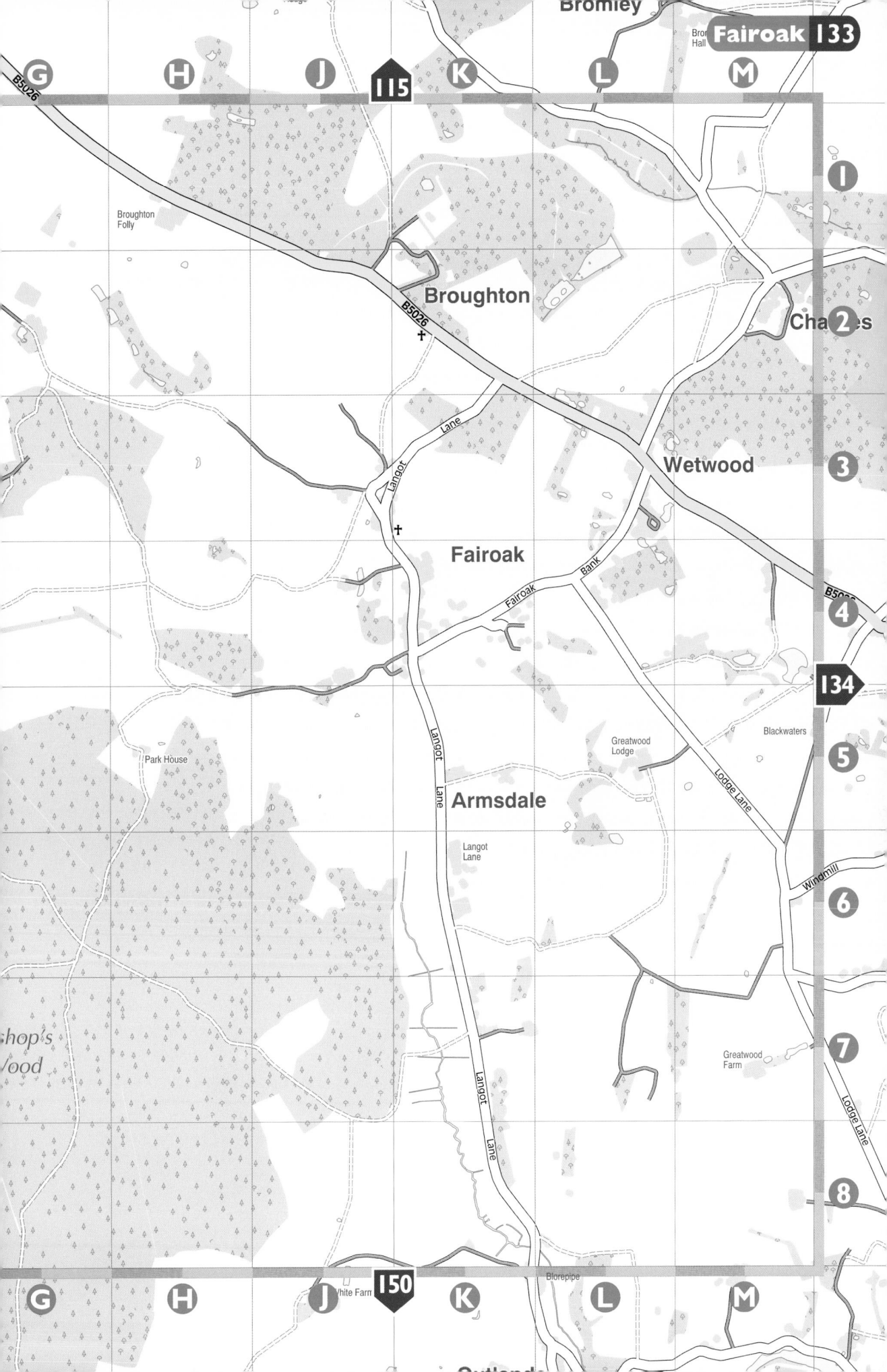

G H J **115** K L M

1

Bromley

Bro
Hall

B5026

Broughton Folly

Broughton

Cha**2**es

Langot Lane

Wetwood **3**

B5026

Fairoak

Bank

Fairoak

4

134

Park House

Greatwood Lodge

Blackwaters **5**

Langot Lane

Armsdale

Langot Lane

Lodge Lane

Windmill **6**

hop's
ood

Greatwood Farm

7

Lodge Lane

8

G H **150** J K L M

hite Farm

Blorepipe

G H J **117** K L M

Cote

I1

2

3

4

136

5

6

7

8

Rock Lane

Rocks

Mill

Meece

Marsh

Walford Back Lane

Walford

Chatcull Brook

Meece Brook

A519

Meadow Lane

Old Hall Lane

Millmeece

Meadow

Aspley

on Brook

A519

Slindon

A519

Brockton

Ankerton

Hilton Drive

Bradley Dr

Paterson AV

Drake Hall
(HM Prison)

Brockton Lane

Lower House
Farm

**Cat's Hill
Cross**

Sturbridge

The Ashtons
Farm

Smithy

M1
1 Alma St
2 Dominic St

M4
1 Birchfields Cl
2 Bushberry Cl
3 Foxwood Cl
4 Newlands Cl

M5
1 Boundary Cl
2 Dutton Wy
3 Goodill Cl
4 Highlands
5 Wood Crs

Darlaston Park

119

G H J K L M

Whitebridge
Industrial
Est

Mount
Industrial

Whitebridge La
Sidings Road
Centre Rd
Canalside

Stone
Station

Station

Mount
Armar st
Victoria
Berkeley
LC Victoria St
Meaford Av
Field Ter

NEWCASTLE ROAD

A34(T)

Trent Road

Stone
Tennis
Club

Stone
Golf Club

Darlaston
Grange

Yarnfield Lane

THE FILLYBROOK

NEWCASTLE ST

B5027

Tunley St
Regent
Trinity Dr
Northesk St

First
Sch
Stone
Police
Stn
Stafford
Borough Council

Stafford
Primary
School 1

The Edward
Practice

Trent
Hosp

Christ Chu
Middle Sch

York St

Princ

Christ Chu

Lichf

St

Gran

High

Cross
St

I

RADFO

STAFFORD ROAD

FILLYBROOKS

Grove
Rd
Woodlands
St Vincent Road
Woodlands Pk Av
Longfield
Churchill
Road
Whitemill
Way
Lane

CROWN
ST
High
St

Trent
Clnc

Stafford
Cl

2

Walton

Tyle's Gv

Manor Hill
First School

Manor
Rise

Orchard
Cl

Walton
Lamb
Lane
Way

PO

3

THE FILLYBROOK

Friars Av
Summing
Stafford

Endid
Gdns

Tillin

Walton
Hill House

Bank Side

Lane

Poplar Ct

Longrope Dr

Pirehill
First
School

Middle
School

4

Moss
Lane
Yarnfield Lane

Moss
House

Micklow
House

Croft
Rd

Meadow
Way

Meadow W

Lea Rd

Lansdown
Close

Crestwood
Dr

Common Drive

B5026

ECCLESHALL ROAD

M6

Walton
Heath

Stuart Cl
Stuart
Tudor

Heath
Gdns

Hill

138

Cold Norton
Farm

Stafford Service Area (northbound)

M6

Walton
Heath

Marlborough
Rd
Essex Dr
Fraser
Redfern Road
Wimpol
Close

Cherry
Tree
Coombe Pk Rd

Wood La

Walton
Industrial
Est

Walton
Industrial Es

Beacon Road

Opal Way

5

6

Coombe Park
Road

Izaak Walton
Golf Club

North
Pirehill
Farm

Pirehill Lane

7

8

Norton
Farm

Stafford Service Area (southbound)

Pirehill
Grange

154

G H J K L M

M6

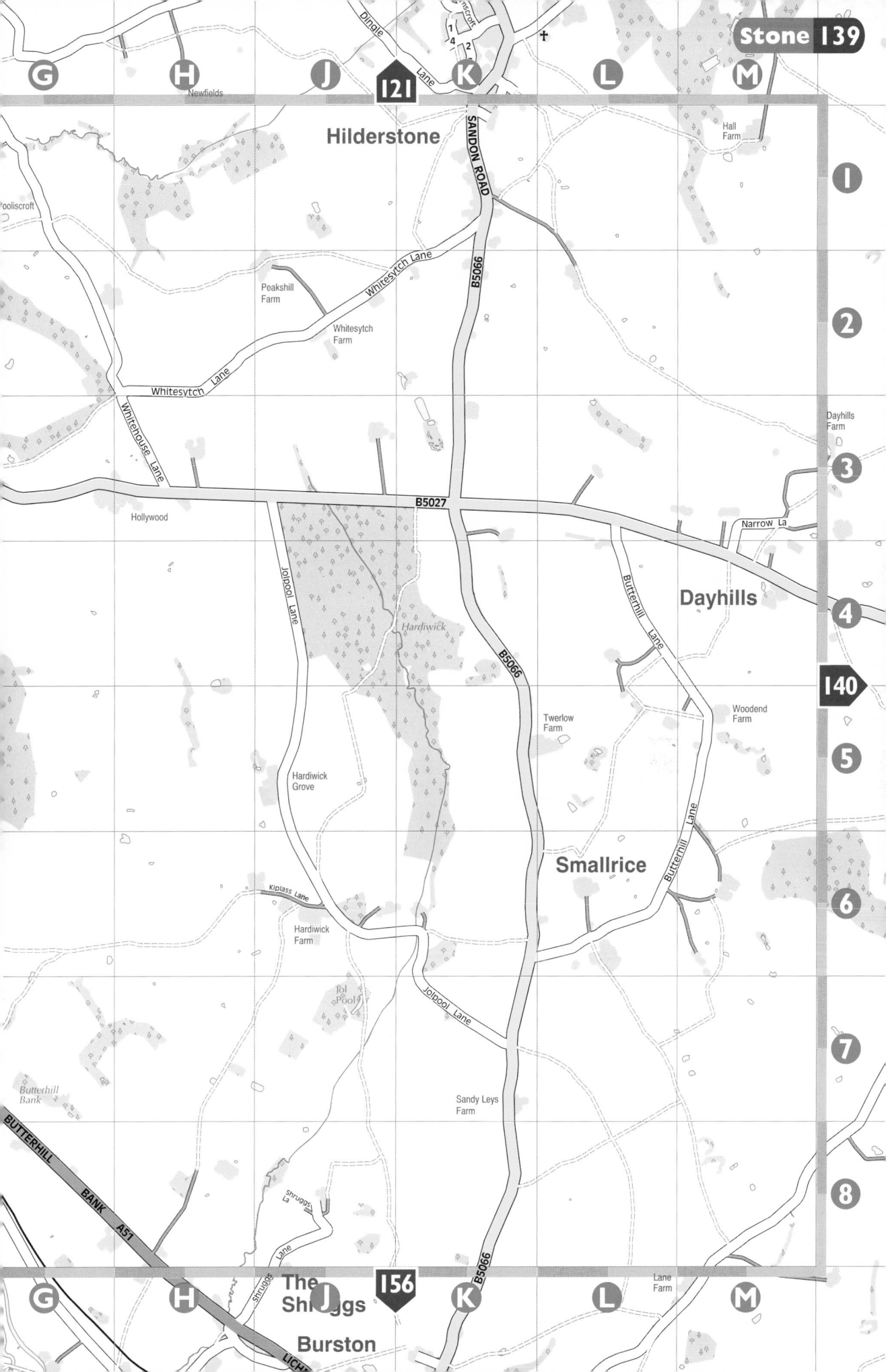

G   H   J   **121**   K   L   M

I

2

3

4

140

5

6

7

8

G   H   J   **156**   K   L   M

Hilderstone

SANDON ROAD

B5066

Newfields

Pooliscroft

Whitesytch Lane

Peakshill Farm

Whitesytch Farm

Whitesytch Lane

Whitehouse Lane

Hollywood

B5027

Jolpool Lane

Hardiwick

Hardiwick Grove

Butterhill Lane

Dayhills

Dayhills Farm

Narrow La

Hall Farm

Woodend Farm

Twerlow Farm

B5066

Smallrice

Butterhill Lane

Kiplass Lane

Hardiwick Farm

Jol Pool

Jolpool Lane

Sandy Leys Farm

Butterhill Bank

BUTTERHILL BANK A51

Shruggs La

Shruggs Lane

The Shruggs

Burston

LICH

B5066

Lane Farm

Dingle Lane

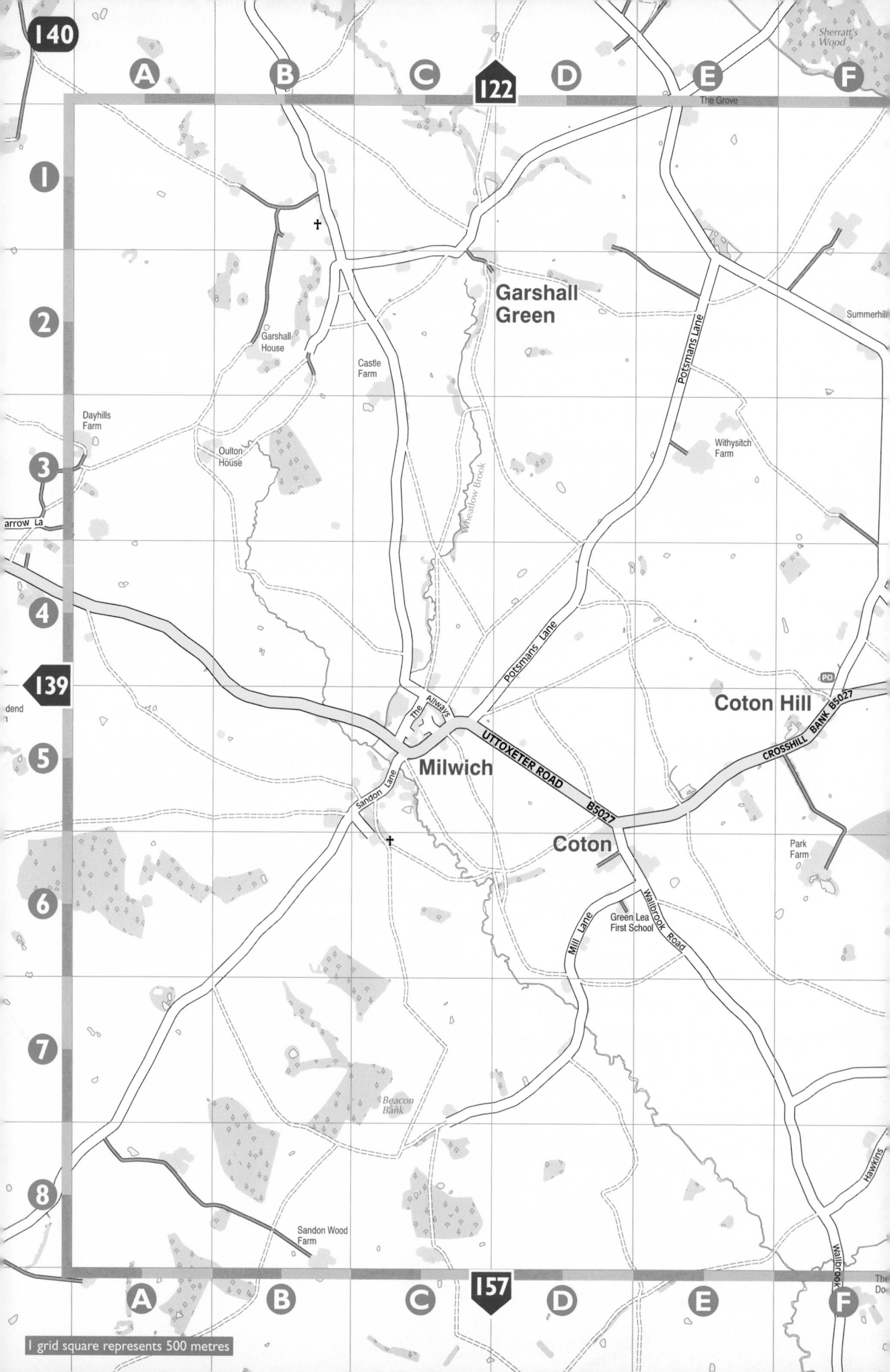

A B C D E F

122

Sherratt's Wood

The Grove

1

2

Garshall Green

Summerhill

Garshall House

Castle Farm

Potsmans Lane

Dayhills Farm

3

Oulton House

Withysitch Farm

arrow La

Wheatlow Brook

4

139

dend

Potsmans Lane

PO

Coton Hill

CROSSHILL BANK B5027

The Allways

5

Milwich

UTTOXETER ROAD

B5027

Coton

Park Farm

Sandon Lane

6

Mill Lane

Green Lea First School

Wallbrook Road

7

Beacon Bank

8

Hawkins

Sandon Wood Farm

Wallbrook

The Do

A B C D E F

157

G H J **123** K L M

Godstone

I

2

Birchwood Park

Myott's Wood

Bearsbrook

B5027

3

Holly Bank Farm

Big Wood

Coton Hayes

4

UTTOXETER ROAD **B5027**

142

5

Fradswell Heath

Shaw Farm

6

Sun Farm

7

Fradswell

8

Fradswell Lane

Lymer's Lane

Road

Yewtree

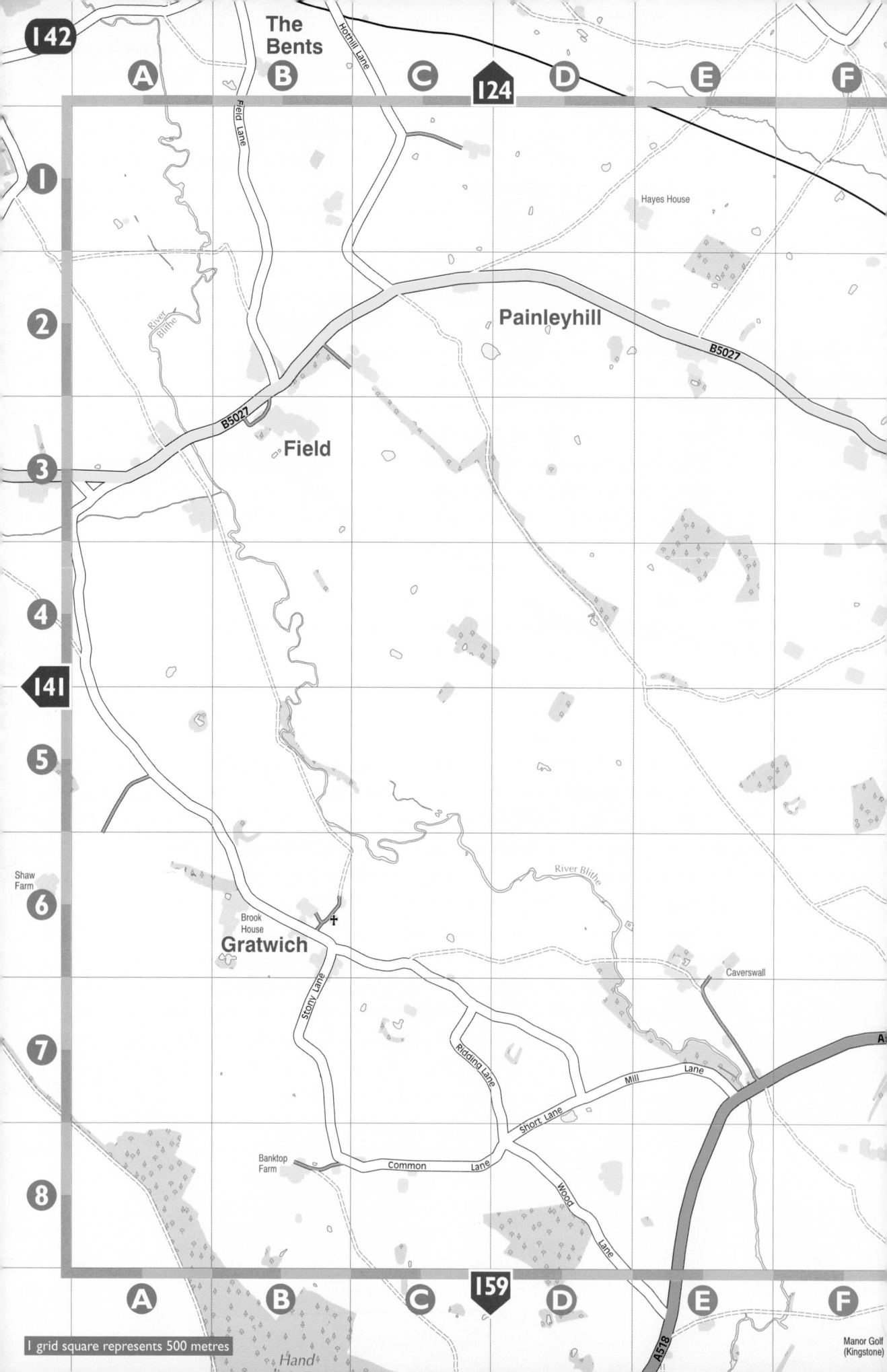

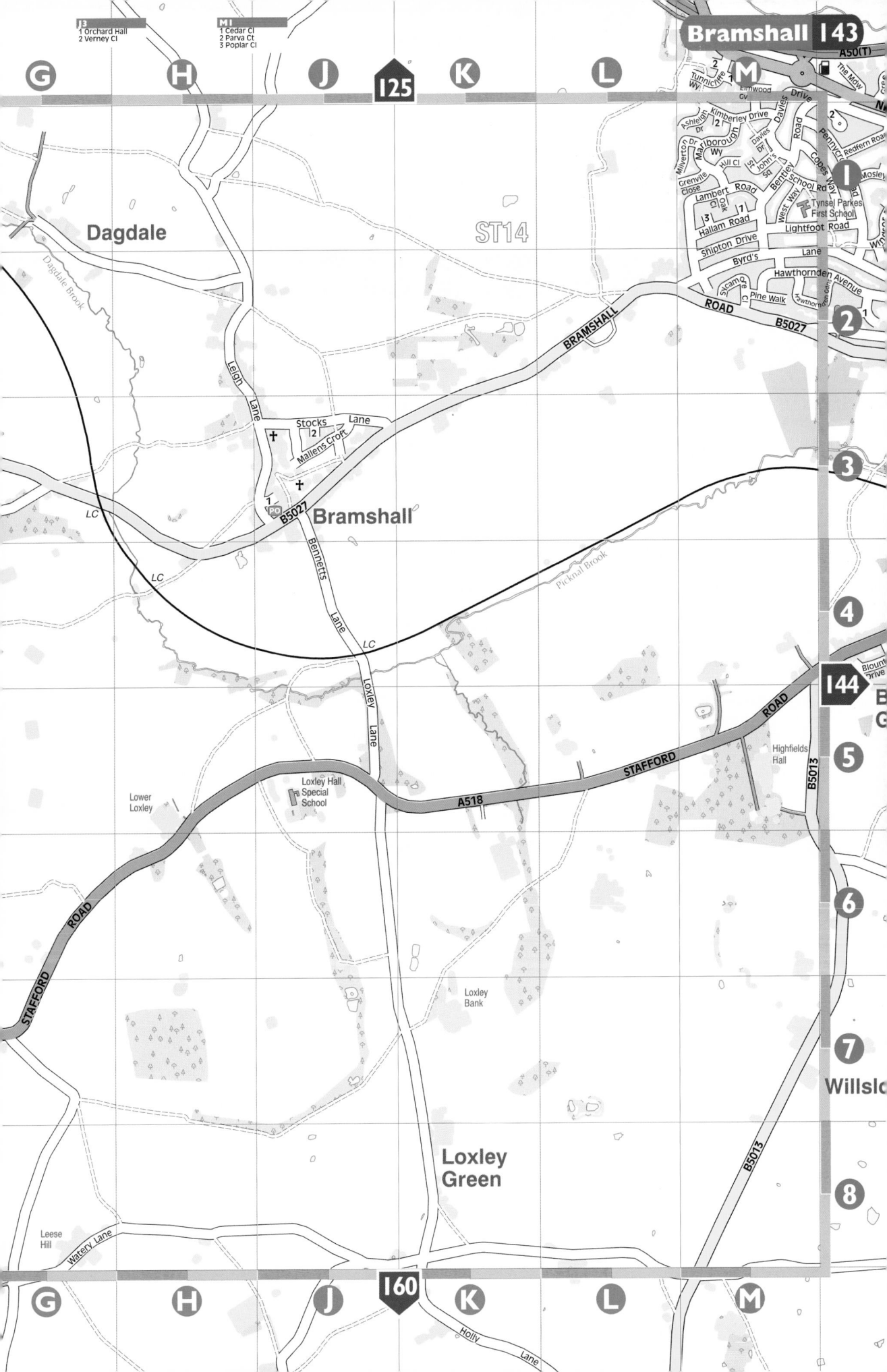

G H J **125** K L M

1 Orchard Hall
2 Verney Cl

M1
1 Cedar Cl
2 Parva Ct
3 Poplar Cl

A50(T)

The Mow

Tunnicliffe Wy

Elmwood Gv

Davies Drive

1

Ashleigh Dr

Kimberley Drive

Milverton Dr

Marlborough Wy

Hill Cl

Davies Road

Penny Cl

Redfern Road

Mosley

St John's Sq

Bentley Rd

Coppice Rd

Grenvile Close

Lambert Road

Oak

Hallam Road

West Way

School Rd

Tynsel Parkes First School

Lightfoot Road

Shipton Drive

Byrd's Lane

Hawthornden Avenue

Sycamore Cl

Pine Walk

Hawthornden Dr

2

ROAD

B5027

Dagdale

ST14

BRAMSHALL

ROAD

3

Dagdale Brook

Leigh Lane

Stocks Lane

Mallens Croft

LC

LC

PO B5027

Bramshall

Bennetts Lane

LC

Picknal Brook

4

144

Blount Drive

5

Highfields Hall

B5013

Loxley Lane

Lower Loxley

Loxley Hall Special School

STAFFORD

ROAD

A518

6

STAFFORD

ROAD

Loxley Bank

7

Willsl

Leese Hill

Watery Lane

Loxley Green

B5013

8

G H J **160** K L M

Holly Lane

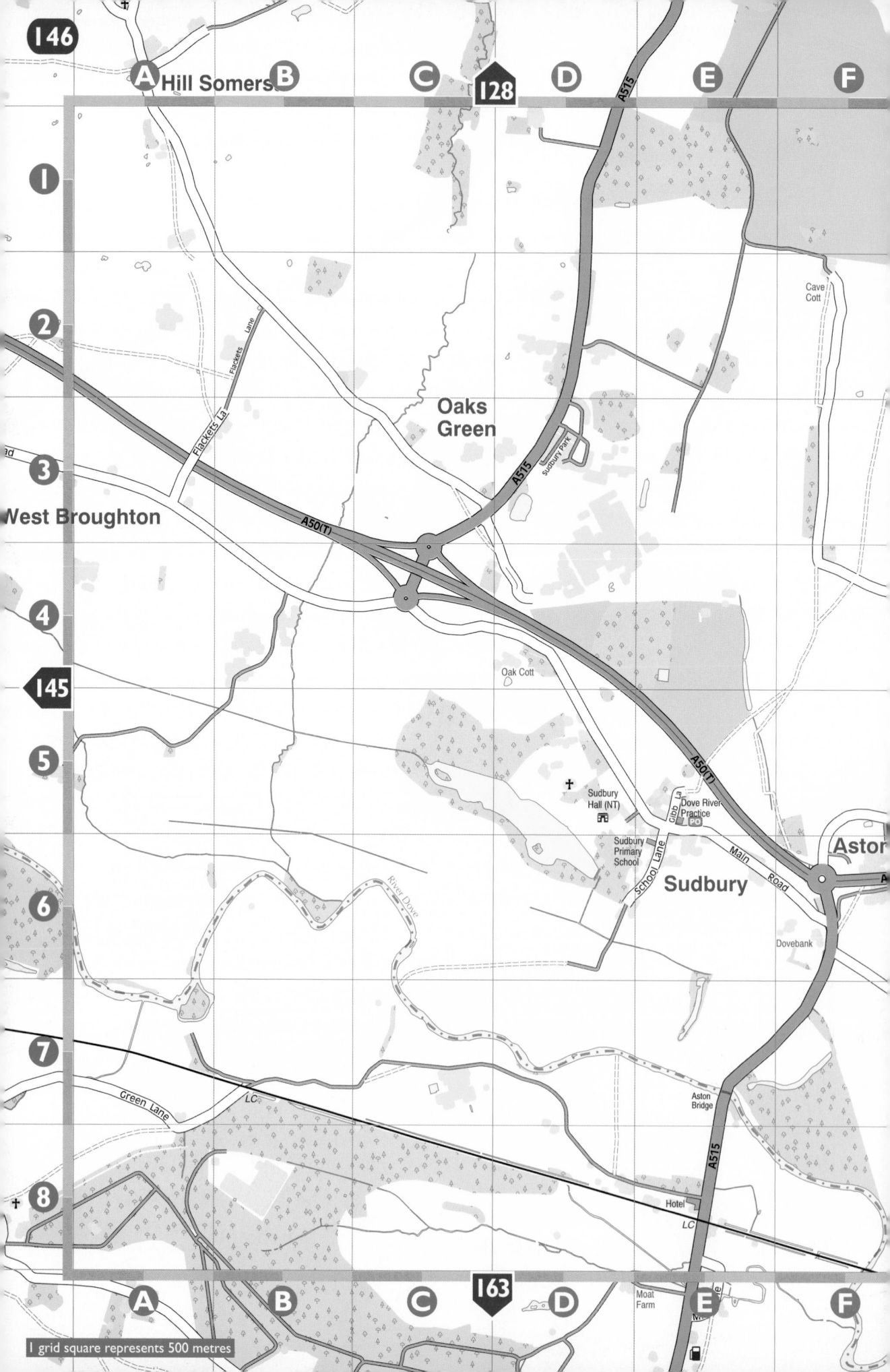

146

A Hill Somerst B   C   128   D   A515 E   F

1

Cave
Cott

2

Flackets Lane

Flackets La

Oaks
Green

A515

Sudbury Park

3

West Broughton

A50(T)

4

145

Oak Cott

A50(T)

5

Sudbury
Hall (NT)

Gibb La

Dove River
Practice
PO

Astor

A

School Lane

Sudbury Primary
School

Sudbury

Main   Road

6

River Dove

Dovebank

7

Green Lane

LC

Aston
Bridge

A515

8

Hotel

LC

Moat
Farm

A   B   C   163   D   E   F

1 grid square represents 500 metres

G H J K L M

129

Sapperton

I

2

Chu
Bro

3

4

5

6

7

8

Gorst
Fields

Ashbourne

Sapperton Lane

Chu

Tipp

Cote Lane

Boggy Lane

Woodhouse Lane

Cotefield

Crowfoot Lane

Muse Lane

Lees Hall
Farm

Marjory Lane

Mackley
House

Foston Mill
Farm

Mill Lane

Dalebrook

Aston
Heath

Breach Lane

Broomhill Farm

Foston Brook

Coplow Lane

Hay Lane

Woodyard Lane

Aston Road

Foston

A50(T)

Uttoxeter Road

Uttoxeter Road

A50(T)

A511

A511

A511

Pa

Pickerton Boulevard

Uttoxeter Road

Watery Lane

Leathersley Lane

Leathersley
Farm

Woodland Drive

Broom's Lane

164

Scropton

PO

LC

Scropton Road

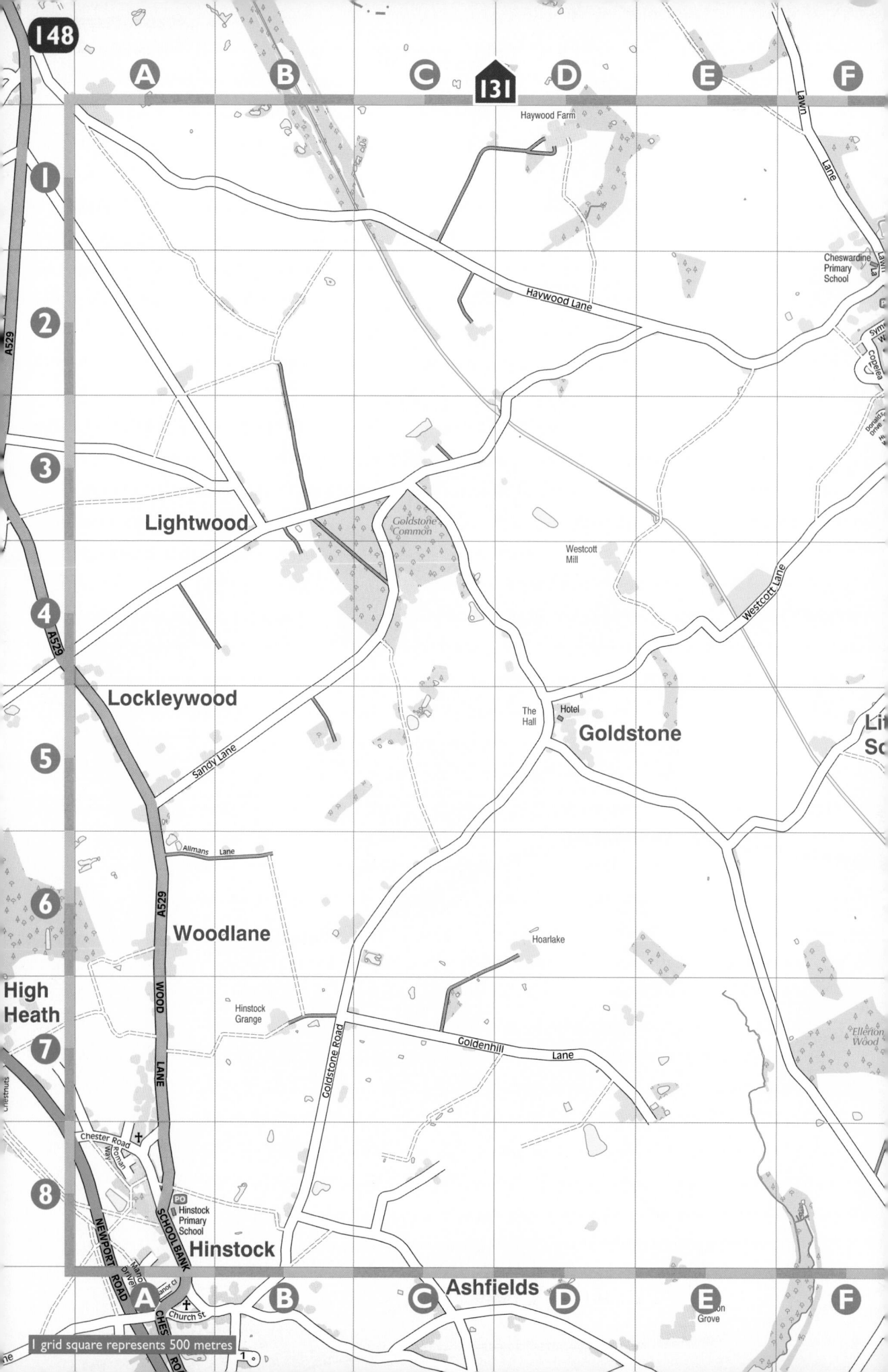

G   H   J   132   K   L   M

Lipley Hall
Farm

I

Doley

2

3

heswardine

Marsh Lane

4

150

Soudley

+

Mossfield

Knighton
Reservoir

5

Hopsnort

Shawbroom

6

Soudley
Park

Knighton Grange
Farm

Shropshire County

Staffordshire County

7

Shropshire Union Canal

Park
Heath

Knighton

8

150

A B C **133** D E F

1

Blorepipe

White Farm

Outlands

New Inn Bank

2
Lower Wood
Corner Farm

Main Road

3
Wood
Farm

Lerridge Lane

4

Adbaston
Farm

149

The
Lea

5

6
Hall
Farm

†

Adbaston

Main Road

Tunstall

7

Offley Grove
Farm

Tunstall Lane

Knighton

8

A B C **169** D E F

Sugnall

Redgreet

G H J K L M

134

B5026

1

Green Farm

2

The

Cop Mere

Offleyrock

Offleyhay

3

Offleymarsh

Mere Rise

PO

Copmere End

Brann Farm

Vinegar Hill

Sandy Lane

4

152

Lea Knowl

5

Villa Farm

Horsley Lane

Horsley Lane

Horsley Farm

Cash Lane

6

Old House Farm

Garmelow

Rue Barn Farm

7

Cash Lane

Park Mill

8

Park Hall Farm

G H J K L M

170

Knightley Eaves

High Offley

Park Lane

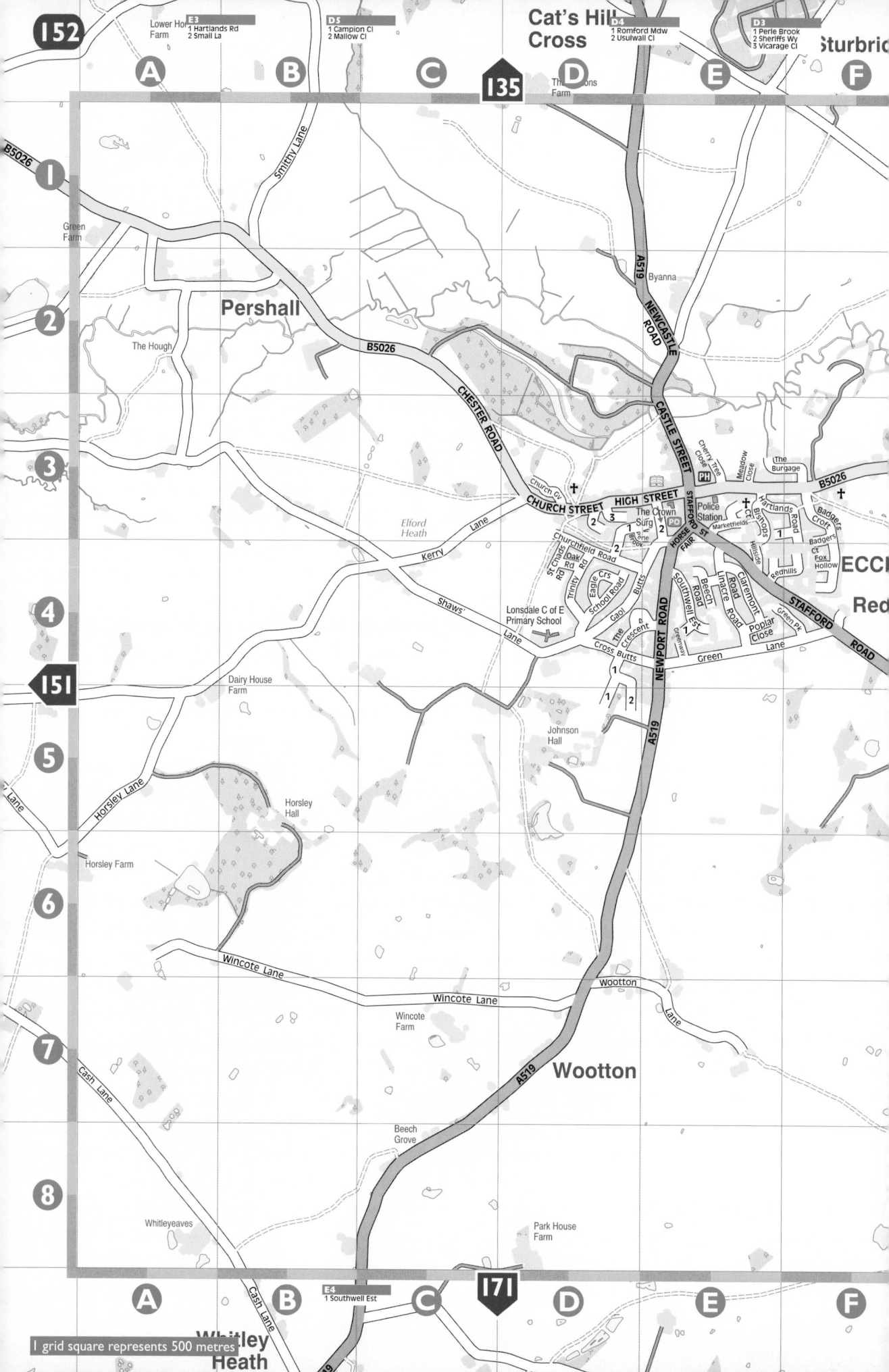

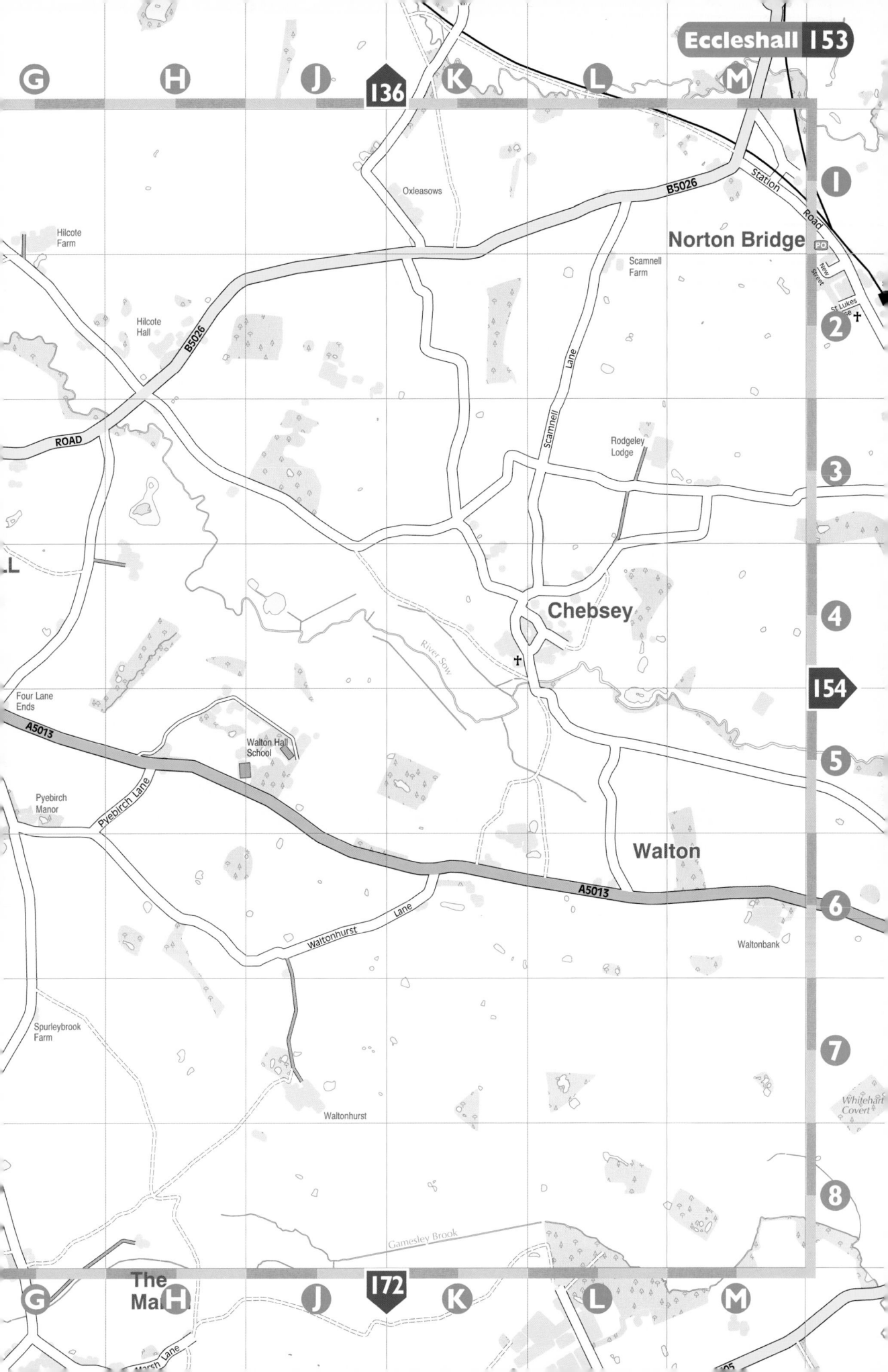

G   H   J   **136**   K   L   M

I

Oxleasows

B5026   Station

Norton Bridge

Hilcote Farm

Scamnell Farm

St Lukes

2

Hilcote Hall

B5026

Scamnell Lane

Rodgeley Lodge

3

ROAD

L

River Sow

Chebsey

4

154

Four Lane Ends

A5013

Walton Hall School

5

Pyebirch Manor

Pyebirch Lane

Walton

A5013

6

Waltonhurst Lane

Waltonbank

Spurleybrook Farm

7

Whitehart Covert

Waltonhurst

8

The Ma   **172**

Gamesley Brook

A B C **137** D E F

1

Stafford Road

PO

New Street

St Lukes Close

Norton Bridge Station

Norton Farm

Greenhill Farm

Pirehill Grange

Hundred-acres

2

Shallowford

3

Izaak Waltons Cottage Museum

Worston Lane

Summerhill

M6

Whitgreav

4

5

Worston Lane

March Lane

Grange Farm

6

Worston Hall

Whitgreave Lane

Waltonbank

A5013

Little Bridgeford

Cherry Lane

7

Whitehart Covert

1

Hawthorn Cl
Clematis Close
Eccleshall Rd
Lilac Close
Jasmine
Magnolia Close
Laburnum Close
Lavender Close
Rose Rd

Newport Rd

PO

River Sow

ECCLESHALL

8

Great Bridgeford

2

NEWPORT ROAD

ROAD

A B C **173** D E F

B5405

Road

A5013

CRES

1 grid square represents 500 metres

G H J **138** K L M

1
2
3
4
156
5
6
7
8

Enson Lane

Enson Lane

Enson Lane

A34(T)

Yarlet Hall
Preparatory
School

New Enson
Farm

Enson Farm

Yarlet PH

Yarlet Lane

Black
Plantation

Park Farm

Grange Farm

Yarlet Lane

Whitgreave
Lane

Upper
Farm

Whitgreave
Manor

Marson

Marston Farm

A34(T)

Marston Lane

Redhill
Farm

Marstongate
Farm

Newbuildings
Farm

Hopton
Farm

G H J **174** K L M

A513 BEACONSIDE

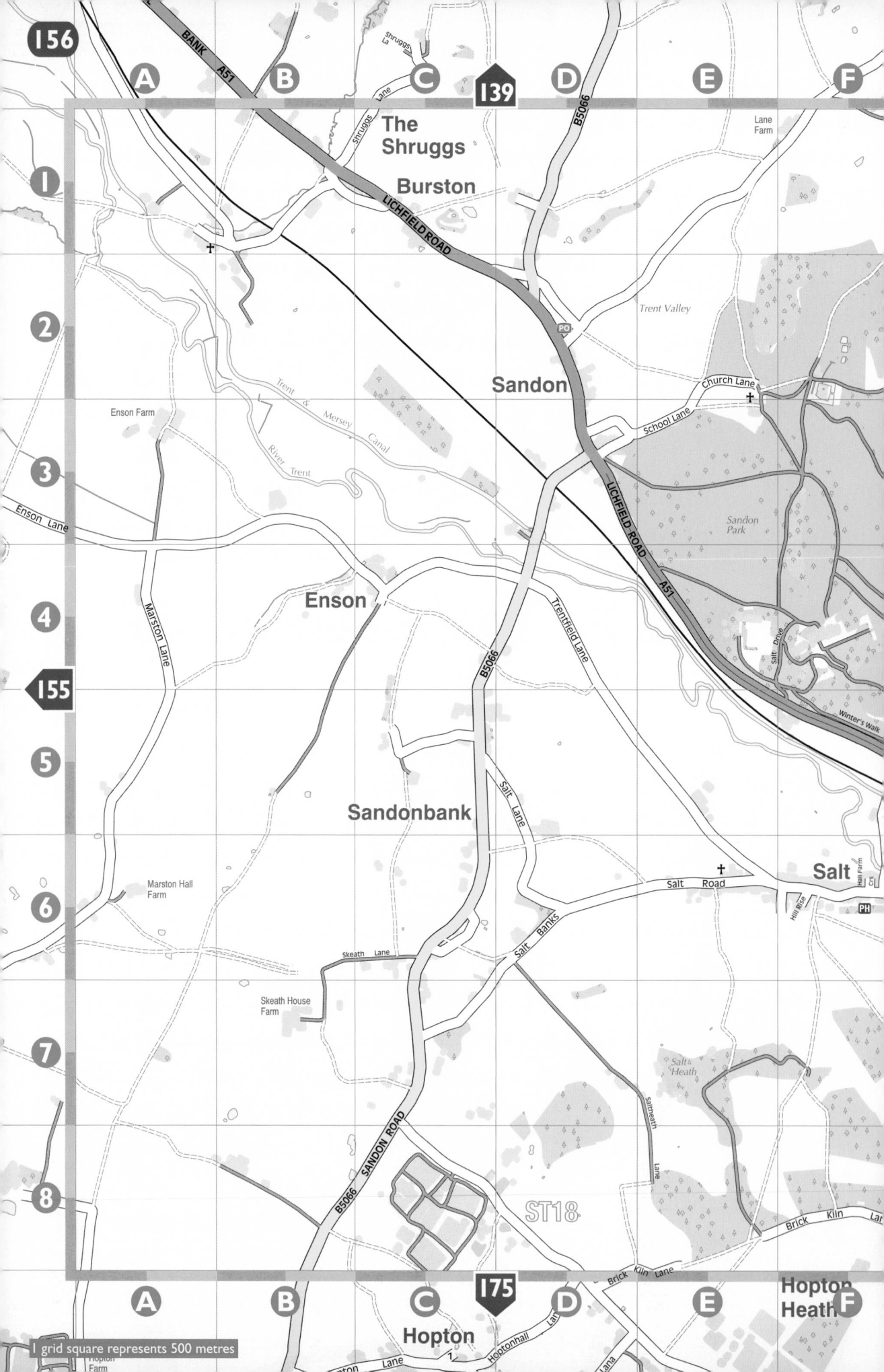

J7
1 Bridge Cl

K7
1 Old School Cl

K8
1 The Bullring
2 Outwoods Cl
3 Outwoods Gn

G H J K L M

140

Sandon Wood Farm

The Doglands

Doglands Road

Hartley Green

Sandon Wood

Westmoor Farm

Parkside Farm

Gayton

158

Vicarage Bank

Church Lane

Moor Leys Farm

Pitt's Column

Gayton Brook

Wadden Lane

Wadden Farm

A518

A51

Sandy Lane

LC

Boat Lane

A518

WESTON BANK

STAFFORD ROAD

St Andrews First School
Cemetery

Meadowbank Avenue

Salt Works Lane

Pellfield Court

Old Road

PO

Wellyard

Manor Cl

Ferrers Road

The Green

Primary Sch

LONDON ROAD

Green Road

Weston

Gayton Brook

G H J K L M

176

G H J **142** K L M

1

Manor Golf Club
(Kingstone)

2

Wanfield
Hall

3

Hand
Leasow
Wood

New Buildings
Farm

A518

Wood
Farm

Grindley

Blythe Bridge Bank

4

Grindley   Lane

160

Stoney Brook

Chartley
Moss

**The
Blythe**

5

Hollyhurst

Lane

Booth Lane

Moss Rise
Farm

Hollyhurst Lane

Upper
Callo

6

River Blythe

7

Booth

Drointon

8

Booth Lane

Callowhill

Lea

Dapple

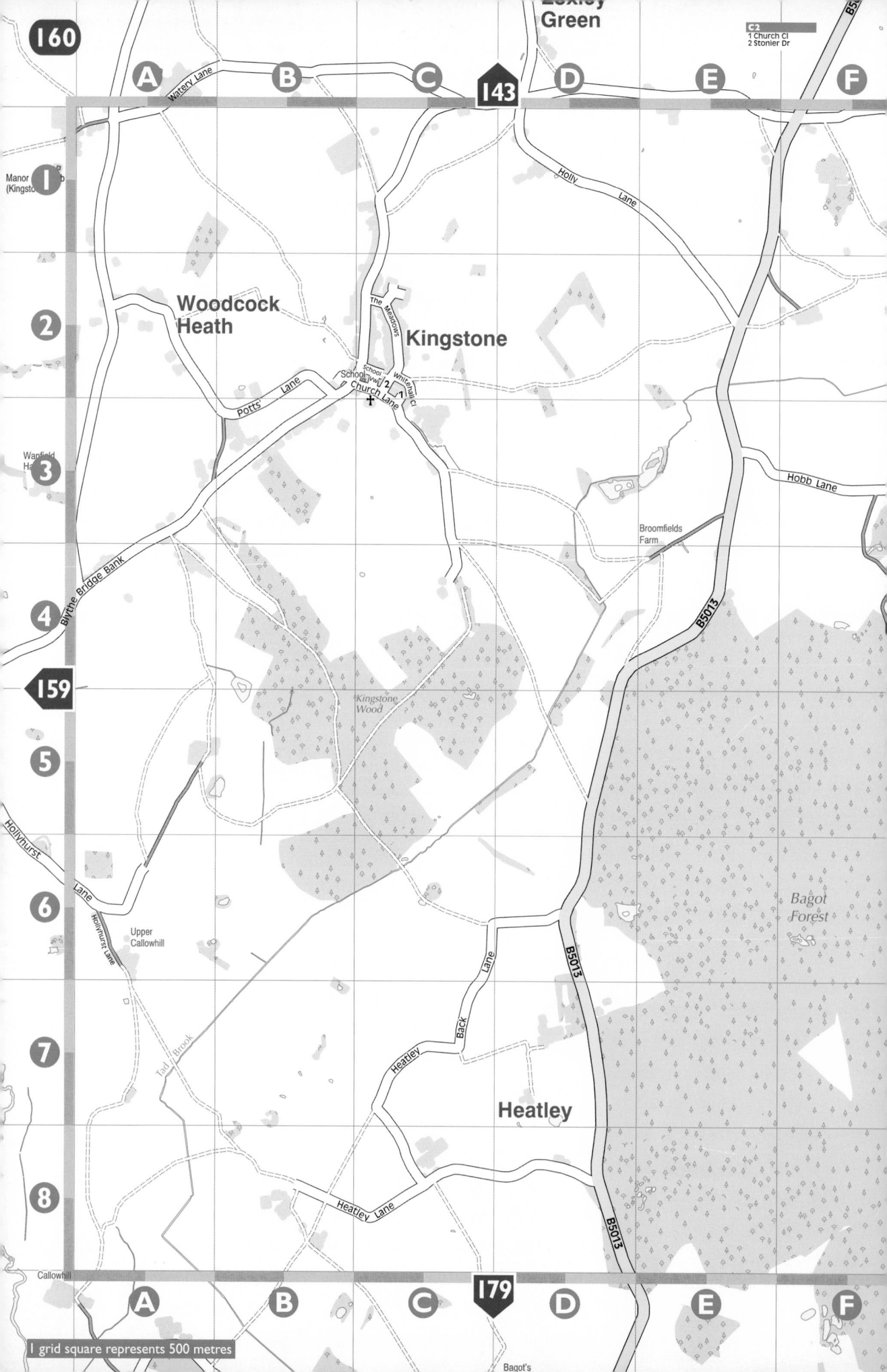

Zoxiey
Green

C2
1 Church Cl
2 Stonier Dr

B5

A Watery Lane B C 143 D E F

Manor
(Kingsto 1

Woodcock
Heath

Holly
Lane

Kingstone

2

The Meadows

Wanfield
Ha 3

School
School 2 1
Church Lane
Whitehall Cl

Potts' Lane

Hobb Lane

Broomfields
Farm

Blythe Bridge Bank

4

B5013

159

Kingstone
Wood

5

Bagot
Forest

Hollyhurst

6 Upper
Callowhill

Hollyhurst Lane

Tad Brook

Back Lane

B5013

7

Heatley

Heatley

B5013

8

Heatley Lane

Callowhill

A B C 179 D E F

1 grid square represents 500 metres

Bagot's

G H J 144 K Netherland Green L M

Brook House Farm

Quee Lane

Scounslow Green

Smallwood Manor

Gorsty Hill

Hobb Lane

Hodge

Tinker's Lane

Thorny Lanes

Marlpit House Farm

Trees

Staffordshire Way

Parkstile

Bagot Forest

Ma Wo

162

Bagot's Park

Park Lodge

Staffordshire Way

Squitch House

G H J 180 K L M

Hart's

I
2
3
4
5
6
7
8

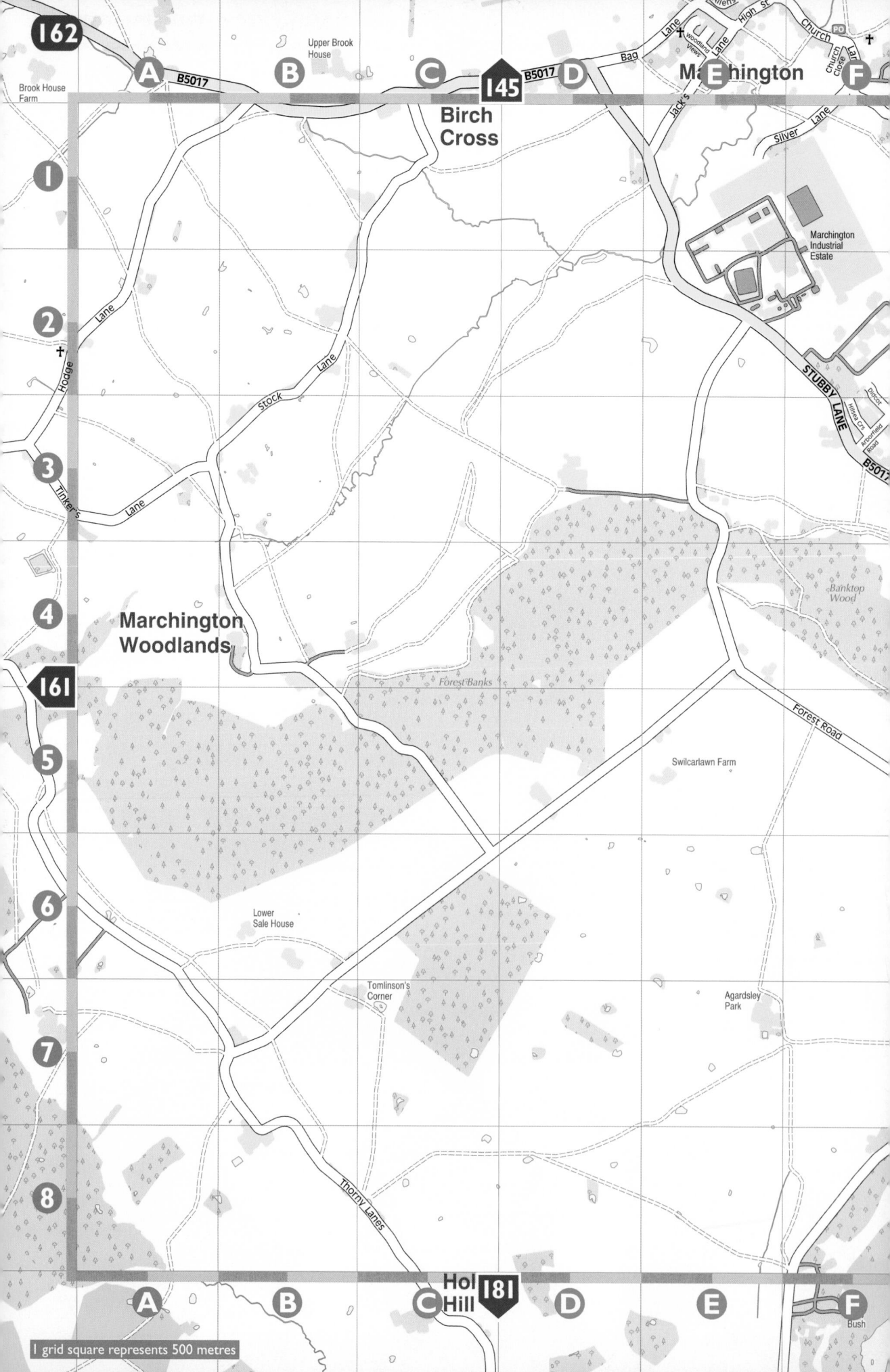

162

A B5017

B

Upper Brook
House

C 145 B5017 D

Bag

Allens High St

Church

Woodland
Lane

PO

Marchington

Church
Close

Birch
Cross

Silver Lane

F

Brook House
Farm

Jack's

E

1

Lane

Marchington
Industrial
Estate

2

Hodge

Stock Lane

STUBBY LANE

3

Tinker's Lane

Hilton Cts
Director
Arborfield
B5017

4

Banktop
Wood

Marchington
Woodlands

161

Forest Banks

Forest Road

5

Swilcarlawn Farm

6

Lower
Sale House

Agardsley
Park

Tomlinson's
Corner

7

8

Thorny Lanes

A B C Hol 181 D E Hill F

Bush

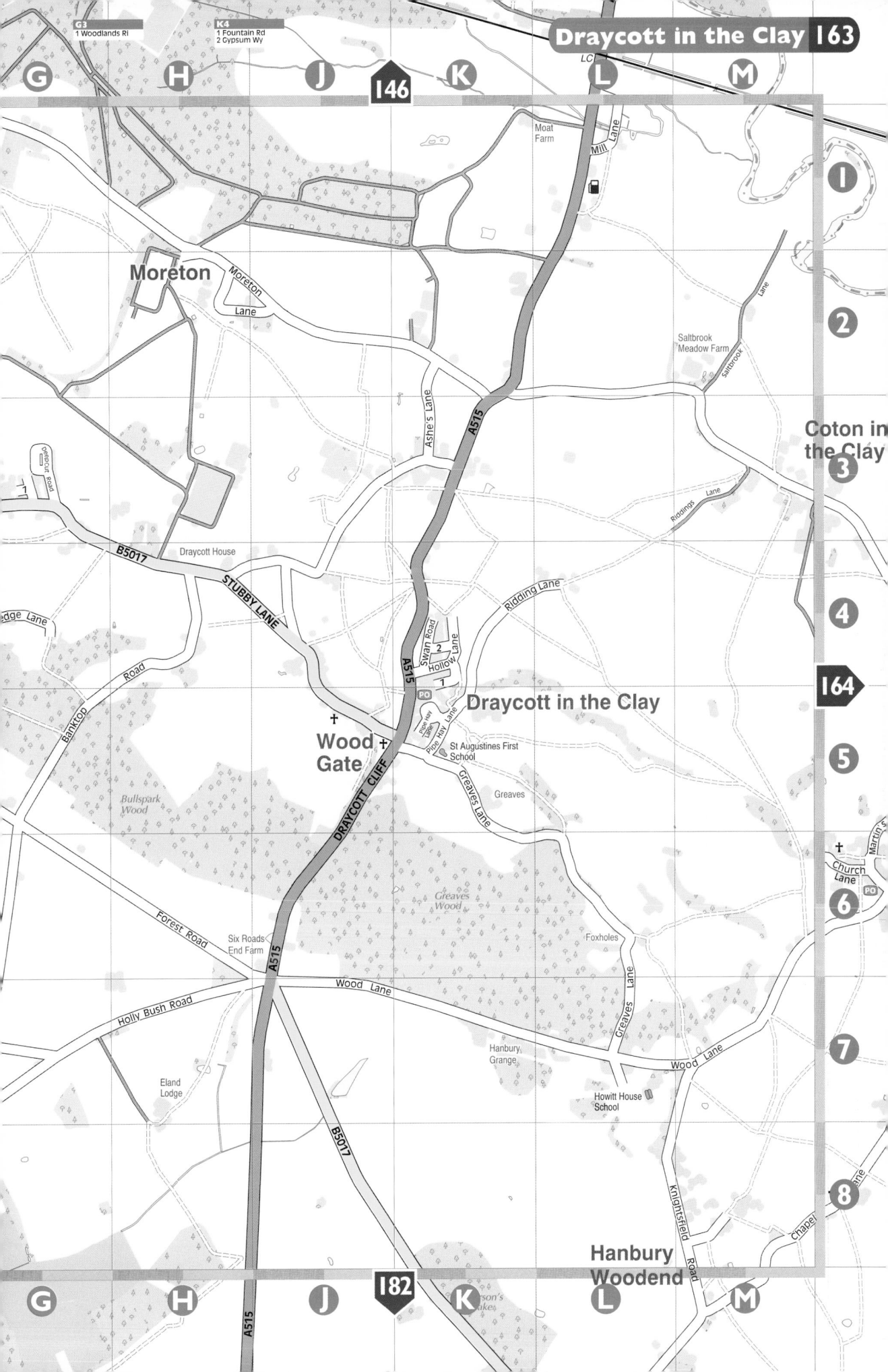

G3
1 Woodlands Ri

K4
1 Fountain Rd
2 Gypsum Wy

G H J 146 K L M

I

Moat
Farm

LC

Mill Lane

2

Saltbrook
Meadow Farm

Saltbrook Lane

Lane

Coton in
the Clay
3

Moreton

Moreton Lane

Ashe's Lane

A515

Riddings Lane

B5017

Draycott House

STUBBY LANE

Swan Road

Hollow Lane

2

Ridding Lane

4

164

Overout Road

Banktop Road

Edge Lane

DRAYCOTT CLIFF

PO
1

Pipe Hay Lane

Pipe Hay Lane

St Augustines First
School

Draycott in the Clay

5

Wood
Gate

Greaves

Martin's

Church
Lane
PO
6

Bullspark
Wood

Greaves Lane

Greaves
Wood

Foxholes

Forest Road

Six Roads
End Farm

A515

Wood Lane

Greaves Lane

Wood Lane

7

Holly Bush Road

Eland
Lodge

Hanbury
Grange

Howitt House
School

Knightsfield Road

B5017

8

Chapel Lane

Hanbury
Woodend

G H J 182 K L M

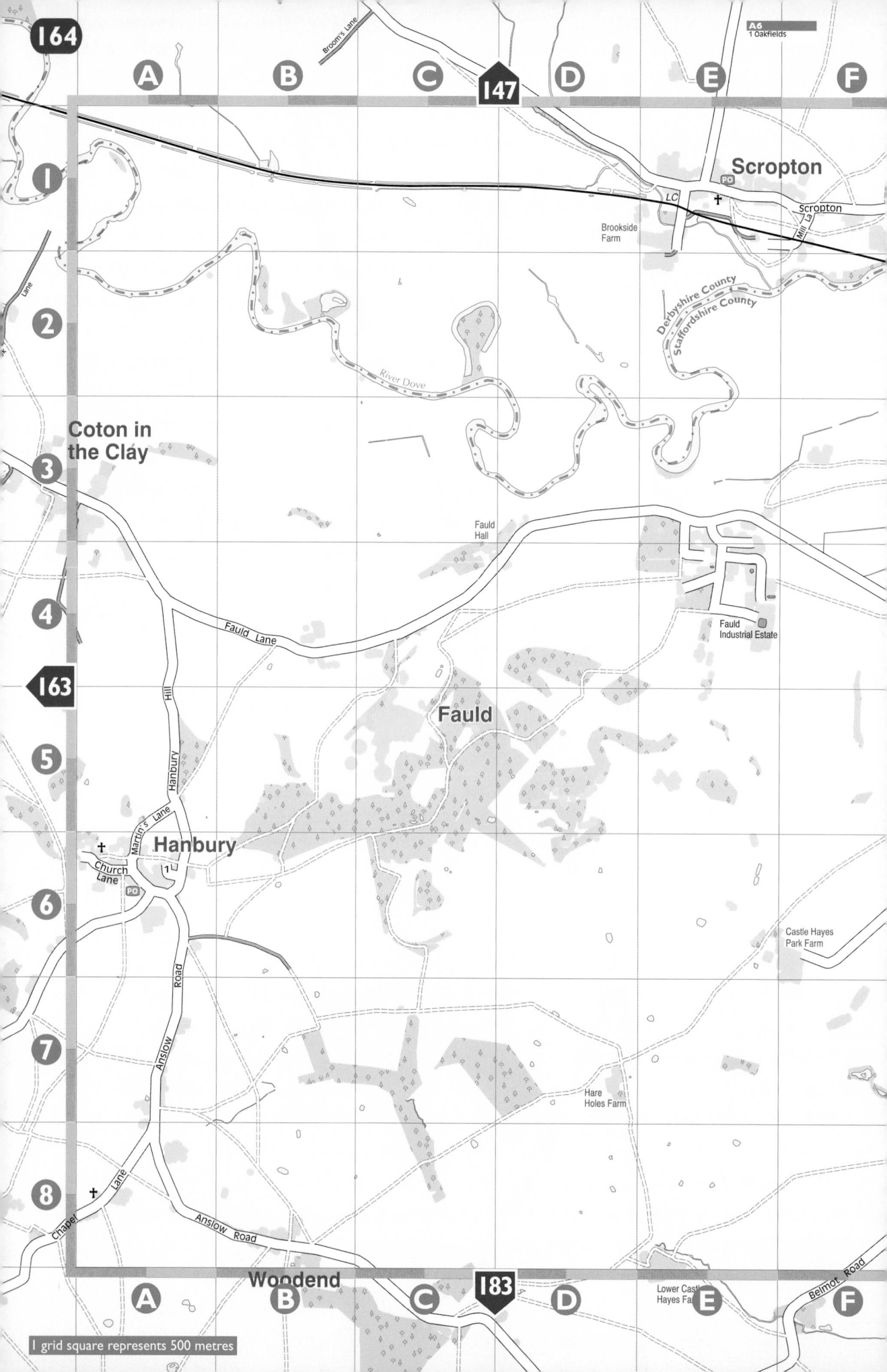

A   B   C   D   E   F

147

A6
1 Oakfields

Scropton
PO
LC
Scropton
Mill La

1

Brookside
Farm

Derbyshire County
Staffordshire County

2

River Dove

**Coton in
the Clay**

3

Fauld
Hall

4

Fauld Lane

Fauld
Industrial Estate

163

Fauld

5

Hill

Hanbury

Martin's Lane

✝ **Hanbury**

Church
Lane   1

PO

6

Castle Hayes
Park Farm

Anslow Road

7

Hare
Holes Farm

8

✝ Chapel Lane

Anslow Road

Woodend

A   B   C   D   E   F

183

Lower Castle
Hayes Fa

Belmot Road

1 grid square represents 500 metres

A B C D E F

E1
1 Bentley Rd
2 Blithe Cl
3 Dale Brook
4 Huntspill Rd
5 Marston Brook
6 Mill Fleam
7 Sandford Brook

D6
1 Twentylands

D7
1 Dodslow Av
2 The Lawns

B6
1 Dove Lea

Main Street

Bembrose Community School

PO Field Cl

Back Lane

Hilton

EGGINGTON ROAD

EGGINGTON ROAD

A5132

DE65

Peacroft Lane

Bloomfield Close

Wyston Brook

Calder Close

Welland Road

Alder's Road

Bancroft Close

Hawthorn Cl

Avon Way

Tinsell Brook

Nene Way

Washford Road

The Mease

A5132

1

Marston Lane

Marston on Dove

The Hall

2

LC

3

Hilton Brook

Mill Fleam

Dove Bridge

4

River Dove

165

5

Snotwoodhill Lane

Church Road

Hall Road

The Paddock

The Lawns

Globe Lane

Marston Lane

Brook Side

The Dower House & Dove Clinic

Alderbrook Cl

Station Road

Rolleston on Dove

Station Road

Dovecliff Road

6

Croft

PH PO Chapel La

John of Rolleston Primary School

Hawksley Dr

Elizabeth Av

School Road

Infant School

Meadow View

Burton Technical College

South Hill

Walford Road

Fairfield Avenue

Burnside

Brick Kiln Lane

Knowles Hill

Newby Close

Beacon Drive

Beacon Road

Craythorne Road

Dovecliff Road

7

Anslow Lane

Cross Lane

Craythorne Road

Craythorne Farm

Tintagel Close

Tristram Grove

Priory Lands

Hall Green Avenue

St Mary Drive

Guinevere Avenue

Shrewsbury Road

Primary School

8

TUTBURY

Beam Rd

Rolleston Road

Nene Way

Athelstan Way

Goodwood

The Belfry

Wentworth Drive

Crown Special

Bitham Lane

Bridge St

Lancelot Drive

Gunmore Dr

Crest

Church

Main Street

Millfield Lane

Jordan

Bridge

Farnham Rd

A B C D E F

E2
1 Stour Cl

D8
1 Arthurs Ct
2 Camelot Cl
3 Galahad Dr
4 Gawain Gv
5 Knights Ct
6 Lohengrin Ct

F8
1 Dovecliff Crs
2 Lovatt Cl

I grid square represents 500 metres

GS
1 Dove Gv

Blakeley Lane

Blakeley Lodge

Eggington Road

Jacksons Lane

Etwall Common

A50(T)

Boundary Road

A50(T)

BURTON ROAD

LC

LC

HILTON ROAD

Egginton Common

A5132 CARRIERS ROAD

Etwall Road

Ash Grove Lane

A38(T)

A5132

THE CASTLE WAY A5132

Ivy Close

smith's Lane

Duck Street

Blacksmith's Lane

Elmhurst

Fishpond Lane

1

PO

Main Street

Grange Court

Smedley Court

William Newton Close

Egginton

Egginton Primary School

Church Road

Rectory Mews

DERBY ROAD

A38(T)

Derbyshire County
Staffordshire County

Clay Mills

DERBY ROAD

A38(T)

DERBY ROAD

Parson'

A5008

BUR

G H J K L M

I
2
3
4
5
6
7
8

168

149

A   B   C   D   E   F

1

2   Ellerton
     Grange

Staffordshire County
The Wrekin

3   Flashbrook
     Manor

     Banqueting
     Farm

     Camp
     Farm

4   Showell
     Grange   Flashbrook
                      Wood

Showell
Mill

5   Mow
     Cop

6   Puleston
                      Common

     Whitleyford
     Bridge

7   Pickstock   Whitley Manor
                      Farm

8   Staffordsh
                      The Wrekin

A   B   C   D   E   F
     River Meese

Puleston

1 grid square represents 500 metres

G H J 150 K L M

1

Batchacre
Park

Shebdon
Farm

Shropshire   Union   Canal

2

Old
Lea

Peggs Lane

Shebdon

Batchacre
Hall

Shay Lane

3

Oldershaws   Lane

Leawood

Kemsey
Manor

Gregory Lane

The   Street

4

170

Loynton
Hall

5

**Weston
Jones**

Gregory Lane

Loynton Sands

Street

eston
nes

Shay Lane

Well Lane

Baker's Lane

6

A519

Lane

7

Warton
Grange

8

Fernhill

Fernhill Road

519

Black Lane

Green
Lane

Cliffs

Sutton

A B C 151 D E F

1

High
Offley

Park Lane

Knightley
Eaves

2 Woodseaves A519

High The Green Back Lane
Offley Road Barn Common
Moss Lane

Dicky's Lane
Woodhaven

3 Glebefields PO Woodseaves C of E
Primary School
B5405

Littleworth Riley Lane
Lane A519

Lodge Lane

4

169 Grange Road

5

Lowton Sands

Knightley
Grange

6 Pinfold Lane

st
Peter's Ct Shropshire Union Canal

High Meadow

Grub Street

Norbury

7

8

Blakemore
House

PH

Norbury
Junction

A B Gulton C 189 D E F

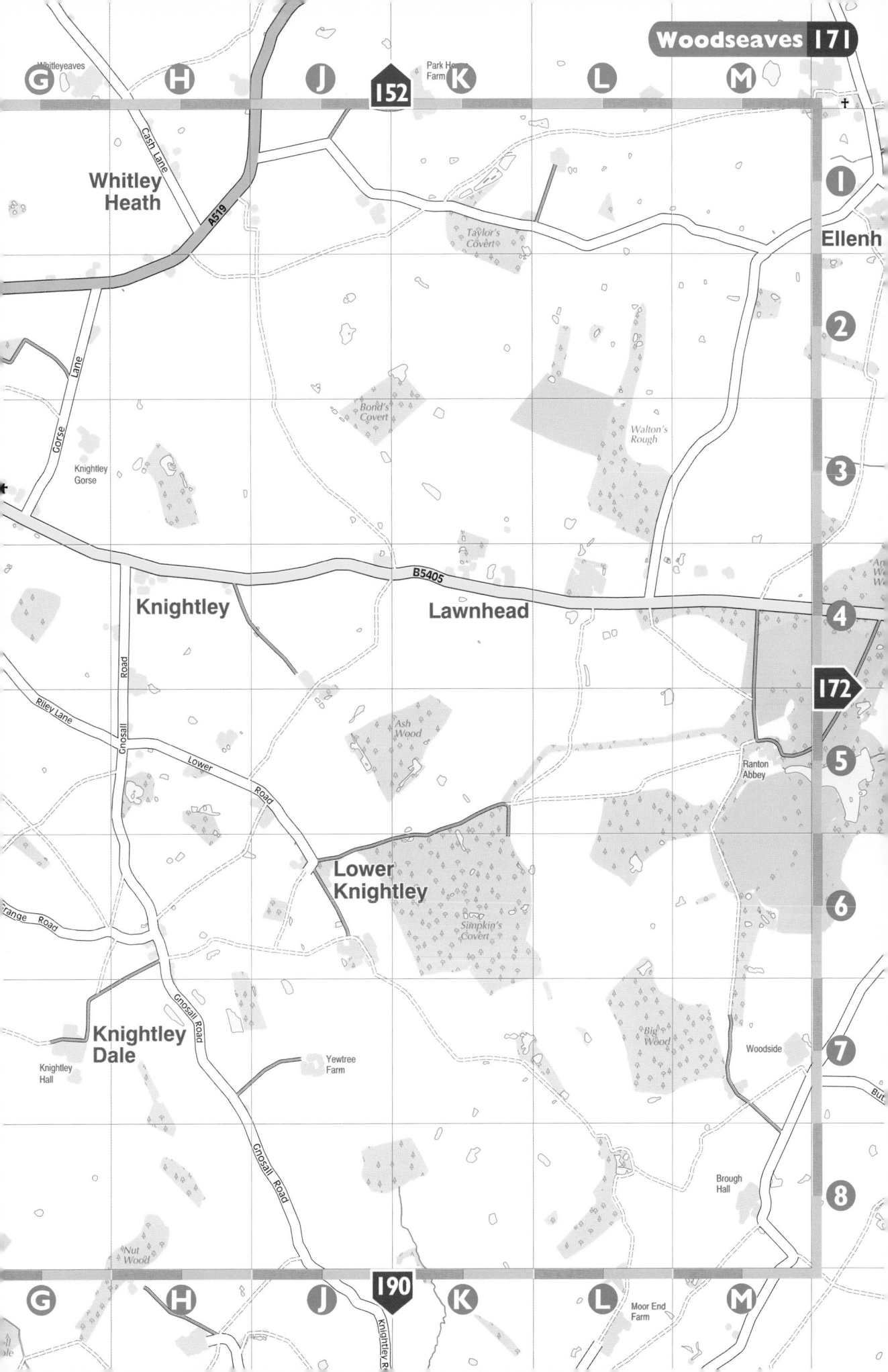

G H J 152 K L M

Whitleyeaves

**Whitley
Heath**

Cash Lane

A519

Gorse Lane

Lane

+

Knightley
Gorse

Park He...
Farm

Taylor's
Covert

Bond's
Covert

Walton's
Rough

Knightley B5405 **Lawnhead**

Riley Lane

Gnosall Road

Lower Road

Ash
Wood

Ranton
Abbey

**Lower
Knightley**

Simpkin's
Covert

...range Road

Gnosall Road

**Knightley
Dale**

Knightley
Hall

Yewtree
Farm

Big
Wood

Woodside

Nut
Wood

Brough
Hall

G H J 190 K L M

Moor End
Farm

Knightley R...

Ellenh

Ellenh

†

1

2

3

4

172

5

6

7

But...

8

An...
W...
W...

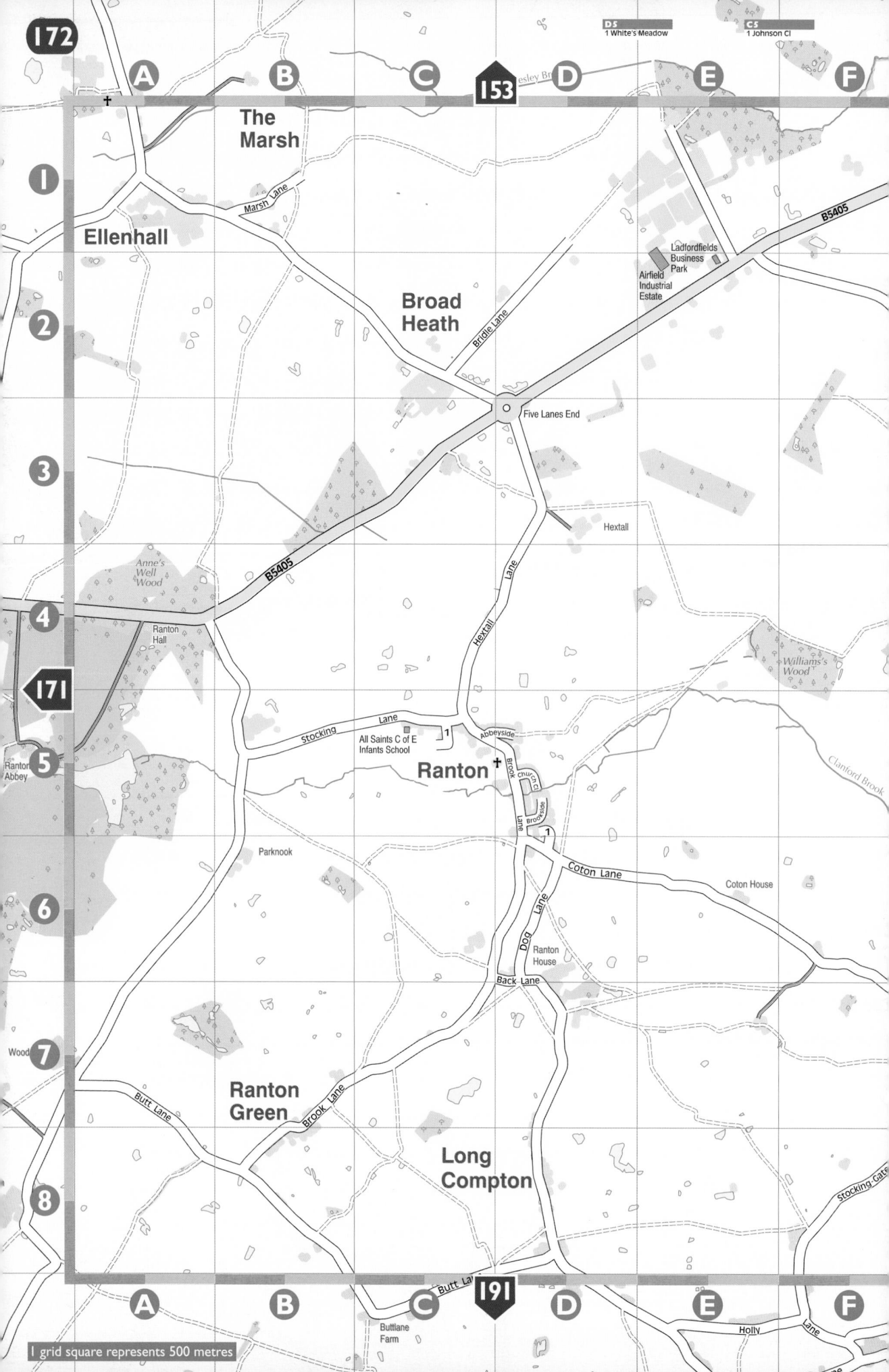

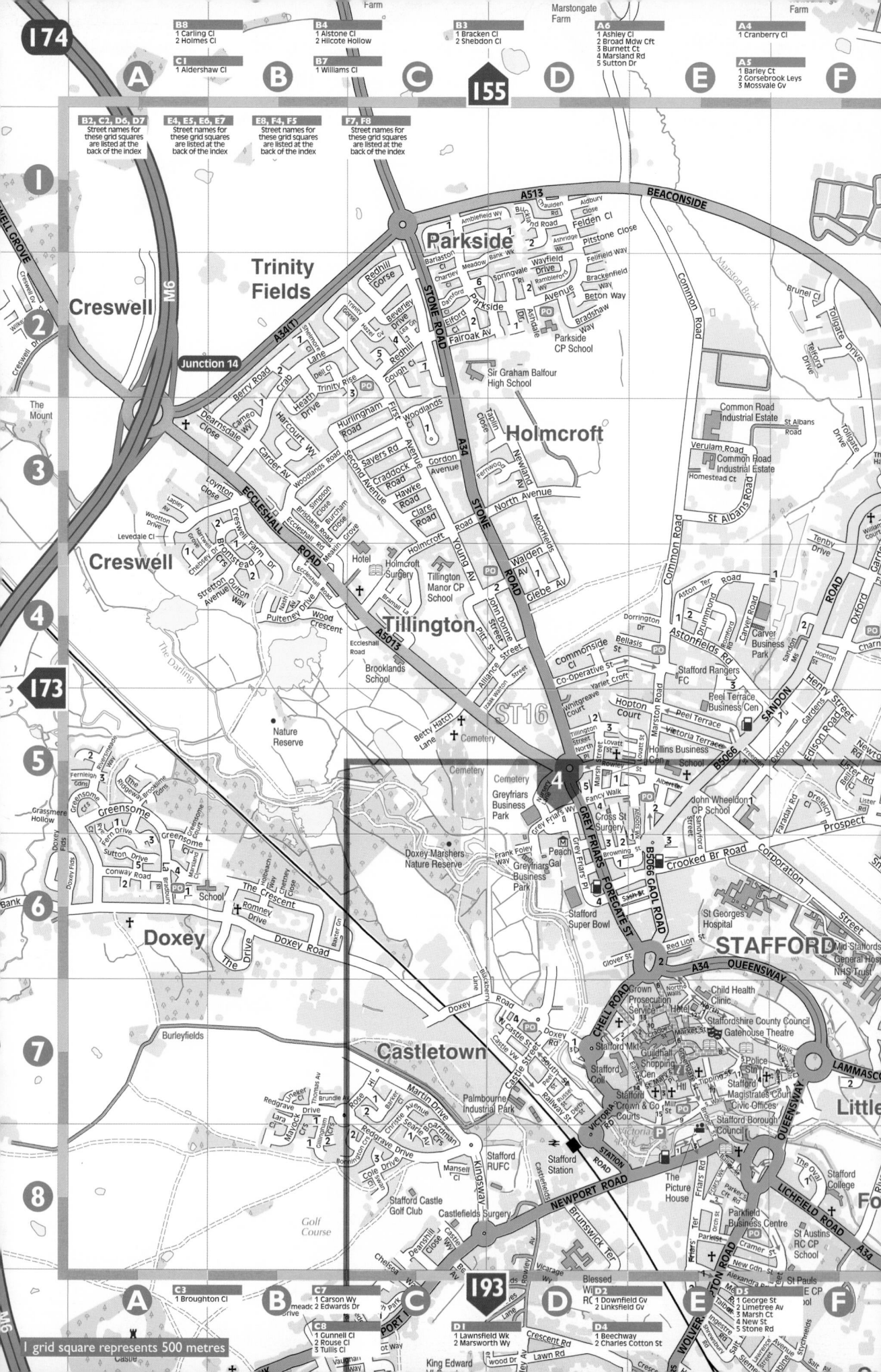

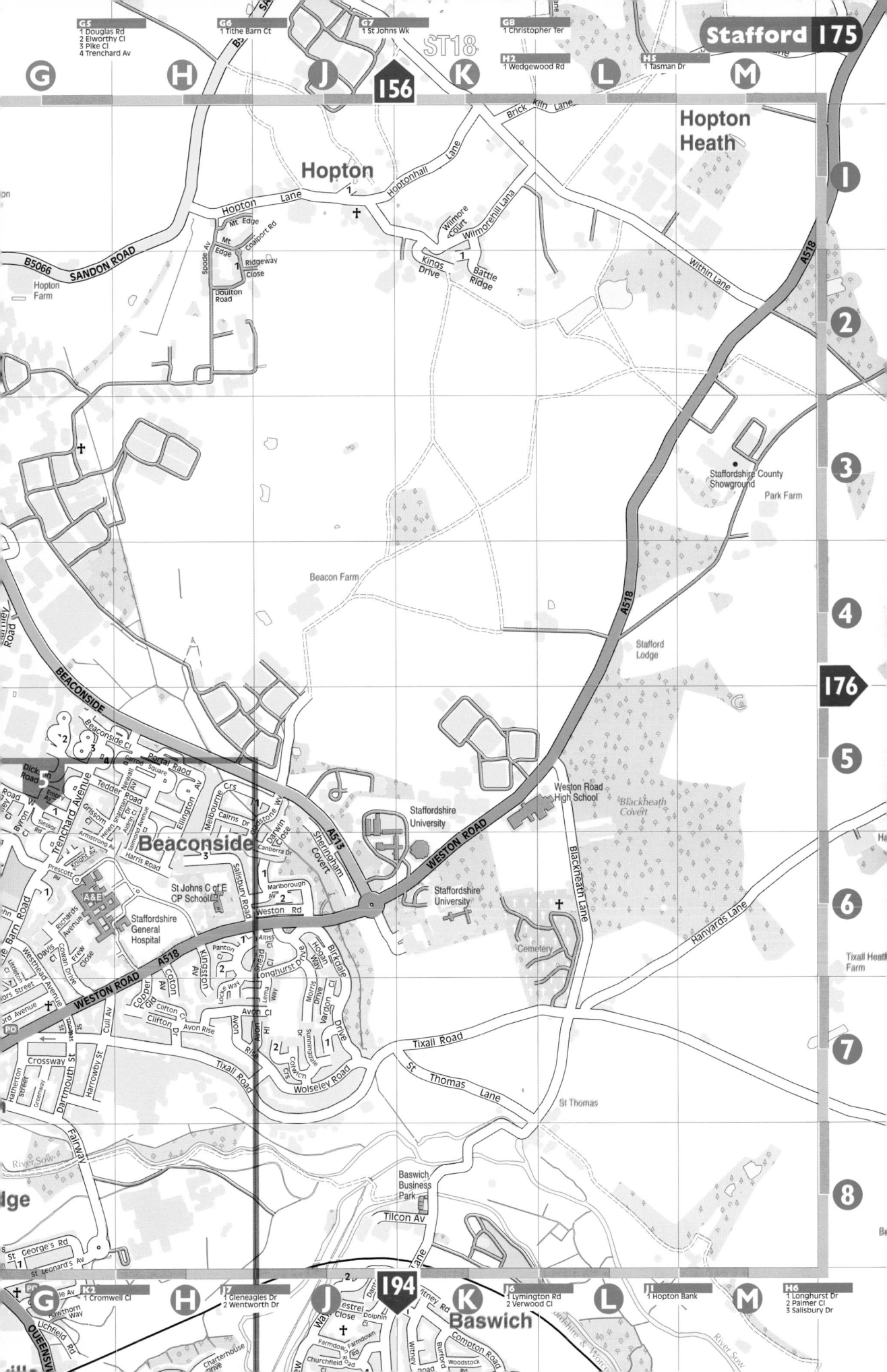

G5
1 Douglas Rd
2 Elworthy Cl
3 Pike Cl
4 Trenchard Av

G6
1 Tithe Barn Ct

G7
1 St Johns Wk

G8
1 Christopher Ter

H2
1 Wedgewood Rd

H5
1 Tasman Dr

G H J K L M

ST18

156

Hopton Heath

Hopton

1

B5066 SANDON ROAD

Hopton Lane

Mt. Edge
Coalport Rd

Spode Av

Hopton Farm

Mt. Edge

Ridgeway Close

Doulton Road

Hoptonhall Lane

Wilmore Court

Wilmorehill Lane

Kings Drive

Battle Ridge

Within Lane

2

A518

3

Staffordshire County Showground

Park Farm

Beacon Farm

4

Stafford Lodge

176

BEACONSIDE

Beaconside Cl

Portal Road

Carroll Square

5

Dickson Road

Trenchard Avenue

Tedder Road

Gresson Cl

Ellington Rd

Melbourne Cl

Cairns Dr

Darwin Close

Canberra Dr

Staffordshire University

Weston Road High School

Blackheath Covert

5

A&E

Richards Avenue

Cowen Drive

Drew Close

Staffordshire General Hospital

St Johns C of E CP School

Salisbury Road

Marlborough Av

Weston Rd

WESTON ROAD

Staffordshire University

Blackheath Lane

Cemetery

Hanyards Lane

6

A518 WESTON ROAD

Kingston Av

Coton Fields

Clifton Cl

Clifton

Avon Rise

Panton

Alliss

Hoban Way

Birkdale

Morris Close

Vardon Drive

Longhurst Drive

Avon Cl

Summerdale

Conich

Wolseley Road

Tixall Road

St Thomas Lane

Tixall Heath Farm

7

Crossway

Harrowby St

Dartmouth St

Tixall Road

St Thomas

River Sow

8

Baswich Business Park

Tilcon Av

G H J K L M

194

Baswich

K2
1 Cromwell Cl

J7
1 Gleneagles Dr
2 Wentworth Dr

J6
1 Lymington Rd
2 Verwood Cl

J1
1 Hopton Bank

H6
1 Longhurst Dr
2 Palmer Cl
3 Salisbury Dr

QUEENSWAY

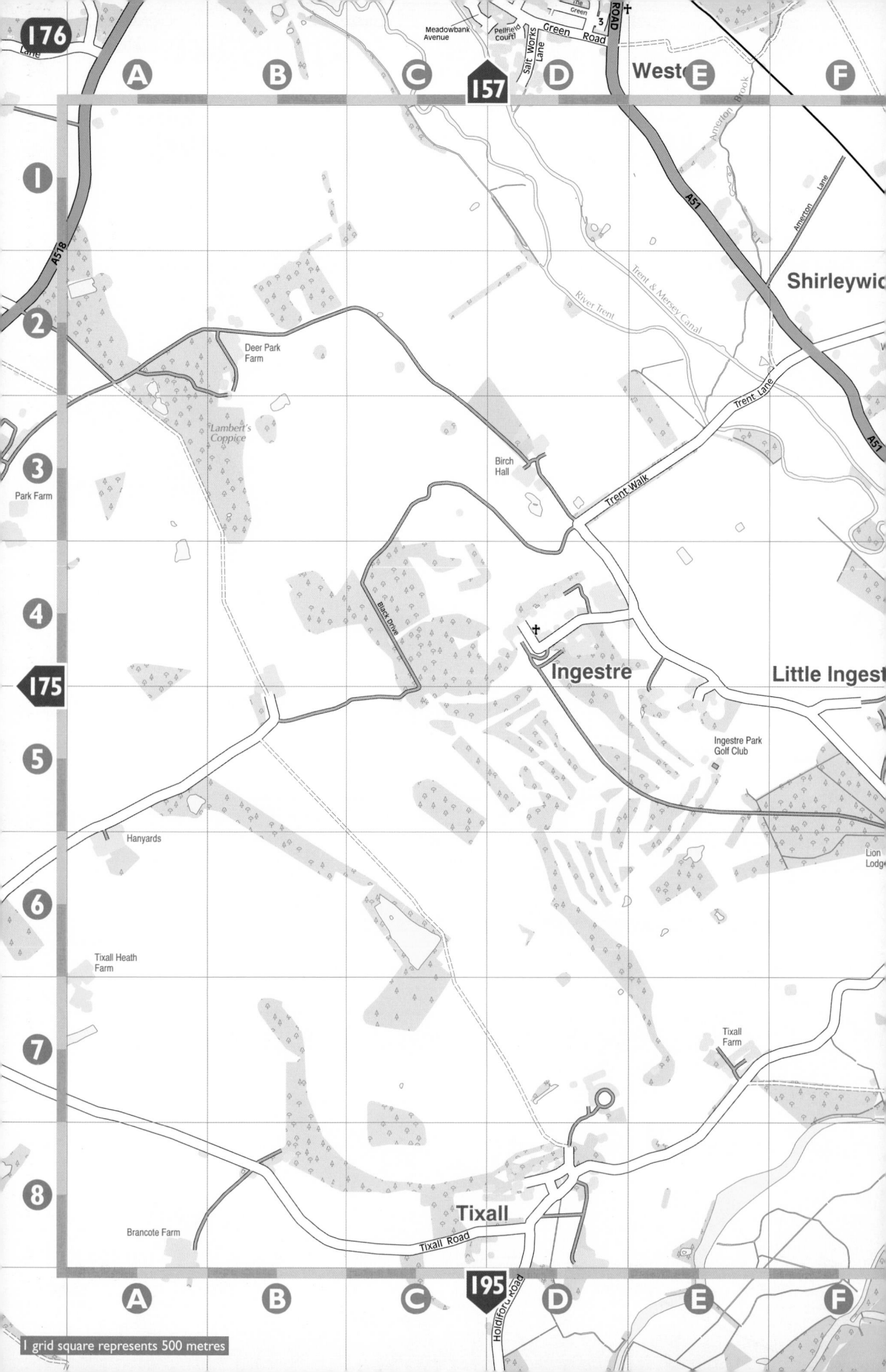

G | H | J | **158** | K | L | M

H7
1 Essex Dr

H8
1 Abbey Flds
2 Brewery La
3 Manor Cl
4 The Stables
5 Trent Cl

J2
1 Baron's Wy
2 Baths La
3 Elm Crs
4 Hammonds Cl
5 Walnut Crest

New Road Industrial Estate

Stowe Lane

Lea Road

Knowle Farm

Church Road

Meadow Gld

Back Lane

Greenfields Rd

Puddle Hill

Ashlands

LC

Road

Featherbed La

Martins Way

Hill Cft

High St

Highfield Rd

Ridgeway

Vine Cl

Sycamore Dr

Smithy Lane

Ivy Ct

The Cft

Church Lane

Hixon

Egg Lane

St Peters C of E CP School

Pasturefields

Hixon Industrial Estate

Pasturefields Industrial Est

Pasturefields Lane

Egg Lane

Egg La

Swansmoor

178

A51

Farley Farm

Hoomill Lane

Tolldish

Moreton Lane

Tolldish Lane

A51

Moreton Lane

Mill Lane

Tithebarn Farm

Oldfields Lane

Mill Court

Oldfields Crs

Earls Wy

Covert

Elm Close

School La

Great Haywood

Little

Tixall Lane

The Uplands

Marlborough Cl

Coley

School

Main Road Surg

Trent La

Main

Nicote Crs

Coley Lane

Primary School

Police Stn

Rockhouse

Oak

Lichfield Dr

Cliff Road

G | H | J | **196** | K | L | M

Drointon

178

Ⓐ   Ⓑ   Ⓒ   **159**   Ⓓ   Ⓔ   Ⓕ

Booth La

Ⓘ

Lea Heath

Lea Road

Heath Lane

Dapple Heath

Knowle Farm

❷

Newbuildings Farm

Bourn Brook

❸

Newton

Vaughan's Lane

❹

◀ **177**

Sw

❺

Rectory Farm

✝

Blithfield Hall

❻

Oakfields

Moreton Lane

❼

Moreton Farm

Lea La

Lea Hall Farm

❽

Ⓐ   Ⓑ   Ⓒ   **197**   Ⓓ   Ⓔ   Ⓕ

Upper Moreton

B5013

1 grid square represents 500 metres

M4
1 Alfred Lyons Cl
2 Cecil Payton Cl
3 Church St
4 Lintake Dr

G   H   J   160   K   B5013   L   M

1

Dunstal

2

Heatley Lane

Bagot's
Bromley

Marsh
Farm

B5013

3

ewton
urst

Harley Lane

UTTOXETER ROAD

B5014

Paget Rise

Salters
Grange

Bagots
VW

The Sur

4

Stansley
Wood

Duckley
Plantation

BAGOT STREET

School

Richa
Clarke
First S

Lintake Dr
4

Mtres Brook

First Ave

St Nicholas Wy

†

180

ST

Goose Lane

Staffordshire Way

Hall Lane

5

Blithfield Reservoir

B5013

Yeatsall Road

Yeatsall

Preebys Cl

Hall Hill

Port   Lane

6

Watery   Lane

Portfields

Waters Road

Seedcroft Lane

7

Admaston

Blithfield
Sailing
Club

B5013

Steenwood   Lane

St Stephen's
Hill Farm

Staffordshire Way

8

acop Lane

G   H   J   198   K   Staffordshire Way   L   Staffordshire Way   M

B5
1 Hillside

A   B   Squitch House   C   D   E   F

1

Dunstal

Hart's Farm

2

Moors Farm

Hobfield Lane

Radmore Lane

Staffordshire Way

3

Woodmill Lane

Radmore Wood

Radmore Lane

Lane

Bagots VW

Salters

2

The Surgery

Paget Rise

Staffordshire Way

Swan

Bagots

4

BAGOT STREET

Schoolhouse

Richard Clarke County First School

St Mary & St Anne School

Abbots Bromley

PH

3

St Thomas

HIGH STREET

PO

Needwood

1

Hall Hill Lane

5

Staff Hill

Hall

ASHBROOK   B5234   LANE

Grange Farm

Bromley Wood

B5234

B5014

Blunts Hollow

Pinfold Lane

6

Mill Green

LICHFIELD

Hart's Farm

Bentilee

Glass Lane

dcroft Lane

ROAD

7

Pinfold Lane

Ash Brook

8

Forge Farm

Cross of the Hand

A   B   C   D   E   F

Orange Lane

Oran

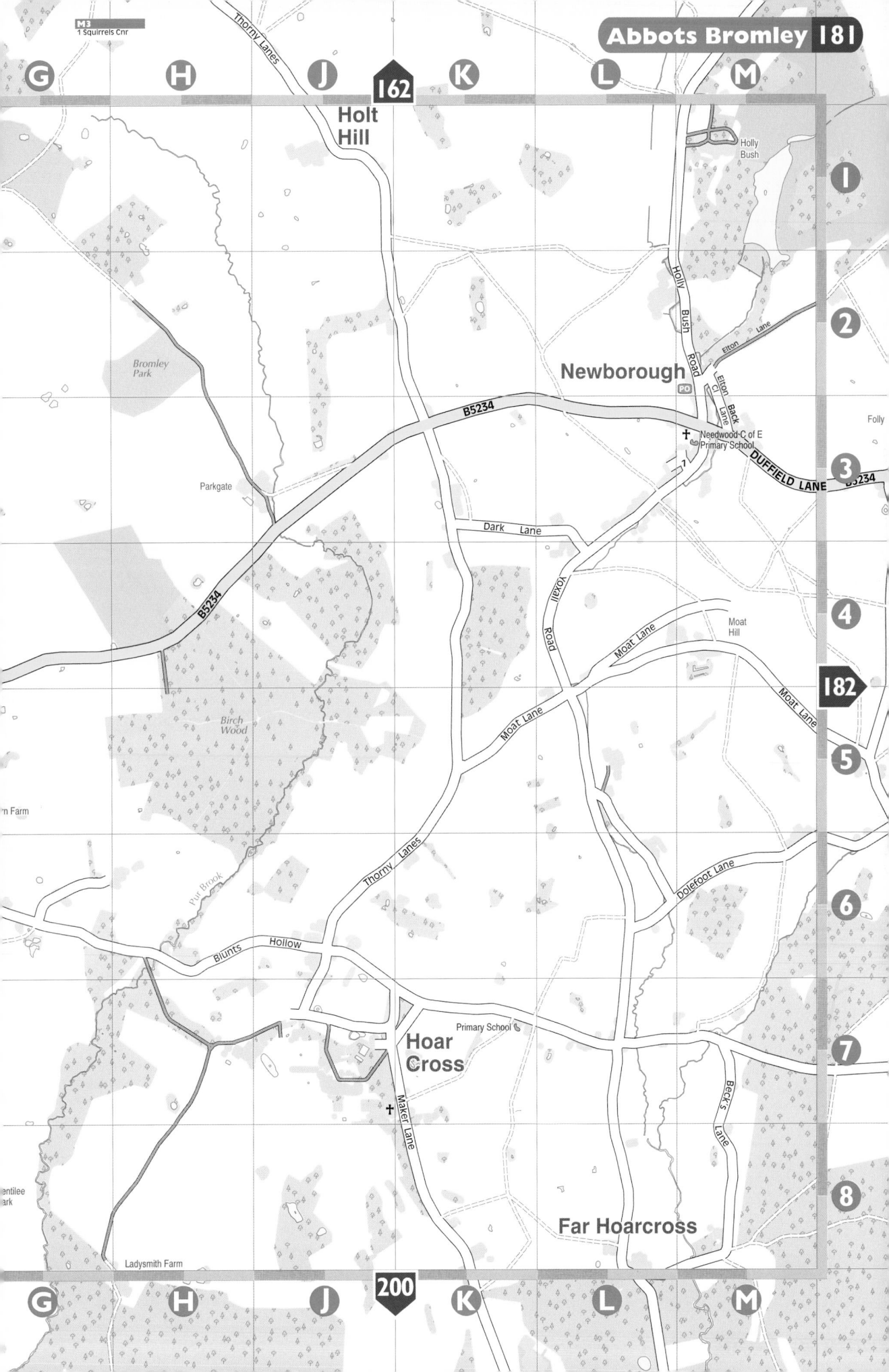

M3
1 Squirrels Cnr

G H J **162** K L M

Holt Hill

Thorny Lanes

Holly Bush

1

Bromley Park

Holly Bush Road

Elton Lane

2

Newborough
PO

Elton Back Lane

Folly

B5234

Needwood C of E Primary School

DUFFIELD LANE

3

B5234

Parkgate

Dark Lane

B5234

Yoxall Road

Moat Lane

Moat Hill

4

182

Birch Wood

Moat Lane

5

Moat Lane

Pur Brook

Thorny Lanes

Dolefoot Lane

6

n Farm

Blunts Hollow

Primary School

Hoar Cross

Beck's Lane

7

Maker Lane

entilee ark

Far Hoarcross

8

Ladysmith Farm

G H J **200** K L M

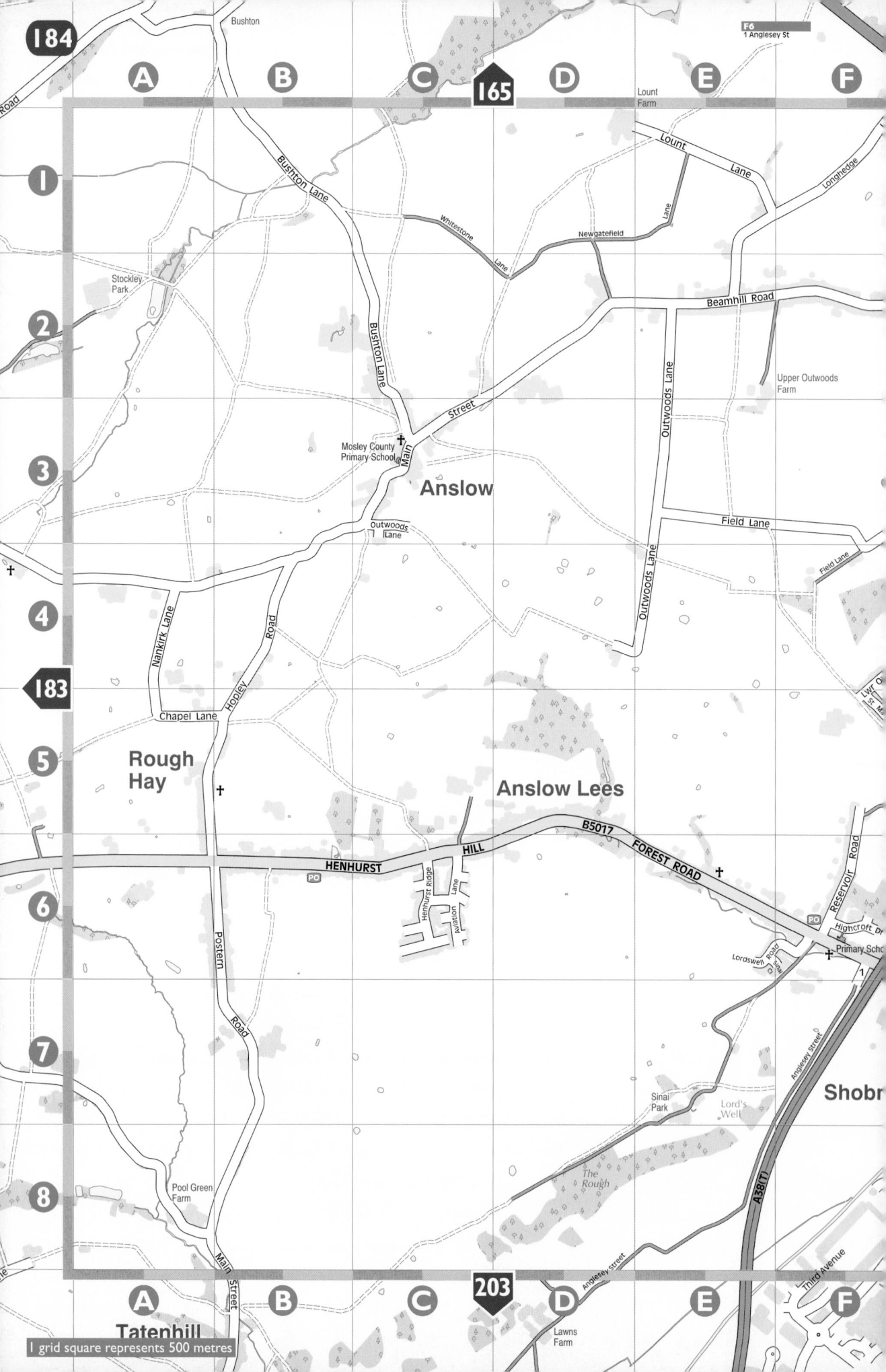

A B C D E F

F6
1 Anglesey St

165

Road

Bushton

Bushton Lane

1

Whitestone Lane

Lount Lane

Newgatefield

Lount Farm

Lount Lane

Longhedge

Beamhill Road

Stockley Park

2

Bushton Lane

Upper Outwoods Farm

Main Street

3

Mosley County Primary School

Anslow

Outwoods Lane

Field Lane

Outwoods Lane

Field Lane

183

Nankirk Lane

Hopley Road

4

Chapel Lane

Rough Hay

5

Anslow Lees

B5017

FOREST ROAD

Henhurst Ridge

HILL

HENHURST

PO

Aviation Lane

Postern Road

6

Reservoir Road

Highcroft Dr

PO

Primary Scho

Lordswell Road

Anglesey Street

7

Sinai Park

Lord's Well

Shobr

Pool Green Farm

8

The Rough

A38(T)

Third Avenue

A B C D E F

203

Anglesey Street

Tatenhill

Lawns Farm

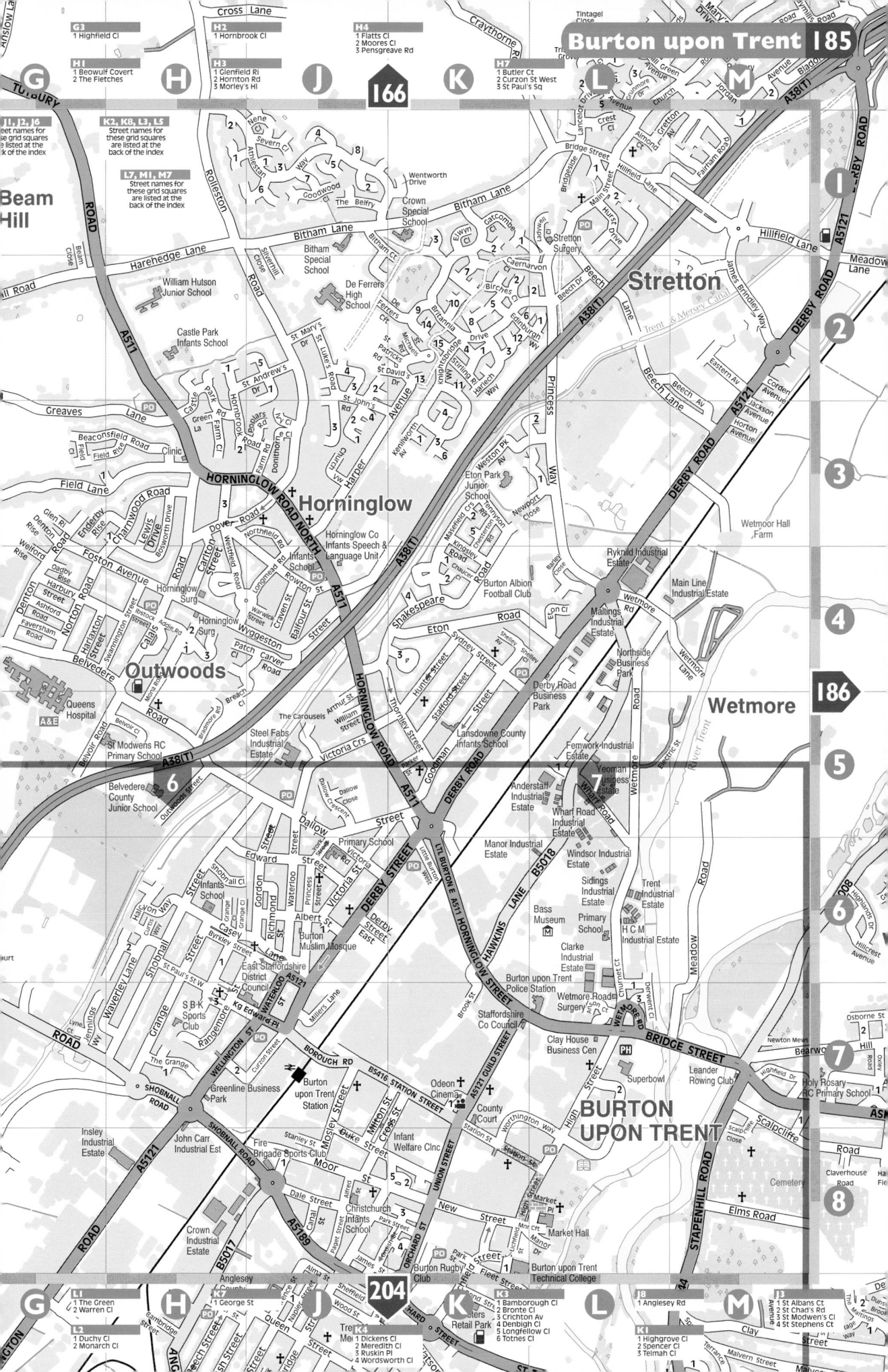

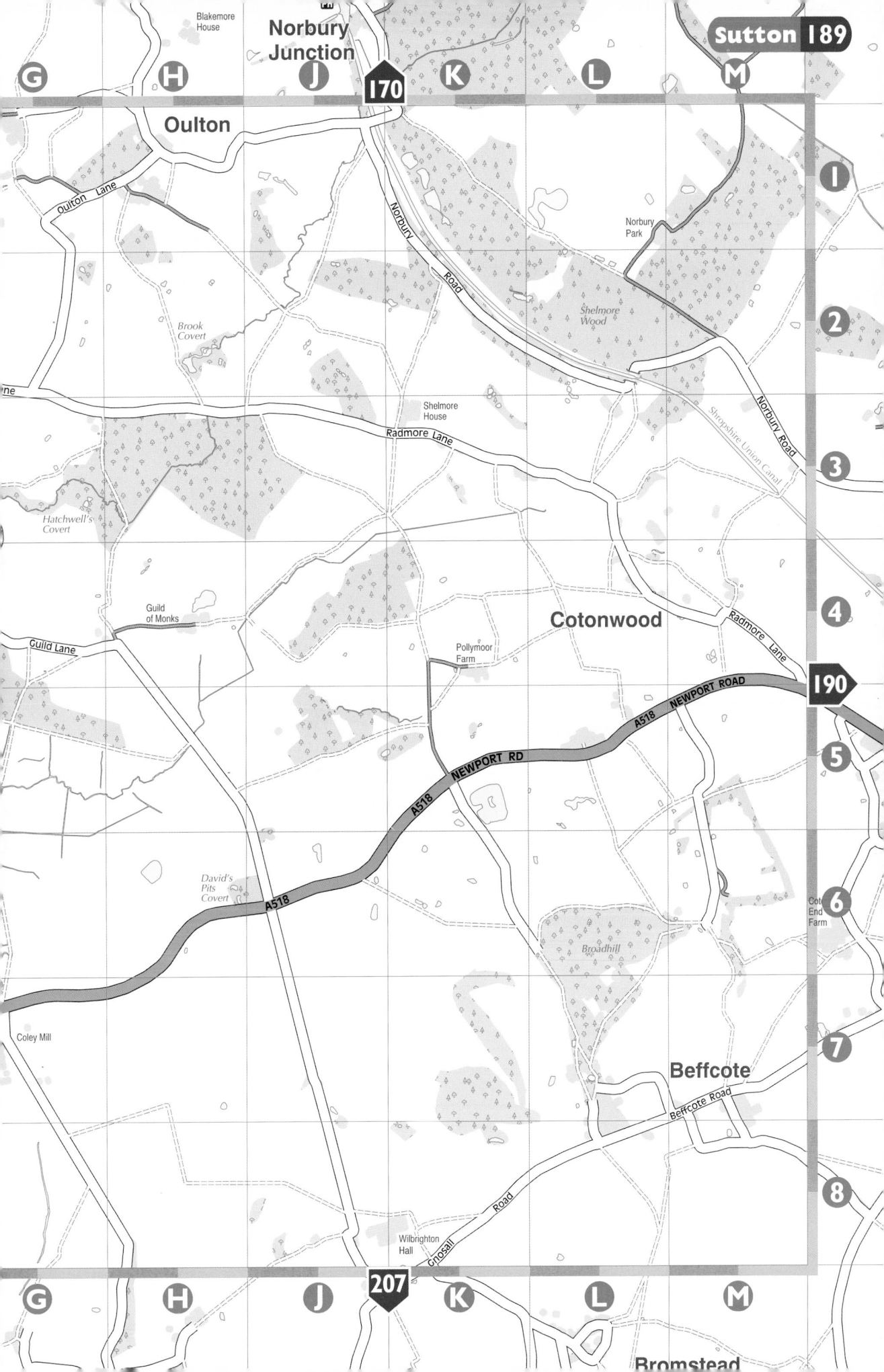

Blakemore
House

**Norbury
Junction**

Oulton

Oulton Lane

Norbury Road

Norbury Park

Norbury Road

Shelmore
Wood

Shropshire Union Canal

Brook Covert

Shelmore
House

Radmore Lane

Hatchwell's
Covert

Cotonwood

Radmore Lane

Guild
of Monks

Guild Lane

Pollymoor
Farm

A518 NEWPORT ROAD

NEWPORT RD

A518

David's
Pits
Covert

A518

Coto
End
Farm

Broadhill

Coley Mill

Beffcote

Beffcote Road

Wilbrighton
Hall

Gnosall Road

Bromstead

170

190

207

G H J K L M

I 2 3 4 5 6 7 8

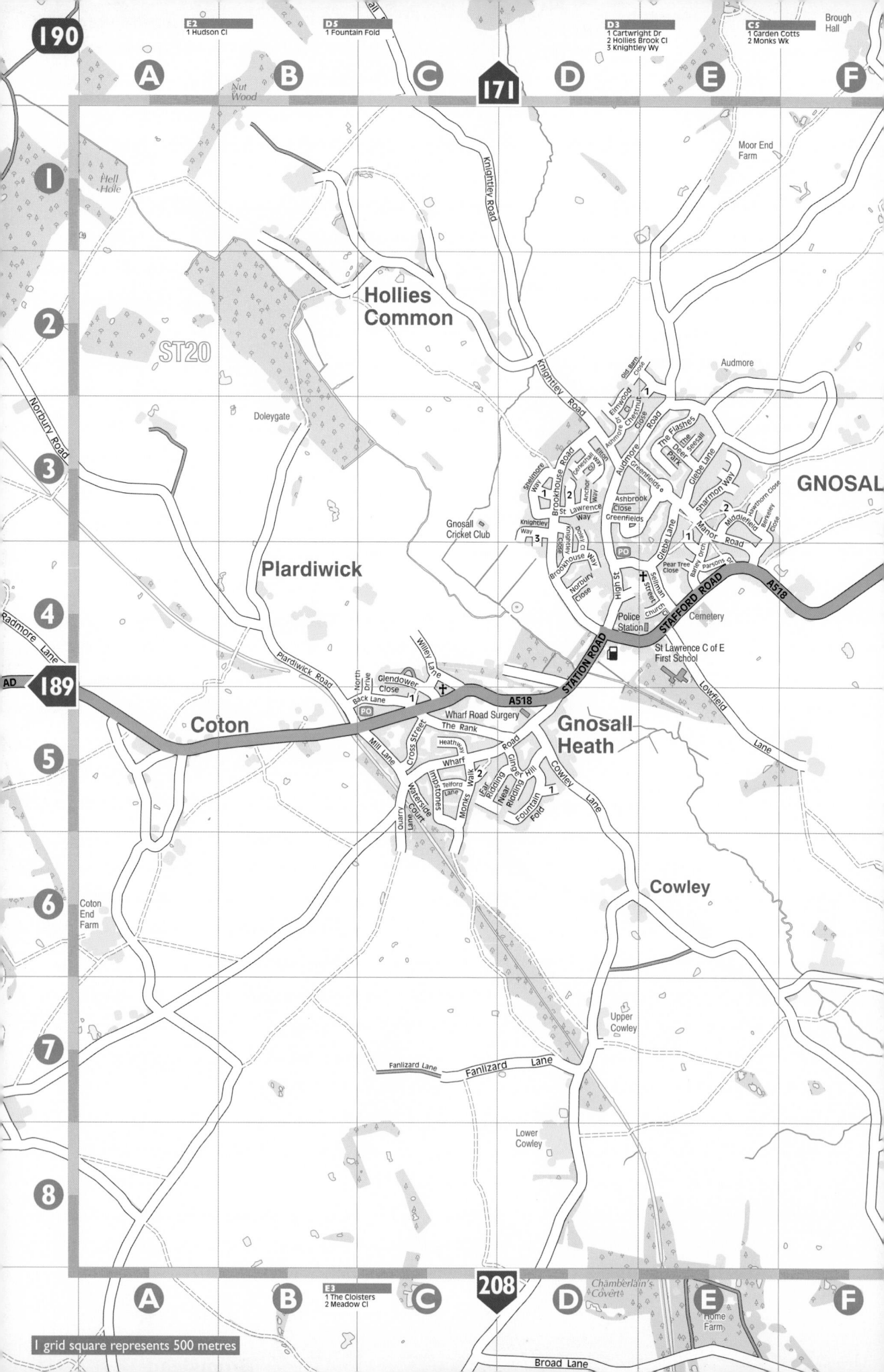

A B C **171** D E F

E2
1 Hudson Cl

D5
1 Fountain Fold

D3
1 Cartwright Dr
2 Hollies Brook Cl
3 Knightley Wy

C5
1 Garden Cotts
2 Monks Wk

Brough Hall

1

Hell Hole

Nut Wood

Moor End Farm

2

ST20

Hollies Common

Audmore

Old Barn

3

Norbury Road

Doleygate

Gnosall Cricket Club

Plardiwick

Knightley Road

Knightley Way

Stafmore Way

Brookhouse Road

Anchor Way

St Lawrence Way

Elmwood Close
Ashmore Chestnut Close

Audmore Road

The Flashes
Deer Park
The Seisall
Glebe Lane

Sharmon Way

GNOSAL

Ashbrook Close
Greenfields

Pear Tree Close

Manor Road

Mundlefield

Hawthorn Close
Berkeley Close

4

Radmore Lane

189 AD

Plardiwick Road

Knightley Close

Brookhouse Road

Norbury Close

Dovey Way

Glebe Lane

PO

High St

Sellman Street

Church
Street
Barley Brook
Parsons Cl

St Lawrence C of E
First School

A518

Stafford Road

Cemetery

5

Coton

Mill Lane

North Drive

Back Lane

Glendower Close

PO

Willey Lane

A518
STATION ROAD

Wharf Road Surgery

The Rank

**Gnosall
Heath**

Police Station

Lowfield Lane

Cross Street

Heathway

Wharf

Waterside Court

Telford Lane

Quarry

Grimstones

Monks Walk

Far Riding

Near Riding

Ginger Hill

Fountain Fold

Cowley Lane

Road

6

Coton End Farm

Cowley

7

Fanlizard Lane

Fanlizard Lane

Upper Cowley

8

Lower Cowley

A B C **208** D E F

E3
1 The Cloisters
2 Meadow Cl

Chamberlain's Covert

Home Farm

Broad Lane

I grid square represents 500 metres

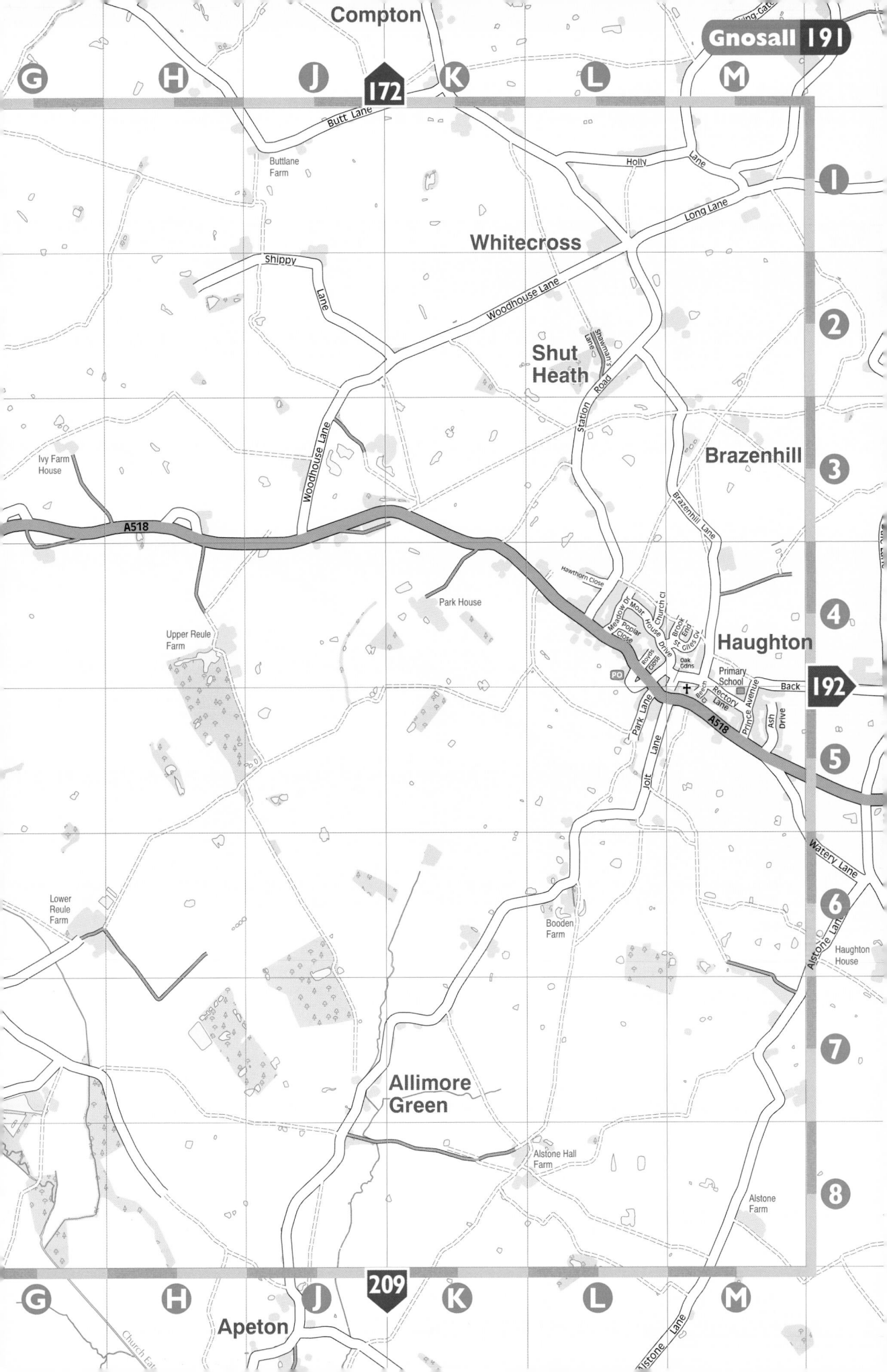

G
H
J
172
K
L
M

I

Butt Lane

Buttlane Farm

Holly Lane

Long Lane

2

Shippy Lane

Whitecross

Woodhouse Lane

Shawnan's Lane

Shut Heath

Station Road

Brazenhill

3

Ivy Farm House

Woodhouse Lane

Brazenhill Lane

A518

Hawthorn Close

Park House

Meadow Dr

Moat House Drive

Church Cl

Brook

St Giles CW

St End

Haughton

4

Upper Reule Farm

PO

Poplar Close

Roads Edge

Oak Gdns

Primary School

Rectory Lane

Beech Gro

Back

192

Park Lane

Jolt Lane

Prince Avenue

Ash Drive

A518

5

Watery Lane

Lower Reule Farm

Booden Farm

Alstone Lane

Haughton House

6

7

Allimore Green

Alstone Hall Farm

Alstone Farm

8

G
H
J
209
K
L
M

Church Eaton

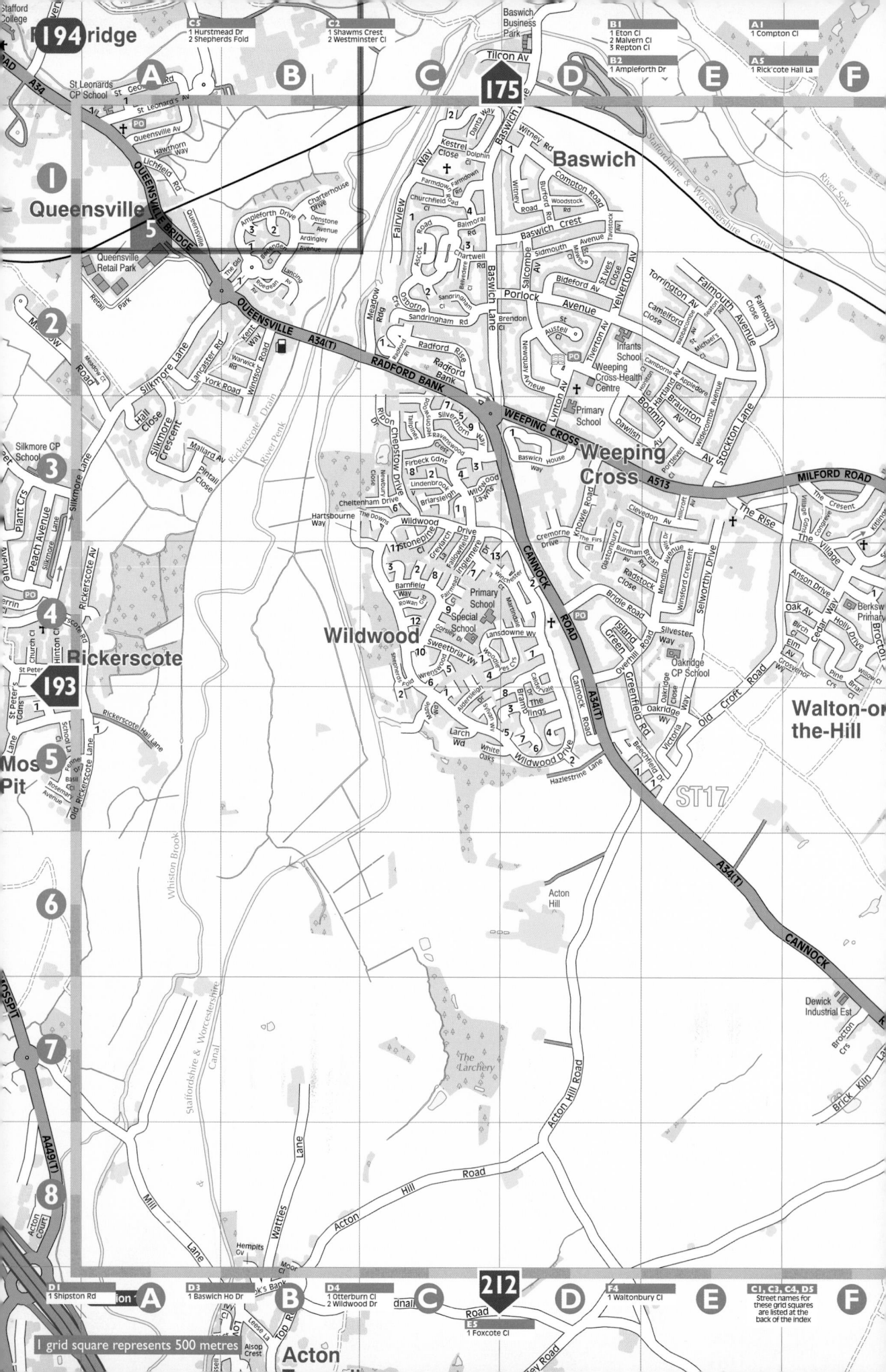

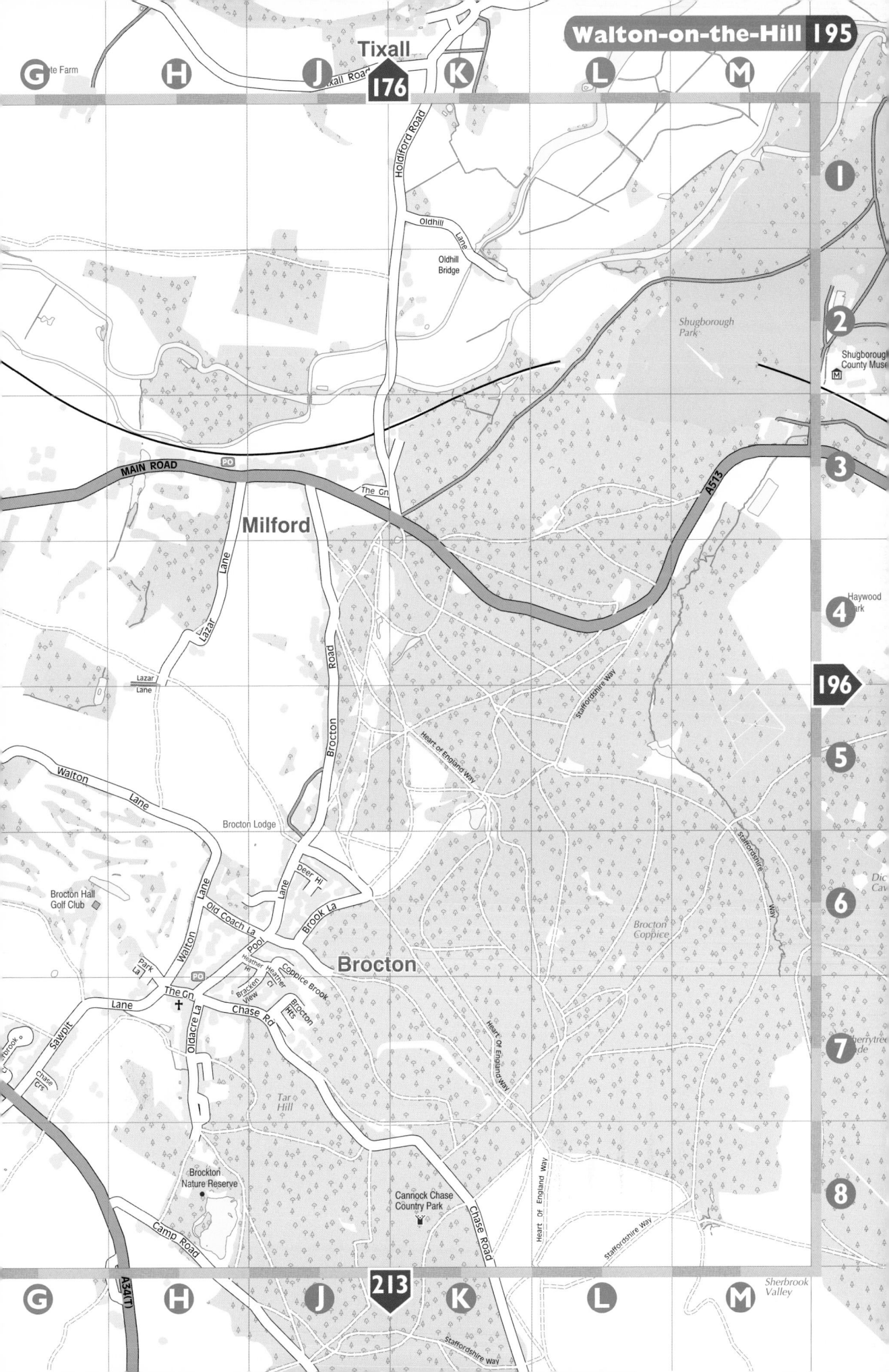

G   H   J   K   L   M

Gate Farm

Tixall

Tixall Road

176

Holdiford Road

Oldhill Lane

Oldhill Bridge

Shugborough Park

I

2

Shugborough County Museum

3

A513

MAIN ROAD   PO

Milford

The Gn

Lazar Lane

Lazar Lane

Brocton Road

Staffordshire Way

Heart of England Way

Haywood Park

4

196

5

Walton Lane

Brocton Lodge

Deer Hi Lane

Lane

Brook La

Staffordshire Way

Brocton Coppice

6

Dick Cav

Brocton Hall Golf Club

Old Coach La

Pool

Brocton

7

berrytree de

Park La

PO

Heather Hi

Heather Cl

Coppice Brook

Brocton Hts

Bracken View

The Gn

Oldacre La

Chase Rd

Heart Of England Way

Walton Lane

Sawpit Lane

Chase Crs

Brook

Tar Hill

Brockton Nature Reserve

Cannock Chase Country Park

Chase Road

Heart of England Way

8

Camp Road

A34(T)

213

Staffordshire Way

Sherbrook Valley

G   H   J   K   L   M

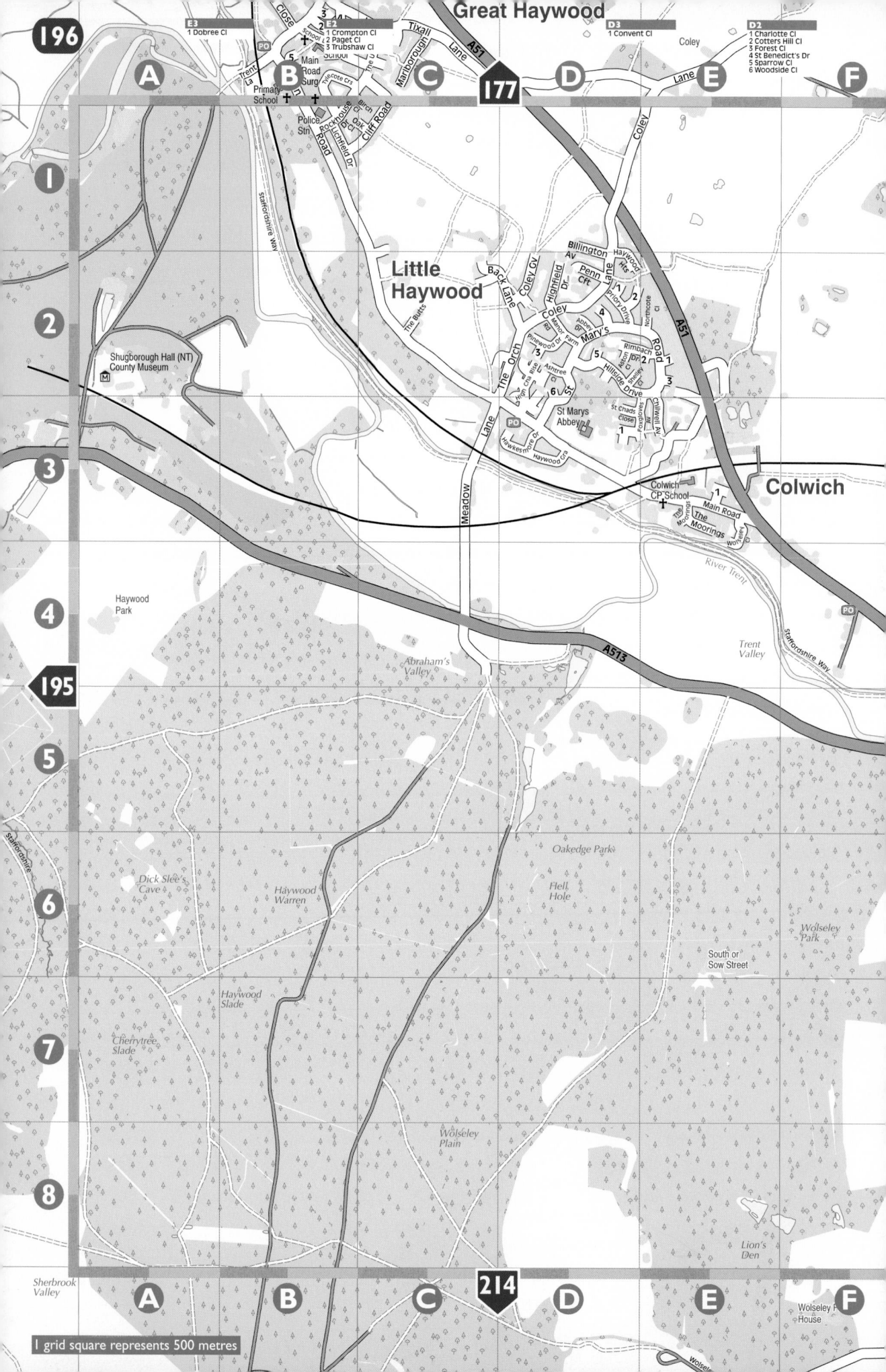

Great Haywood

177

A B C D E F

E3
1 Dobree Cl

E2
1 Crompton Cl
2 Paget Cl
3 Trubshaw Cl

D3
1 Convent Cl

D2
1 Charlotte Cl
2 Cotters Hill Cl
3 Forest Cl
4 St Benedict's Dr
5 Sparrow Cl
6 Woodside Cl

Coley

Little
Haywood

Billington Av

Coley Gv
Highfield
Penn
Crt

Back Lane

The Butts

St Mary's

The Orch

St Marys Abbey

Colwich
CP School

The Moorings
Main Road

Colwich

River Trent

1

2

3

195

Shugborough Hall (NT)
County Museum

Haywood
Park

Abraham's
Valley

Trent
Valley

Staffordshire Way

4

5

Dick Slee's
Cave

Haywood
Warren

Oakedge Park

Hell
Hole

South or
Sow Street

Wolseley
Park

6

Haywood
Slade

Cherrytree
Slade

7

Wolseley
Plain

8

Sherbrook
Valley

Lion's
Den

Wolseley
House

A B C D E F

214

I grid square represents 500 metres

H8
1 Hutchinson Cl
2 Oakfield Cl
3 Waverley Gdns

J7
1 Cheviot Dr
2 Cocketts Nook
3 Spruce Wk

J8
Street names for this grid square are listed at the back of the index

G H J 178 K L M

1

2 Stock

3

4

198

5

6

7

8

G
M8
1 Bishops Gra
2 Deacon Wy
3 Deanery Cl
4 Vicars Cft

H
L8
1 Ch'croft Gdns
2 Lanrick Gdns
3 Old Chancel Rd
4 Rishworth Av

J 215 K

L7
1 Brindley Bank Rd
2 Orchard Cl

L
K8
1 Aneurin Bevan Pl
2 Campbell Cl
3 Frank Rogers Wk
4 Johnson Cl
5 Swallow Cl
6 Winstanley Pl

M
K7
1 Holyoake Pl
2 John Ball Cl
3 Wat Tyler Cl
4 William Morris Ct

A   B   C   179   D   E   F

I

Sherracop Lane

Staffordshire Way

Staffordshire Way

Park Barn
Farm

Newlands

2

Stockwell Heath

Park Lane

Park Lane

Newlands Lane

Hamley
House

Newlands Lane

3

Heatway

Newlands Lane

Moor Cft Way   Manor

Staffordshire Way

High Street

4

St Marys C of E
Pri   School

School Lane

Colton

197

Merlin La

Way   Hollow Lane

Blithbury Road

5

WS15

Blithbu

6

Parchfield
House

Old Wood
Farm

Stonyford Lane

7

Rugeley Trent
Valley Station

Black Flatts
Fam

Blithbury Road

Colton Hall
Farm

B5013

8

Riverside

Stafford
College

Power

Tannery Close

B5014

B5013

Rake End
Court

Back Lane

A   B   C   216   D   E   F

GS
1 Pipe Wd

G

Forge
Farm

H

Cross of the Hand

Pinfold L

J

180

K

L

M

Orange Lane

Orange Lane

Gilleon's
Hall

Glass Lane

1

B5014

Blithford
Farm

Little Blithe

Poplar
Farm

2

Lane

River Blithe

3

Nun's   Lane

Priory
Farm

4

UTTOXETER ROAD

Peartree   Lane

200

Braddocks
Barn

5

thbury

B5014

1

Westwood
School

Pipewood
School

Hayend
Wood

6

Blithbury

7

Pipe   Wood   Lane

Coatfield

Road

8

Bentley Hall
Farm

Goldhayfields

**Hamstall
Ridware**

River Blithe

nd G

Quinton's
rchard

H

J

217

K

L

Lichfield

M

Cowley
Hill
Road

A   B   C   **181**   D   E   F

Bentilee
Park

Far Hoarcross

Ladysmith Farm

1

Cross
Hayes House

River Swarburn

2

3

Rowley
Farms

Redbank
Farm

Maker Lane

Woodmill

4

199

Fawley
Farm

**Hadley
End**

5

Rough
Park

6

Wood
Farm

Hadley   Street

Weaverslake

7

Sandborough

St Peter
Primary

Green Lane

Savey

Morrey

Yoxal

8

River Blithe

**Olive
Green**

Bondfield
Lane

A   B   C   **218**   D   E   F

G8
1 Alwyn Rd
2 Raven Rd
3 Rookery Cl
4 Swainsfield Rd
5 Swarbourn Cl

G **H** **J** **182** **K** **L** **M**

1

2

DE13

3

Darley Oaks

Yoxall Lodge

Lin Brook

Lodge Lane

Whitemere Farm

Thatchmoor Lane

Dunstall

4

Woodlane

Stonyford

Brankley Farm

Sherholt Lodge

202

Whitewood

5

Longcroft Farm

Sich Lane

Longcroft Lane

F Thorn

6

Lucepool

Hollyhurst House

WOOD LANE

A515

DBURY ROAD

Osborne Close

Victoria Street

STREET

Lucepool Lane

Sich Lane

7

B5016

Bar Lane

MAIN STREET

Brown's Lane

PH

B5016 **TOWN HILL**

Upper Blakenhall

Woodhouses

8

nd End Road

G nd End

H **J** **219** **K** **L** **M**

Twichills

Tatenhill

Branston

BURTON

Barton Turn

ton-on-Trent

184

221

204

L3
1 Church Rd
2 Lynwood Rd

M2
1 Cherry Ct
2 Harcourt Rd
3 Warwick Cl

M3
1 Epsom Cl
2 Fontwell Rd
3 Lingfield Rd
4 Lynwood Cl
5 Wetherby Ct

G H J K L M

I
2
3
4
5
6
7
8

Lawns Farm

Hotel

Crown Industrial Estate

WELLINGTON ROAD

A38(T)

A5121

Second Avenue

Eighth Av

Clewley Road

Spinney Rd

Merlin Crs

Harwood Avenue

Festival Road

Cotswold Road

Bridgford Av

Clay's

Rykneld CP School

B5018

A5121

Learnington Rd

Lingfield Road

Arnot Road

Beverley

Sedgefield Rd

Maple Way

Elm Cl

Pine Cl

Hawthorn

MAIN ST B5018

PO

Court Farm Lane

Main Street

Old Road

Warren Lane

Bramell Cl

Holmnick Way

Riverdale Drive

Lansdowne Road

Stewa

Staffordshire County

Derbyshire County

Power Station

Tatenhill Lane

LICHFIELD ROAD

A38(T)

Branston Road

Anglesey street

Main Street

Dark Lane

Manor Croft

PH

The Grove

Tatenhill Lane

The Grove

Gorse Hall

Green Lane

Newbold Manor Farm

River Trent

LICHFIELD ROAD

Graycar Business Park

Warren Farm

Ladle End Lane

Barr Hall

Station Lane

Bells End Rd

Main Street

G H J **189** K L M

brighton
Gnosall Road

I

Bromstead
Common

2

Walton
Grange

Outwoods

Bromstead Heath

Dykes
Lane

Walnut Tree
Lane

Moreton
Park

Church Lane

3

Pooley
Lane

Heath Road

Moreton

Post Office Lane

Church Eaton Road

4

208

5

kton
rs

6

Lynn

Orslow

7

8

Chadwell
Mill

Great
225 hatwell

Wyndford
Mill
Farm

Chatwell
La

King's Street

G H J **225** K L M

adwell

Staffordshire Count
shire Coun

Bu

A   B   C   190   D   E   F

1

2

3

4

207

5

6

7

8

Goosemoor

Chamberlain's Covert

The Home Farm

Broad Lane

Broad Lane

The Hall Farm

Shropshire Union Canal

High Onn Wharf

Church Eaton Road

Walton Fields

High Onn Wood

High Onn

Little Onn

Keepers Cottage

Sweetplace Lane

King's Street

Birchmore Lane

A   B   C   226   D   E   F

New House Farm

G   H   J   191   K   L   M

I

Apeton

2

Alstone Lane

Wood
Eaton

Church Eaton Brook

Church Eaton Endowed
Primary School

Street

3

Malt
House

Alley's La
Wood Eaton Rd
Ashley Cft
Oak Cl
High

The
Oaklands
Parkers
Cl

Church
Eaton

Church
Eaton
Common

ton's Cross

Little Onn Road

4

Shr

210

S
F

Woollaston
Farm

5

Shred
Farm

Church Eaton Brook

6

Woollaston

Slab Lane

7

Shropshire Union Canal

Slab Lane

Mitton
Lodge

8

Slab Lane

Longnor
Gorse
Farm

Gorse Lane

Longnor

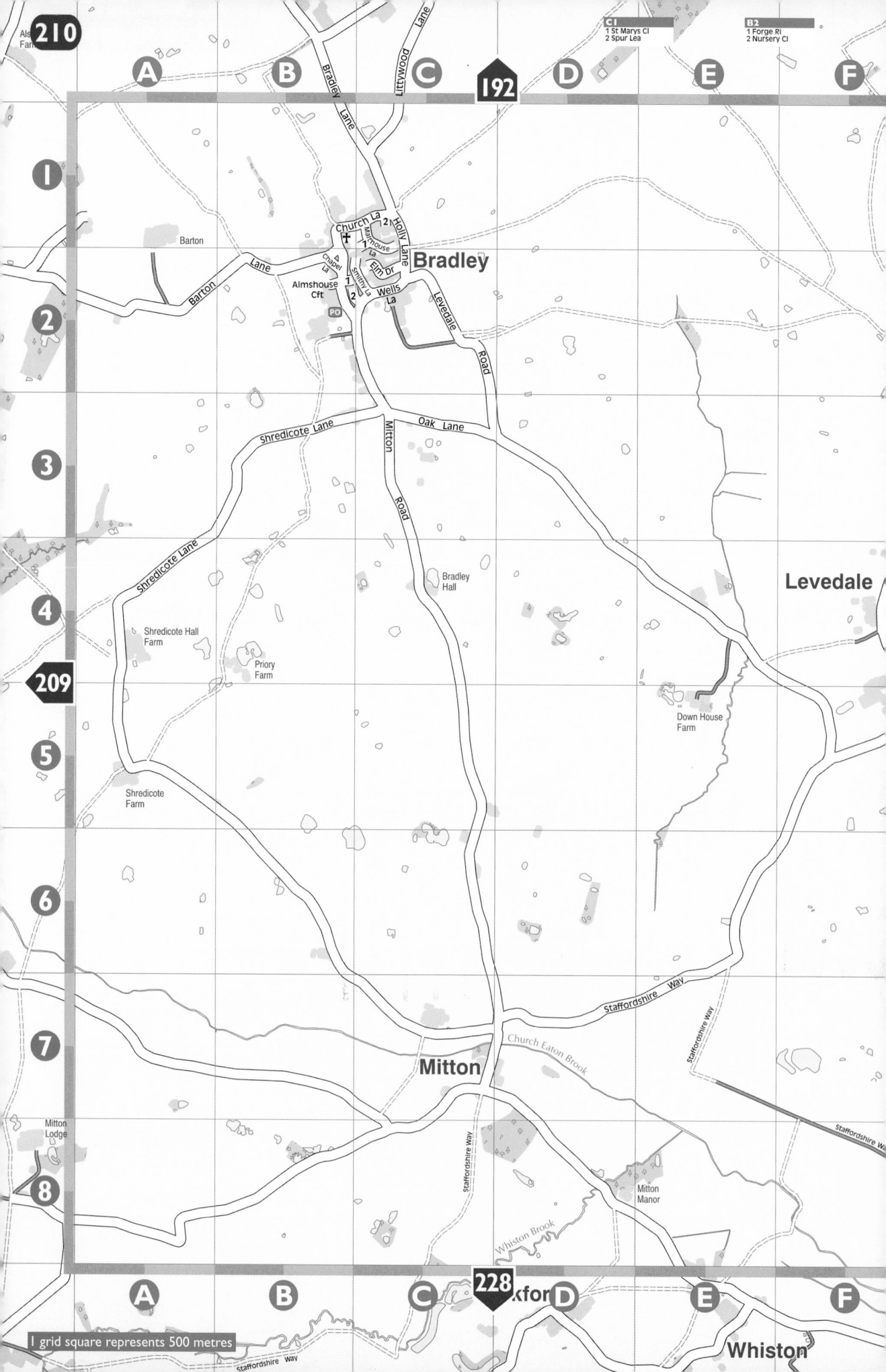

A B C 192 D E F

C1
1 St Marys Cl
2 Spur Lea

B2
1 Forge Ri
2 Nursery Cl

I

2

Barton

Bradley Lane

Littywood Lane

Church La
Mainhouse
Holly Lane
Chapel La
Smithy La
Elm Dr
Almshouse Cft
Wells La
PO

Bradley

Barton Lane

Levedale Road

3

Shredicote Lane

Oak Lane

Mitton Road

4

Shredicote Lane

Bradley Hall

Levedale

209

Shredicote Hall Farm

Priory Farm

Down House Farm

5

Shredicote Farm

6

7

Staffordshire Way

Church Eaton Brook

Staffordshire Way

Mitton

Mitton Lodge

Staffordshire Way

8

Mitton Manor

Whiston Brook

A B C 228 xfor D E F

Staffordshire Way

Whiston

1 grid square represents 500 metres

G   H   J   **193**   K   L   M

Junction 13

The Wheats

Valley Farm

The
Toft

St Leonards C of E
First School

School Lane

Church Cl

Dunston +

Little
Heath

**Dunston
Heath**

Home Farm

Swan Lane

Old Vicarage La

A449(T)

Hay House

Drayton
Manor

212

Hope Farm

The Whittamoors

Honey Pots

Lower

Longridge

Levedale

Road

Chase
View

A449(T)

Whiston Brook

Preston
Vale

Preston
Hill

Nursery Drive
Cooke Cl
Grocott Cl

The Flax Ovens
Goods station
Uplands

STAFFORD ROAD

Penkridge County
Middle School

Preston Vale Lane

Levedale Rd

Teddesley

Road

Marshbrook
First School

Millhouse
Gdns

Marsh La

Frederi

Leacroft Rd

Staffordshire Way

Orchard
Crs

Cherrybrook Dr

Kettmere

Prescott Dr

Haling Rd

G   H   J   **229**   K   L   M

Preston Vale Lane

INECROSS CLO

Hotel

Crown

Mill
First
School

Bellbrook La

Church
Market S

The Saplings

Whiston Brook

A   B   C   D   E   F

Sherbrook
Valley

I

2

Pepper
Slade

Kingsley Wood Road

3   Cannock Chase

Penkridge Bank

Penkridge
Bank

Birches
Forest

Parr's
Warren

4   Penkridge Bank

Birches Valley

nd Way

5   Heart of England Wy

Fairoak Lodge

White
House   Marquis's

6   Drive

Brindley Road

Marquis's Drive

7   Cannock Chase
Forest

Brindley Heath Road

Brindley Valley

8   Brindley Heath

Brindley Road

A   B   C   D   E   F

Broadhurst Green

A460

Slitting Mill River

Wolseley Road

Wolseley Park
House

Lion's
Dep

1 grid square represents 500 metres

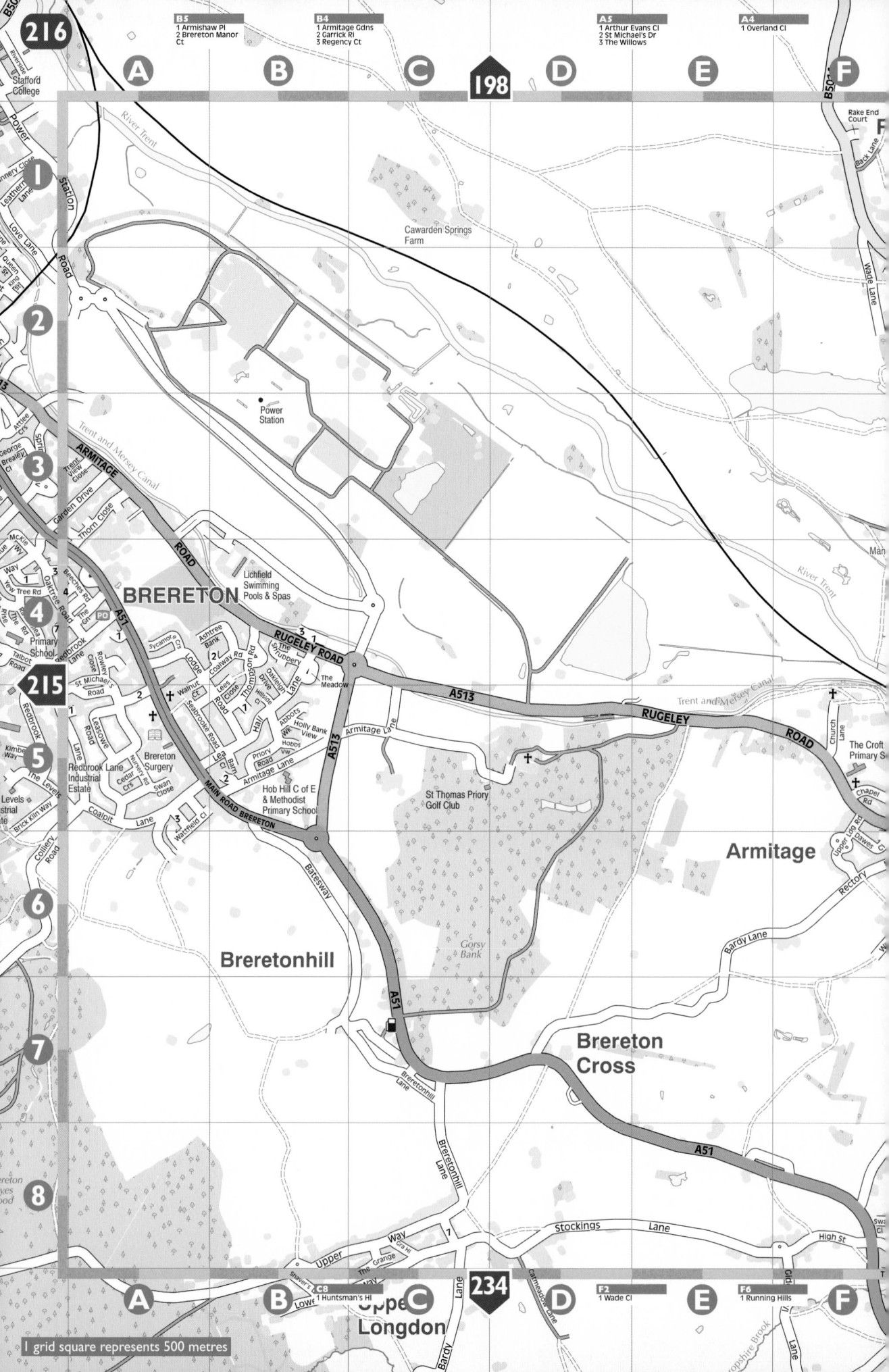

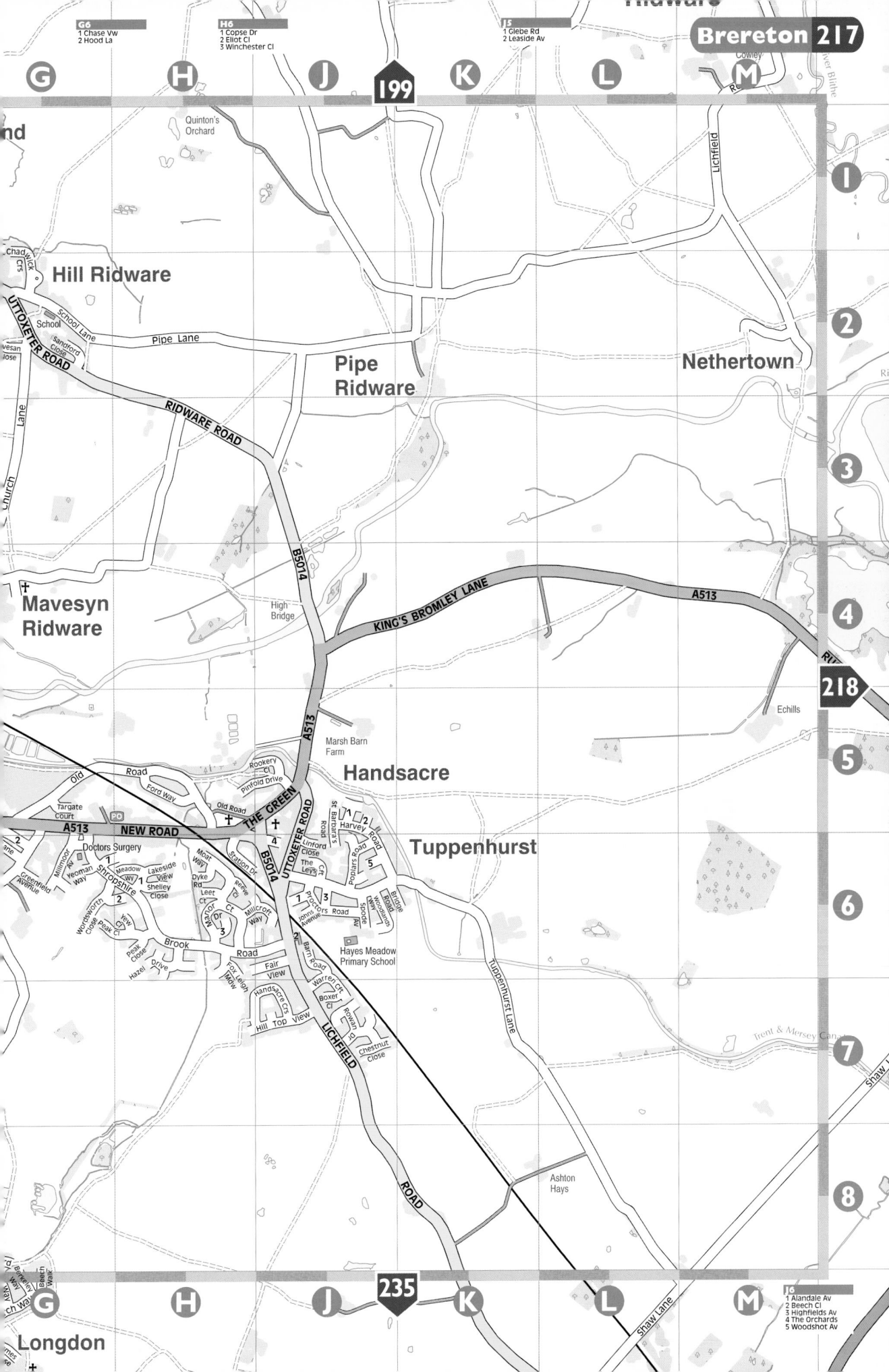

G6
1 Chase Vw
2 Hood La

H6
1 Copse Dr
2 Eliot Cl
3 Winchester Cl

J5
1 Glebe Rd
2 Leaside Av

G H J 199 K L M

I

2

3

4

218

5

6

7

8

Quinton's
Orchard

Hill Ridware

Chadwick Crs

School Lane

School

Sandford Close

Pipe Lane

Pipe
Ridware

Nethertown

Cowley Rd

Lichfield

UTTOXETER ROAD

Yvesan Close

Church Lane

RIDWARE ROAD

Mavesyn
Ridware

B5014

High
Bridge

KING'S BROMLEY LANE

A513

Echills

A513

Marsh Barn
Farm

Handsacre

Tuppenhurst

Old Road

Ford Way

Rookery Cl

Pinfold Drive

Old Road

THE GREEN

UTTOXETER ROAD

St Barbara's
Road

Harvey Close

Linford
Close

The
Leys

Poplars Road

Proctors Road

Spode Av

Bridge Road

Woodlands Way

Targate
Court

PO

A513 NEW ROAD

B5014

Doctors Surgery

Greenfield Avenue

Millmoor Av

Yeoman Way

Shropshire

Meadow View

Lakeside View

Shelley Close

Dyke Rd

Leet Ct

Moat Way

Station Dr

Beeve

Johns Avenue

Wordsworth

Crop Peak Cl

Yew Tree

Scot Dr

Millcroft Way

Brook Road

Peak Close

Hazel Drive

Fox Leigh Walk

Barn Road

Fair View

Warren Ct

Boxer Cl

Rowan Cl

Handsacre Crs

Hill Top View

Hayes Meadow
Primary School

Chestnut
Close

LICHFIELD

Tuppenhurst Lane

Trent & Mersey Canal

Shaw

ROAD

Ashton
Hays

Shaw Lane

Beech Walk

Berkeley Way

G H J 235 K L M

J6
1 Alandale Av
2 Beech Cl
3 Highfields Av
4 The Orchards
5 Woodshot Av

Longdon

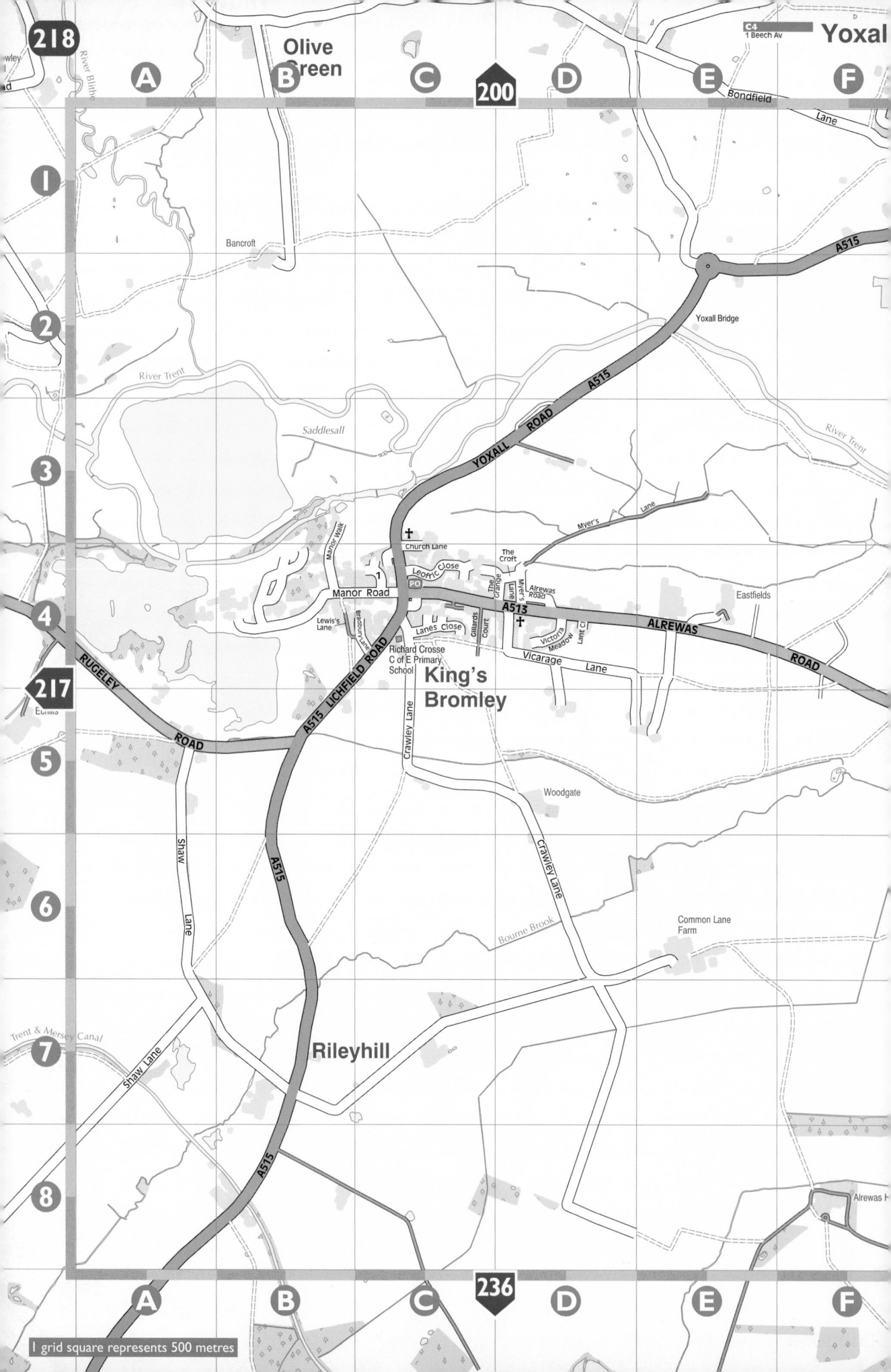

Bond
End

Twichills

The Coppice

River Swarbourn

Meadow Lane

Meadow Lane

Wychnor
Park

River Trent

Wychnor
Park

Orgreave

Overley

A513

Cotton Close
Stafford Lane
Mill End Lane
Church Road

Alrewas

Manor Fields
Audley Cl
William Iv Road
PO
Main

Kings Bromley Road

Walkfield Road

Fox Lane

Hotel
Furlong Lane

Primary Sch

Churchill Crescent

Noon Croft

Anson Road
Somerville Road

Turton Close

Daisy Lane

Trent & Mersey Canal

Bagnall

Daisy

Lane

A513

K2
1 Leedhams Cft

Graycar
Business
Park

LICHFIELD

A38(T)

Barton
Turn

Walton-
on-Trent

Warren
Fa

Barr
Hall

Ladle End
Lane

Main Street

Bells End Road

PO

Orchard
Close

Station Lane

Riverside

Harbin
Road

1

Walton
Hall

Walton-on-
Trent C of E
Primary School

Standing
Butts Close

Fairfield

I

Staffordshire County

Derbyshire County

2

Rosliston

Walton Hill
Farm

Borough
Hill

3

Walton
Wood

Coton Road

4

Oaklands
Farm

Borough
Holme

222

Borough
Fields

5

River Trent

Lads
Grave

6

The
Rough

Catton
Hall

Summerfields

7

Donkhill
Farm

Catton
Wood

Mansditch
Farm

8

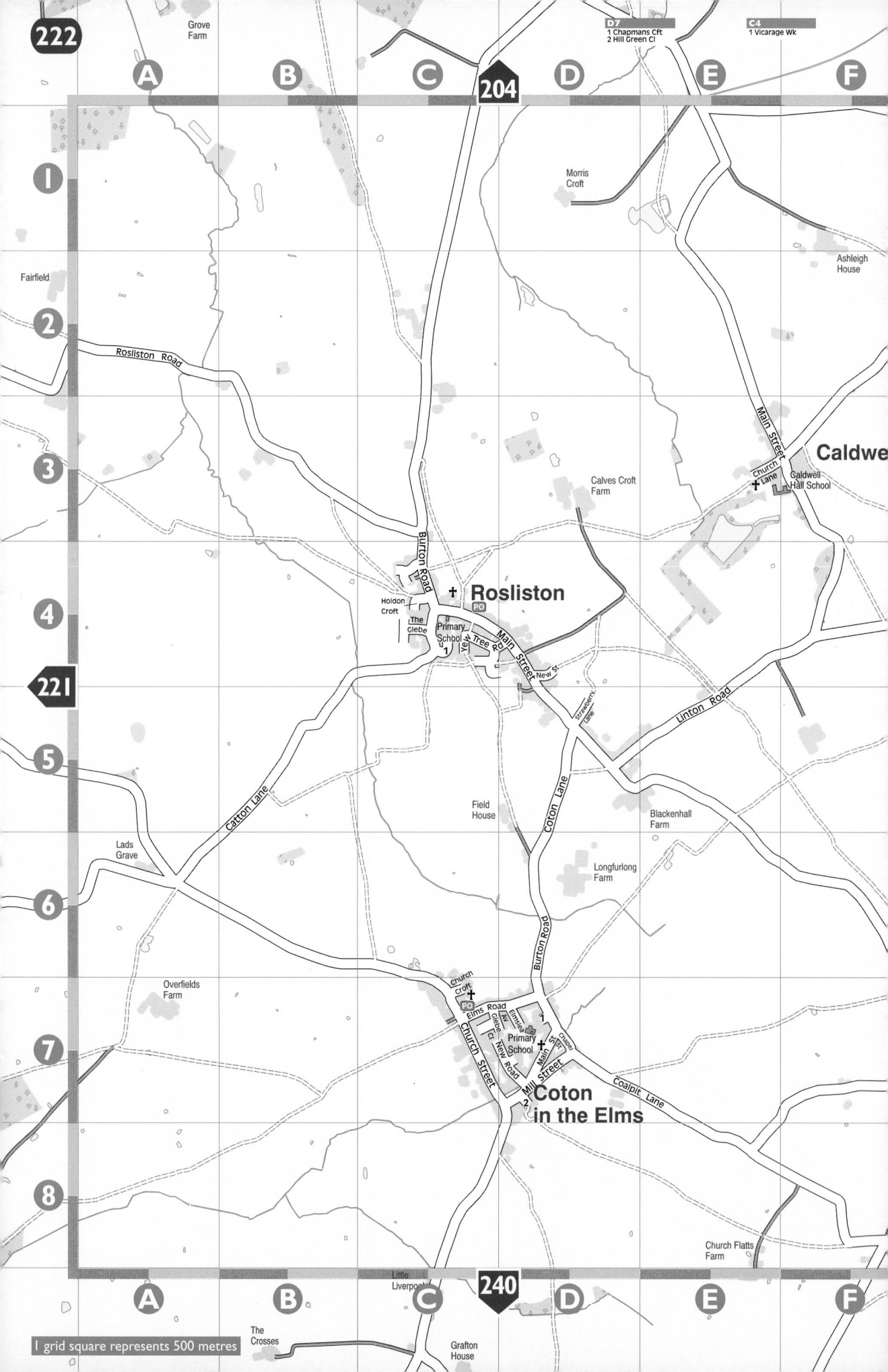

205

Appleby Glade
Industrial Estate

1 Chesterfield Dr

G **H** **J** **K** **L** **M**

Wye Dale
Beresford
Dale

Swadlincote Lane

Home Farm Ct

**Castle
Gresley**

Coton Park

A444

Knob
Fields

**Coton
Park**

Mount Road

The Scotts

Burton Rd

Bridge
Close

Chapel
Street

PO

Linton Road

Arnold
Close

Infant School

Pine
Walk

Arthur St

Cedar
Road

Bass's Crescent

Oak Cl

**Mount
Pleasant**

Mount Pleasant Road

BURTON ROAD

Fields
Lane

Park Rd

Hillside Road

Manor
House

Park Close

Greenfields

Linton

Greenfield Drive

Pear Tree Drive

7

The Crest

Cedar Grove

Warren Drive

Highfields Drive

Main Street

Windsor Rd

PD

St Patrick's Close

**Linton
Heath**

Linton Heath

A444

High Street

The Close

Princess Avenue

Charlton Close

Winchester Drive

Sycamore

Helston Close

Emery
Close

Primary
School

Longlands

Weathern
Field

Colliery Lane

Sealwood Lane

Sealwood Lane

Green Lane

BURTON ROAD

Park
Farm

Overs

Lullington Road

Potter's
Wood

Grangewood Hall

Gunby Hill

241

G **H** **J** **K** **L** **M**

1
2
3
4
5
6
7
8

Ashbourne Drive

1
2

Castle Road

Spring St

Bank St

Spring Close

Colliery Road

Princess Street

Station Street

Old Hall
Gdns

Albert St

Newland

Mount Pleasant Road

G H J K L M

207
Great
Chatwell

Chadwell
Mill

Staffordshire County
Shropshire County

Chadwell

Bun Lane

Chatwell Lane

Chatwell Lane

Wyndford
Mill
Farm

King's Street

Chatwell
La

Brineton

Brockton
Grange

Chatwell
Park Farm

Blymhill
Common

Blymhill
Marsh

Gatherwynd Lane

Gatherwynd

Lower
Beighterton

226

Blymh

School La

PO

White
Sitch

Gorsey Bank

Lodge
Mount

Lodge Farm

Chatwell Lane

B5314

Hatch Lane

Beighterton
House
Farm

Weston-
under-Lizard

Bridgeman Ct

Rectory Dr

A5

A5

WATLING STRE

Mill Lane

Shrewsbury

Drive

G H J K L M

A41(T)

Staffordshire
Shropshire

243
Woodlands

Lane

Tong Drive

Woodside
Farm

Lizard

I

2

3

4

5

6

7

8

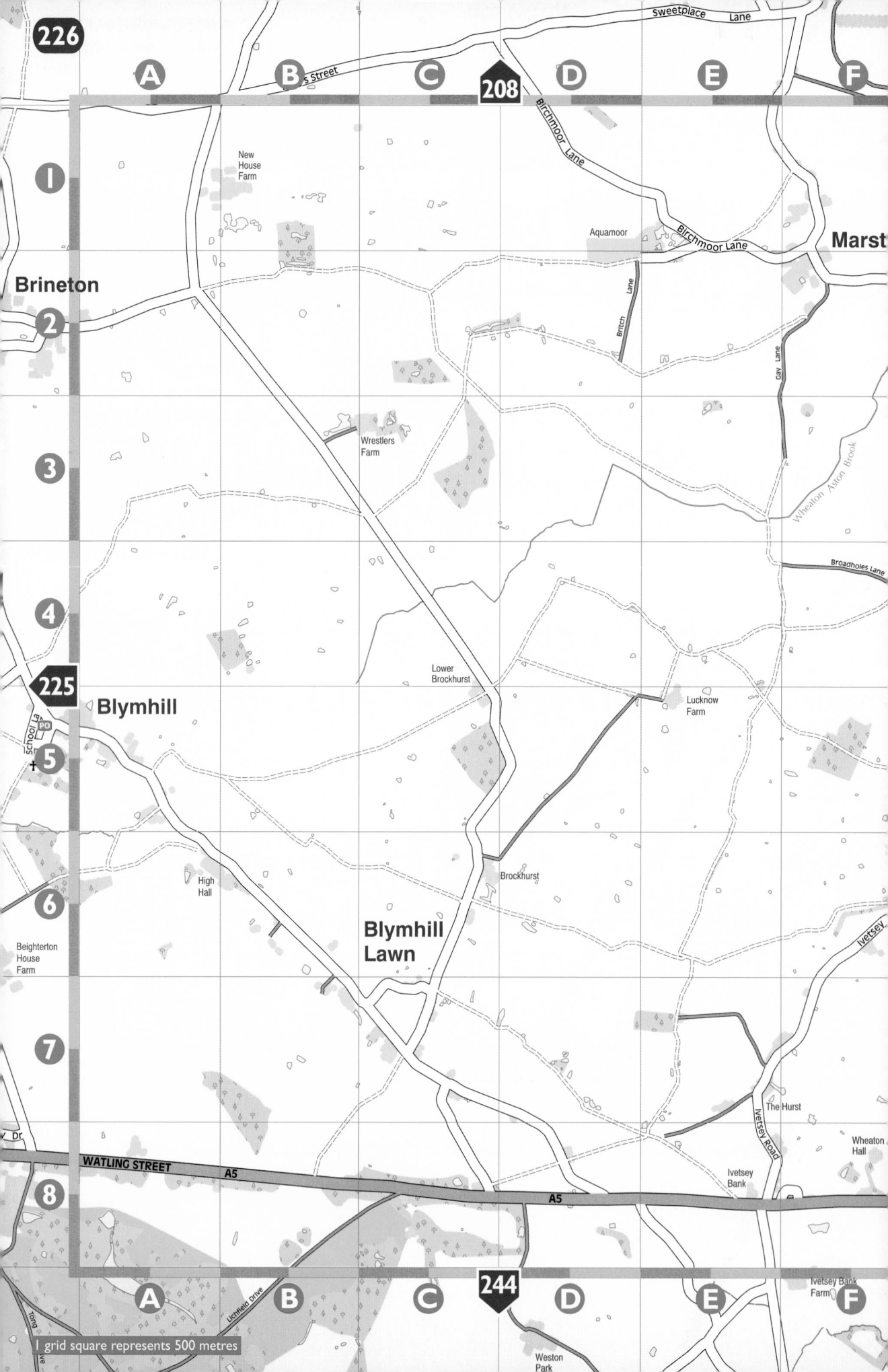

H4
1 Meadow Cl
2 Pinfold Cl

J3
1 Ashleigh Crs
2 Cranbrooks
3 Primrose Cl

J4
1 The Cobbles
2 Downford Cl
3 Marston Cl
4 Oaksmoor Cl

G   H   J   **209**   K   L   M

I
2
3
4
228
5
6
7
8

Longnor

Shushions
Manor

Marston Road

Whitehouse
Farm

Wheaton Aston

Broadholes Lane

Badger's
End

Brick
Kiln Lane

Ivy
Villa

Ivetsey Road

Bellhurst
Lane

Bellhurst
Farm

Timber Pit Lane

Sowdley
Lane

Back Lane

Back Lane

Marston Road

Fenton House Lane

Malthouse
La

Pinfold
La

High St

Burtons
Rd

Ivetsey Cl

Sowdley
Green

Springfield
Dr

Greenhill

Ash Gv

Long St

Caspian

WY Cl

Oak Dr

Beech

Long Street

Yew Tree Dr

Meadowcroft
Gdns

PO

Pinfold
Lane Surg

Hawthorne Rd

Hawthorne
Dr

Frog
La

Mill La

School Road

Starkey's Lane

Downford Lane

Lapley Road

Wheaton
Aston
Cricket Club

Church Lane

Shropshire Union Canal

Staffordshire Way

Lapley
Wood
Farm

Stockings Lane

The
Lights

Leasows
Farm

Staffordshire

WATLING STREET   A5

Whitegate
Farm

White Pump
Farm

A5

G   H   J   **245**   K   L   M

Belvide
Reservoir

228

A   B   C   210   D   E   F

1

Mitton
Manor

Bickford

Whiston

Staffordshire Way

2

Bickford
Grange

Bickford Road

3

Church

Mercian Way

Beacor

Bickford
cl   Lapley

Park   Lane

4

Stretton Road

Staffordshire Way

227

5

Stretton
Wood

ST19

6

Rowleyhill Dr

Sling   Lane

Staffordshire Way

Garden
Lane   Stretton

Wood Lane

Lapley Lane

Stoney Lane

7

Vernon Lodge
Preparatory School
& Kindergarten

PO

Lapley   Lane

School   Lane

The Avenue

Lane

8

A5   WATLING STREET   A5

Horsebrook

A   B   C   246   D   E   F

House

Gisebrook Lane

1 grid square represents 500 metres

L1
1 St Michael's Sq

L3
1 Boscomoor Ct
2 Rendermore Cl

M1
1 Bramdean Dr
2 Hatherton Rd

G   H   Preston Hill   J   211   K   L   STAFFORD ROAD   M

Penkridge County
Middle School

Preston
Vale

Preston Vale Lane

Preston Vale Lane

Levedale Rd

Whiston Brook

Marshbrook
First School

Teddesley

Millhouse
Gdns

Littleton

Leacroft Rd

Staffordshire Way

I

Cuttlestone
Bridge

Hotel

Monkton Recreation
Centre

Pinfold

Lane

Station

Penkridge
Station

Crown

St Michael's
Cl

Mayfield
Av

Church Rd

Dr M Allbeson
& Partners

Police
Station

New Road

Market St

First
School

Cannock Rd

Staffordshire
Co Council

Penkridge
Parish Council

First
School

Haling Rd

Croydon
Dr

Francis Green
Lane

Penkridge

Denefield

WOLGARSTON WAY B5012

PE

Boscomoor

Gardens

Fallowfield

Wheatcroft

Vale

Manorfield

Dene

Lock
Rd

Princefield Av

Bartlett's

Templars
Way

Greville

Druids Way

2

3

Congreve

Water Eaton Lane

The
Deanery

Bungham

Grange Crs

Lane

Wolverhampton Rd

BOSCOMOOR LA

WOLGARSTON WY

Boscomoor
Industrial Est

Commerce Dr

BOSCOMOOR LA

M6

Lyne Hill
Industrial
Estate

WOLVERHAMPTON RD

Lane

Lynehill

Lyne
Hill

Fairfield
Dr

Otherton

Otherton

4

230

5

River Penk

Kinvaston Hall
Farm

A449(T)

Rodbaston

Drive

6

Rowley
Hill

Mere Lane

Mere Lane
Farm

Rodbaston

Staffordshire College of
Agriculture

Worcestershire Canal

M6

7

Water
Eaton

Water Eaton Lane

Gailey

A5

Christ
Church School

A449(T)

Charrisons Lane

**Gailey
Wharf**

8

G   H   J   247   K   L   M

Staffordshire
County Council

M3
1 Cheadle Cl
2 Henney Cl
3 Hussey Cl
4 Willoughby Cl
5 Woodtherne Cl

M2
1 Bitham Cl
2 Bridgewater Cl
3 Edwin Cl
4 Streamside Cl

Croft Farm

Calf Heath

215
234
251

G4
1 Aspen Ct
2 Bentley Brook La
3 Blackthorn Crs
4 Jenkinstown Rd
5 Jesmond Cl
6 Kempton Cl
7 Sandown Cl
8 Saunders Cl

G5
1 Beaudesert Vw
2 Goodwood Cl
3 St Christopher Cl
4 St Francis Cl
5 Warren Cl

G   H   J   K   L   M

Marquis's Drive

1 Summerside Av

Wandon

Startley Lane

Upper Cliff

Beaudesert Old Park

Horsepasture Covert

Heart Of England Way

Sukers Lodge

Beau Desert Golf Club

Rugeley Road

Hazelslade

Hazel Slade CP School

Castle Ring

Road
Baden Powell Close
Gillwell Road
pine side Avenue
The Firs
High Meadow
Chestall Road

Cannock Wood Industrial Estate

Rawnsley

Cannock Wood

Holly Hill

Chapel Lane

Bradhill La
Sycamore Hil
Buds Road

Hornbeam
Alder Wy
Cannock Wood Street
Barnfield Lawns
Charles Valley Road

Eastgate
St Patrick
St David Close
Dr
Old Pk Rd
Matthew
St George
St Thomas
St Andrews
Littleworth Road
Cumberledge Hill

Slang Lane
Ivy Lane

Gentles Primary

Chape

Doctors Surgery
Chetwynd Park
Cannock & Rugeley Cricket Club

Cannock Wood Road

New Hayes

Hayfield Hill

Gen

Windmill Lane

New Hayes Road

St Bernards Close
Danby Dr
Briars Wy
Ironstone

Williamson Av
Longstaff Av
Paints Cl?

Prospect Village

Road

Redmoor Road

Hayfield Hill

Sevens Road

Ironstone Road

Duke Rd

Kingsdown
Littleton Way
Mayor Av
Holly

1 Uplands Cl

Bonny Hay

Squirrels Hollow

G   H   J   K   L   M

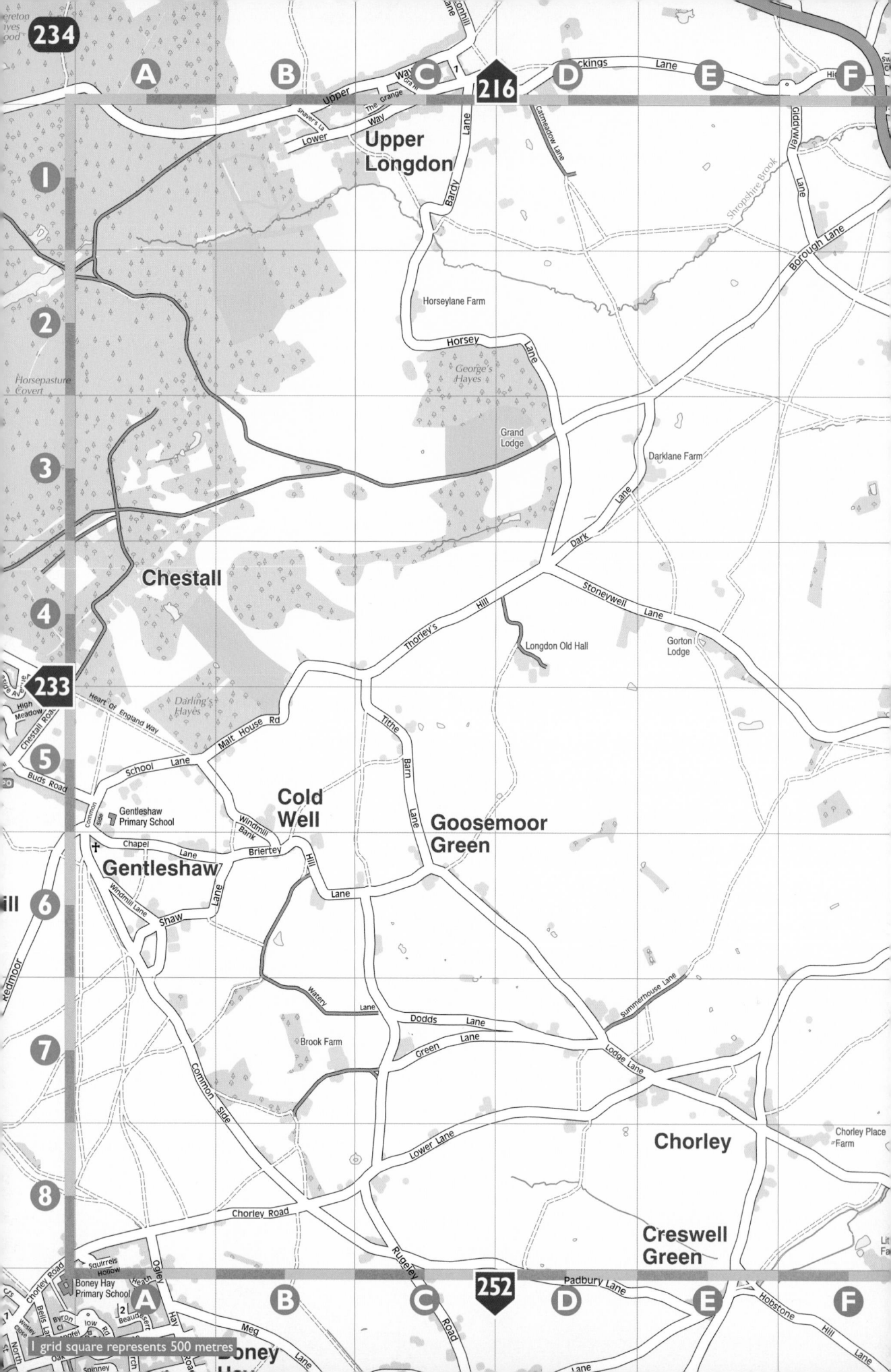

A   B   C   216   D   E   F

1

Upper
Longdon

Horseylane Farm

Horsey   Lane

2

George's
Hayes

3

Grand
Lodge

Darklane Farm

Chestall

Dark   Hill   Lane

Stoneywell   Lane

Gorton
Lodge

4

Thorley's Hill

Longdon Old Hall

Darling's
Hayes

Heart of England Way

Malt House Rd

Tithe

5

School   Lane

Gentleshaw
Primary School

Cold
Well

Barn   Lane

Goosemoor
Green

Common Side

Windmill
Bank

Chapel   Lane   Brierley

Gentleshaw

Hill   Lane

6

Windmill Lane   Shaw   Lane

Watery   Lane

Dodds   Lane

7

Brook Farm

Green   Lane

Summerhouse Lane

Lodge Lane

Common Side

Lower Lane

Chorley

Chorley Place
Farm

8

Chorley Road

Rugeley   Road

Creswell
Green

Squirrels
Hollow

Boney Hay
Primary School

A   B   C   252   D   Padbury Lane   E   F

219

255

238

Fradley Junction

Fradley

Hilliard's Cross

Streethay

Industrial Estate

St Stephens Primary School

The Moor

Willow Close

Holly Drive

Bromwich Drive

Shaw Cl

Ash Close

Statfold Lane

Turner Croft

Old Hall Lane

Long Lane

Church Lane

Fradley Lane

Daisy Lane

Sale Lane

The Sale Farm

Cowhill Lane

Dumore Hay Lane

Roddige Lane

LC

Fox Lane

Hay-End Lane

Corse Lane

Coventry Canal

Common Lane

Beeches Croft

Jordan Close

Blackman Close

Oaklands Close

Worthington Road

Milne Av

Forrester Cl

Jackman Road

Fine Lane
LC

Wood End Lane

Common Lane

Blenheim Way

Lancaster Road

Wood End Lane

Wellington Crescent

East Hill

Brookhay Lane

Ironstone Lane
LC

LC

Coventry Canal

Wetleyhay Wood

Sittles

Williford

Stockford Lane

Brookhay Lane

Bears Hay Farm

Mare Brook

Brookhay

Thatchmoor Farm

Broad Lane

Hurst Farm

Hill Farm

A38(T)

A513

K3
1 Jordan Cft

K4
1 Alexander Cl

L2
1 Edwards Farm Rd

Bagnall

Somerville Road

Turton Close

PO
1

G H J K L M

I

2

3

4

5

6

7

8

1 Woodyard Dr

Catton Wood

G **H** **J** **221** **K** **L** **M**

1

Derbyshire County
Staffordshire County

Homestall Wood

2

Pessall Farm

The Grange

Raddle Farm

Pessall Brook

3

Croxall Road

Pessall Lane

4

Edingale Farm

240

Broadfields Farm

Raddle Lane

Edingale

Lullington Road

5

Pessall Lane

Blakeways Close

Croxall Road

Main Road

PO
1

Mary Howard
C of E Primary
School

Moores Croft

Hatchett Lane

Church Lane

Church Hollow

Schofield Lane

School Lane

Poplars Farm

6

River Mease

Mill Lane

Grange Farm

7

Main Road

Church Side

Harlaston

Main Road

Haselour House

Haselour Hall

PO

Manor Lane

8

Twizles Lane

G **H** **J** **257** **K** **L** **M**

Main Road

M3
1 Holly Bush Cl

G H J 223 K L M

I

2

Grange Wood

Grangewood Hall

Lodge Road

oodfields arm

Grangewood Lodge

Mount Pleasant Lane

Gorsey Lane

West View Farm

Hunts Lane

DE12

Hawthorn Av

Netherseal

3

Croft Close

Hollows Farm

The Grange

Stanley Close

Main Street

Dog Lane

PO

Clifton Road

St Peters C of E Primary School

Church St

4

Yew Tree Farm

5

Netherseal Road

6

Stones Bridge

Seal Fields Farm

Chilcote

Church Lane

No Man's Heath Road

7

Derbyshire County
Staffordshire County

Clifton Hall

8

Cli Lo 259

G H J K L M

Staffordshire County
estershire County

G H J 225 K L M I

Woodside Farm

Lizard Grange

A41(T)

Woodlands

Mill Lane

Staffordshire County
Shropshire County

Lizardmill Farm

Weston Park

2

Havannah

Tong Dr

The Tower

3

Norton Mere

Mill Lane

Tong Knoll

Zard arm

A41(T)

Knoll House

4

244

Tong Norton

Offoxey Road

5

ng Forge

Monarch's Way

Offoxey

Road

Shaw Lane

Tong Hill Farm

Monarch's Way

6

Friar's Lane

Monarch's Way

Tong Priory

Lane

M54

A41(T)

Newport

Hubbal

Tong

Spring Coppice

7

Road

The Hall

Junction 3

M54

Tong Lodge

Tong Park Farm

8

New Building Farm

M54

Neachley Hall

G H J 260 K L M

Neach Hill

Kilsall Hall

Mill La

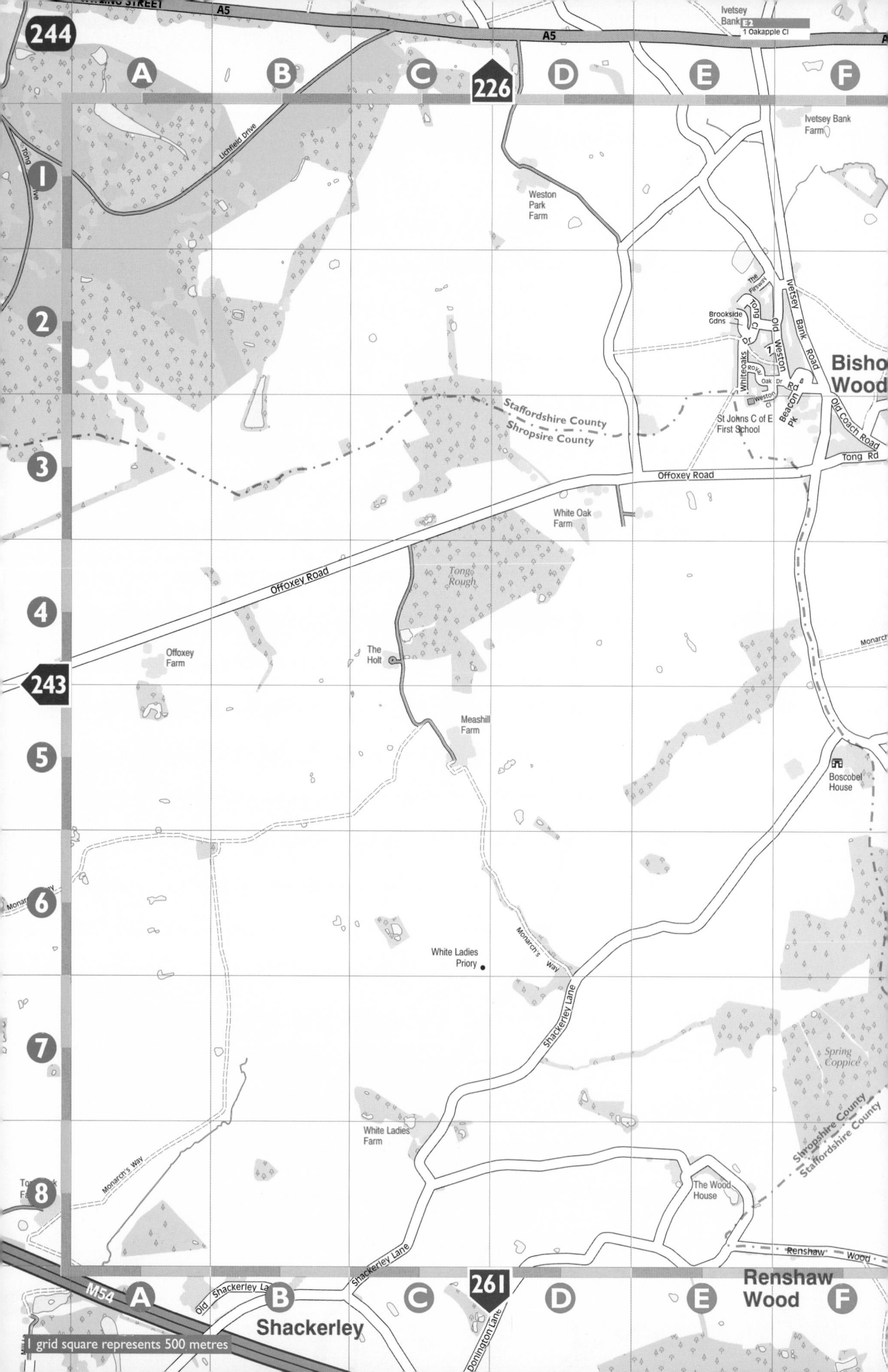

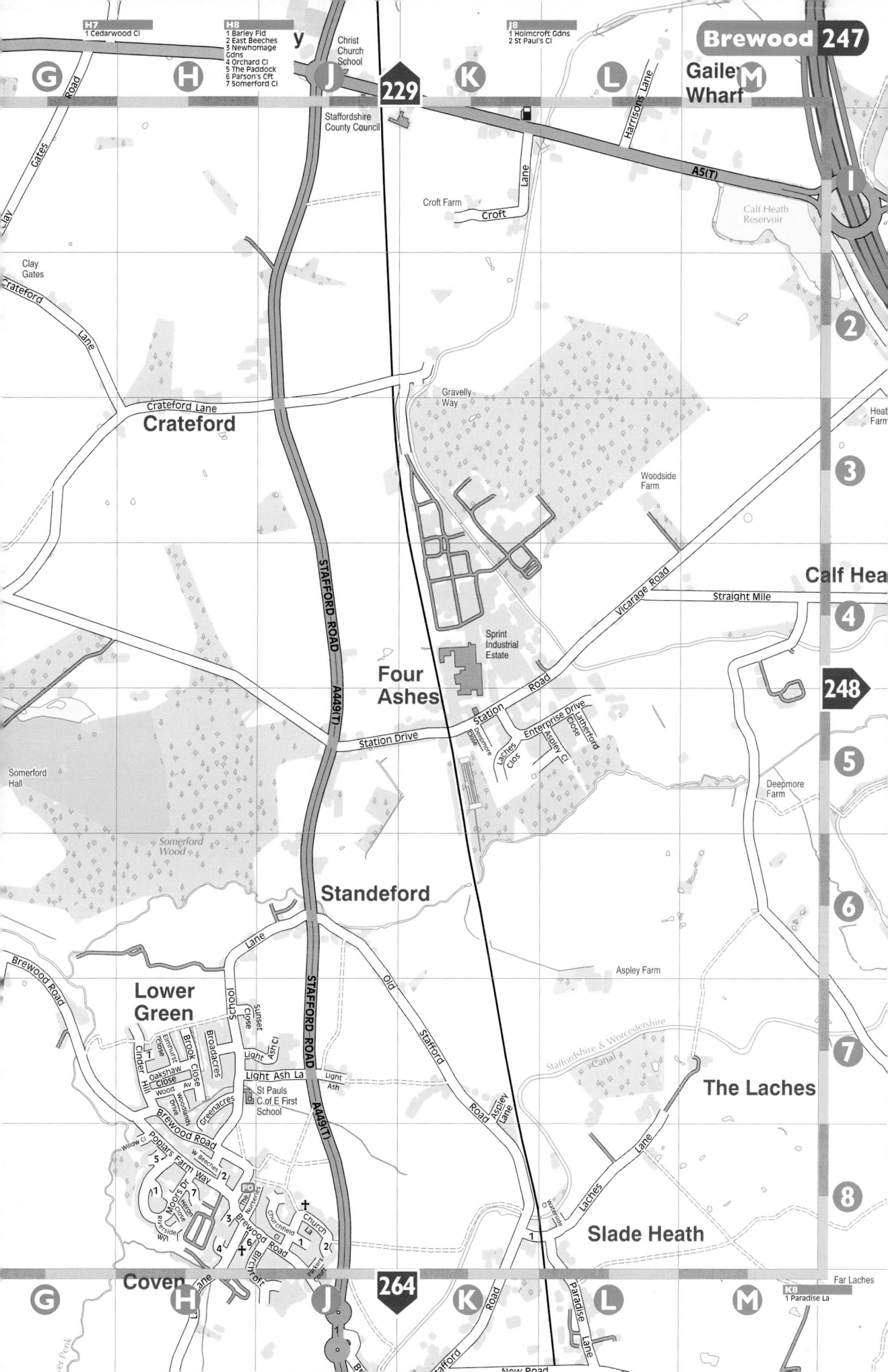

Gailey
Wharf

G   H   J   K   L   M

H7
1 Cedarwood Cl

H8
1 Barley Fld
2 East Beeches
3 Newhomage
Gdns
4 Orchard Cl
5 The Paddock
6 Parson's Cft
7 Somerford Cl

J8
1 Holmcroft Gdns
2 St Paul's Cl

Christ
Church
School

229

Staffordshire
County Council

Croft Farm

Croft   Lane

A5(T)

Calf Heath
Reservoir

I

2

Clay
Gates

Crateford   Lane

Crateford Lane

Crateford

Gravelly
Way

Woodside
Farm

Heath
Farm

3

Calf Hea

Vicarage Road

Straight Mile

4

Sprint
Industrial
Estate

**Four
Ashes**

Station   Road

248

Somerford
Hall

Station Drive

Station

Laches
Clos

Enterprise Drive

Ashley
Close

Latherford
Close

Deepmore
Farm

5

Somerford
Wood

Standeford

Aspley Farm

6

Brewood   Road

Lane

STAFFORD   ROAD

Old

Stafford

Staffordshire & Worcestershire   Canal

7

**Lower
Green**

Sunset
Close

Broadacres

Ash Cl

Light

Aspley   Lane

The Laches

Cinder   Hill

Elmhurst
Close

Brook   Close

School

Oakshaw
Close

Woodlands

Av

Dri

Greenacres

Light Ash La

Light
Ash

St Pauls
C.of E First
School

A449(T)

Willow Cl

W Beeches

Brewood   Road

Popars Farm Way

5

2

1

3

4

Rd

PO

The
Nurseries

Brewood   Road

Birchcroft

Churchfield

Church   La

2

St Leonards

Riverside

Parkes
Court

Waterside
Cl

Laches   Lane

Paradise   Lane

Slade Heath

1

Coven

G   H   J   K   L   M

264

Stafford   Road

New Road

Far Laches

K8
1 Paradise La

7

8

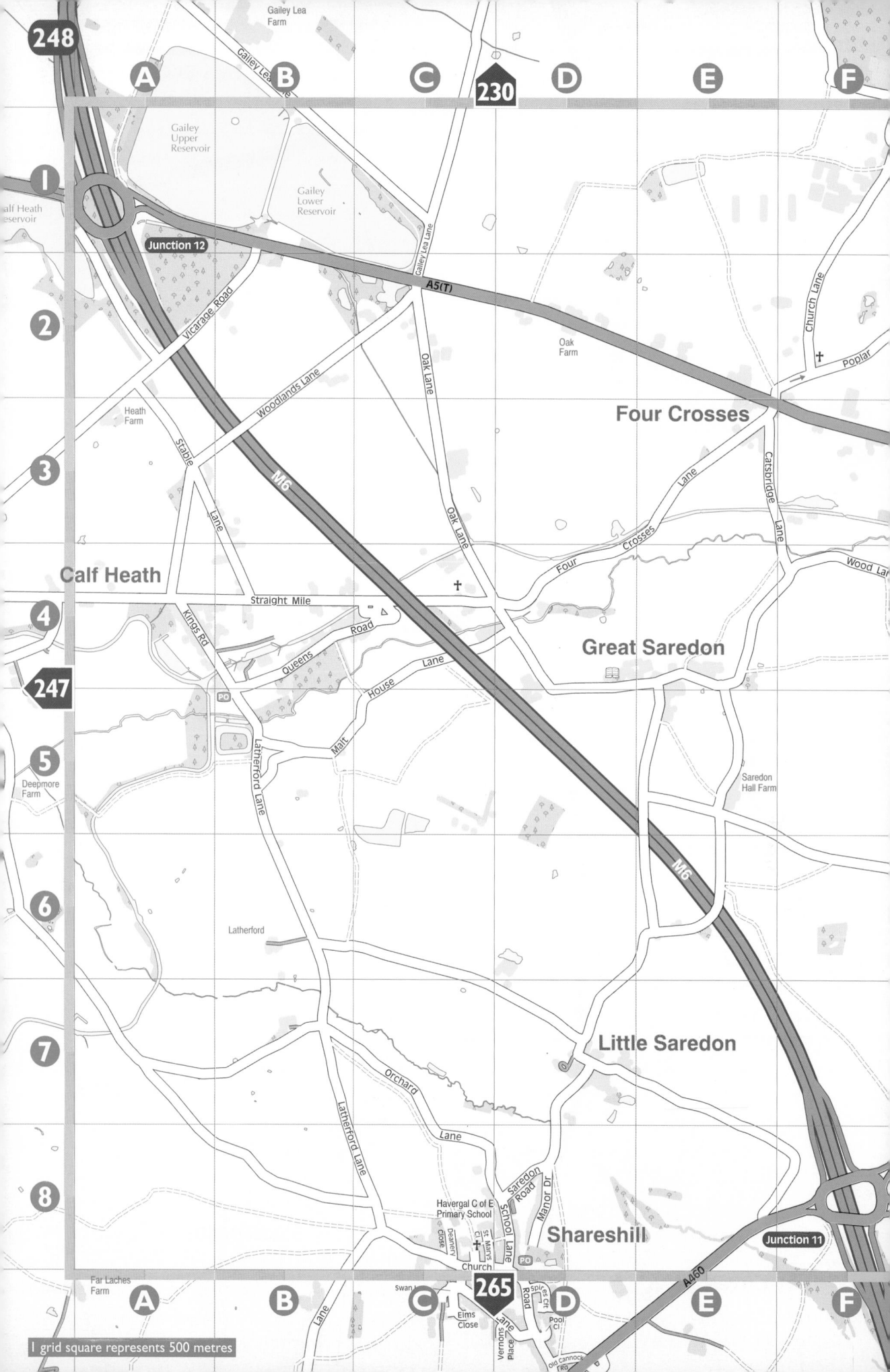

G4
1 Hamilton Lea

K1
1 Coulson Cl

L1
1 Chawner Cl
2 Lodge Rd
3 Sandringham Cl
4 Windsor Cl

G   H   J   233   K   L   M

Boney Hay
Primary School

Squirrels
Hollow

Littleton Way

Mayor Av

Lea Hall
Drive

Kingsdown

Holly Grove
County
Primary
School

The Grovey

The
Valley

Fair Lady
Drive

Bleak
House Dr

Ashley
Rd

School Lane

Radmore
Close

Thorpe Street

Chapel
Street

Lorne
Street

Princess St

Ironstone Road

Eastgate
St

Chase
Terrace

Park
Road

Spencer
Drive

Cross Street

New Street

Water Street

Coppice
Close

Beechen
Grove

Alden
Hurst

Redwood
Drive

Stamford
Crescent

Fieldhouse
Road

Lulworth
Road

Thorpe Av

West
Close

Thorpe
Close

High Street

CANNOCK   ROAD   A5190

Attwood Road

Cobbett Road

Chaselands

Plant Lane

Chase Park
Industrial
Estate

No Name Rd

Cinder Road

Ring Road

Burntwood Town
Shopping Centre

Primary
School

Victory Avenue

Salters Meadow
Health Centre

Cannock
Road

Lichfield
District
Council

Maple Close

Sycamore
Road

Lilac
Gv

High School

BRIDGE

BURNT

Norton Canes
High School

Norton
East

Burntwood

Grange
Road

Lakeside
Dr

Stag
Crs

Norton Canes
Infant School

Primary
School

School
Road

Smith's
Close

Cannel Rd

Robins

Benches
Close

Chase
Vale

Chasewater
Industrial
Estate

St Joseph &
St Theresa
RC Primary School

Hill Street

Burntwood
Baths

HIGH STREET   B5011

Cherry
Close

Poplar Avenue

Beech
Street

Baker
Street

Birch

Bank
Crs

Cedar

Cedar
Close

Chaset

252

Poplar Street

Railway Street

Norton East Road

Pool Av

St James Rd

Breeze Avenue

High Street

Elm Road

Cherry Tree
Road

Silver Birch
Road

Union Street

New St

Doctors
Surgery

Chasetown
CP School

Cem

Church Street

Willett
Av

Cottage
Close

Queen Street

King
Street

Queen Street
Industrial Estate

Belvedere
Close

Eastcote Crs

Ridgeway
Middle School

5

Brownhills Road

Blenheim
Road

Knights
Court

Red Lion
Crs

Braemar Road

Red Lion Lane

Red Lion
Lane

Chasewater

St Anne's
Close

Chasetown
High School

Pool Road

Pavior's Rd

Anglesey
Close

Lawnswood

B5011 HIGHFIELDS RO

6

Albutts Road

Chasewater Light Railway

Chase Watersports
Centre

Beacon Way

Way

Wharf Lane

Wyrley & Essington Canal

7

Little
Norton

A5(T)

Mayfields
Drive

Blithfield Road

Cherwell
Drive

Tyne

Kennet
Close

Shannon
Drive

Severn

Cherwell Drive

Tamar

Medway Rd

Wilkin Road

Peartree
Lane

Poole Crescent

Lawnooks

PO

Beacon Way

Pool Road

Howdle's Lane

Anglesey
Crescent

Hanbury
Rd

White Horse Road

Chapel Ave

Chapel
St

Castle Av

Knaves
Close

Tamworth Close

Castle St

Castle
St

Roundhill
Way

Brownhills West
Primary School

A5(T)

G   H   J   268   K   L   M

M8
1 Old Castle Gv

CHESTER

A452

L8
1 Chorley Rd
2 Mountbatten Cl
3 Robinson Rd
4 Sandown Cl

1 Chapel Dr

Brownhills
Comprehensive
School

Middleton R

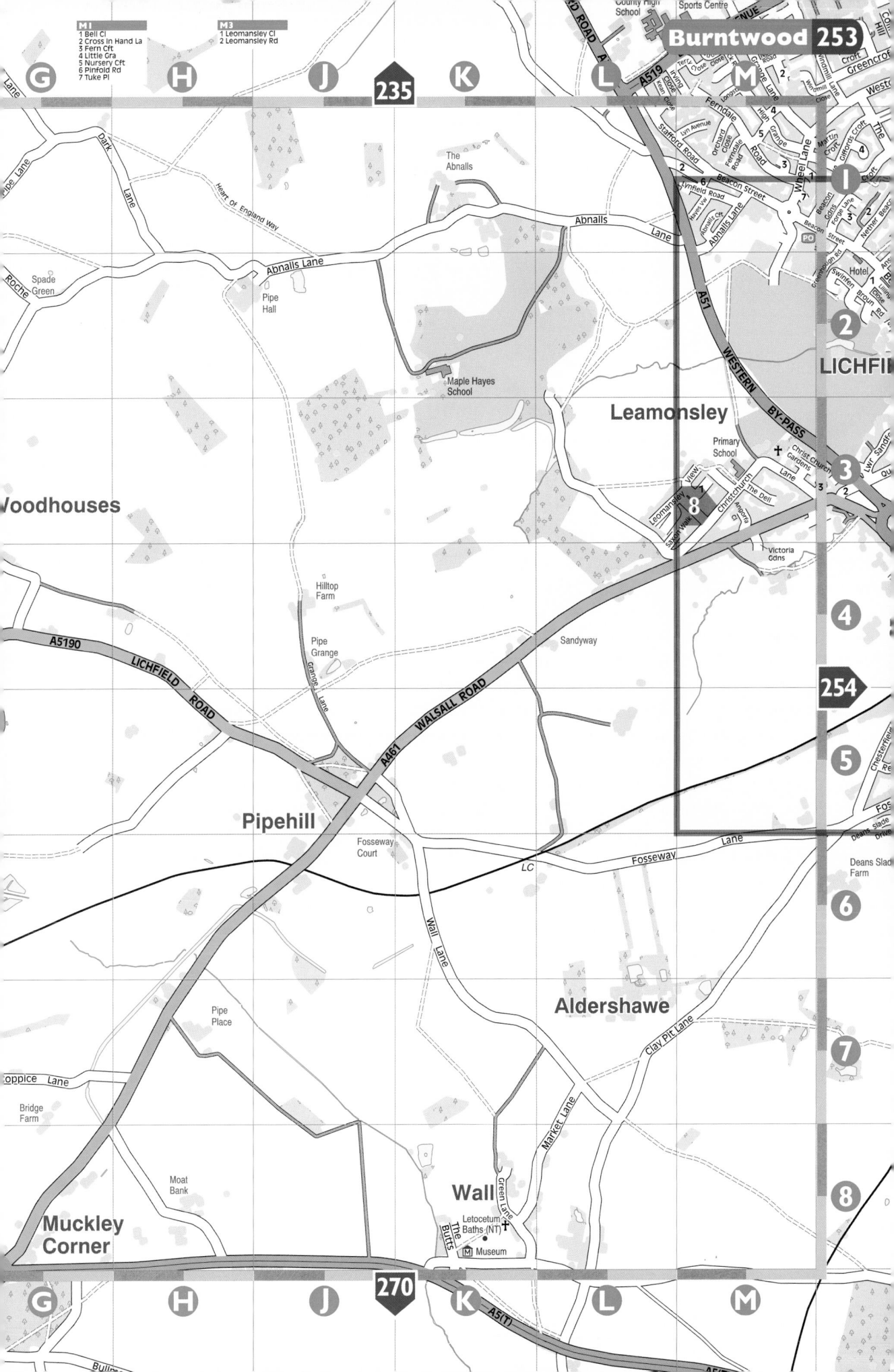

M1
1 Bell Cl
2 Cross In Hand La
3 Fern Cft
4 Little Cra
5 Nursery Cft
6 Pinfold Rd
7 Tuke Pl

M3
1 Leomansley Cl
2 Leomansley Rd

G H J ◆ 235 K L A519 M

The Abnalls

Abnalls Lane

Abnalls Lane

Pipe Hall

Heart of England Way

Spade Green

Roche

Dark Lane

Maple Hayes School

Leamonsley

Primary School

Christ Church

Leomansley View

Christchurch The Dell

Angora

Saxon Walk

Victoria Gdns

A51 WESTERN BY-PASS

LICHFI

Woodhouses

Hilltop Farm

Pipe Grange

A5190

LICHFIELD ROAD

Grange Lane

Sandyway

A461 WALSALL ROAD

254

Deans Slad Farm

Pipehill

Fosseway Court

LC

Fosseway Lane

Aldershawe

Clay Pit Lane

Pipe Place

Wall Lane

Bridge Farm

Coppice Lane

Moat Bank

Muckley Corner

Pipe Place

Wall

Letocetum Baths (NT)

The Burts

Green Lane

Market Lane

Museum

G H J ◆ 270 K A5(T) L M

Street G1
1 Ash Tree La
2 Holland Cl
3 Meadow Cft

L4
1 Baytree Wk
2 Main St

M4
1 Fisherwick Cl

Thatchmoor Farm

G   H   J   237   K   L   M   Broad Hurst Farm

Broad Lane   Whittington Hurst Farm

Hill Farm

Fisherwick Hall

Broad Lane

Park Lane   Park Lane

Burton Road

Huddlesford

Capper's Lane

Huddlesford Lane

Capper's Lane

Whittington Grange School   Swan Road

Noddington Av   Noddington La   Noddington

Burton Road   Darby Av   Dyott Av

Nley Cft   Middleton Road

Pass N   Rock Farm   Spring Lane

Rock 1   PO

Darnford Lane   2

Ellfield House   Back Lane   Blacksmith La   Langton Cres

Bramley Wy   Main St   Barley Cft   Barley Cft Rd

Church   Chapel Lane   The Green   Peregrine Close   Osprey Close

Street   Cloiste Dr   Falcon Dr   1   2

Marsh Lane   Babbington Cl   Fisherwick   Road   5

Common   Road   Beechwood   **Whittington**

Whittington Common   Windmillhill Lane

Sandy   Lane   Whittington Primary School

Common Lane   6

A51   Whittington Heath

Worcester Rd   7

TAMWORTH ROAD   Heath Avenue   Stafford Crescent   Derby Rd

Chester Rd   Nottingham Road

Staffordshire Regiment Museum   8

Heart of England Way

G   H   J   272   K   L   Packington Hall   M
M5
1 Kestrel Cl
2 Merlin Wy

Levett Road

256

Haselour House
Haselour Hall
G H J K L M

Twizles Lane

239

Main Road

Portway

Portway Lane

Dunnimere Farm

1

2

3

Willow Bottom La

258

4

Birdsley Farm

Winterdyne Farm

5

Wigginton Fields

6

Syerscote Manor

Syerscote Lane

7

Syerscote Barn

8

Comberford Lane

Wigginton

St Leonards C of E Primary School

Walrand Cl

Main Street

274

Arka

G H J K L M

Haunton

A B C **240** D E F

Clifton
Campv

Twizles Lane
Smithy Lane
Chestnut Lane
Coppice Lane
CP School

1

Syerscote Lane

2

3

The
Dale

Thorpe
Constanti

4

Highfields

5

Gorse Farm

6

Statfold
Farm

B79

Lonkhills Farm

Staffordshire County
Warwickshire County

Clifton Lane

7

Statfold
Hall

B5493

8

The
Poplars

A B C **275** D E F

Statfold Barn
Farm

New Road

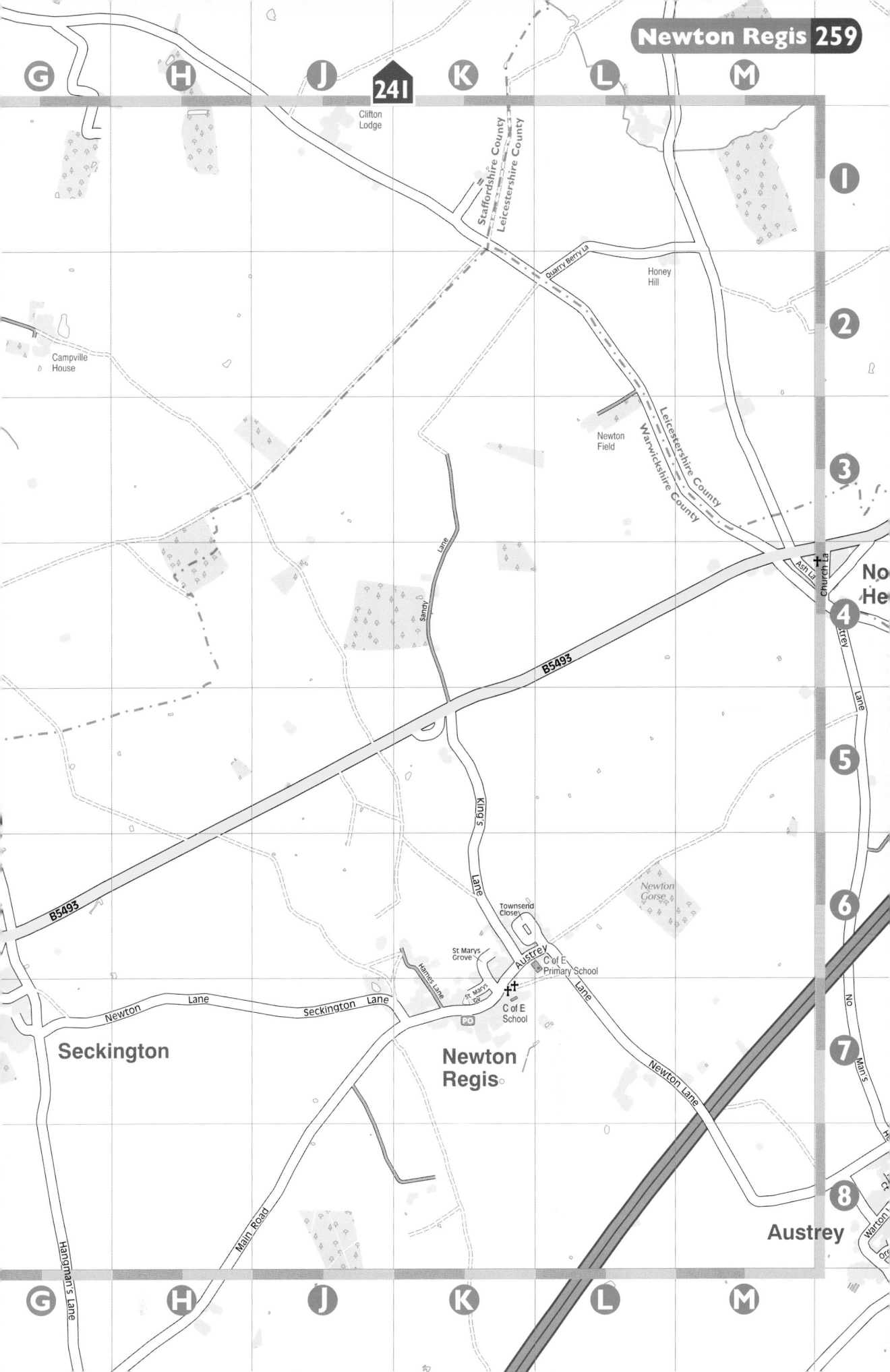

G H J **241** K L M

I
2
3
4
5
6
7
8

Clifton Lodge

Staffordshire County
Leicestershire County

Quarry Berry La

Honey Hill

Campville House

Newton Field

Leicestershire County
Warwickshire County

Ash La

Church La

No He

B5493

Sandy Lane

King's Lane

Newton Gorse

B5493

Townsend Close

Austrey

St Marys Grove

Hames Lane

St Marys Dr

C of E Primary School

C of E School

PO

Newton Lane

Seckington Lane

No Man's

Seckington

Newton Regis

Newton Lane

Warton

Austrey

Hangman's Lane

Main Road

G H J K L M

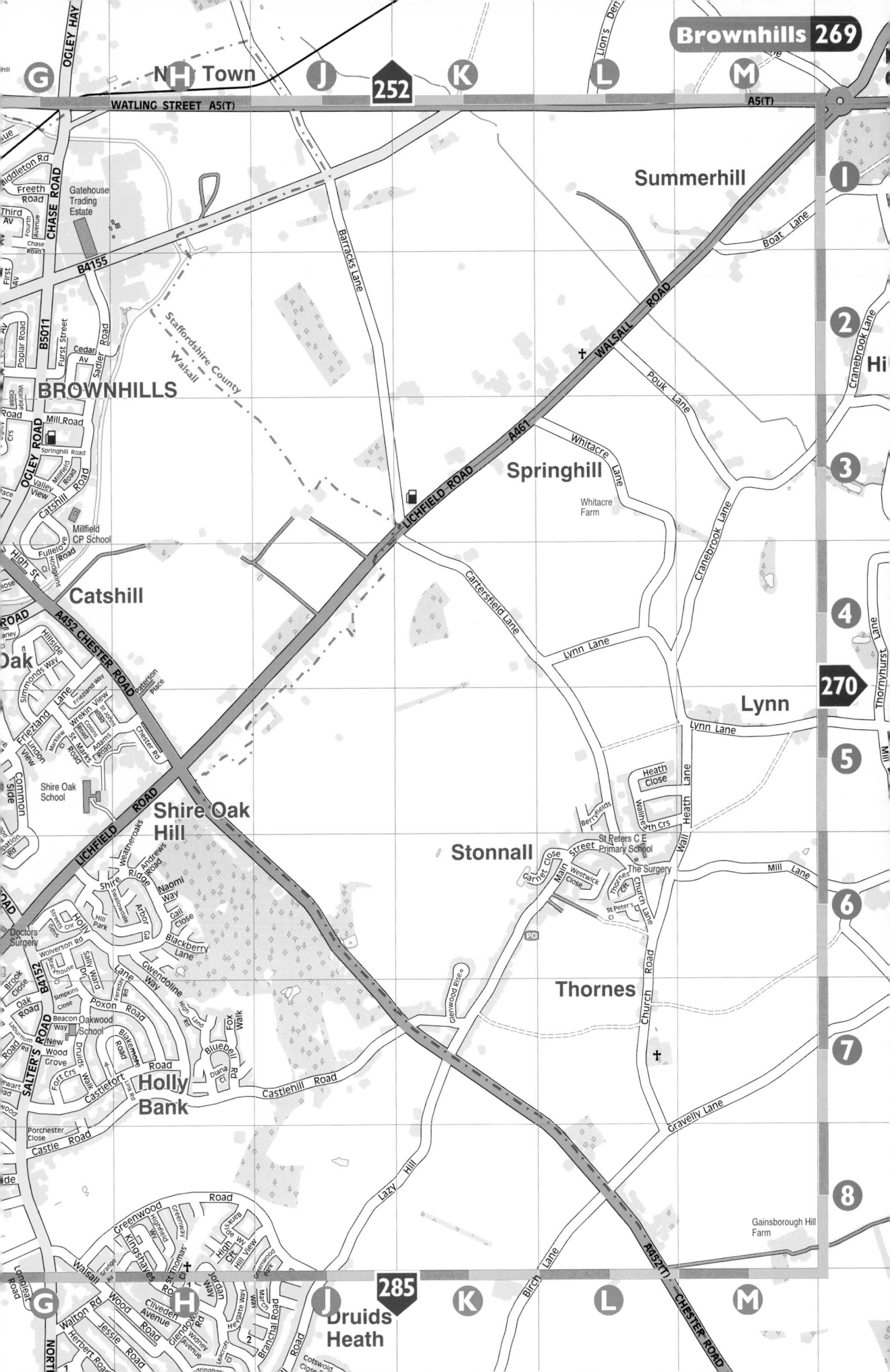

G   H   J   **254**   K   L   M

Swifen
Lake

1

Swifen
Hall

Whitehouse
Farm

Broom Covert
Road
The   Drive

2

Allen Brown
Gallery

A5148

WS14

3

Streetway
Road

Streetway

A5(T)

Streetway
House

Old London Road

A38(T)

BIRMINGHAM ROAD

A5127

4

Mill Lane

Oakwood
Close

Shenstone
Sports Club

272

Greysbrooke
CP School

Barnes
Road

Birmingham Rd

Park Lane

Schoolfields
Road

5

stone

Park Lane

Black Brook

Hungry Lane

LONDON ROAD

6

Thickbroom

Dog Lane

BIRMINGHAM ROAD

Shenstone
Park

Park
Lane

Little Hay Lane

A38(T)

7

Shenstone Lodge
School

Little Hay Lane

8

Shenstone
Woodend

Green
Barn

G   H   J   **256**   K   L   M

K3
1 Gawsworth
2 Glyndebourne
3 Osborne

K4
1 Chalfield
2 Littlecote

L3
1 Fir Tree Cl
2 Lanchester Cl
3 Robinson Cl

River Tame

LC

Comberford Hall

1

Hopwas Hays Wood

Windmill Farm

Windmill Cl

2

Coton Lane

Claremont Rd

Browning Close

Hayworth

St Elizabeths Primary School

The Woodhouse

Kipling Rise

Telford Road

Infants School

Cromwell Rd

Keats Cl

Carlton

Byron Rd

Redhill

3

Thomas Barnes CP School

Coton Hall Farm

Scimitar Close

Bloomfield Wy

School

Libra Cl

Danelagh

Robert Clifton

Byron Rd

Park Special School

Lichfield Crescent

School Lane

Daintry Dr

Coton Lane

Helmingham

Kentwell

Chartwell

Lorton

Longleat

Kepler

Mariner

Ariane

Gerard

Witney

Bentley Wy

Faina Crs

Tamworth District Council

LICHFIELD ROAD A51

Mecca Cl

Normar

Roman

Compton Rd

Edgar Cl

Leyfields

Hopwas

Church Drive

PO

Coton

Godolphin

Buckingham

Browsholme

Road

Meiford

Lichfield Road Industrial Est

Luvs

Wiggington Park

Nursery Lane

Hints Lane

Graham

Newstead

Lichfield Trading Est

4

Hopwas House Farm

Lane

Dunstall Lane

Rufurd

Thoresby

Swallowfield

Shield

The Alders

Mariner

Neander

Armstrong

Lovell

Apollo

274

Hints

LICHFIELD

Main

Oxbridge

Exeter Dr

Borman

Staffs Moor Industrial Estate

Gagarin

The Leys

Neuvil St

5

Hints Lane

Downing Way

ROAD

Bradford Street

Swanmote

Park St

Meadow

Warde

Sunset

LICH

The Bodnets

Broad Meadow

TAMEDRIVE

6

Dunstall Farm

Dunstall Lane

Dunstall Lane

PLANTATION

Kendall's Wood

LANE

Ventura Shopping Cent

7

B5404

Bonehill Farm

Park Road

Ventura Shopping Centre

A57

Ventura Shopping Centre

BONEHILL ROAD A453

angley Farm

A5(T)

Aldin West Cl

Huntington

Hampshire Cl

8

HINTS ROAD B5404

Mile Oak Business Park

Sir Robert Peel Hospital

The Green

Park Lane

County Drive

M7
1 Etchell Rd
2 Winchester Rd

M3
1 Alvis Cl
2 Athelstan Wy

French Ave

Allton Avenue

Affleck Ave

Price Av

M2
1 Campbell Cl
2 Lomond Cl
3 Portland Av

Manor Road

Manor

L5
1 Blackfriars Cl

Park Lane

L4
1 Greyfriars Dr
2 Lagrange
3 Wynyates

Longwood Primary School

George Av

Brookside Rd

Coronation Avenue

B5404

LICHFIELD STREET

Mile Oak

Doctors Surgery

Fazele

Bourne Broc

TON ROAD

G5
1 Crestwood
2 Highfield Av
3 Repington Rd N
4 Repington Rd S

G6
1 Lindera

G8
1 Carisbroke

H4
The
1 The Green

G H J **258** K L M

I

2

Statfold Barn
Farm

The
Decoy

New Road

Shuttington

Pear Tree Cl

Milner
Drive

Church La

School
Lane

1

3

Amington Hall
Farm

Shuttington
Bridge

Shuttington   Road

4

Alvecote

Moor
Lane

Shuttington   Road

Tamworth   Road

Hodge La

Dog La

PO

Coventry Canal

5

Bracklesham
Wy Calster

By Pass
Rd

1
3 2

Primary
School

Chandlers Dr

Tilia Rd

Caister

Woodhouse Lane

Cem

Mercian

Gleneagles

Turnberry

Lytham

Ridgewood
Rd

Wy

1

3 1

Carnoustie

1

Woodland Rd

Warwickshire County
Staffordshire County

6

on

Greenhart

Foxglove

Foxglove

Juniper

Hornbeam

Jasmine

Kernia

Tamworth
Borough
Council

PO

Doctors
Surgery

Road

St Andrews

Troon

Way

Eagle Dr

Golf Club
Bungalow

7

Quince Tree
Special School

Mercian

Pebble Cl

Amington
Industrial
Est

Brookweed

Briar

Briar
Briar

Way

Sandy
Way

Amber Cl Tamworth Business
Centre

Lodge
Farm

Amington Industrial
Est

Robey's Lane

Ankerside

8

Primary
School

Torc
High School

Brain
St

Engine
St

Stephens Cl

Beyer Cl

Pullman

Tamworth
Borough
Council

Silica Rd

Sandy
Wy

Mica
Cl

Amington
Industrial
Est

Pooley
Lane

Pooley

B5000 GLASCOTE ROAD

291

Cheviot

G M3 H J **291** K J5 L H6 M

1 Coronation Crs

Stoneydelph

1 Abberley
2 Correen
3 Crigdon

1 Sunningdale

1 Hoylake
2 Maple Rd

H5
1 Greenacre Cl
2 Levett Rd
3 Muirfield

Ellerbeck
Health Centre

Infants School

B5080

School

WORTH   ROAD   B5000

260

A B C D E F

1

2

Shropshire County
Staffordshire County

Rushey Lane

Bishton
Manor

Farm Road

3

Home Farm Road

Wildicote

Fox Covert

Rous's
Covert

Snowdon Lane

Patshull Hall

Burnhill
Green

Lower
Snowdon

Snowdon Road

4

Church
Pool

Golf
Course

Old
Park

5

Middle Ley

The
Great
Pool

6

Far Ley

Old Park

Hotel

Staffordshire County
Shropshire County

7

Stanlow

Pasford

8

Kingslow

A B C D E F

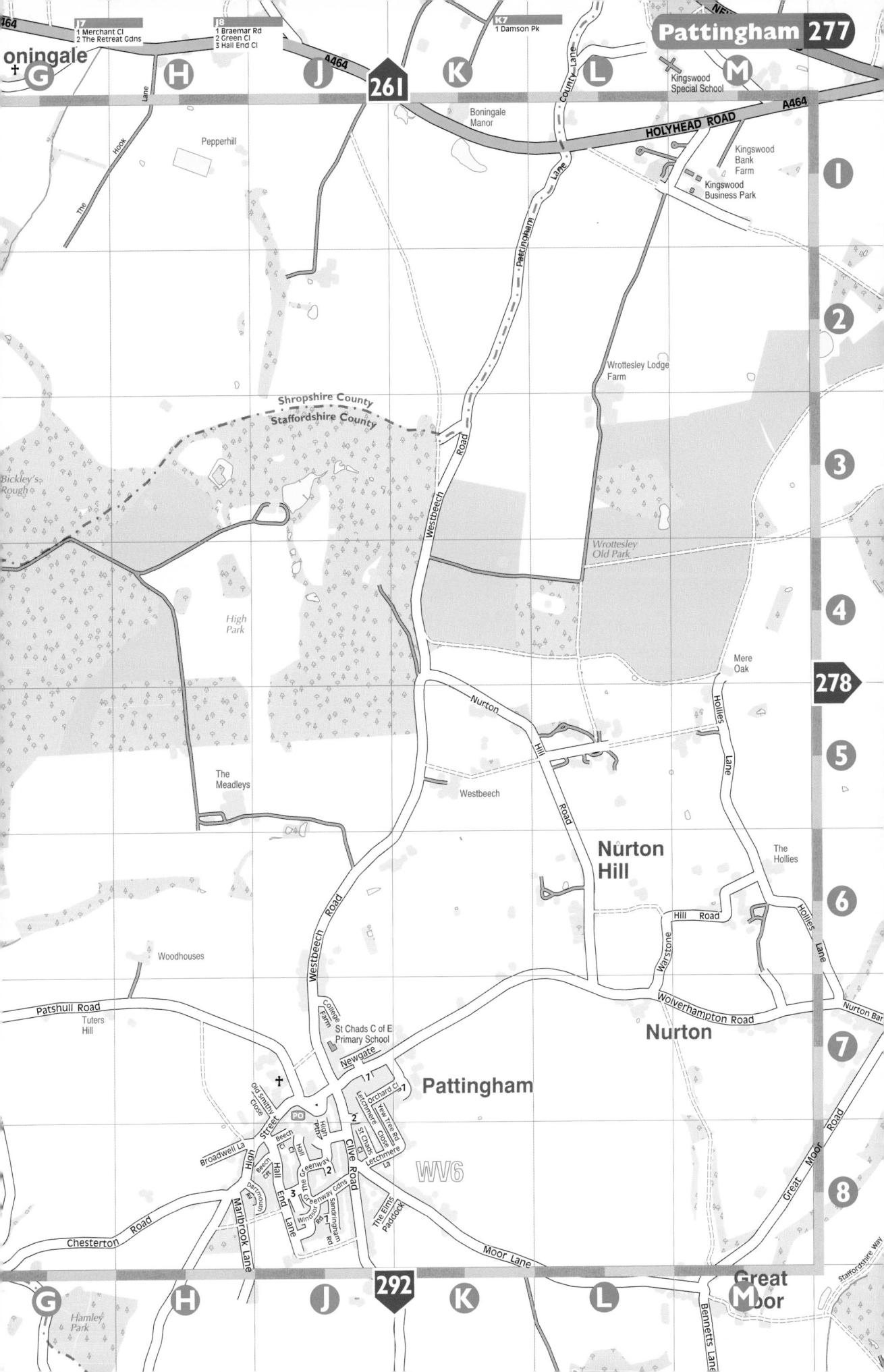

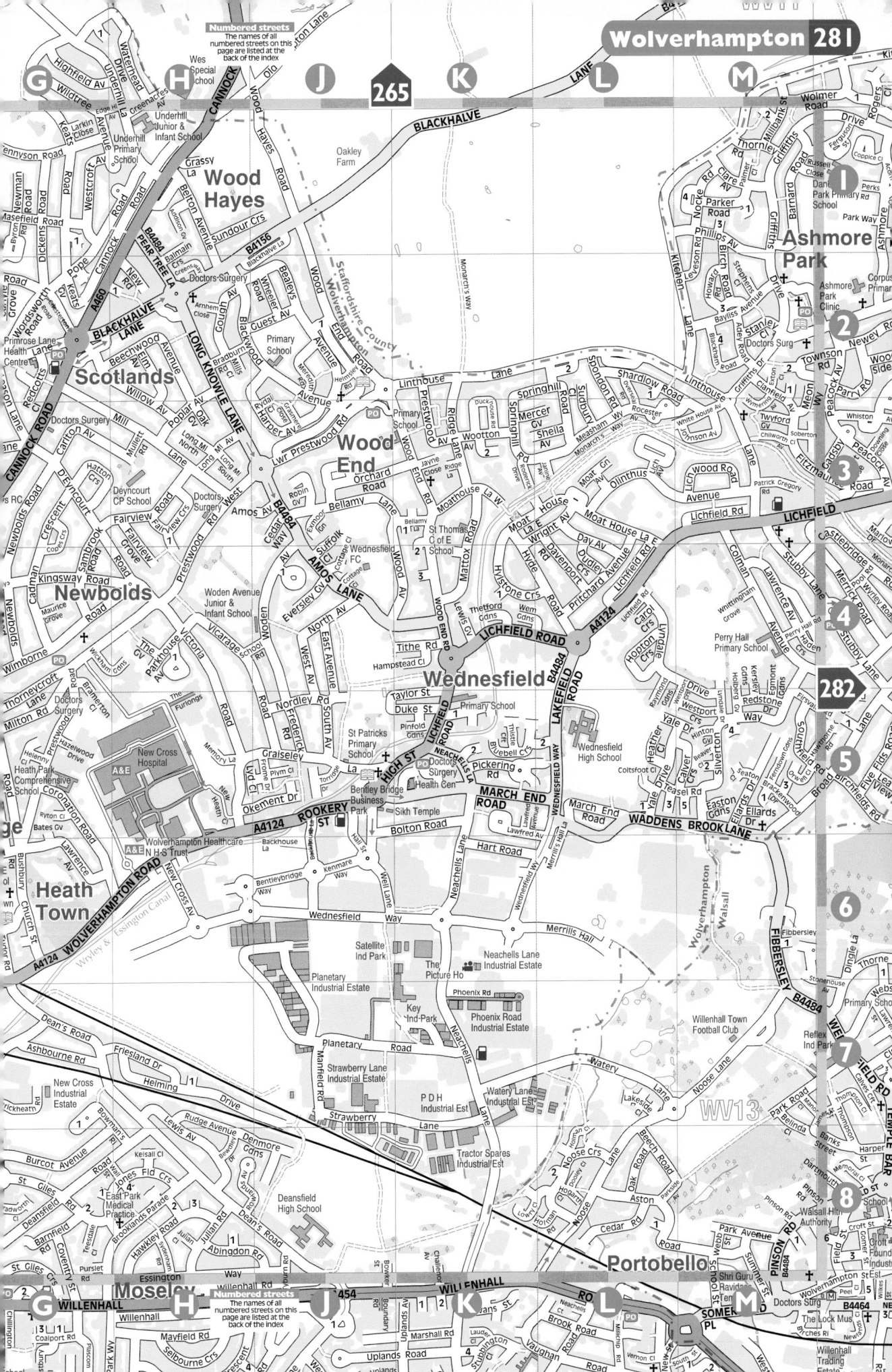

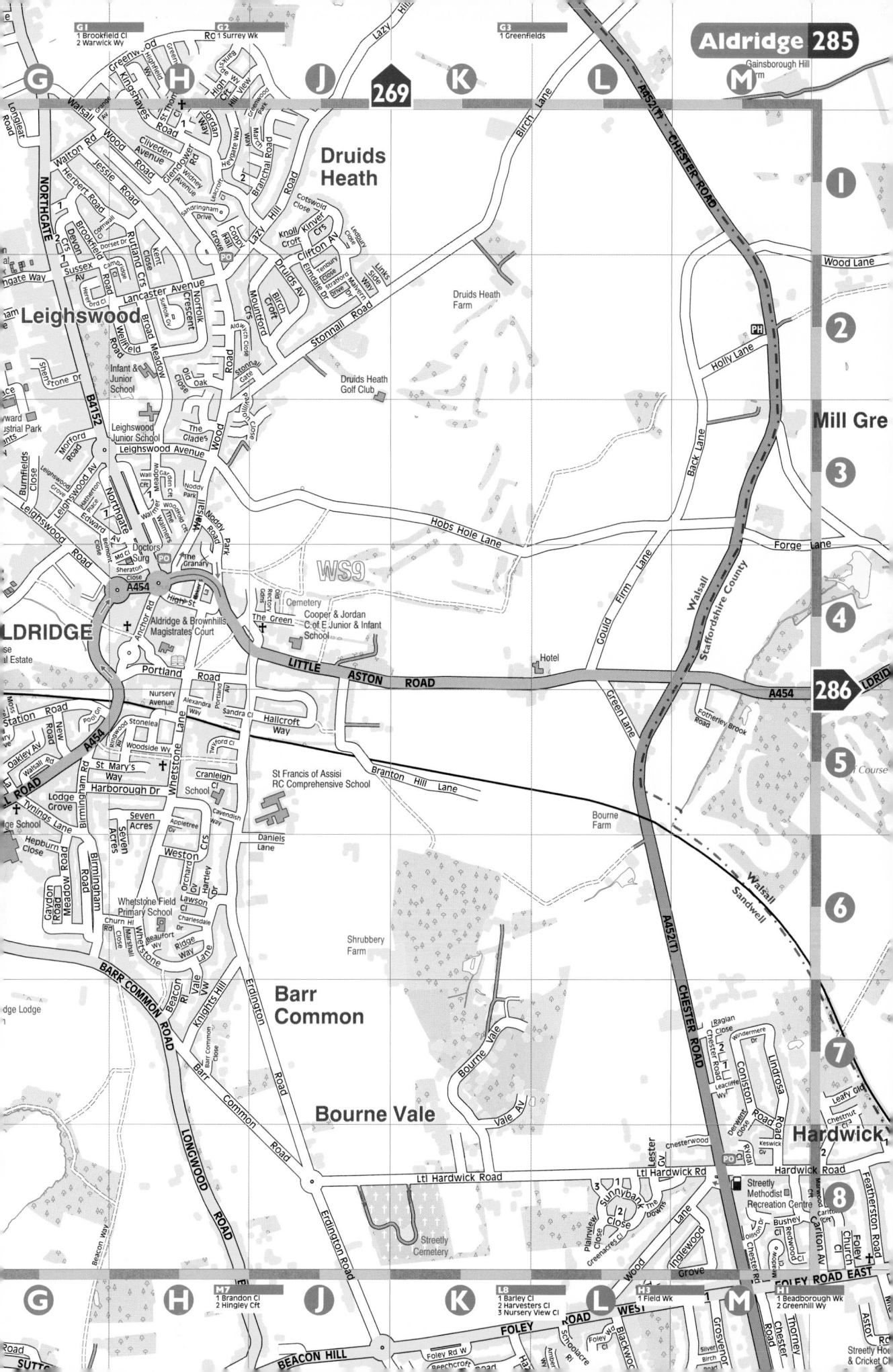

G6
1 Stringer Cl
2 Wardle Cl
3 Westfield Manor

G7
1 Harland Rd
2 Henley Dr

H7
1 The Dovecotes
2 Drayton Cl
3 Sherifoot La
4 Walcot Cl

G · H · J · **271** · K · L · M

1

henstone
Woodend

Little
Hay

Green
Barn

Moneymore

LONDON ROAD

A38(T)

2

Alder Farm

Green Barns Lane

Green Barns Lane

Camp Farm

3

Woodland Ct

smarts Avenue

Gap Road

atford

Staffordshire County

Birmingham

Camp Road

Weeford
Park Farm

4

288

Hillwood Common Road

Wood   Road

Hill Wood

Springhill
Farm

A38(T)

5

Hill

Canwell

Turf Pitts
Lane

London

6

Keating
Gdns

Dutton Close

Dutton
Close

Hill

Hathaway Road

Dawney
Dr

Gresley Dr

Gianville
Dr

Village

Crockford
Road

LICHFIELD

Sara
Close

ROAD

Woodside
Farm

Dutton's   Lane

Weeford   Road

Lane

Turf   Pitts

Lane

Slade
Lane

Mayall Dr

St
John
Cl

Homestead
Dr

Worcester Cl

Duncalfe
Dr

Duggale
Crs

Pudsey
Dr

Randle Dr

Cartwright Rd

Edwards
Road

Darnel Hurst Rd

St Blaise

Little Sutton
Junior &
Infant School

Willmott

Lane

Maripit

Dutton's Lane

Weeford   ROAD

SLADE

SLADE

Bishops
Meadow

7

Gibbons
Road

Tower

Road

Brentnall
Dr

Holly La

Willmcote
Dr

Bodington
Rd

Rednall
Road

Clarendon
Road

Worcester

Willmott   Road

B4151

Bodicote
Gv

Buckton Cl

Blaydon
Av

Aston Rd

Mere Green

Ley Hill
Primary
School

St James
La

Mere Gn Cl

PO

St James

Roughley
Dr

Harvey Dr

Roughley

Coburn
Dr

Little Sutton

Little Sutton   ROAD

Perott
Dr

Sharrat Fld

Holte
Drive

Clive
Rd

Sheperds Pool Rd

Mere Pool

Fox Hill Road

B75

Fox Hill
House

8

BELWELL LANE

Belwell
Lane

Irnham
Road

The
 forry
LB

arthur
berry
chool

Four Oaks
Medical Centre

Cremorne Road

MERE GN RD

Adescote

LITTLE SUTTON

Homer Rd

Devereux
Rd

Little Sutton La

Homer Rd

Grosvenor   Road

Streather
Road

Harwell

Essex Road

Heath

Wyrley
drive

Rowallan
Road

Road

Road

Brockhurst

Ferrers   Rd

WEEFORD

Moor

Moor Hall
Golf Club

Moor Hall

Ashfurlong
Hall

TAMWORTH ROAD

G
Ley Hill

H

J

K

L

M

G8
1 Charnley Dr
2 Mainwaring Dr
3 Mordaunt Dr

H8
1 Bradwell Cft
2 Buckton Cl

K7
1 Amington Cl
2 Woodstile Cl

J8
1 Farnborough Ct

I7
1 Grange Av
2 Wheatley Cl

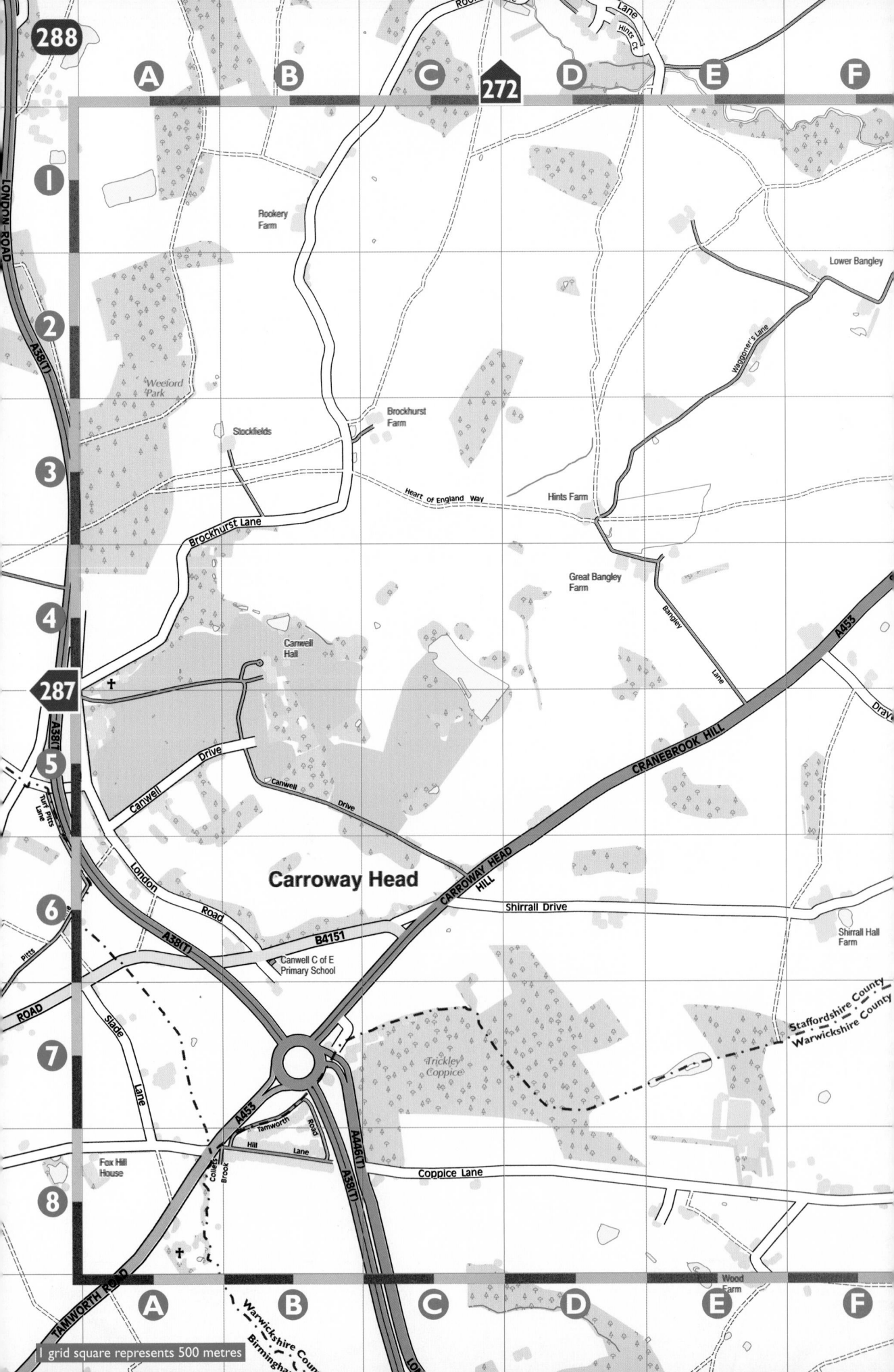

288

A   B   272   C   D   E   F

1

2

3

4

287

5

6

7

8

A   B   C   D   E   F

Rookery Farm

Lower Bangley

Weeford Park

Stockfields

Brockhurst Farm

Waggoner's Lane

Heart of England Way

Hints Farm

Brockhurst Lane

Great Bangley Farm

Canwell Hall

Bangley Lane

A453

Drayt

CRANEBROOK HILL

Canwell Drive

Canwell Drive

Turf Pitts Lane

London Road

Carroway Head

CARROWAY HEAD HILL

Shirrall Drive

Shirrall Hall Farm

A38(T)

B4151

Canwell C of E Primary School

Pitts

ROAD

Slade Lane

Trickley Coppice

Staffordshire County
Warwickshire County

Fox Hill House

Collets Brook

Tamworth Road

A453

Hill Lane

A46(T)

Coppice Lane

TAMWORTH ROAD

Warwickshire Cou
Birmingha

Wood Farm

I grid square represents 500 metres

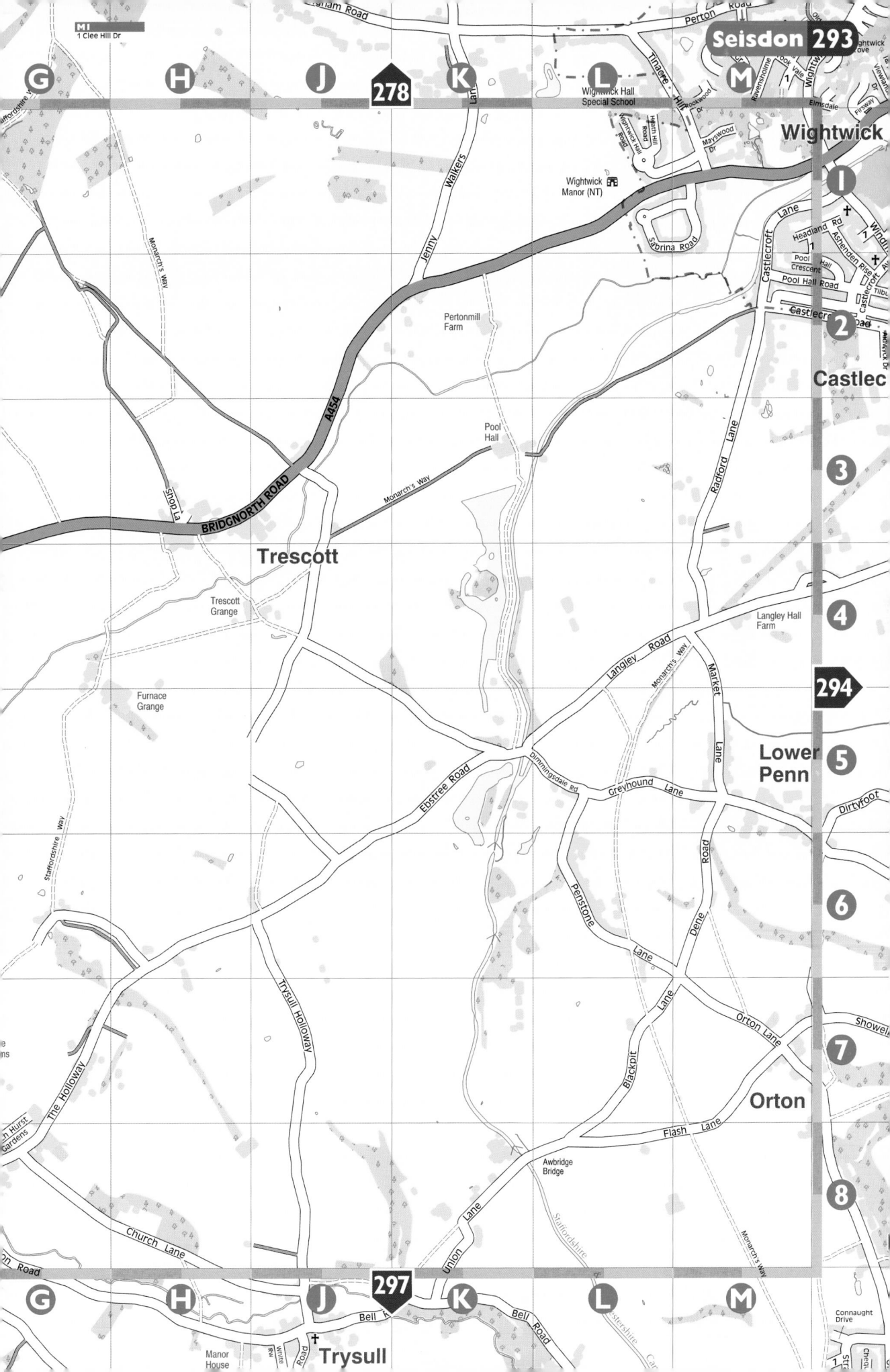

G   H   J   **278**   K   L   M

MI
1 Clee Hill Dr

Wightwick Hall
Special School

Wightwick

Wightwick
Manor (NT)

1

Castlecroft Lane

Headland Rd
Pool
Crescent
Hall

Astenden Rise

Windmill

Castlecroft

Sabrina Road

Pool Hall Road

Castlecroft Road

2

Castlec

Pertonmill
Farm

Radford Lane

3

Pool
Hall

Monarch's Way

A454

Shop La

BRIDGNORTH ROAD

Monarch's Way

Trescott

Trescott
Grange

Langley Hall
Farm

4

Langley Road

Monarch's Way

Market Lane

294

Furnace
Grange

Ebstree Road

Dimmingsdale Rd

Greyhound Lane

**Lower
Penn**

5

Dirtyfoot

Staffordshire Way

Dene Road

6

Penstone Lane

Blackpit Lane

Orton Lane

Showel

7

Trysull Holloway

The Holloway

Hurst
Gardens

Orton

Flash Lane

8

Awbridge
Bridge

Church Lane

Union Lane

Staffordshire

Monarch's Way

Connaught
Drive

Bell Rd

Leicestershire

Bell Road

Check

Manor
House

White

Road

Trysull

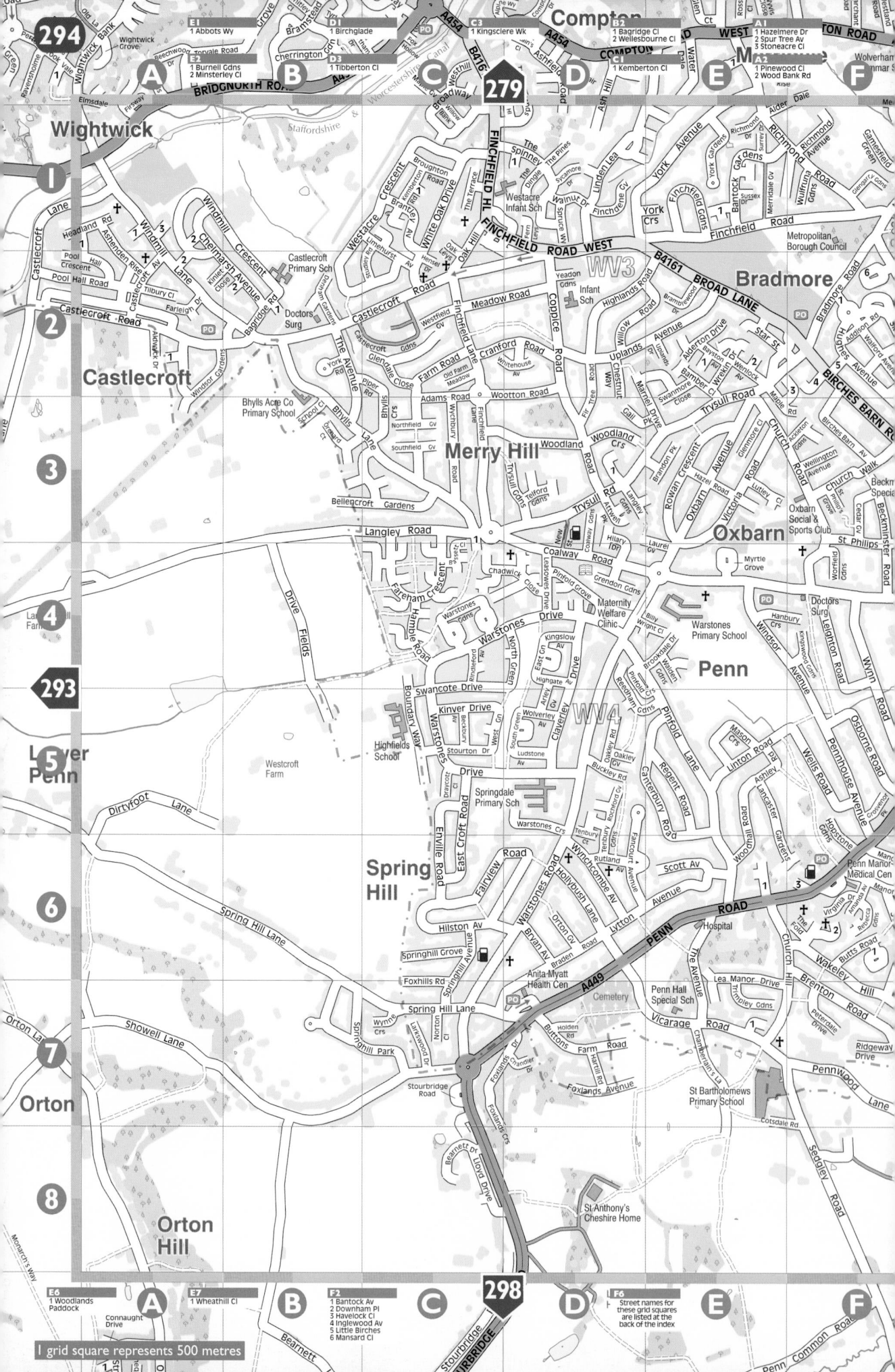

K4
1 Bloomfield Cl
2 Brindley Cl
3 Wombrook Dl

K5
1 The Croft
1 Heathlands
3 Longford Cl

K6
1 Heath Mill Cl

L8
1 The Close

Awbridge
Bridge

G H J **293** K L M

I
1
2

2

The
Bratch

3

Trysull

Manor
House

All Saints C of E
Primary School

Mount
Road

Pennleigh Gdns
Mount Pleasant
Avenue

Ounsdale High School

Ounsdale
Sports Cen

Ounsdale

4

The Beeches

Feashill Road

Crockington Lane

Woodford Lane

Bratch Common Road

Clap Gate Rd

Wombrook
Ind Est

St Bernadettes
RC Primary
School

Spines
Clinic

Sandringham Rd

Kirkstone

Rennison

Feashill Cl

Park
Farm

Gorse Lane

WOMBOURNE

Pool House Road

The Meadlands

Forge va Wy

Quendale

Special
Sch

Brook
Road

298

Blakele

5

Smestow Bridge
Industrial Est

Marburn Wy

Giggetty

Lilac Av

Birch Hl Av

Elm Tree Cl

Smestow Gate

B4176 BRIDGNORTH ROAD

Heathfields
Heath House

Mill's Vale

Milifields Way

Holloway Drive

Furnace Cl

Van Diemans Rd

Calvin Cl

Chapel St

Park Av

Brickbridge

Common Road

Wombourne Park

6

Swindon
Golf Club

Smestow La

Chapel Lane

Monarch's Way

B4176 BRIDGNORTH ROAD

Dickinson Road

Smestow

Heath Mill Road

Amptronik
Trading Est

Smestow Brook

Nature Rese

7

New Road

Feashill Road

Wombourne Road

Himley
Plantation

Whitehouse
Plantation

St Johns
Primary School

Albert
Dr

Stanley Dr

Manor Dr

Fairlands Cl

Swindon

Himley Lane

8

St John's

Church Rd

High Street

Holloway

Reynolds

L4, L5
Street names for
these grid squares
are listed at the
back of the index

M6
1 Green Acres
2 The Warings

M5
1 Chartwell Dr
2 Cranwell Gn
3 Honeybourne Crs
4 The Willows

M4
1 Woodhill Cl

M3
1 Bankside
2 Greenlands
3 Wedgwood Cl

A   B   C   294   D   E   F

294

A5
1 Blakeley Heath Dr
2 Chestnut Dr
3 Hawkswell Av
4 Highfields Dr

A4
1 Maypole Ct
2 Rushford Av
3 Saint Benedicts Rd

A3
1 Sunridge Av
2 Windmill Bank

A1
1 Balmoral Dr
2 Ednam Gv

Orton Hill
St Anth
Cheshire Home

Connaught Drive
Lloyd House

1

Bearnett Lane
Penn Common Road

Strathmore Crs
Chequers Av
Orton Lane

2

The Bratch

Bratch Hollow
Bratch Lane
Billy Buns Lane
Meadow Lane
Bull Lane
Wood Lane
Lane

Gospel End Village

WODEHOUSE LANE

Baggeridge Wood Farm

Victoria Gv
Hazel Grove
Station Road
Mount Road
Bullmeadow Lane

Withymere Lane
A449(T)
STOURBRIDGE ROAD
Stourbridge Road

A463

Wom Brook

3

Bramblewood
St Benedict Biscop Primary School
School Road
Smallbrook Lane
Police Stn
Waverley Gdns

Primary School
Ounsdale Road
Mount Dr

Wombourne Cricket Tennis & Bowling Club
Maypole Gallery
Cannon Rd
Planks Lane
Rennison Drive

Doctors Surg
Church Rd
High Street
Battlefield Hill
Moses Hall Rd
Gilbert La
Sandy
Mt
Battlefield

Ounsdale Sports Cen
Road

4

Spines Clinic
Bramber Dr
Gravel Hill Surg
Civic Cen
PO
Gravel Hill
Redcliffe Drive
Rookery Road
Redhill Dr
Common Road

High Mdw
Copper Beech Dr
Greenhill Road
Sunny Hill Cl

The Foxhills
Woody Park

297

Blakeley
The Longfield
Redhill Av
Glendale Close
The Broadway
Whites Wood Lane
Woodlands Rd
Poplar
Beggars Bush La

Park Farm
Baggeridge Country Park

DY3

5

School
Greenfields Road
Cedars Dr
Sytch Lane
Greenhill Gdns

Spring Pool

Island Pool

6

Calvin Cl
Chapel St
Park Av
Wombourne Park
Dickinson Road
Greenhill Farm

Rock Pool

Higharcal Wood

High Arcal

7

Nature Reserve
Himley Plantation
Bridgnorth Road
Plantation Lane
Churns Hill Lane
Cherry Lane
School Road
Himley La
B4176

Great Pool
Himley Hall

HIMLEY ROAD   B4176

Himley Wood

Himley
Hotel
Hotel
DUDLEY ROAD

Home Farm

PH

8

A449(T)
STOURBRIDGE ROAD

Staffordshire County
Dudley

A   B   F5   C   303   D   E   F

303

F5
1 Sheridan Gdns

Maidensbridge Primary School
Beac Crof
Claydon Road
Maiden
Collingdale
Drive
Monteagle
Oak Lane
St Micha
Jimley Gdns
Camden Way
Copper Beech Dr

| grid square represents 500 metres

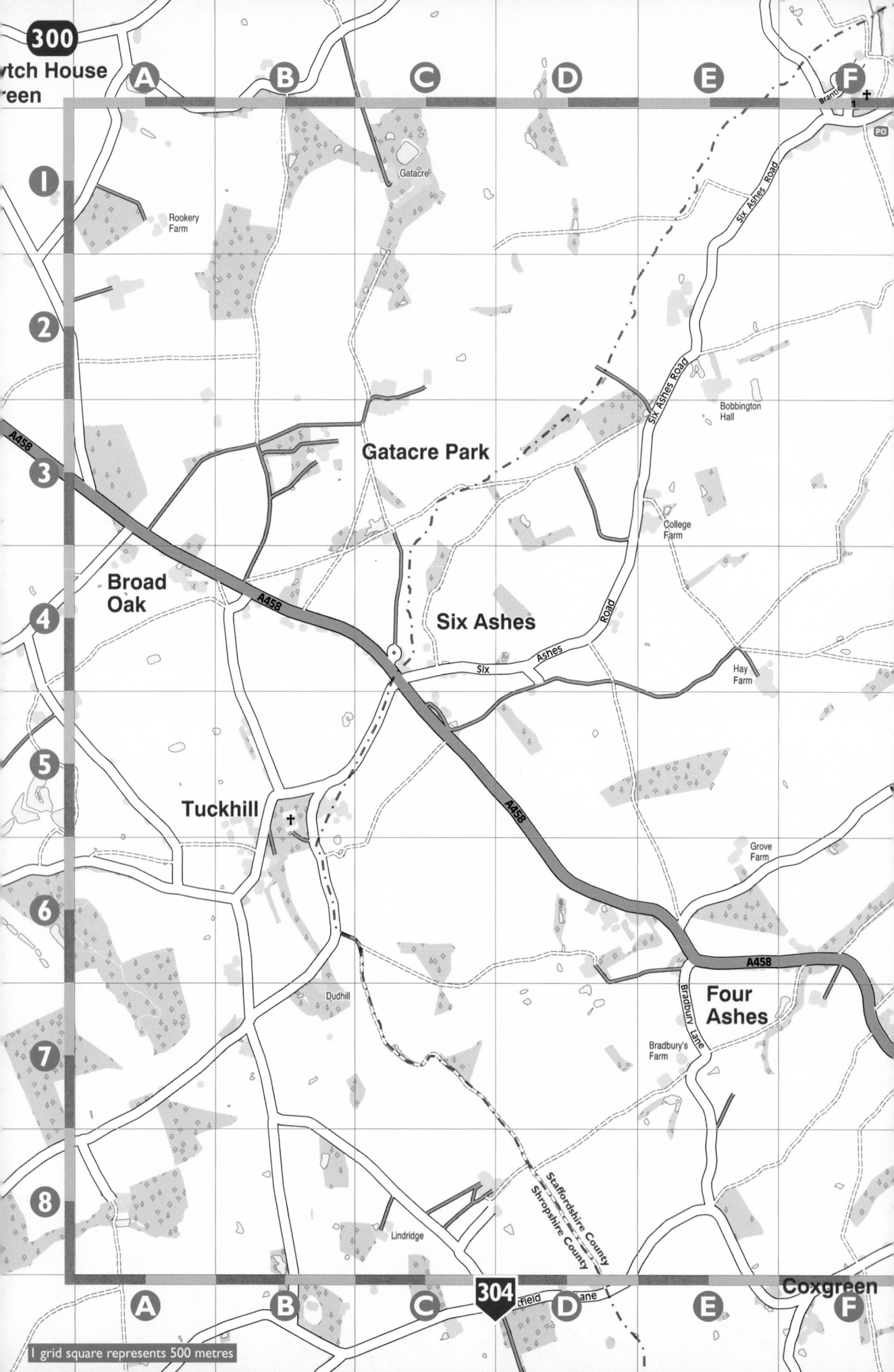

wtch House
reen

A B C D E F

1

†
PO

Brantt

I

Rookery
Farm

Gatacre

2

Bobbington
Hall

A458

3

Gatacre Park

Six Ashes Road

College
Farm

4

Broad
Oak

A458

Six Ashes

Six   Ashes

Ashes

Road

Hay
Farm

5

Tuckhill

†

A458

6

Grove
Farm

A458

Dudhill

Four
Ashes

7

Bradbury Lane

Bradbury's
Farm

8

Lindridge

Staffordshire County

Shropshire County

Coxgreen

A B C D E F

etfield   ane

A **B** **C** 297 **D** **E** **F**

Swindon

Whitehouse Plantation

St John's

Baldwin Way
Swin Forge Way
High St
Church Rd
Stanley Dr
Manor Dr
Falklands Cl
Himley Lane
Reynolds Cl
PO

Staffordshire Way
ghate
untry Park

1

White House Lane

The Holloway

The Brooklands

Monarch's Way

Hinksford Gdns
Hinksford Lane

Hin

2

Chasepool Farm

Swindon

Chasepool Road

3

Camp Hill Road

Camp Farm

Staffordshire & Worcestershire Canal

Mile Flat

My Lady's Farm

4

Greensforge

301

Enville Common Road

Golf Course

5

Smestow Brook

Ashwood

Doctors Lane

6

Great Checkhill Road

Checkhill Farm

Little Checkhill Lane

Greensforge Lane

Mill Lane

7

Ho
Far

8

Gothersley Lane

Gothersley

Monarch's Way

The Million

Gothersley Farm

A **B** **C** 306 **D** **E** **F**

1 grid square represents 500 metres

304

A　B　C　**300**　D　E　F

Coxgreen

Batfield Lane

Staffordshire County
Shropshire ...ny

Hollies Lane

1

Astley

2

The Hollies

Fillets

3

No Man's
Green

No Man's On Lane

4

Bowhills
Dingle

Roughpark
Wood

5

6

Hartsgreen

Compton Park
Farm

Lane

Highfields
Farm

7

Romsley

Beacon Lane

Romsley Lane

Brittle's
Farm

Sturt's Green
Farm

Tudor
House

8

Poolhouse
Farm

Arley Wood

Castlehill
Wood

PH

A　B　C　**308**　D　E　F

1 grid square represents 500 metres

...nshire County

G H J 301 K L M I

2

3

4 306 5

6

7

8

G H 309 J K L M

Kinver 305

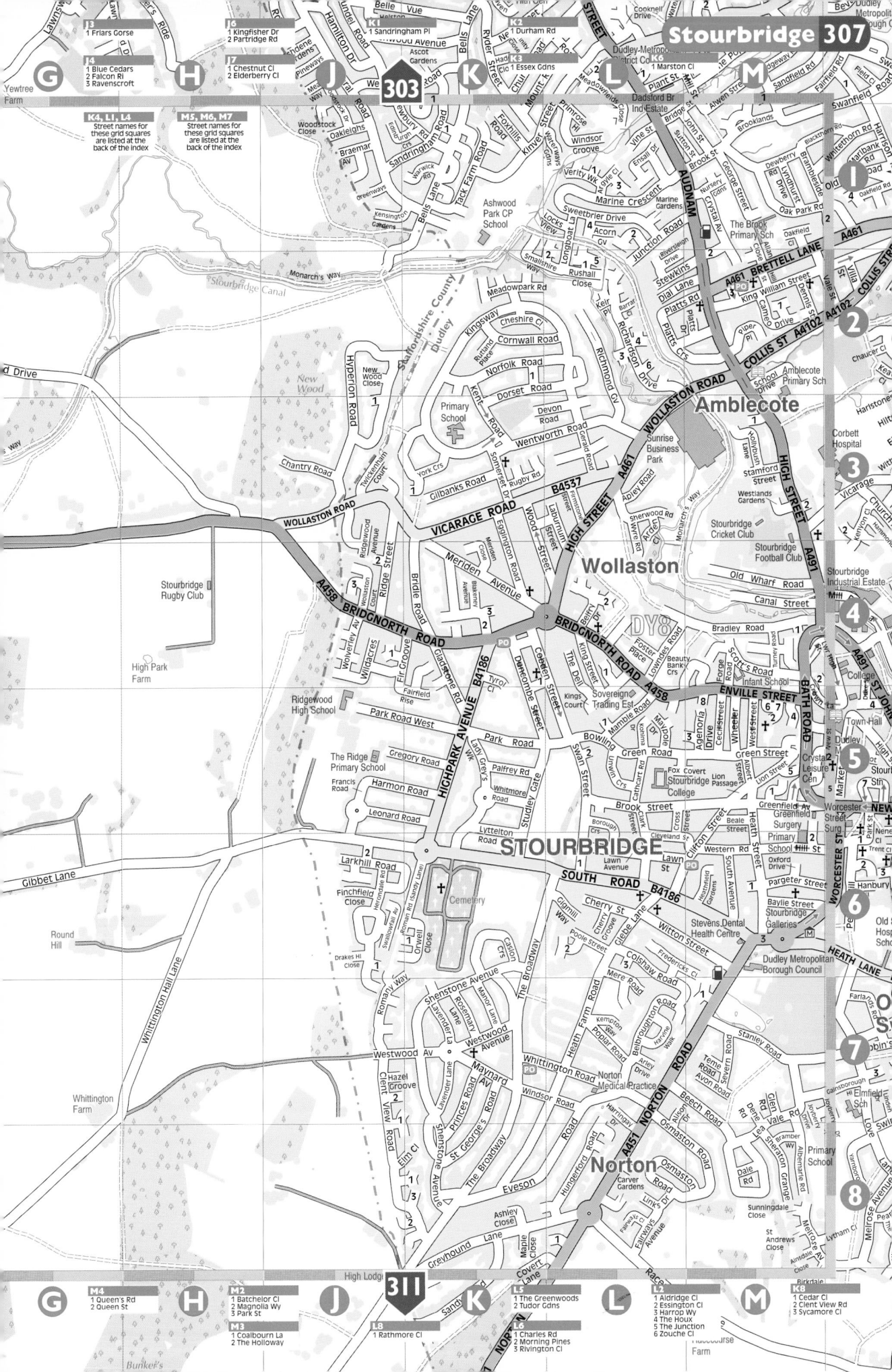

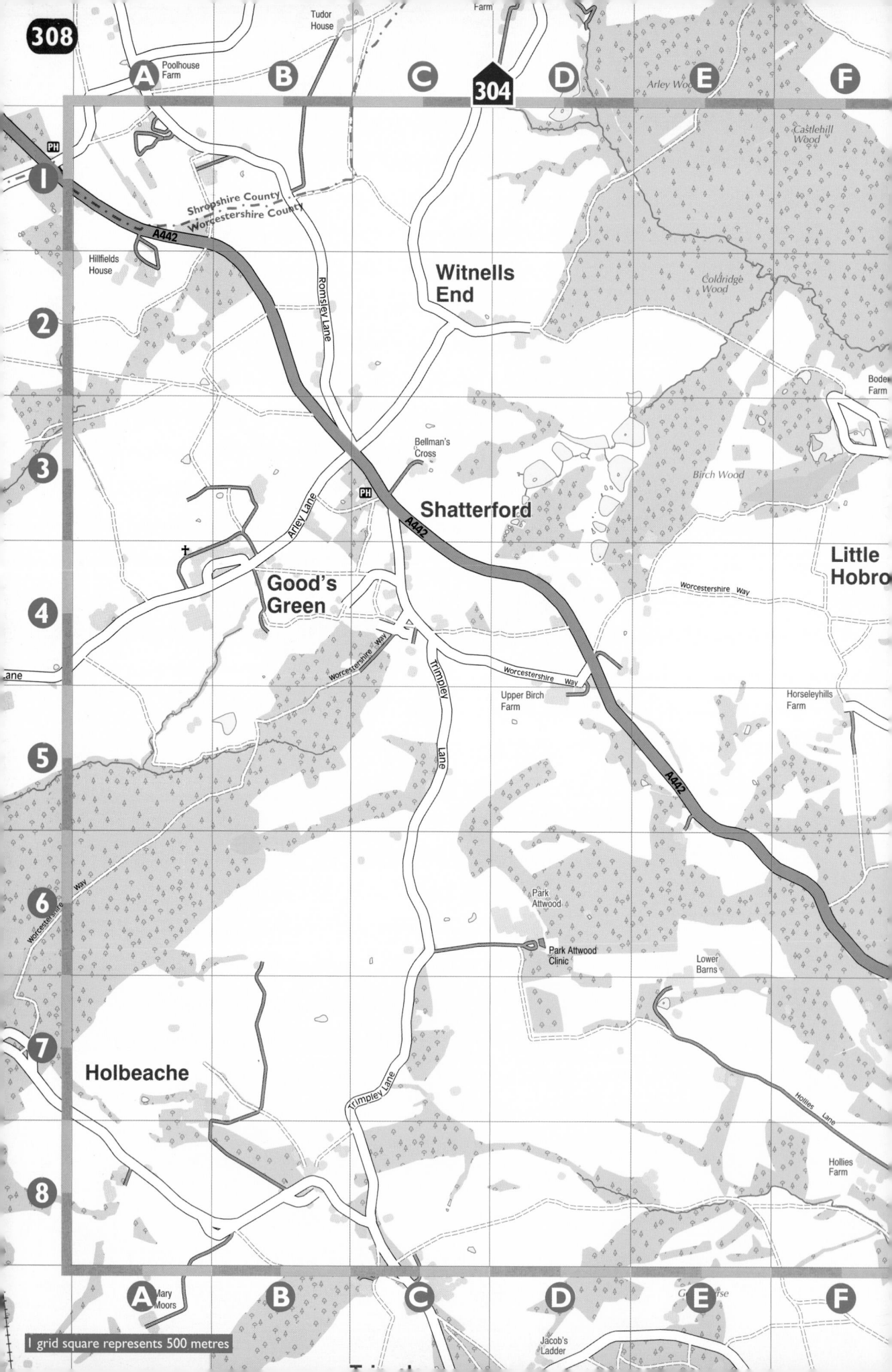

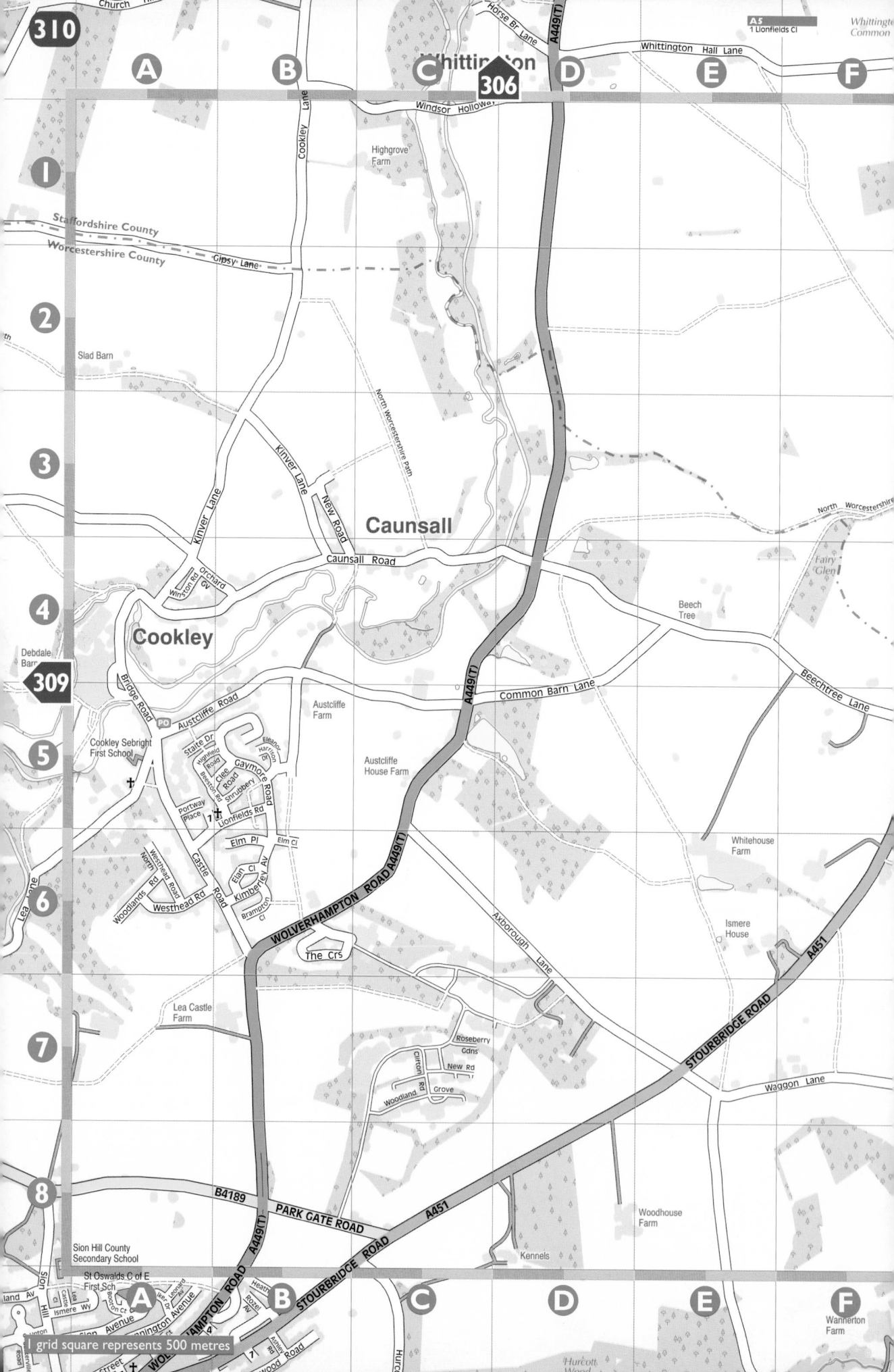

Name	Page	Grid
Abbey Green	43	K2
Abbey Hulton	70	C5
Abbots Bromley	180	A4
Acres Nook	53	G3
Acton	99	K3
Acton Trussell	212	B1
Adbaston	150	C6
Adderley Green	86	D4
Admaston	179	G7
Albrighton	260	F4
Alder Moor	165	M7
Aldershawe	253	L7
The Alders	273	L4
Aldridge	285	G4
Alkmonton	129	J1
Allimore Green	191	K7
Almington	113	J8
Alrewas	219	L7
Alsager	37	H7
Alsagers Bank	66	F5
Alsop en le Dale	49	L7
Alstonefield	48	E6
Alton	107	M1
Alvecote	275	K4
Amblecote	307	M3
Amerton	158	A6
Amington	11	M6
Anslow	184	C3
Anslow Gate	183	L3
Anslow Lees	184	D5
Apedale	67	G3
Apeton	209	H1
Armitage	216	E6
Armsdale	133	K5
Armshead	71	H5
Ash Bank	70	F8
Ashbourne	79	K8
Ashley	115	H5
Ashley Dale	115	G5
Ashley Heath	114	F7
Ashmore Lake	282	B6
Ashmore Park	281	M1
Ashwood	302	E5
Aspley	135	H3
Aston	97	G3
Aston	146	F6
Aston	173	L7
Aston-By-Stone	138	C6
Austrey	259	M8
Back o'th' Brook	60	F5
Baddeley Edge	55	K8
Baddeley Green	55	G7
Bagnall	55	M8
Balance Hill	144	B4
Baldwin's Gate	98	C6
Ball Green	54	D4
Ball Haye Green	43	M3
Balterley	65	J1
Balterley Green	50	B8
Balterley Heath	65	G1
The Bank	39	H3
Bank Top	54	B7
Barlaston	101	L8
Barnfields	43	K7
Barr Common	285	J7
Barrowhill	108	F4
Barthomley	50	D5
Barton Gate	202	B7
Barton Green	220	C2
Barton Turn	221	H1
Barton-under-Needwood	220	B1
Basford	68	C8
Basford Green	58	A6
Baswich	194	D1
Beaconside	5	L2
Beam Hill	185	G1
Beamhurst	125	H4
Beamhurst Lane	125	J6
Beasley	67	M3
Bednall	212	F2
Bednall Head	213	G2
Beechcliff	100	D8
Beffcote	189	M7
Belgrave	290	E1
Bemersley Green	40	D8
Bentilee	86	E1
Bentley	282	D7
The Bents	124	B8
Berry Hill	86	B1
Betley	65	G4
Betley Common	64	E4
Betton	113	G4
Bickford	228	C1
Biddulph	40	B3
Biddulph Moor	41	H1
Biggin	35	J7
Bignall End	51	M7
Bilbrook	263	J6
Billington	192	C4
Birchall	44	A7
Birch Cross	162	C1
Birchendale	107	G8
Birchills	283	K7
Birchmoor	291	L3
Bishop's Offley	150	F2
Bishop's Wood	244	F2
Bishton	197	G4
Bitterscote	10	B8
Blackbrook	97	J8
Blackfords	231	M7
Blackshaw Moor	30	E6
Blackwood Hill	41	M6
Blakedown	311	J8
Blakeley	298	A5
Blakeley Lane	72	C8
Blakenall Heath	283	J2
Blakenhall	64	A7
Blakenhall	295	H3
Blakeshall	309	L3
Blithbury	198	F5
Blore	77	M3
Blore	114	A8
Bloreheath	113	K7
Blount's Green	144	A5
Bloxwich	283	G1
Blundies	301	L7
Blurton	101	M1
Blymhill	226	A5
Blymhill Lawn	226	C6
Blythe Bridge	103	L3
Blythe Marsh	104	B3
The Blythe	159	L5
Bobbington	296	A8
Bolehall	10	F4
Boley Park	254	F3
Bond End	219	G1
Bonehill	289	L1
Boney Hay	252	B1
Boningale	261	G8
Boon Hill	51	M8
Booth	159	L7
Boothen	85	G6
Borough Park	274	B3
Boscomoor	229	L2
Bosley	18	D2
Bottom House	59	L4
Boundary	88	E8
Bourne Vale	285	J7
Bowers	117	H6
Boylestone	129	J6
Boylestonfield	129	L5
Braddocks Hay	40	F2
Bradeley	54	C7
Bradley	210	C2
Bradley in the Moors	107	J3
Bradmore	294	E2
Bradnop	44	E7
Bradshaw	42	E6
Bradwell	68	C3
The Brampton	68	C8
Bramshall	143	J3
Branston	203	L3
The Bratch	297	M2
Brazenhill	191	M3
Brereton	216	A4
Brereton Cross	216	D7
Breretonhill	216	B6
Bretby	187	H6
Brewood	246	E3
Bridgetown	249	K3
Brindley Ford	54	B1
Brineton	225	M2
Brinsford	264	D3
Broad Heath	172	C2
Broad Meadow	67	L4
Broad Oak	300	A4
Brockton	135	H6
Brocton	195	J6
Bromley Wood	180	C5
Bromstead Common	207	L1
Bromstead Heath	207	L2
Brookhouses	89	G7
Broomyshaw	75	J2
Broughton	133	K2
Brown Edge	55	G2
Brownhills	112	C5
Brownhills	269	G2
Brown Lees	40	A5
Brund	33	L3
Bucknall	70	B6
Buckpool	303	M8
Buddileigh	64	F3
Burlington	224	E7
Burnhill Green	276	B4
Burntwood	252	A3
Burntwood Green	252	D4
Burslem	69	G2
Burston	156	C1
Burton Manor	193	K4
Burton upon Trent	7	K5
Burybank	119	H6
Bushbury	264	E7
Butter Bank	173	H7
Butters Green	52	A8
Butterton	46	E4
Butterton	99	K1
Butt Lane	52	C1
Caldwell	222	F3
Calf Heath	247	M3
Callingwood	183	K6
Calton	76	E1
Cannock	231	J7
Cannock Wood	233	L5
Carroway Head	288	B6
Castlecroft	294	A2
Castle Gresley	223	L1
Castletown	4	A5
Cats Edge	56	D4
Catshill	269	G4
Cat's Hill Cross	135	K8
Cauldon	76	A3
Caunsall	310	C3
Caverswall	87	M8
Cellarhead	71	L7
Chadsmoor	231	L6
Chadwell	225	G1
Chapel Chorlton	116	F2
Charnes	133	M2
Chase Terrace	251	L2
Chasetown	251	M4
Chatcull	116	D8
Chatterley	53	H7
Cheadle	89	M7
Cheadle Park	89	K6
Chebsey	153	L4
Checkley	80	D1
Checkley	124	B2
Checkley Green	80	B2
Cheddleton	57	J5
Cheddleton Heath	57	L3
Chell Heath	54	A5
Cheslyn Hay	249	K7
Chestall	234	A4
Chesterfield	270	E2
Chesterton	67	K3
Cheswardine	149	G2
Chetwynd Aston	206	A2
Chilcote	241	M7
Chipnall	132	A2
Chorlton	64	A1
Churchbridge	249	M5
Church Eaton	209	H3
Church Hill	232	D5
Churchill	311	J7
Church Lawton	38	B1
Church Leigh	124	B6
Church Mayfield	94	D4
Churnet Grange	57	L4
Cinder Hill	299	M1
Claregate	279	K4
Clayhanger	268	D4
Clay Mills	167	G7
Clayton	84	C5
Clifton	94	E4
Clifton Campville	240	F8
Cloud Side	18	B7
Clough Hall	52	F2
Coalpit Hill	52	C2
Coal Pool	283	M5
Cobridge	69	J3
Codsall	262	F6
Codsall Wood	262	B3
Cokhay Green	187	G1
Coldeaton	49	H4
Coldham	245	J4
Coldmeece	136	D4
Cold Well	234	B5
Colshaw	15	L6
Colton	198	A4
Colton Hills	295	G7
Colwich	196	E3
Comberford	256	D7
Combridge	126	C2
Compton	95	K1
Compton	279	K8
Compton	305	H4
Congleton Edge	26	C5
Congreve	229	H3
Consall	72	D4
Cookley	310	A4
Cookshill	87	K3
Coombesdale	98	E8
Copmere End	151	L3
Coppenhall	193	H6
Cornhill	54	D5
Cotes	118	A8
Cotes Heath	117	L7
Coton	140	A5
Coton	190	A5
Coton	273	J4
Coton Clanford	173	C6
Coton Hayes	141	G4
Coton Hill	140	E5
Coton in the Clay	163	M5
Coton in the Elms	222	D7
Coton Park	223	J2
Cotonwood	189	L4
Cotton	91	K2
Cotwalton	120	E8
Coven	264	B1
Coven Heath	264	C4
Coven Lawn	264	A2
Cowley	190	E6
Coxgreen	304	F1
Crackley	67	K1
Crackleybank	224	A7
Cracow Moss	65	H6
Crakemarsh	126	B4
Cranberry	117	K5
Crateford	247	H3
Craythorn	166	D8
Creighton	125	M5
Cresswell	104	C7
Cresswell	174	A2
Creswell Green	234	E8
Crossgate	121	K3
Cross Green	264	D1
Cross Heath	67	M7
Crowdecote	24	E3
Croxall	238	F2
Croxden	107	J6
Croxton	134	A5
Croxtonbank	134	B4
Cubley Common	110	E7
Curborough	236	D5
Dagdale	143	G1
Dales Green	39	J5
Dam Mill	279	H1
Danebridge	20	B3
Dane in Shaw	26	C1
Dapple Heath	178	F1
Darley Moor	110	F2
Darnford	9	M7
Daw End	284	B5
Day Green	36	F2
Dayhills	139	M4
Deadman's Green	124	D3
Denford	56	E2
Denstone	108	C4
Derrington	192	E1
Dilhorne	88	D6
Dimsdale	68	A5
Dods Leigh	123	L8
Dogingtree Estate	231	K2
Doley	149	L2
Donington	260	F4
Dordon	291	M5
Dorrington	96	B3
Dosthill	290	B5
Doveridge	145	G2
Doxey	174	A6
Drakelow	309	G5
Draycott	296	A4
Draycott in the Clay	163	K6
Draycott in the Moors	104	D5
Drayton Bassett	289	K5
Dresden	102	B1
Drointon	159	H8
Druids Heath	285	J1
Dudley's Fields	282	F2
Dunkirk	52	A4
Dunsley	306	C6
Dunstal	179	M1
Dunstall	202	C4
Dunstall Hill	280	B5
Dunston	211	L2
Dunston Heath	211	J3
Dunwood	42	C7
Earl Sterndale	17	J7
Eccleshall	152	F4
Ecton	47	K1
Edge Hill	291	J6
Edial	252	E4
Edingale	239	K5
Edlaston	95	H8
Efflinch	220	D3
Egginton	167	J5
Egginton Common	167	J3
Elford	238	D8
Ellastone	93	H7
Ellenhall	172	A1
Elmhurst	236	A5
Endon	55	M3
Endon Bank	55	L2
Englesea-brook	50	A6
Enson	156	B4
Enville	301	K8
Essington	265	M7
Etchinghill	197	H8
Etruria	68	F7
Ettingshall	295	M5
Ettingshall Park	295	K7
Fairfield	309	H7
Fairoak	133	K4
Farewell	235	G6
Far Hoarcross	181	L8
Farley	91	K5
Fauld	164	C5
Fawfieldhead	23	L6
Fazeley	290	A1
Featherstone	265	J3
Fegg Hayes	54	B3
Fenny Bentley	79	H1
Fenton	85	M4
Fenton Low	85	L3
Field	142	B3
Finney Green	82	C1
Fisherwick	256	B5
Fishley	267	J6
Five Ways	311	G5
Flash	15	H7
Florence	102	D1
Fole	124	E3
Footherley	270	E8
Ford	60	C1
Ford Green	54	E8
Fordhouses	264	B7
Forebridge	5	G8
Forsbrook	104	B2
Forton	188	A3
Foston	147	K5
Four Ashes	247	J4
Four Ashes	300	E1
Four Crosses	248	D3
Four Oaks	286	E2
Foxley	51	K3
Foxt	74	D4
Fradley	237	L3
Fradley Junction	237	G2
Fradswell	141	H8
Fradswell Heath	141	J5
Freasley	291	J6
Freehay	105	M3
Friden	35	M4
Froghall	74	A6
Fulford	121	L1
Gailey	229	H8
Gailey Wharf	229	M8
Gallows Green	107	K2
Garmelow	151	K6
Garshall Green	140	D2
Gatacre Park	300	C3
Gayton	157	L4
Gentleshaw	234	A6
Gerrard's Bromley	115	G3
Giggetty	297	L5
Gillow Heath	26	B8
Gillway	274	A3
Glascote	11	G8
Glascote Heath	11	L9
Glutton Bridge	17	H8
Gnosall	190	F3
Gnosall Heath	190	D5
Godleybrook	88	C4
Godstone	141	L1
Goldenhill	53	H4
Goldstone	148	D5
Goldthorn Park	295	K6
Good's Green	308	B4
Goosemoor	208	C2
Goosemoor Green	234	C5
Gornalwood	299	J7
Gorsley Ley	252	C3
Gorstybirch	103	L5
Gorstyhil	105	M5
Gorsty Hill	161	L3
Goscote	283	M2
Gospel Ash	296	D7
Gospel End	298	F2
Gospel End Village	298	E2
Gothersley	302	E8
Gratwich	142	B6
Gravenhunger Moss	80	D8
Great Bridgeford	154	B8
Great Chatwell	207	K8
Great Chell	54	A3
Great Cubley	128	E1
Great Gate	107	G5
Great Haywood	177	J8
Great Moor	292	F1
Great Saredon	248	D4
Great Wyrley	250	A7
Greenhead	72	F8
Green Heath	232	A3
Greensforge	302	D4
Grindley	159	K3
Grindon	47	H3
Gunstone	263	G4
Hademore	256	B5
Hadley End	163	H8
Hales	131	M2
Hales Green	111	H3
Halfpenny Green	296	D6
Hall End	291	M5
Hall Green	38	E5
Halmer End	66	C2
Hammerwich	252	D6
Hamstall Ridware	199	L8
Hanchurch	100	B3
The Handfords	175	H8
Handsacre	217	L8
Hanford	84	D4
Hanley	2	D3
Hansley Cross	91	H4
Harden	283	M4
Hardings Booth	23	L3
Hardings Wood	38	C2
Hardwick	285	M2
Haregate	44	B3
Harehill	129	G4
Harlaston	239	H6
Harper's Gate	42	F4
Harriseahead	39	L2
Hartington	34	D3
Hartley Green	157	L5
Hartsgreen	304	D4
Hartshill	84	C2
Hartwell	102	D1
Hassall	36	E4
Hatherton	248	B3
Hatton	165	J5
Haughton	191	M4
Haunton	240	E6
Hawks Green	250	F1
Hawthorns	82	A4
Hayes	33	M4
Hayfield Hill	233	H4
Hazelslade	252	E1
Hazles	73	L3
Hazlescross	73	J4
Heathcote	35	K2
Heath End	283	K1
Heath Hayes	250	F2
Heath Hill	224	B6
The Heath	144	E4
Heathton	296	C6
Heath Town	281	L8
Heatley	160	C5
Heaton	19	H7
Hednesford	232	B4
Hem Heath	101	K1
Heron Cross	85	H6
Highbridge	268	E4
High Carr	52	F6
Highfields	193	H2
High Heath	268	E2
Highlanes	134	E6
High Offley	170	A5
High Onn	208	E2
High Onn Wharf	208	E1
High Town	231	H5
Highwood	144	C2
Hilderstone	139	J3
Hill	287	G1
Hill Hook	286	D1
Hilliard's Cross	237	K5
Hill Ridware	217	J3
Hill Somersal	128	B1
Hill Top	246	E6
Hill Wood	287	G3
Hilton	270	B1
Himley	298	C7
Hindlow	17	H1
Hinksford	302	F6
Hinstock	148	A8
Hints	272	E6
Hixon	177	K4
Hoar Cross	181	K6
Hobble End	267	J2
Hockley	290	B2
Hodgefield	41	J8
Hoften's Cross	75	H1
Holbeache	308	A2
The Hollands	27	M4
Hollies Common	190	C3
Hollington	107	H6
Hollins	41	M5
Hollins	52	D5
Hollins	73	L3
Hollinsclough	16	B2
Holly Bank	269	J5
Hollybush	85	K7
Holmcroft	174	A2
Holt Hill	181	J2
Hookgate	114	F6
Hope	48	D5
Hopedale	48	C5
Hopton	175	H5
Hopton Heath	175	H4
Hopwas	273	J7
Horninglow	185	J2
Horse Bridge	57	L2
Horsebrook	228	B3
Horton	42	E6
Huddlesford	255	L2
Hulme	87	G1
Hulme End	33	M3
Huntington	231	H3
Huntley	105	J4
Hurst Hill	299	M4
Hyde Lea	193	H3
Ilam	62	A2
Ingestre	176	D7
Ipstones	73	L4
Ireland's Cross	96	D2
Islington	188	A5
Iverley	311	K2
Jack Hayes	70	F2
Jugbank	115	H6
Keele	82	F5
Kerry Hill	70	F5
Kettlebrook	10	C8
Kiddemore Green	245	J3
Kidsgrove	38	C3
King's Bromley	218	C4
Kingsford	309	H2
Kingsley	73	L1
Kingsley Holt	89	M1
Kingsley Moor	89	H7
Kingslow	276	C8
Kingstone	160	D6
Kingswinford	303	M4
Kingswood Common	261	J6
Kinver	305	J2
Knenhall	120	E3
Knightley	171	H4
Knightley Dale	171	G2
Knighton	96	C5

Place	Page	Grid	Place	Page	Grid
nighton	149	M8	Miles Green	66	E2
notbury	14	F5	Milford	195	H3
nowl Bank	65	L3	Mildale	48	F8
nowl Wall	100	B7	Mill Green	286	A3
nutton	67	L8	Millmeece	135	M3
nypersley	40	E5	Milton	70	A1
he Laches	247	M7	Milwich	140	C5
andywood	249	L8	Mitton	210	C7
ane Ends	40	A8	Mixon	45	L3
ane Green	263	J7	Mobberley	105	K3
ane Head	282	C4	Moddershall	120	F5
aney Green	249	C8	Moneystone	91	G1
apley	228	B4	Moor Green	104	A2
ask Edge	41	K3	Moreton	163	H2
awnhead	171	K4	Moreton	207	J3
awns Wood	303	H7	Morrey	200	D8
awton-gate	37	M6	Morridge Side	59	G1
awton Heath	37	L5	Morrilow Heath	122	E6
awton Heath End	37	K4	Mossgate	121	K3
eadendale	102	F8	Mossley	26	B3
ea Heath	178	B1	Moss Pit	193	M5
eamonsley	8	A5	Mount Pleasant	39	H4
eamore	283	G4	Mount Pleasant	85	K5
eek	43	L4	Mount Pleasant	187	L1
eekbrook	57	L2	Mount Pleasant	223	K3
eighswood	285	G2	Mow Cop	39	J3
evedale	210	F4	Mucklestone	114	C3
eycett	66	D8	Muckley Corner	253	C6
eys	74	C7	Napley	113	M2
ichfield	8	C3	Napley Heath	114	A1
ichfield	253	M1	Needwood	183	H5
ight Oaks	70	E1	Netherland Green	144	E8
ightwood	89	M8	Netherseal	241	M3
ightwood	102	E3	Nether Stowe	236	D8
ightwood	148	A3	Nethertown	217	M2
ilyhurst	224	A3	Newbolds	281	G4
inton	223	J4	Newborough	181	L2
inton Heath	223	L4	Newbridge	279	K7
ipley	132	E8	Newcastle-under-Lyme	83	K1
ittle Aston	286	C5	Newchapel	39	L4
ittle Bloxwich	267	K7	Newchurch	182	A7
ittle Bridgeford	154	A7	Newfield	53	J5
ittle Chell	53	M5	Newhall	205	L4
ittle Cubley	128	E2	Newhaven	35	L5
ittle Hay	287	J1	New Invention	282	C2
ittle Haywood	196	C2	Newlands	198	E2
ittle Heath	211	G2	Newpool	40	A4
ittle Hobro	308	F4	Newstead	101	L4
ittle Ingestre	176	F4	New Street	60	B5
ittle Madeley	81	M3	Newton	178	D3
ittle Norton	251	H8	Newton Hurst	179	G2
ittle Onn	208	F6	Newton Regis	259	K7
ittle Saredon	248	D7	Newton Solney	186	E2
ittle Soudley	148	F5	Newtown	23	J8
ittle Stoke	138	D4	Newtown	27	H4
ittle Sugnall	134	L6	New Town	252	B8
ittlewood	249	K6	Newtown	267	G5
ittleworth	5	G5	Nick i'th' Hill	26	A6
ittleworth	232	F6	Norbury	109	K1
Little Wyrley	267	K2	Norbury	170	B7
Lockleywood	148	A5	Norbury Junction	170	C8
Loggerheads	114	E6	Normacot	102	E1
London Fields	299	L8	Northwood	3	H4
Longbridge Hayes	53	L8	Northwood	84	D8
Long Common	296	B2	Norton	307	L8
Long Compton	172	C8	Norton Bridge	153	M1
Longdon	235	G1	Norton Canes	250	E5
Longdon Green	235	G2	Norton East	251	G4
Longnor	24	A4	Norton Green	54	F5
Longnor	227	L1	Norton Green	250	E4
Longport	68	D2	Norton in Hales	113	J1
Longridge	211	H6	Norton-in-the-Moors	54	E7
Longsdon	42	F6	Nurton	277	L7
Longshaw	91	K3	Nurton Hill	277	L6
Longton	85	M6	Oakamoor	90	F4
Lowe Hill	44	A6	Oaken	262	C8
Lower Elkstone	46	D1	Oakhanger	50	D1
Lower Ellastone	93	J8	Oak Hill	84	F5
Lower Gornal	299	L6	Oakley	113	J4
Lower Green	247	H7	Oaks Green	146	C3
Lower Hatton	117	K4	Offleyhay	151	K3
Lower Knightley	171	J6	Offleymarsh	151	G3
Lower Leigh	123	M6	Offleyrock	151	H2
Lower Nobut	124	F8	Old Fallings	280	F3
Lower Penn	293	M5	Oldfallow	231	J7
Lower Stonnall	270	A4	Oldfurnace	90	E6
Lower Tean	106	A8	Old Perton	278	C7
Low Hill	280	D3	Olive Green	200	B8
Loxley Green	143	K8	Onecote	45	L7
Lullington	240	E3	Onneley	80	F8
Lupin	219	G5	Orgreave	219	J5
Lynn	207	H6	Orslow	207	L7
Lynn	269	M5	Orton	293	M7
Madeley	81	L4	Orton Hill	294	A8
Madeley Heath	82	A2	Otherton	229	M5
Maer	116	C1	Oulton	120	C6
Mapleton	78	F6	Oulton	189	H1
Marchington	145	L8	Oultoncross	120	B8
Marchington Woodlands	162	A4	Oulton Grange	120	A6
Market Drayton	130	D2	Oulton Heath	120	B4
Marsh Green	26	D8	Ounsdale	297	M4
The Marsh	172	B1	Outlands	150	D1
Marston	155	K6	Outwoods	185	H4
Marston	226	F1	Outwoods	207	G2
Marston Montgomery	127	M2	Overley	219	K6
Marston on Dove	166	B2	Overmoor	72	B7
Martin Hill	78	A5	Overton	124	F1
Mavesyn Ridware	217	G4	Owen's Bank	165	G5
May Bank	68	C6	Oxbarn	294	E3
Mayfield	94	C3	Oxford	54	B2
Meaford	119	J7	Oxley	280	B2
Meerbrook	29	M4	Packmoor	54	A1
Meir	103	H1	Painleyhill	142	D2
Meir Hay	86	E6	Palmer Moor	145	L3
Meir Heath	102	F6	Palmers Cross	279	H2
Mere Green	287	H7	Park End	51	G6
Merelake	52	A2	Parkfield	295	M5
Meretown	188	B4	Parkgate	92	F5
Merridale	279	L8	Park Lane	246	C8
Merry Hill	294	C3	Parkside	174	C1
Middle Cliff	44	C8	Park Village	280	F5
Middle Hill	249	G6	Pasford	276	E7
Middle Madeley	81	M3	Pasturefields	177	G3
Middle Mayfield	94	B3	Pattingham	277	K7
Middleport	68	D3	Pave Lane	206	B4
Middleton Green	123	G7	Pelsall	268	B7
Mile Oak	289	K1	Pelsall Wood	267	M5
			Pendeford	263	L8

Place	Page	Grid	Place	Page	Grid
Penkhull	84	E4	Slindon	135	K4
Penkridge	230	A2	Slitting Mill	215	J3
Penn	294	E4	Smallrice	139	L6
Perry Crofts	274	C3	Smallthorne	54	D8
Pershall	152	B2	Smestow	297	J6
Perton	278	E6	Smith's Green	50	C3
Pickstock	168	B7	Snelston	94	B7
Pillaton	230	C3	Snelston Common	110	C2
Pilsbury	25	H7	Snelston Hall	94	D7
Pipe Gate	96	D4	Sneyd Green	69	L3
Pipehill	253	H5	Somerford	246	F4
Pipe Ridware	217	J2	Somersal Herbert	127	M7
Pitts Hill	53	M5	Soudley	149	G4
Plardiwick	190	B4	Spath	126	B7
Podmore	116	A6	Spitalhill	95	J3
Poolend	43	H1	Springfield	13	K2
Poolfold	26	F6	Springfields	84	E5
Porthill	68	C4	Springhill	266	D5
Portobello	281	L8	Springhill	269	K3
The Potteries	85	L2	Spring Hill	294	C6
Potter Somersal	128	A5	Stableford	99	G8
Prestwood	108	E1	Stadmorslow	40	A7
Prestwood	306	E1	Stafford	4	F3
Prospect Village	233	H6	Stakenbridge	311	K7
Pye Green	231	M1	Stallington	103	K7
Quarry Heath	230	C2	Standeford	247	J6
Quarry Hill	291	G4	Standon	117	H8
Queensville	5	K9	Stanfield	54	A7
Quixhill	108	E3	Stanhope Brentby	205	M1
Radmore Wood	180	C3	Stanley	56	A5
Radway Green	50	F1	Stanley Moor	55	L6
Rake End	216	F1	Stanlow	276	B7
Rakes Dale	107	J1	Stanshope	62	C1
Rakeway	106	A1	Stanton	93	K1
Ramshorn	92	A3	Stapenhill	204	F2
Rangemore	183	J8	Sterndale Moor	17	L4
Ranton	172	C5	Stockton	206	D4
Ranton Green	172	B7	Stockton Brook	55	J5
Ravenscliffe	53	G5	Stockwell End	279	J5
Ravenshall	65	G6	Stockwell Heath	198	A2
Rawnsley	233	H5	Stoke	84	F2
Red Bull	38	E7	Stoke-on-Trent	2	E7
Red Bull	113	J7	Stone	138	B2
Redhill	152	B5	Stonefield	119	M8
Red Street	52	E7	Stone Heath	122	C7
Renshaw Wood	261	L1	Stonehouses	104	C4
Rickerscote	193	M4	Stoneydelph	291	H1
Ridgeway	54	E2	Stonnall	269	K6
Rileyhill	218	B7	Stonywell	235	G5
Risingbrook	193	M3	Stourbridge	307	K6
Robin Hill	41	G2	Stourton	306	F3
Rocester	108	F7	Stowe	254	C1
Roche Grange	20	F7	Stowe-by-Chartley	158	C7
Rock End	40	F4	The Straits	299	H5
Rodbaston	229	K6	Stramshall	125	M6
Rode Heath	37	M2	Streethay	237	G8
Rolleston on Dove	166	C6	Streetly	286	B8
Romsley	304	A7	Stretton	185	L2
The Rookery	39	J7	Stretton	228	D6
Rosliston	222	C4	Stubber's Green	284	E2
Roston	109	K3	Stubwood	108	C6
Roston Common	110	B4	Sturbridge	135	M8
Rough Close	102	F7	Sudbury	146	E6
Roughcote	87	J4	Sugnall	134	C8
Rough Hay	184	A5	Summerhill	269	L1
Roughley	287	J7	Sutton	130	C6
The Rowe	117	J1	Sutton	188	D1
Rowley Park	4	D9	Swadlincote	205	M6
Rownall	71	L2	Swindon	297	M8
Rudge	292	A3	Swinscoe	77	M5
Rudyard	42	D2	Swynnerton	118	B6
Rugeley	215	K2	Talke	52	C3
Ruiton	299	K6	Talke Pits	52	E5
Rumer Hill	249	L2	Tamworth	11	J8
Rushall	284	C3	Tatenhill	203	G1
Rushton Spencer	28	A1	Tatenhill Common	202	F1
Ryecroft Gate	28	B2	Teanford	105	K4
St Helena	291	M1	Tettenhall	279	J5
Salt	156	F6	Tettenhall Wood	279	K6
Sandborough	200	A7	Thorncliff	30	E8
Sandfields	8	D8	Thornes	269	L7
Sandford Hill	86	C5	Thorpe	78	D1
Sandon	156	C2	Thorpe Constantine	258	F4
Sandonbank	156	B5	Threapwood	90	E8
Sandyford	53	L4	Threelows	91	L1
Sapperton	147	J1	Thurlwood	37	L2
Saverley Green	104	A8	Thurvaston	127	L1
Scholar Green	38	D4	Tillington	174	C4
Scot Hay	66	F8	Tithebarn	107	M2
Scotlands	281	G2	Tittensor	119	H1
Scounslow Green	161	J2	Tixall	176	C8
Scropton	164	E1	The Toft	211	H1
Seabridge	83	M7	Tompkin	56	C7
Seckington	259	G7	Tong	243	K7
Sedgley	299	L2	Tong Forge	243	G5
Seighford	173	H4	Tong Norton	243	J5
Seisdon	292	F8	Toot Hill	107	K1
Shackerley	261	H1	Totmonslow	105	H6
Shaffalong	57	G5	Townend	121	M2
Shallowford	154	B3	Town Head	74	D3
Shareshill	248	D8	Townsend	70	C7
Sharpley Heath	122	A6	Trentham	101	G3
Shatterford	308	C3	Trent Vale	84	F7
Shawfield	32	D2	Trescott	293	J4
Shebdon	169	J2	Triangle	252	B6
Sheen	34	A3	Trinity Fields	174	B2
Shelfield	284	C2	Trysull	297	J1
Shelton	85	J1	Tuckhill	300	A5
Shelton under Harley	99	H6	Tunstall	53	J7
Shenstone	270	F5	Tunstall	150	E7
Shenstone Woodend	287	G1	Tuppenhurst	217	K6
Sherriffhales	224	C5	Turnhurst	53	M2
Shifnal	242	A6	Tutbury	165	G4
Shire Oak	268	F4	Two Gates	290	C2
Shire Oak Hill	269	H5	Ubberley	86	D1
Shirleywich	176	F2	Upper Aston	296	A1
Shobnall	184	F2	Upper Cotton	75	G6
Short Heath	282	D4	Upper Elkstone	32	E7
Shraleybrook	66	A2	Upper Ellastone	93	H6
The Shruggs	156	C1	Upper Gornal	299	L4
Shut Heath	191	L2	Upper Hatton	117	L2
Shutt Green	246	A2	Upper Hulme	30	E3
Shuttington	275	L3	Upper Landywood	266	E3
Sideway	85	H7	Upper Leigh	123	L5
Sidway	97	J6	Upper Longdon	234	C1
Silverdale	83	G1	Upper Nobut	124	E5
Six Ashes	300	C4	Upper Tean	105	L6
Slade Heath	247	L8	Uttoxeter	144	B1

Place	Page	Grid
Vigo	268	F8
The Village	303	L3
Waggersley	118	C2
Wain Lee	39	M6
Waldley	127	L3
Walford	135	H2
Wall	253	K8
Wall Heath	303	H2
Wallington Heath	267	G7
Walsall	284	B8
Walsall Wood	268	F6
Walton	137	L3
Walton	153	L6
Walton-on-the-Hill	194	F5
Walton-on-Trent	221	J1
Warslow	33	H8
Warstone	266	B2
Washerwall	71	G6
Waterfall	61	G7
Waterhouses	76	A1
Watford Gap	286	F3
Weaverslake	200	F7
Wednesfield	281	K4
Weeford	272	A6
Weeping Cross	194	D3
Wereton	66	C1
Wergs	278	F4
Werrington	71	K6
West Broughton	145	M3
West Chadsmoor	231	M4
Westcroft	265	H7
Western Downs	193	G2
West Hill	232	A4
Westlands	83	M4
Weston	157	L8
Weston Coyney	87	G5
Weston Heath	224	F3
Weston Jones	169	J5
Weston Under Lizard	225	L7
Wetley Rocks	72	B3
Wetmore	185	M5
Wetton	47	M7
Wetwood	133	L3
Whateley	290	E7
Wheaton Aston	227	G4
Wheelock Heath	36	A2
Whiston	74	D7
Whiston	228	E1
Whiston Cross	260	C7
Whiston Eaves	90	E1
Whitecross	191	K1
Whitehill	39	J8
Whitehurst	88	C7
Whitemore	26	D4
Whitfield	54	D3
Whitgreave	154	F5
Whitley Heath	171	G1
Whitmore	99	G4
Whittington	134	B2
Whittington	255	L5
Whittington	306	C8
Wigginstall	33	J4
Wigginton	257	H8
Wightwick	293	M1
Wildwood	194	B4
Willenhall	282	B7
Willslock	144	A2
Wilnecote	290	F3
Wimblebury	232	F7
Wincle	19	M2
Winkhill	60	C7
Winnington	114	B2
Winnothdale	106	B4
Winshill	186	A6
Withington	124	B7
Withystakes	71	L5
Witnells End	308	C2
Wollaston	307	L4
Wolstanton	68	D5
Wolverhampton	13	J4
Wolverley	309	L6
Wombourne	297	K4
Woodcock Heath	160	A2
Woodcote	206	D6
Wood Eaton	209	G2
Woodend	183	H1
Wood End	281	J3
Wood Gate	163	J5
Wood Hayes	281	H1
Woodhouse Green	18	C8
Woodhouses	201	J8
Woodhouses	253	G3
Wood Lane	67	G1
Woodlane	148	A6
Woodlane	201	G4
Woodmill	200	F4
Woodseaves	130	E8
Woodseaves	170	D2
Woodsetton	299	L3
Woollaston	209	L8
Woore	96	C1
Wootton	92	E3
Wootton	152	D7
Woottons	107	L8
Wordsley	303	L7
Wrinehill	65	G7
Wyaston	111	K1
Wychnor	220	B1
Wychnor Bridges	220	C5
Yarlet	155	H4
Yarnfield	136	F4
Yeaveley	111	K5
Yoxall	200	F8

USING THE STREET INDEX

Street names are listed alphabetically. Each street name is followed by its postal town or area locality, the Postcode District, the page number, and the reference to the square in which the name is found

Example: **Abberley** *TAM/AM/WIL* B77 .... **275** J8 1

Some entries are followed by a number in a blue box. This number indicates the location of the street within the referenced grid square. The full street name is listed at the side of the map page

GENERAL ABBREVIATIONS

- ACC ACCESS
- ALY ALLEY
- AP APPROACH
- AR ARCADE
- ASS ASSOCIATION
- AV AVENUE
- BCH BEACH
- BLDS BUILDINGS
- BND BEND
- BNK BANK
- BR BRIDGE
- BRK BROOK
- BTM BOTTOM
- BUS BUSINESS
- BVD BOULEVARD
- BY BYPASS
- CATH CATHEDRAL
- CEM CEMETERY
- CEN CENTRE
- CFT CROFT
- CH CHURCH
- CHA CHASE
- CHYD CHURCHYARD
- CIR CIRCLE
- CIRC CIRCUS
- CL CLOSE
- CLFS CLIFFS
- CMP CAMP
- CNR CORNER
- CO COUNTY
- COLL COLLEGE
- COM COMMON
- COMM COMMISSION
- CON CONVENT
- COT COTTAGE
- COTS COTTAGES
- CP CAPE
- CPS COPSE
- CR CREEK
- CREM CREMATORIUM
- CRS CRESCENT
- CSWY CAUSEWAY
- CT COURT
- CTRL CENTRAL
- CTS COURTS
- CTYD COURTYARD
- CUTT CUTTINGS
- CV COVE
- CYN CANYON
- DEPT DEPARTMENT
- DL DALE
- DM DAM
- DR DRIVE
- DRO DROVE
- DRY DRIVEWAY
- DWGS DWELLINGS
- E EAST
- EMB EMBANKMENT
- EMBY EMBASSY
- ESP ESPLANADE
- EST ESTATE
- EX EXCHANGE
- EXPY EXPRESSWAY
- EXT EXTENSION
- F/O FLYOVER
- FC FOOTBALL CLUB
- FK FORK
- FLD FIELD
- FLDS FIELDS
- FLS FALLS
- FLS FLATS
- FM FARM
- FT FORT
- FWY FREEWAY
- FY FERRY
- GA GATE
- GAL GALLERY
- GDN GARDEN
- GDNS GARDENS
- GLD GLADE
- GLN GLEN
- GN GREEN
- GND GROUND
- GRA GRANGE
- GRG GARAGE
- GT GREAT
- GTWY GATEWAY
- GV GROVE
- HGR HIGHER
- HL HILL
- HLS HILLS
- HO HOUSE
- HOL HOLLOW
- HOSP HOSPITAL
- HRB HARBOUR
- HTH HEATH
- HTS HEIGHTS
- HVN HAVEN
- HWY HIGHWAY
- IMP IMPERIAL
- IN INLET
- IND EST INDUSTRIAL ESTATE
- INF INFIRMARY
- INFO INFORMATION
- INT INTERCHANGE
- IS ISLAND
- JCT JUNCTION
- JTY JETTY
- KG KING
- KNL KNOLL
- L LAKE
- LA LANE
- LDG LODGE
- LGT LIGHT
- LK LOCK
- LKS LAKES
- LNDG LANDING
- LTL LITTLE
- LWR LOWER
- MAG MAGISTRATE
- MAN MANSIONS
- MD MEAD
- MDW MEADOWS
- MEM MEMORIAL
- MKT MARKET
- MKTS MARKETS
- ML MALL
- ML MILL
- MNR MANOR
- MS MEWS
- MSN MISSION
- MT MOUNT
- MTN MOUNTAIN
- MTS MOUNTAINS
- MUS MUSEUM
- MWY MOTORWAY
- N NORTH
- NE NORTH EAST
- NW NORTH WEST
- O/P OVERPASS
- OFF OFFICE
- ORCH ORCHARD
- OV OVAL
- PAL PALACE
- PAS PASSAGE
- PAV PAVILION
- PDE PARADE
- PH PUBLIC HOUSE
- PK PARK
- PKWY PARKWAY
- PL PLACE
- PLN PLAIN
- PLNS PLAINS
- PLZ PLAZA
- POL POLICE STATION
- PR PRINCE
- PREC PRECINCT
- PREP PREPARATORY
- PRIM PRIMARY
- PROM PROMENADE
- PRS PRINCESS
- PRT PORT
- PT POINT
- PTH PATH
- PZ PIAZZA
- QD QUADRANT
- QU QUEEN
- QY QUAY
- R RIVER
- RBT ROUNDABOUT
- RD ROAD
- RDG RIDGE
- REP REPUBLIC
- RES RESERVOIR
- RFC RUGBY FOOTBALL CLUB
- RI RISE
- RP RAMP
- RW ROW
- S SOUTH
- SCH SCHOOL
- SE SOUTH EAST
- SER SERVICE AREA
- SH SHORE
- SHOP SHOPPING
- SKWY SKYW
- SMT SUMM
- SOC SOCIE
- SP SP
- SPR SPRI
- SQ SQUA
- ST STRE
- STN STATI
- STR STREA
- STRD STRAN
- SW SOUTH WE
- TDG TRADI
- TER TERRA
- THWY THROUGHW
- TNL TUNN
- TOLL TOLLW
- TPK TURNPI
- TR TRA
- TRL TRA
- TWR TOW
- U/P UNDERPA
- UNI UNIVERSI
- UPR UPP
- V VA
- VA VALL
- VIAD VIADU
- VIL VIL
- VIS VIS
- VLG VILLA
- VLS VILL
- VW VIE
- W WE
- WD WOO
- WHF WHAR
- WK WA
- WKS WAL
- WLS WEL
- WY W
- YD YAR
- YHA YOUTH HOST

POSTCODE TOWNS AND AREA ABBREVIATIONS

- ALBTN Albrighton
- ALDR Aldridge
- ALS/KID Alsager/Kidsgrove
- ASHB Ashbourne
- ATHST Atherstone
- AUD/MAD/W Audlem/Madeley/Woore
- BARL Barlaston
- BDGNE Bridgnorth east
- BDMR/CCFT Bradmore/Castlecroft
- BEWD Bewdley
- BIDD Biddulph
- BILS/COS Bilston/Coseley
- BKHL/PFLD Blakenhall/Priestfield
- BKWL Bakewell
- BLOX/PEL Bloxwich/Pelsall
- BLYBR/FOR Blythe Bridge/Forsbrook
- BNTWD Burntwood
- BRWNH Brownhills
- BUCK/MIL Bucknall/Milton
- BURS/TUN Burslem/Tunstall
- BUT Burton upon Trent
- BUTN/AL/TUT Burton upon Trent north/ Alrewas/Tutbury
- BUX Buxton
- CDLE Cheadle (Staffs)
- CDSL Codsall
- CNCK/NC Cannock/Norton Canes
- CONG Congleton
- COVEN Coven
- CRTAM Central & Rural Tamworth
- CW/HAS Crewe/Haslington
- CW/SHV Crewe/Shavington
- DUDN Dudley north
- DUNHL/THL/PER Dunstall Hill/Tettenhall/Perton
- ECCH Eccleshall
- END/WER Endon/Werrington
- ETTPK/GDPK/PENN Ettingshall Park/ Goldthorn Park/Penn
- FOAKS/STRLY Four Oaks/Streetly
- GNOS Gnosall
- GTWY Great Wyrley
- HAG/WOL Hagley/Wollescote
- HAN Hanley
- HEDN Hednesford
- KGSWFD Kingswinford
- KIDD Kidderminster
- KIDDW Kidderminster west
- KINVER Kinver
- LEEK Leek
- LICH Lichfield
- LICHS Lichfield south
- LNGTN Longton
- MCFLDS Macclesfield south
- MGN/WHC Mere Green/ Whitehouse Common
- MKTDR Market Drayton
- MSHM Measham
- MTLK Matlock
- NANT Nantwich
- NEWUL Newcastle-under-Lyme
- NWPT Newport
- PENK Penkridge
- POL/KGSB/FAZ Polesworth/ Kingsbury/Fazeley
- RDERBYSW Rural Derby southwest
- RSTAF Rural Stafford
- RUGE Rugeley
- RUSH/SHEL Rushall/Shelfield
- SBCH Sandbach
- SEDG Sedgley
- SHHTH Short Heath
- SHIF Shifnal
- STAFN Stafford north
- STAFS Stafford south
- STOKE Stoke-on-Tre
- STONE Stor
- STPNHL/WNHL Stapenhill/Winsh
- STRBR Stourbridg
- SWAD Swadlinco
- TAM/AM/WIL Tamwort Amington/Wilneco
- UTXR Uttoxet
- WLNHL Willenha
- WMBN Wombourr
- WNSFLD Wednesfie
- WOLV Wolverhampto
- WOLVN Wolverhampton nor
- WSL Wals
- WSLW Walsall we

Aar - Ald

Index - streets

A

Aarons Dr *ALS/KID* ST7 **51** M8
Abberley *TAM/AM/WIL* B77 **275** J8 1
Abberley Rd *SEDG* DY3 **299** J6
Abbey Cl *PENK* ST19 **230** A2
UTXR ST14 **109** G7
Abbey Ct *BUCK/MIL* ST2 **70** B5
Abbey Dr *BLOX/PEL* WS3 **268** A5
RSTAF ST18 **196** D2
Abbeyfield Rd *WOLVN* WV10 **264** E6
Abbey Flds *RSTAF* ST18 **177** H8 1
Abbey Green Rd *LEEK* ST13 **43** K1
Abbey La *BUCK/MIL* ST2 **3** M4
Abbey Rd *BUCK/MIL* ST2 **3** M1
BUCK/MIL ST2 **70** B5
END/WER ST9 **72** A5
SEDG DY3 **299** J7
TAM/AM/WIL B77 **11** G8
UTXR ST14 **108** F7
Abbeyside *RSTAF* ST18 **172** C5
Abbey Sq *BLOX/PEL* WS3 **266** E8
Abbey St *BUCK/MIL* ST2 **3** M1
BUT DE14 **7** H8
HEDN WS12 **232** B3
NEWUL ST5 **83** J1
SEDG DY3 **299** J7
STONE ST15 **138** A2
Abbey Wy *MKTDR* TF9 **112** D8
Abbots Cl *RUSH/SHEL* WS4 **284** C4
Abbots Fld *CNCK/NC* WS11 **231** L5
Abbotsford Rd *LICHS* WS14 **9** K4
Abbots Pl *BUCK/MIL* ST2 **70** B4
Abbots Rd *BUCK/MIL* ST2 **70** B4
Abbots Wk *RUGE* WS15 **216** B5
STAFN ST16 **4** E1
Abbots Wy *BDMR/CCFT* WV3 **294** E1 1
NEWUL ST5 **84** B3
Abbott's Cl *CONG* CW12 **26** B2
Abbotts Dr *HAN* ST1 **69** L2
Abbotts Pl *BLOX/PEL* WS3 **283** K1
Abbott's Rd *LEEK* ST13 **44** A4
Abbotts St *BLOX/PEL* WS3 **267** K8
Abercorn St *STOKE* ST4 **85** M5 1
Aberford Cl *SHHTH* WV12 **282** D6
Aberford Gv *HAN* ST1 **3** H2
Abingdon Cl *WOLV* WV1 **281** H8 1
Abingdon Rd *ALBTN* WV7 **260** F2 1
BLOX/PEL WS3 **266** F8
WOLV WV1 **281** H8
Abingdon Wy *BLOX/PEL* WS3 **266** F8
STOKE ST4 **101** H3
Ablon Ct *PENK* ST19 **229** M3
Ablow St *BKHL/PFLD* WV2 **12** E8
Abnalls Cft *LICH* WS13 **8** A1
Abnalls La *LICH* WS13 **8** A1
Abney Av *ALBTN* WV7 **260** F5
Abney Dr *BILS/COS* WV14 **299** M1
Acacia Av *NEWUL* ST5 **67** L8
Acacia Crs *CDSL* WV8 **263** H7
Acacia Gdns *ALS/KID* ST7 **39** J7
Acacia Gv *HEDN* WS12 **232** F7
NEWUL ST5 **67** L8
Achilees Cl *GTWY* WS6 **266** F1
Achilles Wy *BUCK/MIL* ST2 **85** M1 1
Ackleton Gdns
BDMR/CCFT WV3 **294** F3
Acorn Cl *BNTWD* WS7 **252** A1 1
CNCK/NC WS11 **232** C8
GTWY WS6 **267** G1
MKTDR TF9 **114** D5
Acorn Gv *CDSL* WV8 **262** E8
STRBR DY8 **307** L1
Acorn Ri *LNGTN* ST3 **102** D2
Acorn Rd *WNSFLD* WV11 **282** A1
Acorn St *WLNHL* WV13 **282** C8 1
Acre Ri *SHHTH* WV12 **282** B5 1
Acres Nook Rd *BURS/TUN* ST6 **53** G3
Acreswood Rd *BURS/TUN* ST6 **54** B8
Acton Ct *RSTAF* ST18 **193** M8
Acton Dr *SEDG* DY3 **299** H7
Acton Hill Rd *STAFS* ST17 **194** B8
Acton St *HAN* ST1 **2** F1
Acton Wy *ALS/KID* ST7 **37** K4
Adams Av *BURS/TUN* ST6 **53** K5
Adams Gv *LEEK* ST13 **43** H6
Adamson Cl *CNCK/NC* WS11 **249** H1
Adams Rd *BDMR/CCFT* WV3 **294** C3
BRWNH WS8 **269** G5
Adams St *BUCK/MIL* ST2 **70** B1
NEWUL ST5 **68** C6
WSLW WS2 **283** K8
Adamthwaite Dr
BLYBR/FOR ST11 **103** K2
Ada Wrighton Cl
SHHTH WV12 **282** C3 1
Addenbrooke St
BLOX/PEL WS3 **283** J3
Adderley Pl *BARL* ST12 **101** M7
Adderley Rd *BURS/TUN* ST6 **54** E7
MKTDR TF9 **112** C7
Addie Rd *BUTN/AL/TUT* DE13 **185** H4
Addington Wy *LNGTN* ST3 **86** D5
Addison Cl *CNCK/NC* WS11 **231** L5 1
Addison Cft *SEDG* DY3 **299** G5
Addison Gv *WNSFLD* WV11 **281** H1
Addison Rd *BDMR/CCFT* WV3 **294** F2
Addison St *HAN* ST1 **2** F1
Adelaide Crs
STPNHL/WNHL DE15 **186** D8 1
Adelaide Dr *HEDN* WS12 **232** F7
Adelaide St *BURS/TUN* ST6 **69** G3
Adelaide Wk *BKHL/PFLD* WV2 **13** J8
Adey Rd *WNSFLD* WV11 **281** M2
Adkins St *BURS/TUN* ST6 **69** J3
Admiral Parker Dr *LICHS* WS14 **270** F5
Admirals Cl *SHIF* TF11 **242** A4
Admirals Wy *SHIF* TF11 **242** A4
Adonis Cl *CRTAM* B79 **10** E1
Adrian St *STOKE* ST4 **85** L4 1
Adventure Pl *HAN* ST1 **2** C6
Adwalton Rd
DUNHL/THL/PER WV6 **278** F7 1
Aegean Cl *STOKE* ST4 **101** J2
Affleck Av *POL/KGSB/FAZ* B78 **289** K1
Agenoria Dr *STRBR* DY8 **307** M5
Agger Hl *NEWUL* ST5 **82** C2
Ainsdale Cl *LNGTN* ST3 **102** D1 1
STRBR DY8 **307** M8
Ainsley Cl *BUCK/MIL* ST2 **70** B4 1
Ainsworth Av *CDLE* ST10 **73** K8
Ainsworth Rd *WOLVN* WV10 **264** E6
Ainsworth St *STOKE* ST4 **85** J5
Aintree Cl *BUT* DE14 **204** A3 1
HEDN WS12 **232** F4
STOKE ST4 **101** H3 1
Aintree Rd *CDLE* ST10 **105** L6
WOLVN WV10 **264** D6
Aintree Wy *DUDN* DY1 **299** L8
Airdale Gv *STONE* ST15 **120** B8
Airdale Rd *STONE* ST15 **120** B8
Airdale Spinney *STONE* ST15 **120** B8
Airfield Dr *ALDR* WS9 **284** E7
Aitken Cl *POL/KGSB/FAZ* B78 **10** B9
Aitken St *BURS/TUN* ST6 **68** E2
Ajax Cl *GTWY* WS6 **266** F1
Ajax Wy *BUCK/MIL* ST2 **85** M1
Akdene Cl *GTWY* WS6 **249** K8
Akesmoor La *BIDD* ST8 **39** M3
Alanbrooke Gv *LNGTN* ST3 **102** D1
Alan Dl *END/WER* ST9 **71** H6
Alandale Av *RUGE* WS15 **217** J6 1
Alanley Cl *BURS/TUN* ST6 **69** K1 1
Alan Rd *BUCK/MIL* ST2 **70** C7
Alastair Rd *STOKE* ST4 **84** F6 1
Albany Dr *RUGE* WS15 **197** K7
Albany Gv *KGSWFD* DY6 **303** L3
SHHTH WV12 **282** C1
STOKE ST4 **84** D2
Albany Rd *NEWUL* ST5 **68** B8
STOKE ST4 **84** D2
Albany St *BURS/TUN* ST6 **53** J3
Albemarle Rd *STRBR* DY8 **307** M8
Albermarle Rd *NEWUL* ST5 **68** A7
Alberta St *LNGTN* ST3 **86** C8 1
Albert Av *LNGTN* ST3 **86** E7
Albert Clarke Dr
SHHTH WV12 **282** C3 2
Albert Cl *CDSL* WV8 **262** E6
Albert Davie Dr *HEDN* WS12 **232** E6 1
Albert Dr *SEDG* DY3 **297**
Albert Pl *LNGTN* ST3 **102** E
Albert Rd *ALBTN* WV7 **260** F
CRTAM B79 **10** D
POL/KGSB/FAZ B78 **290** A2
STOKE ST4 **101** H
WOLV WV1 **12** A
Albert St *ALS/KID* ST7 **51** L
BIDD ST8 **40** C
BUT DE14 **6** E
CNCK/NC WS11 **231**
HEDN WS12 **232** D
KGSWFD DY6 **303** H
LEEK ST13 **43** L
LNGTN ST3 **86** C
NEWUL ST5 **67** L
NEWUL ST5 **67** J
STOKE ST4 **84** D
STONE ST15 **138** A
STRBR DY8 **307** M
WSL WS1 **283** L
Albert Ter *NEWUL* ST5 **68** C
STAFN ST16 **4** E
Albion Av *WLNHL* WV13 **282** C
Albion Pl *CNCK/NC* WS11 **231** L
Albion Rd *BRWNH* WS8 **268** E
Albion St *CRTAM* B79 **10** E
HAN ST1 **2** C
KGSWFD DY6 **303** H
LEEK ST13 **43** L
RUGE WS15 **215** L
WLNHL WV13 **282** B
WOLV WV1 **13** H
Albrighton By-pass *ALBTN* WV7 **261** G
Albutts Rd *CNCK/NC* WS11 **251** G
Alcester Cl *BURS/TUN* ST6 **54** B
The Alcove *BLOX/PEL* WS3 **267** K
Aldbury Cl *STAFN* ST16 **174** D
Aldbury Pl *LNGTN* ST3 **101** L
Aldeburgh Cl *BLOX/PEL* WS3 **267** G7
Aldeburgh Dr *NEWUL* ST5 **84** B
Alden Hurst *BNTWD* WS7 **251** M

derbrook Cl
 BUTN/AL/TUT DE13 .... 166 C6 ▣
 SEDG DY3 .... 299 H1 ▣
der Cl ALS/KID ST7 .... 53 G2
 LICHS WS14 .... 254 F3
 MKTDR TF9 .... 114 C6
der Coppice SEDG DY3 ...... 295 J8 ▣
derdale Av SEDG DY3 .... 295 J7
derflat Dr STOKE ST4 .... 101 K3
derford Cl CDSL WV8 .... 279 M2
dergate CRTAM B79 .... 10 C4
der Gv NEWUL ST5 .... 67 K2
 STAFS ST17 .... 193 H5
 STPNHL/WNHL DE15 .... 204 F3
derhay La ALS/KID ST7 .... 39 J1
derhithe Gv
 FOAKS/STRLY B74 .... 286 B7
derney Cl STAFN ST16 .... 83 L7
derney Crs LNGTN ST3 .... 85 M7
der Rd KGSWFD DY6 .... 303 M5
 MKTDR TF9 .... 130 A2
ders Brook RDERBYSW DE65 .. 166 D1
dersea Cl BURS/TUN ST6 .... 68 C1
dershaw Cl STAFN ST16 ...... 174 C1 ▣
dersleigh Dr STAFS ST17 ..... 194 C5 ▣
dersley Av
 DUNHL/THL/PER WV6 .... 279 L3
dersley Cl
 DUNHL/THL/PER WV6 .... 279 M1
dersley Rd
 DUNHL/THL/PER WV6 .... 279 M5
ders Rd BIDD ST8 .... 41 H1 ▣
e Alders BUTN/AL/TUT DE13 .. 220 C1
derton Dr BDMR/CCFT WV3 .. 294 E2
derton Gv LNGTN ST3 .... 103 H4
der Wk STOKE ST4 .... 84 E6
der Wy HEDN WS12 .... 232 A8 ▣
derwood Ri SEDG DY3 ...... 299 K5 ▣
din Cl POL/KGSB/FAZ B78 .... 273 L8
dridge Cl POL/KGSB/FAZ B78 .. 291 M2
 STRBR DY8 .... 307 L2 ▣
dridge Rd FOAKS/STRLY B74 .. 286 A7
 RUSH/SHEL WS4 .... 284 B7
drin Cl BLYBR/FOR ST11 ...... 103 J3
 STAFN ST16 .... 5 L1
dwych Cl ALDR WS9 .... 285 H2
dwyck Dr BDMR/CCFT WV3 .. 294 A2
exander Cl LICHS WS14 ...... 237 K4 ▣
exander Rd CDSL WV8 .... 263 J7
 WSLW WS2 .... 282 F8
exander St BDMR/CCFT WV3 .. 12 D6
exandra Crs UTXR ST14 ...... 144 B2
exandra Ms CRTAM B79 ...... 10 E4
exandra Rd
 ETTPK/GDPK/PENN WV4 .... 295 G5
 LNGTN ST3 .... 86 D8
 MKTDR TF9 .... 130 B1
 NEWUL ST5 .... 68 C6
 STAFS ST17 .... 4 F8
 STPNHL/WNHL DE15 .... 186 A7
exandra St STONE ST15 ...... 137 M1
exandra Wy ALDR WS9 ...... 285 H5
fred Dr END/WER ST9 .... 71 C7
fred Lyons Cl RUGE WS15 ... 179 M4 ▣
fred St BLOX/PEL WS3 .... 283 H1
 BUT DE14 .... 6 F6
 CRTAM B79 .... 10 B4
 STOKE ST4 .... 85 L3
freton Rd STOKE ST4 .... 86 A4
gar Rd STOKE ST4 .... 84 E4
gernon St WSLW WS2 .... 283 K8 ▣
icia Wy BUCK/MIL ST2 .... 55 C8
ison Dr STRBR DY8 .... 307 L8
lan Cl STRBR DY8 .... 307 M1
lard TAM/AM/WIL B77 .... 11 K9
 TAM/AM/WIL B77 .... 274 E4
lenby Sq STOKE ST4 .... 84 E6
lendale STAFN ST16 .... 174 E1 ▣
lendale Wk LNGTN ST3 ...... 101 L1
lens Cl SHHTH WV12 .... 282 B5
lens Cft UTXR ST14 .... 145 L1
lens La BLOX/PEL WS3 .... 267 M8
 UTXR ST14 .... 145 L8
lensmead
 TAM/AM/WIL B77 .... 274 C8 ▣
lensmore Av STOKE ST4 ...... 86 B5
len St CDLE ST10 .... 89 L8
 STOKE ST4 .... 84 E2
lensway NEWUL ST5 .... 83 L6
lerdale Rd BRWNH WS8 ...... 268 E4
lerton Rd STOKE ST4 .... 100 F3
leston Rd WOLVN WV10 ..... 280 D1
ley's La GNOS ST20 .... 209 G2
he Alley SEDG DY3 .... 299 H7
lliance St STAFN ST16 .... 174 C4
lliss Cl STAFN ST16 .... 175 J6
llmans La MKTDR TF9 .... 148 A6
llport Rd CNCK/NC WS11 ... 249 L1
llport St CNCK/NC WS11 .... 249 L1
ll Saints Cft BUT DE14 .... 204 C2
ll Saints Dr FOAKS/STRLY B74 .. 286 F4
ll Saints Rd BKHL/PFLD WV2 .. 13 H8
 BUT DE14 .... 6 D9
 STOKE ST4 .... 85 C5
lton Av POL/KGSB/FAZ B78 .. 289 K1
he Allways RSTAF ST18 ...... 140 C5
lma Cl ALS/KID ST7 .... 38 C3
lma Rd SWAD DE11 .... 205 M4
lma St BUT DE14 .... 6 E7
 LEEK ST13 .... 43 K4
 STOKE ST4 .... 85 K4
 STONE ST15 .... 137 M1 ▣
 WLNHL WV13 .... 282 B8 ▣
 WOLVN WV10 .... 13 M3
 WSLW WS2 .... 283 K4
lmond Av WSLW WS2 .... 282 G6
lmond Cl BLOX/PEL WS3 ... 267 M8
lmond Ct BUTN/AL/TUT DE13 .. 185 J1
lmond Gv
 DUNHL/THL/PER WV6 .... 280 C7 ▣
 LNGTN ST3 .... 85 L7
 SWAD DE11 .... 205 M5
lmond Pl NEWUL ST5 .... 67 K1
lmond Rd HEDN WS12 .... 231 K2
 KGSWFD DY6 .... 303 L2 ▣
lmshouse Cft RSTAF ST18 ... 210 B2
lms Rd ASHB DE6 .... 145 J1
lnwick Cl HEDN WS12 .... 232 E8

Alnwick Rd BLOX/PEL WS3 ... 267 G6
Alpha Wy GTWY WS6 .... 267 G2
Alpine Dr HEDN WS12 .... 232 D6
Alpine Wy
 DUNHL/THL/PER WV6 .... 279 J8
Alrewas Rd BUTN/AL/TUT DE13 .. 218 D4
Alsager Rd ALS/KID ST7 .... 51 K7
 SBCH CW11 .... 36 F7
Alsop Crest STAFS ST17 ...... 212 B1
Alsop St LEEK ST13 .... 43 L5
Alston Cl FOAKS/STRLY B74 .. 287 G8
 HEDN WS12 .... 232 E8
Alstone Cl STAFN ST16 ...... 174 B4 ▣
Alstone La RSTAF ST18 ...... 209 L1
Alstonfield Av BUCK/MIL ST2 .. 70 C4
Althorp Wy
 BUTN/AL/TUT DE13 .... 185 K2 ▣
Althrop Gv LNGTN ST3 .... 86 D7
Altona Cl STONE ST15 .... 138 B3
Alton Av SHHTH WV12 .... 282 A5
Alton Cl NEWUL ST5 .... 83 H1
 WOLVN WV10 .... 264 E7
Alton Gv BUCK/MIL ST2 .... 86 D3
 CNCK/NC WS11 .... 249 H1
Alton Rd UTXR ST14 .... 108 D4
Alvaston Cl BLOX/PEL WS3 ... 267 J7
Alverley Cl KGSWFD DY6 .... 303 H2
Alverstoke Cl COVEN WV9 .. 263 M8
Alverton Cl
 TAM/AM/WIL B77 .... 290 C6 ▣
Alvington Cl SHHTH WV12 .. 282 D6
Alvis Cl CRTAM B79 .... 273 M3
Alwen St STRBR DY8 .... 307 M1
Alwyn TAM/AM/WIL B77 ...... 290 E3
Alwyn Cl GTWY WS6 .... 249 K1
Alwyn Crs BURS/TUN ST6 ..... 69 K2
Alwyn Rd
 BUTN/AL/TUT DE13 .... 201 G8 ▣
Amanda Av
 ETTPK/GDPK/PENN WV4 .... 294 F6
Amber Cl TAM/AM/WIL B77 ... 275 H7
Amber Ct END/WER ST9 ...... 55 K5
Amberfield Cl LNGTN ST3 ..... 86 E6
Ambergate Cl BLOX/PEL WS3 .. 267 J7
Ambergate Dr KGSWFD DY6 .. 303 J2 ▣
Amber Gv HEDN WS12 ...... 232 C8 ▣
Amberwood Ri WSLW WS2 .. 282 D7 ▣
Amblecote Dr LNGTN ST3 ..... 86 E6
Amblefield Wy STAFN ST16 .. 174 C1 ▣
Ambleside Pl BURS/TUN ST6 .. 54 A7 ▣
Ambleside Rd KGSWFD DY6 .. 303 K4 ▣
Ambrose Cl WLNHL WV13 ... 281 L8 ▣
Ambrose Crs KGSWFD DY6 .. 303 K2
Ambrose Pl BURS/TUN ST6 ... 53 M3 ▣
Ambury Ct BURS/TUN ST6 .... 53 K7 ▣
Amelia St BURS/TUN ST6 ...... 53 K7 ▣
Amerton La RSTAF ST18 ...... 176 E1 ▣
Amicable St BURS/TUN ST6 .. 68 F3 ▣
Amicombe TAM/AM/WIL B77 .. 291 J1 ▣
Amington Cl MGN/WHC B75 .. 287 K7 ▣
Amington Rd TAM/AM/WIL B77 .. 10 F5
Amison St LNGTN ST3 .... 86 D6
Amos Av WNSFLD WV11 ...... 281 H3
Amos La WNSFLD WV11 ...... 281 J4
Ampleforth Dr STAFS ST17 .... 5 L9
 STAFS ST17 .... 194 B2 ▣
Ampthill Pl STOKE ST4 .... 100 F1
Ancaster St BURS/TUN ST6 ... 53 K3
Anchor Cl TAM/AM/WIL B77 .. 11 J6
Anchor Pl LNGTN ST3 .... 86 C6
Anchor Rd ALDR WS9 .... 285 H4
 LNGTN ST3 .... 86 C6
Anchor Ter STAFN ST16 ...... 86 C6
Anchor Wy GNOS ST20 ...... 190 D3
Anderby Gdns SWAD DE11 .. 205 M8
Anders CRTAM B79 .... 10 A2
Anderson Rd TAM/AM/WIL B77 .. 10 F5
Andover Cft KGSWFD DY6 .. 303 M6
Andover Pl CNCK/NC WS11 .. 232 A6
Andrew Cl SHHTH WV12 ..... 282 D4
Andrew Dr SHHTH WV12 .... 282 D4
Andrew Pl NEWUL ST5 .... 84 C1
Andrew Rd ALDR WS9 .... 269 H6
Andrews Dr BURS/TUN ST6 ... 53 J3
Andrew St
 BUTN/AL/TUT DE13 .... 184 F6 ▣
 BUTN/AL/TUT DE13 .... 203 J2
 HEDN WS12 .... 232 B5
Angle St LEEK ST13 .... 43 K4
Anglian Cl BUTN/AL/TUT DE13 .. 166 M8
Anglia Rd CNCK/NC WS11 .. 231 K7
Angorfa Cl LICH WS13 .... 8 A5
Angus Cl BUCK/MIL ST2 .... 70 C7
Anker Cl BNTWD WS7 .... 252 C3
Ankerdrive CRTAM B79 .... 10 D5
 TAM/AM/WIL B77 .... 10 E6
Annan Av WOLVN WV10 ..... 280 C3
Annan Cl CONG CW12 .... 26 A1
Ann Crs CNCK/NC WS11 .... 231 L4
Ann Ct ALS/KID ST7 .... 52 D5
Annefield Cl MKTDR TF9 ..... 112 D8
Anne Rd
 ETTPK/GDPK/PENN WV4 .... 295 H5
Anne St BURS/TUN ST6 .... 53 J3
Annette Rd STOKE ST4 .... 86 B4
Ann St WLNHL WV13 .... 282 B8
Anslow Gdns WNSFLD WV11 .. 281 M1 ▣
Anslow La BUTN/AL/TUT DE13 .. 166 A8
Anslow Rd BUTN/AL/TUT DE13 .. 164 A7
Ansmede Gv LNGTN ST3 .... 101 M1
Anson Av LICH WS13 .... 8 D2
Anson Cl BNTWD WS7 .... 252 C3
 DUNHL/THL/PER WV6 .... 278 E5 ▣
 GTWY WS6 .... 266 F1
Anson Ct BUT DE14 .... 7 J4
Anson Dr STAFS ST17 .... 194 F4
Anson Rd ALBTN WV7 .... 260 B3
 BUTN/AL/TUT DE13 .... 220 A8
 GTWY WS6 .... 266 F1
 LNGTN ST3 .... 103 G2
 WSLW WS2 .... 282 E8
Anson St RUGE WS15 .... 215 L1

Anston Wy WNSFLD WV11 ... 281 K3 ▣
Anstree Cl GTWY WS6 .... 266 D1
Ansty Dr HEDN WS12 .... 232 D6
Anthony Gv LNGTN ST3 ...... 102 F6
Anthony Pl LNGTN ST3 .... 86 D6
Antler Dr RUGE WS15 .... 197 H8
Apedale Rd ALS/KID ST7 ...... 67 C2
 NEWUL ST5 .... 67 J4
Apex Rd BRWNH WS8 .... 268 C2
Apley Pl STOKE ST4 .... 100 F3
Apley Rd STRBR DY8 .... 307 L3
Apollo CRTAM B79 .... 273 M4
Apollo Cl CNCK/NC WS11 .... 232 A5
Appian Cl TAM/AM/WIL B77 .. 290 C3
Appleby Gdns WNSFLD WV11 .. 266 C8
Appleby Gld SWAD DE11 .... 205 K8
Apple Cft AUD/MAD/W CW3 .. 81 K3
Applecroft NEWUL ST5 .... 67 L1
Appledore Cl GTWY WS6 ..... 250 A7
 HEDN WS12 .... 232 E7
 STAFS ST17 .... 194 E2
Appledore Gv ALS/KID ST7 ... 53 L2
Appleford Pl STOKE ST4 ...... 101 L1
Applegarth Cl STOKE ST4 .... 86 B4 ▣
Appleton Crs
 ETTPK/GDPK/PENN WV4 .... 295 G5
Appleton Dr NEWUL ST5 ...... 98 D5
Appletree Gv ALDR WS9 ..... 285 H5
 DUNHL/THL/PER WV6 .... 280 C5 ▣
Appletree Rd RDERBYSW DE65 .. 165 J1
Apple Wk CNCK/NC WS11 .. 232 C8
Applewood UTXR ST14 .... 144 A1 ▣
Appleyard Ct STAFN ST16 ...... 4 F5
The Appleyard PENK ST19 .. 246 C4 ▣
Apse Cl WMBN WV5 .... 297 M3
Apsley Gv BARL ST12 .... 119 C3
Aqualate Cl NWPT TF10 ..... 188 A6 ▣
Aquinas Cl STOKE ST4 .... 85 L3 ▣
Arbor Cl TAM/AM/WIL B77 .... 11 C7
Arboretum Rd WSL WS1 ..... 283 M8
Arborfield Rd UTXR ST14 ..... 162 F3
Arbor Ga ALDR WS9 .... 269 H6
Arbour Cl AUD/MAD/W CW3 .. 81 L3
Arbourfield Dr BUCK/MIL ST2 .. 3 M9
Arbour St ALS/KID ST7 .... 52 D5
 HAN ST1 .... 2 E4
Arbury Dr STRBR DY8 .... 303 K7 ▣
Arcal St SEDG DY3 .... 299 L3
Archer Rd BLOX/PEL WS3 .... 283 L4
Arch St RUGE WS15 .... 215 M2
Arclid Wy BUCK/MIL ST2 ...... 70 B8 ▣
Arctic Pl STOKE ST4 .... 101 H2
Arden Cl LEEK ST13 .... 44 B6
 RUGE WS15 .... 215 J1
 STRBR DY8 .... 303 J7
 STRBR DY8 .... 307 L4
 TAM/AM/WIL B77 .... 11 K4
Arden Ct CONG CW12 .... 26 B3
Arden Rd BUTN/AL/TUT DE13 .. 220 C2
 TAM/AM/WIL B77 .... 290 F5
Ardgay Dr HEDN WS12 ...... 231 M3 ▣
Ardingley Av WV6 .... 5 M9
Argles Rd LEEK ST13 .... 44 A3
Argosy Cl BLYBR/FOR ST11 .. 103 H3 ▣
Argyle Av TAM/AM/WIL B77 ... 11 C5
Argyle Cl RUSH/SHEL WS4 .. 284 D7
 STRBR DY8 .... 307 L1
Argyle Rd BKHL/PFLD WV2 .. 295 H4
 RUSH/SHEL WS4 .... 284 B7
Argyle St HAN ST1 .... 2 A8
 TAM/AM/WIL B77 .... 11 J6
Argyll Cl BLYBR/FOR ST11 ... 103 L4
Argyll Rd LNGTN ST3 .... 86 D8
Ariane CRTAM B79 .... 273 L3
Aries Cl BURS/TUN ST6 .... 53 M4
Arion Cl TAM/AM/WIL B77 .... 11 H5
Arkall Cl CRTAM B79 .... 274 C3 ▣
Arkle TAM/AM/WIL B77 ...... 290 D6
Arkwright Gv HAN ST1 .... 69 M2
Arkwright Rd WSLW WS2 ... 283 H5
Arlescote Cl MGN/WHC B75 .. 287 J8
Arley Cl ALS/KID ST7 .... 37 J7
Arley Dr STRBR DY8 .... 307 L7
Arley Gv
 ETTPK/GDPK/PENN WV4 .... 294 D5
Arlington Cl KGSWFD DY6 .. 303 K6
Armishaw Pl RUGE WS15 ... 216 B5 ▣
Armitage Gdns RUGE WS15 .. 216 B4 ▣
Armitage Hl
 BUTN/AL/TUT DE13 .... 202 E7 ▣
Armitage La RUGE WS15 .... 216 B5
Armitage Rd RUGE WS15 .... 216 A3
Armshead Rd COVEN WV9 .. 264 A1
Armstrong CRTAM B79 .... 273 M4
Armstrong Av STAFN ST16 .... 5 K1
Armstrong Dr
 DUNHL/THL/PER WV6 .... 280 A4
 WSLW WS2 .... 283 G6
Arnhem Cl WNSFLD WV11 ... 281 H1
Arn Hl ECCH ST21 .... 134 C5
Arnold Cl CRTAM B79 .... 10 A2
 SWAD DE11 .... 223 L3
 WSLW WS2 .... 282 F7
Arnold Gv NEWUL ST5 .... 68 B2
Arnotdale Dr HEDN WS12 ... 231 M3
Arnot Rd BUT DE14 .... 204 A3
Arnwood Cl WSLW WS2 ..... 282 F8 ▣
Arps Rd CDSL WV8 .... 262 F7
Arran Cl CNCK/NC WS11 .... 232 A7
Arran Dr ALS/KID ST7 .... 53 M2
 TAM/AM/WIL B77 .... 290 F3
Arrow Dr ALBTN WV7 .... 261 C5 ▣
Arrow Rd BLOX/PEL WS3 .... 283 L4
Arrowsmith Dr ALS/KID ST7 .. 37 L7
Arthur Evans Cl RUGE WS15 .. 216 A5 ▣
Arthurs Ct
 BUTN/AL/TUT DE13 .... 166 E8 ▣
Arthur St BKHL/PFLD WV2 .. 295 K4
 BURS/TUN ST6 .... 53 L6
 BUT DE14 .... 185 J5
 CNCK/NC WS11 .... 231 M4
 HEDN WS12 .... 232 B7
 NEWUL ST5 .... 83 M1
 STONE ST15 .... 120 A8
 SWAD DE11 .... 223 L3
Arundel TAM/AM/WIL B77 .... 290 C3

Arundel Gv
 DUNHL/THL/PER WV6 .... 279 K5 ▣
Arundel Rd SHHTH WV12 ... 282 F1
 STRBR DY8 .... 303 J8
 WOLVN WV10 .... 264 B8
Arundel Wy LNGTN ST3 .... 86 C4
Ascot Cl LICHS WS14 .... 9 K5
 STPNHL/WNHL DE15 .... 186 A7
Ascot Dr CNCK/NC WS11 .... 249 H2
 DUDN 299 M8
 ETTPK/GDPK/PENN WV4 .... 295 C6
Ascot Gdns STRBR DY8 ..... 303 K8
Ascot Rd STAFS ST17 .... 194 C1 ▣
Ash Bank Rd BUCK/MIL ST2 .. 70 E7
 END/WER ST9 .... 71 J6
Ashbourne Cl
 CNCK/NC WS11 .... 232 A6 ▣
Ashbourne Dr MKTDR TF9 .. 112 C8
 NEWUL ST5 .... 83 H1
 SWAD DE11 .... 223 M1
Ashbourne Gv HAN ST1 .... 2 C2
Ashbourne La ASHB DE6 ..... 48 A7
Ashbourne Rd ASHB DE6 .... 48 A7
 ASHB DE6 .... 94 C3
 ASHB DE6 .... 129 L3
 BLOX/PEL WS3 .... 267 J7
 CDLE ST10 .... 89 M7
 ETTPK/GDPK/PENN WV4 .... 295 L7
 UTXR ST14 .... 108 F6
 UTXR ST14 .... 126 B8
 WOLVN WV1 .... 281 C7
Ashbrook Cl STPNHL/WNHL DE15 .. 205 C1
Ashbrook Cl GNOS ST20 .... 190 D3
Ashbrook La RUGE WS15 ... 180 B5
Ashburn Gv WLNHL WV13 .. 282 C8 ▣
Ashburton Dr BURS/TUN ST6 .. 69 J1
Ashby Crs LNGTN ST3 .... 101 M1
Ashby Rd CRTAM B79 .... 274 C3
 STPNHL/WNHL DE15 .... 7 M5
Ashby Rd East
 CDSL WV8 .... 263 C7
Ash Cl CDLE ST10 .... 89 M8
Ashcombe Gn LNGTN ST3 .. 101 M1
Ashcombe Rd LEEK ST13 .... 57 J6
Ashcombe Wy LEEK ST13 ... 43 M6 ▣
Ash Crs KGSWFD DY6 .... 303 L4
Ashcroft Av STOKE ST4 .... 84 E7
Ashcroft Cl NEWUL ST5 .... 68 A4 ▣
Ashcroft Gv NEWUL ST5 ...... 68 B4 ▣
Ashcroft La LICHS WS14 ..... 270 C2
Ashcroft Pl NEWUL ST5 .... 68 B4 ▣
Ashcroft Rd NEWUL ST5 ...... 68 A4
Ashdale Cl ALS/KID ST7 ...... 37 J5
 HEDN WS12 .... 231 J3 ▣
 KGSWFD DY6 .... 303 C2
 STPNHL/WNHL DE15 .... 205 C2
Ashdale Dr STAFN ST16 .... 174 D2
Ashdale Pk STOKE ST4 ...... 136 F5
Ashdale Ri NEWUL ST5 .... 84 B7
 STOKE ST4 .... 85 J5
 TAM/AM/WIL B77 .... 11 H4
Ashdene Gdns STRBR DY8 .. 303 J8
Ashdown Dr STRBR DY8 .... 303 L1
Ash Dr RSTAF ST18 .... 191 M5
Ashen Cl
 ETTPK/GDPK/PENN WV4 .... 295 C5
Ashendene Gv STOKE ST4 .. 100 F2
Ashenden Ri BDMR/CCFT WV3 .. 294 A1
Ashenhurst Rd ALS/KID ST7 .. 37 M7
Ashenhurst Wy LEEK ST13 ... 43 M6
Ashenough Rd ALS/KID ST7 .. 52 D4
Ashes La ASHB DE6 .... 79 C2
 ASHB DE6 .... 163 K3
Ashfield Cl BLOX/PEL WS3 .. 283 L6
Ashfield Gv WOLVN WV10 .. 264 C7
Ashfield Rd BDMR/CCFT WV3 .. 279 K8
 WOLVN WV10 .... 264 C7
Ashfields New Rd NEWUL ST5 .. 84 A1
Ashfield Sq BUCK/MIL ST2 .... 3 M8
Ash Flats La STAFS ST17 .... 193 L6
Ashford Dr SEDG DY3 .... 299 L3
Ashford Rd BUTN/AL/TUT DE13 .. 185 C2
Ashford St STOKE ST4 .... 85 L2
Ash Green Cl STOKE ST4 .... 101 C3
Ashgrove BNTWD WS7 .... 251 M5
Ash Gv ALBTN WV7 .... 261 C6
 ALS/KID ST7 .... 37 M3
 BARL ST12 .... 119 K1
 BLYBR/FOR ST11 .... 103 J2
 BUCK/MIL ST2 .... 70 F7
 CNCK/NC WS11 .... 231 M6
 LICH WS13 .... 9 L2
 LNGTN ST3 .... 85 L8
 NEWUL ST5 .... 67 H8
 PENK ST19 .... 227 J4
 PENK ST19 .... 246 D4
 SEDG DY3 .... 299 J3
 TAM/AM/WIL B77 .... 290 F5
Ash Grove La RDERBYSW DE65 .. 167 J4
Ash Hl BDMR/CCFT WV3 .... 294 D1
Ashlands RSTAF ST18 .... 177 K1
Ashlands Av STOKE ST4 ...... 84 E2
Ashlands Cl CRTAM B79 .... 274 C3
Ashlands Crs STOKE ST4 .... 84 D3
Ashlands Rd STOKE ST4 ..... 84 D3
Ashland St BDMR/CCFT WV3 .. 12 C7
Ash La CRTAM B79 .... 259 M4
 GTWY WS6 .... 250 A7
 STONE ST15 .... 136 E5
Ashlar Cl BURS/TUN ST6 ..... 54 A2
Ashlea POL/KGSB/FAZ B78 .. 291 M5 ▣
Ashlea Dr ASHB DE6 .... 94 C3
Ashleigh Av NEWUL ST5 .... 205 M5 ▣
Ashleigh Crs PENK ST19 .... 227 J3 ▣
Ashleigh Dr TAM/AM/WIL B77 .. 290 C2
 UTXR ST14 .... 143 M1
Ashleigh Rd CDLE ST10 ..... 105 L6
 RUGE WS15 .... 215 C3
Ashley Cft KGSWFD DY6 ..... 174 A6 ▣
 STAFN ST16 .... 174 A6 ▣
 STPNHL/WNHL DE15 .... 186 A7 ▣
 STRBR DY8 .... 307 K8
Ashley Cft CNCK/NC WS11 .. 209 C2
Ashley Gdns CDSL WV8 ..... 262 F4
Ashley Gv NEWUL ST5 .... 68 C6

Ashley Mt
 DUNHL/THL/PER WV6 .... 279 K5 ▣
Ashley Rd BLOX/PEL WS3 ... 282 F1
 BNTWD WS7 .... 251 K1
 ETTPK/GDPK/PENN WV4 .... 294 E5
Ashley Vw MKTDR TF9 .... 130 C1
Ashmall BNTWD WS7 .... 252 D6 ▣
Ashman St BURS/TUN ST6 ... 54 C8
Ashmead Cl ALS/KID ST7 ..... 37 L7
Ashmead Ms ALS/KID ST7 ... 37 L7
Ashmeadow Ct ASHB DE6 ... 95 K2 ▣
Ashmead Rd BNTWD WS7 .. 252 A5
Ashmole Cl LICHS WS14 .... 9 L7
Ashmore Av WNSFLD WV11 .. 282 A1
Ashmore Dr GNOS ST20 .... 190 D3
Ashmore Lake Rd SHHTH WV12 .. 282 B6
Ashmore Lake Wy
 SHHTH WV12 .... 282 B6
Ashmore's La HAN ST1 .... 2 F5
Ashover Gv BURS/TUN ST6 ... 53 L2
Ashover Rd SWAD DE11 .... 205 L2 ▣
Ashridge Av NEWUL ST5 ...... 84 B8
Ashridge Gv LNGTN ST3 ...... 86 D5
Ashridge Wk STAFN ST16 .. 174 D1
Ash Ri STAFS ST17 .... 193 L6
Ash St BDMR/CCFT WV3 ..... 12 B6
 BLOX/PEL WS3 .... 283 K1
 BUT DE14 .... 6 D9
Ashton Cl CONG CW12 .... 26 B1 ▣
Ashton Ct END/WER ST9 ...... 71 C7
 NEWUL ST5 .... 84 C8 ▣
Ashton Dr RUSH/SHEL WS4 .. 268 C7
Ashtree Bank RUGE WS15 .. 216 A4
Ashtree Cl RSTAF ST18 ...... 196 D2
Ash Tree Cl SWAD DE11 .... 205 M4 ▣
Ash Tree Hl CDLE ST10 .... 89 J8
Ash Tree La LICH WS13 ..... 255 G1 ▣
Ash Tree Rd BLOX/PEL WS3 .. 268 A7
Ash Tree Rd
 BUTN/AL/TUT DE13 .... 220 C1
Ashurst Gv LNGTN ST3 ...... 103 H3
Ash Vw HEDN WS12 .... 231 K2
Ash Wy BUCK/MIL ST2 .... 70 F7
Ashwell Rd STOKE ST4 .... 84 D2 ▣
Ashwells Gv COVEN WV9 ... 263 M8
Ashwood LNGTN ST3 .... 86 B5
Ashwood Av STRBR DY8 .... 303 J8
Ashwood Cl MKTDR TF9 .... 130 A1 ▣
Ashwood Gv BLYBR/FOR ST11 .. 104 A4
 ETTPK/GDPK/PENN WV4 .... 295 C5 ▣
Ashworth Av
 STPNHL/WNHL DE15 .... 186 C8
Ashworth St STOKE ST4 ...... 85 K4
Askerbank La MCFLDS SK11 .. 28 A1
Askern Cl LNGTN ST3 .... 102 E1
Askew Bridge Rd SEDG DY3 .. 299 H7 ▣
Askew Cl SEDG DY3 .... 299 H5
Aspen Cl ALS/KID ST7 .... 39 L7
Aspen Ct HEDN WS12 .... 233 C4 ▣
Aspen Cft STAFS ST17 .... 193 H2 ▣
Aspen Gv BNTWD WS7 ...... 251 M2
 SHHTH WV12 .... 282 D3
Aspen Rd BUTN/AL/TUT DE13 .. 220 C1
Aspen Wy BDMR/CCFT WV3 .. 12 A7
Aspley Cl WOLVN WV10 ..... 247 C5
Aspley La WOLVN WV10 ..... 247 K7
Asquith Cl BIDD ST8 .... 40 E3
Asquith Dr CNCK/NC WS11 .. 232 C8
Astbury Cl BLYBR/FOR ST11 .. 39 J7 ▣
 BLOX/PEL WS3 .... 267 G6
Aster Cl LICHS WS14 .... 87 H4
Aster Wk COVEN WV9 .... 264 A1 ▣
Astil St STPNHL/WNHL DE15 .. 7 M9
Aston Bank STAFN ST16 .... 173 M6
Aston Br ASHB DE6 .... 146 E7
Aston Cha STONE ST15 .... 138 D2
Aston Cl LICHS WS14 .... 270 F4
 PENK ST19 .... 229 M3
 RSTAF ST18 .... 196 D2
Aston Dl SHIF TF11 .... 242 A6
Astonfields Rd STAFN ST16 .. 174 E4
Aston Hl RSTAF ST18 .... 173 L6
 MKTDR TF9 .... 96 F2
 STONE ST15 .... 138 D2
Aston Lodge Pkwy STONE ST15 .. 138 D4
Aston Rd NEWUL ST5 .... 67 K1
 SHIF TF11 .... 242 A6
 WLNHL WV13 .... 281 L8
Aston St BDMR/CCFT WV3 ... 12 B9
Aston Ter STAFN ST16 .... 174 E4
Astoria Cl SHHTH WV12 .... 282 D1
Astoria Dr STAFS ST17 ...... 193 M4 ▣
Astra Rd KGSWFD DY6 ...... 303 M5
Astro Gv LNGTN ST3 .... 86 A6 ▣
Athelstan Cl PENK ST19 .... 230 A2 ▣
Athelstan Gv
 DUNHL/THL/PER WV6 .... 278 C5
Athelstan St BURS/TUN ST6 .. 53 K7 ▣
Athelstan Wy CRTAM B79 .. 273 M3 ▣
Athena Gv HAN ST1 .... 3 J2
Atherstone Rd STOKE ST4 .. 101 C3
 WOLV WV1 .... 281 H8 ▣
Atherstone St
 POL/KGSB/FAZ B78 .... 290 B2
Athelstan Wy
 BUTN/AL/TUT DE13 .... 185 J1
Athlone St BURS/TUN ST6 ... 54 D8
Atholl Rd LNGTN ST3 .... 102 D1
Atkins Wy UTXR ST14 .... 108 F7
Atlam Cl BUCK/MIL ST2 .... 3 L6
Atlantic Gv STOKE ST4 .... 101 J2
Atlas Cft WOLVN WV10 ...... 280 C4
Atlas St STOKE ST4 .... 85 L5
Atlow Brow ASHB DE6 .... 94 C3
Attingham Dr CNCK/NC WS11 .. 250 B1
Attlee Crs RUGE WS15 .... 215 M3
 STAFS ST17 .... 193 L5
Attlee Gv CNCK/NC WS11 .. 232 C8
Attlee Rd CDLE ST10 .... 89 K8
 WSLW WS2 .... 282 F7
Attwell Pk BDMR/CCFT WV3 .. 294 D3
Attwood Gdns
 ETTPK/GDPK/PENN WV4 .... 295 L5
Attwood Rd BNTWD WS7 ... 251 J3
Attwood St ALS/KID ST7 ...... 39 C8
Aubrey St BURS/TUN ST6 .... 53 H3

Auchinleck Dr LICH WS13 254 C1
Auckland Rd KGSWFD DY6 303 L6
Auckland St BURS/TUN ST6 69 G3
Auden Ct DUNHL/THL/PER WV6 278 F6
Auden Pl LNGTN ST3 86 D7
Auden Wy STAFS ST17 193 J2
Audlem Rd AUD/MAD/W CW3 96 B1
Audley Av NWPT TF10 206 B1
Audley Cl BUTN/AL/TUT DE13 220 A7
Audley Pl NEWUL ST5 84 B4
Audley Rd ALS/KID ST7 51 L2
ALS/KID ST7 52 B8
CW/SHV CW2 50 D5
NEWUL ST5 52 C8
Audley St BURS/TUN ST6 53 K7
NEWUL ST5 67 L7
Audmore Rd GNOS ST20 190 D3
Audnam STRBR DY8 307 L1
Augustine Cl STONE ST15 138 C3
Augustine Gv
FOAKS/STRLY B74 286 F5
Aulton Rd MGN/WHC B75 287 L8
Austcliffe Rd KIDD DY10 310 A5
Austen Cl CDLE ST10 89 J8
Austin Cl DUDN DY1 299 M8
Austin Cote La LICHS WS14 9 M4
Austin Friars STAFS ST17 4 E8
Austin St DUNHL/THL/PER WV6 280 B6
HAN ST1 2 F9
Austrey La CRTAM B79 259 K6
Austwick Gv STOKE ST4 84 E5
Autumn Berry Gv SEDG DY3 299 L4
Autumn Cl RUSH/SHEL WS4 268 C8
Autumn Dr LICH WS13 236 D8
RUSH/SHEL WS4 268 C8
SEDG DY3 299 K7
Aveling Rd HAN ST1 69 M2
Avenue Perry WOLVN WV10 280 F2
Avenue Rd
DUNHL/THL/PER WV6 279 L8
HEDN WS12 232 E8
STOKE ST4 85 J1
The Avenue ALS/KID ST7 37 J6
ALS/KID ST7 52 F1
ASHB DE6 92 D6
BDMR/CCFT WV3 294 B2
BLYBR/FOR ST11 104 A4
CDLE ST10 89 K8
END/WER ST9 55 M6
ETTPK/GDPK/PENN WV4 294 E6
KINVER DY7 305 K1
LEEK ST13 57 J6
NEWUL ST5 68 D8
PENK ST19 228 D8
STOKE ST4 84 D3
STONE ST15 138 A1
Averill Dr RUGE WS15 197 K8
Averill Rd STAFS ST17 193 J2
Aviation La BUTN/AL/TUT DE13 184 C6
Avill TAM/AM/WIL B77 291 G5
Avington Cl SEDG DY3 299 K3
Avion Cl BLYBR/FOR ST11 103 J3
Avoca St HAN ST1 2 F2
Avocet Cl UTXR ST14 144 C4
Avon TAM/AM/WIL B77 291 G5
Avon Cl ALS/KID ST7 39 H8
DUNHL/THL/PER WV6 278 F6
NEWUL ST5 84 B6
STAFN ST16 5 M4
Avon Ct ALS/KID ST7 37 J5
Avon Crs BLOX/PEL WS3 284 A1
Avondale Cl KGSWFD DY6 303 L2
Avondale Rd
DUNHL/THL/PER WV6 279 M7
Avondale St BURS/TUN ST6 68 D2
Avon Dr WLNHL WV13 282 C8
Avon Gv CDLE ST10 105 L1
MKTDR TF9 114 E5
Avon Hl STAFN ST16 175 J7
Avonlea Gdns RUGE WS15 215 J1
Avon Ri STAFN ST16 5 M4
Avon Rd BLOX/PEL WS3 283 L1
BNTWD WS7 251 M5
CNCK/NC WS11 249 K2
STRBR DY8 307 M7
Avonside Av BURS/TUN ST6 53 M6
Avon Wy RDERBYSW DE65 166 E1
STPNHL/WNHL DE15 205 G1
Avonwick Gv HAN ST1 3 L1
Awbridge Br WMBN WV5 293 L8
Awdishaw La ASHB DE6 129 H5
Axborough La KIDD DY10 310 C6
Axon Crs LNGTN ST3 87 H7
Aylesbury Rd BUCK/MIL ST2 70 C8
Aylesford Cl SEDG DY3 295 H8
Aylesford Dr FOAKS/STRLY B74 286 E5
Aynsley Av NEWUL ST5 84 B7
Aynsley Cl CDLE ST10 105 J1
Aynsley Rd STOKE ST4 85 H1
Aynsley's Dr BLYBR/FOR ST11 103 L3
Ayr Rd CDLE ST10 89 L5
Ayrshire Wy CONG CW12 26 A1
Ayrton Cl DUNHL/THL/PER WV6 279 G6
Azalea Cl CDSL WV8 263 H7

B

Babbacombe Av STAFS ST17 194 E2
Babbington Cl
BUTN/AL/TUT DE13 165 J5
LICHS WS14 255 L5
Babbs La ASHB DE6 145 J1
Babworth Cl COVEN WV9 264 A8
Back Browning St STAFN ST16 4 D2
Back Bunt's La END/WER ST9 55 J6
Backcester La LICH WS13 8 F3
Backcrofts CNCK/NC WS11 249 L2
Back Ford Green Rd
BURS/TUN ST6 54 D8
Back Garden St NEWUL ST5 84 C2
Back Heathcote St
ALS/KID ST7 39 G8
Backhouse La WLNHL WV13 281 J6
WNSFLD WV11 281 J6
Back La ALDR WS9 285 M3
ASHB DE6 48 D7
ASHB DE6 92 F3
AUD/MAD/W CW3 65 H2
BURS/TUN ST6 55 H3
BUTN/AL/TUT DE13 181 M3
BUX SK17 49 K1
CDLE ST10 76 E1
CDLE ST10 107 M1
ECCH ST21 117 K5
GNOS ST20 170 D2
GNOS ST20 190 B5
LEEK ST13 43 K4
LICHS WS14 255 K5
LICHS WS14 286 D1
MKTDR TF9 115 G6
NWPT TF10 188 D1
PENK ST19 227 H5
RSTAF ST18 172 D6
RSTAF ST18 177 J1
RSTAF ST18 191 M5
RSTAF ST18 196 C2
RUGE WS15 216 F1
Back Rd KGSWFD DY6 303 K3
SHIF TF11 224 C7
Back Westlands Rd UTXR ST14 144 B4
Baddeley Green La
BUCK/MIL ST2 55 H8
Baddeley Hall Rd BUCK/MIL ST2 55 J8
Baddeley Rd BUCK/MIL ST2 70 B1
Baddeley St BURS/TUN ST6 68 F1
CDLE ST10 89 L8
Baden Powell Cl RUGE WS15 233 M4
Baden Rd BURS/TUN ST6 69 J1
Baden St NEWUL ST5 68 B8
Bader Rd DUNHL/THL/PER WV6 278 D7
WSLW WS2 282 F8
Badger Brow Rd MKTDR TF9 114 D5
Badger Cl HEDN WS12 231 J4
Badger Dr WOLVN WV10 13 H1
Badger Gv BLYBR/FOR ST11 103 J3
Badger La MKTDR TF9 97 J7
Badgers Bank Rd
FOAKS/STRLY B74 286 F5
Badgers Brow HAN ST1 3 H6
Badgers Cl BLOX/PEL WS3 268 A5
Badgers Cl ECCH ST21 152 F4
Badgers Cft ECCH ST21 152 F3
STAFS ST17 194 C4
Badger's End PENK ST19 227 H4
Badgers Hollow CDLE ST10 124 A2
Badger St SEDG DY3 299 L5
Badgers Wy HEDN WS12 250 D1
Badgery Cl UTXR ST14 126 A8
Badminton Cl DUDN DY1 299 M7
Badnall St LEEK ST13 43 K4
Baggeridge Cl SEDG DY3 299 G2
Baggott Pl NEWUL ST5 83 M2
Baggott St BKHL/PFLD WV2 295 J3
Bag La ASHB DE6 109 L3
RUGE WS15 178 D3
UTXR ST14 145 K8
Bagnall Rd BUCK/MIL ST2 70 D1
Bagnall St BLOX/PEL WS3 283 J3
HAN ST1 2 D6
Bagot Gv HAN ST1 69 M2
Bagots Oak STAFS ST17 193 J3
Bagot St RUGE WS15 179 M4
Bagots Vw CDLE ST10 124 A6
RUGE WS15 180 A4
Bagridge Cl
BDMR/CCFT WV3 294 B2
Bagridge Rd BDMR/CCFT WV3 294 B2
Bailey Av TAM/AM/WIL B77 290 F5
Bailey Cl CNCK/NC WS11 232 A6
Bailey Ct ALS/KID ST7 37 L7
Bailey Rd LNGTN ST3 85 L6
Bailey's Bank BIDD ST8 26 D7
Bailey St BUT DE14 7 G9
NEWUL ST5 84 A1
STAFS ST17 4 F6
STOKE ST4 84 F1
WOLVN WV10 13 J4
Bainbridge Rd STOKE ST4 101 G3
Bains Gv NEWUL ST5 67 M2
Baker Av BILS/COS WV14 295 M8
Baker Crs BUCK/MIL ST2 55 H7
Baker Crs North BUCK/MIL ST2 55 J7
Baker Crs South BUCK/MIL ST2 55 H8
Bakers Gdns CDSL WV8 262 E6
Baker's La ALDR WS9 285 H4
ASHB DE6 145 J1
LICH WS13 8 F4
NWPT TF10 169 J6
Baker St BNTWD WS7 251 M4
STOKE ST4 85 L4
STPNHL/WNHL DE15 204 E3
Bakers Wy CDSL WV8 262 E6
Bakewell Cl BLOX/PEL WS3 267 J7
NEWUL ST5 83 H1
Bakewell Dr STONE ST15 138 D5
Bakewell Gn SWAD DE11 205 L5
Bakewell St STOKE ST4 84 F5
Bala Gv CDLE ST10 89 M6
Balance St UTXR ST14 144 C3
Balcombe Cl NEWUL ST5 84 B3
Baldwin Gv CNCK/NC WS11 232 C8
Baldwin Wy SEDG DY3 297 L8
Balfour CRTAM B79 10 B5
Balfour Gv BIDD ST8 40 E2
Balfour Rd KGSWFD DY6 303 L2
SHIF TF11 242 A4
Balfour St BUTN/AL/TUT DE13 185 J4
HAN ST1 2 F6
Ballaam's La STONE ST15 121 K5
Ballarat Wk STRBR DY8 307 M5
Ball Haye Gn LEEK ST13 43 M3
Ball Haye Rd LEEK ST13 43 M4
Ball Hayes Rd BURS/TUN ST6 54 C5
Ballington Gdns LEEK ST13 43 M5
Ballington Vw LEEK ST13 43 M6
Ballinson Rd LNGTN ST3 101 L1
Balliol St STOKE ST4 85 G3
Ball La BURS/TUN ST6 55 G5
COVEN WV9 264 C4
LEEK ST13 43 L4
Balloon St STOKE ST4 84 D1
Balls Hl WSL WS1 283 M8
Balls St WSL WS1 283 M8
Balmain Crs WNSFLD WV11 281 H2
Balmoral Cl LICHS WS14 19 M1
RUSH/SHEL WS4 284 D3
STOKE ST4 85 G8
Balmoral Dr HEDN WS12 231 M3
MKTDR TF9 112 E8
SHHTH WV12 282 B3
WMBN WV5 298 A1
Balmoral Rd
ETTPK/GDPK/PENN WV4 295 G6
FOAKS/STRLY B74 286 F5
STAFS ST17 194 C1
STPNHL/WNHL DE15 186 A7
STRBR DY8 303 J8
Balmoral Vw DUDN DY1 299 L8
Balmoral Wy WSLW WS2 283 G6
Baltic Cl CNCK/NC WS11 231 L8
STOKE ST4 101 H3
Balvenie Wy DUDN DY1 299 M7
Bamber Cl BDMR/CCFT WV3 294 E2
Bamber Pl NEWUL ST5 67 M4
Bamber St STOKE ST4 85 H3
Bamborough Cl
BUTN/AL/TUT DE13 185 K3
Bamburgh TAM/AM/WIL B77 290 C3
Bambury St LNGTN ST3 86 C4
Bamford Cl BLOX/PEL WS3 267 J7
Bamford Gv HAN ST1 2 B2
Bamford Rd BDMR/CCFT WV3 12 A9
BLOX/PEL WS3 267 J7
Bamford St TAM/AM/WIL B77 11 H8
Bampton Av BNTWD WS7 252 A2
Banbery Dr WMBN WV5 297 M6
Banbury Cl SEDG DY3 299 L4
Banbury Gv BIDD ST8 40 C2
Banbury Rd CNCK/NC WS11 249 H2
Banbury St ALS/KID ST7 52 D1
Bancroft La BLYBR/FOR ST11 103 M4
Bandridge La MCFLDS SK11 28 A2
Baneberry Dr WOLVN WV10 265 H3
Bangley La POL/KGSB/FAZ B78 289 G2
Bank Cl UTXR ST14 144 C4
Bank Crs BNTWD WS7 251 M5
Bank End BURS/TUN ST6 55 H2
Bankerwall La ASHB DE6 93 J3
Bankfield Gv NEWUL ST5 66 E7
Bankfield Rd LNGTN ST3 102 F2
Bank Hall Rd BURS/TUN ST6 54 B8
Bank House Dr NEWUL ST5 68 E8
Bankhouse Rd
BLYBR/FOR ST11 104 B2
STOKE ST4 100 F2
Bank Rd SEDG DY3 299 J7
Bankside ASHB DE6 93 J1
Bank Side BUX SK17 34 D4
Bankside NEWUL ST5 84 C2
Bank Side STONE ST15 137 M4
Bankside WMBN WV5 297 M3
Bankside Wy ALDR WS9 269 H8
Banks La CDLE ST10 73 L6
Banks St WLNHL WV13 282 A8
Bank St ALS/KID ST7 39 J6
BURS/TUN ST6 53 K6
CDLE ST10 89 K7
HEDN WS12 250 E1
WOLVN WV10 280 E5
The Bank ALS/KID ST7 39 H3
Bank Top RUGE WS15 215 K1
Bank Top Av BURS/TUN ST6 54 A7
Banktop Rd ASHB DE6 163 G5
Banky Brook Cl BURS/TUN ST6 54 C7
Bannut Tree La KINVER DY7 305 J4
Banstead Cl BKHL/PFLD WV2 295 L3
Bantock Av BDMR/CCFT WV3 294 F2
Bantock Gdns
BDMR/CCFT WV3 294 E1
Baonal Wy STONE ST15 136 B4
Barbara St CRTAM B79 10 B3
Barber Cl HEDN WS12 232 E8
Barber Dr ALS/KID ST7 38 E3
Barber Pl BURS/TUN ST6 53 M4
Barber Rd BURS/TUN ST6 53 M4
Barber's Sq NEWUL ST5 68 D6
Barber St BURS/TUN ST6 68 F1
Barbridge Rd NEWUL ST5 52 D8
Barbrook Av LNGTN ST3 86 E6
Barclay Cl ALBTN WV7 261 H4
Barclay St LNGTN ST3 86 C5
Barcliff Av TAM/AM/WIL B77 11 J7
Barcroft WLNHL WV13 282 B7
Bardolph Cl SWAD DE11 205 M7
Bardwell Cl CDSL WV8 279 M2
Bardy La RUGE WS15 234 C1
Barford Rd NEWUL ST5 83 M6
Barford St LNGTN ST3 86 B7
Bargate Dr
DUNHL/THL/PER WV6 12 B1
Bargate La PENK ST19 246 C4
Bargate St PENK ST19 246 C4
Bargery Rd WNSFLD WV11 282 A1
Bargrave St BUCK/MIL ST2 86 D1
Bar Hl AUD/MAD/W CW3 81 J6
Barker Cl STAFN ST16 4 A5
Barker St LNGTN ST3 86 C7
NEWUL ST5 67 M4
Barks Dr BURS/TUN ST6 54 D6
Bar La BUTN/AL/TUT DE13 201 M7
Barlaston Cl STAFN ST16 174 C2
Barlaston Old Rd STOKE ST4 101 H4
Barley Cl ALDR WS9 285 L8
BUT DE14 185 L4
CDSL WV8 279 L1
SEDG DY3 299 M3
Barleycorn Cl
STPNHL/WNHL DE15 205 G1
Barley Ct STAFN ST16 174 A5
Barley Cft ALS/KID ST7 37 L8
Barleycroft CDLE ST10 105 L1
Barley Cft
DUNHL/THL/PER WV6 278 D7
LICHS WS14 255 L5
Barleycroft Ter ALS/KID ST7 38 F3
Barley Fld COVEN WV9 247 H8
Barleyfield Ri KGSWFD DY6 303 G2
Barleyfields ALS/KID ST7 51 K8
BURS/TUN ST6 54 B7
Barleyford Dr LNGTN ST3 86 D4
Barley Green La LICH WS13 238 B2
Barley Orch GNOS ST20 190 E4
Barley Rd CDLE ST10 74 A2
Barlow Cl TAM/AM/WIL B77 11 J5
Barlow Hl MCFLDS SK11 19 M1
Barlow St LNGTN ST3 86 C7
Barlstone Av BLYBR/FOR ST11 103 M4
Barmouth Cl SHHTH WV12 282 C4
Barmouth Gv BIDD ST8 54 B1
Barnaby Sq WOLVN WV10 264 F6
Barnard Pl BKHL/PFLD WV2 295 L4
Barnard Rd WNSFLD WV11 281 M1
Barnard Wy CNCK/NC WS11 231 M8
Barn Av SEDG DY3 299 J3
Barn Bank La RSTAF ST18 193 K5
Barnbridge TAM/AM/WIL B77 274 C8
Barnbridge Cl ALS/KID ST7 38 E3
Barn Cl LICH WS13 236 B7
POL/KGSB/FAZ B78 291 M4
RUGE WS15 216 B5
STAFS ST17 193 L5
Barn Common GNOS ST20 170 D2
Barn Ct NEWUL ST5 84 C7
Barn Cft BNTWD WS7 252 A6
GTWY WS6 250 A7
Barncroft Rd BURS/TUN ST6 54 B4
Barn End Rd STAFS ST17 212 B2
Barnes Rd LICHS WS14 271 G4
STAFS ST17 193 K3
Barnes Wy LNGTN ST3 102 B1
Barnett Cl KGSWFD DY6 303 K6
Barnett Gn KGSWFD DY6 303 K6
Barnett Gv BURS/TUN ST6 53 M5
Barnett La KGSWFD DY6 303 K5
Barnetts La BRWNH WS8 268 F2
Barnett St STRBR DY8 303 K7
Barnfield STOKE ST4 84 F4
Barnfield Cl LICHS WS14 8 F6
Barnfield Rd BURS/TUN ST6 69 G3
CDLE ST10 105 L6
LEEK ST13 43 K6
WOLV WV1 281 G8
Barnfields Cl LEEK ST13 43 K6
Barnfields La CDLE ST10 73 K8
Barnfield Wy HEDN WS12 233 G4
STAFS ST17 194 C4
Barngate St LEEK ST13 43 K4
Barn Gn BDMR/CCFT WV3 294 F3
Barnhurst La CDSL WV8 263 K7
Barn La ECCH ST21 116 C5
PENK ST19 246 C3
Barnlea Gv LNGTN ST3 103 G4
Barnmeadow Cl NWPT TF10 188 A7
Barnmeadow Rd NWPT TF10 188 A7
Barn Owl Dr BLOX/PEL WS3 267 M6
Barn Rd RUGE WS15 217 J6
SHIF TF11 242 A5
Barns Cl ALDR WS9 268 F6
Barns Cft FOAKS/STRLY B74 286 B7
Barnscroft STONE ST15 121 K8
Barnsdale Cl STOKE ST4 101 H5
Barns La RUSH/SHEL WS4 284 C2
Barnswood Cl CNCK/NC WS11 249 H2
Barnwell Cl UTXR ST14 126 A6
Barnwell Gv STOKE ST4 101 G1
Barnwood Rd CDSL WV8 279 L1
Baron Cl BNTWD WS7 251 L1
Baron St STOKE ST4 86 A5
Baron's Wy RSTAF ST18 177 J2
Barracks Cl BLOX/PEL WS3 283 L2
Barracks La BLOX/PEL WS3 283 K2
BRWNH WS8 269 J1
Barracks Rd NEWUL ST5 84 C2
Barracks Wy LEEK ST13 43 K4
Barrage Rd BIDD ST8 41 H4
Barrar Cl STRBR DY8 307 L2
Barratt Gdns BUCK/MIL ST2 70 B2
Barratt Rd ALS/KID ST7 37 M7
Barr Common Cl ALDR WS9 285 H7
Barr Common Rd ALDR WS9 285 G6
Barrett Dr BURS/TUN ST6 69 G4
Barrie Gdns ALS/KID ST7 52 C2
Barrington Cl ALBTN WV7 261 G5
BUTN/AL/TUT DE13 185 J1
WOLVN WV10 280 C1
Barrington Ct NEWUL ST5 68 D7
SHIF TF11 242 A5
Barr St SEDG DY3 299 J7
Barry Av BUCK/MIL ST2 3 L6
Bartholomew Rd LNGTN ST3 102 F2
Barthomley Rd ALS/KID ST7 50 F8
CW/SHV CW2 50 C4
HAN ST1 69 K4
Bartic Av KGSWFD DY6 303 M6
Bartlem St LNGTN ST3 86 D5
Bartlett Cl PENK ST19 229 M2
Barton Crs BURS/TUN ST6 68 E1
Barton La KGSWFD DY6 303 J2
RSTAF ST18 210 A2
Barton Ldg
BUTN/AL/TUT DE13 220 E1
Barton Rd
ETTPK/GDPK/PENN WV4 295 M6
Bartons La MKTDR TF9 130 B2
Barton's Rd MKTDR TF9 130 B2
Barton St BUT DE14 204 C2
Barton Turn
BUTN/AL/TUT DE13 221 G1
Barway ASHB DE6 127 L2
Barwood Av ALS/KID ST7 38 A5
Basalt Cl WSLW WS2 283 G6
Basfordbridge La LEEK ST13 57 K6
Basford La LEEK ST13 57 M2
Basford Park Rd NEWUL ST5 68 D7
Basil Cl STAFS ST17 193 M5
Basildon Gv LNGTN ST3 86 C8
Basin La TAM/AM/WIL B77 11 G7
Baskerville Rd HAN ST1 2 F3
Baskeyfield Cl LICHS WS14 9 K5
Baskeyfield Pl BURS/TUN ST6 54 B5
Baslow Cl BLOX/PEL WS3 267 H7
Baslow Gn SWAD DE11 205 L5
Baslow Rd BLOX/PEL WS3 267 H7
Basnett's Wood Rd
END/WER ST9 55 K4
Bassenthwaite Ct
KGSWFD DY6 303 K4
Bassett Cl CDLE ST10 89 J7
ETTPK/GDPK/PENN WV4 294 C4
SHHTH WV12 282 D6
Bassett St WSLW WS2 283 J8
Bassilow Rd STOKE ST4 85 M3
Bass's Crs SWAD DE11 223 L3
Baswich Crest STAFS ST17 194 D1
Baswich House Dr
STAFS ST17 194 D3
Baswich House Wy STAFS ST17 194 D3
Baswich La STAFS ST17 194 C1
Batchelor Cl STRBR DY8 307 M
Batch La ASHB DE6 145
Bateman Av BIDD ST8 40
Bates Gv WNSFLD WV11 281
Bate St WSLW WS2 283 L
Batesway RUGE WS15 216
Batfield La BDGNE WV15 304
Bath Av WOLV WV1 12
Bath La KINVER DY7 305
Bath Rd CNCK/NC WS11 231
NEWUL ST5 66
STRBR DY8 307
WOLV WV1 12
Baths La RSTAF ST18 177 J
Baths Rd LNGTN ST3 86
Bath St LEEK ST13 43
LNGTN ST3 87
SEDG DY3 299
STOKE ST4 85
WOLV WV1 13 J
Bath Ter STOKE ST4 85 G
Bathurst St LNGTN ST3 86
Batkin Cl BURS/TUN ST6 54
Batten Cl BLYBR/FOR ST11 103
Batten Wk STONE ST15 136
Battisson Crs LNGTN ST3 86
Battlefield Hl WMBN WV5 298
Battlefield La WMBN WV5 298
Battle Rdg RSTAF ST18 175
Battle Rd ALBTN WV7 260 B
Battlesteads CDLE ST10 107
Baulk La BLYBR/FOR ST11 121
Baxter Gn STAFN ST16 174
Baylie St STRBR DY8 307
Bayliss Av WNSFLD WV11 281
Baynton Rd SHHTH WV12 282
Bayston Av BDMR/CCFT WV3 294
Bayswater Rd RUGE WS15 215 K
SEDG DY3 299
Baytree Cl BLOX/PEL WS3 267
HAN ST1 3
Baytree Rd BLOX/PEL WS3 267
Baytree Wk LICHS WS14 255 L
Baywood Cl STAFS ST17 194 C
Beachcroft Rd KGSWFD DY6 303 J
Beachwood Av KGSWFD DY6 303
Beacon Dr BUTN/AL/TUT DE13 166
Beaconfields LICH WS13 8
Beacon Gdns LICH WS13 8
Beacon La BDGNE WV15 304
KINVER DY7 305
SEDG DY3 299
Beacon Pk PENK ST19 244
Beacon Ri ALDR WS9 285
SEDG DY3 299
STONE ST15 138
Beacon Rd BUTN/AL/TUT DE13 166
SHHTH WV12 282 C
STONE ST15 138
Beaconsfield NEWUL ST5 68
Beaconsfield Av
ETTPK/GDPK/PENN WV4 295 K
Beaconsfield Dr
ETTPK/GDPK/PENN WV4 295 K
LNGTN ST3 101
Beaconsfield Rd
BUTN/AL/TUT DE13 185
Beaconside RSTAF ST18 174
Beaconside Cl STAFN ST16 175
Beacon St BILS/COS WV14 299
LICH WS13 8
Beacon Wy ALDR WS9 269
HEDN WS12 232
RUSH/SHEL WS4 284
Beadborough Wk ALDR WS9 285 H
Beadnell Gv LNGTN ST3 102
Beale St STRBR DY8 307
Bealeys Av WNSFLD WV11 281
Bealeys La BLOX/PEL WS3 267
Beam Cl BUTN/AL/TUT DE13 185
Beamhill Rd
BUTN/AL/TUT DE13 184
Beamish La ALBTN WV7 261
Beard Gv BUCK/MIL ST2 70
Bearnett Dr
ETTPK/GDPK/PENN WV4 294
Bearnett La WMBN WV5 298
Bearwood Hill Rd
STPNHL/WNHL DE15 7
Beasley Av NEWUL ST5 67
Beasley Pl NEWUL ST5 67
Beat La MCFLDS SK11 27
Beaton Cl WLNHL WV13 281 L
Beaton Rd FOAKS/STRLY B74 287
Beatrice St BLOX/PEL WS3 283
Beattie Av NEWUL ST5 68
Beatty Cl SHIF TF11 242
Beaubrook Gdns STRBR DY8 303
Beauchamp Rd
TAM/AM/WIL B77 290
Beau Ct CNCK/NC WS11 249
Beaudesert BNTWD WS7 252
Beaudesert Vw HEDN WS12 233 G
Beaufort Av END/WER ST9 71
Beaufort Rd LNGTN ST3 86
STPNHL/WNHL DE15 186
Beaufort Wy ALDR WS9 285
Beaulieu Av KGSWFD DY6 303 M
Beaulieu Cl END/WER ST9 71
Beaumaris Cl DUDN DY1 299
STOKE ST4 84 D2
Beaumont Cl BIDD ST8 26
GTWY WS6 249
Beaumont Gdns STAFS ST17 193 H
Beaumont Rd BURS/TUN ST6 53
GTWY WS6 249
Beauty Bank Crs STRBR DY8 307
Beaver Cl WNSFLD WV11 281
Beaver Dr CDLE ST10 89
Bebington Cl COVEN WV9 279
Beckbury Av
ETTPK/GDPK/PENN WV4 294
Beckdale UTXR ST14 144
Beckenham Cl LNGTN ST3 103
Becket Cl MGN/WHC B75 286
Beckett Av LNGTN ST3 103
Beckfield Cl RUSH/SHEL WS4 284
Beckfields Cl BIDD ST8 41 H1
Beckminster Rd
BDMR/CCFT WV3 294 F

eck Rd AUD/MAD/W CW3 ...... 81 M3
eck's La BUTN/AL/TUT DE13 ...... 181 M7
he Beck CRTAM B79 ...... 256 E1
eckton Av BURS/TUN ST6 ...... 53 L7
edale Pl LNGTN ST3 ...... 101 L1
edcroft Rd STAFS ST17 ...... 101 M7
eddows Rd BLOX/PEL WS3 ...... 283 L5
eddow Wy BURS/TUN ST6 ...... 53 M4
edford Av STAFN ST1 ...... 5 J4
edford Crs NEWUL ST5 ...... 84 C6
edford Ct ALS/KID ST7 ...... 37 H5
edford Pl HEDN WS12 ...... 232 B6
edford Rd ALS/KID ST7 ...... 39 C7
  HAN ST1 ...... 2 A9
  STPNHL/WNHL DE15 ...... 204 D3
edford St HAN ST1 ...... 69 C8
edingstone Dr PENK ST19 ...... 230 A3
ednall Rd STAFS ST17 ...... 212 C1
eecham Ct ALDR WS9 ...... 285 C2
eech Av ALS/KID ST7 ...... 37 M2
  BUTN/AL/TUT DE13 ...... 185 M2
  BUTN/AL/TUT DE13 ...... 218 C4
  LEEK ST13 ...... 57 J6
  TAM/AM/WIL B77 ...... 11 J8
eechcliff La STOKE ST4 ...... 100 C7
eech Cl BIDD ST8 ...... 41 C1
  CDLE ST10 ...... 89 M8
  DUNHL/THL/PER WV6 ...... 277 J1
  KINVER DY7 ...... 306 D6
  LEEK ST13 ...... 43 J8
  PENK ST19 ...... 227 J4
  RSTAF ST18 ...... 191 M5
  RUGE WS15 ...... 217 J2
  SEDG DY3 ...... 299 L1
  UTXR ST14 ...... 144 A2
  WOLVN WV10 ...... 280 B2
eechcote Av KIDDW DY11 ...... 309 K8
eech Ct STONE ST15 ...... 138 B2
eech Crs BNTWD WS7 ...... 251 M4
eech Cft AUD/MAD/W CW3 ...... 81 L3
eech Dr DUNHL/THL/PER WV6 ...... 277 J3
eechcroft Av STAFS ST17 ...... 194 C3
eechcroft Est BARL ST12 ...... 101 M8
eechcroft Pl WOLVN WV10 ...... 280 C4
eechdale La STOKE ST4 ...... 118 D1
eech Dale Rd BARL ST12 ...... 118 F2
eechdale Rd BLOX/PEL WS3 ...... 282 F2
eech Dr ALS/KID ST7 ...... 52 L2
  ASHB DE6 ...... 95 K2
  BUTN/AL/TUT DE13 ...... 185 L2
eechen Gv BNTWD WS7 ...... 251 M2
eeches Cl KGSWFD DY6 ...... 303 K5
eeches Cft LICH WS13 ...... 237 K3
eeches Pl BLOX/PEL WS3 ...... 283 K3
eeches Rd BLOX/PEL WS3 ...... 283 K4
  RUGE WS15 ...... 215 M4
he Beeches NEWUL ST5 ...... 68 C3
  RUGE WS15 ...... 197 J7
  WOLV WV1 ...... 12 A3
eechfield Dr STAFS ST17 ...... 194 D5
eechfield Ri LICH WS13 ...... 9 J3
eechfield Rd STOKE ST4 ...... 101 H4
eechfields BARL ST12 ...... 101 M8
eech Gdns CDSL WV8 ...... 278 F1
  LICHS WS14 ...... 9 C6
eech Ga FOAKS/STRLY B74 ...... 286 B5
eech Gv HEDN WS12 ...... 231 K2
  LEEK ST13 ...... 43 J4
  MKTDR TF9 ...... 114 C5
  NEWUL ST5 ...... 68 C6
  STOKE ST4 ...... 85 J6
  SWAD DE11 ...... 205 M3
eechhouse La WMBN WV5 ...... 297 G2
eech Hurst Gdns WMBN WV5 ...... 293 C8
eech La BUTN/AL/TUT DE13 ...... 185 L2
  RSTAF ST18 ...... 193 J7
eechlawn Dr KINVER DY7 ...... 306 E3
eechmere Ri RUGE WS15 ...... 197 H8
eechmont Gv STAFS ST17 ...... 3 J1
eechmount Ri STAFS ST17 ...... 194 C3
eech Pine Cl HEDN WS12 ...... 232 A2
eech Rd BUTN/AL/TUT DE13 ...... 220 D2
  CRTAM B79 ...... 274 A2
  ECCH ST21 ...... 152 E4
  KGSWFD DY6 ...... 303 K5
  LNGTN ST3 ...... 101 M1
  STRBR DY8 ...... 307 J7
  WLNHL WV13 ...... 281 L8
  WOLVN WV10 ...... 280 B2
eech St BUT DE14 ...... 6 D9
  LNGTN ST3 ...... 86 C7
eech Tree Av WNSFLD WV11 ...... 281 J2
eech Tree Cl KGSWFD DY6 ...... 303 L2
eech Tree La CNCK/NC WS11 ...... 249 K2
eechtree La RUGE WS15 ...... 215 L1
eechtree Rd ALDR WS9 ...... 268 C7
eechurst Gdns ALBTN WV7 ...... 260 F5
eech Wk RUGE WS15 ...... 235 C1
eechway STAFS ST16 ...... 174 D4
eechwood LICHS WS14 ...... 255 L1
eechwood Av WNSFLD WV11 ...... 281 H2
eechwood Cl
  BLOX/PEL WS3 ...... 267 H7
  BLYBR/FOR ST11 ...... 103 M4
  NEWUL ST5 ...... 100 C1
eechwood Crs
  TAM/AM/WIL B77 ...... 11 L5
eechwood Cft
  FOAKS/STRLY B74 ...... 286 D5
eechwood Dr ALS/KID ST7 ...... 37 H6
  DUNHL/THL/PER WV6 ...... 279 C8
  STONE ST15 ...... 138 A4
eecroft Av LICH WS13 ...... 8 D1
eecroft Cl CNCK/NC WS11 ...... 249 L1
ee La WOLVN WV10 ...... 264 D7
eelow La CDLE ST10 ...... 91 K3
ees La RUGE WS15 ...... 215 L1
eeston Av ALS/KID ST7 ...... 53 C3
eeston Rd KIDD DY10 ...... 310 A3
eeston La LNGTN ST3 ...... 86 C5
eeston Rdg STAFS ST17 ...... 193 H3
effcote Rd GNOS ST20 ...... 189 M7
eggars Bush La WMBN WV5 ...... 298 A2
eggars La LEEK ST13 ...... 43 J5
eighton Cl FOAKS/STRLY B74 ...... 286 F4
elbroughton Rd STRBR DY8 ...... 307 L1
elfast Cl BURS/TUN ST6 ...... 54 B8
elfield Av NEWUL ST5 ...... 68 C4
elford Pl STOKE ST4 ...... 84 E1

Belfry Cl BLOX/PEL WS3 ...... 267 G7
Belfry Dr STRBR DY8 ...... 307 L4
The Belfry BUTN/AL/TUT DE13 ...... 185 J1
  DUNHL/THL/PER WV6 ...... 278 D6
Belgrade Rd WOLVN WV10 ...... 264 D8
Belgrave Av ALS/KID ST7 ...... 37 K5
  LNGTN ST3 ...... 86 B8
Belgrave Ct KGSWFD DY6 ...... 303 M6
Belgrave Crs LNGTN ST3 ...... 102 C1
Belgrave Rd NEWUL ST5 ...... 84 C2
  TAM/AM/WIL B77 ...... 290 E2
Belgrave Wk WSLW WS2 ...... 283 H7
Belinda Cl WLNHL WV13 ...... 281 M7
Bellamour La STAFS ST17 ...... 197 C4
Bellamour Wy RUGE WS15 ...... 197 M5
Bellamy La WNSFLD WV11 ...... 281 J3
Bellasis St STAFN ST16 ...... 174 D4
Bellbrook PENK ST19 ...... 229 L1
Bell Cl STAFN ST16 ...... 5 H1
Bell Dr HEDN WS12 ...... 232 C3
Bellefield Vw NEWUL ST5 ...... 68 C7
Bellencroft Gdns
  BDMR/CCFT WV3 ...... 294 B3
Bellerton La BURS/TUN ST6 ...... 54 E8
Belle Vue STRBR DY8 ...... 303 J8
Belle Vue Rd ASHB DE6 ...... 95 C1
  LEEK ST13 ...... 43 K4
Bellevue St BILS/COS WV14 ...... 295 M8
Bellflower Cl WOLVN WV10 ...... 265 C3
Bell Heather Rd BRWNH WS8 ...... 268 D4
Bellhouse La
  BUTN/AL/TUT DE13 ...... 183 L4
Bellhurst La PENK ST19 ...... 227 L7
Bellingham TAM/AM/WIL B77 ...... 291 K1
Bell La ASHB DE6 ...... 145 J2
  BARL ST12 ...... 101 L6
  BLOX/PEL WS3 ...... 283 H1
  BUTN/AL/TUT DE13 ...... 202 D8
Bell Orch MKTDR TF9 ...... 115 J5
Bellringer Cl BIDD ST8 ...... 40 C3
Bells End Rd MSHM DE12 ...... 221 K1
Bell's Hollow NEWUL ST5 ...... 52 E7
Bellsize Cl CNCK/NC WS11 ...... 250 F5
Bells La BNTWD WS7 ...... 251 M1
  STRBR DY8 ...... 307 K1
Bell St WOLV WV1 ...... 12 F6
Bellwood Cl LNGTN ST3 ...... 103 C4
Belmont Av CNCK/NC WS11 ...... 231 J8
Belmont Cl ALDR WS9 ...... 285 C3
  GTWY WS6 ...... 250 A6
Belmont Rd CDLE ST10 ...... 73 K2
  ETTPK/GDPK/PENN WV4 ...... 295 C5
  TAM/AM/WIL B77 ...... 290 E3
Belmont Rd BUTN/AL/TUT DE13 ...... 183 M1
Belper Rd ASHB DE6 ...... 95 K1
  BLOX/PEL WS3 ...... 267 J7
Belsize TAM/AM/WIL B77 ...... 274 E8
Belton Av WNSFLD WV11 ...... 281 H1
Belt Rd HEDN WS12 ...... 232 A5
Belvedere Av
  ETTPK/GDPK/PENN WV4 ...... 295 H5
Belvedere Cl BNTWD WS7 ...... 251 M5
  CRTAM B79 ...... 256 E1
  KGSWFD DY6 ...... 303 M6
  STAFS ST17 ...... 194 C2
Belvedere Gdns
  DUNHL/THL/PER WV6 ...... 279 L3
Belvedere Rd
  BUTN/AL/TUT DE13 ...... 185 C4
  STOKE ST4 ...... 101 C1
Belvedere Ter ALS/KID ST7 ...... 37 M3
Belvoir TAM/AM/WIL B77 ...... 290 C3
Belvoir Av STOKE ST4 ...... 101 H5
Belvoir Cl BUTN/AL/TUT DE13 ...... 185 H5
  DUDN DY1 ...... 299 L8
Belvoir Rd BUTN/AL/TUT DE13 ...... 6 B1
Belwell Dr FOAKS/STRLY B74 ...... 287 C8
Belwell La FOAKS/STRLY B74 ...... 287 C8
Bembridge Cl WNSFLD WV11 ...... 282 B2
Bemersley Rd BIDD ST8 ...... 54 C1
Benches Cl BNTWD WS7 ...... 251 K4
Bend Oak Dr
  STPNHL/WNHL DE15 ...... 186 C6
Benedict Pl BUCK/MIL ST2 ...... 3 L3
Benenden Cl STAFS ST17 ...... 194 B2
Bengal Gv STOKE ST4 ...... 101 J2
Bengry Rd LNGTN ST3 ...... 86 E8
Benion Rd CNCK/NC WS11 ...... 231 M6
Benjamins Wy ALS/KID ST7 ...... 51 M8
Bennett Pl NEWUL ST5 ...... 68 B3
Bennett Rd FOAKS/STRLY B74 ...... 286 D7
Bennett's Fold BKHL/PFLD WV2 ...... 12 E6
Bennetts La
  DUNHL/THL/PER WV6 ...... 292 F1
  MCFLDS SK11 ...... 18 E4
  UTXR ST14 ...... 143 J3
Bennett St BURS/TUN ST6 ...... 68 E3
Bennion Gv UTXR ST14 ...... 108 C5
Bennion St LNGTN ST3 ...... 86 C7
Benson Av
  ETTPK/GDPK/PENN WV4 ...... 295 J5
Benson Cl
  DUNHL/THL/PER WV6 ...... 278 E5
  LICH WS13 ...... 9 H4
Benson Rd BURS/TUN ST6 ...... 53 M5
Bennow Vw CRTAM B79 ...... 274 C2
Bent La NEWUL ST5 ...... 99 H7
Bentley Av NEWUL ST5 ...... 68 B6
Bentleybridge Wy
  WLNHL WV13 ...... 281 J6
Bentley Brook La
  HEDN WS12 ...... 233 G4
Bentley Dr CDSL WV8 ...... 262 F6
  WSLW WS2 ...... 283 H8
Bentley La SHHTH WV12 ...... 282 C6
Bentley New Dr WSLW WS2 ...... 283 H7
Bentley Pl WSLW WS2 ...... 283 J8
Bentley Rd BURS/TUN ST6 ...... 54 C5
  RDERBYSW DE65 ...... 166 E1
  UTXR ST14 ...... 143 M1
  WOLVN WV10 ...... 264 E8
Bentleys St MKTDR TF9 ...... 130 A3
Bentley Wy CRTAM B79 ...... 273 M3
Benton Cl SHHTH WV12 ...... 282 D6

Benton Crs BLOX/PEL WS3 ...... 267 K8
Benton's La GTWY WS6 ...... 267 C1
Bents La CDLE ST10 ...... 124 B7
Bentygrange La LEEK ST13 ...... 60 D6
Beowulf Covert
  BUTN/AL/TUT DE13 ...... 185 H1
Berdmore St STOKE ST4 ...... 86 A5
Beresford Av ASHB DE6 ...... 79 K8
Beresford Crs NEWUL ST5 ...... 84 A4
Beresford Dl AUD/MAD/W CW3 ...... 81 K3
  SWAD DE11 ...... 205 M8
Beresford La BUX SK17 ...... 48 C1
Beresford Rd BLOX/PEL WS3 ...... 283 L2
Beresford St STOKE ST4 ...... 85 H1
Bergamot Dr LNGTN ST3 ...... 103 G4
Berkeley Av ALS/KID ST7 ...... 37 K5
Berkeley Cl
  DUNHL/THL/PER WV6 ...... 278 D6
  GNOS ST20 ...... 190 E3
  WSLW WS2 ...... 282 F7
Berkeley Dr KGSWFD DY6 ...... 303 J3
Berkeley Rd HAN ST1 ...... 2 E7
  STONE ST15 ...... 137 M1
Berkeley Rd RUGE WS15 ...... 217 C8
Berkshire Gv NEWUL ST5 ...... 84 C5
The Berkshire
  BLOX/PEL WS3 ...... 267 C7
Berkswell Cl DUDN DY1 ...... 299 C7
  FOAKS/STRLY B74 ...... 286 E6
Bernard Gv LNGTN ST3 ...... 102 F6
Bernard St HAN ST1 ...... 2 E7
Berne Av NEWUL ST5 ...... 83 L4
Bernwall Ct STRBR DY8 ...... 307 M6
Berrisford Rd MKTDR TF9 ...... 130 D1
Berrybush Gdns SEDG DY3 ...... 299 L3
Berry Dr ALDR WS9 ...... 284 C5
Berryfield Gv LNGTN ST3 ...... 86 F5
Berryfields ALDR WS9 ...... 269 L5
  ALDR WS9 ...... 284 C5
Berry Gdns
  STPNHL/WNHL DE15 ...... 186 C6
Berry Hedge La
  STPNHL/WNHL DE15 ...... 186 C6
Berry Hi Rd HEDN WS12 ...... 232 C6
Berry La LNGTN ST3 ...... 86 B7
Berry Rd STAFN ST16 ...... 174 B3
Berry St STOKE ST4 ...... 85 H3
  WOLV WV1 ...... 13 C5
Bertelin Rd STOKE ST4 ...... 174 F3
Bert Smith Wy MKTDR TF9 ...... 112 C8
Berwick Dr CNCK/NC WS11 ...... 249 H2
Berwick Rd HAN ST1 ...... 69 L2
Berwyn Gv GTWY WS6 ...... 249 M7
Best Av STPNHL/WNHL DE15 ...... 205 H1
Best St STOKE ST4 ...... 85 M4
Beswick Cl CDLE ST10 ...... 105 K1
Beswick Rd BURS/TUN ST6 ...... 53 H4
Bethell Rd BURS/TUN ST6 ...... 69 K3
Bethesda Rd HAN ST1 ...... 2 C6
Bethesda St HAN ST1 ...... 2 C6
Betjeman Pl WOLVN WV10 ...... 281 G1
Betjeman Wk STAFS ST17 ...... 193 J3
Betley Hall Gdns
  AUD/MAD/W CW3 ...... 65 C4
Betley Pl NEWUL ST5 ...... 84 C5
Betlingspring La ASHB DE6 ...... 94 D7
Beton Wy STAFS ST16 ...... 174 D2
Bettany Gld WOLVN WV10 ...... 264 E6
Bettany Rd BURS/TUN ST6 ...... 69 G3
Betton St MKTDR TF9 ...... 112 E8
Betty Hatch La STAFN ST16 ...... 174 C5
Betty's La CNCK/NC WS11 ...... 251 G6
Beulah Dr MKTDR TF9 ...... 130 B1
Bevan Av ALS/KID ST7 ...... 52 D4
  ETTPK/GDPK/PENN WV4 ...... 295 L6
Bevan Cl RUSH/SHEL WS4 ...... 284 C1
Bevandean Cl STOKE ST4 ...... 101 J5
Bevan Lee Rd CNCK/NC WS11 ...... 231 K7
Bevan Rd AUD/MAD/W CW3 ...... 81 L4
Beverley Cl PENK ST19 ...... 229 M3
Beverley Crs BLYBR/FOR ST11 ...... 104 A2
  ETTPK/GDPK/PENN WV4 ...... 295 M6
Beverley Dr BUCK/MIL ST2 ...... 70 B8
  KGSWFD DY6 ...... 303 J3
  STAFN ST16 ...... 174 C2
Beverley Hi HEDN WS12 ...... 232 B8
Beverley Rd BUT DE14 ...... 203 M3
  DUNHL/THL/PER WV6 ...... 279 C6
Beville St STOKE ST4 ...... 85 L4
Bevin Rd WSLW WS2 ...... 282 E7
Bewcastle Gv LNGTN ST3 ...... 103 G3
Bewdley Dr WOLV WV1 ...... 281 H8
Bewley Rd SHHTH WV12 ...... 282 D6
Bew St BURS/TUN ST6 ...... 54 E5
Bexhill Gv HAN ST1 ...... 3 K1
Bexley St HAN ST1 ...... 2 B3
Bexmore Dr LICH WS13 ...... 254 F1
Beyer Cl TAM/AM/WIL B77 ...... 275 C3
Bhylls Gn WOLVN WV10 ...... 264 F6
Bhylls La BDMR/CCFT WV3 ...... 294 C3
Bibbey's Gn WOLVN WV10 ...... 264 F6
Bibby St ALS/KID ST7 ...... 37 L3
Bickford Cl PENK ST19 ...... 228 A4
Bickford Rd PENK ST19 ...... 228 B3
  WOLVN WV10 ...... 280 F5
Bickley Av FOAKS/STRLY B74 ...... 286 E5
Bickley Rd RUSH/SHEL WS4 ...... 284 C3
Bida La CONG CW12 ...... 26 B2
Biddles La ECCH ST21 ...... 117 K5
Biddulph Common Rd BIDD ST8 ...... 27 C3
Biddulph Park Rd BIDD ST8 ...... 27 C5
Biddulph Rd ALS/KID ST7 ...... 39 L4
  BIDD ST8 ...... 26 D5
  BURS/TUN ST6 ...... 54 B3
  CONG CW12 ...... 26 B1
Biddulph St CONG CW12 ...... 26 C3
Bideford Av STAFS ST17 ...... 194 D3
Bideford Rd CNCK/NC WS11 ...... 249 H2
Biggin Cl
  DUNHL/THL/PER WV6 ...... 278 E5
Bignall End Rd ALS/KID ST7 ...... 52 A6
Bigwood La RSTAF ST18 ...... 192 E7
Bilberry Cl RUGE WS15 ...... 215 J1
Bilberry Crs HEDN WS12 ...... 231 J5
Bilbrook Ct CDSL WV8 ...... 263 H7
Bilbrook Gv CDSL WV8 ...... 263 H7
Bilbrook Rd CDSL WV8 ...... 263 G6
Billinge St BURS/TUN ST6 ...... 68 E2

Billington Av RSTAF ST18 ...... 196 D1
Billington Bank RSTAF ST18 ...... 192 D4
Billy Buns La WMBN WV5 ...... 298 A2
Billy Wright Cl
  ETTPK/GDPK/PENN WV4 ...... 294 D4
Bilston Rd BKHL/PFLD WV2 ...... 13 L8
  WOLV WV1 ...... 13 H6
Bilton St STOKE ST4 ...... 85 G4
Bilton Street Island WOLV WV1 ...... 13 H6
Binbrook Rd SHHTH WV12 ...... 282 D6
Bingley St BDMR/CCFT WV3 ...... 12 B9
Birchall Av BURS/TUN ST6 ...... 53 J5
Birchall Cl LEEK ST13 ...... 43 M8
Birchall La LEEK ST13 ...... 43 M8
Birchall Park Av LEEK ST13 ...... 43 M7
Bircham Wk NEWUL ST5 ...... 84 B8
Birch Av ALS/KID ST7 ...... 37 L7
  BIDD ST8 ...... 40 A4
  BNTWD WS7 ...... 251 M4
  BRWNH WS8 ...... 268 E2
  CNCK/NC WS11 ...... 249 J2
Birch Brook La LICHS WS14 ...... 270 E4
Birch Cl BUT DE14 ...... 204 A2
  RSTAF ST18 ...... 177 H8
  STAFS ST17 ...... 194 F4
  UTXR ST14 ...... 108 D4
Birch Coppice WMBN WV5 ...... 297 L4
Birchcoppice Gdns
  SHHTH WV12 ...... 282 E6
Birch Cft ALDR WS9 ...... 285 J2
Birchcroft COVEN WV9 ...... 247 J8
Birch Di AUD/MAD/W CW3 ...... 81 L4
Birchdown Av CDLE ST10 ...... 105 M8
Birch Dr FOAKS/STRLY B74 ...... 286 D5
Birchendale Cl CDLE ST10 ...... 105 K1
Birchenwood Rd BURS/TUN ST6 ...... 53 L2
Birches Av CDSL WV8 ...... 279 J1
Birches Barn Av
  BDMR/CCFT WV3 ...... 294 F3
Birches Barn Rd
  BDMR/CCFT WV3 ...... 294 F2
Birches Cl BUTN/AL/TUT DE13 ...... 185 J1
  HAN ST1 ...... 2 F1
Birches Head Rd BUCK/MIL ST2 ...... 70 A3
  HAN ST1 ...... 2 F1
Birches Park Rd CDSL WV8 ...... 263 G6
Birches Rd CDSL WV8 ...... 263 H8
The Birches CDLE ST10 ...... 89 K8
Birches Va RUGE WS15 ...... 214 D4
Birchfield Av ALS/KID ST7 ...... 37 M3
  DUNHL/THL/PER WV6 ...... 279 H4
  STPNHL/WNHL DE15 ...... 204 D4
Birchfields Dr HEDN WS12 ...... 250 D1
Birchfields Rd SHHTH WV12 ...... 282 A5
Birchgate BUCK/MIL ST2 ...... 70 C6
Birch Green Gv HAN ST1 ...... 69 L3
Birchglade BDMR/CCFT WV3 ...... 294 D1
Birch Gv BLYBR/FOR ST11 ...... 104 A3
  LICH WS13 ...... 9 K3
  LNGTN ST3 ...... 103 C6
  POL/KGSB/FAZ B78 ...... 291 K3
Birch Hill Av WMBN WV5 ...... 297 M5
Birch House La STONE ST15 ...... 136 K1
Birch House Rd NEWUL ST5 ...... 67 K2
  STONE ST15 ...... 136 A3
Birch House Wy STONE ST15 ...... 136 A2
Birchills St WSLW WS2 ...... 283 J8
Birchlands Rd HAN ST1 ...... 3 J1
Birch La ALDR WS9 ...... 285 K1
  RUGE WS15 ...... 215 M5
  RUSH/SHEL WS4 ...... 284 C1
Birchmoor La GNOS ST20 ...... 208 D8
Birchmoor Rd
  POL/KGSB/FAZ B78 ...... 291 L2
Birchover Rd WSLW WS2 ...... 283 C6
Birchover Wy BURS/TUN ST6 ...... 54 A2
Birch Ri MKTDR TF9 ...... 114 E7
Birch Rd ALS/KID ST7 ...... 66 F1
  SEDG DY3 ...... 299 M1
  STONE ST15 ...... 138 B3
  WNSFLD WV11 ...... 281 M1
Birch St HAN ST1 ...... 3 G3
  WOLV WV1 ...... 12 E5
  WSLW WS2 ...... 283 K7
Birchtree Hollow SHHTH WV12 ...... 282 D5
Birch Tree La ALS/KID ST7 ...... 39 H3
  NEWUL ST5 ...... 98 C3
Birchtree La RUGE WS15 ...... 215 L4
Birchwood Cl WNSFLD WV11 ...... 266 A7
Birchwood Rd
  ETTPK/GDPK/PENN WV4 ...... 295 C5
  LICHS WS14 ...... 9 M5
Birchwood Vw ASHB DE6 ...... 79 J7
Bird Cage Wk HAN ST1 ...... 2 C6
Birdhope TAM/AM/WIL B77 ...... 291 J1
Bird Rd LNGTN ST3 ...... 87 H8
Bird's Barn La KINVER DY7 ...... 305 J8
Birds Bush Rd
  TAM/AM/WIL B77 ...... 290 C2
Birdsgrove La ASHB DE6 ...... 78 D7
Bird St LICH WS13 ...... 8 D3
  SEDG DY3 ...... 299 J7
Birkdale Av BUT DE14 ...... 204 A4
Birkdale Cl STRBR DY8 ...... 311 H1
  WOLV WV1 ...... 281 G8
Birkdale Dr ALS/KID ST7 ...... 39 J7
  STAFN ST16 ...... 175 J6
Birkdale Rd BLOX/PEL WS3 ...... 267 G3
Birkholme Dr LNGTN ST3 ...... 103 C5
Birks Dr MKTDR TF9 ...... 114 E5
Birks St STOKE ST4 ...... 85 H5
Birmingham New Rd
  ETTPK/GDPK/PENN WV4 ...... 295 L4
Birmingham Rd ALDR WS9 ...... 285 C5
  BKHL/PFLD WV2 ...... 13 C9
  KIDD DY10 ...... 311 J8
  LICHS WS14 ...... 8 D9
  LICHS WS14 ...... 271 C3
  MGN/WHC B75 ...... 287 C5
Birmingham St WLNHL WV13 ...... 282 B8

Birrell St STOKE ST4 ...... 85 M5
Biscay Gv STOKE ST4 ...... 101 J2
Bishop Rd BURS/TUN ST6 ...... 54 A5
Bishop's Cl ALS/KID ST7 ...... 52 D2
Bishops Ct ECCH ST21 ...... 152 E3
Bishops Dr PENK ST19 ...... 246 D3
Bishops Gra RUGE WS15 ...... 197 M8
Bishops La MKTDR TF9 ...... 130 B1
Bishops Meadow
  MGN/WHC B75 ...... 287 L7
Bishops Wy FOAKS/STRLY B74 ...... 286 F4
Bishton La STAFS ST17 ...... 197 C4
Bishton Rd ALBTN WV7 ...... 260 F6
Bitham Cl PENK ST19 ...... 229 M2
Bitham Ct BUTN/AL/TUT DE13 ...... 185 J1
Bitham La BUTN/AL/TUT DE13 ...... 185 J1
Bittell Cl WOLVN WV10 ...... 264 E6
Bitterne Dr
  DUNHL/THL/PER WV6 ...... 12 B1
Bitterne Pl BUCK/MIL ST2 ...... 86 D2
Bitterscote La
  POL/KGSB/FAZ B78 ...... 274 A8
Black Bank Rd END/WER ST9 ...... 56 D5
Blackbank Rd NEWUL ST5 ...... 67 J6
Blackberry La ALDR WS9 ...... 269 H6
  FOAKS/STRLY B74 ...... 286 B3
  STAFN ST16 ...... 4 B3
Blackbird UTXR ST14 ...... 144 C4
Blackbird Cl UTXR ST14 ...... 144 C4
Blackbird Wy BIDD ST8 ...... 40 E2
Blackbrook Av NEWUL ST5 ...... 67 J2
Blackbrook Wy WOLVN WV10 ...... 264 E6
Blackburn Av
  DUNHL/THL/PER WV6 ...... 279 L3
Blackdown Av HEDN WS12 ...... 291 J1
Black Dr RSTAF ST18 ...... 176 C4
Blackflats Rd STONE ST15 ...... 136 B1
Blackfriars Cl CRTAM B79 ...... 273 L5
Blackfriars Rd NEWUL ST5 ...... 84 B2
Blackhalve La WNSFLD WV11 ...... 281 C2
Blackham Rd WNSFLD WV11 ...... 281 M2
Blackheath La LNGTN ST3 ...... 86 D7
Blackheath La RSTAF ST18 ...... 175 L6
Blackhole La RSTAF ST18 ...... 173 K8
Black Horse La HAN ST1 ...... 2 B5
Blackie's La STONE ST15 ...... 138 D3
Blacklake Dr LNGTN ST3 ...... 103 G6
Black La CDLE ST10 ...... 74 D7
  NWPT TF10 ...... 169 K8
Blackpit La BUTN/AL/TUT DE13 ...... 145 H2
  WMBN WV5 ...... 293 L7
Blackpool St BUT DE14 ...... 204 C2
Blackroot Cl BNTWD WS7 ...... 252 D6
Blackshaw Cl CONG CW12 ...... 26 B1
Blacksmith La LICHS WS14 ...... 255 L4
Blacksmith's La
  RDERBYSW DE65 ...... 167 C5
  STPNHL/WNHL DE15 ...... 186 C2
Blackthorn Av BNTWD WS7 ...... 251 M6
Blackthorn Crs NEWUL ST5 ...... 233 G4
Blackthorne Rd DUDN DY1 ...... 299 M6
  LICHS WS14 ...... 9 M5
Blackthorn Pl NEWUL ST5 ...... 67 L2
Blackthorn Rd
  STPNHL/WNHL DE15 ...... 204 E4
  STRBR DY8 ...... 307 H1
Blackwell's Rw BURS/TUN ST6 ...... 2 B1
Blackwood Av WNSFLD WV11 ...... 281 J1
Blackwood Pl LNGTN ST3 ...... 86 E6
Blackwood Rd
  TAM/AM/WIL B77 ...... 290 C3
Bladon Av NEWUL ST5 ...... 84 B8
Bladon Cl BURS/TUN ST6 ...... 54 A2
Bladon Crs ALS/KID ST7 ...... 37 J5
Bladon St STPNHL/WNHL DE15 ...... 186 C7
Bladon Vw BUTN/AL/TUT DE13 ...... 166 F8
Blaizefield Cl AUD/MAD/W CW3 ...... 80 C8
Blake Cl CNCK/NC WS11 ...... 232 A4
Blakeley Av
  DUNHL/THL/PER WV6 ...... 279 M3
Blakeley Heath Dr
  WMBN WV5 ...... 298 A5
Blakeley La CDLE ST10 ...... 74 F6
Blakeley Ri
  DUNHL/THL/PER WV6 ...... 279 M3
Blakelow La ASHB DE6 ...... 93 H1
Blakelow Rd BUCK/MIL ST2 ...... 70 B4
Blakemore Rd ALDR WS9 ...... 269 K1
Blakenall Cl BLOX/PEL WS3 ...... 283 K1
Blakenall Heath BLOX/PEL WS3 ...... 283 K2
Blakenall La BLOX/PEL WS3 ...... 283 K2
Blakenall Rw BLOX/PEL WS3 ...... 283 K2
Blakeney Av NEWUL ST5 ...... 84 B7
  STRBR DY8 ...... 307 K4
Blakeney Cl SEDG DY3 ...... 299 J2
Blakeshall La KIDDW DY11 ...... 309 K5
Blake St BURS/TUN ST6 ...... 68 L2
  FOAKS/STRLY B74 ...... 286 E4
Blakeways Cl CRTAM B79 ...... 239 J5
Blakiston St STAFN ST16 ...... 5 H2
Blanchard Cl
  BLYBR/FOR ST11 ...... 103 J3
Blandford Dr STRBR DY8 ...... 303 L8
Blandford Gdns BNTWD WS7 ...... 252 C4
Blanefield CDSL WV8 ...... 263 L8
Blantyre St LNGTN ST3 ...... 86 C8
Blay Av WSLW WS2 ...... 283 H8
Blaydon Av MGN/WHC B75 ...... 287 L8
Blaydon Rd COVEN WV9 ...... 280 A1
Blaze Hill Rd KGSWFD DY6 ...... 303 G2
Blaze Pk KGSWFD DY6 ...... 303 H2
Bleak House Dr BNTWD WS7 ...... 252 D3
Bleak Pl BURS/TUN ST6 ...... 69 G3
Bleakridge Av NEWUL ST5 ...... 68 B2
Bleak St NEWUL ST5 ...... 68 B2
Bleeding Wolf La ALS/KID ST7 ...... 38 E5
Blencarn Gv END/WER ST9 ...... 55 J6
Blenheim Cl RUSH/SHEL WS4 ...... 284 D3
  STPNHL/WNHL DE15 ...... 186 C7
  TAM/AM/WIL B77 ...... 10 F6
Blenheim Crs ALBTN WV7 ...... 260 F2
Blenheim Rd ASHB DE6 ...... 95 L3
  BNTWD WS7 ...... 252 A2
  CNCK/NC WS11 ...... 251 H6
  KGSWFD DY6 ...... 303 M4
  SHHTH WV12 ...... 282 B4
Blenheim St STOKE ST4 ...... 85 K5
Blenheim Wy DUDN DY1 ...... 299 L8

LICH WS13 .... 237 H5
Bleriot Cl BLYBR/FOR ST11 ...... 103 J3
Blewitt St HEDN WS12 .... 232 B4
Blithbury Rd RUGE WS15 .... 198 B7
Blithe Cl RDERBYSW DE65 .... 166 E1 🔲
Blithfield Cl END/WER ST9 .... 71 G8
Blithfield Pl CNCK/NC WS11 ...... 250 B1
Blithfield Rd BRWNH WS8 .... 251 J8
Bloomfield Cl RDERBYSW DE65 ... 166 D1
  WMBN WV5 .... 297 K4
Bloomfield Crs LICH WS13 .... 236 A8 🔲
Bloomfield Dr SHTH WV12 .... 282 D1
Bloomfield Wy CRTAM B79 .... 273 M3
Bloomsbury St BKHL/PFLD WV2 ... 12 E7
Bloomsbury Wy LICHS WS14 .... 9 L4
Blore Cl ASHB DE6 .... 95 K2
Blore Rd MKTDR TF9 .... 131 L1
Blossomfield Cl KGSWFD DY6 ..... 303 L2 🔲
Blossom's Fold WOLV WV1 .... 12 F5 🔲
Blount Cl PENK ST19 .... 229 M3
Blount's Dr UTXR ST14 .... 144 A4
Bloxwich La WSLW WS2 .... 283 G4
Bloxwich Rd BLOX/PEL WS3 .... 283 K4
  WSLW WS2 .... 283 K4
Bloxwich Rd North
  SHTH WV12 .... 282 D4
Bloxwich Rd South
  WLNHL WV13 .... 282 A7
Bluebell Cl BIDD ST8 .... 40 E3
  HEDN WS12 .... 232 B4 🔲
  STRBR DY8 .... 303 J8 🔲
Bluebell La CTWY WS6 .... 266 F1
Bluebell Rd ALDR WS9 .... 269 H7
Bluebird Cl LICHS WS14 .... 9 K3
Blue Cedars STRBR DY8 .... 307 L4 🔲
Blue House La ALBTN WV7 .... 261 G3
Blue La East WSLW WS2 .... 283 K8
Blue La West WSLW WS2 .... 283 K8
Bluestone Av BURS/TUN ST6 ...... 54 B8
Bluestone La
  STPNHL/WNHL DE15 ...... 204 F3
Blundies La KINVER DY7 .... 301 L7
Blunts Hollow RUGE WS15 .... 180 E5
Blunt St NEWUL ST5 .... 68 C6
Blurton Rd BARL ST12 .... 102 A8
  LNGTN ST3 .... 85 L7
  LNGTN ST3 .... 102 A5
  STOKE ST4 .... 85 L6
Blythe Av LNGTN ST3 .... 103 C6
Blythe Bridge Bank RSTAF ST18..159 M4
Blythe Bridge Rd
  BLYBR/FOR ST11 .... 87 L8
Blythe Cl BLYBR/FOR ST11 ...... 103 K3
  BNTWD WS7 .... 252 D4
Blythe Gdns CDSL WV8 .... 262 F6
Blythe Mount Pk
  BLYBR/FOR ST11 .... 104 A3 🔲
  STAFS ST17 .... 104 A3 🔲
Blythe Rd BLYBR/FOR ST11 ..... 104 A3 🔲
Blythe St TAM/AM/WIL B77 .... 10 F7
Blythe Vw BLYBR/FOR ST11 ..... 103 M4
Blythfield BUT DE14 .... 7 K3
Boardman Crs STAFN ST16 .... 4 B6
Boardman Rd SWAD DE11 .... 205 L1
Boardmans Bank BURS/TUN ST6.. 55 C1
Board School Gdns
  SEDG DY3 .... 299 L4 🔲
Boathorse Rd ALS/KID ST7 ...... 52 F2
  BURS/TUN ST6 .... 53 C4
Boat La LICHS WS14 .... 269 M1
  RSTAF ST18 .... 157 J7
Boatman's La ALDR WS9 .... 268 E8
Bodicote Gv MGN/WHC B75 ..... 287 L7
Bodington Rd MGN/WHC B75 .... 287 H7
Bodmin Av STAFS ST17 .... 194 D3
Bognop Rd WNSFLD WV11 ...... 265 K6
Bogs La BLYBR/FOR ST11 .... 103 M4
Bolberry Cl LNGTN ST3 .... 102 E1 🔲
Bold St HAN ST1 .... 2 F3
Bolebridge St CRTAM B79 .... 10 D4
Boley Cl LICHS WS14 .... 9 H5
Boley Cottage La LICHS WS14 ..... 9 K5
Boley La LICHS WS14 .... 9 J4
Boleyn Cl CTWY WS6 .... 249 K8
Bolina Gv LNGTN ST3 .... 86 B4 🔲
Bollin Cl ALS/KID ST7 .... 36 F7
Bollin Gv BIDD ST8 .... 40 E1
Bolney Gv HAN ST1 .... 3 J2
Bolsover Cl BURS/TUN ST6 ...... 54 A2
Bolton Pl LNGTN ST3 .... 102 F2
Bolton Rd WNSFLD WV11 ...... 281 J5
Bolton Wy BLOX/PEL WS3 ...... 266 F7 🔲
Boma Rd STOKE ST4 .... 100 F3
Bond End BUTN/AL/TUT DE13 ... 201 G8
Bondfield La
  BUTN/AL/TUT DE13 ...... 200 E8
Bondfield Wy LNGTN ST3 .... 87 H8 🔲
Bond St BKHL/PFLD WV2 .... 12 F7
  BURS/TUN ST6 .... 53 K6
  BUT DE14 .... 7 H8
Bondway HEDN WS12 .... 231 M2
Bonehill Rd POL/KGSBS/FAZ B78 . 10 B6
Bone Mill La WOLV WV1 .... 281 H2
Boney Hay Rd BNTWD WS7 ...... 252 B2
Boningale Wy STAFS ST17 .... 193 H2 🔲
Bonnard Cl BLYBR/FOR ST11 .... 103 J4 🔲
Bonner Gv ALDR WS9 .... 284 F5
Bonnington Crs STAFN ST16 .... 174 B8
Bonville Gdns WOLVN WV10 .... 264 E6 🔲
Boon Av STOKE ST4 .... 85 C4
Boon Gv STAFS ST17 .... 193 L4
Boon Hill Rd ALS/KID ST7 .... 66 F1
Boothby Av ASHB DE6 .... 79 J8 🔲
Booth Cl BLOX/PEL WS3 .... 283 K2
  LICH WS13 .... 236 A8
Boothen Gn STOKE ST4 .... 85 H5
Boothen Old Rd STOKE ST4 ..... 85 H5
Boothen Rd STOKE ST4 .... 85 H4
Boothenwood Ter STOKE ST4 . 85 G5 🔲
Booth La RSTAF ST18 .... 159 L6
  RUGE WS15 .... 159 L6
Boothroyd St HAN ST1 .... 2 D6
Booth St ALS/KID ST7 .... 51 K8
  BLOX/PEL WS3 .... 283 J2
  HEDN WS12 .... 232 B4
  NEWUL ST5 .... 67 H4
  STOKE ST4 .... 85 H5
Bordeaux Cl DUDN DY1 .... 299 L7

Bordeaux Rd LNGTN ST3 .... 103 G2 🔲
Borden Cl CDSL WV8 .... 279 M2
Border Wy STAFS ST17 .... 193 L4
Bore St LICH WS13 .... 8 E4
Borman CRTAM B79 .... 273 M5
Borneo St RUSH/SHEL WS4 ...... 283 M6
Borough Crs STRBR DY8 .... 307 L5
Borough La RUGE WS15 .... 234 F2
Borough Rd BUT DE14 .... 6 E4
  CRTAM B79 .... 274 B3
Borrowcop La LICHS WS14 .... 9 H8
Borrowdale Rd
  BURS/TUN ST6 .... 54 E7 🔲
Borrow St WLNHL WV13 .... 282 A7 🔲
Boscobel Cl DUDN DY1 .... 299 M7
Boscombe Gv STOKE ST4 ...... 101 J5
Boscomoor Ct PENK ST19 ...... 229 L3 🔲
Boscomoor La PENK ST19 .... 229 L3
Bosinney Cl STOKE ST4 .... 86 B5
Bosley Gv BURS/TUN ST6 .... 53 J3
Bosley Vw CONG CW12 .... 26 B1
Bostock Cl STONE ST15 .... 138 D5 🔲
Boston Cl HEDN WS12 .... 250 E1
Bosty La ALDR WS9 .... 284 D5
Boswell Rd CNCK/NC WS11 ...... 231 K6
Boswell St STOKE ST4 .... 84 F1 🔲
Bosworth Cl SEDG DY3 .... 299 M4
Bosworth Dr
  BUTN/AL/TUT DE13 ...... 185 H4
Botany Bay Rd HAN ST1 .... 3 H3
Botany Dr SEDG DY3 .... 299 K5
Botfield Cl ALBTN WV7 .... 261 H4 🔲
Botfield Rd SHIF TF11 .... 242 A5
Botham Dr LEEK ST13 .... 57 K5
Botteslow St HAN ST1 .... 2 F7
Bottom La CDLE ST10 .... 59 J5
  STONE ST15 .... 118 B3
Boucher Rd LEEK ST13 .... 57 J7
Boughey Rd ALS/KID ST7 .... 51 M8
  RUGE WS15 .... 233 M5
Boughey St BURS/TUN ST6 ...... 68 D2
  STOKE ST4 .... 85 C4
The Boulevard BURS/TUN ST6 ... 53 L7
Boulmer Av ALBTN WV7 .... 260 D2
Boulton Cl BNTWD WS7 .... 252 B2
Boulton St HAN ST1 .... 2 F1
  NEWUL ST5 .... 68 C4
Boundary Cl STONE ST15 ...... 137 M5 🔲
Boundary Crs SEDG DY3 .... 299 J7
Boundary Hl SEDG DY3 .... 299 J6
Boundary La CONG CW12 .... 26 A2
Boundary Rd ALDR WS9 .... 268 F7
  RDERBYSW DE65 .... 167 K2
Boundary St HAN ST1 .... 2 C2
Boundary Stret STOKE ST4 ..... 84 D1 🔲
Boundary Vw CDLE ST10 .... 89 H8 🔲
Boundary Wy
  DUNHL/THL/PER WV6 .... 278 F8
  ETTPK/GDPK/PENN WV4 . 294 C4
Bourne Cl
  BUTN/AL/TUT DE13 ..... 165 H4 🔲
  HEDN WS12 .... 232 D8
Bourne Pl LEEK ST13 .... 43 J4
Bourne Rd ALS/KID ST7 .... 38 F8
Bournes Bank BURS/TUN ST6 ... 68 F2
Bourne St ALS/KID ST7 .... 39 J3
  STOKE ST4 .... 85 L6
Bourne V ALDR WS9 .... 285 K7
Bouverie Pde HAN ST1 .... 69 M2
Bowden St BURS/TUN ST6 ...... 69 H1
Bowdler Rd BKHL/PFLD WV2 .... 13 H9
Bowen-cooke Av CDSL WV8 .... 278 E4
Bowen St
  ETTPK/GDPK/PENN WV4 .. 295 L5
Bower Cl LICHS WS14 .... 236 D8
Bower End La AUD/MAD/W CW3.. 81 K4
Bower La RUGE WS15 .... 197 H8
Bowers Ct STONE ST15 .... 138 D3
Bowers La STONE ST15 .... 138 C7
Bower St HAN ST1 .... 2 D8
Bowes Dr CNCK/NC WS11 ...... 231 M6
Bowfell Gv STOKE ST4 .... 86 B3
Bowhill La AUD/MAD/W CW3 .... 65 J4
Bowker St WLNHL WV13 .... 281 J8
Bowland Av NEWUL ST5 .... 67 K7
Bowlers Cl BURS/TUN ST6 ...... 69 C4
Bowlingalley La ASHB DE6 ...... 109 K2
Bowling Alley La LICHS WS14 ... 255 K5
Bowling Alley Or Vicarage La
  STAFS ST17 .... 212 F2
Bowling Green Av
  TAM/AM/WIL B77 .... 290 E3
Bowling Green La ALBTN WV7 .. 260 C5
Bowling Green Rd STRBR DY8 .. 307 L5
Bowman Gv BURS/TUN ST6 ..... 54 B3
Bowman's Ri WOLV WV1 .... 281 C7
Bowmead Cl STOKE ST4 .... 101 J4 🔲
Bowness St HAN ST1 .... 2 A2
Bowood Dr
  DUNHL/THL/PER WV6 .... 279 K5
Bowsey Wood Rd
  AUD/MAD/W CW3 .... 81 K1
Bowstead St STOKE ST4 .... 85 H3 🔲
Bow St RUGE WS15 .... 215 L1
Bowyer Av BURS/TUN ST6 ...... 54 E5 🔲
Boxer Cl RUGE WS15 .... 217 J7
Box La LNGTN ST3 .... 86 F8
Boxwood Rd CDLE ST10 .... 105 L6
Boyden Cl CNCK/NC WS11 ..... 249 H1
  PENK ST19 .... 230 A3
Boyles Hall Rd ALS/KID ST7 ..... 51 L8
Brabazon Cl BLYBR/FOR ST11 .. 103 J3 🔲
Bracken Av MKTDR TF9 .... 114 C5
Brackenberry NEWUL ST5 ...... 68 B7
Bracken Cl ALS/KID ST7 .... 37 M2
  BARL ST12 .... 119 C1
  BNTWD WS7 .... 252 C3
  CDSL WV8 .... 279 L1
  HEDN WS12 .... 232 C2
  LICHS WS14 .... 9 L6
  LNGTN ST3 .... 102 F5
  STAFN ST16 .... 174 B3 🔲
Brackenfield Av BUCK/MIL ST2 .. 86 C1
Brackenfield Wy STAFN ST16 .. 174 D2
Brackenhill Rd BNTWD WS7 ... 252 A2
Bracken Park Gdns STRBR DY8 .303 M8 🔲
Bracken Rd HEDN WS12 ...... 231 J5
The Brackens NEWUL ST5 ...... 84 B8
Bracken St STOKE ST4 .... 85 L6

Bracken Vw STAFS ST17 .... 195 H7
Bracken Wy RUGE WS15 .... 197 J8
Brackenwood Dr
  WNSFLD WV11 .... 281 M5
Brackenwood Rd
  STPNHL/WNHL DE15 .... 204 E4
Bracklesham Wy
  TAM/AM/WIL B77 .... 275 C4
Brackley Av BURS/TUN ST6 ..... 69 H1
Bradburn Rd WNSFLD WV11 ... 281 H2
Bradbury Cl BRWNH WS8 ...... 268 F5
  BURS/TUN ST6 .... 54 E7 🔲
Bradbury La
  BUTN/AL/TUT DE13 ..... 218 C4
  HEDN WS12 .... 232 A2
  KINVER DY7 .... 300 E7
Bradbury Ri STAFN ST16 ...... 174 A6
Braden Rd
  ETTPK/GDPK/PENN WV4 . 294 D6
Bradford Rd BRWNH WS8 ...... 268 E2
Bradford St CNCK/NC WS11 .... 232 A5
  CRTAM B79 .... 273 M5
Bradford Ter HAN ST1 .... 3 C1
Bradgate St SHHTH WV12 ..... 282 C4 🔲
Bradgate Dr FOAKS/STRLY B74 .. 286 C5
Bradley Dr ECCH ST21 .... 135 M7
Bradley La STAFS ST17 .... 192 B8
Bradley Rd BKHL/PFLD WV2 ... 295 L3
  STRBR DY8 .... 307 M4
Bradley St STPNHL/WNHL DE15 . 204 E3
Bradley Vw ASHB DE6 .... 79 K7
Bradmore Rd BDMR/CCFT WV3 . 294 F2
  BUTN/AL/TUT DE13 ..... 185 H5
Bradshaw Meadow
  RDERBYSW DE65 .... 165 J1 🔲
Bradshaw St WOLV WV1 ...... 13 H5 🔲
Bradshaw Wy STAF16 .... 174 D2
Bradwell Cft MGN/WHC B75 .. 287 L7 🔲
Bradwell Gra NEWUL ST5 ...... 68 B4
Bradwell La NEWUL ST5 .... 68 A3
  RUGE WS15 .... 233 M5
Bradwell St BURS/TUN ST6 .... 68 D2
Braemar Av STRBR DY8 .... 307 J1
Braemar Cl BUCK/MIL ST2 ..... 70 D6
  SEDG DY3 .... 299 J1
  SHHTH WV12 .... 282 A4
Braemar Gdns HEDN WS12 .... 231 M3
Braemar Rd CNCK/NC WS11 ... 251 C6
  DUNHL/THL/PER WV6 ... 277 J8 🔲
Braemore Rd BUCK/MIL ST2 .... 70 B4
Braeside Wy BLOX/PEL WS3 .. 267 M4
Braham CRTAM B79 .... 273 K4
Brailsford Cl SWAD DE11 ...... 205 L5 🔲
Brailsford Cl WNSFLD WV11 .. 281 L2 🔲
Brain St TAM/AM/WIL B77 ..... 275 C8
Braithwaite Cl KGSWFD DY6 .. 303 K4 🔲
Braithwell Dr BUCK/MIL ST2 .... 55 C8
Brake La STRBR DY8 .... 311 L4
Brakespeare St BURS/TUN ST6 .. 53 J3
The Brake ALS/KID ST7 .... 39 H3
Brake Village ALS/KID ST7 ...... 39 H5
Bramall La STAFN ST16 .... 174 C4
Bramber Dr WMBN WV5 ...... 297 M4
Bramber Wy STRBR DY8 ...... 307 M3
Bramble Cl BRWNH WS8 ...... 268 E5
  SHHTH WV12 .... 282 C3
Bramble Dr HEDN WS12 ...... 232 C3
Bramble Gv DUDN DY1 .... 299 M5
Bramble Lea AUD/MAD/W CW3 . 81 L4 🔲
Brambleside STAFS ST17 ...... 194 C5 🔲
  STRBR DY8 .... 307 M1
The Brambles LICHS WS14 ...... 9 J6
  NEWUL ST5 .... 84 C8
Bramble Wy RUGE WS15 ...... 215 J1 🔲
Bramblewood WMBN WV5 .... 298 A3 🔲
Bramblewood Dr
  BDMR/CCFT WV3 .... 294 C2
Brambling TAM/AM/WIL B77 .. 291 G3 🔲
Brambling Cl UTXR ST14 ...... 144 C4 🔲
The Bramblings STAFS ST17 .. 194 D5
Bramdean Dr PENK ST19 ...... 229 M1 🔲
Bramell Cl BUT DE14 .... 203 M3
Bramerton Cl WNSFLD WV11 .. 281 C4
Bramfield Dr NEWUL ST5 .... 68 C8
Bramhall Cl RSTAF ST18 ...... 173 H3
Bramley Cl CDLE ST10 .... 89 L8
Bramley Ct RDERBYSW DE65 . 165 J1 🔲
Bramley Dl SWAD DE11 ...... 205 M8
Bramley Pl STOKE ST4 .... 84 E8
Bramley Wy LICHS WS14 ..... 255 K5
Brammall Dr BLYBR/FOR ST11 . 103 L3
Brammer St BURS/TUN ST6 .... 54 C7
Brampton Cl END/WER ST9 .... 55 M2 🔲
  KIDD DY10 .... 310 B6
Brampton Dr HEDN WS12 .... 232 B8
Brampton Gdns NEWUL ST5 .... 68 C7
Brampton Rd NEWUL ST5 ...... 68 C7
Brampton Sidings NEWUL ST5 . 68 B8
Bramshall Rd UTXR ST14 ...... 143 L2
The Bramshaws CDLE ST10 .... 89 L8 🔲
Bramshaw Av
  DUNHL/THL/PER WV6 ... 279 H8
Brancaster Cl TAM/AM/WIL B77..275 C4
Branchal Rd ALDR WS9 ...... 285 J1
Brandon Cl
  FOAKS/STRLY B74 ..... 285 M7 🔲
  SEDG DY3 .... 299 L3
Brandon Gv STOKE ST4 ...... 100 F2
Brandon Pk BDMR/CCFT WV3 . 294 F3
The Brandons STAFS ST17 ... 193 M5 🔲
Bransdale Cl
  DUNHL/THL/PER WV6 ... 280 A5
Bransdale Rd BRWNH WS8 .... 268 E3
Branson Av LNGTN ST3 .... 86 E7
Branston Rd BUT DE14 ...... 204 C2
  BUTN/AL/TUT DE13 .... 203 J2
Bransty Gv STOKE ST4 .... 101 J5 🔲
Brant Av NEWUL ST5 .... 68 A6
Brantley Av BDMR/CCFT WV3 . 294 C1
Brantley La WMBN WV5 ...... 292 A7
Branton Hill La ALDR WS9 .... 285 K1
Brantwood Av BNTWD WS7 .. 252 A5 🔲
Brassington St
  AUD/MAD/W CW3 .... 65 G4 🔲
Brassington Wy BUCK/MIL ST2 .. 86 C1
Bratch Common Rd
  WMBN WV5 .... 297 L3
Bratch Hollow WMBN WV5 .... 298 A2
Bratch La WMBN WV5 .... 298 A2

Bratch Pk WMBN WV5 .... 297 L2
Brattswood Dr ALS/KID ST7 ... 37 M1
Braunton Av STAFS ST17 ..... 194 E3
Braystones Cl ALS/KID ST7 .... 53 L2 🔲
Bray St WLNHL WV13 .... 282 B8 🔲
Brazenhill La RSTAF ST18 ..... 191 M3
Breach Cl ASHB DE6 .... 147 J4
  CDLE ST10 .... 105 H5
Breach Rd BURS/TUN ST6 ..... 55 J3
Breadmarket St LICH WS13 ..... 8 E3 🔲
Bream Cl BRWNH WS8 .... 268 F5
Breamore Crs DUDN DY1 ..... 299 M7
Bream Wy DUDN DY1 .... 54 B8
Bream Rd STAFS ST17 .... 194 E4
Brecon Wy BUCK/MIL ST2 ..... 70 C8 🔲
Bredon Cl ALBTN WV7 .... 261 G5
Breech Cl CDLE ST10 .... 60 F8
Breedon Cl NEWUL ST5 .... 68 A7
Breedon Wy RUSH/SHEL WS4 . 284 C1
Breeze Av RUSH/SHEL WS4 .... 53 L6
  CNCK/NC WS11 .... 251 H5
Brelades Cl DUDN DY1 .... 299 L7
Brempton Cft STONE ST15 ... 121 K8 🔲
Brendale Cl STOKE ST4 ...... 101 C1 🔲
Brendon TAM/AM/WIL B77 .... 291 H1
Brendon Cl STAFS ST17 ...... 194 C2
Brent TAM/AM/WIL B77 ...... 290 E3
Brentmill Cl WOLVN WV10 .... 264 F6
Brentnall Dr MGN/WHC B75 .. 287 H7
Brentnor Cl LNGTN ST3 .... 86 F7
Brenton Rd
  ETTPK/GDPK/PENN WV4 . 294 F6
Brentwood Ct END/WER ST9 .. 71 H6 🔲
Brentwood Cl BUCK/MIL ST2 .. 55 J7 🔲
  END/WER ST9 .... 71 H6 🔲
Brereton Cl KGSWFD DY6 .... 303 H3 🔲
Brereton Manor Ct
  RUGE WS15 .... 216 B5 🔲
Brereton Pl BURS/TUN ST6 .... 68 L1 🔲
Brereton Rd SHHTH WV12 ... 282 C3
Bretby La STPNHL/WNHL DE15 . 186 D8
Bretby Rd SWAD DE11 .... 205 M3
Bretherton Pl BURS/TUN ST6 .. 54 A4
Bretlands Wy
  STPNHL/WNHL DE15 ... 205 C4
Brettell La STRBR DY8 .... 307 M2
Brevitt Rd BKHL/PFLD WV2 ... 295 K4
Brewers Dr BLOX/PEL WS3 ... 284 A1
Brewer St WSLW WS2 .... 283 L6
Brewery La RSTAF ST18 ..... 177 H8 🔲
Brewery St HAN ST1 .... 2 C4
  RUGE WS15 .... 215 L2
Brewester Rd BUCK/MIL ST2 .... 3 K7
Brewood Rd COVEN WV9 ..... 247 G6
  WOLVN WV10 .... 264 C1
Brewster Cl
  POL/KGSBS/FAZ B78 .... 289 L1 🔲
Brianson Av BURS/TUN ST6 .... 69 J3
Briar TAM/AM/WIL B77 .... 275 C7
Briarbank Cl STOKE ST4 ..... 100 F1
Briarbeck RUSH/SHEL WS4 ... 284 C5
Briar Cl HEDN WS12 .... 232 A2
  RUGE WS15 .... 215 J1
  STAFS ST17 .... 194 F4
  SWAD DE11 .... 205 M5
The Briars NEWUL ST5 .... 68 B8
Briars Wy HEDN WS12 .... 233 J6
Briarswood ALS/KID ST7 ...... 53 H1 🔲
Briar Wy ECCH ST21 .... 117 L7
Briarwood Pl LNGTN ST3 .... 103 H1 🔲
Brickbridge La WMBN WV5 ... 297 L3
Brickfield Cl RSTAF ST18 ..... 177 K1 🔲
Brickfield Pl LNGTN ST3 ...... 86 C5
Brickheath Rd WOLV WV1 .... 13 C7
Brickhill La BUTN/AL/TUT DE13 . 182 A3
Brickhouse La CRTAM B79 .... 238 D8
Brick House St BURS/TUN ST6 . 68 F2 🔲
Brickiln St BRWNH WS8 ..... 268 F3
Brick-kiln La
  BUTN/AL/TUT DE13 ... 166 A7
  Brick Kiln La CDSL WV8 .. 245 C7
  Brick Kiln La NEWUL ST5 .. 67 L3
  RSTAF ST18 .... 156 F8
  SEDG DY3 .... 299 C7
  STAFS ST17 .... 194 F7
  STOKE ST4 .... 84 E1
Brick Kiln Wy RUGE WS15 ... 215 M6
Brick St SEDG DY3 .... 299 C9
Brickyard Rd ALDR WS9 ..... 284 F1
Bridestowe Cl LNGTN ST3 .... 103 C3 🔲
Bridge Av CTWY WS6 .... 249 L5
Bridge Cl ALS/KID ST7 .... 51 M8
  RSTAF ST18 .... 157 J7 🔲
Bridge Crs STONE ST15 ...... 138 A3
Bridge Cft BURS/TUN ST6 .... 54 B4
Bridge Cross Rd BNTWD WS7 . 252 A2
Bridge La RSTAF ST18 .... 158 B6
Bridgeman Ct SHIF TF11 ..... 225 M7
Bridgemary Cl WOLVN WV10 . 264 C6
Bridgenorth Rd WMBN WV5 . 296 E5
Bridge Rd KIDDW DY11 ...... 310 A4
  MKTDR TF9 .... 130 A1
  RUGE WS15 .... 217 J6
  RUSH/SHEL WS4 .... 284 B1
  STOKE ST4 .... 84 E7
  UTXR ST14 .... 144 D3
Bridges Crs CNCK/NC WS11 .. 250 D5
Bridgeside BUTN/AL/TUT DE13 . 185 L1
Bridges Rd CNCK/NC WS11 ... 250 C5
Bridge St BIDD ST8 .... 40 B8
  BRWNH WS8 .... 268 E4
  BUT DE14 .... 7 K4
  BUTN/AL/TUT DE13 ... 165 J3
  BUTN/AL/TUT DE13 ... 185 L1
  CNCK/NC WS11 .... 249 L5
  NEWUL ST5 .... 83 J1
  NEWUL ST5 .... 68 B7
  STAFN ST16 .... 4 F5
  STRBR DY8 .... 307 L1
  SWAD DE11 .... 223 L2
  TAM/AM/WIL B77 ...... 11 K4
  UTXR ST14 .... 144 C3
  WOLVN WV10 .... 280 E5
  WSL WS1 .... 283 L5
Bridgewater Cl CONG CW12 .. 26 B1

PENK ST19 .... 229 M
Bridgewater St BURS/TUN ST6 .. 68
  TAM/AM/WIL B77 11
Bridge Wy BRWNH WS8 268
Bridgford Av BUT DE14 203
Bridgnorth Av WMBN WV5 297
Bridgnorth Gv NEWUL ST5 52
  SHHTH WV12 282
Bridgnorth Rd
  DUNHL/THL/PER WV6 .. 292
  KIDDW DY11 308
  KINVER DY7 301
  SEDG DY3 307
  STRBR DY8 307
Bridgwater Cl ALDR WS9 268
Bridgwood Rd
  BLYBR/FOR ST11 104
Bridle La GNOS ST20 172
  STPNHL/WNHL DE15 .. 205
Bridle Pth BUCK/MIL ST2 71
The Bridle Pth
  AUD/MAD/W CW3 81
  NEWUL ST5 83
Bridle Rd STAFS ST17 194
  STRBR DY8 307
Bridle Wk RUGE WS15 197
The Bridleway
  MKTDR TF9 .... 130 B
Brierley Rd CONG CW12 26
Brierley St BURS/TUN ST6 69
Brierley Hill La RUGE WS15 ... 234
Brieryhurst Cl ALS/KID ST7 ... 70
Brieryhurst Rd ALS/KID ST7 .. 39
Bright Crs TAM/AM/WIL B77 . 274
Brightgreen St LNGTN ST3 ... 86
Brighton Cl WSLW WS2 ...... 283 K
Brighton Pl BDMR/CCFT WV3 . 12
Brighton St STOKE ST4 85
The Brighton NEWUL ST5 68
Brights Av ALS/KID ST7 39
Brightstone Cl WOLVN WV10 . 264 F
Bright St LNGTN ST3 103
  STRBR DY8 .... 307 K
  WOLV WV1 13
Brindiwell Gv STOKE ST4 .... 101 J
Brindley Av WNSFLD WV11 .. 282
Brindley Bank Rd
  RUGE WS15 .... 197 L
Brindley Brae KINVER DY7 ... 306
Brindley Cl ALBTN WV7 261
  ALS/KID ST7 53
  PENK ST19 230
  STRBR DY8 .... 307 L
  WMBN WV5 .... 297 K
  WSLW WS2 .... 283 G
Brindley Crs HEDN WS12 232
  LEEK ST13 57
Brindley Heath Rd HEDN WS12 . 232
Brindley La BUCK/MIL ST2 55
Brindley Pl BURS/TUN ST6 54
Brindley Rd HEDN WS12 232
Brindley St NEWUL ST5 ...... 84 B
Brindleys Wy ALS/KID ST7 ... 51
Brindley Wy CONG CW12 26
Brindon Cl LNGTN ST3 87
Brinkburn Pl RUGE WS15 .... 215 H
Brinley Wy KGSWFD DY6 303
Brinsford La WOLVN WV10 ... 264
Brinsford Rd WOLVN WV10 .. 264
Brinsley Av STOKE ST4 101
Brisbane Rd STAFN ST16 174
Brisbane Wy HEDN WS12 232
Brisley Hl STOKE ST4 84
Bristol Cl CNCK/NC WS11 ... 250
Bristol St CNCK/NC WS11 ... 249
  NEWUL ST5 68
Britannia Dr
  BUTN/AL/TUT DE13 ... 185
Britannia St LEEK ST13 ...... 43 L
Britannia Wy LICHS WS14 9
Britch La GNOS ST20 67
Brittain Av NEWUL ST5 67
Brittain Rd LEEK ST13 57
Brittle Pl BURS/TUN ST6 .... 54 D
Britton St STOKE ST4 .... 84 F
Brixham Cl BUCK/MIL ST2 85
Brizlincote La
  STPNHL/WNHL DE15 .. 205
Brizlincote St
  STPNHL/WNHL DE15 7
Broadacres COVEN WV9 247
Broad Eye STAFN ST16 4
Broadfield Cl KGSWFD DY6 .. 303
Broadfield Rd BURS/TUN ST6.. 53
Broadheath Dr
  RUSH/SHEL WS4 284
Broadholes La PENK ST19 ... 226
Broadhurst Gn HEDN WS12 .. 213
Broadhurst Green Rd
  HEDN WS12 213
Broadhurst St BURS/TUN ST6 . 69 H
Broadlands
  BUTN/AL/TUT DE13 .. 185 K
Broadlands Ri LICHS WS14 9
Broad La BDMR/CCFT WV3 .. 294
  BLOX/PEL WS3 283
  BURS/TUN ST6 55
  GNOS ST20 255
  LICH WS13 255
  LICHS WS14 9
  RUSH/SHEL WS4 284
  WNSFLD WV11 284
Broad Lane Gdns
  BLOX/PEL WS3 267
Broad La North SHHTH WV12 . 282
Broad La South
  SHHTH WV12 .... 282 A
Broadlawns Dr STOKE ST4 85
Broadlea TAM/AM/WIL B77 ... 291
Broad Meadow ALDR WS9 ... 285
Broad Meadow Ct
  NEWUL ST5 68
Broad Meadow Cft
  STAFN ST16 .... 174 A
Broad Meadow La GTWY WS6 . 250
Broadmeadows Rd
  SHHTH WV12 .... 282 B2
Broadmine St STOKE ST4 85
Broad Oaks STAFS ST17 .... 193 L
Broadoaks Cl CNCK/NC WS11 .. 250

roadoak Wy LNGTN ST3 ...... 101 L1 ◫
roadsmeath
　TAM/AM/WIL B77 ...... 274 C8 ◫
roadstone Av BLOX/PEL WS3... 283 K3
roadstone Cl
　ETTPK/GDPK/PENN WV4 ...... 295 K5 ◫
road St CNCK/NC WS11 ...... 249 L4
　HAN ST1 ...... 2 C6
　DUDH DY6 ...... 303 K5
　LEEK ST13 ...... 43 L5
　NEWUL ST5 ...... 84 B1
　STAFN ST16 ...... 4 D4
　WOLV WV1 ...... 13 G4
road Street Jct WOLV WV1 .. 13 H4
roadway RUSH/SHEL WS4 ..... 268 C8
roadway BDMR/CCFT WV3 .... 294 C1
　CDSL WV8 ...... 262 E7
　HEDN WS12 ...... 231 M4
　LNGTN ST3 ...... 86 F8
　NWPT TF10 ...... 188 A7
　WOLVN WV10 ...... 264 E8
roadway La CDLE ST10 ...... 61 C7
roadway North WSL 284 A8
roadway St BUT DE14 ...... 204 C2
he Broadway STRBR DY8 ...... 307 K8
　WMBN WV5 ...... 298 A5
roadwell La
　DUNHL/THL/PER WV6 ...... 277 H8
roc CI PENK ST19 ...... 230 A2
rockbank PI BURS/TUN ST6 .. 54 B5
rockeridge CI SHHTH WV12 .. 282 C1 ◫
rockhill MKTDR TF9 ...... 114 D5
rockhurst Dr
　DUNHL/THL/PER WV6 ...... 12 B1
rockhurst La MGN/WHC B75 .. 288 A4
rocklehurst Wy RUSH/SHEL WS1.. 69 L3
rockley Sq HAN ST1 ...... 2 A3
rockley's Wk KINVER DY7 ... 306 B7
rocksford St STOKE ST4 ...... 86 A5
rockton La ECCH ST21 ...... 135 K7
rocton Crs STAFS ST17 ...... 194 C1
rocton Hts STAFS ST17 ...... 195 J2
rocton La STAFS ST17 ...... 194 F4
rocton Rd STAFS ST17 ...... 195 J5
rogan St STOKE ST4 ...... 85 M4 ◫
romfield Ct STONE ST15 ...... 138 L1
romford Ri BDMR/CCFT WV3.. 12 D9
romley Cl WMBN WS12 ...... 232 C3 ◫
romley Ct HAN ST1 ...... 2 A3
romley Gdns CDSL WV8 ...... 263 C6
romley La LEEK ST13 ...... 60 C6
romleyhedge La LEEK ST13 .. 60 C6
romley Hough STOKE ST4..... 84 F5
romley La KGSWFD DY6 ...... 303 L6
romley PI
　ETTPK/GDPK/PENN WV4 .... 295 G5 ◫
romley St BKHL/PFLD WV2... 295 J3
　HAN ST1 ...... 69 G5 ◫
rompton Dr BUCK/MIL ST2 .. 55 H7
rompton Lawns
　DUNHL/THL/PER WV6 ...... 279 G7
romsberrow Wy LNGTN ST3 .. 103 G3
romstead Crs STAFN ST16 .. 174 A5
romwich LICH WS13 ...... 237 K2
romwynd Cl
　BKHL/PFLD WV2 ...... 295 H4 ◫
ronte CI BUT DE14 ...... 185 K3
ronte Dr CRTAM B79 ...... 10 A1
ronte Dr CNCK/NC WS11 .... 232 C8 ◫
ronte Gv BUCK/MIL ST2 ...... 70 A1
ronte Rd BKHL/PFLD WV2 ... 295 M4 ◫
rook Av TAM/AM/WIL B77 ... 290 F3 ◫
rookbank Gdns SEDG DY3 .. 299 H8
rookbank Rd SEDG DY3 ...... 299 H8
rook CI ALDR WS9 ...... 269 C7
　ASHB DE6 ...... 145 J2
　BLYBR/FOR ST11 ...... 104 A3
　COVEN WV9 ...... 247 H7
　END/WER ST9 ...... 56 A2 ◫
　LICH WS13 ...... 8 D1
　PENK ST19 ...... 229 L3
rook Crs KGSWFD DY6 ...... 303 J3
rookdale SEDG DY3 ...... 299 J7
rookdale Dr
　ETTPK/GDPK/PENN WV4 .... 294 D6
rook End BNTWD WS7 ...... 252 A6
　POL/KGSB/FAZ B78 ...... 290 A2
　RSTAF ST18 ...... 191 M4
　RUGE WS15 ...... 234 F1
rooke Rd HEDN WS12 ...... 231 M4
rookes CI STOKE ST4 ...... 85 L4 ◫
rookfield MKTDR TF9 ...... 114 C5
rookfield Cl END/WER ST9 ... 55 L3
rookfield CI ALDR WS9 ...... 285 G1 ◫
　CDLE ST10 ...... 74 D7
rookfield Ct STONE ST15 ...... 138 C4 ◫
rookfield CI ALS/KID ST7 ..... 37 J5 ◫
　CNCK/NC WS11 ...... 249 L3
rookfield Rd ALDR WS9 ...... 285 G1 ◫
　BUCK/MIL ST2 ...... 55 J7 ◫
　CDSL WV8 ...... 263 H7
　STOKE ST4 ...... 84 D5
rookfields Rd CDLE ST10...... 74 D7
rook Gdns BIDD ST8 ...... 26 D8
rookgate BLYBR/FOR ST11 .. 104 B2
rook Glen Rd STAFS ST17 ... 193 L3
rook Gv CDSL WV8 ...... 263 H7
rookhay La LNGTN ST3 ...... 237 K6
rookhill CI SHHTH WV12 ..... 282 C1 ◫
rook House CI WOLVN WV10 .. 265 H4
rookhouse Dr BARL ST12 .... 101 L8
rookhouse La BUCK/MIL ST2 .. 70 E6
　LEEK ST13 ...... 57 C7
　WOLVN WV10 ...... 264 F4
rook House La WOLVN WV10 .. 265 G4
rookhouse Rd ALS/KID ST7 .. 37 K7 ◫
　CDLE ST10 ...... 89 G7
　GNOS ST20 ...... 190 D3
　LNGTN ST3 ...... 87 C8
rookhouse Wy CDLE ST10..... 89 H8
　GNOS ST20 ...... 190 D4
rookland Av LNGTN ST3 ..... 102 A1 ◫
rookland Rd ALDR WS9 ...... 268 F7
　BURS/TUN ST6 ...... 53 M5 ◫
rooklands STRBR DY8 ...... 307 M1
rooklands Av GTWY WS6 ..... 249 M6
rooklands Gv ALDR WS9 ..... 268 F8
rooklands Pde WOLV WV1 .... 281 H8
rooklands Rd ALBTN WV7 ... 261 H5
　CNCK/NC WS11 ...... 232 A6
he Brooklands SEDG DY3 .... 302 E1

Brooklands Wy LEEK ST13 .... 57 M2
Brook La ALDR WS9 ...... 268 F7
　CDLE ST10 ...... 123 M4
　END/WER ST9 ...... 55 M2
　GTWY WS6 ...... 250 A7
　NEWUL ST5 ...... 84 B3
　RSTAF ST18 ...... 172 D5
　STAFS ST17 ...... 195 J6
Brooklime Gdns STAFN ST16 .. 174 A5
Brooklyn Gv KGSWFD DY6... 303 H2
Brooklyn Rd BNTWD WS7 ... 252 A6
　HEDN WS12 ...... 250 D1
Brookmead Gv STOKE ST4 ... 86 B4
Brook Meadow Rd
　RUSH/SHEL WS4 ...... 284 D2
Brook PI NEWUL ST5 ...... 84 C5
　STOKE ST4 ...... 84 F1
Brook Rd GTWY WS6 ...... 249 L5
　STOKE ST4 ...... 101 G3
　WMBN WV5 ...... 297 M4
Brook Side BUT/AL/TUT DE13 .. 166 B6
Brookside ASHB DE6 ...... 79 L8
　BURS/TUN ST6 ...... 68 D2
　CDLE ST10 ...... 74 A7
　KINVER DY7 ...... 301 K7
　RSTAF ST18 ...... 172 D5
　SEDG DY3 ...... 299 K8
　STPNHL/WNHL DE15 ...... 186 B5
Brookside CI NEWUL ST5 ...... 84 A3
　WMBN WV5 ...... 297 L4 ◫
Brookside Ct CDLE ST10 ...... 89 H7 ◫
Brookside Dr END/WER ST9 ... 56 A2
　LNGTN ST3 ...... 85 L8
Brookside Gdns PENK ST19 .. 244 E2
Brookside La STONE ST15 .... 137 L3
Brookside Rd
　BUT/AL/TUT DE13 ...... 220 C1
　POL/KGSB/FAZ B78 ...... 289 K1
　UTXR ST14 ...... 144 D3
Brookside Wy KGSWFD DY6 .. 303 H3
　KIDD 311 H8
　TAM/AM/WIL B77 ...... 290 F4
Brook St BIDD ST8 ...... 40 A5
　BUT DE14 ...... 7 H4
　KGSWFD DY6 ...... 303 H1
　NEWUL ST5 ...... 67 J8
　SEDG DY3 ...... 299 J7
　STOKE ST4 ...... 85 H3
　STRBR DY8 ...... 307 M1
　SWAD DE11 ...... 205 L4 ◫
Brookthorpe Dr SHHTH WV12 .. 282 C6
Brookview Dr LNGTN ST3 .... 86 F7
Brookweed TAM/AM/WIL B77 .. 275 C7
Brookwillows STAFS ST17 ... 194 C3 ◫
Brookwood CI NEWUL ST5 .... 84 A7
Brookwood Dr LNGTN ST3 ... 87 G7
Broom Covert Rd LICHS WS14 .. 271 L2
Broome HI NEWUL ST5 ...... 100 C1
Broome La HAG/WOL DY9 .... 311 L7
Broome Rd WOLVN WV10 .... 280 D3
Broomfield ASHB DE6 ...... 92 F8
Broomfield PI North HAN ST1 .. 69 G7 ◫
Broomfield PI South HAN ST1 .. 69 G7 ◫
Broomfield Rd BURS/TUN ST6 .. 54 D5
Broomfields BIDD ST8 ...... 41 H1
Broomhall Av WNSFLD WV11 .. 281 K4
Broomhill Bank CNCK/NC WS11.. 231 L7
Broomhill CI CNCK/NC WS11 .. 231 L6
Broomhills La RDERBYSW DE65 .. 187 K1
Broomhill St BURS/TUN ST6 .. 53 J6
Broom Hollow MKTDR TF9 .. 114 C5
Broom Lea MKTDR TF9 ...... 114 C6
Broom's La ASHB DE6 ...... 147 H8
Broom St HAN ST1 ...... 2 E3
Broome Rd STONE ST15 ...... 138 A5
The Bullring RSTAF ST18 .... 157 K8 ◫
Broomyclose La UTXR ST14 .. 126 A6
Brough CI BILS/COS WV14.... 295 M7
　LEEK ST13 ...... 43 L4
Brough La STOKE ST4 ...... 101 H3
Brough Rd
　STPNHL/WNHL DE15 ...... 186 C7
Broughton CI STAFN ST16 .. 174 C3 ◫
Broughton Ct
　DUNHL/THL/PER WV6 ...... 279 C7 ◫
Broughton Crs BARL ST12.... 101 L8
Broughton Rd
　BDMR/CCFT WV3 ...... 294 C1
　BUCK/MIL ST2 ...... 55 J6 ◫
　NEWUL ST5 ...... 68 D8
Brown Av ALS/KID ST7 ...... 38 A6
Brownfield Rd LNGTN ST3 ... 87 G8
Brownhill Rd BURS/TUN ST6.. 53 H3
Brownhills Rd BRWNH WS8 .. 268 C5
　BURS/TUN ST6 ...... 53 K8
　CNCK/NC WS11 ...... 251 G5
Browning CI CDLE ST10 ...... 89 J8 ◫
　CRTAM B79 ...... 273 M2
　SHHTH WV12 ...... 282 B2
Browning Crs WOLVN WV10 .. 264 C8
Browning Rd ALS/KID ST7 ... 52 C2
　BNTWD WS7 ...... 252 C2
　LNGTN ST3 ...... 85 M8
　SEDG DY3 ...... 299 G6
Browning St STAFN ST16 ..... 4 D2
Brown La BUX SK17 ...... 24 B3
Brown Lees Rd ALS/KID ST7 .. 39 M6
　BIDD ST8 ...... 26 D8
Brownley Rd BURS/TUN ST6 .. 69 K1
Brownsea PI LNGTN ST3 ..... 85 L6
Brownsfield Rd LICH WS13 .. 236 D8 ◫
Brownshore La WNSFLD WV11 .. 266 A7
Brown's Lake Rd KINVER DY7.. 301 K7
Brown's La BUT/AL/TUT DE13 .. 201 G8
　CRTAM B79 ...... 274 C2
　POL/KGSB/FAZ B78 ...... 291 M5
Brown St BKHL/PFLD WV2 ... 69 G2 ◫
　BURS/TUN ST6 ...... 69 G2 ◫
Brownswall Rd SEDG DY3 .... 299 H3
Brown Westhead Pk
　KIDD 309 M8
Browsholme CRTAM B79 ...... 273 K4
Broxwood Pk
　DUNHL/THL/PER WV6 ...... 279 H7
Bruford St BDMR/CCFT WV3 .. 12 B2
Brundall Ov BUCK/MIL ST2 .. 70 D8
Brund La LEEK ST13 ...... 57 G7
Brundle Av STAFN ST16 ...... 174 B7
Brunel CI BNTWD WS7 ...... 252 B2
　CRTAM B79 ...... 10 B2
　STAFN ST16 ...... 174 F2

Brunel Gv CDSL WV8 ...... 278 E4 ◫
Brunslow CI WOLVN WV10 ... 280 C1
Brunswick PI HAN ST1 ...... 2 D7
Brunswick Rd CNCK/NC WS11 .. 231 L8
Brunswick St HAN ST1 ...... 2 C5
　LEEK ST13 ...... 43 M4
Brunswick Ter STAFS ST17 .... 4 D7
Brunt St BURS/TUN ST6 ...... 68 D3 ◫
Brutus Rd NEWUL ST5 ...... 67 K5
Bryan Av
　ETTPK/GDPK/PENN WV4 .... 294 D5
Bryans La RUGE WS15 ...... 215 M1
Bryan St HAN ST1 ...... 2 D2
Bryans Wy HEDN WS12 ...... 232 F6 ◫
Bryant Rd BUCK/MIL ST2..... 70 B5
Brymbo Rd NEWUL ST5 ...... 67 M5
Brynmawr Rd BILS/COS WV14 .. 295 M7
Bryony BUT DE14 ...... 204 B2
Buccleuch Rd ALS/KID ST7 .. 86 D8
Buchanan Av RUSH/SHEL WS4.. 284 A7
Buchanan Cl
　RUSH/SHEL WS4 ...... 284 A7 ◫
Buchanan Rd RUSH/SHEL WS4.. 284 A7
Buchan Av ALBTN WV7 ...... 260 C5
Buckden TAM/AM/WIL B77 .. 291 J1 ◫
Buckingham CI
　BUTN/AL/TUT DE13 ...... 185 K2 ◫
　STAFS ST17 ...... 194 C1 ◫
Buckingham Crs STOKE ST4 .. 101 G1
Buckingham Dr SHHTH WV12 .. 282 B3
Buckingham Gv KGSWFD DY6 .. 303 J3
Buckingham PI HEDN WS12.. 250 C1 ◫
Buckingham Ri DUDN DY1 ... 299 L8 ◫
Buckingham Rd CRTAM B79 .. 273 K4
　ETTPK/GDPK/PENN WV4 .... 295 G6
Buckland CI HEDN WS12 ..... 250 D1 ◫
Buckland Gv STOKE ST4 ...... 101 J5
Buckland Rd STAFN ST16 .... 174 D1
Buckley Rd BURS/TUN ST6 .. 54 C4
　ETTPK/GDPK/PENN WV4 .... 294 D5
Buckley's Rw NEWUL ST5 ..... 84 C4
Buckmaster Av NEWUL ST5 .. 84 C4
Bucknall New Rd HAN ST1 ..... 2 E5
Bucknall Old Rd HAN ST1..... 2 E5
Bucknall Rd HAN ST1 ...... 3 J6
　WNSFLD WV11 ...... 282 A1
Buckthorn CI HEDN WS12 .. 231 M2 ◫
Buckton CI MGN/WHC B75 .. 287 J7 ◫
Bude Rd ALS/KID ST7 ...... 37 H7 ◫
Buds Rd RUGE WS15 ...... 233 M5
Buildwas CI BLOX/PEL WS3 .. 266 F8 ◫
Bulldog La LICH WS13 ...... 8 E1
Buller St
　ETTPK/GDPK/PENN WV4 .... 295 L5
　HAN ST1 ...... 2 E9
Bullgap La ASHB DE6 ...... 77 J7
Bull HI NEWUL ST5 ...... 4 E3
Bull La BIDD ST8 ...... 40 A8
　WMBN WV5 ...... 298 B3
Bullmeadow La WMBN WV5.. 298 A5
Bullmoor La LICHS WS14 ..... 270 A1
Bullocks House Rd ALS/KID ST7 .. 39 L7
Bullows Rd BRWNH WS8 ...... 268 C4
The Bullring RSTAF ST18 .... 157 K8 ◫
Bull St BEDG DY3 ...... 299 J8 ◫
Bulstrode St BURS/TUN ST6 .. 68 E2 ◫
Bumblehole Mdw WMBN WV5.. 297 M3
Bungham La PENK ST19 ..... 229 K2
Bun La NWPT TF10 ...... 225 J1
Bunny HI NEWUL ST5 ...... 84 C5
Bunting CI UTXR ST14 ...... 144 B4 ◫
Buntingsdale Rd MKTDR TF9 .. 130 B1
Bunt's La END/WER ST9 ...... 56 D8
Bunyan PI CNCK/NC WS11 .. 231 L6 ◫
Burbage CI WOLVN WV10 .... 280 E4 ◫
Burcham CI STAFN ST16...... 174 B3
Burcot Av WOLV WV1 ...... 281 G4
Burdock CI HEDN WS12 ...... 232 B7
Burford Av NEWUL ST5 ...... 67 K1 ◫
Burford Rd PENK ST19 ...... 227 H4
　STAFS ST17 ...... 194 D1
Burford Wy BUCK/MIL ST2 .. 86 A1 ◫
Burgage CI MKTDR TF9 ...... 130 C1 ◫
The Burgage ECCH ST21 ..... 152 E3
　MKTDR TF9 ...... 130 C1
Burgess CI BURS/TUN ST6 .... 68 E3
Burgh Wy WSLW WS2 ...... 283 G6
Burgis CI LEEK ST13 ...... 57 K6
Burgoyne St CNCK/NC WS11 .. 231 K7
Burgundy Gv LNGTN ST3 .... 103 G2 ◫
Burland Av
　DUNHL/THL/PER WV6 ...... 279 K2
Burland CI NEWUL ST5 ...... 52 C8
Burleigh CI HEDN WS12 ...... 232 A7 ◫
　SHHTH WV12 ...... 282 B4 ◫
Burleigh Cft BNTWD WS7 ... 252 A6
Burleigh Gv NEWUL ST5 ...... 68 D7 ◫
Burleigh Rd BDMR/CCFT WV3 .. 295 G3
Burlidge Rd BURS/TUN ST6.. 53 M4
Burlington Av LNGTN ST3 ... 68 D7
Burlington Dr STAFS ST17 .. 193 H2
Burnaby Rd BURS/TUN ST6 .. 53 J4
Burncross Wy WOLVN WV10 .. 280 F4
Burnell Gdns
　BDMR/CCFT WV3 ...... 294 E2 ◫
Burnet Gv WOLVN WV10 ..... 265 H4
Burnett Ct STAFN ST16 ...... 174 A6 ◫
Burnett PI BURS/TUN ST6 ... 54 D6 ◫
Burnett Rd FOAKS/STRLY B74.. 286 D8
Burnfield Dr RUGE WS15 ..... 215 J1
Burnfields CI ALDR WS9 ...... 285 C3
Burnham Av STAFS ST17 ..... 194 D4
　WOLVN WV10 ...... 280 C2
Burnham CI KGSWFD DY6 .. 303 M6 ◫
Burnham Gn CNCK/NC WS11 .. 249 H2 ◫
Burnham St STOKE ST4 ...... 86 A5
Burnhays Rd BURS/TUN ST6.. 53 L8
Burnley St HAN ST1 ...... 2 F1
Burnsall CI COVEN WV9 ...... 264 A7
Burns Av STAFS ST17 ...... 193 H2
　WOLVN WV10 ...... 264 D8
Burns Cl ALS/KID ST7 ...... 37 L2 ◫
　ALS/KID ST7 ...... 53 G2 ◫
　LICHS WS14 ...... 8 E1
Burns Dr BNTWD WS7 ...... 252 C3
Burns PI SEDG DY3 ...... 299 G6
Burnside BUTN/AL/TUT DE13 .. 166 B6
Burnside CI LNGTN ST3 ...... 103 H3 ◫
Burns Rd CRTAM B79 ...... 10 B1

Burns St CNCK/NC WS11 ..... 231 M6
Burnthill La RUGE WS15 ..... 215 L3
Burntwood Rd BNTWD WS7 .. 252 D6
　CNCK/NC WS11 ...... 251 G4
Burnwood Gv ALS/KID ST7 .. 39 H ◫
Burrington Dr STOKE ST4 ... 101 J4 ◫
Burrowes St WSLW WS2 ...... 283 K2
Burrows Rd KGSWFD DY6 ... 303 M6
The Burrows SWAD DE11 .... 205 K5 ◫
Burslem CI BLOX/PEL WS3 .. 267 C6
Bursley CI STAFS ST17 ...... 193 J3
Bursley Rd BURS/TUN ST6 .. 69 C3
Bursley Wy NEWUL ST5 ...... 68 A2
Burslnips Rd WNSFLD WV11 .. 266 C6
Burton Av RUSH/SHEL WS4.. 284 B5
Burton Bank RSTAF ST18 .... 193 J4 ◫
　STAFS ST17 ...... 193 L5
Burton CI CRTAM B79 ...... 274 C3
Burton Crs CDLE ST10 ...... 89 M2 ◫
　HAN ST1 ...... 69 K3 ◫
　WOLVN WV10 ...... 13 J6
Burton Farm Rd
　RUSH/SHEL WS4 ...... 284 B7
Burton Manor Rd STAFS ST17.. 193 L4
Burton Old Rd LICH WS13 ... 254 F1
Burton Old Rd East LICHS WS14 .. 9 L1
Burton Old Rd West LICH WS13 .. 9 H3
Burton PI HAN ST1 ...... 2 D5
Burton Rd BUT DE14 ...... 204 A3
　BUTN/AL/TUT DE13 ...... 165 J4
　BUTN/AL/TUT DE13 ...... 220 A8 ◫
　CRTAM B79 ...... 256 E1
　LICHS WS14 ...... 254 F1
　LICHS WS14 ...... 255 L4
　MSHM DE12 ...... 222 C3
　MSHM DE12 ...... 222 D6
　RDERBYSW DE65 ...... 167 M3
　RDERBYSW DE65 ...... 187 C1
　SWAD DE11 ...... 205 K8
　SWAD DE11 ...... 223 M3
　WOLVN WV10 ...... 13 K2
Burton Sq STAFS ST17 ...... 193 L3
Burton St BUTN/AL/TUT DE13 .. 165 J4
　LEEK ST13 ...... 43 K5
Burt St LNGTN ST3 ...... 87 H1
Burway Meadow
　BUTN/AL/TUT DE13 ...... 220 A8 ◫
Bury Ring RSTAF ST18 ...... 192 D5
Bushberry CI STONE ST15 ... 137 M4 ◫
Bushbury La WOLVN WV10 .. 264 C6
Bushbury Rd WOLVN WV10 .. 281 G4
Bush Dr RUGE WS15 ...... 215 L1
Bushey CI FOAKS/STRLY B74.. 285 M8
Bushfield Rd ALBTN WV7 ... 261 C5
Bush Gv BLOX/PEL WS3 ...... 284 B8
Bushton La BUTN/AL/TUT DE13 .. 165 H7
Bustomley La CDLE ST10...... 123 C6
Bute CI SHHTH WV12 ...... 282 B4
Bute St STOKE ST4 ...... 86 A6
Butler CI BUT DE14 ...... 6 C5
Butlers La FOAKS/STRLY B74.. 286 F7
Butler St STOKE ST4 ...... 85 H4
Butterbank La RSTAF ST18 .. 173 H7
Butterfield Cl
　DUNHL/THL/PER WV6 ...... 278 D7 ◫
Butterfield PI BURS/TUN ST6 .. 53 L7 ◫
Butterhill Bank RSTAF ST18 .. 139 C7
Butterhill La STONE ST15 .... 139 L4
Buttermere
　TAM/AM/WIL B77 ...... 291 H3 ◫
Buttermere CI BURS/TUN ST6 .. 68 E2
　CNCK/NC WS11 ...... 232 A7
　DUNHL/THL/PER WV6 ...... 279 K2
Buttermere Ct
　DUNHL/THL/PER WV6 ...... 278 F6 ◫
Buttermere Gv WNSFLD WV11 .. 266 A8
Butterton La CW/HAS CW1 .... 36 B8
　NEWUL ST5 ...... 83 K7
Butthouse La NEWUL ST5 ... 117 H4
Butt La GNOS ST20 ...... 172 A7
The Butts ALS/KID ST7 ...... 37 K6 ◫
　AUD/MAD/W CW3 ...... 65 C5
　LICHS WS14 ...... 253 K8
　RSTAF ST18 ...... 196 C2
　RUSH/SHEL WS4 ...... 283 M7
Butts Rd
　ETTPK/GDPK/PENN WV4 .... 294 F6
　MKTDR TF9 ...... 130 B1
　RUSH/SHEL WS4 ...... 283 M7
Buxton Av KGSWFD DY6 ...... 67 C8
　POL/KGSB/FAZ B78 ...... 290 D7
Buxton CI BLOX/PEL WS3 .... 267 J7
　STOKE 101 J6
Buxton Rd ASHB DE6 ...... 48 A6
　ASHB DE6 ...... 79 H7
　BLOX/PEL WS3 ...... 267 J7
　BUX SK17 ...... 24 B3
Buxton St HAN ST1 ...... 69 K3
Byatts Gv LNGTN ST3 ...... 86 A8
Bycars CI BURS/TUN ST6 ...... 69 C1
Bycars Rd BURS/TUN ST6 ... 68 F1
Byland TAM/AM/WIL B77 ..... 11 J5 ◫
Byland PI NEWUL ST5 ...... 84 A6
Byland Wy BLOX/PEL WS3 .. 266 F8
By Pass Rd TAM/AM/WIL B77 .. 275 C5
Byrd's La UTXR ST14 ...... 143 M2
Byrkley St BUT DE14 ...... 6 D3
Byrne Rd BKHL/PFLD WV2 ... 295 K3
Byrom St LEEK ST13 ...... 43 K4 ◫
Byron Av LICHS WS14 ...... 8 F3
　STPNHL/WNHL DE15 ...... 204 D3
Byron CI ALS/KID ST7 ...... 37 L3 ◫
　BNTWD WS7 ...... 251 M7
　CDLE ST10 ...... 89 H8
　MKTDR TF9 ...... 130 A3 ◫
　STAFN ST16 ...... 5 J1
Byron Cft FOAKS/STRLY B74.. 286 F4 ◫

　SEDG DY3 ...... 299 G6
Byron PI CNCK/NC WS11 ..... 231 M5
　RUGE WS15 ...... 197 J8 ◫
Byron Rd CRTAM B79 ...... 274 A3
　SHHTH WV12 ...... 282 E3
　WOLVN WV10 ...... 281 C1
Byron St STOKE ST4 ...... 84 D1
Bywater Gv LNGTN ST3 ...... 86 D4 ◫
Byways BLOX/PEL WS3 ...... 267 J7

C

Cable Dr WSLW WS2 ...... 283 J5
Cable St BKHL/PFLD WV2 .... 13 K9
Cabot Gv DUNHL/THL/PER WV6.. 278 E6
Cacklehill La ASHB DE6 ...... 94 C8
Cadeby Gv BUCK/MIL ST2 .... 55 H8
Cadle Rd WOLVN WV10 ...... 280 D3
Cadley Hill Rd SWAD DE11 .. 205 L7
Cadman Crs BURS/TUN ST6 .. 54 E7
　WOLVN WV10 ...... 281 C4
Cadman's La GTWY WS6 ..... 267 J2
Cadogan Rd TAM/AM/WIL B77 .. 290 D5
Caernarvon Av STONE ST15 .. 138 C4 ◫
Caernarvon Cl
　BUTN/AL/TUT DE13 ...... 185 K2
　MKTDR TF9 ...... 112 E8 ◫
　SHHTH WV12 ...... 282 C3 ◫
Caernarvon Wy DUDN DY1 ... 299 L8
Cairn CI BUCK/MIL ST2 ...... 70 C7 ◫
Cairn Dr WSLW WS2 ...... 282 F8
Cairns CI STPNHL/WNHL DE15 .. 186 C7
Cairns Dr STAFN ST16 ...... 5 M1
Cairns St WSLW WS2 ...... 283 J7
Caister TAM/AM/WIL B77 .... 275 G4
Caistor CI BUCK/MIL ST2 ..... 70 A1 ◫
　POL/KGSB/FAZ B78 ...... 289 K2
Calais Rd BUTN/AL/TUT DE13 .. 185 H4
Calcot Dr DUNHL/THL/PER WV6.. 279 L3
Caldbeck PI HAN ST1 ...... 69 K3 ◫
Calder TAM/AM/WIL B77 ..... 275 H8
Calder Av WSL WS1 ...... 284 A8
Calder CI RDERBYSW DE65 .. 166 D1
Calderfields CI
　RUSH/SHEL WS4 ...... 284 A7 ◫
Calder Ri DUDN DY1 ...... 299 M4 ◫
Caldervale Dr STAFS ST17 .. 194 D4
Caldew Gv STOKE ST4 ...... 101 J5
Caldy CI ALS/KID ST7 ...... 37 J6 ◫
Cale CI TAM/AM/WIL B77 ..... 274 C8
Caledonia BKHL/PFLD WV2 .... 13 J9
　HAN ST1 ...... 85 H1
Calgary Crs
　STPNHL/WNHL DE15 ...... 186 D7
Californian Gv BNTWD WS7 .. 251 M7
California St LNGTN ST3 ...... 86 A7
Callaghan Gv CNCK/NC WS11 .. 232 C8 ◫
Callender PI BURS/TUN ST6 .. 69 C2
Callingwood La
　BUTN/AL/TUT DE13 ...... 183 L6
Callow Hill La CDLE ST10 .... 90 B8
Calrofold Dr NEWUL ST5 ...... 67 K1
Calstock Rd SHHTH WV12.... 282 D2
Calvary Crs BUCK/MIL ST2 .. 86 D3
Calveley CI STONE ST15 ...... 136 F4
Calver Crs WNSFLD WV11 ... 281 M5
Calverley St LNGTN ST3 ...... 86 D8
Calvert St BURS/TUN ST6 .... 53 K7 ◫
Calvert Gv NEWUL ST5 ...... 68 B3
Calves Cft WLNHL WV13 .... 282 A7
Calvin CI WMBN WV5 ...... 297 M5
　WOLVN WV10 ...... 264 D7
Calving HI CNCK/NC WS11 .. 231 L8
Camberley Crs
　ETTPK/GDPK/PENN WV4 .... 295 L8
　SEDG DY3 ...... 295 L8
Camberley Dr
　ETTPK/GDPK/PENN WV4 .... 295 G6 ◫
Camberwell Gv STOKE ST4 .. 101 J4 ◫
Camborne CI STAFS ST17 ... 194 C2
Camborne Crs NEWUL ST5 .. 83 M5
Cambrian TAM/AM/WIL B77 .. 274 C8
Cambrian La RUGE WS15..... 197 J7
Cambrian Wy BUCK/MIL ST2 .. 70 C6
Cambria St CNCK/NC WS11 .. 231 K7
Cambridge CI ALDR WS9 ..... 285 C2
　BIDD ST8 ...... 40 C1 ◫
Cambridge Dr NEWUL ST5 ... 84 D6
Cambridge St BUT DE14 ...... 6 C8
　HAN ST1 ...... 2 B7
　STAFN ST16 ...... 5 J3
　WOLVN WV10 ...... 13 H1
Camden St ALDR WS9 ...... 268 E6
Camden St TAM/AM/WIL B77 .. 11 K7 ◫
Camden St ALDR WS9 ...... 268 E6
　STOKE ST4 ...... 85 L6
Camden Wy KGSWFD DY6 .. 303 K1
Camelford St STAFS ST17 ... 194 E2
Camellia Gdns COVEN WV9 .. 263 M7
Camelot Cl
　BUTN/AL/TUT DE13 ...... 166 E8 ◫
　CNCK/NC WS11 ...... 231 M6
　STOKE 101 J6
Cameo Dr STRBR DY8 ...... 307 M2
Cameo Wy STAFN ST16 ...... 174 B3
Cameron Cl
　STPNHL/WNHL DE15 ...... 205 H1 ◫
Cameron Rd RUSH/SHEL WS4.. 284 A7
Camhouses TAM/AM/WIL B77 .. 275 H8
Camillus Rd NEWUL ST5 ...... 67 K5
Camoys St BURS/TUN ST6 ... 69 G3
Campbell Av LEEK ST13 ...... 43 K6
Campbell CI CRTAM B79 ...... 273 M2 ◫
　RUGE WS15 ...... 197 K8 ◫
　RUSH/SHEL WS4 ...... 284 A7
Campbell Rd MKTDR TF9...... 112 D8
　STOKE ST4 ...... 85 H6
Campbell Ter HAN ST1 ...... 3 G1
Campbell Wy NEWUL ST5..... 98 A5
Camp Hill Rd KINVER DY7 ... 302 A3
Campian's Av GTWY WS6 ..... 249 K8
Campion Av NEWUL ST5 ...... 68 D7 ◫
Campion CI ECCH ST21 ...... 152 D5 ◫
　WMBN WV5 ...... 297 L4 ◫
Campion Dr TAM/AM/WIL B77 .. 10 C8
　WOLVN WV10 ...... 265 C3
Camp Rd BURS/TUN ST6 ...... 54 C8
　MGN/WHC B75 ...... 287 K4
　STAFS ST17 ...... 195 H8

Camp St *WOLV* WV1 .... 12 F2
Camrose Gdns *COVEN* WV9 .... 264 A7
Camsey La *BNTWD* WS7 .... 252 E2
Canal La *ALS/KID* ST7 .... 53 K8
The Canal Ms *STOKE* ST4 .... 101 J4
Canal Side *BARL* 119 K1
Canalside Cl *BLOX/PEL* WS3 ...... 283 L1
Canalside Rd *STONE* ST15 .... 119 L8
Canal St *BURS/TUN* ST6 .... 68 D2
   BUT DE14 .... 6 E7
   STRBR DY8 .... 307 H4
Canaway Wk *RUGE* WS15 .... 197 J8 🔲
Canberra Cl *BLYBR/FOR* ST11 .... 103 J4
Canberra Crs *BLYBR/FOR* ST11 .... 103 J4
Canberra Dr *STAFN* ST16 .... 5 M2
Candle La *AUD/MAD/AC* W3 .... 80 B8
Canford Crs *CDSL* WV8 .... 262 E7
Cannel Rd *BNTWD* WS7 .... 251 K3
Canning Rd *WMBN* WV5 .... 298 A4
Canning St *STOKE* ST4 .... 85 M5
Cannock Rd *BNTWD* WS7 .... 251 M5
   CNCK/NC WS11 .... 232 A6
   HEDN WS12 .... 251 C2
   PENK ST19 .... 229 M1
   SHHTH WV12 .... 282 C3
   STAFS ST17 .... 194 D4
   WOLVN WV10 .... 13 H1
   WOLVN WV10 .... 280 F3 🔲
Cannock Wood Rd *HEDN* WS12 .. 233 H5
Cannock Wood St *HEDN* WS12 .. 233 G4
Cannon Pl *HAN* ST1 .... 2 B7
Cannon Rd *WMBN* WV5 .... 298 A4
Cannon St *HAN* ST1 .... 2 C7
   WLNHL WV13 .... 282 B8
   WSLW WS2 .... 283 L6
Cannon St North *WSLW* WS2 .... 283 L6 🔲
Canterbury Av *WLNHL* WV13 .... 282 D8
Canterbury Cl *BLOX/PEL* WS3... 268 A5
Canterbury Dr *BNTWD* WS7 ...... 252 D3
   BURS/TUN ST6 .... 54 B6
   DUNHL/THL/PER WV6 .... 278 D6
Canterbury Rd
   ETTPK/GDPK/PENN WV4 .... 294 D5
   STPNHL/WNHL DE15 .... 186 C7
Canterbury Wy *CNCK/NC* WS11 .. 250 B1
Canvey Gv *LNGTN* ST3 .... 103 H3 🔲
Canwell Dr *MGN/WHC* B75 .... 288 A5
Cape Av *STAFS* ST17 .... 193 H3
Capesthorne Cl *ALS/KID* ST7 ...... 37 J7
   END/WER ST9 .... 71 H7
Cape St *HAN* ST1 .... 2 C3
Capewell St *LNGTN* ST3 .... 86 C6 🔲
Capper Cl *ALS/KID* ST7 .... 39 C8
Cappers La *LICHS* WS14 .... 9 M5
   LICHS WS14 .... 255 C3
Capper St *BURS/TUN* ST6 .... 53 L7 🔲
Capricorn Wy *BURS/TUN* ST6 .... 53 M4
Capstone Av *WOLV* WV10 .... 280 B2
Captain's Cl *BDMR/CCFT* WV3 .. 279 K8
Captain's La
   BUTN/AL/TUT DE13 .... 220 D2
Caradoc *TAM/AM/WIL* B77 ...... 275 G8 🔲
Caraway Pl *LNGTN* ST3 .... 103 G4
Carberry Wy *LNGTN* ST3 .... 86 F6
Carder Av *STAFN* ST16 .... 174 B3
Carder Gn *BUX* SK17 .... 24 B4 🔲
Cardiff Gv *HAN* ST1 .... 2 C8
Cardiff St *BDMR/CCFT* WV3 .... 12 C8
Cardigan Av *RUGE* WS15 .... 215 K4
Cardigan Dr *SHHTH* WV12 .... 282 B4 🔲
Cardigan Gv *STOKE* ST4 .... 101 J4
Cardigan Pl *HEDN* WS12 .... 232 C5
Cardington Cl *NEWUL* ST5 .... 84 A4
Cardlemere La *BUX* SK17 .... 35 M8
Cardoness Pl *DUDN* DY1 .... 299 M8 🔲
Carisbrooke Ct
   DUNHL/THL/PER WV6 .... 279 G7 🔲
Carisbrooke Dr *STAFS* ST17 ...... 193 H3
Carisbrooke Gdns
   WOLVN WV10 .... 264 E7 🔲
Carisbrooke Rd
   DUNHL/THL/PER WV6 .... 279 G7
   WOLVN WV10 .... 264 E7
Carisbrooke Wy *STOKE* ST4 ...... 101 J5
Carlcroft *TAM/AM/WIL* B77 ..... 275 H8
Carling Cl *STAFN* ST16 .... 174 B8 🔲
Carling Gv *STOKE* ST4 .... 86 A5
Carlisle Rd *CNCK/NC* WS11 ...... 249 H3
Carlisle St *LNGTN* ST3 .... 102 B1
Carlos Cl *CDLE* ST10 .... 89 K7 🔲
Carlos Pl *NEWUL* ST5 .... 68 B1
Carl St *WSLW* WS2 .... 283 K5
Carlton Av *BURS/TUN* ST6 .... 55 H4
   FOAKS/STRLY B74 .... 285 M8
   NEWUL ST5 .... 84 B7
   WNSFLD WV11 .... 281 C3
Carlton Cl *BURS/TUN* ST6 .... 55 H4
   CDLE ST10 .... 105 K1
   HEDN WS12 .... 250 D1
Carlton Crs *BNTWD* WS7 .... 252 A2
   CRTAM B79 .... 273 H5
Carlton Cft *FOAKS/STRLY* B74 .. 286 A8
Carlton Rd *BDMR/CCFT* WV3 ... 295 J5
   STOKE ST4 .... 85 J2
Carlton Sq *STAFS* ST17 .... 193 H2 🔲
Carlton St *BUTN/AL/TUT* DE13 .. 185 H4
Carlton Ter *LEEK* ST13 .... 44 A4
Carlyle Cl *ALS/KID* ST7 .... 37 L2
Carlyle Gv *WOLVN* WV10 .... 281 G2
Carlyle Rd *WOLVN* WV10 .... 280 F2
Carlyon Pl *HAN* ST1 .... 69 K2
Carmel Cl *HEDN* WS12 .... 232 C5 🔲
Carmichael Cl *LICHS* WS14........ 9 J5
Carmount Rd *BUCK/MIL* ST2 ..... 70 B3
Carnation Cl *LNGTN* ST3 .... 87 H4
Carnforth Cl *KGSWFD* DY6 .... 303 H5
Carnforth Gv *ALS/KID* ST7 .... 53 L2
Carnoustie Cl *BLOX/PEL* WS3 .. 267 G5
Carol Crs *NEWUL* ST5 .... 281 L4
Caroline Cl *END/WER* ST9 .... 71 H6
Caroline Crs *ALS/KID* ST7 .... 53 M4
Caroline Cl *LNGTN* ST3 .... 86 C6
The Carousels *BUT* DE14 .... 185 J5

Carpenter Cl
   STPNHL/WNHL DE15 .... 205 J1
Carpenter Rd *LNGTN* ST3 .... 86 A6 🔲
Carr Bank *CDLE* ST10 .... 91 C4
Carriage Dr *BIDD* ST8 .... 40 E1
Carrick Cl *BLOX/PEL* WS3 .... 268 A5
Carrick Pl *STOKE* ST4 .... 101 C1
Carriers Rd *RDERBYSW* DE65 .... 167 J3
Carr La *ALS/KID* ST7 .... 66 A1
   ASHB DE6 .... 47 M8
Carroll Dr *LNGTN* ST3 .... 86 D6
Carron St *STOKE* ST4 .... 86 A5
Carroway Head Hl
   MGN/WHC B75 .... 288 C6
Carr St *ALS/KID* ST7 .... 53 M1
Carryer Pl *NEWUL* ST5 .... 83 M2
Carson Rd *BURS/TUN* ST6 .... 53 M8
Carson Wy *STAFN* ST16 .... 4 A5
Cartbridge Cl *BLOX/PEL* WS3 .. 283 M4
   BLOX/PEL WS3 .... 284 A5
Cartbridge La *RUSH/SHEL* WS4 . 284 A5
Cartbridge La South
   RUSH/SHEL WS4 .... 284 A5
Carter Av *CDSL* WV8 .... 263 H7
Carter Rd
   DUNHL/THL/PER WV6 .... 280 B5
Carters Cft *CDLE* ST10 .... 105 L7
Cartersfield La *ALDR* WS9 .... 269 K4
Carter St *UTXR* ST14 .... 144 C3
Cartlich St *BURS/TUN* ST6 .... 53 K5
Cartledge St *STOKE* ST4 .... 84 D1
Cartmel Pl *BURS/TUN* ST6 .... 53 L7
The Cartway
   DUNHL/THL/PER WV6 .... 278 D6 🔲
Cartwright Dr *GNOS* ST20 .... 190 D3 🔲
Cartwright Rd *MGN/WHC* B75 .. 287 J7
Cartwright St *BKHL/PFLD* WV2 . 13 C9
Carver Gdns *STRBR* DY8 .... 307 L8
Carver Rd *BUTN/AL/TUT* DE13 . 185 J4
   STAFN ST16 .... 174 E4
Casewell Rd *BURS/TUN* ST6 ...... 69 J3
   KGSWFD DY6 .... 303 J2
Casey La *BUT* DE14 .... 6 D3
The Casey *LEEK* ST13 .... 75 G1
Cash La *ECCH* ST21 .... 151 K6
Caslon Crs *STRBR* DY8 .... 307 H6
Caspian Gv *STOKE* ST4 .... 101 H3
Caspian Wy *PENK* ST19 .... 227 J4
Castel Cl *NEWUL* ST5 .... 83 L7
Castle Acre *STAFS* ST17 .... 193 H3
Castle Bank *STAFS* ST17 .... 193 H1
Castlebridge Rd *WNSFLD* WV11 . 282 A3
Castle Cl *BRWNH* WS8 .... 251 M8
   TAM/AM/WIL B77 .... 11 J6
Castle Ct *STONE* ST15 .... 138 C4
Castlecroft Av
   BDMR/CCFT WV3 .... 294 A2
Castlecroft Gdns
   BDMR/CCFT WV3 .... 294 B2
Castlecroft La
   BDMR/CCFT WV3 .... 293 M2
Castlecroft Rd
   BDMR/CCFT WV3 .... 294 B2
Castledene Dr *STAFN* ST16 .... 4 A8
Castledine Gv *LNGTN* ST3 .... 86 D6
Castle Dr *SHHTH* WV12 .... 282 B5 🔲
Castle Dyke *LICH* WS13 .... 8 F4 🔲
Castlefields *STAFN* ST16 .... 4 A8
Castlefield St *HAN* ST1 .... 69 G8
Castleford Rd *ALDR* WS9 .... 269 C7
Castle Gv *BUCK/MIL* ST2 .... 70 B5
Castle Hayes La
   BUTN/AL/TUT DE13 .... 165 G6
Castle Hl *STAFN* ST16 .... 4 D4
Castlehill Rd *ALDR* WS9 .... 269 J7
Castle Hill Rd *CDLE* ST10 .... 107 L1
   NEWUL ST5 .... 84 A1
Castle Inn Rd *CONG* CW12 .... 26 C3
Castle Keep Ms *NEWUL* ST5 ...... 84 A2 🔲
Castle La *AUD/MAD/AC* W3 .... 81 L5
Castle Park Rd
   BUTN/AL/TUT DE13 .... 185 H3
Castle Rdg *NEWUL* ST5 .... 83 M2 🔲
Castle St *BRWNH* WS8 .... 251 M8
   BUTN/AL/TUT DE13 .... 165 H3
   ECCH ST21 .... 152 E3
   KINVER DY7 .... 306 A6
   NEWUL ST5 .... 67 L3
   NEWUL ST5 .... 84 C1 🔲
   SEDG DY3 .... 299 K2
   STAFN ST16 .... 4 C5
   WOLV WV1 .... 13 G5
Castleton *BLOX/PEL* WS3 .... 267 J7
   LNGTN ST3 .... 102 C2
Castle Vw *BIDD* ST8 .... 40 C4
Castleview *RDERBYSW* DE65 .... 165 J2 🔲
Castle Vw *RSTAF* ST18 .... 173 L8
   STAFN ST16 .... 4 C4
   TAM/AM/WIL B77 .... 10 E7
Castleview Gv *ALS/KID* ST7 ...... 53 M3 🔲
Castleview Rd *ALS/KID* ST7 .... 39 H7
   STAFN ST16 .... 4 B7
The Castle Wy
   RDERBYSW DE65 .... 167 L5
Caswell Rd *SEDG* DY3 .... 299 J2
Cat And Kittens La
   WOLVN WV10 .... 264 E4
Caterham Dr *STRBR* DY8 .... 303 H7
Caterham Pl *BLYBR/FOR* ST11 . 103 H4
Catesby Dr *KGSWFD* DY6 .... 303 K2
Catharine Rd *BURS/TUN* ST6 ..... 54 B4
Cathcart Rd *STRBR* DY8 .... 307 L5
Cathedral Cl *LICH* WS13 .... 8 E2
Cathedral Rl *LICH* WS13 .... 8 D2
Catherine Ct *ASHB* DE6 .... 79 H8
Catherine St *NEWUL* ST5 .... 68 D6
Catholic La *SEDG* DY3 .... 299 J3
Catholme La
   BUTN/AL/TUT DE13 .... 220 E4
Catisfield Crs *CDSL* WV8 .... 279 M1
Catkin Wk *RUGE* WS15 .... 197 J8
Catmeadow La *RUGE* WS15 ..... 234 D1
Caton Crs *BURS/TUN* ST6 .... 54 F8

Catsbridge La *CNCK/NC* WS11 .. 248 E3
Catshill Rd *BRWNH* WS8 .... 269 G3
Catton Av *MSHM* DE12 .... 222 B5
Cauldon Av *LEEK* ST13 .... 57 K5
   NEWUL ST5 .... 68 B3
Cauldon Cl *LEEK* ST13 .... 43 M5
Cauldon Rd *STOKE* ST4 .... 85 H1
Cauldon Pl *HAN* ST1 .... 85 H1 🔲
Cauldwell Rd *MSHM* DE12 ...... 223 C4
Caulton St *BURS/TUN* ST6 .... 68 F1
Caunsall Rd *KINVER* DY11 .... 310 B4
Causeley Gdns *BUCK/MIL* ST2 .. 70 B7
Causeley Rd *BUCK/MIL* ST2 ...... 70 B7
Causeway Pl *LEEK* ST13 .... 46 F5
Cavalier Circ *WOLVN* WV10 .... 264 E6
Cavan's Cl *CNCK/NC* WS11 ..... 231 L8
Cavell Cl *WSLW* WS2 .... 283 K8
Cavendish Av *ASHB* DE6 .... 145 J1
   KGSWFD DY6 .... 303 K6
Cavendish Crs *ALS/KID* ST7 .... 37 J5
Cavendish Dr *ASHB* DE6 .... 95 K2
   HAG/WOL DY9 .... 313 J1 🔲
Cavendish Gdns *WSLW* WS2 ... 283 G6 🔲
Cavendish Gv *NEWUL* ST5 .... 84 B7
Cavendish Rd *WSLW* WS2 .... 283 G5
Cavendish St *HAN* ST1 .... 69 C7 🔲
Cavendish Wy *ALDR* WS9 .... 285 H5
Caversall La *LNGTN* ST3 .... 103 J2
Caverswall Old Rd
   BLYBR/FOR ST11 .... 103 M2
Caverswall Rd *BLYBR/FOR* ST11 . 103 M3
   CDLE ST10 .... 88 B7
   LNGTN ST3 .... 87 H6
Cavour St *HAN* ST1 .... 68 F8
Caxton St *CNCK/NC* WS11 .... 249 L2
Cayley Pl *BLYBR/FOR* ST11 ..... 103 J4
Cecil Av *HAN* ST1 .... 2 A3
Cecilly St *CDLE* ST10 .... 89 L6
Cecil Payton Cl *RUGE* WS15 .... 179 M4 🔲
Cecil St *CNCK/NC* WS11 .... 231 M6
   RUSH/SHEL WS4 .... 283 M7
   STRBR DY8 .... 307 M5
Cedar Av *ALS/KID* ST7 .... 37 K7
   ALS/KID ST7 .... 52 D1
   BLYBR/FOR ST11 .... 104 A4
   BRWNH WS8 .... 269 C2
Cedar Cl *ASHB* DE6 .... 95 K3
   BNTWD WS7 .... 252 A4
   CDLE ST10 .... 89 L8
   HEDN WS12 .... 232 A1
   LICHS WS14 .... 254 F3
   MKTDR TF9 .... 130 A1 🔲
   STRBR DY8 .... 307 K8 🔲
   UTXR ST14 .... 143 M1 🔲
Cedar Crs *ALS/KID* ST7 .... 66 F1
   END/WER ST9 .... 55 L4
   RUGE WS15 .... 216 A5
Cedar Dr *ALBTN* WV7 .... 261 G5
   CRTAM B79 .... 274 A2
   UTXR ST14 .... 126 A6 🔲
Cedar Gdns *KINVER* DY7 .... 305 M4
Cedar Gv *BDMR/CCFT* WV3 ..... 294 F3
   BIDD ST8 .... 41 G1
   CDSL WV8 .... 263 H7 🔲
   GTWY WS6 .... 250 B6
   LNGTN ST3 .... 85 L7
   MSHM DE12 .... 223 J4
Cedarhill *CDLE* ST10 .... 107 K1
Cedarhill Dr *CNCK/NC* WS11 ... 231 M8 🔲
Cedar Pk *STONE* ST15 .... 138 B2
Cedar Park Rd *SHHTH* WV12 .... 282 C1
Cedars Av *KGSWFD* DY6 .... 303 K6
   WMBN WV5 .... 298 A5
Cedars Dr *STONE* ST15 .... 138 B5
Cedar Wy *STAFS* ST17 .... 194 F4
   WNSFLD WV11 .... 281 L4
Cedarwood Cl *COVEN* WV9 ..... 247 H7 🔲
Cedar Wood Rd *SEDG* DY3 ..... 299 J6
Celandine *TAM/AM/WIL* B77 .... 10 E2
Celandine Cl *BUCK/MIL* ST2 ...... 70 B1
   STRBR DY8 .... 303 J6
The Celandines *WMBN* WV5 .... 297 L4 🔲
Cellarhead Rd *END/WER* ST9 ..... 71 L6
Celtic Av *ALS/KID* ST7 .... 53 M2
Celtic Rd *CNCK/NC* WS11 .... 231 L7
Cemetery Av *LNGTN* ST3 .... 86 B8
Cemetery Rd *CNCK/NC* WS11 .. 231 K6
   HAN ST1 .... 69 G8
   MKTDR TF9 .... 130 B1
   WLNHL WV13 .... 282 A7
Cemetery St *GTWY* WS6 .... 249 J8
   NEWUL ST5 .... 67 L7 🔲
Cemetery Vw *LNGTN* ST3 .... 86 B8 🔲
Cemetery Wy *BLOX/PEL* WS3 ... 283 H1
Cemlyn Av *BUCK/MIL* ST2 .... 85 L7
Central Av *BUCK/MIL* ST2 .... 3 M5
   CNCK/NC WS11 .... 231 M5
   STONE ST15 .... 136 B2
Central Av South *STONE* ST15 .. 136 B3
Central Cl *BLOX/PEL* WS3 .... 283 G1
Central Dr *BLOX/PEL* WS3 .... 282 F2
   LNGTN ST3 .... 85 L7
   SEDG DY3 .... 299 J8 🔲
Central Rd *STONE* ST15 .... 119 L8
Centre Rd *STONE* ST15 .... 119 L8
Centurion Wy
   TAM/AM/WIL B77 .... 291 H4
Century Rd *NEWUL* ST5 .... 52 F8
Century St *HAN* ST1 .... 2 A4
Chad's Ditch *RUGE* WS15 .... 213 L8
Chadsfield Rd *RUGE* WS15 .... 197 L8
Chadswell Hts *LICH* WS13 .... 236 M3
   LICH WS13 .... 236 D8 🔲
Chadwell Gdns *CDSL* WV8 ...... 262 F6
Chadwell Wy *BUCK/MIL* ST2 ..... 86 D1
Chadwick Cl
   ETTPK/GDPK/PENN WV4 ... 294 C7
Chadwick Ct *RUGE* WS15 .... 215 M2 🔲
Chadwick Crs *RUGE* WS15 .... 217 G2
Chadwick St *NEWUL* ST5 .... 68 B3
Chadwyn Dr *BUCK/MIL* ST2 ...... 55 H8 🔲
Chaffinch La *HEDN* WS12 .... 232 B7

   SEDG DY3 .... 295 J8 🔲
Chaffinch Dr *BIDD* ST8 .... 40 E2
   UTXR ST14 .... 144 C4
Chaff La *ASHB* DE6 .... 93 J1
Chain La *STAFS* ST17 .... 193 L6
Chain St *BURS/TUN* ST6 .... 54 C8
Chalcot Dr *HEDN* WS12 .... 231 M3
Chaldon Cl *COVEN* WV9 .... 264 A8
Chalfield *CRTAM* B79 .... 273 K4 🔲
Chalfont Av *CNCK/NC* WS11 ... 249 J2
Challenge Wy *WOLVN* WV10 ... 280 E5
Challenor Av *WLNHL* WV13 ..... 281 K8
Challinor Av *LEEK* ST13 .... 43 L6
Challinor St *BURS/TUN* ST6 .... 53 L7 🔲
Chamberlain Av *STOKE* ST4 ...... 85 G4
Chamberlain's La
   ETTPK/GDPK/PENN WV4 ... 294 E7
Chamberlain St *HAN* ST1 .... 85 J1
Chamberlain Wy *BIDD* ST8 .... 40 E2
Chance Hall La *ALS/KID* ST7 ..... 38 B1
Chancery Dr *HEDN* WS12 .... 232 C3
Chancery St *HAN* ST1 .... 37 H7
   LNGTN ST3 .... 86 C7 🔲
Chandler Av *KINVER* DY7 .... 305 M5
Chandler Dr
   ETTPK/GDPK/PENN WV4 ... 294 D7
Chandlers Cl *COVEN* WV9 .... 280 A1 🔲
Chandlers Dr *TAM/AM/WIL* B77 . 275 H5
Chandlers Keep *BRWNH* WS8 .. 268 F4
Chanterelle Gdns
   ETTPK/GDPK/PENN WV4 ... 295 G6
Chantry Av *BLOX/PEL* WS3 ...... 283 K2
Chantry Rd *KINVER* DY7 .... 307 J3
Chapel Ash *WOLV* WV1 .... 12 C5
Chapel Ash Island *WOLV* WV1 .. 12 D5
Chapel Av *BRWNH* WS8 .... 251 L8
Chapel Bank *ALS/KID* ST7 .... 39 K3
Chapel Cl *ALS/KID* ST7 .... 39 H4 🔲
   WMBN WV5 .... 297 M5
Chapel Dr *BRWNH* WS8 .... 251 L8 🔲
Chapel Gn *WOLVN* WV13 .... 282 B8
Chapel La *ALS/KID* ST7 .... 37 M3
   ALS/KID ST7 .... 39 L6
   ASHB DE6 .... 94 F4
   ASHB DE6 .... 129 G6
   BIDD ST8 .... 41 G6
   BURS/TUN ST6 .... 55 H1
   BURS/TUN ST6 .... 69 G2
   BUTN/AL/TUT DE13 .... 163 M8
   BUTN/AL/TUT DE13 .... 166 B6
   BUTN/AL/TUT DE13 .... 183 J8
   BUTN/AL/TUT DE13 .... 184 A5
   CDLE ST10 .... 90 D8
   CDLE ST10 .... 90 A1
   CDSL WV8 .... 262 F7
   END/WER ST9 .... 42 A5
   LICHS WS14 .... 8 F7
   LICHS WS14 .... 255 L5
   MKTDR TF9 .... 96 C5
   MKTDR TF9 .... 114 E7
   RSTAF ST18 .... 210 B2
   RUGE WS15 .... 233 L5
   RUGE WS15 .... 234 A6
   SEDG DY3 .... 297 J6
Chapel Rd *RUGE* WS15 .... 216 F5
Chapel Sq *GTWY* WS6 .... 249 K7 🔲
Chapel St *ALS/KID* ST7 .... 38 D8
   ALS/KID ST7 .... 39 H4
   ALS/KID ST7 .... 51 L7
   BKHL/PFLD WV2 .... 295 K3
   BLOX/PEL WS3 .... 267 M7
   BLOX/PEL WS3 .... 283 K2
   BLYBR/FOR ST11 .... 104 A2
   BNTWD WS7 .... 251 K2
   BRWNH WS8 .... 251 L8
   BUCK/MIL ST2 .... 70 B6
   BUX SK17 .... 24 B4 🔲
   CDLE ST10 .... 73 K7
   CDLE ST10 .... 89 K7
   CNCK/NC WS11 .... 250 F5
   HEDN WS12 .... 250 E1
   KGSWFD DY6 .... 303 H2
   MSHM DE12 .... 222 D7
   NEWUL ST5 .... 67 J8
   NEWUL ST5 .... 68 D7
   STAFN ST16 .... 4 E4
   STRBR DY8 .... 303 K7
   SWAD DE11 .... 205 M4
   SWAD DE11 .... 223 L2
   WMBN WV5 .... 297 M5
Chapel Wk *SEDG* DY3 .... 299 J8
Chaplain Rd *HEDN* WS12 .... 232 E8
Chaplin Rd *LNGTN* ST3 .... 102 C1
Chapmans Cft *MSHM* DE12 ..... 222 D7 🔲
Charlecote Dr *DUDN* DY1 .... 299 L7
Charlemonte Cl *HEDN* WS12 ... 232 D7
Charles Av *ALBTN* WV7 .... 260 F5
   ETTPK/GDPK/PENN WV4 ... 295 H5
   WNSFLD WV11 .... 265 M6
Charles Cl *GTWY* WS6 .... 266 D1 🔲
Charles Cotton Dr
   AUD/MAD/AC W3 .... 81 K4 🔲
Charles Cotton St
   STAFN ST16 .... 174 C4 🔲
Charles Crs *BLOX/PEL* WS3 ..... 268 A5
Charlesdale Dr *ALDR* WS9 .... 285 H6
Charles Holland St
   WLNHL WV13 .... 282 B8
Charles Rd *STRBR* DY8 .... 307 L6 🔲
Charles St *BIDD* ST8 .... 40 C3
   CDLE ST10 .... 89 K7
   HAN ST1 .... 2 E6
   NEWUL ST5 .... 68 D7
   WLNHL WV13 .... 282 C7
   WSLW WS2 .... 283 K8
Charlesway *MKTDR* TF9 .... 130 B2 🔲
Charlock Gv *NEWUL* ST5 .... 232 C7 🔲
Charlotte Cl *RSTAF* ST18 .... 196 D2 🔲
Charlotte St *BURS/TUN* ST6 ...... 53 J3 🔲
   WSL WS1 .... 284 A5
Charlton Cl *MSHM* DE12 .... 223 J4
Charlton St *STOKE* ST4 .... 85 H2 🔲
Charminster Rd *LNGTN* ST3 ..... 103 G3
Charnes Rd *MKTDR* TF9 .... 115 J5
Charnley Dr *MGN/WHC* B75 .... 287 L8 🔲
Charnley Rd *STAFN* ST16 .... 174 B4

Charnock Pl *BURS/TUN* ST6 ...... 54 A3
Charnsford La *MKTDR* TF9 .... 115 J4
Charnwood Av *SEDG* DY3 .... 295 K6
Charnwood Cl *HEDN* WS12 ...... 232 C7
   LEEK ST13 43
   LICH WS13 9
   LICH WS13 .... 254 C1
   RUGE WS15 215
Charnwood Rd
   BUTN/AL/TUT DE13 .... 185 G6
Charolais Crs *LNGTN* ST3 102
Charter Cl *CNCK/NC* WS11 250
Charterfield Dr *HEDN* WS12 250
   KGSWFD DY6 303
Charterhouse Dr *STAFS* ST17 .... 5 🔲
Charter Rd *NEWUL* ST5 68
The Charters *LICH* WS13 254
Chartley Cl *BLYBR/FOR* ST11 .. 103 L4
   DUNHL/THL/PER WV6 278
   STAFN ST16 174
The Chartway *BLOX/PEL* WS3 .. 268
Chartwell *CRTAM* B79 273
Chartwell Cl *END/WER* ST9 71
   WMBN WV5 .... 297 M5
   WOLVN WV10 280
Chartwell Dr *FOAKS/STRLY* B74 . 286
Chartwell Rd *STAFS* ST17 194
Chartwood *MKTDR* TF9 114
Chase Av *GTWY* WS6 249
Chase Crs *STAFS* ST17 195
Chaselands *BNTWD* WS7 252
Chase La *STONE* ST15 118
Chaseley Av *CNCK/NC* WS11 ... 231
Chaseley Cl *RUGE* WS15 .... 215 H1 🔲
Chaseley Cft *CNCK/NC* WS11 .. 231
Chaseley Gdns *BNTWD* WS7 ... 252
Chaseley Rd *RUGE* WS15 213
Chasepool Rd *SEDG* DY3 302
Chase Rd *BLOX/PEL* WS3 283
   BNTWD WS7 252
   BRWNH WS8 269
   RUGE WS15 213
   STAFS ST17 195
Chaseside Dr *HEDN* WS12 232
Chase Side Dr *RUGE* WS15 216
The Chase
   DUNHL/THL/PER WV6 280
Chase V *BNTWD* WS7 251
Chase Vw
   ETTPK/GDPK/PENN WV4 ... 295
   RUGE WS15 .... 217 G6 🔲
Chase View La *RSTAF* ST18 193
Chaseview Rd
   BUTN/AL/TUT DE13 .... 219 M8
Chase Wk *NEWUL* ST5 102
Chasewater Gv *CDLE* ST10 .... 89 M6 🔲
Chasewater Wy *CNCK/NC* WS11.. 250
Chatcull La *ECCH* ST21 134
Chatfield Cl
   STPNHL/WNHL DE15 205
Chatfield Pl *LNGTN* ST3 86
Chatham St *HAN* ST1 2
Chatsworth Cl *SHHTH* WV12 282
Chatsworth Crs
   RUSH/SHEL WS4 284
Chatsworth Dr *BURS/TUN* ST6 .. 54
   BUTN/AL/TUT DE13 165
   END/WER ST9 55
Chatsworth Pl *LNGTN* ST3 102
   NEWUL ST5 .... 67 M3
Chatteris Cl *BLYBR/FOR* ST11 . 103
Chatterley Cl *NEWUL* ST5 68
Chatterley Dr *ALS/KID* ST7 53
Chatterley Rd *BURS/TUN* ST6 53
Chatterley St *BURS/TUN* ST6 68
Chatterton Pl *LNGTN* ST3 86
Chatwell La *NWPT* TF10 1
   SHIF TF11 1
Chaucer Av *SEDG* DY3 299
   SHHTH WV12 282
Chaucer Cl *BUT* DE14 185
   CRTAM B79 10
   LICHS WS14 8
Chaucer Dr *BNTWD* WS7 252
Chaucer Rd *BLOX/PEL* WS3 283
   STAFS ST17 193
Chaulden Rd *STAFN* ST16 174
Chawner Cl *BNTWD* WS7 .... 251 L1
Cheadle Cl *PENK* ST19 .... 229 M3
Cheadle Rd *BLYBR/FOR* ST11 .. 104
   CDLE ST10 105
   CDLE ST10 107
   END/WER ST9 72
   LEEK ST13 57
   UTXR ST14 144
Cheam Gdns
   DUNHL/THL/PER WV6 279
Cheapside *HAN* ST1 2
   NEWUL ST5 84
Chebsey Cl *BUCK/MIL* ST2 70
Chebsey Dr *STAFN* ST16 174
Checketts St *WSLW* WS2 .... 283 J8
Checkley Cl *HEDN* WS12 .... 40 D1
Checkley La *AUD/MAD/AC* W3 .. 80
Checkley Rd *NEWUL* ST5 67
Cheddar Dr *NEWUL* ST5 66
Cheddleton Heath Rd *LEEK* ST13.. 57
Cheddleton Park Av *LEEK* ST13 .. 57
Cheddleton Rd *LEEK* ST13......... 43
Cheedale Cl
   STPNHL/WNHL DE15 .... 186 A5
Chelford Cl *PENK* ST19 .... 230 A1
Chell Cl *PENK* ST19 .... 229 H1
Chell Green Av *BURS/TUN* ST6 .. 54
Chell Gv *NEWUL* ST5 68
Chell Heath Rd *BURS/TUN* ST6 .. 54
Chell St *STAFN* ST16 4
   STAFN ST16 4
Chell St *HAN* ST1 2
Chelmarsh Av *BDMR/CCFT* WV3.. 294
Chelmorton Dr *LNGTN* ST3 102
Chelmsford Dr *BUCK/MIL* ST2 ... 70
Chelmsford Rd *NEWUL* ST5 ..... 68 C5
Chelsea Cl *BIDD* ST8 .... 40 C1
Chelsea Dr *FOAKS/STRLY* B74 . 286
Chelsea Wy *KGSWFD* DY6 303
   STAFN ST16 4
Chelson St *LNGTN* ST3 86

Chelston Dr DUNHL/THL/PER WV6........279 L6
Cheltenham Av CDLE ST10......89 L5
Cheltenham Dr KGSWFD DY6...303 H4
  STAFS ST17.....................194 B3
Cheltenham Gv HAN ST1.........3 J2
  NEWUL ST5.....................66 F8
Chelwood St HAN ST1............2 B3
Cheniston Rd SHHTH WV12......282 C4
Chepstow Cl BIDD ST8..........40 C1
  DUNHL/THL/PER WV6..........278 F6
Chepstow Dr STAFS ST17........194 C3
Chepstow Pl LNGTN ST3.........86 C1
Chepstow Rd BLOX/PEL WS3.....282 F1
  WOLVN WV10....................264 D5
Chequerfield Dr BDMR/CCFT WV3...295 G4
Chequers Av WMBN WV5.........298 A1
Chequers Ct CNCK/NC WS11.....251 G5
Chequer St BDMR/CCFT WV3.....295 G4
Cheriton Gv DUNHL/THL/PER WV6..278 E7
Cherrington Dr GTWY WS6......249 M6
Cherrington Gdns DUNHL/THL/PER WV6..279 H8
Cherry Bank HEDN WS12........232 C4
Cherrybrook Dr PENK ST19.....229 M1
Cherry Cl BLYBR/FOR ST11.....121 L2
  BNTWD WS7....................251 M3
  NEWUL ST5.....................67 K1
Cherry Ct BUT DE14...........203 M2
Cherry Gn DUDN DY1..........299 M6
Cherry Gv LNGTN ST3..........85 L7
  STRBR DY8.....................307 L6
Cherry Hl AUD/MAD/W CW3......81 L4
  NEWUL ST5.....................67 L8
Cherry Hill Av LNGTN ST3.....87 G8
Cherry Hill La NEWUL ST5.....83 L1
Cherry La ALS/KID ST7.........37 L4
  CDLE ST10.....................90 A5
  CONG CW12.....................26 E2
  RSTAF ST18...................154 C7
  RSTAF ST18...................157 L5
  SEDG DY3.....................298 B7
Cherry Leys STPNHL/WNHL DE15...186 C6
Cherry Orch LICHS WS14........9 G5
  NEWUL ST5.....................84 B1
  STONE ST15...................138 C4
Cherry St BDMR/CCFT WV3......12 C6
  CRTAM B79.....................10 C3
  STRBR DY8....................307 L6
Cherry Tree Av ALS/KID ST7...38 A5
  STOKE ST4.....................101 G4
  STONE ST15...................137 M5
  SWAD DE11....................205 M4
Cherry Tree Crs RSTAF ST18...154 B7
Cherry Tree Gdns CDSL WV8....263 H7
Cherry Tree La AUD/MAD/W CW3..80 B8
  BIDD ST8......................41 H1
  CDSL WV8.....................263 H7
Cherry Tree Rd ALS/KID ST7...66 F1
  CNCK/NC WS11.................251 H6
  HEDN WS12....................231 K2
  KGSWFD DY6...................303 L2
  NEWUL ST5.....................67 L1
  RUGE WS15....................215 M5
Cherrytree Rd STPNHL/WNHL DE15..204 F4
Cherry Tree Wk CRTAM B79.....274 F2
Cherrywood Gv LNGTN ST3.....102 F4
Cherrywood Wy FOAKS/STRLY B74..286 D6
Chertsey Pl HAN ST1...........69 K3
Chervil Cl LNGTN ST3.........103 G4
Chervil Ri WOLVN WV10.........13 L2
Cherwell Dr BRWNH WS8........251 J8
Chesham Gv LNGTN ST3........103 G4
Chesham St STAFN ST16........174 F4
Cheshire Cl STRBR DY8........307 J7
Cheshire Dr PENK ST19........246 D4
Cheshire Gdns MKTDR TF9.....112 C8
Cheshire Gv DUNHL/THL/PER WV6..278 E6
Cheshire Ring Canal Wk ALS/KID ST7..37 K2
Cheshire Rd WSLW WS2.........282 F8
Cheshire St MKTDR TF9........112 C8
Cheslyn Dr GTWY WS6.........249 K8
Chessington Crs STOKE ST4....101 J3
Chestall Rd RUGE WS15.......233 M5
Chester Av DUNHL/THL/PER WV6..279 M3
Chester Cl ALS/KID ST7.......52 D3
  CNCK/NC WS11.................250 B1
  LICH WS13.....................236 C7
  WLNHL WV13...................282 D8
Chester Crs NEWUL ST5........84 B5
Chesterfield Av SWAD DE11....205 L4
Chesterfield Dr MSHM DE12....223 J4
Chesterfield Rd LICHS WS14....8 C9
Chester Rd ALDR WS9..........285 L1
  ALS/KID ST7...................52 D3
  BRWNH WS8....................269 C4
  ECCH ST21.....................152 C2
  FOAKS/STRLY B74..............285 M7
  KINVER DY7....................305 M3
  LICHS WS14....................255 K7
Chester Rd North BRWNH WS8...268 D1
Chester St DUNHL/THL/PER WV6.12 C1
  DUNHL/THL/PER WV6..........277 C8
  WOLVN WV10...................281 G2
Chesterton Wy CRTAM B79.....10 D1
  CRTAM B79.....................274 A3
Chesterwood ALDR WS9........285 L8
Chesterwood Rd BURS/TUN ST6.54 B7
Chestnut Av ALS/KID ST7......37 M3
  CRTAM B79.....................274 B3
Chestnut Cl CDLE ST10........105 M7
  CDSL WV8......................262 F6
  CNCK/NC WS11.................232 C8
  FOAKS/STRLY B74..............286 A8
  GNOS ST20.....................190 D3
  RSTAF ST18...................173 L8
  RUGE WS15....................217 J7
  STRBR DY8.....................307 J7

Chestnut Crs BLYBR/FOR ST11...104 A4
Chestnut Dr ALS/KID ST7......37 L8
  ASHB DE6.......................95 K3
  GTWY WS6......................249 K7
  LICHS WS14...................270 F5
  RUSH/SHEL WS4................284 B2
  WMBN WV5.....................298 A5
Chestnut Gv KGSWFD DY6......303 M4
  KINVER DY7....................305 M5
  NEWUL ST5.....................67 L1
  PENK ST19.....................229 L1
  STONE ST15...................119 M8
Chestnut La CRTAM B79........240 E8
Chestnut Pl BLOX/PEL WS3.....283 K4
Chestnut Rd BLOX/PEL WS3.....283 L4
  BURS/TUN ST6..................55 J3
  MKTDR TF9.....................114 D5
  MKTDR TF9.....................130 C2
  STPNHL/WNHL DE15............204 F3
Chestnut Wy BDMR/CCFT WV3...294 D2
Cheswardine Rd NEWUL ST5.....68 B2
Cheswell Cl DUNHL/THL/PER WV6..279 H8
Chetney Cl STAFN ST16........174 B6
Chetwode Cl MKTDR TF9.......96 C5
Chetwood Cl DUNHL/THL/PER WV6..280 A5
Chetwynd Av BURS/TUN ST6.....54 E5
Chetwynd Cl PENK ST19........229 M3
  RUGE WS15....................215 L4
  WSLW WS2.....................282 C7
Chetwynd Pk HEDN WS12.......233 C5
Chetwynd Rd BKHL/PFLD WV2...295 H4
  NEWUL ST5.....................68 B3
Chetwynd St BURS/TUN ST6.....54 D8
  NEWUL ST5.....................68 D5
Chevening Cl SEDG DY3........299 L3
The Chevin BUTN/AL/TUT DE13..185 J1
Cheviot Av TAM/AM/WIL B77...291 J1
Cheviot Cl NEWUL ST5.........67 L1
Cheviot Dr BURS/TUN ST6......54 A4
  RUGE WS15....................197 J7
Cheviot Hl HEDN WS12........232 C6
Cheviot Rd BKHL/PFLD WV2....295 M3
Cheyney Cl DUNHL/THL/PER WV6..280 A5
Chichester Dr CNCK/NC WS11...250 C1
Chieveley Cl RUGE WS15.......215 J1
Childerplay Rd BIDD ST8......40 B7
Chilgrove Cl HAN ST1..........3 K2
Chilgrove Gdns DUNHL/THL/PER WV6..279 J5
Chillingham TAM/AM/WIL B77...290 C3
Chillington Cl GTWY WS6......266 E1
Chillington Dr CDSL WV8......262 F6
  DUDN DY1......................299 M7
Chillington La CDSL WV8......262 D5
Chillington Rd CDSL WV8......246 A8
  WOLV WV1......................13 L8
Chiltern Cl SEDG DY3........299 K7
Chiltern Pl NEWUL ST5........67 L7
Chiltern Rd TAM/AM/WIL B77...291 J1
Chilton St STOKE ST4.........85 L6
Chilwell Av RSTAF ST18......196 E3
Chilworth Av WNSFLD WV11....281 M3
Chilworth Gv LNGTN ST3......101 M1
China St STOKE ST4...........85 M5
Chingford Cl STRBR DY8......303 J6
Chivelstone Gv STOKE ST4....100 L4
Cholerton Cl STOKE ST4......85 L5
Chorley Av BURS/TUN ST6......54 A4
Chorley Rd BNTWD WS7........251 M1
Chorley St LEEK ST13.........43 L4
Chorlton La CW/SHV CW2......64 A1
Chorlton Rd HAN ST1..........69 K4
Christ Church Gdns LICH WS13..8 A4
Christ Church La MKTDR TF9...130 A2
Christchurch St STOKE ST4....85 L5
Christchurch Wy STONE ST15...138 A2
Christie Av STAFN ST16........4 A6
Christie Pl LNGTN ST3........86 F5
Christine St BUCK/MIL ST2.....3 L7
Christopher Rd BKHL/PFLD WV2..13 J9
Christopher Ter STAFS ST17....5 J7
Chub TAM/AM/WIL B77.........290 D3
Chubb St WOLV WV1...........13 H4
Chubb Wy STOKE ST4..........84 E6
Chumleigh Gv BURS/TUN ST6...54 A8
Church Av BUCK/MIL ST2......55 H8
  RDERBYSW DE65................165 K2
Church Bank ALS/KID ST7......51 K8
  CDLE ST10.....................75 M3
  CDLE ST10.....................91 G5
  NEWUL ST5.....................82 F3
Church Cl BIDD ST8...........40 D4
  GNOS ST20.....................190 E4
  LICHS WS14...................270 F5
  LNGTN ST3.....................102 F5
  POL/KGSB/FAZ B78.............289 L5
  RSTAF ST18...................191 L4
  RSTAF ST18...................211 M2
  RUGE WS15....................215 H3
  STAFS ST17...................193 M4
  STPNHL/WNHL DE15............186 B6
  UTXR ST14.....................145 M8
  UTXR ST14.....................160 C2
Church Cft MSHM DE12........222 C7
Churchcroft Gdns RUGE WS15...197 L8
Church Dr POL/KGSB/FAZ B78...273 H3
Church Eaton Rd NWPT TF10....207 K4
Church Farm MKTDR TF9.......115 J5
  UTXR ST14.....................126 A6
Churchfield La LNGTN ST3.....102 C1
  STAFS ST17...................194 C1
Churchfield Ct CDLE ST10.....73 M1
Churchfield Rd ECCH ST21.....152 D3
  WOLVN WV10...................280 B2
Churchfields BUTN/AL/TUT DE13..201 G8
Church Flds NEWUL ST5........82 F3
Church Gdns WOLVN WV10......281 G6
Church HI CDSL WV8..........262 F5
  ETTPK/GDPK/PENN WV4........294 C6
  HEDN WS12....................232 C5

KINVER DY7...................306 A8
  RUGE WS15....................235 C2
Church Hill Rd DUNHL/THL/PER WV6..279 K4
Church Hill St STPNHL/WNHL DE15..186 B7
Church Hollow CRTAM B79......239 J5
Churchill Cl LEEK ST13........57 K6
  STOKE ST4.....................100 F3
Churchill Cl BLYBR/FOR ST11...103 L4
Churchill Crs BUTN/AL/TUT DE13..219 M8
Churchill Gdns SEDG DY3......299 J3
Churchill La KIDD DY10........311 H8
Churchill Rd CDLE ST10........89 L5
  LICHS WS14....................271 G5
  STONE ST15...................137 M3
  WSLW WS2.....................282 E7
Churchill Wy STAFS ST17......193 L5
  STOKE ST4.....................100 F3
Church La ALBTN WV7.........260 F8
  ALDR WS9......................269 L6
  ALS/KID ST7...................38 B2
  ALS/KID ST7...................39 L3
  ASHB DE6.......................78 D1
  ASHB DE6.......................93 C6
  ASHB DE6.......................145 G1
  AUD/MAD/W CW3................65 K3
  BIDD ST8......................41 H1
  BKHL/PFLD WV2.................12 E7
  BLYBR/FOR ST11...............104 E5
  BNTWD WS7....................252 D6
  BUTN/AL/TUT DE13.............164 A6
  BUTN/AL/TUT DE13.............218 C4
  BUTN/AL/TUT DE13.............220 D1
  CDLE ST10.....................73 M2
  CDLE ST10.....................75 M3
  CDLE ST10.....................124 B2
  CDSL WV8......................262 F6
  CNCK/NC WS11.................248 F2
  COVEN WV9.....................247 J8
  CRTAM B79.....................10 C4
  CRTAM B79.....................239 J5
  CRTAM B79.....................275 L3
  ECCH ST21.....................117 H7
  ECCH ST21.....................134 A5
  END/WER TF9...................55 M2
  KINVER DY7....................300 F1
  LICH WS13.....................237 K3
  MSHM DE12.....................222 E3
  MSHM DE12.....................241 L7
  NEWUL ST5.....................67 L8
  NEWUL ST5.....................68 D6
  NWPT TF10.....................207 K3
  PENK ST19.....................227 M3
  RSTAF ST18...................156 E2
  RSTAF ST18...................157 K5
  RSTAF ST18...................173 L8
  RSTAF ST18...................177 J3
  RSTAF ST18...................210 B1
  RUGE WS15....................197 H8
  RUGE WS15....................216 F5
  RUGE WS15....................217 G3
  SHIF TF11.....................224 B5
  STAFN ST16.....................4 E5
  STOKE ST4.....................84 F8
  STONE ST15...................120 B6
  STPNHL/WNHL DE15............186 D2
  UTXR ST14.....................108 F7
  UTXR ST14.....................145 M8
  UTXR ST14.....................160 B2
  WMBN WV5.....................293 H8
Church Meadow CDLE ST10......73 M1
Church Ms RDERBYSW DE65......165 K2
Church Moat Wy BLOX/PEL WS3..283 H2
Church Pl BLOX/PEL WS3.......283 K4
Church Rd ALBTN WV7..........260 F5
  ALDR WS9......................269 L7
  ALS/KID ST7...................37 H6
  ASHB DE6.......................94 C7
  BDMR/CCFT WV3...............294 E3
  BIDD ST8......................40 D3
  BLOX/PEL WS3.................268 A7
  BNTWD WS7....................252 D3
  BRWNH WS8....................268 F3
  BURS/TUN ST6..................55 H2
  BUT DE14......................203 L3
  BUTN/AL/TUT DE13.............165 M1
  BUTN/AL/TUT DE13.............166 E8
  BUTN/AL/TUT DE13.............219 M7
  CDSL WV8......................262 F6
  CNCK/NC WS11.................249 G1
  CNCK/NC WS11.................250 E6
  CRTAM B79.....................238 D8
  DUNHL/THL/PER WV6..........278 E6
  DUNHL/THL/PER WV6..........279 L5
  DUNHL/THL/PER WV6..........279 H7
  LICHS WS14....................270 F5
  LNGTN ST3.....................101 M1
  MKTDR TF9.....................115 H5
  PENK ST19.....................229 L1
  PENK ST19.....................246 C4
  RDERBYSW DE65................167 H4
  RSTAF ST18...................177 J2
  SEDG DY3.....................297 L8
  SHHTH WV12...................282 D4
  STRBR DY8.....................303 K8
  TAM/AM/WIL B77...............290 C6
  WMBN WV5.....................298 B3
  WOLVN WV10...................248 C8
  WOLVN WV10...................280 C1
Churchside CRTAM B79.........239 J7
Church Sq BURS/TUN ST6.......68 E2
Church St ALS/KID ST7........38 D8
  ALS/KID ST7...................39 H6
  ALS/KID ST7...................39 J4
  ALS/KID ST7...................51 K8
  ALS/KID ST7...................52 D1
  ASHB DE6.......................48 C6
  ASHB DE6.......................79 H8
  BKHL/PFLD WV2.................12 E7
  BLOX/PEL WS3.................283 K4
  BLOX/PEL WS3.................283 J2
  BNTWD WS7....................251 L3
  BRWNH WS8....................268 E5
  BUTN/AL/TUT DE13.............165 J4
  BUX SK17......................24 B4
  BUX SK17......................34 C5
  CDLE ST10.....................73 L8

CDLE ST10......................89 K7
  CNCK/NC WS11.................232 A6
  CNCK/NC WS11.................249 A4
  CNCK/NC WS11.................249 L1
  CRTAM B79.....................10 C4
  CRTAM B79.....................240 E8
  ECCH ST21.....................152 D3
  LICH WS13......................9 G3
  LICHS WS14...................255 K5
  MKTDR TF9.....................130 C2
  MSHM DE12.....................222 C7
  MSHM DE12.....................241 M4
  NEWUL ST5.....................67 J3
  NEWUL ST5.....................67 H8
  NEWUL ST5.....................84 B1
  RUGE WS15....................179 M4
  RUGE WS15....................215 L1
  SEDG DY3.....................299 K7
  STOKE ST4.....................85 H3
  STONE ST15...................138 A2
  UTXR ST14.....................144 C3
  WLNHL WV13...................282 B8
  WOLVN WV10...................281 G6
Church Ter BLYBR/FOR ST11....87 L8
  BURS/TUN ST6...................2 A1
Church V CNCK/NC WS11.......250 E6
Church Vw ALDR WS9..........268 F7
  ASHB DE6.......................94 F4
  BUTN/AL/TUT DE13.............185 J3
  ECCH ST21.....................117 L8
  NEWUL ST5.....................67 J3
Church View Cl BLOX/PEL WS3..283 J2
Church View Gdns KINVER DY7..305 M6
Church Wk BDMR/CCFT WV3.....294 F3
  DUNHL/THL/PER WV6..........279 L5
  NEWUL ST5.....................67 J3
Churchward Gv WMBN WV5.....298 A2
Church Wy RUGE WS15.........235 C1
Churnet Cl ASHB DE6.........94 C2
  LEEK ST13.....................57 H6
Churnet Ct BUT DE14..........7 K4
Churnet Gv DUNHL/THL/PER WV6..278 F6
Churnet Rd BLYBR/FOR ST11....104 A5
  CDLE ST10.....................105 L1
Churnet Valley Rd CDLE ST10...90 A1
Churnet Vw LEEK ST13.........44 A2
Churnet View Rd CDLE ST10....90 F3
Churn Hill Rd ALDR WS9......285 C6
Churns Hill La SEDG DY3......298 E3
Churston Cl BLOX/PEL WS3.....267 C7
  NEWUL ST5.....................84 B8
Churston Pl HAN ST1..........69 K2
Cinder Hl COVEN WV9.........247 H2
Cinder-hill La ALS/KID ST7...38 E4
Cinderhill La LNGTN ST3......86 D7
Cinder Rd BNTWD WS7.........251 L3
Circuit Cl WLNHL WV13........282 B7
Circular Rd ALBTN WV7.......42 F6
City La ALDR WS9............42 H2
City Rd STOKE ST4............85 K4
Clamgoose La CDLE ST10......89 H4
Clanbrook Rd KINVER DY7.....305 M3
Clandon Av BURS/TUN ST6......53 L6
Clanfield Av WNSFLD WV11....281 M1
Clanford Ct STAFS ST17......193 M5
Clanford La RSTAF ST18......173 G6
Clanford Rd RSTAF ST18......173 J2
Clanway St BURS/TUN ST6......53 K5
Clap Gate Gv WMBN WV5......297 L4
Clap Gate Rd WMBN WV5......297 J5
Clare Av NEWUL ST5..........68 B4
  WNSFLD WV11..................281 M1
Clare Crs BILS/COS WV14......295 M8
Claremont Cl NEWUL ST5.......68 B5
Claremont Gv STAFS ST17.....193 H2
Claremont Rd BDMR/CCFT WV3...295 C3
  CRTAM B79.....................273 M2
  ECCH ST21.....................152 E4
  SEDG DY3.....................299 L2
Clarence Gdns FOAKS/STRLY B74..286 F8
Clarence Rd FOAKS/STRLY B74..286 E5
  LNGTN ST3.....................86 B6
  WOLV WV1......................12 E4
Clarence St BUT DE14.........6 E8
  NEWUL ST5.....................68 B5
  NEWUL ST5.....................84 D1
  SEDG DY3.....................299 L5
  STOKE ST4.....................85 L3
  WOLV WV1......................12 C5
Clarendon Dr STAFS ST17.....193 H2
Clarendon Pl BLOX/PEL WS3...267 M6
Clarendon Rd MGN/WHC B75....287 J7
  RUSH/SHEL WS4................268 C8
Clarendon St BDMR/CCFT WV3..12 B5
  BLOX/PEL WS3.................283 H1
  STOKE ST4.....................85 J4
  STAFN ST16....................174 C3
  WOLVN WV10...................280 E3
Clare St ALS/KID ST7.........39 J4
  STOKE ST4.....................84 D1
Claridge Rd STOKE ST4........84 E1
Clarion Wy CNCK/NC WS11.....231 L5
Clarke's Av HEDN WS12.......232 E7
Clarke's Cl UTXR ST14.......144 B1
Clarkes La WLNHL WV13.......282 C7
Clarke St HAN ST1............2 A8
Clark Rd BDMR/CCFT WV3......279 M8
Clark's Crs RUGE WS15.......180 A4
Clark St STAFN ST16..........5 C5
Claud St STOKE ST4...........85 K6
Claverdon Dr FOAKS/STRLY B74.286 E5
Claverhouse Rd STPNHL/WNHL DE15..186 A8
Claverley Dr ETTPK/GDPK/PENN WV4..294 D5
Clayalders Bank ECCH ST21....116 C4
Claydon Crs NEWUL ST5.......84 B8
Claydon Rd KGSWFD DY6.......303 J1
Clayfield Gv LNGTN ST3.......86 C4
Clayfield Gv West LNGTN ST3..86 B4
Claygate Rd HEDN WS12.......232 E7
Claygates Rd PENK ST19......246 C1
Clay Gates Rd PENK ST19.....247 C1
Clayhanger Cl NEWUL ST5.....68 A2

Clayhanger La BRWNH WS8.....268 D4
Clayhanger Rd BRWNH WS8.....268 F4
Clayhanger St BURS/TUN ST6...68 F2
Clay Hills BURS/TUN ST6......53 J7
Clay Lake END/WER ST9.......55 K2
Claymills Rd BUTN/AL/TUT DE13..166 F5
Claymore TAM/AM/WIL B77.....290 D4
Clay Pit La LICHS WS14.......253 L7
Clay's La BUT DE14...........203 M3
Clay St PENK ST19............229 L1
  STPNHL/WNHL DE15..............7 M8
Clay St East STPNHL/WNHL DE15..205 G1
Clayton Cl BKHL/PFLD WV2....295 J3
Clayton La NEWUL ST5.........84 C6
Clayton Rd NEWUL ST5........84 B3
Clayton St LNGTN ST3.........86 B7
Claytonwood Rd STOKE ST4....84 E7
Cleadon Pl BUCK/MIL ST2.....70 B4
Clear Vw KGSWFD DY6.........303 H4
Clearwell Gdns DUDN DY1.....299 L7
Cleasby TAM/AM/WIL B77......291 J1
Cleave Rd BUT DE14..........204 A2
Clee Hill Dr BDMR/CCFT WV3..295 M1
Clee Hill Rd SEDG DY3.......299 J6
Clee Rd KIDD DY10...........310 B5
Cleeton St HEDN WS12.........250 D1
Cleeve TAM/AM/WIL B77.......11 H7
Cleeve Dr FOAKS/STRLY B74...286 F4
Cleeve Rd BLOX/PEL WS3.....266 F7
Cleeve Wy BLOX/PEL WS3......266 F8
Clee View Meadow SEDG DY3...295 K8
Clee View Rd WMBN WV5......297 L5
Clematis TAM/AM/WIL B77.....11 M7
Clematis Av BLYBR/FOR ST11..103 M4
Clematis Cl RSTAF ST18......154 B3
Clematis Crs STPNHL/WNHL DE15..205 G2
Clematis Dr COVEN WV9......263 M7
Clement Cl STAFN ST16.........5 H1
Clement Pl BURS/TUN ST6.....54 E7
Clement Rd BURS/TUN ST6.....54 A5
Clemson St WLNHL WV13......282 A8
Clent View Rd STRBR DY8.....307 K8
Clerk Bank LEEK ST13.........43 L4
Clermont Av STAFS ST17......194 D3
Clevedon Av STAFS ST17......194 D3
Cleveland Cl WNSFLD WV11....281 M1
Cleveland Dr CNCK/NC WS11...232 B4
Cleveland Pas WOLV WV1......12 F6
Cleveland Rd BKHL/PFLD WV2..13 H7
  HAN ST1........................2 C9
  NEWUL ST5.....................67 L7
Cleveland St BKHL/PFLD WV2..12 F6
  BURS/TUN ST6..................68 F2
  STRBR DY8.....................307 L6
Cleveland Wk STAFS ST17.....193 H2
Cleves Crs GTWY WS6.........266 D1
Clewley Dr COVEN WV9.......264 A7
Clewley Rd BUT DE14.........203 M2
Clewlow Pl LNGTN ST3........86 C5
Clews St BURS/TUN ST6.......68 E3
Clews Wk NEWUL ST5..........68 E3
Cley Gv NEWUL ST5...........84 B8
Cliffe Pl BURS/TUN ST6......54 A7
Clifford Av BURS/TUN ST6.....54 F5
Clifford Cl TAM/AM/WIL B77...11 K7
Clifford Rd MKTDR TF9.......130 C2
Clifford St DUNHL/THL/PER WV6.12 A2
  HAN ST1........................2 E8
  TAM/AM/WIL B77...............11 K7
Cliff Rd RSTAF ST18.........196 B1
Cliffs La NWPT TF10..........188 E1
Cliff St BURS/TUN ST6.......69 J1
Cliff Vale Pl STOKE ST4.....84 F1
Clift Av SHHTH WV12.........282 D3
Clift Cl SHHTH WV12.........282 C4
Clifton Av ALDR WS9.........285 J2
  BRWNH WS8....................268 D4
  CNCK/NC WS11.................249 J3
  CRTAM B79.....................273 M3
Clifton Cl STAFN ST16.........5 L4
  STOKE ST4.....................85 L5
  SWAD DE11....................205 M8
Clifton Dr STAFN ST16.........5 L4
Clifton Gdns CDSL WV8.......263 J7
Clifton La CRTAM B79........258 B7
Clifton Rd ASHB DE6.........94 F4
  DUNHL/THL/PER WV6..........279 K5
  MSHM DE12....................241 K4
Clifton St BDMR/CCFT WV3....12 C5
  BILS/COS WV14................299 M1
  NEWUL ST5.....................68 D6
  STOKE ST4.....................85 K5
  STRBR DY8.....................307 M6
Clinton Crs BNTWD WS7.......252 B2
Clinton Sq HAN ST1...........2 B7
Clive Av BUCK/MIL ST2.......55 H7
Clive Cl MGN/WHC B75........287 K8
Cliveden Av ALDR WS9........285 H1
Cliveden Rd BUCK/MIL ST2....70 B5
Clive Rd BNTWD WS7.........252 A3
  DUNHL/THL/PER WV6..........277 J8
  MKTDR TF9.....................130 C1
  NEWUL ST5.....................68 D4
Clive St BURS/TUN ST6.......53 L6
Clockmill Av BLOX/PEL WS3...267 M7
Clockmill Pl BLOX/PEL WS3...267 M7
Clockmill Rd BLOX/PEL WS3...267 M7
The Cloisters GNOS ST20.....190 E3
  STPNHL/WNHL DE15............7 J9
Cloister Wk LICHS WS14.....255 L5
Close La ALS/KID ST7.........37 G8
  ALS/KID ST7...................39 K3
The Close ALS/KID ST7........37 G7
  BUTN/AL/TUT DE13.............165 H4
  KINVER DY7....................301 K2
  LNGTN ST3.....................87 H5
  MSHM DE12.....................223 J5
  SEDG DY3.....................297 L8
  SEDG DY3.....................299 J6
  STAFS ST17....................4 A8
  STAFS ST17...................193 L5
Clothier Gdns WLNHL WV13....282 A7
Clothier St WLNHL WV13......282 A7
Clough Hall Dr ALS/KID ST7..52 E3
Clough Hall Rd ALS/KID ST7..52 E3
Clough La END/WER ST9.......71 G7

Clough St HAN ST1 69 G7
Cloverdale
DUNHL/THL/PER WV6 278 D6
STAFS ST17 194 C3 4
Cloverdale Pl LNGTN ST3 86 F7 1
Cloverdale Rd NEWUL ST5 68 B7
Clover La KGSWFD DY6 303 G3
Clover Ley WOLVN WV10 13 L3
Clover Mdw HEDN WS12 250 C1 2
Clover Rdg GTWY WS6 249 J7
Clover Rd NEWUL ST5 68 D4
Clowes Av ALS/KID ST7 37 M7
Clowes Rd BUCK/MIL ST2 3 L7
Club La WOLVN WV10 264 C4
Club Rw SEDG DY3 299 L5
Club St STOKE ST4 85 G4 1
Clumber Av NEWUL ST5 84 C4
Clumber Gv NEWUL ST5 84 C5
Cluny Pl BUCK/MIL ST2 3 L3
Clyde Av BIDD ST8 40 E1
Clyde Pl NEWUL ST5 84 A6 1
Clyde Rd BURS/TUN ST6 69 G3
Clyde St HAN ST1 2 A7
Clynes Wy LNGTN ST3 87 H7 1
Coach House La RUGE WS15 215 L1 1
Coach House Ri
TAM/AM/WIL B77 290 F3 2
Coalbourn La STRBR DY8 307 M3 1
Coalheath La RUSH/SHEL WS4 284 C2
Coalpitford La LEEK ST13 56 E6
Coalpit Hl ALS/KID ST7 52 D3
Coalpit La MSHM DE12 222 D7
RUGE WS15 216 A5
Coal Pool La BLOX/PEL WS3 283 M3 1
Coalport Cl CDLE ST10 105 J1
Coalport Rd RSTAF ST18 175 H2
Coalway Av
ETTPK/GDPK/PENN WV4 295 G4
Coalway Gdns
BDMR/CCFT WV3 294 D4
Coalway Rd BLOX/PEL WS3 283 G1
ETTPK/GDPK/PENN WV4 294 D4
RUGE WS15 216 B4
Coates Pl BURS/TUN ST6 54 B2 1
Cobbett Rd BNTWD WS7 251 J3
The Cobbles PENK ST19 227 J4 1
Cobden Cl HEDN WS12 232 C3
Cobden St LNGTN ST3 102 B1
NEWUL ST5 68 D4
STRBR DY8 307 K4
Cobham Cl STONE ST15 136 F4 1
Cobham Pl LNGTN ST3 103 G2 3
Cobia TAM/AM/WIL B77 290 D3
Cob Moor Rd ALS/KID ST7 39 G6
Cobridge Rd HAN ST1 2 A2
Coburn Dr MGN/WHC B75 287 K8
Cocketts Nook RUGE WS15 197 J7 2
Cock Hl ASHB DE6 94 F4
Cock La STAFS ST17 212 E3
Cocknage Rd LNGTN ST3 102 C2
Cockshead La ASHB DE6 110 C3
Cockshutts La BKHL/PFLD WV2 295 K3
Cocks La BUCK/MIL ST2 55 J7
Cocksparrow La
CNCK/NC WS11 231 G6
Cockspur St POL/KGSB/FAZ B78 291 L3
Cockster Brook La LNGTN ST3 85 L8
Cockster Rd LNGTN ST3 85 M7
Cockstubbles UTXR ST14 144 B2
Cocton Cl
DUNHL/THL/PER WV6 278 E5
Codsall Gdns CDSL WV8 262 E6
Codsall Rd CDSL WV8 279 J1
DUNHL/THL/PER WV6 279 L3
Coghlan Rd STAFS ST17 193 J2
Cokayne Av ASHB DE6 79 J8
Colaton Cl WOLVN WV10 280 E6
Colbourne Rd
POL/KGSB/FAZ B78 274 A8
Colclough Av NEWUL ST5 68 A2 1
Colclough La BURS/TUN ST6 53 K3
Colclough Rd LNGTN ST3 103 G1
Coldridge Cl COVEN WV9 279 M1
Coldstream Dr STRBR DY8 303 L7
Coldwall Br ASHB DE6 78 B2
Cole Dr STAFN ST16 4 A6
Coleford Cl STRBR DY8 303 J8
Colehill CRTAM B79 10 D4
Colenso Wy NEWUL ST5 68 B2
Coleridge Cl BLOX/PEL WS3 268 A5 1
CRTAM B79 10 B1
SHHTH WV12 282 E3 1
Coleridge Dr CDLE ST10 89 J8
DUNHL/THL/PER WV6 278 E6
STAFS ST17 193 J2
Coleridge Ri SEDG DY3 299 G6
Coleridge Rd LNGTN ST3 85 M8
Coleshill Rd POL/KGSB/FAZ B78 290 A3
Cole St BIDD ST8 40 C3
Coley Gv RSTAF ST18 196 D2
Coley La RSTAF ST18 196 D2
Colin Crs LNGTN ST3 87 H6
Colindene Gv STOKE ST4 84 F4
Colinwood Cl GTWY WS6 266 F1 1
Collard Av NEWUL ST5 68 B7
College Cl AUD/MAD/W CW3 81 L2
College Farm
DUNHL/THL/PER WV6 277 J7
College Flds STONE ST15 136 F4 2
College La CRTAM B79 10 D4
College Rd ALS/KID ST7 37 H5
DUNHL/THL/PER WV6 279 K6
HAN ST1 2 C9
STOKE ST4 85 H2
UTXR ST14 108 C4
College Vw
DUNHL/THL/PER WV6 279 K7
Collet Rd CDSL WV8 278 E5
Collets Brook MGN/WHC B75 288 A8
Colley Av WOLVN WV10 280 F2
Colley Rd BURS/TUN ST6 53 M4
Collier Cl BRWNH WS8 268 C3
GTWY WS6 249 K8
Colliers Cl SHHTH WV12 282 B4
Colliery Dr BLOX/PEL WS3 266 F7
Colliery La MSHM DE12 223 K5
Colliery Rd RUGE WS15 215 M6
WOLV WV1 13 M5
Collindale Ct KGSWFD DY6 303 K1
Collingwood Gv STOKE ST4 84 E2
Collingwood Rd WOLVN WV10 264 E8
Collin Rd STOKE ST4 84 F5
Collins Hl LICH WS13 236 A8
Collinson Rd BURS/TUN ST6 53 K3
BUTN/AL/TUT DE13 220 D1
Collins Rd BRWNH WS8 269 G5
Collin St UTXR ST14 144 B3
Collis Av STOKE ST4 84 D1
Collis St STRBR DY8 307 M2
Colman Av WNSFLD WV11 281 M4
Colne Mt UTXR ST14 144 B3
Colshaw Rd STRBR DY8 307 L6
Coltham Rd SHHTH WV12 282 C4
Coltman Cl LICHS WS14 9 K5
Colton Rd RUGE WS15 197 L6
Coltsfoot Cl WNSFLD WV11 281 L5
Coltsfoot Vw GTWY WS6 249 L8
Columbian Crs BNTWD WS7 251 M2
Columbian Dr CNCK/NC WS11 231 M7
Columbian Wy CNCK/NC WS11 231 M7
Colville St STOKE ST4 85 M4
Colwall Rd SEDG DY3 299 K6
Colwich Crs STAFN ST16 175 J7
Colwyn Dr BIDD ST8 40 D5
Combe Dr LNGTN ST3 103 G5
Comberford La CRTAM B79 257 G8
Comberford Rd CRTAM B79 274 A3
Comber Gv KINVER DY7 306 A7
Comber Rd KINVER DY7 305 M8
Comfrey Cl LNGTN ST3 103 G4
Commerce Dr PENK ST19 229 L3
Commerce St LNGTN ST3 86 C7 4
Commercial Rd HAN ST1 2 F6
WOLV WV1 13 K6
WSLW WS2 283 G3
Commercial St BURS/TUN ST6 69 G3
Common Barn La KIDD DY10 310 D5
Common La AUD/MAD/W CW3 64 E4
BUX SK17 17 M1
CDLE ST10 76 E4
CNCK/NC WS11 232 A7
CRTAM B79 10 D5 1
ECCH ST21 117 L4
LICH WS13 237 H5
LICHS WS14 255 K7
LNGTN ST3 102 F5
NEWUL ST5 98 D4
STAFS ST17 212 F2
STONE ST15 137 L4
UTXR ST14 142 C8
Common Rd STAFN ST16 174 E2
WMBN WV5 297 M6
Commonside BLOX/PEL WS3 268 A8
Common Side BRWNH WS8 269 G5
RUGE WS15 234 A5
Commonside Cl STAFN ST16 174 D4
The Common CDLE ST10 88 D7
Common Vw BNTWD WS7 252 A1 2
HEDN WS12 232 B3 1
Community Dr BURS/TUN ST6 69 K1
Como Pl NEWUL ST5 83 L4
The Compa KINVER DY7 306 A7
Compton LEEK ST13 43 L5
Compton Cl KINVER DY7 305 M6
STAFS ST17 5 J8
Compton Dr KGSWFD DY6 303 K5
Compton Gdns KINVER DY7 305 M6
Compton Gv KGSWFD DY6 303 K5
Compton Hill Dr
DUNHL/THL/PER WV6 279 K8
Compton Rd BDMR/CCFT WV3 279 M8
CRTAM B79 273 M3
KINVER DY7 305 K6
STAFS ST17 194 D1
Compton Rd West
BDMR/CCFT WV3 279 K8
The Comptons MKTDR TF9 149 G2
Compton St ASHB DE6 79 J8
HAN ST1 2 A7
Comwall Cl BLOX/PEL WS3 283 J3 1
Condlyffe Rd LEEK ST13 43 L6 1
Condor Gv CNCK/NC WS11 250 C1
Condover Cl WSLW WS2 282 D7
Conduit Rd CNCK/NC WS11 251 G6
Conduit St LICH WS13 8 F3
Conewood Pl LNGTN ST3 101 L1
Coneybere Gdns PENK ST19 246 D4
Coneygreave Cl CDLE ST10 105 K1 1
Coneygreave La NEWUL ST5 98 D4
Conford Cl BUCK/MIL ST2 3 K9
Congleton Edge Rd CONG CW12 26 B5
Congleton Rd ALS/KID ST7 39 L2
ALS/KID ST7 52 D1
BIDD ST8 40 D1
Congleton Rd North
ALS/KID ST7 38 E6
Congleton Rd South
ALS/KID ST7 38 D8
Congreve Cl STAFS ST17 194 F3
Congreve Rd LNGTN ST3 85 M8 1
Conifer Cl HEDN WS12 232 A2
Conifer Gv LNGTN ST3 85 M8
STAFS ST17 193 H3 2
The Conifers ALS/KID ST7 37 H7
Coningsby Rd ALBTN WV7 260 D2
Coniston TAM/AM/WIL B77 291 H3 2
Coniston Dr CDLE ST10 89 L6
KGSWFD DY6 303 H3
Coniston Gv NEWUL ST5 84 B6
Coniston Pl STOKE ST4 100 F3
Coniston Rd
DUNHL/THL/PER WV6 279 K2
FOAKS/STRLY B74 285 M7
Coniston Wy CNCK/NC WS11 249 L1
Connaught Dr WMBN WV5 298 A1
Connaught Rd WOLV WV1 12 B4
Connaught St BURS/TUN ST6 53 K8
Conrad Cl LNGTN ST3 86 D7
Consall Gv STOKE ST4 101 J4
Consall La END/WER ST9 72 C4
Consett Rd LNGTN ST3 101 M2
Consort St STOKE ST4 85 H3 5
Constable Av NEWUL ST5 67 L4
Constable Cl LNGTN ST3 103 H3 4
Constance Av STOKE ST4 101 H2
Convent Cl CNCK/NC WS11 249 K2
RSTAF ST18 196 D3 1
STPNHL/WNHL DE15 204 F2
Convent Court Cl STOKE ST4 85 G2
Convent La STONE ST15 120 B6
Conway Cl
BUTN/AL/TUT DE13 185 K2 4
KGSWFD DY6 303 M6
Conway Crs SHHTH WV12 282 C3
Conway Gv CDLE ST10 105 L1
Conway Rd BIDD ST8 40 C4
CNCK/NC WS11 249 H2
DUNHL/THL/PER WV6 278 F7
STAFN ST16 174 A6
Conway St STOKE ST4 85 J2
Conwy Cl WSLW WS2 283 G6 2
Conygree La ASHB DE6 94 D3
Cook Cl
DUNHL/THL/PER WV6 278 E6 2
Cooke Cl PENK ST19 211 L8
Cooke St BKHL/PFLD WV2 295 J3
Cook La ASHB DE6 145 H1
Cookley La KINVER DY7 310 B1
Cooknell Dr STRBR DY8 303 L8
Cook Rd BLOX/PEL WS3 267 K8
Cook's Bank STAFS ST17 212 B1
Cook's Hollow LEEK ST13 59 G2
Cook's La LEEK ST13 58 F1
Cookson Av LNGTN ST3 102 C1
Coombe Cft COVEN WV9 264 A7 3
Coombe Park Rd STONE ST15 137 M5
Coombesdale NEWUL ST5 116 E1
Co-operative La ALS/KID ST7 66 D3 1
Co-operative St STAFN ST16 174 D4
Cooper Av NEWUL ST5 68 E8 2
Cooper Cl STONE ST15 138 D3
Cooper's Cl ASHB DE6 79 J8
LEEK ST13 43 J5
Coopers Cft RDERBYSW DE65 165 J1
Cooper St HAN ST1 2 B8
NEWUL ST5 67 L4 1
WOLV WV1 13 M9
Coopers Wy BIDD ST8 40 B2
Copeland Av BARL ST12 119 G1
NEWUL ST5 84 B7 3
Copeland Cl CDLE ST10 105 K1
Copeland Dr STONE ST15 138 D4
The Copelands KINVER DY7 306 A7
Copeland St STOKE ST4 85 H3
Copelea MKTDR TF9 148 F2
Cope's Av BURS/TUN ST6 53 L6
Copes Crs WOLVN WV10 281 G4
Cope's Dr CRTAM B79 274 A3
Cope St BLOX/PEL WS3 283 J4
BUCK/MIL ST2 70 A1
STAFN ST16 4 F5
Copes Wy UTXR ST14 143 M1
Copley Cft ASHB DE6 79 K7 1
Copley La
DUNHL/THL/PER WV6 277 G7
Coplow Av CDLE ST10 105 J6
Coplow La RDERBYSW DE65 147 K4
Copperas Rd SWAD DE11 205 K5
Copper Beech Dr KGSWFD DY6 303 K1
WMBN WV5 298 B4
Copperfields LICHS WS14 9 J4
Copper Gld STAFN ST16 5 L4
Copperhill Rd CONG CW12 26 B3
Copperkins Rd HEDN WS12 232 D6
Coppermill Cl HEDN WS12 231 M3
Coppice Av NEWUL ST5 83 G1
Coppice Brook STAFS ST17 195 J6
Coppice Cl BIDD ST8 40 D3 1
BNTWD WS7 251 M2
GTWY WS6 249 K6
SEDG DY3 299 J3
WNSFLD WV11 282 A1
Coppice Ct CNCK/NC WS11 249 H3 1
Coppice Crs BRWNH WS8 268 D3
Coppice Dr POL/KGSB/FAZ B78 291 M3
Coppice Farm Wy SHHTH WV12 282 B3
Coppice Gdns STONE ST15 138 B1 1
Coppice Gv LICHS WS14 254 F3
LNGTN ST3 86 F7
Coppice La ALDR WS9 284 F1
BNTWD WS7 253 G7
BRWNH WS8 268 D2
CNCK/NC WS11 249 K6
CRTAM B79 258 F1
DUNHL/THL/PER WV6 279 H4
POL/KGSB/FAZ B78 288 C8
SHHTH WV12 282 C4
Coppice Rd ALDR WS9 268 F6
ALS/KID ST7 52 C2
BDMR/CCFT WV3 294 D2
RUGE WS15 215 L4
SHIF TF11 242 A4 1
STONE ST15 138 B1
Coppice Side BRWNH WS8 268 D2
The Coppice BURS/TUN ST6 69 J3 1
HEDN WS12 250 E1 1
MKTDR TF9 130 B1 4
SHHTH WV12 282 C4
Coppice Vw NEWUL ST5 68 A6
The Coppins STAFS ST17 194 C3 5
Copp La BURS/TUN ST6 53 J8
Copplestone Gv LNGTN ST3 86 E7
Coppull Pl BURS/TUN ST6 54 A3 2
Coppy Hall Gv ALDR WS9 285 H1
Coppy Nook La BNTWD WS7 252 B5
Copse Crs BLOX/PEL WS3 268 A6
Copse Dr RUGE WS15 217 H6 1
Copthorne Av BNTWD WS7 251 M6
Copthorne Rd
BDMR/CCFT WV3 295 G3
Coral Gv STOKE ST4 101 H3
Corbin Rd POL/KGSB/FAZ B78 291 M4
Corden Av BUTN/AL/TUT DE13 185 M2
Cordy La ALBTN WV7 261 H2
Corfe Cl DUNHL/THL/PER WV6 278 F7
Corfield Pl BURS/TUN ST6 54 D5
Corfton Dr
DUNHL/THL/PER WV6 279 J7
Corina Wy LNGTN ST3 86 D6
Cormie Cl BURS/TUN ST6 54 B5
Corncrake Rd SEDG DY3 299 K7
Cornel TAM/AM/WIL B77 11 M6
Cornelious St LNGTN ST3 103 G1 1
Corneville Rd BUCK/MIL ST2 70 B7
Cornfield CDSL WV8 279 L1
Cornfield Cl KGSWFD DY6 303 G2
Cornfield Dr LICHS WS14 9 M4
Cornfield Rd BIDD ST8 40 D3
Cornflower Cl WOLVN WV10 265 G3 1
Cornflower Rd BRWNH WS8 268 D4
Cornhill CNCK/NC WS11 231 L5
Corn Hl WOLV WV1 13 H5
Cornhill Cl NEWUL ST5 67 K1 2
Cornhill Gdns LEEK ST13 43 L6
Cornhill Rd BURS/TUN ST6 54 C5
Cornhill St LEEK ST13 43 L5 1
Cornmill Bank
BUTN/AL/TUT DE13 165 K4
Cornmill Gv
DUNHL/THL/PER WV6 278 D7 3
Corn Mill La BUTN/AL/TUT DE13 165 K4
Cornmill La BUTN/AL/TUT DE13 165 J4
Cornovian Cl
DUNHL/THL/PER WV6 278 E5 3
Corns Gv WMBN WV5 297 M5
Cornwall Av NEWUL ST5 84 C6
POL/KGSB/FAZ B78 290 A1
Cornwall Cl ALDR WS9 285 G1
CONG CW12 26 A2
KGSWFD DY6 303 K2 1
Cornwall Ga SHHTH WV12 282 B5 3
Cornwallis Dr SHIF TF11 242 A5
Cornwallis St STOKE ST4 85 H4
Cornwall Pl WSLW WS2 282 E7
Cornwall Rd
DUNHL/THL/PER WV6 279 J6
HEDN WS12 232 B5
STPNHL/WNHL DE15 204 E4
STRBR DY8 307 K2
Cornwall St LNGTN ST3 86 C6
Cornwood Gv LNGTN ST3 102 E2
Coronation Av ALS/KID ST7 37 G7
BIDD ST8 40 B5
LNGTN ST3 86 B7
POL/KGSB/FAZ B78 289 K1
WLNHL WV13 282 D8
Coronation Crs CRTAM B79 275 M3 1
UTXR ST14 109 G6 1
Coronation Rd ALDR WS9 268 F7
NEWUL ST5 84 C2 3
RUSH/SHEL WS4 268 B8
STAFN ST16 175 G4
STOKE ST4 84 E2
WNSFLD WV11 281 G5
Coronation St BURS/TUN ST6 53 L6
CRTAM B79 10 B3
Corporation St CRTAM B79 10 C4
NEWUL ST5 84 B1 3
STAFN ST16 4 F1
STOKE ST4 85 G4
WOLV WV1 12 E5 1
Corran Rd STAFS ST17 193 K4
Correen TAM/AM/WIL B77 275 J8 2
Corrin Gv KGSWFD DY6 303 J2
Corser St DUDN DY1 299 M8
WOLV WV1 13 L6
Corsican Cl BNTWD WS7 251 M2
SHHTH WV12 282 E3 2
Corsican Dr HEDN WS12 232 A2
Cort Dr BNTWD WS7 252 B2
Corve Gdns
DUNHL/THL/PER WV6 279 L5
Corve Vw SEDG DY3 299 J1 1
Corwell Rd LNGTN ST3 86 B7
Coseley St BURS/TUN ST6 69 J1
Cotehill Rd END/WER ST9 71 H7
Cote La KINVER DY7 305 L1
Cotesheath St STOKE ST4 85 K1
Cotes La ECCH ST21 117 M8
Cot La STRBR DY8 303 K6
Coton Av STAFN ST16 5 L3
Coton La CRTAM B79 273 K3
MSHM DE12 222 D6
RSTAF ST18 172 D6
Coton Pk MSHM DE12 223 J1
Coton Ri BARL ST12 119 L1
Coton Rd
ETTPK/GDPK/PENN WV4 295 H5
MSHM DE12 221 L4
Cotsdale Rd
ETTPK/GDPK/PENN WV4 294 E7
Cotswold Av GTWY WS6 249 M7 1
NEWUL ST5 67 L7
Cotswold Cl ALDR WS9 285 J1
Cotswold Ct
BKHL/PFLD WV2 295 G4 2
Cotswold Crs BUCK/MIL ST2 70 A1
Cotswold Dr ALBTN WV7 261 H5
Cotswold Gv SHHTH WV12 282 B1 1
Cotswold Rd BKHL/PFLD WV2 295 M3
BUT DE14 203 M3
HEDN WS12 232 A2
Cottage Cl BNTWD WS7 251 M5
HEDN WS12 232 D6
LNGTN ST3 102 E1
WNSFLD WV11 281 J4
Cottage Farm Rd
TAM/AM/WIL B77 290 D3
Cottage La BIDD ST8 41 G1
BNTWD WS7 251 M5
WOLVN WV10 264 D7
Cottage St KGSWFD DY6 303 K3
Cottage Vw CDSL WV8 263 H6 1
Cotterill Dr NEWUL ST5 68 B2
Cotterill Gv BURS/TUN ST6 68 F3
Cotters Hill Cl RSTAF ST18 196 D2 2
Cottesmore Rd
STPNHL/WNHL DE15 205 G1
Cottle Cl WSLW WS2 282 F7 1
Cotton Cl BUTN/AL/TUT DE13 219 M7
Cotton Gv HEDN WS12 232 A1
Cotton La CDLE ST10 75 H7
LEEK ST13 75 G5
Cotton Rd BURS/TUN ST6 53 J4
Cottonwood Gv ALS/KID ST7 39 L7
LNGTN ST3 86 C6 3
Cotwall End Rd SEDG DY3 299 H6
Coulson Cl BNTWD WS7 251 K1 1
Coulter Gv
DUNHL/THL/PER WV6 278 D6
Coulter La BNTWD WS7 252 E2
Coulthwaite Wy RUGE WS15 215 M4 1
Countess Dr RUSH/SHEL WS4 284 D3
County Dr POL/KGSB/FAZ B78 289 M1
County La ALBTN WV7 277 L1
KINVER DY7 311 K2
County Rd STAFN ST16 4 D3
Coupe Dr LNGTN ST3 87 G5
Court Crs KGSWFD DY6 303 J5
Court Dr LICHS WS14 270 F6
Court Farm La BUT DE14 203 L
Courtland Rd KGSWFD DY6 303 L
The Courtlands
DUNHL/THL/PER WV6 279 L
Court La NEWUL ST5 68 E
Courtney Pl LNGTN ST3 102 E
Court Rd DUNHL/THL/PER WV6 279 M
Court Wy WSLW WS2 283 K
Courtway Dr HAN ST1 69 K
Cousins St BKHL/PFLD WV2 295 K
Coven Cl BLOX/PEL WS3 268 A
Coven Rd PENK ST19 246 D
Coven St WOLVN WV10 13 H
Coventry St WOLV WV1 281 C
Coverdale Cl LNGTN ST3 103 C
Coverley Pl STOKE ST4 84 F4
Covert Cl RSTAF ST18 177 H
Covert Gdns ALS/KID ST7 52 D
Covert La STRBR DY8 311 K
The Covert CDSL WV8 279 L
NEWUL ST5 83 H
NEWUL ST5 84 C
Covey Cl LICH WS13 9 J
Cowallmoor La BURS/TUN ST6 41 J
Cowan Dr STAFN ST16 5 K
Cowan St BURS/TUN ST6 54 D
Cowhill La LICH WS13 237 L
Cowhouse La CDLE ST10 124 B
Cow La CDLE ST10 75 M
POL/KGSB/FAZ B78 290 F
Cowley TAM/AM/WIL B77 274 E
Cowley Cl PENK ST19 229 M
STAFS ST17 193 J2
Cowley Dr DUDN DY1 299 M
Cowley Gn HEDN WS12 231 M
Cowley La GNOS ST20 190 D
Cowley Wy BUCK/MIL ST2 86 E3
Cowlishaw Cl BIDD ST8 40 A
Cowlishaw Rd BURS/TUN ST6 54 E
Cowlow La BUX SK17 33
Cowper Cl SHHTH WV12 282 E
Cowper St STOKE ST4 85 M
Coxmoor Cl BLOX/PEL WS3 266 F7
Coxwell Av WOLVN WV10 280 C
Coyney Gv LNGTN ST3 87 C
Crabbery St STAFN ST16 4 E
Crab La CNCK/NC WS11 232 A
KINVER DY7 296 E
SHHTH WV12 282 D
STAFN ST16 174 E
Crabtree Av BIDD ST8 40 C
Crabtree Wy RUGE WS15 215 J
Crackley La NEWUL ST5 66 E
Cracow Moss AUD/MAD/W CW3 65 C
Craddock Rd STAFN ST16 174 C
Craddock St
DUNHL/THL/PER WV6 280 A
Craftdown Cl STAFS ST17 193 M
Craigside BIDD ST8 40 C
Craig Wk ALS/KID ST7 37 M
Cramer St STAFS ST17 4 F
Cranberry Av CDLE ST10 124 E
Cranberry Cl STAFN ST16 174 A4
Cranberry Dr NEWUL ST5 67 K1
Cranberry La ALS/KID ST7 37 C
Cranberry Marsh ECCH ST21 117 K
Cranberry Moss La
ALS/KID ST7 37 G7
Cranborne Av BUCK/MIL ST2 55 H8
Cranbourne Av
ETTPK/GDPK/PENN WV4 295
Cranbrook Cl STOKE ST4 101 G3
Cranbrook Gv
DUNHL/THL/PER WV6 278 F
Cranbrooks PENK ST19 227 J3
Cranbrook Wk STAFS ST17 193 H2
Cranebrook Hl
POL/KGSB/FAZ B78 288 D
Cranebrook La LICHS WS14 269 M
Crane Dr BNTWD WS7 252 A
Crane Fld LICH WS13 254 A
Crane Hollow WMBN WV5 297 L5
Cranesbill Cl WOLVN WV10 265 J3
Crane St HAN ST1 2 A
Crane Ter
DUNHL/THL/PER WV6 279
Cranfield Dr ALS/KID ST7 37 C
Cranfield Pl BUCK/MIL ST2 70 B8
Cranfield Rd BNTWD WS7 252 A
Cranford Ms ALS/KID ST7 37 C
Cranford Rd BDMR/CCFT WV3 294 C
Cranford Wy BUCK/MIL ST2 70 D
Cranham Dr KGSWFD DY6 303 K
Cranleigh Av HAN ST1 69 K
Cranleigh Cl ALDR WS9 285 H
SHHTH WV12 282 C1
Cranleigh Wy LICHS WS14 9
Cranley Dr CDSL WV8 262 F
Cranmer Av SHHTH WV12 282 D
Cranmer Cl GTWY WS6 266 C
Cranmere Av
DUNHL/THL/PER WV6 279 C
Cranmer Gv FOAKS/STRLY B74 286 F
Cranmer St STOKE ST4 85 H
Cranmore Rd BDMR/CCFT WV3 279 M
Cranswick Gv BUCK/MIL ST2 86 D
Crantock Cl SHHTH WV12 282 C
Cranwell Gn WMBN WV5 297 M5
Cranwell Pl LNGTN ST3 102 F
Cranwood Rd BARL ST12 119 G1
Cranworth Gv LNGTN ST3 102 E
Crateford La PENK ST19 247 H
Crathorne Av WOLVN WV10 280 C
Craven TAM/AM/WIL B77 291 H
Craven Cl STOKE ST4 101 C
Craven St BKHL/PFLD WV2 295 M
BUTN/AL/TUT DE13 185
Crawford Av
ETTPK/GDPK/PENN WV4 295 M
Crawford Rd BDMR/CCFT WV3 12 A
Crawfurd St STOKE ST4 85 H
Crawley La BUTN/AL/TUT DE13 218 C
Craythorne Rd
BUTN/AL/TUT DE13 166 C
Crediton Av BURS/TUN ST6 54 C
Creighton La UTXR ST14 126 A
Cremorne Dr STAFS ST17 194 D
Cremorne Rd MGN/WHC B75 287 H
Crescent Gv STOKE ST4 84
Crescent Rd STAFS ST17 4 C

WLNHL WV13 .... 282 C8
The Crescent ASHB DE6 .... 94 D3
  BNTWD WS7 .... 251 M1
  DUNHL/THL/PER WV6 .... 279 H7
  ECCH ST21 .... 152 D4
  END/WER ST9 .... 42 D1
  GTWY WS6 .... 250 A8
  HAG/WOL DY9 .... 311 M5
  KIDD DY10 .... 310 B6
  LEEK ST13 .... 44 A4
  MKTDR TF9 .... 115 J5
  NEWUL WS2 .... 67 H8
  NEWUL ST5 .... 84 A4
  SHIF TF11 .... 224 C5
  STAFN ST17 .... 174 B6
  STONE ST15 .... 138 A1
  SWAD DE11 .... 205 L4
The Cresent STAFS ST17 .... 194 F3
Cresswell Av NEWUL WS2 .... 67 K1
Cresswell Crs BLOX/PEL WS3 .... 266 F8
Cresswell La BLYBR/FOR ST11 .... 104 D5
  PENK ST19 .... 246 C4
Cresswell Old Rd
  BLYBR/FOR ST11 .... 104 D7
Cresswell Rd HAN ST1 .... 3 C6
  STONE ST15 .... 121 L8
Cresswellshawe Rd
  ALS/KID ST7 .... 37 K5
Crestbrook Rd BUCK/MIL ST2 .... 70 B3
Crest Cl BUTN/AL/TUT DE13 .... 185 L1
Crestfield Rd LNGTN ST3 .... 102 F2
The Crest MSHM DE12 .... 223 J4
Crestway Rd BUCK/MIL ST2 .... 55 J8
Crestwood
  TAM/AM/WIL B77 .... 275 G5
Crestwood Cl
  BUTN/AL/TUT DE13 .... 185 K2
Crestwood Dr STONE ST15 .... 137 L4
Crestwood Gln
  DUNHL/THL/PER WV6 .... 279 L3
Crestwood Pk PENK ST19 .... 246 D3
Crestwood Ri RUGE WS15 .... 197 J8
Creswell Dr RSTAF ST18 .... 173 M2
Creswell Farm Dr STAFN ST16 .... 174 B3
Creswell Gv RSTAF ST18 .... 173 M2
Crewe Rd ALS/KID ST7 .... 37 H7
Crichton Av
  BUTN/AL/TUT DE13 .... 185 K3
Crich Wy SWAD DE11 .... 205 L5
Cricket Cl STPNHL/WNHL DE15 .... 186 E2
Cricketers Cl
  STPNHL/WNHL DE15 .... 204 F2
Cricket La LICHS WS14 .... 9 H9
Cricket Meadow SEDG DY3 .... 299 L5
  WOLVN WV10 .... 264 D6
Crick Rd HAN ST1 .... 2 F9
Crigdon PI POL/KGSB/FAZ B78 .... 275 J8
Crinan St STAFS ST17 .... 193 J4
Cringlebrook TAM/AM/WIL B77 .. 290 D1
Cripps Rd WSLW WS2 .... 282 E7
Crispin Cl STAFN ST16 .... 174 C2
Critchlow Av LNGTN ST3 .... 102 A1
Crockford Dr MGN/WHC ST7 .... 287 C7
Crockington La WMBN WV5 .... 292 F8
Crockington La WMBN WV5 .... 297 C1
Crocus Crs COVEN WV9 .... 264 A7
Croft Av HEDN WS12 .... 232 A1
  NEWUL ST5 .... 68 A4
Croft Ct BUTN/AL/TUT DE13 .... 166 B6
  CRTAM B79 .... 238 E8
  MSHM DE12 .... 241 M3
Croft Crs BRWNH WS8 .... 268 C3
  STOKE ST4 .... 85 C4
Crofter Cl BIDD ST8 .... 40 B2
Crofters Cl NEWUL ST5 .... 52 D7
Croftfield St BUCK/MIL ST2 .... 86 D2
Croft Gdns BNTWD WS7 .... 252 A2
Croft Gv UTXR ST14 .... 144 B1
Croft La WOLVN WV10 .... 247 K1
  WOLVN WV10 .... 280 F3
The Croft Leys RUGE WS15 .... 217 J6
Croft Rd CDLE ST10 .... 89 K7
  NEWUL ST5 .... 68 B8
  STONE ST15 .... 137 M4
Croftstead Av UTXR ST14 .... 108 D4
Croft St BURS/TUN ST6 .... 68 F2
  CRTAM B79 .... 10 C2
  WLNHL WV13 .... 282 A8
  WSLW WS3 .... 283 K7
The Croft BUTN/AL/TUT DE13 .. 218 D4
  CDLE ST10 .... 89 L4
  GTWY WS6 .... 249 L8
  KIDD DY10 .... 311 J8
  LEEK ST13 .... 57 J6
  RSTAF ST18 .... 177 J2
  RUGE WS15 .... 234 F1
  SEDG DY3 .... 299 L1
  STOKE ST4 .... 84 F5
  STPNHL/WNHL DE15 .... 7 M9
  SWAD DE11 .... 205 L4
  WLNHL WV13 .... 282 A8
  WMBN WV5 .... 297 K5
Croft Wy MKTDR TF9 .... 130 B1
Cromartie St LNGTN ST3 .... 86 C8
Cromdale TAM/AM/WIL B77 .. 291 J1
Cromer Av HAN ST1 .... 3 H4
Cromer Gdns
  DUNHL/THL/PER WV6 .... 279 M5
Cromer Rd HAN ST1 .... 3 H4
Cromers St NEWUL ST5 .... 68 D6
Crompton Cl RSTAF ST18 .... 196 E2
  WSLW WS2 .... 283 C5
Crompton Gv STOKE ST4 .... 101 J5
Crompton Rd STONE ST15 .... 138 B3
Cromwell Cl
  BUTN/AL/TUT DE13 .... 165 L1
  RSTAF ST18 .... 175 K2
  WSLW WS2 .... 282 E6
Cromwell Rd CRTAM B79 .... 273 L2
  HEDN WS12 .... 250 D1
  WOLVN WV10 .... 264 E6
Cromwells Meadow LICHS WS14 .... 9 H9
Cromwell St BIDD ST8 .... 40 C1
  HAN ST1 .... 69 K4
Crony Cl LEEK ST13 .... 57 J6
Crooked Bridge Rd STAFN ST16 .... 4 E2
Crosby Cl
  DUNHL/THL/PER WV6 .... 279 M5
Crosby Rd STOKE ST4 .... 84 E7

Cross Butts ECCH ST21 .... 152 D4
Crossdale Av BUCK/MIL ST2 ..... 55 G8
Cross Edge BURS/TUN ST6 ..... 55 H3
Crossfell TAM/AM/WIL B77 .... 291 H1
Crossfield Av BIDD ST8 .... 40 C4
  BLYBR/FOR ST11 .... 103 M4
Crossfield Rd LICH WS13 .... 9 M2
Cross Hi BURS/TUN ST6 .... 68 F2
Crosshill Bank RSTAF ST18 .... 140 E5
Crossing La RSTAF ST18 .... 173 H6
Cross in Hand La LICH WS13 ... 253 M1
Cross Keys LICH WS13 .... 8 F3
Crossland Crs
  DUNHL/THL/PER WV6 .... 279 M1
Crossland PI East
  LNGTN ST3 .... 103 G2
Crossland PI West
  LNGTN ST3 .... 103 G1
Crosslands CONG CW12 .... 26 A1
Cross La ALS/KID ST7 .... 51 L6
  BUTN/AL/TUT DE13 .... 166 B8
  CONG CW12 .... 26 A2
  LEEK ST13 .... 60 E6
  LICHS WS14 .... 9 K6
  SEDG DY3 .... 299 K2
  STONE ST15 .... 120 C4
Crossley Rd BURS/TUN ST6 ..... 54 A7
Crossley Stone RUGE WS15 .... 215 L1
Crosslow La ASHB DE6 .... 49 L6
Cross May St NEWUL ST5 .... 84 A2
Crossmead Gv HAN ST1 .... 3 K1
Cross PI SEDG DY3 .... 299 L1
Cross Rd ALBTN WV7 .... 260 E7
  RUGE WS15 .... 215 L3
  UTXR ST14 .... 144 B1
Cross Side ASHB DE6 .... 94 F3
Cross St ALS/KID ST7 .... 37 J7
  BIDD ST8 .... 40 C2
  BLOX/PEL WS3 .... 284 A1
  BNTWD WS7 .... 251 L2
  BURS/TUN ST6 .... 68 C2
  BUT DE14 .... 6 F6
  CDLE ST10 .... 73 K7
  CDLE ST10 .... 89 K7
  CNCK/NC WS11 .... 249 L5
  GNOS ST20 .... 190 C5
  GTWY WS6 .... 249 K8
  HEDN WS12 .... 250 E1
  KGSWFD DY6 .... 303 J4
  LEEK ST13 .... 43 M5
  LNGTN ST3 .... 86 C6
  MKTDR TF9 .... 130 D1
  NEWUL ST5 .... 67 K2
  STONE ST15 .... 138 A1
  STRBR DY8 .... 303 K7
  STRBR DY8 .... 307 L5
  SWAD DE11 .... 223 L2
  TAM/AM/WIL B77 .... 10 E7
  WOLV WV1 .... 13 M6
Cross St South BKHL/PFLD WV2.. 295 J3
Crossway STAFN ST16 .... 5 J5
Crossway Rd BURS/TUN ST6 ..... 69 J3
Crossways BIDD ST8 .... 40 E1
Crossways Rd ALS/KID ST7 .... 38 A6
The Crossway NEWUL ST5 .... 68 C7
Croston St HAN ST1 .... 2 B9
Crouch Av BURS/TUN ST6 ..... 54 A6
Crowberry Cl BRWNH WS8 .... 268 C4
Crowborough Rd BIDD ST8 .... 40 F4
  BURS/TUN ST6 .... 41 H4
Crowcrofts Rd STOKE ST4 .... 101 L3
Crowden Rd TAM/AM/WIL B77 .. 291 G1
Crowfoot La RDERBYSW DE65 .. 147 L1
Crowland Av
  DUNHL/THL/PER WV6 .... 278 E6
Crown Bank BURS/TUN ST6 ..... 52 D3
Crown Bank Crs ALS/KID ST7 ..... 52 D4
Crown Br PENK ST19 .... 229 L1
Crown Cl SEDG DY3 .... 299 K1
Crowndale PI BURS/TUN ST6 ..... 53 L2
Crown La FOAKS/STRLY B74 .... 286 E8
  STRBR DY8 .... 307 M4
Crown St HAN ST1 .... 2 C6
  NEWUL ST5 .... 83 J1
  STONE ST15 .... 138 A2
  WOLV WV1 .... 280 D6
Crowther Gv
  DUNHL/THL/PER WV6 .... 279 M6
Crowther Rd
  DUNHL/THL/PER WV6 .... 279 M5
  WOLVN WV10 .... 280 E6
Crowther St STOKE ST4 .... 85 J2
Croxall Rd BUTN/AL/TUT DE13 .. 220 B8
  LICH WS13 .... 238 F2
Croxden Cl CDLE ST10 .... 105 K2
Croxdene Av BLOX/PEL WS3 ..... 282 F1
Croxden Rd BUCK/MIL ST2 ..... 70 B4
Croxstalls Av BLOX/PEL WS3 ..... 283 G2
Croxstalls Cl BLOX/PEL WS3 ..... 283 G1
Croxstalls PI BLOX/PEL WS3 ..... 283 G1
Croxstalls Rd BLOX/PEL WS3 ..... 283 G1
Croyde PI LNGTN ST3 .... 103 G4
Croydon Dr PENK ST19 .... 229 L2
Cruso St LEEK ST13 .... 43 K5
Crutchley Av
  POL/KGSB/FAZ B78 .... 274 A8
Crystal Av STRBR DY8 .... 307 M1
Crystal St BURS/TUN ST6 .... 2 A1
Cubley La ASHB DE6 .... 127 M1
Cuckoo Cage La
  BUTN/AL/TUT DE13 .... 202 F1
Cuckoo Cl HEDN WS12 .... 232 D2
Cullamore La UTXR ST14 .... 144 A6
Culland Rd BUT DE14 .... 204 B3
Cull Av BUT DE14 .... 6 D1
Cullen Av BLOX/PEL WS3 .... 95 J1
Culmore Cl SHHTH WV12 .... 282 D6
Culwell St WOLVN WV10 .... 13 H3
Cumberbatch Av BURS/TUN ST6.. 54 B3
Cumberland Cl ALS/KID ST7 ..... 52 E3
  KGSWFD DY6 .... 303 J5
Cumberland Crs
  BNTWD WS7 .... 252 A2
Cumberland Dr
  POL/KGSB/FAZ B78 .... 290 A1
Cumberland Rd
  CNCK/NC WS11 .... 232 A6
  STPNHL/WNHL DE15 .... 204 D4
  WLNHL WV13 .... 282 D8
Cumberland St STOKE ST4 .... 84 D1

STOKE ST4 .... 85 L3
Cumberledge Hl RUGE WS15 .... 233 L5
Cumming St STOKE ST4 .... 84 E1
Cunningham Rd
  DUNHL/THL/PER WV6 .... 278 E6
  WSLW WS2 .... 282 E8
Curborough Rd LICH WS13 ...... 236 B7
Curland PI LNGTN ST3 .... 86 F8
Curlew TAM/AM/WIL B77 .... 291 G5
Curlew Cl LICHS WS14 .... 9 M5
  UTXR ST14 .... 144 C4
Curlew Hl CNCK/NC WS11 ...... 232 A7
Curriers La SHIF TF11 .... 242 A5
Curtiss PI BLYBR/FOR ST11 ...... 103 H4
Curtis Wy BUT DE14 .... 6 C3
Curzon Av ALS/KID ST7 .... 37 K5
  BUTN/AL/TUT DE13 .... 203 C1
  BUTN/AL/TUT DE13 .... 220 A7
  GTWY WS6 .... 267 J1
  KINVER DY7 .... 306 C7
  LICH WS13 .... 8 A5
  POL/KGSB/FAZ B78 .... 291 L2
  RUGE WS15 .... 234 D4
  WNSFLD WV11 .... 265 K3
  WOLVN WV10 .... 264 D2
Curzon Ri HEDN WS12 .... 233 G4
Curzon Rd BURS/TUN ST6 ..... 54 A8
Curzon St BKHL/PFLD WV2 .... 295 K3
  BUT DE14 .... 6 D3
  NEWUL ST5 .... 68 D8
Curzon St West BUT DE14 .... 6 D4
The Cutting
  RUSH/SHEL WS4 .... 283 M6
Cutts St HAN ST1 .... 2 B9
Cygnet Cl AUD/MAD/W CW3 ...... 82 A2
  HEDN WS12 .... 232 C3
Cynthia Gv BURS/TUN ST6 ..... 54 A8
Cypress Av SEDG DY3 .... 299 K5
Cypress Cl MKTDR TF9 .... 130 A1
Cypress Gdns KGSWFD DY6 ..... 303 K6
Cypress Gv BLYBR/FOR ST11 .... 104 A3
  NEWUL ST5 .... 67 K2
Cypress Ri HEDN WS12 .... 233 G4
Cyprus St BKHL/PFLD WV2 .... 295 H3

D

Dace TAM/AM/WIL B77 .... 290 D3
Dace Gv BURS/TUN ST6 .... 54 D3
Daffodil Cl SEDG DY3 .... 299 L3
Daffodil Wk RUGE WS15 .... 197 J8
Dag La MSHM DE12 .... 240 D3
Dahlia Cl LNGTN ST3 .... 87 H4
Dain PI NEWUL ST5 .... 68 B4
Dain St BURS/TUN ST6 .... 68 E3
Daintry Cl LEEK ST13 .... 43 L6
Daintry Dr POL/KGSB/FAZ B78 .. 273 H3
Daintry St LEEK ST13 .... 43 L5
  STOKE ST4 .... 84 F6
Dairy Cl LEEK ST13 .... 44 A4
Dairyfields Wy BURS/TUN ST6 .. 69 J3
Dairyhouse La CDLE ST10 .... 72 B8
Dairylands Rd ALS/KID ST7 ..... 38 A6
Daisy Av CDLE ST10 .... 74 A2
Daisy Bank HEDN WS12 .... 231 M2
  LEEK ST13 .... 43 L4
Daisy Bank Cl BLOX/PEL WS3 ..... 268 B8
Daisy La BUTN/AL/TUT DE13 ..... 237 K1
Daisy PI STOKE ST4 .... 85 L6
Daisy St
  DUNHL/THL/PER WV6 .... 280 A6
Daisy Wk COVEN WV9 .... 264 A7
Dalbeg Cl CDSL WV8 .... 279 L2
Dalby Rd BLOX/PEL WS3 .... 283 M4
Dale Av BURS/TUN ST6 .... 54 E4
Dale Brook RDERBYSW DE65 .. 166 F1
Dalebrook Rd
  STPNHL/WNHL DE15 .... 186 A5
Dale Cl CDLE ST10 .... 89 L8
  NEWUL ST5 .... 98 C5
Dale Dr BNTWD WS7 .... 252 B3
Dalegarth Gv LNGTN ST3 .... 102 L2
Dalehouse Rd LEEK ST13 .... 57 H6
Dalelands Est MKTDR TF9 .... 130 B2
Dale La ASHB DE6 .... 76 E5
  CDLE ST10 .... 76 D4
  RSTAF ST18 .... 192 A1
Dales Cl BIDD ST8 .... 41 H2
Dales Cl
  DUNHL/THL/PER WV6 .... 280 A6
  SWAD DE11 .... 205 L5
Dales Green Rd ALS/KID ST7 ..... 39 J5
Daleside
  STPNHL/WNHL DE15 .... 205 H1
Dalesman Cl KGSWFD DY6 ..... 303 M5
Dale St BDMR/CCFT WV3 .... 12 D7
  BURS/TUN ST6 .... 68 E2
  BUT DE14 .... 6 E6
The Dale BUX SK17 .... 33 J8
  MKTDR TF9 .... 115 H5
Dale Vw ALS/KID ST7 .... 39 J5
  BUX SK17 .... 17 H7
  LNGTN ST3 .... 87 H7
Dale View Ct
  BLYBR/FOR ST11 .... 121 L1
Daleview Dr NEWUL ST5 .... 83 J1
Dalkeith St WSLW WS2 .... 283 J7
Dallow Cl BUT DE14 .... 6 F1
Dallow Crs BUT DE14 .... 6 F1
Dallow St BUT DE14 .... 6 D1
Dalton Av STPNHL/WNHL DE15 .. 205 H1
Dalton Cl BUCK/MIL ST2 .... 86 D1
Dalton Rd WSLW WS2 .... 283 G7
Dalton St BDMR/CCFT WV3 ..... 12 C9
Daltry Wy AUD/MAD/W CW3 .. 81 M3
Daly Crs NEWUL ST5 .... 83 H1
Dama Rd POL/KGSB/FAZ B78 .... 289 M2
Dam La ASHB DE6 .... 27 G8
Dampier St LEEK ST13 .... 43 L5
Damson Cl WNSFLD WV11 ...... 282 A4
Damson La SHIF TF11 .... 224 E3
Damson Pk
  DUNHL/THL/PER WV6 .... 277 K7
The Dams BLYBR/FOR ST11 .... 87 K8
Dam St LICH WS13 .... 8 E3
Danby Crest STAFS ST17 .... 193 G2
Danby Dr HEDN WS12 .... 233 J6
Dandillion Av CDLE ST10 .... 105 K2
Danebower Rd STOKE ST4 ...... 101 H4
Dane Cl ALS/KID ST7 .... 37 G7
Dane Dr BIDD ST8 .... 40 E5
Dane Gdns ALS/KID ST7 .... 39 J8
Dane Gv CDLE ST10 .... 105 J3
Danehill Gv STOKE ST4 .... 100 F1

Danelagh Cl CRTAM B79 .... 273 M3
Danemead Cl LNGTN ST3 .... 103 G3
Danes Cl WNSFLD WV11 .... 265 M6
Danescourt Rd
  DUNHL/THL/PER WV6 .... 279 G4
Danes Cft STOKE ST4 .... 101 H3
Daneswood Dr ALDR WS9 ...... 268 F7
Dane Wk HAN ST1 .... 2 F5
Daniels Cross NWPT TF10 ...... 188 A6
Daniels La ALDR WS9 .... 285 J6
Danilo Rd CNCK/NC WS11 ...... 249 K1
Danta Wy STAFS ST17 .... 194 C1
Darby Av ALS/KID ST7 .... 55 L4
Darges La GTWY WS6 .... 249 M6
Darius Cl NEWUL ST5 .... 68 B2
Dark La BUTN/AL/TUT DE13 ..... 181 K3
  BUTN/AL/TUT DE13 .... 203 C1
  BUTN/AL/TUT DE13 .... 220 A7
  GTWY WS6 .... 267 J1
  KINVER DY7 .... 306 C7
  LICH WS13 .... 8 A5
  POL/KGSB/FAZ B78 .... 291 L2
  RUGE WS15 .... 234 D4
  WNSFLD WV11 .... 265 K3
  WOLVN WV10 .... 264 D2
Darley Cl STPNHL/WNHL DE15 .. 205 J1
Darley Dl SWAD DE11 .... 205 M8
Darley Dr
  DUNHL/THL/PER WV6 .... 280 B5
Darley Gv CDLE ST10 .... 105 L1
Darlington St WOLV WV1 .... 12 E5
Darlington Yd WOLV WV1 ...... 12 E5
Darnbrook TAM/AM/WIL B77 .. 291 G1
Darnel Hurst Rd
  MGN/WHC B75 .... 287 J7
Darnford Cl STAFN ST16 .... 174 C2
Darnford La LICHS WS14 .... 9 M6
Darnford Moors LICHS WS14 .... 9 M7
Darnford Vw LICH WS13 .... 9 L1
Darnley St STOKE ST4 .... 85 J2
Darrall Gdns STOKE ST4 .... 84 E7
Darsham Gdns NEWUL ST5 ..... 84 C8
Dart TAM/AM/WIL B77 .... 291 G5
Dart Av BURS/TUN ST6 .... 54 A6
  STAFS ST17 .... 193 H2
Dart Cl ALS/KID ST7 .... 37 G6
  BIDD ST8 .... 40 D1
Dartford PI BURS/TUN ST6 ..... 54 C6
Dartford Rd BLOX/PEL WS3 ..... 282 F1
Dart Gv CDLE ST10 .... 105 L1
Dartmouth Av BLOX/PEL WS3 .. 283 L5
  CNCK/NC WS11 .... 249 J2
  DUNHL/THL/PER WV6 .... 277 H8
  NEWUL ST5 .... 84 A5
  STRBR DY8 .... 303 K7
  WLNHL WV13 .... 281 M8
Dartmouth Dr ALDR WS9 ...... 284 F5
Dartmouth PI BLOX/PEL WS3 .. 283 L4
  LNGTN ST3 .... 102 F2
Dartmouth Rd CNCK/NC WS11 .. 249 K1
Dartmouth St
  BKHL/PFLD WV2 .... 13 H8
  BURS/TUN ST6 .... 69 H1
  STAFN ST16 .... 5 K5
Dart PI NEWUL ST5 .... 84 A6
Darvel Rd SHHTH WV12 .... 282 D6
Darwall St WSL WS1 .... 283 L8
Darwin Cl BNTWD WS7 .... 252 B3
  HEDN WS12 .... 250 E1
  LICH WS13 .... 8 D1
  STAFN ST16 .... 175 J6
  STPNHL/WNHL DE15 .... 205 J1
Darwin Ct
  DUNHL/THL/PER WV6 .... 278 E6
Darwin PI WSLW WS2 .... 283 H4
Darwin Rd WSLW WS2 .... 283 H4
Datteln Rd CNCK/NC WS11 ...... 232 A6
Davenport Cl LEEK ST13 .... 43 H6
Davenport Rd
  DUNHL/THL/PER WV6 .... 279 H5
  WNSFLD WV11 .... 281 L4
Davenport St BURS/TUN ST6 .. 68 D1
Davenport Wy NEWUL ST5 .... 83 M7
Daventry Cl BUCK/MIL ST2 ..... 3 K8
David Rd LNGTN ST3 .... 102 F1
Davidson Rd LICHS WS14 ...... 8 F7
Davies Dr UTXR ST14 .... 143 M1
Davis Cl ALS/KID ST7 .... 37 L6
  STAFN ST16 .... 5 K3
Davison St BURS/TUN ST6 ..... 69 C3
Davis Rd SHHTH WV12 .... 282 D2
  TAM/AM/WIL B77 .... 11 L6
Davis St HAN ST1 .... 69 G8
Davy Cl RUGE WS15 .... 215 K4
Davy Rd WSLW WS2 .... 283 C5
Daw End RUSH/SHEL WS4 ..... 284 C4
Daw End La RUSH/SHEL WS4 .. 284 B3
Dawes Cl RUGE WS15 .... 216 F6
Dawley Brook Rd KGSWFD DY6.. 303 K3
Dawley Rd KGSWFD DY6 ...... 303 J2
Dawlish Av STAFS ST17 .... 194 D3
Dawlish Dr BUCK/MIL ST2 ..... 70 B8
Dawn Av BURS/TUN ST6 .... 54 A6
Dawney Dr MGN/WHC B75 ..... 287 G6
Dawn Vw LNGTN ST3 .... 87 H7
Dawson Av BILS/COS WV14 ..... 295 M8
Dawson St BLOX/PEL WS3 ..... 283 K2
Day Av WNSFLD WV11 .... 281 L3
Dayton Dr NEWUL ST5 .... 68 A3
Daywell Ri RUGE WS15 .... 197 J3
Deacon Wy RUGE WS15 .... 197 M8
Deakin Av BRWNH WS8 .... 268 F1
Deakin Gv NEWUL ST5 .... 84 C5
Deakin Rd BURS/TUN ST6 ..... 54 D5
Deal Av RUGE WS15 .... 197 M8
Dean Cl CDSL WV8 .... 278 E5
Dean Hollow ALS/KID ST7 ..... 51 K8
Dean PI GTWY WS6 .... 2 F9
Dean Rd RUSH/SHEL WS4 ..... 284 C3
  WMBN WV5 .... 297 M5
Deansberry Cl STOKE ST4 .... 101 C2
Deans Cft LICH WS13 .... 9 C4
Deanscroft Wy LNGTN ST3 ...... 86 D6

Deansfield Cl PENK ST19 .... 246 D4
Deansfield Rd PENK ST19 ...... 246 C4
  WOLV WV1 .... 281 G8
Deansgate LEEK ST13 .... 43 M4
Deanshill Cl STAFN ST16 .... 4 B7
Deans La CW/SHV CW2 .... 50 C8
  CW/SHV CW2 .... 50 C8
  NEWUL ST5 .... 52 C8
Deans PI BLOX/PEL WS3 .... 283 M4
Dean's Rd WOLV WV1 .... 281 G7
Deans Slade Dr LICHS WS14 .... 8 D9
Dean St BUCK/MIL ST2 .... 70 C6
  PENK ST19 .... 246 C4
  SEDG DY3 .... 299 K2
Deansway STOKE ST4 .... 101 H4
Dearnsdale Cl STAFN ST16 ...... 174 A3
Deavall Wy CNCK/NC WS11 ..... 232 B8
Deaville Rd BUCK/MIL ST2 ..... 70 C7
Debenham Crs BUCK/MIL ST2 .. 3 L9
Deborah Cl
  ETTPK/GDPK/PENN WV4 ..... 295 J4
Decade Cl NEWUL ST5 .... 52 F8
Deebank Av LEEK ST13 .... 44 B4
Dee Cl ALS/KID ST7 .... 52 E3
  BIDD ST8 .... 40 L1
Dee Gv CNCK/NC WS11 .... 249 K3
Dee La NEWUL ST5 .... 84 B6
Deeley TAM/AM/WIL B77 .... 291 G1
Deeley PI BLOX/PEL WS3 .... 283 H2
Deeley St BLOX/PEL WS3 .... 283 H2
Deep Cut Rd ASHB DE6 .... 163 G3
Deepdale POL/KGSB/FAZ B78 .. 291 K1
Deepdale Cl BURS/TUN ST6 ..... 54 E8
  STPNHL/WNHL DE15 .... 186 B5
Deepdale La ASHB DE6 .... 94 B8
  DUDN DY1 .... 299 L7
Deepdales STAFS ST17 .... 194 C4
  WMBN WV5 .... 297 L4
Deepmore Av WSLW WS2 ...... 283 H8
Deepmore Cl
  BUTN/AL/TUT DE13 .... 220 A8
  WOLVN WV10 .... 247 K5
Deepwood Cl RUSH/SHEL WS4... 284 B4
Deer Cl BLOX/PEL WS3 .... 283 J1
  CNCK/NC WS11 .... 251 G3
Deerfold Crs BNTWD WS7 ...... 252 B3
Deerhill TAM/AM/WIL B77 .... 291 J1
Deerhurst Ri HEDN WS12 .... 232 F4
Deerleap Wy RUGE WS15 .... 215 J1
Dee Rd BLOX/PEL WS3 .... 283 L1
Deer Pk GNOS ST20 .... 190 C3
Deer Park Rd
  POL/KGSB/FAZ B78 .... 289 L1
De Ferrers Cft
  BUTN/AL/TUT DE13 .... 185 K2
Defford Rd RUSH/SHEL WS4 .... 284 C1
Defoe Dr LNGTN ST3 .... 86 E6
De Havilland Dr STONE ST15..... 136 F5
Delafield Wy RUGE WS15 .... 197 J8
Delamere Ct ALS/KID ST7 .... 36 F6
Delamere Gv NEWUL ST5 .... 84 B1
  STOKE ST4 .... 101 G3
Delamere La STAFS ST17 .... 193 G2
Delamere Rd SHHTH WV12 ...... 282 C3
Delaney Dr LNGTN ST3 .... 86 F6
Delaware Av ALBTN WV7 ...... 260 F5
Delhi Cl STPNHL/WNHL DE15 .. 186 C7
Delhurst Av
  ETTPK/GDPK/PENN WV4 ..... 295 L7
Delius Gv HAN ST1 .... 3 K2
Dell Cl STAFN ST16 .... 174 B2
The Dell CRTAM B79 .... 10 C2
  HEDN WS12 .... 232 F6
  LICH WS13 .... 8 A5
  STRBR DY8 .... 307 L4
Dellwood Gv LNGTN ST3 .... 86 D4
Delphouse Rd CDLE ST10 .... 88 F8
Delphside ALS/KID ST7 .... 51 M8
Delta Wy CNCK/NC WS11 ...... 249 K4
Deltic TAM/AM/WIL B77 .... 291 G1
Delves St NEWUL ST5 .... 84 B5
Denbigh Cl BIDD ST8 .... 40 C4
  BUTN/AL/TUT DE13 .... 185 K3
  DUDN DY1 .... 299 L8
  NEWUL ST5 .... 84 D6
Denbigh St HAN ST1 .... 2 A3
Denbury Cl HEDN WS12 .... 250 D1
Denby Av LNGTN ST3 .... 86 C9
Dency Gv BURS/TUN ST6 ..... 54 A7
Dene Av KGSWFD DY6 .... 303 J6
Dene Cl PENK ST19 .... 229 M2
Denefield PENK ST19 .... 229 M2
Dene Rd
  ETTPK/GDPK/PENN WV4 ..... 293 M6
  STRBR DY8 .... 307 M7
Dene Side NEWUL ST5 .... 84 A2
Denewood Rd LNGTN ST3 ...... 103 H1
Denford PI ALS/KID ST7 .... 37 K4
Denford Rd LEEK ST13 .... 56 F7
Denham Gdns
  BDMR/CCFT WV3 .... 294 B2
Den La NANT CW5 .... 64 A4
Denleigh Rd KGSWFD DY6 ...... 303 M6
Denmark Ri HEDN WS12 .... 232 D3
Denmead Dr WNSFLD WV11 .... 281 M2
Denmore Gdns WOLV WV1 ...... 281 H8
Dennington Crs LNGTN ST3 ..... 101 L1
Dennis TAM/AM/WIL B77 .... 11 K9
Dennis St STOKE ST4 .... 85 M5
  STRBR DY8 .... 307 M2
Denry Crs NEWUL ST5 .... 68 A2
Denshaw Wk LNGTN ST3 .... 86 D6
Denstone Av STAFS ST17 .... 5 M9
Denstone Crs LNGTN ST3 .... 85 M8
Denstone La UTXR ST14 .... 108 C3
Dentdale Cl LNGTN ST3 .... 103 G3
Denton Cl NEWUL ST5 .... 84 B7
Denton Gv LNGTN ST3 .... 86 E7
Denton Ri BUTN/AL/TUT DE13 .. 185 G3
Dent St CRTAM B79 .... 10 E4
Denver Fold STAFS ST17 .... 193 G2
Denzil Gn STAFS ST17 .... 193 G2
Derby Dr DUNHL/THL/PER WV6.. 279 L3
Derby La ASHB DE6 .... 128 F1
Derby PI NEWUL ST5 .... 84 C6
Derby Rd ALS/KID ST7 .... 52 D3
  ASHB DE6 .... 95 K2
  ASHB DE6 .... 127 G8

ASHB DE6 ... 145 M3
BUT DE14 ... 7 H1
BUTN/AL/TUT DE13 ... 185 M3
LICHS WS14 ... 255 K7
RDERBYSW DE65 ... 167 H7
UTXR ST14 ... 144 D2
Derby St BUT DE14 ... 6 F3
  HAN ST1 ... 2 E7
  LEEK ST13 ... 43 M5
  STAFN ST16 ... 4 D5
  WSLW WS2 ... 283 K6
Dereham Wy BUCK/MIL ST2 ... 86 D1
Derek Dr HAN ST1 ... 69 L4
Derrington La RSTAF ST18 ... 192 E1
Derry St BKHL/PFLD WV2 ... 13 C9
  STOKE ST4 ... 85 L6
Derwent Av STONE ST15 ... 138 D3
Derwent Cl ALS/KID ST7 ... 37 C6
  BUT ... 7 K4
  FOAKS/STRLY B74 ... 285 M8
  WLNHL WV13 ... 282 C8
Derwent Crs ALS/KID ST7 ... 39 J8
Derwent Dr BIDD ST8 ... 40 E1
  CDLE ST10 ... 105 L1
  MKTDR TF9 ... 114 E5
Derwent Gdns ASHB DE6 ... 95 K2
Derwent Gv BNTWD WV7 ... 252 D4
  CNCK/NC WS11 ... 249 K3
Derwent Pl NEWUL ST5 ... 68 A7
Derwent Rd
  DUNHL/THL/PER WV6 ... 279 K2
  STPNHL/WNHL DE15 ... 205 C1
Derwent St HAN ST1 ... 2 A2
Devall Cl RUGE WS15 ... 215 L3
Deveron Cl
  BUTN/AL/TUT DE13 ... 185 J1
Devil's La END/WER ST9 ... 42 E5
  STPNHL/WNHL DE15 ... 204 E4
Devon Cl NEWUL ST5 ... 84 C6
Devon Crs ALDR WS9 ... 285 J1
Devon Gv BIDD ST8 ... 40 C1
Devon Rd CNCK/NC WS11 ... 249 K2
  STRBR DY8 ... 307 K3
  WOLV WV1 ... 12 D2
Devonshire Dr
  POL/KGSB/FAZ B78 ... 290 A1
Devon Wy LNGTN ST3 ... 102 D1
  STAFN ST17 ... 193 K4
Devoran Cl
  DUNHL/THL/PER WV6 ... 280 B6
Dewberry Rd STRBR DY8 ... 307 M1
De-wint Rd STONE ST15 ... 138 B3
Dewsbury Cl STRBR DY8 ... 303 L7
Dewsbury Dr BNTWD WV7 ... 252 C4
  ETTPK/GDPK/PENN WV4 ... 295 C7
Dewsbury Rd STOKE ST4 ... 85 L2
Dexter Wy POL/KGSB/FAZ B78... 291 M2
Dexton Ri STAFS ST17 ... 193 C2
D'eyncourt Rd WNSFLD WV11 ... 281 C3
Dial La CONG CW12 ... 27 C1
  STRBR DY8 ... 307 L2
Diamond Av ALS/KID ST7 ... 39 H8
Diamond Cl BARL ST12 ... 119 J2
  BIDD ST8 ... 40 C2
  LNGTN ST3 ... 103 C6
Diamond Gv HEDN WS12 ... 232 C8
Diamond Park Dr STRBR DY8 . 307 L1
Diamond Rdg BARL ST12 ... 119 J2
Diamond Wy STONE ST15 ... 138 B5
Diana Cl ALDR WS9 ... 269 H7
Diana Rd HAN ST1 ... 3 J1
Diarmid Wy STOKE ST4 ... 100 F1
Dibble Cl SHHTH WV12 ... 282 D5
Dibble Rd BUT DE14 ... 204 A3
Dibdale Rd DUDN DY1 ... 299 M7
Dibdale St DUDN DY1 ... 299 M8
Dickens Cl BUT DE14 ... 185 K4
  SEDG DY3 ... 299 H5
Dickenson Rd East
  BURS/TUN ST6 ... 69 J3
Dickens Rd WOLVN WV10 ... 281 C2
Dickens St BUCK/MIL ST2 ... 70 C6
Dickinson Av WOLVN WV10 ... 280 E2
Dickinson Rd WMBN WV5 ... 298 A6
Dickson Rd STAFN ST16 ... 5 K1
Dicky's La GNOS ST20 ... 170 D3
Didcot Dr UTXR ST14 ... 162 F2
Digby Rd KGSWFD DY6 ... 303 K2
Diglake Cl ALS/KID ST7 ... 52 C4
Diglake St ALS/KID ST7 ... 51 M7
Digmire La ASHB DE6 ... 78 C1
Dig St ASHB DE6 ... 79 H8
  BUX SK17 ... 34 C4
Dilhorne Gv LNGTN ST3 ... 102 C1
Dilhorne La BLYBR/FOR ST11 ... 87 M8
  CDLE ST10 ... 89 H7
Dilke Rd ALDR WS9 ... 284 F5
Dilke St HAN ST1 ... 2 E2
Dill Gv LNGTN ST3 ... 103 H4
Dimble La CDLE ST10 ... 107 L2
Dimbles HI LICH WS13 ... 254 B1
Dimbles La LICH WS13 ... 236 A8
Dimmelow St LNGTN ST3 ... 87 H5
Dimmingsdale Rd
  ETTPK/GDPK/PENN WV4 ... 293 K5
Dimmock St
  ETTPK/GDPK/PENN WV4 ... 295 L5
Dimsdale Pde East NEWUL ST5 .. 68 B5
Dimsdale Pde West
  NEWUL ST5 ... 68 A4
Dimsdale Vw BURS/TUN ST6 ... 68 E3
Dimsdale Vw East NEWUL ST5 ... 68 B4
Dimsdale Vw West NEWUL ST5... 68 B4
Dingle Cl BIDD ST8 ... 27 K5
  STONE ST15 ... 121 J8
  WLNHL WV13 ... 282 A6
Dingle Rd BRWNH WS8 ... 268 C5
  WMBN WV5 ... 297 M5
The Dingle BDMR/CCFT WV3 ... 294 D1
  BURS/TUN ST6 ... 55 H3
  STPNHL/WNHL DE15 ... 204 E2
Dingle Vw SEDG DY3 ... 299 J3
Dinham Gdns DUDN DY1 ... 299 L7
Dippons Dr
  DUNHL/THL/PER WV6 ... 279 G7
Dippons Mill Cl
  DUNHL/THL/PER WV6 ... 279 G7

Dirtyfoot La
  ETTPK/GDPK/PENN WV4 ... 294 A5
Dirty La PENK ST19 ... 246 C4
The Ditch BUX SK17 ... 17 L2
Dividy Rd BUCK/MIL ST2 ... 3 L7
Dixon's Rw NEWUL ST5 ... 67 K3
Dixon St BKHL/PFLD WV2 ... 295 L4
Dobbinhorse La ASHB DE6 ... 95 H5
Dobbs St BKHL/PFLD WV2 ... 12 F8
Dobell Gv LNGTN ST3 ... 86 D6
Dobree Cl STAFS ST17 ... 196 E5
Dobson St BURS/TUN ST6 ... 69 J3
Dock Rd STRBR DY8 ... 303 M8
Doctor's Bank MKTDR TF9 ... 115 J5
Doctors Cl BIDD ST8 ... 40 C2
Doctors La KGSWFD DY6 ... 302 F5
Doctor's Piece WLNHL WV13 ... 282 B8
Doddington Pl NEWUL ST5 ... 84 B4
Dodds La LICH WS13 ... 234 C7
Dodslow Av
  BUTN/AL/TUT DE13 ... 166 B7
Dogcroft Rd BURS/TUN ST6 ... 54 C5
Dog Kennel La MKTDR TF9 ... 130 D2
  WSL WS1 ... 283 M8
Doglands Rd RSTAF ST18 ... 157 M2
Dog La CDLE ST10 ... 77 C2
  LEEK ST13 ... 46 E3
  LICHS WS14 ... 272 A6
  MSHM DE12 ... 241 M4
  NEWUL ST5 ... 99 J7
  RSTAF ST18 ... 172 D6
  TAM/AM/WIL B77 ... 275 H4
Dogmoor La CDLE ST10 ... 76 F2
Dogshead La
  BUTN/AL/TUT DE13 ... 220 C2
Dolefoot La
  BUTN/AL/TUT DE13 ... 181 M6
Doles La ASHB DE6 ... 94 F3
Dolespring Cl
  BLYBR/FOR ST11 ... 104 A2
Doley Cl GNOS ST20 ... 190 D3
Dolly's La BURS/TUN ST6 ... 54 A8
Dolphin Cl BLOX/PEL WS3 ... 283 M1
  STAFS ST17 ... 194 C1
Dominic Dr LNGTN ST3 ... 85 M6
Dominic St STOKE ST4 ... 85 G2
  STONE ST15 ... 137 M1
Donald Rd HAN ST1 ... 69 L4
Donaldson Dr MKTDR TF9 ... 148 F3
Doncaster La STOKE ST4 ... 84 F3
Don Gv CNCK/NC WS11 ... 249 K3
Donington La ALBTN WV7 ... 261 G3
Donithorne Cl
  BUTN/AL/TUT DE13 ... 185 J3
Donkey La CDLE ST10 ... 89 L5
Dooley Cl WLNHL WV13 ... 281 L8
Dorado Dr TAM/AM/WIL B77 ... 290 D4
Dorcas Dr LNGTN ST3 ... 85 M6
Dorchester Cl ALS/KID ST7 ... 39 C7
  SHHTH WV12 ... 282 C2
Dorchester Rd CNCK/NC WS11 . 249 H1
  SHHTH WV12 ... 282 C2
Dorchester Wk BUCK/MIL ST2 ... 70 C8
Dordon Rd POL/KGSB/FAZ B78... 291 M2
Doreen Av CONG CW12 ... 26 B2
Dorian Wy END/WER ST9 ... 55 M3
Dorlan Cl BUCK/MIL ST2 ... 3 J9
Dorlan Cl END/WER ST9 ... 55 J7
Dormer Av TAM/AM/WIL B77 ... 11 J3
Dormston Dr SEDG DY3 ... 299 K2
Dorridge Gv NEWUL ST5 ... 68 E6
Dorrington Cl BUCK/MIL ST2 ... 55 C8
Dorrington Dr STAFN ST16 ... 174 C4
Dorrington Rd NEWUL ST5 ... 68 C4
Dorset Cl BUCK/MIL ST2 ... 70 C7
  POL/KGSB/FAZ B78 ... 290 A1
  STPNHL/WNHL DE15 ... 204 E4
Dorset Dr ALDR WS9 ... 285 J1
  BIDD ST8 ... 40 C2
Dorset Pl ALS/KID ST7 ... 39 G7
  BLOX/PEL WS3 ... 283 J3
  NEWUL ST5 ... 84 D6
Dorset Rd HEDN WS12 ... 250 E1
  STRBR DY8 ... 307 K3
Dosthill Rd (Two Gates)
  TAM/AM/WIL B77 ... 290 D4
Douglas Av BIDD ST8 ... 40 C3
  STOKE ST4 ... 84 F6
Douglas Davies Cl
  SHHTH WV12 ... 282 C6
Douglas Pl HAN ST1 ... 2 F9
  WOLVN WV10 ... 280 C4
Douglas Rd NEWUL ST5 ... 68 A7
  STAFN ST16 ... 5 H1
Douglas Rd West STAFN ST16... 5 H1
Douglas St HAN ST1 ... 2 A1
Doulton Cl CDLE ST10 ... 105 K1
Doulton Dr NEWUL ST5 ... 68 B3
Doulton Rd RSTAF ST18 ... 175 H2
Doulton St BURS/TUN ST6 ... 69 G2
Douse La LEEK ST13 ... 45 G6
Dovebank Gv LNGTN ST3 ... 103 G4
Dovecliff Crs
  BUTN/AL/TUT DE13 ... 166 F8
Dovecliff Rd
  BUTN/AL/TUT DE13 ... 166 E6
  STAFS ST17 ... 193 M4
Dove Cl BNTWD WV7 ... 252 D4
Dovecote Cl
  DUNHL/THL/PER WV6 ... 279 J5
Dovecote Pl LNGTN ST3 ... 102 E2
The Dovecotes
  MGN/WHC B75 ... 287 H7
Dovedale CNCK/NC WS11 ... 232 A5
Dovedale Av ASHB DE6 ... 95 K1
  BLOX/PEL WS3 ... 268 A5
  SHHTH WV12 ... 282 A6
Dovedale Cl BURS/TUN ST6 ... 53 H3
  CDLE ST10 ... 89 L4
  STPNHL/WNHL DE15 ... 186 A6
Dovedale Ct
  ETTPK/GDPK/PENN WV4 ... 295 M8
Dovedale Pl NEWUL ST5 ... 83 C1
Dovedale Rd CDLE ST10 ... 73 L8
  ETTPK/GDPK/PENN WV4 ... 295 L7
  KGSWFD DY6 ... 303 L2
Dovefields UTXR ST14 ... 108 F7
Dove Flds UTXR ST14 ... 144 D2
Dove Gv BIDD ST8 ... 40 D1
  RDERBYSW DE65 ... 167 G5
Dove Hollow GTWY WS6 ... 266 F1

HEDN WS12 ... 232 E6
Dovehouse Flds LICHS WS14 ... 8 E7
Dove House Gn ASHB DE6 ... 79 H8
Dove La UTXR ST14 ... 109 C6
Dove Lea BUTN/AL/TUT DE13 ... 166 B6
Dover Farm Cl
  TAM/AM/WIL B77 ... 291 H2
Doveridge Rd
  STPNHL/WNHL DE15 ... 186 B8
Dove Rd BLYBR/FOR ST11 ... 104 A3
Dove Rd BUTN/AL/TUT DE13 ... 185 H3
Dover St HAN ST1 ... 2 F2
Dove Side RDERBYSW DE65 ... 165 K2
Dovestone
  POL/KGSB/FAZ B78 ... 291 K1
Dove St ASHB DE6 ... 93 H8
Dove Vw BUTN/AL/TUT DE13 ... 165 J4
Dove Wk UTXR ST14 ... 144 D2
The Dove Wy UTXR ST14 ... 126 C8
Dowells Gdns STRBR DY8 ... 303 K7
Downderry Cl STAFS ST17 ... 193 C2
Downend Cl WOLVN WV10 ... 264 C6
Downesway CNCK/NC WS11 ... 231 J8
Downey St HAN ST1 ... 2 D7
Downfield Cl BLOX/PEL WS3 ... 267 C6
Downfield Dr SEDG DY3 ... 299 L4
Downfield Gv STAFN ST16 ... 174 D2
Downfield Pl BUCK/MIL ST2 ... 69M1
Downford Cl PENK ST19 ... 227 J4
Downford La PENK ST19 ... 227 J2
Downham Pl
  BDMR/CCFT WV3 ... 294 F2
Downham Rd NEWUL ST5 ... 67 L8
Downie Rd CDSL WV8 ... 263 J7
Downing Av WNSFLD WV11 ... 282 A3
Downing Cl WNSFLD WV11 ... 282 A3
The Downs FOAKS/STRLY B74 .. 285 L8
  STAFS ST17 ... 194 B3
  WOLVN WV10 ... 280 C4
Downsview Gv LNGTN ST3 ... 85 M7
Dowty Wy COVEN WV9 ... 264 A7
Doxey Flds STAFN ST16 ... 173 M6
Doxey Rd STAFN ST16 ... 4 C4
Dragon Sq NEWUL ST5 ... 67 L2
Drake Cl BLOX/PEL WS3 ... 283 H1
  BUCK/MIL ST2 ... 85M1
Drakeford Gv BURS/TUN ST6 ... 54 E6
Drakelow La KIDDW DY11 ... 309 H4
Drake Rd BLOX/PEL WS3 ... 283 J1
Drakes Hill Cl KINVER DY7 ... 307 J6
Drancy Av SHHTH WV12 ... 282 D4
Draw-well La END/WER ST9 ... 71 H6
Draycott Cliff ASHB DE6 ... 163 J5
Draycott Cl
  ETTPK/GDPK/PENN WV4 ... 294 C5
Draycott Crs
  TAM/AM/WIL B77 ... 290 D1
Draycott Cross Rd CDLE ST10... 104 F2
Draycott Dr CDLE ST10 ... 105 K1
  NEWUL ST5 ... 52 D7
Draycott Old Rd
  BLYBR/FOR ST11 ... 104 B3
Draycott Rd CDLE ST10 ... 105 H6
Drayton Cl MGN/WHC B75 ... 287 H7
Drayton Gv MKTDR TF9 ... 130 C1
Drayton La POL/KGSB/FAZ B78 .. 288 F5
Drayton Manor Dr
  POL/KGSB/FAZ B78 ... 289M1
Drayton Rd LNGTN ST3 ... 86 B6
  SHIF TF11 ... 242 A4
  STOKE ST4 ... 100 B5
Drayton St BKHL/PFLD WV2 ... 12 F9
  NEWUL ST5 ... 84 A2
  WSLW WS2 ... 283 J8
Drayton St East WSLW WS2 ... 283 J8
Dreieich Cl STAFN ST16 ... 5 G1
Drenfell Rd ALS/KID ST7 ... 38 F3
Dresden St HAN ST1 ... 2 D7
The Dreys STOKE ST4 ... 101 H3
Drive Flds
  ETTPK/GDPK/PENN WV4 ... 294 B4
The Drive ALS/KID ST7 ... 67 C4
  BLOX/PEL WS3 ... 267 L8
  CDSL WV8 ... 262 F7
  DUNHL/THL/PER WV6 ... 279 J5
  LICHS WS14 ... 271 L2
  RUSH/SHEL WS4 ... 284 C1
  STAFN ST16 ... 174 B6
Drointon La RSTAF ST18 ... 158 D7
Droitwich Cl HAN ST1 ... 66 F8
Drovers Wy NWPT TF10 ... 188 A6
The Droveway COVEN WV9 ... 263 M8
Drubbery La LNGTN ST3 ... 102 A1
Druid Park Rd SHHTH WV12 ... 282 C1
Druids Av ALDR WS9 ... 285 J2
Druids Wk ALDR WS9 ... 269 C7
Druids Wy PENK ST19 ... 229 M3
Drumber La ALS/KID ST7 ... 39 H2
Drumburn Cl BURS/TUN ST6 ... 53 M3
Drummond Cl
  WNSFLD WV11 ... 266 A8
Drummond Rd STAFN ST16 ... 174 F4
Drummond St BURS/TUN ST6 .. 53 K3
  WOLV WV1 ... 12 E3
Drury La BUX SK17 ... 35 J8
  CDSL WV8 ... 262 F6
Dryburgh Cl STAFS ST17 ... 193 H3
Dryden Cl SHHTH WV12 ... 282 C6
Dryden Crs STAFS ST17 ... 4 A9
Dryden Pl BLOX/PEL WS3 ... 283 L3
Dryden Rd BLOX/PEL WS3 ... 283 L3
  BURS/TUN ST6 ... 69 C4
  CRTAM B79 ... 10 B1
  WOLVN WV10 ... 280 F1
Dryden Wy CDLE ST10 ... 89 J8
Dual Wy HEDN WS12 ... 231 J2
Dubarry Av KGSWFD DY6 ... 303 J3
Duchy Cl BUTN/AL/TUT DE13 ... 185 L2
Duckhouse Rd WNSFLD WV11 ... 281 K3
Duck La CDSL WV8 ... 263 H8
Duck St RDERBYSW DE65 ... 167 G4
Duddell Rd BURS/TUN ST6 ... 54 C8
Dudding Rd
  ETTPK/GDPK/PENN WV4 ... 295 K5
Dudley Crs WNSFLD WV11 ... 281 L4
Dudley Pl LNGTN ST3 ... 103 G2
Dudley Rd BKHL/PFLD WV2 ... 13 G8
  BKHL/PFLD WV2 ... 295 K3

KGSWFD DY6 ... 303 J2
  SEDG DY3 ... 299 K3
Dudley St SEDG DY3 ... 299 K2
  WOLV WV1 ... 12 F5
Dudley Wk
  ETTPK/GDPK/PENN WV4 ... 295 J5
Dudmaston Wy DUDN DY1 ... 299 L7
Duffield Cl CDSL WV8 ... 279M1
Duffield La BUTN/AL/TUT DE13 .. 185M3
Dugdale Cl HEDN WS12 ... 232 F7
Dugdale Gv MGN/WHC B75 ... 287 J7
Duke Bank Ter BURS/TUN ST6 .. 54 F5
Duke Pl NEWUL ST5 ... 83 J1
Duke Rd BNTWD WV7 ... 251 L1
Duke's La LEEK ST13 ... 75 J3
Duke St BDMR/CCFT WV3 ... 295 C3
  BUT DE14 ... 6 D3
  BUTN/AL/TUT DE13 ... 165 J4
  LEEK ST13 ... 43 L5
  NEWUL ST5 ... 84 C3
  SEDG DY3 ... 299 K5
  STOKE ST4 ... 85 L6
  WNSFLD WV11 ... 281 K5
  WOLV WV1 ... 13 J6
Dulverton Av NEWUL ST5 ... 84 A5
Dumbleberry Av SEDG DY3 ... 299 J3
Dumbleberry La ALDR WS9 ... 284 E2
Dumolo's La TAM/AM/WIL B77 .. 11 K7
Dumore Hay La LICH WS13 ... 237 L2
Duncalfe Dr NEWUL ST5 ... 68 B3
Duncalf St BURS/TUN ST6 ... 68 E2
Duncan St BKHL/PFLD WV2 ... 295 J3
  STOKE ST4 ... 85 L4
Duncombe Dr ASHB DE6 ... 95 J2
Duncombe St STRBR DY8 ... 307 K4
Dundalk La GTWY WS6 ... 266 D1
Dundas Cl HAN ST1 ... 69 C7
Dundee Rd HAN ST1 ... 69 C7
Dundee St LNGTN ST3 ... 86 B8
Dunedin Crs
  STPNHL/WNHL DE15 ... 186 A8
Dunham Cl ALS/KID ST7 ... 37 J7
Dunkirk Cl NEWUL ST5 ... 84 A1
Dunkirk Ct NEWUL ST5 ... 84 A1
Dunkley St WOLV WV1 ... 12 E2
Dunlin Cl WOLVN WV10 ... 265 C3
Dunnerdale Rd BRWNH WS8 ... 268 D4
Dunning St BURS/TUN ST6 ... 53 K6
Dunnocksfold Rd ALS/KID ST7 .. 36 F6
Dunnock Wy BIDD ST8 ... 40 E2
Dunrobin St LNGTN ST3 ... 102 C1
Dunsany Gv HAN ST1 ... 69 L4
Dunsford Av BUCK/MIL ST2 ... 55 C8
Dunsley Dr KINVER DY7 ... 306 D2
  STRBR DY8 ... 303 L7
Dunsley Gv
  ETTPK/GDPK/PENN WV4 ... 295 G6
Dunsley Rd KINVER DY7 ... 306 B7
Dunstall Av
  DUNHL/THL/PER WV6 ... 280 C6
Dunstall Brook
  STPNHL/WNHL DE15 ... 205 G1
Dunstall Cross
  BUTN/AL/TUT DE13 ... 202 A4
Dunstall Hi BUTN/AL/TUT DE13 .. 202 B4
  DUNHL/THL/PER WV6 ... 280 C5
Dunstall La
  DUNHL/THL/PER WV6 ... 280 C3
  POL/KGSB/FAZ B78 ... 273 J4
Dunstall Rd
  DUNHL/THL/PER WV6 ... 280 B6
  DUNHL/THL/PER WV6 ... 280 C5
Dunster TAM/AM/WIL B77 ... 290 C3
Dunster Cl STAFS ST17 ... 193 H3
Dunster Gv
  DUNHL/THL/PER WV6 ... 278 F7
Dunster Rd LNGTN ST3 ... 86 B5
Dunston Cl GTWY WS6 ... 266 E2
  KGSWFD DY6 ... 303 K5
Dunston Dr BNTWD WV7 ... 252 A2
Dunton Cl MGN/WHC B75 ... 287 C6
Dunwood Dr ALS/KID ST7 ... 37 K4
Dunwood La END/WER ST9 ... 42 E2
Durban Cl
  STPNHL/WNHL DE15 ... 186 C7
Durber Cl ALS/KID ST7 ... 66 D1
  STOKE ST4 ... 84 E6
D'urberville Rd
  BKHL/PFLD WV2 ... 295 M3
Durham Av WLNHL WV13 ... 282 C7
Durham Cl
  POL/KGSB/FAZ B78 ... 274 A8
  RUGE WS15 ... 215 K4
Durham Dr LNGTN ST3 ... 102 C2
Durham Gv NEWUL ST5 ... 84 D6
Durham Rd STRBR DY8 ... 307 K2
Durlston Cl TAM/AM/WIL B77 ... 11 M2
Dursley Cl SHHTH WV12 ... 282 D6
Dursley Dr CNCK/NC WS11 ... 231 K4
Dursley Rd BNTWD WV7 ... 252 A3
Durston Pl LNGTN ST3 ... 86 E7
Dutton's La MGN/WHC B75 ... 287 L6
Dutton Wy STONE ST15 ... 137 M5
Dyke Rd RUGE WS15 ... 217 H6
Dykes La NWPT TF10 ... 207 K2
Dyke St HAN ST1 ... 2 E4
Dylan Rd LNGTN ST3 ... 86 D7
Dyott Av LICHS WS14 ... 255 L4
Dyott Cl LICH WS13 ... 255 G1
Dyson Cl WSLW WS2 ... 282 F7

E

Eagle Cl GTWY WS6 ... 249 K8
  UTXR ST14 ... 144 B4
Eagle Crs ECCH ST21 ... 152 D4
Eagle Dr TAM/AM/WIL B77 ... 275 H6
Eagle Gv HEDN WS12 ... 250 C1
Eagle Hts STPNHL/WNHL DE15 .. 186 D7
Eagle St BDMR/CCFT WV3 ... 295 C3
  BKHL/PFLD WV2 ... 13 K8
  HAN ST1 ... 3 C5
Ealingham TAM/AM/WIL B77 ... 275 H8
Eamont Av BURS/TUN ST6 ... 54 A6
Eardleyend Rd ALS/KID ST7 ... 51 L3

Earl Dr BNTWD WS7 ... 251 L
Earlsbrook Dr NEWUL ST5 ... 101 J3
Earls Ct BUTN/AL/TUT DE13 ... 185 K7
Earl's Dr NEWUL ST5 ... 84 B
Earls Rd RUSH/SHEL WS4 ... 284 C
  STOKE ST4 ... 101 H
Earl St KGSWFD DY6 ... 303 K
  LEEK ST13 ... 43 M
  NEWUL ST5 ... 83 J
  NEWUL ST5 ... 84 D
  STAFN ST16 ... 4 F
Earlsway CDLE ST10 ... 76 E3
Earls Wy RSTAF ST18 ... 177 J
Earlswood Crs COVEN WV9 ... 264 A
Earlswood Rd HAN ST1 ... 2 E
  KGSWFD DY6 ... 303 L2
Early La STONE ST15 ... 118 C
Easby Cl STAFS ST17 ... 193 H
Easby Wy BLOX/PEL WS3 ... 266 F
Easdale Pl NEWUL ST5 ... 84 B
Easedale Cl BUCK/MIL ST2 ... 55 C8
Easing La LEEK ST13 ... 44 F
East Av WNSFLD WV11 ... 281 J
East Bank Ride
  BLYBR/FOR ST11 ... 104 A
Eastbank Rd HAN ST1 ... 2 A
East Beeches COVEN WV9 ... 247 H8
Eastbourne La LEEK ST13 ... 43 K
Eastbourne Rd HAN ST1 ... 2 E
Eastbourne St RUSH/SHEL WS4.. 283 M
Eastbridge Av NEWUL ST5 ... 69 K2
East Butts Rd RUGE WS15 ... 215 H
East Cannock Rd HEDN WS12 ... 232 C
Eastcote Crs BNTWD WS7 ... 251 M5
Eastcote Rd WOLVN WV10 ... 280 F
East Ct ALS/KID ST7 ... 39 G
East Crs HAN ST1 ... 69 L
  NEWUL ST5 ... 68 D7
East Croft Rd
  ETTPK/GDPK/PENN WV4 ... 294 C
Eastdean Av BUCK/MIL ST2 ... 3 L
East Dr ASHB DE6 ... 79 J
  BIDD ST8 ... 40 D
  LEEK ST13 ... 57 J
Eastern Av ALBTN WV7 ... 260 F
  BUTN/AL/TUT DE13 ... 185M
  LICH WS13 ... 235M
Eastern Wy CNCK/NC WS11 ... 249M
  HEDN WS12 ... 232 B
Easters Gv BUCK/MIL ST2 ... 70 E1
Eastfield Gv WOLV WV1 ... 13 M
Eastfield Retreat WOLV WV1 ... 13 M
Eastfields Rd UTXR ST14 ... 144 D
Eastgate HEDN WS12 ... 233 C
  PENK ST19 ... 246 D3
Eastgate St BNTWD WS7 ... 251 L
  STAFN ST16 ... 4 F
East Gn
  ETTPK/GDPK/PENN WV4 ... 294 D
East Gv LNGTN ST3 ... 103 C
Easthall Cl PENK ST19 ... 246 D4
Eastlands STAFS ST17 ... 193 L
Eastlands Gv STAFS ST17 ... 193 L2
East Lawns AUD/MAD/W CW3 ... 65 C
Eastleigh SEDG DY3 ... 299 H
Eastmoor Cl FOAKS/STRLY B74.. 286 B
Eastney Crs CDSL WV8 ... 279 L
Easton Gdns WNSFLD WV11 ... 281 M
Eastridge Cft LICHS WS14 ... 271 C
East Rd WOLVN WV10 ... 265 C
East St CNCK/NC WS11 ... 249 L
  LEEK ST13 ... 43 M
  LNGTN ST3 ... 87 H
  SEDG DY3 ... 299 J
  STPNHL/WNHL DE15 ... 186 B
  TAM/AM/WIL B77 ... 290 D5
  WOLV WV1 ... 13 J
  TAM/AM/WIL B77 ... 11 J
Eastward Gln CDSL WV8 ... 279 J
Eastwick Crs STOKE ST4 ... 101 C
Eastwood Av BNTWD WS7 ... 252 A
  BURS/TUN ST6 ... 54 A
Eastwood Pl HAN ST1 ... 2 D
Eastwood Ri NEWUL ST5 ... 98 A
Eastwood Rd HAN ST1 ... 3 C
Eaton Cl RDERBYSW DE65 ... 165 K
Eaton Crs SEDG DY3 ... 299 H
Eaton Pl KGSWFD DY6 ... 303 L
Eaton Ri SHHTH WV12 ... 282 B
Eaton Rd ALS/KID ST7 ... 37 J
  UTXR ST14 ... 108 F7
Eaton St HAN ST1 ... 2 A
  UTXR ST14 ... 144 C
Eaves Court Dr SEDG DY3 ... 295 J
Eaves La BUCK/MIL ST2 ... 70 C
  CDLE ST10 ... 105 L
  CDLE ST10 ... 105 L
Eaveswood Rd BUCK/MIL ST2 ... 70 C
Ebenezer St HEDN WS12 ... 232 A
Ebstree Rd
  ETTPK/GDPK/PENN WV4 ... 293 K
  WMBN WV5 ... 292 F
Ebury Gv LNGTN ST3 ... 102 F
Eccleshall Rd MKTDR TF9 ... 114 C
  RSTAF ST18 ... 174 B
  STAFN ST16 ... 174 B
  STONE ST15 ... 137 K
Ecclestone Rd WNSFLD WV11 ... 282 A
Eccleston Pl BURS/TUN ST6 ... 54 A
Edale TAM/AM/WIL B77 ... 291 H
Edale Cl BURS/TUN ST6 ... 53 H
  ETTPK/GDPK/PENN WV4 ... 295 J7
  KGSWFD DY6 ... 303 H
  STAFS ST17 ... 193 H
Eddenswood Cl
  POL/KGSB/FAZ B78 ... 289 L3
Eddies La CRTAM B79 ... 256 E
Eddisbury Dr NEWUL ST5 ... 52 D
Eden Cl ALS/KID ST7 ... 39 H
  BIDD ST8 ... 40 E
  HEDN WS12 ... 232 E8
Eden Gv CDLE ST10 ... 105 L1
  LNGTN ST3 ... 102 F1
  MKTDR TF9 ... 114 E
Edenhurst Av LNGTN ST3 ... 103 H
Edensor Cl WOLVN WV10 ... 13 M

Edensor Rd *LNGTN* ST3 .... 86 B7
Edensor St *NEWUL* ST5 .... 67 L3
Edensor Ter *NEWUL* ST5 .... 86 B8
Edes Farm Dr *UTXR* ST14 .... 108 F6
Edgar Cl *CRTAM* B79 .... 273 M3
Edgar Pl *LNGTN* ST3 .... 86 C4
Edge Av *BURS/TUN* ST6 .... 54 A4
Edgefield La *BURS/TUN* ST6 .... 55 J5
Edgefield Rd *LNGTN* ST3 .... 86 C5
Edge Hl *KINVER* DY7 .... 305 M6
  POL/KGSB/FAZ B78 .... 291 H8
Edge Hill Dr
  DUNHL/THL/PER WV6 .... 278 E7
  SEDG DY3 .... 295 J8
Edge Hill Rd *FOAKS/STRLY* B74... 286 E6
Edgehill Rd *LEEK* ST13 .... 43 J5
Edge La *END/WER* ST9 .... 55 K5
Edgeley Rd *BIDD* ST8 .... 40 D4
Edgemoor Meadow
  HEDN WS12 .... 250 C1
Edge St *BURS/TUN* ST6 .... 53 M8
  KINVER DY7 .... 305 M5
Edge View Cl *BUCK/MIL* ST2 .... 55 J8
  KINVER DY7 .... 305 M5
Edge View Ct *BIDD* ST8 .... 40 C3
Edge View Wk *KINVER* DY7 .... 55 J8
Edgeview Rd *CONG* CW12 .... 26 B3
Edge View Wk *KINVER* DY7 .... 305 M5
Edgeware Rd *HAN* ST1 .... 2 A2
Edgeworth Cl *SHHTH* WV12 .... 282 C6
Edinburgh Av *WSLW* WS2 .... 282 E7
Edinburgh Crs *STRBR* DY8 .... 307 J1
Edinburgh Dr *RUSH/SHEL* WS4 ... 284 D3
  SHHTH WV12 .... 282 B4
Edinburgh La *WSLW* WS2 .... 283 G6
Edinburgh Wy
  BUTN/AL/TUT DE13 .... 185 K2
Edison Cl *HEDN* WS12 .... 232 C3
Edison Rd *STAFN* ST16 .... 174 F5
  WSLW WS2 .... 283 C5
Edison St *STOKE* ST4 .... 85 K4
Edlaston La *ASHB* DE6 .... 95 C7
Edmonton Cl *CNCK/NC* WS11 ... 232 B8
Edmonton Gv *BUCK/MIL* ST2 ... 69 M1
Edmonton Pl
  STPNHL/WNHL DE15 .... 186 D7
Edmoor Cl *SHHTH* WV12 .... 282 C4
Edmund Av *STAFS* ST17 .... 193 H1
Edmund Rd *SEDG* DY3 .... 299 L4
Ednam Gv *WMBN* WV5 .... 298 A1
Ednam Pl *LNGTN* ST3 .... 103 G1
Ednam Rd
  ETTPK/GDPK/PENN WV4 .... 295 J4
Edwal Rd *LNGTN* ST3 .... 87 G5
Edward Av *ALDR* WS9 .... 285 G3
  NEWUL ST5 .... 84 B4
  STOKE ST4 .... 101 H4
Edward Ct *TAM/AM/WIL* B77 .... 11 L6
Edward Davies Rd
  BURS/TUN ST6 .... 54 C8
Edward Rd
  DUNHL/THL/PER WV6 .... 278 E5
Edwards Dr *STAFN* ST16 .... 4 A5
Edwards Farm Rd *LICH* WS13 ... 237 L2
Edwards Rd *BNTWD* WS7 .... 251 M5
  MGN/WHC B75 .... 287 K7
Edward St *ALS/KID* ST7 .... 51 M7
  BUT DE14 .... 6 E2
  CNCK/NC WS11 .... 231 L6
  CRTAM B79 .... 10 B4
  ETTPK/GDPK/PENN WV4 .... 295 M4
  NEWUL ST5 .... 68 D6
  STOKE ST4 .... 85 L3
  STONE ST15 .... 137 M1
  WSLW WS2 .... 283 H7
Edwards Wy *ALS/KID* ST7 .... 37 L3
Edwin Cl *PENK* ST19 .... 229 M2
  STAFS ST17 .... 193 H2
Efflinch La *BUTN/AL/TUT* DE13... 220 E5
Egelwin Cl
  DUNHL/THL/PER WV6 .... 278 E5
Egerton Rd *STOKE* ST4 .... 84 C2
  WOLVN WV10 .... 264 C7
Egerton St *STOKE* ST4 .... 85 K1
Eggington Rd *PENK* ST19 .... 229 M3
Eggington Rd *RDERBYSW* DE65... 167 H1
  STRBR DY8 .... 307 K3
Egg La *RSTAF* ST18 .... 177 L2
Egmont Gdns *WNSFLD* WV11 ... 281 M5
Eighth Av *BUT* DE14 .... 203 M2
Elaine Av *BURS/TUN* ST6 .... 69 H1
Elan Cl *KIDD* DY10 .... 310 B6
  SEDG DY3 .... 299 J2
Elan Rd *SEDG* DY3 .... 299 J2
Elburton Rd *STOKE* ST4 .... 86 A4
Elderberry Cl *STRBR* DY8 .... 307 J7
Elder Cl *CNCK/NC* WS11 .... 232 C8
  UTXR ST14 .... 144 B4
Elder Gv *WMBN* WV5 .... 297 M4
Elder La *BNTWD* WS7 .... 252 C3
Elder Pl *BURS/TUN* ST6 .... 69 H4
Elder Rd *BURS/TUN* ST6 .... 2 A1
Eldertree La *MKTDR* TF9 .... 115 J4
Eldon St *HAN* ST1 .... 2 E1
  STPNHL/WNHL DE15 .... 186 B7
Eldridge Cl *COVEN* WV9 .... 263 M8
Eleanor Crs *NEWUL* ST5 .... 84 B4
Eleanor Harrison Dr *KIDD* DY10.. 310 B5
Eleanor Pl *NEWUL* ST5 .... 84 A4
Eleanor Vw *NEWUL* ST5 .... 84 B4
Electric St *BUT* DE14 .... 7 K1
Elenora St *STOKE* ST4 .... 85 H3
Elers Gv *BURS/TUN* ST6 .... 68 E3
Elford Cl *STAFN* ST16 .... 174 C2
Elgar Cl *CNCK/NC* WS11 .... 231 L5
  LICH WS13 .... 236 B3
Elgar Crs *HAN* ST1 .... 3 K2
Elgin Cl *SEDG* DY3 .... 299 L1
Elgin Ct *DUNHL/THL/PER* WV6... 278 E6
Elgin Rd *BLOX/PEL* WS3 .... 267 G6
Elgin St *STOKE* ST4 .... 85 H1
Elgood La *BURS/TUN* ST6 .... 53 J3
Elias Cl *LICHS* WS14 .... 9 L7
Eliases La *BIDD* ST8 .... 27 H8
Eliot Cl *CRTAM* B79 .... 274 A3
  RUGE WS15 .... 217 H6
Eliot Wy *STAFS* ST17 .... 4 A9
Elizabeth Av
  BUTN/AL/TUT DE13 .... 166 B7
  ETTPK/GDPK/PENN WV4 .... 295 H5

Elizabeth Ct *ALS/KID* ST7 .... 52 D5
  MKTDR TF9 .... 130 C1
Elizabeth Dr *CRTAM* B79 .... 10 A1
  CRTAM B79 .... 274 A3
  NEWUL ST5 .... 67 L3
Elizabeth Rd *CNCK/NC* WS11 ... 231 L4
Elizabeth St *HAN* ST1 .... 3 G5
Elkes Gv *UTXR* ST14 .... 125 M8
Elkington Ri
  AUD/MAD/W CW3 .... 81 M3
Elkstone Cl *BURS/TUN* ST6 .... 53 L6
Ellam's Pl *NEWUL* ST5 .... 83 L1
Ellards Dr *WNSFLD* WV11 .... 281 M5
Ellastone Cl *BURS/TUN* ST6 .... 84 F4
Ellastone Rd *CDLE* ST10 .... 75 K6
  LEEK ST13 .... 60 B8
Elldawn Av *BURS/TUN* ST6 .... 54 F8
Ellerbeck *TAM/AM/WIL* B77 ... 291 H1
Ellerby Rd *LNGTN* ST3 .... 101 L2
Ellerton Wk *WOLVN* WV10 .... 280 F5
Ellesmere Rd *CNCK/NC* WS11 ... 249 H2
Ellgreave St *BURS/TUN* ST6 .... 68 C2
Ellington Av *STAFN* ST16 .... 5 L2
Ellington Cl *BUCK/MIL* ST2 .... 3 L8
Elliot Dr *END/WER* ST9 .... 71 H6
Elliot Rd *STOKE* ST4 .... 85 M4
Elliott Cl *CNCK/NC* WS11 .... 231 M5
Elliotts La *CDSL* WV8 .... 263 G7
Elliott St *STOKE* ST4 .... 84 D1
Ellison St *NEWUL* ST5 .... 68 D3
Ellis St *BURS/TUN* ST6 .... 69 J3
Ellis Wk *CNCK/NC* WS11 .... 249 M2
Ellowes Rd *SEDG* DY3 .... 299 J6
Elm Av *STAFS* ST17 .... 194 F4
  WNSFLD WV11 .... 281 M2
Elmbridge Wy *SEDG* DY3 .... 299 L4
Elmbrook Cl *LNGTN* ST3 .... 102 E2
Elm Cl *ALS/KID* ST7 .... 53 H2
  ASHB DE6 .... 145 J1
  BUT DE14 .... 203 M2
  KIDD DY10 .... 310 B6
  LEEK ST13 .... 43 J5
  RSTAF ST18 .... 177 H8
  SEDG DY3 .... 299 H6
  STRBR DY8 .... 307 J8
Elm Ct *RSTAF* ST18 .... 193 J5
Elm Crs *RSTAF* ST18 .... 177 J2
Elmcroft Gdns *WOLVN* WV10 ... 264 E7
Elmcroft Rd *BUCK/MIL* ST2 .... 70 B4
Elmdale Dr *ALDR* WS9 .... 285 J2
Elm Dale Rd
  ETTPK/GDPK/PENN WV4 .... 295 C5
Elmdon Cl *PENK* ST19 .... 230 A2
  WOLVN WV10 .... 280 A1
Elmdon Pl *LNGTN* ST3 .... 103 H3
Elmdon Rd *WOLVN* WV10 .... 280 A1
Elm Dr *CDLE* ST10 .... 89 M8
  KIDD DY10 .... 311 H8
  MKTDR TF9 .... 130 A2
  RSTAF ST18 .... 210 C2
Elm Farm Rd *BKHL/PFLD* WV2 ... 295 K3
Elm Gdns *LICHS* WS14 .... 9 G5
Elm Gv *ALS/KID* ST7 .... 37 L6
  CDSL WV8 .... 263 G7
  HEDN WS12 .... 231 K2
  KINVER DY7 .... 306 C7
Elmhurst *RDERBYSW* DE65 .... 167 G5
Elmhurst Cl *BUCK/MIL* ST2 .... 3 K8
  COVEN WV9 .... 247 H7
  STAFN ST16 .... 174 C2
Elmhurst Dr *BNTWD* WS7 .... 252 A6
  KGSWFD DY6 .... 303 M6
Elmley Gv
  DUNHL/THL/PER WV6 .... 278 F7
Elmore Green Cl *BLOX/PEL* WS3.. 283 G1
Elmore Green Rd
  BLOX/PEL WS3 .... 283 G1
Elmore La *RUGE* WS15 .... 215 L1
Elmore Rw *BLOX/PEL* WS3 .... 283 H1
Elm Pl *KIDD* DY10 .... 310 B6
  LNGTN ST3 .... 101 M1
Elm Rd *ALBTN* WV7 .... 260 E5
  BLOX/PEL WS3 .... 283 K4
  CNCK/NC WS11 .... 251 H5
  KGSWFD DY6 .... 303 L4
  STONE ST15 .... 138 C2
Elms Cl *WOLVN* WV10 .... 265 J1
Elmsdale *DUNHL/THL/PER* WV6.. 278 F8
Elms Dr *CNCK/NC* WS11 .... 249 J1
Elms La *WOLVN* WV10 .... 265 J1
Elmslea Av *MSHM* DE12 .... 222 D7
Elmsmere Av *LNGTN* ST3 .... 102 A1
Elmsmere Rd *BUCK/MIL* ST2 ... 70 B4
The Elms Paddock
  DUNHL/THL/PER WV6 .... 277 J8
Elms Rd *MSHM* DE12 .... 222 C7
  STPNHL/WNHL DE15 .... 7 L7
Elmstead Cl *STOKE* ST4 .... 100 F1
The Elms *NEWUL* ST5 .... 68 D6
Elmstone St *STAFS* ST17 .... 194 D5
Elm St *BDMR/CCFT* WV3 .... 12 A6
  BURS/TUN ST6 .... 69 H3
  NEWUL ST5 .... 68 D3
  WLNHL WV13 .... 282 B8
Elms Wy *LNGTN* ST3 .... 87 C8
Elm Tree Cl *WMBN* WV5 .... 297 M5
Elm Tree Dr *ALS/KID* ST7 .... 66 F1
Elmwood Av *WNSFLD* WV11 ...... 266 A7
Elmwood Cl *ALS/KID* ST7 .... 37 M6
  CNCK/NC WS11 .... 232 A7
  GNOS ST20 .... 190 D3
Elmwood Dr *BLYBR/FOR* ST11 ... 104 A4
Elmwood Gv *UTXR* ST14 .... 125 M8
Elmwood Ri *SEDG* DY3 .... 299 H1
Elmwood Rd *STRBR* DY8 .... 303 J7
Elphinstone Rd *STOKE* ST4 .... 84 F7
Elsby Pl *BURS/TUN* ST6 .... 54 A4
Elsby Rd *ALS/KID* ST7 .... 37 M8
Elsdon Rd *STAFS* ST17 .... 193 J4
Elsing St *STOKE* ST4 .... 85 K4
Elston Hall La *WOLVN* WV10 ...... 280 E1
Elstree Cl *LNGTN* ST3 .... 86 F8
Elstree Gv *HAN* ST1 .... 3 L1
Eltham Gdns *NEWUL* ST5 .... 68 D6
Elton Cl *BUTN/AL/TUT* DE13 ... 181 M2
  WOLVN WV10 .... 264 E6
Elton La *BUTN/AL/TUT* DE13 ... 181 M2
Elton Ter *BURS/TUN* ST6 .... 53 J3
Elton Wy *GNOS* ST20 .... 190 D3
Elunda Gv *BNTWD* WS7 .... 251 L4

Elviron Dr
  DUNHL/THL/PER WV6 .... 279 H5
Elworthy Cl *STAFN* ST16 .... 175 G5
Elwyn Cl *BUTN/AL/TUT* DE13 ... 185 K1
Ely Cl *CNCK/NC* WS11 .... 250 B1
Embers Wy *END/WER* ST9 .... 56 A2
Emberton St *NEWUL* ST5 .... 67 L3
Emberton Wy *TAM/AM/WIL* B77 ... 11 L3
Embry Av *STAFN* ST16 .... 5 K1
Emerald Wy *STONE* ST15 .... 138 B6
Emerson Cl *SEDG* DY3 .... 299 G6
Emerson Gv *WOLVN* WV10 ...... 280 F2
Emerson Rd *BURS/TUN* ST6 .... 69 G4
  WOLVN WV10 .... 280 F1
Emery Av *HAN* ST1 .... 69 L2
Emery Cl *MSHM* DE12 .... 223 K5
Emery St *BURS/TUN* ST6 .... 2 A1
Emmanuel Rd *BNTWD* WS7 ...... 252 A1
Empire Cl *ALDR* WS9 .... 284 F2
Empire Pas *STOKE* ST4 .... 85 G4
Empire Rd *STPNHL/WNHL* DE15.. 186 D7
Empire St *STOKE* ST4 .... 85 G4
Emsworth Crs *BURS/TUN* ST6 ... 69 C3
Emsworth Rd *LNGTN* ST3 .... 101 L2
Encounter Pl *HAN* ST1 .... 3 H3
Enderby Dr
  ETTPK/GDPK/PENN WV4 .... 294 F6
Enderby Ri *BUTN/AL/TUT* DE13.. 185 C3
Enderley Cl *BLOX/PEL* WS3 ...... 267 H7
Enderley Dr *BLOX/PEL* WS3 ...... 267 H7
Enderley Rd *NEWUL* ST5 .... 84 B1
End Hall Rd
  DUNHL/THL/PER WV6 .... 279 G7
Endon Dr *BIDD* ST8 .... 40 B5
Endon Rd *BURS/TUN* ST6 .... 54 F5
The End *STPNHL/WNHL* DE15 .. 185 G3
Endwood Dr *FOAKS/STRLY* B74... 286 C6
Engine La *BRWNH* WS8 .... 268 C2
  TAM/AM/WIL B77 .... 275 G8
Englesea Av *LNGTN* ST3 .... 87 G5
Engleton La *PENK* ST19 .... 246 D3
Engleton Mill La *PENK* ST19 ... 246 E2
Ennerdale Cl *BURS/TUN* ST6 ... 68 E2
Ennerdale Dr
  DUNHL/THL/PER WV6 .... 278 F6
Ennerdale Rd
  DUNHL/THL/PER WV6 .... 279 K2
Enoch St *BURS/TUN* ST6 .... 68 F3
Ensall Dr *STRBR* DY8 .... 307 L1
Ensbury Cl *SHHTH* WV12 .... 282 B4
Ensford Cl *FOAKS/STRLY* B74 ... 286 A3
Ensor Rd *POL/KGSB/FAZ* B78.... 291 M1
Enstone Cl *LNGTN* ST3 .... 101 M2
Enstone Ct *NEWUL* ST5 .... 84 B7
Enterprise Dr *WOLVN* WV10 ...... 247 K5
Enterprise Gv *BLOX/PEL* WS3 .. 268 B5
Enville Cl *BLOX/PEL* WS3 .... 267 G7
Enville Common Rd
  KINVER DY7 .... 301 M5
Enville Pl *STRBR* DY8 .... 307 M5
Enville Rd
  ETTPK/GDPK/PENN WV4 .... 294 C5
  KGSWFD DY6 .... 303 J2
  KINVER DY7 .... 305 M4
  SEDG DY3 .... 299 K6
Enville St *STRBR* DY8 .... 307 M5
Ephraim St *HAN* ST1 .... 2 D8
Epping Cl *BLOX/PEL* WS3............ 283 M4
Epping Rd *BURS/TUN* ST6 .... 84 E7
Epsley's Yd *STAFS* ST17 .... 4 E6
Epsom Cl *BUT* DE14 .... 203 M3
  CDLE ST10 .... 89 L5
  DUNHL/THL/PER WV6 .... 278 F6
  LICHS WS14 .... 9 K4
Epsom Dr *STAFS* ST17 .... 194 C3
Epworth St *STOKE* ST4 .... 85 G3
Erasmus Wy *LICH* WS13 .... 8 C2
Erdington Av *ALDR* WS9 .... 285 H7
Eringden *TAM/AM/WIL* B77 ... 291 H1
Ermington Rd
  ETTPK/GDPK/PENN WV4 .... 295 K5
Ernald Gdns *STONE* ST15 .... 138 A3
Ernest Clarke Cl
  SHHTH WV12 .... 282 C6
Eros Crs *HAN* ST1 .... 3 H1
Errill Cl *STOKE* ST4 .... 85 J4
Erskine St *LNGTN* ST3 .... 86 C8
Esdaile Cl *WOLV* WV1 .... 281 G8
Esdaile Pl *NEWUL* ST5 .... 84 B5
  STOKE ST4 .... 100 F3
Eskrett St *HEDN* WS12 .... 232 B3
Esperanto Wy *BURS/TUN* ST6 ... 68 F2
Esselie Av *MKTDR* TF9 .... 115 J5
Essex Av *KGSWFD* DY6 .... 303 H5
Essex Dr *ALS/KID* ST7 .... 38 F8
  BIDD ST8 .... 26 D8
  HEDN WS12 .... 232 B6
  RSTAF ST18 .... 177 H7
  RUGE WS15 .... 215 K4
  STONE ST15 .... 137 M5
Essex Gdns *STRBR* DY8 .... 307 K3
Essex Pl *NEWUL* ST5 .... 84 A4
Essex St *STPNHL/WNHL* DE15 ... 204 D4
Essex St *WSLW* WS2 .... 283 K5
Essington Cl
  BUTN/AL/TUT DE13 .... 220 A7
  LICHS WS14 .... 8 D8
  STRBR DY8 .... 307 L2
Essington Rd *SHHTH* WV12 ...... 282 B1
Estridge La *GTWY* WS6 .... 250 A8
Etchell Rd
  POL/KGSB/FAZ B78 .... 273 M7
Etching Hill Rd *RUGE* WS15 ...... 215 G1
Ethelfleda Rd
  TAM/AM/WIL B77 .... 290 F5
Ethelred Cl *FOAKS/STRLY* B74... 287 G7
Eton Av *BURS/TUN* ST6............ 83 M6
Eton Cl *BUT* DE14 .... 185 L4
Eton Rd *BUT* DE14 .... 185 K4
Etruria Old Rd *HAN* ST1 .... 2 A5
Etruria Rd *HAN* ST1 .... 69 G7
Etruria Vale Rd *HAN* ST1 .... 69 G7
Etruria Wy *NEWUL* ST5 .... 68 E7
Etruscan St *HAN* ST1 .... 68 F8
Etruscan Wk *BARL* ST12 .... 101 M6

Ettingshall Park Farm La
  ETTPK/GDPK/PENN WV4 .... 295 K6
Ettymore Rd *SEDG* DY3 .... 299 K2
Ettymore Rd West *SEDG* DY3.... 299 K2
Etwall Rd *RDERBYSW* DE65 ...... 167 H4
Europa Wy *LICHS* WS14 .... 254 F2
Eva Gv *NEWUL* ST5 .... 100 C3
Evans Cl *KIDD* DY11 .... 309 J7
Evans Cft *POL/KGSB/FAZ* B78... 290 A1
Evans St *BILS/COS* WV14 .... 299 M1
  BURS/TUN ST6 .... 68 F1
  DUNHL/THL/PER WV6 .... 12 C1
Eve La *DUDN* DY1 .... 299 M5
Evelyn St *STOKE* ST4 .... 85 K5
Everest Rd *ALS/KID* ST7 .... 39 J7
  WSLW WS2 .... 282 F7
Everglade Rd
  POL/KGSB/FAZ B78 .... 291 H8
Evergreen Hts *HEDN* WS12 ...... 232 A2
The Evergreens *SHIF* TF11 ...... 224 B5
Eversley Av *LICHS* WS14 .... 43 L5
Eversley Gv *SEDG* DY3 .... 295 J8
  WNSFLD WV11 .... 281 J4
Eversley Rd *LNGTN* ST3 .... 86 E8
Evesham Crs *BLOX/PEL* WS3 ... 266 F7
Evesham Wy *LNGTN* ST3 .... 86 E7
Eveson Rd *STRBR* DY8 .... 307 K8
Ewart Rd *WSLW* WS2 .... 282 F7
Ewe Dale La *ASHB* DE6 .... 48 A7
Exbury Cl *COVEN* WV9 .... 263 M8
Excelsior Gv *BLOX/PEL* WS3 ...... 268 B5
Exchange Rd
  BUTN/AL/TUT DE13 .... 220 A7
The Exchange
  BLOX/PEL WS3 .... 283 H1
Exeter Dr *CRTAM* B79 .... 273 L5
Exeter Rd *CNCK/NC* WS11 ...... 249 H2
Exeter St *STAFS* ST17 .... 193 M2
Exmoor Gn *WNSFLD* WV11 ...... 281 J3
Exmouth Cl *BURS/TUN* ST6 ... 69 C3
Exton Cl *WNSFLD* WV11 .... 281 M2
Eyam Cl *STPNHL/WNHL* DE15 .. 186 B8
Eyland Gv *WSL* WS1 .... 283 M8
Eyre St *BURS/TUN* ST6 .... 68 B1
The Eyrie
  STPNHL/WNHL DE15 .... 186 C7
Ezekiel La *SHHTH* WV12 .... 282 C4

F

Faceby Gv *BLYBR/FOR* ST11 ...... 103 J3
Fairbank Av *STOKE* ST4 .... 84 F5
Fairbanks Wk *STONE* ST15 ...... 118 B6
Fairburn Crescent
  BLOX/PEL WS3 .... 268 B5
Fairclough Pl *BURS/TUN* ST6 ... 54 A7
Fairfax Rd *WOLVN* WV10 .... 264 D7
Fairfax St *HAN* ST1 .... 2 F1
Fairfield Av *BURS/TUN* ST6 ...... 55 H3
  BUTN/AL/TUT DE13 .... 166 D6
  LNGTN ST3 .... 102 C2
  NEWUL ST5 .... 68 C6
  STONE ST15 .... 121 K8
Fairfield Ct *STAFN* ST16 .... 174 F2
Fairfield Crs *SWAD* DE11 .... 205 L5
Fairfield Dr *BLOX/PEL* WS3 ...... 268 B6
  CDSL WV8 .... 262 E7
  KINVER DY7 .... 306 A7
  PENK ST19 .... 229 L4
Fairfield La *KIDDW* DY11 .... 309 H7
Fairfield Ri *STRBR* DY8 .... 307 J5
Fairfield Rd *STRBR* DY8 .... 303 M8
  UTXR ST14 .... 144 B2
Fairfields *ALS/KID* ST7 .... 51 M8
Fairfields Hl *BIDD* ST8 .... 41 G1
Fairfields Rd *BIDD* ST8 .... 41 G1
Fairford Gdns *BNTWD* WS7 ...... 252 C4
  STRBR DY8 .... 303 L7
Fairham Rd *BUTN/AL/TUT* DE13.. 185 M1
Fairhaven Gv *HAN* ST1 .... 3 G1
Fairhills *SEDG* DY3 .... 299 K2
Fair Lady Dr *BNTWD* WS7 .... 251 K2
Fair Lawn *ALBTN* WV7 .... 261 C5
Fairlawn Cl *LNGTN* ST3 .... 102 E2
  SHHTH WV12 .... 282 C1
Fairlawn Dr *KGSWFD* DY6 .... 303 K6
Fairlawns *NEWUL* ST5 .... 68 B8
Fairlight Gv *STAFS* ST17 .... 103 C3
Fairmead Cl *STAFS* ST17 .... 194 C4
Fairmount Dr *CNCK/NC* WS11 ... 249 L2
Fairmount Wy *RUGE* WS15 ...... 215 J1
Fairoak Av *STAFN* ST16 .... 174 C2
Fairoak Bank *ECCH* ST21 .... 133 K4
Fairoak Dr
  DUNHL/THL/PER WV6 .... 279 C7
Fair Oak Rd *NEWUL* ST5 .... 67 K1
Fair Oaks Dr *GTWY* WS6 .... 267 C2
Fair Vw *RUGE* WS15 .... 217 J6
Fairview Av *ALS/KID* ST7 .... 37 K6
Fairview Cl *GTWY* WS6 .... 249 K8
  TAM/AM/WIL B77 .... 11 M4
  WNSFLD WV11 .... 281 H3
Fairview Crs *KGSWFD* DY6 ...... 303 M4
  WNSFLD WV11 .... 281 H3
Fairview Gv *WNSFLD* WV11 ...... 281 H3
Fairview Rd
  ETTPK/GDPK/PENN WV4 .... 294 C6
Fair View Rd *LEEK* ST13 .... 44 A5
Fairview Rd *WNSFLD* WV11 ...... 281 H3
Fairview Wy *STAFS* ST17 .... 194 C1
Fairway *BUT* DE14 .... 204 B4
  CNCK/NC WS11 .... 249 G4
  RUSH/SHEL WS4 .... 284 D1
  STAFN ST16 .... 5 J5
  STOKE ST4 .... 100 E5
  TAM/AM/WIL B77 .... 290 E5
Fairway Av *STRBR* DY8 .... 307 L8
Fairway Rd *STRBR* DY8 .... 307 L8
Fairways Av *STRBR* DY8 .... 307 L8
Fairways Cl *STRBR* DY8 .... 307 L8
The Fairway *ALS/KID* ST7 .... 37 L5
  SWAD DE11 .... 205 L5
Falcon *TAM/AM/WIL* B77 .... 291 C4
Falcon Cl *CNCK/NC* WS11 .... 231 J8
  GTWY WS6 .... 295 M8
Falcondale Rd *SHHTH* WV12 ...... 282 C1
Falcon Dr *LICHS* WS14 .... 255 L5

Falcon Ri *STRBR* DY8 .... 307 J4
Falcon Rd *LNGTN* ST3 .... 103 G4
Faldo Cl *BUT* DE14 .... 204 B4
Falklands Cl *SEDG* DY3 .... 297 L8
Fallowfield *CDSL* WV8 .... 263 L8
Fallow Fld *CNCK/NC* WS11 ...... 231 L5
Fallowfield
  DUNHL/THL/PER WV6 .... 278 D6
Fallow Fld *FOAKS/STRLY* B74 ... 286 B7
  LICH WS13 .... 236 B7
  LNGTN ST3 .... 101 M2
Fallowfield *STAFS* ST17 .... 194 C4
Fallowfield Cl *PENK* ST19 .... 229 L2
  STONE ST15 .... 138 C4
Fallowfield Dr
  BUTN/AL/TUT DE13 .... 202 C8
Falmouth Av *STAFS* ST17 .... 194 E2
Falmouth Cl *STAFS* ST17 .... 194 E2
Falmouth Dr *TAM/AM/WIL* B77 ... 11 M3
Falna Crs *CRTAM* B79 .... 273 M3
Fancourt Av
  ETTPK/GDPK/PENN WV4 .... 294 D5
Fancy Wk *STAFN* ST16 .... 4 D1
Fane Rd *WNSFLD* WV11 .... 282 A1
Fanlizard La *GNOS* ST20 .... 190 C7
Fanny's Cft *ALS/KID* ST7 .... 37 K8
Faraday Dr
  BUTN/AL/TUT DE13 .... 185 K2
Faraday Rd *STAFN* ST16 .... 5 C2
  WSLW WS2 .... 283 H4
Farams Rd *ALS/KID* ST7 .... 37 L3
Farbrook Wy *SHHTH* WV12 ...... 282 B4
Farcroft Av *NEWUL* ST5 .... 67 M3
Farcroft Dr *MKTDR* TF9 .... 130 A1
Fareham Crs
  ETTPK/GDPK/PENN WV4 .... 294 C4
Fareham Gv *LNGTN* ST3 .... 102 E3
Farewell La *BNTWD* WS7 .... 252 E4
Farifields Rd *MKTDR* TF9 .... 112 D8
Farington Pl *BURS/TUN* ST6 ... 54 A4
Farland Gv *BURS/TUN* ST6 ...... 54 A4
Farleigh Dr *BDMR/CCFT* WV3 ... 294 A2
Farleigh Gv *BUCK/MIL* ST2 ...... 86 C1
Farleigh Rd
  DUNHL/THL/PER WV6 .... 279 G7
Farley La *CDLE* ST10 .... 91 K7
Farley Rd *CDLE* ST10 .... 91 H4
Farmadine *STOKE* ST4 .... 101 H3
Farman Cl *BLYBR/FOR* ST11 ...... 103 J3
Farmbridge Cl *WSLW* WS2 ...... 282 D7
Farmbridge Rd *WSLW* WS2 ...... 282 D7
Farmbrook Av *WOLVN* WV10 ... 264 C6
Farm Cl *BUTN/AL/TUT* DE13 ... 185 H3
  CDSL WV8 .... 263 H8
  CRTAM B79 .... 274 C3
  HEDN WS12 .... 232 C7
  RUGE WS15 .... 197 J8
  SEDG DY3 .... 299 H3
Farmdown Rd *STAFS* ST17 ...... 194 C1
Farmers Bank *NEWUL* ST5 ...... 83 J1
Farmer St *LNGTN* ST3 .... 86 C8
Farmfields Ri *AUD/MAD/W* CW3 .. 96 C1
Farmhouse Rd *SHHTH* WV12 ... 282 D5
Farm La *STPNHL/WNHL* DE15 ... 186 D4
Farm Lea *BURS/TUN* ST6 .... 54 E4
  STONE ST15 .... 121 K8
Farmoor Wy *WOLVN* WV10 ...... 264 E6
Farm Rd *BDMR/CCFT* WV3 ...... 294 C2
  BUTN/AL/TUT DE13 .... 185 J3
  DUNHL/THL/PER WV6 .... 276 D3
Farm Side *SWAD* DE11 .... 205 M5
Farmside Gn *COVEN* WV9 ...... 263 M8
Farmside La *BIDD* ST8 .... 41 H1
Farm St *WSLW* WS2 .... 283 L6
Farm Vw *STONE* ST15 .... 121 K8
Farmwood Cl *LNGTN* ST3 ...... 103 H1
Farnborough Ct
  MGN/WHC B75 .... 287 J8
Farnborough Dr
  BLYBR/FOR ST11 .... 103 J3
Farncote Dr *FOAKS/STRLY* B74... 286 B7
Farndale Av
  DUNHL/THL/PER WV6 .... 280 C5
Farndale St *BURS/TUN* ST6 ...... 53 K7
Farne Gv *LNGTN* ST3 .... 86 A7
Farnham Dr *BIDD* ST8 .... 40 B5
Farnworth Cl *BIDD* ST8 .... 40 B4
Farnworth Rd *LNGTN* ST3 ...... 86 B7
Far Ridding *GNOS* ST20 .... 190 C5
Farrier Cl *STONE* ST15 .... 138 D3
Farriers Gn *NWPT* TF10 .... 188 B7
Farriers Ml *BLOX/PEL* WS3 ...... 267 L6
Farrier Wy *KGSWFD* DY6 .... 303 C5
Farringdon St *WSLW* WS2 ...... 283 K8
Farrington Cl *BURS/TUN* ST6 ... 54 E7
Farrington Rd
  ETTPK/GDPK/PENN WV4 .... 295 L8
Farwall La *CDLE* ST10 .... 61 L7
Farway Gdns *CDSL* WV8 .... 262 F8
Fauld La *BUTN/AL/TUT* DE13 ... 164 D3
Faulkland Crs *WOLV* WV1 .... 13 G3
Faulkner Cl *STRBR* DY8 .... 307 M6
Faulkner Pl *LNGTN* ST3 .... 86 F6
Faversham Cl *CDSL* WV8 .... 279 L2
  WSLW WS2 .... 282 D7
Faversham Rd
  BUTN/AL/TUT DE13 .... 185 G4
Fawdry St *WOLV* WV1 .... 12 D2
Fawfield Dr *BURS/TUN* ST6 ...... 53 J4
Fawn Cl *LNGTN* ST3 .... 103 G2
Fazeley Rd *POL/KGSB/FAZ* B78... 10 A1
  RSTAF ST18 .... 177 L2
Featherbed La *LICH* WS13 ...... 235 L7
  RUGE WS15 .... 215 G3
Featherstone Gv *STOKE* ST4 ... 85 C3
Featherstone La *WOLVN* WV10 .. 265 H2
Featherston Rd
  FOAKS/STRLY B74 .... 286 A8
Fecknam Wy *LICH* WS13 .... 236 C8
Federation Rd *BURS/TUN* ST6 ... 68 L1
Fegg Hayes Rd *BURS/TUN* ST6 ... 54 A4
Feiashill Cl *WMBN* WV5 .... 297 H3
Feiashill Rd *WMBN* WV5 .... 297 K3
  WMBN WV5 .... 297 H3
Felcourt Gdns *HAN* ST1 .... 3 G3
Felden St *STAFN* ST16 .... 174 D1
Fellbrook La *BUCK/MIL* ST2 ...... 3 M5
Fellfield Wy *STAFN* ST16 .... 174 D2
Fellmeadow Wy *SEDG* DY3 ...... 299 L3
Fellows Av *KGSWFD* DY6 .... 303 J2
Fellows St *BKHL/PFLD* WV2 ...... 12 E9

Fell St BURS/TUN ST6 69 J1
Felspar Rd TAM/AM/WIL B77 275 G7
Felstead Cl TAM/AM/WIL B77 290 C6
Felsted St BUCK/MIL ST2 55 H7
Felthouse La LEEK ST13 57 H8
Fenbourne Cl RUSH/SHEL WS4 284 C2
Fenchurch Cl WSLW WS2 283 K6
Fenlow Av BUCK/MIL ST2 3 K9
Fenmere Cl
ETTPK/GDPK/PENN WV4 295 K5
Fennel Cl GTWY WS6 249 K7
Fennel Dr STAFS ST17 193 M5
Fennel Gv LNGTN ST3 103 H4
Fenn Ri SHHTH WV12 282 B4
STRBR DY8 303 J7
Fenn St TAM/AM/WIL B77 290 D1
Fenpark Rd STOKE ST4 86 A4
Fenton Cl CONG CW12 26 A1
Fenton Cft PENK ST19 227 H4
Fenton House La PENK ST19 227 H4
Fenton Pk STOKE ST4 86 A4
Fenton Rd BUCK/MIL ST2 3 L7
Fereday Rd ALDR WS9 269 H7
Fereday's Cft SEDG DY3 299 K3
Ferguson St WNSFLD WV11 282 A1
Fermain Cl NEWUL ST5 83 L7
Fern Cl RUSH/SHEL WS4 284 C1
Ferncombe Dr RUGE WS15 197 J8
Fern Cft LICH WS13 253 M1 3
Ferncroft Cl STOKE ST4 101 H3 3
Ferndale Cl BLYBR/FOR ST11 103 M4 1
BNTWD WS7 252 A4
END/WER ST9 71 G6
Ferndale Rd LICH WS13 253 M1
WNSFLD WV11 266 B7
Fern Dell Cl CNCK/NC WS11 231 J8 1
Fern Dene AUD/MAD/W CW3 81 K3 1
Ferndown Av SEDG DY3 299 J3
Ferndown Cl BLOX/PEL WS3 267 H6
LNGTN ST3 102 D1 2
Ferndown Dr NEWUL ST5 84 C8
Ferndown Dr South
NEWUL ST5 100 C1
Ferndown Gdns WNSFLD WV11 281 M5
Fern Dr GTWY WS6 250 A6
STAFN ST16 174 A6
Ferney Pl BURS/TUN ST6 53 J4 1
Fernhill Rd NWPT TF10 188 C1
Fernhurst Cl STONE ST15 138 C3 1
Fernhurst Gv LNGTN ST3 102 E2
Fernie Cl STONE ST15 138 C4 1
Fernlea Crs END/WER ST9 55 M2
Fernleaf Cl ALS/KID ST7 37 M2 1
Fernlea Gv LNGTN ST3 87 H5
LNGTN ST3 103 G6
Fernleigh Av BNTWD WS7 252 A2
Fernleigh Gdns STAFN ST16 174 A5
STRBR DY8 303 J7
Fernleigh Rd RUSH/SHEL WS4 284 B7
Fern Leys BDMR/CCFT WV3 294 D1
Fern Pl LNGTN ST3 86 B8
Fern Rd BDMR/CCFT WV3 12 D8 1
HEDN WS12 231 K5
Fernwood STAFN ST16 174 C3
Fernwood Cft LEEK ST13 43 J6 1
Fernwood Dr LEEK ST13 43 J6
RUGE WS15 197 K8
Fernwood Gn STOKE ST4 101 J3
Ferrand Cl STOKE ST4 85 G8
Ferrers Av BUTN/AL/TUT DE13 165 H5
Ferrers Cl MGN/WHC B75 287 K8
Ferrers Rd BUTN/AL/TUT DE13 200 F8
RSTAF ST18 157 K8
TAM/AM/WIL B77 11 H5
Ferrie Gv BRWNH WS8 268 E2
Ferry St STPNHL/WNHL DE15 204 E2 1
Ferry Vale Cl
STPNHL/WNHL DE15 204 E2
Festing St HAN ST1 2 E3
Festival Ms HEDN WS12 231 M4
Festival Rd BUT DE14 203 L3
Festival Wy BURS/TUN ST6 68 F5
DUNHL/THL/PER WV6 280 B5
Fibbersley WLNHL WV13 281 M6
WNSFLD WV11 281 M6
Fibbersley Bank
WLNHL WV13 281 M6 1
Fiddlers Bank BURS/TUN ST6 55 H2
Fiddler's La BUTN/AL/TUT DE13 165 L7
Field Av BUCK/MIL ST2 55 H8
RDERBYSW DE65 165 J1
Field Cl BLOX/PEL WS3 268 B8
BLOX/PEL WS3 283 J2
BLYBR/FOR ST11 103 L4
BUTN/AL/TUT DE13 185 G3
NEWUL ST5 98 C5 2
Field Crs RSTAF ST18 173 K8
Fielden Cl BURS/TUN ST6 54 F8
Field End Cl STOKE ST4 101 H3
Fieldfare BNTWD WS7 252 D5
Field Farm Rd
TAM/AM/WIL B77 274 D8
Field Head Pl
DUNHL/THL/PER WV6 279 H6
Field House Ct STONE ST15 119 M8 1
Fieldhouse Rd BNTWD WS7 252 A3
ETTPK/GDPK/PENN WV4 295 L6
HEDN WS12 231 M3
Fielding St STOKE ST4 85 H5
Field La ASHB DE6 93 J2
BUTN/AL/TUT DE13 184 E3
CDLE ST10 124 B8
GTWY WS6 249 M7
RUSH/SHEL WS4 268 B8
Field Pl LNGTN ST3 86 C5
RUGE WS15 215 H3 2
STAFN ST16 174 E4 1
Field Ri BUTN/AL/TUT DE13 185 G3
Field Rd BLOX/PEL WS3 283 J1
LICH WS13 236 B7
Fields Cl ALS/KID ST7 37 L6
Fieldside STAFS ST17 194 D5 2
STONE ST15 136 E3
Fields La SWAD DE11 223 M4
Fields Rd ALS/KID ST7 37 K7
Field St CNCK/NC WS11 231 M7
LEEK ST13 43 L5 2
WLNHL WV13 282 A8
WOLVN WV10 13 J2
Fieldsway STONE ST15 137 L2
Field Ter STONE ST15 138 A1
Field Vw BIDD ST8 40 C2
LNGTN ST3 87 H6
Field Wk ALDR WS9 285 H3 1
Field Wy ALS/KID ST7 37 L6
Fieldway BLYBR/FOR ST11 103 K3
BUCK/MIL ST2 70 F7
LNGTN ST3 85 L7
The Fieldway STOKE ST4 100 E3
Fife St STOKE ST4 86 A6
Fifth Av ALS/KID ST7 52 E1
WOLVN WV10 280 F3
Filance Cl PENK ST19 229 M3
Filance La PENK ST19 229 M3
Filey TAM/AM/WIL B77 11 M3
Filey Cl CNCK/NC WS11 249 J2
Filey Rd WOLVN WV10 264 B8
Fillybrooks Cl STONE ST15 137 M2
The Fillybrooks STONE ST15 137 L2
Filton Av BNTWD WS7 252 A2
Fincham Cl COVEN WV9 264 A7 3
Finchdean Cl LNGTN ST3 103 G4
Finchdene Gv BDMR/CCFT WV3 294 D1
Finches Hl RUGE WS15 197 J8
Finchfield Cl STRBR DY8 307 J6
Finchfield Gdns
BDMR/CCFT WV3 294 E1
Finchfield Hl BDMR/CCFT WV3 294 C1
Finchfield La BDMR/CCFT WV3 294 C2
Finchfield Rd BDMR/CCFT WV3 294 E1
Finchfield Rd West
BDMR/CCFT WV3 294 C1
Finchley Cl SEDG DY3 299 K8 1
Finch Pl BIDD ST8 40 B8
Finchsmith Pl LNGTN ST3 86 B8
Finch St BIDD ST8 54 B1
Fine La LICH WS13 237 L4
Finger Post Dr BLOX/PEL WS3 268 A5
Finney Gn BUCK/MIL ST2 3 L5
Finstock Av LNGTN ST3 101 L2
Firbank Pl LNGTN ST3 86 F6
Firbank Wy BLOX/PEL WS3 267 M8
Firbeck Gdns STAFS ST17 194 C3
Firbob La CDLE ST10 106 F7
Fir Cl HEDN WS12 231 K2
Fircroft Cl CNCK/NC WS11 232 A7 1
Firecrest Cl HEDN WS12 232 C8 3
Fir Gv BDMR/CCFT WV3 12 A7
STRBR DY8 307 J4
Firmstone St STRBR DY8 307 L3
Firsbrook Cl
DUNHL/THL/PER WV6 280 A6 2
The Firs Cl STAFS ST17 194 D3
Firs Rd KGSWFD DY6 303 L4
First Av ALS/KID ST7 52 E1
BRWNH WS8 269 G2
BUCK/MIL ST2 70 D6
NEWUL ST5 68 C3
STAFN ST16 174 C3
WOLVN WV10 280 E3
The Firs ASHB DE6 95 J1
RUGE WS15 233 M5
Fir St SEDG DY3 298 F3
Firsvale Rd WNSFLD WV11 281 M5
Firsway DUNHL/THL/PER WV6 294 A1
The Firsway PENK ST19 244 E2
Fir Tree Cl CRTAM B79 273 L3 1
Firtree Cl RSTAF ST18 193 H7
Fir Tree Dr SEDG DY3 299 L3
Fir Tree Rd BDMR/CCFT WV3 294 D3
LNGTN ST3 102 E2
Firwood Rd BIDD ST8 40 E1
Fisher Rd BLOX/PEL WS3 266 F8
Fisher St BDMR/CCFT WV3 12 C8
BIDD ST8 40 B8
HEDN WS12 231 M2
WLNHL WV13 282 C8
Fisherwick Cl LICHS WS14 255 M4 1
Fisherwick Rd LICHS WS14 255 L5
Fishley Cl BLOX/PEL WS3 267 J6
Fishley La BLOX/PEL WS3 267 L4
Fishpond La
BUTN/AL/TUT DE13 165 J4
RDERBYSW DE65 167 G5
Fishpond Wy BUCK/MIL ST2 70 A4
Fistral Cl LNGTN ST3 86 D6
Fitzgerald Cl LNGTN ST3 87 H6
Fitzherbert Cl STONE ST15 118 B6 1
Fitzherbert Rd HAN ST1 69 M2
Fitzmaurice Rd WNSFLD WV11 281 M3
Five Fields Rd SHHTH WV12 282 A5
Five Lands Rd
STPNHL/WNHL DE15 204 F2
Five Lanes Ends GNOS ST20 172 D3
Five Oaks Cl NEWUL ST5 83 L7
Flackets La ASHB DE6 146 A3
Flackett St LNGTN ST3 86 C5 3
Flamborough Gv BURS/TUN ST6 68 E3
Flanders Dr KGSWFD DY6 303 K2 2
The Flashes GNOS ST20 190 E3
Flash La BUCK/MIL ST2 55 J8
MKTDR TF9 131 M1
STOKE ST4 84 E7
WMBN WV5 293 L8
Flather La ASHB DE6 93 K1
Flats La LICHS WS14 272 A4
Flatts Cl BUTN/AL/TUT DE13 185 H4 1
Flatts Rd BURS/TUN ST6 54 E5
Flavells La SEDG DY3 299 H8
Flax Cft STONE ST15 138 B3
Flaxley Rd RUGE WS15 215 K4
Flaxman Cl BARL ST12 101 L6
The Flax Ovens PENK ST19 211 L8
Flax St STOKE ST4 85 H4
Fleckney Av LNGTN ST3 86 E7 1
Fleets La LEEK ST13 61 H2
Fleet St BUT DE14 7 H8
Fleming Pl WSLW WS2 283 G4
Fleming Rd STOKE ST4 85 H3
WSLW WS2 283 G4
Flemmynge Cl CDSL WV8 262 E6 1
Fletcher Bank NEWUL ST5 84 A1 1
Fletcher Crs BUCK/MIL ST2 55 H8
Fletcher Rd SHHTH WV12 282 D1
STOKE ST4 85 H5
Fletcher's La WLNHL WV13 282 C8
Fletcher St HAN ST1 2 B8
The Fletches
BUTN/AL/TUT DE13 185 H1 2
Fleur Gv STOKE ST4 86 B4
Flinn Cl LICHS WS14 9 K5
Flintsham Gv HAN ST1 2 C2
Flint St LNGTN ST3 87 H5
Flora Cl CRTAM B79 274 C3
Florence Av
ETTPK/GDPK/PENN WV4 295 M6
Florence Dr ASHB DE6 145 H2
Florence Rd CDSL WV8 263 J7
STOKE ST4 100 F1
Florence St HEDN WS12 232 A3
NEWUL ST5 84 B1
Florendine St TAM/AM/WIL B77 11 M4
Florida Cl BURS/TUN ST6 69 H2
Floyds La RUSH/SHEL WS4 284 C4
Floyd St STOKE ST4 85 H2 2
Flynn Rw STOKE ST4 85 L2
Foden Av ALS/KID ST7 37 M7
Foden Cl LICHS WS14 270 F4
Foden St STOKE ST4 85 G5
Fogg St West NEWUL ST5 84 B1 1
Fold La BIDD ST8 26 E6
Fold St WOLV WV1 12 E6
The Fold
ETTPK/GDPK/PENN WV4 294 F6
Fole La UTXR ST14 124 F2
Foley Av DUNHL/THL/PER WV6 279 H7
Foley Church Cl
FOAKS/STRLY B74 286 A8
Foley Dr DUNHL/THL/PER WV6 279 J7
Foley Gv WMBN WV5 297 L5
Foley Pl STOKE ST4 86 A6 3
Foley Rd LNGTN ST3 86 A7
Foley St KINVER DY7 306 B6
STOKE ST4 86 B6
Folly Flds LEEK ST13 72 B1
Folly La END/WER ST9 72 C3
LEEK ST13 72 B1
Fontaine Pl STOKE ST4 85 G5 2
Fontenaye Rd CRTAM B79 273 L3
Fonthill Rd STAFN ST16 174 F4
Fontwell Rd BUT DE14 203 M3 2
WOLVN WV10 264 D6
Footherley La LICHS WS14 270 C6
Footherley Rd LICHS WS14 270 F5
Forber Rd STOKE ST4 84 F6
Ford Av BURS/TUN ST6 54 B5
Ford Brook La BLOX/PEL WS3 284 B1
Ford Cl STONE ST15 138 A3
Ford Dr STONE ST15 136 E4
Ford Green Rd BURS/TUN ST6 54 D8
Fordham Gv COVEN WV9 264 A7
Fordhouse Rd WOLVN WV10 280 D1
Ford La LICH WS13 235 G8
RUGE WS15 217 G8
Fords La ALS/KID ST7 39 K4
Ford St LEEK ST13 43 M4
NEWUL ST5 67 H8
STOKE ST4 84 E1
STPNHL/WNHL DE15 204 E3
Ford Wy RUGE WS15 217 H5
Foregate St STAFN ST16 4 D2
Forest Av BLOX/PEL WS3 283 K3
Forest Cl NEWUL ST5 83 L6
RSTAF ST18 196 D2 3
Forest Dr KINVER DY7 305 M7
Forest Ga SHHTH WV12 282 D2 1
Forest Gld GTWY WS6 249 M8 1
Forest La BLOX/PEL WS3 283 L5
KINVER DY7 296 E8
Forest Pl BLOX/PEL WS3 283 L4
Forest Rd BUTN/AL/TUT DE13 184 D6
BUTN/AL/TUT DE13 202 B5
LNGTN ST3 102 F3
MKTDR TF9 130 A2
UTXR ST14 162 F5
Forestside Gv STOKE ST4 84 F8
Forest Wy GTWY WS6 267 G1
Forge Cl BNTWD WS7 252 D5
CDSL WV8 279 L1
Forge La ALDR WS9 285 M4
BNTWD WS7 252 F4
BUTN/AL/TUT DE13 166 F8
FOAKS/STRLY B74 286 C4
HAN ST1 68 F7
KGSWFD DY6 303 G2
LICH WS13 8 C1
LICHS WS14 286 B2
MKTDR TF9 113 J1
Forge Leys WMBN WV5 297 L4 7
Forge Ri RSTAF ST18 210 B2 1
Forge Rd BLOX/PEL WS3 267 M5
RUGE WS15 215 M1
SHHTH WV12 282 C6
STRBR DY8 307 M4
Forge Side END/WER ST9 56 A2 3
Forge St HEDN WS12 232 C6
Forge Valley Wy WMBN WV5 297 L4
Forge Wy BIDD ST8 40 B6
Formby Av
DUNHL/THL/PER WV6 278 D6
Formby Wy BLOX/PEL WS3 267 G7
Forrest Av CNCK/NC WS11 249 L3
WNSFLD WV11 266 A6
Forrester Cl BIDD ST8 40 C2 2
LICH WS13 237 K4
Forrester Rd STONE ST15 138 B3
Forresters Bank BUCK/MIL ST2 55 J7
Forrester St WSLW WS2 283 J8
Forrester Street Prec
WSLW WS2 283 J8
Forrister St LNGTN ST3 86 C6
Forshaw Cl ASHB DE6 95 J2
Forster St BURS/TUN ST6 53 K7
Forsyte Rd LNGTN ST3 86 B4
Forsythia Gv CDSL WV8 263 G7 1
Fort Crs ALDR WS9 269 G7
Fortescue La RUGE WS15 197 L8
Forties TAM/AM/WIL B77 290 E3
Forton Cl
DUNHL/THL/PER WV6 279 H8
Forty Acre Cl MKTDR TF9 114 E5 1
Forum Rd NEWUL ST5 67 K5
Fosbrooke Pl STOKE ST4 84 D2
Fossdale Rd TAM/AM/WIL B77 291 G2
Fosseway LICHS WS14 8 C9
Fosseway La LICHS WS14 253 L6
Foster Av HEDN WS12 231 M4
Foster Ct LNGTN ST3 85 M8
Foster Crs KINVER DY7 306 A6
Foster Gn
DUNHL/THL/PER WV6 278 E7
Foster Pl STRBR DY8 307 L4
Foster Rd WOLVN WV10 280 E4
Foster St BLOX/PEL WS3 283 K2
KINVER DY7 306 A6
Foston Av BUTN/AL/TUT DE13 185 G4
Foston Cl RDERBYSW DE65 165 J1
Fotherley Brook Rd ALDR WS9 285 M5
Foundry La ALS/KID ST7 38 F3
BLOX/PEL WS3 267 L7
BUCK/MIL ST2 3 M7
Foundry Rd KGSWFD DY6 303 H2
Foundry St HAN ST1 2 C5
KGSWFD DY6 303 H2
Fountain Ct BIDD ST8 40 D1
Fountain Fold GNOS ST20 190 D5 1
Fountain Rd ASHB DE6 163 K4 1
Fountains Av NEWUL ST5 84 B6
Fountains Rd BLOX/PEL WS3 266 E8
Fountain St LEEK ST13 43 M4
STOKE ST4 85 L4
Fountains Wy
BLOX/PEL WS3 266 E8 1
Four Ashes Rd PENK ST19 246 D3
Four Crosses La WOLVN WV10 248 D4
Four Crosses Rd
RUSH/SHEL WS4 284 C1
Four Oaks Common Rd
FOAKS/STRLY B74 286 E7
Four Oaks Rd
FOAKS/STRLY B74 286 F8
Fourth Av ALS/KID ST7 52 F1
BRWNH WS8 269 G1
BUCK/MIL ST2 70 D6
WOLVN WV10 280 D4
Fowlchurch Rd LEEK ST13 43 M3
Fowler Cl CDSL WV8 278 E4
Fowler's La BUCK/MIL ST2 55 K8
Fowler St BKHL/PFLD WV2 295 J4 2
Fox Cl BUT DE14 204 B2 1
WMBN WV5 292 F8
Foxcote Cl STAFS ST17 194 E5 1
Fox Covert STRBR DY8 307 L5
Foxcroft Cl BNTWD WS7 252 A5
Foxes La PENK ST19 245 J4
Foxes Rake CNCK/NC WS11 231 L7
Foxfield Cl CDLE ST10 89 L4
Foxfields Wy HEDN WS12 231 J3
Foxfield Wy LNGTN ST3 101 M2 1
Fox Gdns ALS/KID ST7 52 D2
Foxglove TAM/AM/WIL B77 275 G6
Foxglove Av
STPNHL/WNHL DE15 205 G2
UTXR ST14 144 B4
Foxglove Cl BLOX/PEL WS3 268 A5 2
LNGTN ST3 87 H5
RUGE WS15 215 J1
WNSFLD WV11 281 L5 1
WOLVN WV10 265 H3 1
Foxglove La NEWUL ST5 100 C1
Foxglove Rd DUDN DY1 299 M6
Foxgloves Av RSTAF ST18 196 E3
Fox Gv NEWUL ST5 84 C8
Foxhill Cl HEDN WS12 232 D8
Fox Hill Rd MGN/WHC B75 287 M8
Foxhill's Cl BNTWD WS7 252 A5
Foxhills Rd
ETTPK/GDPK/PENN WV4 294 C7
STRBR DY8 307 K1
Fox Hollow
DUNHL/THL/PER WV6 279 J8
ECCH ST21 152 F4
MKTDR TF9 114 D5
Foxland Av GTWY WS6 250 A7 1
Foxlands Av
ETTPK/GDPK/PENN WV4 294 D7
Foxlands Cl BUCK/MIL ST2 70 D7
Foxlands Crs
ETTPK/GDPK/PENN WV4 294 C7
Foxlands Dr
ETTPK/GDPK/PENN WV4 294 C7
SEDG DY3 299 K5
Fox La BUTN/AL/TUT DE13 219 M8
LICH WS13 236 A6
LICH WS13 237 M1
Fox Leigh Mdw RUGE WS15 217 H6
Foxley La BUCK/MIL ST2 70 A1
Foxmeadow Cl SEDG DY3 299 L3 3
Fox Rd WMBN WV5 292 E7
Fox's La WOLV WV1 280 D5
Fox Wk ALDR WS9 269 H7
Foxwood Cl STONE ST15 137 M4 3
Foxwood Rd
POL/KGSB/FAZ B78 291 M2
Fradley La LICH WS13 237 L3
Fradswell La RSTAF ST18 158 A1
Framlingham Gv
DUNHL/THL/PER WV6 279 G7 3
Frampton Gv BURS/TUN ST6 53 L4
Frances Dr BLOX/PEL WS3 267 H8 1
Franche Rd KIDDW DY11 309 J8
Francis Cl KGSWFD DY6 303 K2 3
PENK ST19 229 M2
Francis Green La PENK ST19 229 M1
Francis Rd LICH WS13 236 A8
STRBR DY8 307 J5
Francis St BURS/TUN ST6 53 M5
WOLV WV1 12 E1
Frank Foley Wy STAFN ST16 4 C2
Frank Gee Cl RUGE WS15 215 K1 2
Franklin Cl STPNHL/WNHL DE15 205 H1
Franklin Dr BNTWD WS7 252 B4
Franklin Rd STOKE ST4 84 F3
Franklyn Cl
DUNHL/THL/PER WV6 278 E5
Franklyn St HAN ST1 2 F8
Frank Rogers Wk
RUGE WS15 197 K8 3
Frank St STOKE ST4 85 G4
Fraser Cl STONE ST15 137 M5
Fraser St BURS/TUN ST6 69 H3
Frayne Av KGSWFD DY6 303 J3
Freckleton Pl
BLYBR/FOR ST11 103 J3 4
Frederick Av STOKE ST4 85 G3
Frederick Rd PENK ST19 211 M8
WNSFLD WV11 281 J5
Fredericks Cl STRBR DY8 307 L6
Frederick St BKHL/PFLD WV2 12 F8
STOKE ST4 85 L4
STPNHL/WNHL DE15 204 E2
Frederick William St
WLNHL WV13 282 B8 3
Freebridge Cl LNGTN ST3 86 E6 3
Freeford Gdns LICHS WS14 9 M6
Freehold St NEWUL ST5 84 C2
Freeland Gv KGSWFD DY6 303 M6 2
Freeman St WOLVN WV10 13 L4
Freemen St STAFN ST16 174 E5
Freer St WSL WS1 283 L8
Freeth Rd BRWNH WS8 269 G1
Free Trade St HAN ST1 2 E3
Fremantle Dr HEDN WS12 232 E8
Fremantle Rd STOKE ST4 84 F6
Fremont Dr DUDN DY1 299 L7
French Av POL/KGSB/FAZ B78 289 J1
Frenchmore Gv LNGTN ST3 102 E1
Frensham Cl GTWY WS6 249 L6
Freshwater Gv BUCK/MIL ST2 3 K7
Freville Cl CRTAM B79 10 B2
Frew Cl STAFN ST16 5 K3
Friars Av STONE ST15 138 A3
Friars Cl CDLE ST10 89 K6
STRBR DY8 303 J7
Friars Gorse KINVER DY7 307 J3 1
Friar's La SHIF TF11 243 K6
Friars Pl BUCK/MIL ST2 70 B3
Friars Rd BUCK/MIL ST2 70 B3
STAFS ST17 4 F7
Friars' St NEWUL ST5 84 B2
Friars' Ter STAFS ST17 4 E7
Friar St LNGTN ST3 86 C6
STAFN ST16 4 D1
Friars' Wk NEWUL ST5 84 B4
STAFS ST17 4 F6
Friarswood Rd NEWUL ST5 84 B2
Friary Av LICH WS13 8 D5
RUGE WS15 179 M5
Friary Crs RUSH/SHEL WS4 284 C4
Friary Gdns LICH WS13 8 C5
Friary Rd LICH WS13 8 C5
The Friary LICH WS13 8 D6
Friday Acre LICH WS13 254 A1
Friendly Av NEWUL ST5 68 B2
Friesian Gdns NEWUL ST5 52 C8
Friesland Dr WOLV WV1 281 H7
Friezeland Rd WSLW WS2 283 H8
Friezland La BRWNH WS8 269 G5
Friezland Wy BRWNH WS8 269 G5
Frinton Cl STAFN ST16 174 F4
Frith St LEEK ST13 43 K4
Frobisher Cl GTWY WS6 266 F1
Frobisher Dr STONE ST15 118 B6
Frodingham Rd BUCK/MIL ST2 86 D1
Froghall NEWUL ST5 84 B1 2
Froghall Rd CDLE ST10 74 A2
Frog La LICH WS13 8 F4
MKTDR TF9 130 C1 2
PENK ST19 227 J4
Frogmore Rd MKTDR TF9 130 C1
Frome Dr WNSFLD WV11 281 J5
Frome Wk BURS/TUN ST6 54 A5
Froyle Cl DUNHL/THL/PER WV6 279 J5
Froysell St WLNHL WV13 282 B8
Fryers Cl BLOX/PEL WS3 283 H3
Fryers Rd WSLW WS2 283 G4
Fryer St WOLV WV1 13 G4
Fuchsia Dr COVEN WV9 263 M7
Fulford Rd STONE ST15 121 K2
Fullbrook Av
BUTN/AL/TUT DE13 220 D2
Fullelove Rd BRWNH WS8 269 G4
Fuller St BURS/TUN ST6 53 L6 2
Fullerton Cl CDSL WV8 279 L1
Fullmore Cl PENK ST19 229 M3
Fulmer Pl LNGTN ST3 103 H3
Furber Pl KGSWFD DY6 303 M4
Furlong Av CDLE ST10 105 L7
Furlong Cl
BUTN/AL/TUT DE13 220 A8 2
RSTAF ST18 157 J8
Furlong Dr CDLE ST10 105 L7
Furlong La ASHB DE6 48 C6
BURS/TUN ST6 68 E3
BUTN/AL/TUT DE13 219 M8
RSTAF ST18 192 D7
Furlong Pde BURS/TUN ST6 68 F2 2
Furlong Pas BURS/TUN ST6 68 F2 2
Furlong Rd BURS/TUN ST6 53 L6
Furlongs Rd SEDG DY3 299 K4
The Furlongs WOLVN WV10 281 H5
The Furlong STONE ST15 136 F4
Furlong Wk SEDG DY3 299 K6
Furmston Pl LEEK ST13 44 A2
Furnace Cl WMBN WV5 297 L5
Furnace La AUD/MAD/W CW3 81 K3
Furnace Rd LNGTN ST3 86 D8
Furness TAM/AM/WIL B77 11 H8
Furness Cl BLOX/PEL WS3 266 F7 3
Furness Gv STAFS ST17 193 H8
Furnival St BURS/TUN ST6 69 H4
Furst St BRWNH WS8 269 G2
Furzebank Wy SHHTH WV12 282 E6
Fyfield Rd STPNHL/WNHL DE15 204 E3
Fynney Flds LEEK ST13 57 M2
Fynney St LEEK ST13 43 M5

G

Gable Cft LICHS WS14 9 M6
The Gables ALS/KID ST7 37 J7
SWAD DE11 205 L5 2
Gable St STOKE ST4 85 H4 2
Gadsby Av WNSFLD WV11 282 A3
Gaelic Rd CNCK/NC WS11 231 K6
Gagarin CRTAM B79 273 M5
Gag La ASHB DE6 63 K1
Gaiafields Rd LICH WS13 8 E1
Gaialands Crs LICH WS13 8 E1
Gaia La LICH WS13 8 F1
Gaiastowe LICH WS13 8 F1
Gail Cl ALDR WS9 269 H6
Gailey Lea La PENK ST19 248 C2
Gail Pk BDMR/CCFT WV3 294 D3
Gainford Cl COVEN WV9 279 M1
Gainsborough Dr
DUNHL/THL/PER WV6 278 F6

Gainsborough Pl *DUDN* DY1 .... 299 L8
Gainsborough Rd *LNGTN* ST5 .... 101 L2
   NEWUL ST5 .... 67 L4
Gainsborough Wy
   STPNHL/WNHL DE15 .... 186 B7
Gainsbrook Cl *CNCK/NC* WS11 .... 250 F5
Gains La *BLOX/PEL* WS3 .... 250 D8
Gairloch Rd *WNSFLD* WV11 .... 282 B1 ⬚
Galahad Dr
   BUTN/AL/TUT DE13 .... 166 E8 ⬚
Galleys Bank *ALS/KID* ST7 .... 39 H7
Galliers Cl *TAM/AM/WIL* B77 ...... 290 F5 ⬚
Gallimore Cl *BURS/TUN* ST6 .... 68 E1
Galloway Rd *BUCK/MIL* ST2 .... 86 E2
Gallowstree La *ASHB* DE6 .... 94 C1
   NEWUL ST5 .... 83 L3
Galsworthy Rd *STOKE* ST4 .... 86 B4
Galway Rd *BNTWD* WS7 .... 252 A2
Gamesfield Gn
   BDMR/CCFT WV3 .... 294 F1
Gandy Rd *SHHTH* WV12 .... 282 A4
Ganton Rd *BLOX/PEL* WS3 .... 267 C6
Gaol Butts *ECCH* ST21 .... 152 D4
Gaolgate St *STAFN* ST16 .... 4 E4
Gaol Rd *STAFN* ST16 .... 4 E2
Gaol Sq *STAFN* ST16 .... 4 E3
Garbett St *BURS/TUN* ST6 .... 53 J3
Garden Cotts *GNOS* ST20 .... 190 C5 ⬚
Garden Crs *BLOX/PEL* WS3 .... 267 M7
Garden Cft *ALDR* WS9 .... 285 H3
Garden Dr *RUGE* WS15 .... 215 M3
Gardeners Cl *BIDD* ST8 .... 40 A5
Gardeners Wy *WMBN* WV5 .... 297 M6
Gardenholm Cl *LNGTN* ST3 .... 102 C2
Garden La *PENK* ST19 .... 228 D6
Garden Pl *STOKE* ST4 .... 84 D2
The Gardens *CRTAM* B79 .... 238 D8
Garden St *LEEK* ST13 .... 43 K4
   NEWUL ST5 .... 84 C2
   STAFS ST17 .... 4 F7
   STOKE ST4 .... 84 F4
   WSLW WS2 .... 283 L7
Garden Vw *RUGE* WS15 .... 215 K1
Garden Village *CDLE* ST10 .... 105 K7
Gardiner Dr *LNGTN* ST3 .... 86 A3
Gardner Pl *UTXR* ST14 .... 144 A1 ⬚
Garfield Av *STOKE* ST4 .... 100 F1
Garfield Crs *STOKE* ST4 .... 100 F1
Garfield St *HAN* ST1 .... 2 A8
Garibaldi St *HAN* ST1 .... 68 F7
Garlick St *BURS/TUN* ST6 .... 69 H1 ⬚
Garner St *HAN* ST1 .... 68 F8
Garners Wk
   AUD/MAD/W CW3 .... 81 M3 ⬚
Garnet Cl *ALDR* WS9 .... 269 K6
Garnet St *HAN* ST1 .... 69 G7 ⬚
Garnett Rd East *NEWUL* ST5 .... 68 B5
Garnett Rd West *NEWUL* ST5 .... 68 B4
Garret Cl *KGSWFD* DY6 .... 303 K1
Garrick Ri *BNTWD* WS7 .... 252 B3
   RUGE WS15 .... 216 B4 ⬚
Garrick St *CNCK/NC* WS11 .... 231 K6
   LICH WS13 .... 235 M8
Garrick St *WOLV* WV1 .... 13 G6
Garrigill *TAM/AM/WIL* B77 .... 291 G1
Garrod Sq *STAFN* ST16 .... 5 L1
Garsdale Crs *LNGTN* ST3 .... 101 L2
Gartan Rd *BUT* DE14 .... 204 A2
Garth Cl *STAFS* ST17 .... 193 L5
Garth Rd *STAFS* ST17 .... 193M5
Garth St *HAN* ST1 .... 2 E4
The Garth *LICH* WS13 .... 236 B8
Gaskell Rd *BUCK/MIL* ST2 .... 70 D7
Gas St *UTXR* ST14 .... 144 C2
Gatacre St *SEDG* DY3 .... 299 K7 ⬚
Gatcombe Cl
   BUTN/AL/TUT DE13 .... 185 K1
   WOLV WV10 .... 264 F6
Gatcombe Rd *DUDN* DY1 .... 299 L8 ⬚
Gate Cl *WMBN* WV5 .... 298 A5
Gate St *LNGTN* ST3 .... 87 H5
   SEDG DY3 .... 299 L3 ⬚
Gateway *NEWUL* ST5 .... 52 D8
Gateway Av *NEWUL* ST5 .... 98 C5
Gatherwynd La *SHIF* TF11 .... 225 L4
Gatis St *DUNHL/THL/PER* WV6 ... 280 A6
Gatley Gv *LNGTN* ST3 .... 103 H4
Gauledge La *LEEK* ST13 .... 43 L3
Gawain Gv
   BUTN/AL/TUT DE13 .... 166 E8 ⬚
Gawsworth *CRTAM* B79 .... 273 K3 ⬚
Gawsworth Cl *ALS/KID* ST7 .... 37 J7 ⬚
   LNGTN ST3 .... 86 C4
Gaydon Cl
   DUNHL/THL/PER WV6 .... 278 D5
Gaydon Rd *ALDR* WS9 .... 285 C6
Gay La *GNOS* ST20 .... 226 E2
Gayle *TAM/AM/WIL* B77 .... 291 C1
Gaymore Rd *KIDD* DY10 .... 310 B5
Gayton Av *BUCK/MIL* ST2 .... 55 H8
Geary La *STPNHL/WNHL* DE15 ... 186 F8
Gedney Gv *NEWUL* ST5 .... 84 B8
Geen St *STOKE* ST4 .... 85 H3
Gemini Dr *CNCK/NC* WS11 .... 249 M4
Gemini Gv *BURS/TUN* ST6 .... 53 L4
Geneshall Cl *GNOS* ST20 .... 190 D3
Geneva Dr *HAN* ST1 .... 69 M4
   NEWUL ST5 .... 83 L4
Genge Av
   ETTPK/GDPK/PENN WV4 ... 295 L6 ⬚
Genista Cl *STPNHL/WNHL* DE15 .. 205 L2 ⬚
Genthorn Cl
   ETTPK/GDPK/PENN WV4 ... 295 M6 ⬚
Geoffrey Av *LEEK* ST13 .... 43 K5
Geoffrey Gv *LNGTN* ST3 .... 87 C6
George Av *NEWUL* ST5 .... 103 H1
   POL/KGSB/FAZ B78 .... 289 J1
George Bates Cl *ALS/KID* ST7 ..... 37 J7
George Brealey Cl *RUGE* WS15 .. 215M3
George Elliott Cl *UTXR* ST14 .... 144 C4
George La *LICH* WS13 .... 9 C3
   STONE ST15 .... 138 C3
George's Ct *LNGTN* ST3 .... 86 B7
George's Pde *BKHL/PFLD* WV2 .... 13 C6
George St *ALS/KID* ST7 .... 37 H2
   ASHB DE6 .... 95 H2
   BKHL/PFLD WV2 .... 12 F7
   BUT DE14 .... 7 G5

   HEDN WS12 .... 232 C6
   NEWUL ST5 .... 67 L3
   NEWUL ST5 .... 85 J1
   NEWUL ST5 .... 83 H1 ⬚
   NEWUL ST5 .... 84 C1
   STAFN ST16 .... 4 D1 ⬚
   STOKE ST4 .... 85 L3
   STRBR DY8 .... 307 M1
   WLNHL WV13 .... 282 A6 ⬚
Georges Wy *ALS/KID* ST7 .... 51 M8
Georgian Pl *CNCK/NC* WS11 ..... 231 L8
Gerald Rd *STRBR* DY8 .... 307 L3
Gerard *CRTAM* B79 .... 273 L3
Gerards Wy *MKTDR* TF9 .... 115 J3
Gerrard St *STOKE* ST4 .... 85 G2
Gibbet La *KINVER* DY7 .... 307 C6
Gibbins St *HAN* ST1 .... 2 F7
Gibb La *ASHB* DE6 .... 146 E5
Gibbons Gv
   DUNHL/THL/PER WV6 .... 279 L6
Gibbons Hill Rd *SEDG* DY3 .... 295 K8
Gibbons Rd
   DUNHL/THL/PER WV6 .... 279 M6
   MGN/WHC B75 .... 287 H7
Gibraltar *KINVER* DY7 .... 306 B6
Gibson Av *NEWUL* ST5 .... 67 K2
Gibson Pl *LNGTN* ST3 .... 87 C8
Gibson Rd
   DUNHL/THL/PER WV6 .... 278 E7 ⬚
Gibson St *BURS/TUN* ST6 .... 53 L8
Giddywell La *RUGE* WS15 .... 234 F3
Gideons Cl *SEDG* DY3 .... 299 K5
Giffard Rd *WOLV* WV10 .... 264 F7
Gifford Pl *STOKE* ST4 .... 84 F4
Giffords Cft *LICH* WS13 .... 254 A1
Giggetty La *WMBN* WV5 .... 297 L4
Gigmill Wy *STRBR* DY8 .... 307 K3
Gilbanks Rd *STRBR* DY8 .... 307 K3
Gilbern Dr *BIDD* ST8 .... 40 D5
Gilbert Cl *ALS/KID* ST7 .... 39 C8
   WNSFLD WV11 .... 282 A3
Gilbert La *WMBN* WV5 .... 298 B3
Gilbert Rd *LICH* WS13 .... 236 C3
Gilbert St *BURS/TUN* ST6 .... 53 J5
   BURS/TUN ST6 .... 53 J5
Gilbeys Ct *STRBR* DY8 .... 307 L1 ⬚
Giles Cl *CDLE* ST10 .... 89 K7
Giles Rd *LICH* WS13 .... 236 A7
Gillards Ct *BUTN/AL/TUT* DE13 .. 218 C4
Gill Bank Rd *ALS/KID* ST7 .... 53 H2
   BURS/TUN ST6 .... 53 H5
Gillingham Crs *STAFN* ST16 .... 174 D8
Gillway *CRTAM* B79 .... 274 D2
Gilman Av *BUCK/MIL* ST2 .... 55 H8
Gilman Pl *HAN* ST1 .... 2 E5
Gilman St *HAN* ST1 .... 2 E5
Gilpin Crs *BLOX/PEL* WS3 .... 268 A6
Gilpins Cft *GTWY* WS6 .... 266 D1
Gilwell Rd *RUGE* WS15 .... 233M4
Gimson St *STOKE* ST4 .... 85 L4
Ginger Hl *GNOS* ST20 .... 190 D5
Ginger La *ECCH* ST21 .... 134 B6
Gipsy La *KIDDW* DY11 .... 310 A2
Girsby Cl *STOKE* ST4 .... 101 J5
Girton Rd *CNCK/NC* WS11 .... 249M2
Gisborne Cl *BUTN/AL/TUT* DE13 . 201 C7
Gitana St *HAN* ST1 .... 2 C5
Gladeside Cl *RUSH/SHEL* WS4 .. 284 C2
The Glades *ALDR* WS9 .... 285 H3
The Glade *CDSL* WV8 .... 279 L1 ⬚
   CNCK/NC WS11 .... 231 J8
   NEWUL ST5 .... 84 B4
   STAFS ST17 .... 194 B2
Gladstone Gv *BIDD* ST8 .... 40 D2
   KGSWFD DY6 .... 303 K2 ⬚
Gladstone Pl *STOKE* ST4 .... 84 F5
Gladstone Rd *HEDN* WS12 .... 250 E1
   STRBR DY8 .... 307 K4
Gladstone St *LEEK* ST13 .... 43 L4
   STOKE ST4 .... 68 E8
   WSLW WS2 .... 283 K6
Gladstone Wy *STAFN* ST16 .... 5 M2
Gladwyn St *BUCK/MIL* ST2 .... 70 C6
Glaisdale Gdns
   DUNHL/THL/PER WV6 .... 280 A5 ⬚
Glaisedale Gv *WLNHL* WV13 ..... 282 A6 ⬚
Glaisher Dr *BLYBR/FOR* ST11 ... 103 J5
   WOLV WV10 .... 280 C4
Glamis Cl *BUTN/AL/TUT* DE13 .. 185 K2 ⬚
Glamis Dr *STONE* ST15 .... 138 C5
Glamis Rd *SHHTH* WV12 .... 282 B3
Glandore Rd *LNGTN* ST3 .... 86 F6
Glanville Dr *MGN/WHC* B75 .... 287 C6
Glascote La *TAM/AM/WIL* B77 ... 290 F3
Glascote Rd *TAM/AM/WIL* B77 ... 10 F6
Glasscroft Cottages
   BNTWD WS7 .... 252 A3
Glass La *RUGE* WS15 .... 199 L1
Glass St *HAN* ST1 .... 2 D4
Glastonbury Cl *END/WER* ST9 ..... 55 K7
   STAFS ST17 .... 194 B4
Glastonbury Crs
   BLOX/PEL WS3 .... 266 E3
Glastonbury Wy
   BLOX/PEL WS3 .... 282 E1 ⬚
Glebe Av *STAFN* ST16 .... 174 D4
Glebe Cl *ASHB* DE6 .... 145 J2 ⬚
   BLYBR/FOR ST11 .... 104 A4
   BUTN/AL/TUT DE13 .... 166 A6
   MKTDR TF9 .... 149 G2
   MSHM DE12 .... 222 C7
Glebe Ct *STOKE* ST4 .... 85 J3 ⬚
Glebedale Rd *STOKE* ST4 .... 85 L4
Glebefields *GNOS* ST20 .... 170 D5
Glebelands *STAFS* ST17 .... 193 M4 ⬚
Glebe La *GNOS* ST20 .... 190 E4
   STRBR DY8 .... 307 L5
Glebe Rd *CDLE* ST10 .... 73 K8
   CDLE ST10 .... 89 H8
   RUGE WS15 .... 217 J3 ⬚
The Glebe *ALBTN* WV7 .... 261 C5 ⬚
   MSHM DE12 .... 222 C4
Glebeville *LEEK* ST13 .... 43 L6
Gledhill Pk *LICHS* WS14 .... 9 C8
Glencastle Wy *STOKE* ST4 .... 101 J5
Glen Cl *HEDN* WS12 .... 231 K5
   RUSH/SHEL WS4 .... 284 A7
Glencoe Dr *CNCK/NC* WS11 ..... 232 A6
Glencoe St *LNGTN* ST3 .... 86 B8

Glen Ct *DUNHL/THL/PER* WV6 ... 279 L8
Glencroft Cl *BUT* DE14 .... 204 B3 ⬚
Glendale Cl *BDMR/CCFT* WV3 ... 294 C2
Glendale Ct *NEWUL* ST5 .... 100 C1
   TAM/AM/WIL B77 .... 291 H4 ⬚
Glendale Dr *WMBN* WV5 .... 298 A4
Glendale Rd *BURS/TUN* ST6 .... 69 G3
Glendawn Cl *CNCK/NC* WS11 ... 232 A7 ⬚
Glendower Cl *GNOS* ST20 .... 190 C4
Glendower Rd *ALDR* WS9 .... 285 H1
Glen Dr *CDLE* ST10 .... 107 L2
Glendue Gv *STOKE* ST4 .... 101 J4
Gleneagles *BLOX/PEL* WS3 .... 266 F7
Gleneagles Cl *HAN* ST1 .... 69 K4
Gleneagles Dr
   BUTN/AL/TUT DE13 .... 185 J1 ⬚
   STAFN ST16 .... 175 J7 ⬚
Gleneagles Rd *BLOX/PEL* WS3 .. 266 F7 ⬚
   DUNHL/THL/PER WV6 .... 278 D5
Glenfield CDSL WV8 .... 263 L8 ⬚
Glenfield Ri
   BUTN/AL/TUT DE13 .... 185 H3 ⬚
Glenfield Wy *BUCK/MIL* ST2 .... 86 E3 ⬚
Glengarry Gdns
   BDMR/CCFT WV3 .... 294 F1
Glenhaven *RUGE* WS15 .... 197 J8
Glenhurst Cl *WSLW* WS2 .... 282 D7
Glenmore Av *BNTWD* WS7 .... 252 D7
Glenmore Cl *BDMR/CCFT* WV3 .. 294 E3
Glen Park Rd *SEDG* DY3 .... 299 K8
Glen Ri *BUTN/AL/TUT* DE13 .... 185 C5
Glen Rd *SEDG* DY3 .... 299 L4
   STRBR DY8 .... 307 M7
Glenroyd Av *BUCK/MIL* ST2 .... 86 A1
Glenthorne Cl *STAFS* ST17 .... 194 D5 ⬚
Glenthorne Dr *GTWY* WS6 .... 249 L7 ⬚
Glentworth Gdns
   DUNHL/THL/PER WV6 .... 280 B5
Glenwood Cl *LNGTN* ST3 .... 86 B6 ⬚
   NEWUL ST5 .... 83 J1
Glenwood Ri *ALDR* WS9 .... 269 K7
Globe Av *STAFS* ST17 .... 193 L4
Globe St *BURS/TUN* ST6 .... 68 E2
Gloucester Cl *LICH* WS13 .... 236 B7 ⬚
Gloucester Gra *NEWUL* ST5 .... 84 C5 ⬚
Gloucester Rd *ALS/KID* ST7 .... 38 F8
   STPNHL/WNHL DE15 .... 205 H1
Gloucester Wy *CNCK/NC* WS11 . 250 B1
Glovers Cl *HEDN* WS12 .... 233 C5
Glover St *HAN* ST1 .... 2 F2
   HEDN WS12 .... 232 F7
   STAFN ST16 .... 4 D3
Glyme Dr
   DUNHL/THL/PER WV6 .... 279 L5 ⬚
Glyndebourne *CRTAM* B79 ...... 273 K3 ⬚
Glynne Av *KGSWFD* DY6 .... 303 K6
Glyn Pl *BURS/TUN* ST6 .... 53 M7
Gnosall Rd *GNOS* ST20 .... 171 H5
   NWPT TF10 .... 207 K1
Goddard St *LNGTN* ST3 .... 86 C6
Godfrey Rd *BUCK/MIL* ST2 .... 70 B7
Godleybarn La *CDLE* ST10 .... 88 E4
Godley La *CDLE* ST10 .... 88 D6
Godolphin *CRTAM* B79 .... 273 K4
Gofton *TAM/AM/WIL* B77 .... 291 C2
Golborn Av *LNGTN* ST3 .... 103 H5 ⬚
Golborn Cl *LNGTN* ST3 .... 103 H6
Goldcrest *TAM/AM/WIL* B77 ..... 291 G4
Goldcrest Wy *BIDD* ST8 .... 40 E2 ⬚
Goldenhill La *MKTDR* TF9 .... 148 C7
Goldenhill Rd *STOKE* ST4 .... 86 B6
Goldfinch Vw *MKTDR* TF9 .... 114 C7
Goldhurst Dr *CDLE* ST10 .... 105 M8
Goldsborough
   TAM/AM/WIL B77 .... 291 G1
Goldsmith Pl *CRTAM* B79 .... 274 A3 ⬚
   LNGTN ST3 .... 86 D6 ⬚
Goldsmith Rd *BLOX/PEL* WS3 ... 268 A2
Goldstone Rd *MKTDR* TF9 .... 148 B7
Gold St *LNGTN* ST3 .... 86 B7 ⬚
Goldthorn Av
   ETTPK/GDPK/PENN WV4 ... 295 H5
Goldthorn Crs
   ETTPK/GDPK/PENN WV4 ... 295 G4
Goldthorne Av *CNCK/NC* WS11 . 231 M8
Goldthorn Hl
   ETTPK/GDPK/PENN WV4 ... 295 H4
Goldthorn Rd
   ETTPK/GDPK/PENN WV4 ... 295 H4
Golf Links Cl *BURS/TUN* ST6 .... 53 J3
Gomer St *WLNHL* WV13 .... 282 A8
Gomer St West *WLNHL* WV13 ... 282 A8 ⬚
Goms Mill Rd *LNGTN* ST3 .... 86 A8
   LNGTN ST3 .... 102 A1
Goodfellow St *BURS/TUN* ST6 ... 53 K7 ⬚
Goodill Cl *STONE* ST15 .... 137 M5 ⬚
Goodrich Av
   DUNHL/THL/PER WV6 .... 279 C7
Goodson St *HAN* ST1 .... 2 D5
Goods Station La *PENK* ST19 .... 211 L8
Goodwick Cl *STOKE* ST4 .... 101 J5 ⬚
Goodwin Av *NEWUL* ST5 .... 68 B8
Goodwin Rd *LNGTN* ST3 .... 87 H7
Goodwood Av *CDLE* ST10 .... 89 M6
Goodwood Cl
   BUTN/AL/TUT DE13 .... 185 J1 ⬚
   HEDN WS12 .... 233 C5 ⬚
   LICHS WS14 .... 9 K4
Goodwood Pl *STOKE* ST4 .... 101 G3
Goosebridge La *WOLV* WV10 ... 280 C2 ⬚
Goosefield Cl *MKTDR* TF9 .... 130 B1
Goose La *RUGE* WS15 .... 179 M4
Goosemoor Gv *LNGTN* ST3 ...... 103 G3 ⬚
Goose St *NEWUL* ST5 .... 84 B3
Goostry Cl *TAM/AM/WIL* B77 ...... 11 H5
Goostry Rd *TAM/AM/WIL* B77 .... 11 H4
Gordon Av *BURS/TUN* ST6 .... 69 J3 ⬚
   CDLE ST10 .... 89 H7 ⬚
   ETTPK/GDPK/PENN WV4 ... 295 M7
Gordon Crs *HAN* ST1 .... 69 K3
Gordon Rd *BURS/TUN* ST6 .... 53 J4
Gordon St *BKHL/PFLD* WV2 .... 13 H8
   BURS/TUN ST6 .... 69 H1
   BUT DE14 .... 6 E2
   NEWUL ST5 .... 67 L7 ⬚
   WNSFLD WV11 .... 282 B2
Gorey Cl *WNSFLD* WV11 .... 282 B2

Gorge Rd *SEDG* DY3 .... 299 L2
Gorsebrook Leys *STAFN* ST16 .. 174 A5 ⬚
Gorsebrook Rd
   DUNHL/THL/PER WV6 .... 280 C5 ⬚
Gorseburn Wy *RUGE* WS15 .... 197 J3
Gorse Crs *MKTDR* TF9 .... 114 E5
Gorse Dr *HEDN* WS12 .... 231 K5
Gorse La *GNOS* ST20 .... 171 G3
   GNOS ST20 .... 209 K8
   LICH WS13 .... 237 C3
   LICHS WS14 .... 9 L3
   RUGE WS15 .... 215M4
   WMBN WV5 .... 297 C4
Gorsemoor Rd *HEDN* WS12 ...... 250 C1 ⬚
Gorsemoor Wy
   WNSFLD WV11 .... 266 B7 ⬚
Gorse Rd *RUGE* WS15 .... 215M4
   WNSFLD WV11 .... 282 A2
Gorse St *STOKE* ST4 .... 85 L6
Gorseway *BNTWD* WS7 .... 252 B5
Gorsey Bank *BURS/TUN* ST6 .... 54 E4
Gorsey La *CNCK/NC* WS11 .... 249 H1
   CNCK/NC WS11 .... 250 C8
   GTWY WS6 .... 266 F2
Gorsey Wy *ALDR* WS9 .... 284 E5
Gorsley Dl *STAFS* ST17 .... 194 C4
Gorstey Lea *BNTWD* WS7 .... 252 C3
Gorsty Bank *LICHS* WS14 .... 9 L3
Gorsty Hayes *CDSL* WV8 .... 262 F7
Gorsty Hill Rd *CDLE* ST10 .... 105 K6
Gorsty La *RSTAF* ST18 .... 173 C7
Gorsy Bank Rd
   TAM/AM/WIL B77 .... 290 F5
Gorsy La *NWPT* TF10 .... 168 F6
Gort Rd *NEWUL* ST5 .... 67 M6
Gosberryhole La *CONG* CW12 .... 18 A3
Goscote La *BLOX/PEL* WS3 .... 283 M1
Goscote La *BLOX/PEL* WS3 .... 284 A3
Goscote Lodge Crs
   BLOX/PEL WS3 .... 284 A3
Goscote Pl *BLOX/PEL* WS3 .... 284 A3
Goscote Rd *BLOX/PEL* WS3 ..... 283M1
Gosforth Gv *BLYBR/FOR* ST11 .. 103 J3
Gospel Ash Rd *KINVER* DY7 ..... 301 L2
Gospel End Rd *SEDG* DY3 .... 299 H2
Gospel End St *SEDG* DY3 .... 299 K3
Gothersley La *KINVER* DY7 .... 302 D8
Gough Av *WNSFLD* WV11 .... 281 H2
Gough Cl *STAFS* ST16 .... 174 C2
Gough Side *BUT* DE14 .... 7 C6 ⬚
Gough St *WLNHL* WV13 .... 282 C8
   WOLV WV1 .... 13 J5
Gould Firm La *ALDR* WS9 .... 285 L4
Govan Rd *STOKE* ST4 .... 85 L2
Gowan Av *BURS/TUN* ST6 .... 54 A6 ⬚
Gower Rd *SEDG* DY3 .... 299 H1
   STONE ST15 .... 138 B3
Gower St *BKHL/PFLD* WV2 .... 13 J8
   NEWUL ST5 .... 84 C1
   WLNHL WV13 .... 282 A8 ⬚
Gowland Dr *CNCK/NC* WS11 .... 249 H1
Gowy Cl *ALS/KID* ST7 .... 36 F7
Goya Cl *HEDN* WS12 .... 232 C8
Grace St *LEEK* ST13 .... 43 J4 ⬚
Graffam Gv *CDLE* ST10 .... 89M6
Grafton Av *BURS/TUN* ST6 .... 69 H1 ⬚
Grafton Gdns *SEDG* DY3 .... 299 H7
Grafton Rd *LNGTN* ST3 .... 86 C6 ⬚
   STPNHL/WNHL DE15 .... 205 H1
Grafton St *HAN* ST1 .... 2 E3
Graham Cl *BUT* DE14 .... 204 A7
Graham Rd *STRBR* DY8 .... 303 K6
Graham St *BUCK/MIL* ST2 .... 3 L7
Graiseley Hl *BKHL/PFLD* WV2 ... 12 D9
Graiseley La *WNSFLD* WV11 ..... 281 J5
Graiseley Rw *BKHL/PFLD* WV2 .. 12 E9
Graiseley St *BDMR/CCFT* WV3 ... 12 D7
Granary Cl *HEDN* WS12 .... 232 B5
   KGSWFD DY6 .... 303 C2 ⬚
Granary Rd *CDSL* WV8 .... 279 L1
The Granary *ALDR* WS9 .... 285 H3
Granbourne Rd *WSLW* WS2 ...... 282 D6 ⬚
Granchester Cl *LNGTN* ST3 .... 103 H4 ⬚
Grange Av *ALDR* WS9 .... 285 C1
   CNCK/NC WS11 .... 231 M8
   MGN/WHC B75 .... 287 J7 ⬚
   PENK ST19 .... 229 L3
Grange Cl *BUT* DE14 .... 26 C8
   TAM/AM/WIL B77 .... 290 C2 ⬚
Grange Ct *BIDD* ST8 .... 26 C8
   RDERBYSW DE65 .... 167 H5
Grange Crs *PENK* ST19 .... 229 K3
   RUSH/SHEL WS4 .... 284 B2
Grangefield Cl *CDSL* WV8 .... 279 M1 ⬚
   LEEK ST13 .... 57 K6 ⬚
Grangefields *BIDD* ST8 .... 26 E7
Grange Hl *RUGE* WS15 .... 216 C8
Grange La *KGSWFD* DY6 .... 303M6
   LICH WS13 .... 253 J4
   MGN/WHC B75 .... 287 J7
   NEWUL ST5 .... 68 D6
Grange Pk *ALBTN* WV7 .... 260 F4
Grange Rd *ALBTN* WV7 .... 260 F5
   BIDD ST8 .... 26 E7
   BKHL/PFLD WV2 .... 295 H4
   BNTWD WS7 .... 252 A5
   CNCK/NC WS11 .... 251 H4
   DUNHL/THL/PER WV6 .... 279 J5
   GNOS ST20 .... 170 F5
   LEEK ST13 .... 57 J6
   LNGTN ST3 .... 102 F4
   PENK ST19 .... 229 K3
   STONE ST15 .... 138 C3
   SWAD DE11 .... 205 L5
   UTXR ST14 .... 144 A1
Grange St *BURS/TUN* ST6 .... 2 A1
   BUT DE14 .... 6 C4
The Grange *BUT* DE14 .... 6 C5
   BUTN/AL/TUT DE13 .... 218 C4
   LNGTN ST3 .... 87 C8
   RUGE WS15 .... 234 C1
   WMBN WV5 .... 298 A3
Grangewood Av *LNGTN* ST3 ..... 102 F4
Grangewood Rd *LNGTN* ST3 ..... 103 C2
Granstone Cl *BURS/TUN* ST6 ..... 53M3
Grant Cl *KGSWFD* DY6 .... 303 K2
Grantham Pl *BUCK/MIL* ST2 .... 3 M1
Grantley Cl *LNGTN* ST3 .... 102 F1 ⬚

Grantley Crs *KGSWFD* DY6 .... 303 J3
Grantown Gv *GTWY* WS6 .... 267 C6 ⬚
Grant St *BLOX/PEL* WS3 .... 283 H2 ⬚
   STOKE ST4 .... 85 J3 ⬚
Granville Av *BURS/TUN* ST6 .... 69 K3
   NEWUL ST5 .... 84 C1
Granville Cl *BKHL/PFLD* WV2 ...... 13 H8 ⬚
   RDERBYSW DE65 .... 165 K1
Granville Dr *KGSWFD* DY6 .... 303M6
Granville Rd *BUCK/MIL* ST2 .... 70 B6
Granville St *BKHL/PFLD* WV2 ...... 13 H8
   WLNHL WV13 .... 282 A7
Granville Ter *STONE* ST15 .... 138 A1
Grasmere Av
   DUNHL/THL/PER WV6 .... 278 F6 ⬚
   FOAKS/STRLY B74 .... 286 A7
   NEWUL ST5 .... 84 B6
Grasmere Cl
   DUNHL/THL/PER WV6 .... 279 K2
   KGSWFD DY6 .... 303 H3
   STPNHL/WNHL DE15 .... 205 H1
   WNSFLD WV11 .... 281 J3
Grasmere Pl *CNCK/NC* WS11 ... 231 L5
Grasmere Ter *BURS/TUN* ST6 ...... 54 A7
Grassholme *TAM/AM/WIL* B77 ... 291 G2
Grassmere Ct *GTWY* WS6 .... 249 K7 ⬚
Grassmere Dr *STRBR* DY8 .... 307 M7 ⬚
Grassmere Hollow *STAFN* ST16 .. 173M5
Grassygreen La *ALS/KID* ST7 ..... 66 E1
Grassy La *WOLVN* WV10 .... 281 H1
Gratley Cft *HEDN* WS12 .... 231 J6
Gratton La *END/WER* ST9 .... 42 A8
Gratton Rd *BUCK/MIL* ST2 .... 70 D7
Gravel Hl *WMBN* WV5 .... 298 B4
Gravel La *HAN* ST1 .... 231 H4
   STAFS ST17 .... 193 C2
Gravelly Bank Ms *ASHB* DE6 .... 111 K5
Gravelly Hl *MKTDR* TF9 .... 115 C5
Gravelly La *ALDR* WS9 .... 269 L8
Grayling *TAM/AM/WIL* B77 .... 290 D4
Grayling Gv *BURS/TUN* ST6 .... 54 B7
Grayling Willows
   AUD/MAD/W CW3 .... 81 L4 ⬚
Gray Rd *HEDN* WS12 .... 231 M4
Gray's Cl *ALS/KID* ST7 .... 39 H3
Grayshott Rd *BURS/TUN* ST6 ...... 53 L5
Grayston Gv *TAM/AM/WIL* B77 ... 11 J6
Gray Wk *STAFS* ST17 .... 193 J3 ⬚
Grazewood Cl *SHHTH* WV12 .... 282 B5 ⬚
The Grazings *KINVER* DY7 .... 306 C2 ⬚
Greadier St *SHHTH* WV12 .... 282 C5
Greasley Rd *BUCK/MIL* ST2 .... 70 B4
Greatbatch Av *STOKE* ST4 .... 84 F3
Great Brickkiln St
   BDMR/CCFT WV3 .... 12 C7
Great Charles St *BRWNH* WS8 ... 268 F2
Great Checkhill Rd *KINVER* DY7 .. 302 B6
Great Furlong
   BUTN/AL/TUT DE13 .... 220 A8 ⬚
Great Hales St *MKTDR* TF9 .... 130 D1
Great Hampton St *WOLV* WV1 ... 12 D2
Greatmead *TAM/AM/WIL* B77 ... 290 C1
Great Moor Rd
   DUNHL/THL/PER WV6 .... 277 M8
Greatoak Rd *ALS/KID* ST7 .... 51 M6
Great Western St *WOLV* WV1 ..... 13 G3
Great Wood Rd *CDLE* ST10 ...... 105 L6
Greaves Crs *SHHTH* WV12 .... 282 C2
Greaves La *ASHB* DE6 .... 163 K5
   BUTN/AL/TUT DE13 .... 163 L7
Greenacre Cl
   TAM/AM/WIL B77 .... 275 H5 ⬚
Greenacre Dr *CDSL* WV8 .... 263 H8
Greenacres *WMBN* WV5 .... 297 M6 ⬚
Greenacres Av
   BLYBR/FOR ST11 .... 103 J2
   WOLVN WV10 .... 281 H1
Greenacres Cl
   FOAKS/STRLY B74 .... 285 L8
Greenacres Dr *UTXR* ST14 .... 126 A6
The Greenacre *ASHB* DE6 .... 94 F3
Greenbank Gdns *STRBR* DY8 ... 303 L8 ⬚
Greenbank Rd *BURS/TUN* ST6 .... 53 M7
   NEWUL ST5 .... 68 C7
Green Barns La *LICHS* WS14 .... 287 H2
Green Brook Ct *NEWUL* ST5 .... 68 B7 ⬚
Green Cl *BARL* ST12 .... 119 K1
   BLYBR/FOR ST11 .... 103 K3
   DUNHL/THL/PER WV6 .... 277 J8 ⬚
Greencroft *KGSWFD* DY6 .... 303 K6
   LICH WS13 .... 236 A3
Greendale Dr *NEWUL* ST5 .... 67 K1 ⬚
Greendale La *CDLE* ST10 .... 90 D7
Greendock St *LNGTN* ST3 .... 86 B7
Green Dr *ALS/KID* ST7 .... 37 K6
   WOLVN WV10 .... 280 C3
Green Ends La
   RDERBYSW DE65 .... 165 C2
Greenfield *BIDD* ST8 .... 40 D4 ⬚
Greenfield Av *BURS/TUN* ST6 ...... 55 J3 ⬚
   RUGE WS15 .... 217 C6
   STRBR DY8 .... 307 M5
Greenfield Cl *BURS/TUN* ST6 ...... 55 J3 ⬚
Greenfield Crs *CDLE* ST10 .... 89 L6
Greenfield Dr *MSHM* DE12 .... 223 J4
   UTXR ST14 .... 144 A2
Greenfield La *WOLVN* WV10 ..... 264 D5 ⬚
Greenfield Rd *BURS/TUN* ST6 ..... 53 L5
   STAFS ST17 .... 194 D4
Greenfields *ALDR* WS9 .... 285 C3 ⬚
   CNCK/NC WS11 .... 231 L8
   GNOS ST20 .... 190 D3
   SHIF TF11 .... 225 L4
   UTXR ST14 .... 108 D4 ⬚
Greenfields Crs *SHIF* TF11 .... 242 A6 ⬚
Greenfields Rd *END/WER* ST9 ..... 55 L2
   KGSWFD DY6 .... 303 L5
   RSTAF ST18 .... 177 J1
   RUSH/SHEL WS4 .... 268 C4
   WMBN WV5 .... 298 A5
Greenfield Vw *SEDG* DY3 .... 299 H3
Greenfinch Cl *UTXR* ST14 .... 144 C4

Greengate Rd ALS/KID ST7 .... 37 M5
Greengates St BURS/TUN ST6 .... 53 L6
Greengate St STAFN ST16 .... 4 E5
Greenhart TAM/AM/WIL B77 .... 275 C6
Greenhead Crs BUX SK17 .... 35 J8
Greenhead St BURS/TUN ST6 .... 68 F2
Green Heath Rd HEDN WS12 .... 232 A2
Greenhill LICH WS13 .... 9 G3
  WMBN WV5 .... 298 B4
Greenhill Cl SHHTH WV12 .... 282 B5
  TAM/AM/WIL ST2 .... 290 C5
Greenhill Gdns WMBN WV5 .... 298 B5
Greenhill La PENK ST19 .... 227 J4
Greenhill Rd BURS/TUN ST6 .... 54 E4
  SEDG DY3 .... 299 M5 ❶
Greenhill Wy ALDR WS9 .... 285 H1 ❷
Greenhough Rd LICH WS13 .... 8 C2
Greenland Cl KGSWFD DY6 .... 303 L2 ❷
Greenlands WMBN WV5 .... 297 M3 ❷
Green La ALBTN WV7 .... 260 E6
  ALDR WS9 .... 285 L5
  ASHB DE6 .... 49 J8
  ASHB DE6 .... 94 E2
  ASHB DE6 .... 109 M2
  BLOX/PEL WS3 .... 268 A6
  BLOX/PEL WS3 .... 283 J3
  BLYBR/FOR ST11 .... 104 A4
  BNTWD WS7 .... 252 B8
  BNTWD WS7 .... 252 D1
  BUTN/AL/TUT DE13 .... 165 J5
  BUTN/AL/TUT DE13 .... 185 H3
  BUTN/AL/TUT DE13 .... 203 K6
  CDLE ST10 .... 77 C2
  CNCK/NC WS11 .... 249 L4
  DUDN DY1 .... 299 M5
  DUNHL/THL/PER WV6 .... 279 L3
  ECCH ST21 .... 152 E4
  KGSWFD DY6 .... 303 K3
  LEEK ST13 .... 28 F8
  LICH WS13 .... 234 C7
  LICHS WS14 .... 253 K8
  MKTDR TF9 .... 115 J5
  MSHM DE12 .... 223 M6
  MSHM DE12 .... 240 B4
  NWPT TF10 .... 188 E1
  POL/KGSB/FAZ B78 .... 291 K3
  RSTAF ST18 .... 154 F2
  RSTAF ST18 .... 193 J6
  RUGE WS15 .... 197 K8
  RUGE WS15 .... 200 B7
  RUSH/SHEL WS4 .... 268 C7
  UTXR ST14 .... 146 A7
  WSLW WS2 .... 283 J4
Green Lea TAM/AM/WIL B77 .... 291 C3
Greenlea Cl STOKE ST4 .... 101 J5 ❸
Greenleighs SEDG DY3 .... 295 M7
Greenly Rd
  ETTPK/GDPK/PENN WV4 .... 295 K5
Green Meadow
  WNSFLD WV11 .... 281 L5 ❷
Green Meadow Cl WMBN WV5 .... 297 L4
Greenmeadow Gv
  END/WER ST9 .... 55 L4
Green Meadow Rd
  SHHTH WV12 .... 282 B3 ❷
  Green Mdw HEDN WS12 .... 250 C1
Greenmeadows Rd
  AUD/MAD/W CW3 .... 81 L3
Greenmoor Rd BURS/TUN ST6 ..... 54 A2
Green Oak Rd CDSL WV8 .... 263 H8
Greenock Cl NEWUL ST5 .... 83 M3
Green Pk BLYBR/FOR ST11 .... 121 C2 ❶
  CDLE ST10 .... 124 C2 ❸
  ECCH ST21 .... 152 E4
Green Rd RSTAF ST18 .... 157 K8
  STOKE ST4 .... 84 E7
The Green BUT DE14 .... 7 H8
  STRBR DY8 .... 307 M5
  WSLW WS2 .... 283 J7
Greensforge La KINVER DY7 ..... 306 D2
Greenside NEWUL ST5 .... 84 A1
  STONE ST15 .... 136 E4
Greenside Av BUCK/MIL ST2 .... 55 J7
Greenside Cl ALS/KID ST7 .... 53 G3 ❶
Green Slade Gv HEDN WS12 .... 232 C3
Greenslade Rd SEDG DY3 .... 295 H8
Green's La BUCK/MIL ST2 .... 70 E7
Greensleeves FOAKS/STRLY B74.. 286 F8
Greensome Cl STAFN ST16 .... 174 A6
Greensome Crs STAFN ST16 .... 174 A6
Greensome La STAFN ST16 .... 174 A5
Green St BUT DE14 .... 7 H8
  STRBR DY8 .... 307 M5
  WSLW WS2 .... 283 J7
Greensway WNSFLD WV11 .... 281 H2
The Green ALDR WS9 .... 285 J4
  BLOX/PEL WS3 .... 283 H1
  BLYBR/FOR ST11 .... 87 K7
  BLYBR/FOR ST11 .... 121 L1
  BURS/TUN ST6 .... 185 L1 ❶
  BUTN/AL/TUT DE13 .... 220 C1
  CDLE ST10 .... 73 K8
  CDLE ST10 .... 89 H8
  GNOS ST20 .... 170 C2
  LICHS WS14 .... 255 L5
  POL/KGSB/FAZ B78 .... 273 L8
  POL/KGSB/FAZ B78 .... 291 H6
  RSTAF ST18 .... 157 K8
  RUGE WS15 .... 216 A4
  RUGE WS15 .... 217 H5
  STAFS ST17 .... 195 H7
  STAFS ST17 .... 195 J3
  STOKE ST4 .... 84 E2
  STRBR DY8 .... 307 K8
  TAM/AM/WIL B77 .... 275 H4 ❶
Greenvale Cl
  STPNHL/WNHL DE15 .... 204 F2
Greenway ALDR WS9 .... 269 H8
  ALS/KID ST7 .... 37 H5
  ASHB DE6 .... 79 J7
  ECCH ST21 .... 152 E4
  LNGTN ST3 .... 85 L7
  SEDG DY3 .... 299 L1
  STAFN ST16 .... 5 J5
  STOKE ST4 .... 100 E3
  STPNHL/WNHL DE15 .... 186 A6
Greenway Av BURS/TUN ST6 ..... 54 B8

Greenway Bank BIDD ST8 .... 40 D7
  BUCK/MIL ST2 .... 55 H8
Greenway Cl ALS/KID ST7 .... 37 M3
Greenway Gdns
  DUNHL/THL/PER WV6 .... 277 J8
  SEDG DY3 .... 299 L1
Greenway Hall Rd BUCK/MIL ST2.. 55 K7
Greenway Pl BUCK/MIL ST2 .... 70 B3
Greenway Rd BIDD ST8 .... 26 E8
Greenways ALS/KID ST7 .... 51 M8 ❸
  PENK ST19 .... 230 A2
  RSTAF ST18 .... 193 J5
  STOKE ST4 .... 307 J1
Greenways Dr CDLE ST10 .... 89 K6
The Greenway
  DUNHL/THL/PER WV6 .... 277 J8
  HAG/WOL DY9 .... 311 M5
  NEWUL ST5 .... 68 C7
Greenwood Av STOKE ST4 .... 84 E8
Greenwood Cl LICHS WS14 .... 8 F6
Greenwood Gv STAFS ST17 ..... 193 J3 ❶
Greenwood Pk ALDR WS9 .... 285 J1
  HEDN WS12 .... 232 B2
Greenwood Rd ALDR WS9 .... 269 H8
  BLYBR/FOR ST11 .... 104 A2 ❷
  STPNHL/WNHL DE15 .... 204 E2
  WOLVN WV10 .... 280 C3
The Greenwoods STRBR DY8 ... 307 L5 ❸
Gregory La NWPT TF10 .... 169 K5
Gregory Rd STRBR DY8 .... 307 J5
Gregory St LNGTN ST3 .... 86 A6
Greig Ct CNCK/NC WS11 .... 232 C8
Grenadier Cl STOKE ST4 .... 101 J6
Grendon Gdns
  ETTPK/GDPK/PENN WV4 .... 294 D4
Grenfell Rd BLOX/PEL WS3 .... 267 K7
Grenville Cl UTXR ST14 .... 143 M1
  WSLW WS2 .... 282 D7
Grenville Ct SHIF TF11 .... 242 A5 ❶
Grenville St WSLW WS1 .... 2 E2
Gresham Rd CNCK/NC WS11 ..... 231 L1
Gresley Cl MGN/WHC B75 .... 287 G6
Gresley Rw LICH WS13 .... 9 G3
Gresley Wy ALS/KID ST7 .... 51 L8
Gresley Wood Rd SWAD DE11 .. 205 M7
Gresty St STOKE ST4 .... 85 G3
Gretton Av BUTN/AL/TUT DE13 .. 185 L1
Gretton Crs ALDR WS9 .... 284 F5
Gretton Rd ALDR WS9 .... 284 F5
Greville Cl PENK ST19 .... 229 M2
Grey Friars STAFN ST16 .... 4 D1
Greyfriars Cl DUDN DY1 .... 299 L7
Greyfriars Dr CRTAM B79 .... 273 L4 ❶
Grey Friars' Pl STAFN ST16 .... 4 D1
Greyfriars Rd BUCK/MIL ST2 .... 3 L3
Grey Friars Wy STAFN ST16 .... 4 C1
Greyhound La
  ETTPK/GDPK/PENN WV4 .... 293 L5
  STRBR DY8 .... 307 K8
Greyhound Wy HAN ST1 .... 69 C5
Greylarch La STAFS ST17 .... 194 C4
Greysan Av ALS/KID ST7 .... 53 M2 ❷
Greystoke Dr KGSWFD DY6 .... 303 K4
Greyswood Rd STOKE ST4 .... 84 E7 ❷
Grice Rd STOKE ST4 .... 84 E7 ❸
Griffin Cl BNTWD WS7 .... 251 L2
Griffin St LNGTN ST3 .... 86 B6
  WOLV WV1 .... 13 M6
Griffiths Dr WMBN WV5 .... 298 A5
  WNSFLD WV11 .... 281 M1
Griffiths Rd SHHTH WV12 .... 282 D2
Griffiths Wy STONE ST15 .... 138 D4
Grig Pl ALS/KID ST7 .... 37 J5
Grimley Wy CNCK/NC WS11 ..... 231 M6 ❶
Grimstone St WOLVN WV10 .... 13 H3
Grindcobbe Gv RUGE WS15 ..... 197 K8
Grindley Hill Ct STOKE ST4 .... 84 D3
Grindley La BLYBR/FOR ST11 .... 103 L3
  LNGTN ST3 .... 103 G5
  RSTAF ST18 .... 103 G5
Grindsbrook TAM/AM/WIL B77 .. 291 G2
Grisedale Cl LNGTN ST3 .... 103 C3
Grissom Cl STAFN ST16 .... 5 K1
Gristhorpe Wy BUCK/MIL ST2 .. 86 D1 ❶
Gritstone Trail MCFLDS SK11 ..... 19 G7
Gritton St BURS/TUN ST6 .... 53 K8
Grocott Cl PENK ST19 .... 211 L8
Grosvenor Av ALS/KID ST7 .... 37 K5
  STOKE ST4 .... 84 F6
Grosvenor Cl END/WER ST9 .... 55 M2 ❸
  LICHS WS14 .... 9 J7
  PENK ST19 .... 229 M1
  WOLVN WV10 .... 264 D8
Grosvenor Ct MKTDR TF9 ..... 112 D8 ❷
Grosvenor Crs WOLVN WV10 .. 264 D8
Grosvenor Gdns NEWUL ST5 .... 84 C2 ❸
Grosvenor Pk
  ETTPK/GDPK/PENN WV4 .... 294 E4
Grosvenor Pl BURS/TUN ST6 .. 53 K6 ❷
  NEWUL ST5 .... 68 C7
Grosvenor Rd
  ETTPK/GDPK/PENN WV4 .... 295 L7
  LNGTN ST3 .... 102 F1
  MKTDR TF9 .... 112 D8
  NEWUL ST5 .... 84 C2
  SEDG DY3 .... 299 K8
  WOLVN WV10 .... 264 D8
Grosvenor St LEEK ST13 .... 43 M5
  LNGTN ST3 .... 86 B7
  WOLV WV1 .... 13 L3
Grosvenor Wy STAFS ST17 ..... 194 E4
Grotto La
  DUNHL/THL/PER WV6 .... 279 L5
Grotto Rd MKTDR TF9 .... 130 A1
Grounds Dr
  FOAKS/STRLY B74 .... 286 F7 ❶
Grounds Rd FOAKS/STRLY B74.. 286 F7 ❷
Grove Av ALS/KID ST7 .... 38 A6
  ALS/KID ST7 .... 52 E2
  STOKE ST4 .... 85 L5
Grovebank Rd STOKE ST4 .... 84 E7 ❸
  LNGTN ST3 .... 85 L7
Grove Crs AUD/MAD/W CW3 .... 96 C2
Grove Gdns MKTDR TF9 .... 130 D1
Grovelands Crs WOLVN WV10.. 264 D7
Grove La ASHB DE6 .... 145 L1
  BLOX/PEL WS3 .... 267 L1

DUNHL/THL/PER WV6 .... 279 H8
Grove Pk KGSWFD DY6 .... 303 J2
Grove Park Av ALS/KID ST7 .... 38 A6
Grove Pl HAN ST1 .... 2 A8
Grove Rd STOKE ST4 .... 85 K6
  STONE ST15 .... 137 L2
Groveside Wy WNSFLD WV11 .. 281 J2 ❶
Grove St BURS/TUN ST6 .... 69 G4
  LEEK ST13 .... 43 K4
  NEWUL ST5 .... 67 L7
  WOLVN WV10 .... 13 M2
The Grove ALS/KID ST7 .... 38 A6
  BLYBR/FOR ST11 .... 103 L4
  BNTWD WS7 .... 251 K2
  BURS/TUN ST6 .... 54 B8
  BUTN/AL/TUT DE13 .... 203 C3
  ETTPK/GDPK/PENN WV4 .... 295 L5
  FOAKS/STRLY B74 .... 286 D5
  NEWUL ST5 .... 84 B4
  STONE ST15 .... 138 C7
  WNSFLD WV11 .... 281 H4
Grub St GNOS ST20 .... 170 A5
Grunmore Dr
  BUTN/AL/TUT DE13 .... 166 E8
Guernsey Dr NEWUL ST5 .... 83 L6
Guest Av WNSFLD WV11 .... 281 J2
Guild Av BLOX/PEL WS3 .... 283 K3
Guildford St STOKE ST4 .... 85 J2
Guild La NWPT TF10 .... 188 E1
Guild St BUT DE14 .... 7 H5
Guinevere Av
  BUTN/AL/TUT DE13 .... 166 E8
Gun Battery La BIDD ST8 .... 41 C2
Gunby Hl MSHM DE12 .... 241 M1
Gungate CRTAM B79 .... 10 D3
Gunnell Cl STAFN ST16 .... 4 A6
Gunn St BIDD ST8 .... 40 C2
Gunstone La CDSL WV8 .... 262 F5
Gurnard TAM/AM/WIL B77 .... 290 D4 ❶
Gurnard Cl WNSFLD WV11 .... 282 B1
Gurney Pl WSLW WS2 .... 283 C5
Gurney Rd WSLW WS2 .... 283 C5
Guthrum Cl
  DUNHL/THL/PER WV6 .... 278 F5 ❶
Guy Av WOLVN WV10 .... 280 D4
Guy La CRTAM B79 .... 273 M3 ❷
Guy's La SEDG DY3 .... 299 H8
Guy St BUCK/MIL ST2 .... 70 B6
Gwendoline Wy ALDR WS9 .... 269 H6
Gwenys Crs LNGTN ST3 .... 85 L6
Gwyn Av BIDD ST8 .... 40 D4
Gypsum Wy ASHB DE6 .... 163 K4 ❷

H

Hackett Cl BILS/COS WV14 .... 299 M1
Hackford Rd
  ETTPK/GDPK/PENN WV4 .... 295 M6
Hackwood Cl BARL ST12 .... 101 M6 ❶
Hadden Cl END/WER ST9 .... 71 H8
Hadden Ct ASHB DE6 .... 95 K2
Hadden Crs SHHTH WV12 .... 282 C3
Haddon Gv NEWUL ST5 .... 67 M4 ❸
Haddon La NEWUL ST5 .... 116 D1
Haddon Pl BUCK/MIL ST2 .... 70 C5
  STONE ST15 .... 138 D3
Haden Cl STRBR DY8 .... 303 K8
Haden Crs WNSFLD WV11 .... 281 M4
Haden Hl BDMR/CCFT WV3 .... 12 A5
Hadleigh Cl NEWUL ST5 .... 84 B8 ❸
Hadleigh Rd BUCK/MIL ST2 .... 70 B4
Hadley Av STOKE ST4 .... 84 A8
Hadley St BUTN/AL/TUT DE13 .. 200 F7
Hadrians Cl
  TAM/AM/WIL B77 .... 290 D2 ❶
Hadrian Wy NEWUL ST5 .... 67 K4
Haggar St BKHL/PFLD WV2 .... 295 J4
Hagley Dr RUGE WS15 .... 215 K1
Hagley Park Gdns
  RUGE WS15 .... 215 K3 ❶
Hagley Rd RUGE WS15 .... 215 K1
Haig Cl CNCK/NC WS11 .... 232 A5
Haigh Ct LEEK ST13 .... 57 K5
Haig Rd LEEK ST13 .... 44 A3
Haig St LNGTN ST3 .... 86 D8
Hailes Park Cl BKHL/PFLD WV2 .. 295 K4
Hailsham Cl BURS/TUN ST6 .... 53 L5
Hainult Cl STRBR DY8 .... 303 K6
Halcyon Wy BUT DE14 .... 6 C3
Halecroft Av WNSFLD WV11 ... 281 K5 ❶
Hales Cl SHIF TF11 .... 224 B5
Hales Hall Rd CDLE ST10 .... 89 L6
Hales Pl LNGTN ST3 .... 102 C1
Halesworth Crs NEWUL ST5 .... 84 B8
Halesworth Rd COVEN WV9 ..... 263 M8
Haley St SHHTH WV12 .... 282 C5
Halford Crs BLOX/PEL WS3 .... 283 M5
Halford St CRTAM B79 .... 10 A4
Halfway Pl NEWUL ST5 .... 67 L8
Halifax Cl BLYBR/FOR ST11 .... 103 J3
Halifax Rd ALBTN WV7 .... 260 F1
Haliford Av HAN ST1 .... 69 K3
Haling Cl PENK ST19 .... 229 M2
Haling Rd PENK ST19 .... 229 M1
Hallahan Cl STONE ST15 .... 138 C4
Hallam Crs WOLVN WV10 .... 280 E4
Hallam Rd UTXR ST14 .... 143 M1
Hallams Rw BUT DE14 .... 6 F3
Hallam St STOKE ST4 .... 85 K4
Hall Av LEEK ST13 .... 44 A3
Hall Bank BUX SK17 .... 34 D5
Hallbridge Cl BLOX/PEL WS3 ... 267 M8
Hall Cl DUNHL/THL/PER WV6 ... 277 J8 ❶
  STAFS ST17 .... 194 A3
Hallcourt Cl CNCK/NC WS11 ... 249 L2 ❷
Hallcourt Crs CNCK/NC WS11 .. 249 L2
Hallcourt La CNCK/NC WS11 ... 249 L2
Halldearn Av BLYBR/FOR ST11 .. 87 K7 ❶
Hall End Cl
  DUNHL/THL/PER WV6 .... 277 J8 ❷
Hall End La
  DUNHL/THL/PER WV6 .... 277 J8

Hallet Dr BDMR/CCFT WV3 .... 12 D7
Hallfarm Cl PENK ST19 .... 246 D4 ❷
Hall Farm Crs RSTAF ST18 .... 156 F6
Hallfarm Rd PENK ST19 .... 246 D4
Hallfield Gv BLOX/PEL WS3 .... 53 L5
Hallfields Rd SWAD DE11 .... 205 K6
Hall Gdns UTXR ST14 .... 145 L8
Hall Green Av
  BUTN/AL/TUT DE13 .... 166 E8
Hall Hill Dr BUCK/MIL ST2 .... 86 D2
Hall Hill La RUGE WS15 .... 180 A5
Hall La ALDR WS9 .... 268 E8
  ASHB DE6 .... 79 J8
  ASHB DE6 .... 92 F3
  ASHB DE6 .... 145 H1
  BILS/COS WV14 .... 299 M1
  BLOX/PEL WS3 .... 267 M7
  BNTWD WS7 .... 252 E6
  ECCH ST21 .... 117 K7
  GTWY WS6 .... 249 M6
  STONE ST15 .... 118 D7
  STONE ST15 .... 122 A7
Hall Meadow CNCK/NC WS11 .. 249 H4
Hall Orch CDLE ST10 .... 89 K7
Hall Pl NEWUL ST5 .... 68 D5
Hall Ri ASHB DE6 .... 79 K7
Hall Rd BUTN/AL/TUT DE13 .... 166 A6
  UTXR ST14 .... 144 A2
  UTXR ST14 .... 145 L7
Halls Rd ALS/KID ST7 .... 39 J4
  BIDD ST8 .... 40 C1
Hall St ALS/KID ST7 .... 51 K8
  BURS/TUN ST6 .... 68 E2
  NEWUL ST5 .... 68 C3
  SEDG DY3 .... 299 K2 ❸
  WNSFLD WV11 .... 281 J5
  WSLW WS2 .... 283 K7
Halston Rd BNTWD WS7 .... 252 B2 ❷
Halton Gn LNGTN ST3 .... 101 L2
Haltonlea TAM/AM/WIL B77 ..... 291 G2
Hambledon Cl COVEN WV9 ..... 264 A8 ❸
  COVEN WV9 .... 264 A8 ❷
Hamble Gv
  DUNHL/THL/PER WV6 .... 278 E6
Hamble Rd
  ETTPK/GDPK/PENN WV4 .... 294 C4
Hambleton Cl ASHB DE6 .... 95 J2
Hambleton Pl BIDD ST8 .... 40 B5 ❶
Hamble Wy BUCK/MIL ST2 ..... 86 D1 ❶
Hambridge Cl STAFS ST17 .... 193 K3
Hambrook Cl
  DUNHL/THL/PER WV6 .... 280 A1
Hambro Pl BURS/TUN ST6 .... 54 B3
Hamelin St CNCK/NC WS11 ..... 231 L7
Hames La CRTAM B79 .... 259 K6
Hamil Dr LEEK ST13 .... 43 K4
Hamil Rd BURS/TUN ST6 .... 69 J1
Hamilton Av STRBR DY8 .... 307 K4 ❸
Hamilton Cl HEDN WS12 .... 232 F6 ❶
  SEDG DY3 .... 299 J2 ❸
  STRBR DY8 .... 303 J8
Hamilton Dr STRBR DY8 .... 303 J8
Hamilton Flds
  STPNHL/WNHL DE15 .... 186 A8
Hamilton Gdns WOLVN WV10 .. 264 E7 ❸
Hamilton Lea CNCK/NC WS11 .. 251 C4 ❶
Hamilton Ri BUCK/MIL ST2 .... 55 H8
Hamilton Rd LNGTN ST3 .... 86 D8
  STPNHL/WNHL DE15 .... 186 A8 ❶
Hamilton St BLOX/PEL WS3 ..... 283 J7
  STOKE ST4 .... 85 J5 ❸
Ham La KGSWFD DY6 .... 303 L1
The Hamlet CNCK/NC WS11 ..... 250 A8
Hamlett Pl BURS/TUN ST6 .... 54 E7
Hammersley Hayes Rd
  CDLE ST10 .... 89 L4
Hammersley St HAN ST1 .... 3 G1
Hammerton Av BUCK/MIL ST2 ..... 3 K9
Hammerwich La BNTWD WS7 .. 252 D7
Hammerwich Rd BNTWD WS7 .. 252 D4
Hammond Av BURS/TUN ST6 ..... 55 H3
  WOLVN WV10 .... 280 C2
Hammond Rd NEWUL ST5 .... 67 L2
Hammonds Cl RSTAF ST18 ..... 177 J2 ❸
Hammoon Gv BURS/TUN ST6 .. 70 B8 ❸
Hamps Cl BNTWD WS7 .... 252 B2
Hampshire Cl END/WER ST9 ..... 55 M3
  POL/KGSB/FAZ B78 .... 273 M6
Hampstead Cl WNSFLD WV11 .. 281 J4
Hampstead Gv STOKE ST4 ..... 101 J3 ❸
Hamps Valley Rd CDLE ST10 ..... 60 F8
Hampton Dr NWPT TF10 .... 188 A7
Hampton Gn CNCK/NC WS11 .. 249 K3
Hampton Gv BLOX/PEL WS3 ... 267 M6
  KINVER DY7 .... 306 B6
Hampton Rd WOLVN WV10 ..... 280 B1
Hampton St CNCK/NC WS11 ... 249 K3
  HAN ST1 .... 2 E9
Hams Cl BIDD ST8 .... 40 C3
Hanbridge Av NEWUL ST5 .... 68 A3
Hanbury Crs
  ETTPK/GDPK/PENN WV4 .... 294 E4
Hanbury Hl BUTN/AL/TUT DE13.. 164 A5 ❶
Hanbury Rd BRWNH WS8 .... 251 L8
  CNCK/NC WS11 .... 250 F5
  TAM/AM/WIL B77 .... 275 L4
Hanchurch Cl
  STPNHL/WNHL DE15 .... 186 A6 ❶
Hancock St STOKE ST4 .... 85 J3 ❸
Handel Ct CNCK/NC WS11 .... 232 C8
Handel Gv HAN ST1 .... 3 L1
Hand La SHIF TF11 .... 224 B5
Handley Banks BLYBR/FOR ST11.. 87 L7 ❶
Handley Dr BIDD ST8 .... 40 B8
Handley St ALS/KID ST7 .... 40 A8
Handsacre Cl SWAD DE11 .... 205 M7
Handsacre Crs RUGE WS15 ..... 217 C3 ❶
Handscross Rd NEWUL ST5 .... 86 C5
Hand St BURS/TUN ST6 .... 53 L8
Hangman's La CRTAM B79 .... 259 G8
Hanley Rd BURS/TUN ST6 .... 69 J1
Hanlith TAM/AM/WIL B77 .... 291 C2
Hannaford Wy CNCK/NC WS11.. 231 M8
Hanney Hay Rd BNTWD WS7 .. 252 B7
Hanover Ct
  DUNHL/THL/PER WV6 .... 279 J6

Hanover Pl CNCK/NC WS11 ... 231 L8 ❷
Hanover St HAN ST1 .... 2 C5
  HAN ST1 .... 84 C7
Hanyards La RSTAF ST18 .... 175 M6 ❶
Harald Cl DUNHL/THL/PER WV6.. 278 E5 ❶
Harber St BUT DE14 .... 86 C7
Harbin Rd MSHM DE12 .... 221 K2
Harborne Rd CDLE ST10 .... 89 K6
Harborough Dr ALDR WS9 .... 285 C5
Harbourne Crs CDLE ST10 .... 89 L6 ❶
Harbury St BUTN/AL/TUT DE13 .. 185 C4
Harcourt Av LNGTN ST3 .... 102 F1
Harcourt Dr DUDN DY1 .... 299 K8
  FOAKS/STRLY B74 .... 286 E6
  NWPT TF10 .... 188 A6
Harcourt Rd BUT DE14 .... 203 M2 ❶
Harcourt St HAN ST1 .... 85 H7
Harcourt Wy STAFN ST16 .... 174 A8 ❶
Harden Cl BLOX/PEL WS3 .... 283 J3
Harden Gv BLOX/PEL WS3 .... 283 J3
Harden Rd BLOX/PEL WS3 .... 283 K3
Hardie Av RUGE WS15 .... 215 L3
Hardie Gn CNCK/NC WS11 .... 231 M7 ❷
Hardinge St STOKE ST4 .... 85 K4
Harding Rd HAN ST1 .... 2 E8
Harding's La BUX SK17 .... 35 G5
Hardings Meadow ALS/KID ST7 .. 38 C5
Hardingswood Rd ALS/KID ST7.. 38 C4
Hardings Ter STOKE ST4 .... 85 G4 ❶
Hardman St BUCK/MIL ST2 .... 70 A7
Hardon Rd
  ETTPK/GDPK/PENN WV4 .... 295 M5
Hardwick Cl STOKE ST4 .... 101 J6
Hardwick Rd FOAKS/STRLY B74.. 285 M6
Hardy Cl BUTN/AL/TUT DE13 ... 220 E7
  CDLE ST10 .... 89 J8
Hardy Rd BLOX/PEL WS3 .... 283 L2
Hardy Sq BKHL/PFLD WV2 ..... 295 M4 ❸
Hardy St BURS/TUN ST6 .... 53 K6
Harebell TAM/AM/WIL B77 .... 275 G6
Harebell Cl HEDN WS12 .... 232 D8
  WOLVN WV10 .... 265 G3 ❸
Harecastle Av ALS/KID ST7 ..... 52 D1 ❸
Haregate Rd LEEK ST13 .... 44 A3
Harehedge La
  BUTN/AL/TUT DE13 .... 185 H2
Hareshaw Gv BURS/TUN ST6 .. 54 A2
Harewood Cl CDLE ST10 .... 89 K6 ❶
Harewood Rd BURS/TUN ST6 .. 53 K3
Hargate Rd
  STPNHL/WNHL DE15 .... 205 J1
Hargreave Rd LEEK ST13 .... 43 M7
Hargreaves La STAFS ST17 .... 4 C8
Harington Dr LNGTN ST3 .... 86 E5
Harland Rd
  FOAKS/STRLY B74 .... 287 G7 ❶
Harlaxton St
  BUTN/AL/TUT DE13 .... 185 G4
Harlech Av LNGTN ST3 .... 102 F1
Harlech Dr BIDD ST8 .... 40 C4
Harlech Rd SHHTH WV12 .... 282 C4
Harlech Wy BUTN/AL/TUT DE13.. 185 K2
  DUDN DY1 .... 299 M6
Harlequin Dr BURS/TUN ST6 ..... 54 F8
Harley Cl BRWNH WS8 .... 285 J2
  RUGE WS15 .... 215 M4 ❸
Harley La RUGE WS15 .... 179 M2 ❸
  STOKE ST4 .... 118 C7 ❸
Harley St HAN ST1 .... 2 E6
Harley Thorn La STOKE ST4 ... 99 M6 ❸
Harmon Rd STRBR DY8 .... 307 J3
Harmony Gn STAFS ST17 .... 193 H2
Harney Ct RUGE WS15 .... 197 K2 ❸
Harold St BURS/TUN ST6 .... 69 J1
Harper Av BUTN/AL/TUT DE13 .. 185 J3
  NEWUL ST5 .... 68 B6
  WNSFLD WV11 .... 281 J2
Harper St BURS/TUN ST6 .... 68 E3
  WLNHL WV13 .... 282 A8
Harplow La CDLE ST10 .... 105 G7
Harpur Cl RUSH/SHEL WS4 ..... 284 A6
Harpur Crs ALS/KID ST7 .... 37 H5
Harpur Rd RUSH/SHEL WS4 ... 284 A6
Harrier Cl LNGTN ST3 .... 103 G4
Harrietts Hayes Rd CDSL WV8 .. 261 L4
Harringay Dr STRBR DY8 .... 307 L3 ❸
Harrington St LNGTN ST3 .... 86 E5 ❸
Harriseahead La ALS/KID ST7 .. 39 K7
Harrison Cl ALS/KID ST7 .... 66 D1 ❸
  BLOX/PEL WS3 .... 283 J1
  BUT DE14 .... 204 B2
  GTWY WS6 .... 266 D1 ❶
Harrison Rd BURS/TUN ST6 ..... 54 E7
  CNCK/NC WS11 .... 249 L3
  FOAKS/STRLY B74 .... 286 E5
  RUSH/SHEL WS4 .... 268 C4
Harrisons La PENK ST19 .... 247 L1 ❶
Harrison St BLOX/PEL WS3 ..... 283 J1
  NEWUL ST5 .... 84 C2 ❸
Harrison Wy LEEK ST13 .... 57 K5
Harris St STAFN ST16 .... 5 K5
Harrogate Gv NEWUL ST5 ...... 66 F8 ❶
Harrop St HAN ST1 .... 2 F8
Harrop Wy STRBR DY8 .... 307 L2 ❸
Harrots La BUX SK17 .... 34 D4
Harrowby Dr NEWUL ST5 .... 83 M6 ❸
Harrowby Rd LNGTN ST3 .... 103 G2
  WOLVN WV10 .... 264 B7
Harrowby St STAFN ST16 .... 5 K5
Harrow Crs ALBTN WV7 .... 260 B8
Harrow Dr BUT DE14 .... 204 C3
Harrow Pl STONE ST15 .... 138 C3
Harrow Rd KGSWFD DY6 .... 303 K1 ❶
Harrow St WOLV WV1 .... 12 D7 ❶
Harry Perks St WLNHL WV13 .. 282 A7
Hart Cl NEWUL ST5 .... 84 B1 ❶
Hartill Rd
  ETTPK/GDPK/PENN WV4 .... 294 D7
Hartill St STOKE ST4 .... 85 J5
Hartington St LEEK ST13 .... 43 L5
  NEWUL ST5 .... 67 L8
Hartland Av BURS/TUN ST6 .... 54 C6
Hartland St LEEK ST13 .... 194 E3
Hartlands Rd ECCH ST21 .... 152 E3 ❸
Hartley Cl HEDN WS12 .... 232 C7 ❶
Hartleyburn
  TAM/AM/WIL B77 .... 291 G2 ❶
Hartley Dr ALDR WS9 .... 285 H6
Hartley St BDMR/CCFT WV3 ..... 12 D1 ❶

Hart Rd *WNSFLD* WV11 .... 281 K6
Hartsbourne Rd *STAFS* ST17 ...... 194 B3
Hartshill Rd *STOKE* ST4 .... 84 E2
Hartshorne Rd
  RDERBYSW DE65 .... 187 L2
Hartslade *LICHS* WS14 .... 9 M6
Hartwell Cl *STAFN* ST16 .... 174 A3
  STONE ST15 .... 102 A8
Hartwell La *GTWY* WS6 .... 250 A7 🔒
  STONE ST15 .... 102 A8
Hartwell Rd *LNGTN* ST3 .... 103 G1
Harvard Cl *DUDN* DY1 .... 299 M6 🔒
Harvest Cl *SEDG* DY3 .... 299 L5
Harvesters Cl
  FOAKS/STRLY B74 .... 285 L8 🔒
Harvesters Rd *SHHTH* WV12 ...... 282 D5
Harvester Wy *KGSWFD* DY6 ...... 303 G2 🔒
Harvey Av *MGN/WHC* B75 .... 287 J8
Harvey Pl *UTXR* ST14 .... 144 B1
Harvey Rd *BUT* DE14 .... 204 A2
  LNGTN ST3 .... 87 H8
  RUGE WS15 .... 217 J3
  WSLW WS2 .... 283 H5
Harvine Wk *STRBR* DY8 .... 307 L7
Harwell Cl *CRTAM* B79 .... 274 C3 🔒
Harwin Cl
  DUNHL/THL/PER WV6 .... 279 M3
Harwood Av *BUT* DE14 .... 203 M2
Harwood Drive
  TAM/AM/WIL B77 .... 290 D6
Harwood Rd *LICH* WS13 .... 236 B7
Haslemere Av *BUCK/MIL* ST2 ..... 70 B1
Haslington Cl *STAFS* ST17 .... 67 K1 🔒
Hassall Rd *ALS/KID* ST7 .... 37 H4
  RDERBYSW DE65 .... 165 K1
  SBCH CW11 .... 36 E2
  SBCH CW11 .... 36 A3
Hassall St *HAN* ST1 .... 2 E6
Hassam Av *NEWUL* ST5 .... 68 A3
Hassam Pde *NEWUL* ST5 .... 68 B5
Hassell St *NEWUL* ST5 .... 84 C2
Haste Hill La *CDLE* ST10 .... 73 M8
Hastings Cl *TAM/AM/WIL* B77 .... 290 F4
Hastings Ct *DUDN* DY1 .... 299 L8 🔒
Hatchett La *CRTAM* B79 .... 239 J5
Hatch Heath Cl *WMBN* WV5 ..... 297 M3
Hatch La *SHIF* TF11 .... 225 K7
Hateley Dr
  ETTPK/GDPK/PENN WV4 ..... 295 L6
Hatfield Crs *NEWUL* ST5 .... 84 C2
Hathaway Rd *MGN/WHC* B75 .... 287 G6
Hathersage Cl *LICH* WS13 .... 86 C5 🔒
Hatherton Cl *NEWUL* ST5 .... 52 D8
Hatherton Cft *CNCK/NC* WS11 ... 249 L1
Hatherton Gdns
  WOLVN WV10 .... 264 E8 🔒
Hatherton Pl *ALDR* WS9 .... 285 C5
Hatherton Rd *CNCK/NC* WS11 ... 249 H1
  PENK ST19 .... 229 M1 🔒
  WSL WS1 .... 283 L8 🔒
Hatherton St *GTWY* WS6 .... 249 J8
  RUSH/SHEL WS4 .... 283 L7
  STAFN ST16 .... 5 J5
Hatrell St *NEWUL* ST5 .... 84 C2
Hatton Crs *WNSFLD* WV11 .... 281 C3
Hatton Rd *BDMR/CCFT* WV3 .... 279 M7 🔒
  CNCK/NC WS11 .... 249 C1
Hattons Gv *CDSL* WV8 .... 263 H8 🔒
Havefield Av *LICHS* WS14 .... 9 K4
Havelet Dr *NEWUL* ST5 .... 83 M7
Havelock Cl
  BDMR/CCFT WV3 .... 294 F2 🔒
Havelock Gv *BIDD* ST8 .... 40 C3
Havelock Pl *HAN* ST1 .... 2 A9
Haven Av *BURS/TUN* ST6 .... 69 K2
Haven Crs *END/WER* ST9 .... 71 H6 🔒
Haven Gv *NEWUL* ST5 .... 68 C3
The Haven *BKHL/PFLD* WV2 .... 12 F9
  STRBR DY8 .... 303 K8
Haverhill Cl *BLOX/PEL* WS3 ...... 267 C7
Hawbush Rd *BLOX/PEL* WS3 .... 283 L4
Hawcroft *RUGE* WS15 .... 216 F8
Hawes St *BURS/TUN* ST6 .... 53 K6
Haweswater Dr
  KGSWFD DY6 .... 303 K4 🔒
Hawfield La
  STPNHL/WNHL DE15 .... 186 D6
Hawfinch *TAM/AM/WIL* B77 ..... 291 C5 🔒
Hawfinch Rd *CDLE* ST10 .... 89 L7
Hawk Cl *LNGTN* ST3 .... 103 C5
Hawke Rd *STAFN* ST16 .... 174 C3
Hawkesmoor Dr *LICHS* WS14 ...... 9 K4
Hawkesmore Dr *RSTAF* ST18 ..... 196 D3
Hawkestone Cl *NEWUL* ST5 ...... 84 C2 🔒
Hawkins Cl *LICH* WS13 .... 236 B8 🔒
Hawkins Cl *CNCK/NC* WS11 ..... 249 J6
Hawkins La *BUT* DE14 .... 7 H3
  RSTAF ST18 .... 140 F8
Hawkins St *STOKE* ST4 .... 85 J4
Hawkley Cl *WOLV* WV1 .... 281 H8 🔒
Hawkley Rd *WOLV* WV1 .... 281 H8
Hawks Cl *GTWY* WS6 .... 249 K8
Hawksdale Cl *LNGTN* ST3 .... 103 C5
Hawk's Dr *STPNHL/WNHL* DE15 .. 186 D7
Hawksford Crs *WOLVN* WV10 .... 280 D3
Hawks Green La
  CNCK/NC WS11 .... 232 A8
Hawkside *TAM/AM/WIL* B77 ..... 291 H2
Hawksley Dr
  BUTN/AL/TUT DE13 .... 166 B6
Hawksmoor Cl *LNGTN* ST3 ...... 102 E3
Hawksmoor Dr
  DUNHL/THL/PER WV6 .... 278 D7
Hawksmoor Rd *STAFS* ST17 ..... 193 L3
Hawkstone Cl *CDSL* WV8 .... 278 D5
Hawkswell *WMBN* WV5 .... 298 A5 🔒
Hawksworth Av *LICHS* WS14 ...... 43 K6
Hawksworth Cl *LEEK* ST13 .... 43 K6 🔒
Hawkyard Cl *CNCK/NC* WS11 ... 232 A6 🔒
Hawley Cl *STONE* ST15 .... 138 C5 🔒
Hawksford Crs *WOLVN* WV10 .... 280 D3
Hawthorn Av *GTWY* WS6 .... 267 G1 🔒
  MSHM DE12 .... 241 M3
  STONE ST15 .... 137 M5
Hawthorn Cl *ASHB* DE6 .... 95 K2 🔒
  ASHB DE6 .... 145 H1
  GNOS ST20 .... 190 E3
  LICH WS13 .... 9 J3
  RDERBYSW DE65 .... 166 D1
  RSTAF ST18 .... 154 B8
  RSTAF ST18 .... 191 L4

Hawthorn Crs
  STPNHL/WNHL DE15 .... 204 F4
Hawthornden Av *UTXR* ST14 ..... 143 M2
Hawthornden Cl *UTXR* ST14 ..... 144 A2 🔒
Hawthornden Gdns *UTXR* ST14 .. 143 M2
Hawthorne Av *ALS/KID* ST7 .... 66 F1 🔒
  CRTAM B79 .... 274 A2
  STOKE ST4 .... 84 E5
Hawthorne Cl *CDLE* ST10 .... 105 L7
Hawthorne Crs *BNTWD* WS7 .... 252 A4
Hawthorne Dr *PENK* ST19 .... 227 J4
Hawthorne Gv *SEDG* DY3 .... 299 K8 🔒
Hawthorne La *CDSL* WV8 .... 278 E1
Hawthorne Rd
  BKHL/PFLD WV2 .... 295 K4 🔒
  GTWY WS6 .... 249 L6
  HEDN WS12 .... 231 K2
  HEDN WS12 .... 232 F7
  PENK ST19 .... 227 J4
  SHHTH WV12 .... 282 D3
  WNSFLD WV11 .... 266 A7 🔒
  WNSFLD WV11 .... 281 M5
Hawthorne Wy *KINVER* DY7 ..... 306 C7
Hawthorn Gdns *ALS/KID* ST7 .... 52 D7
Hawthorn Pl *LNGTN* ST3 .... 102 F1
  WSLW WS2 .... 282 E7
Hawthorn Ri *SWAD* DE11 .... 205 M3 🔒
Hawthorn Rd *NEWUL* ST5 .... 67 L1
  RUSH/SHEL WS4 .... 284 B2
Hawthorn St *BURS/TUN* ST6 ...... 69 C4
Hawthorn Wy *RUGE* WS15 ...... 215 K1
  STAFS ST17 .... 5 K8
Haybank La *CDLE* ST10 .... 91 L5
The Hay Barns *STONE* ST15 ...... 118 B6
The Haybarn *STAFS* ST16 .... 174 F3
Haybridge Av *STRBR* DY8 .... 311 M5
Haycroft Dr *MGN/WHC* B75 ..... 287 G6
Haydock Cl *BUT* DE14 .... 204 A3 🔒
  CDLE ST10 .... 89 L5
  DUNHL/THL/PER WV6 .... 280 B5 🔒
Haydon St *STOKE* ST4 .... 68 E8
Hay End La *BUTN/AL/TUT* DE13 .. 237 H2
Hayes Cl *LEEK* ST13 .... 43 M4
Hayes Rd *KIDDW* DY11 .... 309 J7
Hayes St *BURS/TUN* ST6 .... 54 C8
The Hayes *SHHTH* WV12 .... 282 B4
Hayes Vw *LICH* WS13 .... 8 A1
Hayes View Dr *GTWY* WS6 .... 249 L6
Hayes Wy *CNCK/NC* WS11 ...... 250 A1
  HEDN WS12 .... 250 C1
Hayeswood La *ALS/KID* ST7 .... 66 E4 🔒
Hayfield Crs *STOKE* ST4 .... 85 L3
Hayfield Hl *RUGE* WS15 .... 233 M6
Hayfield Rd *NEWUL* ST5 .... 83 H1
Hayhead Cl *ALS/KID* ST7 .... 39 H8
Hay La *ASHB* DE6 .... 92 E6
  RDERBYSW DE65 .... 147 L4
  RUGE WS15 .... 235 C3
Hayling Cv *BKHL/PFLD* WV2 .... 295 H4 🔒
Haymarket *BURS/TUN* ST6 .... 53 K7 🔒
Haymoor *LICHS* WS14 .... 9 L5
Hayner Gv *LNGTN* ST3 .... 87 H6
Hayrick Dr *KGSWFD* DY6 .... 303 H3 🔒
Hays La *LEEK* ST13 .... 60 F7
Haywain Cl *COVEN* WV9 .... 263 M8 🔒
Haywards Cl *BLOX/PEL* WS3 .... 267 M7
Haywood Dr
  DUNHL/THL/PER WV6 .... 279 J6
Haywood Gra *RSTAF* ST18 .... 196 D3
Haywood Hts *RSTAF* ST18 .... 196 D3
Haywood La *MKTDR* TF9 .... 148 D2
Haywood Rd *BURS/TUN* ST6 .... 54 A8
Haywood St *LEEK* ST13 .... 43 L5
  STOKE ST4 .... 85 H1
Hayworth Cl *CRTAM* B79 .... 273 M7
Hayworth Rd *LICH* WS13 .... 236 C8 🔒
Hazel Cl *ALS/KID* ST7 .... 39 H7
  ASHB DE6 .... 95 K2
  STOKE ST4 .... 84 F5
  UTXR ST14 .... 144 B4
Hazeldene Rd *STOKE* ST4 .... 101 J3
Hazel Dr *HEDN* WS12 .... 233 C4
  RUGE WS15 .... 217 H6
Hazel Gdns *CDSL* WV8 .... 263 C6 🔒
Hazelgarth *TAM/AM/WIL* B77 ... 291 C2
Hazel Gv *ALS/KID* ST7 .... 38 A7
  BIDD ST8 .... 41 H1 🔒
  LEEK ST13 .... 43 J5
  LICHS WS14 .... 9 C5
  LNGTN ST3 .... 86 F8
  STAFN ST16 .... 174 C2
  STRBR DY8 .... 307 J7
  WMBN WV5 .... 298 A3
Hazelhurst Dr *LEEK* ST13 .... 57 K5
Hazelhurst Rd *BURS/TUN* ST6 ... 53 M4
Hazelhurst St *HAN* ST1 .... 2 E8
Hazel La *GTWY* WS6 .... 250 B8
Hazelmere Dr
  BDMR/CCFT WV3 .... 294 A1 🔒
  BNTWD WS7 .... 251 M6
Hazel Rd *BDMR/CCFT* WV3 ..... 294 C3
  KGSWFD DY6 .... 303 L5
  NEWUL ST5 .... 67 K2
Hazelwood Cl *BURS/TUN* ST6 ... 69 J4
  GTWY WS6 .... 249 K8 🔒
Hazelwood Dr *WNSFLD* WV11 .. 281 C5
Hazelwood Gv *SHHTH* WV12 .... 282 D5
Hazelwood Rd *DUDN* DY1 ...... 299 M5 🔒
  END/WER ST9 .... 71 J6
  STPNHL/WNHL DE15 .... 204 E4 🔒
Hazlemere Gv *CNCK/NC* WS11 .. 249 H2
Hazlescross Rd *CDLE* ST10 .... 73 K7
Hazlestrine La *STAFS* ST17 .... 194 D5
Hazleton Gn *STAFS* ST17 .... 193 K4
Hazlitt Wy *LNGTN* ST3 .... 86 E5
Headland Rd *BDMR/CCFT* WV3 . 293 M1
The Headlands
  FOAKS/STRLY B74 .... 286 C7
Headland Wy *CDLE* ST10 .... 107 M1 🔒
Heakley Av *SWAD* DE11 .... 205 M4
Healey La *AUD/MAD/W* CW3 ... 65 L2
The Heights *LEEK* ST13 .... 43 H8
Helenny Cl *WOLVN* WV10 .... 281 H2
Healey Av *BIDD* ST8 .... 40 B3
Hearthcote Rd *SWAD* DE11 ..... 205 M7
Heart of England Wy
  LICH WS13 .... 253 H1
  POL/KGSB/FAZ B78 .... 289 M5
  STAFS ST17 .... 195 K7
  STAFS ST17 .... 195 K5
Heath Av *ALS/KID* ST7 .... 37 M3
  END/WER ST9 .... 71 L4

  LICHS WS14 .... 255 J7
  WS 68 C7
Heathbank Dr *HEDN* WS12 .... 231 J4
Heath Bridge Cl *BLOX/PEL* WS3 . 284 A2
Heathbrook Av *KGSWFD* DY6 ... 303 H5
Heath Cl *ALDR* WS9 .... 269 L5
Heathcote Ri *LNGTN* ST3 .... 87 H6
Heathcote Rd *ALS/KID* ST7 .... 66 B2
  LNGTN ST3 .... 86 B7
Heathcote St *LNGTN* ST3 .... 52 F1
  LNGTN ST3 .... 86 C4
  NEWUL ST5 .... 67 L2 🔒
Heath Ct *ALS/KID* ST7 .... 37 L4
Heathdene Cl *LNGTN* ST3 .... 86 B6 🔒
Heath Dr *STAFN* ST16 .... 174 B3
Heath End Rd *ALS/KID* ST7 .... 37 H4
Heather Cl *END/WER* ST9 .... 71 C6 🔒
  RSTAF ST18 .... 154 C3 🔒
  RUGE WS15 .... 215 M4
  STAFS ST17 .... 195 J6
  WNSFLD WV11 .... 281 L5
Heather Crs *LNGTN* ST3 .... 103 C6 🔒
  KINVER DY7 .... 305 M6
Heather Dr *HEDN* WS12 .... 231 K5
  KINVER DY7 .... 305 M6
Heather Gld
  AUD/MAD/W CW3 .... 81 K3 🔒
Heather Gv *SHHTH* WV12 .... 282 E6
Heather Hills *END/WER* ST9 ...... 55 K5
Heatherleigh Gv *HAN* ST1 .... 3 J1
Heather Ms *HEDN* WS12 .... 232 A2
Heather Rd *BLOX/PEL* WS3 ..... 282 F2
  HEDN WS12 .... 232 A1
Heatherside *ALS/KID* ST7 .... 39 J5
Heather Va *HEDN* WS12 .... 232 D4
Heather Vw *BURS/TUN* ST6 ...... 54 L4
Heath Farm Rd *CDSL* WV8 ...... 263 H8 🔒
  STRBR DY8 .... 307 L7
Heathfield Dr *BLOX/PEL* WS3 ... 267 H8 🔒
  NEWUL ST5 .... 67 K1
Heathfield Gdns *STRBR* DY8 .... 307 M6
Heathfield Gv *LNGTN* ST3 .... 102 F4
Heathfield Rd *BURS/TUN* ST6 ... 54 C5
  FOAKS/STRLY B74 .... 286 F7
  UTXR ST14 .... 144 B2
Heath Gap Rd *CNCK/NC* WS11 . 231 M7
Heath Gdns *STONE* ST15 .... 137 M4
Heath Gn *DUDN* DY1 .... 299 M5
Heath Gv *CDSL* WV8 .... 263 H7 🔒
  LNGTN ST3 .... 103 C5
  MKTDR TF9 .... 114 E6
Heath Hill Rd
  DUNHL/THL/PER WV6 .... 293 L1
Heath House Dr *WMBN* WV5 ... 297 K5
Heath House La *CDLE* ST10 ..... 105 M8
  CDSL WV8 .... 278 E2
  END/WER ST9 .... 42 C1
  HAN ST1 .... 3 K4
Heathland Cl *HEDN* WS12 .... 232 D8 🔒
Heathlands *WMBN* WV5 .... 297 K5 🔒
Heathlands Cl *KGSWFD* DY6 .... 303 L2 🔒
Heathlands Dr *UTXR* ST14 .... 144 B1 🔒
The Heathlands *WMBN* WV5 .... 297 K5
Heath La *RUGE* WS15 .... 178 E1
Heathley La *POL/KGSB/FAZ* B78.. 289 K4
Heath Mill Cl *SEDG* DY3 .... 297 K6 🔒
Heath Pl *NEWUL* ST5 .... 68 C7
Heath Rd *NEWUL* ST5 .... 98 D4
  NWPT TF10 .... 188 A6 🔒
  RUGE WS15 .... 215 M4 🔒
  SHHTH WV12 .... 282 D2
  STPNHL/WNHL DE15 .... 204 E3
  UTXR ST14 .... 144 B1
Heath Rw *AUD/MAD/W* CW3 ... 82 A2
Heathside Dr *BLOX/PEL* WS3 ... 268 A6 🔒
Heathside La *BURS/TUN* ST6 .... 53 H3
Heath's Pas *LNGTN* ST3 .... 86 D7 🔒
Heath St *BIDD* ST8 .... 40 C3
  BURS/TUN ST6 .... 53 J3
  CRTAM B79 .... 10 E4
  HEDN WS12 .... 232 B3
  NEWUL ST5 .... 67 M4
  NEWUL ST5 .... 84 B1
  STRBR DY8 .... 307 M5
Heath Top *MKTDR* TF9 .... 114 E6
Heath Vw *BNTWD* WS7 .... 252 A4
Heathview *LEEK* ST13 .... 57 L3
Heath Wy *CNCK/NC* WS11 ...... 232 C8
  CNCK/NC WS11 .... 250 C1
  RDERBYSW DE65 .... 165 K1
Heathway *GNOS* ST20 .... 190 C5
  RUGE WS15 .... 198 A3
Heathwood Dr *ALS/KID* ST7 ...... 37 H5
Heatley Back La *RUGE* WS15 ... 160 C7
Heatley La *RUGE* WS15 .... 160 B8
Heaton Cl *WOLVN* WV10 .... 264 E5
Heaton Ter *NEWUL* ST5 .... 68 B4
Hebden *TAM/AM/WIL* B77 ...... 291 H2
Hebden Gv *WNSFLD* WV11 ...... 282 B1
Heber St *LNGTN* ST3 .... 86 C5
Hedgerow Cl *HEDN* WS12 .... 231 M3
Hedgerow Dr *KGSWFD* DY6 .... 303 K1
The Hedgerows
  TAM/AM/WIL B77 .... 290 F2 🔒
The Hedges *WMBN* WV5 .... 297 L4 🔒
Hedging La *TAM/AM/WIL* B77 .. 290 E5
Hedley Pl *NEWUL* ST5 .... 83 M2
Hednesford Rd *BRWNH* WS8 ... 251 J7
  CNCK/NC WS11 .... 249 L1
  HEDN WS12 .... 232 D8
  HEDN WS12 .... 250 A5
Hednesford St *CNCK/NC* WS11 . 249 L1
Heenan Gv *LICH* WS13 .... 235 M8 🔒
  STAFS ST17 .... 193 L5 🔒
Heighley Castle Wy
  AUD/MAD/W CW3 .... 81 L1
Helen Sharman Dr *STAFN* ST16.. 5 K2
Helford Gv *STAFS* ST17 .... 193 H2
Hellier Rd *WOLVN* WV10 .... 264 E8
Hellyar-brook Rd *ALS/KID* ST7 .. 37 H6
Helming Dr *WOLV* WV1 .... 281 H7
Helmingham *CRTAM* B79 .... 273 J3
Helmsley Rd *WNSFLD* WV11 .... 281 J1
Helston Av *LNGTN* ST3 .... 86 D7

Helston Cl *CRTAM* B79 .... 274 C2 🔒
  MSHM DE12 .... 223 K5
  STRBR DY8 .... 303 J8
Heming Pl *BUCK/MIL* ST2 .... 3 L6
Hemingway Rd *LNGTN* ST3 .... 86 D6
Hemlock Av *LNGTN* ST3 .... 86 C6 🔒
Hemlock Wy *CNCK/NC* WS11 ... 232 B8
  HEDN WS12 .... 232 C7
Hemmings Cl *STRBR* DY8 .... 307 M5 🔒
  WOLVN WV10 .... 13 C3
The Hempbutts *STONE* ST15 .... 138 B2
Hempits Gv *STAFS* ST17 .... 194 B8
Hemplands Rd *STRBR* DY8 ...... 307 M5 🔒
Hempstalls Gv *NEWUL* ST5 .... 68 C7
Hempstalls La *NEWUL* ST5 .... 68 B8
Hemsby Wy *NEWUL* ST5 .... 84 B8
Hencroft *LEEK* ST13 .... 43 L4
Henderson Cl *LICHS* WS14 .... 9 K4
Henderson Gv *LNGTN* ST3 .... 87 H7
Hendon Cl *SEDG* DY3 .... 299 K8 🔒
Henfield Cl *WNSFLD* WV11 ...... 281 K4 🔒
Henhurst Hl
  BUTN/AL/TUT DE13 .... 184 B6
Henhurst Rdg
  BUTN/AL/TUT DE13 .... 184 C6
Hen La *CDLE* ST10 .... 123 K4
Henley Av *BIDD* ST8 .... 40 A4
Henley Cl *BLOX/PEL* WS3 .... 283 L1
  BNTWD WS7 .... 252 B5
  CRTAM B79 .... 10 F1
  STOKE ST4 .... 101 L5
Henley Dr *MGN/WHC* B75 .... 287 G7 🔒
  NWPT TF10 .... 188 A6
Henley Gra *RUGE* WS15 .... 215 H1
Henley Rd *WOLVN* WV10 .... 280 B1
Henmore Pl *ASHB* DE6 .... 79 J8 🔒
Henney Cl *PENK* ST19 .... 229 M3 🔒
Henry St *BURS/TUN* ST6 .... 53 K6
  STAFN ST16 .... 174 F4
Hensel Dr *BDMR/CCFT* WV3 ... 294 C2
Henshall Hall Dr *CONG* CW12 ... 26 B1
Henshall Pl *BURS/TUN* ST6 .... 53 K4
Henshall Rd *NEWUL* ST5 .... 67 L2
Henshaw Wy *STONE* ST15 .... 136 F4
Henwood Cl
  DUNHL/THL/PER WV6 .... 279 K7 🔒
Henwood Rd
  DUNHL/THL/PER WV6 .... 279 J7
Hepburn Cl *ALDR* WS9 .... 285 C6
Hepworth Cl
  DUNHL/THL/PER WV6 .... 278 F6 🔒
Herbert Rd *ALS/KID* ST7 .... 285 C1
  STAFS ST17 .... 4 E9
Herbert St *STOKE* ST4 .... 85 K4
  STPNHL/WNHL DE15 .... 186 B7
  WOLV WV1 .... 13 C3
Herbhill Cl
  ETTPK/GDPK/PENN WV4 ..... 295 K6
Herdsmans Cl *ASHB* DE6 .... 79 L4
Herd St *BURS/TUN* ST6 .... 68 F1
Hereford Av *NEWUL* ST5 .... 84 C6
Hereford Cl *ALBTN* WV7 .... 260 F2
  ALDR WS9 .... 285 C2
Hereford Gv *BUCK/MIL* ST2 ...... 70 D8
Hereford Rd *HEDN* WS12 .... 232 B6
Hereford St *WSLW* WS2 .... 283 L6
Hereford Wy
  POL/KGSB/FAZ B78 .... 274 A8 🔒
Herenswood *STAFS* ST17 .... 194 C3
Heritage Ct *LICHS* WS14 .... 9 K6
Heritage Wy
  STPNHL/WNHL DE15 .... 205 C1
Herm Cl *NEWUL* ST5 .... 83 L6
Hermes Cl *BLYBR/FOR* ST11 ... 103 J4
Hermes Rd *LICH* WS13 .... 236 D8
Hermitage La *ASHB* DE6 .... 94 B4
  POL/KGSB/FAZ B78 .... 291 L1
Hermit St *SEDG* DY3 .... 299 K6
Heron Cl *AUD/MAD/W* CW3 ..... 81 M3 🔒
  COVEN WV9 .... 247 H8
Herondale *HEDN* WS12 .... 232 B6
Herondale Rd *STRBR* DY8 .... 307 J6
Heron Dr *UTXR* ST14 .... 144 C4
Heron Ml *BLOX/PEL* WS3 .... 267 L7
Heron Pool Dr *NEWUL* ST5 .... 98 C6
The Heronry
  DUNHL/THL/PER WV6 .... 278 F3 🔒
Herons Gate Rd *KINVER* DY7 ... 305 C5
Heron St *RUGE* WS15 .... 215 M2
  STOKE ST4 .... 85 L5
Herrick St *BDMR/CCFT* WV3 ..... 12 D6
Hertford Gv *NEWUL* ST5 .... 84 D7
Hertford St *STOKE* ST4 .... 85 L6 🔒
Hesketh Av *BURS/TUN* ST6 .... 54 C5
Hesketh Rd *STAFS* ST17 .... 193 L4
Heskin Wy *BURS/TUN* ST6 .... 54 A4
Hexham Wy *DUDN* DY1 .... 299 M8 🔒
Hextall La *RSTAF* ST18 .... 172 C4
Heybridge Cl *CDLE* ST10 .... 105 M8
Heyburn Crs *BURS/TUN* ST6 ..... 68 C2
Heygate Wy *ALDR* WS9 .... 285 H1
Heysham Cl *LNGTN* ST3 .... 87 H6
Hickman St *NEWUL* ST5 .... 84 B1 🔒
Hickmerelands La *SEDG* DY3 ... 299 K7 🔒
Hickory Ct *CNCK/NC* WS11 ..... 232 C8 🔒
Hick St *NEWUL* ST5 .... 84 B2
Hidden Hills *AUD/MAD/W* CW3 .. 81 L2 🔒
Hide La *BUX* SK17 .... 34 D4
Hide St *STOKE* ST4 .... 85 C3
Higgins Rd *SWAD* DE11 .... 205 M4
Higgott Cl *BUT* DE14 .... 204 A3
Higgs Rd *WNSFLD* WV11 .... 282 A1
Higham Wy *WOLVN* WV10 ...... 280 E4
High Arcal Dr *SEDG* DY3 .... 299 M3
High Arcal Rd *SEDG* DY3 .... 298 F6
High Bank *CNCK/NC* WS11 ..... 249 L2
High Bank Pl *BURS/TUN* ST6 .... 69 J1 🔒
High Bank Rd
  STPNHL/WNHL DE15 .... 186 B7
Highbrook Cl *COVEN* WV9 ...... 264 A8

Highbury Rd *END/WER* ST9 .... 71 J6 🔒
  FOAKS/STRLY B74 .... 286 C7
High Chase Ri *RSTAF* ST18 ...... 196 D5
Highcliffe Rd *TAM/AM/WIL* B77 . 290 D2
High Cft *ALDR* WS9 .... 269 H8
Highcroft *BLOX/PEL* WS3 .... 268 B5 🔒
Highcroft Av *STRBR* DY8 .... 303 H7
Highcroft Crs *LICHS* WS14 .... 9 C5 🔒
Highcroft Dr
  BUTN/AL/TUT DE13 .... 184 F6
  FOAKS/STRLY B74 .... 286 E7
High Cross *BUX* SK17 .... 34 F5
Higher Ash Rd *ALS/KID* ST7 ...... 52 D2
Higherland *NEWUL* ST5 .... 84 A2
Highfield Av *ALS/KID* ST7 .... 39 H8
  BNTWD WS7 .... 252 B3
  CDLE ST10 .... 89 K6
  LNGTN ST3 .... 102 F1
  NEWUL ST5 .... 68 D6
  RUSH/SHEL WS4 .... 284 C2
  TAM/AM/WIL B77 .... 275 C5 🔒
  WOLVN WV10 .... 265 C8
Highfield Cl *BLYBR/FOR* ST11 .. 103 K3
  BNTWD WS7 .... 252 B3
  BUTN/AL/TUT DE13 .... 185 C3 🔒
  STAFS ST17 .... 212 B2
Highfield Ct *NEWUL* ST5 .... 84 C4
Highfield Crs *CDLE* ST10 .... 89 K6
  WOLVN WV10 .... 281 H4 🔒
Highfield Dr *LNGTN* ST3 .... 85 L6
  RSTAF ST18 .... 196 D2
  STPNHL/WNHL DE15 .... 7 M5
Highfield Gdns *LICHS* WS14 .... 9 J4
Highfield Gra *NEWUL* ST5 .... 68 D6
Highfield Gv *STAFS* ST17 .... 193 K2
Highfield La *BUX* SK17 .... 34 E5
Highfield Ri *STOKE* ST4 .... 100 F2
Highfield Rd *ASHB* DE6 .... 95 C2
  BLOX/PEL WS3 .... 268 A6
  BNTWD WS7 .... 252 B3
  HEDN WS12 .... 250 E1
  KIDD DY10 .... 310 A5
  RSTAF ST18 .... 177 J2
  SEDG DY3 .... 299 K1
Highfield Rd East *BIDD* ST8 .... 40 D3
Highfield Rd North
  BLOX/PEL WS3 .... 267 M5
Highfield Rd West *BIDD* ST8 ...... 40 D2
Highfields *BNTWD* WS7 .... 252 B3
Highfields Av *RUGE* WS15 .... 217 J6 🔒
Highfields Dr *MSHM* DE12 .... 223 H8
  WMBN WV5 .... 298 A5 🔒
Highfields Gra *GTWY* WS6 .... 266 D1
Highfields Pk *GTWY* WS6 .... 266 D1
Highfields Rd *BNTWD* WS7 ...... 251 M6
The Highfields
  DUNHL/THL/PER WV6 .... 279 C8
Highfield Wy *ALDR* WS9 .... 269 H8
Highgate *SEDG* DY3 .... 299 L5
Highgate Av
  ETTPK/GDPK/PENN WV4 ..... 294 D4
Highgate Cl *BURS/TUN* ST6 ...... 54 E7
Highgate Rd *KINVER* DY7 .... 301 L2
High Gra *LICH* WS13 .... 253 H1
High Gn *CNCK/NC* WS11 .... 249 K1
  PENK ST19 .... 246 B4
Highgrove
  DUNHL/THL/PER WV6 .... 279 J7 🔒
  STONE ST15 .... 138 C5 🔒
Highgrove Cl
  BUTN/AL/TUT DE13 .... 185 K1 🔒
  SHHTH WV12 .... 282 B4
Highgrove Pl *DUDN* DY1 .... 299 M8
Highgrove Rd *STOKE* ST4 .... 84 F7
High Hl *WNSFLD* WV11 .... 266 A8
High Holborn *SEDG* DY3 .... 299 K3
High House La *ALBTN* WV7 ...... 261 J6
Highland Cl *BIDD* ST8 .... 41 H2
  BLYBR/FOR ST11 .... 103 L4
Highland Dr *LNGTN* ST3 .... 102 D1
High Land Rd *ALDR* WS9 .... 269 H7
Highland Rd *NEWUL* ST5 .... 231 J6
Highlands *STAFS* ST17 .... 193 K2
  STONE ST15 .... 137 M5 🔒
Highlands Dr
  STPNHL/WNHL DE15 .... 186 A6
Highlands Rd *BDMR/CCFT* WV3 . 294 C2
Highland Wy *RUGE* WS15 .... 197 J7
High La *ALS/KID* ST7 .... 66 L4
  BURS/TUN ST6 .... 55 C4
  LEEK ST13 .... 55 L5
  NEWUL ST5 .... 67 C6
Highlanes *ECCH* ST21 .... 134 D4
High Lows La *STONE* ST15 ...... 136 E4
High Meadow *GNOS* ST20 ...... 170 B7
  RUGE WS15 .... 233 M5 🔒
High Mdw
  DUNHL/THL/PER WV6 .... 279 J8
  NWPT TF10 .... 188 A7 🔒
  WMBN WV5 .... 298 A4
Highmoor Cl *SHHTH* WV12 ..... 282 B3
High Mount St *HEDN* WS12 ..... 232 B4
High Offley Rd *GNOS* ST20 ...... 170 D2
High Pk *STAFS* ST17 .... 4 A8
Highpark Av *STRBR* DY8 .... 307 K5
High Park Cl *SEDG* DY3 .... 299 K1
High Park Crs *SEDG* DY3 .... 299 K1
High Pth *DUNHL/THL/PER* WV6 . 277 J7
High Rdg *ALDR* WS9 .... 284 F5
  RUGE WS15 .... 197 J7
High Ridge Cl *ALDR* WS9 .... 284 E5 🔒
High Rd *SHHTH* WV12 .... 282 C5
High St *ALBTN* WV7 .... 260 F5
  ALDR WS9 .... 268 F7
  ALDR WS9 .... 285 H4
  ALS/KID ST7 .... 39 K5
  ALS/KID ST7 .... 39 J7
  ALS/KID ST7 .... 39 L6
  ALS/KID ST7 .... 52 D5
  ALS/KID ST7 .... 66 D3
  ALS/KID ST7 .... 67 C1
  ASHB DE6 .... 145 H1
  BIDD ST8 .... 40 C3
  BLOX/PEL WS3 .... 268 A2
  BLOX/PEL WS3 .... 283 H2
  BLYBR/FOR ST11 .... 87 L7
  BNTWD WS7 .... 251 M5
  BRWNH WS8 .... 268 F3
  BURS/TUN ST6 .... 53 K6
  BUT DE14 .... 7 J5

330 Hig - Hun

BUTN/AL/TUT DE13 ... 165 J4
BUX SK17 ... 24 B4
CDLE ST10 ... 73 L8
CDLE ST10 ... 74 A1
CDLE ST10 ... 88 C6
CDLE ST10 ... 89 K7
CDLE ST10 ... 107 L1
CNCK/NC WS11 ... 251 H5
DUNHL/THL/PER WV6 ... 277 H8
DUNHL/THL/PER WV6 ... 279 K6
ECCH ST21 ... 152 D3
GNOS ST20 ... 190 D4
GNOS ST20 ... 209 H3
GTWY WS6 ... 249 J8
KGSWFD DY6 ... 303 K4
KGSWFD DY6 ... 303 H2
KINVER DY7 ... 306 B7
LEEK ST13 ... 43 L4
MKTDR TF9 ... 130 D1
MKTDR TF9 ... 148 F2
MSHM DE12 ... 223 H5
NEWUL ST5 ... 67 L3
NEWUL ST5 ... 67 L7
NEWUL ST5 ... 68 C4
NEWUL ST5 ... 83 H1
NEWUL ST5 ... 84 B1 3
PENK ST19 ... 227 H4
RSTAF ST18 ... 177 J2
RUGE WS15 ... 180 A4
RUGE WS15 ... 198 A4
RUGE WS15 ... 216 F8
SEDG DY3 ... 297 L8
SEDG DY3 ... 299 K1
STONE ST15 ... 138 A2
STRBR DY8 ... 303 L8
STRBR DY8 ... 307 M3
TAM/AM/WIL B77 ... 290 C6
UTXR ST14 ... 108 F7
UTXR ST14 ... 144 C2
UTXR ST14 ... 145 L8
WMBN WV5 ... 298 B4
WNSFLD WV11 ... 281 J5
High Street (Sandyford)
BURS/TUN ST6 ... 53 K5
Highton St BUCK/MIL ST2 ... 70 C1
Highup Rd LEEK ST13 ... 43 J2
High Vw ALS/KID ST7 ... 39 H5
BILS/COS WV14 ... 299 M1
LNGTN ST3 ... 103 G5
Highview Dr KGSWFD DY6 ... 303 M6
High View Rd LEEK ST13 ... 44 B5
END/WER ST9 ... 55 M2
Highview Rd BLYBR/FOR ST11 ... 121 L2
Highway La NEWUL ST5 ... 82 D4
High Wood Cl KGSWFD DY6 ... 303 J4 1
Highwood Rd UTXR ST14 ... 144 D5
Higson Av STOKE ST4 ... 85 G2
Hilary Dr ALDR WS9 ... 285 G5
BDMR/CCFT WV3 ... 294 D3
Hilcote Hollow STAFN ST16 ... 174 B4 2
Hilderstone Rd LNGTN ST3 ... 102 F5
Hildicks Crs BLOX/PEL WS3 ... 283 M3
Hildicks Pl BLOX/PEL WS3 ... 283 M3
Hillary Crest RUGE WS15 ... 215 L4
SEDG DY3 ... 299 L5 1
Hillary Rd ALS/KID ST7 ... 39 H7
Hillary St BURS/TUN ST6 ... 69 H4
Hill Av ETTPK/GDPK/PENN WV4 ... 295 M7
Hillberry Cl BUCK/MIL ST2 ... 3 M9
Hillboro Ri KINVER DY7 ... 306 A5
Hillbury Dr SHHTH WV12 ... 282 B2
Hillchurch St HAN ST1 ... 2 D4
Hill Cl SEDG DY3 ... 299 L1
UTXR ST14 ... 143 M1
Hill Crs ALS/KID ST7 ... 66 F4
STONE ST15 ... 138 A4
Hillcrest BUTN/AL/TUT DE13 ... 165 H5
LEEK ST13 ... 43 K4
PENK ST19 ... 246 D3
Hill Crest SEDG DY3 ... 299 H6
STAFS ST17 ... 193 J2
Hillcrest Av CDLE ST10 ... 74 A8
STPNHL/WNHL DE15 ... 186 A6
WOLVN WV10 ... 280 E2
Hillcrest Cl CDLE ST10 ... 74 A8
Hill Crest Dr LICH WS13 ... 8 C1
Hillcrest Gdns SHHTH WV12 ... 282 D5
Hillcrest Ri BNTWD WS7 ... 252 B6
Hillcrest Rd POL/KGSB/FAZ B78 ... 291 M3
Hillcrest St HAN ST1 ... 2 E5
Hill Cft RSTAF ST18 ... 177 J2
Hillcroft Av STAFS ST17 ... 194 E3
Hillcroft Rd KGSWFD DY6 ... 303 L3
Hilldene Rd KGSWFD DY6 ... 303 J6
Hill Dr CNCK/NC WS11 ... 232 A7
STONE ST15 ... 138 A4
Hillfarm Cl STAFS ST17 ... 193 M5
Hillfield Av STOKE ST4 ... 84 E6
Hillfield La BUTN/AL/TUT DE13 ... 185 M1
Hill Green Cl MSHM DE12 ... 222 D7 2
Hillgreen Rd LNGTN ST3 ... 86 D5
Hillhead La BUX SK17 ... 16 E1
Hill Hook Rd FOAKS/STRLY B74 ... 286 E4
Hill La BNTWD WS7 ... 251 L1
CDLE ST10 ... 123 G7
MGN/WHC B75 ... 288 B8
Hillman TAM/AM/WIL B77 ... 11 J9
Hillman St BUCK/MIL ST2 ... 70 B1
Hillmorton Rd
FOAKS/STRLY B74 ... 286 F6
Hill Pk ALDR WS9 ... 269 G6
Hill Pl WNSFLD WV11 ... 282 A1
Hillport Av NEWUL ST5 ... 68 B3
Hillrise CDLE ST10 ... 107 L2
Hill Ri RSTAF ST18 ... 156 F6
Hillsdale La LEEK ST13 ... 46 E7
Hillsdale Rd
STPNHL/WNHL DE15 ... 186 B5
Hillside BRWNH WS8 ... 269 G4
BUTN/AL/TUT DE13 ... 165 H4
ECCH ST21 ... 152 E3
LICHS WS14 ... 9 J7
NEWUL ST5 ... 84 A2
RUGE WS15 ... 180 B5 1
Hill Side SEDG DY3 ... 299 J6
Hillside Av ALS/KID ST7 ... 53 G3
ASHB DE6 ... 79 J7
BLYBR/FOR ST11 ... 104 A2
END/WER ST9 ... 55 M3
LNGTN ST3 ... 102 F1
Hillside Cl ALS/KID ST7 ... 39 K3
BIDD ST8 ... 41 H1
BLYBR/FOR ST11 ... 121 L2
BUCK/MIL ST2 ... 55 J8
HEDN WS12 ... 232 A3
RUGE WS15 ... 216 B5
Hillside Crs BLOX/PEL WS3 ... 267 M8
Hillside Dr LEEK ST13 ... 43 J6
RSTAF ST18 ... 196 D2
Hillside Gdns SWAD DE11 ... 205 M8
WOLV WV1 ... 281 G7 1
Hillside Rd BUCK/MIL ST2 ... 55 J7
END/WER ST9 ... 71 H6
FOAKS/STRLY B74 ... 286 F6
LEEK ST13 ... 57 J6
MSHM DE12 ... 223 J4
Hillside Wk STOKE ST4 ... 84 D2
Hillstone Gdns WOLVN WV10 ... 280 F2
Hill St BNTWD WS7 ... 251 L5
CNCK/NC WS11 ... 250 F4
GTWY WS6 ... 249 J8
HEDN WS12 ... 232 C7
NEWUL ST5 ... 68 A8
RUGE WS15 ... 215 L2
SEDG DY3 ... 299 L5
STOKE ST4 ... 85 H3
STPNHL/WNHL DE15 ... 204 E3
STRBR DY8 ... 307 M2
STRBR DY8 ... 307 M6
WNSFLD WV11 ... 265 M7
Hillswood Av LEEK ST13 ... 43 K4
Hillswood Dr END/WER ST9 ... 55 L2
Hill Ter ALS/KID ST7 ... 51 K8
Hilltop RUGE WS15 ... 215 M3
Hill Top Av CRTAM B79 ... 274 B2
Hilltop Av NEWUL ST5 ... 68 E8
Hill Top Cl BURS/TUN ST6 ... 55 H1
Hill Top Crs LNGTN ST3 ... 103 G5
Hill Top Vw RUGE WS15 ... 217 J7
Hill Vw ALDR WS9 ... 269 H8
BUCK/MIL ST2 ... 55 H8
Hillview Crs NEWUL ST5 ... 98 C5
Hill Village Rd MGN/WHC B75 ... 287 G6
Hillway Cl RUGE WS15 ... 215 J1
Hill Wd BLOX/PEL WS3 ... 267 M8
Hillwood Cl STRBR DY8 ... 303 J6
Hillwood Common Rd
MGN/WHC B75 ... 287 H5
Hillwood Rd AUD/MAD/W CW3 ... 82 A2
Hill Wood Rd MGN/WHC B75 ... 287 J5
Hilmore Wy TAM/AM/WIL B77 ... 290 E2
Hilsea Cl COVEN WV9 ... 279 M1
Hilsea Crs UTXR ST14 ... 162 F3
Hilston Av
ETTPK/GDPK/PENN WV4 ... 294 C6
Hilton Cl BLOX/PEL WS3 ... 282 F1
Hilton Cross WOLVN WV10 ... 265 H5
Hilton Dr ECCH ST21 ... 135 M7
Hilton La GTWY WS6 ... 250 A8
WOLVN WV10 ... 265 K2
Hilton Rd
ETTPK/GDPK/PENN WV4 ... 295 M6
RDERBYSW DE65 ... 167 G3
SHHTH WV12 ... 282 C2
STOKE ST4 ... 84 D3
WOLVN WV10 ... 265 H3
Hilton St WOLVN WV10 ... 13 J2
Himley Av DUDN DY1 ... 299 M8
Himley Cl SHHTH WV12 ... 282 A5
Himley Crs
ETTPK/GDPK/PENN WV4 ... 295 J5
Himley Gdns SEDG DY3 ... 298 F6
Himley La SEDG DY3 ... 298 B7
Himley Rd SEDG DY3 ... 298 F7
Hinchco Pl BURS/TUN ST6 ... 54 E6
Hinckes Rd
DUNHL/THL/PER WV6 ... 279 H5
Hinckley Gv STOKE ST4 ... 101 H5
Hinde St HAN ST1 ... 2 C8
Hines St STOKE ST4 ... 85 L5
Hingley Cft
FOAKS/STRLY B74 ... 285 M7 2
Hinksford Gdns SEDG DY3 ... 297 L8
Hinksford La SEDG DY3 ... 302 E1
Hinsford Cl KGSWFD DY6 ... 303 L2
Hinsley Mill La MKTDR TF9 ... 112 E8
Hinstock Cl
ETTPK/GDPK/PENN WV4 ... 295 G6
Hinton Cl STAFS ST17 ... 193 M4
Hinton Gv WNSFLD WV11 ... 281 M5
Hints Ct POL/KGSB/FAZ B78 ... 272 D8
Hints La POL/KGSB/FAZ B78 ... 273 H4
Hints Rd POL/KGSB/FAZ B78 ... 273 H8
Hislop Rd RUGE WS15 ... 215 L4
Histons Dr CDSL WV8 ... 262 F7
Histons Hl CDSL WV8 ... 262 F8
Hitchman St STOKE ST4 ... 85 L4 3
Hoarstone STRBR DY8 ... 311 M5 1
Hobart Cl STPNHL/WNHL DE15 ... 186 C8
Hobart Rd HEDN WS12 ... 232 E8
Hobart St BURS/TUN ST6 ... 69 G3
Hobb La UTXR ST14 ... 160 F3
Hobble End La GTWY WS6 ... 267 G4
Hobbs Vw RUGE WS15 ... 216 B5
Hobby Cl LNGTN ST3 ... 103 G3
Hobfield La RUGE WS15 ... 180 B2
Hobgate Rd WOLVN WV10 ... 13 L1
Hobley St WLNHL WV13 ... 282 C8 3
Hobnock Rd WNSFLD WV11 ... 266 A6
Hobs Hole La ALDR WS9 ... 285 K3
Hobson St BURS/TUN ST6 ... 69 G2
Hob's Rd LICH WS13 ... 9 L1
Hobstone Hill La BNTWD WS7 ... 252 E1
Hockley Rd TAM/AM/WIL B77 ... 290 F3
Hodge La TAM/AM/WIL B77 ... 275 H4
UTXR ST14 ... 161 M2
Hodgkins Cl BRWNH WS8 ... 269 G4
Hodgkinson St NEWUL ST5 ... 67 M4
Hodnet Gv HAN ST1 ... 2 B2
Hodnet Pl CNCK/NC WS11 ... 232 B8
Hodson Cl WNSFLD WV11 ... 281 M2 2
Hogan Wy STAFN ST16 ... 175 J6
Hogarth Cl WLNHL WV13 ... 281 L8
Hogarth Pl NEWUL ST5 ... 67 L4 2
Holbeach Av BUCK/MIL ST2 ... 3 L9
Holbeache La KGSWFD DY6 ... 303 K1
Holbeache Rd KGSWFD DY6 ... 303 J2
KINVER DY7 ... 302 G6
Holbeach Wy STAFN ST16 ... 174 B6
Holberg Gv WNSFLD WV11 ... 281 M4
Holborn NEWUL ST5 ... 84 B1
The Holborn AUD/MAD/W CW3 ... 81 L4
Holbury Cl COVEN WV9 ... 264 A8
Holcroft Rd KGSWFD DY6 ... 303 J1
Holdcroft Rd BUCK/MIL ST2 ... 70 B5
Holden Av NEWUL ST5 ... 68 D7
Holden Av North BURS/TUN ST6 ... 69 K2
Holden Av South
BURS/TUN ST6 ... 69 K2 2
Holden Crs BLOX/PEL WS3 ... 283 L5
Holden Pl BLOX/PEL WS3 ... 283 L6
Holden Rd
ETTPK/GDPK/PENN WV4 ... 294 D7
Holder Dr CNCK/NC WS11 ... 231 H8
Holdiford Rd RSTAF ST18 ... 195 K1
Holding Crs ALS/KID ST7 ... 66 D3 2
Holdings La AUD/MAD/W CW3 ... 80 F6
Holditch Rd NEWUL ST5 ... 67 M5
Holdon Cft MSHM DE12 ... 222 C4
Holehouse La ALS/KID ST7 ... 38 D2
END/WER ST9 ... 41 K8
Holehouse Rd BUCK/MIL ST2 ... 70 B4
Holland Cl LICH WS13 ... 255 G1 2
Holland Pk BUTN/AL/TUT DE13 ... 202 E8
Hollands Pl BLOX/PEL WS3 ... 283 K1
Hollands Rd BLOX/PEL WS3 ... 283 K1
The Hollands BIDD ST8 ... 27 J7
Holland St BURS/TUN ST6 ... 53 K7 2
Hollemeadow Av
BLOX/PEL WS3 ... 283 K3
Hollies Av CNCK/NC WS11 ... 249 M1
Hollies Brook Cl GNOS ST20 ... 190 D3 2
Hollies Cl ASHB DE6 ... 94 F4
STPNHL/WNHL DE15 ... 186 E2
Hollies Dr LNGTN ST3 ... 102 F5
Hollies La ASHB DE6 ... 110 C6
DUNHL/THL/PER WV6 ... 277 M5
KIDDW DY11 ... 308 F7
KINVER DY7 ... 304 E2
The Hollies BKHL/PFLD WV2 ... 12 E8
NEWUL ST5 ... 68 C8
Hollings St STOKE ST4 ... 86 A5
Hollington Dr BURS/TUN ST6 ... 54 A2
Hollington La UTXR ST14 ... 125 M5
Hollington Rd CDLE ST10 ... 105 M7
Hollinscloughs Rake BUX SK17 ... 15 M7
Hollins Crs ALS/KID ST7 ... 52 E1
Hollins Gra ALS/KID ST7 ... 52 D2 1
Hollinshead Av NEWUL ST5 ... 68 A6
Hollinshead Cl ALS/KID ST7 ... 38 F3 1
Hollins La CDLE ST10 ... 73 H6
Hollinwell Cl BLOX/PEL WS3 ... 267 G7 3
Hollinwood Cl ALS/KID ST7 ... 52 E2
Hollinwood Rd ALS/KID ST7 ... 52 E2
Hollis La UTXR ST14 ... 108 B4
Holloway CRTAM B79 ... 10 C5
Holloway Dr WMBN WV5 ... 297 L5
Holloway La NEWUL ST5 ... 97 J4
Holloway St SEDG DY3 ... 299 K6
Holloway St West SEDG DY3 ... 299 K5
The Holloway
DUNHL/THL/PER WV6 ... 279 H8
SEDG DY3 ... 302 D1
STRBR DY8 ... 307 M3 2
WMBN WV5 ... 293 G7
Hollow Crs
STPNHL/WNHL DE15 ... 186 C6 1
Hollow Croft Rd SHHTH WV12 ... 282 B3
Hollow La ASHB DE6 ... 94 C1
ASHB DE6 ... 163 K4
LEEK ST13 ... 57 H5
RUGE WS15 ... 198 A4
STPNHL/WNHL DE15 ... 186 C6 2
Hollowood Pl BURS/TUN ST6 ... 54 D5
The Hollow ALS/KID ST7 ... 39 H5
ASHB DE6 ... 109 L4
BLYBR/FOR ST11 ... 87 L8
UTXR ST14 ... 144 C4 3
Holly Av LEEK ST13 ... 57 J6
Hollybank Av WNSFLD WV11 ... 266 A7
Hollybank Cl BLOX/PEL WS3 ... 267 G8 1
Hollybank Crs STOKE ST4 ... 85 G5
Holly Bank Vw RUGE WS15 ... 216 B5
Holly Bush Cl MSHM DE12 ... 241 M3 1
Hollybush Crs LNGTN ST3 ... 85 L6
Hollybush La CDSL WV8 ... 262 D8
ETTPK/GDPK/PENN WV4 ... 294 D6
Holly Bush La NEWUL ST5 ... 98 B6
Hollybush La STRBR DY8 ... 307 M3
Holly Bush Rd
BUTN/AL/TUT DE13 ... 163 H7
BUTN/AL/TUT DE13 ... 181 L2
Hollybush Rd LNGTN ST3 ... 85 L7
Holly Cl ASHB DE6 ... 95 K2 1
CRTAM B79 ... 274 B3
KINVER DY7 ... 305 M5
MKTDR TF9 ... 130 A2 1
SHHTH WV12 ... 282 C4
Holly Ct BUCK/MIL ST2 ... 86 E3 1
Holly Dr END/WER ST9 ... 71 G7 1
LICH WS13 ... 237 K2
STAFS ST17 ... 194 F4
Holly Flds STONE ST15 ... 136 E4 1
Holly Gn STPNHL/WNHL DE15 ... 204 F2
Holly Gv BDMR/CCFT WV3 ... 294 F3
STONE ST15 ... 138 B3 2
STRBR DY8 ... 307 M5 1
Holly Grove La BNTWD WS7 ... 251 L1
Hollyhedge Cl WSLW WS2 ... 283 J8
Hollyhedge La WSLW WS2 ... 283 J7
Hollyhill La LICHS WS14 ... 270 E6
Holly Hill Rd LICHS WS14 ... 270 F5
RUGE WS15 ... 233 L5
Hollyhock Wy BUT DE14 ... 203 L3
Hollyhurst STAFS ST17 ... 194 D5 1
Hollyhurst Dr STRBR DY8 ... 303 L7 3
Hollyhurst La ASHB DE6 ... 128 B3
RSTAF ST18 ... 160 A6
Holly La ALDR WS9 ... 269 G6
ALDR WS9 ... 285 M2
ALS/KID ST7 ... 37 L7
ALS/KID ST7 ... 39 L5
GTWY WS6 ... 266 F2
HEDN WS12 ... 231 J3
MGN/WHC B75 ... 287 G7
RSTAF ST18 ... 191 L1
RSTAF ST18 ... 210 C1
UTXR ST14 ... 160 D1
Holly Pl STOKE ST4 ... 85 L6
Holly Rd BUTN/AL/TUT DE13 ... 220 D1
NEWUL ST5 ... 67 K1
UTXR ST14 ... 144 A2
Hollys Rd BUTN/AL/TUT DE13 ... 200 F8
Holly St CNCK/NC WS11 ... 231 M4
STPNHL/WNHL DE15 ... 204 F2
Holly Tree Dr BIDD ST8 ... 26 C8
Hollywall La BURS/TUN ST6 ... 53 J5
Hollywood La NEWUL ST5 ... 82 D1
Holman Cl WLNHL WV13 ... 281 L8
Holman Rd WLNHL WV13 ... 281 K8
Holmcroft Gdns COVEN WV9 ... 247 J8 1
Holmcroft Rd STAFN ST16 ... 174 C4
Holme Cl RDERBYSW DE65 ... 165 J1
Holme Farm Av
STPNHL/WNHL DE15 ... 204 F2
Holme Ml WOLVN WV10 ... 264 D6
Holme Ri PENK ST19 ... 230 A1
Holmes Cl STAFN ST16 ... 174 B8 2
Holmes Rd SHHTH WV12 ... 282 D3
The Holmes WOLVN WV10 ... 264 D7
Holmes Wy BURS/TUN ST6 ... 54 B2
Holme Wy RUSH/SHEL WS4 ... 284 B3
Holm Oak Dr AUD/MAD/W CW3 ... 81 L3
Holm Rd CDLE ST10 ... 91 J8
Holm Vw Cl LICHS WS14 ... 270 F4 1
Holst Dr HAN ST1 ... 3 L1
Holston Cl HEDN WS12 ... 250 F1 1
Holsworth Cl
TAM/AM/WIL B77 ... 290 D1 2
Holt Crs CNCK/NC WS11 ... 232 B8
Holte Dr MGN/WHC B75 ... 287 K8
Holt La CDLE ST10 ... 73 L8
Holtshill La WSL WS1 ... 283 M8
Holt's La BUTN/AL/TUT DE13 ... 165 H5
Holwick TAM/AM/WIL B77 ... 291 H2 2
Holyhead Crs LNGTN ST3 ... 87 H6
Holyhead Rd ALBTN WV7 ... 260 F8
CDSL WV8 ... 278 D2
Holyoake Pl RUGE WS15 ... 197 K7 1
Holyrood Cl STONE ST15 ... 138 C5 2
Holywell Ri LICHS WS14 ... 9 J6
Home Farm Ct SWAD DE11 ... 223 K1
Home Farm Rd
DUNHL/THL/PER WV6 ... 276 C3
Homefield Rd CDSL WV8 ... 263 H7
Homer Pl BURS/TUN ST6 ... 54 B5
Homer Rd MGN/WHC B75 ... 287 J8
Homer St HAN ST1 ... 3 G5
Homestead Cl SEDG DY3 ... 299 L5 2
Homestead Ct STAFN ST16 ... 174 E3
Homestead Dr MGN/WHC B75 ... 287 J7
Homestead St BUCK/MIL ST2 ... 86 D2
The Homestead
BUCK/MIL ST2 ... 55 J7 2
Honesty Cl BRWNH WS8 ... 268 D3
Honeybourne Crs
WMBN WV5 ... 297 M5 3
Honeybourne Wy
WLNHL WV13 ... 282 C8
Honeybrook Cl KIDDW DY11 ... 309 K8
Honeysuckle Av
BLYBR/FOR ST11 ... 103 M4 2
KGSWFD DY6 ... 303 L3
Honeysuckle Cl CDLE ST10 ... 105 M7
Honeysuckle Dr WOLVN WV10 ... 265 H3
Honeysuckle La END/WER ST9 ... 42 D8
Honeysuckle Vw
STPNHL/WNHL DE15 ... 205 G3 1
Honeytree Cl KGSWFD DY6 ... 303 M7
Honeywall STOKE ST4 ... 85 G3
Honeywall La ASHB DE6 ... 93 L2
AUD/MAD/W CW3 ... 82 B2
Honeywood NEWUL ST5 ... 68 B7
Honington Av ALBTN WV7 ... 260 C2
Honiton Cl STAFS ST17 ... 194 D2
Honiton Wy ALDR WS9 ... 284 F5
Honor Av
ETTPK/GDPK/PENN WV4 ... 295 J5
Hood La RUGE WS15 ... 217 G6 2
Hook Dr FOAKS/STRLY B74 ... 286 E6
Hook La LICHS WS14 ... 270 C7
UTXR ST14 ... 126 A3
The Hook La ALBTN WV7 ... 277 G1
Hoo La KINVER DY7 ... 301 M6
Hoomill La RSTAF ST18 ... 177 G6
Hoon Av NEWUL ST5 ... 68 B6
Hoon Rd RDERBYSW DE65 ... 165 K2
Hoover St BURS/TUN ST6 ... 53 K7 3
Hopedale Cl NEWUL ST5 ... 84 B7
STOKE ST4 ... 86 B3
Hope St ALS/KID ST7 ... 51 M7
HAN ST1 ... 2 C3
STRBR DY8 ... 303 K7
Hopley Rd BUTN/AL/TUT DE13 ... 184 B5
Hopleys Cl TAM/AM/WIL B77 ... 11 K6
Hopmeadow La
STPNHL/WNHL DE15 ... 205 G1 2
Hopstone Gdns
ETTPK/GDPK/PENN WV4 ... 294 F5
Hopton Bank RSTAF ST18 ... 175 J1 1
Hopton Cl
DUNHL/THL/PER WV6 ... 278 F7
Hopton Ct STAFN ST16 ... 174 D5
Hopton Crs WNSFLD WV11 ... 281 L4
Hoptonhall La RSTAF ST18 ... 175 J1
Hopton La RSTAF ST18 ... 175 H1
Hopton Meadow
HEDN WS12 ... 250 C1 2
Hopton St STAFN ST16 ... 174 F4
Hopton Wy BURS/TUN ST6 ... 54 A2
Hopwas Hl POL/KGSB/FAZ B78 ... 273 G4
Hopwood Pl BUCK/MIL ST2 ... 70 B7
Hopyard Cl SEDG DY3 ... 299 H7 2
Hopyard La SEDG DY3 ... 299 H7
Hopyard Rd WSLW WS2 ... 282 E8
Horatius Rd NEWUL ST5 ... 67 K4
Hordern Cl
DUNHL/THL/PER WV6 ... 279 M5
Hordern Gv
DUNHL/THL/PER WV6 ... 279 M5
Hordern Rd
DUNHL/THL/PER WV6 ... 280 A6
Hordley St HAN ST1 ... 2 E6
Hornbeam TAM/AM/WIL B77 ... 275 G6
Hornbeam Crs HEDN WS12 ... 233 G4
The Hornbeams UTXR ST14 ... 144 A1 3
Hornbrook Cl
BUTN/AL/TUT DE13 ... 185 H2 1
Hornbrook Rd
BUTN/AL/TUT DE13 ... 185 H2
Hornby Rd
ETTPK/GDPK/PENN WV4 ... 295
Hornby Rw STOKE ST4 ... 85
Horninglow Rd BUT DE14 ... 185
Horninglow Rd North
BUTN/AL/TUT DE13 ... 185
Horninglow St BUT DE14 ... 7
Horns Cft RUGE WS15 ... 215 H3
Hornton Cl FOAKS/STRLY B74 ... 286
Hornton Rd
BUTN/AL/TUT DE13 ... 185 H3
Horsa Wy ALBTN WV7 ... 260
Horse Bridge La KINVER DY7 ... 306
Horsebrook La PENK ST19 ... 246
Horsecroft Crs LEEK ST13 ... 44
Horsecroft Gv LEEK ST13 ... 44 B3
Horse Fair ECCH ST21 ... 152
RUGE WS15 ... 215
Horsehills Dr
BDMR/CCFT WV3 ... 279 L8
Horseley Flds WOLV WV1 ... 13
Horse Rd CDLE ST10 ... 107
Horseshoe Dr RUGE WS15 ... 215 H1
Horsey La RUGE WS15 ... 234
Horsham Av STRBR DY8 ... 303
Horsley Gv LNGTN ST3 ... 101
Horsley La ECCH ST21 ... 151
LICHS WS14 ... 270
Horsley Rd STONE ST15 ... 136
Horsley Wy STONE ST15 ... 136
Horton Av BUTN/AL/TUT DE13 ... 185
Horton Cl SEDG DY3 ... 299
Horton Dr LNGTN ST3 ... 87
Horton Rd KINVER DY7 ... 305
Horton St LEEK ST13 ... 43 M4
STOKE ST4 ... 84 D1
Hose St BURS/TUN ST6 ... 53
Hoskins Rd BURS/TUN ST6 ... 53
Hospital La MKTDR TF9 ... 130
Hospital Rd BNTWD WS7 ... 252
Hospital St CRTAM B79 ... 10
WOLV WV1 ... 13
WSLW WS2 ... 283
Hothill La CDLE ST10 ... 124
Hot La BIDD ST8 ... 27
BURS/TUN ST6 ... 69
Hougher Wall Rd ALS/KID ST7 ... 51
Hough Hl BURS/TUN ST6 ... 55
Houghton St HAN ST1 ... 2
Houghwood La END/WER ST9 ... 55
Houldsworth Dr BURS/TUN ST6 ... 54
Housefield Rd BUCK/MIL ST2 ... 86
Houseman Dr LNGTN ST3 ... 86
Houston Av END/WER ST9 ... 55
Houting TAM/AM/WIL B77 ... 290
The Houx STRBR DY8 ... 307 L2
Hoveringham Dr BUCK/MIL ST2 ... 85
Howard Cl END/WER ST9 ... 71
LEEK ST13 ... 43 J6
Howard Crs HAN ST1 ... 3
HEDN WS12 ... 232
Howard Gv NEWUL ST5 ... 83
Howard Pl HAN ST1 ... 2
NEWUL ST5 ... 84
Howard Rd STAFS ST17 ... 193
WNSFLD WV11 ... 281
Howard St BKHL/PFLD WV2 ... 13
LNGTN ST3 ... 86 C8
Howdle's La BRWNH WS8 ... 251
Howe Crs SHHTH WV12 ... 282
Howe Gv NEWUL ST5 ... 67 L8
Howell Rd BKHL/PFLD WV2 ... 295
Howitt Crs UTXR ST14 ... 144
Howland Cl COVEN WV9 ... 263
Howson St HAN ST1 ... 2
Hoylake TAM/AM/WIL B77 ... 275 H6
Hoylake Cl BLOX/PEL WS3 ... 267
Hoylake Rd
DUNHL/THL/PER WV6 ... 278
Hubbal La SHIF TF11 ... 243
Huddale La CDLE ST10 ... 76
Huddlesford La LICH WS13 ... 255
Huddlestone Cl WOLVN WV10 ... 265
Huddocks Vw BLOX/PEL WS3 ... 267
Hudson Cl CNCK/NC WS11 ... 232
GNOS ST20 ... 190 E2
Hudson Dr BNTWD WS7 ... 252
Hudson Gv
DUNHL/THL/PER WV6 ... 278 E5
Hudson Rd ALBTN WV7 ... 260 B3
Hudson Wy MKTDR TF9 ... 148
Hugh Bourne Pl BIDD ST8 ... 40
Hughes Av BDMR/CCFT WV3 ... 294
NEWUL ST5 ... 68
Hughes St BURS/TUN ST6 ... 69
Hughson Gv BURS/TUN ST6 ... 54 E7
Hugo St LEEK ST13 ... 43
Hulland Cl NEWUL ST5 ... 83 H1
Hullock's Pool Rd ALS/KID ST7 ... 51
Hulme Cl NEWUL ST5 ... 83
Hulme La END/WER ST9 ... 71
Hulme Rd LNGTN ST3 ... 86
Hulme St STOKE ST4 ... 84 E2
Hulse St STOKE ST4 ... 86
Hulton Cl CONG CW12 ... 26
Hulton Rd BUCK/MIL ST2 ... 70
Hulton St HAN ST1 ... 2
Humber Dr BIDD ST8 ... 40
Humber Rd BDMR/CCFT WV3 ... 12
Humbert St HAN ST1 ... 68
Humber Wy NEWUL ST5 ... 84
Humphreys Rd WOLVN WV10 ... 280
Humphrey St SEDG DY3 ... 299
Hungerford La
AUD/MAD/W CW3 ... 81
Hungerford Rd STRBR DY8 ... 307
Hungry La LICHS WS14 ... 271
Hunslet Rd BNTWD WS7 ... 252
Huntbach St HAN ST1 ... 2
Hunter Av BNTWD WS7 ... 252
Hunter Cl LICHS WS14 ... 9
Hunter Crs BLOX/PEL WS3 ... 283
Hunter Rd CNCK/NC WS11 ... 249
Hunters Cl BIDD ST8 ... 40
Hunters Dr STOKE ST4 ... 84
Hunter's Point MKTDR TF9 ... 114 D5
Hunter's Ride KINVER DY7 ... 303
STAFS ST17 ... 193 L6
Hunter St BUT DE14 ... 185
DUNHL/THL/PER WV6 ... 12

Hunters Wy STOKE ST4 .... 84 F4
Huntilee Rd BURS/TUN ST6 .... 53 M7
Huntingdon Cl
 POL/KGSB/FAZ B78 .... 273 M8
Huntingdon Pl HAN ST1 .... 69 M4
Huntingdon Rd
 STPNHL/WNHL DE15 .... 204 D4
Huntington Rd SHHTH WV12 .... 282 D5
Huntington Terrace Rd
 CNCK/NC WS11 .... 231 M6
Huntley Av STOKE ST4 .... 85 G4
Huntley Cl CDLE ST10 .... 105 K2
Huntley Rd LEEK ST13 .... 56 E3
Huntsbank Dr NEWUL ST5 .... 67 K1
Hunts La MSHM DE12 .... 241 L2
 SHHTH WV12 .... 282 D4
Huntsmans Dr KINVER DY7 .... 305 M5
Huntsmans Ga BNTWD WS7 .... 252 B2
Huntsman's Hl RUGE WS15 .... 216 C8
Huntsmans Ri HEDN WS12 .... 231 J2
Huntsmans Wk RUGE WS15 .... 215 J1
Huntspill Rd
 RDERBYSW DE65 .... 166 E1
Hunt St BURS/TUN ST6 .... 53 L7
Hurlingham Rd STAFN ST16 .... 174 B3
Huron Cl CNCK/NC WS11 .... 232 B8
Huron Gv STOKE ST4 .... 101 G2
Hurstbourne Cl RUGE WS15 .... 197 J8
Hurst Cl ALS/KID ST7 .... 52 D4
Hurst Dr BUT/AL/TUT DE13 .... 185 L1
Hurstmead Dr STAFS ST17 .... 194 C5
Hurstons La CDLE ST10 .... 107 L1
Hurst Rd BIDD ST8 .... 27 C7
 BILS/COS WV14 .... 299 M1
Husphins La CDSL WV8 .... 262 A5
Hussey Cl PENK ST19 .... 229 M3
Hussey Rd BRWNH WS8 .... 268 C2
 CNCK/NC WS11 .... 250 F5
Hutchinson Cl RUGE WS15 .... 197 H8
Hut Hill La UTXR WS14 .... 250 A6
Hutton Wy BUCK/MIL ST2 .... 70 D8
Huxley Cl COVEN WV9 .... 264 A7
Huxley Pl LNGTN ST3 .... 86 D6
Hyacinth Ct NEWUL ST5 .... 68 C8
Hyde La KINVER DY7 .... 306 A5
Hyde La KINVER DY7 .... 306 A5
Hyde Lea Bank RSTAF ST18 .... 193 J5
Hyde Mill Cft PENK ST19 .... 246 C5
Hyde Mill La PENK ST19 .... 246 B5
Hyde Rd WNSFLD WV11 .... 281 K4
Hylstone Crs WNSFLD WV11 .... 281 K4
Hylton Cl BUT DE14 .... 204 A3
Hyndley Cl BUCK/MIL ST2 .... 3 M7
Hyperion Dr
 ETTPK/GDPK/PENN WV4 .... 295 G7
Hyperion Rd KINVER DY7 .... 307 L3
Hyssop Cl CNCK/NC WS11 .... 232 B8

Ian Rd ALS/KID ST7 .... 39 K8
Ibsen Rd LNGTN ST3 .... 87 G6
Ibstock St BUTN/AL/TUT DE13 ..... 185 H4
Idonia Rd
 DUNHL/THL/PER WV6 .... 278 E5
Idsall Crs SHIF TF11 .... 242 A5
Ikins Dr ALS/KID ST7 .... 51 M8
Ilam Cl NEWUL ST5 .... 83 H1
Ilam Ct ASHB DE6 .... 95 K2
Ilam Moor La ASHB DE6 .... 62 D2
Ilford Side LNGTN ST3 .... 101 L2
Ilkley Pl NEWUL ST5 .... 66 F8
Illshaw COVEN WV9 .... 264 A7
Imandra Cl STOKE ST4 .... 101 G2
Imogen Cl STOKE ST4 .... 86 B4
Imperial Ct HAN ST1 .... 2 E8
Impstones GNOS ST20 .... 190 C5
Inchlaggan Rd WOLVN WV10 ...... 280 F4
Ingatestine Dr STRBR DY8 .... 303 J7
Inge Dr BUTN/AL/TUT DE13 .... 220 A8
Ingelow Cl LNGTN ST3 .... 86 A8
Ingestre Cl BLOX/PEL WS3 .... 266 F7
 WOLVN WV10 .... 250 B1
Ingestre Rd STAFS ST17 .... 4 F8
 WOLVN WV10 .... 280 C1
Ingestre Sq LNGTN ST3 .... 101 L2
Ingleborough Pl
 BUCK/MIL ST2 .... 70 D1
Ingleby Cl SWAD DE11 .... 205 M7
Ingleby Gdns
 DUNHL/THL/PER WV6 .... 280 A5
Ingleby Rd LNGTN ST3 .... 101 L2
Ingledew Cl WSLW WS2 .... 282 D7
Inglefield Av BURS/TUN ST6 ...... 69 H1
Inglemere Dr STAFS ST17 .... 194 C4
Ingleside RUGE WS15 .... 215 J1
Ingleton Gv LNGTN ST3 .... 103 G3
Inglewood STAFS ST17 .... 4 C8
Inglewood Av
 BDMR/CCFT WV3 .... 294 F2
Inglewood Cl KGSWFD DY6 .... 303 K5
Inglewood Dr NEWUL ST5 .... 68 C4
Inglewood Gv
 FOAKS/STRLY B74 .... 285 M8
 NEWUL ST5 .... 68 C4
Inglis St STOKE ST4 .... 85 J2
Ingot Cl WSLW WS2 .... 283 H4
Ingram Pit La TAM/AM/WIL B77 ... 275 G5
Ingram Pl BLOX/PEL WS3 .... 283 K1
Ingram Rd BLOX/PEL WS3 .... 283 K1
Inhedge St SEDG DY3 .... 299 L5
Inkerman Gv WOLVN WV10 .... 13 L4
Inkerman St WOLVN WV10 .... 13 L4
Instow Cl WNSFLD WV11 .... 282 B2
Intake La BURS/TUN ST6 .... 54 D6
Intake Rd BURS/TUN ST6 .... 54 D6
Intakes La CDLE ST10 .... 123 L7
Intown WSL WS1 .... 283 M8
Intown Rw WSL WS1 .... 283 M8
Inworth COVEN WV9 .... 264 B7
Iona Pl LNGTN ST3 .... 85 M7
Irene Av BURS/TUN ST6 .... 53 M7
 NEWUL ST5 .... 68 D8
Ireton Rd WOLVN WV10 .... 264 D7
Iris Cl CRTAM B79 .... 10 E1
 LNGTN ST3 .... 87 J5
Irnham Rd FOAKS/STRLY B74 ..... 287 C8
Ironbridge Dr NEWUL ST5 .... 67 M8

Ironmarket NEWUL ST5 .... 84 B1
Ironstone La LICH WS13 .... 237 L5
Ironstone Rd BNTWD WS7 .... 251 L2
 HEDN WS12 .... 233 J6
Ironwalls La
 BUTN/AL/TUT DE13 .... 165 J5
Irvine Rd BLOX/PEL WS3 .... 283 H3
Irvine Rd BLOX/PEL WS3 .... 283 H2
 END/WER ST9 .... 71 J6
Irving Cl LICH WS13 .... 235 L8
 SEDG DY3 .... 299 G6
Isabel Cl STOKE ST4 .... 85 G4
Isherwood Pl LNGTN ST3 .... 86 D6
Isis Gv WLNHL WV13 .... 282 C8
Island Gn STAFS ST17 .... 194 D4
The Island CDLE ST10 .... 105 K6
Itchen Gv
 DUNHL/THL/PER WV6 .... 278 E7
Ivanhoe Rd LICH WS13 .... 8 E6
Ivatt Cl RUSH/SHEL WS4 .... 284 B3
Iverley La BLOX/PEL WS3 .... 311 J5
Ivetsey Bank Rd PENK ST19 ...... 244 F2
Ivetsey Cl PENK ST19 .... 227 H5
Ivetsey Rd PENK ST19 .... 226 E7
Ivy Ct BLYBR/FOR ST11 .... 103 M4
 BUTN/AL/TUT DE13 .... 185 J3
 CNCK/NC WS11 .... 249 J2
 STAFS ST17 .... 212 B1
 UTXR ST14 .... 144 A2
Ivy Ct RDERBYSW DE65 .... 166 D1
 RSTAF ST18 .... 177 H2
 STAFS ST17 .... 212 A1
Ivy Cft COVEN WV9 .... 263 M7
Ivy Gv STOKE ST4 .... 100 F2
Ivyhouse Dr BARL ST12 .... 101 L6
Ivy House La PENK ST19 .... 246 E1
Ivy House Rd BIDD ST8 .... 26 C8
 HAN ST1 .... 3 H6
Ivy La ALS/KID ST7 .... 37 L8
 RUGE WS15 .... 233 M5
Ivy Lodge Cl
 STPNHL/WNHL DE15 .... 204 E3
Izaac Walton Wy
 AUD/MAD/W CW3 .... 81 L5
Izaak Walton St STAFN ST16 ..... 174 C5

Jackdaw Cl SEDG DY3 .... 295 J8
Jackfield St BURS/TUN ST6 .... 69 H1
Jack Haye La BUCK/MIL ST2 ...... 70 E2
Jacklin Cl BUT DE14 .... 204 A4
Jackman Cl LICH WS13 .... 237 K4
Jackman Rd LICH WS13 .... 237 K4
Jack's La UTXR ST14 .... 162 E1
Jackson Av BUTN/AL/TUT DE13 .. 185 M3
Jackson Cl CNCK/NC WS11 ...... 250 B1
 WOLVN WV10 .... 265 G4
Jackson Rd LICH WS13 .... 236 B7
Jackson St BURS/TUN ST6 .... 69 G2
 DUNHL/THL/PER WV6 .... 280 B6
Jacobean Ct
 STPNHL/WNHL DE15 .... 186 C6
Jacob's Hall La GTWY WS6 ...... 267 G1
Jacqueline St BURS/TUN ST6 .... 53 J6
Jade Ct LNGTN ST3 .... 86 D6
Jade Gv HEDN WS12 .... 232 C8
Jaguar TAM/AM/WIL B77 .... 11 J9
Jamage Rd ALS/KID ST7 .... 52 D5
James Brindley Cl HAN ST1 ..... 69 G8
James Brindley Wy
 BUTN/AL/TUT DE13 .... 185 M2
James Cl SHIF TF11 .... 224 C4
James Crs END/WER ST9 .... 71 J6
Jameson St
 DUNHL/THL/PER WV6 .... 280 B6
James St BUT DE14 .... 6 F7
 CNCK/NC WS11 .... 231 M6
 KINVER DY7 .... 306 A6
 LEEK ST13 .... 43 K5
 NEWUL ST5 .... 68 C5
 STOKE ST4 .... 85 G5
 UTXR ST14 .... 144 B2
 WLNHL WV13 .... 282 A8
James Warner Cl RUGE WS15 ... 215 K1
James Wy BIDD ST8 .... 40 A4
Jamieson Cl ALS/KID ST7 .... 37 L6
Jane Lane Cl WSLW WS2 .... 282 F6
Janet Pl HAN ST1 .... 3 G4
Janine Av WNSFLD WV11 ...... 281 L3
Janson St STOKE ST4 .... 100 F1
Jasmine Cl COVEN WV9 .... 263 M7
 STPNHL/WNHL DE15 .... 205 G3
Jasmine Ct BLYBR/FOR ST11 .... 103 M4
Jasmine Gv CDSL WV8 .... 263 H7
Jasmine Rd RSTAF ST18 .... 154 B8
 TAM/AM/WIL B77 .... 275 G6
Jasmin Wy ALS/KID ST7 .... 39 M8
Jason Cl TAM/AM/WIL B77 ...... 11 H3
Jason St NEWUL ST5 .... 68 A4
Jasper Cl BARL ST12 .... 101 M6
 NEWUL ST5 .... 68 B3
Jasper St HAN ST1 .... 2 D7
Java Crs STOKE ST4 .... 101 H3
Jaycean Av BURS/TUN ST6 ..... 53 L6
Jayne Cl WNSFLD WV11 .... 281 K3
Jay Rd KGSWFD DY6 .... 303 K2
Jean Cl BURS/TUN ST6 .... 54 A8
Jedburgh Av
 DUNHL/THL/PER WV6 .... 278 E6
Jeddo St BURS/TUN ST6 .... 53 K6
Jefferson St BURS/TUN ST6 .... 53 K6
Jeffery Cl RUGE WS15 .... 197 K7
Jeffrey Av
 ETTPK/GDPK/PENN WV4 ..... 295 M4
Jeffs Av BURS/TUN ST6 .... 53 H9
Jellicoe Crs SHIF TF11 .... 242 A4
Jenkinson Cl NEWUL ST5 ...... 83 M2
Jenkins St BURS/TUN ST6 ...... 68 F2
Jenkinstown Rd HEDN WS12 ... 233 G4
Jenks Av WOLVN WV10 .... 280 C2
Jenks Rd WMBN WV5 .... 297 M5
Jenner Av WSLW WS2 .... 282 F4
Jenner Rd WSLW WS2 .... 282 F4
Jenner St BKHL/PFLD WV2 ..... 13 J7
Jennings Wy BUT DE14 .... 6 B4
Jenny Walkers La
 DUNHL/THL/PER WV6 .... 293 K2

Jensen TAM/AM/WIL B77 .... 11 J9
Jephson Rd BUT DE14 .... 204 B3
Jerbourg Cl NEWUL ST5 .... 83 L6
Jeremy Cl STOKE ST4 .... 84 F4
Jeremy Rd
 ETTPK/GDPK/PENN WV4 ..... 295 J5
Jerningham St STAFN ST16 .... 4 C4
Jerome Dr CNCK/NC WS11 .... 251 G5
Jerome Rd CNCK/NC WS11 .... 250 F5
Jerome Wy BNTWD WS7 ...... 252 B3
Jerry's La LICHS WS14 .... 272 C2
Jersey Cl CONG CW12 .... 26 A1
 NEWUL ST5 .... 83 L6
Jervis Crs FOAKS/STRLY B74 .. 286 D7
Jervis La STONE ST15 .... 119 J7
Jervison St LNGTN ST3 .... 86 D4
Jervis Rd STONE ST15 .... 138 B3
Jervis St HAN ST1 .... 2 F3
Jesmond Cl HEDN WS12 ...... 233 G4
Jesmond Gv LNGTN ST3 ...... 101 L2
Jessel Rd WSLW WS2 .... 283 J8
Jessie Rd ALDR WS9 .... 285 C1
Jew's La DUDN DY1 .... 299 L6
Joanhurst Crs HAN ST1 .... 2 A8
Joan St BKHL/PFLD WV2 ...... 295 L4
Jockey Fld SEDG DY3 .... 299 L4
Jodrell Vw ALS/KID ST7 .... 53 H2
Joeys La CDSL WV8 .... 263 J7
John Amery Dr STAFS ST17 ... 193 K5
John Ball St RUGE WS15 ...... 197 K7
John Bright St HAN ST1 .... 2 F3
John Donne St STAFN ST16 ... 174 D4
Johndory TAM/AM/WIL B77 ... 290 D4
John Harper St WLNHL WV13 . 282 B8
John Offley Rd
 AUD/MAD/W CW3 .... 81 K4
John O'gaunt's Rd
 NEWUL ST5 .... 84 A1
John Riley Dr SHHTH WV12 ... 282 C2
Johns Av RUGE WS15 .... 217 J6
Johnsgate PENK ST19 .... 246 D3
Johns La GTWY WS6 .... 249 M7
Johnson Av WNSFLD WV11 ... 281 M3
Johnson Cl CONG CW12 ...... 26 B1
 LICH WS13 .... 8 F6
 RSTAF ST18 .... 172 C5
 RUGE WS15 .... 197 K8
Johnson Crs CDLE ST10 ...... 73 K8
Johnson Pl BURS/TUN ST6 .... 54 B4
Johnson Rd BNTWD WS7 ..... 251 M2
 CNCK/NC WS11 .... 231 K6
 SHHTH WV12 .... 282 D1
 UTXR ST14 .... 144 B1
Johnson St BILS/COS WV14 .. 299 M1
 BKHL/PFLD WV2 .... 13 G9
 NEWUL ST5 .... 67 K3
 HAN ST1 .... 2 D6
 HEDN WS12 .... 232 F7
 LEEK ST13 .... 43 L5
 NEWUL ST5 .... 67 L8
 NEWUL ST5 .... 84 D1
 STAFN ST16 .... 5 J3
 STRBR DY8 .... 307 M1
 SWAD DE11 .... 205 L4
 TAM/AM/WIL B77 .... 11 J7
 UTXR ST14 .... 144 B2
 WSLW WS2 .... 283 L7
John Till Cl RUGE WS15 ...... 215 L1
Jolley St BURS/TUN ST6 ...... 69 J1
Jolliffe St LEEK ST13 .... 43 L5
Jolpool La RSTAF ST18 .... 139 J4
Jolt La RSTAF ST18 .... 191 L5
Jolyon Cl LNGTN ST3 .... 86 B3
Jonathan Rd STOKE ST4 ...... 101 J5
Jones Cl STAFS ST17 .... 193 K3
Jones Field Crs WOLV WV1 ... 281 H8
Jones' La BNTWD WS7 .... 252 F3
 GTWY WS6 .... 267 H1
 RUGE WS15 .... 215 J2
 WOLVN WV10 .... 280 C4
Jones Rd SHHTH WV12 ...... 282 D1
Jonkel Av TAM/AM/WIL B77 .. 290 F5
Jordan Av BUTN/AL/TUT DE13 166 F8
Jordan Cl LICH WS13 .... 8 C2
 LICH WS13 .... 237 K4
Jordan Cft LICH WS13 .... 237 K3
 STONE ST15 .... 138 B3
Jordan Wy ALDR WS9 .... 285 H1
Jordon St HAN ST1 .... 2 A8
Joseph Crs ALS/KID ST7 ...... 37 L8
Joseph Dewsbury Cl
 BNTWD WS7 .... 251 L2
Joseph Dix Dr RUGE WS15 ... 197 K8
Joseph St BURS/TUN ST6 ..... 68 E2
Josiah Wedgwood St HAN ST1 . 69 G7
Jowett La BUTN/AL/TUT DE13 . 11 H9
Joyberry Dr STRBR DY8 .... 307 M7
Joyce Av BURS/TUN ST6 ...... 54 B8
Joyce's La STAFS ST17 .... 213 G2
Jubilee Av HAN ST1 .... 69 C7
Jubilee Cl BIDD ST8 .... 40 D3
 BLOX/PEL WS3 .... 283 L4
 GTWY WS6 .... 266 F1
Jubilee Dr CDLE ST10 .... 74 D7
Jubilee Rd NEWUL ST5 .... 68 D7
 STOKE ST4 .... 100 F2
Jubilee Sq ASHB DE6 .... 95 J5
Jubilee St RUGE WS15 .... 215 K1
Jubilee Ter LEEK ST13 .... 43 K4
Judgefield La BURS/TUN ST6 . 40 F8
Judith Gv STOKE ST4 .... 85 J5
Jug Bank MKTDR TF9 .... 115 H6
Julian Cl GTWY WS6 .... 250 A7
 WOLV WV1 .... 281 H8
Julian Rd WOLV WV1 .... 281 H8
Junction St LEEK ST13 .... 43 L5
 STRBR DY8 .... 307 L2
The Junction STRBR DY8 ...... 307 L2
June Crs TAM/AM/WIL B77 .... 11 J4
June Rd STOKE ST4 .... 86 B4
Juniper TAM/AM/WIL B77 ...... 275 C6
Juniper Cl HEDN WS12 .... 233 J4
Juniper Dr HEDN WS12 .... 233 C3
Jupiter St BURS/TUN ST6 ..... 69 J1
Justin Cl NEWUL ST5 .... 68 D4

K

Kara Pl STOKE ST4 .... 101 H2
Kaydor Cl END/WER ST9 ...... 71 H6
Kay Dr SWAD DE11 .... 205 M3
Kayne Cl KGSWFD DY6 .... 303 J3
Kean Cl LICH WS13 .... 235 L8
Kearsley Av LNGTN ST3 ...... 101 L2
Keary St STOKE ST4 .... 85 H4
Keasdon Gv WLNHL WV13 ... 282 C7
Keates Av CNCK/NC WS11 ... 231 L5
 STAFS ST17 .... 193 J3
Keats Cl CRTAM B79 .... 273 M2
 FOAKS/STRLY B74 .... 286 F4
 SEDG DY3 .... 299 C5
Keats Dr ALS/KID ST7 .... 37 L2
Keats Gdns ALS/KID ST7 ..... 53 C2
Keats Gv WOLVN WV10 ...... 281 C2
Keats Rd BLOX/PEL WS3 ..... 283 L3
 SHHTH WV12 .... 282 E3
 WOLVN WV10 .... 281 C1
Keble Cl BNTWD WS7 .... 252 C3
 CNCK/NC WS11 .... 249 L1
 STPNHL/WNHL DE15 .... 186 C8
Keble Wy LNGTN ST3 .... 86 A8
Kedleston Cl BLOX/PEL WS3 . 267 G7
 BUTN/AL/TUT DE13 .... 185 J1
Kedleston Rd BURS/TUN ST6 . 54 A8
Keele Rd AUD/MAD/W CW3 .. 82 A2
 NEWUL ST5 .... 83 C3
Keele St BURS/TUN ST6 ...... 53 K6
Keeling Dr CNCK/NC WS11 ... 249 H1
Keeling Rd CDLE ST10 .... 89 L7
Keelings Dr HAN ST1 .... 3 C3
Keelings Rd HAN ST1 .... 3 C3
Keene Cl STAFN ST16 .... 174 D4
Keepers Cl ALDR WS9 .... 268 F7
 BNTWD WS7 .... 252 A4
 KGSWFD DY6 .... 303 H2
 LICHS WS14 .... 9 L5
Keepers La CDSL WV8 .... 279 C2
Keepers Rd FOAKS/STRLY B74 286 C5
Keir Pl STRBR DY8 .... 307 L2
Keld Av UTXR ST14 .... 193 H2
Keldy Cl DUNHL/THL/PER WV6 279 M5
Kelland Rd STOKE ST4 .... 86 A4
Kelly Av RUGE WS15 .... 215 M4
Kelmore Cl LNGTN ST3 ...... 86 B6
Kelsall Cl WOLV WV1 .... 281 H8
Kelsall St STAFN ST16 .... 69 H1
Kelsall Wy ALS/KID ST7 ...... 66 D1
Kelso Gdns
 DUNHL/THL/PER WV6 ...... 278 D6
Kelvedon Wy RUGE WS15 ... 215 J1
Kelvin Av HAN ST1 .... 69 K4
Kelvin Dr CNCK/NC WS11 ... 232 A7
Kelvin Rd BLOX/PEL WS3 .... 283 H4
Kelvin Rd WSLW WS2 .... 283 C4
Kelvin St NEWUL ST5 .... 68 D6
Kemball Av STOKE ST4 .... 85 J5
Kemberton Cl
 BDMR/CCFT WV3 .... 294 C1
Kemberton Rd
 BDMR/CCFT WV3 .... 294 C1
Kemble Cl SHHTH WV12 ..... 282 D6
Kemnay Av BURS/TUN ST6 .. 54 A2
Kempson Rd PENK ST19 ..... 229 L2
Kempthorne Av WOLVN WV10 280 E2
Kempthorne Gdns
 BLOX/PEL WS3 .... 267 G8
Kempthorne Rd HAN ST1 .... 2 F7
Kempton Dr GTWY WS6 ..... 249 M8
Kempton Gv CDLE ST10 ..... 89 L5
Kempton Rd
 STPNHL/WNHL DE15 .... 186 A7
Kempton Wy STRBR DY8 .... 307 L7
Kendal Cl
 DUNHL/THL/PER WV6 ...... 279 M4
 STAFS ST17 .... 193 H3
Kendal Ct CNCK/NC WS11 .. 249 H2
Kendal Gv BUCK/MIL ST2 ... 70 D8
Kendall Ri KGSWFD DY6 .... 303 M5
Kendall Pl NEWUL ST5 ...... 84 B4
Kendal Ri
 DUNHL/THL/PER WV6 ...... 279 M4
Kenderdine Cl STAFS ST17 .. 212 F2
Kendrick Rd WOLVN WV10 .. 280 E4
Kendrick St LNGTN ST3 ..... 86 D7
Kenelyn Crs ALS/KID ST7 .... 85 L6
Kenilworth Av
 BUTN/AL/TUT DE13 .... 185 K3
 PENK ST19 .... 230 A2
 STRBR DY8 .... 303 K8
Kenilworth Cl MKTDR TF9 ... 112 E8
Kenilworth Crs
 ETTPK/GDPK/PENN WV4 ... 295 L6
 WSLW WS2 .... 283 C6
Kenilworth Dr CNCK/NC WS11 231 K6
Kenilworth Gv NEWUL ST5 .. 68 E7
Kenilworth Rd
 DUNHL/THL/PER WV6 ...... 278 F6
 LICHS WS14 .... 8 F6
 TAM/AM/WIL B77 .... 11 K5
Kenley Av END/WER ST9 .... 55 M2
Kenmare Wy WNSFLD WV11 . 281 J2
Kenmore Av HEDN WS12 .... 231 M3
Kennedy Cl
 TAM/AM/WIL B77 .... 290 C1
Kennedy Crs SEDG DY3 ..... 299 K6
Kennedy Rd STOKE ST4 ..... 101 H3
 WOLVN WV10 .... 13 H3
Kennedy Wk END/WER ST9 .. 71 H6
Kennedy Wy STAFN ST16 .... 174 B2
Kennel La ALBTN WV7 .... 260 D6
Kennermont Rd
 BUCK/MIL ST2 .... 70 C5
Kennet Cl BRWNH WS8 ...... 251 J8
Kennington Rd
 WOLVN WV10 .... 280 F5
Kenrick Cl AUD/MAD/W CW3 . 96 C1
Kensington Ct ALS/KID ST7 .. 36 F7
 BURS/TUN ST6 .... 53 L6
 STOKE ST4 .... 84 E7

Kensington Dr
 FOAKS/STRLY B74 .... 286 F5
Kensington Gdns STRBR DY8 . 307 J1
Kensington Rd SHHTH WV12 . 282 B3
 STOKE ST4 .... 84 F6
 STPNHL/WNHL DE15 .... 186 A7
Kensworth Cl NEWUL ST5 ... 84 A7
Kent Av ALDR WS9 .... 285 H1
 BLOX/PEL WS3 .... 283 L5
Kent Cl ALDR WS9 .... 285 H1
 BLOX/PEL WS3 .... 283 L5
Kent Dr END/WER ST9 ...... 55 L4
Kent Gv NEWUL ST5 .... 67 K2
 STONE ST15 .... 119 M8
Kentish Cl STAFS ST17 ...... 193 C2
Kentmere Cl PENK ST19 ..... 230 A1
 STAFS ST17 .... 193 H2
 STOKE ST4 .... 86 B5
Kentmere Pl NEWUL ST5 .... 84 B4
Kenton Av
 DUNHL/THL/PER WV6 ...... 279 M6
Kent Pl HEDN WS12 .... 250 F1
 STOKE ST4 .... 85 L4
Kent Rd BKHL/PFLD WV2 .... 295 L3
 STPNHL/WNHL DE15 .... 204 D4
 STRBR DY8 .... 307 K2
Kent St SEDG DY3 .... 299 L5
 WSLW WS2 .... 283 L5
Kent Wy STAFS ST17 .... 194 B2
Kentwell CRTAM B79 .... 273 K3
Kenworthy Rd STAFN ST16 .. 174 E4
Kenworthy St BURS/TUN ST6 . 53 L6
Kepler CRTAM B79 .... 273 L3
Kerria Rd TAM/AM/WIL B77 .. 275 H6
Kerridge Cl COVEN WV9 ..... 264 A8
Kerry La ECCH ST21 .... 152 C4
Kersbrook Cl STOKE ST4 .... 101 J4
Kersley Gdns WNSFLD WV11 . 281 M4
Kervis Gv BLYBR/FOR ST11 .. 103 H4
Kesterton Rd FOAKS/STRLY B74 286 E5
Kestrel TAM/AM/WIL B77 .... 291 C4
Kestrel Av BLYBR/FOR ST11 .. 103 J3
Kestrel Cl BIDD ST8 .... 40 B4
 LICHS WS14 .... 255 M5
 NWPT TF10 .... 188 A5
 STAFS ST17 .... 194 C1
 UTXR ST14 .... 144 A1
Kestrel Dr FOAKS/STRLY B74 . 286 F5
 MKTDR TF9 .... 114 D6
Kestrel Gv HEDN WS12 ...... 250 C1
 SHHTH WV12 .... 282 C2
Kestrel La CDLE ST10 .... 89 L7
Kestrel Ri
 DUNHL/THL/PER WV6 ...... 279 M3
Kestrel Wy GTWY WS6 ...... 249 J8
 STPNHL/WNHL DE15 .... 186 C6
Keswick Dr KGSWFD DY6 .... 303 K4
Keswick Gv FOAKS/STRLY B74 285 M8
 STAFS ST17 .... 193 C2
Ketley Rd KGSWFD DY6 ..... 303 M4
Kettlebrook Rd
 TAM/AM/WIL B77 .... 10 F9
Kettlemore La SHIF TF11 ..... 224 C5
Kettlesbank Rd SEDG DY3 ... 299 H8
Ketton Cl BURS/TUN ST6 ..... 54 A2
Kewstoke Cl WNSFLD WV11 .. 282 B1
Kewstoke Rd SHHTH WV12 ... 282 C1
Keyes Dr KGSWFD DY6 ...... 303 K1
Keystone Rd RUGE WS15 .... 215 M2
Kibblestone Rd STONE ST15 .. 120 B6
Kibworth Gv HAN ST1 .... 2 C2
Kiddemore Green Rd
 PENK ST19 .... 245 H4
Kidderminster Rd KGSWFD DY6 303 C4
 KIDD DY10 .... 311 J3
Kidderminster Rd South
 KIDD DY10 .... 311 L7
Kidsgrove Bank ALS/KID ST7 . 53 L2
Kidsgrove Rd BURS/TUN ST6 . 53 J2
Kielder Cl HEDN WS12 .... 232 E8
Kilburn Cl HEDN WS12 .... 232 E8
Kilburn Pl BUCK/MIL ST2 .... 3 K8
Kilburn Wy SWAD DE11 ...... 205 M5
Kilbye Cl TAM/AM/WIL B77 ... 290 F5
Kildare St LNGTN ST3 .... 86 C8
Kilmorie Rd CNCK/NC WS11 . 231 J8
Kilnbank Crs MKTDR TF9 .... 130 C2
Kilnbank Rd MKTDR TF9 ..... 130 C2
Kilndown Cl HAN ST1 .... 69 C8
Kiln La LEEK ST13 .... 43 J4
Kiln Wy POL/KGSB/FAZ B78 .. 291 M1
Kilsby Gv BUCK/MIL ST2 ..... 55 H8
Kimberley TAM/AM/WIL B77 .. 290 F3
Kimberley Av KIDD DY10 ..... 310 B6
Kimberley Cl
 FOAKS/STRLY B74 .... 286 A8
Kimberley Dr
 STPNHL/WNHL DE15 .... 186 C7
 UTXR ST14 .... 143 M1
Kimberley Rd HAN ST1 ...... 69 C7
 NEWUL ST5 .... 68 B3
Kimberley St BDMR/CCFT WV3 12 B7
 HAN ST1 .... 86 A8
Kimberley Wy RUGE WS15 ... 215 M5
 STAFS ST17 .... 193 C2
Kinder Pl NEWUL ST5 .... 83 H1
Kineton Ri SEDG DY3 .... 295 J8
Kinfare Dr
 DUNHL/THL/PER WV6 ...... 279 H6
Kinfare Ri SEDG DY3 .... 299 L6
King Charles Av WSLW WS2 .. 282 E8
Kingcross St LNGTN ST3 .... 86 C7
Kingcup Rd STAFS ST17 ..... 193 L5
King Edward Pl BUT DE14 ... 6 D4
King Edward's Rw
 BKHL/PFLD WV2 .... 12 F9
King Edward St CDLE ST10 .. 89 L6
Kingfisher TAM/AM/WIL B77 .. 291 C4
Kingfisher Cl
 AUD/MAD/W CW3 .... 81 M3
 SEDG DY3 .... 295 J8
Kingfisher Crs STONE ST15 ... 121 J4
Kingfisher Cresent CDLE ST10 . 89 L7
Kingfisher Dr HEDN WS12 ... 232 C6
 STRBR DY8 .... 307 J1
Kingfisher Gv BURS/TUN ST6 . 54 C7
 SHHTH WV12 .... 282 B2
Kingfisher Wk PENK ST19 .... 229 M2
Kingfisher Wy UTXR ST14 .... 144 B4

King George Crs
 RUSH/SHEL WS4 .... 284 B4
King George Pl
 RUSH/SHEL WS4 .... 284 B4
King George St HAN ST1 ...... 2 F3
Kingham Cl SEDG DY3 .... 299 J8
Kings Av
 MKTDR TF9 .... 130 A2
 NEWUL ST5 .... 68 C5
 STONE ST15 .... 138 A1
Kingsbridge Av NEWUL ST5 .. 84 B5
King's Bromley La RUGE WS15... 217 J4
Kings Bromley Rd
 BUTN/AL/TUT DE13 .... 219 L8
Kingsbury Cl RUSH/SHEL WS4 ... 284 B6
 STPNHL/WNHL DE15 .... 186 A6
Kingsbury Gv HAN ST1 .... 69 M4
Kingsclere Gv HAN ST1 ...... 69 L3
Kingsclere Wk
 ETTPK/GDPK/PENN WV4 ...... 294 C3
Kings Ct STRBR DY8 .... 307 L5
King's Cft STOKE ST4 .... 84 D1
Kingsdale Cl LNGTN ST3 ..... 103 C3
Kingsdale Cft
 BUTN/AL/TUT DE13 .... 185 K2
Kingsdene Av STRBR DY8 ..... 303 J6
Kingsdown Rd BNTWD WS7 ..... 251 L1
Kings Dr RSTAF ST18......... 175 K2
Kingsfield Crs BIDD ST8 .... 40 D2
Kingsfield Rd BIDD ST8 ..... 40 C3
 STOKE ST4................. 84 D1
Kingsford La KIDDW DY11..... 309 H4
Kingsford Pl LNGTN ST3 ..... 103 C3
Kingshayes Rd ALDR WS9 ..... 269 H8
King's Hill Rd LICHS WS14 ... 9 G7
Kingside Gv STOKE ST4 ...... 101 J5
Kingsland Av STOKE ST4 ..... 84 F6
Kingsland Rd STONE ST15 .... 138 C3
 WOLV WV1 .... 12 C3
King's La CRTAM B79 .... 259 K5
Kingsley Av
 DUNHL/THL/PER WV6 .... 279 H6
 HEDN WS12 .... 232 C3
Kingsley Cl ALS/KID ST7 .... 52 D4
 CRTAM B79 .... 10 A1
 STAFS ST17 .... 193 L2
Kingsley Gdns CDSL WV8 ..... 262 F7
Kingsley Pl SEDG DY3 .... 299 G5
Kingsley Rd ALS/KID ST7 .... 52 D4
 BUT DE14 .... 185 K3
 END/WER ST9.............. 72 A7
 KGSWFD DY6 .... 303 J5
 STAFS ST17 .... 193 L2
Kingsley St LNGTN ST3 ...... 103 C3
Kingsley Vw LEEK ST13 ...... 57 K5
Kingsley Wood Rd RUGE WS15 .. 214 B3
Kingslow Av
 ETTPK/GDPK/PENN WV4 ...... 294 D4
Kingsmead Rd LNGTN ST3...... 102 F3
Kingsnorth Pl BLYBR/FOR ST11 ... 103 H4
Kings Pl STOKE ST4 .... 68 D8
Kings Rd RUSH/SHEL WS4 ..... 284 C3
 SEDG DY3 .... 299 L2
 STOKE ST4................. 101 C1
 WOLV WV10 .... 248 A4
King's NWPT TF10 .... 225 L1
 SHIF TF11 .... 224 E8
Kings Ter NEWUL ST5 .... 84 D1
 STAFN ST16 .... 5 M3
Kingston Av HAN ST1 .... 69 L3
Kingston Cl CRTAM B79 ...... 274 C3
Kingston Pl STOKE ST8 ...... 26 E8
 BURS/TUN ST6 .... 54 E7
Kingston Rd
 STPNHL/WNHL DE15 .... 186 C8
Kingston Rd KGSWFD DY6 ..... 303 J3
King St ALDR WS9 .... 268 F8
 ALS/KID ST7 .... 39 G8
 ALS/KID ST7 .... 52 D5
 ALS/KID ST7 .... 66 D1
 ASHB DE6 .... 79 G4
 BIDD ST8 .... 40 C2
 BNTWD WS7 .... 251 M5
 BUT DE14 .... 6 F9
 BUTN/AL/TUT DE13 .... 201 C7
 CRTAM B79 .... 10 C5
 LEEK ST13 .... 43 L5
 NEWUL ST5 .... 67 L3
 NEWUL ST5 .... 68 A7
 RUGE WS15 .... 215 M2
 STOKE ST4................ 86 A5
 STRBR DY8 .... 307 L4
 WLNHL WV13 .... 282 B8
 WOLV WV1 .... 12 F5
Kingsway BUT DE14 .... 204 B2
 CNCK/NC WS11 .... 232 A6
 STAFN ST16 .... 4 B6
 STOKE ST4................ 85 H3
 STRBR DY8 .... 307 K2
 WNSFLD WV11 .... 266 A6
 WOLV WV10 .... 281 C4
Kingsway East NEWUL ST5 .... 84 B4
Kingsway Rd WOLV WV10 ..... 281 C4
Kingsway West NEWUL ST5 .... 84 A4
Kingswear Av
 DUNHL/THL/PER WV6 .... 278 F7
Kingswell Rd STOKE ST4 ..... 84 D1
Kingswinford Pl
 BURS/TUN ST6 .... 69 K3
Kingswood Av
 CNCK/NC WS11 .... 249 J5
Kingswood Dr CNCK/NC WS11 ... 250 F5
 GTWY WS6 .... 250 A6
Kingswood Gdns
 ETTPK/GDPK/PENN WV4 ..... 294 F4
Kingswood Rd ALBTN WV7 .... 261 J6
 STRBR DY8 .... 303 J6
Kington Cl SHHTH WV12 ..... 282 B2
King William St BURS/TUN ST6... 53 L7
 STRBR DY8 .... 307 M2
Kinlet Cl BDMR/CCFT WV3..... 294 A2
Kinloch Dr DUDN DY1 .... 299 M7
Kinloss Av WLNHL WV13 ..... 260 D2
Kinnersley Av ALS/KID ST7 ... 52 E3
Kinnersley St ALS/KID ST7 ... 39 C8
Kinross Av HEDN WS12 ...... 231 M3
Kinsall Gn TAM/AM/WIL B77 ... 291 J4
Kinsey St NEWUL ST5 .... 67 H8
Kinver Av SHHTH WV12 ...... 282 B5

Kinver Cl ASHB DE6 .... 94 C2
Kinver Crs ALDR WS9 .... 285 J1
Kinverdale KIDDW DY11 ...... 309 H4
Kinver Dr
 ETTPK/GDPK/PENN WV4 ..... 294 C5
Kinver La KIDDW DY11 ...... 310 A1
Kinver Rd KINVER DY7 ...... 305 L3
 STPNHL/WNHL DE15 .... 186 A6
Kinver St BURS/TUN ST6 ..... 69 J1
 STRBR DY8 .... 307 K1
Kiplass La RSTAF ST18 ...... 139 J6
Kipling Ri CRTAM B79 .... 273 M2
Kipling Rd SEDG DY3 .... 299 G5
 SHHTH WV12 .... 282 E3
 WOLV WV10 .... 264 D8
Kipling Wy BUCK/MIL ST2 .... 86 D1
Kirby St BURS/TUN ST6 ...... 54 D6
Kirkbride Cl LNGTN ST3 ..... 86 D6
Kirkham St STOKE ST4 ...... 85 G4
Kirkland La STOKE ST4 ...... 85 G3
Kirkland Wy
 POL/KCSB/FAZ B78 .... 289 H2
Kirkside Gv BRWNH WS8 ..... 268 F3
Kirkstall BLOX/PEL WS3 ..... 266 F3
Kirkstall Av STAFS ST17 .... 193 H3
Kirkstall Crs BLOX/PEL WS3 ... 266 F8
Kirkstone Crs WMBN WV5 .... 297 M4
Kirk St BURS/TUN ST6 ...... 69 J1
Kirkwall Gv BUCK/MIL ST2 ... 55 H8
Kirstead Gdns
 DUNHL/THL/PER WV6 ...... 279 H7
Kirtley TAM/AM/WIL B77 ..... 274 E8
Kirton Gv
 DUNHL/THL/PER WV6 ...... 279 J6
Kitchen La WNSFLD WV11 .... 281 L2
Kite Gv ALS/KID ST7 .... 39 K7
 LNGTN ST3 .... 103 G4
Kitling Greaves La
 BUTN/AL/TUT DE13 .... 185 G2
Kitlings La STAFS ST17 ..... 194 F3
Kittoe Rd FOAKS/STRLY B74 .. 286 F7
Kitwood Av POL/KCSB/FAZ B78... 291 M4
Knarsdale Cl LNGTN ST3 ..... 86 D5
Knaves Castle Av BRWNH WS8 ... 251 M8
Knenhall STONE ST15 .... 120 D1
Knenhall La STONE ST15 ..... 121 G1
Knight Av STAFN ST16 ...... 5 K2
Knight La CDLE ST10 .... 107 L1
Knightley AUD/MAD/W CW3 .... 81 M5
Knightley Cl GNOS ST20 ..... 190 D3
Knightley Rd GNOS ST20 ..... 190 C1
Knightley Wy GNOS ST20 ..... 190 D3
Knighton Cl
 FOAKS/STRLY B74 .... 286 F7
Knighton Dr FOAKS/STRLY B74... 286 F8
Knighton Rd FOAKS/STRLY B74... 286 D5
 HEDN WS12 .... 232 E7
Knight Rd BNTWD WS7 ...... 251 L1
 KIDDW DY11 .... 309 J7
Knights Av
 DUNHL/THL/PER WV6 ...... 279 L4
Knightsbridge Cl
 FOAKS/STRLY B74 .... 286 F6
Knightsbridge La SHHTH WV12... 282 B4
Knightsbridge Wy
 BUTN/AL/TUT DE13 .... 185 K2
Knights Cl PENK ST19 ...... 229 M3
Knights Ct
 BUTN/AL/TUT DE13 .... 166 E8
 CNCK/NC WS11 .... 251 G6
Knights Crs
 DUNHL/THL/PER WV6 ...... 279 L3
Knightsfield Rd Cl NEWUL ST5... 82 F3
Knightsfield Rd
 BUTN/AL/TUT DE13 .... 163 L8
Knights Hl ALDR WS9 .... 285 H7
Knight's La RDERBYSW DE65... 187 J4
Knights St BURS/TUN ST6 .... 53 K6
Kniveden La LEEK ST13 ..... 44 A5
Knob Flds SWAD DE11 ...... 223 L2
Knoll Cl BNTWD WS7 .... 252 A5
Knoll Cft ALDR WS9 .... 285 J1
The Knoll KGSWFD DY6 ..... 303 L5
Knotty La CRTAM B79 ...... 27 G2
Knowlbank Rd ALS/KID ST7 .. 65 M4
Knowle La LICHS WS14 ..... 254 B8
Knowle Rd BIDD ST8 .... 40 C3
Knowle St STOKE ST4 ...... 85 G2
Knowle Wood Vw LNGTN ST3... 85 H7
Knowsley Av ALS/KID ST7 ... 38 E6
Knowsley Rd LEEK ST13 .... 56 D7
Knox Rd BKHL/PFLD WV2 .... 295 J4
Knox's Grave La LICHS WS14... 272 B3
Knutsford Rd ALS/KID ST7 ... 37 M5
Knutton Rd NEWUL ST5 ..... 68 C5
Knype Cl NEWUL ST5 ...... 68 A3
Knypersley Rd BURS/TUN ST6... 54 E6
Knype Wy BIDD ST8 .... 40 B4
 NEWUL ST5 .... 68 A3
Kohima Dr STRBR DY8 ...... 307 L5
Kurtus TAM/AM/WIL B77 ..... 290 D4
Kyffin Rd BUCK/MIL ST2 .... 70 B4
Kyle Cl WOLV WV10 .... 280 B1
Kynaston Crs CDSL WV8 .... 263 H8

L

Laburnum Cl ALS/KID ST7 .... 52 E2
Laburnham Rd KGSWFD DY6 ... 303 L4
Laburnum Av CNCK/NC WS11 ... 249 K3
 CRTAM B79 .... 274 D2
Laburnum Cl BLOX/PEL WS3 ... 267 M8
 BLYBR/FOR ST11 .... 104 A4
 CNCK/NC WS11 .... 249 L3
 KINVER DY7 .... 305 M5
 MKTDR TF9 .... 112 D8
 RSTAF ST18 .... 154 M4
Laburnum Gv BNTWD WS7 .... 251 M4
 LNGTN ST3 .... 85 L7
 WSLW WS2 .... 282 F7
Laburnum Pl LNGTN ST3 .... 102 F2
 NEWUL ST5 .... 67 K1
Laburnum Rd ALDR WS9 ..... 269 G7
 ETTPK/GDPK/PENN WV4 ... 295 L7
 STPNHL/WNHL DE15 ..... 204 F4
 SWAD DE11 .... 205 M4
Laburnum St BDMR/CCFT WV3... 12 L7
 STRBR DY8 .... 307 L3
Laches Cl WOLV WV10 ...... 247 K5
Laches La WOLV WV10 ...... 247 L8
Ladbrook Gv SEDG DY3 ..... 299 G7
Lad La AW/WIL ST1 .... 84 B1
Ladle End La MSHM DE12 .... 221 K1
Ladybank Gv LNGTN ST3 .... 101 L2
Ladydale Cl LEEK ST13 ..... 43 M6
Ladygates AUD/MAD/W CW3... 65 G4
Lady Grey's Wk STRBR DY8 ... 307 K5
Lady Meadow Cl UTXR ST14... 108 E5
Ladymoor La BURS/TUN ST6 ... 41 H7
Ladypool Pl RUSH/SHEL WS4... 284 A5
Ladysmith Rd HAN ST1 ...... 69 C7
Ladysmith St LNGTN ST3 .... 86 B8
Ladywell Cl BUTN/AL/TUT DE13... 185 L1
 WMBN WV5 .... 298 A2
Ladywell Rd BURS/TUN ST6 ... 53 K7
Lagonda TAM/AM/WIL B77 .... 11 H8
Lagonda Cl BIDD ST8 .... 40 B5
Lagrange CRTAM B79 .... 273 L4
The Lair POL/KCSB/FAZ B78... 291 M2
Lake Dr ASHB DE6........... 145 C1
Lakefield Rd WNSFLD WV11 ... 281 L5
Lakeland Dr TAM/AM/WIL B77... 291 C3
Lake Rd END/WER ST9 ...... 42 E1
Lakeside ASHB DE6......... 79 J8
Lakeside Cl NEWUL ST5 ..... 98 C6
Lakeside Dr CNCK/NC WS11... 251 C4
Lakeside Vw RUGE WS15 .... 217 H6
Lake St SEDG DY3 .... 299 K7
Lakewood Dr BARL ST10 .... 68 F6
Lakewood Gv HAN ST1 ...... 68 F6
Lally Pl SEDG DY3 .... 40 B8
Lamb Crs WMBN WV5 ...... 297 M5
Lambert Cl ALS/KID ST7 .... 39 K7
Lambert Dr BNTWD WS7 ..... 252 A3
Lambert Rd UTXR ST14 ..... 143 M1
 WOLV WV10 .... 280 F4
Lambert St BURS/TUN ST6 ... 53 L7
Lamb La STONE ST15 ...... 137 M3
Lambourne Av ALS/KID ST7 ... 39 K6
Lambourne Cl GTWY WS6 .... 249 M7
 LICHS WS14 .... 9 L3
Lambourne Dr BUCK/MIL ST2... 70 C1
Lambourn Pl LNGTN ST3 .... 101 K2
Lamb St ALS/KID ST7 ...... 39 C8
Lamerton Gv LNGTN ST3 .... 86 F8
Lame St HAN ST1 .... 2 D5
Lameledge La SHIF TF11 .... 242 B6
Lammascote Rd STAFN ST16... 5 H5
Lammas St STRBR DY8 ..... 303 J7
Lamotte Cl STOKE ST4 ..... 86 B5
Lamprey TAM/AM/WIL B77 ... 290 D4
Lancaster Av ALDR WS9 .... 285 H2
 BLYBR/FOR ST11 .... 121 L2
 LEEK ST13 .... 43 M3
 STOKE ST4............. 84 D2
Lancaster Crs STOKE ST4 ... 84 D2
Lancaster Dr BURS/TUN ST6... 54 F6
 BUTN/AL/TUT DE13 ...... 165 H5
Lancaster Gdns
 ETTPK/GDPK/PENN WV4 ... 294 E5
Lancaster Pl BLOX/PEL WS3... 267 J8
Lancaster Rd LICH WS13 ... 237 J5
 STAFS ST17 .... 194 A2
 STOKE ST4............. 84 D2
Lance Dr BNTWD WS7 ...... 251 L1
Lancelot Dr BUTN/AL/TUT DE13... 185 L1
Lanchester Cl BIDD ST8 .... 40 B4
 CRTAM B79 .... 273 L3
Lancia Cl BIDD ST8 .... 40 B5
Lancing Av STAFS ST17 .... 194 B3
Landau Cl WSLW WS2 ...... 283 J5
Landon Gv LNGTN ST3 ..... 86 C7
Landor Crs RUGE WS15 .... 215 L4
Landport Rd WOLV WV1 .... 13 L8
Landrake Gv BURS/TUN ST6... 53 L3
Landrake Rd KGSWFD DY6 ... 303 M5
Landseer Pl NEWUL ST5 .... 67 L4
Landywood Gn GTWY WS6 ... 249 L8
Landywood La GTWY WS6 ... 249 K8
Lane Av WSLW WS2 .... 283 H7
Lane Cl WSLW WS2 .... 283 H7
Lane Farm Gv HAN ST1 .... 69 L3
Lane Green Av CDSL WV8 ... 279 J1
Lane Green Rd CDSL WV8 ... 263 J8
Lane Head BUX SK17 ...... 24 B3
Lanehead Rd HAN ST1 ..... 68 F7
Lanehead Wk RUGE WS15 ... 197 J8
Lanes Cl BUTN/AL/TUT DE13... 218 C4
 WMBN WV5 .... 297 K5
Laneside Gdns WSLW WS2 ... 283 C8
The Lane RSTAF ST18 ..... 193 J7
Langdale Ct TAM/AM/WIL B77... 275 C4
Langdale Dr CNCK/NC WS11... 249 H3
Langdale Rd NEWUL ST5 .... 85 B5
Langer Cl BUT DE14 ...... 204 A4
Langford Rd BUCK/MIL ST2... 70 C7
 NEWUL ST5 .... 84 A7
Langford St LEEK ST13 .... 43 K5
Langham Rd BUCK/MIL ST2... 70 A1
Langholm Dr HEDN WS12 ... 232 E8
Langland Dr LNGTN ST3 .... 85 M8
 SEDG DY3 .... 299 J5
Langley Cl NEWUL ST5 .... 52 D8
Langley Gdns BDMR/CCFT WV3... 294 D3
Langley Rd
 ETTPK/GDPK/PENN WV4 ... 293 C2
Langley St STOKE ST4 .... 84 D1
Langmead Pl WSLW WS2 ... 282 D7
Langot La ECCH ST21 ..... 133 K3
Langsett Rd WOLV WV10 ... 13 J1
Langton Crs LICHS WS14 ... 255 L4
Langton Ct END/WER ST9 ... 71 C6
Langtree Gv HEDN WS12 ... 250 D1
Lanrick Gdns RUGE WS15 ... 197 L8
Lansbury Cl STAFS ST17 ... 193 L2

Lansbury Dr CNCK/NC WS11... 231 L6
Lansbury Gv LNGTN ST3 .... 87 H7
Lansbury Rd RUGE WS15 ... 215 L4
Landsell Av NEWUL ST5 .... 68 B4
Lansdown Cl STONE ST15 ... 137 M4
Lansdowne Av CDSL WV8 ... 262 E8
Lansdowne Cl END/WER ST9... 71 H6
 TAM/AM/WIL B77 .... 290 D1
Lansdowne Rd BUT DE14 ... 203 M3
 STOKE ST4............. 84 E2
 WOLV WV1 .... 12 D3
Lansdowne St LNGTN ST3 ... 102 B1
Lansdowne Wy RUGE WS15 ... 197 J8
 STAFS ST17 .... 194 C4
Lant Cl BUTN/AL/TUT DE13 ... 218 D4
Lapley Av STAFS ST16 ..... 174 A3
Lapley Cl WOLV WV1 .... 281 H8
Lapley La PENK ST19 ...... 228 C6
Lapley Rd PENK ST19 ...... 227 K3
Lapper Av
 ETTPK/GDPK/PENN WV4 ... 295 M8
Lapwing Cl BIDD ST8 ...... 40 D2
Lapwing Ct CTWY WS6 ..... 266 C1
Lapwing Rd ALS/KID ST7 ... 39 K8
Lapworth Wy NWPT TF10 ... 188 A7
Lara Cl STAFN ST16 ...... 174 B7
Larch Cl ALS/KID ST7 ..... 53 G2
 KINVER DY7 .... 306 C2
 LICHS WS14 .... 9 M5
Larches La BDMR/CCFT WV3... 12 A5
Larchfields STONE ST15 ... 138 B4
Larch Gv LNGTN ST3 ...... 85 L8
 SEDG DY3 .... 299 L3
Larchmere Dr WNSFLD WV11... 266 A7
Larchmount Cl STOKE ST4 ... 101 H3
Larch Rd KGSWFD DY6 ..... 303 L3
 RUGE WS15 .... 215 M4
 SWAD DE11 .... 205 M3
Larch Wd STAFS ST17 ..... 194 C5
Larchwood Dr
 CNCK/NC WS11 .... 232 A6
Larcombe Dr
 ETTPK/GDPK/PENN WV4 ... 295 K5
Lark Av ALS/KID ST7 ...... 39 K7
Larkfield Av NEWUL ST5 ... 53 G1
Larkhill La RSTAF ST18 .... 115 G6
Larkhill Rd STRBR DY8 .... 307 J6
Larkholme Cl RUGE WS15 ... 215 L5
Larkin Av LNGTN ST3 ...... 86 D6
Larkin Cl STAFS ST17 ..... 193 J3
 WOLV WV10 .... 281 G1
Lark Ri UTXR ST14 .... 144 B4
Larksfield Rd BURS/TUN ST6... 69 K1
Larksmeadow V STAFS ST17... 194 C4
Larkspur TAM/AM/WIL B77 ... 290 C4
Larkspur Av BNTWD WS7 .... 252 A5
Larkspur Dr WOLV WV10 ... 265 H3
Larkspur Gv NEWUL ST5 ... 68 C8
Larkspur Wy BRWNH WS8 ... 268 C4
Larkstone La ASHB DE6 .... 61 M1
Larkswood Dr
 ETTPK/GDPK/PENN WV4 ... 294 C7
 SEDG DY3 .... 299 K3
Lascelles St BURS/TUN ST6... 53 K7
Lask Edge Rd BIDD ST8 .... 41 J2
Laski Crs LNGTN ST3 ...... 87 H3
Latebrook Cl BURS/TUN ST6... 53 J3
Latham Cl
 STPNHL/WNHL DE15 ...... 186 C8
Latham Gv BURS/TUN ST6 ... 54 E8
Latherford Cl WOLV WV10 ... 247 L5
Latherford La WOLV WV10 ... 248 B1
Lathkill Dl SWAD DE11 .... 205 M8
Lathkill Dr ASHB DE6 ..... 95 L2
Latimer St WLNHL WV13 ... 282 A7
Latimer Wy BUCK/MIL ST2 ... 70 C8
Lauder Cl SEDG DY3 ...... 299 J1
Lauderdale Gdns
 WOLV WV10 .... 264 E7
Lauder Pl North BUCK/MIL ST2... 86 E2
Lauder Pl South BUCK/MIL ST2... 86 E3
Launceston Cl
 TAM/AM/WIL B77 .... 274 D8
Laurel Bank CRTAM B79 .... 10 C2
Laurel Cl LICH WS13 ..... 9 J3
Laurel Crs END/WER ST9 ... 71 C7
Laurel Dr ALS/KID ST7 .... 39 L7
 BNTWD WS7 .... 252 C3
 HEDN WS12 .... 232 E6
Laurel Gv BDMR/CCFT WV3... 294 E4
 LNGTN ST3 .... 85 K8
 STAFS ST17 .... 193 M3
 STPNHL/WNHL DE15 ..... 204 C5
The Laurels RUGE WS15 ... 215 M3
Laurence Gv
 DUNHL/THL/PER WV6 ..... 279 L3
Lauren Cl STOKE ST4 ..... 85 L4
Lauriston Cl DUDN DY1 ... 299 M7
Lavender Av COVEN WV9 ... 263 M7
 LNGTN ST3 .... 87 H5
 RSTAF ST18 .... 154 C8
Lavender La STRBR DY8 ... 307 K7
Lavender Rd TAM/AM/WIL B77... 11 K5
Laverock Gv
 AUD/MAD/W CW3 .... 81 L4
Lawford Av LICHS WS14 ... 9 L4
Lawfred Av WNSFLD WV11 ... 281 K5
Lawley Cl RUSH/SHEL WS4... 284 B1
Lawley St LNGTN ST3 ..... 86 D7
Lawn Av STRBR DY8 ...... 307 L6
Lawn La COVEN WV9 ..... 264 A4
 MKTDR TF9 .... 148 F2
Lawnoaks Cl BRWNH WS8 ... 251 K8
Lawn Rd BKHL/PFLD WV2 ... 295 L4
 STAFS ST17 .... 4 C9
Lawnswood Wk STAFN ST16... 174 D1
The Lawns
 BUTN/AL/TUT DE13 ...... 166 B7
 UTXR ST14............. 126 A8
Lawn St STRBR DY8 ...... 307 L6
Lawnswood KINVER DY7 ... 303 G6
Lawnswood Av BNTWD WS7... 251 M6
 DUNHL/THL/PER WV6 ..... 279 L2
 ETTPK/GDPK/PENN WV4 ... 295 L6
 STRBR DY8 .... 303 J6
Lawnswood Cl HEDN WS12 ... 250 D1
Lawnswood Dr ALDR WS9 ... 269 C7
 KINVER DY7 .... 303 G6

Lawnswood Ri
 DUNHL/THL/PER WV6 ..... 279 L6
Lawnswood Rd SEDG DY3 ... 299 K7
 STRBR DY8 .... 303 J4
Lawrence Av WNSFLD WV11... 281 M4
 WOLV WV10 .... 281 L6
Lawrence Ct BTRM 10 A7
 STAFS ST17 .... 4 F7
Lawrence Dr STONE ST15 ... 118 D6
Lawrence St HAN ST1 ..... 2 B6
 STAFS ST17 .... 4 F7
 WLNHL WV13 .... 282 A6
Lawson Cl ALDR WS9 ..... 285 H6
Lawson Ter NEWUL ST5 ... 68 B3
Lawton Av ALS/KID ST7 ... 38 C3
Lawton Coppice ALS/KID ST7... 38 B8
Lawton Crs BIDD ST8 ..... 40 D2
Lawton Heath Rd ALS/KID ST7... 37 K4
Lawton Rd ALS/KID ST7 ... 37 K5
 ALS/KID ST7 .... 39 J4
 BIDD ST8 .... 40 D7
 BURS/TUN ST6 .... 54 A4
Laxley Rd NEWUL ST5 .... 101 J8
Laxton Gv STOKE ST4 .... 101 J7
Lazar La STAFS ST17 .... 195 H4
Lazy Hi ALDR WS9 .... 269 J4
Lazy Hill Rd ALDR WS9 ... 285 J2
Leacliffe Wy FOAKS/STRLY B74... 285 M4
Lea Cl NEWUL ST5 .... 98 D5
Leacote Dr
 DUNHL/THL/PER WV6 ..... 279 J4
 STONE ST15 .... 138 D6
Leacroft SHHTH WV12 .... 282 C2
 STONE ST15 .... 138 D6
Leacroft Av WOLV WV10 ... 280 E1
Leacroft Cl ALDR WS9 ... 285 H6
Leacroft La CNCK/NC WS11... 249 M4
Leacroft Rd KGSWFD DY6 ... 303 L2
 LNGTN ST3 .... 103 C6
 PENK ST19 .... 211 M4
Leadbeater Av STOKE ST4 ... 84 F7
Leadendale La LNGTN ST3 ... 102 E5
Leafenden Av BNTWD WS7 ... 252 A5
Leaford Wy KGSWFD DY6 ... 303 M4
Leafy Gld FOAKS/STRLY B74... 286 A4
Leafy Ri SEDG DY3 ...... 299 J4
Lea Gn STAFN ST16 ..... 174 C2
Lea Hall Av RUGE WS15 ... 251 K6
Lea Hall La RUGE WS15 ... 216 B3
Leahurst Cl STAFS ST17 ... 194 C4
Leaks Aly LNGTN ST3 .... 86 B8
Lea La GTWY WS6 .... 250 A4
 KIDD DY10 .... 309 L4
 RUGE WS15 .... 309 H2
Lea Manor Dr
 ETTPK/GDPK/PENN WV4 ... 294 C3
Leam Dr BNTWD WS7 ..... 252 D3
Leamington Cl CNCK/NC WS11... 249 J2
Leamington Gdns NEWUL ST5... 68 E3
Leamington Rd BUT DE14 ... 203 L2
Leamore Cl WSLW WS2 ... 283 G3
Leamore La BLOX/PEL WS3... 283 J2
 WSLW WS2 .... 283 G3
Leander Cl BNTWD WS7 ... 294 E3
 GTWY WS6 .... 266 F1
Leander Ri STPNHL/WNHL DE15... 205 C4
Lea Pl LNGTN ST3 ...... 85 K8
Leapley La ASHB DE6 .... 111 J4
Lea Rd BDMR/CCFT WV3 ... 295 G3
 RSTAF ST18 .... 177 K2
 STONE ST15 .... 137 M4
Lear Rd WMBN WV5 ..... 298 B2
Leasawe Cl RSTAF ST18 ... 177 J8
Leaside Av RUGE WS15 ... 217 J5
Leaside Rd STOKE ST4 ... 84 E7
Leason La WOLV WV10 ... 281 C8
Leason Rd LNGTN ST3 ... 84 D3
Leason St STOKE ST4 .... 85 H4
Leasowe Rd RUGE WS15 ... 216 A7
Leasowes Dr
 DUNHL/THL/PER WV6 ..... 278 D7
 ETTPK/GDPK/PENN WV4 ... 294 C5
The Leasowe WSLW WS2 ... 254 A7
The Leasow ALDR WS9 ... 284 E7
The Leas WOLV WV10 .... 265 J6
Leaswood Cl NEWUL ST5 ... 84 C7
Leaswood Pl NEWUL ST5 ... 84 C7
Lea St STOKE ST4 .... 101 H3
Leathermill La RUGE WS15... 215 M3
Leathersley La ASHB DE6 ... 147 H4
Lea Vale Rd STRBR DY8 ... 307 M5
Lea Vw ALDR WS9 .... 284 E2
 SHHTH WV12 .... 282 A7
Lea Wy ALS/KID ST7 .... 37 K8
Leawood Rd STOKE ST4 ... 84 E6
Lebanon Gv BNTWD WS7 ... 251 M4
Leckie Rd WSLW WS2 .... 283 H1
Ledbury Cl ALDR WS9 .... 285 J1
Ledbury Crs HAN ST1 .... 3 J1
Ledstone Wy LNGTN ST3 ... 103 C3
Leech Av NEWUL ST5 .... 67 M4
Leedham Av TAM/AM/WIL B77... 11 C3
Leedhams Cft MSHM DE12... 221 K2
Leeds St STOKE ST4 ..... 85 M5
Lee Gv NEWUL ST5 ...... 84 B6
Leekbrook Wy LEEK ST13... 57 H4
Leek La BIDD ST8 .... 41 H6
Leek New Rd BUCK/MIL ST2... 55 H6
Leek Rd ASHB DE6 ...... 47 K4
 BURS/TUN ST6 .... 72 D6
 CDLE ST10 .... 72 C3
 CONG SK12 .... 55 J8
 END/WER ST9 .... 55 L8
 HAN ST1 .... 57 K4
 LEEK ST13 .... 57 H4
 LNGTN ST3 .... 85 M8
 STOKE ST4........... 85 L4
Leeming Rd ALBTN WV7 ... 260 D2
Lees Cl RUGE WS15 ..... 216 E3
Leese La STAFS ST17 .... 157 H4
 STONE ST15 .... 120 F7
Lees La STOKE ST4 ...... 85 H5
Lees La CDLE ST10 ...... 123 H4
Leett Ct WSLW WS2 ..... 55 M4
Legge La RSTAF ST18 .... 177 J2
Legge St BKHL/PFLD WV2... 295 J3
 NEWUL ST5 .... 84 C2
Legion Cl CNCK/NC WS11... 251 C3
Legs La WOLV WV10 ..... 264 F7
Leicester Av ALS/KID ST7 ... 37 L5

eicester Cl NEWUL ST5 .... 84 C5
eicester Rd BUCK/MIL ST2 ...... 70 C8
eicester St BUT DE14 .... 12 C1
  DUNHL/THL/PER WV6 .... 283 L8
  WSL WS1 .... 283 L8
eigh Av BNTWD WS7 .... 252 B5
eigh Bank CDLE ST10 .... 123 M2
eigh Cl RUSH/SHEL WS4 .... 284 A6
  STAFS ST17 .... 193 M5
eigh La BURS/TUN ST6 .... 68 C1
  CDLE ST10 .... 123 H6
  CDLE ST10 .... 123 M1
  UTXR ST14 .... 143 H2
eigh Rd RUSH/SHEL WS4 .... 284 A4
eighs Cl RUSH/SHEL WS4 .... 284 C1
eighs Rd RUSH/SHEL WS4 .... 284 B1
eigh St RUSH/SHEL WS4 .... 54 A8
eighswood STAFS ST17 .... 194 A7
eighswood Av ALDR WS9 .... 285 G3
eighswood Cl CNCK/NC WS11 .... 250 F5
eighswood Gv ALDR WS9 .... 285 G3
eighswood Rd ALDR WS9 .... 285 H4
eighton Cl DUDN DY1 .... 299 L8
  END/WER WV... .... 55 J6
eighton Rd
  ETTPK/GDPK/PENN WV4 .... 294 F4
  UTXR ST14 .... 144 C4
ema Wy STAFN ST16 .... 5 M4
e More FOAKS/STRLY B74 .... 287 F5
en Davies Rd SHHTH WV12 ..... 232 A8
ennox Gdns BDMR/CCFT WV3 .... 12 A3
ennox Rd LNGTN ST3 .... 86 D8
eofric Cl BUTN/AL/TUT DE13 ... 218 C4
eomansley Cl WSL WS13 .... 8 A5
eomansley Rd LICH WS13 .... 8 A5
eomansley Vw LICH WS13 .... 253 L3
eonard Av BUCK/MIL ST2 .... 55 H7
eonard Dr BURS/TUN ST6 .... 55 H4
eonard Rd STRBR DY8 .... 307 J5
eonard St BURS/TUN ST6 .... 69 H1
  LEEK ST13 .... 43 M5
eonora St BURS/TUN ST6 .... 68 F3
eopold St STOKE ST4 .... 85 L4
erdington Cl GNOS ST20 .... 150 E4
erryn Cl KGSWFD DY6 .... 303 M5
erwick Cl KGSWFD DY6 .... 303 H5
esley Dr KGSWFD DY6 .... 303 L6
eslie Rd FOAKS/STRLY B74 .... 286 B8
  WOLVN WV10 .... 280 F6
essort Cl COVEN WV9 .... 264 A7
essways Cl NEWUL ST5 .... 68 A2
ester Cl ALS/KID ST7 .... 37 K6
ester Gv ALDR WS9 .... 285 L8
etchmere Cl
  DUNHL/THL/PER WV6 .... 277 J7
etchmere La
  DUNHL/THL/PER WV6 .... 277 J8
etheridge Gdns STAFS ST17 .... 193 G2
euchers La ALBTN WV7 .... 260 D2
evedale Cl STAFN ST16 .... 174 A1
evedale Rd PENK ST19 .... 229 K1
  RSTAF ST18 .... 210 C2
  RSTAF ST18 .... 211 J7
he Levels RUGE WS15 .... 215 M5
even Dr WNSFLD WV11 .... 282 B1
ever St BKHL/PFLD WV2 .... 13 C8
everton Ri WOLVN WV10 .... 280 C4
eveson Av GTWY WS6 .... 249 L8
eveson Rd STOKE ST4 .... 100 F1
  WNSFLD WV11 .... 281 M4
eveson St LNGTN ST3 .... 86 C8
  WLNHL WV13 .... 282 A8
evett Rd LICHS WS14 .... 272 C1
  TAM/AM/WIL B77 .... 275 H5
evetts Flds LICH WS13 .... 9 G4
evetts Hollow HEDN WS12 ..... 232 D7
evington Cl
  DUNHL/THL/PER WV6 .... 278 F6
evita Rd STOKE ST4 .... 84 F6
ewis Av WOLV WV1 .... 281 H7
ewis Cl LICHS WS14 .... 9 M4
  SHHTH WV12 .... 282 D5
ewis Dr BUTN/AL/TUT DE13 ... 185 H3
ewis Gv WNSFLD WV11 .... 281 K4
ewisham Dr BURS/TUN ST6 ...... 53 J3
ewisham Rd WOLVN WV10 ...... 264 B8
ewis's La BUTN/AL/TUT DE13 .. 218 B4
ewis St STOKE ST4 .... 85 H2
  WSLW WS2 .... 283 K7
ewthorn Ri
  ETTPK/GDPK/PENN WV4 .... 295 K6
exham Pl LNGTN ST3 .... 86 E8
exington Gn LNGTN ST3 .... 193 G2
eybourne Crs COVEN WV9 ...... 263 M8
eyburn Cl WNSFLD WV12 .... 282 D6
eycett La NEWUL ST5 .... 66 E7
eycett Rd NEWUL ST5 .... 66 D6
ey Cft RDERBYSW DE65 .... 165 J1
eyfield Rd STOKE ST4 .... 101 H4
eyfields LICH WS13 .... 236 B8
ey Gdns LNGTN ST3 .... 86 A7
eyland Av BDMR/CCFT WV3 .... 294 A1
eyland Cl BLOX/PEL WS3 .... 267 M6
eyland Dr RUGE WS15 .... 197 L3
eyland Rd TAM/AM/WIL B77 ..... 11 J9
ey Ri SEDG DY3 .... 299 J1
eys Dr NEWUL ST5 .... 83 L6
eys La BUCK/MIL ST2 .... 55 J8
he Leys SWAD DE11 .... 205 L4
iberty Pk STAFS ST17 .... 193 G2
iberty Rd TAM/AM/WIL B77 .... 290 F7
ibra Cl CRTAM B79 .... 273 M3
ibra Pl BURS/TUN ST6 .... 53 M4
ich Av WNSFLD WV11 .... 281 L3
ichen Cl HEDN WS12 .... 231 J5
ichfield Crs
  POL/KGSB/FAZ B78 .... 273 H3
ichfield Dr RSTAF ST18 .... 196 B1
  SHIF TF11 .... 244 B1
ichfield Rd ALDR WS9 .... 269 G6
  ALDR WS9 .... 269 K3
  ALS/KID ST7 .... 52 D3
  BLOX/PEL WS3 .... 267 J8
  BRWNH WS8 .... 268 F4
  BURS/TUN ST6 .... 203 J6
  BUTN/AL/TUT DE13 .... 220 D7
  CNCK/NC WS11 .... 250 B2

FOAKS/STRLY B74 .... 286 F5
  LICH WS13 .... 235 M2
  MGN/WHC B75 .... 287 G5
  POL/KGSB/FAZ B78 .... 273 H5
  RSTAF ST18 .... 156 D3
  RUGE WS15 .... 180 A6
  RUSH/SHEL WS4 .... 284 B3
  SHHTH WV12 .... 282 B3
  STAFS ST17 .... 4 F6
  STAFS ST17 .... 5 K8
  STONE ST15 .... 138 C3
  WNSFLD WV11 .... 281 L4
ichfield St BUT DE14 .... 7 G8
  CRTAM B79 .... 10 A4
  HAN ST1 .... 2 D6
  POL/KGSB/FAZ B78 .... 289 M1
  RUGE WS15 .... 215 M2
  RUSH/SHEL WS4 .... 283 M7
  STONE ST15 .... 138 A2
  WOLV WV1 .... 12 F5
  WSL WS1 .... 283 L8
ichwood Rd WNSFLD WV11 ..... 281 M3
iddle St STOKE ST4 .... 85 G4
idgate Gv LNGTN ST3 .... 85 M8
idgate Wk NEWUL ST5 .... 100 B1
id La ASHB DE6 .... 109 L3
  CDLE ST10 .... 89 J8
iffs Rd BUX SK17 .... 35 H7
ifton Cft KGSWFD DY6 .... 303 M5
ight Ash WOLVN WV10 .... 247 J7
ight Ash Cl COVEN WV9 .... 247 H7
ight Ash La COVEN WV9 .... 247 H7
ightfoot Gv UTXR ST14 .... 143 M1
ight Oaks Av BUCK/MIL ST2 ...... 69 M1
ightwater Gv BUCK/MIL ST2 ..... 69 M1
ightwood Rd
  BUTN/AL/TUT DE13 .... 218 F1
  LNGTN ST3 .... 86 C8
  NEWUL ST5 .... 67 K1
ilac Av CNCK/NC WS11 .... 249 K3
ilac Cl LNGTN ST3 .... 87 J5
  RSTAF ST18 .... 154 B7
  UTXR ST14 .... 144 B4
ilac Dr WMBN WV5 .... 297 M4
ilac Gv BNTWD WS7 .... 251 M3
  LNGTN ST3 .... 85 L7
  STAFS ST17 .... 193 M3
  STPNHW/WNHL DE15 .... 204 F4
  WSLW WS2 .... 282 E7
ilac La GTWY WS6 .... 266 F2
ilac Rd CRTAM B79 .... 274 A2
  SHHTH WV12 .... 282 E3
ilchurch Av STAFN ST16 .... 174 D2
ileshall Crs BKHL/PFLD WV2 ..... 295 K3
ileshall Rd NEWUL ST5 .... 84 C5
ileshall St LNGTN ST3 .... 86 C8
ileshall Wy STAFS ST17 .... 193 H3
illeshall Cl LICH WS13 .... 8 C2
illydale Rd BUCK/MIL ST2 .... 70 B7
illy St NEWUL ST5 .... 68 D5
imbrick Cl ALS/KID ST7 .... 65 M1
imepit La HEDN WS12 .... 231 L4
ime Rd BILS/COS WV14 .... 299 M1
  HEDN WS12 .... 231 M3
  SEDG DY3 .... 299 M1
imes Av LEEK ST13 .... 57 G1
imes Rd DUNHL/THL/PER WV6 . 279 J6
he Limes ALBTN WV7 .... 261 G6
  NEWUL ST5 .... 68 C3
imestone Wy ASHB DE6 .... 78 B2
  UTXR ST14 .... 109 C6
ime St BDMR/CCFT WV3 .... 12 B8
  STOKE ST4 .... 85 H5
imes Vw SEDG DY3 .... 299 K3
ime Tree Av
  DUNHL/THL/PER WV6 .... 279 G7
imetree Av STAFN ST16 .... 174 D5
ime Tree Gdns CDSL WV8 ...... 263 H4
ime Tree Rd CDSL WV8 .... 263 H7
imewood Cl BLYBR/FOR TF11 . 104 A4
inacre Rd ECCH ST21 .... 152 E4
inacre Wy LNGTN ST3 .... 86 E5
incoln Av NEWUL ST5 .... 84 C5
  WLNHL WV13 .... 282 D8
incoln Cl LICH WS13 .... 236 C7
incoln Cft LICHS WS14 .... 270 F4
incoln Dr CNCK/NC WS11 .... 249 M2
incoln Gn WOLVN WV10 .... 264 D8
incoln Gv WOLVN WV10 .... 264 D8
incoln Meadow STAFS ST17 .. 193 G2
incoln Rd ALS/KID ST7 .... 38 F8
  BURS/TUN ST6 .... 69 G3
  STPNHW/WNHL DE15 .... 204 D3
  WSL WS1 .... 284 A8
incoln St HAN ST1 .... 2 F6
  WOLVN WV10 .... 13 K3
indale Dr WMBN WV5 .... 297 M4
indale Gv LNGTN ST3 .... 103 H3
inda Rd BURS/TUN ST6 .... 53 L5
inden Av BNTWD WS7 .... 251 M2
inden Cl CONG CW12 .... 26 A2
inden Ct NEWUL ST5 .... 68 B7
  STAFS ST17 .... 193 H2
  TAM/AM/WIL B77 .... 11 L5
inden Dr BIDD ST8 .... 40 C1
inden La NEWUL ST5 .... 68 B7
inden La SHHTH WV12 .... 282 E3
inden Lea BDMR/CCFT WV3 .... 294 D1
inden Pl LNGTN ST3 .... 101 M1

Linden Rd BUTN/AL/TUT DE13 ... 220 D1
The Lindens
  DUNHL/THL/PER WV6 .... 279 L7
  STONE ST15 .... 138 B5
Lindera TAM/AM/WIL B77 .... 275 G6
Lindisfarne TAM/AM/WIL B77 ... 11 H9
Lindley Pl LNGTN ST3 .... 103 G6
Lindley St BURS/TUN ST6 .... 69 H3
Lindon Cl BRWNH WS8 .... 269 G4
Lindon Dr BRWNH WS8 .... 268 F4
Lindon Rd BRWNH WS8 .... 269 G4
Lindon Vw BRWNH WS8 .... 269 G5
Lindops La AUD/MAD/W CW3 ... 81 M3
Lindop St HAN ST1 .... 2 D6
Lindrick Cl BLOX/PEL WS3 .... 266 F7
Lindrosa Rd FOAKS/STRLY B74 .. 285 M7
Lindsay St HAN ST1 .... 2 B7
Lindsay Wy ALS/KID ST7 .... 37 G6
Lindum Av STOKE ST4 .... 101 J3
Lineker Cl STAFN ST16 .... 174 B7
Linfield Gdns SEDG DY3 .... 299 J1
Linfield Rd HAN ST1 .... 2 E5
Linford Cl RUGE WS15 .... 217 J6
Lingard St BURS/TUN ST6 .... 69 G2
Lingfield Av BURS/TUN ST6 .... 55 G2
  WOLVN WV10 .... 264 D5
Lingfield Cl GTWY WS6 .... 249 M8
Lingfield Dr GTWY WS6 .... 249 M8
Lingfield Gv
  DUNHL/THL/PER WV6 .... 278 F6
Lingfield Rd BUT DE14 .... 203 M3
Ling Rd HEDN WS12 .... 231 J5
Linhope Gv LNGTN ST3 .... 103 H3
Linkend Cl HAN ST1 .... 3 K3
Link Rd ALDR WS9 .... 269 H7
  WMBN WV5 .... 298 A1
Links Av DUNHL/THL/PER WV6 .. 279 K3
  NEWUL ST5 .... 68 B6
Links Dr STRBR DY8 .... 307 L8
Linksfield Gv STAFN ST16 .... 174 D2
Links Rd
  ETTPK/GDPK/PENN WV4 .... 295 C1
Links Side Wy ALDR WS9 .... 285 J2
Linley Dr ALDR WS9 .... 284 C5
Linley Gv WOLVN WV10 .... 280 E1
Linley Gv ALS/KID ST7 .... 37 M7
  SEDG DY3 .... 299 H8
Linley La ALS/KID ST7 .... 38 A7
Linley Rd ALS/KID ST7 .... 37 M8
  RUSH/SHEL WS4 .... 284 D3
  STOKE ST4 .... 84 D2
Linley Wood Rd ALDR WS9 ..... 284 E5
Linnburn Rd LNGTN ST3 .... 86 E6
Linnet Cl HEDN WS12 .... 231 K3
Linnet Gv SHHTH WV12 .... 282 C2
Linnet Wy BIDD ST8 .... 40 E2
Linslade Cl
  ETTPK/GDPK/PENN WV4 .... 295 K6
Lintake Dr RUGE WS15 .... 179 M4
Linthouse La WNSFLD WV11 ... 281 L2
Lintly TAM/AM/WIL B77 .... 291 H1
Linton Heath MSHM DE12 ...... 223 L5
Linton Rd
  ETTPK/GDPK/PENN WV4 .... 294 E5
  MSHM DE12 .... 222 D5
  SWAD DE11 .... 223 L3
Linwood Dr HEDN WS12 .... 231 M3
Linwood Wy BURS/TUN ST6 ...... 53 L5
Lionel Gv STOKE ST4 .... 84 E3
Lionfields Cl KIDD DY10 .... 310 A5
Lionfields Rd KIDD DY10 .... 310 B5
Lion Gv NEWUL ST5 .... 67 L2
Lion Pas STRBR DY8 .... 307 M5
Lion's Den LICHS WS14 .... 252 F8
Lion St RUGE WS15 .... 215 L1
  STOKE ST4 .... 85 G3
  STRBR DY8 .... 307 M5
Lisbon Pl NEWUL ST5 .... 83 L3
Liskeard Cl BUCK/MIL ST2 .... 86 A1
Lister Cl WSLW WS2 .... 283 H5
Lister Rd STAFN ST16 .... 5 H1
  WSLW WS2 .... 283 H5
Litley Dr CDLE ST10 .... 105 K2
Little Albert St WSL WS1 .... 283 L8
Little Aston Hall Dr
  FOAKS/STRLY B74 .... 286 A5
Little Aston La
  FOAKS/STRLY B74 .... 286 D4
Little Aston Park Rd
  FOAKS/STRLY B74 .... 286 A7
Little Aston Rd ALDR WS9 .... 285 J4
Little Birches
  BDMR/CCFT WV3 .... 294 F2
Little Bricklin St
  BKHL/PFLD WV2 .... 12 E7
Little Burton East BUT DE14 ...... 7 G1
Little Burton West BUT DE14 ...... 7 G2
Little Checkhill La KINVER DY7 . 302 D6
Little Chell La BURS/TUN ST6 .... 53 M5
Little Church La CRTAM B79 ...... 10 D4
Little Cliffe Rd LNGTN ST3 .... 85 L6
Little Clothier St
  WLNHL WV13 .... 282 A7
Littlecote CRTAM B79 .... 273 K4
Little Eaves La BUCK/MIL ST2 .... 70 C4
Little-field STOKE ST4 .... 84 E6
Littlefield La ASHB DE6 .... 92 F8
  ASHB DE6 .... 93 G1
Little Gra LICH WS13 .... 253 M1
Littlehales Rd NWPT TF10 .... 206 A3
Little Hardwick Rd ALDR WS9 .. 285 K3
Little Hayes KIDDW DY11 .... 309 J7
Little Hay La LICHS WS14 .... 271 J8
Little La LNGTN ST3 .... 102 E6
  SHHTH WV12 .... 282 D1
Little Lawns Cl BRWNH WS8 ... 268 F5
Little Marsh Gv PENK ST19 ..... 229 M1
Little Moss Cl ALS/KID ST7 ...... 38 C5
Little Moss La ALS/KID ST7 ...... 38 E5
Little Onn Rd GNOS ST20 .... 209 C4
Little Orch RUGE WS15 .... 197 L8
Little Park St WOLV WV1 .... 13 H5
Little Pipe La LICH WS13 .... 253 C1
Little Pountney St
  BKHL/PFLD WV2 .... 12 F7
Little Rd CDLE ST10 .... 88 C8
Little Rw STOKE ST4 .... 85 J5
Little's La WOLV WV1 .... 13 G3
Little Station St WSL WS1 .... 283 L8

Little Sutton Rd MGN/WHC B75 . 287 J8
Little Tixall La RSTAF ST18 ...... 177 J8
Littleton Cl STAFN ST16 .... 5 J3
Littleton Crs PENK ST19 .... 229 M1
Littleton Dr HEDN WS12 .... 231 J3
Littleton Rd SHHTH WV12 .... 282 C3
Littleton St East WSL WS1 .... 283 L8
Littleton St West WSLW WS2 ... 283 L8
Littleton Wy BNTWD WS7 .... 251 K1
Littlewood Cl LNGTN ST3 .... 249 L6
Littlewood Rd GTWY WS6 .... 249 L6
Littleworth Hl HEDN WS12 ...... 232 B8
Littleworth Rd HEDN WS12 ..... 232 D6
Litton TAM/AM/WIL B77 .... 291 J1
Littywood La RSTAF ST18 .... 192 C3
Liverpool Rd ALS/KID ST7 .... 53 C1
  NEWUL ST5 .... 52 D8
Liverpool Rd East ALS/KID ST7 .. 38 D7
Liverpool Rd West ALS/KID ST7 . 38 A6
Livingstone Av
  DUNHL/THL/PER WV6 .... 278 E5
Livingstone Rd BLOX/PEL WS3 .. 267 L8
Livingstone St BURS/TUN ST6 .. 54 C8
  LEEK ST13 .... 43 M5
Lizard La SHIF TF11 .... 242 F5
Llewellyn Roberts Wy
  MKTDR TF9 .... 112 D7
Lloyd Dr
  ETTPK/GDPK/PENN WV4 .... 294 C8
Lloyd George Gv
  CNCK/NC WS11 .... 232 C8
Lloyd Rd DUNHL/THL/PER WV6 . 279 K5
Lloyd St CNCK/NC WS11 .... 249 K1
  DUNHL/THL/PER WV6 .... 279 M6
  LNGTN ST3 .... 86 D8
Loak Rd ALBTN WV7 .... 260 E5
Lochalsh Gv WNSFLD WV11 .... 282 B1
Lochsong Cl TAM/AM/WIL B77 . 290 D1
Lockerbie Cl LEEK ST13 .... 44 B5
Lockers Bank CDLE ST10 .... 106 E6
Lockett Cl WSL WS2 .... 282 F6
Lockett St HAN ST1 .... 2 F1
Locke Wy STAFN ST16 .... 5 M4
Lockfield Cl STRBR DY8 .... 303 M8
Lockington Av BUCK/MIL ST2 .... 70 D8
Lock Keepers Cl CNCK/NC WS11 . 250 F5
Lockley Cl WOLVN WV10 .... 280 F6
Lockley St HAN ST1 .... 3 G3
Lock Rd PENK ST19 .... 229 M2
Lockside ALDR WS9 .... 284 F3
  WMBN WV5 .... 297 L3
Locksmith Cl WLNHL WV13 .... 282 B8
Lock St WOLV WV1 .... 13 H3
Locks Vw STRBR DY8 .... 307 K1
Lockwood Cl CDLE ST10 .... 90 A1
Lockwood Gv CDLE ST10 .... 90 A2
Lockwood Rd BUCK/MIL ST2 .... 54 D7
  STOKE ST4 .... 84 D1
Lode La ASHB DE6 .... 48 E6
Lodge Av ASHB DE6 .... 95 F2
Lodge Barn Rd ASHB DE6 .... 95 H2
Lodge Cl ASHB DE6 .... 95 H2
  NEWUL ST5 .... 68 C4
Lodge Crs ALDR WS9 .... 285 G5
Lodge Farm Cha ASHB DE6 ...... 95 H2
  NEWUL ST5 .... 68 C4
Lodge Hl BUTN/AL/TUT DE13 .. 165 L7
Lodge La ASHB DE6 .... 48 B7
  ASHB DE6 .... 62 D6
  BUTN/AL/TUT DE13 .... 201 H2
  CNCK/NC WS11 .... 249 H6
  ECCH ST21 .... 133 M5
  GNOS ST20 .... 170 D4
  KGSWFD DY6 .... 303 H4
  LICH WS13 .... 234 D7
Lodge Rd ALS/KID ST7 .... 37 J6
  ALS/KID ST7 .... 52 D4
  BNTWD WS7 .... 251 L1
  MSHM DE12 .... 241 K1
  RUGE WS15 .... 216 A4
  RUSH/SHEL WS4 .... 284 B1
  STOKE ST4 .... 84 E3
  WOLVN WV10 .... 280 B2
Lodge St SHHTH WV12 .... 282 C5
Lodge Vw GTWY WS6 .... 249 J7
Loftus Ct BNTWD WS7 .... 251 M5
Loftus St HAN ST1 .... 2 B3
Loganbeck Gv LNGTN ST3 .... 86 E5
Logan Cl WOLVN WV10 .... 280 C4
Lohengrin Cl
  BUTN/AL/TUT DE13 .... 166 E8
Lomas St HAN ST1 .... 69 C8
  WOLV WV1 .... 12 F1
Lomax Cl LICH WS13 .... 8 D1
Lomax Rd HEDN WS12 .... 232 B3
Lombard Ct ALS/KID ST7 .... 37 L6
Lombard St ALS/KID ST7 .... 8 F3
Lombardy Gdns
  SHHTH WV12 .... 282 E3
Lombardy Gv BNTWD WS7 ...... 251 M2
  LNGTN ST3 .... 87 G8
Lomita Crs TAM/AM/WIL B77 ... 290 D2
Lomond Cl CRTAM B79 .... 273 M2
Lomond Gv CDLE ST10 .... 89 L6
Lomond Rd SEDG DY3 .... 299 J1
London Rd AUD/MAD/W CW3 ... 96 C2
  LICHS WS14 .... 9 G9
  MKTDR TF9 .... 96 F5
  NEWUL ST5 .... 67 L2
  NEWUL ST5 .... 84 C2
  RSTAF ST18 .... 157 K8
  STOKE ST4 .... 85 C5
London St LEEK ST13 .... 43 L5
Long Acre CDSL WV8 .... 262 E8
Longacres HEDN WS12 .... 232 F5
Long Acre St WSLW WS2 .... 283 K7
Longboat La STRBR DY8 .... 307 L2
Longbow Cl
  BUTN/AL/TUT DE13 .... 185 J1
Longbridge Hayes Rd
  BURS/TUN ST6 .... 68 C2
Long Bridge Rd LICHS WS14 .... 253 M1
Longbrook Av LNGTN ST3 .... 86 A8
Long Cft HEDN WS12 .... 231 J6
Longclough Rd NEWUL ST5 ...... 52 B8

Longdoles Av LNGTN ST3 .... 86 E7
Longdon Av
  ETTPK/GDPK/PENN WV4 .... 295 K5
Longdon Dr FOAKS/STRLY B74 . 286 E6
Longfellow Cl BUT DE14 .... 185 K3
Longfellow Pl
  CNCK/NC WS11 .... 231 L6
Longfellow Rd BNTWD WS7 .... 251 M1
  SEDG DY3 .... 299 G5
Longfield Av LNGTN ST3 .... 137 M2
Longfield Cl TAM/AM/WIL B77 .. 11 J5
Longfield Rd STOKE ST4 .... 84 D3
Longford Cl WMBN WV5 .... 297 K5
Longford Rd CNCK/NC WS11 ... 249 K4
  WOLVN WV10 .... 280 F6
Longhedge La
  BUTN/AL/TUT DE13 .... 184 F1
Longhope Dr STONE ST15 ...... 137 M3
Longhurst Dr STONE ST15 ...... 137 M3
Long Knowle La WNSFLD WV11 . 281 H2
Longlake Av
  DUNHL/THL/PER WV6 .... 279 G7
Longlands Dr TAM/AM/WIL B77 . 11 M6
Longlands La MKTDR TF9 .... 130 C3
The Longlands WMBN WV5 ..... 298 A4
Long La ALBTN WV7 .... 260 C2
  ALS/KID ST7 .... 39 L6
  ASHB DE6 .... 48 B5
  LICH WS13 .... 237 L2
  RSTAF ST18 .... 191 M1
  WNSFLD WV11 .... 266 D5
Longleat CRTAM B79 .... 273 K3
Longleat Dr DUDN DY1 .... 299 L8
Longleat Rd ALDR WS9 .... 269 G8
Long Ley WOLVN WV10 .... 13 M3
Longley Rd LNGTN ST3 .... 86 C5
Long Meadow NEWUL ST5 .... 84 C7
  STAFS ST17 .... 193 L6
Long Meadow Dr SEDG DY3 ... 299 H1
Longmead Rd
  BUTN/AL/TUT DE13 .... 185 J4
Long Mill Av WNSFLD WV11 .... 281 H3
Long Ml North WNSFLD WV11 .. 281 H3
Long Ml South WNSFLD WV11 .. 281 H3
Longmoor Cl WNSFLD WV11 ... 281 M5
Long Mynd Cl SHHTH WV12 .... 282 B1
Longnor Pl BUCK/MIL ST2 .... 3 L9
Longport Rd BURS/TUN ST6 ...... 68 D3
Long Rw ALS/KID ST7 .... 53 G1
Longsdon Cl NEWUL ST5 .... 53 G1
Longsdon Gv LNGTN ST3 .... 86 E6
Longshaw Av NEWUL ST5 .... 68 B3
Longshaw La CDLE ST10 .... 91 L4
Longshaw St BURS/TUN ST6 .... 68 D2
Longshore St STAFS ST17 .... 193 J4
Longslow Cl NEWUL ST5 .... 68 A3
Longslow Rd MKTDR TF9 .... 130 B1
Longstaff Av HEDN WS12 .... 233 J3
Longstaff Cft LICH WS13 .... 235 M8
Long St PENK ST19 .... 227 J4
  STPNHW/WNHL DE15 .... 204 E3
  WOLV WV1 .... 13 G4
Longton Rd STOKE ST4 .... 101 C4
  STONE ST15 .... 102 D8
  STONE ST15 .... 138 B1
Long Valley Rd BIDD ST8 .... 26 C8
Longview Av ALS/KID ST7 .... 37 K6
Longview Cl LNGTN ST3 .... 86 D5
Longwood La RUSH/SHEL WS4 . 284 E6
Longwood Ri SHHTH WV12 .... 282 D5
Longwood Rd ALDR WS9 .... 285 H8
Lonsdale Cl SHHTH WV12 .... 282 B5
Lonsdale Rd BDMR/CCFT WV3 .. 12 C9
  BUT DE14 .... 204 B2
Lonsdale St STOKE ST4 .... 85 H4
Loomer Rd NEWUL ST5 .... 67 K5
Loop Rd STONE ST15 .... 136 C3
Lord's Dr WSLW WS2 .... 283 L7
Lordship La STOKE ST4 .... 85 K3
Lordshire Pl ALS/KID ST7 .... 53 M1
Lordsley La MKTDR TF9 .... 115 C2
Lord St BDMR/CCFT WV3 .... 12 C6
  BIDD ST8 .... 40 D5
  BURS/TUN ST6 .... 69 J1
Lordswell Rd
  BUTN/AL/TUT DE13 .... 184 E6
Lorien Cl LEEK ST13 .... 43 J6
Loring Rd NEWUL ST5 .... 68 C4
Loring Ter South NEWUL ST5 .... 68 C4
Lorne St BNTWD WS7 .... 251 L2
  BURS/TUN ST6 .... 69 G1
Lorraine St ALS/KID ST7 .... 53 M1
Lorton CRTAM B79 .... 273 K2
Lothersdale TAM/AM/WIL B77 . 291 H2
Lothians Rd BLOX/PEL WS3 ..... 268 A5
  DUNHL/THL/PER WV6 .... 279 K4
Lotus TAM/AM/WIL B77 .... 11 J3
Lotus Av BIDD ST8 .... 40 B4
Lotus Ct STONE ST15 .... 120 B3
Lotus Dr CNCK/NC WS11 .... 231 L5
Loughborough Wk
  LNGTN ST3 .... 86 C9
Loughshaw TAM/AM/WIL B77 . 291 J1
Louise Dr LNGTN ST3 .... 85 M7
Louise St BURS/TUN ST6 .... 69 G1
  SEDG DY3 .... 299 H7
Lount La BUTN/AL/TUT DE13 .. 184 E1
Louvain Av HAN ST1 .... 69 K3
Lovage Gv BUCK/MIL ST2 .... 3 M6
  BUCK/MIL ST2 .... 70 B7
Lovat St WOLV WV1 .... 12 C5
Lovatt Av NEWUL ST5 .... 68 A6
Lovatt Cl BUTN/AL/TUT DE13 .. 166 F8
Lovatt Pl CNCK/NC WS11 .... 231 L5
Lovatt St CNCK/NC WS11 .... 231 L5
  STAFN ST16 .... 174 C5
  STOKE ST4 .... 85 C5
Lovelace Cl STAFS ST17 .... 193 J2
Love La DUNHL/THL/PER WV6 .. 279 K4
  GTWY WS6 .... 250 B6
  RUGE WS15 .... 215 M1
Lovell CRTAM B79 .... 273 M4
Lovell Cl SHIF TF11 .... 242 A4
Lovell Rd BUTN/AL/TUT DE13 . 218 F1
Loveridge Cl CDSL WV8 .... 262 E7
Lovers La MKTDR TF9 .... 114 F6
Loveston Gv LNGTN ST3 .... 86 D6
Lovett Ct RUGE WS15 .... 197 K8
Lowbridge Cl SHHTH WV12 .... 282 C5
Lowdham TAM/AM/WIL B77 ... 291 J1

Lowe Dr *KGSWFD* DY6 .... 303 L6
Lowe La *KIDDW* DY11 .... 309 H7
Lowell Dr *LNGTN* ST3 .... 86 F6
Lower Ash Rd *ALS/KID* ST7 .... 52 E2
Lower Av *COVEN* WV9 .... 246 D6
Lower Bedford St *HAN* ST1 .... 69 G8
Lower Bethesda St *HAN* ST1........ 2 D7
Lower Brook St *RUGE* WS15 ...... 215 L1 ⑧
Lower Bryan St *HAN* ST1 .... 2 C2
Lowercroft Wy
 FOAKS/STRLY B74 .... 286 E4
Lower Forster St *WSL* WS1 .... 283 M8
Lower Foundry St *HAN* ST1 .... 2 C5
Lower Hadderidge
 BURS/TUN ST6 .... 68 F2
Lower High St *ALS/KID* ST7 .... 39 K3
 BUTN/AL/TUT DE13 .... 165 J3
 STRBR DY8 .... 307 M4
Lower Horseley Flds *WOLV* WV1 .. 13 L5
Lower House La *ATHST* CV9 ...... 291 M8
Lower La *LICH* WS13 .... 234 C8
Lower Lichfield St
 WLNHL WV13 .... 282 B8
Lower Mayer St *HAN* ST1 .... 2 E3
Lower Milehouse La *NEWUL* ST5 .. 67 M7
Lower North St
 RUSH/SHEL WS4 .... 283 L7
Lower Outwoods Rd
 BUTN/AL/TUT DE13 .... 184 F5
Lower Oxford Rd *NEWUL* ST5....68 E8
Lowerpark Rd *TAM/AM/WIL* B77 .. 290 C1 ⑫
Lower Penkridge Rd
 STAFS ST17 .... 212 B1
Lower Prestwood Rd
 WNSFLD WV11 .... 281 J3
Lower Rd *GNOS* ST20 .... 171 H5
 HEDN WS12 .... 232 F2
 MKTDR TF9 .... 114 E8
Lower Rookery Rd *STONE* ST15 .. 136 B3
Lower Rushall St *WSL* WS1 .... 283 M8
Lower Sandford St *LICH* WS13 .... 8 C4
Lower Spring Rd *LNGTN* ST3 ...... 86 D8 ⑧
Lower St *ASHB* DE6 .... 145 H2
 BURS/TUN ST6 .... 69 G3
 DUNHL/THL/PER WV6 .... 279 L5
 NEWUL ST5 .... 84 B2
Lower Vauxhall *WOLV* WV1........12 A4
Lower Villiers St
 BKHL/PFLD WV2 .... 295 J3
Lower Walsall St *WOLV* WV1........13 L6
Lower Wy *RUGE* WS15 .... 234 B1
Lowe St *DUNHL/THL/PER* WV6 .... 12 B1
 STOKE ST4 .... 85 H3
Lowfield La *GNOS* ST20 .... 190 E4
Lowforce *TAM/AM/WIL* B77........ 291 J1
Low Hill Crs *WOLVN* WV10 .... 280 E2
Lowhurst Dr *BURS/TUN* ST6 .... 54 A3
Lowland Rd *HEDN* WS12 .... 231 J5
Lowlands Av
 DUNHL/THL/PER WV6 .... 279 L4
Lowlands Rd *BURS/TUN* ST6 ...... 53 G6
Lowndes Cl *STOKE* ST4............ 84 F4
Lowndes Rd *STRBR* DY8 .... 307 L4
Lowry Cl *DUNHL/THL/PER* WV6 .. 278 F6
 WLNHL WV13 .... 281 K8
Low St *ALS/KID* ST7 .... 37 L2
 GTWY WS6 .... 249 J7
Lowther Pl *LEEK* ST13 .... 44 A5
Lowther St *HAN* ST1 .... 2 A3
Lowthorpe Wy *BUCK/MIL* ST2 .... 86 E1 ⑥
Loxley La *UTXR* ST14 .... 143 J4
Loxley Pl *LNGTN* ST3 .... 102 F3
Loxley Rd *MGN/WHC* B75 .... 287 K7
Loxton Cl *FOAKS/STRLY* B74 ...... 286 D5
Loynton Cl *STAFN* ST16 .... 174 A3
Loynton Sands *GNOS* ST20 ...... 170 A5
Lucas St *BURS/TUN* ST6 .... 68 E3
Lucepool La
 BUTN/AL/TUT DE13 .... 201 K7
Lucerne Pl *NEWUL* ST5............ 83 L3
Luce Rd *WOLVN* WV10 .... 280 E4
Lucknow Rd *SHHTH* WV12 ...... 282 C4
Ludbrook Rd *STOKE* ST4.......... 86 B5
Ludford Cl *NEWUL* ST5............ 52 D8
Ludgate *CRTAM* B79.............. 10 B3
Ludgate St *BUTN/AL/TUT* DE13 .. 165 J4
 SHHTH WV12 .... 282 B4
Ludlow Cl *HEDN* WS12 .... 232 C8
Ludlow La *WSLW* WS2.......... 283 G6 ⑥
Ludlow St *HAN* ST1 .... 2 F5
Ludlow Wy *DUDN* DY1 .... 299 L8
Ludstone Av
 ETTPK/GDPK/PENN WV4 ...... 294 D5
Ludwall Rd *LNGTN* ST3 .... 102 E1
Lugano Cl *NEWUL* ST5............ 83 L4
Lukesland Av *STOKE* ST4........ 84 E4 ⑫
Luke St *BURS/TUN* ST6............ 68 E3
Lullington Rd *CRTAM* B79 .... 239 L5
Lulworth Gv *BURS/TUN* ST6 ...... 53 L4 ⑫
Lulworth Rd *BNTWD* WS7 .... 252 A3
Lundy Rd *LNGTN* ST3 .... 85 M7
Lune Cl *CONG* CW12 .... 26 A1
Lunns Cft *LICH* WS13 .... 9 G2
Lutley Cl *BDMR/CCFT* WV3 ...... 294 E3
Lutley La *KINVER* DY7 .... 301 G2
Lyd Cl *WNSFLD* WV11 .... 281 H5
Lydford Pl *LNGTN* ST3 .... 86 F7
Lydford Rd *BLOX/PEL* WS3 ...... 267 H8
Lydgate Rd *KGSWFD* DY6.......... 303 M5
Lydia Cft *FOAKS/STRLY* B74........ 286 E4
Lydia Dr *HAN* ST1................ 69 M4
Lydian Cl *DUNHL/THL/PER* WV6 .. 12 D1
Lydiates Cl *SEDG* DY3 .... 299 H3
Lydney Cl *SHHTH* WV12 .... 282 D6
Lyme Brook Pl *STOKE* ST4 .... 84 E7 ⑫
Lyme Gv *NEWUL* ST5............ 68 C7
Lyme Rd *LNGTN* ST3 .... 103 H1
Lymer Rd *WOLVN* WV10 .... 280 C1
Lymer's La *RSTAF* ST18.......... 158 A1
Lymes Rd *NEWUL* ST5............ 83 G5
Lymevale Rd *STOKE* ST4 .... 84 E6 ⑫
Lyme Valley Rd *NEWUL* ST5........ 84 B3
Lymewood Cl *NEWUL* ST5........ 84 B2
Lyme Wood Gv *NEWUL* ST5........ 84 B3
Lymington Rd *BNTWD* WS7........ 251 M1
 STAFN ST16 .... 173 J6 ⑥
 WLNHL WV13 .... 282 B8 ⑫
Lymsey Cft *STRBR* DY8 .... 303 J7

Lynam St *STOKE* ST4............ 85 G3
Lynam Wy *AUD/MAD/W* CW3 .... 81 L3 ⑫
Lyn Av *LICH* WS13 .... 253 M1
The Lynch *POL/KGSB/FAZ* B78 .. 291 M1
Lyncroft *ALBTN* WV7 .... 261 G5
Lyndale Cft *TAM/AM/WIL* B77 ...... 290 F4
Lyndale Dr *WNSFLD* WV11 .... 281 L4
Lyndale Rd *SEDG* DY3 .... 295 H8
Lyndham Av *STPNHL/WNHL* DE15 .. 7 M8
Lyndhurst Dr *BIDD* ST8 .... 40 A5
Lyndhurst Gv *STONE* ST15........ 138 D4
Lyndhurst Rd *BDMR/CCFT* WV3 .. 295 G3
 HEDN WS12 .... 250 D1
Lyndhurst St *BURS/TUN* ST6...... 68 E2
Lyndon Cl *SEDG* DY3 .... 299 L1
Lyndon Gv *KGSWFD* DY6 .... 303 H2
Lyne Ct *BUT* DE14 .... 6 B4
Lyneham Av *ALBTN* WV7 .... 260 C2
Lyneham Cl *CRTAM* B79.......... 274 B2
Lynehill La *PENK* ST19 .... 229 K4
Lyneside Rd *BIDD* ST8 .... 40 B4
Lynfield Rd *LICH* WS13 .... 253 M8
Lynmouth Gv *ALDR* WS9........ 284 F5
 BIDD ST8 .... 40 C4
Lynmouth Gv *BURS/TUN* ST6 .... 53 L3
Lynn Av *ALS/KID* ST7............ 52 C2
Lynn La *ALDR* WS9 .... 269 L4
Lynn St *LNGTN* ST3 .... 87 H5
Lynsey Cl *ALS/KID* ST7............ 66 E3
Lynton Av
 DUNHL/THL/PER WV6 .... 279 L3
 STAFS ST17 .... 194 D3
Lynton Gv *LNGTN* ST3............ 102 E2
Lynton Rd *NEWUL* ST5............ 83 M5 ⑫
Lynwood Av *KGSWFD* DY6 .... 303 H2
Lynwood Cl *BUT* DE14 .... 203 M3 ⑫
 SHHTH WV12 .... 282 E2 ⑫
Lynwood Dr *KIDD* DY10 .... 311 H8
Lynwood Rd *BUT* DE14 .... 203 L3 ⑫
Lyric Cl *STAFS* ST17 .... 193 M4
Lysander Av *ALBTN* WV7........ 260 B3
Lysander Rd *BLYBR/FOR* ST11 .. 103 H5
 LNGTN ST3 .... 103 G3
Lysander Wy *CNCK/NC* WS11 .... 231 L2
Lysways La *LICH* WS13 .... 235 K2
Lytham *TAM/AM/WIL* B77 .... 275 J5
Lytham *BLOX/PEL* WS3 .... 267 G6 ⑧
Lytham Rd
 DUNHL/THL/PER WV6 .... 278 D6
Lyttelton Rd *STRBR* DY8 .... 307 K5
Lytton Av
 ETTPK/GDPK/PENN WV4 ...... 294 D4
Lytton St *STOKE* ST4............ 85 J3

M

Macadam Cl *BNTWD* WS7 .... 252 B2
Macclesfield Rd *LEEK* ST13 .... 43 H1
Macclesfield St *BURS/TUN* ST6.... 69 H1
Macdonald Crs *LNGTN* ST3 ...... 87 G7
Mace St *STOKE* ST4.............. 84 F6
Mac Gregor Crs
 TAM/AM/WIL B77 .... 11 L6
Macgregor Tithe *CRTAM* B79 ...... 10 C3
Machin Crs *NEWUL* ST5.......... 68 A3
Macintyre St *BURS/TUN* ST6 ...... 69 G3
Mackay Rd *BLOX/PEL* WS3 ...... 267 K8
Mackenzie Crs *CDLE* ST10........ 105 K1
Maclagan St *NEWUL* ST5.......... 85 H4
Macrome Rd
 DUNHL/THL/PER WV6 .... 279 L2
Madden Cl *ALS/KID* ST7 .... 66 D1
Maddock St *ALS/KID* ST7.......... 66 D1
 BURS/TUN ST6 .... 68 E3
Madeira Cl *CDSL* WV8 .... 263 G8
Madeira Pl *BURS/TUN* ST6........ 53 K7
Madeley St *BURS/TUN* ST6........ 53 K6
 NEWUL ST5 .... 83 H1
Madison Av *WSLW* WS2.......... 283 M8 ⑫
Madison St *BURS/TUN* ST6........ 53 K6
Madox Cl *CRTAM* B79............ 273 L2
Madras Rd
 STPNHL/WNHL DE15 .... 186 C7 ⑧
Maer La *ECCH* ST21 .... 116 D4
 MKTDR TF9 .... 112 C8
Maerway La *MKTDR* TF9 .... 97 H5
Mafeking St *LNGTN* ST3 .... 86 B8
Magdalen Rd *ALBTN* WV7 .... 260 B3 ⑫
Magister Rd *ALBTN* WV7 .... 260 B3 ⑫
Magna Cl *GTWY* WS6 .... 249 L7
Magness Crs *SHHTH* WV12 ...... 282 C5
Magnolia Cl *RSTAF* ST18.......... 154 B8
Magnolia Dr *BURS/TUN* ST6 ...... 54 F8 ⑧
Magnolia Gv *CDSL* WV8 .... 263 G7 ⑧
Magnolia Wy *STRBR* DY8 .... 307 M2 ⑧
Magnus Cl *TAM/AM/WIL* B77 .... 290 E4
Magpie Crs *ALS/KID* ST7 .... 39 H8 ⑫
Maidendale Rd *KGSWFD* DY6 .... 303 H3
Maidensbridge Gdns
 KGSWFD DY6 .... 303 H1 ⑧
Maidensbridge Rd
 KGSWFD DY6 .... 303 H1
Maidstone Dr *BNTWD* WS7 ...... 252 D4
 STRBR DY8 .... 303 L7
Maidstone Gv *BUCK/MIL* ST2 .... 70 C8
Main Rd *ASHB* DE6 .... 94 D2
 ASHB DE6 .... 146 E6
 AUD/MAD/W CW3 .... 65 G4
 CDLE ST10 .... 75 L6
 CRTAM B79 .... 239 K5
 CRTAM B79 .... 257 J7
 CRTAM B79 .... 259 H8
 END/WER ST9.................. 72 B3
 GNOS ST20 .... 150 D3
 MKTDR TF9 .... 113 J1
 RSTAF ST18 .... 177 H8
 STAFS ST17 .... 195 H3
 STONE ST15 .... 136 B3
Main Road Brereton
 RUGE WS15 .... 216 A4
Main St *ALDR* WS9 .... 269 L6
 BUT DE14 .... 203 M3
 BUTN/AL/TUT DE13 .... 184 B8
 BUTN/AL/TUT DE13 .... 184 C3
 BUTN/AL/TUT DE13 .... 185 L1
 BUTN/AL/TUT DE13 .... 201 G8
 BUTN/AL/TUT DE13 .... 202 C8

 BUTN/AL/TUT DE13 .... 219 M7
 CRTAM B79 .... 240 E8
 CRTAM B79 .... 274 B1
 LICHS WS14 .... 255 L4 ⑧
 LICHS WS14 .... 270 F4
 STAFS ST17 .... 87 H5
 BUTN/AL/TUT DE13 .... 200 E1
 MSHM DE12 .... 221 K1
 MSHM DE12 .... 222 C4
 MSHM DE12 .... 222 D7
 MSHM DE12 .... 222 K4
 MSHM DE12 .... 223 K4
 MSHM DE12 .... 241 M3
 RDERBYSW DE65 .... 167 H5
 RDERBYSW DE65 .... 187 K1
 STPNHL/WNHL DE15 .... 204 F2
 SWAD DE11 .... 205 L4
Mainwaring Dr
 MGN/WHC B75 .... 287 L8 ⑦
Majors Barn *CDLE* ST10 .... 89 J8
Major St *BKHL/PFLD* WV2 .... 295 L3
Maker La *BUTN/AL/TUT* DE13 .... 181 K7
 BUTN/AL/TUT DE13 .... 200 C1
Malam St *HAN* ST1 .... 2 B3
Malbon's Yd *ASHB* DE6 .... 95 H1
Malcolm Cl *BUCK/MIL* ST2 ...... 55 H8
Malcolm Dr *BUCK/MIL* ST2 ...... 70 C5
Malcolm Rd *STAFS* ST17 .... 193 K4
Maldale *TAM/AM/WIL* B77 .... 291 J1
Malham Rd *NEWUL* ST5.......... 67 L8
 TAM/AM/WIL B77 .... 291 J1
Malins Rd
 ETTPK/GDPK/PENN WV4 ...... 295 K5
Malkin Wy *BURS/TUN* ST6........ 68 E4
Malkit Cl *WSLW* WS2 .... 282 E6
Mallard Av *STAFS* ST17 .... 194 A3
Mallard Cl *BLOX/PEL* WS3 ...... 268 A5 ⑧
 UTXR ST14 .... 144 C4
Mallard Wy *BURS/TUN* ST6 ...... 54 C7
Mallens Cft *UTXR* ST14.......... 143 J3
Mallicot Cl *LICH* WS13 .... 9 J1
Mallorie Rd *BURS/TUN* ST6 ...... 54 D6
Mallory Crs *BLOX/PEL* WS3 ...... 267 K8
Mallory Rd
 DUNHL/THL/PER WV6 .... 278 C7
Mallory Wy *CDLE* ST10.......... 89 M7
Mallow Cl *ECCH* ST21 .... 152 D5 ⑧
Mallowdale Cl *STOKE* ST4 ...... 101 J4 ⑫
Malpass Gdns *CDSL* WV8.......... 262 E6
Malstone Av *BUCK/MIL* ST2 ...... 55 J8
Malthouse La *BARL* ST12 .... 101 L8
 DUNHL/THL/PER WV6 .... 279 K4
Malt House La *GNOS* ST20 ...... 209 G2
Malthouse La *LNGTN* ST3........ 87 H2
 PENK ST19 .... 227 H4
 RSTAF ST18 .... 210 C1
Malt House La *WOLVN* WV10 .... 248 B5
Malthouse Rd *BUCK/MIL* ST2 .... 70 B7
 CDLE ST10 .... 107 L1
Malt House Rd *RUGE* WS15 ...... 234 B5
The Maltings
 STPNHL/WNHL DE15 .... 205 G1
 WOLV WV1 .... 13 G2
Malt La *LNGTN* ST3 .... 86 D8 ⑧
Malt Mill La *STAFN* ST16 .... 4 F4 ⑧
Malton Gv *BURS/TUN* ST6........ 53 K6
Malvern Av *NEWUL* ST5.......... 66 F8 ⑫
Malvern Cl *SHHTH* WV12 .... 282 B6
 STAFS ST17 .... 5 L1
 STOKE ST4 .... 101 C3
Malvern Ct *WOLVN* WV10........ 280 D2 ⑥
Malvern Dr *ALDR* WS9 .... 285 J2
 RUGE WS15 .... 197 J8 ⑧
Malvern St *STPNHL/WNHL* DE15 .. 7 J1
Malvern View Rd *SEDG* DY3 .... 299 K6 ⑧
Mamble Gv *STRBR* DY8 .... 307 L5
Mancroft Cl *KGSWFD* DY6 ...... 303 H3 ⑧
Mancroft Gdns
 DUNHL/THL/PER WV6 .... 279 J5
Mancroft Rd
 DUNHL/THL/PER WV6 .... 279 L2
Mandale Rd *WOLVN* WV10........ 280 F4
Mandela Wy *LNGTN* ST3 .... 86 C8
Manderley Cl *SEDG* DY3 .... 295 J8
Mander St *BDMR/CCFT* WV3 .... 12 D8
Manderville Gdns *KGSWFD* DY6 .. 303 J4
Mandeville Cl *BURS/TUN* ST6 .... 54 C7 ⑧
Manfield Rd *WLNHL* WV13 ...... 281 J7
Manifold Av *ASHB* DE6.......... 95 J1
Manifold Cl *BNTWD* WS7 .... 252 D4 ⑧
 NEWUL ST5 .... 83 H1
Manifold Dr *CDLE* ST10 .... 105 L1
Manifold Rd *BLYBR/FOR* ST11 .. 103 M2
Manifold Wy *BUX* SK17........ 47 J2
 CDLE ST10 .... 76 C1
 LEEK ST13 .... 61 L2
Manley Rd *LICH* WS13 .... 9 K1
Manlove St *BDMR/CCFT* WV3 .... 12 B8
Mann St *LNGTN* ST3 .... 87 J3
Manor Av *CNCK/NC* WS11 ...... 249 K1
 GTWY WS6 .... 250 A6
Manor Cl *BLYBR/FOR* ST11 ...... 104 C4 ⑫
 CDSL WV8 .... 263 H7 ⑦
 CONG CW12 .... 26 A1
 ETTPK/GDPK/PENN WV4 ...... 294 D5 ⑥
 MKTDR TF9 .... 130 C1 ⑦
 RSTAF ST18 .... 157 K7
 RSTAF ST18 .... 177 H8 ⑧
 STPNHL/WNHL DE15 .... 205 G4
 UTXR ST14 .... 144 C2 ⑫
 WLNHL WV13 .... 281 M7
Manor Court Dr *RUGE* WS15 .... 217 H6
Manor Court St *STOKE* ST4 ...... 84 F4
Manor Crs *STPNHL/WNHL* DE15 .. 205 G4
Manor Cft *BUT* DE14 .... 7 J7
 BUTN/AL/TUT DE13 .... 203 G2
Manor Dr *BUT* DE14 .... 7 J7
 SEDG DY3 .... 297 J3
 WOLVN WV10 .... 248 B6
Manor Farm Crs *STAFS* ST17 .... 193 L5
Manor Farm Dr *MKTDR* TF9 .... 148 A8
 SHHTH WV12 .... 282 D5
Manor Farm Rd *RSTAF* ST18 .... 196 D2
Manor Flds *BUTN/AL/TUT* DE13 .. 219 M7
Manor Fold *CDSL* WV8 .... 262 D8
Manor Gdns *ALBTN* WV7 .... 261 G5 ⑫
 MKTDR TF9 .... 130 C1
Manor Gld *NEWUL* ST5.......... 98 A3
Manor Gn *STAFS* ST17............ 193 K3 ⑦
Manor House Pk *CDSL* WV8 .... 263 H6

Manor La *CRTAM* B79............ 239 K8
 CRTAM B79 .... 256 E7
 KINVER DY7 .... 296 D7
 STRBR DY8 .... 307 K7
Manor Pk *KGSWFD* DY6 .... 303 L4
Manor Ri *BNTWD* WS7 .... 252 A5
 LICHS WS14 .... 9 H6
 STONE ST15 .... 137 M3
Manor Rd *ALS/KID* ST7............ 39 K3
 ASHB DE6 .... 79 J7
 AUD/MAD/W CW3 .... 81 L7
 BUTN/AL/TUT DE13 .... 218 B4
 ETTPK/GDPK/PENN WV4 ...... 294 F6
 GNOS ST20 .... 190 E3
 POL/KGSB/FAZ B78 .... 289 K1
 STPNHL/WNHL DE15 .... 205 G4
 STRBR DY8 .... 303 K8
 TAM/AM/WIL B77 .... 10 F5
 UTXR ST14 .... 144 B2
 WOLVN WV10 .... 280 C3
 WSLW WS2 .... 283 J8
Manor Road Prec *WSLW* WS2 .. 283 J8 ⑫
Manor Sq *STAFS* ST17............ 193 K3
Manor St *DUNHL/THL/PER* WV6 .. 279 J5
 STOKE ST4 .... 84 F4
Manor Wk *BUTN/AL/TUT* DE13 .. 218 B4
Manor Wy *RUGE* WS15 .... 198 A4
Mansard Cl *BDMR/CCFT* WV3 .. 294 F2 ⑦
 WNSFLD WV11 .... 281 H2 ⑫
Manse Cl *LNGTN* ST3 .... 86 C6 ⑫
Mansell Cl *STAFN* ST16.......... 4 B6
Mansfield Cl *CRTAM* B79........ 273 L4
 NEWUL ST5 .... 84 C8
Mansfield Dr *STRBR* DY8.......... 40 A5
Mansion Cl *CDLE* ST10.......... 89 L8
 DUDN DY1 .... 299 M7 ⑧
Mansion Dr *BNTWD* WS7 .... 252 D6
Manston Dr
 DUNHL/THL/PER WV6 .... 278 E5
Manston Hl *PENK* ST19 .... 229 L3
Manston Vw *CRTAM* B79........ 274 C2
Manta Rd *TAM/AM/WIL* B77 .... 290 D4
Manton Cl *SWAD* DE11.......... 205 M4 ⑫
Maple Av *ALS/KID* ST7............ 37 L8
 ALS/KID ST7 .... 52 D2
 NEWUL ST5 .... 67 K1
Maple Cl *BNTWD* WS7 .... 251 M3
 BURS/TUN ST6 .... 55 G5
 CDLE ST10 .... 89 L8
 KINVER DY7 .... 306 A5
 STONE ST15 .... 136 F5
 STRBR DY8 .... 307 K8
Maple Crs *BLYBR/FOR* ST11 ...... 104 A4
 CNCK/NC WS11 .... 249 J2
Mapledene Cl *STAFS* ST17 ...... 194 D5 ⑧
Maple Dr *ASHB* DE6 .... 95 K2 ⑧
 HEDN WS12 .... 231 K2
 MKTDR TF9 .... 114 D8
 RSTAF ST18 .... 192 D1
 RUSH/SHEL WS4 .... 284 D2
 SEDG DY3 .... 299 H8
Maple Gdns *STONE* ST15........ 138 A4
Maple Gv *BDMR/CCFT* WV3 .... 279 J8
 KGSWFD DY6 .... 303 L4
 LICHS WS14 .... 9 M4
 STAFS ST17 .... 193 L3
 STPNHL/WNHL DE15 .... 204 E5
Maplehurst Cl *BURS/TUN* ST6.... 69 H2
Maple Pl *ALS/KID* ST7............ 37 M3 ⑧
 ALS/KID ST7 .... 87 H8
Maple Ri *TAM/AM/WIL* B77 .... 275 H6 ⑧
Maple Rd *BDMR/CCFT* WV3...... 294 E2
 BLOX/PEL WS3 .... 267 M8
Maple St *BLOX/PEL* WS3 .... 267 K8
Mapleton Rd *ASHB* DE6.......... 79 G8
Maple Wd *STAFS* ST17 .... 194 C5
Marcel Cl *STOKE* ST4............ 85 G8
Marchant Cl *BDMR/CCFT* WV3 .. 279 M8
March Banks *RUGE* WS15 ...... 215 K1
March End Rd *WNSFLD* WV11.... 281 L5
March La *END/WER* ST9........ 72 A7
 RSTAF ST18 .... 154 F5
March Rd *LNGTN* ST3 .... 86 B6 ⑫
 WOLV WV1 .... 13 H5
Marchwood Ct *STOKE* ST4 ...... 84 E4
Marconi Pl *HEDN* WS12 .... 232 C3
Maree Gv *WNSFLD* WV11 .... 282 B1
Margam Crs *BLOX/PEL* WS3 .... 266 F8
Margam Ter *BLOX/PEL* WS3 .... 266 F8
Margam Wy *BLOX/PEL* WS3 .... 266 F8
Margaret Av *WSLW* WS2 .... 282 E7
Margaret Dr *CNCK/NC* WS11 .... 231 L2 ⑧
Margaret Rd *WSLW* WS2........ 282 E7
Margaret St *HAN* ST1............ 3 G5
 STONE ST15 .... 137 M1
 WSLW WS2 .... 283 K8
Margery Av *ALS/KID* ST7 .... 38 E3
Margery Cl *ASHB* DE6............ 95 H2
Margill Cl *HAN* ST1 .... 2 A7
Marholm Cl *COVEN* WV9........ 263 M8 ⑧
Marigold Cl *HEDN* WS12 .... 232 C7 ⑧
Marina Cl *HEDN* WS12 .... 232 A5
Marina Dr *HAN* ST1.............. 68 F6
 NEWUL ST5 .... 68 C7
Marine Crs *STRBR* DY8 .... 307 L1
Marine Gdns *STRBR* DY8 .... 307 L1
Mariner *CRTAM* B79............ 273 L3
Marjory La *ASHB* DE6............ 129 J8
Market Drayton Rd *MKTDR* TF9 .. 114 C6
Marketfields *ECCH* ST21 .... 152 E3
Market Hall St *CNCK/NC* WS11 .. 249 L1
Market La
 ETTPK/GDPK/PENN WV4 ...... 293 M4
 LICHS WS14 .... 253 J8
 NEWUL ST5 .... 68 C7
Market Pl *BLOX/PEL* WS3 .... 283 H1 ⑧
 BURS/TUN ST6 .... 68 F2
 BUT DE14 .... 7 J7
 BUX SK17 .... 24 B4 ⑧
 CNCK/NC WS11 .... 249 K1
 PENK ST19 .... 246 C4 ⑧
 UTXR ST14 .... 144 C2
 WLNHL WV13 .... 282 A8
Market Sq *RUGE* WS15 .... 215 L1 ⑧
Market St *ALS/KID* ST7............ 53 G1
 CRTAM B79 .... 10 C3
 HEDN WS12 .... 232 B4

 LEEK ST13 43
 LICH WS13 8
 LNGTN ST3 229
 PENK ST19 229
 RUGE WS15 215
 STAFN ST16 .... 4 E6
 UTXR ST14 144
 WOLV WV1 13
Markham Cft *COVEN* WV9........ 264
Markham Dr *KGSWFD* DY6 ...... 303 L4
Marklew Cl *BRWNH* WS8........ 269
Marklin Av *WOLVN* WV10........ 280
Marksbury Cl
 DUNHL/THL/PER WV6............ 280
Marlborough Av *STAFN* ST16 175
Marlborough Cl *END/WER* ST9 .. 55 L2
 FOAKS/STRLY B74 .... 286 E4
 RSTAF ST18 177
Marlborough Ct *LICH* WS13 8
Marlborough Crs
 STPNHL/WNHL DE15 204
Marlborough Gdns
 DUNHL/THL/PER WV6............ 279
 STRBR DY8 .... 303 K6
Marlborough Rd *SEDG* DY3 299
 STONE ST15 137
Marlborough St *BLOX/PEL* WS3 .. 283
 STOKE ST4 85
Marlborough Wy
 TAM/AM/WIL B77 11
 UTXR ST14 143
Marlbrook Dr
 ETTPK/GDPK/PENN WV4 295
Marlbrook La
 DUNHL/THL/PER WV6............ 277
Marlburn Wy *WMBN* WV5........ 297
Marldon Pl *BURS/TUN* ST6 ...... 53 J2
Marlin *TAM/AM/WIL* B77 290
Marlow Cl *LNGTN* ST3.......... 102
Marlowe Dr *SHHTH* WV12 282
Marlowe Rd *STAFS* ST17 193
Marlow Rd *LNGTN* ST3.......... 86
 TAM/AM/WIL B77 291
Marlow St *WOLV* WV2 283
Marlpit La *ASHB* DE6 93
 MGN/WHC B75................ 287
 STONE ST15 108
 UTXR ST14 108
Marlpool Dr *BLOX/PEL* WS3 .... 283 H
Marmion St *CRTAM* B79.......... 10
Marnel Dr *BDMR/CCFT* WV3 294
Marquis's Dr *HEDN* WS12 215
 RUGE WS15 215
Marrick *TAM/AM/WIL* B77 291
Marriott St *STOKE* ST4............ 86
Marsden St *HAN* ST1............ 2
Marsett *TAM/AM/WIL* B77 291
Marshall Av *BURS/TUN* ST6 55
Marshall Cl *ALDR* WS9 285
Marshall St *BURS/TUN* ST6 ...... 68 F1
 TAM/AM/WIL B77 11
Marsh Av *ALS/KID* ST7............ 39
 BURS/TUN ST6 69
 NEWUL ST5 69
Marsh Cl *ALS/KID* ST7............ 37 G7
 END/WER ST9.................. 71
Marsh Ct *STAFN* ST16............ 174 D
Marsh Crs *STRBR* DY8 .... 303 K7
Marshfield La *BIDD* ST8.......... 26
Marsh Green Cl *BIDD* ST8........ 26
Marshgreen Rd *BIDD* ST8 26
Marsh Gv *BIDD* ST8.............. 26
Marshland Gv *BURS/TUN* ST6 .. 54
Marsh La *ALS/KID* ST7............ 37 G7
 ASHB DE6 93
 ECCH ST21 151
 LICHS WS14 8
 MKTDR TF9 149
 PENK ST19 211
 SHIF TF11 224
 WOLVN WV10 264
 WSLW WS2 283
Marsh Lane Pde *WOLVN* WV10 .. 264
Marsh Pde *NEWUL* ST5.......... 68
Marsh Rd *SHIF* TF11 224
Marsh St *STAFN* ST16............ 4
 WSL WS1 .... 283 L8
 WSLW WS2 283
Marsh St North *HAN* ST1 2
Marsh St South *HAN* ST1 2
Marsh Vw *LNGTN* ST3............ 103
Marsh Wy *NEWUL* ST5.......... 68
Marshwood Cl
 CNCK/NC WS11 .... 232 A4
Marsland Cl *STAFN* ST16........ 174 A
Marsland Rd *STAFN* ST16........ 174 A6
Mars St *BURS/TUN* ST6 .... 69 J2
Marston Brook
 RDERBYSW DE65 .... 166 E1
Marston Cl *PENK* ST19 .... 227 J4
 STRBR DY8 .... 307 K6
Marston Gv *HAN* ST1............ 69 J7
Marston La *ASHB* DE6............ 79 J7
 BUTN/AL/TUT DE13 .... 166 A1
 RDERBYSW DE65 .... 166 E1
 RDERBYSW DE65 .... 166 E1
 RSTAF ST18 .... 155 J1
Marston Old La
 RDERBYSW DE65 165
Marston Ri
 STPNHL/WNHL DE15 .... 204 F7
Marston Rd *BKHL/PFLD* WV2 295
 GNOS ST20 227
 HEDN WS12 .... 231 M
 STAFN ST16 .... 4 E8
Marston St *WLNHL* WV13 .... 282 C
Marsworth Wy *STAFN* ST16 .... 174 D1
Martham Dr
 DUNHL/THL/PER WV6............ 279
Martin Cft *LICH* WS13 .... 254 A8
Martindale *CNCK/NC* WS11 .... 232 A4
Martin Dl *MKTDR* TF9............ 114 D
Martindale *STAFS* ST17.......... 194 D1
Martindale Cl *LNGTN* ST3 ...... 102 F
Martin Dr *SHHTH* WV12 .... 282 C
Martin's La *BUTN/AL/TUT* DE13 .. 164 A
Martinslow La *LEEK* ST13 .... 60 E
Martin St *BURS/TUN* ST6.......... 68 F
 ETTPK/GDPK/PENN WV4 ...... 295 M

Milne Av *LICH* WS13 .... 237 K4
Milner Dr *CRTAM* B79 .... 275 L3
Milner Ter *LEEK* ST13 .... 44 A3
Milnes Cl *LNGTN* ST3 .... 86 A8
Milton Av *CRTAM* B79 .... 274 A3
Milton Cl *SHHTH* WV12 .... 282 E3
Milton Ct *DUNHL/THL/PER* WV6.. 278 E6
Milton Crs *ALS/KID* ST7 .... 52 C2
SEDG DY3 .... 299 G5
Milton Dr *MKTDR* TF9 .... 112 C8
Milton Gv *STAFS* ST17 .... 193 H3
Milton Rd *BUCK/MIL* ST2 .... 69 M1
CNCK/NC WS11 .... 231 L6
HAN ST1 .... 69 L2
WOLVN WV10 .... 281 G5
Milton St *BUT* DE14 .... 6 F6
HAN ST1 .... 2 A7
Milvale St *BURS/TUN* ST6 .... 68 C8
Milverton Dr *UTXR* ST14 .... 143 M1
Milward Cl *ALS/KID* ST7 .... 102 F4
Mimosa Wk *KGSWFD* DY6 .... 303 L2 2
Minard Cl *LNGTN* ST3 .... 87 G6
Minden Gv *BURS/TUN* ST6 .... 69 K2
Minehead Rd *WOLVN* WV10 .... 264 B8
Miner St *WSLW* WS2 .... 283 J7
Miners Wk
POL/KGSB/FAZ B78 .... 291 M1 4
Minerva Cl *BIDD* ST8 .... 40 B5
SHHTH WV12 .... 282 E6
TAM/AM/WIL B77 .... 11 H3
Minerva Rd *STOKE* ST4 .... 85 M4
Minewood Cl *BLOX/PEL* WS3 ... 266 F7 2
Minfield Cl *ALS/KID* ST7 .... 53 G2
Minn-end-lane *MCFLDS* SK11 .. 19 G4
Minors HI *LICHS* WS14 .... 9 J7
Minshall St *STOKE* ST4 .... 85 J5
Minsterley Cl
BDMR/CCFT WV3 .... 294 E2 5
Minster St *BURS/TUN* ST6 .... 69 H1
The Minster *BDMR/CCFT* WV3 .. 294 F3
Minton Cl *CDLE* ST10 .... 105 K1
CONG CW12 .... 26 B1
Minton St *NEWUL* ST5 .... 68 D5
STOKE ST4 .... 84 E2
Miranda Gv *BURS/TUN* ST6 .... 69 K1
Mires Brook La *RUGE* WS15 .... 179 M4
The Mires *ASHB* DE6 .... 48 A7
Mirfield Cl *COVEN* WV9 .... 264 A7 2
Miss Pickerings Fld *STAFS* ST17 .. 212 B1
Mitcham Gv *HEDN* WS12 .... 231 M3 5
Mitchell Av *ALS/KID* ST7 .... 52 D1
Mitchell Dr *ALS/KID* ST7 .... 52 D1
Mitchell Ri *STOKE* ST15 .... 136 F4
Mitchell St *BURS/TUN* ST6 .... 68 F1
Mitchel Rd *KGSWFD* DY6 .... 303 M6
Mitre Cl *SHHTH* WV12 .... 282 D3
WNSFLD WV11 .... 266 A7
Mitre Fold *WOLV* WV1 .... 12 E4
Mitre Gv *GTWY* WS6 .... 249 K8
Mitton Rd *RSTAF* ST18 .... 210 C3
Moat Bank
STPNHL/WNHL DE15 .... 186 D8
Moat Brook Av *CDSL* WV8 .... 262 E6
Moatbrook La *CDSL* WV8 .... 262 D6
Moat Dr *POL/KGSB/FAZ* B78 .... 289 L5
Moat Farm Wy *BLOX/PEL* WS3.. 268 A5
Moat Green Av *WNSFLD* WV11 .. 281 L3
Moathouse Cl *STAFS* ST17 .... 212 A2
Moat House Ct *RSTAF* ST18 .... 191 L4
Moat House La East
WNSFLD WV11 .... 281 L3
Moathouse La West
WNSFLD WV11 .... 281 K3
Moat La *ALS/KID* ST7 .... 51 G8
BUTN/AL/TUT DE13 .... 181 K5
GTWY WS6 .... 250 A8
Moat Rd *WSLW* WS2 .... 283 J8
Moatside Cl *BLOX/PEL* WS3 ... 268 A5 4
Moat St *WLNHL* WV13 .... 282 A8
The Moat *LNGTN* ST3 .... 87 H6
Moat Wy *RUGE* WS15 .... 217 H6
Mobberley Rd *BURS/TUN* ST6 .. 53 J3
Mob La *RUSH/SHEL* WS4 .... 268 C8
Moddershall Oaks *STONE* ST15 .. 120 F2
Moden Cl *SEDG* DY3 .... 299 K5
Moden HI *SEDG* DY3 .... 299 J4
Moffat Gv *BUCK/MIL* ST2 .... 86 E3
Moffatt Wy *NEWUL* ST5 .... 66 F8
Moises Hall Rd *WMBN* WV5 .... 298 B4
Moisty La *UTXR* ST14 .... 145 H7
Molineux St *WOLV* WV1 .... 12 F3
Molineux Wy *WOLV* WV1 .... 12 F2
Mollatts Cl *LEEK* ST13 .... 43 H8
Mollatts Wood Rd *LEEK* ST13 .. 43 H8
Mollison Rd *LNGTN* ST3 .... 103 G2
Monaco PI *NEWUL* ST5 .... 83 L3
Monarch Cl
BUTN/AL/TUT DE13 .... 185 L2 6
Monarch's Wy *ALBTN* WV7 .... 244 A8
COVEN WV9 .... 263 L3
DUNHL/THL/PER WV6 .... 278 A7
KGSWFD DY6 .... 302 E4
SHIF TF11 .... 243 H5
WNSFLD WV11 .... 265 K7
WSLW WS2 .... 283 G6
Mona Rd *BUTN/AL/TUT* DE13 .. 185 H5
Monkhouse *CDLE* ST10 .... 89 K7
Monkleigh Cl *STOKE* ST4 .... 101 H5 2
Monks Cl *NEWUL* ST5 .... 84 C4
WMBN WV5 .... 297 L4 2
Monks Wk *GNOS* ST20 .... 190 C5 2
Monk St *BUTN/AL/TUT* DE13 .. 165 J4
TAM/AM/WIL B77 .... 11 M4
Monkton Cl *LNGTN* ST3 .... 102 A1 3
Monmer La *WLNHL* WV13 .... 102 A1 3
Monmouth PI *NEWUL* ST5 .... 84 D6
Monmouth Rd *WSLW* WS2 .... 282 E7
Monsal Av *WOLV* WV1 .... 13 J1
Monsaldale Cl *BRWNH* WS8 .... 268 D3 5
STPNHL/WNHL DE15 .... 186 B6 6
Monsal Gv *HAN* ST1 .... 3 J3
Monteagle Dr *KGSWFD* DY6 .... 303 K1
Montford Gv *SEDG* DY3 .... 299 K3 6
Montfort PI *HAN* ST1 .... 84 B4
Montgomery PI *LNGTN* ST3 .... 87 H8 4
Montgomery Rd *WSLW* WS2 .... 282 E8
Montley *TAM/AM/WIL* B77 .... 291 J2
Montpelier Cl *BUT* DE14 .... 204 A3 1

Montpellier Gdns *DUDN* DY1 .. 299 L8
Montrose Cl *CNCK/NC* WS11 .. 231 M5
Montrose Dr *STOKE* ST4 .... 85 M5
Montville Dr *STAFS* ST17 .... 193 H2
Monty PI *STOKE* ST4 .... 86 B5
Monument Dr *WOLVN* WV10 .... 265 J2
Monument La *BARL* ST12 .... 101 G8
SEDG DY3 .... 299 L1
Monument Rd *ALS/KID* ST7 .... 52 D4
Monument Vw *ALS/KID* ST7 .... 51 M8
Monyash Cl *BLYBR/FOR* ST11 .. 103 J3
Monyash Dr *LEEK* ST13 .... 44 A5
Moon's La *GTWY* WS6 .... 249 K8
Moor Cl *BIDD* ST8 .... 40 E1
STAFS ST17 .... 194 B8
Moor Cft *RUGE* WS15 .... 198 A3
Moorcroft Av *NEWUL* ST5 .... 84 B7
Moorcroft Cl *CDLE* ST10 .... 105 J1
Moore Cl *DUNHL/THL/PER* WV6 .. 278 F7
FOAKS/STRLY B74 .... 286 F4 6
Moore Rd *SHHTH* WV12 .... 282 D2
Moores Cl
BUTN/AL/TUT DE13 .... 185 H4 3
Moores Cft *CRTAM* B79 .... 239 J5
Moore St *BURS/TUN* ST6 .... 69 G3
HEDN WS12 .... 232 C3
WOLV WV1 .... 13 G5
Moor Farm Rd (East) *ASHB* DE6.. 95 L3
Moor Farm Rd (West) *ASHB* DE6 .. 95 L2
Moorfield Av *BIDD* ST8 .... 40 C2
Moorfield Rd *BKHL/PFLD* WV2 .. 295 H3
Moorfields *LEEK* ST13 .... 43 M5 5
Moorfields Cl *CDLE* ST10 .... 75 L6
Moorgate *CRTAM* B79 .... 10 B3
Moor Gv *UTXR* ST14 .... 144 A2
Moor Hall La *PENK* ST19 .... 230 A3
Moorhead Dr *END/WER* ST9 .... 55 M6
Moorhouse Av *ALS/KID* ST7 .... 37 L6
Moorhouse Ct *STONE* ST15 .... 137 G4
Moorhouse St *LEEK* ST13 .... 43 M5 5
The Moorings
BUTN/AL/TUT DE13 .... 219 M7 3
COVEN WV9 .... 263 M8 3
STAFS ST17 .... 196 E3
Moorland Av *END/WER* ST9 .... 71 J6
WOLVN WV10 .... 280 C4
Moorland Cl *END/WER* ST9 .... 71 H6
RUGE WS15 .... 215 J1
Moorland Rd *ALS/KID* ST7 .... 39 K3
BIDD ST8 .... 40 D2
BLOX/PEL WS3 .... 283 G2
BURS/TUN ST6 .... 69 H1
CNCK/NC WS11 .... 231 L5
LEEK ST13 .... 44 B5
LEEK ST13 .... 57 J5
Moorlands Dr *ASHB* DE6 .... 94 C3
Moorland Vw *BURS/TUN* ST6 .. 54 C7
Moor La *ASHB* DE6 .... 95 L4
CDLE ST10 .... 89 M6
CDLE ST10 .... 123 L5
CRTAM B79 .... 275 G4
DUNHL/THL/PER WV6 .... 277 K8
LICHS WS14 .... 286 E1
RSTAF ST18 .... 173 K2
RUGE WS15 .... 197 M3
TAM/AM/WIL B77 .... 11 G4
Moorleys La *RSTAF* ST18 .... 158 A5
Moor Pk *BLOX/PEL* WS3 .... 267 H7
DUNHL/THL/PER WV6 .... 278 D5
Moors Dr *COVEN* WV9 .... 247 H8
Moorside Gdns *WSLW* WS2 .... 283 H7
Moorside Rd *END/WER* ST9 .... 71 K6
Moorson Av *ALS/KID* ST7 .... 38 F2
Moor St *BUT* DE14 .... 6 F6
CRTAM B79 .... 10 A4
Moor St South *BKHL/PFLD* WV2.. 295 J3
Moorsyde Rd *STOKE* ST4 .... 84 E5
Moorthorne Crs *NEWUL* ST5 .. 68 A4
Moran Cv *BURS/TUN* ST6 .... 68 E3
Moran Rd *NEWUL* ST5 .... 67 M8
Mordaunt Dr *MGN/WHC* B75 .. 287 L8 5
Moresby Cl *BUCK/MIL* ST2 .... 70 B1
Moreton Av *CDLE* ST10 .... 73 K8
ETTPK/GDPK/PENN WV4 .... 295 K5
NEWUL ST5 .... 100 D2
Moreton Cl *ALS/KID* ST7 .... 53 H2
END/WER ST9 .... 71 G8
Moreton Dr *ALS/KID* ST7 .... 37 H7
Moreton La *ASHB* DE6 .... 163 H2
RSTAF ST18 .... 177 L6
RUGE WS15 .... 197 J2
Moreton Pde *NEWUL* ST5 .... 68 D6
Moreton Rd *WOLVN* WV10 .... 280 D1
Moreton St *CNCK/NC* WS11 .. 231 M6
Morfe Hall La *KINVER* DY7 .... 301 K7
Morfe La *KINVER* DY7 .... 301 G8
Morford Rd *ALDR* WS9 .... 285 M8
Morgan Cl *WLNHL* WV13 .... 282 B6
Morgan Rd *POL/KGSB/FAZ* B78 .. 274 A8
Morgan Wy *NEWUL* ST5 .... 54 A4
Morland Ct *STONE* ST15 .... 138 B5
Morley Dr *CONG* CW12 .... 26 A1
Morley Gv
DUNHL/THL/PER WV6 .... 280 C6
Morley Rd *BNTWD* WS7 .... 252 B3
Morley's HI
BUTN/AL/TUT DE13 .... 185 H3 3
Morley St *HAN* ST1 .... 2 B6
LEEK ST13 .... 43 M5
Morlings Dr *BNTWD* WS7 .... 252 B2 2
Morning Pines *STRBR* DY8 .... 307 L6 5
Morningside *AUD/MAD/W* CW3 .. 81 L4
Mornington Rd *HAN* ST1 .... 69 K2
Morpeth *TAM/AM/WIL* B77 .... 290 C3
Morpeth St *LNGTN* ST3 .... 86 C7
Morridge Vw *WSLW* WS2 .... 57 J6 2
Morris Av *WSLW* WS2 .... 282 E8
Morris Dr *STAFN* ST16 .... 175 J7
Morris HI *POL/KGSB/FAZ* B78 .. 291 M3
Morrison Av *WOLVN* WV10 .... 280 E2
Morston Dr *TAM/AM/WIL* B77 .. 290 D6 1
Morston St *NEWUL* ST5 .... 84 B8
Mortimer PI *LNGTN* ST3 .... 86 F6 1
Morton Rd *STAFS* ST17 .... 193 K4
Morton St *STOKE* ST4 .... 85 L3
Morville Cl *STOKE* ST4 .... 85 J3
Mosedale Av *LNGTN* ST3 .... 102 E3
Mosedale Dr *WNSFLD* WV11 .. 281 M5 2

Moseley Ct *WNSFLD* WV11 .... 265 M7
Moseley Old Hall La
WOLVN WV10 .... 265 G5
Moseley Rd *WOLVN* WV10 .... 265 G5
Moseley St
DUNHL/THL/PER WV6 .... 280 C6
Mosley Dr *UTXR* ST14 .... 144 A1
Mosley St *BUT* DE14 .... 6 F6
Mossbank Av *BNTWD* WS7 .... 252 A4
Moss Cl *ALDR* WS9 .... 285 G5
END/WER ST9 .... 71 H6
HEDN WS12 .... 231 H5
RUSH/SHEL WS4 .... 284 A7
Mossdale *TAM/AM/WIL* B77 .... 291 J2 3
Mossdale Wy *SEDG* DY3 .... 299 L3
Mossfield *MKTDR* TF9 .... 149 G4
Mossfield Crs *ALS/KID* ST7 .... 39 H8 3
Mossfield Rd *LNGTN* ST3 .... 86 C3
Moss Flds *ALS/KID* ST7 .... 37 G7
Moss Gn *RUGE* WS15 .... 197 J8
Moss Gv *KGSWFD* DY6 .... 303 K3
NEWUL ST5 .... 52 D7
Moss HI *END/WER* ST9 .... 55 K5
Mossland Rd *LNGTN* ST3 .... 86 C5
Moss La *ALS/KID* ST7 .... 38 E6
AUD/MAD/W CW3 .... 81 K4
CDLE ST10 .... 106 A1
GNOS ST20 .... 170 F2
MKTDR TF9 .... 112 F4
NEWUL ST5 .... 98 C5
STONE ST15 .... 115 M1
STONE ST15 .... 121 K3
STONE ST15 .... 137 G3
Mossley Cl *BLOX/PEL* WS3 .... 282 F1 1
Mossley Garth Cl *CONG* CW12 .. 26 A1
Mossley La *BLOX/PEL* WS3 .... 266 F8
Moss Park Av *END/WER* ST9 .... 71 G6
Mosspit *STAFS* ST17 .... 193 M7
Moss PI *ALS/KID* ST7 .... 39 H7
Moss Rd *CNCK/NC* WS11 .... 232 A7
Moss Ri *NEWUL* ST5 .... 100 C3
Moss Side *HAN* ST1 .... 69 L2 3
Moss St *BURS/TUN* ST6 .... 54 E5
CNCK/NC WS11 .... 232 A6
Mossvale Gv *STAFS* ST16 .... 174 A5 3
Mosswood Cl *CNCK/NC* WS11 .. 249 K3
Moston St *HAN* ST1 .... 2 F2
Mostyn St *WOLV* WV1 .... 12 D1
Mott PI *BURS/TUN* ST6 .... 68 D2 3
Moulton Rd *LNGTN* ST3 .... 86 B6
Mounfield PI *STOKE* ST4 .... 85 K4
Mountain Ash Rd *BRWNH* WS8.. 268 C5
Mountain Pine Cl
HEDN WS12 .... 232 A2 2
Mount Av *HEDN* WS12 .... 232 B3
STOKE ST4 .... 84 F3
STONE ST15 .... 119 M8
Mountbatten Cl *SHIF* TF11 .... 242 A4
BNTWD WS7 .... 251 M1 2
BUTN/AL/TUT DE13 .... 185 K2 1
Mountbatten Rd *WSLW* WS2 .... 282 F8
Mount Cl *END/WER* ST9 .... 71 J6
GTWY WS6 .... 249 K8
SEDG DY3 .... 299 J8
STONE ST15 .... 138 D4
WMBN WV5 .... 298 A3
Mount Crs *STONE* ST15 .... 119 M8
Mount Dr *WMBN* WV5 .... 298 A3
Mount Edge *RSTAF* ST18 .... 175 H7
Mountford Crs *ALDR* WS9 .... 285 H2
Mountford St *BURS/TUN* ST6 .. 68 F1
Mount Gdns *CDSL* WV8 .... 262 F6
Mount La *MKTDR* TF9 .... 130 C2
SEDG DY3 .... 299 J8
Mount PI *BLYBR/FOR* ST11 .... 104 A3
Mount Pleasant *ALS/KID* ST7 .. 249 L8
GTWY WS6 .... 249 L8
HAN ST1 .... 2 A7
KGSWFD DY6 .... 303 J6
LEEK ST13 .... 43 M5
MKTDR TF9 .... 114 F5 1
NEWUL ST5 .... 67 L4
RSTAF ST18 .... 173 L8
STOKE ST4 .... 84 D2
TAM/AM/WIL B77 .... 290 C1
Mount Pleasant Av
WMBN WV5 .... 297 M3
Mount Pleasant Rd *ALS/KID* ST7 .. 39 H3
SWAD DE11 .... 223 L3
Mount Rd *ALS/KID* ST7 .... 53 H1
BLOX/PEL WS3 .... 268 A6
BLYBR/FOR ST11 .... 104 A3
BNTWD WS7 .... 252 B4
DUNHL/THL/PER WV6 .... 279 G8
ETTPK/GDPK/PENN WV4 .... 295 M8
ETTPK/GDPK/PENN WV4 .... 295 G6
LEEK ST13 .... 44 B4
RUGE WS15 .... 197 H6
STONE ST15 .... 119 L7
STPNHL/WNHL DE15 .... 187 G7
STRBR DY8 .... 307 K1
SWAD DE11 .... 223 K2
WMBN WV5 .... 298 A3
Mountside Gdns *LEEK* ST13 .. 44 B4
Mountside St *HEDN* WS12 .... 232 B3
Mountsorrel Cl *STOKE* ST4 .... 101 J4 3
Mount St *HAN* ST1 .... 2 F3
HEDN WS12 .... 232 B3
NEWUL ST5 .... 67 L4 3
STAFN ST16 .... 4 E4
STPNHL/WNHL DE15 .... 186 A7
The Mount *ALS/KID* ST7 .... 38 E3
ALS/KID ST7 .... 53 G1
NEWUL ST5 .... 67 L4
Mountwood Covert
DUNHL/THL/PER WV6 .... 279 H7
Mouse HI *BLOX/PEL* WS3 .... 267 H7
Mousley St *BURS/TUN* ST6 .... 68 D2
Mowbray Cft *BNTWD* WS7 .... 251 L1
Mow Cop Rd *ALS/KID* ST7 .... 39 J4
Mow Cop Trail *MCFLDS* SK11 .. 19 G7
Mow La *ALS/KID* ST7 .... 26 A3
ALS/KID ST7 .... 39 G5
Moxhull Cl *SHHTH* WV12 .... 282 C1
Moxhull Gdns *SHHTH* WV12 .. 282 C1 1
Moxley Av *HAN* ST1 .... 69 K3
Mozart Ct *CNCK/NC* WS11 .... 232 C8

Moseley Rd
ETTPK/GDPK/PENN WV4 .... 295 G5
Mucklestone Rd *MKTDR* TF9 .. 114 D5
Mucklestone Wood La
MKTDR TF9 .... 114 D5
Muirfield *TAM/AM/WIL* B77 .... 275 H5 3
Muirfield Cl *BLOX/PEL* WS3 .... 267 G7
Muirville Cl *STRBR* DY8 .... 303 K7 3
Mulberry Dr *BLYBR/FOR* ST11 .. 104 A3
Mulberry Gn *DUDN* DY1 .... 299 M5 3
Mulberry PI *BLOX/PEL* WS3 .... 282 F1 2
Mulberry Rd *BLOX/PEL* WS3 .... 282 F1
Mulberry St *HAN* ST1 .... 2 F6
Muldoon Cl *CNCK/NC* WS11 .. 232 A6
Mulgrave St *HAN* ST1 .... 2 A2
Mullett Rd *WNSFLD* WV11 .... 281 H3
Mulliner Cl *BUCK/MIL* ST2 .... 70 D7 3
Mumford Dr *ASHB* DE6 .... 95 K2
Munro St *STOKE* ST4 .... 85 G5
Munster Ter *STOKE* ST4 .... 84 F5
Murdock Wy *WSLW* WS2 .... 282 F5
Murhall St *BURS/TUN* ST6 .... 68 E2
Murray St *BURS/TUN* ST6 .... 53 J3
Murton *TAM/AM/WIL* B77 .... 291 J2 3
Muse La *ASHB* DE6 .... 147 G1
Musk La *SEDG* DY3 .... 299 H7
Musk La West *SEDG* DY3 .... 299 H7
Muxloe Cl *BLOX/PEL* WS3 .... 267 G7
Myatt Av *ALDR* WS9 .... 284 F5
BKHL/PFLD WV2 .... 295 L4
BNTWD WS7 .... 252 A3
Myatt Cl *BKHL/PFLD* WV2 .... 295 L4
Myatt St *HAN* ST1 .... 2 F2
Myer's La *BUTN/AL/TUT* DE13 .. 218 D4
Mynors St *HAN* ST1 .... 2 F4
STAFN ST16 .... 5 J4
Myott Av *NEWUL* ST5 .... 84 A3
Myrtle Av *LNGTN* ST3 .... 87 H7
Myrtle Cl *SHHTH* WV12 .... 282 E5
Myrtle Gv *BDMR/CCFT* WV3 .... 294 E4
PENK ST19 .... 246 D4
Myrtle St *BKHL/PFLD* WV2 .... 295 M4

N

Nabb La *CDLE* ST10 .... 107 L2
Nabbs Cl *ALS/KID* ST7 .... 39 H8 3
Nabbswood Rd *ALS/KID* ST7 .. 39 H8
Nab Hill Av *LEEK* ST13 .... 43 J4
Nab Hill Ct *LEEK* ST13 .... 43 J4
Naesby Rd
DUNHL/THL/PER WV6 .... 278 F7 2
Nagington Dr *PENK* ST19 .... 229 M3
Nailers Dr *BNTWD* WS7 .... 252 C4
Nairn Rd *BLOX/PEL* WS3 .... 267 G6
Nankirk La *BUTN/AL/TUT* DE13 .. 184 A4
Nanny Goat La *STONE* ST15 .. 138 A1
Nanny Murphy's La *SHIF* TF11 .. 242 D2
Nantwich Rd *ALS/KID* ST7 .... 65 L1
AUD/MAD/W CW3 .... 80 B8
Naomi Wy *ALDR* WS9 .... 269 H6
Napier *TAM/AM/WIL* B77 .... 11 J8
Napier *BKHL/PFLD* WV2 .... 295 K3
WSLW WS2 .... 283 G5
Napier St *BUT* DE14 .... 6 E8
STOKE ST4 .... 85 K4
Naples Cl *LNGTN* ST3 .... 86 E6 3
Naples Dr *NEWUL* ST5 .... 83 M4
Napley Rd *MKTDR* TF9 .... 113 K1
Narlow La *ASHB* DE6 .... 63 M8
Narrow La *BRWNH* WS8 .... 268 C8
STONE ST15 .... 139 M3
UTXR ST14 .... 108 D4
Narvik Crs *BURS/TUN* ST6 .... 54 B8
Nash Av *DUNHL/THL/PER* WV6 .. 278 E7
STAFN ST16 .... 174 B4
Nashe Dr *LNGTN* ST3 .... 85 M8
Nash La *LICHS* WS14 .... 236 A5
STAFS ST17 .... 212 B2
Nash Peake St *BURS/TUN* ST6 .. 53 J7
Nash St *NEWUL* ST5 .... 67 L8
Naunton Rd *WSLW* WS2 .... 283 G7
Navigation Rd *BURS/TUN* ST6 .. 68 F3
Navigation St *BURS/TUN* ST6 .. 68 E3
WOLV WV1 .... 13 J7
Naylors Gv *SEDG* DY3 .... 299 L6
Naylor St *BURS/TUN* ST6 .... 53 M5 3
Naylor Yd *LEEK* ST13 .... 43 L4 3
Neachells La *WLNHL* WV13 .... 281 K6
WNSFLD WV11 .... 281 K5
Neachless Av *WMBN* WV5 .... 298 A5
Neachley La *SHIF* TF11 .... 242 F6
Neal Cft *LICHS* WS14 .... 255 L4
Neale PI *BUCK/MIL* ST2 .... 70 B5
Neale St *WSLW* WS2 .... 283 J8
Neander *CRTAM* B79 .... 273 M4
Near Ridding *GNOS* ST20 .... 190 D5
Neath Cl *LNGTN* ST3 .... 86 D7
Neath Rd *BLOX/PEL* WS3 .... 266 F8
Neath Wy *BLOX/PEL* WS3 .... 266 F8
Needwood Dr
ETTPK/GDPK/PENN WV4 .... 295 M6 3
Needwood Gra *RUGE* WS15 .... 180 A3
Needwood HI *LICHS* WS14 .... 236 A8 3
Needwood St *BUT* DE14 .... 6 D3
Nellan Crs *BURS/TUN* ST6 .... 69 K1
Nelson Bank *ALS/KID* ST7 .... 53 G3
Nelson Ct *SHIF* TF11 .... 242 A4 2
Nelson Crs *ECCH* ST21 .... 117 L8
Nelson Dr *HEDN* WS12 .... 232 E6
Nelson La *ALS/KID* ST7 .... 37 M8
Nelson PI *HAN* ST1 .... 2 F6
Nelson Rd *STOKE* ST4 .... 84 E2
Nelson St *LEEK* ST13 .... 43 M3
NEWUL ST5 .... 68 C5 3
STOKE ST4 .... 85 K5 3
STPNHL/WNHL DE15 .... 186 C7 3
WLNHL WV13 .... 282 A7
Nelson Wy *STAFS* ST17 .... 193 L4
Nene Cl *BUTN/AL/TUT* DE13 .. 185 J1
Nene Wy *RDERBYSW* DE65 .... 166 D2 3
Nephew St *BURS/TUN* ST6 .... 68 E2 3
Neptune Gv *HAN* ST1 .... 3 H1
Ness Gv *CDLE* ST10 .... 89 J3
Nest Common *BLOX/PEL* WS3 .. 267 M5
Nether Beacon *LICH* WS13 .... 8 C1
Netherbridge Av *LICHS* WS14 .. 9 M3

Netherby Rd *SEDG* DY3 299
Nethercote PI *BUCK/MIL* ST2 .. 86
Nethergate *BNTWD* WS7 299
Nether La *BNTWD* WS7 299
Netherseal Rd *CRTAM* B79 240
MSHM DE12 241
Netherset Hey La
AUD/MAD/W CW3 81
Netherstone Gv
FOAKS/STRLY B74 286
Netherstowe *LICH* WS13 236
Netherstowe La *LICH* WS13 .. 236
Netherton Gv *BUCK/MIL* ST2 .. 55
Nethy Dr *DUNHL/THL/PER* WV6 .. 279
Netley PI *LNGTN* ST3 101
Netley Rd *BLOX/PEL* WS3 266
Netley Wy *BLOX/PEL* WS3 266
Nevada La *BURS/TUN* ST6 69
Neve Av *WOLVN* WV10 280
Neville Av
ETTPK/GDPK/PENN WV4 295
Neville Cl *BUTN/AL/TUT* DE13 .. 166
Neville St *STOKE* ST4 84
TAM/AM/WIL B77 11
Nevill St *CRTAM* B79 10
Nevin Av *BIDD* ST8 40
Nevis Ct *DUNHL/THL/PER* WV6 .. 279
Nevis Gv *SHHTH* WV12 282
Newall Av *STAFN* ST16 5
Newark Gv *BURS/TUN* ST6 .... 53 J
Newark Rd *SHHTH* WV12 .... 282 C
New Av *BLYBR/FOR* ST11 104
New Barns La *LICHS* WS14 270
Newbolds Rd *WOLVN* WV10 281
Newborough Cl *HAN* ST1 69
Newbridge Av
DUNHL/THL/PER WV6 279
Newbridge Crs
DUNHL/THL/PER WV6 279
Newbridge Gdns
DUNHL/THL/PER WV6 .... 279 L
Newbridge Rd
KGSWFD DY6 303
Newbridge St
DUNHL/THL/PER WV6 279
Newburn Gv *STOKE* ST4 101
Newbury Cl *GTWY* WS6 249
STAFS ST17 194
Newbury Dr
BUTN/AL/TUT DE13 .... 185 J
Newbury Gv *LNGTN* ST3 101
Newbury Rd *STRBR* DY8 307
WOLVN WV10 264
Newcastle La *STOKE* ST4 100
Newcastle Rd *ALS/KID* ST7 52
AUD/MAD/W CW3 81
AUD/MAD/W CW3 96
ECCH ST21 117
ECCH ST21 152
LEEK ST13 57
MKTDR TF9 112
MKTDR TF9 113
NEWUL ST5 100
STOKE ST4 84
STONE ST15 137
Newcastle St *BURS/TUN* ST6 .. 68
NEWUL ST5 67
STONE ST15 .... 137 H
New Century St *HAN* ST1 2
New Chapel Ct *BURS/TUN* ST6 .. 53
Newchapel Rd *ALS/KID* ST7 53
New Close Av *BLYBR/FOR* ST11 .. 104
Newcomen Rd *BNTWD* WS7 252
Newcott Cl *COVEN* WV9 263
New Cross Av *WOLVN* WV10 281
New Dudley Rd *KGSWFD* DY6 .. 303
Newent Cl *SHHTH* WV12 282
Newey Rd *WNSFLD* WV11 281
Newfield Cl *WSLW* WS2 283
Newfield Dr *KGSWFD* DY6 303
Newfield Rd
STPNHL/WNHL DE15 186
Newfield St *BURS/TUN* ST6 55
Newfold Crs *BURS/TUN* ST6 .. 55
Newford Crs *BUCK/MIL* ST2 .. 69
New Forest Rd *BLOX/PEL* WS3.. 283
New Garden St *STAFS* ST17 4
Newgate *DUNHL/THL/PER* WV6.. 277
Newgatefield La
BUTN/AL/TUT DE13 184
Newgate St *BNTWD* WS7 252
New Haden Rd *CDLE* ST10 89
Newhall Crs *HEDN* WS12 232
New Hall Rd *LNGTN* ST3 86
Newhall St *CDLE* ST10 .... 73 K7
CNCK/NC WS11 249
New Hall St *HAN* ST1 2
WLNHL WV13 282
New Hampton Rd East
WOLV WV1 12
Newhaven Gv *STOKE* ST4 101
New Hayes Rd *BURS/TUN* ST6 .. 53
HEDN WS12 233
New Homage Gdns
COVEN WV9 247
New Horse Rd *GTWY* WS6 249
Newhouse La *ALBTN* WV7 261
Newhouse Rd *BUCK/MIL* ST2 .. 70
Newick Av *FOAKS/STRLY* B74 .. 286
Newington Gv *STOKE* ST4 101
New Inn Bank *ECCH* ST21 150
New Inn La *STOKE* ST4 100
New King St *ALS/KID* ST7 66
New Kingsway *LNGTN* ST3 87
Newland Av *STAFN* ST16 174
Newland Cl *RUSH/SHEL* WS4 .. 268
Newlands Cl *NEWUL* ST5 84
PENK ST19 229
STONE ST15 137
Newlands Ct *HEDN* WS12 232
Newlands La *CNCK/NC* WS11 .. 250
RUGE WS15 198
Newlands St *STOKE* ST4 85
New Landwood La
WNSFLD WV11 266
New La *BURS/TUN* ST6 55
Newleigh St *BUCK/MIL* ST2 .... 70 B1
Newlyn Cl *LICHS* WS14 9
Newman Av
ETTPK/GDPK/PENN WV4 .... 295 M

wman Cl STONE ST15 .... 138 C3
wman Dr BUT DE14 .... 204 B2
wman Gv WILS WS15 .... 215 M3
wman Rd WOLVN WV10 .... 281 G1
wmarket Cl
  DUNHL/THL/PER WV6 .... 280 A5 ▣
wmarket Wy CDLE ST10 .... 89 L5 ▣
w Mill La POL/KGSB/FAZ B78 .. 290 D2
wmill St BUCK/MIL ST2 .... 70 A1
wmount Rd STOKE ST4 .... 86 B5
w Penkridge Rd
  CNCK/NC WS11 .... 231 H8
wpool Rd BIDD ST8 .... 40 A4
wpool Ter BIDD ST8 .... 40 B5
wport Cl TAM/AM/WIL B77 .... 11 L3
wport Cl BUT DE14 .... 185 K3
wport Cft PENK ST19 .... 246 C4 ▣
wport Gv NEWLV ST5 .... 52 E8
wport La BURS/TUN ST6 .... 68 C3
wport Rd ALBTN WV7 .... 260 F4
  ECCH ST21 .... 152 E4
  GNOS ST20 .... 189 K5
  MKTDR TF9 .... 130 C3
  MKTDR TF9 .... 148 A8
  RSTAF ST18 .... 154 C8 ▣
  SHIF TF11 .... 243 K7
  STAFS ST17 .... 4 D7
wport St BURS/TUN ST6 .... 68 E3
  PENK ST19 .... 246 C4
  WOLVN WV10 .... 280 E6 ▣
wquay Av STAFS ST17 .... 194 D2
w Rd ALDR WS9 .... 285 G5
  ALS/KID ST7 .... 51 L8
  ASHB DE6 .... 129 G7
  AUD/MAD/W CW3 .... 81 L3
  BNTWD WS7 .... 252 B4
  BRWNH WS8 .... 268 F5
  BUCK/MIL ST2 .... 70 F7
  CDLE ST10 .... 88 C7
  CDLE ST10 .... 107 L1
  CRTAM B79 .... 275 L1
  DUNHL/THL/PER WV6 .... 279 L6
  KIDDW DY11 .... 310 B3
  KINVER DY7 .... 296 F5
  LICHS WS14 .... 270 F4
  MKTDR TF9 .... 131 M2
  MSHM DE12 .... 222 C7
  PENK ST19 .... 229 L1
  RSTAF ST18 .... 177 C2
  RUGE WS15 .... 217 H5
  SWAD DE11 .... 205 L4
  TAM/AM/WIL B77 .... 290 F3
  UTXR ST14 .... 144 A1
  WNSFLD WV11 .... 281 H2
  WOLVN WV10 .... 264 D1
  WOLVN WV10 .... 265 J2
wstead CRTAM B79 .... 273 K4
wstead Rd BUCK/MIL ST2 .... 70 B5
ew St BDMR/CCFT WV3 .... 294 C4
  BLOX/PEL WS3 .... 283 H1
  BNTWD WS7 .... 251 J3
  BURS/TUN ST6 .... 68 F2
  BUT DE14 .... 7 G6
  CNCK/NC WS11 .... 249 L1 ▣
  ETTPK/GDPK/PENN WV4 .... 295 L5
  GTWY WS6 .... 267 G1
  HEDN WS12 .... 232 C6
  KGSWFD DY6 .... 303 K6
  LEEK ST13 .... 43 M4
  MSHM DE12 .... 222 D4
  NEWUL ST5 .... 68 D5
  POL/KGSB/FAZ B78 .... 290 B2
  POL/KGSB/FAZ B78 .... 291 K2
  RUSH/SHEL WS4 .... 284 D1
  RUSH/SHEL WS4 .... 284 B3
  SEDG DY3 .... 299 J2
  STAFN ST16 .... 4 D1
  STONE ST15 .... 154 A4
  STRBR DY8 .... 303 K8
  TAM/AM/WIL B77 .... 11 J7
  UTXR ST14 .... 144 B2
  WNSFLD WV11 .... 266 A7
ewton Cl STPNHL/WNHL DE15 .. 186 E2
ewton Ct END/WER ST9 .... 71 G6 ▣
ewton Ct CRTAM B79 .... 259 G7
  STPNHL/WNHL DE15 .... 186 E2
ewton Leys
  STPNHL/WNHL DE15 .... 186 C6
ewton Ms STPNHL/WNHL DE15 .. 7 M4
ewton Pl WSLW WS2 .... 283 H4 ▣
ewton Rd LICH WS13 .... 235 M8
  NEWUL ST5 .... 68 B4
  STAFN ST16 .... 174 C5
  STPNHL/WNHL DE15 .... 7 M3
  WSLW WS2 .... 283 L6
ewton St STOKE ST4 .... 68 E8
ewtown ALS/KID ST7 .... 39 L8
  MKTDR TF9 .... 130 C2
ew Wood Cl KINVER DY7 .... 307 J2
ew Wood Gv ALDR WS9 .... 269 G7
all Rd STOKE ST4 .... 100 F1
cholas St STONE ST15 .... 43 H6
cholas St BURS/TUN ST6 .... 68 F2 ▣
cholls La STONE ST15.......... 120 B8
cholls St STOKE ST4 .... 85 H5
cholls Wy HEDN WS12 .... 250 E1
cholson Wy LEEK ST13 .... 43 M4
cklaus Cl BUT DE14 .... 204 A3 ▣
gel Rd DUDN DY1 .... 299 M8
ghtingale
  TAM/AM/WIL B77 .... 290 E2 ▣
ghtingale Cl HEDN WS12 .... 231 J5 ▣
ghtingale Crs SHHTH WV12 .... 282 B2
ghtingale Rd CDLE ST10 .... 123 M1
le St BURS/TUN ST6 .... 69 G2
mbus TAM/AM/WIL B77 .... 290 D6
ne Elms La WOLVN WV10 .... 280 E6
nefoot La
  TAM/AM/WIL B77 .... 290 E2 ▣
nian Wy TAM/AM/WIL B77 .... 290 E4
rvana Wy CNCK/NC WS11 .... 231 J8
oblett Rd HAN ST1 .... 69 L3
ocke Rd WNSFLD WV11 .... 281 M1
oddington Av LICHS WS14 .... 255 L4
oddington La LICHS WS14 .... 255 L4
oddy Pk ALDR WS9 .... 285 H3
oddy Park Rd ALDR WS9.......... 285 H3
o Man's Green La KINVER DY7 .. 304 E4

No Man's Heath Rd
  MSHM DE12 .... 241 L7
No Name Rd BNTWD WS7 .... 251 L3
The Nook GTWY WS6 .... 266 C1
Noon Cft BUTN/AL/TUT DE13 ...... 219 M8
Noose Cl WLNHL WV13 .... 281 L8
Noose La WLNHL WV13 .... 281 L8
Norbroom Ct NWPT TF10 .... 188 A7 ▣
  NWPT TF10 .... 188 A6 ▣
Norbroom Dr NWPT TF10 .... 188 A7
Norbury Av BLOX/PEL WS3 .... 267 M7
  BUCK/MIL ST2 .... 70 B1
Norbury Cl GNOS ST20 .... 190 D4
Norbury Crs
  ETTPK/GDPK/PENN WV4 .... 295 M6
Norbury Hollow ASHB DE6 .... 109 K1
Norbury Rd GNOS ST20 .... 189 K1
  WOLVN WV10 .... 280 F4
Nordley Rd WNSFLD WV11 .... 281 J5
Norfolk Cl NEWUL ST5 .... 84 A8
Norfolk Crs ALDR WS9 .... 285 H2
Norfolk Dr POL/KGSB/FAZ B78 .. 289 M1
Norfolk Gv BIDD ST8 .... 40 C1
  GTWY WS6 .... 266 F1
Norfolk New Rd WSLW WS2 .... 283 G6
Norfolk Pl WSLW WS2 .... 283 K5
Norfolk Rd ALS/KID ST7 .... 38 F8
  BDMR/CCFT WV3 .... 12 A9
  STPNHL/WNHL DE15 .... 204 D3
  STRBR DY8 .... 307 K2
Norfolk St HAN ST1 .... 2 B9
Norfolk Wy STAFS ST17 .... 193 J3
Normacot Grange Rd
  LNGTN ST3 .... 102 F3
Normacot Rd LNGTN ST3.......... 86 D8
Norman Av BURS/TUN ST6 .... 53 M7
Normanbrook Ct MKTDR TF9 .. 130 C1
Norman Cl CRTAM B79 .... 273 L3
Normandy Gv BUCK/MIL ST2 .. 55 G8 ▣
Norman Gv NEWUL ST5 .... 68 D8
Norman Keep
  BUTN/AL/TUT DE13 .... 165 J4 ▣
Norman Rd BUTN/AL/TUT DE13 .. 165 J4
  PENK ST19 .... 229 M2
Normanton Gv LNGTN ST3 .... 86 D4
Norris Cl MKTDR TF9 .... 115 J5
Norris Rd BURS/TUN ST6 .... 53 M7
Northam Rd HAN ST1 .... 69 K4
North Av ASHB DE6 .... 79 H8
  .... 43 K5
  STAFN ST16 .... 174 D3
  WNSFLD WV11 .... 281 J4
North Castle St STAFN ST16 ...... 4 C4
Northcliffe Rd ASHB DE6.......... 79 H4
Northcote Av STOKE ST4 .... 85 G2 ▣
Northcote Cl RSTAF ST18 .... 196 F1
Northcote Pl NEWUL ST5 .... 84 C1 ▣
Northcote St STOKE ST4 .... 85 H1 ▣
  WSLW WS2 .... 283 K6
North Crs WOLVN WV10 .... 265 H3
North Dr GNOS ST20 .... 190 C5
Northesk Pl NEWUL ST5 .... 84 A5
Northesk St STONE ST15 .... 137 M1
Northfield Av UTXR ST14 .... 108 F6
Northfield Cl UTXR ST14 .... 126 A8
Northfield Dr BIDD ST8 .... 40 E1
Northfield Gv BDMR/CCFT WV3 .. 294 C3
Northfield Rd
  BUTN/AL/TUT DE13 .... 185 H3
Northfields Wy BRWNH WS8 .. 268 D3
Northfleet St BUCK/MIL ST2 .... 3 L6
Northgate ALDR WS9 .... 285 G3
Northgate Cl STOKE ST4 .... 100 F1
Northgate Wy ALDR WS9 .... 285 G2
North Gn
  ETTPK/GDPK/PENN WV4 .... 294 D4
Northlands AUD/MAD/W CW3 .. 96 C1
North Leys ASHB DE6.......... 95 H1
North Ov SEDG DY3 .... 299 L5
North Pl BUCK/MIL ST2 .... 70 B4
  STAFN ST16 .... 174 D5
North Rd BURS/TUN ST6 .... 69 H3
  STONE ST15 .... 136 D4 ▣
  WOLV WV1 .... 12 F1
North Springfield SEDG DY3.......... 299 L1
North St ALS/KID ST7 .... 39 H4
  BNTWD WS7 .... 251 M1
  CNCK/NC WS11 .... 249 L4
  LEEK ST13 .... 43 J4
  NEWUL ST5 .... 67 H8
  NEWUL ST5 .... 84 C1 ▣
  STOKE ST4. .... 85 G2
  STPNHL/WNHL DE15 .... 186 B7
  WOLV WV1 .... 12 F4
  WSLW WS2 .... 283 L6
North Ter NEWUL ST5.......... 68 B5
Northumberland Cl
  POL/KGSB/FAZ B78 .... 290 A1 ▣
Northumberland Rd
  STPNHL/WNHL DE15 .... 204 D3
North Wk LNGTN ST3 .... 103 H1
North Walls STAFN ST16.......... 4 F4
Northway SEDG DY3 .... 299 J3
North West Ter BURS/TUN ST6.. 69 J1
Northwood St NEWUL ST5 .... 84 D8
Northwood Gn HAN ST1 .... 3 G5
Northwood La ASHB DE6 .... 93 J6
  NEWUL ST5 .... 84 C8
Northwood Park Cl
  WOLVN WV10 .... 264 E7 ▣
Northwood Park Rd HAN ST1 .... 2 F3
  WOLVN WV10 .... 264 E8
Northwood Ri ASHB DE6.......... 95 H2
North Worcestershire Pth
  KIDDW DY11 .... 309 L2
Northycote La WOLVN WV10 .. 264 F6
Norton Av BURS/TUN ST6 .... 54 A7
Norton Cl CRTAM B79 .... 274 C3
  ETTPK/GDPK/PENN WV4 .... 295 K2
Norton Crs BURS/TUN ST6 .... 69 K2
Norton Dr BURS/TUN ST6 .... 69 K2
Norton East Rd CNCK/NC WS11 .. 251 H5
Norton Gra CNCK/NC WS11 .... 250 F6
Norton Green La
  CNCK/NC WS11 .... 250 E6
Norton Hall Cl BURS/TUN ST6.. 54 E7
Norton Hall La CNCK/NC WS11 .. 250 D7
Norton La BNTWD WS7 .... 252 D4
  BURS/TUN ST6 .... 54 E7

CNCK/NC WS11 .... 250 B3
  GTWY WS6 .... 250 A6
Norton Rd BLOX/PEL WS3 .... 268 A5
  BUTN/AL/TUT DE13 .... 185 G4
  HEDN WS12 .... 250 F2
  STRBR DY8 .... 311 K1
Norton Springs CNCK/NC WS11 .. 250 F5
Norton St BUCK/MIL ST2 .... 70 B1
Norton Ter CNCK/NC WS11 .... 250 F4
Norwich Cl LICH WS13 .... 236 C2
Norwich Pl NEWUL ST5 .... 84 C5 ▣
Norwich Rd BUCK/MIL ST2 .... 70 B8
Nottingham Dr SHHTH WV12 .. 282 C3
Nottingham Rd LICHS WS14 .... 255 J7
Novi La LEEK ST13 .... 44 A3
Nunn's Cl LNGTN ST3 .... 87 H5
Nunn St LEEK ST13 .... 43 K4
Nun's La RUGE WS15 .... 199 H4
The Nurseries COVEN WV9 .... 247 H8
Nursery Av ALDR WS9 .... 285 H5
  END/WER ST9 .... 55 J7
Nursery Cl ALS/KID ST7 .... 52 D1
  CDLE ST10 .... 89 J7
  RSTAF ST18 .... 210 B2 ▣
Nursery Cft LICH WS13 .... 253 M1 ▣
Nursery Dr BIDD ST8 .... 26 C8
  PENK ST19 .... 211 L8
  WMBN WV5 .... 297 M6
Nursery Gdns CDSL WV8 .... 262 F6 ▣
  STRBR DY8 .... 307 M1
Nursery La ALS/KID ST7 .... 52 D1
  BLOX/PEL WS3 .... 283 H2
  CW/HAS CW1 .... 36 D8
  RUGE WS15 .... 216 A5
Nursery St STOKE ST4 .... 85 J6
Nursery View Cl ALDR WS9 .. 285 L8 ▣
Nursery Wk
  DUNHL/THL/PER WV6 .... 279 K5
Nurton Bank
  DUNHL/THL/PER WV6 .... 278 A7
Nurton Hill Rd
  DUNHL/THL/PER WV6 .... 277 K5
Nutbrook Av STOKE ST4 .... 85 J6
Nuthurst Dr CNCK/NC WS11 .. 249 M6
Nyewood Av LNGTN ST3 .... 86 D5
Nymet TAM/AM/WIL B77 .... 290 E2

Oadby Ri BUTN/AL/TUT DE13 .... 185 L4 ▣
Oakamoor Rd CDLE ST10 .... 89 M6
Oakapple Cl PENK ST19 .... 244 E2 ▣
Oak Av ALS/KID ST7 .... 37 L8
  GTWY WS6 .... 266 F1
  HEDN WS12 .... 231 K2
  LEEK ST13 .... 57 J6
  STAFS ST17 .... 194 F4
  WSLW WS2 .... 282 E7
Oak Cl GNOS ST20 .... 209 G3
  KINVER DY7 .... 306 C7
  RSTAF ST18 .... 196 F1
  SWAD DE11 .... 223 J3
  UTXR ST14 .... 143 M1
Oak Crs ASHB DE6.......... 95 J2
  BLOX/PEL WS3 .... 283 K4
Oakdale NEWUL ST5 .... 84 C7 ▣
Oakdene Av NEWUL ST5 .... 68 A4
Oakdene Cl BLYBR/FOR ST11 .. 104 A4
  NEWUL ST5 .... 68 A4 ▣
Oakdene Gv NEWUL ST5 .... 68 A4
Oakdene Rd BNTWD WS7 .... 252 A4
Oakdene Wy BIDD ST8 .... 40 D3
Oak Dr ASHB DE6 .... 145 H1
  PENK ST19 .... 227 J4
  WMBN WV5 .... 297 F8
Oaken Covert CDSL WV8 .... 262 E7 ▣
Oaken Dr CDSL WV8 .... 262 E7
  SHHTH WV12 .... 282 E3
Oakenfield LICH WS13 .... 235 M8
Oaken Gdns BNTWD WS7 .... 252 A2
Oaken Gv CDSL WV8 .... 262 E8 ▣
Oakenhayes Crs BRWNH WS8 .. 268 F1
Oakenhayes Dr BRWNH WS8 .. 268 F1
Oaken La CDSL WV8 .... 262 C7
  CDSL WV8 .... 262 E7
Oaken Pk CDSL WV8 .... 263 G8
Oakfield Av KGSWFD DY6 .... 303 J5
Oakfield Cl RUGE WS15 .... 197 H8 ▣
  STRBR DY8 .... 307 M1
Oakfield Dr BLOX/PEL WS3 .... 268 A5
Oakfield Rd BUTN/AL/TUT DE13.. 220 A4
  CDSL WV8 .... 263 H8
  MKTDR TF9 .... 130 B2
Oakfields
  BUTN/AL/TUT DE13 .... 164 A6 ▣
Oak Gdns RSTAF ST18 .... 191 M4
Oak Gn DUNHL/THL/PER WV6 .. 279 H7
Oak Gv WNSFLD WV11 .... 281 H3
Oakham Wy BUCK/MIL ST2 .... 70 C8 ▣
Oakhill Av STOKE ST4 .... 84 F6
Oakhill Cl CDLE ST10 .... 105 J6
Oakhill Rd CNCK/NC WS11 .... 231 M8
Oakhurst LICHS WS14 .... 9 H5
Oakhurst Crs LNGTN ST3 .... 103 G4
Oakland Cl END/WER ST9 .... 72 A4
Oakland Dr SEDG DY3 .... 299 H8
Oakland Rd BLOX/PEL WS3 .... 283 L4
Oaklands Av NEWUL ST5 .... 68 C4
Oaklands Cl HEDN WS12 .... 231 J4 ▣
  LICH WS13 .... 237 K4
  RUGE WS15 .... 217 G2
Oaklands Dr STAFS ST17 .... 4 C8
Oaklands Rd BDMR/CCFT WV3.. 12 C9
The Oaklands GNOS ST20 .... 209 G3
  RUGE WS15.......... 215 J1
Oaklands Wy BLOX/PEL WS3 .. 268 A5
Oak La ASHB DE6 .... 128 D6
  BNTWD WS7 .... 251 M1
  KGSWFD DY6 .... 303 L1
  PENK ST19 .... 248 C2
  RSTAF ST18 .... 210 C3
Oak Lea LEEK ST13 .... 43 H6 ▣
Oakleigh Av SWAD DE11 .... 205 M5
Oakleigh St STONE ST15 .... 138 C6

Oakleigh Dr CDSL WV8 .... 263 C7
  RUGE WS15 .... 216 B4
Oakleighs STRBR DY8.......... 307 J1
Oakley Av ALDR WS9 .... 285 G5
Oakley Cl PENK ST19 .... 230 A1
Oakley Copse RUGE WS15 .... 215 H3
Oakley Gv
  ETTPK/GDPK/PENN WV4 .... 294 D5
Oakley La MKTDR TF9 .... 113 G5
Oakley Pl BURS/TUN ST6 .... 54 A2
Oakley Rd
  ETTPK/GDPK/PENN WV4 .... 294 D5
Oak Leys BDMR/CCFT WV3 .... 294 C1
Oakleys PENK ST19 .... 246 D4
Oakmount Cl BLOX/PEL WS3 .. 267 M7
Oak Mount Rd END/WER ST9 .. 71 H6
Oak Park Rd STRBR DY8 .... 307 M1
Oak Pl UTXR ST14 .... 126 A8
Oakridge Cl SHHTH WV12 .... 282 C6 ▣
  STAFS ST17 .... 194 C5
Oakridge Dr GTWY WS6 .... 249 L8 ▣
  SHHTH WV12 .... 282 C6
Oak Rd ALDR WS9 .... 269 C7
  BLOX/PEL WS3 .... 267 M5
  BUTN/AL/TUT DE13 .... 220 D1
  ECCH ST21 .... 152 D4
  NEWUL ST5 .... 67 K8
  PENK ST19 .... 246 D4
  RUSH/SHEL WS4 .... 284 C2
  STONE ST15 .... 138 B2
  UTXR ST14 .... 108 E4
  WLNHL WV13 .... 281 L8
Oaks Crs BDMR/CCFT WV3 .... 12 B6
Oaks Dr BDMR/CCFT WV3 .... 12 B5
  CNCK/NC WS11 .... 249 J1
  WMBN WV5 .... 298 A5
  WOLVN WV10 .... 264 F2
Oakshaw Cl COVEN WV9 .... 247 H7
Oakshaw Gv STOKE ST4 .... 101 H2
Oaksmoor Cl PENK ST19 .... 227 J4 ▣
Oak St ALS/KID ST7 .... 37 L2
  BDMR/CCFT WV3 .... 12 B6
  BUT DE14 .... 6 D9
  CDLE ST10 .... 89 K7 ▣
  HAN ST1 .... 3 C1
  KGSWFD DY6 .... 303 J5
  NEWUL ST5 .... 68 D7
Oaktree Cl STAFS ST17 .... 193 H3 ▣
Oaktree La ALS/KID ST7 .... 52 D5
Oaktree Rd RUGE WS15 .... 215 M4
  STOKE ST4 .... 101 H4
Oakville Av BURS/TUN ST6 .... 54 B8
Oakwall Gv LNGTN ST3 .... 102 C1 ▣
Oakwood RUGE WS15 .... 215 H1
Oakwood Cl ALDR WS9 .... 268 E6
  LICHS WS14 .... 271 C4
  RDERBYSW DE65 .... 165 J2 ▣
  WNSFLD WV11 .... 266 B7 ▣
Oakwood Rd BLOX/PEL WS3 .... 283 L3
  LEEK ST13 .... 43 J4
  LNGTN ST3 .... 101 L1
Oakwoods CNCK/NC WS11 .... 249 J2
Oasthouse Cl KGSWFD DY6 .... 303 J3
Oatfield Cl BNTWD WS7 .... 252 A6
Oatlands Wy
  DUNHL/THL/PER WV6 .... 278 D7
Oban Cl NEWUL ST5 .... 83 M2
Oberon Cl BURS/TUN ST6 .... 69 K1
Occupation Rd BRWNH WS8 .. 269 G6
Occupation St NEWUL ST5 .... 84 C3
Odell Crs BLOX/PEL WS3 .... 283 J1
Odell Cv BURS/TUN ST6 .... 68 E1
Odell Rd BLOX/PEL WS3 .... 283 H1
Odiham Cl CRTAM B79 .... 274 C2
Odin Cl HEDN WS12 .... 232 A5
Offadrive CRTAM B79 .... 10 E3
Offa's Dr DUNHL/THL/PER WV6 .. 278 E5
Offa St CRTAM B79 .... 10 C3
Offcote Crs ASHB DE6 .... 79 J7
Offoxey Rd SHIF TF11 .... 243 J5
Ogden Rd HAN ST1 .... 2 D7
Ogley Crs BRWNH WS8 .... 269 C3
Ogley Hay Rd BNTWD WS7 .... 234 A8
  BRWNH WS8 .... 252 A8
Ogley Rd BRWNH WS8 .... 269 C5
Ogmore Gv LNGTN ST3 .... 103 G2 ▣
Ohio Gv BURS/TUN ST6 .... 69 H2
Okement Dr WNSFLD WV11 .. 281 H5
Okeover Av ASHB DE6 .... 95 K1
Oldacre La STAFS ST17 .... 195 H7
Oldacres Rd STOKE ST4 .... 101 H5
The Old Armoury MKTDR TF9 .. 130 C2
Old Bank ASHB DE6 .... 94 D2
Old Barn Cl GNOS ST20 .... 190 D2
Old Birchills WSLW WS2 .... 283 J7
Old Butt La ALS/KID ST7 .... 38 D8
Old Cannock Rd WOLVN WV10 .. 265 K1
Oldcastle Av NEWUL ST5 .... 68 A4
Old Castle Gv BRWNH WS8 .. 251 M8 ▣
Old Chancel Rd RUGE WS15 .. 197 L8 ▣
Old Chapel Cl RUGE WS15 .... 82 E2
Old Coach La STAFS ST17 .... 195 H6
Old Coach Rd PENK ST19 .... 244 F3
Old Coalpit La BUX SK17 .... 17 L1
Oldcott Cl ALS/KID ST7 .... 53 J2
Oldcott Dr ALS/KID ST7 .... 53 J2
Old Croft Rd STAFS ST17 .... 194 E5
Old Derby Rd ASHB DE6 .... 95 J1 ▣
Old Eaton Rd RUGE WS15 .... 197 L2
Olde Hall La WOLVN WV10 .... 265 K1
Oldershaws La GNOS ST20 .... 169 L3
Old Fallings Crs WOLVN WV10 .. 280 F4
Old Fallings La WOLVN WV10 .. 280 F1
Old Fallow Av CNCK/NC WS11 .. 231 H1
Old Fallow Rd CNCK/NC WS11 .. 231 L7
Old Falls Cl GTWY WS6 .... 249 L7 ▣
Old Farm Meadow
  BDMR/CCFT WV3 .... 294 C2
Oldfield Av BURS/TUN ST6 .... 54 D5
Oldfield Dr STONE ST15 .... 138 C4
Oldfields La RSTAF ST18 .... 177 J8
Oldfield St STOKE ST4 .... 86 A5
Oldford La RSTAF ST18 .... 173 C3
Old Hall Cl ALBTN WV7 .... 260 D4

Old Hall Dr CRTAM B79 .... 238 D8
Old Hall St HAN ST1 .... 68 A2 ▣
Old Hall La CNCK/NC WS11 .... 250 B3
  ECCH ST21 .... 135 M3
  LICH WS13 .... 237 K2
Old Hampton La WNSFLD WV11.. 265 J8
Oldham St HAN ST1 .... 2 E6
Old Heath Rd WOLV WV1 .... 281 G8
Old Hedging La
  TAM/AM/WIL B77 .... 290 D5 ▣
Old Hednesford Rd
  CNCK/NC WS11 .... 232 A8
  HEDN WS12 .... 232 B7
Old Hl ASHB DE6 .... 95 J1
  HEDN WS12 .... 279 K5
Oldhall Br RSTAF ST18 .... 195 K3
Oldhill Cl ALS/KID ST7 .... 52 E5
Oldhill La RSTAF ST18 .... 195 K1
Oldicote La
  STPNHL/WNHL DE15 .... 186 E7
Old Landywood La
  WNSFLD WV11 .... 266 C4
Old La BLOX/PEL WS3.......... 283 J3
  BURS/TUN ST6 .... 55 C1
  CDLE ST10 .... 124 C2
  DUNHL/THL/PER WV6 .... 278 F8
  STOKE ST4. .... 118 B1
  WOLVN WV10 .... 265 J3
Old London Rd LICHS WS14.......... 271 K1
Old Manor Cl
  POL/KGSB/FAZ B78 .... 289 L5
Old Mill Gdns RUSH/SHEL WS4 .. 268 E8
Old Mill La END/WER ST9 .... 56 B7
Oldmill St STOKE ST4 .... 85 J3
Old Oak Cl ALDR WS9 .... 285 H2
Old Park Rd DUDN DY1 .... 299 M6
  HEDN WS12 .... 233 G5
Old Penkridge Rd
  CNCK/NC WS11 .... 231 J8
Old Quarry Dr SEDG DY3 .... 299 K5
Old Rectory Gdns ALDR WS9 .. 285 J4
Old Rectory Rd STONE ST15 .. 138 B2
Old Rickerscote La STAFS ST17 .. 193 M5
Old Rd ALS/KID ST7 .... 51 L7
  AUD/MAD/W CW3 .... 65 C7
  BARL ST12 .... 101 J8
  BUT DE14 .... 203 L3
  RSTAF ST18 .... 157 K8
  RUGE WS15 .... 217 G5
  STONE ST15 .... 120 A8
Old Rd Cl STONE ST15 .... 138 A1 ▣
Old School Cl RSTAF ST18 .... 157 K7 ▣
  WLNHL WV13 .... 282 A8 ▣
Old Shackerley La ALBTN WV7 .. 261 G1
Old Smithy Cl
  DUNHL/THL/PER WV6 .... 277 H7
Old Stafford Rd WOLVN WV10 .. 247 J6
Old Town La BLOX/PEL WS3 .... 267 M7
Old Town Rd HAN ST1 .... 3 G8
Old Tramway STOKE ST4 .... 85 M5
Old Vicarage Cl BLOX/PEL WS3 .. 268 A8
Old Vicarage La RSTAF ST18 .. 211 M4
Old Warstone La
  WNSFLD WV11 .... 266 B2
Oldway Pl LNGTN ST3 .... 86 C5
Old Well Cl RUSH/SHEL WS4 .. 284 B3
Old Weston Rd PENK ST19 .... 244 E2
Old Wharf Pl HAN ST1 .... 3 C8
Old Wharf Rd STRBR DY8 .... 307 M4
Old Whieldon Rd STOKE ST4...... 85 J4
Old Worcester Rd ALBTN WV7 .. 260 D4
Olinthus Av WNSFLD WV11 .... 281 L3
Olive Av
  ETTPK/GDPK/PENN WV4 .... 295 L5 ▣
Oliver Rd STOKE ST4 .... 84 E3
Ollison Dr FOAKS/STRLY B74 .. 285 M8
Olof Palme Gv LNGTN ST3 .... 86 C8 ▣
Omega Wy STOKE ST4 .... 101 G2
One Oak Ri STAFS ST17 .... 193 M5 ▣
Onslow Dr NEWUL ST5 .... 68 B2 ▣
Ontario Cl STOKE ST4 .... 101 G2
Opal Rd STOKE ST4 .... 85 L5
Opal Wy STONE ST15 .... 138 A6
Oram's La PENK ST19 .... 246 C3
Orange La RUGE WS15 .... 199 J1
Orbital Wy CNCK/NC WS11 .... 250 A4 ▣
Orb St HAN ST1 .... 2 C7
Orchard Av CNCK/NC WS11.......... 231 J8
Orchard Cl COVEN WV9 .... 247 H8 ▣
  DUNHL/THL/PER WV6 .... 277 J7
  GTWY WS6 .... 249 L7 ▣
  LICH WS13 .... 253 J7
  MKTDR TF9 .... 115 J5 ▣
  MSHM DE12 .... 221 K3
  PENK ST19 .... 229 M1
  RUGE WS15 .... 197 L7 ▣
  RUSH/SHEL WS4 .... 284 C4
  STONE ST15 .... 120 C6 ▣
  STONE ST15 .... 137 M3
  TAM/AM/WIL B77 .... 290 C5
Orchard Ct BDMR/CCFT WV3 .. 294 B3
  KGSWFD DY6 .... 303 K4
Orchard Crs ALS/KID ST7 .... 52 D1
  PENK ST19 .... 229 M1
Orchard Gdns LEEK ST13 .... 43 J4 ▣
Orchard Gv ALDR WS9 .... 285 H6
  ETTPK/GDPK/PENN WV4 .... 295 G6
  FOAKS/STRLY B74 .... 286 F7
  KIDDW DY11 .... 310 A4
  KINVER DY7 .... 306 B6
  SEDG DY3 .... 299 H7
Orchard La ASHB DE6 .... 111 K1
  CDSL WV8 .... 263 H7
  RSTAF ST18 .... 193 J5
  WOLVN WV10 .... 248 C7
Orchard Pk BUT DE14 .... 7 C7
Orchard Pl BARL ST12 .... 119 K1
Orchard Ri BLYBR/FOR ST11 .. 103 L3
  MKTDR TF9 .... 130 A2
Orchard St SHIF TF11 .... 242 A5
  WNSFLD WV11 .... 281 J3
The Orchards RUGE WS15 .... 217 J6 ▣
Orchard St BUT DE14 .... 7 C7
  CRTAM B79 .... 10 C4
  NEWUL ST5 .... 68 C5
  STAFS ST17 .... 4 F7
  SWAD DE11 .... 205 M4

P

ch Rd WSLW WS2 .... 283 G6
cival Cl BUX SK17 .... 35 K7
cival Dr END/WER ST9 .... 55 J7
cy James Cl ALS/KID ST7 .... 37 L6
cy St HAN ST1 .... 2 D5
egrine Cl LICHS WS14 .... 255 M5
rPNHL/WNHL DE15 .... 186 D7
egrine Gv LNGTN ST3 .... 103 G4
vale Cl HAN ST1 .... 3 L1
winkle Cl BRWNH WS8 .... 268 D4
kins St BURS/TUN ST6 .... 53 J3
rs Rd WNSFLD WV11 .... 282 A1
le Brook ECCH S21 .... 152 D5
ott Dr MGN/WHC B75 .... 287 K8
rin Cl STAFS ST17 .... 193 M4
ry Cl HAN ST1 .... 2 E6
rycrofts Dr CRTAM B79 .... 274 C3
ry Hall Dr SHHTH WV12 .... 282 B5
ry Hall Rd WNSFLD WV11 .... 281 M4
sehouse St WSL WS1 .... 283 M8
shore Cl BLOX/PEL WS3 .... 266 F8
shore Dr BUT DE14 .... 204 A2
shore Rd BLOX/PEL WS3 .... 266 F8
shore Wy BLOX/PEL WS3 .... 266 F8
th Cl STPNHL/WNHL DE15 .... 186 C8
th Rd SHHTH WV12 .... 282 B4
th St STOKE ST4 .... 86 A5
ton St STOKE ST4 .... 100 F3
ton Brook V
rUNHL/THL/PER WV6 .... 278 F8
ton Gv
rUNHL/THL/PER WV6 .... 278 F8
ton Rd
rUNHL/THL/PER WV6 .... 278 F8
ton Wood Vw LNGTN ST3 .... 85 M7
sall La CRTAM B79 .... 239 J3
erborough Dr
rCK/NC WS11 .... 250 C1
erdale Dr
TTPK/GDPK/PENN WV4 .... 294 F7
erhead Gv TAM/AM/WIL B77 .... 11 L3
er James Ct STAFN ST16 .... 174 E4
ers Ct RDERBYSW DE65 .... 165 K1
ersfield CNCK/NC WS11 .... 231 M6
ersfield Rd BURS/TUN ST6 .... 54 A3
ershouse Dr
rOAKS/STRLY B74 .... 286 F5
er's La BNTWD WS7 .... 253 J5
er St ASHB DE6 .... 95 J1
hills La LEEK ST13 .... 60 B4
rrel Gv LNGTN ST3 .... 103 H3
vensey Gv LNGTN ST3 .... 86 C4
erill Rd
rUNHL/THL/PER WV6 .... 278 F6
TTPK/GDPK/PENN WV4 .... 295 L7
easant Wk MKTDR TF9 .... 114 D7
lip Gv CNCK/NC WS11 .... 231 L4
lip La END/WER ST9 .... 71 H6
lip St STOKE ST4 .... 85 L4
lips Av WNSFLD WV11 .... 281 M1
lips Cl STONE ST15 .... 138 D3
lipson Wy BURS/TUN ST6 .... 69 K2
penix Cl ALS/KID ST7 .... 39 J8
GV WS15 .... 215 M1
penix Rd CNCK/NC WS11 .... 232 A8
rLNLH WV13 .... 281 K7
penix St BKHL/PFLD WV2 .... 295 K4
rURS/TUN ST6 .... 53 K7
adilly HAN ST1 .... 2 D5
asso Cl CNCK/NC WS11 .... 232 D8
asso Ri LNGTN ST3 .... 103 H4
cadilly HAN ST1 .... 2 C6
cadilly La ASHB DE6 .... 94 C1
cadilly St BURS/TUN ST6 .... 53 K7
kering Cl LNGTN ST3 .... 102 A1
kering Rd WNSFLD WV11 .... 281 K5
kford Pl LNGTN ST3 .... 102 F1
kleys La ASHB DE6 .... 145 J2
kmere Cl BUCK/MIL ST2 .... 55 H7
knalls UTXR ST14 .... 144 B3
kwick Pl ALS/KID ST7 .... 38 D8
kwood Av LEEK ST13 .... 44 A5
kwood Cl LEEK ST13 .... 44 A5
kon St HAN ST1 .... 2 F6
EEK ST13 .... 43 K4
ldocks Rd
TPNHL/WNHL DE15 .... 205 H4
lduck St BURS/TUN ST6 .... 68 E3
lrce St BURS/TUN ST6 .... 53 K7
leonhay La UTXR ST14 .... 125 K7
lgott Gv BUCK/MIL ST2 .... 3 M6
le Cl STAFN ST16 .... 175 D5
le La RUGE WS15 .... 217 G6
elow La CDLE ST10 .... 61 G7
lemere Rd ALS/KID ST7 .... 37 H5
le Rd WSLW WS2 .... 283 G6
sden Pl BLYBR/FOR ST11 .... 103 J3
stones Rd STONE ST15 .... 136 B1
stones Wy STONE ST15 .... 136 C1
sbury Rd SHHTH WV12 .... 282 D3
lnico Ct SEDG DY3 .... 299 K7
e Pinch ASHB DE6 .... 49 H7
le Cl ALS/KID ST7 .... 52 C3
3DMR/CCFT WV3 .... 12 A6
3UT DE14 .... 204 A2
CRTAM B79 .... 274 B2
GTWY WS6 .... 249 M6
KGSWFD DY6 .... 303 K5
KINVER DY7 .... 306 C7
le Ct BLYBR/FOR ST11 .... 103 K2
MKTDR TF9 .... 114 D6
le Crs STAFS ST17 .... 194 F4
le Cft ASHB DE6 .... 95 J3
le Gv BNTWD WS7 .... 251 M4
SWAD DE11 .... 205 M4
ehurst Cl NEWUL ST5 .... 84 B7
eneedle Cft SHHTH WV12 .... 282 C6
e Rd STOKE ST4 .... 85 J4
eside Av RUGE WS15 .... 233 M4
e Pines BDMR/CCFT WV3 .... 294 D1
JCHS WS14 .... 254 F3
e St BLOX/PEL WS3 .... 283 J1
e Tree Cl HEDN WS12 .... 232 A1

Pinetree Dr BLYBR/FOR ST11 .... 103 K3
Pinetrees La MKTDR TF9 .... 114 F5
Pine Vw RUGE WS15 .... 197 J5
Pine Wk CDSL WV8 .... 262 F8
rSWAD DE11 .... 223 L3
rUTXR ST14 .... 143 M2
Pineways FOAKS/STRLY B74 .... 286 C7
rSTRBR DY8 .... 303 J8
Pineways Dr
rDUNHL/THL/PER WV6 .... 279 L7
Pinewood Av CNCK/NC WS11 .... 231 K6
Pinewood Cl
rBDMR/CCFT WV3 .... 294 A2
rBRWNH WS8 .... 251 L8
rSHHTH WV12 .... 282 D3
rWMBN WV5 .... 298 A4
Pinewood Crs LNGTN ST3 .... 103 H1
Pinewood Dr MKTDR TF9 .... 114 F6
rRSTAF ST18 .... 196 D2
Pinewood Gv BLYBR/FOR ST11 .... 104 A4
rNEWUL ST5 .... 67 L1
Pinewood Rd MKTDR TF9 .... 114 F7
rSTPNHL/WNHL DE15 .... 204 F4
Pinewoods Av HAG/WOL DY9 .... 311 M6
Pinewoods Cl HAG/WOL DY9 .... 311 M6
Pinfold BLOX/PEL WS3 .... 283 J2
rSHIF TF11 .... 224 C5
Pinfold Av BURS/TUN ST6 .... 54 D6
Pinfold Cl BUTN/AL/TUT DE13 .... 165 H1
rPENK ST19 .... 227 H4
Pinfold Crs
ETTPK/GDPK/PENN WV4 .... 294 D4
Pinfold Dr RUGE WS15 .... 217 H5
Pinfold Gdns WNSFLD WV11 .... 281 K5
Pinfold Gv
rETTPK/GDPK/PENN WV4 .... 294 D4
Pinfold Hl LICHS WS14 .... 270 F4
Pinfold La CNCK/NC WS11 .... 250 E6
ETTPK/GDPK/PENN WV4 .... 294 C5
rGNOS ST20 .... 170 B6
rGTWY WS6 .... 249 J8
rMKTDR TF9 .... 113 J8
rPENK ST19 .... 227 H4
rPENK ST19 .... 229 K2
rRUGE WS15 .... 180 E3
rRUGE WS15 .... 180 E6
Pinfold Rd LICH WS13 .... 8 A1
Pinfold St UTXR ST14 .... 144 C3
Pingle Farm Rd SWAD DE11 .... 205 M5
Pingle La BNTWD WS7 .... 252 D6
rSTOKE ST15 .... 138 B3
The Pingle RUGE WS15 .... 215 H3
Pinhoe Pl LNGTN ST3 .... 86 F7
Pinnox St BURS/TUN ST6 .... 53 L8
Pinson Rd WLNHL WV13 .... 281 M8
Pintail Cl STAFS ST17 .... 194 A3
Pipe Hay La ASHB DE6 .... 163 K5
Pipe La RUGE WS15 .... 217 H2
Piper Cl DUNHL/THL/PER WV6 .... 278 F6
Piper Pl STRBR DY8 .... 307 M2
Piper Rd BDMR/CCFT WV3 .... 294 B2
Pipers Cft LICH WS13 .... 236 A8
Piper's Rw WOLV WV1 .... 14 E3
Pipe Wd RUGE WS15 .... 199 G5
Pipe Wood La RUGE WS15 .... 199 H7
The Pippins NEWUL ST5 .... 84 C7
rSTAFS ST17 .... 193 L5
Pireford Pl NEWUL ST5 .... 68 A1
Pirehill Hl STONE ST15 .... 137 M6
Pirehill Rd NEWUL ST5 .... 68 B1
Pitcairn St BURS/TUN ST6 .... 53 L7
Pitcher La LEEK ST13 .... 44 B5
Pitchford Rd ALBTN WV7 .... 260 F6
Pitfield Av NEWUL ST5 .... 68 D7
Pitgreen La NEWUL ST5 .... 68 C4
Pit La ALS/KID ST7 .... 52 C5
Pitsford St LNGTN ST3 .... 86 B8
Pitstone Cl STAFN ST16 .... 174 D1
Pitts Hill Bank BURS/TUN ST6 .... 53 M5
Pitt St STAFN ST16 .... 174 C4
Plainfield Gv BUCK/MIL ST2 .... 86 D2
Plainview Cl FOAKS/STRLY B74 .... 285 L8
The Plaisaunce NEWUL ST5 .... 84 B4
Plane Gv NEWUL ST5 .... 67 L1
Planetary Rd WLNHL WV13 .... 281 J7
Planks La WMBN WV5 .... 297 M4
Plantation La
rPOL/KGSB/FAZ B78 .... 273 H5
rSEDG DY3 .... 298 D5
Plantation Rd HEDN WS12 .... 231 M1
rSTOKE ST15 .... 101 K4
Plant Crs STAFS ST17 .... 193 M3
Plant La BNTWD WS7 .... 251 K3
Plants Cl GTWY WS6 .... 267 G2
Plant St CDLE ST10 .... 89 L7
rLNGTN ST3 .... 86 C6
rSTRBR DY8 .... 303 L8
Plant Wy BLOX/PEL WS3 .... 267 M6
Plardiwick Rd GNOS ST20 .... 190 B4
Platts Av END/WER ST9 .... 55 L4
Platts Crs STRBR DY8 .... 307 L2
Platts Dr STRBR DY8 .... 307 M2
Platts Rd STRBR DY8 .... 307 L2
Platt St CNCK/NC WS11 .... 232 A5
Pleasant Cl KGSWFD DY6 .... 303 J6
Pleasant Md ALDR WS9 .... 284 E5
Pleasant St BURS/TUN ST6 .... 68 F3
Pleasant Vw SEDG DY3 .... 299 K8
Plex St ALS/KID ST7 .... 53 J7
The Plex ALS/KID ST7 .... 37 K6
Pleydell St HAN ST1 .... 69 M3
Plough Bank END/WER ST9 .... 72 B3
Plough Cft ALS/KID ST7 .... 37 G7
Plough La NWPT TF10 .... 188 A5
Ploughmans Cft NWPT TF10 .... 188 A6
Ploughmans Wk
rKGSWFD DY6 .... 303 G3
rLICH WS13 .... 236 C7
Plough St HAN ST1 .... 2 E2
Plover Cl LNGTN ST3 .... 103 G3
rWOLVN WV10 .... 265 G3
Plover Fld AUD/MAD/W CW3 .... 81 K4
Plover Ri RUGE WS15 .... 215 K1
Plummer Rd SWAD DE11 .... 205 M4
Plumtree Gv HAN ST1 .... 69 M4
Plym Cl WNSFLD WV11 .... 281 J5
Plymouth Gv NEWUL ST5 .... 67 M3
Pochard Cl BURS/TUN ST6 .... 54 C7
Podmore Av ALS/KID ST7 .... 66 F4

Podmore La ALS/KID ST7 .... 66 D4
Podmore Rd MKTDR TF9 .... 148 F2
Podmore St BURS/TUN ST6 .... 69 G3
Pointon Gv BURS/TUN ST6 .... 55 G5
Polperro Wy LNGTN ST3 .... 103 G3
Pomona Rd BUTN/AL/TUT DE13 .... 166 E2
Pond Crs BKHL/PFLD WV2 .... 295 L3
Pond Gv BKHL/PFLD WV2 .... 295 L3
Pond La BKHL/PFLD WV2 .... 13 H9
rBKHL/PFLD WV2 .... 295 L3
Ponesfield Rd LICH WS13 .... 236 B8
Ponesgreen LICH WS13 .... 236 B8
Ponton Cl WNSFLD WV11 .... 251 H5
Pool Av CNCK/NC WS11 .... 251 H5
Pool Cl WOLVN WV10 .... 265 K1
Pooldam NEWUL ST5 .... 84 B2
Poole Av BUCK/MIL ST2 .... 55 H8
Poole Crs BRWNH WS8 .... 251 J8
Pooles La SHHTH WV12 .... 282 E3
Pooles Rd BIDD ST8 .... 307 L6
Poole's Wy BNTWD WS7 .... 252 B4
Pooley Ct NWPT TF10 .... 207 J3
rPOL/KGSB/FAZ B78 .... 275 M8
Poolfield Av NEWUL ST5 .... 83 M2
Poolfield Rd North
rNEWUL ST5 .... 84 A2
Poolfields Cl NEWUL ST5 .... 83 M2
Pool Gn ALDR WS9 .... 285 G5
Pool Hall Crs BDMR/CCFT WV3 .... 293 M2
Pool Hall Rd BDMR/CCFT WV3 .... 293 M2
Pool Hayes La SHHTH WV12 .... 282 A5
Pool House Rd WMBN WV5 .... 297 K4
Pool La STAFS ST17 .... 195 J6
Pool Meadow Cl RUGE WS15 .... 215 K2
Pool Rd BRWNH WS8 .... 251 J8
rWNSFLD WV11 .... 282 A4
Pool Side ALS/KID ST7 .... 38 B2
Poolside AUD/MAD/W CW3 .... 81 L4
Pool Side NEWUL ST5 .... 84 A1
Pool St BKHL/PFLD WV2 .... 12 E9
rNEWUL ST5 .... 84 A2
rSTOKE ST4 .... 86 B4
Pool Vw GTWY WS6 .... 250 A6
rRUSH/SHEL WS4 .... 284 D3
Pope Gdns STAFS ST17 .... 193 J5
Pope Gv HEDN WS12 .... 231 M4
Pope Rd WOLVN WV10 .... 281 G2
Poplar Av ALBTN WV7 .... 260 F2
rBNTWD WS7 .... 251 M4
rBRWNH WS8 .... 269 G2
rCNCK/NC WS11 .... 231 M6
rNEWUL ST5 .... 68 A7
rWNSFLD WV11 .... 281 H3
rWSLW WS2 .... 282 D6
Poplar Ct BLYBR/FOR ST11 .... 104 A4
rECCH S21 .... 152 E4
rNEWUL ST5 .... 68 A7
rRSTAF ST18 .... 191 L4
rSTONE ST15 .... 137 M3
rUTXR ST14 .... 143 M1
rWMBN WV5 .... 298 B4
rWSLW WS2 .... 282 E6
Poplar Ct CNCK/NC WS11 .... 231 L6
Poplar Crs ASHB DE6 .... 95 J2
Poplar Dr ALS/KID ST7 .... 37 L8
rALS/KID ST7 .... 53 G2
rLNGTN ST3 .... 85 L8
Poplar Gv CNCK/NC WS11 .... 102 A1
rNEWUL ST5 .... 84 D1
Poplar La CNCK/NC WS11 .... 248 F2
Poplar Ri FOAKS/STRLY B74 .... 286 D5
Poplar Rd BDMR/CCFT WV3 .... 295 G4
rBRWNH WS8 .... 269 G2
rGTWY WS6 .... 266 F1
rKGSWFD DY6 .... 303 L5
rSTOKE ST4 .... 307 L7
Poplars Dr CDSL WV8 .... 262 F8
Poplars Farm Wy COVEN WV9 .... 247 H8
Poplars Rd BUTN/AL/TUT DE13 .... 185 J3
rRUGE WS15 .... 217 J6
The Poplars CNCK/NC WS11 .... 231 L6
rSTRBR DY8 .... 303 M8
Poplar St BKHL/PFLD WV2 .... 295 K4
rCNCK/NC WS11 .... 251 G4
Poplar Wy STAFS ST17 .... 193 L4
Poppit's La UTXR ST14 .... 125 M6
Poppy Gdns
rBUTN/AL/TUT DE13 .... 220 A8
Porchester Cl ALDR WS9 .... 269 G8
Porlock Av STAFS ST17 .... 194 D2
Porlock Gv STOKE ST4 .... 101 H4
Portal Rd STAFN ST16 .... 175 H5
rWSLW WS2 .... 282 F8
Portchester Dr
rWNSFLD WV11 .... 281 K5
Porters La LEEK ST13 .... 44 F7
Porthill Bank NEWUL ST5 .... 68 C4
Porthill Gn NEWUL ST5 .... 68 C4
Porthkerry Gv SEDG DY3 .... 299 H3
Portland Av ALDR WS9 .... 285 H5
rBUT DE14 .... 204 A3
rCRTAM B79 .... 273 M2
Portland Cl BLYBR/FOR ST11 .... 103 K3
Portland Dr ALS/KID ST7 .... 38 E4
rBIDD ST8 .... 26 D8
rBLYBR/FOR ST11 .... 104 B2
rMKTDR TF9 .... 130 A1
Portland Gv NEWUL ST5 .... 84 B7
Portland Ms NEWUL ST5 .... 68 B4
Portland Pl BARL ST12 .... 101 M6
rCDLE ST10 .... 60 F7
rCNCK/NC WS11 .... 249 J3
Portland Rd ALDR WS9 .... 285 H4
rLNGTN ST3 .... 86 B6
Portland St HAN ST1 .... 2 A3
rLEEK ST13 .... 43 M4
rWSLW WS2 .... 283 L7
Portland St North LEEK ST13 .... 43 M4
Portland St South LEEK ST13 .... 43 M5
Port La CDSL WV8 .... 263 H4
rRUGE WS15 .... 179 L6
Portleven Cl STAFS ST17 .... 194 E3
Portleys La POL/KGSB/FAZ B78 .... 289 K4
Portrush Rd
rDUNHL/THL/PER WV6 .... 278 D6
Portsdown Cl WOLVN WV10 .... 280 F3
Portsea St BLOX/PEL WS3 .... 283 J4

Port St BURS/TUN ST6 .... 68 E3
Portswood Cl COVEN WV9 .... 279 M1
Port Vale St BURS/TUN ST6 .... 68 E3
Portway Cl KGSWFD DY6 .... 303 L5
Portway Dr BUTN/AL/TUT DE13 .... 165 J5
Portway La CRTAM B79 .... 257 J3
Portway Pl KIDD DY10 .... 310 A5
The Portway KGSWFD DY6 .... 303 L5
Postern Rd BUTN/AL/TUT DE13 .... 184 B6
Post La END/WER ST9 .... 55 M4
Post Office Cl CW/SHV CW2 .... 64 F1
rNWPT TF10 .... 207 K3
rRUGE WS15 .... 215 H3
Post Office Rd
rBUTN/AL/TUT DE13 .... 220 A7
rWMBN WV5 .... 292 F7
Pothooks La RSTAF ST18 .... 140 D4
Potsmans La RSTAF ST18 .... 140 D4
Potteries Wy HAN ST1 .... 2 D3
Potters Av STONE ST15 .... 136 F4
Potters End BIDD ST8 .... 40 B1
Potts' La UTXR ST14 .... 160 B3
Pouk Hill Cl WSLW WS2 .... 283 G7
Pouk La LICHS WS14 .... 269 L2
Poulson St STOKE ST4 .... 85 H3
Pound Gdns BURS/TUN ST6 .... 54 D6
Poundsgate Gv STOKE ST4 .... 101 H2
Pountney St BKHL/PFLD WV2 .... 12 F8
Povey Pl NEWUL ST5 .... 68 B1
Powderham Cl BURS/TUN ST6 .... 53 L2
Powell St HAN ST1 .... 2 A3
rWOLVN WV10 .... 280 F6
Power Gv LNGTN ST3 .... 86 A6
Power Station Rd RUGE WS15 .... 215 M1
Powlett St BKHL/PFLD WV2 .... 13 G7
Pownt St BUX SK17 .... 34 A4
Powy Dr ALS/KID ST7 .... 39 G8
Poxon Rd ALDR WS9 .... 269 G7
The Poynings
rDUNHL/THL/PER WV6 .... 279 J5
Preedys Cl RUGE WS15 .... 179 M5
Premier Av ASHB DE6 .... 95 H2
Premier Gdns ALS/KID ST7 .... 38 F8
Prescott Av STAFN ST16 .... 5 K2
Prescott Dr PENK ST19 .... 230 A1
Prestbury Av NEWUL ST5 .... 100 B1
Preston St BURS/TUN ST6 .... 69 J2
Preston Vale La PENK ST19 .... 229 G1
Prestwick Rd KGSWFD DY6 .... 303 J4
Prestwood Av WNSFLD WV11 .... 281 K2
Prestwood End Dr KINVER DY7 .... 306 F2
Prestwood La UTXR ST14 .... 108 E1
Prestwood Rd KINVER DY7 .... 306 E4
rWNSFLD WV11 .... 281 C5
Prestwood Rd West
rWNSFLD WV11 .... 281 H4
Pretoria Rd HAN ST1 .... 69 G8
Priam Cl NEWUL ST5 .... 68 B1
Priam Gv BLOX/PEL WS3 .... 268 B5
Price Av MKTDR TF9 .... 114 D6
Price Cl BURS/TUN ST6 .... 68 F1
rCNCK/NC WS11 .... 249 L1
Prices Rd SEDG DY3 .... 299 J7
Price St BURS/TUN ST6 .... 68 F1
rCNCK/NC WS11 .... 231 L4
rLEEK ST13 .... 43 M4
Priestley Dr LNGTN ST3 .... 86 D6
Priestley Rd WSLW WS2 .... 283 C5
Prime St HAN ST1 .... 3 H2
Primitive St ALS/KID ST7 .... 39 J3
Primley Av TAM/AM/WIL B77 .... 290 F5
Primley Cl WSLW WS2 .... 283 H8
Primrose Av WOLVN WV10 .... 264 D7
Primrose Cl BLOX/PEL WS3 .... 268 A8
rPENK ST19 .... 227 J3
Primrose Dell AUD/MAD/W CW3 .... 81 K4
Primrose Gdns CDSL WV8 .... 263 G7
rWOLVN WV10 .... 265 H3
Primrose Gv NEWUL ST5 .... 68 C8
Primrose Hl STOKE ST4 .... 85 L8
rSTRBR DY8 .... 303 L8
Primrose La WOLVN WV10 .... 280 F2
Primrose Meadow
rCNCK/NC WS11 .... 232 C8
Primrose Wy UTXR ST14 .... 144 B2
Prince Av RSTAF ST18 .... 191 M5
Prince Charles Av LEEK ST13 .... 44 B3
Princefield Av PENK ST19 .... 229 M2
Prince George St CDLE ST10 .... 89 K7
Prince's Av WSL WS1 .... 284 A8
Princes Dr CDSL WV8 .... 263 G7
Princes Gdns CDSL WV8 .... 262 F7
Prince's Rd STOKE ST4 .... 84 F2
rSTRBR DY8 .... 307 K8
Princess Aly WOLV WV1 .... 13 C5
Princess Anne Rd WSLW WS2 .... 282 F7
Princess Av ALS/KID ST7 .... 66 D1
rLEEK ST13 .... 44 B2
rMSHM SE22 .... 223 J5
Princess Dr LNGTN ST3 .... 87 G7
Princess Sq BURS/TUN ST6 .... 68 D2
Princess Rd UTXR ST14 .... 144 A1
Princess St ALS/KID ST7 .... 52 D5
rBIDD ST8 .... 40 D3
rBNTWD WS7 .... 251 L2
rBUT DE14 .... 6 E3
rCNCK/NC WS11 .... 231 L5
rNEWUL ST5 .... 84 C2
rSWAD DE11 .... 223 M2
rWOLV WV1 .... 13 C5
Princes St STAFN ST16 .... 4 E4
rSTONE ST15 .... 120 A8
Princess Wy
rBUTN/AL/TUT DE13 .... 185 L2
Prince St ALDR WS9 .... 268 F8

NEWUL ST5 .... 84 A3
RUGE WS15 .... 216 B5
STONE ST15 .... 138 B3
The Priory END/WER ST9 .... 56 A2
rSEDG DY3 .... 299 K2
Pritchard Av WNSFLD WV11 .... 281 L4
Pritchett Av
ETTPK/GDPK/PENN WV4 .... 295 M7
Probert Rd WOLVN WV10 .... 280 B1
Proctors Rd RUGE WS15 .... 217 J6
Proffitt Cl WSLW WS2 .... 283 L6
Proffitt St WSLW WS2 .... 283 L6
Progress Dr CNCK/NC WS11 .... 249 L3
Prole St WOLVN WV10 .... 280 E6
Prospect Dr LICHS WS14 .... 254 F2
Prospect Rd BNTWD WS7 .... 252 B4
rLEEK ST13 .... 44 A5
rMKTDR TF9 .... 130 B1
rSEDG DY3 .... 299 H8
rSTAFN ST16 .... 5 G2
Prospect St BURS/TUN ST6 .... 68 E4
rCRTAM B79 .... 10 A3
Prospect Ter NEWUL ST5 .... 84 A1
Prosper Meadow KGSWFD DY6 .... 303 L3
Prosser St WOLVN WV10 .... 280 E5
Provence Cl WOLVN WV10 .... 280 F6
Providence Cl BLOX/PEL WS3 .... 283 J3
Providence La BLOX/PEL WS3 .... 283 J3
Providence St HAN ST1 .... 2 E2
Provost Pl LEEK ST13 .... 44 A3
Pruden Av
ETTPK/GDPK/PENN WV4 .... 295 M7
Puddle Hl RSTAF ST18 .... 177 K1
Puddy La END/WER ST9 .... 56 A5
Pudsey Dr MGN/WHC B75 .... 287 J7
Pugh Crs WSLW WS2 .... 282 E8
Pugh Rd BILS/COS WV14 .... 295 M8
Pugin Cl
rDUNHL/THL/PER WV6 .... 278 D7
Pullman Cl TAM/AM/WIL B77 .... 275 G8
Pullman Ct CDLE ST10 .... 89 J8
Pulteney Dr STAFN ST16 .... 174 B4
Pump Bank NEWUL ST5 .... 82 F3
Pump La ASHB DE6 .... 145 H2
rRUGE WS15 .... 197 J7
Pump St LEEK ST13 .... 44 A3
rSTOKE ST4 .... 85 G3
Purbeck Cl BURS/TUN ST6 .... 69 H3
Purbrook TAM/AM/WIL B77 .... 290 E2
Purbrook Gv WOLV WV1 .... 13 M8
Purcell Av LICH WS13 .... 236 B8
Purcell Rd WOLVN WV10 .... 280 D2
Purser Crs NEWUL ST5 .... 68 B5
Purslet Rd WOLV WV1 .... 281 J4
Pyebirch La ECCH S21 .... 153 G5
Pye Green Rd CNCK/NC WS11 .... 231 L5
rHEDN WS12 .... 231 M2
Pyenest St HAN ST1 .... 2 A9

Q

The Quadrangle END/WER ST9 .... 55 M3
Quadrant Rd HAN ST1 .... 2 C4
The Quadrant SEDG DY3 .... 299 K1

Quadrille Lawns
rCOVEN WV9 .... 263 M8
Quail Gn DUNHL/THL/PER WV6 .... 278 F8
Quail Gv LNGTN ST3 .... 103 G3
Qualcast Rd WOLVN WV10 .... 13 L4
Quarry Av STOKE ST4 .... 84 F2
Quarry Bank CDLE ST10 .... 107 G6
Quarry Bank Rd MKTDR TF9 .... 130 A3
rNEWUL ST5 .... 82 F2
Quarry Berry La CRTAM B79 .... 259 L2
Quarry Brow SEDG DY3 .... 299 L5
Quarry Cl BUCK/MIL ST2 .... 55 J7
rEND/WER ST9 .... 71 G6
rGTWY WS6 .... 249 L7
rRUGE WS15 .... 215 H2
Quarry Hills La LICHS WS14 .... 9 J8
Quarry House La MKTDR TF9 .... 130 A3
Quarry La GNOS ST20 .... 190 C5
Quarry Rd STOKE ST4 .... 84 F2
Quarry Ter ALS/KID ST7 .... 53 G1
Quayle Gv STRBR DY8 .... 303 K7
Quee La UTXR ST14 .... 161 H1
Queen Anne St STOKE ST4 .... 85 H2
Queen Elizabeth Av WSLW WS2 .... 282 F8
Queen Margaret's Rd
rMKTDR TF9 .... 114 D5
Queen Mary Rd STOKE ST4 .... 101 G1
Queen Mary's Dr BARL ST12 .... 101 L6
Queen's Av BURS/TUN ST6 .... 53 L7
Queensberry Rd LNGTN ST3 .... 86 D8
Queens Ct BUT DE14 .... 204 B2
rNEWUL ST5 .... 84 C1
Queens Cft MKTDR TF9 .... 148 F2
Queen's Dr BIDD ST8 .... 40 D4
rBNTWD WS7 .... 251 M5
rLEEK ST13 .... 44 A2
Queens Gdns CDSL WV8 .... 262 F7
Queensland Crs
rSTPNHL/WNHL DE15 .... 186 C8
Queen's Lea SHHTH WV12 .... 282 C5
Queensmead Rd LNGTN ST3 .... 102 F3
Queens Park Av LNGTN ST3 .... 102 B1
Queen Sq WOLV WV1 .... 12 F5
Queens Ri
rBUTN/AL/TUT DE13 .... 165 J4
rRUSH/SHEL WS4 .... 284 C3
rSEDG DY3 .... 299 L2
rSTOKE ST4 .... 84 F2
rSTRBR DY8 .... 307 M4
rWOLVN WV10 .... 288 B4
Queens Sq STONE ST15 .... 120 A8
Queen St ALDR WS9 .... 268 F8
rALS/KID ST7 .... 39 G8
rALS/KID ST7 .... 66 C1
rBNTWD WS7 .... 251 M5
rBURS/TUN ST6 .... 68 F2
rBUT DE14 .... 6 E8
rBUX SK17 .... 24 B4
rCDLE ST10 .... 89 L7
rCNCK/NC WS11 .... 232 A5
rCNCK/NC WS11 .... 249 K1
rGTWY WS6 .... 249 K8
rKGSWFD DY6 .... 303 K5
rLEEK ST13 .... 43 M4

LICH WS13 8 D4
MKTDR TF9 130 C1
NEWUL ST5 68 B4
NEWUL ST5 84 C1
RUGE WS15 215 M2
STRBR DY8 303 K7
STRBR DY8 307 M4
WOLV WV1 13 G5
Queensville *STAFS* ST17 5 K9
Queensville Av *STAFS* ST17 5 J8
Queensville Br *STAFS* ST17 5 J9
Queens Wy *POL/KGSB/FAZ* B78 291 M4
Queensway *ALS/KID* ST7 37 H5
BURS/TUN ST6 68 D4
CRTAM B79 274 A2
RUGE WS15 215 L3
STAFN ST16 4 F3
STAFN ST16 5 G5
STOKE ST4 85 H2
Quendale *WMBN* WV5 297 L4
Quicksand La *ALDR* WS9 284 F6
Quillets Rd *STRBR* DY8 303 J7
Quilow La *ASHB* DE6 95 K7
Quilter Cl *WSLW* WS2 282 F7
Quinton Av *GTWY* WS6 249 M7
Quinton Gv *NEWUL* ST5 68 B6
Quinton Wk *BURS/TUN* ST6 54 C8
Quixhill Bank *UTXR* ST14 108 F2
Quixhill Cl *ASHB* DE6 95 H2
Quixhill La *UTXR* ST14 108 D2
Quonians La *LICH* WS13 8 F3
Quorn Cl *STPNHL/WNHL* DE15 205 G1
Quorn Crs *STRBR* DY8 303 J7

R

Rabbit La *WOLVN* WV10 265 G3
Rabone St *BURS/TUN* ST6 53 L7
Raby St *BKHL/PFLD* WV2 13 H8
Race Course *NEWUL* ST5 83 J1
Racecourse La *STRBR* DY8 311 L1
Racecourse Rd
DUNHL/THL/PER WV6 280 A5
STOKE ST4 85 G6
Rachel Gv *STOKE* ST4 86 B4
Raddle La *CRTAM* B79 239 K4
Radford Bank *STAFS* ST17 194 C2
Radford Cl *STONE* ST15 138 A1
Radford Dr *RUSH/SHEL* WS4 268 C8
Radford La
ETTPK/GDPK/PENN WV4 293 M3
Radford Ri *STAFS* ST17 194 C2
Radford Rd *STOKE* ST4 84 E1
Radford St *STONE* ST15 138 A2
Radhurst Ri
BUTN/AL/TUT DE13 202 C8
Radley Rd *RUSH/SHEL* WS4 284 C4
Radley Wy *END/WER* ST9 71 H7
Radmore Cl *BNTWD* WS7 251 K2
Radmore La *GNOS* ST20 189 M4
NWPT TF10 188 F2
RUGE WS15 180 C3
Radnor Ri *HEDN* WS12 232 B6
Radnor Rd *SEDG* DY3 299 J2
Radstock Cl *STAFS* ST17 194 D4
Radstock Rd *SHHTH* WV12 282 C1
Radstone Ri *NEWUL* ST5 84 B7
Radway Green Rd *CW/SHV* CW2 50 D4
Ragees Rd *STRBR* DY8 303 M7
Raglan Av
DUNHL/THL/PER WV6 278 F7
Raglan Cl
BUTN/AL/TUT DE13 185 K2
FOAKS/STRLY B74 285 M7
SEDG DY3 299 H3
Raglan St *BDMR/CCFT* WV3 12 D5
STOKE ST4 85 K4
Ragley Cl *BLOX/PEL* WS3 283 G1
Raikes La *LICHS* WS14 270 B4
Railswood Dr *BLOX/PEL* WS3 268 A7
Railton Av *LNGTN* ST3 102 A1
Railway Ct *END/WER* ST9 55 M3
Railway Dr *WOLV* WV1 13 H4
Railway La *BNTWD* WS7 251 L1
Railway Pas *LNGTN* ST3 86 C6
Railway Rd *LNGTN* ST3 86 E8
Railway St *BURS/TUN* ST6 53 L8
CNCK/NC WS11 249 L2
STAFN ST16 4 C5
WOLV WV1 13 H4
Railway Ter *LNGTN* ST3 86 C7
Rainbow St *BKHL/PFLD* WV2 13 G9
Rainford Cl *ALS/KID* ST7 53 M1
Rainham Gv *BURS/TUN* ST6 54 A2
Rainscar *TAM/AM/WIL* B77 291 H3
Rake End Ct *RUGE* WS15 216 F1
Rake Hl *BNTWD* WS7 252 B2
Rakeway Rd *CDLE* ST10 105 L1
Raleigh St *WSLW* WS2 283 J8
Ralph Ct *STAFS* ST17 193 H2
Ralph Dr *HAN* ST1 69 L3
Ralston Cl *BLOX/PEL* WS3 267 G6
Ramage Gv *LNGTN* ST3 102 D1
Rambleford Wy *STAFN* ST16 174 D2
Ramillies Crs *GTWY* WS6 266 F1
Ramsay Cl *BARL* ST12 101 L5
Ramsay Rd *WSLW* WS2 283 G5
Ramsey Rd *NEWUL* ST5 68 A8
Ramsey St *STOKE* ST4 85 J5
Ramshaw Dr *LNGTN* ST3 86 D4
Ramshaw Vw *LEEK* ST13 44 A2
Ramshorn Rd *CDLE* ST10 91 K2
Randall Cl *KGSWFD* DY6 303 M6
Randle Dr *MGN/WHC* B75 287 J7
Randles La *END/WER* ST9 72 B4
Ranelagh Rd *BKHL/PFLD* WV2 295 J4
Ranelagh St *HAN* ST1 2 C7
Rangemoor La *ASHB* DE6 93 J4
Rangemore Hl
BUTN/AL/TUT DE13 202 B4
Rangemore St *BUT* DE14 6 D4
Rangemore Ter *NEWUL* ST5 68 D7
Ranger's Wk *RUGE* WS15 215 H1
Rangeways Rd *KGSWFD* DY6 303 M7
Rangifer Rd
POL/KGSB/FAZ B78 289 M1
The Rank *GNOS* ST20 190 C5
Ranleigh Av *KGSWFD* DY6 303 M6
Ranscombe Dr *SEDG* DY3 299 K8
Ransome Pl *LNGTN* ST3 86 E6
Ranworth Cl *NEWUL* ST5 84 B8
Ranworth Ri
ETTPK/GDPK/PENN WV4 295 K6
Ratcliffe Av *BUT* DE14 204 B2
Ratcliffe Cl *SEDG* DY3 299 M3
Ratcliffe Rd *WNSFLD* WV11 282 A4
Rathbone Av *NEWUL* ST5 68 D7
Rathlin Cl *COVEN* WV9 264 A7
Rathmore Cl *STRBR* DY8 307 L8
Rathwell Cl *COVEN* WV9 264 A8
Rattigan Dr *LNGTN* ST3 86 F6
Ratton St *HAN* ST1 2 E4
Raven Cl *GTWY* WS6 249 K8
HEDN WS12 231 J3
HEDN WS12 232 E6
Raven Crs *WNSFLD* WV11 281 M2
Ravenhill Cl *RUGE* WS15 215 M4
Ravenhill Dr *CDSL* WV8 263 G7
Ravenhill Ter *RUGE* WS15 215 M4
Raven Rd
BUTN/AL/TUT DE13 201 G8
Ravensbourne Gv
WLNHL WV13 282 C8
Ravenscliffe Rd *ALS/KID* ST7 53 G2
Ravens Cl *ALS/KID* ST7 51 L7
Ravenscroft *STRBR* DY8 307 J4
Ravenscroft Rd *SHHTH* WV12 282 B5
Ravensholme
DUNHL/THL/PER WV6 278 F8
Raven's La *ALS/KID* ST7 51 M7
Ravenslea Rd *RUGE* WS15 215 M4
Ravenstone
TAM/AM/WIL B77 291 H2
Ravens Wy *BUT* DE14 6 C3
Ravenswood Cl *NEWUL* ST5 84 A7
Ravenswood Crest *STAFS* ST17 194 C3
Rawle Cl *CDLE* ST10 89 J7
Rawlins St *HAN* ST1 3 G3
Rawnsley Rd *HEDN* WS12 232 E3
Raybolds Bridge St
WSLW WS2 283 J6
Raygill *TAM/AM/WIL* B77 291 H2
Rayleigh Rd *BDMR/CCFT* WV3 12 A9
Rayleigh Wy *BUCK/MIL* ST2 86 D1
Raymond Av *HAN* ST1 69 K3
Raymond Cl *WSLW* WS2 283 K5
Raymond Gdns *WNSFLD* WV11 281 L5
Raymond St *HAN* ST1 2 C8
Raynor Rd *WOLVN* WV10 280 F4
Reacliffe Rd *END/WER* ST9 28 D7
MCFLDS SK11 28 B3
Read Av *STAFN* ST16 5 H1
Reade's La *CONG* CW12 26 E2
CONG CW12 26 B2
Reading Wy *BUCK/MIL* ST2 70 D8
Reads Rd *STOKE* ST4 85 M2
Reansway Sq
DUNHL/THL/PER WV6 280 A6
Reapers Cl *SHHTH* WV12 282 D5
Reason Rd *STAFS* ST17 193 M5
Reaymer Cl *WSLW* WS2 283 H3
Rebecca Gdns
ETTPK/GDPK/PENN WV4 294 F6
Rebecca St *STOKE* ST4 85 H2
Recorder Gv *BURS/TUN* ST6 54 B4
Recreation Rd *LNGTN* ST3 86 E8
Rectory Cl *CDLE* ST10 124 A5
POL/KGSB/FAZ B78 289 L5
Rectory Dr *SHIF* TF11 225 M8
Rectory Gdns *RUGE* WS15 217 G6
Rectory La *RSTAF* ST18 191 M5
RUGE WS15 216 F6
Rectory Ms *RDERBYSW* DE65 167 H6
Rectory Rd *ALBTN* WV7 260 F4
CDLE ST10 107 H8
HAN ST1 2 A8
Rectory St *HAN* ST1 2 A8
STRBR DY8 303 K7
Rectory Vw *ALS/KID* ST7 52 D4
Redacres *DUNHL/THL/PER* WV6 279 L4
Red Bank *LNGTN* ST3 102 C1
MKTDR TF9 130 B2
Red Bank La *MKTDR* TF9 130 B2
Redbourn Rd *BLOX/PEL* WS3 267 G6
Redbridge Cl *STOKE* ST4 100 F1
Redbrook Cl *HEDN* WS12 250 D1
Redbrook La *RUGE* WS15 215 M4
Red Brook Rd *WSLW* WS2 283 G5
Redcar Rd *STOKE* ST4 101 G3
WOLVN WV10 264 D6
Redcliff *TAM/AM/WIL* B77 11 L3
Redcliffe Dr *WMBN* WV5 298 B4
Redcotts Cl *WOLVN* WV10 281 G3
Redfern Dr *BNTWD* WS7 252 B5
Redfern Rd *STONE* ST15 137 M5
UTXR ST14 144 A1
Redford Dr *ALBTN* WV7 261 G5
Redgrave Dr *STAFN* ST16 4 A6
Red Hall La *ALS/KID* ST7 66 B5
Redhall Rd *SEDG* DY3 299 J8
Redheath Cl *NEWUL* ST5 66 F8
Redhill *STAFN* ST16 174 C2
Redhill Av *WMBN* WV5 298 A4
Redhill Cl *CRTAM* B79 274 A3
Redhill Gorse *STAFN* ST16 174 C2
Redhill La *BUTN/AL/TUT* DE13 165 H5
Redhill Rd *CNCK/NC* WS11 231 M6
STONE ST15 138 B1
Redhills *ECCH* ST21 152 E4
Red Hill St *WOLV* WV1 12 F2
Red House Crs *LNGTN* ST3 86 A7
Red House La *ALDR* WS9 284 E5
Redhouse Rd
DUNHL/THL/PER WV6 279 H5
Redhurst Dr *WOLVN* WV10 264 B7
Redlake *TAM/AM/WIL* B77 290 E2
Redland Dr *BUCK/MIL* ST2 70 D7
The Redlands *STONE* ST15 138 C3
Red La *AUD/MAD/W* CW3 81 K5
BUCK/MIL ST2 55 J8
RDERBYSW DE65 187 M4
SEDG DY3 299 H2
WNSFLD WV11 266 C8
Red Lion Av *CNCK/NC* WS11 251 G6
Red Lion Cl *ALS/KID* ST7 52 D3
Red Lion Crs *CNCK/NC* WS11 251 G6
Red Lion La *CNCK/NC* WS11 251 G6
Red Lion Pas *HAN* ST1 2 B7
Red Lion St *STAFN* ST16 4 E3
WOLV WV1 12 E4
Redlock Fld *LICHS* WS14 8 D9
Redman Gv *BURS/TUN* ST6 69 J3
Redmine Cl *NEWUL* ST5 67 M6
Redmond Cl *RUGE* WS15 197 J8
Redmoor Cl
STPNHL/WNHL DE15 186 B6
Redmoor Gdns
ETTPK/GDPK/PENN WV4 295 G5
Redmoor Rd *RUGE* WS15 233 M7
Rednall Dr *MGN/WHC* B75 287 J7
Redpine Crest *SHHTH* WV12 282 D6
Red River Rd *WSLW* WS2 283 G5
Red Rd *CDLE* ST10 91 H6
Red Rock Dr *CDSL* WV8 262 F8
Redruth Cl *KGSWFD* DY6 303 K2
Redstone Dr *WNSFLD* WV11 281 M5
Redwell Cl *TAM/AM/WIL* B77 11 H4
Redwing *TAM/AM/WIL* B77 291 G4
Redwing Cl *BNTWD* WS7 252 D5
Redwing Dr *BIDD* ST8 40 E2
HEDN WS12 231 J3
Redwood Av *DUDN* DY1 299 M5
STONE ST15 138 B4
Redwood Cl *FOAKS/STRLY* B74 285 M8
Redwood Dr *BNTWD* WS7 251 M2
CNCK/NC WS11 231 M7
STPNHL/WNHL DE15 205 G2
Redwood Pl *LNGTN* ST3 103 G1
Redwood Rd *KINVER* DY7 306 C7
Redwood Wy *WNSFLD* WV11 282 B2
Reedbed Cl *BURS/TUN* ST6 54 C7
Reedham Gdns
ETTPK/GDPK/PENN WV4 294 D4
Reedham Wy *BUCK/MIL* ST2 70 D8
Reedly Rd *SHHTH* WV12 282 C1
Reedmace *TAM/AM/WIL* B77 10 E9
Reedswood Cl *WSLW* WS2 283 J7
Reedswood Gdns *WSLW* WS2 283 J7
WSLW WS2 283 J7
Reedswood La *WSLW* WS2 283 J7
Reedswood Wy *WSLW* WS2 283 J6
Rees Dr *WMBN* WV5 298 B3
Reeve Cl *RUGE* WS15 217 H6
Reeve La *LICH* WS13 8 E2
Reeves Av *BURS/TUN* ST6 54 A7
NEWUL ST5 68 B7
Reeves Gdns *CDSL* WV8 263 G6
Reeves St *BLOX/PEL* WS3 283 H2
Regency Cl *ALS/KID* ST7 52 D5
Regency Ct *RUGE* WS15 216 B4
Regency Wk *FOAKS/STRLY* B74 286 D5
Regency Wy
BUTN/AL/TUT DE13 185 K2
Regent Av *BURS/TUN* ST6 53 M7
Regent Cl *KGSWFD* DY6 303 J4
Regent Ct *CDLE* ST10 74 A2
Regent Rd
ETTPK/GDPK/PENN WV4 294 E5
HAN ST1 2 D8
Regent St *LEEK* ST13 43 M4
STOKE ST4 84 F5
STONE ST15 137 M1
WLNHL WV13 282 A7
Regina Crs
DUNHL/THL/PER WV6 279 H6
Regina Dr *RUSH/SHEL* WS4 284 A6
Reginald Mitchell Wy
BURS/TUN ST6 53 J6
Reginald St *BURS/TUN* ST6 69 G2
Regina St *BURS/TUN* ST6 54 D8
Regis Rd *DUNHL/THL/PER* WV6 279 H5
Registry St *STOKE* ST4 85 H2
Reid Av *SHHTH* WV12 282 D4
Reid St *BURS/TUN* ST6 68 E2
Reindeer Rd
POL/KGSB/FAZ B78 289 L1
Relay Dr *TAM/AM/WIL* B77 291 J3
Rembrandt Cl *HEDN* WS12 232 D8
Rembrandt Wy *LNGTN* ST3 103 H4
Remer St *BURS/TUN* ST6 2 A1
Remington Dr *CNCK/NC* WS11 249 M2
Remington Pl *WSLW* WS2 283 J5
Remington Rd *WSLW* WS2 283 H4
Renard Wy *BLYBR/FOR* ST11 103 H3
Rendermore Cl *PENK* ST19 229 L3
Rene Rd *TAM/AM/WIL* B77 11 J4
Renfrew Cl *NEWUL* ST5 83 M2
STRBR DY8 303 J7
Renfrew Pl *STOKE* ST4 101 G1
Rennie Crs *LEEK* ST13 57 K6
Rennison Dr *WMBN* WV5 298 A4
Renown Cl *BUCK/MIL* ST2 85 M1
Renshaw Dr *SWAD* DE11 205 M5
Renshaw Wood La *CDSL* WV8 244 F8
Renton Gv *WOLVN* WV10 280 A1
Renton Rd *WOLVN* WV10 280 A1
Repington Rd *HAN* ST1 69 L2
Repington Rd North
TAM/AM/WIL B77 275 G5
Repington Rd South
TAM/AM/WIL B77 275 G5
Repton Av *DUNHL/*
THL/PER WV6 278 D7
Repton Cl *CNCK/NC* WS11 249 H2
STAFS ST17 5 L9
Repton Dr *NEWUL* ST5 83 M5
Reservoir Rd
BUTN/AL/TUT DE13 184 F6
HEDN WS12 232 D6
LNGTN ST3 86 E8
Retreat Gdns *SEDG* DY3 299 L3
The Retreat Gdns
DUNHL/THL/PER WV6 277 J7
Reva Rd *STAFS* ST17 193 L2
Revival St *BLOX/PEL* WS3 283 H1
Reynards La *BUX* SK17 34 D5
Reynards Ri *MKTDR* TF9 114 D5
Reynolds Av *NEWUL* ST5 67 L4
Reynolds Cl *LICH* WS13 236 B8
SEDG DY3 297 L8
Reynolds Gv
DUNHL/THL/PER WV6 278 F5
Reynolds Rd *BURS/TUN* ST6 54 A7
Reynolds Wk *WNSFLD* WV11 282 A2
Rhodes Cl *SEDG* DY3 299 G6
Rhodes St *HAN* ST1 2 F1
Rhondda Av *BURS/TUN* ST6 69 J3
Rhys Thomas Cl
SHHTH WV12 282 D6
Rialto Pl *BURS/TUN* ST6 53 K7
Ribbesford Av *WOLVN* WV10 280 B2
Ribble Cl *NEWUL* ST5 84 B7
Ribble Dr *BIDD* ST8 40 E2
Ribblesdale
TAM/AM/WIL B77 291 H2
Ricardo St *LNGTN* ST3 102 B1
Riceyman Rd *NEWUL* ST5 68 B1
Richard Cooper Rd *LICHS* WS14 270 F5
Richards Av *BURS/TUN* ST6 53 L7
STAFN ST16 5 K3
Richardson Dr *STRBR* DY8 307 L2
Richardson Pl *BURS/TUN* ST6 54 B4
Richborough Dr *DUDN* DY1 299 L7
Riches St *DUNHL/THL/PER* WV6 279 M7
Richfield La *STAFS* ST17 212 F2
Richmond Av *BDMR/CCFT* WV3 294 F1
HAN ST1 69 K2
Richmond Cl *CNCK/NC* WS11 232 A5
CRTAM B79 10 A4
STAFS ST17 193 L2
Richmond Dr *BDMR/CCFT* WV3 294 E1
DUNHL/THL/PER WV6 278 F7
LICHS WS14 9 K5
Richmond Gdns *WMBN* WV5 298 A5
Richmond Gv *NEWUL* ST5 68 D7
STRBR DY8 307 L2
Richmond Pk *KGSWFD* DY6 303 J2
Richmond Rd *BDMR/CCFT* WV3 294 E1
SEDG DY3 299 L3
STOKE ST4 100 F1
Richmond St *BUT* DE14 6 E3
STOKE ST4 85 G2
Richmond Ter *HAN* ST1 2 B9
Rickerscote Av *STAFS* ST17 194 A4
Rickerscote Hall La
STAFS ST17 194 A5
Rickerscote Rd *STAFS* ST17 193 L4
Ridding Bank *STOKE* ST4 100 B3
Ridding La *UTXR* ST14 92 E8
UTXR ST14 142 C7
Riddings Crs *BLOX/PEL* WS3 267 M6
Riddings La *ASHB* DE6 163 K4
The Riddings *TAM/AM/WIL* B77 11 K4
WOLVN WV10 281 G3
Rider's Wy *RUGE* WS15 215 H1
Ridge Cl *BARL* ST12 119 J2
WSLW WS2 282 D7
Ridge Crs *LNGTN* ST3 102 F4
Ridge Cft *STONE* ST15 138 B3
Ridgefields *BIDD* ST8 41 H1
Ridgehouse Dr *HAN* ST1 69 G5
Ridge La *WNSFLD* WV11 281 K3
Ridge Rd *BURS/TUN* ST6 53 K4
KGSWFD DY6 303 J5
Ridge St *STRBR* DY8 307 J4
Ridget La *LICH* WS13 238 B2
Ridge Wy *ALDR* WS9 285 H6
Ridgeway *RSTAF* ST18 177 J2
SEDG DY3 299 K3
Ridgeway Cl *RSTAF* ST18 175 H2
RSTAF ST18 193 J5
Ridgeway Dr
ETTPK/GDPK/PENN WV4 294 F7
Ridgeway Rd
STPNHL/WNHL DE15 204 E4
STRBR DY8 303 M8
The Ridgeway *BNTWD* WS7 252 A5
STAFN ST16 174 A5
Ridgewood Av *STRBR* DY8 307 J4
Ridgewood Ri
TAM/AM/WIL B77 275 G5
Ridgmont Rd *NEWUL* ST5 83 M6
Ridgway Dr *BLYBR/FOR* ST11 103 K3
Ridgway Pl *NEWUL* ST5 68 D4
Ridgway Rd *STOKE* ST4 85 J1
Ridings Brook Dr
CNCK/NC WS11 232 A8
Riding Wy *SHHTH* WV12 282 D4
Ridley St *STOKE* ST4 85 J5
Ridware Rd *RUGE* WS15 217 H3
Rigby Dr *CNCK/NC* WS11 231 L6
Rigby Rd *ALS/KID* ST7 39 H7
Riggs La *ASHB* DE6 128 A3
Riley *TAM/AM/WIL* B77 11 J8
Riley Av *BURS/TUN* ST6 54 B8
Riley Crs *BDMR/CCFT* WV3 294 F4
Riley La *GNOS* ST20 170 E3
Riley St *WLNHL* WV13 282 B8
Riley St North *BURS/TUN* ST6 68 E2
Riley St South *BURS/TUN* ST6 68 F2
Rileys Wy *ALS/KID* ST7 51 M8
Rill St *LNGTN* ST3 86 B6
Rimbach Dr *RSTAF* ST18 196 D2
Rimini Cl *LNGTN* ST3 86 E5
Rindleford Av
ETTPK/GDPK/PENN WV4 294 C4
Ringhills Rd *CDSL* WV8 263 H8
Ringland Cl *HAN* ST1 2 F5
Ring Rd *BNTWD* WS7 251 K3
Ring Road St Andrews
WOLV WV1 12 D5
Ring Road St Davids *WOLV* WV1 13 H4
Ring Road St Georges
BKHL/PFLD WV2 13 G7
Ring Road St Johns
BKHL/PFLD WV2 12 E7
Ring Road St Marks
BDMR/CCFT WV3 12 D6
Ring Road St Patricks
WOLV WV1 13 G3
Ring Road St Peters *WOLV* WV1 12 E4
Ringway *CNCK/NC* WS11 249 L1
Ringwood Av *ALDR* WS9 285 H5
Ringwood Rd *WOLVN* WV10 280 D1
Ripon Av *NEWUL* ST5 67 L3
Ripon Dr *STAFS* ST17 194 C3
Ripon Rd *LNGTN* ST3 101 M2
WOLVN WV10 280 C3
WSLW WS2 283 H8
Rischale Wy *RUSH/SHEL* WS4 284 C2
Riseley Rd *STOKE* ST4 84 D2
The Rise *KGSWFD* DY6 303 L5
RUGE WS15 215 M4
STAFS ST17 194 E3
SWAD DE11 205 M5
Rishworth Av *RUGE* WS15 197 L8
Rising Brook
DUNHL/THL/PER WV6 279
STAFS ST17 19
Rivendell Gdns
DUNHL/THL/PER WV6 27
Rivendell La *LEEK* ST13 4
Riverbank Rd *WLNHL* WV13 28
Rivercroft Cl *UTXR* ST14 10
Riverdale Cl
STPNHL/WNHL DE15 18
Riverdale Dr *BURS/TUN* ST6 5
Riverdrive *POL/KGSB/FAZ* B78 1
Riverfield Gv *TAM/AM/WIL* B77 1
River Lea Ms
AUD/MAD/W CW3 81
Riversfield Dr *UTXR* ST14 10
Riverside *MSHM* DE12 22
RUGE WS15 19
Riverside Dr *BUT* DE14 20
Riverside Rd *CDLE* ST10 10
STOKE ST4 8
Riverside Wy *COVEN* WV9 24
Riversleigh Dr *STRBR* DY8 30
Riversmead *NEWUL* ST5 84
Riversmeade Wy *STAFN* ST16 17
Riverway *STAFS* ST17
River Wy *STONE* ST15 13
Rivington Cl *STRBR* DY8 307
Rivington Crs *BURS/TUN* ST6 5
Rixdale Cl *HAN* ST1
Roach *TAM/AM/WIL* B77 29
Roach Crs *WNSFLD* WV11 281
Roadmeadow Cl *ASHB* DE6 95
Robert Cl *CRTAM* B79 27
Robert Heath St
BURS/TUN ST6 54
Roberts Av *NEWUL* ST5 6
Roberts Cl *ALDR* WS9 26
ALS/KID ST7 66
Roberts Green Rd *SEDG* DY3 29
Robertson Dr *NEWUL* ST5 6
Robertson Sq *STOKE* ST4 8
Roberts Rd *BLOX/PEL* WS3 28
Robert St *BURS/TUN* ST6 53
SEDG DY3 29
Robertville Rd *BUCK/MIL* ST2 7
Robert Wynd *BILS/COS* WV14 29
Robey's La *POL/KGSB/FAZ* B78 27
Robina Dr *CDLE* ST10 8
Robin Cl *HEDN* WS12 23
UTXR ST14 14
Robin Gv *WNSFLD* WV11 28
Robin Hl *BIDD* ST8 4
Robin Hill Gv *STOKE* ST4 8
Robins Cl *GTWY* WS6 24
Robin's Cross La
RDERBYSW DE65 18
Robinson Av *BURS/TUN* ST6 69
Robinson Cl *CRTAM* B79 273
Robinson Rd *BNTWD* WS7 251
STOKE ST4 10
SWAD DE11 20
Robins Rd *BNTWD* WS7 25
The Robins *MKTDR* TF9 11
Robinswood *STAFS* ST17 194
Robottom Cl *WSLW* WS2 28
Robson St *HAN* ST1 2
Rocester Av *WNSFLD* WV11 28
Rocester La *CDLE* ST10 6
Roche Av *LEEK* ST13 4
Roche Rd *BLOX/PEL* WS3 28
Rochester Av *BNTWD* WS7 25
Rochester Cft *WSLW* WS2 283
Rochester Rd *LNGTN* ST3 8
Rochester Wy *HEDN* WS12 25
The Roche *BNTWD* WS7 25
LEEK ST13 57
Roche Wy *BLOX/PEL* WS3 28
Rochford Cl *LEEK* ST13 43
Rochford Gv
ETTPK/GDPK/PENN WV4 29
Rock Crs *STONE* ST15 12
Rock End Dr *LEEK* ST13 7
Rock Farm Rd *LICHS* WS14 25
Rockfield Av *BUCK/MIL* ST2 7
Rock Hl *POL/KGSB/FAZ* B78 27
Rock House Dr *BARL* ST12 11
Rockhouse Dr *RSTAF* ST18 19
Rockhouse La *ALS/KID* ST7 5
Rockingham Cl
BLOX/PEL WS3 283
SEDG DY3 299
Rockingham Dr
DUNHL/THL/PER WV6 27
Rocklands Crs *LICH* WS13 9
Rock La *ECCH* ST21 117
MKTDR TF9 11
MKTDR TF9 11
Rock Rd *BILS/COS* WV14 29
Rockrose Gdns *WOLVN* WV10 265
Rockside *ALS/KID* ST7 3
The Rocks *ECCH* ST21 11
Rock St *SEDG* DY3 29
The Rock *DUNHL/THL/PER* WV6 27
SHIF TF11 22
Rocky Wall *KINVER* DY7 30
Rodbaston Dr *PENK* ST19 22
Rodbridge La *LICH* WS13 23
Rode House Cl *ALS/KID* ST7 3
Roderick Dr *WNSFLD* WV11 281
The Rode *ALS/KID* ST7 3
Rodger Av *AUD/MAD/W* CW3 6
Rodgers St *BURS/TUN* ST6 5
Rodney Cl *SHIF* TF11 242
Rodsley La *ASHB* DE6 111
Rodway Cl
ETTPK/GDPK/PENN WV4 29
Roebuck Gld *SHHTH* WV12 28
Roebuck Pl *BLOX/PEL* WS3 283
Roebuck Rd *BLOX/PEL* WS3 28
Roebuck St *STOKE* ST4 8
Roedean Av *STAFS* ST17 19
Roe La *NEWUL* ST5 8
Roe Pk *CONG* CW12 3
Roford Ct *SEDG* DY3 299
Rogate Cl *STOKE* ST4 86
Rogers Av *NEWUL* ST5 6
Rogers Cl *WNSFLD* WV11 28
Rogerstone Av *STOKE* ST4 84
Rokewood Cl *KGSWFD* DY6 30

holt Crs *CNCK/NC* WS11 .... 249 J1
fe Cl *STOKE* ST4 .... 85 G8
eston La
UTN/AL/TUT DE13 .... 165 K5
eston Rd
UTN/AL/TUT DE13 .... 185 H1
nan Cl *BRWNH* WS8 .... 251 L8
nan Dr *NEWUL* ST5 .... 67 K5
nan La *FOAKS/STRLY* B74 .... 286 B6
nan Pk *FOAKS/STRLY* B74 .... 286 B6
nan Rd *FOAKS/STRLY* B74 .... 286 C5
nan Rd (Sandy Lane)
STRBR DY8 .... 307 L1
nan Vw *CNCK/NC* WS11 .... 249 M5
nan Wy *CRTAM* B79 .... 273 L3
CHS WS14 .... 9 K4
MKTDR TF9 .... 148 A8
nany Wy *STRBR* DY8 .... 307 J7
ner Side *BUCK/MIL* ST2 .... 86 C2
nford Meadow
CCH ST21 .... 152 D4
nford Pl *LNGTN* ST3 .... 103 H3
nford Rd *STAFN* ST16 .... 174 E4
nilly Cl *LICHS* WS14 .... 9 L4
STRBR DY8 .... 307 L4
nney *TAM/AM/WIL* B77 .... 290 F2
nney Av *NEWUL* ST5 .... 67 L4
nney Dr *STAFN* ST16 .... 174 B6
nsey Gv *WOLVN* WV10 .... 264 C7
nsey Rd *WOLVN* WV10 .... 264 C7
nsey Wy *BLOX/PEL* WS3 .... 266 F7
nsley La *BDGNE* WV15 .... 304 A7
nsley La *BDGNE* WV15 .... 304 A7
EWD DY12 .... 308 B2
nald St *LNGTN* ST3 .... 86 C8
nson Av *STOKE* ST4 .... 84 E6
ker Av *BKHL/PFLD* WV2 .... 295 L4
ker Crs *BKHL/PFLD* WV2 .... 295 M4
kery Av *LNGTN* ST3 .... 102 A1
kery Cl
UTN/AL/TUT DE13 .... 201 G8
UGE WS15 .... 217 H5
kery Crs *BLYBR/FOR* ST11 .... 104 C8
ker La *BKHL/PFLD* WV2 .... 295 G4
OL/KGSB/FAZ B78 .... 272 C8
TOKE ST4 .... 84 F7
kery Ri *WMBN* WV5 .... 298 B4
kery Rd *ALS/KID* ST7 .... 39 J7
TONE ST15 .... 136 B3
/MBN WV5 .... 298 B4
kery St *WNSFLD* WV11 .... 281 J5
e Rookery *NEWUL* ST5 .... 83 J1
kwood Copse
TAFS ST17 .... 194 C4
kwood Dr
UNHL/THL/PER WV6 .... 293 M1
er Wy *SEDG* DY3 .... 299 M4
e St *STOKE* ST4 .... 84 D1
e Ropewalk *BUT* DE14 .... 6 E9
salind *WNSFLD* WV11 .... 282 A5
seacre *NEWUL* ST5 .... 83 M3
seacre Gv *LNGTN* ST3 .... 102 F4
seacre La *LNGTN* ST3 .... 103 M4
se Av *BUTN/AL/TUT* DE13 .... 167 G8
se Bank Cresent *CDLE* ST10 ...... 91 H4
se Bank Dr *BLOX/PEL* WS3 ...... 283 L6
se Bank St *LEEK* ST13 .... 43 M4
se Bay Meadow
NCK/NC WS11 .... 232 C8
seberry Dr
UD/MAD/W CW3 .... 81 L3
sebery Cl *BIDD* ST8 .... 40 E2
sebery Rd *TAM/AM/WIL* B77 ... 290 C6
sebery St *BDMR/CCFT* WV3 ... 12 C7
URS/TUN ST6 .... 53 M5
sebury Gv *WMBN* WV5 .... 297 L4
se Cottage Gdns *BUT* DE14 .... 6 F9
se Dr *BRWNH* WS8 .... 268 C5
sehill *HEDN* WS12 .... 231 M2
se Hl *STAFN* ST16 .... 4 A6
seland Crs *BUCK/MIL* ST2 .... 70 B1
se La *BNTWD* WS7 .... 252 C3
seleigh Crs *SWAD* DE11 .... 205 M4
semary Av
TTPK/GDPK/PENN WV4 .... 295 J4
GTWY WS6 .... 249 K7
TAFS ST17 .... 193 M5
semary Cl *BRWNH* WS8 .... 268 D4
semary Cl *DUDN* DY1 .... 299 M4
semary Crs
TTPK/GDPK/PENN WV4 .... 295 J5
semary Crs West
TTPK/GDPK/PENN WV4 .... 295 H5
semary Dr *FOAKS/STRLY* B74 .. 286 C7
HEDN WS12 .... 231 K5
UTXR ST14 .... 144 B4
semary Hill Rd
FOAKS/STRLY B74 .... 286 C8
semary La *STRBR* DY8 .... 307 K7
semary Nook
FOAKS/STRLY B74 .... 286 D5
semary Pl *HAN* ST1 .... 69 L3
semary Rd *CNCK/NC* WS11 ..... 249 K6
TAM/AM/WIL B77 .... 11 K5
se Ml *MKTDR* TF9 .... 114 E5
semount Rd
STPNHL/WNHL DE15 .... 7 M6
sendale Av *NEWUL* ST5 .... 67 M4
se St *HAN* ST1 .... 3 G3
se Tree Av *STOKE* ST4 .... 84 E8
se Tree La
STPNHL/WNHL DE15 .... 205 M3
sevale Ct *NEWUL* ST5 .... 67 L2
sevale Rd *NEWUL* ST5 .... 67 L2
sevale St *BUCK/MIL* ST2 .... 70 B1
seville Dr *CONG* CW12 .... 26 B2
seville Gdns *CDSL* WV8 .... 262 F6
se Wy *RUGE* WS15 .... 197 J8
sewood Av *END/WER* ST9 .... 55 J6
sewood Cl *TAM/AM/WIL* B77 ... 11 H6
sewood Ct *TAM/AM/WIL* B77 ... 11 H6
sewood Dr *SHHTH* WV12 .... 282 B2
sewood Gdns *WNSFLD* WV11 ... 266 B7
sewood Pk *GTWY* WS6 .... 249 K8
sewood Rd
STPNHL/WNHL DE15 .... 204 L4
sliston Rd *MSHM* DE12 .... 222 A2
STPNHL/WNHL DE15 .... 204 D7

Rosliston Rd South
STPNHL/WNHL DE15 .... 204 E6
Rossall Av *NEWUL* ST5 .... 83 M6
Ross Cl *DUNHL/THL/PER* WV6 .. 279 L8
Ross Dr *KGSWFD* DY6 .... 303 J3
Rossett Gv *ALS/KID* ST7 .... 53 M2
Ross Rd *BLOX/PEL* WS3 .... 283 M4
CDLE ST10 .... 74 C8
Rosvean Cl *HAN* ST1 .... 2 C3
Rosy Bank *BUCK/MIL* ST2 .... 55 J7
Rosy Cross *CRTAM* B79 .... 10 D3
Rothay *TAM/AM/WIL* B77 .... 290 F2
Rothbury Gn *HEDN* WS12 .... 232 E8
Rother Wk *BURS/TUN* ST6 .... 54 A6
Rotherwood Dr *STAFS* ST17 .... 4 B8
Rothesay Av *NEWUL* ST5 .... 83 M3
Rothesay Dr *STRBR* DY8 .... 303 J7
Rothesay Rd *LNGTN* ST3 .... 86 C8
Rothesay Wy *SHHTH* WV12 ...... 282 B4
Rothley Gn *LNGTN* ST3 .... 101 M2
Rothley Gn *LNGTN* ST3 .... 101 M2
Rothsay Av *HAN* ST1 .... 69 K2
Rothwell St *STOKE* ST4 .... 84 F4
Rotten Rw *LICHS* WS13 .... 9 G3
Rotterdam Rd *NEWUL* ST5 .... 83 M1
Rotterdam Rd *NEWUL* ST5 .... 83 M1
Rough Bank *CONG* CW12 .... 26 E2
Roughcote La *LNGTN* ST3 .... 87 J4
Rough Hills Rd *BKHL/PFLD* WV2 . 295 M4
Roughley Dr *MGN/WHC* B75 ...... 287 J8
Roughlow La *ASHB* DE6 .... 109 K1
Roughwood La *SBCH* CW11 .... 37 C1
Round Cft *WLNHL* WV13 .... 282 A8
Round Hl *SEDG* DY3 .... 299 K8
Roundhill Wy *BRWNH* WS8 .... 252 A8
Round House Rd *SEDG* DY3 .... 299 L6
Roundlea Cl *SHHTH* WV12 .... 282 B3
Roundway *LNGTN* ST3 .... 85 K3
Roundway Down
DUNHL/THL/PER WV6 .... 278 E7
Roundwell St *BURS/TUN* ST6 ..... 53 K7
Rouse Cl *STAFN* ST16 .... 4 A6
Rowallan Rd *MGN/WHC* B75 ...... 287 K8
Rowanburn Cl *LNGTN* ST3 .... 86 D5
Rowan Cl *ALS/KID* ST7 .... 37 K7
ALS/KID ST7 .... 53 G2
BIDD ST8 .... 41 J7
LICH WS13 .... 9 K2
STONE ST15 .... 138 A4
Rowan Ct *BDMR/CCFT* WV3 .... 294 E3
Rowan Dr *RUGE* WS15 .... 217 J2
WNSFLD WV11 .... 266 B7
Rowan Gld *STAFS* ST17 .... 194 C4
Rowan Gv *BNTWD* WS7 .... 251 M4
LNGTN ST3 .... 85 K7
PENK ST19 .... 246 D4
Rowan La *MKTDR* TF9 .... 114 F5
Rowan Ri *KGSWFD* DY6 .... 303 L4
Rowan Rd *CNCK/NC* WS11 .... 231 J8
MKTDR TF9 .... 112 D8
SEDG DY3 .... 299 L1
Rowan Tree Cl *ASHB* DE6 .... 95 J2
Rowbury Dr
STPNHL/WNHL DE15 .... 186 B8
Rowena Gdns *SEDG* DY3 .... 295 J8
Rowhurst Cl *NEWUL* ST5 .... 67 J3
Rowhurst Pl *BURS/TUN* ST6 ..... 54 C5
Rowland Gdns *WSLW* WS2 .... 283 J7
Rowlands Av *WOLV* WV1 .... 281 H8
WSLW WS2 .... 282 E7
Rowlands Cl *WSLW* WS2 .... 282 E6
Rowland St *LNGTN* ST3 .... 102 B1
WSLW WS2 .... 283 J7
Rowley Av *NEWUL* ST5 .... 67 M3
STAFS ST17 .... 193 L2
Rowley Bank *STAFS* ST17 .... 193 L2
Rowley Bank Gdns *STAFS* ST17 . 193 L2
Rowley Cl *HEDN* WS12 .... 232 A2
RUGE WS15 .... 216 A4
Rowley Gv *STAFS* ST17 .... 193 L2
Rowley Hall Cl *STAFS* ST17 .... 4 C9
Rowley Hall Dr *STAFS* ST17 .... 193 K2
Rowleyhill Dr *PENK* ST19 .... 228 F6
Rowley Pl *RUSH/SHEL* WS4 ...... 284 B3
Rowley St *STAFN* ST16 .... 4 D1
WSL WS1 .... 284 A8
Rownall Pl *LNGTN* ST3 .... 87 G8
Rownall Rd *END/WER* ST9 .... 71 L4
LNGTN ST3 .... 87 G8
Rownall Vw *LEEK* ST13 .... 43 J6
Rowney Cl *MKTDR* TF9 .... 114 D6
Rowton Av
DUNHL/THL/PER WV6 .... 278 E7
Rowton St *BUTN/AL/TUT* DE13 . 185 J2
Roxall Cl *KIDD* DY10 .... 311 J8
Roxburghe Av *LNGTN* ST3 .... 86 D8
Roxby Gdns
DUNHL/THL/PER WV6 .... 280 A5
Royal Oak Dr *PENK* ST19 .... 244 F2
Royal St *STOKE* ST4 .... 86 A5
Royce Av *BIDD* ST8 .... 40 B5
Roycroft Cl *NEWUL* ST5 .... 68 B2
Royden Av *HAN* ST1 .... 3 J6
Royds Cl *RSTAF* ST18 .... 191 L4
Roylance St *BURS/TUN* ST6 .... 53 K6
Royville Pl *BURS/TUN* ST6 .... 69 K2
Rubens Cl *SEDG* DY3 .... 299 K5
Rubens Wy *LNGTN* ST3 .... 103 H4
Rubian St *STOKE* ST4 .... 85 M4
Rudge Av *WOLV* WV1 .... 281 H7
Rudge Cl *BUCK/MIL* ST2 .... 70 B1
Rudge Dale Rd *MKTDR* TF9 ...... 115 C6
Rudge Rd
DUNHL/THL/PER WV6 .... 292 A2
Rudyard Cl *WOLVN* WV10 .... 264 C6
Rudyard Gv *NEWUL* ST5 .... 68 C6
Rudyard Rd *BIDD* ST8 .... 41 H1
Rudyard Wy *CDLE* ST10 .... 89 M6
Ruffin Ct *STONE* ST15 .... 138 C3
Rufford Cl *CRTAM* B79 .... 273 L4
Rufford Wy *ALDR* WS9 .... 284 C3
Rugby Cl *BUT* DE14 .... 204 C2
NEWUL ST5 .... 83 M5

Rugby Dr *LNGTN* ST3 .... 102 B1
Rugby Rd *STRBR* DY8 .... 307 K3
Rugby St *WOLV* WV1 .... 12 C1
Rugeley Av *STRBR* DY8 .... 282 D2
Rugeley Rd *BNTWD* WS7 .... 251 M2
BUTN/AL/TUT DE13 .... 218 A4
HEDN WS12 .... 232 C4
RUGE WS15 .... 216 B4
Ruiton St *SEDG* DY3 .... 299 K6
Rumer Hill Rd *CNCK/NC* WS11 .. 249 L3
Running Hills *RUGE* WS15 .... 216 F6
Runnymede *STONE* ST15 .... 138 A4
Runnymede Cl *BUCK/MIL* ST2 ... 70 B7
Rupert St *BDMR/CCFT* WV3 ...... 12 C2
BIDD ST8 .... 40 C2
Rushall Cl *RUSH/SHEL* WS4 ..... 284 B6
Rushall Cl *RUSH/SHEL* WS4 ..... 284 B6
STRBR DY8 .... 307 L2
Rushall Manor Cl
RUSH/SHEL WS4 .... 284 B6
Rushall Manor Rd
RUSH/SHEL WS4 .... 284 B6
Rushall Rd *WOLVN* WV10 .... 264 E8
Rushbrook Cl *BRWNH* WS8 ...... 268 E4
Rushcliffe Dr *LNGTN* ST3 .... 103 H3
Rushes Ml *BLOX/PEL* WS3 .... 267 L7
Rushey La *ALBTN* WV7 .... 276 D2
Rushford Av *WOLVN* WV5 .... 298 A4
Rush La *MKTDR* TF9 .... 112 A8
TAM/AM/WIL B77 .... 290 D7
Rushmoor Gv
BLYBR/FOR ST11 .... 103 H3
Rushton Av *CDLE* ST10 .... 73 K8
Rushton Cl
BUTN/AL/TUT DE13 .... 165 J4
Rushton Gv *BURS/TUN* ST6 .... 69 G3
Rushton Rd *BURS/TUN* ST6 .... 69 G4
Rushtons La *STONE* ST15 .... 120 F4
Rushton Wy
BLYBR/FOR ST11 .... 104 A2
Rushwater Cl *WMBN* WV5 .... 297 L4
Rushwood Cl *RUSH/SHEL* WS4 . 284 A7
Ruskin Av
ETTPK/GDPK/PENN WV4 .... 295 M8
SEDG DY3 .... 299 G5
Ruskin Cl *LNGTN* ST3 .... 86 D5
Ruskin Cl *RSTAF* ST18 .... 173 L8
Ruskin Pl *BUT* DE14 .... 185 K4
Ruskin Rd *WOLVN* WV10 .... 280 F2
Rusper Cl *HAN* ST1 .... 69 M4
Russell Av *ALS/KID* ST7 .... 37 J5
Russell Bank Rd
FOAKS/STRLY B74 .... 286 E6
Russell Cl *WNSFLD* WV11 .... 281 M1
Russell Gv *END/WER* ST9 .... 71 H6
Russell Pl *BURS/TUN* ST6 .... 53 L4
Russell Rd *BURS/TUN* ST6 .... 53 K4
Russell St *BDMR/CCFT* WV3 ...... 12 D7
BUT DE14 .... 6 F7
LEEK ST13 .... 43 L5
LNGTN ST3 .... 102 B1
NEWUL ST5 .... 68 C5
WLNHL WV13 .... 282 B8
Russel St *STAFN* ST16 .... 4 C5
Russet Cl *LNGTN* ST3 .... 103 G2
RDERBYSW DE65 .... 165 J1
Russett Cl *BNTWD* WS7 .... 252 A4
The Russetts *STAFS* ST17 .... 193 M4
Rustington Av *LNGTN* ST3 .... 86 E7
Ruston Av *BURS/TUN* ST6 .... 54 B4
Rutherford Av *NEWUL* ST5 .... 84 B7
Rutherford Rd *WSLW* WS2 .... 283 G4
Rutherglen Cl *RUGE* WS15 .... 215 J1
Ruthin Rd *BUCK/MIL* ST2 .... 70 D8
Rutland Av
ETTPK/GDPK/PENN WV4 .... 294 D6
RUGE WS15 .... 215 K4
Rutland Cl *STPNHL/WNHL* DE15 . 204 D4
Rutland Crs *ALDR* WS9 .... 285 H1
Rutland Dr *POL/KGSB/FAZ* B78 . 290 A1
Rutland Pl *NEWUL* ST5 .... 84 C6
STRBR DY8 .... 307 K2
Rutland Rd *ALS/KID* ST7 .... 39 G8
HEDN WS12 .... 250 E1
LNGTN ST3 .... 86 B6
Rutland St *BLOX/PEL* WS3 .... 283 L5
HAN ST1 .... 2 A3
Ruxley Rd *BUCK/MIL* ST2 .... 3 L6
Ryan Av *WNSFLD* WV11 .... 282 A3
Rydal *TAM/AM/WIL* B77 .... 291 G3
Rydal Cl *FOAKS/STRLY* B74 ..... 285 M8
HEDN WS12 .... 232 A2
WNSFLD WV11 .... 281 J3
Rydal Dr *DUNHL/THL/PER* WV6 . 278 F6
Rydal Wy *ALS/KID* ST7 .... 37 J5
NEWUL ST5 .... 84 B6
Ryder Cl *SWAD* DE11 .... 205 K8
Ryder Rd *LNGTN* ST3 .... 103 C2
Ryders Hayes La
BLOX/PEL WS3 .... 268 A6
Ryder St *STRBR* DY8 .... 303 K8
Rye Bank *NEWUL* ST5 .... 84 B1
Rye Bank Crs *NEWUL* ST5 .... 84 B1
Ryebrook Gv *BURS/TUN* ST6 ..... 55 M3
Rye Cl *ALS/KID* ST7 .... 37 H7
Rye Cft *STAFN* ST16 .... 174 A5
Ryecroft *NEWUL* ST5 .... 84 B1
Ryecroft Av
ETTPK/GDPK/PENN WV4 .... 295 H5
Ryecroft Cl *CDLE* ST10 .... 105 M7
SEDG DY3 .... 299 J2
Ryecroft Pk *WSLW* WS2 .... 283 L7
Ryecroft Pl *BLOX/PEL* WS3 ...... 283 M4
Ryecroft Rd *BURS/TUN* ST6 .... 54 E7
Ryecroft St *WSLW* WS2 .... 283 L7
Ryefield *CDSL* WV8 .... 279 L1
Rye Flatts La *RDERBYSW* DE65 . 165 K1
Ryehills *ALS/KID* ST7 .... 66 E1
Ryknild Cl *FOAKS/STRLY* B74 ... 286 F4
Ryknild St *LICHS* WS14 .... 9 L7
Rylands Dr
ETTPK/GDPK/PENN WV4 .... 295 G6
Ryle St *BLOX/PEL* WS3 .... 267 K8
Ryton *TAM/AM/WIL* B77 .... 290 D5
Ryton Cl *WNSFLD* WV11 .... 281 G5

S

Sabine St *STAFS* ST17 .... 5 G9
Sabrina Rd
DUNHL/THL/PER WV6 .... 293 L1
Sackville St *STAFS* ST17 .... 68 D8
Saddler Av *STONE* ST15 .... 138 C3
The Saddlestones
DUNHL/THL/PER WV6 .... 278 D6
Saddleworth Cl *GTWY* WS6 ...... 267 G6
Sadler Br *BRWNH* WS8 .... 269 G2
Saffron Cl
BUTN/AL/TUT DE13 .... 220 C1
LNGTN ST3 .... 103 G4
Saffron Gdns
ETTPK/GDPK/PENN WV4 .... 295 G6
Sage Cl *HAN* ST1 .... 2 D8
St Aidan's Cl
BUTN/AL/TUT DE13 .... 185 J2
St Aidan's Rd *CNCK/NC* WS11 .. 231 L5
St Aidan's St *BURS/TUN* ST6 ...... 53 K6
St Albans Cl *WNSFLD* WV11 ..... 282 A2
St Albans Ct
BUTN/AL/TUT DE13 .... 185 J3
St Albans Rd *STAFN* ST16 .... 174 F3
St Andrew Cl *HEDN* WS12 .... 233 G5
St Andrews *TAM/AM/WIL* B77 .. 275 H6
St Andrews Av *BLOX/PEL* WS3 . 268 A5
St Andrew's Cl *CRTAM* B79 ...... 240 F8
SEDG DY3 .... 299 C7
STRBR DY8 .... 307 M8
St Andrews Crs *BURS/TUN* ST6 . 69 K3
St Andrews Dr *ALS/KID* ST7 .... 39 J7
BUTN/AL/TUT DE13 .... 185 H2
DUNHL/THL/PER WV6 .... 278 D5
NEWUL ST5 .... 83 M2
St Andrews Gdns *ALS/KID* ST7 ... 37 L8
St Andrews Rd *STAFS* ST17 ...... 193 L3
St Andrew's Sq *STOKE* ST4 .... 85 G3
St Anne's Cl *BNTWD* WS7 .... 251 L6
St Annes Rd *LICH* WS13 .... 236 B7
WLNHL WV13 .... 282 B7
WOLVN WV10 .... 280 B1
St Anne's V *BURS/TUN* ST6 .... 55 H2
St Ann St *HAN* ST1 .... 2 F5
St Anthonys Cl *RUGE* WS15 ..... 215 M2
St Anthonys Dr *BLOX/PEL* WS3 . 268 B5
St Augustine's Rd
RUGE WS15 .... 215 L4
St Austell Cl *CRTAM* B79 .... 10 B2
STAFS ST17 .... 194 D2
St Barbara's Rd *RUGE* WS15 .... 217 J3
St Bartholomews Cl
BURS/TUN ST6 .... 54 E6
St Benedict's Dr *RSTAF* ST18 .... 196 D2
St Benedict's Rd *BNTWD* WS7 .. 252 B4
St Bernard Pl *BUCK/MIL* ST2 ...... 3 M3
St Bernards Cl *HEDN* WS12 ...... 233 J6
St Bernard's Rd *NEWUL* ST5 ..... 67 M8
St Blaise Rd *MGN/WHC* B75 .... 287 K7
St Brides Cl *SEDG* DY3 .... 299 J2
WMBN WV5 .... 297 M4
St Catherine's Crs
ETTPK/GDPK/PENN WV4 .... 294 F6
St Catherines Rd *LICH* WS13 .... 236 B7
SWAD DE11 .... 205 M5
St Chad's Cl
BUTN/AL/TUT DE13 .... 185 J2
CNCK/NC WS11 .... 232 A6
DUNHL/THL/PER WV6 .... 277 J8
PENK ST19 .... 246 C4
RSTAF ST18 .... 196 D3
SEDG DY3 .... 299 H7
STONE ST15 .... 138 C3
UTXR ST14 .... 108 D4
St Chad's Pl *STAFN* ST16 .... 4 F5
St Chads Rd *BURS/TUN* ST6 ...... 53 L7
BUTN/AL/TUT DE13 .... 185 J3
ECCH ST21 .... 152 D4
LICH WS13 .... 8 F1
WOLVN WV10 .... 280 F2
St Christopher Av *STOKE* ST4 .... 84 E3
St Christopher Cl
HEDN WS12 .... 233 G5
St Christopher's Dr
TAM/AM/WIL B77 .... 290 C1
St Clair St *LNGTN* ST3 .... 86 C8
St Clement's Av *BLOX/PEL* WS3 . 283 J3
St Cuthberth's Crs *ALBTN* WV7 . 260 E4
St David Cl *HEDN* WS12 .... 233 G4
St Davids Cl *BLOX/PEL* WS3 .... 268 B5
St David's Dr
BUTN/AL/TUT DE13 .... 185 J2
St Davids Pl *BLOX/PEL* WS3 .... 267 K8
St Davids Rd *CRTAM* B79 .... 240 F8
STAFS ST17 .... 193 K3
St Editha's Cl *CRTAM* B79 .... 10 C4
St Edmund's Av *NEWUL* ST5 ...... 68 D3
St Edmund's Cl
DUNHL/THL/PER WV6 .... 279 M7
St Edwards Ct *SWAD* DE11 ...... 205 L5
St Edwards Gn *RUGE* WS15 ..... 215 L3
St Edward's Rd *LEEK* ST13 .... 57 J6
St Edward St *LEEK* ST13 .... 43 L4
St Francis Cl *BLOX/PEL* WS3 .... 268 B5
BUTN/AL/TUT DE13 .... 185 K2
HEDN WS12 .... 233 G5
St George Dr *HEDN* WS12 .... 233 G5
St Georges Av *BURS/TUN* ST6 .... 54 A6
END/WER ST9 .... 55 L4
St George's Av North
NEWUL ST5 .... 68 B5
St George's Av South
NEWUL ST5 .... 68 B5
St George's Av West *NEWUL* ST5 . 68 B5
St Georges Cl
FOAKS/STRLY B74 .... 286 E5
St George's Cs *STOKE* ST4 .... 101 G1
St George's Rd
BUTN/AL/TUT DE13 .... 184 F5
NEWUL ST5 .... 84 A2
STAFS ST17 .... 5 J7
STONE ST15 .... 138 D2
STRBR DY8 .... 307 K8

St George's Wy
TAM/AM/WIL B77 .... 11 K6
St Giles Crs *WOLV* WV1 .... 281 G8
St Giles Gv *RSTAF* ST18 .... 191 M4
St Giles Rd *BNTWD* WS7 .... 252 B4
NEWUL ST5 .... 67 M8
WOLV WV1 .... 281 G8
St Gregory's Rd *LNGTN* ST3 ...... 86 A7
St Helens Rd *LICH* WS13 .... 236 B7
St Helier Cl *NEWUL* ST5 .... 83 M7
St Hilda's Av *LEEK* ST13 .... 57 J6
St Ives Cl *CRTAM* B79 .... 10 C1
STAFS ST17 .... 194 D2
St James Cl *BLOX/PEL* WS3 .... 268 B5
RUGE WS15 .... 235 G1
St James Crs *STAFS* ST17 .... 212 B2
St James Pl *STOKE* ST4 .... 101 G1
St James'
BUTN/AL/TUT DE13 .... 220 D1
CNCK/NC WS11 .... 249 J2
CNCK/NC WS11 .... 251 H5
MGN/WHC B75 .... 287 J8
St James St *HAN* ST1 .... 2 B7
SEDG DY3 .... 299 K7
WOLV WV1 .... 13 J6
Saint James Wk *BRWNH* WS8 .. 268 F3
St John Cl *MGN/WHC* B75 .... 287 K6
St John's Av *NEWUL* ST5 .... 68 C6
STOKE ST15 .... 120 C7
St John's Cl *ALDR* WS9 .... 268 F7
CNCK/NC WS11 .... 249 K2
LICH WS13 .... 8 E6
RSTAF ST18 .... 158 C7
RUGE WS15 .... 215 J2
SEDG DY3 .... 297 K8
St John's Ct *HEDN* WS12 .... 250 E1
St John's Dr *LICHS* WS14 .... 270 F5
SWAD DE11 .... 205 L5
St John's Hl *LICHS* WS14 .... 270 F5
St Johns Pl *BIDD* ST8 .... 40 D3
NEWUL ST5 .... 67 M8
St John's Rd *BIDD* ST8 .... 40 C4
BLOX/PEL WS3 .... 268 B5
BRWNH WS8 .... 269 G5
BUTN/AL/TUT DE13 .... 185 J2
CNCK/NC WS11 .... 249 K2
MKTDR TF9 .... 115 J5
STAFS ST17 .... 193 J5
WNSFLD WV11 .... 266 A7
St John's Sq *BKHL/PFLD* WV2 ... 12 F7
BURS/TUN ST6 .... 68 F2
UTXR ST14 .... 143 M1
St John's St *ASHB* DE6 .... 79 J8
St John St *CRTAM* B79 .... 10 C4
HAN ST1 .... 2 E3
LICH WS13 .... 8 E4
St Johns Wy *MKTDR* TF9 .... 115 J5
St John's Wd *ALS/KID* ST7 .... 52 F1
St Josephs Cl *BLOX/PEL* WS3 .. 268 A6
St Joseph St *BURS/TUN* ST6 ...... 53 K5
St Jude's Rd
DUNHL/THL/PER WV6 .... 279 M7
St Jude's Rd West
DUNHL/THL/PER WV6 .... 279 M7
St Jude's Wy
BUTN/AL/TUT DE13 .... 185 J2
St Lawrence Dr *CNCK/NC* WS11 . 232 B8
St Lawrence Vw *BUX* SK17 .... 33 G8
St Leonard's Av *CDLE* ST10 .... 74 A2
STAFS ST17 .... 5 J8
St Leonards Vw
POL/KGSB/FAZ B78 .... 291 M2
St Leonard's Wy
AUD/MAD/W CW3 .... 80 C8
St Lucy's Dr *NEWUL* ST5 .... 68 C3
St Luke's Cl *CNCK/NC* WS11 .... 249 J2
NEWUL ST5 .... 67 H8
STONE ST15 .... 154 A2
St Luke's Rd *BNTWD* WS7 .... 252 C4
BUTN/AL/TUT DE13 .... 185 J2
BUTN/AL/TUT DE13 .... 220 D1
St Luke St *HAN* ST1 .... 2 F6
St Margarets
BUTN/AL/TUT DE13 .... 184 F5
FOAKS/STRLY B74 .... 286 C7
St Margarets Ct
AUD/MAD/W CW3 .... 65 G4
St Margaret's Dr *HAN* ST1 .... 69 L2
St Margarets Gv *LNGTN* ST3 ...... 85 L7
St Margarets Rd
BLOX/PEL WS3 .... 268 A6
LICH WS13 .... 236 B7
St Mark's Cl *HAN* ST1 .... 2 B8
St Mark's Rd *BDMR/CCFT* WV3 . 12 B6
BLOX/PEL WS3 .... 268 A6
BNTWD WS7 .... 252 C4
BRWNH WS8 .... 269 G5
BUTN/AL/TUT DE13 .... 185 J2
St Mark's St *BDMR/CCFT* WV3 . 12 D6
HAN ST1 .... 2 B8
St Martin's Cl
BKHL/PFLD WV2 .... 295 L4
BUTN/AL/TUT DE13 .... 185 J2
St Martin's La *LNGTN* ST3 .... 86 C6
St Martin's Pl *STAFN* ST16 .... 4 E2
St Martin's Rd *ALS/KID* ST7 .... 52 E5
NEWUL ST5 .... 83 M2
St Mary's Cl *ALBTN* WV7 .... 260 C1
ALS/KID ST7 .... 37 J5
BILS/COS WV14 .... 299 J2
RSTAF ST18 .... 210 C1
Saint Mary's Cl
STPNHL/WNHL DE15 .... 186 E2
St Marys Cl *WOLVN* WV10 .... 248 C8
St Mary's Crs *UTXR* ST14 .... 144 B1
St Mary's Dr
BUTN/AL/TUT DE13 .... 166 F8
NEWUL ST5 .... 84 A2
St Marys Gv *CRTAM* B79 .... 259 K7
St Mary's Pl *STAFN* ST16 .... 4 E5
St Mary's Rd *LICH* WS13 .... 236 B7
LNGTN ST3 .... 86 D5
MKTDR TF9 .... 114 D5
NEWUL ST5 .... 68 D4
RSTAF ST18 .... 196 D2
St Mary's St *MKTDR* TF9 .... 130 C1
St Mary's Wy *ALDR* WS9 .... 285 G5
TAM/AM/WIL B77 .... 11 K5

St Matthew Cl HEDN WS12 233 G5
St Matthew's Av BNTWD WS7 252 F3
St Matthews Cl
BLOX/PEL WS3 268 B5 4
St Matthews Dr RSTAF ST18 173 L8 2
St Matthew's Rd BNTWD WS7 252 F2
St Matthew's St BUT DE14 204 C2
St Matthew St STOKE ST4 85 M4
WOLV WV1 13 M6
St Mawes Cl STAFS ST17 194 D1
St Mawes Rd
DUNHL/THL/PER WV6 278 F7
St Michael Rd LICH WS13 9 H2
St Michael's Cl BLOX/PEL WS3 267 M8
PENK ST19 229 L2
STAFS ST17 194 E2
STONE ST15 138 B2 2
St Michael's Ct
DUNHL/THL/PER WV6 279 L5
St Michaels Dr HEDN WS12 233 G5
RUGE WS15 216 A5 2
St Michaels Mt STONE ST15 138 C4
St Michael's Rd BURS/TUN ST6 53 M5
BUTN/AL/TUT DE13 185 K2
NEWUL ST5 68 B7
PENK ST19 229 L2
RUGE WS15 216 A5
SEDG DY3 298 F5
UTXR ST14 125 M6
St Michael's Sq PENK ST19 229 L1 1
St Modwena Wy PENK ST19 229 M3
St Modwen's Cl
BUTN/AL/TUT DE13 185 J3 3
St Nicholas Av BURS/TUN ST6 54 E6
St Nicholas Cl BLOX/PEL WS3 268 A6 3
St Nicholas Wy RUGE WS15 179 M4
St Oswald Crs ASHB DE6 95 J1
St Patrick Cl HEDN WS12 233 G5
St Patrick's Dr NEWUL ST5 83 M2
St Patricks Rd
BUTN/AL/TUT DE13 185 J2
St Patrick's St STAFN ST16 4 D2
St Paul's Cl CNCK/NC WS11 250 B1
COVEN WV9 247 J8 2
WSL WS1 283 L8
St Paul's Ct LNGTN ST3 85 M8
TAM/AM/WIL B77 290 C6 2
St Pauls Crs BLOX/PEL WS3 268 B5
St Paul's Rd BNTWD WS7 252 C4
HEDN WS12 232 E7
NEWUL ST5 84 A1
RUGE WS15 215 M2 4
St Paul's Sq BUT DE14 6 D4
St Paul's St WSL WS1 283 L8
St Paul's St West BUT DE14 6 C3
St Paul St BURS/TUN ST6 68 E2
St Peter's Br BUT DE14 7 H9
St Peter's Cl ALDR WS9 269 L6
TAM/AM/WIL B77 290 C1
St Peters Ct BLOX/PEL WS3 283 H1
GNOS ST20 170 A6
STPNHL/WNHL DE15 7 L9
St Peters Dr BLOX/PEL WS3 268 A6
St Peter's Gdns STAFS ST17 193 M4
St Peter's Rd BNTWD WS7 252 C4
HEDN WS12 232 D6
St Peter's St STPNHL/WNHL DE15 7 L9
St Peters Ter WSLW WS2 283 L6 6
St Philips Av BDMR/CCFT WV3 295 G3
St Philip's Gv BDMR/CCFT WV3 294 F3
St Saviour's Cl
BKHL/PFLD WV2 295 M4 3
St Saviour's St ALS/KID ST7 52 D1
St Stephen's Av
WLNHL WV13 281 M8 1
St Stephens Ct
BUTN/AL/TUT DE13 185 J3 4
St Stephen's Rd BNTWD WS7 252 B4
St Thomas' Cl ALDR WS9 285 H1
BLOX/PEL WS3 283 L4
St Thomas Dr HEDN WS12 233 G5
St Thomas La RSTAF ST18 175 K7
St Thomas Pl STOKE ST4 84 F4
St Thomas's Rd CDLE ST10 105 K6
St Thomas St ALS/KID ST7 39 K3
STAFN ST16 5 K4
St Vincent Pl NEWUL ST5 67 L8 2
St Vincent Rd STONE ST15 137 L2
Salcombe Av STAFS ST17 194 D2
Salcombe Cl CNCK/NC WS11 249 H2
Salcombe Pl HAN ST1 69 K3 4
Sale La BUTN/AL/TUT DE13 237 H1
Salem St HAN ST1 68 F7
Sales La STPNHL/WNHL DE15 186 C7
Salisbury Av HAN ST1 85 J1
STPNHL/WNHL DE15 186 C7
Salisbury Cl AUD/MAD/W CW3 81 M3
DUDN DY1 299 M7
LICH WS13 236 C7 2
Salisbury Dr CNCK/NC WS11 250 B2
STAFN ST16 5 L2
Salisbury Hill Vw MKTDR TF9 130 B3
Salisbury Rd MKTDR TF9 130 B2
STAFN ST16 5 M2
Salisbury St BDMR/CCFT WV3 12 C7
BURS/TUN ST6 53 L7
LEEK ST13 43 L4
Salkeld Pl BURS/TUN ST6 54 B5
Sallow Gv BRWNH WS8 268 F1
Sallyfield La ASHB DE6 93 L1
Sally Ward Dr ALDR WS9 269 G6
Salmond Av STAFN ST16 5 L1
Salop Dr CNCK/NC WS11 249 M2
Salop Gv NEWUL ST5 84 C6
Salop Pl ALS/KID ST7 39 G7
Salop St BKHL/PFLD WV2 12 E6
Salt Av STAFS ST17 4 F8
Salt Banks RSTAF ST18 156 D6
Saltbrook La ASHB DE6 163 M2
Saltdean Cl LNGTN ST3 86 E8 2
Salt Dr RSTAF ST18 156 E4
Salters Cl END/WER ST9 71 H7
Saltersford La CDLE ST10 107 L2
Salters Gra RUGE WS15 179 M4
Salter's La CRTAM B79 10 C2
END/WER ST9 71 H7
Salter's Rd ALDR WS9 269 G7
Salter St STAFN ST16 4 E4
Saltheath La RSTAF ST18 156 E7
Salt La RSTAF ST18 156 D5
Salt Rd RSTAF ST18 156 E6
STAFS ST17 4 F9
Salts La POL/KGSB/FAZ B78 289 M6
Salt Works La RSTAF ST18 157 K8
Sam Barber Ct HEDN WS12 232 E8 2
Sambar Rd POL/KGSB/FAZ B78 289 M1
Sambrook Crs MKTDR TF9 112 E8
Sambrook Rd WOLVN WV10 281 G4
Sampson St HAN ST1 2 C4
Samuel Cl LICH WS13 236 C8
Samuel St ALS/KID ST7 53 M1
BLOX/PEL WS3 283 H1
Sandalwood Cl SHHTH WV12 282 B2 3
Sandalwood Dr STAFN ST16 174 F5 1
Sandalwood Gv LNGTN ST3 101 M2
Sandalwood Rd
STPNHL/WNHL DE15 204 E4
Sandbach Rd ALS/KID ST7 37 L2
BURS/TUN ST6 69 H3
SBCH CW11 37 K1
Sandbach Rd North ALS/KID ST7 37 J5
Sandbach Rd South ALS/KID ST7 37 K7
Sand Bank BLOX/PEL WS3 283 G1 1
BLOX/PEL WS3 283 H1 3
Sandbeds Rd SHHTH WV12 282 C6
Sandcrest Pl LNGTN ST3 102 E1
Sanderling Cl WOLVN WV10 265 H3
Sanderling Ri BNTWD WS7 252 B2
Sandfield Gv SEDG DY3 299 H8
Sandfield Rd STRBR DY8 303 M8
Sandford Brook
RDERBYSW DE65 166 E1 7
Sandford Cl RUGE WS15 217 G2
Sandford Ri
DUNHL/THL/PER WV6 279 L4
Sandford St LICH WS13 8 D4
LNGTN ST3 86 C5 5
NEWUL ST5 67 L2
Sandgate St LNGTN ST3 86 D7
Sandhill St BLOX/PEL WS3 283 G1 1
Sandhurst Av LNGTN ST3 102 F1
Sandhurst Cl NEWUL ST5 68 B5
Sandhurst Dr
ETTPK/GDPK/PENN WV4 295 G6
Sandhurst Gv STRBR DY8 303 L7
Sandhurst Pl LNGTN ST3 102 F2
Sandhurst Rd
FOAKS/STRLY B74 286 F5
Sandiway BUTN/AL/TUT DE13 220 E2
Sandiway Pl HAN ST1 69 L4 5
Sandland Rd SHHTH WV12 282 C2
Sand La ASHB DE6 145 H1
Sandmere Ri WOLVN WV10 280 E1 1
Sandon Av NEWUL ST5 84 A5
Sandon Cl BLYBR/FOR ST11 104 C8 1
Sandon La RSTAF ST18 140 C5
Sandon Ms STAFN ST16 174 F4
Sandon Old Rd LNGTN ST3 102 F3
Sandon Rd BLYBR/FOR ST11 104 C8
LNGTN ST3 102 F3
RSTAF ST18 175 G2
STAFN ST16 174 E5
STONE ST15 139 K1
WOLVN WV10 264 B8
Sandon St HAN ST1 69 G7
LEEK ST13 43 L6
Sandown TAM/AM/WIL B77 11 L3
Sandown Av GTWY WS6 249 K7
Sandown Cl BNTWD WS7 251 M1 2
BUT DE14 204 A3 6
CDLE ST10 89 L5
HEDN WS12 233 G4 7
Sandown Dr
DUNHL/THL/PER WV6 278 F6
Sandown Pl BUCK/MIL ST2 55 J8 3
Sandpiper TAM/AM/WIL B77 291 G5
Sandpiper Cl HEDN WS12 232 C3
Sandpiper Dr UTXR ST14 144 B4 5
Sandra Cl ALDR WS9 285 H5
BURS/TUN ST6 54 A8
Sandringham Av SHHTH WV12 282 B4
STPNHL/WNHL DE15 205 G1
Sandringham Cl BNTWD WS7 251 L1 3
MKTDR TF9 112 D8
STAFS ST17 194 C2
Sandringham Crs STOKE ST4 101 G1
Sandringham Dr ALDR WS9 285 H1
Sandringham Pl STRBR DY8 307 K1 1
Sandringham Rd
DUNHL/THL/PER WV6 277 J8
ETTPK/GDPK/PENN WV4 295 H5 1
STAFS ST17 194 C2
STRBR DY8 307 J1
WMBN WV5 297 M4
Sand Rd BUTN/AL/TUT DE13 183 H3
Sandsdown Cl BIDD ST8 40 C1
Sandside Rd ALS/KID ST7 37 H7 2
Sands La BURS/TUN ST6 41 G7
Sands Rd ALS/KID ST7 39 L4
Sandstone Cl SEDG DY3 299 K6
Sandwell Pl LNGTN ST3 102 E2
SHHTH WV12 282 D3
Sandwell Rd WOLVN WV10 280 B1
Sandwick Crs HAN ST1 3 K1
Sandwood Crs LNGTN ST3 86 C5
Sandy Bank ECCH ST21 117 J6
Sandybrook Cl ASHB DE6 79 J6 1
LEEK ST13 43 M8
Sandybrook La LEEK ST13 43 M8
Sandy Crs WNSFLD WV11 282 A2
Sandyfield Rd HAN ST1 3 H3
Sandyfields NEWUL ST5 98 C5
Sandyfields Rd SEDG DY3 299 G4
Sandyford St STAFN ST16 4 E1
Sandy Gv BRWNH WS8 268 F1
Sandy Hl END/WER ST9 71 J6
Sandy Hollow
DUNHL/THL/PER WV6 279 J8
Sandylands Crs ALS/KID ST7 37 M5
Sandy La ALBTN WV7 260 F3
BUCK/MIL ST2 55 J8
BURS/TUN ST6 55 H2
CDLE ST10 106 D1
CDSL WV8 262 F6
CNCK/NC WS11 249 G1
CRTAM B79 259 K4
DUNHL/THL/PER WV6 279 L4
ECCH ST21 117 K6
ECCH ST21 151 K3
KIDDW DY11 309 M1
LEEK ST13 56 F2
LICHS WS14 255 J6
MKTDR TF9 113 J7
MKTDR TF9 115 H3
MKTDR TF9 130 D5
MKTDR TF9 148 A5
MSHM DE12 223 G2
NEWUL ST5 68 C8
NEWUL ST5 98 C6
PENK ST19 246 C4
RSTAF ST18 157 J6
RUGE WS15 215 L3
SBCH CW11 36 A3
WOLVN WV10 280 E1
Sandy Mt WMBN WV5 298 B3
Sandy Rd BIDD ST8 26 C8
BURS/TUN ST6 53 K3
STRBR DY8 311 K1
Sandy Wy TAM/AM/WIL B77 275 G7
Sangster La BURS/TUN ST6 54 D8
Sankey Crs RUGE WS15 215 L3 3
Sankey Rd CNCK/NC WS11 231 M7
Sanstone Cl BLOX/PEL WS3 267 J7
Sanstone Rd BLOX/PEL WS3 267 H7
Sant St BURS/TUN ST6 68 E2
The Saplings NEWUL ST5 84 C7
PENK ST19 229 M1
Sappertonfield La ASHB DE6 129 J6
Sapperton La RDERBYSW DE65 147 M1
Sapphire Dr HEDN WS12 232 C7
Saracen Wy LNGTN ST3 103 G1 5
Sara Cl FOAKS/STRLY B74 287 G7
Sarah Challinor Cl
RUGE WS15 215 L2 1
Saredon Cl BLOX/PEL WS3 284 A1
Saredon Rd CNCK/NC WS11 249 H6
GTWY WS6 249 J7 1
WOLVN WV10 248 D8
Sargeant Av BURS/TUN ST6 54 A4
Sark Cl NEWUL ST5 83 L6
Sark Pl LNGTN ST3 86 D4 4
Sarver La CDLE ST10 88 C6
Sash St STAFN ST16 4 D2
Saturn Rd BURS/TUN ST6 69 J1
CNCK/NC WS11 232 A5
Saunders Cl HEDN WS12 233 G4 8
Saunders Rd NEWUL ST5 68 B6
Saverley Green Rd
BLYBR/FOR ST11 121 L2
Savey La BUTN/AL/TUT DE13 200 F8
Saw Mill Cl RUSH/SHEL WS4 283 L7
Sawpit La STAFS ST17 195 G7
Sawyer Dr BIDD ST8 40 C1
Saxifrage Dr STONE ST15 138 C4
Saxon Cl GTWY WS6 250 A8
POL/KGSB/FAZ B78 291 M1
STPNHL/WNHL DE15 204 F3
TAM/AM/WIL B77 290 F4
Saxoncourt
DUNHL/THL/PER WV6 279 J5
Saxondrive CRTAM B79 10 E5
Saxonfields
DUNHL/THL/PER WV6 279 J5 3
Saxon Mill La CRTAM B79 10 E5
Saxon Rd PENK ST19 229 M2
Saxon St STPNHL/WNHL DE15 204 F3
Saxon Wk LICH WS13 253 L4
Saxton Dr FOAKS/STRLY B74 286 F4
Sayers Rd STAFN ST16 174 C3
Scalpcliffe Cl STPNHL/WNHL DE15 7 L6
Scalpcliffe Rd
STPNHL/WNHL DE15 7 M5
Scammerton TAM/AM/WIL B77 291 H3
Scamnell La ECCH ST21 153 L3
Scampton Cl
DUNHL/THL/PER WV6 278 E5 5
Scampton Wy CRTAM B79 274 C2 3
Scarlett St NEWUL ST5 84 B2 1
Scarratt Cl BLYBR/FOR ST11 104 B2
Scarratt Dr BLYBR/FOR ST11 104 B3
Sceptre St HAN ST1 2 C7
Schofield La CRTAM B79 239 K5
Scholars Ga BNTWD WS7 252 D4
School Av BRWNH WS8 268 F2
School Bank MKTDR TF9 148 A8
School Cl ALS/KID ST7 67 G1
ASHB DE6 79 G1
BDMR/CCFT WV3 294 B3
BNTWD WS7 251 K2
CDSL WV8 263 G6
CNCK/NC WS11 251 G4
LEEK ST13 43 J6
WMBN WV5 297 J1
School Crs CNCK/NC WS11 251 G4
School Dr CDLE ST10 91 G4 1
STRBR DY8 307 M2
Schoolfields Rd LICHS WS14 271 G5
Schoolgate Cl RUSH/SHEL WS4 284 D1
School Ground La
NWPT TF10 188 A7 3
Schoolhouse La RUGE WS15 180 A4
School La ASHB DE6 95 H1
ASHB DE6 146 E6
AUD/MAD/W CW3 80 F6
BIDD ST8 27 H8
BLOX/PEL WS3 250 E8
BLOX/PEL WS3 267 M6
BLYBR/FOR ST11 87 K8
BNTWD WS7 251 K2
BUTN/AL/TUT DE13 166 B6
CDLE ST10 88 D6
COVEN WV9 247 H7
CRTAM B79 239 J6
CRTAM B79 275 M3
END/WER ST9 42 F7
LEEK ST13 44 E7
LNGTN ST3 102 A2
MKTDR TF9 97 G3
MKTDR TF9 115 H4
MKTDR TF9 130 A2
PENK ST19 228 C7
POL/KGSB/FAZ B78 272 D7
POL/KGSB/FAZ B78 273 H3
RSTAF ST18 156 E3
RSTAF ST18 177 H8
RSTAF ST18 211 J3
RUGE WS15 178 F7
RUGE WS15 197 M4
RUGE WS15 217 G2
RUGE WS15 234 A5
SHIF TF11 225 M5
STAFS ST17 193 M5
STAFS ST17 194 F4
TAM/AM/WIL B77 290 D5
WOLVN WV10 248 D8
WOLVN WV10 264 D8
School Lane Cl STAFS ST17 193 M5
School Pl STAFN ST16 4 F1
School Rd BUCK/MIL ST2 3 M2
CNCK/NC WS11 251 G4
DUNHL/THL/PER WV6 279 G7
ECCH ST21 152 D4
PENK ST19 227 J4
PENK ST19 246 C4
SEDG DY3 298 B7
UTXR ST14 143 M1
WMBN WV5 297 J1
WMBN WV5 298 B3
WNSFLD WV11 281 H4
School St BKHL/PFLD WV2 12 E7
LEEK ST13 43 L4 3
NEWUL ST5 67 M4
NEWUL ST5 84 C1
RUSH/SHEL WS4 284 D1
SEDG DY3 299 L2
STOKE ST4 84 E7 6
STRBR DY8 307 M5 6
TAM/AM/WIL B77 11 J6
WLNHL WV13 281 M8
WOLV WV1 12 E6
School Vw UTXR ST14 160 C2
School Wk BNTWD WS7 251 K2
Scimitar Cl CRTAM B79 273 L3
Scotch Orch LICH WS13 254 D1
Scot Hay Rd ALS/KID ST7 66 E6
NEWUL ST5 66 F7
Scotia Rd BURS/TUN ST6 53 L7
CNCK/NC WS11 231 K7
Scott Av
ETTPK/GDPK/PENN WV4 294 E6
Scott Cl ALS/KID ST7 37 L2 2
LICHS WS14 8 F6
Scott Lidgett Rd BURS/TUN ST6 68 D3
Scott Rd BURS/TUN ST6 53 M5
TAM/AM/WIL B77 11 K5
Scott's Rd STRBR DY8 307 M4
The Scotts SWAD DE11 223 K3
Scott St HEDN WS12 232 F7
NEWUL ST5 84 C1 5
Scragg St ALS/KID ST7 53 M2
Scrimshaw Dr BURS/TUN ST6 54 B7
Scrivener Rd STOKE ST4 84 F1
Scropton Old Rd
RDERBYSW DE65 165 J2
Scropton Rd RDERBYSW DE65 164 F1
Sculthorpe Rd KIDD DY10 311 H8
Seabridge La NEWUL ST5 83 L6
Seabridge Rd NEWUL ST5 84 A3
Seabrooke Rd RUGE WS15 216 A5
Seafield TAM/AM/WIL B77 11 M3
Seafield Cl KGSWFD DY6 303 L6 2
Seaford St STOKE ST4 85 H1
Seaforth Gv WNSFLD WV11 282 B1 3
Seagram Wy UTXR ST14 144 D3
Seagrave Pl NEWUL ST5 84 A4
Seagrave St NEWUL ST5 84 C1 6
Seal Vw MSHM DE12 223 J4
Sealwood La MSHM DE12 223 L5
Seal Wood La MSHM DE12 223 K5
Searle Av STAFN ST16 4 A5
Seaton TAM/AM/WIL B77 290 F2
Seaton Av STAFS ST17 194 E2
Seaton Cl LNGTN ST3 102 E2
WNSFLD WV11 281 M5
Seaton Pl STRBR DY8 303 J8
Sebright Gn KIDDW DY11 309 J7 1
Sebright Rd KIDDW DY11 309 J7
Sebring Av LNGTN ST3 102 E2
Seckham Rd LICH WS13 8 C2
Seckington La CRTAM B79 259 J7
Second Av ALS/KID ST7 52 E1
BRWNH WS8 269 G2
BUCK/MIL ST2 70 D6
BUT DE14 203 L1
NEWUL ST5 68 C3
STAFN ST16 174 B3
WOLVN WV10 280 E3
Sedbergh Cl NEWUL ST5 83 L6
Seddon Rd LNGTN ST3 102 F2
Sedgefield Cl DUDN DY1 299 L7 5
Sedgefield Gv
DUNHL/THL/PER WV6 278 F6 2
Sedgefield Rd BUT DE14 203 M3
Sedgemere Gv
RUSH/SHEL WS4 284 C2
Sedgemoor Av BNTWD WS7 252 B5
Sedgley Hall Av SEDG DY3 299 J2
Sedgley Rd
ETTPK/GDPK/PENN WV4 294 F8
Sedgley St BKHL/PFLD WV2 295 J3
Seedcroft La RUGE WS15 179 M6
Seedfields Rd LNGTN ST3 85 L7
Seeds La BRWNH WS8 268 F2
Seedymill La LICH WS13 235 L3
The Seesall GNOS ST20 190 E3
Sefton Av CONG CW12 26 A1
HAN ST1 69 L3
Sefton Cl STPNHL/WNHL DE15 205 H1
Sefton Rd LNGTN ST3 86 E8
TAM/AM/WIL B77 290 D6
Sefton St HAN ST1 69 G7
Seighford Rd RSTAF ST18 173 K5
Seisdon Common Rd
WMBN WV5 296 D2
Seisdon Rd WMBN WV5 293 G8
Selborne Rd LEEK ST13 43 L6
Selbourne Dr BURS/TUN ST6 53 L3
Selby Cl NEWUL ST5 84 A5
Selby St LNGTN ST3 87 H5
Selby Wk LNGTN ST3 101 L3
Selby Wy BLOX/PEL WS3 266 E8
Selker Dr TAM/AM/WIL B77 11 K3
Sellman St GNOS ST20 190 E4
Selmans Hl BLOX/PEL WS3 267 J7
Selsdon Rd BLOX/PEL WS3 266 F7
Selworthy Dr STAFS ST17 194 E4
Selworthy Rd BURS/TUN ST6 55 G5
Selwyn Cl BKHL/PFLD WV2 295 J3
BUTN/AL/TUT DE13 220 A7
Selwyn St STOKE ST4 85 H4
Selwyn Wk FOAKS/STRLY B74 2
Serin Cl UTXR ST14 144
Setterfield Wy RUGE WS15 215
Settle Gv LNGTN ST3 1
Setton Dr SEDG DY3 29
Seven Acres ALDR WS9 28
Seven Arches Wy STOKE ST4 8
Sevenoaks Gv LNGTN ST3 10
Sevens Rd HEDN WS12 23
Severn Cl BIDD ST8 4
BUTN/AL/TUT DE13 18
SHHTH WV12 28
Severn Dr BNTWD WS7 25
BUT DE14 7
DUNHL/THL/PER WV6 27
NEWUL ST5 8
Severn Rd BLOX/PEL WS3 28
BRWNH WS8 25
STRBR DY8 30
Severn St HAN ST1
Seward Cl LICHS WS14
Seymour Av
BUTN/AL/TUT DE13 185
Seymour Cl GTWY WS6 266
Seymour Gdns
FOAKS/STRLY B74 286
Seymour St HAN ST1
Shackerley La ALBTN WV7 26
Shackleton Dr
DUNHL/THL/PER WV6 27
Shackleton Rd BLOX/PEL WS3 26
Shackson Cl HAN ST1
Shadwell Dr SEDG DY3 29
Shady Gv ALS/KID ST7 3
Shaffalong La LEEK ST13 5
Shaftesbury Av BURS/TUN ST6 5
Shaftesbury Dr HEDN WS12 23
Shaftsbury Rd RUGE WS15 21
Shakespeare Av LICHS WS14
Shakespeare Cl ALS/KID ST7 5
BUCK/MIL ST2 5
CRTAM B79 1
Shakespeare Ct BIDD ST8 40
Shakespeare Crs
BLOX/PEL WS3 28
Shakespeare Gv
CNCK/NC WS11 231
Shakespeare Pl BLOX/PEL WS3 28
Shakespeare Rd BNTWD WS7 25
BUT DE14 18
SEDG DY3 29
STAFS ST17 193
Shakespeare St WOLV WV1 1
Shaldon Av END/WER ST9 5
The Shales WMBN WV5 297
Shallcross La SEDG DY3 29
Shallowford Ct HAN ST1 69
Shanklin Cl GTWY WS6 24
Shannon TAM/AM/WIL B77 29
Shannon Dr BRWNH WS8 25
BURS/TUN ST6 5
Shannon Rd STAFS ST17 19
Shardlow Cl STOKE ST4 8
STONE ST15 138
Shardlow Rd WNSFLD WV11 28
Sharesacre St WLNHL WV13 28
Sharman Cl STOKE ST4 8
Sharman Rd WOLVN WV10 28
Sharmon Wy GNOS ST20 19
Sharnbrook Dr RUGE WS15 19
Sharnbrook Gv STAFS ST17 194
Sharon Cl
ETTPK/GDPK/PENN WV4 29
Sharon Wy HEDN WS12 23
Sharpe St TAM/AM/WIL B77 27
Sharplands MKTDR TF9 11
Sharrat Fld MGN/WHC B75 28
Sharrocks St WOLV WV1 1
Sharron Dr LEEK ST13 4
Shaver's La RUGE WS15 23
Shawbury Gv
DUNHL/THL/PER WV6 27
Shawbury Rd WOLVN WV10 28
Shaw Cl LICH WS13 23
Shawcroft ASHB DE6 79
Shaw Cft SHIF TF11 22
Shaw Dr BNTWD WS7 252
Shawe Park Rd CDLE ST10 8
Shaw Gdns STAFS ST17 19
Shaw Hall La COVEN WV9 26
Shaw La ALBTN WV7 26
ASHB DE6 12
BUTN/AL/TUT DE13 21
DUNHL/THL/PER WV6 27
LICH WS13
RUGE WS15 23
SHIF TF11 24
Shawman's La RSTAF ST18 19
Shawms Crest STAFS ST17 194
Shaw Pl LEEK ST13 4
Shawport Av NEWUL ST5 6
Shaw Rd BKHL/PFLD WV2 29
WOLVN WV10 280
Shaws' La ECCH ST21 15
GTWY WS6 25
Shaw St BIDD ST8 4
HAN ST1 6
NEWUL ST5 8
WSLW WS2 283
Shaw-wall La LEEK ST13 7
Shay La CDLE ST10 7
NWPT TF10 18
Shayler Gv BKHL/PFLD WV2 29
Sheaf Pas LNGTN ST3 8
Sheaf St HAN ST1
Shearer St HAN ST1
Shebdon Cl STAFN ST16 174
Sheepcote La TAM/AM/WIL B77 1
Sheep Fair RUGE WS15 21
Sheepwalks La KINVER DY7 30
Sheepwash La KIDDW DY11 30
Sheffield St BUT DE14
Shefford Rd NEWUL ST5 8
Sheila Av WNSFLD WV11 28
Shelburne St STOKE ST4 8
Sheldon Av CONG CW12 2
Sheldon Gv NEWUL ST5 6
Sheldon Rd WOLVN WV10 28
Sheldrake Gv STOKE ST4 8
Shelford Rd BURS/TUN ST6 5

elley Av BUT DE14 185 K4
elley Cl ALS/KID ST7 37 L2
LS/KID ST7 53 G2
BUT DE14 185 K4
STAF ST18 196 D2
UGE WS15 217 H6
EDG DY3 299 G5
TAFN ST16 5 J1
elley Dr CDLE ST10 89 J8
OAKS/STRLY B74 286 F4
elley Rd BNTWD WS7 252 A1
UCK/MIL ST2 70 B4
NCK/NC WS11 231 L5
RTAM B79 273 M3
HHTH WV12 282 E3
VOLVN WV10 264 D8
elmore Cl STAFN ST16 174 B2
elmore Wy GNOS ST20 190 D3
elsley Cl PENK ST19 230 A1
elsley Rd CDLE ST10 89 L6
elton Farm Rd HAN ST1 2 B9
elton New Rd STOKE ST4 84 E1
elton Old Rd STOKE ST4 85 H2
elton St TAM/AM/WIL B77 290 F3 4
emilt Crs BURS/TUN ST6 54 C7
enley Gv STAFS ST17 193 K4 1
enstone Av STRBR DY8 307 K8
enstone Cl
OAKS/STRLY B74 286 E4 2
enstone Ct
BDMR/CCFT WV3 295 G4 3
enstone Dr ALDR WS9 285 G2
enton St LNGTN ST3 86 D5
epherd Cl LICH WS13 236 C8
epherd Dr SHHTH WV12 282 B5 4
epherds Bush St STAFN ST16 4 E1
epherds Ct NWPT TF10 188 A7
epherds Fold STAFS ST17 194 C5 2
epherds Pool Rd
MGN/WHC B75 287 L8
epherd St BIDD ST8 40 C3
epley Cl STONE ST15 138 C3 3
epley Gv LNGTN ST3 101 L3
eppard St STOKE ST4 85 G4
epwell Gdns WOLVN WV10 265 J2
eraton Cl ALDR WS9 285 H4
HEDN WS12 231 M3 3
eraton Gra STRBR DY8 307 M8
erborne Cl BLOX/PEL WS3 283 J3 3
STOKE ST4 101 L3
erborne Dr NEWUL ST5 84 A5
erborne Gdns CDSL WV8 263 G7
erborne Rd WOLVN WV10 280 D1
erbourne Av HEDN WS12 232 E6
erbourne Dr BUT DE14 204 A3 7
erbrook Cl STAFS ST17 195 G7
erbrooke Av
TAM/AM/WIL B77 290 E4
erbrook Rd CNCK/NC WS11 249 J1
eridan Gdns LNGTN ST3 85 M8
SEDG DY3 298 F5 1
eridan St STAFN ST16 5 H2
eridan Wy STONE ST15 138 D3
eriffhales Dr NWPT TF10 224 A2
eriffs Cl LICHS WS14 9 M6
eriffs Wy ECCH ST21 152 D3 2
erifoot La MGN/WHC B75 287 H7 3
eringham Covert
STAFN ST16 175 J6
eringham Dr RUGE WS15 197 H8
eringham Pl NEWUL ST5 68 D6 2
erington Dr
ETTPK/GDPK/PENN WV4 295 K5 5
erlock Cl SHHTH WV12 282 D5
erracop La RUGE WS15 198 A1
errans Dell
ETTPK/GDPK/PENN WV4 295 K7 1
erratt St BURS/TUN ST6 54 C7
erringham Dr SHHTH WV12 282 C1
ervale Cl
ETTPK/GDPK/PENN WV4 295 G4 4
erwin Rd BURS/TUN ST6 53 M7
erwood Av STAFS ST17 193 L3
erwood Dr CNCK/NC WS11 232 A7
erwood Rd LNGTN ST3 102 F3
STRBR DY8 307 L3
erwood St WOLV WV1 12 E2
erwood Wk RUSH/SHEL WS4 284 D3
etland Cl
DUNHL/THL/PER WV6 280 B5 3
etland Rd LNGTN ST3 85 M7 2
illingford Dr STOKE ST4 101 H2
ilton Cl STOKE ST4 84 F5 1
inwell Gv LNGTN ST3 103 G2
ipley Cl BUT DE14 204 B2
ipley Pl BURS/TUN ST6 54 C8
ippy La RSTAF ST18 191 J2
ipston Rd STAFS ST17 194 D1 1
ipton Cl DUDN DY1 299 L7
ipton Dr UTXR ST14 143 M2
irburn Rd LEEK ST13 44 A4
irehall Pl CNCK/NC WS11 232 B8
irelea Cl BNTWD WS7 252 B2
ireoaks Dr STAFS ST17 194 C4 10
ire Rdg ALDR WS9 269 G6
ireview Rd BLOX/PEL WS3 268 B6
irley Dr CDLE ST10 107 L2
irley Rd HAN ST1 2 C9
irley St BURS/TUN ST6 68 D2
LEEK ST13 43 K5
irrall Dr POL/KGSB/FAZ B78 288 D6
oal Hill Cl CNCK/NC WS11 249 H1
obnall Cl BUT DE14 6 D2
obnall Rd BUT DE14 6 C5
BUTN/AL/TUT DE13 184 F6
obnall St BUT DE14 6 C4
oling Cl CDSL WV8 279 M1
oobridge St LEEK ST13 43 M5
ooting Butts Rd RUGE WS15 215 G2
op La CDSL WV8 278 D1
DUNHL/THL/PER WV6 293 H3
PENK ST19 246 C3
ort Acre St WSLW WS2 283 K7
ort Bambury St LNGTN ST3 86 D4
ortbutts La LICHS WS14 8 E9
ortlands La BLOX/PEL WS3 267 M6
ort La BUTN/AL/TUT DE13 220 D1
GTWY WS6 249 L7 3
UTXR ST14 142 D8
ort Rd WOLVN WV10 280 E1
Short St BRWNH WS8 268 F3
CNCK/NC WS11 231 M7
LNGTN ST3 86 C7
SHHTH WV12 282 C5
STPNHL/WNHL DE15 204 E3
STRBR DY8 307 M5 7
UTXR ST14 144 B2
WOLV WV1 13 G4 1
The Shortyard KIDDW DY11 309 K6
Shorwell Gv BURS/TUN ST6 53 L2
Shotsfield Pl BUCK/MIL ST2 70 A1
Shotsfield St BUCK/MIL ST2 70 A1
Shotwoodhill La
BUTN/AL/TUT DE13 165 M5
Showan Av NEWUL ST5 68 D7
Showell Circ WOLVN WV10 280 E3
Showell La
ETTPK/GDPK/PENN WV4 294 A7
Showell Rd WOLVN WV10 280 C4
Shraleybrook Rd ALS/KID ST7 66 A3
Shredicote La RSTAF ST18 210 A4
Shrewsbury Cl BLOX/PEL WS3 282 F1
Shrewsbury Dr NEWUL ST5 52 E8
SHIF TF11 225 L8
Shrewsbury Rd
BUTN/AL/TUT DE13 166 F8
MKTDR TF9 130 A2
STAFS ST17 4 F8
Shropshire Brook Rd
RUGE WS15 217 G6
Shropshire St MKTDR TF9 130 C1
Shrubbery KIDD DY10 310 B5
The Shrubbery CRTAM B79 256 D1
RUGE WS15 216 B4
Shruggs La RSTAF ST18 139 J8
Shugborough Dr DUDN DY1 299 L8
Shugborough Rd RUGE WS15 197 J7
Shugborough Wy
CNCK/NC WS11 250 B1
Shughborough Cl END/WER ST9 71 G8
Shuker's Cl NWPT TF10 188 A8
Shut La ECCH ST21 134 B4
Shutt Green La PENK ST19 245 M2
Shuttington Br CRTAM B79 275 K3
Shuttington Rd CRTAM B79 275 H4
Sich La BUTN/AL/TUT DE13 201 K7
Sidcot Pl HAN ST1 69 K3
Siddalls St STPNHL/WNHL DE15 186 B7
Siddons Cl LICH WS13 235 M8
Sides La ASHB DE6 94 A8
Sideway Rd STOKE ST4 85 H6
Sidings Pl LNGTN ST3 86 B6
Sidings Rd STONE ST15 119 L8
The Sidings CDLE ST10 89 K8
Sidlaw Cl WOLVN WV10 280 B4
Sidmouth Av NEWUL ST5 84 C1
STAFS ST17 194 D2
Sidney Av STAFS ST17 193 M3
Sidney Dr CDLE ST10 74 A8
Sidney St BKHL/PFLD WV2 12 E8
Sidon Hill Wy HEDN WS12 232 C7
Siemens Rd STAFS ST17 4 F9
Sigmund Cl WOLV WV1 281 H7 1
Signal Gv BLOX/PEL WS3 283 G1
Silica Rd TAM/AM/WIL B77 275 H8
Silk Mill La
BUTN/AL/TUT DE13 165 J4 4
Silkmore Crs STAFS ST17 194 A3
Silkmore La STAFS ST17 193 M4
Silk St LEEK ST13 43 L4
Sillitoe Pl STOKE ST4 85 G4
Silsden Gv LNGTN ST3 87 J8
Silva Av KGSWFD DY6 303 M6
Silver Birch Coppice
FOAKS/STRLY B74 286 D5
Silver Birch Dr KINVER DY7 305 M5
Silver Birch Rd BKHL/PFLD WV2 295 K3
CNCK/NC WS11 251 H6
HEDN WS12 231 K2
Silver Cl BIDD ST8 40 C2
Silverdale Dr WOLVN WV10 280 E6
Silverdale Gdns STRBR DY8 303 J7
Silverdale Rd NEWUL ST5 68 C5
NEWUL ST5 83 L1
Silverdale St NEWUL ST5 67 L7 5
Silver Fir Cl HEDN WS12 232 A2
Silverhill Cl BUTN/AL/TUT DE13 185 J1
Silver La UTXR ST14 162 E1
Silver Link Rd TAM/AM/WIL B77 11 M9
Silvermere Pk SHIF TF11 242 A7
Silvermine Cl ALS/KID ST7 39 H8 5
Silver Rdg BARL ST12 119 J2
Silver's Cl BLOX/PEL WS3 267 M5
Silverster St BURS/TUN ST6 69 G2
Silverstone Av CDLE ST10 89 L6
Silverstone Cl WSLW WS2 282 D7
Silverstone Crs BURS/TUN ST6 53 L3
Silver St BRWNH WS8 268 E3
BURS/TUN ST6 54 E6
CDLE ST10 89 L4
CRTAM B79 10 C4
Silverthorn Wy STAFS ST17 194 C3
Silverton Cl NEWUL ST5 68 A2
Silverton Wy WNSFLD WV11 281 M5
Silverwood ALS/KID ST7 53 H1 3
Silvester Wy STAFS ST17 194 E4
Simcox St HEDN WS12 232 D6 1
Simeon Wy STONE ST15 138 C4
Simmonds Cl BLOX/PEL WS3 267 K7
Simmonds Rd BLOX/PEL WS3 267 K7
Simmonds Wy BRWNH WS8 269 G5
Simmons Rd WNSFLD WV11 282 B1
Simonburn Av STOKE ST4 84 E3
Simon Pl HAN ST1 85 H1 3
Simons Rd MKTDR TF9 130 B2
Simpkins Cl ALDR WS9 269 G7
Simpson Cl STAFN ST16 174 B3
Simpson Gv WOLVN WV10 280 E4
Simpson Rd LICH WS13 236 B7
WOLVN WV10 280 E4
WSLW WS2 283 H5
Simpson St HAN ST1 2 F9
NEWUL ST5 68 B5
Sinai Cl BUTN/AL/TUT DE13 184 E6
Sinclair Av ALS/KID ST7 37 H7
Siskin Cl BNTWD WS7 252 D5
Siskin Pl LNGTN ST3 103 H3
Sitwell Gv LNGTN ST3 86 D6
Six Ashes Rd BDGNE WV15 300 C4
KINVER DY7 300 E3
Skeath La RSTAF ST18 156 B6
Skellern Av BURS/TUN ST6 54 C7
Skellern St ALS/KID ST7 38 D8
Skidmore Av BDMR/CCFT WV3 294 F2
TAM/AM/WIL B77 290 C6
Skinner St WOLV WV1 12 E5
Skipacre Av BURS/TUN ST6 69 J1
Skipness TAM/AM/WIL B77 11 K3
Skipton Gn
DUNHL/THL/PER WV6 280 A5 3
Skipton Pl CNCK/NC WS11 249 H3
Skye Cl LNGTN ST3 86 E7
Skylark Cl HEDN WS12 231 J3
UTXR ST14 144 C4
Slab La GNOS ST20 209 G6
Slacken La ALS/KID ST7 38 D8
Slack La ASHB DE6 94 C2
Slacky La BLOX/PEL WS3 283 M1
Sladd La KIDDW DY11 309 H6
Slade Av BNTWD WS7 252 A2
Slade Flds UTXR ST14 144 B1
Slade Gdns CDSL WV8 263 G6
Sladehollow La ASHB DE6 93 J1
Slade La LEEK ST13 61 G5
MGN/WHC B75 288 A7
TAM/AM/WIL B77 290 C6
Slade Rd MGN/WHC B75 287 L7
WOLVN WV10 264 C7
Slade View Ri HEDN WS12 233 G4
Slaidburn Gv HAN ST1 3 J3
STAFS ST17 194 C4 11
Slaney St NEWUL ST5 84 C3
Slang La RUGE WS15 233 L5
Slapton Cl BUCK/MIL ST2 85 M1
Slate La CDSL WV8 262 D5
Slater St BIDD ST8 40 C3
BURS/TUN ST6 68 E3
WLNHL WV13 282 C7
The Sleeve LEEK ST13 43 J6
Slessor Rd STAFN ST16 5 J1
Slim Rd WSLW WS2 282 E8
Slindon Cl NEWUL ST5 67 K1
Sling La PENK ST19 228 B6
Slingsby TAM/AM/WIL B77 290 C3
Slippery La HAN ST1 2 B6
Slitting Mill Rd RUGE WS15 215 H3
Sloane Wy STOKE ST4 86 B4
Smallbrook La WMBN WV5 298 B3
Smalley Cl CNCK/NC WS11 232 A5
Small La ECCH ST21 152 E3 2
Smallman St STAFN ST16 5 H2
Smallridge LICH WS13 235 M8 2
Smallshire Wy STRBR DY8 307 K2
Smallwood Cl NEWUL ST5 67 K1
Smallwood Gv HAN ST1 3 K1
Smallwood Rd CDSL WV8 263 L8
Smarts Av LICHS WS14 287 G3
Smedley Ct RDERBYSW DE65 167 H5
Smestow La SEDG DY3 297 J6
Smestow St WOLVN WV10 13 H1
Smillie Pl CNCK/NC WS11 231 M7
Smith Child St BURS/TUN ST6 53 K6
Smith Cl ALS/KID ST7 37 H6 1
Smithfield Cl MKTDR TF9 112 D8 3
Smithfield Ri LICH WS13 9 G2
Smithfield Rd BLOX/PEL WS3 283 K1
MKTDR TF9 112 C8
UTXR ST14 144 B2
Smithpool Rd STOKE ST4 85 K5
Smith's Cl BNTWD WS7 251 K3
Smiths Pas STOKE ST4 86 A5
Smith St LNGTN ST3 86 C6
Smithy Bank CDLE ST10 107 L1
Smithy Dr BLOX/PEL WS3 268 A6
Smithyfield Rd BURS/TUN ST6 54 D6
Smithy La BIDD ST8 26 D8
CDLE ST10 105 K2
CRTAM B79 240 E8
CW/SHV CW2 50 D4
ECCH ST21 152 B1
LICH WS13 8 C1
LNGTN ST3 86 C7 9
MCFLDS SK11 18 E4
MKTDR TF9 96 B5
NEWUL ST5 98 F4
RSTAF ST18 173 H4
RSTAF ST18 177 J2
RSTAF ST18 210 B2
RUGE WS15 234 F2
STAFS ST17 212 F2
TAM/AM/WIL B77 290 F3
Smokies Wy BIDD ST8 40 C1
Smout Crs BILS/COS WV14 295 M8 2
Snape Hall Cl NEWUL ST5 98 D4
Snape Hall Rd NEWUL ST5 98 C3
Snape Rd WNSFLD WV11 282 A1
Snapes La ASHB DE6 110 B2
Snead Cl STAFN ST16 175 J6
Sneyd Av LEEK ST13 43 L5
NEWUL ST5 83 M3
Sneyd Cl LEEK ST13 57 H6
Sneyd Crs NEWUL ST5 83 M3
Sneyd Hall Cl BLOX/PEL WS3 283 G2 2
Sneyd Hall Rd BLOX/PEL WS3 282 F1
Sneyd Hl BURS/TUN ST6 69 H2
Sneyd La BLOX/PEL WS3 282 F1
WNSFLD WV11 282 C1
Sneyd Pl BURS/TUN ST6 53 J4
Sneyd St BURS/TUN ST6 69 H4
LEEK ST13 43 L5
Sneyd Ter NEWUL ST5 67 H8
Sneyd Wood Vw BURS/TUN ST6 69 J3
Snipe Cl WOLVN WV10 265 H3 3
Snipesmoor La ASHB DE6 95 M3
Snowden Wy LNGTN ST3 87 H8 4
Snowdon Ri SEDG DY3 299 K4 2
Snowdon Rd CNCK/NC WS11 231 L4
DUNHL/THL/PER WV6 276 B4
Snowdon Wy SHHTH WV12 282 B1
WOLVN WV10 280 B4
Snowdrop Cl BRWNH WS8 268 D4
Snow Hl BKHL/PFLD WV2 13 G6
HAN ST1 2 B8
STAFN ST16 4 E3
Snow Hill Jct BKHL/PFLD WV2 13 G7
Snowshill Gdns DUDN DY1 299 M6
Snows Yd STAFN ST16 4 D2 1
Soames Crs LNGTN ST3 86 B4
Soberton Cl WNSFLD WV11 281 M3
Solcum La KIDDW DY11 309 K4
Solent Cl COVEN WV9 263 M8 3
Solney Cl SWAD DE11 205 M7
Solway Cl CRTAM B79 274 A3
Solway Gv LNGTN ST3 86 E6 5
Somerfield Cl RUSH/SHEL WS4 284 C1
Somerfield Rd BLOX/PEL WS3 283 H2
Somerford Cl COVEN WV9 247 H8 7
Somerford Gdns
WOLVN WV10 264 E8 2
Somerford La PENK ST19 246 E4
Somerley Rd HAN ST1 3 K1
Somerset Av ALS/KID ST7 38 F8
RUGE WS15 215 K4
Somerset Cl
POL/KGSB/FAZ B78 290 A1 4
Somerset Dr STRBR DY8 307 K3
Somerset Pl CNCK/NC WS11 231 L6
Somerset Rd HAN ST1 3 G5
RUSH/SHEL WS4 284 A6
STAFS ST17 193 J3
STPNHL/WNHL DE15 204 D4
WLNHL WV13 282 D8
Somerton Rd END/WER ST9 71 G7
Somerton Wy LNGTN ST3 86 D5 4
Somervale STAFS ST17 194 C4 12
Somerville Av NEWUL ST5 68 D7
Somerville Rd
BUTN/AL/TUT DE13 219 M8
Sonning Dr COVEN WV9 263 M8
Sopwith Cl STONE ST15 136 F4 3
Sorrel Ave CDLE ST10 105 L7
Sorrel Cl BUCK/MIL ST2 3 M6
UTXR ST14 144 B4
WOLVN WV10 265 H3
Sorrento Gv LNGTN ST3 86 E6 6
Souldern Wy LNGTN ST3 86 D6
Southall Rd WNSFLD WV11 282 A2
Southall Wy BUCK/MIL ST2 86 A1
Southampton St HAN ST1 2 D3
WOLV WV1 13 G3
South Av STRBR DY8 307 M6
WNSFLD WV11 281 J5
Southbank St LEEK ST13 43 M5
Southbank Vw KGSWFD DY6 303 L6 3
Southborough Crs
BURS/TUN ST6 54 B6
Southbourne Pl
CNCK/NC WS11 231 K8 1
Southbourne Rd WOLVN WV10 264 C7
South Broadway St
BUT DE14 204 C2 2
South Cheshire Wy ALS/KID ST7 37 L1
South Cl CNCK/NC WS11 249 J2
South Crs WOLVN WV10 265 J4
South Dr SWAD DE11 205 M4
Southern Cl KGSWFD DY6 303 M7
Southern Cross LICH WS13 9 H4
Southerndown Rd SEDG DY3 299 H2
Southern Wy BURS/TUN ST6 69 K1
Southey Cl SHHTH WV12 282 E2
Southfield Cl STAFS ST17 193 K5
Southfield Gv BDMR/CCFT WV3 294 C3
Southfield Rd WNSFLD WV11 281 M5
Southfields Rd STAFS ST17 193 K4
Southfield Wy GTWY WS6 249 M8
Southgate CNCK/NC WS11 249 H3
PENK ST19 246 D3 3
WOLV WV1 12 D4 1
Southgate Av STOKE ST4 101 J4 6
Southgate End
CNCK/NC WS11 249 H3 2
South Gn
ETTPK/GDPK/PENN WV4 294 D5
South Hl BUTN/AL/TUT DE13 166 D6
Southlands Av LNGTN ST3 102 B1
NEWUL ST5 68 C5
Southlands Cl LEEK ST13 43 J4
Southlands Rd CONG CW12 26 A1
Southlowe Av END/WER ST9 71 L6
Southlowe Rd END/WER ST9 71 L6
South Oak St BUT DE14 204 B2
South Ov SEDG DY3 299 L5
South Pl BURS/TUN ST6 54 D4
South Rd BUCK/MIL ST2 70 B5 1
STONE ST15 136 D4
STRBR DY8 307 M6 3
South St ALS/KID ST7 39 H4
ASHB DE6 95 J1
BURS/TUN ST6 54 D4
STAFN ST16 4 C5
WOLVN WV10 280 C4
South Ter NEWUL ST5 68 C5
STOKE ST4 85 G6
South Uxbridge St BUT DE14 204 B2
South Vw BIDD ST8 40 C2
South View Cl CDSL WV8 263 H8
WOLVN WV10 265 H4
South View Rd SEDG DY3 299 H2
South Wk LNGTN ST3 103 H1
South Walls STAFN ST16 4 F5
Southwark Cl LICH WS13 236 C7 3
Southway Ct KGSWFD DY6 303 M6
Southwell Est ECCH ST21 152 E4 1
South Wolfe St STOKE ST4 85 H3
South Wd NEWUL ST5 98 A3
Southwood Cl KGSWFD DY6 303 L5
Sovereign Dr BUT DE14 204 B2 4
DUDN DY1 299 K8
Sovereign La MKTDR TF9 115 J5
Sowdley Gn PENK ST19 227 H5
Sowdley La PENK ST19 227 H6
Sowers Cl SHHTH WV12 282 D5
Sowers Gdns SHHTH WV12 282 D5 1
Spalden Av ASHB DE6 79 J7
Spalding Pl BUCK/MIL ST2 86 E2
Sparch Av NEWUL ST5 68 C6
Sparch Gv NEWUL ST5 68 C6
Sparch Hollow NEWUL ST5 68 C7
Spark St STOKE ST4 85 G3
Spark Ter STOKE ST4 85 G3
Sparrowbutts Gv ALS/KID ST7 39 J8 2
Sparrow Cl RSTAF ST18 196 D2 5
Sparrows End La PENK ST19 246 D4
Sparrow St BURS/TUN ST6 54 D8
Sparrow Ter NEWUL ST5 68 B4
Spa St BURS/TUN ST6 69 J3
Speakman St LNGTN ST3 86 D8 4
Spearhill LICHS WS14 9 L4
Spedding Rd STOKE ST4 85 L2
Spedding Wy BIDD ST8 40 E2 5
Speechly Dr RUGE WS15 197 K8
Speedwall St LNGTN ST3 86 C5
Speedwell Cl ALDR WS9 284 F5
WNSFLD WV11 281 L5 3
Speedwell Gdns WOLVN WV10 265 H2
Speedwell Rd NEWUL ST5 67 M1
Speedy Cl CNCK/NC WS11 231 L5
Spencer Av END/WER ST9 55 L4
LEEK ST13 43 L6
Spencer Cl ALS/KID ST7 36 F6
ASHB DE6 95 J2
BUTN/AL/TUT DE13 185 K1 2
SEDG DY3 299 G6
Spencer Dr BNTWD WS7 251 L2
Spencer Pl NEWUL ST5 67 L4
Spencer Rd LICHS WS14 8 F7
STOKE ST4 85 J2
Spencroft Rd NEWUL ST5 67 M5
Spend La ASHB DE6 79 G4
Spenser Av
DUNHL/THL/PER WV6 278 E6
Spenser Cl CRTAM B79 10 A2 1
STAFS ST17 193 J2
Spens St BURS/TUN ST6 68 F2
Sperry Cl BLYBR/FOR ST11 103 H3
Spey Dr ALS/KID ST7 39 J8
Spills Meadow SEDG DY3 299 L5 5
Spindlewood Cl HEDN WS12 250 D1 5
Spinney Cl BLOX/PEL WS3 268 A8
BNTWD WS7 252 A1
CNCK/NC WS11 250 F5
END/WER ST9 55 L2
POL/KGSB/FAZ B78 291 M2
STRBR DY8 303 H7
Spinney Farm Rd
CNCK/NC WS11 249 H3 3
Spinney Flds STAFS ST17 194 D5 6
Spinney La BNTWD WS7 251 M1
Spinney Rd BUT DE14 203 M2
The Spinney ALS/KID ST7 38 E6 1
AUD/MAD/W CW3 82 A2 1
BDMR/CCFT WV3 294 D1
FOAKS/STRLY B74 286 B4
SEDG DY3 299 J8
Spinning School La CRTAM B79 10 D4
Spire Cl BURS/TUN ST6 54 E7
Spires Cft WOLVN WV10 265 K1
The Spires LICHS WS14 9 L6
Spitfire Av ALBTN WV7 260 A3
Splash La HEDN WS12 232 C7
Spode Av RSTAF ST18 175 H2
RUGE WS15 217 J6
Spode Cl CDLE ST10 89 J8
Spode Gv NEWUL ST5 84 B7
Spode Pl CNCK/NC WS11 232 B8
Spode St STOKE ST4 85 H5
Spondon Rd WNSFLD WV11 281 L2
Spoutfield Rd STOKE ST4 84 F1
Spout La BUCK/MIL ST2 70 C1
Spragg House La BURS/TUN ST6 54 D8
Spratslade Dr LNGTN ST3 86 B8
Spreadoaks Dr STAFS ST17 194 D5 7
Sprengers Cl PENK ST19 230 A1
Spring Bank ALS/KID ST7 39 G3
Springbank Av END/WER ST9 55 L4
Spring Cl ALS/KID ST7 37 L2
HAG/WOL DY9 311 M6
KINVER DY7 305 M5 2
RUSH/SHEL WS4 268 C8
SWAD DE11 223 M1
Spring Crs BURS/TUN ST6 55 J3 4
Springcroft
BLYBR/FOR ST11 103 M4 4
Springfarm Rd
STPNHL/WNHL DE15 205 G1
Springfield BLYBR/FOR ST11 103 L4 4
MKTDR TF9 114 E5
Springfield Av ASHB DE6 95 K2
RUGE WS15 215 M3
SEDG DY3 299 L1
Springfield Cl LEEK ST13 44 A5
NEWUL ST5 67 M4
Springfield Ct LEEK ST13 44 A4 1
Springfield Crs LNGTN ST3 86 B8 3
Springfield Dr BLYBR/FOR ST11 104 A2
LEEK ST13 44 A4
PENK ST19 227 J3
STAFS ST17 193 L5 3
Springfield Gv BIDD ST8 40 D3 3
SEDG DY3 299 K1
Springfield La WOLVN WV10 264 D6
Springfield Ri HEDN WS12 232 C4
Springfield Rd BIDD ST8 40 D3
LEEK ST13 44 A5
TAM/AM/WIL B77 290 D2 3
UTXR ST14 144 B2
WOLVN WV10 13 J1
Springfields RUSH/SHEL WS4 284 B3
Springfields Rd RUGE WS15 197 K7
STOKE ST4 84 E4
Spring Garden Rd LNGTN ST3 86 B8
Spring Gdns BLYBR/FOR ST11 104 B2
LEEK ST13 43 K5
STONE ST15 138 A5
Springhead Cl ALS/KID ST7 52 D4
Springhill Av
ETTPK/GDPK/PENN WV4 294 C7
Springhill Cl RUSH/SHEL WS4 284 D1
SHHTH WV12 282 D3
Springhill Gv
ETTPK/GDPK/PENN WV4 294 C6
Spring Hill La
ETTPK/GDPK/PENN WV4 294 A6
Springhill Pk
ETTPK/GDPK/PENN WV4 294 B7
Springhill Rd BNTWD WS7 252 A4
BRWNH WS8 269 G3
WNSFLD WV11 281 K2
Springhill Ter RUGE WS15 215 M4
Spring La LICHS WS14 255 L4
RUSH/SHEL WS4 268 C8
SHHTH WV12 282 B6
Springle Styche La
BNTWD WS7 252 C1
Spring Meadow GTWY WS6 266 D1 5
Springpool NEWUL ST5 83 J4
Spring Rd LICH WS13 236 D8
LNGTN ST3 86 E8
RUSH/SHEL WS4 284 D1
Springs Bank END/WER ST9 56 A8

Springside Pl *LNGTN* ST3 .... 101 L3
Spring St *CNCK/NC* WS11 .... 249 L2
  STOKE ST4 .... 84 D1 ⑤
Spring Terrace Rd
  STPNHL/WNHL DE15 .... 7 L8
Springvale Ri *STAFS* ST16 .... 174 D2
Springvale St *WLNHL* WV13 .... 282 B7
Spring Wk *WSLW* WS2 .... 283 H7
Springwood Dr *STONE* ST15 .... 138 D3
Springwood Rd *NEWUL* ST5 .... 67 J2
Sprink Bank Rd *BURS/TUN* ST6 .... 54 A5
Sprinkswoods La *ASHB* DE6 .... 94 E5
Sprinkwood Gv *LNGTN* ST3 .... 87 C7
Sproston Rd *BURS/TUN* ST6 .... 53 M5
Spruce Gv *ALS/KID* ST7 .... 37 M3
Spruce Rd *WSL* WS3 .... 231 M1
Spruce Wk *RUGE* WS15 .... 197 J7 ①
Spruce Wy *BDMR/CCFT* WV3 .... 294 D1
Spur Lea *RSTAF* ST18 .... 210 C1 ①
Spur St *HAN* ST1 .... 2 F9
Spur Tree Av
  BDMR/CCFT WV3 .... 294 A1 ②
The Square *BKHL/PFLD* WV2 .... 13 H9
  BLYBR/FOR ST11 .... 87 L8
  CRTAM B79 .... 256 D1
  NEWUL ST5 .... 84 A4
  STPNHL/WNHL DE15 .... 187 H7
  UTXR ST14 .... 145 L8
Squires Ga *BNTWD* WS7 .... 252 C2
Squires Vw *STOKE* ST4 .... 85 J3
Squirrel Cl *HEDN* WS12 .... 231 J4
  HEDN WS12 .... 232 D8 ①
Squirrel Hayes Av *BIDD* ST8 .... 40 E4
Squirrels Cnr
  BUTN/AL/TUT DE13 .... 181 M3 ⑤
Squirrels Hollow *BNTWD* WS7 .... 252 A1
The Squirrels *NEWUL* ST5 .... 84 C7
Squirrel Wk
  ETTPK/GDPK/PENN WV4 .... 295 C6
  FOAKS/STRLY B74 .... 286 C5
  STAFS ST17 .... 193 L6 ③
Stable Ct *SEDG* DY3 .... 299 L4
Stable Rd *ASHB* DE6 .... 62 B1
  MKTDR TF9 .... 130 B1 ③
  WOLVN WV10 .... 248 A3
The Stables *RSTAF* ST18 .... 177 H8 ③
Stacey Cl *BUX* SK17 .... 33 H8
Stackhouse Cl *ALDR* WS9 .... 269 G6
Stackhouse Dr
  BLOX/PEL WS3 .... 268 A6 ②
Stadium Cl *WLNHL* WV13 .... 282 B6 ②
Stadium Ct *BURS/TUN* ST6 .... 69 G4
Stadmorslow La *ALS/KID* ST7 .... 39 M6
Stafford Av *NEWUL* ST5 .... 84 C5
Stafford Brook Rd *RUGE* WS15 .... 215 C1 ①
Stafford Cl *BLOX/PEL* WS3 .... 267 J8
  STONE ST15 .... 138 A3
Stafford Crs *LICHS* WS14 .... 255 K7
  NEWUL ST5 .... 84 C6
Stafford La *CDSL* WV8 .... 278 D1
  CNCK/NC WS11 .... 232 B5
  HAN ST1 .... 2 D5
  HEDN WS12 .... 232 C6
Stafford Rd *CNCK/NC* WS11 .... 249 K1 ③
  COVEN WV9 .... 264 C2
  ECCH ST21 .... 152 F4
  GNOS ST20 .... 190 E4
  GTWY WS6 .... 267 G4
  HEDN WS12 .... 231 J3
  LICH WS13 .... 235 L8
  PENK ST19 .... 229 L1
  RSTAF ST18 .... 157 J7
  STONE ST15 .... 138 A3
  UTXR ST14 .... 142 F7
  WOLVN WV10 .... 264 C1 ③
  WOLVN WV10 .... 280 C2
Staffordshire Moorlands Wks
  LEEK ST13 .... 58 B4
  BIDD ST8 .... 26 D6
  BURS/TUN ST6 .... 54 F4
  CDLE ST10 .... 58 D6
  CDLE ST10 .... 89 H5
  CDLE ST10 .... 91 C7
  CDLE ST10 .... 105 H2
  CONG CW12 .... 26 A7
  END/WER ST9 .... 72 B4
  END/WER ST9 .... 73 H5
  LEEK ST13 .... 30 A2
  LEEK ST13 .... 58 A5
Staffordshire Wy *ALS/KID* ST7 .... 39 L2
  CDLE ST10 .... 73 M8
  CDSL WV8 .... 262 F5
  END/WER ST9 .... 73 C2
  KINVER DY7 .... 301 M1
  LEEK ST13 .... 43 H8
  PENK ST19 .... 230 A1
  RUGE WS15 .... 198 A4
  STAFS ST17 .... 195 L5
  UTXR ST14 .... 108 F4
Stafford St *BUT* DE14 .... 185 K5
  ECCH ST21 .... 152 E4
  HAN ST1 .... 2 C5
  HEDN WS12 .... 250 E1
  MKTDR TF9 .... 130 D1
  NEWUL ST5 .... 84 B2 ③
  PENK ST19 .... 246 C4
  STAFN ST16 .... 4 E4
  WLNHL WV13 .... 282 A8 ②
  WOLV WV1 .... 12 F1
  WSLW WS2 .... 283 L6
Stafford Street Jct *WOLV* WV1 .... 12 F1
Stagborough Wy *HEDN* WS12 .... 232 B6
Stag Cl *RUGE* WS15 .... 215 H1 ③
Stag Crs *BLOX/PEL* WS3 .... 283 L4
  CNCK/NC WS11 .... 251 G4
Stag Dr *HEDN* WS12 .... 231 J4
Stag Hill Rd *BLOX/PEL* WS3 .... 283 L3
Staines Ct *STONE* ST15 .... 138 C3
Staite Dr *KIDD* DY10 .... 310 A5
Stakenbridge La *KIDD* DY10 .... 311 J6
Staley Cft *BURS/TUN* ST6 .... 54 A6
Stalling's La *KGSWFD* DY6 .... 303 K2
  KGSWFD DY6 .... 303 M1
Stallington Cl
  BLYBR/FOR ST11 .... 103 K6 ③
Stallington Gdns
  BLYBR/FOR ST11 .... 103 M4 ③
Stallington Rd *BLYBR/FOR* ST11 .... 103 L5
  LNGTN ST3 .... 103 H8
Stamer St *STOKE* ST4 .... 85 H4 ④

Stamford Crs *BNTWD* WS7 .... 252 A2
Stamford St *STRBR* DY8 .... 307 M3
Stamps Cl
  STPNHL/WNHL DE15 .... 186 C7 ③
Standard St *STOKE* ST4 .... 85 K4 ③
Standedge *TAM/AM/WIL* B77 .... 291 G3
Standersfoot Pl *BURS/TUN* ST6 .... 54 B4
Standhills Rd *KGSWFD* DY6 .... 303 L4
Stanfield Crs *CDLE* ST10 .... 105 K1
Stanfield Rd *BURS/TUN* ST6 .... 69 G1
Stanfield St *LNGTN* ST3 .... 86 D4
Stanford Cl *PENK* ST19 .... 229 L1
Stanford Rd *BKHL/PFLD* WV2 .... 295 J3
Stanhope Rd *BDMR/CCFT* WV3 .... 12 D6 ③
  HAN ST1 .... 2 A8
  STPNHL/WNHL DE15 .... 186 B7
Stanier Cl *RUSH/SHEL* WS4 .... 284 B3
Stanier St *NEWUL* ST5 .... 84 A1
  STOKE ST4 .... 85 L4
Stanley Bank *END/WER* ST9 .... 55 M5
Stanley Cl *MSHM* DE12 .... 241 M3
  WNSFLD WV11 .... 281 M2
Stanley Ct *ALS/KID* ST7 .... 37 J6
  DUNHL/THL/PER WV6 .... 278 E6
Stanley Crs *UTXR* ST14 .... 126 A8
Stanley Dr *NEWUL* ST5 .... 67 J1 ③
  SEDG DY3 .... 297 L8
Stanley Gv *BUCK/MIL* ST2 .... 55 M4
  NEWUL ST5 .... 68 D8 ③
Stanley Matthews Wy
  STOKE ST4 .... 85 J7
Stanley Moss La *END/WER* ST9 .... 55 J1
Stanley Moss Rd *END/WER* ST9 .... 55 L5
Stanley Pl *RUSH/SHEL* WS4 .... 284 B4
  END/WER ST9 .... 55 K6
  HEDN WS12 .... 232 B4
  NEWUL ST5 .... 68 D8
  RUSH/SHEL WS4 .... 284 B4
  STOKE ST4 .... 84 E2
  STRBR DY8 .... 307 M7
  WOLVN WV10 .... 280 D1
Stanley St *BIDD* ST8 .... 40 C2
  BLOX/PEL WS3 .... 283 J2
  BURS/TUN ST6 .... 53 L6
  BUT DE14 .... 6 E6
  LEEK ST13 .... 43 L5
Stansgate Pl *HAN* ST1 .... 2 A3
Stanshope La *ASHB* DE6 .... 48 D8
Stansmore Rd *LNGTN* ST3 .... 87 H3
Stanton Av *DUDN* DY1 .... 299 M4
Stanton Cl *NEWUL* ST5 .... 67 M8
Stanton La *ASHB* DE6 .... 93 M1
Stanton Rd *ASHB* DE6 .... 95 K2
  LNGTN ST3 .... 103 G1
  SHIF TF11 .... 242 E6
  STPNHL/WNHL DE15 .... 204 F2
  WOLV WV1 .... 13 M5
Stanway Av *BURS/TUN* ST6 .... 69 J3
Stanways La *BIDD* ST8 .... 27 H8
Stapenhill Rd
  STPNHL/WNHL DE15 .... 7 L7
Stapleford Gdns
  BNTWD WS7 .... 252 D4 ③
Stapleford Gv *STRBR* DY8 .... 303 L8
Stapleton Crs *LNGTN* ST3 .... 102 A1
Stapleton Rd *ALDR* WS9 .... 284 F5
Star And Garter Rd *LNGTN* ST3 .... 102 E2
Star Bank *CDLE* ST10 .... 91 K1
Star Cl *WSLW* WS2 .... 282 F6
Starkey's La *PENK* ST19 .... 227 K3
Starling Cl *ALS/KID* ST7 .... 39 K7
Star St *BDMR/CCFT* WV3 .... 294 C2
Startley La *RUGE* WS15 .... 215 L8
Starwood Rd *LNGTN* ST3 .... 102 E2
Statfold La *BUTN/AL/TUT* DE13 .... 219 M6
  LICH WS13 .... 237 K2
Statham St *HAN* ST1 .... 2 B7
Station Ap *FOAKS/STRLY* B74 .... 286 F4
  STONE ST15 .... 119 M8
Station Bridge Rd *STOKE* ST4 .... 85 L5
Station Cl *BLOX/PEL* WS3 .... 283 H2
  CDSL WV8 .... 262 E7
Station Ct *NWPT* TF10 .... 206 A1
Station Crs *BURS/TUN* ST6 .... 54 B8
Station Dr *KIDD* DY10 .... 311 H8 ④
  NEWUL ST5 .... 82 D2
  RUGE WS15 .... 217 H6
  WOLVN WV10 .... 247 J5
Station Gv *BUCK/MIL* ST2 .... 70 A1
Station La *MSHM* DE12 .... 221 J1
Station Pl *BLOX/PEL* WS3 .... 283 H2
Station Rd *ALBTN* WV7 .... 261 G5
  ALDR WS9 .... 285 G5
  ALS/KID ST7 .... 37 J7
  ALS/KID ST7 .... 38 E3
  ALS/KID ST7 .... 48 E3
  ALS/KID ST7 .... 52 F1 ①
  ALS/KID ST7 .... 53 L1
  ALS/KID ST7 .... 66 D3
  ASHB DE6 .... 79 H8
  AUD/MAD/W CW3 .... 81 L5
  AUD/MAD/W CW3 .... 81 G8
  BARL 119 K1
  BIDD ST8 .... 40 C1
  BLOX/PEL WS3 .... 268 A7
  BNTWD WS7 .... 252 E7
  BUTN/AL/TUT DE13 .... 166 B6
  BUTN/AL/TUT DE13 .... 202 E8
  CDLE ST10 .... 89 K8
  CDLE ST10 .... 91 L8
  CDSL WV8 .... 262 E7
  ECCH ST21 .... 117 K7
  END/WER ST9 .... 55 M3
  GNOS ST20 .... 190 D5
  GTWY WS6 .... 249 M6
  HEDN WS12 .... 232 C4
  LEEK ST13 .... 57 K4
  LICH WS13 .... 8 F4
  LICHS WS14 .... 270 F4
  NEWUL ST5 .... 67 H8
  NEWUL ST5 .... 82 C2
  NEWUL ST5 .... 82 E2
  PENK ST19 .... 229 L1
  RDERBYSW DE65 .... 165 K2
  RSTAF ST18 .... 158 C7
  RSTAF ST18 .... 191 L3
  RUGE WS15 .... 215 L1
  RUSH/SHEL WS4 .... 284 A4

  STAFN ST16 .... 4 D6
  STOKE ST4 .... 85 H2
  STONE ST15 .... 136 C4
  STONE ST15 .... 137 M1
  STONE ST15 .... 153 M1
  UTXR ST14 .... 144 C3
  WMBN WV5 .... 298 A2
  WOLVN WV10 .... 13 M1
Station St *ASHB* DE6 .... 95 H1
  BLOX/PEL WS3 .... 283 H2
  BURS/TUN ST6 .... 68 D3
  BUT DE14 .... 6 F4
  GTWY WS6 .... 249 L7
  LEEK ST13 .... 43 K5
  SWAD DE11 .... 223M2
Station Vw *LNGTN* ST3 .... 103 G1
Station Wks *ALS/KID* ST7 .... 66 D3
Staunton Rd *BLOX/PEL* WS3 .... 267 G7
Staveley Cl *BUCK/MIL* ST2 .... 3M7
Staveley Pl *NEWUL* ST5 .... 83 C1
Staveley Rd
  STEAD Dr WOLVN WV10 .... 280 D2
Steel Dr *WOLVN* WV10 .... 12 D1
Stead Cl *WSLW* WS2 .... 283 J5
Stedman Crs *STAFS* ST17 .... 193 M4
Stedman St *HAN* ST1 .... 2 F2
Steele Av *BURS/TUN* ST6 .... 54 B8
Steele Cl *LEEK* ST13 .... 57 K5 ③
Steele St *STOKE* ST4 .... 84 E2 ③
Steelhouse La *BKHL/PFLD* WV2 .... 13 J8
Steenwood La *RUGE* WS15 .... 179 C7
Steere Av *CRTAM* B79 .... 274 C3
Stellar St *WOLVN* WV10 .... 69 J1 ③
Stenbury Cl *WOLVN* WV10 .... 264 F6 ③
Stencills Dr *RUSH/SHEL* WS4 .... 284 B7
Stencills Rd *RUSH/SHEL* WS4 .... 284 B6
Stephen Av *CDLE* ST10 .... 73 K8
Stephens Cl *WNSFLD* WV11 .... 281 M2
Stephenson Av *WSLW* WS2 .... 283 C4
Stephenson Cl
  TAM/AM/WIL B77 .... 275 C8
Stephenson Dr
  DUNHL/THL/PER WV6 .... 278 E5
Stephenson Sq *WSLW* WS2 .... 283 H5 ①
Stephenson St *BDMR/CCFT* WV3 .... 12 D8
Stephens Wy *ALS/KID* ST7 .... 51M8
Stepping Stone Cl *WSLW* WS2 .... 282 F6
Sterndale Dr *NEWUL* ST5 .... 84 B7
  STOKE ST4 .... 86 B4
Sterrymere Gdns *KINVER* DY7 .... 306 A6
Stevens Dr *HEDN* WS12 .... 232 D4 ①
Stevens Ga *BKHL/PFLD* WV2 .... 12 F9
Stevenson Dr *STAFS* ST17 .... 193 J3
Stevenson Rd *ASHB* DE6 .... 145 H2
  BUCK/MIL ST2 .... 3M5
  CRTAM B79 .... 10 B1
Stevenson Wk *LICHS* WS14 .... 8 F7
Steventon Pl *BURS/TUN* ST6 .... 68 F2
Stewart Cl *BUT* DE14 .... 204 A4
Stewart Rd *ALDR* WS9 .... 269 G7
  KGSWFD DY6 .... 303 K6
Stewart St *BKHL/PFLD* WV2 .... 12 F8
  STOKE ST4 .... 85 K4
Stewkins *STRBR* DY8 .... 307 L2
Stickley La *SEDG* DY3 .... 299 J6
Stile Cl *BIDD* ST8 .... 40 B5
  RUGE WS15 .... 215M4
Stile Cop Rd *RUGE* WS15 .... 215 K6
Stirling Cl *BUCK/MIL* ST2 .... 86 E3
Stirling Crs *SHHTH* WV12 .... 282 B5
Stirling Pl *CNCK/NC* WS11 .... 249 H2
Stirling Ri *BUTN/AL/TUT* DE13 .... 185 K2
Stirling Rd *ALBTN* WV7 .... 260 F2 ①
The Stitchings *ASHB* DE6 .... 93 J1
Stockbridge Cl
  DUNHL/THL/PER WV6 .... 278 F8 ③
Stockfield Rd *LNGTN* ST3 .... 102 F3
Stockford La *LICH* WS13 .... 238 A8
Stockhay La *RUGE* WS15 .... 252 D5
Stockholm Gv *HAN* ST1 .... 69 L3
Stocking-gate La *RSTAF* ST18 .... 172 F8
Stocking La *RSTAF* ST18 .... 172 B5
Stockings La *PENK* ST19 .... 227 K5
  RUGE WS15 .... 216 D8
Stock La *UTXR* ST14 .... 162 B3
Stocks La *UTXR* ST14 .... 143 J3
Stockton Cl *WSLW* WS2 .... 283 K6
Stockton La *STAFS* ST17 .... 194 E3
Stockwell End
  DUNHL/THL/PER WV6 .... 279 K4
Stockwell Gv *LNGTN* ST3 .... 86 D7 ③
Stockwell Rd
  DUNHL/THL/PER WV6 .... 279 K5
Stockwell St *LEEK* ST13 .... 43 L4
Stockwood Rd *NEWUL* ST5 .... 83M6
Stoke Old Rd *STOKE* ST4 .... 84 D1
Stoke Rd *HAN* ST1 .... 85 H1
Stokesay Av
  DUNHL/THL/PER WV6 .... 278 F7
Stokesay Gv *BURS/TUN* ST6 .... 69 G3 ③
Stokesay Ri *DUDN* DY1 .... 299 L7 ③
Stoke's La *CNCK/NC* WS11 .... 250 E3
Stokes St *BLOX/PEL* WS3 .... 283 H2
Stoneacre Cl
  BDMR/CCFT WV3 .... 294 A1 ③
Stone Bank Rd *ALS/KID* ST7 .... 53 C2
Stone Chair La *ALS/KID* ST7 .... 38 C8
Stonecrop Cl *BRWNH* WS8 .... 268 D4 ③
Stone Cross *PENK* ST19 .... 229 L1
Stonehaven *TAM/AM/WIL* B77 .... 11 L4
Stonehaven Gv *HAN* ST1 .... 2 E9
Stonehouse Av *WLNHL* WV13 .... 281 M7
Stonehouse Dr
  FOAKS/STRLY B74 .... 286 B6
Stonehouse Rd *END/WER* ST9 .... 71 H7
  RUGE WS15 .... 215 G2
Stone La *KINVER* DY7 .... 306 A6
Stonelea *ALDR* WS9 .... 285 H5
Stoneleigh Ct *RSTAF* ST18 .... 193 J5
Stoneleigh Gdns *CDSL* WV8 .... 262 F7
Stoneleigh Rd *BURS/TUN* ST6 .... 54 A5
Stoneleigh Wy *SEDG* DY3 .... 299 K4
Stone Pine Cl *HEDN* WS12 .... 231M2
Stonepine Cl *STAFS* ST17 .... 194 C4
Stonepit *TAM/AM/WIL* B77 .... 290 C1
Stone Rd *BARL* ST12 .... 101 G7
  ECCH ST21 .... 152 F3
  STAFN ST16 .... 4 D1

Stoke *ST4* 84 E7
  STOKE ST4 .... 100 F3
  STONE ST15 .... 119 J3
  UTXR ST14 .... 144 A2
Stone St *STOKE* ST4 .... 85 C3
Stonewall Rd *NEWUL* ST5 .... 83 K1
Stonewell La *BUX* SK17 .... 34 C5
Stonewood St *STOKE* ST4 .... 84 E7 ③
Stoney Brook Leys *WMBN* WV5 .... 297 C5
Stoneycroft *BUCK/MIL* ST2 .... 55 H8
Stoney Cft *CNCK/NC* WS11 .... 249 M1
Stoney Dl *CDLE* ST10 .... 90 F5
Stoneydale Cl *SWAD* DE11 .... 205 M5 ③
Stoneyfields *BIDD* ST8 .... 41 H1
Stoneyfields *BUCK/MIL* ST2 .... 55 H8
Stoneyfields
  CNCK/NC WS11 .... 231 M8 ①
Stoney La *BLOX/PEL* WS3 .... 267 K7
  CDLE ST10 .... 75 K4
  END/WER ST9 .... 55 L3
  HAG/WOL DY9 .... 311 C7
  PENK ST19 .... 228 D7
Stoney Lea Rd *CNCK/NC* WS11 .... 231 M8
Stoneywell La *RUGE* WS15 .... 234 D4
Stonier Dr *UTXR* ST14 .... 160 C2 ③
Stonnall Ga *ALDR* WS9 .... 285 H2
Stonnall Rd *ALDR* WS9 .... 285 J2
Stonor Rd *BURS/TUN* ST6 .... 69 G4
Stonydelph La
  TAM/AM/WIL B77 .... 291 G3
Stonyford La *RUGE* WS15 .... 198 E6
Stony La *CDLE* ST10 .... 76 D1
  UTXR ST14 .... 142 B7
Stormont Cl *BURS/TUN* ST6 .... 54 C8 ③
Stour *TAM/AM/WIL* B77 .... 291 G5
Stourbridge Rd
  ETTPK/GDPK/PENN WV4 .... 294 C7
  KIDD DY10 .... 311 G5
  SEDG DY3 .... 298 C6
  WMBN WV5 .... 298 C1
Stour Cl *BNTWD* WS7 .... 252 D4
  RDERBYSW DE65 .... 166 E2 ③
Stourmore Cl *SHHTH* WV12 .... 282 D4
Stourton Crs *KINVER* DY7 .... 306 F4
Stourton Dr
  ETTPK/GDPK/PENN WV4 .... 294 C5
Stowecroft *LICH* WS13 .... 254 C1
Stowe Hill Gdns *LICH* WS13 .... 254 C1 ③
Stowe La *RSTAF* ST18 .... 158 C8
Stowe Rd *LICH* WS13 .... 9 C2 ③
Stowe St *BLOX/PEL* WS3 .... 283 J3
  LICH WS13 .... 9 C2 ③
  LICH WS13 .... 9 C2 ③
Stowford Gv *STOKE* ST4 .... 101 H2 ③
Stradbroke Dr *LNGTN* ST3 .... 102 A1
Straight Mile *WOLVN* WV10 .... 247 M4
Straight Rd *SHHTH* WV12 .... 282 C4
Straits Gn *SEDG* DY3 .... 299 H6
Straits Rd *SEDG* DY3 .... 299 H7
The Straits *SEDG* DY3 .... 299 G6
Strangman St *LEEK* ST13 .... 43 L5
Stranraer Cl *STOKE* ST4 .... 87 H6 ③
Stratford Av *NEWUL* ST5 .... 68 D7
Stratford Cl *BLYBR/FOR* ST11 .... 104 A2 ③
  BURS/TUN ST6 .... 54 F8
  DUDN DY1 .... 299 L8
  RDERBYSW DE65 .... 187 K1
Stratford Dr *ALDR* WS9 .... 285 J2
Stratford Wy *CNCK/NC* WS11 .... 231 M5
Strathleden Rd *BURS/TUN* ST6 .... 54 B8
Strathmore Crs *WMBN* WV5 .... 298 A1
Strathmore Pl *CNCK/NC* WS11 .... 231 M8
Stratton St *WOLVN* WV10 .... 280 E6
Strawberry La *GTWY* WS6 .... 266 E2
  MSHM DE12 .... 222 D5
  WLNHL WV13 .... 281 J7
Strawmoor La *CDSL* WV8 .... 262 B8
Stream Meadow
  RUSH/SHEL WS4 .... 284 C1
Stream Pk *KGSWFD* DY6 .... 303 K6
Stream Rd *KGSWFD* DY6 .... 303 K6
Streamside Cl *PENK* ST19 .... 229 M2 ③
Streamside Wy
  RUSH/SHEL WS4 .... 284 D2
Streetly Crs *FOAKS/STRLY* B74 .... 286 D7
Streetly Dr *FOAKS/STRLY* B74 .... 286 D7
Streetly La *FOAKS/STRLY* B74 .... 286 D6
Streetly Wd *FOAKS/STRLY* B74 .... 286 A8
Streets Corner Gdns *ALDR* WS9 .... 269 G6
Streets La *GTWY* WS6 .... 266 C2
The Street *GNOS* ST20 .... 169 M4
Streetway Rd *LICHS* WS14 .... 271 H3
Stretton Av *STAFN* ST16 .... 174 A4
Stretton Gdns *CDSL* WV8 .... 262 F6
Stretton Rd *NEWUL* ST5 .... 66 F8 ③
  PENK ST19 .... 228 A4
  SHHTH WV12 .... 282 C2
Stretton St *TAM/AM/WIL* B77 .... 11 J7
Stringer Cl *MGN/WHC* B75 .... 287 C6 ③
Stringer Ct *BURS/TUN* ST6 .... 53 K7 ⑤⑤
Stringers Hl *HEDN* WS12 .... 232 D3
Stringer's Pl *BIDD* ST8 .... 40 C2
Stringes La *WLNHL* WV13 .... 282 B8
Strode Rd *BKHL/PFLD* WV2 .... 295 J4
Stroma Cl *BURS/TUN* ST6 .... 68 F3 ③
Stross Av *BURS/TUN* ST6 .... 53 M5
Stroud Av *SHHTH* WV12 .... 282 C6 ③
Stroud Cl *LNGTN* ST3 .... 103 H3
  SHHTH WV12 .... 282 C6 ③
Stuart Av *BLYBR/FOR* ST11 .... 104 C4
  STOKE ST4 .... 101 G3
Stuart Cl *STONE* ST15 .... 137 M4
Stuart Cl (North) *STONE* ST15 .... 137 M4
Stuart Gv *NEWUL* ST5 .... 68 C6
Stuart Rd *HAN* ST1 .... 2 F9
Stuart St *BLOX/PEL* WS3 .... 283 H2
Stubbers Green Rd *ALDR* WS9 .... 284 D2
Stubbs Gn *SEDG* DY3 .... 299 C6
Stubbsfield Rd *NEWUL* ST5 .... 84 C3
Stubbs' Ga *NEWUL* ST5 .... 84 B2
Stubbs La *ASHB* DE6 .... 77 J8
  HAN ST1 .... 2 E7
Stubbs Rd *BDMR/CCFT* WV3 .... 295 C3
Stubbs St *BURS/TUN* ST6 .... 68 E2
  NEWUL ST5 .... 84 C2 ③
Stubby La *UTXR* ST14 .... 162 F2
  WNSFLD WV11 .... 281 M4
Stubley Dr *WOLVN* WV10 .... 280 E5 ③
Stubwood Hollow *UTXR* ST14 .... 108 D5

Stubwood La *UTXR* ST14 108
Studley Ga *STRBR* DY8 307
Studley Rd *BDMR/CCFT* WV3 ....
Stump La *SHIF* TF11 224
Sturgeon's Hl *LICH* WS13 ....
Sturgess St *STOKE* ST6 85
Sturston Rd *ASHB* DE6 ....
Stychbrook Gdns *LICH* WS13 236
Stychfields *STAFS* ST17 ....
Suckling Green La *CDSL* WV8 262
Sudbourne Cl *ALS/KID* ST7 53
Sudbury Cl *WNSFLD* WV11 281
Sudbury Pk *ASHB* DE6 146
Sudbury Pl *NEWUL* ST5 67
Sudbury Rd
  BUTN/AL/TUT DE13 201
Sudeley Cl *TAM/AM/WIL* B77 290
Sudgrove Pl *LNGTN* ST3 103
Sudlow St *BURS/TUN* ST6 69
Suffolk Cl *NEWUL* ST5 84
  WNSFLD WV11 281
Suffolk Gv *ALDR* WS9 285
Suffolk Pl *WSLW* WS2 283
Suffolk Rd *STPNHL/WNHL* DE15 204
Suffolk Wy
  POL/KGSB/FAZ B78 .... 290 A
Sugar Loaf La *KINVER* DY7 311
Sugar St *MCFLDS* SK11 28
Summerbane Rd *BURS/TUN* ST6 53
Summercourt Dr *KGSWFD* DY6 303
Summercourt Sq *KGSWFD* DY6 303
Summer Dr *SEDG* DY3 299
Summerfield *ALS/KID* ST7 .... 53 H
Summerfield Av
  TAM/AM/WIL B77 11
Summerfield Dr *UTXR* ST14 .... 144 A
Summerfield Rd *BNTWD* WS7 252
  TAM/AM/WIL B77 11
  WOLV WV1 .... 12 C
Summerfields *STONE* ST15 136
Summergate *SEDG* DY3 299
Summer Gv *LICH* WS13 .... 236 D
Summer Hl *KGSWFD* DY6 303
Summerhill Dr *NEWUL* ST5 67
Summerhill Gdns *MKTDR* TF9 130
Summerhouse La *LICH* WS13 234
Summer La *RUSH/SHEL* WS4 268
  SEDG DY3 ....
Summer Rw *BKHL/PFLD* WV2 12
  LNGTN ST3 ....
Summerside *HEDN* WS12 .... 233 J
Summerset St *KGSWFD* DY6 303
  STOKE ST4 ....
  STRBR DY8 .... 307 M
  WLNHL WV13 281
Summerville Rd *STOKE* ST4 84
Summit Pl *SEDG* DY3 299
Sunbeam *TAM/AM/WIL* B77 11
Sunbeam Dr *GTWY* WS6 249
Sunbeam St *BKHL/PFLD* WV2 295
Sunbury Av *LICHS* WS14 9
Sunbury Cl *STOKE* ST4 101
Sundorne Pl *BUCK/MIL* ST2 70
Sundour Crs *WNSFLD* WV11 281
Sundown Dr *STAFS* ST17 193
Sunfield Rd *CNCK/NC* WS11 249
Sunningdale
  BUTN/AL/TUT DE13 .... 185 J
Sunley Dr *HEDN* WS12 232
Sunningdale *STONE* ST15 138
  TAM/AM/WIL B77 .... 275 J
Sunningdale Av
  DUNHL/THL/PER WV6 .... 278 D
Sunningdale Cl *BURS/TUN* ST6 54
  STRBR DY8 307
Sunningdale Dr *STAFN* ST16 173
Sunningdale Gv *NEWUL* ST5 .... 67 K
Sunningdale Rd *SEDG* DY3 299
Sunningdale Wy
  BLOX/PEL WS3 267
Sunny Bank *BURS/TUN* ST6 68
Sunnybank Cl
  FOAKS/STRLY B74 285
Sunnybank Rd *SEDG* DY3 299
Sunnycroft Av *LNGTN* ST3 102
Sunnyfield Ov *BUCK/MIL* ST2 55
Sunny Hill Cl *WMBN* WV5 298
Sunnyhills Rd *LEEK* ST13 58
Sunny Hollow *NEWUL* ST5 68
Sunnyside *ALDR* WS9 268
  ALS/KID ST7 37
Sunny Side *CDLE* ST10 73
Sunnyside *STPNHL/WNHL* DE15 205
  SWAD DE11 ....
Sunnyside Av *BURS/TUN* ST6 53
Sunnyside Rd *UTXR* ST14 145
Sunridge Av *WMBN* WV5 .... 298 A
Sunridge Cl *BUCK/MIL* ST2 .... 55 H
Sunrise Hl *HEDN* WS12 232
Sunset Cl *COVEN* WV9 247
  CRTAM B79 ....
  GTWY WS6 249
Sunset Pl
  ETTPK/GDPK/PENN WV4 .... 295 H
Sun St *CDLE* ST10 89
  HAN ST1 13
  WOLVN WV10 ....
Sunwell Gdns *CDLE* ST10 89
Surrey Cl *CNCK/NC* WS11 249
  RUGE WS15 215
Surrey Dr *BDMR/CCFT* WV3 294
  POL/KGSB/FAZ B78 .... 290 A
  STRBR DY8 ....
Surrey Rd *ALS/KID* ST7 53
  STAFS ST17 193
Surrey Wk *ALDR* WS9 .... 285 G
Surtees Gv *STOKE* ST4 85
Sussex Av *ALDR* WS9 285
Sussex Dr *ALS/KID* ST7 37
  BDMR/CCFT WV3 294
  HEDN WS12 ....
Sussex Rd *STPNHL/WNHL* DE15 .... 204 D
Sutherland Av *LNGTN* ST3 102
Sutherland Crs
  BLYBR/FOR ST11 103
Sutherland Dr *NEWUL* ST5 83
  WMBN WV5 298
Sutherland Gv
  DUNHL/THL/PER WV6 .... 278 F

therland Pl *BKHL/PFLD* WV2 ... 13 H7
  NGTN ST3 ... 86 D8
therland Rd *BARL* ST12 ... 101 G8
  TTPK/GDPK/PENN WV4 ... 295 H5
  TWY WS6 ... 249 L8
  LEEK ST13 ... 57 G2
  NGTN ST3 ... 86 C7
  STONE ... 138 B4
therland St *STOKE* ST4 ... 85 J4
tton Av *POL/KGSB/FAZ* B78 ... 10 B9
tton Cl *RUGE* WS15 ... 215 M4
tton Ct
  TTPK/GDPK/PENN WV4 ... 295 L8
tton Dr *STAFN* ST16 ... 174 A6
  STOKE ST4 ... 84 F6
tton La *MKTDR* TF9 ... 130 C6
tton Pl *BURS/TUN* ST6 ... 54 B5
tton Rd *POL/KGSB/FAZ* B78 ... 288 F4
tton St *NEWUL* ST5 ... 67 L4
  STRBR DY8 ... 307 L1
tton Wy *MKTDR* TF9 ... 130 B3
vadlincote La *SWAD* DE11 ... 223 K1
vaffham Wy *BUCK/MIL* ST2 ... 70 D8
vainsfield Rd
  BUTN/AL/TUT DE13 ... 201 G8
vainsley Cl *BURS/TUN* ST6 ... 69 G3
vale Gv *WLNHL* WV13 ... 282 D8
vallow Cl *ALS/KID* ST7 ... 39 C8
  NGTN ST3 ... 103 C3
  RUGE WS15 ... 197 K8
  LICH ... 254 A1
vallowdale *ALDR* WS9 ... 269 G6
  DUNHL/THL/PER WV6 ... 278 F8
  STAFS ST17 ... 194 C1
vallowfall Av *STRBR* DY8 ... 307 J6
vallow Cl *RUGE* WS15 ... 273 L4
vallowfields Dr *HEDN* WS12 ... 232 B7
  SEDG DY3 ... 295 J7
vallomore Vw
  ALS/KID ST7 ... 52 C2
vallows Cl *BLOX/PEL* WS3 ... 268 A5
vallow Wk *BIDD* ST8 ... 40 D3
vanage Cl *LNGTN* ST3 ... 103 H3
van Bank *ALS/KID* ST7 ... 52 C3
  TTPK/GDPK/PENN WV4 ... 294 F6
van Cl *ALS/KID* ST7 ... 52 D2
  TWY WS6 ... 249 J8
  RUGE WS15 ... 216 F8
  RUGE WS15 ... 216 A5
  STAFN ST16 ... 4 A6
vancote Dr
  TTPK/GDPK/PENN WV4 ... 294 C5
van Farm La
  AUD/MAD/W CW3 ... 96 B1
vanfields *BDMR/CCFT* WV3 ... 294 E3
vanland Gv *LNGTN* ST3 ... 86 D6
van La *RSTAF* ST18 ... 211 M4
  RUGE WS15 ... 180 A4
  STOKE ST4 ... 84 E7
  WOLVN WV10 ... 265 J1
van Ms *LICH* WS13 ... 8 D4
vanmore Cl *BDMR/CCFT* WV3 ... 294 E3
vanmote *CRTAM* B79 ... 273 M5
vannington St
  BUTN/AL/TUT DE13 ... 185 H4
van Pas *BLYBR/FOR* ST11 ... 103 L3
van Pool Gv
  RUSH/SHEL WS4 ... 284 D1
van Rd *ASHB* DE6 ... 163 K4
  LICH WS13 ... 8 D4
  LICHS WS14 ... 255 L4
van Sq *STOKE* ST4 ... 85 G2
  STRBR DY8 ... 307 L5
  WOLV WV1 ... 13 L5
vanton Pl *STOKE* ST4 ... 100 F3
varbourn Cl
  BUTN/AL/TUT DE13 ... 201 G8
vaything Gv *BUCK/MIL* ST2 ... 86 D1
veetbriar La *SHHTH* WV12 ... 282 D5
veetbriar Wy *STAFS* ST17 ... 194 C4
veetbriar Dr *STRBR* DY8 ... 307 L1
veetman Pl
  DUNHL/THL/PER WV6 ... 12 B2
veetpeace La *GNOS* ST20 ... 208 E8
veetpool La *HAG/WOL* DY9 ... 311 H5
vettenham Cl *ALS/KID* ST7 ... 37 J7
vift *TAM/AM/WIL* B77 ... 11 K8
vift Cl *ALS/KID* ST7 ... 39 H8
vift Dr *BIDD* ST8 ... 40 E2
vift Pl *LNGTN* ST3 ... 86 F5
vinburne Cl *LNGTN* ST3 ... 85 M8
  STAFS ST17 ... 193 J2
vindale *TAM/AM/WIL* B77 ... 291 H4
vindon Rd *KGSWFD* DY6 ... 302 F2
vinfen Broun Rd *LICH* WS13 ... 8 C2
vinford Leys *WMBN* WV5 ... 297 K5
vinford Rd *WOLVN* WV10 ... 280 E5
vin Forge Wy *STAFS* ST17 ... 297 L8
vingle Hill Rd *LNGTN* ST3 ... 85 M7
vinscoe Hl *ASHB* DE6 ... 77 M6
vinson Cl *UTXR* ST14 ... 109 C7
viss Dr *STRBR* DY8 ... 303 M8
viss Lodge Dr
  POL/KGSB/FAZ B78 ... 289 M2
vithin Cl *STOKE* ST4 ... 86 B4
vynnerton Dr *WNSFLD* WV11 ... 265 M6
vcamore *TAM/AM/WIL* B77 ... 290 C3
vcamore Av *ALS/KID* ST7 ... 37 L8
  ALS/KID ST7 ... 37 M3
vcamore Cl *ALS/KID* ST7 ... 52 E2
  BIDD ST8 ... 26 E8
  LNGTN ST3 ... 103 C5
  MSHM DE12 ... 223 K5
  RUSH/SHEL WS4 ... 284 B2
  STRBR DY8 ... 307 K8
  UTXR ST14 ... 143 M2
vcamore Crs *RUGE* WS15 ... 216 A4
vcamore Dr *BDMR/CCFT* WV3 ... 294 D1
  RSTAF ST18 ... 177 J2
vcamore Gn *CNCK/NC* WS11 ... 231 J8
  DUDN ST3 ... 299 M5
vcamore Gv *LNGTN* ST3 ... 85 K7
  NEWUL ST5 ... 68 D7
vcamore Hl *RUGE* WS15 ... 233 M5
vcamore La *STAFS* ST17 ... 193 H3
vcamore Rd *ASHB* DE6 ... 94 C3
  BNTWD WS7 ... 251 M3

HEDN WS12 ... 232 F6
KGSWFD DY6 ... 303 L4
RUSH/SHEL WS4 ... 284 D1
STONE ST15 ... 138 B2
STPNHL/WNHL DE15 ... 204 E5
The Sycamores *LICHS* WS14 ... 8 E9
  WOLVN WV10 ... 280 F7
Sycamore Wy *HEDN* WS12 ... 231 K2
Sydenham Pl *BUCK/MIL* ST2 ... 86 D2
Sydenham Rd *WOLVN* WV1 ... 281 H8
Sydnal La *ALBTN* WV7 ... 260 E2
Sydney St *BUT* DE14 ... 185 K4
  NEWUL ST5 ... 68 D8
Syerscote La *CRTAM* B79 ... 240 B8
  CRTAM B79 ... 257 K7
Sykesmoor
  TAM/AM/WIL B77 ... 291 H3
Sylvan Gv *STOKE* ST4 ... 84 E7
Sylvan Wy *STAFS* ST17 ... 194 C5
Symons Wy *MKTDR* TF9 ... 148 F2
Sytch La *WMBN* WV5 ... 298 A5
Sytch Rd *BURS/TUN* ST6 ... 55 G2

T

Tack Farm Rd *STRBR* DY8 ... 307 K1
Tadgedale Av *MKTDR* TF9 ... 114 D6
Tadworth Cl *WOLV* WV1 ... 281 L6
Tag La *MKTDR* TF9 ... 131 L7
Talaton Cl *COVEN* WV9 ... 264 A8
Talbot *TAM/AM/WIL* B77 ... 11 K8
Talbot Av *FOAKS/STRLY* B74 ... 286 A7
Talbot Cl *WSLW* WS2 ... 283 J4
Talbot Dr *WOLV* WV1 ... 260 E5
  BKHL/PFLD WV2 ... 295 J4
  RUGE WS15 ... 215 M4
  STAFS ST17 ... 4 F8
Talbot St *HAN* ST1 ... 2 E8
  LEEK ST13 ... 43 M5
  RUGE WS15 ... 215 M2
Talbot Wy *MKTDR* TF9 ... 112 C8
Talke Rd *ALS/KID* ST7 ... 37 L7
  NEWUL ST5 ... 52 D7
Talland Av *TAM/AM/WIL* B77 ... 11 K4
Tallis Gv *HAN* ST1 ... 3 K2
Tallpines *STAFS* ST17 ... 194 C3
Tall Trees Cl
  FOAKS/STRLY B74 ... 286 D6
  SHHTH WV12 ... 282 D4
Talsarn Gv *STOKE* ST4 ... 101 J4
Tamar Cl *BRWNH* WS8 ... 251 J8
Tamar Dr *SEDG* DY3 ... 299 M4
  DUNHL/THL/PER WV6 ... 278 E6
  STAFS ST17 ... 193 H2
  WLNHL WV13 ... 282 C8
Tamar Rd *ALS/KID* ST7 ... 39 H8
  TAM/AM/WIL B77 ... 291 G5
Tame Av *BNTWD* WS7 ... 252 D4
Tame Cl *BIDD* ST8 ... 40 D1
Tame Dr *BLOX/PEL* WS3 ... 284 A1
Tamedrive *POL/KGSB/FAZ* B78 ... 10 A5
Tame Gv *CNCK/NC* WS11 ... 249 K2
Tame St *TAM/AM/WIL* B77 ... 10 E7
Tamworth Cl *BRWNH* WS8 ... 251 M8
Tamworth Rd *CRTAM* B79 ... 256 C7
  LICHS WS14 ... 9 M8
  POL/KGSB/FAZ B78 ... 291 L1
  TAM/AM/WIL B77 ... 275 H4
Tamworth Rd (Amington)
  TAM/AM/WIL B77 ... 11 K4
Tamworth Rd (Dosthill)
  TAM/AM/WIL B77 ... 290 C4
Tamworth St *LICH* WS13 ... 8 F3
Tanfield Cl
  DUNHL/THL/PER WV6 ... 279 H7
Tanglewood Gv *SEDG* DY3 ... 295 J8
Tangmere Cl
  DUNHL/THL/PER WV6 ... 278 E5
Tanhill *TAM/AM/WIL* B77 ... 291 H3
Tanners Rd *BUCK/MIL* ST2 ... 70 B3
Tannery Cl *RUGE* WS15 ... 215 M1
  WSLW WS2 ... 283 K7
Tansey Cl *BUCK/MIL* ST2 ... 3 M6
Tansley Vw *BKHL/PFLD* WV2 ... 295 K3
Tansy *TAM/AM/WIL* B77 ... 10 F8
Tanyard *LICH* WS13 ... 8 F2
Tape St *CDLE* ST10 ... 89 K7
Taplin Cl *STAFN* ST16 ... 174 C3
Taplow Pl *CNCK/NC* WS11 ... 231 M6
Tapton Cl *BLOX/PEL* WS3 ... 267 J7
Tara Gv *BUCK/MIL* ST2 ... 55 G8
Targate Ct *RUGE* WS15 ... 217 G5
Target Cl *ALS/KID* ST7 ... 52 E4
Tarleton Rd *HAN* ST1 ... 3 G5
Tarporley Gv *STOKE* ST4 ... 84 E5
Tarragon Dr *LNGTN* ST3 ... 103 C4
Tarvin Gv *BURS/TUN* ST6 ... 53 M4
Tasman Gv
  DUNHL/THL/PER WV6 ... 278 E5
Tatenhill Common
  BUTN/AL/TUT DE13 ... 183 K8
Tatenhill La *BUTN/AL/TUT* DE13 ... 183 K7
Tatlowfold La *LEEK* ST13 ... 60 F6
Tatton Cl *ALS/KID* ST7 ... 37 J7
  LEEK ST13 ... 43 H6
Tatton St *LNGTN* ST3 ... 86 C1
Taunton Av *WOLVN* WV10 ... 264 D6
Taunton Rd *NEWUL* ST5 ... 67 M3
Taunton Wy *BUCK/MIL* ST2 ... 70 D8
Taurus Gv *BURS/TUN* ST6 ... 53 M4
Taverners Cl *SHHTH* WV12 ... 282 C1
Tavistock Av *STAFS* ST17 ... 194 D1
Tavistock Cl *CRTAM* B79 ... 274 C3
Tavistock Crs *NEWUL* ST5 ... 84 A5
Tavistock Pl *STOKE* ST4 ... 84 E1
Tavistock Rd *ALS/KID* ST7 ... 39 H8
Tawney Cl *RUGE* WS15 ... 216 A4
Tawney Crs *LNGTN* ST3 ... 87 H7
Tay Cl *BIDD* ST8 ... 40 E1
  CDLE ST10 ... 89 L5
  LNGTN ST3 ... 86 L5
Taylor Av *BLOX/PEL* WS3 ... 283 K2
  NEWUL ST5 ... 68 C6
Taylor Rd *BUCK/MIL* ST2 ... 70 B4
  TTPK/GDPK/PENN WV4 ... 295 M5
Taylor's La *CW/HAS* CW1 ... 36 C7
  RUGE WS15 ... 215 L1
Taylor St *BURS/TUN* ST6 ... 53 J3

NEWUL ST5 ... 68 C6
WNSFLD WV11 ... 281 J5
Taylor Wk *STAFS* ST17 ... 193 J3
Teal Cl *NEWUL* ST5 ... 98 C5
Teal Vw *BURS/TUN* ST6 ... 54 A2
Tean Cl *BNTWD* WS7 ... 252 D4
  STPNHL/WNHL DE15 ... 205 G1
Teanhurst Rd *CDLE* ST10 ... 105 M8
Tean Rd *CDLE* ST10 ... 105 K2
Teasel Gv *WOLVN* WV10 ... 265 H5
Teasel Rd *WNSFLD* WV11 ... 281 L5
Tebworth Cl *COVEN* WV9 ... 263 M8
Tedder Rd *STAFN* ST16 ... 5 K1
Teddesley Ct *CNCK/NC* WS11 ... 231 L7
Teddesley Rd *HEDN* WS12 ... 229 M1
Teddesley St *RUSH/SHEL* WS4 ... 283 M7
Teddesley Wy *HEDN* WS12 ... 231 J4
Teesdale Cl *WOLV* WV1 ... 281 G8
Teign *TAM/AM/WIL* B77 ... 291 G6
Telegraph St *STAFS* ST17 ... 4 E7
Telford Av *ALBTN* WV7 ... 261 G4
  GTWY WS6 ... 249 M7
Telford Cl *ALS/KID* ST7 ... 52 E2
  BNTWD WS7 ... 252 B2
  WSLW WS2 ... 283 G5
Telford Dr *STAFN* ST16 ... 174 F2
Telford Gdns *BDMR/CCFT* WV3 ... 294 D3
  PENK ST19 ... 246 C3
Telford Gv *HEDN* WS12 ... 232 B3
Telford La *GNOS* ST20 ... 190 C5
Telford Rd *CRTAM* B79 ... 273 M2
  WSLW WS2 ... 283 G5
Telford Wy *BURS/TUN* ST6 ... 54 A6
Tellwright Gv *NEWUL* ST5 ... 68 A4
Tellwright St *BURS/TUN* ST6 ... 54 A8
Telmah Cl
  BUTN/AL/TUT DE13 ... 185 K1
Teme Gv *WLNHL* WV13 ... 282 D8
Teme Rd *STRBR* DY8 ... 307 M7
Tempest St *BKHL/PFLD* WV2 ... 13 G6
  CRTAM B79 ... 10 B3
Templar Crs *NEWUL* ST5 ... 68 A4
Templars Wy *PENK* ST19 ... 229 M2
Templar Ter *NEWUL* ST5 ... 68 A4
Temple Bar *WLNHL* WV13 ... 282 A7
Temple Cl *BUTN/AL/TUT* DE13 ... 185 L3
Temple Rd *WLNHL* WV13 ... 282 A7
Temple Sq *WOLV* WV1 ... 13 G5
Temple St *BKHL/PFLD* WV2 ... 12 F6
  SEDG DY3 ... 299 K7
  STOKE ST4 ... 85 K4
Templeton Av *BUCK/MIL* ST2 ... 86 C2
Tenacre La *SEDG* DY3 ... 299 L5
Tenbury Cl *ALDR* WS9 ... 285 J2
  WSLW WS2 ... 282 D7
Tenbury Ct
  TTPK/GDPK/PENN WV4 ... 294 D5
Tenbury Gdns
  TTPK/GDPK/PENN WV4 ... 294 D5
Ten Butts Crs *STAFS* ST17 ... 193 M5
Tenby Dr *STAFN* ST16 ... 174 F3
Tenby Gv *NEWUL* ST5 ... 67 L3
Tenford La *CDLE* ST10 ... 105 K5
Tennant Pl *NEWUL* ST5 ... 68 B3
Tennscore Av *GTWY* WS6 ... 249 L7
Tennyson Av *ALS/KID* ST7 ... 53 G2
  BNTWD WS7 ... 252 A1
  CRTAM B79 ... 10 B2
  FOAKS/STRLY B74 ... 286 F4
Tennyson Cl *ALS/KID* ST7 ... 37 L2
  CDLE ST10 ... 89 H8
  MKTDR TF9 ... 130 K3
Tennyson Gdns *LNGTN* ST3 ... 85 M8
Tennyson Rd *BLOX/PEL* WS3 ... 283 L2
  BUT DE14 ... 185 K3
  SEDG DY3 ... 299 G5
  SHHTH WV12 ... 282 E2
  STAFS ST17 ... 193 G1
  WOLVN WV10 ... 281 G1
Tenterbanks *STAFN* ST16 ... 4 D5
Tercel Gv *LNGTN* ST3 ... 103 C3
Tern Cl *ALS/KID* ST7 ... 39 J8
Tern Cl *BIDD* ST8 ... 40 E2
  TTPK/GDPK/PENN WV4 ... 295 K7
Tern Gv *MKTDR* TF9 ... 114 F5
Tern Vw *MKTDR* TF9 ... 130 K3
The Terrace *BDMR/CCFT* WV3 ... 294 C1
  CDLE ST10 ... 89 J7
Terrington Dr *NEWUL* ST5 ... 84 B8
Terry Cl *LICH* WS13 ... 235 M8
  LNGTN ST3 ... 87 H7
Terson Wy *STOKE* ST4 ... 86 F6
Tetley Av *RUSH/SHEL* WS4 ... 284 A6
Tettenhall Rd
  DUNHL/THL/PER WV6 ... 279 M7
Teveray Dr *PENK* ST19 ... 229 M3
Tewkesbury Cl *STAFS* ST17 ... 3 M4
Tewkesbury Rd *BLOX/PEL* WS3 ... 266 E8
Tewnals La *LICH* WS13 ... 235 L4
Thackeray Dr *CRTAM* B79 ... 274 A3
  LNGTN ST3 ... 86 A8
Thackeray Wk *STAFS* ST17 ... 193 J3
Thames Cl *BIDD* ST8 ... 40 E1
  CDLE ST10 ... 105 L1
Thames Rd *BLOX/PEL* WS3 ... 283 K2
  NEWUL ST5 ... 84 A7
Thames Wy *STAFS* ST17 ... 193 H2
Thanet Cl *KGSWFD* DY6 ... 303 J4
Thanet Gv *NEWUL* ST5 ... 84 A7
Thatcham Gn *LNGTN* ST3 ... 101 J3
Thatcher Gv *BIDD* ST8 ... 40 B2
Thatchmoor La
  BUTN/AL/TUT DE13 ... 201 J3
Thelma Av *BURS/TUN* ST6 ... 55 H3
Theodore Rd *BUCK/MIL* ST2 ... 70 B7
Theresa Cl *STOKE* ST4 ... 85 G8
The Roaches *LEEK* ST13 ... 21 J7
Thetford Gdns *WNSFLD* WV11 ... 281 K4
Third Av *ALS/KID* ST7 ... 52 L1
  BRWNH WS8 ... 269 G1
  BUCK/MIL ST2 ... 70 D6
  BUT DE14 ... 203 M1
  WOLVN WV10 ... 280 E3
Thirlmere Cl *CNCK/NC* WS11 ... 249 L1
  DUNHL/THL/PER WV6 ... 279 K2
Thirlmere Dr *WNSFLD* WV11 ... 266 A8
Thirlmere Gv
  DUNHL/THL/PER WV6 ... 278 F6

LNGTN ST3 ... 86 E7
Thirlmere Rd *NEWUL* ST5 ... 67 G8
Thirsk Pl *NEWUL* ST5 ... 67 G8
Thirston Cl *WNSFLD* WV11 ... 282 A5
Thistleberry Av *NEWUL* ST5 ... 83 M3
Thistle Cl *RUGE* WS15 ... 197 J3
  SEDG DY3 ... 299 M4
Thistle Cft *WNSFLD* WV11 ... 281 K5
Thistledown Av *BNTWD* WS7 ... 252 A4
Thistle Down Cl
  FOAKS/STRLY B74 ... 286 A8
Thistledown Dr *HEDN* WS12 ... 250 D1
  WOLVN WV10 ... 265 G3
The Thistles *NEWUL* ST5 ... 83 M3
Thistley Hough *STOKE* ST4 ... 84 F4
Thistley Nook *LICH* WS13 ... 254 A1
Thomas Av *NEWUL* ST5 ... 68 A6
  STAFN ST16 ... 174 B7
  STONE ST15 ... 138 C4
Thomas Cl *ALS/KID* ST7 ... 37 L6
Thomas Mason Cl
  WNSFLD WV11 ... 281 K3
Thomas St *ALS/KID* ST7 ... 52 D2
  ALS/KID ST7 ... 53 M1
  BIDD ST8 ... 40 C1
  BKHL/PFLD WV2 ... 12 F8
  LEEK ST13 ... 43 K3
  TAM/AM/WIL B77 ... 11 H6
  WSLW WS2 ... 283 K8
Thompson Av *BKHL/PFLD* WV2 ... 295 K3
Thompson Cl *STAFS* ST17 ... 193 J3
  WLNHL WV13 ... 282 A7
Thompson Rd *RUGE* WS15 ... 216 B5
Thompson St *WLNHL* WV13 ... 282 A7
Thompstone Av *NEWUL* ST5 ... 67 M7
Thor Cl *CNCK/NC* WS11 ... 232 A5
Thoresby *CRTAM* B79 ... 273 L4
Thorley Dr *CDLE* ST10 ... 89 M8
Thorley's Hl *RUGE* WS15 ... 234 C4
Thornburrow Dr *STOKE* ST4 ... 84 E3
Thornbury Ct
  DUNHL/THL/PER WV6 ... 279 G7
Thornby Av
  TAM/AM/WIL B77 ... 290 F2
Thorncliffe Vw *LEEK* ST13 ... 44 B2
Thorncliff Gv *HAN* ST1 ... 3 H2
Thorncliff Rd *LEEK* ST13 ... 44 B3
Thorn Cl *RUGE* WS15 ... 216 A4
Thorndyke Cl *HAN* ST1 ... 2 A1
Thorne Av *WOLVN* WV10 ... 280 E3
Thorne Rd *WLNHL* WV13 ... 282 A6
Thornes Cft *ALDR* WS9 ... 269 L6
Thornescroft Gdns *BUT* DE14 ... 204 B3
Thornewill Dr
  BUTN/AL/TUT DE13 ... 185 M1
Thorneycroft Av
  BURS/TUN ST6 ... 54 B8
Thorneycroft La *WOLVN* WV10 ... 281 G5
Thorneyfields La *RSTAF* ST18 ... 193 G4
  STAFS ST17 ... 193 G4
Thornfield Av *LEEK* ST13 ... 44 B5
Thornfield Crs *BNTWD* WS7 ... 252 A2
Thornfield Cft *SEDG* DY3 ... 299 L3
Thornham Cl *NEWUL* ST5 ... 84 B8
Thornhill Cl *BUTN/AL/TUT* DE13 ... 202 C8
Thornhill Dr *AUD/MAD/W* CW3 ... 81 L3
Thornhill Rd *BUCK/MIL* ST2 ... 86 C2
  HEDN WS12 ... 231 M3
  LEEK ST13 ... 43 J6
Thornleigh *SEDG* DY3 ... 299 K5
Thornley Cl *WNSFLD* WV11 ... 281 M1
Thornley Rd *BURS/TUN* ST6 ... 53 M7
  WNSFLD WV11 ... 281 M1
Thornley St *BUT* DE14 ... 185 K5
  WOLV WV1 ... 13 G3
Thornton Rd *STOKE* ST4 ... 85 J2
Thorn Tree La
  STPNHL/WNHL DE15 ... 205 M2
Thornyedge Rd *END/WER* WS9 ... 56 A8
Thornyhurst La *LICHS* WS14 ... 270 A5
Thorny La *BUTN/AL/TUT* DE13 ... 181 M2
  UTXR ST14 ... 161 L4
Thorny Rd *STONE* ST15 ... 136 M3
Thorpe Av *BNTWD* WS7 ... 251 K2
Thorpe Cl *BNTWD* WS7 ... 251 K2
  STPNHL/WNHL DE15 ... 205 J1
Thorpe Gn *LNGTN* ST3 ... 101 M3
Thorpe Ri *CDLE* ST10 ... 89 L4
Thorpe St *BNTWD* WS7 ... 251 K2
Thorswood La *ASHB* DE6 ... 77 H8
Three Mile La *NEWUL* ST5 ... 82 F4
Three Tuns La *WOLVN* WV10 ... 264 C8
Threshers Dr *SHHTH* WV12 ... 282 D4
Thrift Rd *BUT* DE14 ... 204 B2
Thurlstone Dr
  TTPK/GDPK/PENN WV4 ... 294 F6
Thurlstone Rd *BLOX/PEL* WS3 ... 267 H7
Thurlwood Dr *BURS/TUN* ST6 ... 54 F8
Thursfield Av *ALS/KID* ST7 ... 39 J7
Thursfield Pl *BURS/TUN* ST6 ... 54 D6
Thurso *TAM/AM/WIL* B77 ... 11 K4
Thurston Wy *BUCK/MIL* ST2 ... 86 C2
Thurvaston Rd *ASHB* DE6 ... 127 M1
Thyme Gv *LNGTN* ST3 ... 103 H4
Tibberton Cl
  BDMR/CCFT WV3 ... 294 D3
Tibb St *ALS/KID* ST7 ... 51 M8
Tiber Dr *NEWUL* ST5 ... 67 K5
Tickhill La *BLYBR/FOR* ST11 ... 88 A4
Tidebrook Pl *BURS/TUN* ST6 ... 53 L3
Tideswell Gn *SWAD* DE11 ... 205 L5
Tideswell Rd *LNGTN* ST3 ... 86 C5
Tierney St *HAN* ST1 ... 2 F5
Tiffany La *COVEN* WV9 ... 263 M8
Tilbrook Cl *BUCK/MIL* ST2 ... 86 C2
Tilbury Pl *BDMR/CCFT* WV3 ... 294 A2
Tilcon Av *RSTAF* ST18 ... 175 J8
Tildesley Cl *PENK* ST19 ... 229 L2
Tildesley Dr *SHHTH* WV12 ... 282 B5
Tilehurst Pl *LNGTN* ST3 ... 101 L1
Tilery La *LNGTN* ST3 ... 101 L1
Tilewright Cl *ALS/KID* ST7 ... 39 H8
Tilia Rd *TAM/AM/WIL* B77 ... 275 C4
Tilling Dr *STONE* ST15 ... 138 A4
Tillington St *STAFN* ST16 ... 174 D5
Tilson Av *STOKE* ST4 ... 84 F3
Tilstone Cl *ALS/KID* ST7 ... 53 C2
Timberfields Rd *STONE* ST15 ... 136 E4
Timber Gv *PENK* ST19 ... 246 D4
Timber La *UTXR* ST14 ... 144 B4

Timber Pit La *PENK* ST19 ... 227 H6
Timble Cl *BUCK/MIL* ST2 ... 86 C2
Timmis Cl *HAN* ST1 ... 69 G7
Timor Gv *STOKE* ST4 ... 101 H2
Timothy Cl *LNGTN* ST3 ... 86 C4
Tinacre Hl
  DUNHL/THL/PER WV6 ... 278 E8
Tinker's Castle Rd *WMBN* WV5 ... 296 F1
Tinkers Green Rd
  TAM/AM/WIL B77 ... 291 G4
Tinkers La *MKTDR* TF9 ... 114 F5
  PENK ST19 ... 246 D5
  UTXR ST14 ... 161 M3
Tinsell Brook *RDERBYSW* DE65 ... 166 D1
Tintagel Cl *BUTN/AL/TUT* DE13 ... 166 E8
  DUNHL/THL/PER WV6 ... 278 F7
Tintagel Dr *DUDN* ST3 ... 299 L8
Tintagel Pl *BUCK/MIL* ST2 ... 86 D2
Tintern Ct
  DUNHL/THL/PER WV6 ... 278 E6
Tintern Crs *BLOX/PEL* WS3 ... 266 F8
Tintern Pl *NEWUL* ST5 ... 67 M3
Tintern St *HAN* ST1 ... 3 G6
Tintern Wy *BLOX/PEL* WS3 ... 266 F8
Tipping Av *LNGTN* ST3 ... 103 H1
Tipping St *STAFN* ST16 ... 4 F5
Tipton Rd *SEDG* DY3 ... 299 L3
Tirley St *STOKE* ST4 ... 85 L5
Tissington Pl *BLYBR/FOR* ST11 ... 103 J3
Tissington Trail *ASHB* DE6 ... 78 F2
  BUX SK17 ... 35 K6
Titan Wy *LICHS* WS14 ... 254 F2
Titchfield Cl *WOLVN* WV10 ... 264 E6
Tithe Barn Ct *STAFN* ST16 ... 5 J2
Tithe Barn La *RUGE* WS15 ... 234 C5
Tithebarn Rd *RUGE* WS15 ... 197 L8
Tithe Barn Rd *STAFN* ST16 ... 5 J4
Tithe Cft *WOLV* WV10 ... 13 M2
Tithe Rd *WNSFLD* WV11 ... 281 K4
Tittensor Rd *BARL* ST12 ... 119 H2
  NEWUL ST5 ... 84 C5
Titterton La *LEEK* ST13 ... 46 B6
Titterton St *STOKE* ST4 ... 85 J4
Tittesworth Av *LEEK* ST13 ... 44 A3
Tiverton Av *STAFS* ST17 ... 194 C3
Tiverton Rd *BUCK/MIL* ST2 ... 86 C1
Tixall Rd *STAFN* ST16 ... 5 L4
Toft End Rd *NEWUL* ST5 ... 68 B1
Tolkien Wy *STOKE* ST4 ... 85 C2
Toll Bar Rd *END/WER* ST9 ... 71 K6
Tolldish La *RSTAF* ST18 ... 177 J7
Tollgate Av *NEWUL* ST5 ... 98 D5
Tollgate Cl *ALS/KID* ST7 ... 52 C2
Tollgate Dr *STAFS* ST17 ... 174 F3
Tollgate Rd *UTXR* ST14 ... 125 M8
Tolman Dr *TAM/AM/WIL* B77 ... 10 F7
Tolson Av *POL/KGSB/FAZ* B78 ... 290 B2
Tolson Cl *TAM/AM/WIL* B77 ... 290 C5
Tolworth Gdns
  BKHL/PFLD WV2 ... 295 L3
Tomfields *ALS/KID* ST7 ... 66 F2
Tom La *KINVER* DY7 ... 296 D5
Tomlinson St *BURS/TUN* ST6 ... 68 D2
Tompkin Rd *END/WER* ST9 ... 56 A5
Tonadine Cl *WNSFLD* WV11 ... 282 A1
Tonbridge Av *BURS/TUN* ST6 ... 54 B6
Tong Cl *PENK* ST19 ... 244 F3
Tong Dr *SHIF* TF11 ... 243 K2
Tong Rd *PENK* ST19 ... 244 F3
Tongue La *BURS/TUN* ST6 ... 54 F5
Tontine St *HAN* ST1 ... 2 D5
Toothill Rd *UTXR* ST14 ... 144 E6
Top Chapel La *BURS/TUN* ST6 ... 55 H1
Top La *STOKE* ST4 ... 118 C1
Top Rd *BIDD* ST8 ... 27 J8
  STAFS ST17 ... 212 B2
Top Station Rd *ALS/KID* ST7 ... 39 J3
Torbay *TAM/AM/WIL* B77 ... 11 K4
Torc Av *TAM/AM/WIL* B77 ... 11 H6
Torfield *CDSL* WV8 ... 263 L8
Torquoise Gv *WOLVN* WV10 ... 232 C7
Torrance Cl *BUT* DE14 ... 204 A4
Torrance Gv *UTXR* ST14 ... 125 M8
Torridge *TAM/AM/WIL* B77 ... 291 G5
Torridge Dr *STAFS* ST17 ... 193 H2
  WNSFLD WV11 ... 281 J5
Torridon Cl *STOKE* ST4 ... 101 J4
Torridon Rd *WNSFLD* WV11 ... 282 A1
Torrington Av *STAFS* ST17 ... 194 C2
Torside *TAM/AM/WIL* B77 ... 291 H3
Tor St *HAN* ST1 ... 69 K3
Torvale Rd
  DUNHL/THL/PER WV6 ... 279 G8
Torville Dr *BIDD* ST8 ... 40 E2
Tor W Wy *BLOX/PEL* WS3 ... 267 M7
Totnes Cl *BUTN/AL/TUT* DE13 ... 185 K3
Tower Cl *BIDD* ST8 ... 40 A4
  MKTDR TF9 ... 130 B1
  BIDD ST8 ... 39 M4
Tower Rd *HEDN* WS12 ... 231 M1
  MCN/WHC B75 ... 287 H7
  MKTDR TF9 ... 114 F6
  STPNHL/WNHL DE15 ... 186 B8
Tower Sq *BURS/TUN* ST6 ... 53 K7
Tower St *SEDG* DY3 ... 299 L1
  WOLV WV1 ... 13 G5
  WSL WS1 ... 283 L8
Tower View Rd *GTWY* WS6 ... 266 F2
Townend *BLYBR/FOR* ST11 ... 121 L2
Town End *CDLE* ST10 ... 89 J7
Town La *ASHB* DE6 ... 77 L5
  CDLE ST10 ... 60 F6
Townfield Cl *ALS/KID* ST7 ... 38 D8
Townfields *LICH* WS13 ... 8 C5
Townfold *BLOX/PEL* WS3 ... 268 A6
Town Hall Yd *ASHB* DE6 ... 79 J8
Town Head *CDLE* ST10 ... 107 L1
Town Hl *BUTN/AL/TUT* DE13 ... 201 J8
Town Rd *HAN* ST1 ... 2 D5
Townsend Av *SEDG* DY3 ... 299 J3
Townsend Cl *CRTAM* B79 ... 259 K6
Townsend La *ALS/KID* ST7 ... 38 A2
Townsend Rd *BUCK/MIL* ST2 ... 70 B7
Townwell Fold *WOLV* WV1 ... 12 E5
Toy Cl *RUGE* WS15 ... 215 K1
Trade St *STOKE* ST4 ... 85 H3

Trafalgar Cl HEDN WS12 .... 232 E6 2
Trafalgar Rd STOKE ST4 .... 84 E2
Trafalgar St HAN WS1 .... 2 C3
Trafford Cl LEEK ST13 .... 44 A5
Transport La LNGTN ST3 .... 86 B7
Tranter Crs HEDN WS12 .... 232 B8
Tranter Rd BUCK/MIL ST2 .... 70 B4
Tranwell Cl COVEN WV9 .... 263 M8 2
Travellers Cl BNTWD WS7 .... 252 A5
Travers St BURS/TUN ST6 .... 68 E3
Treasure Cl TAM/AM/WIL B77 .... 11 J6
Trecastle Gv LNGTN ST3 .... 102 E1
Treetops STAFS ST17 .... 194 C3 2
Treetops Dr SHHTH WV12 .... 282 E5
Tregaron Ct BUCK/MIL ST2 .... 71 G7
Tregenna Ct LNGTN ST3 .... 103 G3
Tregew Pl NEWUL ST5 .... 67 K8
Tregony Ri LICHS WS14 .... 9 J6
Tregowan St BURS/TUN ST6 .... 54 B1
Tremaine Gdns WOLVN WV10 .... 13 H1
Tremont St WOLVN WV10 .... 13 K3
Trenance Cl LICHS WS14 .... 9 J5
Trenchard Av STAFN ST16 .... 5 K2
Trentfield La RSTAF ST18 .... 156 D4
Trentfields Rd BUCK/MIL ST2 .... 55 G8
Trent Gv BIDD ST8 .... 40 D4
NEWUL ST5 .... 84 A7
Trentham Av SHHTH WV12 .... 282 A5
Trentham Cl CNCK/NC WS11 .... 250 B1
Trentham Gardens Cl
STOKE ST4 .... 100 F3 2
Trentham Gv NEWUL ST5 .... 68 C6
Trentham Ri
BKHL/PFLD WV2 .... 295 M3 2
Trentham Rd LNGTN ST3 .... 102 A1
NEWUL ST5 .... 99 K2
STOKE ST4 .... 101 L3
Trent La RSTAF ST18 .... 176 E3
STPNHL/WHNL DE15 .... 186 D2
Trentley Dr BIDD ST8 .... 41 H2
Trentley Rd STOKE ST4 .... 101 G3
Trentmill Rd HAN ST1 .... 3 C8
Trent Pl BLOX/PEL WS3 .... 283 K2
Trent Rd BLOX/PEL WS3 .... 284 A1
BLYBR/FOR ST11 .... 104 A2
CNCK/NC WS11 .... 231 L5
STONE ST15 .... 137 L1
Trentside Rd BURS/TUN ST6 .... 55 C5
Trent St BUCK/MIL ST2 .... 3 K7
BUT DE14 .... 6 F9
Trent Valley Rd LICH WS13 .... 9 J3
STOKE ST4 .... 84 F5
Trent View Cl RUGE WS15 .... 215 M3
Trent Wk HAN ST1 .... 4 E9
RSTAF ST18 .... 176 D3
Trentway Cl RSTAF ST18 .... 176 D3
Tresham Rd KGSWFD DY6 .... 303 K2 2
Trevelyan's Gn STAFN ST16 .... 174 C2 1
Trevelyn Cl
STPNHL/WHNL DE15 .... 205 J1
Trevithick Cl BNTWD WS7 .... 252 C2
Trevor Av GTWY WS6 .... 250 A7
Trevor Dr BLYBR/FOR ST11 .... 87 K7
Trevor Rd BLOX/PEL WS3 .... 267 M6
Trevose Cl BLOX/PEL WS3 .... 266 F7 2
Trimley Wy BUCK/MIL ST2 .... 70 B8
Trimpley Gdns
ETTPK/GDPK/PENN WV4 .... 294 E7
Trimpley La BEWD DY12 .... 308 C3
Trimpos CDLE ST10 .... 89 C6
Triner Pl BURS/TUN ST6 .... 54 E6
Tring Ct DUNHL/THL/PER WV6 .... 279 M6
STRBR DY8 .... 303 K8
Trinity Cl CNCK/NC WS11 .... 249 L2
STRBR DY8 .... 303 K8
Trinity Dr STONE ST15 .... 137 M1
Trinity Gorse STAFN ST16 .... 174 B2
Trinity Pl BUCK/MIL ST2 .... 70 B6
CONG CW12 .... 26 B2
Trinity Ri STAFN ST16 .... 174 B2
Trinity Rd ECCH ST21 .... 152 D4
SHHTH WV12 .... 282 D4
UTXR ST14 .... 144 C3
Trinity St HAN ST1 .... 2 C5
Tristram Gv BUTN/AL/TUT DE13 .... 166 E8
Triton Cl GTWY WS6 .... 266 F1
Triumph TAM/AM/WIL B77 .... 11 K9
Trojan TAM/AM/WIL B77 .... 11 K9
Troon TAM/AM/WIL B77 .... 275 J6
Troon Cl BLOX/PEL WS3 .... 267 G7
Troon Ct DUNHL/THL/PER WV6 .... 278 D5
Troon Pl STRBR DY8 .... 303 J7
Troutdale Cl STOKE ST4 .... 86 B3
Trowbridge Crs BUCK/MIL ST2 .... 70 C8
Trubshaw Cl RSTAF ST18 .... 196 E2 2
Trubshaw St BURS/TUN ST6 .... 68 D2 2
Trubshaw Pl ALS/KID ST7 .... 39 H7
Truro Cl LICH WS13 .... 236 E7
Truro Pl BUCK/MIL ST2 .... 70 B8
Trussell Cl STAFS ST17 .... 212 A1
Trustley Cl BUT DE14 .... 204 B3 3
Trysull Gdns BDMR/CCFT WV3 .... 294 D3
Trysull Holloway WMBN WV5 .... 293 J7
Trysull Rd BDMR/CCFT WV3 .... 294 D3
WMBN WV5 .... 297 L1
Tudor Cl BDMR/CCFT WV3 .... 252 B4
GTWY WS6 .... 249 L7
LICHS WS14 .... 254 F4
NWPT TF10 .... 188 A6 2
STOKE ST4 .... 85 G4
STONE ST15 .... 137 M4
Tudor Ct WNSFLD WV11 .... 265 M7
Tudor Crs BKHL/PFLD WV2 .... 295 H4
TAM/AM/WIL B77 .... 11 L6
Tudor Gdns NEWUL ST5 .... 68 C6
Tudor Hollow BLYBR/FOR ST11 .... 121 L1
BUTN/AL/TUT DE13 .... 185 KJ 11
Tudor Pl SEDG DY3 .... 299 L4 2
Tudor Ri CRTAM B79 .... 240 E8
STAFN ST16 .... 174 C2 2
Tudor Rd BNTWD WS7 .... 252 C4
HEDN WS12 .... 231 M2
SEDG DY3 .... 299 L4
WOLVN WV10 .... 281 G6

The Tudors BURS/TUN ST6 .... 53 M6
Tudor V SEDG DY3 .... 299 L4
Tudor Wy GTWY WS6 .... 266 D1
STAFS ST17 .... 193 H1
Tuke Pl LICH WS13 .... 8 B1
Tulip Gv NEWUL ST5 .... 68 C8
Tulley Pl BUCK/MIL ST2 .... 3 M7
Tullis Cl STAFN ST16 .... 4 A6
Tulsa Ct BUCK/MIL ST2 .... 86 A1
Tunbridge NEWUL ST5 .... 66 F8
Tunley St STONE ST15 .... 137 M1
Tunnicliffe Cl LNGTN ST3 .... 86 E7
Tunnicliffe Dr RUGE WS15 .... 215 K1
Tunnicliffe Wy UTXR ST14 .... 125 M8
Tunstall La GNOS ST20 .... 150 E7
Tunstall Rd BIDD ST8 .... 40 C5
CONG CW12 .... 26 E2
Tuppenhurst La RUGE WS15 .... 217 K6
Turf Pitts La MGN/WHC B75 .... 287 M5
Turin Dr NEWUL ST5 .... 83 L4
Turls Hill Rd SEDG DY3 .... 299 L2
Turls St SEDG DY3 .... 299 L3
Turnberry NEWUL ST5 .... 83 K4 2
Turnberry Dr STOKE ST4 .... 100 F2
Turnberry Gv CDSL WV8 .... 278 D5
Turnberry Rd BLOX/PEL WS3 .... 267 G7
Turnbury Cl BUT DE14 .... 204 A3
Turner Av ALS/KID ST7 .... 67 G1
ETTPK/GDPK/PENN WV4 .... 295 M8
Turner Cl CNCK/NC WS11 .... 232 D8
Turner Crs NEWUL ST5 .... 67 L4
Turner Cft LICH WS13 .... 237 K2
Turner Gv
DUNHL/THL/PER WV6 .... 279 G6
Turner's Gv SEDG DY3 .... 299 J6 2
Turner's Hill Rd SEDG DY3 .... 299 J6
Turner St HAN WS1 .... 2 F2
SEDG DY3 .... 299 K2
Turney Gv STAFS ST17 .... 193 J2
Turney Rd STRBR DY8 .... 307 M4
Turnham Gn
DUNHL/THL/PER WV6 .... 278 E7
Turnhill Cl STAFS ST17 .... 193 J4
Turnhill Gv NEWUL ST5 .... 68 B3
Turnhurst Rd BURS/TUN ST6 .... 53 M3
Turnlea Cl BIDD ST8 .... 40 B4
Turnock St BUCK/MIL ST2 .... 70 C6
Turnstone Dr WOLVN WV10 .... 265 H3
Turton Cl BLOX/PEL WS3 .... 267 G6
BUTN/AL/TUT DE13 .... 220 A8
Tuscan Cl CDLE ST10 .... 105 J1 11
Tuscan St LNGTN ST3 .... 86 C6
Tuscan Wy NEWUL ST5 .... 67 K4
Tutbury TAM/AM/WIL B77 .... 290 C3
Tutbury Av
DUNHL/THL/PER WV6 .... 278 F7
Tutbury Cl HEDN WS12 .... 232 C7
Tutbury Gv LNGTN ST3 .... 86 D6 2
Tutbury Rd BUTN/AL/TUT DE13 .... 166 A8
Tutehill TAM/AM/WIL B77 .... 291 H3 2
Tuxford Cl WOLVN WV10 .... 13 J1
Twayblade BUT DE14 .... 204 B2
Tweed Gv NEWUL ST5 .... 84 A6 2
Tweed St STOKE ST4 .... 85 L6 2
Twemlow Cl RSTAF ST18 .... 173 K8
Twemlow St HAN ST1 .... 69 C7 2
Twentylands
BUTN/AL/TUT DE13 .... 166 D6 1
Twickenham Ct STRBR DY8 .... 307 J3
Twigg St BUCK/MIL ST2 .... 70 B8
Twisses Bank ASHB DE6 .... 129 C8
Twizles La CRTAM B79 .... 258 A1
Twyford Cl ALDR WS9 .... 285 H5
SWAD DE11 .... 205 M8
Twyford Gv WNSFLD WV11 .... 281 M3
Twyning Gn LNGTN ST3 .... 101 M3
Tylecote Crs RSTAF ST18 .... 177 H8
Tyler Gv BURS/TUN ST6 .... 68 E2
STONE ST15 .... 137 L3
Tyne Cl BRWNH WS8 .... 251 J8
Tynedale Crs
ETTPK/GDPK/PENN WV4 .... 295 L7
Tyneham Gv BUCK/MIL ST2 .... 55 C8 4
Tyne Wy NEWUL ST5 .... 84 A6
Tyning Cl COVEN WV9 .... 264 A8
Tyninghame Av
DUNHL/THL/PER WV6 .... 279 K4
Tynings La ALDR WS9 .... 285 C5
Tynwald Gra NEWUL ST5 .... 68 A8
Tyrell Gv HAN ST1 .... 69 M2
Tyrley Cl DUNHL/THL/PER WV6 .... 279 H8
Tyrley Rd MKTDR TF9 .... 130 F5
Tyrol Cl STRBR DY8 .... 307 K4
Tythebarn Dr KGSWFD DY6 .... 303 G3

U

Ubberley Rd BUCK/MIL ST2 .... 70 B8
Uffington Pde BUCK/MIL ST2 .... 86 B2
Ufton Cl LNGTN ST3 .... 101 M4
Ullswater TAM/AM/WIL B77 .... 291 H3 2
Ullswater Av BURS/TUN ST6 .... 68 E2
Ullswater Dr CDLE ST10 .... 89 L6
STONE ST15 .... 138 D3
Ullswater Gdns KGSWFD DY6 .... 303 K4 2
Ullswater Pl CNCK/NC WS11 .... 249 L1
Ullswater Rd WNSFLD WV11 .... 282 B1
Ulster Cl CNCK/NC WS11 .... 232 A7
Ulster Dr KGSWFD DY6 .... 303 L6
Ulster Ter STOKE ST4 .... 85 G5
Ulverston Rd LNGTN ST3 .... 101 M3
Umberleigh Rd LNGTN ST3 .... 101 L3
Underhill La WOLVN WV10 .... 265 G7
Underley Cl KGSWFD DY6 .... 303 H3 2
Under Rainow Rd CONG CW12 .... 26 E1
Under the Hi BIDD ST8 .... 41 G1
Undertown La ASHB DE6 .... 109 J4
Underwood Cl STAFN ST16 .... 174 C2 2
Underwood Rd NEWUL ST5 .... 82 F1
Unicorn Pl BUCK/MIL ST2 .... 53 M5
Union La WMBN WV5 .... 297 K1
Union Mill St WOLV WV1 .... 13 J3
Union St ASHB DE6 .... 79 H8
BNTWD WS7 .... 251 L5
BUT DE14 .... 7 G6
CNCK/NC WS11 .... 249 L4
HAN ST1 .... 2 C3
LEEK ST13 .... 43 M4

WLNHL WV13 .... 282 A8
WOLV WV1 .... 13 H5
WSL WS1 .... 283 M8
Unity Av BURS/TUN ST6 .... 69 K3
Unity Wy ALS/KID ST7 .... 52 D2
Unwin Crs STRBR DY8 .... 307 L5
Unwin St BURS/TUN ST6 .... 54 B7
Upfield Wy RUGE WS15 .... 197 J8
Uplands Av BDMR/CCFT WV3 .... 294 D2
BRWN/TUN ST9 .... 53 M4
END/WER ST9 .... 71 G7
Uplands Cl PENK ST19 .... 211 L8
WNSFLD WV11 .... 233 M5 1
Uplands Cft END/WER ST9 .... 71 G6
Uplands Dr BDMR/CCFT WV3 .... 294 C2
END/WER ST9 .... 71 G7
SEDG DY3 .... 299 K2
Uplands Gn RUGE WS15 .... 215 K4
Uplands Rd BUCK/MIL ST2 .... 70 B3
STAFS ST17 .... 193 K4
The Uplands BIDD ST8 .... 26 E8
RSTAF ST18 .... 177 J8
Upmeadows Dr STAFN ST16 .... 193 H1
Upper Av CDSL WV8 .... 246 A7
Upper Belgrave Rd LNGTN ST3 .... 102 D1
Upper Brook St RUGE WS15 .... 215 L2
Upper Cross Rd RUGE WS15 .... 215 L3 2
Upper Cross St LNGTN ST3 .... 86 C6 10
Upper Forster St
RUSH/SHEL WS4 .... 283 M7
Upper Furlong St STOKE ST4 .... 85 K4 2
Upper Gn
DUNHL/THL/PER WV6 .... 279 K5
Upper Green La WSLW WS2 .... 283 J6
Upper Gungate CRTAM B79 .... 10 D2
Upper Hillchurch St HAN ST1 .... 2 E4
Upper Huntbach St HAN ST1 .... 2 E4
Upper Landywood La
GTWY WS6 .... 266 E2
Upper Lichfield St
WLNHL WV13 .... 282 A8
Upper Lodge Rd RUGE WS15 .... 216 F6
Upper Marsh NEWUL ST5 .... 68 D7
Upper Navigation St
WSLW WS2 .... 283 K3
Upper Normacot Rd LNGTN ST3 .... 86 E3
Upper St John St LICHS WS14 .... 8 F6
Upper Sneyd Rd WNSFLD WV11 .... 282 B2
Upper St DUNHL/THL/PER WV6 .... 279 K5
Upper Vauxhall WOLV WV1 .... 12 B4
Upper Villiers St
ETTPK/GDPK/PENN WV4 .... 295 H4
Upper Wy RUGE WS15 .... 234 B1
Upper Zoar St BDMR/CCFT WV3 .... 12 C8
Upton Pl RUGE WS15 .... 197 K8
Upwoods Rd ASHB DE6 .... 127 H8
Urmston Pl LNGTN ST3 .... 86 C5
Usulwall Cl ECCH ST21 .... 152 D4 2
Utterby Side BUCK/MIL ST2 .... 86 C2
Uttoxeter Cl
DUNHL/THL/PER WV6 .... 280 B5 1
Uttoxeter Rd ASHB DE6 .... 147 J6
CDLE ST10 .... 107 L2
LNGTN ST3 .... 86 C7
RDERBYSW DE65 .... 147 M6
RSTAF ST18 .... 141 C4
RUGE WS15 .... 179 L3
STONE ST15 .... 138 E4
UTXR ST14 .... 125 K6
Uxbridge Cl SEDG DY3 .... 299 K8 2
Uxbridge St BUT DE14 .... 6 E9
HEDN WS12 .... 232 C6

V

Vale Av ALDR WS9 .... 285 K8
Vale Cl LICH WS13 .... 8 E1
Vale Gdns PENK ST19 .... 229 L2
Valentine La ALS/KID ST7 .... 53 G1
Vale Pleasant NEWUL ST5 .... 67 J8
Valerian Wy LNGTN ST3 .... 103 G4 2
Vale Ri PENK ST19 .... 229 L2
Vale Rw SEDG DY3 .... 299 K5 2
Vale St NEWUL ST5 .... 67 H8
NEWUL ST5 .... 67 L2
SEDG DY3 .... 299 K5
STOKE ST4 .... 85 H3
STRBR DY8 .... 307 M2
Vale Vw ALDR WS9 .... 285 H7
NEWUL ST5 .... 68 D3
Valiant Rd ALBTN WV7 .... 260 E3
Valley Cl ALS/KID ST7 .... 36 F7
Valley Dr LEEK ST13 .... 43 H5
Valley Gn GTWY WS6 .... 249 L8
Valley La LICH WS13 .... 9 K2
TAM/AM/WIL B77 .... 290 K2
Valley Park Vw LNGTN ST3 .... 85 M7
Valley Rd BLOX/PEL WS3 .... 283 K2
HEDN WS12 .... 232 D4
LNGTN ST3 .... 87 H7
SEDG DY3 .... 299 L4
STONE ST15 .... 136 B3
STONE ST15 .... 138 A3
WOLVN WV10 .... 280 F5
Valley Side BLOX/PEL WS3 .... 267 M8
The Valley BNTWD WS7 .... 251 K2
Valley Vw BRWNH WS8 .... 269 G3
MKTDR TF9 .... 130 A3
Vanbrugh Ct
DUNHL/THL/PER WV6 .... 278 E7
Vancouver Dr
STPNHL/WHNL DE15 .... 186 C7
Van Diemans Rd WMBN WV5 .... 297 L5
Van Gogh Cl CNCK/NC WS11 .... 232 D8
Vanguard TAM/AM/WIL B77 .... 290 D4
Vanity Cl STONE ST15 .... 120 C6
Vanity La STONE ST15 .... 120 C6
Vardon Cl STAFN ST16 .... 175 J7
Vaughan Cl FOAKS/STRLY B74 .... 286 F7
Vaughan Gdns CDSL WV8 .... 262 F6 3
Vaughan's La RUGE WS15 .... 178 C4
Vaughan Wy STAFS ST17 .... 193 H1
Vauxhall Av WOLV WV1 .... 12 B4
Venn Pl HAN ST1 .... 4 C6
Ventnor Gv LNGTN ST3 .... 101 M4 11
Venton Cl BURS/TUN ST6 .... 54 E6
Ventura Park Rd
POL/KGSB/FAZ B78 .... 10 A3

Vercourt FOAKS/STRLY B74 .... 286 B7
Verdi Ct LICH WS13 .... 236 C8
Verdon Dr PENK ST19 .... 230 A3 2
Verity Wk STRBR DY8 .... 307 L1
Vermont Gn CNCK/NC WS11 .... 232 A7 2
Verney Cl UTXR ST14 .... 143 J3 2
Vernon Av ALS/KID ST7 .... 51 K8
BRWNH WS8 .... 269 G3
Vernon Cl ALS/KID ST7 .... 51 K8
FOAKS/STRLY B74 .... 286 E5
WNSFLD WV11 .... 265 M6 2
Vernon Rd STOKE ST4 .... 85 H2
Vernons Pl WOLVN WV10 .... 265 K1
Vernon Wy BLOX/PEL WS3 .... 282 E1
Veronica Av
ETTPK/GDPK/PENN WV4 .... 295 L5
Verulam Rd STAFN ST16 .... 174 C3
Verwood Cl STAFS ST16 .... 175 J6 2
Vesey Cl FOAKS/STRLY B74 .... 286 F8
Vessey Ter NEWUL ST5 .... 84 C2
Vestry Ct STRBR DY8 .... 307 L4 2
Viaduct Dr
DUNHL/THL/PER WV6 .... 280 B4
Vicarage Bank RSTAF ST18 .... 157 L3
Vicarage Cl BRWNH WS8 .... 269 G2
ECCH ST21 .... 152 D3 2
POL/KGSB/FAZ B78 .... 291 M5
STPNHL/WHNL DE15 .... 186 B6
Vicarage Crs
BLYBR/FOR ST11 .... 87 K7
NEWUL ST5 .... 84 C3
Vicarage Dr KINVER DY7 .... 306 A7
UTXR ST14 .... 125 M6
Vicarage La AUD/MAD/W CW3 .... 81 L5
BARL ST12 .... 101 L8
BUTN/AL/TUT DE13 .... 218 D4
STOKE ST4 .... 84 E6
Vicarage Rd BKHL/PFLD WV2 .... 13 H8
BLOX/PEL WS3 .... 268 A8
BRWNH WS8 .... 268 F3
CDLE ST10 .... 105 L6
ETTPK/GDPK/PENN WV4 .... 294 E7
LEEK ST13 .... 43 M4
PENK ST19 .... 246 D4
SEDG DY3 .... 299 L5
STOKE ST4 .... 84 F2
STRBR DY8 .... 307 K3
WNSFLD WV11 .... 281 H4
WOLVN WV10 .... 247 L4
Vicarage Wk MSHM DE12 .... 222 C4 1
Vicarage Wy STAFS ST17 .... 4 C7
Vicar's Cl STONE ST15 .... 120 C6 2
Vicars Cft RUGE WS15 .... 197 M8 2
Vicar St SEDG DY3 .... 299 K2
Vichy Cl NEWUL ST5 .... 83 L3
Vickers Rd BURS/TUN ST6 .... 54 A5
Victor Cl ALBTN WV7 .... 260 E3 2
Victoria Av ALS/KID ST7 .... 38 F8
ALS/KID ST7 .... 66 E3
BLOX/PEL WS3 .... 283 J1
HAN ST1 .... 2 C9
Victoria Crs BUT DE14 .... 6 E1
Victoria Dr
POL/KGSB/FAZ B78 .... 290 A2 2
Victoria Gdns LICH WS13 .... 8 B5
Victoria Gv WMBN WV5 .... 298 A2
Victoria Meadow
BUTN/AL/TUT DE13 .... 218 D4
Victoria Ms RUSH/SHEL WS4 .... 284 A7 2
Victoria Park Rd BURS/TUN ST6 .... 53 L6
Victoria Pas WOLV WV1 .... 12 F5
Victoria Pl NEWUL ST5 .... 67 L3 2
STOKE ST4 .... 85 L4
Victoria Rd ALBTN WV7 .... 260 E2 2
BDMR/CCFT WV3 .... 294 E3
BLOX/PEL WS3 .... 268 A7
BUT DE14 .... 6 F2
CRTAM B79 .... 10 E4
DUNHL/THL/PER WV6 .... 279 L5
MKTDR TF9 .... 130 B1
NEWUL ST5 .... 84 C2
SEDG DY3 .... 299 L2 8
STAFN ST16 .... 4 D5
STOKE ST4 .... 85 K2
WNSFLD WV11 .... 281 H4
WOLVN WV10 .... 280 F5
Victoria Sq HAN ST1 .... 2 B7
Victoria St BUT DE14 .... 6 F2
BUTN/AL/TUT DE13 .... 201 G7
CNCK/NC WS11 .... 249 K2
HEDN WS12 .... 232 C4
KCSWFD DY6 .... 303 H1
LEEK ST13 .... 44 A3 2
NEWUL ST5 .... 67 J8
NEWUL ST5 .... 67 L3
NEWUL ST5 .... 84 C2
STAFN ST16 .... 4 E2
STONE ST15 .... 120 A8
STONE ST15 .... 138 A3
WLNHL WV13 .... 282 A7
WOLV WV1 .... 12 F6
Victoria Ter RUSH/SHEL WS4 .... 283 M7
STAFN ST16 .... 174 C5
Victoria Wy STAFS ST17 .... 194 E5
Victor St BLOX/PEL WS3 .... 284 A1
STONE ST15 .... 137 M1
Victory Av BNTWD WS7 .... 251 M3
Victory Cl HEDN WS12 .... 232 E6
Victory Crs CDLE ST10 .... 89 L6
Victory La WSLW WS2 .... 283 G6
Vienna Pl NEWUL ST5 .... 83 L4
Viewfield Av HEDN WS12 .... 231 M3
Viewfield Crs SEDG DY3 .... 299 K3
Viewlands Dr
DUNHL/THL/PER WV6 .... 279 G8
View St HEDN WS12 .... 231 M4
Viggars Pl NEWUL ST5 .... 67 M8
Vigo Cl ALDR WS9 .... 268 E8
Vigo Pl ALDR WS9 .... 285 G3
Vigo Rd ALDR WS9 .... 268 E8
Vigo Ter ALDR WS9 .... 268 F7
Villa Cl BIDD ST8 .... 40 C4
Village Gdns STAFS ST17 .... 194 F3
The Village END/WER ST9 .... 56 A1
KGSWFD DY6 .... 303 H1

STAFS ST17 194
Villa Rd LEEK ST13 57
The Villas STOKE ST4 85
Villa St STOKE ST4 85
Villiers St LNGTN ST3 87
WLNHL WV13 282
Vincent Cl ALBTN WV7 260
Vincent St HAN ST1 3
Vine Bank Rd ALS/KID ST7 39
Vinebank St STOKE ST4 85
Vine Cl RSTAF ST18 177
Vine St STRBR DY8 307
Vinegar HI ECCH ST21 151
Vine La CNCK/NC WS11 249
Vine Rw STOKE ST4 85
Vine St STRBR DY8 307
Violet Wy STPNHL/WHNL DE15 204
Virginia Dr
ETTPK/GDPK/PENN WV4 294
Virginia Rd ALBTN WV7 260
Virginsalley La ASHB DE6 110
Viscount Rd BNTWD WS7 251
Viscount Wk LNGTN ST3 102
The Vista SEDG DY3 299
Vivian Rd STOKE ST4 85
Vowchurch Wy BUCK/MIL ST2 .... 86 C
Voyager Dr CNCK/NC WS11 249
Vulcan Rd LICH WS13 254

W

Waddell Cl BILS/COS WV14 299
Wadden La RSTAF ST18 157
Waddens Brook La
WNSFLD WV11 281
Waddington Rd ALBTN WV7 260
Wade Av NEWUL ST5 68
Wadebridge Rd BUCK/MIL ST2 70
Wade Cl CDLE ST10 105
RUGE WS15 .... 216 F
Wade La RUGE WS15 216
Wadesmill Lawns
WOLVN WV10 .... 264 E
Wade St BURS/TUN ST6 69
LICH WS13 9
Wadham St STOKE ST4 85
Waggoner's La
POL/KGSB/FAZ B78 288
Waggon La KIDD DY10 310
Wain Av NEWUL ST5 54
NEWUL ST5 68
Wain Dr STOKE ST4 85
Wainrigg TAM/AM/WIL B77 .... 291 H
Wain St BURS/TUN ST6 68
Wainwright Cl KGSWFD DY6 .... 303 G
Wakefield Cl
BUTN/AL/TUT DE13 165
Wakefield Rd STOKE ST4 84
Wakeley HI
ETTPK/GDPK/PENN WV4 294
Walcot Cl MGN/WHC B75 .... 287 H
Walcot Gv BUCK/MIL ST2 3
Waldale Cl SHHTH WV12 282
Walden Av STAFN ST16 174
Walden Gdns
ETTPK/GDPK/PENN WV4 294
Waldley La ASHB DE6 127
Wales La BUTN/AL/TUT DE13 220
Walford Av BDMR/CCFT WV3 294
Walford Back La ECCH ST21 166
Walford Rd BUTN/AL/TUT DE13 166
Walhouse Cl WSL WS1 .... 283 M
Walhouse Dr PENK ST19 229
Walhouse Rd WSL WS1 283
Walhouse St CNCK/NC WS11 249
Walker Av WOLVN WV10 280
Walker Pl BLOX/PEL WS3 283
Walker Rd BLOX/PEL WS3 283
BURS/TUN ST6 53
Walkers Cft LICH WS13 236
Walkers Fold SHHTH WV12 282
Walkersgreen Rd NEWUL ST5 .... 52 D
Walkers Ri HEDN WS12 232
Walker St BURS/TUN ST6 68
BUT DE14 6
Walkfield Rd
BUTN/AL/TUT DE13 219
Walk La WMBN WV5 298
Walklate Av NEWUL ST5 .... 68 C
Walkley Bank NWPT TF10 188
Walkmill La CNCK/NC WS11 249
Walkmill Rd MKTDR TF9 130
Walkmill Wy CNCK/NC WS11 249
The Walks HAN ST1 43
The Walk SEDG DY3 299
Wallace Cl CNCK/NC WS11 250
Wallace Ct GTWY WS6 266
Wallace Rd BRWNH WS8 268
Wallbridge Cl LEEK ST13 43
Wallbridge Dr LEEK ST13 43
Wallbrook Rd RSTAF ST18 140
Wall Cft ALDR WS9 285
Wall Ditch ASHB DE6 108
Wall Dr FOAKS/STRLY B74 286
Wall End Cl WSLW WS2 283
Walley Dr BURS/TUN ST6 53
Walley's Dr NEWUL ST5 .... 69 C
Walley's Dr NEWUL ST5 68
Walley St BIDD ST8 40
BURS/TUN ST6 69
Wallfield Cl CDLE ST10 105
Wallheath Crs ALDR WS9 269
Wall Heath La ALDR WS9 269
Wallington Cl BLOX/PEL WS3 .... 267 H
Wallington Heath
BLOX/PEL WS3 .... 267 H
Wallis Pl BUCK/MIL ST2 70
Wallis St STOKE ST4 85
Wallis Wy BUCK/MIL ST2 86
Wall La LICHS WS14 253
Wall Lane Ter LEEK ST13 57
Wallows Wd SEDG DY3 299
Wall Rd BUT DE14 6
Wall St WOLV WV1 281
Walls Wd ALDR WS9 285
Walmer Meadow ALDR WS9 285
Walmer Pl LNGTN ST3 86
The Walmers ALDR WS9 285
Walney Gv HAN ST1 3

alnut Av *CDSL* WV8 263 H7 9
alnut Cl *CNCK/NC* WS11 231 M7 1
alnut Ct *RUGE* WS15 216 A5
alnut Crest *RSTAF* ST18 177 J2 5
alnut Dr *BDMR/CCFT* WV3 294 D1
CNCK/NC WS11 231 M8
alnut Gv *LICHS* WS14 254 F3
NEWUL ST5 67 K2
alnut Tree La *NWPT* TF10 207 H3
alpole St
DUNHL/THL/PER WV6 12 B2
LNGTN ST3 86 D5
alrand Cl *CRTAM* B79 274 B1
alsall Rd *ALDR* WS9 268 E8
BLOX/PEL WS3 268 A8
CNCK/NC WS11 249 L4 1
FOAKS/STRLY B74 286 C4
GTWY WS6 250 A6
LICH WS13 8 C5
LICHS WS14 269 L2
WLNHL WV13 282 B8
alsall St *WOLV* WV1 13 J6
alsall Wood Rd *ALDR* WS9 285 H3
alsingham Gdns *NEWUL* ST5 84 B8 4
alter St *BLOX/PEL* WS3 284 A1
altonbury Cl *STAFS* ST17 194 F4 1
alton Crs *ASHB* DE6 95 K1
ETTPK/GDPK/PENN WV4 295 L5 3
STOKE ST4 85 J5
alton Gdns *CDSL* WV8 262 F6
alton Gv *ALS/KID* ST7 52 C2
alton Heath *BLOX/PEL* WS3 266 F7
altonhurst La *ECCH* ST21 153 J6
alton La *STAFS* ST17 195 H6
alton Mead Cl *STAFS* ST17 194 F3
alton Pl *NEWUL* ST5 67 M4
alton Rd *ALDR* WS9 285 G1
ETTPK/GDPK/PENN WV4 295 M5 1
STOKE ST4 84 F7
STPNHL/WNHL DE15 204 D5
alton Wy *ALS/KID* ST7 52 C2
STONE ST15 137 M3
anderers Av *BKHL/PFLD* WV2 295 J4
ansbeck Wk *SEDG* DY3 299 M4
arburton St *BURS/TUN* ST6 69 G3
ard Gv
ETTPK/GDPK/PENN WV4 295 M7
ardle Cl *MGN/WHC* B75 287 G6 2
ardle Crs *LEEK* ST13 43 L6
ardle La *BUCK/MIL* ST2 70 C1
ardle Pl *HEDN* WS12 231 K5
ardles La *GTWY* WS6 249 M8
ardle St *BURS/TUN* ST6 53 L7
CRTAM B79 10 A4
ardle Wy *KIDDW* DY11 309 H7
ardlow Cl
ETTPK/GDPK/PENN WV4 295 H4
ard Pl *BURS/TUN* ST6 54 B5
ard Rd *CDSL* WV8 262 F7
ETTPK/GDPK/PENN WV4 295 K5
ards La *CONG* CW12 26 C2
ard St *HEDN* WS12 231 M4
WLNHL WV13 282 B7
WOLV WV1 13 J5
WSL WS1 283 M8
arewell St *WSL* WS1 283 M8 3
e Warings *WMBN* WV5 297 M6 2
arm Cft *STONE* ST15 138 C3
armley Cl
DUNHL/THL/PER WV6 280 B5
armson Cl *LNGTN* ST3 86 C4
arner Pl *BLOX/PEL* WS3 283 M4
arner Rd *BLOX/PEL* WS3 284 A4
CDSL WV8 262 F7
arner St *HAN* ST1 2 C7
arren Av *WOLVN* WV10 280 F5
arren Cl
BUTN/AL/TUT DE13 185 L1 2
HEDN WS12 233 G5 5
LICHS WS14 9 M5
arren Cft *RUGE* WS15 217 J7
arren Dr *MSHM* DE12 223 H4
SEDG DY3 295 J8
arren Gdns *KGSWFD* DY6 303 J4
arren La *BUT* DE14 203 M3
arren Pl *BRWNH* WS8 269 G3
arren Rd *BNTWD* WS7 252 A5
BURS/TUN ST6 54 B4
arren St *LNGTN* ST3 86 C8
arrilowheath Rd *NEWUL* ST5 67 J1 2
arrington Dr *LEEK* ST13 43 H4
arrington Rd *STOKE* ST4 85 K1
arrington St *STOKE* ST4 85 L4
arsill Gv *LNGTN* ST3 86 D6 9
arstone Hill Rd
DUNHL/THL/PER WV6 277 L6
arstone Rd *WOLVN* WV10 266 B1
arstones Crs
ETTPK/GDPK/PENN WV4 294 D5
arstones Dr
ETTPK/GDPK/PENN WV4 294 C5
arstones Gdns
ETTPK/GDPK/PENN WV4 294 C4
arstones Rd
ETTPK/GDPK/PENN WV4 294 D6
artell Bank *KGSWFD* DY6 303 K3
arwick Av
DUNHL/THL/PER WV6 278 F7
LNGTN ST3 102 F1 2
NEWUL ST5 84 C6
WLNHL WV13 282 D8 5
arwick Cl *ALS/KID* ST7 39 G8
BUT DE14 203 M2 3
CNCK/NC WS11 249 M2
MKTDR TF9 112 D8
arwick Dr *CDSL* WV8 262 E7
arwick Gv *NEWUL* ST5 68 E7
arwick Rd *STAFS* ST17 194 B2
STRBR DY8 307 K1
TAM/AM/WIL B77 11 K5
arwick St *BIDD* ST8 40 C3
BUTN/AL/TUT DE13 185 J4
HAN ST1 69 G8
NEWUL ST5 67 L4
RUSH/SHEL WS4 283 M7
WOLV WV1 13 J6
arwick Wy *ALDR* WS9 285 G1 2
asdale Dr *KGSWFD* DY6 303 L4
asdale Rd *BRWNH* WS8 268 D4 2
ashbrook La *ASHB* DE6 63 M7
CNCK/NC WS11 250 D6
Wash Dale La *STONE* ST15 119 M5
Washerwall La *END/WER* ST9 71 G5
Washerwall St *BUCK/MIL* ST2 86 D2 1
Washford Rd *RDERBYSW* DE65 166 E2
Washington Cl *BIDD* ST8 26 C8
Washington St *BURS/TUN* ST6 53 L8 1
Waste La *ASHB* DE6 92 D6
Wastwater Ct
DUNHL/THL/PER WV6 278 F6 10
Watchfield Cl *LNGTN* ST3 86 F8
Waterbeck Gv *STOKE* ST4 101 J5 6
Waterbrook Cl *PENK* ST19 229 L3
Water Dl *BDMR/CCFT* WV3 279 L8
Waterdale *WMBN* WV5 297 L5
Waterdale Gv *LNGTN* ST3 86 E7
Water Eaton La *PENK* ST19 229 H8
Waterfall La *CDLE* ST10 60 F8
Waterford Rd *KGSWFD* DY6 303 K3 2
Waterfowl Wk *NEWUL* ST5 98 D6
Watergate St *BURS/TUN* ST6 53 K8
Waterhead Cl *WOLVN* WV10 265 G8 1
Waterhead Dr *WOLVN* WV10 265 H8
Waterhead Rd *LNGTN* ST3 102 F1
Watering Cl *NEWUL* ST5 98 C6
Watering Trough Bank
AUD/MAD/W CW3 82 B2
Water La *KINVER* DY7 301 K1
Waterloo Bvd *HEDN* WS12 232 E6
Waterloo Gv *ALS/KID* ST7 53 G1 1
Waterloo Rd *BURS/TUN* ST6 69 G4
WOLV WV1 12 E4
Waterloo St *BUT* DE14 6 E2
HAN ST1 2 F6
LEEK ST13 43 K5
Watermeadow Dr
RUSH/SHEL WS4 284 D1
Watermere *RUSH/SHEL* WS4 284 D2
Watermill Cl *WOLVN* WV10 264 D7
Waterpark Rd *ASHB* DE6 145 H2 1
Water Rd *SEDG* DY3 299 J8
Waters Dr *FOAKS/STRLY* B74 286 D7
Waterside *RUGE* WS15 215 M4 7
STPNHL/WNHL DE15 204 E3
Waterside Cl *AUD/MAD/W* CW3 81 L4
WOLVN WV10 247 L8
Waterside Ct *GNOS* ST20 190 C5
Waterside Dr *LNGTN* ST3 101 L3
MKTDR TF9 112 E8
Waterside Rd
STPNHL/WNHL DE15 204 D3
Waterside Wy *BRWNH* WS8 251 J8
Water Side Wy *COVEN* WV9 264 A8
Watersmead Cl *HEDN* WS12 232 E6
Watersmeet Ct *STONE* ST15 138 C4 7
Waters Rd *RUGE* WS15 179 M7
Water St *BNTWD* WS7 251 L2
KGSWFD DY6 303 K3
NEWUL ST5 52 D8
NEWUL ST5 84 C1 7
STAFN ST16 4 E5
STOKE ST4 85 G5
WOLVN WV10 13 H2
Waters Vw *BLOX/PEL* WS3 268 B5
Waterways Gdns *STRBR* DY8 307 L1
Watery La *ASHB* DE6 93 H7
ASHB DE6 94 F1
CDSL WV8 263 G5
LICH WS13 234 B7
LICH WS13 236 C7
LNGTN ST3 102 D1
RDERBYSW DE65 147 L7
RSTAF ST18 192 A6
RUGE WS15 179 J6
STPNHL/WNHL DE15 187 J7
STRBR DY8 303 L8
SWAD DE11 205 K5
UTXR ST14 143 G8
WLNHL WV13 281 L7
Watford Gap Rd
MGN/WHC B75 287 G3
Watford St *STOKE* ST4 85 J2
Wathan Av *BILS/COS* WV14 295 M8
Watkins Rd *SHHTH* WV12 282 C5
Watkin St *STOKE* ST4 85 K5
Watkiss Dr *RUGE* WS15 215 K1
Watlands Av *NEWUL* ST5 68 C5
Watlands Rd *ALS/KID* ST7 51 L8
Watlands Vw *NEWUL* ST5 68 B4
Watling St *BRWNH* WS8 269 H1
PENK ST19 227 G8
POL/KGSB/FAZ B78 291 L5
SHIF TF11 226 A8
TAM/AM/WIL B77 290 C2
Watson Cl *RUGE* WS15 197 K7
Watson Rd *BILS/COS* WV14 295 M8
STOKE ST4 84 F6
WOLVN WV10 264 B8
Watson St *BUT* DE14 7 G9
STOKE ST4 84 F2
Wattfield Cl *RUGE* WS15 216 A6
Wattisham Wy *ALBTN* WV7 260 D2
Wattles La *STAFS* ST17 194 B8
Watt Pl *CDLE* ST10 89 K7
Wat Tyler Cl *RUGE* WS15 197 K7 3
Wavell Rd *WSLW* WS2 282 E8
Waveney Av
DUNHL/THL/PER WV6 278 E6
Waveney Gv *CNCK/NC* WS11 249 H1
NEWUL ST5 84 B6
Waverley Crs
ETTPK/GDPK/PENN WV4 295 G4 5
ETTPK/GDPK/PENN WV4 295 M7 1
Waverley Gdns *RUGE* WS15 197 H8 3
WMBN WV5 298 B3
Waverley La *BUT* DE14 6 C4
Waverley Pl *NEWUL* ST5 84 A5 1
Waverley Rd *BLOX/PEL* WS3 266 F8
Waverton Rd *BUCK/MIL* ST2 86 E3
Wavertree Av *ALS/KID* ST7 38 E3
Waybutt La *CW/SHV* CW2 64 D3
Wayfield Dr *STAFN* ST16 174 D2
Wayfield Gv *STOKE* ST4 84 D2
Wayside Acres *CDSL* WV8 262 F8
Wayside Av *NEWUL* ST5 68 C6
Wayside Dr *FOAKS/STRLY* B74 286 C7
Wayside Gdns *SHHTH* WV12 282 E5
Wayside Linley *ALS/KID* ST7 37 M8
Wayside Wk *WSLW* WS2 283 G7
Wayte St *HAN* ST1 2 B2
Wealden Hatch
WOLVN WV10 264 E6 5
Wealdstone Dr *SEDG* DY3 299 K8
Weathern Fld *MSHM* DE12 223 K5
Weatheroaks *ALDR* WS9 269 H6
Weaver Cl *ALS/KID* ST7 37 G7 4
ASHB DE6 95 J2
BIDD ST8 40 D1
CDLE ST10 89 L5
Weaver Dr *STAFS* ST17 193 H2
Weaver Gv *WLNHL* WV13 282 D8
Weaver Pl *NEWUL* ST5 84 B6
Weaver Rd *UTXR* ST14 144 B1
Weavers La *STONE* ST15 138 C4
The Weavers *UTXR* ST14 108 D4
Weaver St *HAN* ST1 2 C5
Weavers Wk *STONE* ST15 118 C7
Webb Av *DUNHL/THL/PER* WV6 278 E5
Webberley La *LNGTN* ST3 86 C7 11
Webb St *LNGTN* ST3 87 H7 2
WLNHL WV13 281 M8
Webley Ri *WOLVN* WV10 264 F6
Webster Av *LNGTN* ST3 86 E5
Webster Rd *WLNHL* WV13 282 A7
WSLW WS2 283 K5
Webster St *NEWUL* ST5 84 C2 9
Wedge St *WSL* WS1 283 M8 4
Wedgewood Av *ALS/KID* ST7 66 F1
Wedgewood Cl *BNTWD* WS7 252 C3
STPNHL/WNHL DE15 205 H1 3
Wedgewood Rd *RSTAF* ST18 175 H2 1
Wedgwood Av *NEWUL* ST5 83 M4
Wedgwood Cl *WMBN* WV5 297 M3 3
Wedgwood Dr *BARL* ST12 101 K6
Wedgwood La *BARL* ST12 101 L6
BIDD ST8 26 C7
Wedgwood Pl *BURS/TUN* ST6 68 F1
Wedgwood Rd *ALS/KID* ST7 52 D4
CDLE ST10 105 J1
STOKE ST4 85 M4
Wedgwood St *NEWUL* ST5 68 D5
Wednesfield Rd *WLNHL* WV13 282 A7
WOLVN WV10 13 K3
Wednesfield Wy *WLNHL* WV13 281 K6
WNSFLD WV11 281 L5
Weeping Cross *STAFS* ST17 194 D3
Weighton Gv *BUCK/MIL* ST2 86 E1
Weir Bank *STPNHL/WNHL* DE15 204 E4
Weir Gv *ALS/KID* ST7 39 G8
Welbeck Av *WOLVN* WV10 280 D3
Welbeck Dr *RUSH/SHEL* WS4 284 D3 2
Welbeck Pl *BUCK/MIL* ST2 70 C5
Welbury Gdns
DUNHL/THL/PER WV6 279 M5
Welby St *STOKE* ST4 85 K4
Welch St *STOKE* ST4 85 H3 8
Weldon Av *LNGTN* ST3 87 H6 2
Welford Gv *FOAKS/STRLY* B74 286 F7
Welford Ri *BUTN/AL/TUT* DE13 185 G3
Welford Rd *TAM/AM/WIL* B77 290 C5
Welland Cl *STPNHL/WNHL* DE15 186 A5
Welland Gv *NEWUL* ST5 84 A7
WLNHL WV13 282 C8
Welland Rd *RDERBYSW* DE65 166 D1
Wellbury Cl *STOKE* ST4 101 J5
Weller St *STOKE* ST4 84 E2 3
Wellesbourne *CRTAM* B79 274 C2 4
Wellesbourne Cl
BDMR/CCFT WV3 294 B2 2
Wellesley St *HAN* ST1 2 B9
Wellfield Cl *CNCK/NC* WS11 249 H3 4
Wellfield Rd *ALDR* WS9 285 H2
BUCK/MIL ST2 86 C1
BUTN/AL/TUT DE13 220 A8
Wellington Av
BDMR/CCFT WV3 294 F3
Wellington Cl *KGSWFD* DY6 303 L6
Wellington Crs *LICH* WS13 237 H6
Wellington Dr *CNCK/NC* WS11 249 H2
RUGE WS15 215 L2
Wellington Pl *WLNHL* WV13 281 M7
Wellington Rd *ALBTN* WV7 260 F2
ALS/KID ST7 53 G1
BUT DE14 6 B7
HAN ST1 2 F5
Wellington St *BUT* DE14 6 D5
HAN ST1 2 E5
LEEK ST13 43 L4
NEWUL ST5 68 C5
Wellington St East *BUT* DE14 6 D5
Wellington Ter *HAN* ST1 2 F6
Well La *ALS/KID* ST7 37 J7
BIDD ST8 26 C8
BLOX/PEL WS3 283 K3
BUX SK17 32 B8
GTWY WS6 267 G1
NWPT TF10 169 J6
RDERBYSW DE65 187 J1
WNSFLD WV11 281 J6
Well Pl *BLOX/PEL* WS3 283 L2
Wells Cl *BIDD* ST8 40 D2
CNCK/NC WS11 231 L5
DUNHL/THL/PER WV6 278 D6 8
Wells Dr *STAFS* ST17 194 E4
Wells La *RSTAF* ST18 210 C2
Wells Rd
ETTPK/GDPK/PENN WV4 294 F5
Well St *ALS/KID* ST7 39 K3
BIDD ST8 40 C3
BLYBR/FOR ST11 104 A2
CDLE ST10 89 L7
HAN ST1 2 E6
LEEK ST13 43 M5
NEWUL ST5 84 C2
Wellyards Cl *RSTAF* ST18 157 K8
Welney Gdns *COVEN* WV9 264 A7
Wembury *TAM/AM/WIL* B77 11 K4
Wem Gdns *WNSFLD* WV11 281 K4
Wem Gv *NEWUL* ST5 52 E8
Wendell Crest *WOLVN* WV10 264 F7 1
Wendover Gv *BUCK/MIL* ST2 86 B1
Wendover Rd
ETTPK/GDPK/PENN WV4 295 L8
Wendy Cl *BUCK/MIL* ST2 86 B1
Wenger Crs *STOKE* ST4 100 F3
Wenham Dr *LNGTN* ST3 103 H3
Wenlock *TAM/AM/WIL* B77 11 H7
Wenlock Av *BDMR/CCFT* WV3 294 E2
Wenlock Cl *BURS/TUN* ST6 54 B2
NEWUL ST5 52 E8
SEDG DY3 299 J3 2
Wenlock Gdns *BLOX/PEL* WS3 283 L5
Wensleydale Cl
BURS/TUN ST6 69 K3 5
Wentlows Av *CDLE* ST10 105 K5
Wentlows Rd *CDLE* ST10 105 K5
Wentworth Cl *BNTWD* WS7 252 C3
Wentworth Dr *ALS/KID* ST7 39 J7
BUTN/AL/TUT DE13 185 K1
LICHS WS14 9 K8
STAFN ST16 175 J7 2
Wentworth Gv *CDSL* WV8 278 D5 2
HAN ST1 69 M3
Wentworth Rd
BLOX/PEL WS3 266 F7 9
STRBR DY8 307 K3
WOLVN WV10 264 F8
Werburgh Dr *STOKE* ST4 100 F3
Wereton Rd *ALS/KID* ST7 66 D1
Wergs Dr *DUNHL/THL/PER* WV6 279 G3
Wergs Hall Rd *CDSL* WV8 278 F1
Wergs Rd
DUNHL/THL/PER WV6 279 G4
Werneth Gv *BLOX/PEL* WS3 267 G6
Werrington Rd *BUCK/MIL* ST2 3 M6
Wesker Pl *LNGTN* ST3 86 F6
Wesleyan Rd *MKTDR* TF9 115 G4
Wesley Av *ALS/KID* ST7 37 K6
CDSL WV8 263 H8
GTWY WS6 249 K7
Wesley Cl *BNTWD* WS7 251 M1
Wesley Dr *STONE* ST15 138 C4
Wesley Pl *ALS/KID* ST7 66 D3 3
HEDN WS12 232 C3 6
NEWUL ST5 83 M2
Wesley Rd *CDSL* WV8 263 H8
Wesley St *ALS/KID* ST7 67 G2
BLYBR/FOR ST11 104 A3
BURS/TUN ST6 53 K7
Wesley Wy *TAM/AM/WIL* B77 11 K5
Wessenden
TAM/AM/WIL B77 291 H3 8
Wessex Cl *BRWNH* WS8 268 F3
Wessex Dr *CNCK/NC* WS11 231 M8
STOKE ST4 101 G2
Wessex Rd *BKHL/PFLD* WV2 295 M4
Westacre *HAN* ST1 3 K6
Westacre Crs *BDMR/CCFT* WV3 294 B2
Westacre Dr *SWAD* DE11 205 M8
West Av *ALS/KID* ST7 52 C1
NEWUL ST5 68 D8
STOKE ST4 84 F2
WNSFLD WV11 281 J4
West Bank *STOKE* ST4 85 G4
West Beeches *COVEN* WV9 247 H8
Westbeech Rd *ALBTN* WV7 277 K3
DUNHL/THL/PER WV6 277 J7
Westbook Wy *WMBN* WV5 297 M5
Westbourne Av *CNCK/NC* WS11 231 K8
GTWY WS6 249 L6
Westbourne Cl *LEEK* ST13 43 J4 3
Westbourne Cresent
BNTWD WS7 252 B3 1
Westbourne Dr *BURS/TUN* ST6 53 L5
Westbourne Rd
ETTPK/GDPK/PENN WV4 295 G5
RUSH/SHEL WS4 284 A6 1
Westbourne St
RUSH/SHEL WS4 283 M7
West Brampton *NEWUL* ST5 84 B1
Westbrook Av *ALDR* WS9 284 F5
Westbury Cl *HAN* ST1 3 J2
Westbury Hayes *STAFS* ST17 193 G2 8
Westbury Rd *NEWUL* ST5 84 B7 6
Westbury St *WOLV* WV1 13 G4
West Butts Rd *RUGE* WS15 215 H1
Westcliffe Av *NEWUL* ST5 84 A7
West Cl *STAFN* ST16 5 J5
West Coppice Rd *BRWNH* WS8 268 C2
Westcott Cl *STRBR* DY8 303 M7 1
Westcott La *MKTDR* TF9 148 E4
West Crs *HAN* ST1 69 L2
Westcroft Av *WOLVN* WV10 281 G1
Westcroft Rd *CDSL* WV8 278 F4
SEDG DY3 295 H8
West Dr *ASHB* DE6 145 G1
LEEK ST13 57 J3
POL/KGSB/FAZ B78 273 L8
West End Av *LEEK* ST13 43 K5
Westerby Dr *END/WER* ST9 71 G7
Westerham Cl *STOKE* ST4 100 F3 4
Westering Pkwy *WOLVN* WV10 264 E6
Western Av *ALBTN* WV7 260 E2
SEDG DY3 299 H2
WSLW WS2 282 D7
Western Cl *WSLW* WS2 282 D7 6
Western Rd *HEDN* WS12 232 B4
STRBR DY8 307 M6
Western Springs Rd
RUGE WS15 197 K8
Westfield Av *ALS/KID* ST7 51 J8
Westfield Dr *WMBN* WV5 297 M3
Westfield Gv *BDMR/CCFT* WV3 294 C2
Westfield Mnr
MGN/WHC B75 287 G6 3
Westfield Rd *ALS/KID* ST7 39 J3
BUCK/MIL ST2 70 B7
BUTN/AL/TUT DE13 185 H3
SEDG DY3 299 K1
Westfields *CDLE* ST10 75 L6
LEEK ST13 43 M5
Westfields Ri *AUD/MAD/W* CW3 96 C1
Westfields Rd *RUGE* WS15 216 F6
The Westfields *MKTDR* TF9 148 F3
Westgate *ALDR* WS9 284 E3
HEDN WS12 232 F4
PENK ST19 246 D3
Westgate Cl *SEDG* DY3 299 L3 8
West Gn
ETTPK/GDPK/PENN WV4 294 C5
West Gv *ALS/KID* ST7 37 L6
Westhall Cl *PENK* ST19 246 D4 3
Westhead Av *STAFN* ST16 5 J3
Westhead Rd *KIDD* DY10 310 A6
Westhead Rd North *KIDD* DY10 310 A6
Westhill *BDMR/CCFT* WV3 279 J8
West Hl *UTXR* ST14 144 C4
West Hill Av *HEDN* WS12 232 B5
Westhouse La *ASHB* DE6 92 E7
Westland Gdns
BDMR/CCFT WV3 279 M8
STRBR DY8 307 M3
Westland Rd *BDMR/CCFT* WV3 279 M8
MKTDR TF9 130 B1
Westlands *ALS/KID* ST7 51 M8 4
Westlands Av *NEWUL* ST5 83 M3
Westlands Rd *UTXR* ST14 144 B4
Westland St *STOKE* ST4 85 G3
Westleigh Rd *WMBN* WV5 297 M5
Westmarsh Gv *BURS/TUN* ST6 54 A6
Westmead Rd
BUTN/AL/TUT DE13 220 C1 2
Westmill St *HAN* ST1 2 E9
Westminster Av
ETTPK/GDPK/PENN WV4 295 H5
Westminster Cl *STAFS* ST17 194 C2 2
Westminster Dr
BUTN/AL/TUT DE13 185 K2 15
MKTDR TF9 130 A3 3
Westminster Pl *STOKE* ST4 101 G1 3
Westminster Rd
CNCK/NC WS11 231 L4
LEEK ST13 44 A3
RUSH/SHEL WS4 284 B3
STRBR DY8 303 J8
Westmorland Av *ALS/KID* ST7 52 F3
Westmorland Cl *BURS/TUN* ST6 54 A2
POL/KGSB/FAZ B78 290 A1 7
Weston Bank *ASHB* DE6 127 M2
RSTAF ST18 157 G8
Weston Cl *BUCK/MIL* ST2 71 G7
CNCK/NC WS11 250 C1
NEWUL ST5 67 M7
PENK ST19 244 E3
Weston Coyney Rd *LNGTN* ST3 86 E7
Weston Crs *ALDR* WS9 285 H6
Weston Dr *GTWY* WS6 266 E2
LNGTN ST3 87 G6
Westonfields Dr *LNGTN* ST3 86 E7
Weston La *ECCH* ST21 117 G5
Weston Park Av *BUT* DE14 185 K3
Weston Rd *ALBTN* WV7 261 H5
LICH WS13 236 A8
LNGTN ST3 87 G7
RSTAF ST18 175 K6
STAFN ST16 5 J4
Weston St *LEEK* ST13 44 A4
LNGTN ST3 86 D5
Westonview Av *LNGTN* ST3 86 D5
West Pde *STOKE* ST4 85 J5
Westport Crs *WNSFLD* WV11 281 M5
Westport Greenway
BURS/TUN ST6 68 D1
Westport Rd *BURS/TUN* ST6 68 E1
Westridge *SEDG* DY3 299 J2
Westsprink Crs *LNGTN* ST3 86 E7
West St *ALS/KID* ST7 39 H4
BIDD ST8 40 C3
BLOX/PEL WS3 283 J3
CNCK/NC WS11 249 L4
CRTAM B79 10 E5
DUNHL/THL/PER WV6 280 C5
LEEK ST13 43 K4
LNGTN ST3 87 H5
NEWUL ST5 68 D3
NEWUL ST5 83 H1 5
NEWUL ST5 84 C2
STPNHL/WNHL DE15 186 B7
STRBR DY8 307 M5
TAM/AM/WIL B77 10 E8
West Vw *LNGTN* ST3 102 F6
NEWUL ST5 68 B5
UTXR ST14 109 G7
WOLVN WV10 265 H4 1
Westview Cl *LEEK* ST13 43 J4
West View Dr *KGSWFD* DY6 303 L5
Westville Rd *WSLW* WS2 283 G7
Westward Cl *UTXR* ST14 144 B1
West Wy *RUSH/SHEL* WS4 268 B8
STAFS ST17 4 A9
UTXR ST14 143 M1
Westwick Cl *ALDR* WS9 269 L6
Westwood Av *STRBR* DY8 307 J7
Westwood Cl *LEEK* ST13 57 J6 3
Westwood Gv *LEEK* ST13 43 K4 4
Westwood Heath Rd *LEEK* ST13 43 J5
Westwood Pk *SWAD* DE11 205 M5
Westwood Park Av *LEEK* ST13 43 H5
Westwood Park Dr *LEEK* ST13 43 H5
Westwood Rd *LEEK* ST13 43 J5
LNGTN ST3 87 H8
NEWUL ST5 68 D4
Westwoods Hollow
BNTWD WS7 252 B2
Wetenhall Dr *LEEK* ST13 43 H5
Wetherall Cl *RUGE* WS15 197 K8
Wetherby Cl *CDLE* ST10 89 L5
NEWUL ST5 67 L3 3
WOLVN WV10 264 D6
Wetherby Ct *BUT* DE14 203 M3 5
Wetherby Rd *BLOX/PEL* WS3 267 G6
STOKE ST4 101 H3
Wetherel Rd
STPNHL/WNHL DE15 205 J1
Wetley Av *END/WER* ST9 71 M6
Wetley La *LEEK* ST13 45 M8
Wetmore La *BUT* DE14 185 M4
Wetmore Rd *BUT* DE14 7 K3
Wetton Rd *LEEK* ST13 47 H5
Wexford Cl *DUDN* DY1 299 M8
Weybourne Av *BUCK/MIL* ST2 55 H7
Weyhill Cl *COVEN* WV9 263 L8
Weymouth Dr
FOAKS/STRLY B74 286 F6
Whalley Av *STOKE* ST4 84 E3
Wharf Ap *ALDR* WS9 284 F3
Wharf Cl *LICHS* WS14 9 G5
Wharfedale Cl *KGSWFD* DY6 303 H3
Wharf La *BNTWD* WS7 251 M7
Wharf Pl *STOKE* ST4 85 J3
Wharf Rd *BIDD* ST8 40 C2
BUT DE14 7 J1
GNOS ST20 190 C5
RUGE WS15 215 L3
Wharf St *NEWUL* ST5 84 C1
WOLV WV1 13 J6
Wharf Ter *AUD/MAD/W* CW3 82 B2
Wharmadine La *MKTDR* TF9 115 K3
NEWUL ST5 97 M8

Wharwell La GTWY WS6 ...... 267 G1
Whateley Av BLOX/PEL WS3 ...... 283 M4
Whateley La TAM/AM/WIL B77 ...... 290 F6
Whateley Pl BLOX/PEL WS3 ...... 283 M4
Whateley Rd BLOX/PEL WS3 ...... 283 M4
Wheatmore St BURS/TUN ST6 ...... 69 J1
  PENK ST19 ...... 229 L2
Wheatcroft Cl BNTWD WS7 ...... 252 A5
Wheathill Cl
  ETTPK/GDPK/PENN WV4 ...... 294 E7
Wheatlands Cl HEDN WS12 ...... 250 C1
Wheatlands Rd
  STPNHL/WNHL DE15 ...... 204 E3
The Wheatlands
  DUNHL/THL/PER WV6 ...... 278 D7
Wheatley Cl MGN/WHC B75 ...... 287 J7
Wheatley La
  STPNHL/WNHL DE15 ...... 186 B6
Wheatly Av WOLVN WV10 ...... 280 C3
Wheatmill Cl KIDD DY10 ...... 311 H8
Wheaton Cl WOLVN WV10 ...... 280 C3
Wheatridge Rd KGSWFD DY6 ...... 303 G2
Wheatsheaf Rd CDSL WV8 ...... 279 L1
Wheatstone Cl SEDG DY3 ...... 299 L4
Wheel Av CDSL WV8 ...... 262 F7
Wheeler Cl CDSL WV8 ...... 262 E6
Wheeler Rd WNSFLD WV11 ...... 281 J2
Wheeler St STRBR DY8 ...... 307 M5
Wheel La LICH WS13 ...... 8 B1
Wheelock Cl ALS/KID ST7 ...... 37 G7
Wheelock Wy ALS/KID ST7 ...... 39 H8
Whernside Dr
  DUNHL/THL/PER WV6 ...... 280 A5
Whetstone La ALDR WS9 ...... 285 H5
Whetstone Rd BIDD 26 C8
  WOLVN WV10 ...... 280 D2
Whieldon Crs STOKE ST4 ...... 85 J5
Whieldon Rd STOKE ST4 ...... 85 J4
Whilmot Cl WOLVN WV10 ...... 265 H4
Whimster Sq STAFS ST17 ...... 193 L2
Whinyates Ri
  CNCK/NC WS11 ...... 249 M2
Whisper La NEWUL ST5 ...... 99 L3
Whiston Av WNSFLD WV11 ...... 282 A3
Whiston Cl ALBTN WV7 ...... 261 G5
Whiston Eaves La CDLE ST10 ...... 74 D7
Whitacre La LICHS WS14 ...... 269 L3
Whitaker Rd LNGTN ST3 ...... 85 L7
Whitbread Dr BIDD ST8 ...... 40 E2
Whitburn Cl COVEN WV9 ...... 264 A8
Whitby Cl BLOX/PEL WS3 ...... 266 F7
  STAFS 193 J3
Whitby Wy CNCK/NC WS11 ...... 249 J2
Whitchurch Gv NEWUL ST5 ...... 52 E8
Whitcliffe Pl LNGTN ST3 ...... 85 M7
Whitcombe Rd LNGTN ST3 ...... 87 G8
White Bark Rd NEWUL ST5 ...... 232 A2
Whitebeam Cl BRWNH WS8 ...... 268 E4
Whitebeams SEDG DY3 ...... 299 J6
Whitebridge La STONE ST15 ...... 119 L8
White Farm Rd
  FOAKS/STRLY B74 ...... 286 E6
Whitefield Cl CDSL WV8 ...... 263 H8
Whitefield La CDLE ST10 ...... 61 G7
Whitehall Cl ALS/KID ST7 ...... 38 F8
White Hall Rd ALS/KID ST7 ...... 38 F8
Whitehall Rd
  ETTPK/GDPK/PENN WV4 ...... 295 H6
  KGSWFD DY6 ...... 303 J4
Whitehaven Dr HAN ST1 ...... 2 B2
Whitehead Rd BURS/TUN ST6 ...... 54 B5
White Hl KINVER DY7 ...... 305 M5
Whitehill Rd ALS/KID ST7 ...... 39 G8
White Horse Rd BRWNH WS8 ...... 251 L8
Whitehouse Av
  BDMR/CCFT WV3 ...... 294 C2
White House Av WNSFLD WV11 ...... 281 M3
Whitehouse Crs
  WNSFLD WV11 ...... 281 M1
Whitehouse Cresent
  BNTWD WS7 ...... 252 B3
Whitehouse La CDSL WV8 ...... 262 C3
White House La KINVER DY7 ...... 302 A1
Whitehouse La STONE ST15 ...... 139 H3
Whitehouse Rd NEWUL ST5 ...... 68 B7
  POL/KGSB/FAZ B78 ...... 291 M3
Whitehouse Rd North
  NEWUL ST5 ...... 68 B6
White Houses La WOLVN WV10 ...... 265 G4
Whitehouse St WSLW WS2 ...... 283 K7
Whitehouse Wy ALDR WS9 ...... 284 F6
Whitehurst La CDLE ST10 ...... 88 D3
White Ladies Ct ALBTN WV7 ...... 260 F5
White Lion St STAFS ST17 ...... 4 F6
Whitemill La STONE ST15 ...... 137 M3
White Oak Dr BDMR/CCFT WV3 ...... 294 C1
  KGSWFD DY6 ...... 303 J4
White Oaks STAFS ST17 ...... 194 C5
Whiteridge Rd ALS/KID ST7 ...... 39 G8
White Rw WMBN WV5 ...... 297 J1
Whitesands Cl TAM/AM/WIL B77 ...... 291 J5
Whitesands Rd LNGTN ST3 ...... 103 H4
White's Dr SEDG DY3 ...... 299 L2
White's Meadow RSTAF ST18 ...... 172 D5
Whitesmith Cl SEDG DY3 ...... 299 K2
Whitestone La
  BUTN/AL/TUT DE13 ...... 184 C1
Whitestone Rd LNGTN ST3 ...... 103 H4
Whites Wd WMBN WV5 ...... 298 A5
Whitesytch La STONE ST15 ...... 139 H2
Whitethorn Av BARL ST12 ...... 119 K1
Whitethorn Cl HEDN WS12 ...... 232 A2
Whitethorn Wy NEWUL ST5 ...... 67 L1
Whitewood Gld
  SHHTH WV12 ...... 282 C6
Whitfield Av NEWUL ST5 ...... 84 A2
Whitfield Rd ALS/KID ST7 ...... 39 H8
  BURS/TUN ST6 ...... 54 D4
  HEDN WS12 ...... 232 C3
Whitfield St LEEK ST13 ...... 43 L6
  WOLVN WV10 ...... 280 A2
Whitgreave Av WOLVN WV10 ...... 265 H3
Whitgreave Ct STAFN ST16 ...... 174 C5
Whitgreave St RSTAF ST18 ...... 154 D7

RUGE WS15 ...... 215 L4
Whiting TAM/AM/WIL B77 ...... 290 D3
Whitley Av TAM/AM/WIL B77 ...... 11 K3
Whitley Cl
  DUNHL/THL/PER WV6 ...... 279 H8
Whitley Rd ALBTN WV7 ...... 260 B3
  BURS/TUN ST6 ...... 54 D4
Whitley Wy ASHB DE6 ...... 95 L2
Whitminster Cl SHHTH WV12 ...... 282 C6
Whitmore Av END/WER ST9 ...... 71 H6
Whitmore Hl WOLV WV1 ...... 12 E4
Whitmore Rd STOKE ST4 ...... 100 E3
  STRBR DY8 ...... 307 K5
  WOLV WV1 ...... 13 G4
Whitney Av STRBR DY8 ...... 307 K4
Whitridge Gv BUCK/MIL ST2 ...... 86 D2
Whittaker St WSL WS1 ...... 283 M8
Whittingham Dr STAFS ST17 ...... 193 H2
Whittingham Gv
  WNSFLD WV11 ...... 281 M4
Whittington Common Rd
  LICHS WS14 ...... 255 C6
Whittington Hall La
  KINVER DY7 ...... 306 E8
Whittington Hall La RUGE WS15 ...... 307 K7
Whittle Rd LNGTN ST3 ...... 103 H2
Whitty La LEEK ST13 ...... 30 D2
Whitworth St RUGE WS15 ...... 215 H1
Whygate Gv HAN ST1 ...... 3 K1
Wickham Gdns WNSFLD WV11 ...... 281 G4
Widecombe Av STAFS ST17 ...... 194 E3
Widecombe Rd HAN ST1 ...... 69 M4
Widney Av ALDR WS9 ...... 285 H1
Wigeon Gv WOLVN WV10 ...... 265 H3
Wigford Rd TAM/AM/WIL B77 ...... 290 C5
Wightman St LICHS WS14 ...... 9 L7
Wightwick Bank
  DUNHL/THL/PER WV6 ...... 278 F8
Wightwick Gv
  DUNHL/THL/PER WV6 ...... 279 G8
Wightwick Hall Rd
  DUNHL/THL/PER WV6 ...... 293 L1
Wigley Bank Rd KINVER DY7 ...... 305 J4
Wigmore Pl LNGTN ST3 ...... 86 C4
Wignall Rd BURS/TUN ST6 ...... 53 K4
Wilbraham's Wk ALS/KID ST7 ...... 51 K8
Wilbrahams Wy ALS/KID ST7 ...... 37 K6
Wilcox Av HEDN WS12 ...... 232 B3
Wild Goose Av ALS/KID ST7 ...... 39 K7
Wildhay La ASHB DE6 ...... 93 G3
Wilding Rd BURS/TUN ST6 ...... 54 D4
Wildtree Av WOLVN WV10 ...... 265 G8
Wildwood Dr STAFS ST17 ...... 194 D4
Wildwood Lawns STAFS ST17 ...... 194 C3
Wileman Pl STOKE ST4 ...... 85 L4
Wileman St STOKE ST4 ...... 85 L4
Wilfred Pl STOKE ST4 ...... 84 E2
Wilkes Cl BLOX/PEL WS3 ...... 267 L7
Wilkes Cft SEDG DY3 ...... 299 K3
Wilkes Rd CDSL WV8 ...... 262 F7
Wilke's Wd RSTAF ST18 ...... 173 M2
Wilkin Rd BRWNH WS8 ...... 251 J8
Wilkins Cft
  BUTN/AL/TUT DE13 ...... 219 M8
Wilkinson Cl BNTWD WS7 ...... 252 B2
Wilkinson St BURS/TUN ST6 ...... 53 K8
Wilks St BURS/TUN ST6 ...... 53 L6
Willatt Pl BUCK/MIL ST2 ...... 70 A1
  BUT DE14 ...... 204 A3
Willcock Rd BKHL/PFLD WV2 ...... 295 L3
Wildale Gv HAN ST1 ...... 3 K3
Willenhall La WSLW WS2 ...... 282 F5
Willerby Fold WOLVN WV10 ...... 264 F6
Willeton St BUCK/MIL ST2 ...... 3 M7
Willett Av BNTWD WS7 ...... 251 L5
Willey La GNOS ST20 ...... 190 C4
Willfield La BURS/TUN ST6 ...... 55 J4
William Av BIDD ST8 ...... 40 E3
  LNGTN ST3 ...... 103 J2
William Birch Rd
  BUCK/MIL ST2 ...... 86 A1
William Cl BLYBR/FOR ST11 ...... 104 B3
William Clowes St
  BURS/TUN ST6 ...... 68 F2
William Fiske St STOKE ST4 ...... 84 F6
William Iv Rd
  BUTN/AL/TUT DE13 ...... 220 A7
William Morris Ct
  RUGE WS15 ...... 197 K7
William Morris Gv
  CNCK/NC WS11 ...... 231 L6
William Nadin Wy SWAD DE11 ...... 205 M6
William Newton Cl
  RDERBYSW DE65 ...... 167 H5
William Rd ALS/KID ST7 ...... 39 G8
William Ruston Rd
  BURS/TUN ST6 ...... 54 D8
Williams Cl SHHTH WV12 ...... 282 C5
  STAFN ST16 ...... 174 B7
Williams Ct STAFS ST17 ...... 174 F3
Williamson Av BURS/TUN ST6 ...... 54 D4
  HEDN 233 J6
Williamson St BDMR/CCFT WV3 ...... 12 D8
  BURS/TUN ST6 ...... 53 L8
William St BUT DE14 ...... 185 J5
  RUSH/SHEL WS4 ...... 283 M7
  STOKE ST4 ...... 85 L4
William Wiggin Av
  BLOX/PEL WS3 ...... 267 H8
Willington Rd CRTAM B79 ...... 274 B3
Willmer Crs ALS/KID ST7 ...... 39 H4
Willmott Cl MGN/WHC B75 ...... 287 K7
Willmott Rd MGN/WHC B75 ...... 287 K7
Willotts Hill Rd NEWUL ST5 ...... 67 K1
Willoughby Cl PENK ST19 ...... 229 M3
Willoughby Rd CRTAM B79 ...... 273 J2
Willoughby St BURS/TUN ST6 ...... 53 K3
Willow Av BNTWD WS7 ...... 252 C4
  WNSFLD WV11 ...... 281 H2
Willow Bank BDMR/CCFT WV3 ...... 294 C1
Willowbank POL/KGSB/FAZ B78 ...... 290 B1
Willow Bottom La CRTAM B79 ...... 257 H4
Willowbrook RSTAF ST18 ...... 173 L8
Willow Cl ALS/KID ST7 ...... 53 G3
  CDLE ST10 ...... 105 K5

COVEN WV9 ...... 247 H8
HAG/WOL DY9 ...... 311 H5
LICH WS13 ...... 237 L2
STAFS ST17 ...... 194 D4
Willowcroft Wy ALS/KID ST7 ...... 39 L6
Willow Di STONE ST15 ...... 138 C7
Willowdale Rd STOKE ST4 ...... 85 J5
Willowdale Gra
  DUNHL/THL/PER WV6 ...... 279 L5
Willow Dr CDSL WV8 ...... 263 H7
  SWAD DE11 ...... 205 M3
Willow Gv LNGTN ST3 ...... 85 L7
  WNSFLD WV11 ...... 266 B7
Willowherb Cl
  CNCK/NC WS11 ...... 232 C8
Willow La LNGTN ST3 ...... 103 G7
Willow Meadow Rd ASHB DE6 ...... 95 J2
Willowmoor STAFS ST17 ...... 193 L5
Willowood Gv LNGTN ST3 ...... 103 J2
Willow Pl BIDD ST8 ...... 41 H1
  STPNHL/WNHL DE15 ...... 204 E3
Willow Rd BDMR/CCFT WV3 ...... 294 D2
  BUTN/AL/TUT DE13 ...... 220 D1
  KINVER DY7 ...... 306 D7
  STOKE ST4 ...... 138 B3
Willow Rw LNGTN ST3 ...... 86 B7
Willows Dr LNGTN ST3 ...... 103 G6
Willowside RUSH/SHEL WS4 ...... 284 C2
Willowsmere Dr LICHS WS14 ...... 254 F3
Willows Rd RUSH/SHEL WS4 ...... 284 C2
The Willows CNCK/NC WS11 ...... 249 J1
  LEEK ST13 ...... 43 J5
  RUGE WS15 ...... 216 A5
  STONE ST15 ...... 136 E4
  STONE ST15 ...... 138 B4
  WSL WS1 ...... 297 M5
Willowtree Cl LICH WS13 ...... 236 B8
Willow Tree Gv ALS/KID ST7 ...... 37 M3
Willow Wy BLYBR/FOR ST11 ...... 104 A2
Willridding La ASHB DE6 ...... 93 J3
Wilmcote Dr MGN/WHC B75 ...... 287 H7
Wilmore La RSTAF ST18 ...... 175 K1
Wilmorehill La RSTAF ST18 ...... 175 K1
Wilmot Cl NEWUL ST5 ...... 67 M7
Wilmot Dr NEWUL ST5 ...... 67 M7
Wilmot Rd NEWUL ST5 ...... 86 C4
Wilmott Cl LICH WS13 ...... 8 B5
Wilncote La
  TAM/AM/WIL B77 ...... 290 E2
Wilner's Vw BLOX/PEL WS3 ...... 267 M5
Wilsford Cl RUSH/SHEL WS4 ...... 284 C2
Wilson Gv CNCK/NC WS11 ...... 232 C8
Wilson St BURS/TUN ST6 ...... 54 B8
  STOKE ST4 ...... 84 B1
Wilson Wy BURS/TUN ST6 ...... 53 J4
Wiltell Rd LICHS WS14 ...... 8 F6
Wilton Av END/WER ST9 ...... 71 H6
Wilton Cl SEDG DY3 ...... 299 L3
Wilton St NEWUL ST5 ...... 68 A8
Wiltshire Gv NEWUL ST5 ...... 84 C6
Wiltshire Cl WSLW WS2 ...... 283 K6
Wimberry Dr NEWUL ST5 ...... 67 K1
Wimblebury Rd HEDN WS12 ...... 232 F6
Wimborne Av LNGTN ST3 ...... 101 M3
Wimborne Cl WOLVN WV10 ...... 281 G4
Wimshurst Meadow
  WOLVN WV10 ...... 264 F6
Winceby Rd
  DUNHL/THL/PER WV6 ...... 278 F7
Winchcombe Cl DUDN DY1 ...... 299 L7
Winchcombe Dr
  STPNHL/WNHL DE15 ...... 205 H1
Winchester Av BUCK/MIL ST2 ...... 70 C8
Winchester Cl LICH WS13 ...... 236 C7
  RUGE WS15 ...... 217 H6
Winchester Ct STAFS ST17 ...... 194 C4
Winchester Dr BUT DE14 ...... 204 C2
  MSHM DE12 ...... 223 K5
  NEWUL ST5 ...... 83 M6
Wincote Dr
  DUNHL/THL/PER WV6 ...... 279 J6
Wincote La ECCH ST21 ...... 152 J6
Windermere Wy CDLE ST10 ...... 89 M6
Windermere
  TAM/AM/WIL B77 ...... 291 G3
Windermere Dr
  FOAKS/STRLY B74 ...... 285 M7
  KGSWFD DY6 ...... 303 K4
Windermere Pl
  CNCK/NC WS11 ...... 249 L1
Windermere Rd
  DUNHL/THL/PER WV6 ...... 279 K2
  NEWUL ST5 ...... 84 B6
Windermere St HAN ST1 ...... 2 A2
The Windings LICH WS13 ...... 8 D1
Windmill Av ALS/KID ST7 ...... 53 G2
Windmill Bank RUGE WS15 ...... 234 B5
  WMBN WV5 ...... 298 A3
Windmill Cl CRTAM B79 ...... 274 A2
  LICH WS13 ...... 235 M8
  LNGTN ST3 ...... 102 F6
  UTXR ST14 ...... 144 B1
Windmill Crs BDMR/CCFT WV3 ...... 294 A1
Windmill Dr UTXR ST14 ...... 145 L7
Windmill Gv KGSWFD DY6 ...... 303 G2
Windmill Hl LA LICHS WS14 ...... 255 L5
Windmill La ALBTN WV7 ...... 260 E5
  ASHB DE6 ...... 79 J7
  ASHB DE6 ...... 94 E7
  BDMR/CCFT WV3 ...... 294 A1
  ECCH ST21 ...... 133 M6
  LICH WS13 ...... 236 A8
  RUGE WS15 ...... 234 A6
Windmill St HAN ST1 ...... 2 E4
  SEDG DY3 ...... 299 K5
Windmill Vw END/WER ST9 ...... 71 J6
The Windrow
  DUNHL/THL/PER WV6 ...... 278 D6
Windrush Cl STOKE ST4 ...... 101 J3
Windsmoor St STOKE ST4 ...... 85 H1
Windsor Av
  ETTPK/GDPK/PENN WV4 ...... 294 E4
  LNGTN ST3 ...... 86 D3
Windsor Cl ASHB DE6 ...... 79 K7
  BNTWD WS7 ...... 251 L1

CRTAM B79 ...... 274 C3
STONE ST15 ...... 137 M5
Windsor Crs KINVER DY7 ...... 305 M6
Windsor Dr ALS/KID ST7 ...... 36 F6
  LEEK ST13 ...... 44 B3
  MKTDR TF9 ...... 112 E8
  STPNHL/WNHL DE15 ...... 7 M8
Windsor Gdns
  BDMR/CCFT WV3 ...... 294 A3
  CDSL WV8 ...... 262 F7
Windsor Ga SHHTH WV12 ...... 282 C6
Windsor Gv RUSH/SHEL WS4 ...... 268 C3
  STRBR DY8 ...... 307 L1
Windsor Holloway KINVER DY7 ...... 310 C1
Windsor Rd ALBTN WV7 ...... 261 G5
  DUNHL/THL/PER WV6 ...... 277 J3
  ETTPK/GDPK/PENN WV4 ...... 295 M5
  GTWY WS6 ...... 249 L6
  MSHM DE12 ...... 223 K5
  STAFS ST17 ...... 194 B3
  STOKE ST4 ...... 101 G1
  STRBR DY8 ...... 307 K7
  WMBN WV5 ...... 297 M4
Windsor St NEWUL ST5 ...... 84 C1
Windsor Wy RUSH/SHEL WS4 ...... 284 D3
Windy Arbour CDLE ST10 ...... 89 K6
Windycote La END/WER ST9 ...... 72 A8
Windyridge BUX SK17 ...... 24 B4
Winford Av KGSWFD DY6 ...... 303 L6
Wingate Rd WSLW WS2 ...... 282 B5
Wing Cl WSLW WS2 ...... 282 F6
Winghay Cl STOKE ST4 ...... 68 C2
Winghay Pl BURS/TUN ST6 ...... 54 B5
Winghay Rd ALS/KID ST7 ...... 39 H8
Winghouse La BARL ST12 ...... 118 F3
Wingrove Av LNGTN ST3 ...... 102 D1
Winifred St HAN ST1 ...... 2 B3
Winnipeg Cl STOKE ST4 ...... 101 H2
Winpenny Rd NEWUL ST5 ...... 67 M2
Winsford Av LNGTN ST3 ...... 86 E8
Winsford Crs STAFS ST17 ...... 194 E4
Winslow Dr
  DUNHL/THL/PER WV6 ...... 279 L6
Winsor Av HEDN WS12 ...... 232 B4
Winstanley Pl RUGE WS15 ...... 197 K8
Winster Gn SWAD DE11 ...... 205 L5
Winston Av ALS/KID ST7 ...... 37 J6
Winston Pl BUCK/MIL ST2 ...... 3 M6
Winston Rd KIDDW DY11 ...... 310 A4
  SEDG DY3 ...... 297 L8
Winston Ter NEWUL ST5 ...... 68 C4
Winterbourne Gv LNGTN ST3 ...... 86 E7
Winter Cl LICH WS13 ...... 236 D8
Wintercroft La ASHB DE6 ...... 78 D1
Winterfield La LNGTN ST3 ...... 87 H3
Winterley Gdns SEDG DY3 ...... 299 L4
Winterley La RUSH/SHEL WS4 ...... 284 C3
Winterside Cl NEWUL ST5 ...... 67 K1
Winter's Wk RSTAF ST18 ...... 156 F5
Wintonfield St STOKE ST4 ...... 85 J3
Wiscombe Av PENK ST19 ...... 229 M1
Wisemore WSL WS1 ...... 283 L8
  WSL WS1 ...... 283 L8
  WSLW WS2 ...... 283 L7
Wise St LNGTN ST3 ...... 102 C1
Wissage Ct LICH WS13 ...... 9 J3
Wissage La LICH WS13 ...... 9 J2
Wissage Rd LICH WS13 ...... 9 H1
Wistwood Hayes WOLVN WV10 ...... 264 F6
Witchford Crs LNGTN ST3 ...... 101 M3
Witham Wy BIDD ST8 ...... 40 E1
Withern Wy SEDG DY3 ...... 299 K7
Withers Rd CDSL WV8 ...... 263 H7
Withies Rd STOKE ST4 ...... 84 E6
Withington Rd BURS/TUN ST6 ...... 54 A4
Within La RSTAF ST18 ...... 175 M2
Withymere La WMBN WV5 ...... 298 C2
Withystakes Rd END/WER ST9 ...... 71 K6
Withywood Cl SHHTH WV12 ...... 282 B1
Witney Cl CRTAM B79 ...... 273 M3
Witney Rd STAFS ST17 ...... 194 D1
Wittering Rd ALBTN WV7 ...... 260 C2
Witton Rd
  ETTPK/GDPK/PENN WV4 ...... 295 G4
Witton St STRBR DY8 ...... 307 L6
Wobaston Rd CDSL WV8 ...... 263 K7
  COVEN WV9 ...... 263 L6
  WOLVN WV10 ...... 264 B6
Woburn Av SHHTH WV12 ...... 282 B4
Woburn Ct STOKE ST4 ...... 101 J5
Wodehouse Av WMBN WV5 ...... 297 L5
Wodehouse La SEDG DY3 ...... 298 E2
Woden Av WNSFLD WV11 ...... 281 J4
Woden Cl WMBN WV5 ...... 297 M3
Woden Crs WNSFLD WV11 ...... 281 J4
Woden Rd WOLVN WV10 ...... 13 L1
Wogan St STAFN ST16 ...... 4 E1
Wolfe St STOKE ST4 ...... 85 H4
Wolfscote Di SWAD DE11 ...... 205 M8
Wolgarston Wy PENK ST19 ...... 229 L3
Wollaston Cl STRBR DY8 ...... 307 J3
Wollaston Crs WNSFLD WV11 ...... 281 K4
Wollaston Rd KINVER DY7 ...... 307 L3
  STRBR DY8 ...... 307 L3
Wolmer Rd WNSFLD WV11 ...... 265 M8
Wolmore La WMBN WV5 ...... 292 A8
Wolseley Bank WOLVN WV10 ...... 280 D3
Wolseley Cl STAFS ST17 ...... 196 E4
  WOLVN WV10 ...... 280 D3
Wolseley Ga WOLVN WV10 ...... 280 F3
Wolseley Rd NEWUL ST5 ...... 68 B5
  RUGE WS15 ...... 214 E1
  STAFN ST16 ...... 175 J7
  STOKE ST4 ...... 84 F6
Wolsey Rd LICH WS13 ...... 235 M8
Wolstanton Rd NEWUL ST5 ...... 67 M4
Wolston St LNGTN ST3 ...... 86 D5
Wolverhampton Rd
  BLOX/PEL WS3 ...... 267 L2
  CDSL WV8 ...... 262 F6
  CNCK/NC WS11 ...... 249 H3
  DUNHL/THL/PER WV6 ...... 277 L7
  KGSWFD DY6 ...... 303 J2
  KIDD DY10 ...... 310 B6
  KINVER DY7 ...... 306 F3

PENK ST19 22
SEDG DY3 29
STAFS ST17 17
WNSFLD WV11 26
WOLVN WV10 28
WOLVN WV10 28
WSLW WS2 29
Wolverhampton Rd East
  ETTPK/GDPK/PENN WV4 29
Wolverhampton Rd West
  WSLW WS2 28
Wolverhampton St
  WSLW WS2 283
  WSLW WS2 283
Wolverley Av
  ETTPK/GDPK/PENN WV4 29
  STRBR DY8 30
Wolverley Ct ALBTN WV7 26
Wolverley Rd DY10 30
Wolverly Rd KIDD DY10 31
Wolverson Cl SHHTH WV12 28
Wolverson Rd ALDR WS9 26
Wombourne Cl SEDG DY3 299
Wombourne Pk WMBN WV5 29
Wombourne Rd SEDG DY3 29
Wombrook Di WMBN WV5 297
Woodall St BLOX/PEL WS3 283
  HAN ST1 ......
Wood Av CDLE ST10 73
  COVEN WV9 24
  SEDG DY3 299
  WNSFLD WV11 28
Wood Bank La PENK ST19 21
Wood Bank Rd
  BDMR/CCFT WV3 294
Woodbank Rd SEDG DY3 299
Woodbank St BURS/TUN ST6 6
Woodberry Av RUGE WS15 ......
Woodberry Cl STAFS ST17 193
Woodbridge Cl BLOX/PEL WS3 267
  RUSH/SHEL WS4 ......
Woodbridge Rd NEWUL ST5 8
Woodcock Gdns
  WOLVN WV10 265
Woodcock La ALS/KID ST7 3
Woodcock Rd RUGE WS15 215
Wood Common Gra
  BLOX/PEL WS3 267
Woodcote Rd
  DUNHL/THL/PER WV6 279
The Woodcote STAFS ST17 194
Wood Ct BUT DE14 ......
Wood Crs STAFN ST16 174
  STONE ST15 137
Woodcroft ALS/KID ST7 6
Woodcroft Av CRTAM B79 1
  LEEK ST13 43
Woodcroft Rd LEEK ST13 4
Woodcross St BILS/COS WV14 295
Wooddisse La LEEK ST13 4
Wood Dr ALS/KID ST7 3
Wood Eaton Rd GNOS ST20 209
Woodedge La UTXR ST14 163
Wood End La LICH WS13 236
  LICH WS13 237
Woodend Pl
  DUNHL/THL/PER WV6 279
Wood End Rd WNSFLD WV11 281
Woodend St STOKE ST4 85
Woodfield Av
  ETTPK/GDPK/PENN WV4 294
Woodfield Cl CNCK/NC WS11 25
Woodfield Ct LEEK ST13 44
Woodfield Dr CNCK/NC WS11 250
Woodfield Hts
  DUNHL/THL/PER WV6 279
Woodfield Rd SEDG DY3 299
Woodfields Dr LICHS WS14 9
Woodfold Cft ALDR WS9 285
Woodford Cl COVEN WV9 263
Woodford Crs BNTWD WS7 25
Woodford End
  CNCK/NC WS11 231
Woodford La WMBN WV5 297
Woodford Wy HEDN WS12 25
Woodgate Av ALS/KID ST7 3
Woodgate St LNGTN ST3 103
Woodgreen GTWY WS6 249
Woodhall Pl NEWUL ST5 66
Woodhall Rd ALS/KID ST7 39
  ETTPK/GDPK/PENN WV4 294
Woodhaven CNCK/NC WS11 249
  GNOS ST20 170
  RUSH/SHEL WS4 284
Wood Hayes Rd WOLVN WV10 265
Woodhead Rd BUCK/MIL ST2 70
Woodheyes Lawns RUGE WS15 215
Woodhill Cl WMBN WV5 ...... 297 M
Wood Hill Dr WMBN WV5 297
Woodhouse La ALBTN WV7 ......
  BIDD ST8 26
  BURS/TUN ST6 55
  RDERBYSW DE65 147
  RSTAF ST18 191
  TAM/AM/WIL B77 275
Woodhouse Rd
  DUNHL/THL/PER WV6 279
Woodhouse Rd North
  DUNHL/THL/PER WV6 279
Woodhouses La BNTWD WS7 252
Woodhouses Rd BNTWD WS7 253
Woodhouse St STOKE ST4 85
Woodhurst Cl TAM/AM/WIL B77 11
Woodingdean Cl LNGTN ST3 ...... 86 D
Woodkirk Cl BURS/TUN ST6 54
Woodland Av BURS/TUN ST6 54
  DUNHL/THL/PER WV6 279
  LEEK ST13 72
  NEWUL ST5 68
  STRBR DY8 311
Woodland Cl ALBTN WV7 260
  HEDN WS12 232
  LEEK ST13 43
  SHHTH WV12 282
Woodland Crs
  BDMR/CCFT WV3 294
Woodland Dr ASHB DE6 147

odland Gv *BURS/TUN* ST6 .... 54 B8
EDG DY3 .... 299 H7 🔳
odland Hills
UD/MAD/W CW3 .... 81 L1
odland Rd *ALS/KID* ST7 .... 37 L2
DMR/CCFT WV3 .... 294 D3
TPNHL/WNHL DE15 .... 205 J6
AM/AM/WIL B77 .... 275 G6
odlands Av *ALS/KID* ST7 .... 38 D8
STONE ST15 .... 137 L2
odlands Brow *ASHB* DE6 ...... 79 K6 🔳
odlands Crs *BLOX/PEL* WS3... 267 M5
odlands Dr *COVEN* WV9 .... 247 H7
odlands La *BLYBR/FOR* ST11.. 104 B5
WOLVN WV10 .... 248 D3
odlands Paddock
ETTPK/GDPK/PENN WV4 .... 294 F6 🔳
odlands Ri *BLOX/PEL* WS3...... 267 M5
odlands Rd *KIDD* DY10 .... 310 A6
STAFN ST16 .... 174 B3
STOKE ST4 .... 84 E6
WOLVN WV10 .... 298 A5
e Woodlands *LICH* WS13 .... 9 J1
odland St *BIDD* ST8 .... 40 D3
BURS/TUN ST6 .... 53 L7
odlands Vw *RUGE* WS15 .... 217 J6
odland Views *UTXR* ST14 ...... 145 L8
odland Wy *BNTWD* WS7 .... 252 A4
POL/KGSB/FAZ B78 .... 291 M2
ood La *ALDR* WS9 .... 286 A2
BLOX/PEL WS3 .... 267 M5
BUTN/AL/TUT DE13 .... 163 J7
BUTN/AL/TUT DE13 .... 201 G5
HEDN WS12 .... 232 C6
MKTDR TF9 .... 97 K7
MKTDR TF9 .... 148 A7
PENK ST19 .... 228 C6
SHHTH WV12 .... 282 E3
STONE ST15 .... 137 M5
SWAD DE11 .... 205 M3
UTXR ST14 .... 142 D8
UTXR ST14 .... 144 E4
WOLVN WV10 .... 248 F4
WOLVN WV10 .... 264 D8
ood Lane CI *SHHTH* WV12 .... 282 E3 🔳
odlawn Gv *KGSWFD* DY6 .... 303 K5 🔳
odleighton Gv *UTXR* ST14 ... 144 C4 🔳
odleyes Crs *STAFS* ST17 ...... 194 C4
odman La *GTWY* WS6 .... 249 L6
odmans Cft
RDERBYSW DE65 .... 165 J1
odman St *BUCK/MIL* ST2 ...... 70 B1 🔳
odmill La *RUGE* WS15.......... 180 A3
odpark La *LNGTN* ST3 .... 102 D3
odpecker Vw *MKTDR* TF9 ... 114 C7
odpecker Wy *HEDN* WS12 ... 232 C7
ood PI *LNGTN* ST3 .... 87 H8
ood Ridings *LICH* WS13 .... 254 A1
ood Rd *CDSL* WV8 .... 262 D6
DUNHL/THL/PER WV6 .... 279 H7
LEEK ST13 .... 57 G2
SEDG DY3 .... 299 J7
WMBN WV5 .... 298 B3
odrow Wy *MKTDR* TF9 ...... 115 J5 🔳
odruff CI *ALS/KID* ST7 .... 53 M1 🔳
ods Cft *LICH* WS13 .... 8 D1
odshot Av *RUGE* WS15 .... 217 J6 🔳
odshutt's St *ALS/KID* ST7 ... 52 D1
odside *ALS/KID* ST7 .... 38 E6
AUD/MAD/W CW3 .... 81 L3
FOAKS/STRLY B74 .... 286 E8
NEWUL ST5 .... 98 C6

Wood Side *WNSFLD* WV11 .... 282 A2
Woodside Av *ALS/KID* ST7 ...... 37 L6
ALS/KID WV3 .... 52 F1
BURS/TUN ST6 .... 55 M4
Woodside Dr *RSTAF* ST18 ..... 196 D2 🔳
Woodside Crs *NEWUL* ST5 ..... 84 C8
Woodside Dr *FOAKS/STRLY* B74.. 286 C5
LNGTN ST3 .... 103 G6
Woodside La *LEEK* ST13 .... 43 J8
Woodside PI *BUCK/MIL* ST2 .... 70 B1 🔳
HEDN WS12 .... 231 K5
Woodside Wy *ALDR* WS9 ...... 285 H5
SHHTH WV12 .... 282 E3
Woods La *STPNHL/WNHL* DE15.. 204 F2
STPNHL/WNHL DE15 .... 205 G1 🔳
Woodsorrel Rd *DUDN* DY1 ..... 299 M6
Woodstile CI *MGN/WHC* B75 .. 287 K7 🔳
Woodstock CI *NEWUL* ST5 ...... 68 C7 🔳
STRBR DY8 .... 307 J1
Woodstock Dr
FOAKS/STRLY B74 .... 286 D6
HEDN WS12 .... 231 J3
STRBR DY8 .... 303 J8
Woodstock Rd *BURS/TUN* ST6.. 53 G3
STAFS ST17 .... 194 D1
Woodstock St *BURS/TUN* ST6... 53 H2
Wood St *ALS/KID* ST7 .... 39 J3
ALS/KID ST7 .... 51 L7
BUT DE14 .... 6 F8
LEEK ST13 .... 43 M5
LNGTN ST3 .... 86 C6
STRBR DY8 .... 307 K3
WLNHL WV13 .... 282 A4
WOLVN WV10 .... 280 E5
Wood Ter *HAN* ST1 .... 2 B8
The Wood *LNGTN* ST3 .... 87 H8
Woodtherne CI *PENK* ST19 .... 229 M3 🔳
Woodthorne CI *RUGE* WS15 ... 197 J8 🔳
SEDG DY3 .... 299 K8 🔳
Woodthorne Rd
DUNHL/THL/PER WV6 .... 279 G4
Woodthorne Rd South
DUNHL/THL/PER WV6 .... 279 G5
Woodvale Crs *END/WER* ST9 .. 55 L4 🔳
Wood Vw *ALS/KID* ST7 .... 67 G1
RUGE WS15 .... 215 M4 🔳
Woodview Rd *SWAD* DE11 ...... 205 K5
Woodville Gdns *SEDG* DY3 ..... 299 M1 🔳
Woodville PI *LNGTN* ST3 .... 87 G8 🔳
Woodville Rd *LNGTN* ST3 .... 87 G8
Woodward St *HAN* ST1 .... 2 F1
HAN ST1 .... 69 K4 🔳
Woodyard Dr *CRTAM* B79 .... 239 J5 🔳
Woodyard La *RDERBYSW* DE65.. 147 M6
Woody Bank *GTWY* WS6 .... 249 L8
Woolaston Dr *ALS/KID* ST7 ..... 37 K7 🔳
Woollaton La *BUX* SK17 .... 35 K8
Woolliscroft Av *NEWUL* ST5 ..... 68 D7
Woolliscroft Rd *BUCK/MIL* ST2.. 70 B7
Woolrich St *BURS/TUN* ST6 ..... 68 E3
Woosnam CI *BUT* DE14 .... 204 A4 🔳
Wootton Av *WNSFLD* WV11 ..... 281 K3
Wootton CI *HEDN* WS12 .... 232 B8 🔳
Wootton Dr *STAFN* ST16 .... 174 A3
Wootton La *CDLE* ST10 .... 91 K5
ECCH ST21 .... 152 D7
Wootton Rd *BDMR/CCFT* WV3.. 294 C3
Woottons Ct *CNCK/NC* WS11 .. 249 M1
Worcester Av *ALS/KID* ST7 ...... 52 D3
CNCK/NC WS11 .... 249 M2 🔳
LICH WS13 .... 236 D7
MGN/WHC B75 .... 287 K7
Worcester Ct
BDMR/CCFT WV3 .... 295 G4 🔳
Worcester Gv
DUNHL/THL/PER WV6 .... 278 D6 🔳

Worcester La *MGN/WHC* B75 ... 287 K7
Worcester PI *ASHB* DE6 .... 79 J8
Worcester Rd *ALBTN* WV7 ...... 260 D3
HAG/WOL DY9 .... 311 M7
LICHS WS14 .... 255 J7
STPNHL/WNHL DE15 .... 204 E4
WLNHL WV13 .... 282 D8
Worcestershire Wy
BEWD DY12 .... 308 B4
Worcester St *BKHL/PFLD* WV2 .. 12 E7
Wordsworth Av *CRTAM* B79 .... 10 L2
ETTPK/GDPK/PENN WV4 .... 295 L6
STAFS ST17 .... 193 H2
Wordsworth CI *BUT* DE14 ...... 185 K4 🔳
CDLE ST10 .... 89 J8
CNCK/NC WS11 .... 231 K6 🔳
LICHS WS14 .... 8 F9
RUGE WS15 .... 217 G6
Wordsworth Ct
DUNHL/THL/PER WV6 .... 278 E6 🔳
Wordsworth Dr *MKTDR* TF9 ... 130 A3
Wordsworth Rd *BLOX/PEL* WS3.. 283 L2
BNTWD WS7 .... 252 A2
SEDG DY3 .... 299 H5
SHHTH WV12 .... 282 E3
WOLVN WV10 .... 281 G2
Wordsworth Wy *ALS/KID* ST7 .. 37 K6
Worfield CI *RUSH/SHEL* WS4 .. 284 A6
Worfield Gdns
BDMR/CCFT WV3 .... 294 F4
Works Dr *AUD/MAD/W* CW3 .... 82 B3
Worsley Dr *CONG* CW12 .... 26 B1
Worston La *STONE* ST15 .... 154 B4
Worth CI *LNGTN* ST3 .... 86 D6
Worthington Dr *ALBTN* WV7 ... 260 E4
Worthington Rd *LICH* WS13 .... 237 J4
Worthington Wy *BUT* DE14 ..... 7 H5
Worthy Down
WNSFLD WV11 .... 281 M5 🔳
Wortley Av *WOLVN* WV10 ...... 280 E4 🔳
Wragby CI *COVEN* WV9 .... 264 B7
Wraggs La *BIDD* ST8 .... 41 H1
Wrekin Dr *BDMR/CCFT* WV3 ... 294 E2
DUNHL/THL/PER WV6 .... 279 C5
Wrekin Gv *SHHTH* WV12 .... 282 B1 🔳
Wrekin La
DUNHL/THL/PER WV6 .... 279 G5
Wrekin Vw *BRWNH* WS8 .... 269 G5
HEDN WS12 .... 231 J2
Wrekin View Rd *SEDG* DY3 .... 299 J2
Wren Av *DUNHL/THL/PER* WV6 .. 278 D7
Wrenbury CI *NEWUL* ST5 .... 67 K1 🔳
Wren CI *BIDD* ST8 .... 40 E2 🔳
Wrenswood *STAFS* ST17 .... 194 E2
Wren Vw *LNGTN* ST3 .... 86 D8 🔳
MKTDR TF9 .... 114 C6
Wrexham CI *BIDD* ST8 .... 40 D1
Wright Av *NEWUL* ST5 .... 67 L3
WNSFLD WV11 .... 281 K3
Wrighton CI *BUCK/MIL* ST2 ..... 3 K9
SHHTH WV12 .... 282 C2
Wright's Av *CNCK/NC* WS11 ... 231 M6
Wright St *ALS/KID* ST7 .... 52 D1
STAFN ST16 .... 4 E1
WOLVN WV10 .... 280 D6 🔳
Wrottesley Park Rd *CDSL* WV8 .. 278 D4
DUNHL/THL/PER WV6 .... 278 D5
Wrottesley Rd
DUNHL/THL/PER WV6 .... 279 H5
Wrottesley Rd West
DUNHL/THL/PER WV6 .... 278 F4
Wroxham Wy *NEWUL* ST5 ...... 84 B8
Wulfad Ct *STONE* ST15 .... 138 C3 🔳
Wulfric CI *PENK* ST19 .... 230 A2
Wulfruna Gdns
BDMR/CCFT WV3 .... 294 F1
Wulfruna St *WOLV* WV1 .... 12 F4
Wulstan Dr *NEWUL* ST5 .... 68 C7

Wulstan Rd *BURS/TUN* ST6 ..... 69 G4
Wyaston Rd *ASHB* DE6 .... 95 J2
Wyatt CI *BURS/TUN* ST6 .... 53 J3
Wychall Dr *WOLVN* WV10 ...... 264 E6
Wychbold CI *SHHTH* WV12 ..... 282 D1
Wychbury Rd *BDMR/CCFT* WV3.. 294 C3
Wych Elm Rd *BRWNH* WS8 .... 268 D5
Wycherwood Gdns
STAFS ST17 .... 194 D5 🔳
Wycliffe Rd *BURS/TUN* ST6...... 68 F2
Wye CI *CDLE* ST10 .... 105 L1 🔳
DUNHL/THL/PER WV6 .... 278 F6 🔳
Wye DI *SWAD* DE11 .... 205 M8
Wye Rd *BLOX/PEL* WS3 .... 283 L1
NEWUL ST5 .... 84 A7
Wyggeston St
BUTN/AL/TUT DE13 .... 185 H4
Wykeham Gv
DUNHL/THL/PER WV6 .... 278 D7
Wymering Av *WNSFLD* WV11 .. 281 M3
Wymondley Gv *STOKE* ST4 .... 101 H4
Wynbank CI *ALS/KID* ST7 .... 66 C2 🔳
Wynchcombe Av
ETTPK/GDPK/PENN WV4 .... 294 D6
Wyndham Crs
STPNHL/WNHL DE15 .... 186 C7 🔳
Wyndham Rd *LNGTN* ST3 ...... 101 M3
The Wynd *SEDG* DY3 .... 299 K1
Wynford PI *BUCK/MIL* ST2 ...... 86 B1 🔳
Wynne Crs
ETTPK/GDPK/PENN WV4 .... 294 C7
Wynn Rd
ETTPK/GDPK/PENN WV4 .... 294 F4
Wynstay Ct *NEWUL* ST5 .... 100 C1 🔳
Wynyates *CRTAM* B79 .... 273 L4 🔳
Wyre CI *ALDR* WS9 .... 268 F6
Wyre Rd *STRBR* DY8 .... 307 L3
Wyrley CI *BRWNH* WS8 .... 251 M7
LICHS WS14 .... 8 D8
SHHTH WV12 .... 282 C3
Wyrley La *BLOX/PEL* WS3 ...... 267 L1
Wyrley Rd *WNSFLD* WV11 ..... 282 A4
Wyrley St *WOLVN* WV10 .... 13 L4
Wyston Brook
RDERBYSW DE65 .... 166 D1
Wyton Av *ALBTN* WV7 .... 260 D2
Wyvern CI *SHHTH* WV12 .... 282 A3
Wyvern Gv *HEDN* WS12 .... 232 A5
Wyvis CI *DUNHL/THL/PER* WV6.. 279 L8

Y

Yale Dr *WNSFLD* WV11 .... 281 L5
Yale St *BURS/TUN* ST6 .... 68 E3
Yardley PI *LNGTN* ST3............ 101 M4
Yardley St *BURS/TUN* ST6 ...... 54 F5
Yarlet Cft *STAFN* ST16 .... 174 D5
Yarlet La *RSTAF* ST18 .... 155 J4
Yarnbrook Gv *BURS/TUN* ST6 .. 54 D7 🔳
Yarnfield CI *LNGTN* ST3 .... 87 G8
Yarnfield La *STONE* ST15 .... 136 E5
Yarrow CI *BLOX/PEL* WS3 .... 268 A5
WNSFLD WV11 .... 281 M5 🔳
Yarwell CI *WOLVN* WV10 .... 13 H1
Yateley CI *BUCK/MIL* ST2 .... 70 B8
Yates Cft *FOAKS/STRLY* B74 .. 286 F4
Yates St *HAN* ST1 .... 2 B7
Yaxley Ct *NEWUL* ST5 .... 84 B8
Yaxley PI *LNGTN* ST3 .... 101 M4
Yeadon Gdns *BDMR/CCFT* WV3.. 294 D2
Yeager Ct *STONE* ST15 .... 136 F4
Yeaman St *STOKE* ST4 .... 85 H4
Yeatsall Rd *RUGE* WS15 .... 179 K5
Yeldham PI *LNGTN* ST3 .... 101 M4
Yelt La *ASHB* DE6 .... 145 K2

Yelverton Av *STAFS* ST17 .... 194 D2
Yelverton CI *BLOX/PEL* WS3 ... 267 H6 🔳
Yemscroft *GTWY* WS6 .... 267 G2 🔳
Yenton CI *POL/KGSB/FAZ* B78.. 290 A1
Yeoman Wy *RUGE* WS15 .... 217 G6
Yeovil PI *LNGTN* ST3 .... 101 M4
Yeovilton *CRTAM* B79 .... 274 C2 🔳
Yerley HI *ASHB* DE6 .... 78 A3
Yew CI *RUGE* WS15 .... 217 H6
Yew Tree Av *LICHS* WS14 .... 9 L4
LNGTN ST3 .... 85 L8
Yew Tree Ct *ALS/KID* ST7 .... 37 L8
CNCK/NC WS11 .... 251 G5
RSTAF ST18 .... 173 K8
STAFS ST17 .... 193 L6 🔳
Yewtree Crs
STPNHL/WNHL DE15 .... 204 F3
Yew Tree Dr *PENK* ST19 .... 227 J4
Yew Tree Gdns *CDSL* WV8 ..... 263 G6 🔳
Yew Tree La
DUNHL/THL/PER WV6 .... 278 F4
Yew Tree Rd
DUNHL/THL/PER WV6 .... 277 J7
MSHM DE12 .... 222 C4
RUGE WS15 .... 215 M4
RUSH/SHEL WS4 .... 284 B1
Yewtree Rd *SWAD* DE11 .... 205 M3
Yew Tree Ter *ALS/KID* ST7 ..... 53 G2
York Av *BDMR/CCFT* WV3 ...... 294 E1
BLYBR/FOR ST11 .... 121 L1
WLNHL WV13 .... 282 D8
WSLW WS2 .... 283 H8
York CI *ALS/KID* ST7 .... 52 D3
BIDD ST8 .... 26 D8
BLYBR/FOR ST11 .... 104 B2
LICH WS13 .... 236 C7
York Crs *BDMR/CCFT* WV3 ..... 294 D1
STRBR DY8 .... 307 K3
Yorkdale CI *SEDG* DY3 .... 299 K7 🔳
York Gdns *BDMR/CCFT* WV3 ... 294 E1
York Rd *BDMR/CCFT* WV3 ...... 294 D2
CNCK/NC WS11 .... 249 M3
LNGTN ST3 .... 87 H7
RUSH/SHEL WS4 .... 284 D3
STAFS ST17 .... 194 A2
Yorksand Rd
POL/KGSB/FAZ B78 .... 289 M2
York St *BUT* DE14 .... 6 E2
HAN ST1 .... 2 B3
LEEK ST13 .... 43 M4
NEWUL ST5 .... 84 C1
STONE ST15 .... 120 A8
WOLV WV1 .... 13 J6
Youlgreave Av *BUCK/MIL* ST2.. 70 B8
Youlton PI *BUCK/MIL* ST2 .... 86 B1 🔳
Young Av *STAFN* ST16 .... 174 C3
Younger St *STOKE* ST4 .... 85 K4 🔳
Young St *BURS/TUN* ST6 .... 53 M4
CDLE ST10 .... 89 L7 🔳
Yoxall Av *STOKE* ST4 .... 84 C7
Yoxall Rd *BUTN/AL/TUT* DE13... 181 L4
BUTN/AL/TUT DE13 .... 218 C3

Z

Zamenhof Gv *BURS/TUN* ST6 .. 69 J1
Zennor Gv *BUCK/MIL* ST2 .... 70 B8
Zetland PI *LNGTN* ST3 .... 101 M4
Zion CI *GTWY* WS6 .... 249 K7
Zoar St *BDMR/CCFT* WV3 .... 12 C7
SEDG DY3 .... 299 J7
Zodiac Dr *BURS/TUN* ST6........ 53 M4
Zouche CI *STRBR* DY8 .... 307 L2 🔳

Index - featured places

obey CP School
BLOX/PEL WS3 .... 266 E7
obey Hill Special School
BUCK/MIL ST2 .... 70 C5
obey Hulton CP School
BUCK/MIL ST2 .... 3 M2
obey Surgery
BUCK/MIL ST2 .... 70 B3
obey Vue Tennis Club
LEEK ST13 .... 43 L3
botsholme School
UTXR ST14 .... 109 H8
B C Cinemas
HAN ST1 .... 2 C6
dderley Green County
Infants School
LNGTN ST3 .... 86 D3
dvance Business Park
HEDN WS12 .... 232 B7
elfgar School
RUGE WS15 .... 215 L1
erospace
ALBTN WV7 .... 260 D1
rfield Industrial Estate
RSTAF ST18 .... 172 E2
an Cotterell Practice
BKHL/PFLD WV2 .... 13 G7
bion Road Junior School
WLNHL WV13 .... 282 C8
brighton C of E School
ALBTN WV7 .... 261 H5
brighton County
Infant School
ALBTN WV7 .... 261 G6
brighton County
Junior School
ALBTN WV7 .... 261 G6
dergate Medical Centre
CRTAM B79 .... 10 C2
dersley High School
CDSL WV8 .... 279 L1

Aldridge & Brownhills
Magistrates Court
ALDR WS9 .... 285 H4
Aldridge School
ALDR WS9 .... 285 G5
Alexander Trading Estate
HAN ST1 .... 69 G8
Alexandra County
Infants School
LNGTN ST3 .... 86 E8
Alexandra Junior School
LNGTN ST3 .... 102 E1
Allen Brown Gallery
LICHS WS14 .... 271 L2
Allens Rough Community
Primary School
SHHTH WV12 .... 282 C1
Allen Street Surgery
CDLE ST10 .... 89 L7
Alleynes School
STONE ST15 .... 120 B8
All Saints C E Primary School
WMBN WV5 .... 297 J2
All Saints C of E First School
CDLE ST10 .... 124 A6
All Saints C of E First School
LEEK ST13 .... 43 M6
All Saints C of E First School
UTXR ST14 .... 108 E4
All Saints C of E
Infants School
RSTAF ST18 .... 172 C5
All Saints C of E
Primary School
BUTN/AL/TUT DE13 .... 183 J8
All Saints C of E
Primary School
BUTN/AL/TUT DE13 .... 220 A8
All Saints C of E
Primary School
STAFS ST17 .... 212 E2

All Saints First School
ECCH ST21 .... 117 J7
All Saints Road Surgery
BUT DE14 .... 204 C2
All Saints School
BKHL/PFLD WV2 .... 13 J9
Alsager Cricket Club
ALS/KID ST7 .... 37 K6
Alsager Dental Clinic
ALS/KID ST7 .... 37 K7
Alsager Highfields CP School
ALS/KID ST7 .... 37 K6
Alsager Leisure Centre
ALS/KID ST7 .... 37 H6
Alsager School
ALS/KID ST7 .... 37 H6
Amblecote Primary School
STRBR DY8 .... 307 M2
Amington Industrial Estate
TAM/AM/WIL B77 .... 275 G7
Amison Street Surgery
LNGTN ST3 .... 86 D6
Amptronik Trading Estate
SEDG DY3 .... 297 K6
Anderstaff Industrial Estate
BUT DE14 .... 7 J1
Anglesey Business Park
HEDN WS12 .... 232 E6
Anglesey County
Primary School
BUT DE14 .... 6 E8
Anita Myatt Health Centre
ETTPK/GDPK/PENN WV4 .... 294 D6
Ankermoor County
Primary School
TAM/AM/WIL B77 .... 11 J3
Ankerside Shopping Centre
CRTAM B79 .... 10 D5
Anson C of E Primary School
RSTAF ST18 .... 177 H8
Apedale Business Park
NEWUL ST5 .... 67 J3

Apex Business Park
CNCK/NC WS11 .... 251 G5
Appleby Glade
Industrial Estate
SWAD DE11 .... 205 K8
Argyle Street Clinic
TAM/AM/WIL B77 .... 11 J5
Arthur Terry School
FOAKS/STRLY B74 .... 287 J5
Ashbourne Business Centre
ASHB DE6 .... 79 H8
Ashbourne Golf Club
ASHB DE6 .... 94 F4
Ashbourne Leisure Centre
ASHB DE6 .... 95 H1
Ashbourne P N E U School
ASHB DE6 .... 79 J7
Ashcombe Park Cricket Club
LEEK ST13 .... 57 J6
Ashcroft County
Infants School
CRTAM B79 .... 274 C2
Ashford Industrial Estate
BKHL/PFLD WV2 .... 295 M3
Ash Green CP School
STOKE ST4 .... 101 H5
Ashlands Medical Centre
NEWUL ST5 .... 84 C1
Ashmore Industrial Estate
WSLW WS2 .... 283 K7
Ashmore Park Clinic
WNSFLD WV11 .... 282 A1
Ashwood Park CP School
STRBR DY8 .... 307 K1
Audley Avenue
Business Park
NWPT TF10 .... 188 D2
Audley Cricket Club
ALS/KID ST7 .... 51 J8
Avon Business Park
CNCK/NC WS11 .... 249 J3

Aynsley Special School
BLYBR/FOR ST11 .... 103 K3
Baddeley Green Surgery
END/WER ST9 .... 55 J6
Baker Street Surgery
STOKE ST4 .... 85 L4
Baldwins Gate C of E
Primary School
NEWUL ST5 .... 98 D5
Ball Green CP School
BURS/TUN ST6 .... 54 D5
Balliol Business Park
COVEN WV9 .... 263 L7
Barlaston C of E First School
BARL ST12 .... 101 L8
Barlaston Cricket Club
BARL ST12 .... 101 M8
Barnfields Primary School
STAFS ST17 .... 194 C4
Barons Court Industrial Estate
ALDR WS9 .... 268 E8
Barton Under Needwood
Cottage Hospital
BUTN/AL/TUT DE13 .... 220 C1
Bass Museum
BUT DE14 .... 7 J3
Baswich Business Park
RSTAF ST18 .... 175 K8
Beacon CP School
SHHTH WV12 .... 282 D2
Beacon Trading Estate
ALDR WS9 .... 285 G4
Beauchamp Industrial Park
TAM/AM/WIL B77 .... 290 D2
Beau Desert Golf Club
HEDN WS12 .... 233 H2
Beauty Bank County
Primary Junior
& Infant School
STRBR DY8 .... 307 M4
Beckminster Special School
BDMR/CCFT WV3 .... 294 F3

Beechdale Centre Surgery
WSLW WS2 .... 283 G5
Beechdale CP School
WSLW WS2 .... 283 J5
Beeches County Junior School
BLYBR/FOR ST11 .... 104 A3
Beeches Hospital
WOLV WV1 .... 12 A3
Beechwood Business Park
HEDN WS12 .... 232 B7
The Beechwood Surgery
ALS/KID ST7 .... 53 G1
Beecroft Hill Special School
CNCK/NC WS11 .... 231 K8
Belgrave County High School
TAM/AM/WIL B77 .... 290 F1
Belgrave Medical Centre
LNGTN ST3 .... 102 C1
Belgrave Recreation Centre
TAM/AM/WIL B77 .... 290 E1
Belle Vue Primary School
STRBR DY8 .... 303 J7
Belmont Infants School
HAN ST1 .... 69 G7
Belvedere County
Junior School
BUT DE14 .... 6 C1
Bend Oak County
Junior School
STPNHL/WNHL DE15 .... 186 C7
Bennick Trading Estate
CNCK/NC WS11 .... 249 L4
Bentilee CP School
BUCK/MIL ST2 .... 86 E2
Bentley Bridge Business Park
WNSFLD ST3 .... 281 J5
Bentley Drive JMI School
WSLW WS2 .... 283 H7
Bentley Lane Industrial Park
WSLW WS2 .... 283 H7
Bentley West Primary School
WSLW WS2 .... 282 E7
Beresford Memorial
C of E First School
LEEK ST13 .... 44 B3
Berkswich C of E
Primary School
STAFS ST17 .... 194 F4
Betley C of E Primary School
AUD/MAD/W CW3 .... 65 H4
Bhylls Acre County
Primary School
BDMR/CCFT WV3 .... 294 B3
Biddulph Community
Health Centre
BIDD ST8 .... 40 D3
Biddulph High School
BIDD ST8 .... 40 D5
Biddulph Medical Centre
BIDD ST8 .... 40 D3
Biddulph Valley Leisure Centre
BIDD ST8 .... 40 D1
Biggin C of E School
BUX SK17 .... 35 K7
Bilbrook C of E Middle School
CDSL WV8 .... 263 H7
Bilbrook Medical Centre
CDSL WV8 .... 263 H7
Bilston Community College
BKHL/PFLD WV2 .... 295 M3
Bingley Junior School
BDMR/CCFT WV3 .... 12 B9
Birchbrook Industrial Park
LICHS WS14 .... 270 E4
Birch Business Park
CNCK/NC WS11 .... 249 M4
Birch Coppice
Industrial Estate
POL/KGSB/FAZ B78 .... 291 L5
Birches First School
CDSL WV8 .... 279 H1
Birches Head County
High School
HAN ST1 .... 69 M3
Birches Head Medical Centre
HAN ST1 .... 3 J1
The Birches High School
HAN ST1 .... 2 F2
Birchfield School
ALBTN WV7 .... 261 K5
Birchills C of E School
WSLW WS2 .... 283 K8
Birchills Health Centre
WSLW WS2 .... 283 J7
Birchwood Primary School
Polesworth
POL/KGSB/FAZ B78 .... 291 M3
Birds Bush County
Primary School
TAM/AM/WIL B77 .... 290 E2
Bishop Rawle C of E
Primary School
CDLE ST10 .... 89 K8
Bitham Special School
BUTN/AL/TUT DE13 .... 185 J1
Blackfriars Special School
NEWUL ST5 .... 84 B2
Blackshaw Moor C of E
First School
LEEK ST13 .... 30 E6
Bladon House School
STPNHL/WNHL DE15 .... 186 B4
Blake County High School
HEDN WS12 .... 231 M4
Blakedown C of E
Primary School
KIDD DY10 .... 311 J8
Blakeley Heath CP School
WMBN WV5 .... 298 A5
Blakenhall Industrial Estate
BKHL/PFLD WV2 .... 295 H3
Blandford Mere
Primary School
KGSWFD DY6 .... 303 L3
Blessed William
Howard RC High School
STAFS ST17 .... 4 D8

Blithfield Sailing Club
RUGE WS15 .... 179 L7
Bloxwich Business Park
WSLW WS2 .... 283 H3
Bloxwich C of E
Primary School
BLOX/PEL WS3 .... 283 H1
Bloxwich Hospital
BLOX/PEL WS3 .... 283 H2
Bloxwich Lane
Industrial Estate
WSLW WS2 .... 283 G7
Bloxwich Leisure Centre
BLOX/PEL WS3 .... 283 J2
Blurton County High School
LNGTN ST3 .... 101 K2
Blurton CP School
LNGTN ST3 .... 85 L8
Blurton & Newstead
Health Centre
LNGTN ST3 .... 101 M2
Blythe Bridge High School
BLYBR/FOR ST11 .... 104 A3
Boardman Industrial Estate
SWAD DE11 .... 205 L7
Boney Hay Primary School
BNTWD WS7 .... 252 A1
Boothen C of E Primary School
STOKE ST4 .... 85 G5
Boscobel House
PENK ST19 .... 244 F5
Boscomoor Industrial Estate
PENK ST19 .... 229 L3
Boston Industrial Estate
RUGE WS15 .... 197 M8
Boundary Industrial Estate
WOLVN WV10 .... 264 C5
Bower Norris RC
Primary School
STAFS ST17 .... 193 J3
Brackendale Shopping Centre
SHHTH WV12 .... 282 D6
Bradwell CP School
NEWUL ST5 .... 68 A3
Bradwell Hospital
NEWUL ST5 .... 68 A3
Brampton House
Business Centre
NEWUL ST5 .... 84 C1
Brampton Sidings
Industrial Estate
NEWUL ST5 .... 68 B8
Branston Golf & Country Club
BUT DE14 .... 204 B4
Brereton Surgery
RUGE WS15 .... 216 A5
Brewery
WOLV WV1 .... 12 D5
Brewood Cricket Club
PENK ST19 .... 246 D3
Brewood Farm Centre School
PENK ST19 .... 246 B4
Brewood Middle School
PENK ST19 .... 246 C4
Brickkiln Primary School
BDMR/CCFT WV3 .... 12 C1
Bridge Industrial Estate
BURS/TUN ST6 .... 69 H3
Bridgeman Street
Trading Estate
WSLW WS2 .... 283 K8
Bridgeside Industrial Estate
TAM/AM/WIL B77 .... 10 F9
Bridgeside Trading Estate
TAM/AM/WIL B77 .... 10 F9
Bridge Surgery
STPNHL/WNHL DE15 .... 204 E2
Bridgetown Primary School
CNCK/NC WS11 .... 249 L4
Bridgtown Business Centre
CNCK/NC WS11 .... 249 L4
Bridgtown Gallery
CNCK/NC WS11 .... 249 K4
Brindley Business Park
HEDN WS12 .... 232 B7
Brindley Heath Junior School
KINVER DY7 .... 306 A5
Brindley Mill
LEEK ST13 .... 43 K3
Britannia Park Industrial Estate
BURS/TUN ST6 .... 69 H3
Brittania Stadium
(Stoke City FC)
STOKE ST4 .... 85 J6
Broad Street Gallery
WOLV WV1 .... 13 G4
Brocton Hall Golf Club
STAFS ST17 .... 195 G6
Bromley Hills Primary School
KGSWFD DY6 .... 303 M5
Brookfields Surgery
LNGTN ST3 .... 86 B8
Brooklands School
STAFN ST16 .... 174 C4
Brook Medical Centre
BURS/TUN ST6 .... 54 C7
The Brook Primary School
STRBR DY8 .... 307 M1
Brookside Business Park
ECCH ST21 .... 136 A5
Brookside Business Park
UTXR ST14 .... 144 D2
Brough Park Leisure Centre
LEEK ST13 .... 43 M3
Brownhills Business Park
BRWNH WS8 .... 268 F5
Brownhills Business Park
BURS/TUN ST6 .... 53 K8
Brownhills Clinic
BRWNH WS8 .... 268 F3
Brownhills Comprehensive
School
BRWNH WS8 .... 268 F1
Brownhills High School
BURS/TUN ST6 .... 68 E1
Brownhills West Primary
School
BRWNH WS8 .... 251 J8

Brown Lees Road
Industrial Estate
BIDD ST8 .... 40 B6
Brunswick Industrial Estate
BURS/TUN ST6 .... 68 D1
Buckpool Comprehensive
School
STRBR DY8 .... 303 M7
Burntwood Baths
BNTWD WS7 .... 251 M4
Burntwood Health Centre
BNTWD WS7 .... 252 C4
Burntwood Town
Shopping Centre
BNTWD WS7 .... 251 L3
Burnwood County
Primary School
BURS/TUN ST6 .... 54 B6
Burslem Cricket Club
BURS/TUN ST6 .... 69 G4
Burslem Health Centre
Pharmacy Ltd
BURS/TUN ST6 .... 69 G2
Burslem Town Hall
BURS/TUN ST6 .... 68 F2
Bursley CP School
NEWUL ST5 .... 68 B2
Burton Albion Football Club
BUT DE14 .... 185 K4
Burton Borough School
NWPT TF10 .... 188 A8
Burton Manor CP School
STAFS ST17 .... 193 K4
Burton Muslim Mosque
BUT DE14 .... 6 E3
Burton-upon-Trent
Police Station
BUT DE14 .... 7 J4
Burton Rugby Club
BUT DE14 .... 7 G8
Burton Technical College
BUTN/AL/TUT DE13 .... 166 C6
Burton Tennis & Squash Club
STPNHL/WNHL DE15 .... 186 B8
Burton upon Trent Golf Club
STPNHL/WNHL DE15 .... 205 M1
Burton-upon-Trent
Technical College
BUT DE14 .... 7 J7
Bushbury Baths
WOLVN WV10 .... 280 E1
Bushbury Health Centre
WOLVN WV10 .... 264 E8
Bushbury Infant School
WOLVN WV10 .... 280 F1
Busill Jones JMI School
BLOX/PEL WS3 .... 282 F2
The Business Centre
BURS/TUN ST6 .... 69 H3
Butts Primary School
RUSH/SHEL WS4 .... 283 M7
CAB
HAN ST1 .... 2 D5
Cadmans Leisure Centre
BURS/TUN ST6 .... 54 C8
Calderfields Golf Club
RUSH/SHEL WS4 .... 284 C8
Caldwell Hall School
MSHM DE12 .... 222 F3
Camargue Gallery
STOKE ST4 .... 85 L3
Cannock Chase Council
CNCK/NC WS11 .... 249 K4
Cannock Chase Football Club
HEDN WS12 .... 232 A2
Cannock Chase High School
CNCK/NC WS11 .... 231 L8
Cannock Chase Hospital
CNCK/NC WS11 .... 231 L8
Cannock Chase
Technical College
CNCK/NC WS11 .... 249 L7
Cannock Chase
Technical College
CNCK/NC WS11 .... 249 K1
Cannock Industrial Centre
CNCK/NC WS11 .... 249 K5
Cannock & Rugeley Cricket Club
HEDN WS12 .... 233 G5
Cannock Wood
Industrial Estate
HEDN WS12 .... 233 J4
Canwell C of E Primary School
MGN/WHC B75 .... 288 B6
Cardinal Griffin RC School
CNCK/NC WS11 .... 231 K7
Carmountside CP School
BUCK/MIL ST2 .... 70 C3
Carver Business Park
STAFN ST16 .... 174 E4
Castle
BUTN/AL/TUT DE13 .... 165 H3
Castlechurch CP School
STAFS ST17 .... 193 H2
Castle CP School
ALS/KID ST7 .... 39 K4
Castlecroft Primary School
BDMR/CCFT WV3 .... 294 B2
Castlefields Surgery
STAFN ST16 .... 4 B7
Castle Gresley Infant School
SWAD DE11 .... 223 L2
Castle Meadows Surgery
SEDG DY3 .... 299 K8
Castle Park Infants School
BUTN/AL/TUT DE13 .... 185 H2
Castle School
BLOX/PEL WS3 .... 283 H3
Castle View Industrial Estate
RDERBYSW DE65 .... 165 J2
Cathedral Gallery
LICH WS13 .... 8 E3
Cauldon County
Secondary School
STOKE ST4 .... 85 J1
Cauldon CP School
STOKE ST4 .... 85 J1

Caverswall Cricket Club
LNGTN ST3 .... 87 J6
Cedars Medical Centre
ALS/KID ST7 .... 37 K7
Central Forest Park
HAN ST1 .... 2 D1
Central Trading Estate
KGSWFD DY6 .... 303 M1
Century Retail Park
HAN ST1 .... 2 A5
Chadsmead County
Primary School
LICH WS13 .... 254 A1
Chadsmoor C E Junior School
CNCK/NC WS11 .... 232 A6
Chadsmoor County
Infants School
CNCK/NC WS11 .... 232 A6
Chadsmoor Medical Practice
CNCK/NC WS11 .... 231 L5
Chamber of Commerce
and Industry
BDMR/CCFT WV3 .... 12 A4
Chancel County Infants School
RUGE WS15 .... 197 L8
Chancel Industrial Estate
KGSWFD DY6 .... 303 L2
Chancel Industrial Estate
WLNHL WV13 .... 282 B8
Chapel Museum
ALS/KID ST7 .... 39 K4
Charles Street Surgery
HAN ST1 .... 2 E6
Charnwood County
Primary School
LICH WS13 .... 236 C7
Chartley Castle (Remains of)
RSTAF ST18 .... 158 D4
Chase Park Industrial Estate
BNTWD WS7 .... 251 K3
Chaseside Industrial Estate
HEDN WS12 .... 232 B7
Chase Terrace County
Primary School
BNTWD WS7 .... 251 M2
Chasetown CP School
BNTWD WS7 .... 251 L5
Chasetown High School
BNTWD WS7 .... 251 L6
Chasewater Industrial Estate
BNTWD WS7 .... 251 L4
Chase Watersports Centre
BRWNH WS8 .... 251 J7
Chasewood Park
Business Centre
HEDN WS12 .... 250 E1
Cheadle Council Offices
CDLE ST10 .... 89 K6
Cheadle CP School
CDLE ST10 .... 89 K8
Cheadle Cricket Club
CDLE ST10 .... 105 L1
Cheadle High School
CDLE ST10 .... 89 K8
Checkley Cricket Club
CDLE ST10 .... 124 A1
Cherry Trees Special School
WMBN WV5 .... 297 M4
Cheslyn Hay CP School
GTWY WS6 .... 249 J7
Cheslyn Hay High School
GTWY WS6 .... 249 J7
Chesterton Clinic
NEWUL ST5 .... 67 L4
Chesterton CP School
NEWUL ST5 .... 67 M3
Chesterton High School
NEWUL ST5 .... 67 L3
Cheswardine Primary School
MKTDR TF9 .... 148 F2
Child Health Clinic
STAFN ST16 .... 4 F4
Childrens Clinic
HAN ST1 .... 2 A9
Chillington Works
Industrial Estate
WOLV WV1 .... 13 M7
Christ Church C of E
First School
STONE ST15 .... 138 A1
Christ Church C of E
Infant School
DUNHL/THL/PER WV6 .... 12 D1
Christ Church C of E
Infant School
DUNHL/THL/PER WV6 .... 279 H7
Christ Church C of E
Middle School
STONE ST15 .... 120 A8
Christ Church C of E
Primary School
BLOX/PEL WS3 .... 283 K3
Christ Church C of E
Primary School
LICH WS13 .... 8 A4
Christchurch C of E
Primary School
STOKE ST4 .... 85 L4
Christchurch Infants School
BUT DE14 .... 6 F6
Christ Church School
DUNHL/THL/PER WV6 .... 279 J6
Christ Church School
PENK ST19 .... 229 J8
Chuckery Primary School
WSL WS1 .... 284 A8
Church Eaton Endowed
Primary School
GNOS ST20 .... 209 H2
Churchfield C E Junior School
RUGE WS15 .... 215 L2
Churchfields CP School
NEWUL ST5 .... 67 M4
Church Lawton Gate CP School
ALS/KID ST7 .... 38 A5
Church of the Ascension C of E
Primary School
KGSWFD DY6 .... 303 J2

Churnetside Business Park
LEEK ST13 57
Churnetside Gallery
END/WER ST9 43
Churnet View County
Middle School
LEEK ST13 57
Cicely Haughton School
END/WER ST9 56
Cinderhill Industrial Estate
LNGTN ST3 86
Cinderhill Lane Surgery
ALS/KID ST7 38
City General Hospital
STOKE ST4 84
Civic Centre
WMBN WV5 298
Civic Centre
WOLV WV1 12
Civic Hall
WOLV WV1 12
Claregate Primary School
DUNHL/THL/PER WV6 279
Clarke Industrial Estate
BUT DE14 7
Clay House Business Centre
BUT DE14 7
Clayton County High School
NEWUL ST5 84
Cleveland Trading Estate
HAN ST1 2
Clifton C of E Primary School
ASHB DE6 94
Close County Junior School
STOKE ST4 84
Clothier Street Primary School
WLNHL WV13 282
Clough Hall County
High School
ALS/KID ST7 52
Club House
WOLVN WV10 280
Coalpool Clinic
BLOX/PEL WS3 283
Cobridge Industrial Estate
BURS/TUN ST6 69
Cobridge Mosque
BURS/TUN ST6 69
Cockshute Industrial Estate
STOKE ST4 84
Codsall Clinic
CDSL WV8 263
Codsall County High School
CDSL WV8 263
Codsall County Middle School
CDSL WV8 263
College of Adult Education
WOLV WV1 13
Collingwood Junior School
WOLVN WV10 264
Colwich CP School
RSTAF ST18 196
Combined Health Centre
BURS/TUN ST6 53
Common Road
Industrial Estate
STAFN ST16 174
Congleton Borough Council
ALS/KID ST7 37
Congleton Golf Club
CONG CW12 26
Cookley Sebright First School
KIDDW DY11 310
Cooper & Jordan C of E
Junior & Infant School
ALDR WS9 285
Cooper Perry CP School
RSTAF ST18 173
Coppice High School
WNSFLD WV11 282
Coppice Special School
NEWUL ST5 84
Corbett C E Primary School
WMBN WV5 296
Corpus Christi Primary School
WNSFLD WV11 282
Coton-in-the-elms C of E
Primary School
MSHM DE12 222
Cotton Green CP School
CRTAM B79 273
Cotwell End County
Primary School
SEDG DY3 299
County & Crown Courts
HAN ST1 2
Crackley Bank CP School
NEWUL ST5 67
Cranberry CP School
ALS/KID ST7 37
Crescent Clinic
STAFS ST17 193
Crestwood School
KGSWFD DY6 303
Crewe Road Surgery
ALS/KID ST7 37
Croft Foundry
Industrial Estate
WLNHL WV13 282
Croft Infant School
WSLW WS2 283
The Croft Primary School
RUGE WS15 216
Cromartie Street Surgery
LNGTN ST3 86
Crossfield Industrial Estate
LICH WS13 9
Crossings Industrial Estate
BLOX/PEL WS3 283
Cross Street Surgery
STAFN ST16 4
Crown Industrial Estate
BUT DE14 6
Crown Medical Practice
TAM/AM/WIL B77 275
Crown Prosecution Service
STAFN ST16 4

own Special School
BUTN/AL/TUT DE13 .... 185 K1
e Crown Surgery
ECCH ST21 .... 152 D3
owtrees Farm
Industrial Estate
ECCH ST10 .... 60 F8
oxdon Abbey
UTXR ST14 .... 107 K6
llwell Industrial Park
WOLVN WV10 .... 13 J3
llwell Trading Estate
WOLVN WV10 .... 13 L1
ru Nanak Sikh Temple
WOLVN WV10 .... 280 E6
adsford Bridge
Industrial Estate
STRBR DY8 .... 303 L8
anesmore Park
Primary School
WNSFLD WV11 .... 281 M1
avelanie Clinic
ASHB DE6 .... 79 J1
aw End School
RUSH/SHEL WS4 .... 284 B4
awley Brook CP School
KGSWFD DY6 .... 303 J3
awley Trading Estate
KGSWFD DY6 .... 303 K2
ay Hospital
CRTAM B79 .... 10 C3
eansfield High School
WOLV WV1 .... 281 J8
eeleys Industrial Estate
WSLW WS2 .... 283 H4
eepdale Industrial Estate
DUDN DY1 .... 299 L7
e Ferrers High School
BUTN/AL/TUT DE13 .... 185 J2
elta Business Centre
CNCK/NC WS11 .... 249 K4
enstone College
UTXR ST14 .... 108 B5
epartment of Pharmacy
Policy & Practice
NEWUL ST5 .... 83 H3
erby Road Business Park
BUT DE14 .... 185 L4
erwick Industrial Estate
STAFS ST17 .... 194 F7
eyncourt CP School
WNSFLD WV11 .... 281 H3
lhorne Endowed
Primary School
CDLE ST10 .... 88 D5
lhorne Recreation Centre
CDLE ST10 .... 88 C7
mensions Leisure Complex
BURS/TUN ST6 .... 53 M8
vidy Road Surgery
BUCK/MIL ST2 .... 70 B8
e Dormston School
SEDG DY3 .... 299 L2
ormston Trading Estate
DUDN DY1 .... 299 M6
osthill School
TAM/AM/WIL B77 .... 290 C5
oval Works Industrial Estate
CDLE ST10 .... 105 L6
ove Bank CP School
ALS/KID ST7 .... 39 C8
ovecote Junior
& Infant School
CDSL WV8 .... 279 J2
ovefields Industrial Estate
UTXR ST14 .... 144 D3
ove First School
UTXR ST14 .... 109 G6
overidge CP School
ASHB DE6 .... 145 J2
ove River Practice
ASHB DE6 .... 146 E5
e Dower House
& Dove Clinic
BUTN/AL/TUT DE13 .... 166 M2
oxey CP School
STAFN ST16 .... 174 A6
raycott Manor CP School
BLYBR/FOR ST11 .... 104 C3
raycott Sports Centre
BLYBR/FOR ST11 .... 104 C4
resden C of E Primary School
LNGTN ST3 .... 102 C1
r K A Jafri & Partner
LNGTN ST3 .... 86 C6
r M Allbeson & Partners
PENK ST19 .... 229 L1
r M El Shaw & Partners
BURS/TUN ST6 .... 54 C8
rs Suxena Page & Turner
ALS/KID ST7 .... 51 K8
ruids Heath Golf Club
ALDR WS9 .... 285 J2
udley Kingswinford
Rugby Football Club
KGSWFD DY6 .... 303 G3
udley Metropolitan
Borough Council
DUDN DY1 .... 299 M5
udley Metropolitan
Borough Council
SEDG DY3 .... 299 K1
udley Metropolitan
Borough Council
STRBR DY8 .... 307 G6
udley Metropolitan
District Council
STRBR DY8 .... 303 L8
udley Priority Health
N H S Trust
KGSWFD DY6 .... 303 L4
umolos County
Primary School
TAM/AM/WIL B77 .... 274 F8
uncan Street Surgery
BKHL/PFLD WV2 .... 295 K3

Dunrobin Street
Medical Centre
LNGTN ST3 .... 86 C8
Dunstall Hill Industrial Estate
DUNHL/PER WV6 .... 280 C5
Durberville Road
Industrial Estate
BKHL/PFLD WV2 .... 295 M3
Earl Sterndale School
BUX SK17 .... 17 J7
East Cannock Industrial Estate
HEDN WS12 .... 232 B7
Eastfield Junior
& Infant School
WOLV WV1 .... 13 M5
East Park Medical Practice
WOLV WV1 .... 281 G8
East Park Trading Estate
WOLV WV1 .... 13 M8
East Staffordshire
District Council
BUT DE14 .... 6 D3
East Staffordshire
District Council
UTXR ST14 .... 144 C2
Eaton Park CP School
BUCK/MIL ST2 .... 3 M8
Eaton Park Health Centre
BUCK/MIL ST2 .... 86 A1
Edenhurst Preparatory School
NEWUL ST5 .... 83 M3
Edensor C of E Primary School
LNGTN ST3 .... 86 A8
Edensor County High School
LNGTN ST3 .... 86 B7
Edgar Stammers Junior
& Infant School
BLOX/PEL WS3 .... 283 M3
Edgecliff County High School
KINVER DY7 .... 306 A6
Edgecliff County School
KINVER DY7 .... 306 A6
Edge Hill Junior School
STPNHL/WNHL DE15 .... 204 F3
The Edward
Anderson Practice
STONE ST15 .... 138 A2
Egginton Primary School
RDERBYSW DE65 .... 167 H5
Ellison CP School
NEWUL ST5 .... 68 D5
The Ellowes Hall Gm School
SEDG DY3 .... 299 J5
Elmore Green Primary School
BLOX/PEL WS3 .... 283 G1
Elm Street Infant School
WLNHL WV13 .... 282 C7
Elston Hall Primary School
WOLVN WV10 .... 264 D8
Empire Industrial Park
ALDR WS9 .... 284 F2
Endon Hall CP School
END/WER ST9 .... 55 M2
Endon High School
END/WER ST9 .... 55 L4
Englands Gallery
LEEK ST13 .... 43 M4
English Martyrs RC
Primary School
BIDD ST8 .... 40 D3
Essington Light
Industrial Estate
WNSFLD WV11 .... 265 M6
Etching Hill C E Primary School
RUGE WS15 .... 197 J8
Eton Park Junior School
BUT DE14 .... 185 K3
Etruria Industrial Museum
HAN ST1 .... 69 G8
Etruria Trading Estate
NEWUL ST5 .... 68 E7
Etruscan Trading Estate
HAN ST1 .... 2 A5
Excalibur CP School
ALS/KID ST7 .... 37 L8
Excalibur Industrial Estate
ALS/KID ST7 .... 37 L7
Exchange Industrial Estate
CNCK/NC WS11 .... 249 L4
Eye Infirmary
BDMR/CCFT WV3 .... 12 B5
Faber RC Primary School
CDLE ST10 .... 91 J2
Fairey Industrial Estate
TAM/AM/WIL B77 .... 290 D2
Fairhaven Primary School
STRBR DY8 .... 303 K7
Fairmeadows Gm
Primary School
SWAD DE11 .... 205 L5
Fair Oaks High School
RUGE WS15 .... 215 J2
Fallings Park Industrial Estate
WOLVN WV10 .... 280 F5
Far Green Industrial Estate
HAN ST1 .... 2 E1
Farndale Junior School
DUNHL/THL/PER WV6 .... 280 A6
Fauld Industrial Estate
BUTN/AL/TUT DE13 .... 164 E4
Fazeley Health Centre
POL/KGSB/FAZ B78 .... 290 A2
Featherstone Health Centre
WOLVN WV10 .... 265 H3
Fegg Hayes Health Centre
BURS/TUN ST6 .... 54 B4
Femwork Industrial Estate
HAN ST1 .... 185 L5
Fenpark Industrial Estate
STOKE ST4 .... 85 M5
Fenton Clinic
STOKE ST4 .... 85 L4
Fenton Manor Swimming Pool
STOKE ST4 .... 85 K3
Festival Heights Retail Park
HAN ST1 .... 69 G5
Finney Gardens Sports Ground
HAN ST1 .... 3 K6

Fire Brigade Sports Club
BUT DE14 .... 6 E6
Fire Station
HAN ST1 .... 2 D7
First Community Health
GTWY WS6 .... 249 M8
The Fitzherbert C of E
Primary School
HEDN WS12 .... 79 G1
Five Ways CP School
HEDN WS12 .... 232 D8
Flash Ce C Primary School
BUX SK17 .... 15 H7
Flash Ley CP School
STAFS ST17 .... 193 L3
Flax Hill Junior School
CRTAM B79 .... 274 B3
Flaxley County Primary School
RUGE WS15 .... 215 L4
Flint Mill Museum
LEEK ST13 .... 57 J4
Florence CP School
LNGTN ST3 .... 86 C8
Florendine County
Primary School
TAM/AM/WIL B77 .... 11 M4
Foden Street Surgery
STOKE ST4 .... 85 C5
Foley Infants School
KINVER DY7 .... 306 A7
Fordhouse Road
Industrial Estate
WOLVN WV10 .... 280 C2
Fordhouses Cricket Club
WOLVN WV10 .... 264 D6
Forest Park County
Primary School
HAN ST1 .... 2 B4
Forest Park CP School
HAN ST1 .... 2 B2
Forsbrook C of E
Infants School
BLYBR/FOR ST11 .... 103 M3
Four Oaks Junior
& Infant School
FOAKS/STRLY B74 .... 286 E6
Four Oaks Medical Centre
MGN/WHC B75 .... 287 H8
Four Oaks Saints Cricket Club
FOAKS/STRLY B74 .... 286 E6
Frank F Harrison
Community School
WSLW WS2 .... 282 F3
Friarswood Primary School
NEWUL ST5 .... 84 B3
The Friary County High School
LICH WS13 .... 235 L8
Friary Grange Sports Centre
LICH WS13 .... 235 M8
Fulfen County Primary School
BNTWD WS7 .... 252 D3
Fulford CP School
BLYBR/FOR ST11 .... 121 K2
Furlong Industrial Estate
BURS/TUN ST6 .... 68 E3
Furlong Medical Centre
BURS/TUN ST6 .... 53 K6
The Galleria Group Ltd
NEWUL ST5 .... 84 B1
The Gallery
ASHB DE6 .... 79 H8
Gas Works Industrial Estate
ALS/KID ST7 .... 38 E8
Gatehouse Theatre
STAFN ST16 .... 4 F4
Gatehouse Trading Estate
BRWNH WS8 .... 269 G1
Gentleshaw Primary School
RUGE WS15 .... 234 A5
Gilani Noor Mosque
LNGTN ST3 .... 86 D6
Gladstone Pottery Museum
LNGTN ST3 .... 86 C7
Glascote Heath Primary School
TAM/AM/WIL B77 .... 11 M9
Glebe CP School
STOKE ST4 .... 85 L4
Glenthorne CP School
GTWY WS6 .... 249 L7
Glynne Primary School
KGSWFD DY6 .... 303 J6
Gnosall Cricket Club
GNOS ST20 .... 190 C3
Goldenhill Primary School
BURS/TUN ST6 .... 53 J3
Goldthorne Medical Centre
ETTPK/GDPK/PENN WV4 .... 295 J4
Goldthorn Park
Primary School
ETTPK/GDPK/PENN WV4 .... 295 K5
Golf Club Bungalow
TAM/AM/WIL B77 .... 275 G2
Golf Clubhouse
LICHS WS14 .... 286 E4
Gorsemoor CP School
HEDN WS12 .... 250 D1
Goscote Hospital
BLOX/PEL WS3 .... 283 M2
Goscote Industrial Estate
BLOX/PEL WS3 .... 283 L1
Grafton County Infants School
LNGTN ST3 .... 86 C6
Graiseley Primary School
BKHL/PFLD WV2 .... 12 E9
Grand Theatre
WOLV WV1 .... 13 G4
Grange County Infants School
BUT DE14 .... 6 D2
Grange CP School
LNGTN ST3 .... 103 C3
Gravel Hill Surgery
WMBN WV5 .... 298 B4
Graycar Business Park
BUTN/AL/TUT DE13 .... 203 H8
Great Fenton Business Park
STOKE ST4 .... 85 K6
Great Wood CP School
CDLE ST10 .... 105 L7

Great Wyrley County
High School
GTWY WS6 .... 249 M6
The Grecian Temple
CDSL WV8 .... 262 C3
Greenacres County
Primary School
TAM/AM/WIL B77 .... 275 H5
Greenfield Primary School
STRBR DY8 .... 307 M6
Greenfield Surgery
STRBR DY8 .... 307 M5
Greenhill Health Centre
LICH WS13 .... 9 G5
Green Industrial Estate
HEDN WS12 .... 232 C3
Green Lea First School
RSTAF ST18 .... 140 D6
Greenline Business Park
BUT DE14 .... 6 D5
Green Rock Junior
& Infant School
BLOX/PEL WS3 .... 283 L1
Greenways CP School
END/WER ST9 .... 55 J9
Greyfriars Business Park
STAFN ST16 .... 4 C1
Greysbrooke CP School
LICHS WS14 .... 271 K4
The Grove CP School
STAFS ST17 .... 193 L6
Grove House Clinic
NEWUL ST5 .... 84 C1
Grove Junior School
HAN ST1 .... 2 F2
Grove Medical Centre
BKHL/PFLD WV2 .... 13 K9
Grove Park Industrial Estate
CNCK/NC WS11 .... 249 L4
Grove Road Industrial Estate
STOKE ST4 .... 85 K6
Grove Upper
Comprehensive School
MKTDR TF9 .... 130 E1
Guildhall Shopping Centre
STAFN ST16 .... 4 E5
Guru Nanak Sikh Temple
BDMR/CCFT WV3 .... 12 C9
Guru Nanak Sikh Temple
BKHL/PFLD WV2 .... 295 J3
Guy Motors Industrial Park
WOLVN WV10 .... 280 C5
Hagley Park County
High School
RUGE WS15 .... 215 K2
Hagley RC High School
STRBR DY8 .... 311 M5
Hamilton County
Infants School
HAN ST1 .... 2 E1
Hammerwich Hospital
BNTWD WS7 .... 252 B5
Hanburys Farm
Primary School
TAM/AM/WIL B77 .... 290 D1
Hanford Clinic
STOKE ST4 .... 100 F2
Hanley Business Park
HAN ST1 .... 2 C8
Hanley Health Centre
HAN ST1 .... 2 E4
Hanley Shopping Centre
HAN ST1 .... 2 D5
Hanley Town Football Club
BUCK/MIL ST2 .... 3 L4
Hanley Town Hall
HAN ST1 .... 2 D6
Harden Primary School
BLOX/PEL WS3 .... 283 L3
Harden Surgery
BLOX/PEL WS3 .... 283 L3
Harley Street Medical Centre
HAN ST1 .... 2 E7
Harpfields Primary School
STOKE ST4 .... 84 D2
Harrisons Institute
& Sports Club
GTWY WS6 .... 267 G1
Hartington C of E School
BUX SK17 .... 34 E5
Hartshill Business Park
STOKE ST4 .... 84 D1
Hartshill & Newcastle
Cricket Club
NEWUL ST5 .... 84 D5
Hassell CP School
NEWUL ST5 .... 84 C2
Hatherton Lane Junior
Mixed & Infant School
WSLW WS2 .... 282 F4
Hatton School
RDERBYSW DE65 .... 165 K1
Haughton C of E
Primary School
RSTAF ST18 .... 191 M4
Havergal C of E
Primary School
WOLVN WV10 .... 248 C8
Hawkes Green Medical Centre
CNCK/NC WS11 .... 232 C8
Hawkins Colliery Sports Club
GTWY WS6 .... 249 K6
Hawkins Sports Club
GTWY WS6 .... 249 K6
Haybridge High School
STRBR DY8 .... 311 M4
Hayes Meadow
Primary School
RUGE WS15 .... 217 J6
Hayward Industrial Park
ALDR WS9 .... 285 G3
Haywood High School
BURS/TUN ST6 .... 54 A8
The Haywood Hospital
BURS/TUN ST6 .... 54 A7
Hazel Slade CP School
HEDN WS12 .... 233 G4

H C M Industrial Estate
BUT DE14 .... 7 K3
The Health Centre
MKTDR TF9 .... 130 C1
Heathcote CP School
ALS/KID ST7 .... 66 E4
Heathfields County
Infants School
TAM/AM/WIL B77 .... 290 F4
Heath Fields Primary School
RDERBYSW DE65 .... 165 J1
Heath Hayes CP School
HEDN WS12 .... 232 F8
Heath House Clinic
UTXR ST14 .... 144 B1
Heath Park
Comprehensive School
WOLVN WV10 .... 281 G5
Heath Town Leisure Centre
WOLVN WV10 .... 280 F6
Hempstalls CP School
NEWUL ST5 .... 68 B7
Henmore Trading Estate
ASHB DE6 .... 95 G2
Henry Chadwick CP School
RUGE WS15 .... 217 G2
The Henry Prince School
ASHB DE6 .... 94 D3
Heron Cross CP School
STOKE ST4 .... 85 L6
H Hayes Clinic
HEDN WS12 .... 250 E1
High Arcal School
SEDG DY3 .... 299 M4
Higherland Surgery
NEWUL ST5 .... 84 A2
Highfields Primary School
BNTWD WS7 .... 252 C3
Highfields School
ETTPK/GDPK/PENN WV4 .... 294 C5
High School
BNTWD WS7 .... 252 A3
High Street Surgery
ALS/KID ST7 .... 52 D4
High Street Surgery
NEWUL ST5 .... 68 C5
High Street Surgery
STONE ST15 .... 138 A2
Hill Avenue Primary School
ETTPK/GDPK/PENN WV4 .... 295 M7
Hillcrest Close
CRTAM B79 .... 10 C1
Hillcrest School
NEWUL ST5 .... 68 C4
Hillside CP School
BUCK/MIL ST2 .... 55 J8
Hillsprings Clinic
RUGE WS15 .... 197 J8
Hill Street School
STPNHL/WNHL DE15 .... 204 E2
Hill Top CP School
ALS/KID ST7 .... 52 D3
Hill Top CP School
BURS/TUN ST6 .... 68 F2
Hilltop School
ASHB DE6 .... 95 J2
Hill West Junior
& Infant School
FOAKS/STRLY B74 .... 286 F6
Hilton Cross Business Park
WOLVN WV10 .... 265 H4
Hilton Main Industrial Estate
WNSFLD WV11 .... 265 J5
Hilton Trading Estate
ETTPK/GDPK/PENN WV4 .... 295 M6
Himley Hall
SEDG DY3 .... 298 D7
Hingorani Clinic
STPNHL/WNHL DE15 .... 186 A7
Hinstock Primary School
MKTDR TF9 .... 148 A8
Hixon Industrial Estate
RSTAF ST18 .... 177 H3
HM Prison
WOLVN WV10 .... 264 F3
Hob Hill C of E &
Methodist Primary School
RUGE WS15 .... 216 B5
Holden Lane County
High School
BUCK/MIL ST2 .... 69 M2
Holden Lane CP School
HAN ST1 .... 69 M3
Holditch Industrial Estate
NEWUL ST5 .... 67 M5
Hollies Business Park
CNCK/NC WS11 .... 249 M1
Hollies Industrial Estate
BKHL/PFLD WV2 .... 12 E8
Hollins Business Centre
STAFN ST16 .... 4 D1
Hollinsclough County
BUX SK17 .... 16 D8
Holly Grove County
Primary School
BNTWD WS7 .... 251 L1
Hollywall CP School
BURS/TUN ST6 .... 53 J4
Holmcroft Surgery
STAFN ST16 .... 174 C4
Holy Trinity C E Primary School
BUT DE14 .... 7 J3
Holy Trinity C of E
Infant School
BRWNH WS8 .... 268 D4
Horninglow Clinic
BUTN/AL/TUT DE13 .... 185 H4
Horninglow County
Infants Speech
& Language Unit
BUTN/AL/TUT DE13 .... 185 J3
Horninglow Infants School
BUTN/AL/TUT DE13 .... 185 J4
Horning Low Surgery
BUTN/AL/TUT DE13 .... 185 H4
Horton Lodge Special School
END/WER ST9 .... 28 D8

Howard County
Primary School
CRTAM B79 .... 238 D8
Howitt House School
BUTN/AL/TUT DE13 .... 163 L7
Hugo Meynell C of E
Primary School
MKTDR TF9 .... 114 E6
Huntington CP School
HEDN WS12 .... 231 K2
Hussani Mosque
DUNHL/THL/PER WV6 .... 279 M6
Hutchinson Memorial
C of E First School
CDLE ST10 .... 124 B1
Hyde Park Trading Estate
STOKE ST4 .... 85 J4
Idsall School
SHIF TF11 .... 242 A5
Ilam C of E Primary School
ASHB DE6 .... 62 E8
Imex Business Park
BKHL/PFLD WV2 .... 295 H3
Imex Business Park
STOKE ST4 .... 85 M5
Industrial Estate
LICH WS13 .... 237 H4
Infant Welfare Clinic
BUT DE14 .... 6 F5
Ingestre Park Golf Club
RSTAF ST18 .... 176 E5
Insley Industrial Estate
BUT DE14 .... 6 C6
Izaak Walton Golf Club
STONE ST15 .... 137 G7
Izaak Waltons
Cottage Museum
STONE ST15 .... 154 B4
Jackfield County
Infants School
BURS/TUN ST6 .... 69 H1
James Brindley High School
BURS/TUN ST6 .... 53 M4
Jamia Mosque
DUNHL/THL/PER WV6 .... 12 A2
Jane Lane School
WSLW WS2 .... 282 F7
Jerome CP School
CNCK/NC WS11 .... 250 F5
Jewish Synagogue
HAN ST1 .... 2 E6
John Arnold Galleries
BIDD ST8 .... 40 C2
John Bamford County
Primary School
RUGE WS15 .... 215 J1
John Carr Industrial Estate
BUT DE14 .... 6 D6
John of Rolleston
Primary School
BUTN/AL/TUT DE13 .... 166 B6
John Taylor High School
BUTN/AL/TUT DE13 .... 202 E8
John Wheeldon CP School
STAFN ST16 .... 4 F1
John Wood C of E
Infants School
CNCK/NC WS11 .... 249 K2
John Worthy Gallery
LEEK ST13 .... 43 L4
Joiners Square CP School
HAN ST1 .... 2 F8
J W Green Swimming Pools
BDMR/CCFT WV3 .... 12 B7
Keele Sports Ground
NEWUL ST5 .... 83 G2
Keele University
NEWUL ST5 .... 83 H3
Kemball Special School
STOKE ST4 .... 85 M5
Key Industrial Park
WLNHL WV13 .... 281 K7
Kidsgrove Medical Centre
ALS/KID ST7 .... 39 J8
Kidsgrove Sports Centre
ALS/KID ST7 .... 52 F1
King Charles Primary School
WSLW WS2 .... 282 F8
King Edward VI County
High School
STAFS ST17 .... 4 B9
King Edward VI County School
LICHS WS14 .... 9 G6
King Edward VI Leisure Centre
LICHS WS14 .... 9 H7
Kingsfield Co First & Secondary
School
BIDD ST8 .... 40 D2
Kingsmead County
High School
HEDN WS12 .... 232 C6
The Kingswinford Gm School
KGSWFD DY6 .... 303 K3
Kingswood Business Park
ALBTN WV7 .... 277 M1
Kingswood Special School
ALBTN WV7 .... 261 M8
Kinver Health Centre
KINVER DY7 .... 306 B7
Knutton Infants School
NEWUL ST5 .... 67 L8
Knutton Infant Welfare
Centre & Clinic
NEWUL ST5 .... 67 M8
Knutton St Mary's
C of E School
NEWUL ST5 .... 67 L8
Knypersley First School
BIDD ST8 .... 40 B4
Knypersley Sports Club
BIDD ST8 .... 40 C5
Krishna Temple
BKHL/PFLD WV2 .... 295 H3
Ladfordfields Business Park
RSTAF ST18 .... 172 E1
Lakeside Medical Centre
DUNHL/THL/PER WV6 .... 278 E6

Lakeside Primary School
TAM/AM/WIL B77 .... 11 K9
Landywood County
Primary School
GTWY WS6 .... 266 F2
Lane End Gallery
END/WER ST9 .... 55 M4
Lane Green County
First School
CDSL WV8 .... 263 H6
Langdale County Junior
& Infants School
NEWUL ST5 .... 84 B5
Langton Medical Group
LICH WS13 .... 236 A8
Lansdowne County
Infants School
BUT DE14 .... 185 K5
Lark Hall County
Infants School
CRTAM B79 .... 274 A2
Laurel House Surgery
CRTAM B79 .... 10 D3
Leamore Industrial Estate
BLOX/PEL WS3 .... 283 G3
Leamore Primary School
BLOX/PEL WS3 .... 283 J3
Leander Rowing Club
BUT DE14 .... 7 L5
Lea Road Medical Practice
BDMR/CCFT WV3 .... 12 C9
Leasowes County Junior
& Infants School
STAFS ST17 .... 194 D2
Leekbrook Industrial Estate
LEEK ST13 .... 57 M1
Leek College of Further
Education & School of Art
LEEK ST13 .... 43 L4
Leek County First School
LEEK ST13 .... 44 A5
Leek County High School
LEEK ST13 .... 44 A4
Leek Golf Club
LEEK ST13 .... 43 M8
Leek Health Centre
LEEK ST13 .... 43 M4
Leek Moorlands Hospital
LEEK ST13 .... 44 A5
Leek Road Industrial Estate
BUX SK17 .... 33 G8
Leek Road Surgery
BUCK/MIL ST2 .... 70 A4
Leek Town Football Club
LEEK ST13 .... 43 J4
Leighswood Infant
& Junior School
ALDR WS9 .... 285 H2
Leighswood Junior School
ALDR WS9 .... 285 H3
Leisure Centre
PENK ST19 .... 230 B2
The Levels Industrial Estate
RUGE WS15 .... 215 M5
Ley Hill Primary School
MGN/WHC B75 .... 287 H8
Lichfield College
LICH WS13 .... 8 E4
Lichfield County Court
LICH WS13 .... 8 E4
Lichfield Cricket Club
LICH WS13 .... 8 D7
Lichfield District Council
BNTWD WS7 .... 251 M3
Lichfield District Council
LICH WS13 .... 8 F4
Lichfield District Council
POL/KGSB/FAZ B78 .... 290 A1
Lichfield Rd Industrial Estate
CRTAM B79 .... 10 A2
Lichfield Road Industrial Estate
CRTAM B79 .... 273 L3
Lichfield Rugby Union
Football Club
LICHS WS14 .... 254 F5
Lichfield Swimming
Pools & Spas
RUGE WS15 .... 216 B4
Lichfield Trading Estate
CRTAM B79 .... 273 L4
Lilleshall Golf Club
NWPT TF10 .... 224 A2
The Limes Industrial Estate
LEEK ST13 .... 44 A3
Linkway Retail Park
CNCK/NC WS11 .... 249 H4
Linley Trading Estate
ALS/KID ST7 .... 52 C1
Linton Primary School
MSHM DE12 .... 223 K5
Lion Industrial Park
ALDR WS9 .... 285 G1
Little Aston CP School
FOAKS/STRLY B74 .... 286 C4
Little London JMI School
WLNHL WV13 .... 282 A8
Little Stoke Cricket Club
STONE ST15 .... 138 E4
Little Sutton Junior &
Infant School
MGN/WHC B75 .... 287 K7
Little Theatre Co
STPNHL/WNHL DE15 .... 204 F2
Littleworth Business Park
HEDN WS12 .... 231 J3
Lodgefarm Junior School
WSLW WS2 .... 282 E6
Longbridge Hayes
Industrial Estate
BURS/TUN ST6 .... 68 C2
Longdon Hall School
RUGE WS15 .... 235 G2
Longfield County Road Surgery
STOKE ST4 .... 84 E2
Longford County
Primary School
CNCK/NC WS11 .... 249 J2

Longford Industrial Estate
CNCK/NC WS11 .... 249 K4
Long Knowle Primary School
WNSFLD WV11 .... 281 J2
Longlands Primary School
MKTDR TF9 .... 112 D8
Long Ley Primary School
WOLVN WV10 .... 13 M2
Longton Cricket Club
LNGTN ST3 .... 101 M2
Longton Hall Road Surgery
LNGTN ST3 .... 85 M3
Longton High School
LNGTN ST3 .... 86 F8
Longton Leisure Centre
LNGTN ST3 .... 86 B7
Longton Town Hall
LNGTN ST3 .... 86 B6
Longwood Primary School
POL/KGSB/FAZ B78 .... 289 J1
Lonpark Industrial Estate
CRTAM B79 .... 10 C3
Lonsdale C of E Primary School
ECCH ST21 .... 152 D4
Loomer Road Industrial Estate
NEWUL ST5 .... 67 K5
Lord Nelson Industrial Estate
HAN ST1 .... 2 F7
Lower Farm JMI School
BLOX/PEL WS3 .... 267 J6
Lower Gornal Health Centre
SEDG DY3 .... 299 H8
Low Hill Medical Centre
WOLVN WV10 .... 280 E3
Loxley Hall Special School
UTXR ST14 .... 143 J5
Lucy Wedgwood Health Centre
BURS/TUN ST6 .... 69 C2
Lyme Brook Mental
Health Centre
NEWUL ST5 .... 68 A3
Lyne Hill Industrial Estate
PENK ST19 .... 229 L3
Madeley High School
AUD/MAD/W CW3 .... 81 L4
Maer Lane Industrial Estate
MKTDR TF9 .... 112 D8
Maidensbridge Primary School
KGSWFD DY6 .... 303 H1
Main Line Industrial Estate
BUTN/AL/TUT DE13 .... 185 M4
Main Road Surgery
RSTAF ST18 .... 177 M3
Maltings Industrial Estate
BUT DE14 .... 185 L4
Manchester
Metropolitan University
ALS/KID ST7 .... 37 H6
Mander Shopping Centre
WOLV WV1 .... 12 F5
Manifold County
Primary School
BUX SK17 .... 33 G7
Manor CP School
POL/KGSB/FAZ B78 .... 289 L5
Manor Farm
Comprehensive School
RUSH/SHEL WS4 .... 284 B4
Manor Golf Club (Kingstone)
UTXR ST14 .... 159 M1
Manor Hill First School
STONE ST15 .... 137 L3
Manor Industrial Estate
BUT DE14 .... 7 H2
Mansion House Surgery
STONE ST15 .... 138 A2
Maple Hayes School
LICH WS13 .... 253 K2
Maple Leaf Industrial Estate
WSLW WS2 .... 283 H7
Marchington Industrial Estate
UTXR ST14 .... 162 F1
Marcus Industrial Estate
HAN ST1 .... 3 J6
Market Drayton Golf Club
MKTDR TF9 .... 130 B5
Market Drayton Junior School
MKTDR TF9 .... 130 B2
Market Drayton
Swimming Centre
MKTDR TF9 .... 130 D2
Market Hall
BUT DE14 .... 7 J7
Market Hall
CDLE ST10 .... 89 K7
Market Street Surgery
KGSWFD DY6 .... 303 K5
Marmion Junior School
CRTAM B79 .... 10 C1
Marshalls Industrial Estate
BKHL/PFLD WV2 .... 295 J3
Marshbrook First School
PENK ST19 .... 229 L1
Marsh CP School
BLYBR/FOR ST11 .... 103 M4
Marshlands Special School
STAFS ST17 .... 194 C4
Marston Montgomery
C of E Primary School
ASHB DE6 .... 127 L1
Marston Road Industrial Estate
BKHL/PFLD WV2 .... 295 J3
Martindale Trading Estate
CNCK/NC WS11 .... 232 A8
Marychurch C of E
Primary School
BUCK/MIL ST2 .... 3 M6
Mary Elliot School
WSLW WS2 .... 283 L6
Maryhill CP School
ALS/KID ST7 .... 39 H7
Mary Howard C of E
Primary School
CRTAM B79 .... 239 H5
Masterton Street Surgery
STOKE ST4 .... 85 K4
Maternity Welfare Clinic
ETTPK/GDPK/PENN WV4 ..... 294 D4

May Bank Business Centre
NEWUL ST5 .... 68 D6
May Bank County
Infants School
NEWUL ST5 .... 68 D7
Maybrook Industrial Estate
BRWNH WS8 .... 268 F5
Mayfield Surgery
LNGTN ST3 .... 86 B8
Maypole Gallery
WMBN WV5 .... 298 A3
Meadows County
Primary School
AUD/MAD/W CW3 .... 82 A2
Meadows Special School
BIDD ST8 .... 40 C3
Media Centre
WOLV WV1 .... 13 G4
Meir CP School
LNGTN ST3 .... 103 H1
Meir Health Centre
LNGTN ST3 .... 102 F1
Meir Heath CP School
LNGTN ST3 .... 103 G6
Meir Heath Cricket Club
LNGTN ST3 .... 103 G7
Meir Park Surgery
LNGTN ST3 .... 103 H3
Members Business Centre
NEWUL ST5 .... 68 C8
Memorial Hall School
SWAD DE11 .... 205 L4
Merridale Primary School
BDMR/CCFT WV3 .... 12 A7
Merryfields School
NEWUL ST5 .... 68 B6
Mesnes Green Industrial Estate
LICHS WS14 .... 9 G5
Metro Business Park
HAN ST1 .... 2 A6
Michelin Sports Centre
STOKE ST4 .... 84 E8
Middlehurst Special School
ALS/KID ST7 .... 53 M3
Middlemore Business Park
ALDR WS9 .... 284 E3
Middleport Infants School
BURS/TUN ST6 .... 68 E3
Midland House Dawley
Trading Estate
KGSWFD DY6 .... 303 K2
Mid Staffordshire
General Hospital NHS Trust
STAFN ST16 .... 5 G3
Mile Oak Business Park
POL/KGSB/FAZ B78 .... 273 J8
Milking Bank Primary School
DUDN DY1 .... 299 L8
Millbuck Industrial Estate
WOLVN WV10 .... 280 D3
Miller Street Surgery
NEWUL ST5 .... 84 C1
Millfield County
Primary School
POL/KGSB/FAZ B78 .... 290 A2
Millfield CP School
BRWNH WS8 .... 269 G3
Mill Hill CP School
BURS/TUN ST6 .... 53 M6
Milton CP School
BUCK/MIL ST2 .... 70 B1
Mitchell County High School
BUCK/MIL ST2 .... 70 C7
Mitchell Memorial
Youth Centre & Theatre
HAN ST1 .... 2 B6
Moat Hall County
Primary School
GTWY WS6 .... 249 M7
Molineux Youth
& Sports Centre
WOLV WV1 .... 12 E3
Monkton Recreation Centre
PENK ST19 .... 229 K1
Monmore Park
Industrial Estate
BKHL/PFLD WV2 .... 295 M3
Moorcroft Medical Centre
HAN ST1 .... 2 F7
Moorfields Industrial Estate
STONE ST15 .... 118 A6
Moor First School
BIDD ST8 .... 41 H1
Moorgate County
Primary School
CRTAM B79 .... 10 C3
Moor Hall Junior
& Infant School
MGN/WHC B75 .... 287 K8
Moorhill County
Primary School
CNCK/NC WS11 .... 231 L5
Moorhill Primary School
CNCK/NC WS11 .... 231 L6
Moorland Medical Centre
LEEK ST13 .... 43 M4
Moorpark County
Junior School
BURS/TUN ST6 .... 69 G1
Moorside High School
END/WER ST9 .... 71 L6
Moreton Community School
WOLVN WV10 .... 280 F1
Morley Road Shopping Centre
BNTWD WS7 .... 252 B3
Mosley County Primary School
BUTN/AL/TUT DE13 .... 184 B3
Mosque
BURS/TUN ST6 .... 53 K6
Mosque
BUT DE14 .... 6 E9
Mosque Taiyyibah
BDMR/CCFT WV3 .... 12 B8
Mossely Junior School
BLOX/PEL WS3 .... 266 F8
Moss Grove Surgery
KGSWFD DY6 .... 303 K4

Moss Lane Surgery
AUD/MAD/W CW3 81
Mossley Clinic
BLOX/PEL WS3 283
Mossley C of E Primary School
CONG CW12 26
Mossley Primary School
BLOX/PEL WS3 266
Mount Industrial Estate
STONE ST15 119
Mount Pleasant CP School
STOKE ST4 85
Mount Special School
STOKE ST4 84
Mow Cap Castle (Nt)
ALS/KID ST7 39
Municipal Art Gallery
WOLV WV1 12
Museum
LICHS WS14 253
The Museum
of Cannock Chase
HEDN WS12 232
Naqshbandia Mosque
HAN ST1 2
Neachells Lane
Industrial Estate
WLNHL WV13 281
Needwood C of E
Primary School
BUTN/AL/TUT DE13 181
Nelson Industrial Estate
STOKE ST4 84
Nether Stowe County
High School
LICH WS13 254
The New Abbey Friar
BUCK/MIL ST2 3
Newbridge Doctors Surgery
DUNHL/THL/PER WV6 279
Newbridge
Preparatory School
DUNHL/THL/PER WV6 279
Newcastle Borough Council
NEWUL ST5 84
Newcastle Business Centre
NEWUL ST5 68
Newcastle College of Further
Education
NEWUL ST5 68
Newcastle Museum
& Art Gallery
NEWUL ST5 68
Newcastle Secondary School
NEWUL ST5 84
Newcastle Town Football Club
NEWUL ST5 84
Newcastle-under-Lyme
Borough Council
NEWUL ST5 84
Newcastle-under-Lyme
Borough Council
NEWUL ST5 84
Newcastle-under-Lyme
Boys School
NEWUL ST5 84
Newcastle-under-Lyme
Girls School
NEWUL ST5 84
New Cheadle Hospital
CDLE ST10 89
New Cross Hospital
WOLVN WV10 281
New Cross Industrial Estate
WOLV WV1 281
Newfields Industrial Estate
BURS/TUN ST6 53
New Ford CP School
BURS/TUN ST6 69
Newhall County Infant School
SWAD DE11 205
Newhall County Junior School
SWAD DE11 205
Newhall Surgery
SWAD DE11 205
Newhampton Open
Door Theatre
WOLV WV1 12
Newhouse Special School
BUCK/MIL ST2 70
New Invention CP School
SHHTH WV12 282
New Parkhall Industrial Estate
LNGTN ST3 86
New Road Industrial Estate
RSTAF ST18 177
Newstead CP School
LNGTN ST3 101
Newton Regis C of E
Primary School
CRTAM B79 259
Newton Regis C of E School
CRTAM B79 259
Newton Solney C of E
Infant School
STPNHL/WNHL DE15 186
New Victoria Theatre
NEWUL ST5 68
Norbury C of E Primary School
ASHB DE6 109
North CP School
BURS/TUN ST6 69
Northgate Surgery
UTXR ST14 144
Northside Business Park
BUT DE14 185
North Staffordshire Combined
Healthcare N H S Trust
BUCK/MIL ST2 70
North Staffordshire Combined
Healthcare N H S Trust
NEWUL ST5 68
North Staffordshire
Health Authority
LNGTN ST3 102
North Staffordshire
Health Authority
STOKE ST4 84

orth Staffordshire
Health Authority
STOKE ST4 .... 85 H3
orth Staffordshire Hospital
STOKE ST4 .... 84 E2
orth Staffordshire Hospital
Management
STOKE ST4 .... 84 E2
e North Staffordshire
Nuffield Hospital
NEWUL ST5 .... 84 C7
orth Staffordshire
Royal Infirmary
STOKE ST4 .... 84 F3
orth Staffs Hospital
STOKE ST4 .... 84 E3
orth Staffs Hospital
Management Committee
STOKE ST4 .... 84 E3
orth Staffs Maternity Hospital
STOKE ST4 .... 84 D3
orth Staffs Regional
Film Theatre
STOKE ST4 .... 85 H2
orth Walsall Junior
& Infant School
WSLW WS2 .... 283 L6
orthwood County
Infants School
HAN ST1 .... 3 C3
orthycote High School
WOLVN WV10 .... 264 E7
orton Canes Business Park
CNCK/NC WS11 .... 251 C6
orton Canes High School
CNCK/NC WS11 .... 251 C5
orton Canes Infant School
CNCK/NC WS11 .... 251 C6
orton Canes Primary School
CNCK/NC WS11 .... 251 C6
orton CP School
BURS/TUN ST6 .... 54 F7
orton Industrial Estate
BURS/TUN ST6 .... 54 E8
orton In Hales C of E
(VC) Primary School
MKTDR TF9 .... 113 J1
orton Medical Practice
STRBR DY8 .... 307 L7
akdale Trading Estate
KGSWFD DY6 .... 303 K3
akhill CP School
STOKE ST4 .... 84 F7
akland Industrial Estate
HEDN WS12 .... 232 B7
aklands Academy
of Theatre Dance
BLOX/PEL WS3 .... 268 A6
akmeadow Junior School
WNSFLD WV11 .... 282 A3
akridge CP School
STAFS ST17 .... 194 E4
akwood School
ALDR WS9 .... 269 G7
ctagon Retail Park
HAN ST1 .... 69 G6
deon Cinema
BUT DE14 .... 7 G5
deon Cinema
& Hot Shots Snooker
HAN ST1 .... 69 G6
gley Hay Infant School
BRWNH WS8 .... 268 F2
d Colehurst Manor
MKTDR TF9 .... 130 A7
d Fallings Junior School
WOLVN WV10 .... 280 F1
dfields Business Park
STOKE ST4 .... 85 M5
dfields Hall School
UTXR ST14 .... 144 A3
d Grammar School
MKTDR TF9 .... 130 D1
d Hall Industrial Estate
BLOX/PEL WS3 .... 283 J2
d Hall School
WSLW WS2 .... 282 E5
d Road Surgery
CDLE ST10 .... 105 K6
lympia Sports Centre
CNCK/NC WS11 .... 249 L1
necote CP School
LEEK ST13 .... 45 M7
nneley Golf Club
AUD/MAD/W CW3 .... 81 H7
pen Market
BDMR/CCFT WV3 .... 12 E6
rchard Surgery
BURS/TUN ST6 .... 54 E6
smaston C of E
Primary School
ASHB DE6 .... 95 M4
ulton C of E First School
STONE ST15 .... 120 C6
unsdale High School
WMBN WV5 .... 297 M3
unsdale Sports Centre
WMBN WV5 .... 297 M3
ur Lady & St Benedict RC
Primary School
BUCK/MIL ST2 .... 3 M3
ur Lady St Chads RC School
WOLVN WV10 .... 280 F2
ur Lady & St Werburghs
RC Primary School
STOKE ST4 .... 84 B6
xbarn Social & Sports Club
BDMR/CCFT WV3 .... 294 F3
xhey First School
BIDD ST8 .... 40 E1
ackmoor CP School
ALS/KID ST7 .... 53 M1
aget County High School
BUT DE14 .... 204 A4
ainsley RC High School
CDLE ST10 .... 89 K8
almbourne Industrial Park
STAFN ST16 .... 4 C5

Palmers Cross Primary School
DUNHL/THL/PER WV6 .... 279 K2
Paramount Business Park
BURS/TUN ST6 .... 69 G2
Park Attwood Clinic
BEWD DY12 .... 308 D6
Park County Middle School
BIDD ST8 .... 40 C4
Parkfield Business Centre
STAFS ST17 .... 4 F7
Parkfield Clinic
BKHL/PFLD WV2 .... 295 K4
Parkfield High School
ETTPK/GDPK/PENN WV4 .... 295 L5
Parkfield Primary School
ETTPK/GDPK/PENN WV4 .... 295 L5
Parkfield Primary School
TAM/AM/WIL B77 .... 290 C1
Parkfield Surgery
ETTPK/GDPK/PENN WV4 .... 295 K4
Park Hall CP School
LNGTN ST3 .... 87 G6
Parkhall Industrial Estate
LNGTN ST3 .... 86 E5
Park Lane Trading Estate
WOLVN WV10 .... 280 E5
Parkside County Junior School
ASHB DE6 .... 79 J8
Parkside CP School
STAFN ST16 .... 174 D2
Parkside Industrial Estate
WOLV WV1 .... 13 M7
Park Special School
CRTAM B79 .... 274 A3
Pasturefields Industrial Estate
RSTAF ST18 .... 177 H3
Paulet County High School
STPNHL/WNHL DE15 .... 204 F3
P D H Industrial Estate
WLNHL WV13 .... 281 K7
Peach Gallery
STAFN ST16 .... 4 C2
Pear Tree County
Primary School
RUGE WS15 .... 215 L3
The Peel Medical Centre
CRTAM B79 .... 10 C4
Peel Terrace Business Centre
STAFN ST16 .... 174 E5
Pelsall Clinic
BLOX/PEL WS3 .... 268 A6
Pelsall Comprehensive School
RUSH/SHEL WS4 .... 284 B1
Pelsall Village JMI School
BLOX/PEL WS3 .... 267 M6
Pendeford Business Park
COVEN WV9 .... 263 M7
Pendeford Health Centre
COVEN WV9 .... 264 A8
Pendene Complimentary
Medical Centre
WOLV WV1 .... 12 C4
Penkhull County
Infants School
STOKE ST4 .... 84 F3
Penkridge County
Middle School
PENK ST19 .... 212 A8
Penkridge Parish Council
PENK ST19 .... 229 M1
Pennfields Health Centre
BDMR/CCFT WV3 .... 12 C8
Penn Hall Special School
ETTPK/GDPK/PENN WV4 .... 294 E7
Penn Hospital
ETTPK/GDPK/PENN WV4 .... 294 E6
Penn Manor Medical Centre
ETTPK/GDPK/PENN WV4 .... 294 F6
Pens Meadow School
STRBR DY8 .... 303 M7
Perry Hall Primary School
WNSFLD WV11 .... 281 M4
Perton Clinic
DUNHL/THL/PER WV6 .... 278 E6
Perton County First School
DUNHL/THL/PER WV6 .... 278 E5
Perton County Middle School
DUNHL/THL/PER WV6 .... 279 G6
Perton Parish Council
DUNHL/THL/PER WV6 .... 278 E6
Phoenix Road
Industrial Estate
WLNHL WV13 .... 281 K7
Picknalls County First School
UTXR ST14 .... 144 B3
The Picture House
BURS/TUN ST6 .... 54 D8
The Picture House
STAFN ST16 .... 4 E6
The Picture House
WLNHL WV13 .... 281 K6
Pikemere County
Primary School
ALS/KID ST7 .... 37 H5
The Pine Gallery
STOKE ST4 .... 85 L4
Pinewood CP School
LNGTN ST3 .... 87 J8
Pinfold Industrial Estate
BLOX/PEL WS3 .... 283 J2
Pinfold Lane Surgery
RUGE WS15 .... 227 J4
Pipewood School
RUGE WS15 .... 199 H6
Pirehill First School
STONE ST15 .... 137 M4
Planetary Industrial Estate
WLNHL WV13 .... 281 J6
Polesworth High School
POL/KGSB/FAZ B78 .... 291 M2
The Police Station
ECCH ST21 .... 152 E3
Pool Hayes Comprehensive
School
SHHTH WV12 .... 282 B5
Pool Hayes Primary School
SHHTH WV12 .... 282 B4

Portfolio Gallery
CRTAM B79 .... 10 D4
Porthill Clinic
NEWUL ST5 .... 68 C4
Porthill Park Cricket Club
NEWUL ST5 .... 68 C6
Port Vale Football Club Co Ltd
BURS/TUN ST6 .... 69 G1
The Potteries Business Centre
HAN ST1 .... 69 G6
The Potteries Museum
& Art Gallery
HAN ST1 .... 2 C6
Potteries Shopping Centre
HAN ST1 .... 2 D4
Power Wash Trading Estate
BIDD ST8 .... 40 B6
Primrose Lane Health Centre
WOLVN WV10 .... 281 G2
Princefield First School
PENK ST19 .... 229 M2
Priory C of E Infants
& Junior School
STOKE ST4 .... 100 F2
Priory Green Junior
& Infants School
COVEN WV9 .... 264 A8
Priory Junior Mixed
& Infants School
BLOX/PEL WS3 .... 283 H3
Progress Business Centre
CNCK/NC WS11 .... 249 L3
Prospect Business Park
CNCK/NC WS11 .... 249 J3
Public Baths
BURS/TUN ST6 .... 53 L7
Pye Green Valley CP School
HEDN WS12 .... 232 A3
Queen Anne Street Surgery
STOKE ST4 .... 85 H2
Queen Elizabeth Lower School
ASHB DE6 .... 95 J2
Queen Elizabeth
Mercian High School
CRTAM B79 .... 10 D1
Queen Elizabeth's
Grammar School
ASHB DE6 .... 79 J7
Queen Marys High School
RUSH/SHEL WS4 .... 283 M7
Queens County Primary School
STOKE ST4 .... 86 A5
Queens Croft Special School
LICH WS13 .... 8 E5
Queens Hospital
BUTN/AL/TUT DE13 .... 185 G5
Queen Street Industrial Estate
BNTWD WS7 .... 251 M5
Queensville Retail Park
STAFS ST17 .... 194 A2
Queensway Industrial Estate
BURS/TUN ST6 .... 68 C2
Queen Victoria Primary School
SEDG DY3 .... 299 K2
Quince Tree Special School
TAM/AM/WIL B77 .... 275 G6
The Racecourse Gallery
UTXR ST14 .... 144 C3
Racecourse Road
Industrial Estate
DUNHL/THL/PER WV6 .... 280 A5
Radleys Primary School
RUSH/SHEL WS4 .... 284 C3
Rafferty Business Park
BURS/TUN ST6 .... 69 H2
Rakegate Infant School
WOLVN WV10 .... 280 B1
Rakegate Junior School
WOLVN WV10 .... 280 B1
Ramgarhia Sabha Sikh Temple
WOLV WV1 .... 12 D3
Ravenhill County
Primary School
RUGE WS15 .... 215 M4
Ravenside Retail Park
STOKE ST4 .... 85 K2
Ravensmead CP
Primary School
ALS/KID ST7 .... 51 L7
Rawlett High School
CRTAM B79 .... 274 A1
Redbrook Lane
Industrial Estate
RUGE WS15 .... 215 M5
Redhall Junior & Infant School
SEDG DY3 .... 299 J7
Redhill Primary School
CNCK/NC WS11 .... 231 L5
Red Hill Street Clinic
WOLV WV1 .... 12 F1
Red House Football Club
BLYBR/FOR ST11 .... 87 K7
Redhouse Industrial Estate
ALDR WS9 .... 284 E4
Redhouse Industrial Estate
ALDR WS9 .... 285 G4
Redhouse JMI School
ALDR WS9 .... 284 E5
Red Rooster Industrial Estate
ALDR WS9 .... 284 E4
Red Rose Theatre
RUGE WS15 .... 215 L1
Reflex Industrial Park
WLNHL WV13 .... 281 M7
Regent Theatre
HAN ST1 .... 2 C6
The Reginald Mitchell
County Primary School
ALS/KID ST7 .... 52 D1
Regional Health Authority
BKHL/PFLD WV2 .... 295 K3
The Regional Heart Study
NEWUL ST5 .... 83 H1
Regis Comprehensive School
DUNHL/THL/PER WV6 .... 279 H5
Ribble Industrial Estate
BURS/TUN ST6 .... 68 F3

Richard Clarke County
First School
RUGE WS15 .... 180 A4
Richard Crosse C E
Primary School
BUTN/AL/TUT DE13 .... 218 C4
Richard Wakefield C of E
Primary School
BUTN/AL/TUT DE13 .... 165 J4
The Ridge Primary School
STRBR DY8 .... 307 J5
Ridgeway Middle School
BNTWD WS7 .... 252 A5
Ridgeway Surgery
SEDG DY3 .... 299 K3
Ridgewood High School
KINVER DY7 .... 307 J5
Ringway Industrial Estate
LICH WS13 .... 236 C7
Rising Brook County
High School
STAFS ST17 .... 193 L4
Riverside Industrial Estate
POL/KGSB/FAZ B78 .... 290 B1
The Roaches School
BIDD ST8 .... 40 B4
Robert Sherborne
Infant School
BUTN/AL/TUT DE13 .... 166 C5
Roberts Infant School
SEDG DY3 .... 299 K7
Roberts Primary School
SEDG DY3 .... 299 L6
Robert Sutton RC High School
STPNHL/WNHL DE15 .... 205 G3
Robirch Sports Centre
BUT DE14 .... 6 A4
Rocklands Special School
LICH WS13 .... 9 J2
Rode Heath CP School
ALS/KID ST7 .... 37 M3
Rosedale C of E School
SHHTH WV12 .... 282 D5
Rosliston C of E
Primary School
MSHM DE12 .... 222 C4
Rosslyn Road Surgery
LNGTN ST3 .... 86 C8
Rough Close C of E
Primary School
LNGTN ST3 .... 102 E5
Roundwell Place Day Hospital
BURS/TUN ST6 .... 53 K7
Rowhurst Industrial Estate
NEWUL ST5 .... 67 J3
Rowley Hall Hospital &
Nursing Home
STAFS ST17 .... 193 K2
Royal Wolverhampton
Junior School
BDMR/CCFT WV3 .... 295 G3
The Royal Wolverhampton
School
BKHL/PFLD WV2 .... 295 H3
Rugby Industrial Estate
BUT DE14 .... 6 D6
Rugeley Health Centre
RUGE WS15 .... 215 L2
Rugeley Tennis Club
RUGE WS15 .... 215 J1
Rushall Primary School
RUSH/SHEL WS4 .... 284 B3
Rushton C of E Primary School
MCFLDS SK11 .... 28 C1
Ryandra Business Park
CDLE ST10 .... 89 H8
Rydal Estate
RUGE WS15 .... 197 M7
Ryders Hayes Junior
Mixed & Infants School
BLOX/PEL WS3 .... 268 A5
Ryecroft Middle School
UTXR ST14 .... 108 E6
Ryecroft Surgery
NEWUL ST5 .... 84 B1
Rykneld CP School
BUT DE14 .... 203 L3
Ryknild Industrial Estate
BUTN/AL/TUT DE13 .... 185 L4
Sai Medical Centre
WSLW WS2 .... 283 J8
St Albans C of E
Primary School
WNSFLD WV11 .... 282 B2
St Andrews C of E CP School
CRTAM B79 .... 240 E8
St Andrews C of E
Infant School
DUNHL/THL/PER WV6 .... 279 M6
St Andrews C of E
Primary School
RSTAF ST18 .... 157 K8
St Andrews C of E
Primary School
SHIF TF11 .... 242 A8
St Andrews First School
RSTAF ST18 .... 157 J7
St Annes C of E CP School
BURS/TUN ST6 .... 55 H1
St Annes Industrial Estate
WLNHL WV13 .... 282 B7
St Annes RC Primary School
STAFS ST17 .... 194 D3
St Anthonys Junior
& Infant School
WOLVN WV10 .... 264 D7
St Augustines First School
ASHB DE6 .... 163 K5
St Augustines RC
Primary School
LNGTN ST3 .... 102 F2
St Austins RC CP School
STAFS ST17 .... 5 C7
St Bartholomews
C of E Primary School
BUX SK17 .... 24 B3

St Bartholomews
Primary School
ETTPK/GDPK/PENN WV4 .... 294 E7
St Bedes Preparatory School
STAFS ST17 .... 197 G4
St Benedict Biscop
Primary School
WMBN WV5 .... 298 B3
St Bernadettes RC JMI School
BRWNH WS8 .... 268 F2
St Bernadettes RC
Primary School
WMBN WV5 .... 297 M4
St Chads Cathedral School
LICH WS13 .... 8 C2
St Chads Catholic
Primary School
SEDG DY3 .... 299 K3
St Chads C E Primary School
DUNHL/THL/PER WV6 .... 277 J7
St Chads C of E CP School
NEWUL ST5 .... 52 D8
St Chads Stowe Primary School
LICH WS13 .... 9 H2
St Christophers RC
Primary School
CDSL WV8 .... 263 G7
St Dominics Independent
Junior School
STOKE ST4 .... 85 G2
St Dominics Priory School
STONE ST15 .... 137 M1
St Dominics RC Primary School
STONE ST15 .... 137 M2
St Dominics School
PENK ST19 .... 246 C4
St Edmunds RC School
DUNHL/THL/PER WV6 .... 279 L7
St Edwards C of E First School
LEEK ST13 .... 57 H5
St Edwards C of E
Middle School
LEEK ST13 .... 43 J5
St Edwards Hospital
LEEK ST13 .... 57 J2
St Elizabeths Primary School
CRTAM B79 .... 274 A2
St Filumenas RC CP School
BLYBR/FOR ST11 .... 87 L8
St Francis Junior
& Infant School
RUSH/SHEL WS4 .... 284 C1
St Francis of Assisi RC
Comprehensive School
ALDR WS9 .... 285 J5
St Gabriels RC CP School
ALS/KID ST7 .... 37 J7
St Gabriels RC Primary School
TAM/AM/WIL B77 .... 290 E1
St George & St. Martins
RC CP School
HAN ST1 .... 2 F2
St Georges Hospital
STAFN ST16 .... 4 F2
St Giles C of E Junior School
WLNHL WV13 .... 282 B8
St Giles RC CP School
CDLE ST10 .... 89 K7
St Giles & St. Georges
C of E CP School
NEWUL ST5 .... 84 B1
St Gregorys RC Junior & Infants
School
LNGTN ST3 .... 86 B8
St James C E Primary School
RUGE WS15 .... 217 G8
St James C of E
Primary School
STRBR DY8 .... 307 K3
St James Primary School
BRWNH WS8 .... 268 F2
St John Fisher RC High School
NEWUL ST5 .... 68 A8
St Johns C E Primary School
WNSFLD WV11 .... 266 A6
St Johns C of E CP School
END/WER ST9 .... 72 A3
St Johns C of E CP School
NEWUL ST5 .... 82 F3
St Johns C of E CP School
STAFN ST16 .... 5 M2
St Johns C of E First School
PENK ST19 .... 244 E3
St Johns C of E Infants School
BURS/TUN ST6 .... 68 F3
St Johns Hospital
LICH WS13 .... 8 E3
St Johns Preparatory School
LICH WS13 .... 8 E5
St Johns Primary School
SEDG DY3 .... 297 L8
St Johns RC CP School
ALS/KID ST7 .... 52 F1
St Johns RC CP School
CDLE ST10 .... 91 L8
St Johns RC CP School
RSTAF ST18 .... 177 H8
St Joseph & St Theresa
RC Primary School
BNTWD WS7 .... 251 L4
St Joseph's College Gm School
STOKE ST4 .... 84 F7
St Josephs Convent
Preparatory School
DUNHL/THL/PER WV6 .... 279 L4
St Josephs Primary School
RUGE WS15 .... 215 L3
St Josephs RC CP School
BURS/TUN ST6 .... 53 K3
St Josephs RC CP School
UTXR ST14 .... 144 B2
St Josephs RC Primary School
HEDN WS12 .... 232 C6
St Josephs RC Primary School
LICHS WS14 .... 9 H5
St Josephs RC Primary School
STRBR DY8 .... 307 M8

St Judes Junior
& Infant School
DUNHL/THL/PER WV6 .... 279 M6
St Judes Junior School
BDMR/CCFT WV3 .... 279 M8
St Lawrence C of E
First School
GNOS ST20 .... 190 E4
St Leonards C of E
Primary School
CRTAM B79 .... 257 J8
St Leonards C of E
First School
CDLE ST10 .... 74 A2
St Leonards C of E
First School
RSTAF ST18 .... 211 M2
St Leonards CP School
STAFS ST17 .... 5 J7
St Lukes C of E CP School
END/WER ST9 .... 55 L3
St Lukes C of E CP School
HAN ST1 .... 2 F5
St Lukes Infant School
BKHL/PFLD WV2 .... 295 J3
St Lukes Junior School
BKHL/PFLD WV2 .... 295 H3
St Margarets C of E
Junior School
NEWUL ST5 .... 68 D6
St Margaret Ward RC
High School
BURS/TUN ST6 .... 53 M5
St Maria Goretti RC
Primary School
BUCK/MIL ST2 .... 70 C8
St Marks C of E
Primary School
HAN ST1 .... 2 B8
St Mary of the Angels RC
School
ALDR WS9 .... 285 H5
St Marys Abbey
RSTAF ST18 .... 196 D3
St Mary & St Anne School
RUGE WS15 .... 180 A4
St Mary & St Chads C of E
First School
PENK ST19 .... 246 C4
St Marys C of E CP School
BURS/TUN ST6 .... 53 K7
St Marys C of E First School
UTXR ST14 .... 144 B1
St Marys C of E Primary School
KGSWFD DY6 .... 303 K3
St Marys C of E Primary School
MCFLDS SK11 .... 18 D2
St Marys C of E Primary School
MKTDR TF9 .... 114 A3
St Marys C of E Primary School
RUGE WS15 .... 197 M4
St Marys RC CP School
BURS/TUN ST6 .... 54 D7
St Marys RC CP School
LEEK ST13 .... 43 L6
St Marys RC CP School
NEWUL ST5 .... 84 A1
St Marys RC CP School
PENK ST19 .... 246 B4
St Marys RC Primary School
CNCK/NC WS11 .... 249 L2
St Marys RC School
WOLV WV10 .... 281 G3
St Marys & St Johns RC School
BKHL/PFLD WV2 .... 13 H9
St Michaels C of E First School
PENK ST19 .... 229 L1
St Michaels C of E First School
STONE ST15 .... 138 C4
St Michaels C of E Primary School
LICH WS13 .... 9 H3
St Michaels C of E Primary School
LICHS WS14 .... 9 H4
St Michaels C of E School
BLOX/PEL WS3 .... 267 M8
St Michaels First School
END/WER ST9 .... 28 C8
St Mildreds C of E CP School
CDLE ST10 .... 74 D7
St Modwens Primary School
BUTN/AL/TUT DE13 .... 185 H5
St Nicholas's C E First School
CDSL WV8 .... 262 F6
St Oswalds C of E Infant School
ASHB DE6 .... 79 H8
St Oswalds Hospital
ASHB DE6 .... 79 G8
St Patricks Junior Middle
& Infant RC School
WSLW WS2 .... 283 K7
St Patricks Primary School
WNSFLD WV11 .... 281 J5
St Pauls C E First School
COVEN WV9 .... 247 J7
St Pauls C of E CP School
STAFS ST17 .... 5 G8
St Pauls C of E Junior School
BURS/TUN ST6 .... 68 E2
St Peters C E Primary School
ALDR WS9 .... 269 L6
St Peters C E Primary School
BUTN/AL/TUT DE13 .... 200 F7
St Peters C E Primary School
HEDN WS12 .... 232 D6
St Peters C of E CP School
RSTAF ST18 .... 177 H3
St Peters C of E CP School
STOKE ST4 .... 85 H4
St Peters C of E First School
CDLE ST10 .... 107 L1
St Peters C of E First School
UTXR ST14 .... 145 M8
St Peters C of E
Primary School
MSHM DE12 .... 241 M4
St Peters C of E School
BLYBR/FOR ST11 .... 87 K7

St Peters Collegiate School
DUNHL/THL/PER WV6 .... 279 L7
St Peters High School
STOKE ST4 .... 84 F3
St Peters RC CP School
BURS/TUN ST6 .... 69 G4
St Peters Retail Park
BUT DE14 .... 7 H8
St Peters & St. Pauls RC
Primary School
LICH WS13 .... 254 B1
St Peters Surgery
WSLW WS2 .... 283 K6
St Saviours C of E (C)
Primary School
ALS/KID ST7 .... 52 C1
St Stephens C of E
Primary School
WOLVN WV10 .... 280 E6
St Stephens Primary School
LICH WS13 .... 237 K3
St Teresas RC CP School
STOKE ST4 .... 84 E8
St Teresas RC Primary School
ETTPK/GDPK/PENN WV4 ..... 295 L5
St Thomas C of E School
WNSFLD WV11 .... 281 K3
St Thomas More
Catholic College
LNGTN ST3 .... 86 A7
St Thomas More RC
Primary School
CNCK/NC WS11 .... 250 A6
St Thomas of Canterbury
School
BLOX/PEL WS3 .... 283 M4
St Thomas Priory Golf Club
RUGE WS15 .... 216 C5
St Thomas RC CP School
CDLE ST10 .... 105 L6
St Thomas RC CP School
STOKE ST4 .... 84 F1
St Thomas's C of E
Primary School
ALS/KID ST7 .... 53 G2
St Werburghs C of E CP School
CDLE ST10 .... 73 L8
St Wilfreds RC CP School
BURS/TUN ST6 .... 53 M7
St Wulstans RC CP School
NEWUL ST5 .... 68 D5
Salisbury Place
Industrial Estate
BDMR/CCFT WV3 .... 12 C7
Salters Meadow Health Centre
BNTWD WS7 .... 251 M3
Saltery County Junior School
END/WER ST9 .... 71 H7
Saltery School
END/WER ST9 .... 71 H8
Salvation Army
HAN ST1 .... 2 D4
Sandon High School
LNGTN ST3 .... 102 F2
Sandon Road Surgery
LNGTN ST3 .... 102 F1
Sandown County First School
DUNHL/THL/PER WV6 .... 278 F6
Sandy Lane Surgery
PENK ST19 .... 246 C4
Satellite Industrial Park
WLNHL WV13 .... 281 J6
Saxon Hill Special School
LICHS WS14 .... 9 H6
S B K Sports Club
BUT DE14 .... 6 D4
Scholar Green CP School
ALS/KID ST7 .... 38 E4
Scotch Orchard County
Primary School
LICH WS13 .... 254 D1
Scotia Business Park
BURS/TUN ST6 .... 53 L8
Scott Lidgett Industrial Estate
BURS/TUN ST6 .... 68 D3
Seabridge County
Junior & Infants School
NEWUL ST5 .... 84 A6
Shelfield Clinic
RUSH/SHEL WS4 .... 284 C2
Shelfield Community School
RUSH/SHEL WS4 .... 268 C8
Shelton Swimming Pool
STOKE ST4 .... 85 H1
Shenstone Lodge School
LICHS WS14 .... 271 G8
Shenstone Parish Council
FOAKS/STRLY B74 .... 286 D4
Shenstone Sports Club
LICHS WS14 .... 271 G4
Sheriffhales Primary School
SHIF TF11 .... 224 B6
Shifnal Golf Club
SHIF TF11 .... 242 A2
Shifnal Industrial Estate
SHIF TF11 .... 242 B7
Shifnal Primary School
SHIF TF11 .... 242 A5
Shifnal Sports Centre
SHIF TF11 .... 242 A6
Shire Oak School
BRWNH WS8 .... 269 G5
Shires Industrial Estate
LICHS WS14 .... 8 D7
Shobnall County
Primary School
BUTN/AL/TUT DE13 .... 184 F6
Short Heath Clinic
SHHTH WV12 .... 282 D4
Shorth Heath Junior School
SHHTH WV12 .... 282 D5
Short Street Infants School
STPNHL/WNHL DE15 .... 204 E3
Showell Road Industrial Estate
WOLVN WV10 .... 280 D4
Shri Guru Ravidass Temple
BKHL/PFLD WV2 .... 295 K3

Shugborough Hall
County Museum
RSTAF ST18 .... 196 A2
Sidings Industrial Estate
BUT DE14 .... 7 K2
Sikh Temple
STAFN ST16 .... 5 J4
Sikh Temple
WLNHL WV13 .... 282 C8
Sikh Temple
WNSFLD WV11 .... 281 K5
Sikh Temple
WOLV WV1 .... 13 G4
Silkmore CP School
STAFS ST17 .... 193 M3
Silverdale CP School
NEWUL ST5 .... 83 J1
Silverdale Cricket Club
NEWUL ST5 .... 83 G1
Silverdale Health Centre
NEWUL ST5 .... 83 J1
Silverdale Surgery
NEWUL ST5 .... 67 J8
Sion Hill County
Secondary School
KIDD DY10 .... 310 A8
Sir Graham Balfour High School
STAFN ST16 .... 174 C2
Sir John Offley C of E (C)
Primary School
AUD/MAD/W CW3 .... 81 L5
Sir Robert Peel Hospital
POL/KGSB/FAZ B78 .... 273 K8
Sir Thomas Boughey
High School
ALS/KID ST7 .... 66 D3
Sixth Form College
STOKE ST4 .... 85 K3
Smallthorne CP School
BURS/TUN ST6 .... 54 D8
Smestow Bridge
Industrial Estate
WMBN WV5 .... 297 J4
Sneyd Community School
BLOX/PEL WS3 .... 266 E8
Sneyd Cricket Club
BURS/TUN ST6 .... 69 H3
Sneyd Green CP School
BURS/TUN ST6 .... 69 J3
Sneyd High School
NEWUL ST5 .... 83 M1
Sneyd Street Surgery
BURS/TUN ST6 .... 69 K3
Snow Hill Clinic
BKHL/PFLD WV2 .... 13 G6
Sofer Gallery
CNCK/NC WS11 .... 249 L5
Somerset Surgery
HAN ST1 .... 3 C5
South Staffordshire Council
CDSL WV8 .... 263 C2
South Staffs Business Park
CNCK/NC WS11 .... 249 J6
Sovereign Trading Estate
STRBR DY8 .... 307 L5
Spines Clinic
WMBN WV5 .... 297 M4
Sports Centre
NEWUL ST5 .... 67 L8
Sports Stadium
BURS/TUN ST6 .... 53 L5
Springcroft CP School
BLYBR/FOR ST11 .... 103 K3
Springdale Primary School
ETTPK/GDPK/PENN WV4 ..... 294 C5
Springfield CP School
STOKE ST4 .... 84 E4
Springfields County
First School
STONE ST15 .... 136 F4
Springfield Special School
LEEK ST13 .... 44 A5
Springhead CP School
ALS/KID ST7 .... 52 D4
Springhill CP School
BNTWD WS7 .... 252 B4
Springhill Medical Centre
BNTWD WS7 .... 252 A3
Springhill Trading Estate
SHIF TF11 .... 242 A6
Spring Lane Industrial Estate
SHHTH WV12 .... 282 C6
Springvale Primary School
CNCK/NC WS11 .... 249 L2
Sprint Industrial Estate
WOLVN WV10 .... 247 K4
Squirrel Hayes County
First School
BIDD ST8 .... 40 D3
Stafford Borough Council
STONE ST15 .... 138 A1
Stafford Castle Golf Club
STAFN ST16 .... 4 A6
Stafford College
RUGE WS15 .... 197 M8
Stafford College
STAFN ST16 .... 4 D5
Stafford College
STAFS ST17 .... 5 H6
Stafford Crown & County Courts
STAFN ST16 .... 4 E4
Stafford Grammar School
RSTAF ST18 .... 193 J4
Stafford Magistrates Court
STAFN ST16 .... 4 F5
Stafford Market
STAFN ST16 .... 4 D4
Stafford Rangers Football Club
STAFN ST16 .... 174 C4
Stafford Road Sports Club
BLOX/PEL WS3 .... 267 H4
Stafford Rugby Union
Football Club
STAFN ST16 .... 4 C6
Staffordshire College
of Agriculture
PENK ST19 .... 229 L6

Staffordshire County Council
AUD/MAD/W CW3 .... 81 L3
Staffordshire County Council
BURS/TUN ST6 .... 53 J3
Staffordshire County Council
BUT DE14 .... 7 H4
Staffordshire County Council
CNCK/NC WS11 .... 249 J2
Staffordshire County Council
CRTAM B79 .... 10 E3
Staffordshire County Council
HAN ST1 .... 2 C8
Staffordshire County Council
LEEK ST13 .... 43 M5
Staffordshire County Council
LICH WS13 .... 8 F5
Staffordshire County Council
LNGTN ST3 .... 102 F4
Staffordshire County Council
NEWUL ST5 .... 84 C3
Staffordshire County Council
NEWUL ST5 .... 84 B1
Staffordshire County Council
PENK ST19 .... 229 M1
Staffordshire County Council
PENK ST19 .... 247 J1
Staffordshire County Council
STOKE ST4 .... 84 F2
Staffordshire County Council
STOKE ST4 .... 84 D2
Staffordshire County Council
STOKE ST4 .... 85 K4
Staffordshire General Hospital
STAFN ST16 .... 5 K2
Staffordshire Magistrates Court
NEWUL ST5 .... 84 B1
Staffordshire Moorlands District
Council
LEEK ST13 .... 43 L4
Staffordshire
Regiment Museum
LICHS WS14 .... 255 J8
Staffordshire University
HAN ST1 .... 2 D6
Staffordshire University
HAN ST1 .... 2 A9
Staffordshire University
RSTAF ST18 .... 175 K5
Staffordshire University
STOKE ST4 .... 85 H2
Stafford Super Bowl
STAFN ST16 .... 4 D2
Staffs Moor Industrial Estate
CRTAM B79 .... 10 A2
Stallington Hospital
BLYBR/FOR ST11 .... 103 K7
Stanfield Hospital
BURS/TUN ST6 .... 54 A7
Stanton County Primary School
STPNHL/WNHL DE15 .... 205 H5
Stapenhill Football Club
STPNHL/WNHL DE15 .... 204 E5
Station Industrial Estate
HAN ST1 .... 3 K6
Station Road Industrial Estate
RDERBYSW DE65 .... 165 J2
Station Road Surgery
END/WER ST9 .... 55 M3
Steel Fabs Industrial Estate
BUT DE14 .... 185 J5
Steps to Health
WOLVN WV10 .... 280 E3
Stevens Dental Health Centre
STRBR DY8 .... 307 M6
Stockwell Surgery
LEEK ST13 .... 43 M4
Stoke Business Park
STOKE ST4 .... 85 H3
Stoke Health Centre
STOKE ST4 .... 85 G3
Stoke-on-Trent College
BURS/TUN ST6 .... 68 F2
Stoke-on-Trent College
BURS/TUN ST6 .... 69 H1
Stoke-on-Trent College
HAN ST1 .... 2 D4
Stoke-on-Trent College
HAN ST1 .... 2 A9
Stoke-on-Trent College
STOKE ST4 .... 85 H1
Stoke-on-Trent College of Art
STOKE ST4 .... 85 H2
Stoke-on-Trent
Magistrates Court
STOKE ST4 .... 85 K4
Stoke-on-Trent Rugby
Football Club
STONE ST15 .... 102 C8
Stoke Superbowl
HAN ST1 .... 69 G6
Stone Cricket Club
STONE ST15 .... 138 B3
Stone Golf Club
STONE ST15 .... 137 L2
Stonehouse Hotel
& Leisure Centre
STONE ST15 .... 138 B5
Stone Police Station
STONE ST15 .... 138 A1
Stone Tennis Club
STONE ST15 .... 137 M1
Stonewall Industrial Estate
NEWUL ST5 .... 67 K8
Stoneydelph County
Junior School
TAM/AM/WIL B77 .... 291 G1
Stoneydelph Infants School
TAM/AM/WIL B77 .... 291 G1
Stourbridge College
STRBR DY8 .... 307 L5
Stourbridge Cricket Club
STRBR DY8 .... 307 M3
Stourbridge Football Club
STRBR DY8 .... 307 M4
Stourbridge Galleries
STRBR DY8 .... 307 M6
Stourbridge Rugby Club
KINVER DY7 .... 307 H4

Stowe C of E School
LICH WS13 9
The Straits Primary School
SEDG DY3 299
Strawberry Lane
Industrial Estate
WLNHL WV13 281
Streetly Methodist
Recreation Centre
FOAKS/STRLY B74 285
Stretton Surgery
BUTN/AL/TUT DE13 185
Studio 1 Health Centre
LNGTN ST3 86
Sudbury Primary School
ASHB DE6 146
Sugnall Business Centre
ECCH ST21 134
Summerbank
Central CP School
BURS/TUN ST6 53
Summerhill School
KGSWFD DY6 303
Sunrise Business Park
STRBR DY8 307
Sunshine Infant School
BLOX/PEL WS3 283
Superbowl
BUT DE14 7
Sutherland CP School
LNGTN ST3 101
Swimming Baths
CDLE ST10 89
Swimming Baths
WOLV WV1 12
Swindon Golf Club
SEDG DY3 297
Swynnerton RC
Primary School
STONE ST15 118
Sycamore Green CP School
DUDN DY1 299
Talbot County First School
UTXR ST14 160
Talke Clinic
ALS/KID ST7 52
Tamar Medical Centre
DUNHL/THL/PER WV6 278
Tame Valley Small
Business Centre
TAM/AM/WIL B77 290
Tamworth Borough Council
CRTAM B79 10
Tamworth Borough Council
TAM/AM/WIL B77 275
Tamworth Borough Council
TAM/AM/WIL B77 290
Tamworth Business Centre
TAM/AM/WIL B77 275
Tamworth College of Further
Education
CRTAM B79 10
Tamworth District Council
CRTAM B79 273
Tandon Medical Centre
SEDG DY3 299
Tardis Surgery
CDLE ST10 89
Telford United Football Club
CNCK/NC WS11 251
Tettenhall College
DUNHL/THL/PER WV6 279
Theatre Royal
HAN ST1 2
Thistley Hough High School
STOKE ST4 84
Thomas Alleynes High School
UTXR ST14 144
Thomas Barnes CP School
POL/KGSB/FAZ B78 273
Thomas Russell Infants School
BUTN/AL/TUT DE13 202
Thomas Russell Junior School
BUTN/AL/TUT DE13 220
Thursfield CP School
ALS/KID ST7 39
Tillington Manor CP School
STAFN ST16 174
Tittensor C of E First School
BARL ST12 119
Tolson Industrial Estate
POL/KGSB/FAZ B78 290
Tolsons Mill Industrial Estate
POL/KGSB/FAZ B78 290
Torc High School
TAM/AM/WIL B77 275
The Towerview
Primary School
STPNHL/WNHL DE15 186
Tower Works Industrial Estate
BDMR/CCFT WV3 12
Townsend Primary School
BUCK/MIL ST2 70
Town Yard Industrial Estate
LEEK ST13 43
T P Riley
Comprehensive School
BLOX/PEL WS3 267
Tractor Spares
Industrial Estate
WLNHL WV13 281
Trent Business Park
RUGE WS15 215
Trentham High School
STOKE ST4 101
Trentham Rugby
Football Club
STOKE ST4 101
Trent Hospital
STONE ST15 137
Trent Industrial Estate
BUT DE14 7
Trent Meadows
Medical Centre
BUT DE14 7
Trent Rowing Club
BUT DE14 7

ntside Clinic
STONE ST15 .... 138 A2
ntside Cricket Club
BUT DE14 .... 204 B3
nt Vale C of E
Primary School
STOKE ST4 .... 84 E7
nt Vale Health Centre
STOKE ST4 .... 84 F7
nt Valley Trading Estate
WV13 .... 236 C7
nt Valley Trading Estate
RUGE WS15 .... 197 M7
ity C of E Junior School
WOLVN WV10 .... 280 F6
bury Cricket Club
BUTN/AL/TUT DE13 .... 165 J3
bury Health Centre
BUTN/AL/TUT DE13 .... 165 J4
o Gates County
Primary School
TAM/AM/WIL B77 .... 290 C2
o Gates Trading Estate
TAM/AM/WIL B77 .... 290 D3
sel Parkes First School
.... 143 M1
erley Health Centre
BURS/TUN ST6 .... 86 C1
derhill Junior
& Infant School
WOLVN WV10 .... 281 H1
derhill Primary School
WOLVN WV10 .... 281 H1
icorn Industrial Estate
BURS/TUN ST6 .... 68 D2
iversity (North Site)
WOLV WV1 .... 12 F3
iversity of Keele
STOKE ST4 .... 84 C2
iversity (South Site)
WOLV WV1 .... 12 F4
lands Junior & Infant School
BDMR/CCFT WV3 .... 294 D2
S A M Trading Estate
WOLVN WV10 .... 264 D8
toxeter Golf Club
UTXR ST14 .... 144 E4
toxeter Leisure Centre
UTXR ST14 .... 144 B3
erie Bettany Clinic
HAN ST1 .... 2 D5
ley CP School
CDLE ST10 .... 91 G3
ntura Retail Park
POL/KGSB/FAZ B78 .... 10 B7
ntura Shopping Centre
POL/KGSB/FAZ B78 .... 10 A7
rnon Lodge Preparatory
School & Kindergarten
PENK ST19 .... 228 C7
ctoria Gallery
ASHB DE6 .... 79 H8
ctoria Hall
HAN ST1 .... 2 D6
ctoria Primary School
BUT DE14 .... 6 F2
ctoria Surgery
HAN ST1 .... 2 B7
e Village Surgery
NEWUL ST5 .... 68 C4
liers Trading Estate
BKHL/PFLD WV2 .... 295 H3
olet Lane County
Infants School
STPNHL/WNHL DE15 .... 204 F2

Walkmill Business Park
CNCK/NC WS11 .... 249 J5
Walsall College of Technology
WSL WS1 .... 283 L8
Walsall & District Doctors
on Call
BLOX/PEL WS3 .... 283 M2
Walsall Health Authority
WLNHL WV13 .... 281 M8
Walsall Health Authority
WSL WS1 .... 283 M8
Walsall Metropolitan
Borough Council
ALDR WS9 .... 268 F7
Walsall Metropolitan
Borough Council
WSL WS1 .... 283 L8
Walsall Wood Junior
& Infant School
ALDR WS9 .... 269 G6
Walton Hall Sch
ECCH ST21 .... 153 J5
Walton Industrial Estate
STONE ST15 .... 137 M5
Walton on Trent C of E
Primary School
MSHM DE12 .... 221 K2
Walton Priory County
Middle School
STONE ST15 .... 137 M4
Warslow Middle School
BUX SK17 .... 33 G8
Warstones Primary School
ETTPK/GDPK/PENN WV4 .... 294 E4
Wartell Bank Industrial Estate
KGSWFD DY6 .... 303 K3
Waterhouses C of E
Primary School
CDLE ST10 .... 60 F8
Waterhouses Medical Practice
CDLE ST10 .... 61 G8
Waterloo Road Jamia Mosque
DUNHL/THL/PER WV6 .... 280 C6
Waterloo Road Surgery
BURS/TUN ST6 .... 69 G3
Waterside County
Junior School
STPNHL/WNHL DE15 .... 204 D3
Watery Lane Industrial Estate
WLNHL WV13 .... 281 K7
Watling Junior & Infant School
BRWNH WS8 .... 268 E1
Wayside Farm Equine Hospital
MKTDR TF9 .... 97 J7
Wedgwood Memorial College
BARL ST12 .... 101 K8
Wednesfield Football Club
WNSFLD WV11 .... 281 J4
Wednesfield High School
WNSFLD WV11 .... 281 L5
Wednesfield Village
Primary School
WNSFLD WV11 .... 281 K5
Weeping Cross Health Centre
STAFS ST17 .... 194 D2
Wellesley Street Surgery
HAN ST1 .... 2 B9
Well Street Medical Centre
CDLE ST10 .... 89 L7
Werrington County
Infants School
END/WER ST9 .... 71 H6
Werrington Village Surgery
END/WER ST9 .... 71 H7

Westacre Infant School
BDMR/CCFT WV3 .... 294 D1
West Chadsmoor Clinic
CNCK/NC WS11 .... 231 L5
Westcliffe Hospital
BURS/TUN ST6 .... 53 M3
Westcroft Special School
WOLVN WV10 .... 265 H8
Western Springs County
Primary School
RUGE WS15 .... 197 K8
Westfield County
Primary School
WMBN WV5 .... 298 A3
Westgate Trading Estate
ALDR WS9 .... 284 E4
West Hill Primary School
HEDN WS12 .... 232 B4
Westlake Trading Estate
BURS/TUN ST6 .... 53 K8
Westlands CP School
NEWUL ST5 .... 83 M4
Weston Coyney Infants School
LNGTN ST3 .... 87 H5
Weston Coyney Junior School
LNGTN ST3 .... 87 H7
Weston Road High School
RSTAF ST18 .... 175 L5
West Park Hospital
WOLV WV1 .... 12 C4
West Park Infant School
WOLV WV1 .... 12 D3
West Park Junior School
WOLV WV1 .... 12 D2
Westwood County First School
LEEK ST13 .... 43 J5
Westwood Golf Club
LEEK ST13 .... 43 J7
Westwood High School
LEEK ST13 .... 43 H5
Westwood School
RUGE WS15 .... 199 G6
Wetmore Road Surgery
BUT DE14 .... 7 K4
Wharf Road Industrial Estate
BUT DE14 .... 7 J1
Wharf Road Surgery
GNOS ST20 .... 190 C5
Wheaton Aston Cricket Club
PENK ST19 .... 227 K3
Whetstone Field
Primary School
ALDR WS9 .... 285 H6
Whieldon Industrial Estate
STOKE ST4 .... 85 K4
Whiston Hall Golf Club
CDLE ST10 .... 74 E7
Whitebridge Industrial Estate
STONE ST15 .... 119 L8
Whitfield Valley CP School
BURS/TUN ST6 .... 54 B3
Whitgreave Infant School
WOLVN WV10 .... 280 E2
Whitgreave Junior School
WOLVN WV10 .... 280 E2
Whitgreave Primary School
WOLVN WV10 .... 265 H3
Whitmore Medical Centre
WOLV WV1 .... 12 E2
Whitmore & Newcastle
Cricket Club
NEWUL ST5 .... 98 F4

Whitmore Reans Health Centre
DUNHL/THL/PER WV6 .... 12 B1
Whittington Grange School
LICHS WS14 .... 255 K4
Whittington Primary School
LICHS WS14 .... 255 L6
Wightwick Hall Special School
DUNHL/THL/PER WV6 .... 278 E8
Willenhall Lane
Industrial Estate
BLOX/PEL WS3 .... 283 G2
Willenhall Town Football Club
WLNHL WV13 .... 281 M7
William Allitt School
SWAD DE11 .... 205 L3
William Baxter Special School
HEDN WS12 .... 232 A4
William Hutson Junior School
BUTN/AL/TUT DE13 .... 185 H2
William Macgregor
Primary School
TAM/AM/WIL B77 .... 11 G6
William Shrewsbury
County Primary School
BUTN/AL/TUT DE13 .... 166 F8
Willows County
Primary School
LICH WS14 .... 236 B8
Wilnecote Health Centre
TAM/AM/WIL B77 .... 290 F3
Wilnecote High School
TAM/AM/WIL B77 .... 290 F4
Wilnecote Junior School
TAM/AM/WIL B77 .... 290 F3
Wiltell Road Industrial Estate
LICHS WS14 .... 8 F5
Wincle C of E Primary School
MCFLDS SK11 .... 19 M1
Windsor Industrial Estate
BUT DE14 .... 7 J2
Windsor Park C of E
Middle School
UTXR ST14 .... 144 B2
Winshill Clinic
STPNHL/WNHL DE15 .... 186 B7
Winshill Infants School
STPNHL/WNHL DE15 .... 186 B6
Woden Avenue Junior
& Infant School
WNSFLD WV11 .... 281 H4
Woden Junior School
WOLVN WV10 .... 13 J1
Wolgarston High School
PENK ST19 .... 230 A2
Wolstanton C of E School
NEWUL ST5 .... 68 C5
Wolstanton High School
NEWUL ST5 .... 68 C6
Wolverhampton
& Bilston Athletic Club
DUNHL/THL/PER WV6 .... 279 M4
Wolverhampton
Borough Council
WOLV WV1 .... 12 F3
Wolverhampton
Borough Council
WOLV WV1 .... 12 E5
Wolverhampton Cricket Club
DUNHL/THL/PER WV6 .... 279 J4
Wolverhampton
Grammar School
BDMR/CCFT WV3 .... 279 M8

Wolverhampton
Healthcare N H S Trust
WOLVN WV10 .... 281 H6
Wolverhampton Metropolitan
Borough Council
BDMR/CCFT WV3 .... 294 E1
Wolverhampton Metropolitan
Borough Council
WOLV WV1 .... 13 G3
Wolverhampton University
WOLVN WV10 .... 280 C4
Wolverhampton
Wanderers Football Club
WOLV WV1 .... 12 E2
Wolverley High School
KIDDW DY11 .... 309 K6
Wolverley Sebright First School
KIDDW DY11 .... 309 K7
Wombourne Cricket Tennis
& Bowling Club
WMBN WV5 .... 298 A3
Wombrook Industrial Estate
WMBN WV5 .... 297 L4
Woodcocks Weel C of E
Primary School
ALS/KID ST7 .... 39 J4
Woodcroft County First School
LEEK ST13 .... 43 J6
Wood End Primary School
WNSFLD WV11 .... 281 K3
Woodlands JMI School
SHHTH WV12 .... 282 D4
Woodlands Primary School
TAM/AM/WIL B77 .... 11 K6
Wood Lane CP School
ALS/KID ST7 .... 66 F1
Woodseaves C of E
Primary School
GNOS ST20 .... 170 E3
The Woodsetton School
SEDG DY3 .... 299 M3
Woodthorne Primary School
DUNHL/THL/PER WV6 .... 279 H6
Woore County Primary School
AUD/MAD/W CW3 .... 96 C1
Worcester Street Surgery
STRBR DY8 .... 307 M5
Wordsley Green Health Centre
STRBR DY8 .... 303 K8
Wordsley Hospital
STRBR DY8 .... 303 L7
Wrottesley Hall
CDSL WV8 .... 278 B2
Wulfrun College
BDMR/CCFT WV3 .... 279 M8
Wulfrun College
WOLV WV1 .... 12 E3
Wulfrun Shopping Centre
WOLV WV1 .... 12 F6
Wulfrun Trading Estate
DUNHL/THL/PER WV6 .... 280 C5
Yarlet Hall Preparatory School
RSTAF ST18 .... 155 J3
Yeoman Business Estate
BUT DE14 .... 7 K1
Yew Tree Gallery
ASHB DE6 .... 93 H7
Yoxall Health Centre
BUTN/AL/TUT DE13 .... 201 G7
Zip Theatre
WOLV WV1 .... 12 E2

Page 37

C7
1 Cranberry Moss La
2 Marsh Cl
3 Marsh La
4 Weaver Cl
5 Wheelock Cl

K5
1 Cresswellshawe Rd

Page 43

K6
1 Hawksworth Cl
2 Woodcroft Av

L5
1 Cornhill Cl
2 Field St
3 Jolliffe St
4 Mayers Ct

M6
1 Ashcombe Wy

Page 53

H1
1 Briarswood
2 Charnwood
3 Silverwood
4 Summerfield

J3
1 Charlotte St
2 Elton Ter
3 Latebrook Cl
4 Newark Gv

K3
1 Drummond St
2 Park Farm Vw
3 St Joseph St
4 Willoughby St

K6
1 Dunning Cl
2 Grosvenor Pl
3 Mc Kinley St
4 Robert St

K7
1 America St
2 Athelstan St
3 Calver St
4 Farndale St
5 Goodfellow St
6 Haymarket
7 Holland St
8 Hoover St
9 Ladywell Rd
10 Mcgough St
11 Oldcourt St
12 Paradise St
13 Phoenix St
14 Piccadilly St
15 Rialto Pl
16 Stringer Ct

J5
1 Butterfield Cl
2 Capper St
3 Challinor St
4 Melfont St
5 Pitcairn St
6 Rabone St

Page 54

A7
1 Ambleside Pl
2 Bank Top Av
3 Dunwood Dr
4 Reeves Av

C8
1 Livingstone St
2 Quinton Wk
3 Robert Heath St
4 Stormont Cl

D8
1 Athlone St
2 Back Ford Green Rd
3 Brittle Pl
4 William Ruston Cl

E6
1 Knypersley Rd
2 St Bartholomews Cl

E7
1 Borrowdale Rd
2 Bradbury Cl
3 Clement Pl
4 Hughson Gv
5 Keene Cl
6 Kingston Pl
7 Meere Cl

F8
1 Magnolia Dr
2 Thurlwood Dr

Page 67

K1
1 Burford Av
2 Cornhill Cl
3 Cranberry Dr
4 Greendale Dr
5 Haslington Cl
6 Huntsbank Dr
7 Laburnum Pl
8 Wrenburry Cl

L3
1 Edensor St
2 Victoria Av
3 Wetherby Cl

L4
1 Cooper St
2 Hogarth Pl
3 Mount St
4 Reynolds Av

L1
1 Howe Gv
2 St Vincent Pl

M4
1 Barker St
2 Broad Meadow Ct
3 Haddon Cl

Page 68

A2
1 Colclough Av

A4
1 Ashcroft Cl
2 Dimsdale Pde West
3 Oakdene Cl
4 Oakdene Gv

A5
1 Onslow Dr

B4
1 Ashcroft Rd
2 Chetwynd Rd
3 Portland Ms

B5
1 St George's Av South

B6
1 Whitehouse Rd North

B7
1 Green Brook Ct

B8
1 Fairlawns

C2
1 Winghay Cl

C3
1 The Beeches
2 Michaels Cl

C4
1 George St
2 Inglewood Gv
3 Loring Ter South
4 Porthill Gn
5 Winston Ter

C5
1 Chelmsford Rd
2 Nelson St
3 Palmerston St
4 Peel St
5 Russell St

C6
1 Rudyard Gv

C7
1 Bellefield Vw
2 Brampton Gdns
3 Woodstock St

D2
1 Avondale St
2 Mott Pl
3 Princes Sq
4 Tomlinson St
5 Trubshawe Cl

D3
1 Brunt St

D6
1 Barber's Sq
2 Sheringham Pl

D7
1 Burleigh Gv
2 Campion Av
3 East Crs
4 Parkside Gv
5 Rangemore Ter
6 Sycamore Gv
7 Walklate Av

D8
1 Kings Pl
2 Stanley Gv

E1
1 Barton Crs

E2
1 Billinge St
2 Bulstrode St
3 Joseph St
4 Neushew St
5 Reid St

E8
1 Bank House Dr
2 Cooper Av

F1
1 Barber St
2 Marshall St
3 Overhouse St

F2
1 Brick House Ct
2 Clayhanger St
3 Cleveland St
4 Furlong Pde
5 Furlong Pas
6 Jenkins St
7 Keates St
8 Nicholas St
9 Riley St South
10 St John's Sq
11 Swan Sq
12 William Clowes St

F3
1 Stroma Cl

Page 69

C1
1 Brown St
2 Doulton St
3 Jackson St
4 Mayer Bank
5 Reginald St

G3
1 Bleak Pl
2 Lower St
3 Macintyre St
4 Orgreave St
5 Rushton Gv
6 Stokesay Gv
7 Swainsley Cl
8 Walley Pl

G5
1 Bromley St

G7
1 Broomfield Pl North
2 Broomfield Pl South
3 Cavendish St
4 Garnet St
5 Shallowford Ct
6 Twemlow St

H1
1 Broadhurst St
2 Garlick St
3 Grafton Av
4 Inglefield Av
5 Jackfield St

H4
1 Church Ter
2 Emery St
3 Mawdesley St
4 Remer St

H5
1 Bowness St
2 Bromley Ct

H7
1 Cambridge St
2 Clinton Sq
3 Crompton St
4 Lindsay St
5 Mersey St
6 Morley St
7 Red Lion Pas
8 Statham St
9 Victoria Sq

H8
1 Croston St
2 Cutts St
3 Garfield St
4 Joanhurst Crs
5 Jordon St
6 Parkhouse St
7 Rectory St
8 Richmond Ter
9 St Mark's Ct
10 Shelton Farm Rd
11 Stanhope St
12 Thorndyke St

J1
1 High Bank Pl
2 Stellar St
3 Whatmore St

J3
1 The Coppice
2 Ellis St
3 Gordon Av
4 Rhondda Av

J7
1 Adventure Pl
2 Albion St
3 Bagnall St
4 Boothroyd St
5 Downey St
6 Eastwood Pl
7 Lower Bethesda St
8 Orb St
9 Pall Mall
10 Ranelagh St
11 Sceptre St

J8
1 Raymond St
2 Victoria Av

K1
1 Alanley Cl

K3
1 Kingswinford Pl
2 Melrose Av
3 Raymond Av
4 Salcombe Pl
5 Wensleydale Cl

K5
1 Dover St
2 Free Trade St
3 Grenville St
4 Myatt St
5 Providence St
6 Southampton St
7 Stedman St

K7
1 Hassall St
2 Hordley St
3 Howson St
4 Lincoln St
5 Mulberry St
6 Perry Cl
7 Wellington Ter

K8
1 Imperial Ct
2 Oldham St
3 Stonehaven Gv
4 Westmill St

L2
1 Moss Side

L3
1 Rosemary St

L4
1 Donald Rd
2 Dunsany Gv
3 Sandiway Rd

L6
1 Cromer Crs
2 Elizabeth St
3 Mayfield Crs
4 Northwood Gn
5 Sandyfield Rd

L8
1 Douglas Pl

M1
1 Edmonton Gv
2 Lightwater Cl

M4
1 Baytree Cl
2 Beechmont Gv
3 Crosshead Gv
4 Huntingdon Rd
5 Kingsbury Gv
6 Neptune Gv
7 Pandora Gv
8 Smallwood Gv
9 Whygate Gv

M5
1 Linkend Cl
2 Slaidburn Gv
3 Westbury Cl
4 Wildale Gv

H1
1 Freshwater Gv

H4
1 Conford Cl
2 Daventry Cl
3 Elmhurst Cl
4 Wrighton Cl

Page 70

A8
1 Ellington Cl
2 Elmhurst Cl
3 Hillberry Cl
4 Strand Cl

B1
1 Easters Gv
2 Lyminster Gv
3 Newleigh St
4 Woodman St
5 Woodside Pl

D8
1 Hutton Wy
2 Reading Wy
3 Reedham Wy
4 Swaffham Wy
5 Taunton Wy

Page 84

A1
1 Fletcher Bank
2 John O'Gaunt's Rd
3 Pool Side

A2
1 Buckley's Rw
2 Castle Keep Ms
3 Poolfield Av North

A5
1 Penarth Pl

A6
1 Waverley Pl

A7
1 Cape St
2 Flintsham Gv
3 Rosvean St
4 Trafalgar St

J6
1 Brewery St
2 Church St
3 Burton Pl
4 Gitana St
5 Goodson St
6 Lower Foundry St
7 New Hall St
8 Parliament Sq
9 Stafford La
10 Weaver St

B6
1 Avon Cl
2 Dee La
3 Lee Gv
4 Medway Cl
5 Riversmead

B7
1 Aynsley Av
2 Blakeney St
3 Copeland Av
4 Ribble Cl
5 Westbury Rd

B8
1 Claydon Crs
2 Hadleigh Cl
3 Thornham Cl
4 Walsingham Gdns

C1
1 Castle St
2 Northcote St
3 North St
4 Queens Ct
5 Scott St
6 Seagrave St
7 Water St
8 Windsor St

K3
1 Back Garden St
2 Belgrave St
3 Coronation St
4 Grosvenor Gdns
5 Harrison St
6 Hawkestone Cl
7 Legge St
8 Stubbs' St
9 Webster St

C3
1 Duke St
2 Leech St
3 Vicarage St

K6
1 Gloucester Gra
2 Leicester Ct
3 Norwich Pl

C7
1 Barn Ct
2 Oakdale

C8
1 Ashton Ct

D1
1 Balloon St
2 Boundary Street
3 Clarence St
4 Cumberland St
5 Horton St
6 Kingswell Rd
7 Lockwood St
8 Spring St

D8
1 Ashwell Pl
2 Beaumaris Cl
3 Lancaster Av
4 Lancaster Crs

L2
1 Moss Side

L3
1 Ashlands Cl

L4
1 Hulme St
2 Steel St
3 Weller St
4 Wilfred Pl

E3
1 Ashlands Crs

E4
1 Lukesland Av
2 Rogerstone Av

E5
1 Mayfield Pl West

E6
1 Lymevale Av
2 St John's Av

E7
1 Darrall Rd
2 Greyswood Rd
3 Huntingdon Rd
4 Kensington Cl
5 Lyme Brook Pl
6 School St
7 Stonewood Cl
8 Swan La

E8
1 Bramley Pl

F1
1 Boswell St
2 Britton St

C2
1 Coverley Pl
2 Ellastone Gv

F5
1 Shilton Cl

F6
1 Alastair Rd
2 William Fiske St

F7
1 Elphinstone Rd

Page 85

G2
1 Hallahan Cl
2 Northcote Av

G3
1 Balliol St
2 Bath Ter
3 Featherstone Gv

C4
1 Club St
2 Empire Pas
3 Harding Ter
4 Liddle St

G5
1 Boothenwood Ter
2 Fontaine Pl

H2
1 Charlton St
2 Floyd St
3 Rebecca St

H3
1 Aquinas St
2 Bamber St
3 Berry St
4 Bowstead St
5 Consort St
6 Lesse St
7 Trade St
8 Welch St

D2
1 Washerwall St

D4
1 Dywater Gv
2 Dellwood Gv
3 Ramshaw Gv
4 Sark Pl
5 Stanfield Rd

J5
1 Hamilton St
2 Whieldon Crs

K1
1 Egerton St
2 Mawson Gv

B7
1 Raglan St
2 Standard St
3 Upper Furlong St
4 Younger St

K5
1 Blenheim St

L1
1 Maud St

L2
1 Adrian St
2 Brookes St
3 Duncan St
4 Gimson St
5 Hitchman St
6 Kent Pl
7 Leopold St
8 Victoria Pl
9 Wileman Pl

L5
1 Cholerton Cl
2 Clifton Cl

L6
1 Camden St
2 Derry St
3 Hertford St
4 Tweed St

M1
1 St Margarets Cl

M3
1 Achilles Wy

M4
1 Brogan St
2 Rubian St
3 Woodend St

M5
1 Abercorn St
2 Canning St
3 Dennis St
4 Leeds St
5 Paynter St

M7
1 Downsview St
2 Shetland Rd
3 Whitcliffe Pl

F7
1 Congreve Rd
2 Lidgate St

Page 86

A1
1 Burford Wy
2 William Birch Rd

A6
1 Astro Gv
2 Carpenter Rd
3 Foley Pl

A8
1 Longbrook Av

B1
1 Wynford Rd
2 Youlton Gv

E2
1 Applegarth Cl
2 Bolina Gv
3 Jolyon Cl
4 Rogate Cl

B5
1 Kentmere Cl

B6
1 Glenwood Cl
2 Heathdene Cl
3 Kelmore Cl
4 March Rd

B7
1 Clayton St
2 Edensor Rd
3 Gold St
4 Grosvenor St

E8
1 Cemetery Vw
2 Leaks Alley
3 Springfield Crs

C1
1 Vowchurch Wy

C2
1 Romer Side
2 Thurston Wy

F5
1 Wilmot Gv

F6
1 Beeston Av
2 Denby Av
3 Fleet St
4 Hathersage Gv
5 Sandford St
6 Tideswell Rd

F7
1 Belsay Cl
2 Caswell St
3 Cottonwood Gv
4 Cross St
5 Grafton Rd
6 Hemlock Av
7 Loughborough Wk
8 Manse Cl
9 Upper Cross St

G3
1 Barlow St
2 Bennion St
3 Chancery La
4 Commerce St
5 Kingcross St
6 Landon St
7 Millbank St
8 Royston Wk
9 Smithy La
10 The Strand
11 Webberley La

Page 101

H5
1 Meerbrook Cl
2 Monkleigh Cl

J3
1 Hampstead Gv

J4
1 Bowmead Cl
2 Brindiwell Gv
3 Camberwell Gv
4 Mallowdale Cl
5 Mountserrel Cl
6 Southgate Av
7 Torridon Cl

L1
1 Broadoak Wy
2 Tilehurst Rd

Page 103

G2
1 Bordeaux Rd
2 Burgundy Gv
3 Cobham Pl
4 Crossland Pl East
5 Dudley Pl
6 Fawn Cl
7 Kingsford Pl
8 Ogmore Cl
9 Russet Cl

C4
1 Bergamot Dr
2 Chesham Gv
3 Dovebank Gv
4 Juniper Cl
5 Peregrine Gv
6 Valerian Wy

G6
1 Heather Crs
2 Lindley Pl
3 Melrose Av
4 Woodlands Gv

H3
1 Argosy Cl
2 Burnside Cl
3 Canvey Gv
4 Constable Cl
5 Linhope Gv
6 Renard Wy
7 Rushcliffe Dr
8 Rushmoor Gv

J1
1 Granchester Cl
2 Kervis Gv
3 Rembrandt Wy
4 Rubens Wy
5 Whitesands Gv

J3
1 Blanchard Cl
2 Brabazon Cl
3 Farman Cl
4 Freckleton Pl

L4
1 Chartley Cl
2 Churchill Cl
3 Park Vw
4 Springfield

M4
1 Ferndale Cl
2 Honeysuckle Av
3 Jasmine Cl
4 Springcroft
5 Stallangton Gdns

D5
1 Knarsdale Cres
2 Melbourne St
3 Rowanburn Cl
4 Somerton Wy
5 Woodingdean Cl

D6
1 Denshaw Wk
2 Goldsmith Rd
3 Isherwood Pl
4 Larkin Av
5 Loveston Gv
6 Palmer St
7 Swanland Gv
8 Tutbury Gv
9 Warsill Gv

D7
1 Blackheath Cl
2 Cinderhill La
3 Heath's Pas
4 Stockwell Gv

D8
1 Lower Spring Rd
2 Malt La
3 Roxburghe Av
4 Speakman St
5 Sutherland Pl
6 Windsor Av
7 Wren Vw

E1
1 Lowthorpe Wk

E3
1 Cowley Wy
2 Glenfield Wy
3 Holly Ct

E5
1 Loganbeck Gv

E6
1 Amberfield Pl
2 Blackwood Pl
3 Freebridge Cl
4 Naples Cl
5 Solway Gv
6 Sorrento Gv

E7
1 Fleckney Av
2 Winterbourne Gv

E8
1 Lexham Pl
2 Saltdean Cl

F5
1 Christie Pl
2 Swift Pl

F6
1 Mortimer Pl
2 Parker-jervis Gv

F7
1 Cloverdale Pl

Page 174

B2
1 Allendale
2 Kennedy Wy

C1
1 Crispin Cl
2 Elmhurst Cl
3 Paddock Cl
4 Trelawny's Gn
5 Tudor Ri
6 Underwood Cl

D6
1 Back Browning St
2 Friar St
3 New St
4 Snows Yd

D7
1 Broad Eye
2 Broad St
3 Castle Hi
4 Gingham St

Page 185

H6
1 Needwood Cl
2 Ravens Wy

J1
1 Barrington Rd
2 The Chevin
3 Deveron Cl
4 Gleneagles Dr
5 Kedleston Ct
6 Longbow Cl
7 Newbury Dr
8 Suningdale Cl

J2
1 St Aidan's Cl
2 St Chad's Ct
3 St Jude's Wk
4 St Mark's Ct

J6
1 Hallams Rw

K2
1 Althorp Wy
2 Broadlands
3 Buckingham Cl
4 Conway Cl
5 Crestwood Cl
6 Earls Ct
7 Faraday Av
8 Glamis Cl
9 Kingsdale Cft
10 Mountbatten Cl
11 Raglan Cl
12 Regency Wy
13 St Francis Cl
14 Tudor Hollow
15 Westminster Dr

K8
1 Abbey St
2 Gough Side
3 Orchard Pk
4 Ordish Ct
5 Russell St

Page 186

B1
1 Blenheim Cl
2 Delhi Cl
3 Durban Cl
4 The Eyrie
5 Madras Rd
6 Stamps Ct
7 Wyndham Crs

Page 193

G2
1 Denver Fold
2 Kentish Cl
3 Keswick Gv
4 Letheridge Gdns
5 Lexington Av
6 Rembrandt Wy
7 Rubens Wy
8 Westbury Hayes
9 Whimster Sq

H2
1 Beaumont Gdns
2 Boningale Wy
3 Carlton Sq
4 Cleveland Wk
5 Cranbrook Wk
6 Dart Av
7 Edwin Cl
8 Keld Av
9 Kentmere Cl
10 Ralph Ct

J1
1 The Close

J3
1 Betjeman Wk
2 Cray Wk
3 Greenwood Gv
4 Matthews Rd
5 St Andrews Rd
6 Stevenson Dr
7 Taylor Wk
8 Thompson Cl
9 Whitby Cl

K1
1 Inglewood

K4
1 Shenley Wy

Page 194

C1
1 Ascot Rd
2 Baywood Cl
3 Buckingham Rd
4 Mayfield Rd

E4
1 Field Pl
2 Kenworthy Rd
3 Peter James Ct

E5
1 School Pl
2 Wogan St

E6
1 Abbots Wk
2 Gaol Sq
3 Lloyd St

E7
1 Appleyard St
2 Chapel St
3 Church La
4 Cope St
5 Eastgate St
6 Gaolgate St
7 Malt Mill La
8 Martin St
9 Mill Bank
10 Princes St
11 St Chad's Pl
12 Salter St
13 Stafford St
14 Victoria Rd
15 Water St

E8
1 Epsley's Yd
2 Middle Friars
3 Pilgrim St

F4
1 Drummond Rd
2 Fairfield Cl

F5
1 Sandalwood Dr

F7
1 Corporation St
2 Lammascote Rd

F8
1 Lichfield Ct

Page 197

J8
1 Byron Pl
2 Canaway Wk
3 Crestwood Ri
4 Daffodil Wk
5 Dayton Dr
6 Hurstbourne Ct
7 Lanehead Wk
8 Lansdowne Wy
9 Malvern Dr
10 Redmond Cl
11 Thistle Cl
12 Woodthorne Cl

Page 204

A3
1 Aintree Cl
2 Haydock Cl
3 Hylton Cl
4 Montpellier Cl
5 Nicklaus Cl
6 Sandown Cl
7 Sherbourne St

B2
1 Fox Cl
2 Queens Ct
3 Ratcliffe Av
4 Sovereign Ct

B3
1 Culland Rd
2 Glencroft Cl
3 Jephson Rd
4 Trustley Cl

H7
1 Billbrook Cl
2 Billbrook Gv
3 Cedar Gv
4 Cherry Tree Gdns
5 Heath Gv
6 Jasmine Gv
7 Lavender Cl
8 Manor Cl
9 Pendinas Dr
10 Walnut Av
11 Willow Gv

M8
1 Exbury Cl
2 Farmside Gn
3 Haywain Cl
4 Marholm Cl
5 The Moorings
6 Princeton Gdns
7 Quadrille Lawns
8 Solent Cl
9 Tranwell Cl
10 Woodford Cl

Page 205

E6
1 Bonville Gdns
2 Farmoor Wy
3 Titchfield Cl
4 Wadesmill Lawns
5 Wealden Hatch

Page 215

H3
1 Church Cl
2 Field Pl
3 Horns Cft

J2
1 St Johns St

K1
1 Bayswater Rd
2 Frank Gee Ct
3 Jubilee St
4 Toy Cl

K4
1 Davy Pl
2 Rutland Av

L1
1 Coach House La
2 Crossley Stone
3 Lower Brook St
4 Market Sq
5 Penny Bank Ct

L2
1 Sarah Challinor Cl

M2
1 Chadwick Cl
2 Keystone Rd
3 St Anthonys Cl
4 St Pauls Rd

Page 231

L5
1 Addison Cl
2 Lotus Dr
3 Pye Green Rd

L6
1 Bunyan Pl
2 Longfellow Pl
3 Masefield Gv
4 The Poplars
5 William Morris Gv

M8
1 Cedarhill Dr
2 Meadow Hill Dr
3 Millbrook Cl
4 Stoneyfields Cl

Page 232

A5
1 Richmond Cl

A7
1 Fircroft Cl
2 Glendawn Cl
3 Vermont Gn

C5
1 Bell Dr
2 Bromley Cl
3 Cygnet Cl
4 Kingsley Av
5 Passfield Av
6 Wesley Pl

C7
1 Charnwood Cl
2 Farm Cl
3 Hartlebury Cl
4 Marigold Cl
5 Meadway Cl
6 Torquoise Gv

C8
1 Amber Gv
2 Bronte Dr
3 Callaghan Cl
4 Chestnut Cl
5 Diamond Gv
6 Firecrest Cl
7 Hickory Cl
8 Ludlow Cl
9 Rose Bay Meadow
10 Willowherb Cl
11 Wilson Gv

C3
1 Brambleside
2 Brookwillows
3 Cloverdale
4 The Coppins
5 Epsom Dr
6 Leighswood
7 Treetops
8 The Woodcote

C4
1 Badgers Cft
2 Cherrywood Cl
3 Deepdales
4 Larksmeadow V
5 Learhurst Cl
6 Meadway Dr
7 Robinswood
8 Rockswood Copse
9 Sharnbrook Gv
10 Shireoaks Dr
11 Slaidburn Gv
12 Somervale
13 Swallowdale

D5
1 Elmstone Cl
2 Fieldside
3 Glenthorne Cl
4 Hollyhurst
5 Mapledene Cl
6 Spinney Flds
7 Spreadoaks Dr
8 Wycherwood Gdns

Page 249

H3
1 Coppice Cl
2 Southgate End
3 Spinney Farm Rd
4 Wellfield Ct

K7
1 Chapel Sq
2 Grasmere Ct
3 Old Falls Cl

K8
1 Boleyn Cl
2 Cheslyn Dr
3 Vauxhall Wy
4 Raven Cl

Page 254

A2
1 Beaconsfields
2 Cathedral Ri
3 Swan Ms

D2
1 Beechfield Ri
2 Birch Gv
3 Rocklands Crs
4 Rowan Cl
5 The Woodlands

Page 263

C1
1 Ingestre Rd

C4
1 Beechcroft Pl
2 Logan Ct
3 Shaw Rd

C5
1 Appletree Gv
2 Gorsebrook Rd

C6
1 Almond Gv
2 Boscobel Crs

E6
1 Deanery Rw
2 Drummond St
3 Nursery St
4 Red Hill St

Page 264

E6
1 Carisbrooke Gdns
2 Elmcroft Gdns
3 Hamilton Gdns
4 Lauderdale Gdns
5 Northwood Park Cl

Page 274

B6
1 Bolebridge St
2 College La
3 Common La

C3
1 Arkall Cl
2 Harwell Cl

D5
1 Arion Cl
2 Garaget St
3 Goostry Rd
4 Minerva Cl
5 Rodwell Cl

E6
1 Hopleys Cl
2 John St
3 Kenilworth Rd
4 School St

E7
1 Talbot
2 Triumph
3 Trojan

M8
1 Newport
2 Padstow
3 Redcliff
4 Modhurst Cl

Page 278

D6
1 The Belfry
2 The Cartway
3 Fallowfield
4 Kelso Gdns
5 The Paddock
6 The Pastures
7 The Saddlestones
8 Wells Cl
9 The Windrow
10 Worcester Dr

D7
1 Barley Cft
2 Butterfield Cl
3 Cornhill Cl
4 Meadow Cft
5 Pugin Cl

E6
1 Cheshire Gv
2 Cook Cl
3 Cunningham Rd
4 Jedburgh Av
5 Tintern Cl
6 Wordsworth Cl

D8
1 Heathland Cl
2 Picasso Cl
3 Rembrandt Cl
4 Squirrel Cl
5 Turner Cl

E6
1 Albert Davie Dr
2 Trafalgar St

E8
1 Appledore St

E8
1 Eden Cl
2 Sam Barber Ct

F4
1 Deerhurst Ri

F6
1 Bryans Wy
2 Hamilton Cl

F7
1 Dugdale St

F8
1 Melbourne Crs

F6
1 Avon Cl
2 Buttermere Cl
3 Chepstow Cl
4 Grasmere Av
5 Hepworth Cl
6 Kenilworth Rd
7 Sedgefield Gv
8 Sutherland Gv
9 Thirlmere Gv
10 Wastwater Cl
11 Wye Cl

Page 279

H6
1 Rising Brook
2 Woodend Pl

Page 280

A1
1 Chandlers Cl

A5
1 Chetwood Cl
2 Glaisdale Gdns
3 Ingleby Gdns
4 Newmarket Cl
5 Skipton Gn

A7
1 The Beeches

A8
1 Merridale Crs
2 Middle Vauxhall
3 Vauxhall Wy
4 Westland Av

B4
1 Dales Cl

B7
1 Kingsland Rd

B8
1 Albany Rd
2 Lovatt St
3 Meadow St
4 Park Crs
5 Southgate
6 Summerfield Rd

G6
1 Church Gdns

G7
1 Hillside Gdns

G8
1 Birkdale Cl
2 Eskdale Cl

H2
1 Mansard Cl

H3
1 Fairview Cl

H4
1 Highfield Crs

H7
1 Sigmund Cl

H8
1 Abingdon Cl
2 Atherstone Rd
3 Hawkley Cl
4 Lapley Cl

J2
1 Beech Tree Av

J3
1 Woden Crs

K3
1 Anston Wy
2 Thomas Mason Cl

K4
1 Broomhall Cl
2 Henfield Cl
3 Wollaston Crs

K5
1 Halecroft Av
2 Portchester Dr

L2
1 Brailsford Cl
2 Linthouse La

L5
1 Foxglove Cl
2 Green Meadow
3 Speedwell Cl

L8
1 Ambrose Cl
2 Beaton Cl

M1
1 Anslow Gdns
2 Cleveland Cl
3 Thornley Cl
4 Whitehouse Rd

M2
1 Denmead Dr
2 Hodson Cl
3 Raven Crs
4 Roach Crs

M5
1 Longmoor Cl
2 Mosedale Dr
3 Oxted Cl
4 Worthy Down
5 Yarrow Cl

M6
1 Fibbersley Bank

M8
1 St Stephen's Av

Page 281

G1
1 Betjeman Pl

Page 282

A4
1 Broad La South
2 Damson Cl
3 Ratcliffe Rd

A5
1 Thirston Cl

A6
1 George St

A7
1 Borrow St
2 Clothier Gdns
3 Little Clothier St
4 Regent St
5 Temple St

A8
1 Clemson St
2 The Croft
3 Gomer St West
4 Gomer St East
5 Old School Cl
6 Round Cft
7 Stafford St

B1
1 Cotswold Cl
2 Gairloch Rd
3 Long Mynd Cl
4 Seaforth Cl
5 Wrekin Cl

B2
1 Bembridge Cl
2 Rosewood Dr
3 Sandalwood Cl

B3
1 Grazewood Cl
2 Green Meadow Rd
3 Meadow Grange Dr
4 Roundlea Cl

B4
1 Burleigh Cl
2 Cardigan Dr
3 Rothesay Wy

B5
1 Acre Ri
2 Castle Dr
3 Cornwall La
4 Shepherd Dr

B7
1 Nelson St
2 Stadium Cl

B8
1 Alma St
2 Bray St
3 Frederick William St
4 John Harper St
5 Locksmith Cl
6 Middle Gdns

C1
1 Brockeridge Cl
2 Crockhall Cl
3 Marchall Gdns
4 Taverners Cl

C2
1 Beacon Rd
2 Dorchester Cl

C3
1 Ada Wrighton Cl
2 Albert Clarke Dr
3 Caernarvon Cl
4 Newark Rd

C4
1 Bradgate Cl
2 Edmoor Cl
3 Lucknow Rd

C6
1 Douglas Davies Cl
2 Edgeworth Cl
3 Ernest Clarke Cl
4 Stroud Av
5 Stroud Cl
6 Whitminster Cl
7 Windsor Gv

C3
Acorn St
Ashburn Gv
Hobley St
Tamar Gv

D2
Forest Ga

D4
Drancy Av

D5
Sowers Gdns

D6
Bassett Cl
Granbourne Rd
Rhys Thomas Av

D7
Amberwood Cl
Farmbridge Cl
Farmbridge Rd
Faversham Cl
Ridge Cl
Western Cl

D8
Chester Cl
Gloucester Pl
Lymington Rd
Teme Gv
Warwick Av

E1
Glastonbury Wy

E2
Broadmeadows Rd
Lynwood Cl

E3
Coleridge Cl
Corsican Cl
Lombardy Gdns
Oregon Dr
Wood Lane Cl

E6
Whitewood Gld

E7
Bevin Rd

F1
Mossley Cl

F2
Beechdale Rd

F7
Cottle Cl
Everest Rd

F8
Arnwood Cl
Cheshire Rd
Tedder Rd

Page 283

G1
Sand Bank
Sandhill St

G2
Croxstalls Pl
Sneyd Hall Cl

G5
Brindley Cl
Red River Rd
Telford Cl

G6
Cavendish Gdns
Conwy Cl
Edinburgh La
Ludlow La
Perch Rd
Rochester Cft

H1
Drake Cl
The Exchange
Market Pl
Rockingham Cl
Sand Bank
Wightwick Cl

H2
Church Moat Wy
Deeley St
Grant St

H4
Newton Pl

H5
Stephenson Sq

H7
Belgrave Wk

H8
Madison Av

J3
Cornwall Cl
Dorset Pl
Sherborne Cl

J5
Remington Pl

J6
Raybolds Bridge St
Reedswood Wy

J7
Reedswood Gdns
Rowland Gdns

J8
Checketts St
Manor Road Prec

K6
Wiltshire Cl

K7
Brighton Cl
Long Acre St
Tannery Cl
Whitehouse St

K8
Algernon St
Shaw St
Wolverhampton St

L4
Roebuck Pl

L6
Cannon St North
Farm St
Rose Bank Dr
St Peters Ter

L7
Ryecroft Pk
Ryecroft St
Wisemore

L8
Bate St
Hatherton Rd
Leicester St
Little Albert St
Little Station St
Marsh St
Townend St
Wisemore
Wolverhampton St

M3
Coal Pool La

M4
Whateley Pl

M6
The Cutting

M8
Balls St
Walhouse Cl
Warewell St
Wedge St

Page 290

A2
1 Albert Rd
2 Victoria Dr

C2
1 Grange Cl

F3
1 Brook Av
2 Coach House Ri
3 Kimberley
4 Shelton St

Page 291

G5
1 Hawfinch

H2
1 Dover Farm Cl
2 Holwick
3 Ravenstone
4 Ribblesdale

H4
1 Glendale Ct

J1
1 Amicombe
2 Birdhope
3 Buckden
4 Cromdale
5 Darnbrook

Page 294

F6
1 St Catherine's Crs
2 Thurlstone Dr
3 Woodlands Cottages

Page 295

G1
1 Kimberley St
2 Melbury Cl

G3
1 Duke St

G4
1 Chequerfield Dr
2 Cotswold Cl
3 Shenstone Ct
4 Shervale Cl
5 Waverley Crs
6 Worcester Ct

G5
1 Ashwood Gv
2 Bromley Pl
3 Redmoor Gdns

G6
1 Balmoral Rd
2 Camberley Dr

H1
1 Laburnum St
2 Rosebery St
3 Salisbury St
4 Stanhope St
5 Williamson St

H2
1 Fern Rd

H4
1 Bromwynd Cl

H5
1 Sandringham Rd

J1
1 Bennett's Fold
2 Bond St
3 Cleveland Pas
4 Fold St
5 Little Brickiln St
6 Summer Rw
7 Victoria Fold

J2
1 Bloomsbury St
2 Frederick St
3 The Haven
4 The Hollies
5 King Edward's Rw
6 Little Pountney St
7 Stevens Ga

J3
1 Baggott St
2 Duncan St
3 Mason St

J4
1 Deborah Cl
2 Fowler St

J8
1 Alder Coppice
2 Chaffinch Cl
3 Tanglewood Gv

K1
1 Bilston St
2 George's Pde
3 George St
4 Hospital St
5 King Road St Georges

K2
1 Dartmouth St
2 Granville Cl
3 Rainbow St

K3
1 Lilleshall Crs

K4
1 Hawthorne Rd
2 Parkfield Rd

K5
1 Beaconsfield Av
2 Beaconsfield Dr
3 Broadstone Cl
4 Larcombe Dr
5 Sherington Dr

K7
1 Sherrans Dell

K8
1 Charnwood Av

L1
1 Bath St
2 East St
3 Mary Ann St
4 Oxford St

L2
1 Adelaide Wk
2 Christopher Rd
3 Dartmouth St

L3
1 Pond La
2 Tolworth Gdns

L4
1 St Martin's Cl

L5
1 Olive Av
2 Penhallow Dr
3 Walton Crs

L6
1 Genge Av

L7
1 Edale Cl

M1
1 Corser St

M3
1 Trentham Ri

M4
1 Bronte Rd
2 Hardy Sq
3 St Saviour's Cl

M5
1 Walton Rd

M6
1 Barton Rd
2 Genthorn Cl
3 Needwood Dr

M7
1 Waverley Crs

M8
1 Dovedale Ct
2 Smout Crs

Page 297

L4
1 Birch Coppice
2 Brookside Cl
3 Campion Cl
4 The Celandines
5 Clap Gate Gv
6 Deepdales
7 Forge Leys
8 The Hedges
9 Monks Cl
10 The Paddock
11 Rosebury Gv
12 Rushwater Cl

L5
1 Crane Hollow
2 Millside
3 The Shales
4 Wodehouse Cl

Page 299

G6
1 Emerson Cl

H1
1 Alderbrook Cl

H5
1 Dickens Cl

H7
1 Askew Bridge Rd
2 Hopyard Cl
3 Rockingham Cl
4 Woodland Gv

H8
1 Kettlesbank Rd
2 Linley Gv

J1
1 Corve Vw
2 Ley Ri
3 Meadow Vw

J2
1 Blakeney Cl
2 Hamilton Cl
3 Ryecroft Cl
4 St Brides Cl
5 Wombourne Cl

J5
1 Oakleigh Dr
2 Wenlock Cl

J6
1 Parkhouse Gdns
2 Turner's Gv
3 Whitebeams Cl

J7
1 Prices Rd

J8
1 Central Dr
2 Overbrook Cl

K2
1 Dean St
2 Fairhills
3 Hall St
4 Whitesmith Cl

K3
1 Avington Cl
2 Montford Gv
3 Wilkes Cft

K4
1 Mill Cl
2 Snowdon Ri

K5
1 Alderwood Ri
2 Vale Rw

K6
1 Malvern View Rd

K7
1 Chiltern Cl
2 Gatacre St
3 Withern Wy
4 Yorkdale Cl

K8
1 Finchley Cl
2 Hawthorne Gv
3 Hendon Cl
4 Penny Royal Cl
5 Ranscombe Dr
6 Uxbridge Cl
7 Woodthorne Cl

L1
1 The Croft
2 Cross Pl

L2
1 Victoria Rd

L3
1 Berrybush Gdns
2 Chevening Cl
3 Fellmeadow Wy
4 Foxmeadow Cl
5 Gate St
6 Thornfield Cft
7 Tipton Rd
8 Westgate Cl

L4
1 Autumn Berry Gv
2 Banbury Cl
3 Board School Gdns
4 Elmbridge Wy
5 Tudor Pl
6 Wheatstone Cl
7 Winterley Gdns

L5
1 Hillary Crest
2 Homestead Cl
3 The Paddock
4 Roford Ct
5 Spills Meadow

L7
1 Clearwell Gdns
2 Dinham Gdns
3 Dudmaston Wy
4 Hever Cl
5 Sedgefield Cl
6 Stokesay Ri
7 Winchcombe Cl

L8
1 Blenheim Wy
2 Buckingham Ri
3 Gatcombe Rd
4 Hastings Ct
5 Leighton Cl
6 Longleat Gv

M1
1 Woodville Gdns

M3
1 Barley Cl

M4
1 Thistle Cl

M5
1 Greenhill Rd
2 Mulberry Gn
3 Sycamore Gn

M6
1 Harvard Cl

M7
1 Badminton Cl
2 Lauriston Cl
3 Mansion Cl

M8
1 Cardoness Pl
2 Hexham Wy

Page 303

H3
1 Brenwood Cl
2 Hayrick Dr
3 Mancroft Cl
4 The Parade
5 Underley Cl

J3
1 Maygrove Rd

K3
1 Dunston Cl
2 Waterford Rd

K4
1 Ambleside Wy
2 Bassenthwaite Ct
3 Braithwaite Cl
4 Haweswater Dr
5 Ullswater Gdns

K8
1 Kenilworth Cl
2 Marlborough Gdns

L1
1 Kilburn Dr

L2
1 Almond Rd
2 Beech Tree Cl
3 Blossomfield Cl
4 Earlswood Rd
5 Greenland Cl
6 Heathlands Cl
7 Leacroft Rd
8 Mimosa Wk

L6
1 Markham Dr
2 Seafield Cl
3 Southbank Vw

L7
1 Dunsley Dr
2 Fairford Gdns
3 Hollyhurst Dr

L8
1 Greenbank Gdns
2 Meadowhill Dr

M4
1 Blenheim Rd
2 Metfield Cft

M6
1 Beaulieu Av
2 Freeland Gv

M7
1 Westcott Cl

M8
1 Lockfield Cl
2 Swiss Dr

Page 307

K4
1 Bright St
2 Hamilton Av
3 Whitney Av

L1
1 Brindley Cl
2 Diamond Park Dr
3 Gilbeys Cl
4 Greenway Av

L4
1 Romilly Cl
2 Vestry Ct

M5
1 Ballarat Wk
2 Enville Pl
3 Hemmings Cl
4 Hemplands Rd
5 Holly Gv
6 School St
7 Short St
8 Summer St

M6
1 Bernwall Cl
2 Faulkner Cl
3 South Rd

M7
1 Grassmere Dr

Notes

Notes

Notes

Notes

Notes

Notes